This book is due for return not later than the last date stamped below, unless recalled sooner.

POLITICAL PARTIES OF
EASTERN EUROPE

POLITICAL PARTIES OF EASTERN EUROPE

A Guide to Politics in the Post-Communist Era

JANUSZ BUGAJSKI

The Center for Strategic and International Studies

M.E.Sharpe

Armonk, New York
London, England

Library of Congress Cataloging-in-Publication Data

Bugajski, Janusz, 1954–
    Political parties of Eastern Europe: a guide to politics in the post-Communist era / by
Janusz Bugajski.
      p.cm.
    Includes bibliographical references and indexes.
    ISBN 1-56324-676-7 (alk. paper)
     1. Political parties—Europe, Eastern—Directories. 2. Political parties—Former
Soviet republics—Directories. 3. Post-communism—Europe, Eastern.
4. Post-communism—Former Soviet republics. I. Title.

JN96.A979 B84 2002
320.947′09′049—dc21   2001032823

I dedicate this book to Margarita,
who finally saw me emerge from a stack of paper and
a pile of airline tickets and still recognized me.
For the life and love we share.

Contents

Author's Note

This guide provides detailed coverage of political developments in eighteen countries of Eastern Europe as well as two distinct political entities—Montenegro and Kosova—that were not internationally recognized states at the beginning of the twenty-first century. Both territories were still technically part of the Federal Republic of Yugoslavia—Montenegro as the sole remaining federal partner of Serbia, and Kosova as a province of Serbia. However, developments in the two territories in the late 1990s had effectively severed their political systems from that of Serbia, and so they will be treated separately here.

Acknowledgments

This encyclopedic volume took much longer to complete than was initially envisaged. The breadth and scope of the undertaking, spanning twenty countries and aspiring states, has involved extensive and intensive research, data gathering, fact sifting, and the condensing of pertinent material. Unlike in communist times, when a little information often went a long way, since the collapse of the single-party regimes, the sheer volume of information available has necessitated long hours of careful reading, analysis, and selection. Moreover, the rapidity and complexity of developments throughout Eastern Europe continue to perplex the layperson and specialist alike and invariably undermine conclusions and predictions. Work on this book also was slowed by my frequent trips to the region and by the various programs on behalf of the region conducted at the East European department at the Center for Strategic and International Studies (CSIS), in Washington, D.C.

The completion of this monumental endeavor would not have been possible without the encouragement and assistance that I have received at CSIS over the years. In particular, I am most indebted to Ilona Teleki, my research associate for her outstanding research skills and determination to bring this volume to fruition. Sudabeh Koochekzadeh also played a pivotal role in the various book-related projects. Among the legion of interns and research assistants who painstakingly gathered and processed the raw material, I must mention: Vesna Grujicic, Dominika Dabrowska, Lada Trifonova, Paul Nemes, Zlatica Sandels, Lana Skrtic, Ioana Copil-Popovici, Darko Pavlovic, Zuzana Jasenovkova, Marketa Houskova, Admirela Balic, Marusa Jamnik, Andrew Astapov, Karolina Ristova, Sonja Andonova, Thomas Hessel, Neven Crvenkovic, and Nevena Assenova. I would also like to thank all my interlocutors in the region, who are too many to mention, as well as the helpful staffs at several embassies in Washington, D.C., especially the Albanian, Macedonian, Czech, Ukrainian, Belarusian, Estonian, Lithuanian, Montenegrin, Slovak, Bulgarian, and Latvian missions.

Introduction: Pluralism and Democratization

More than a decade has passed since the one-party communist regimes in Eastern Europe collapsed like a row of dominos. The "demonstration effect" and the prospects of "democratic diffusion" helped scholars account for the rapid unraveling of communism. However, the "demonstration" that communist rule was brittle throughout the region did not automatically ensure the expected "effect" of crystallization of liberal democracies. Some of the new political leaders sought to preserve certain autocratic elements and even to weaken many initial democratic gains. Early predictions of rapid democratization and economic liberalism proved too optimistic, and warnings about the imminent rise of ultranationalism and perpetual ethnic conflicts proved too pessimistic. Instead, the eastern half of Europe has witnessed enormous diversification in the pace and content of political and economic transformation, and numerous challenges to the "completion" or consolidation of the democratization process. Indeed, the region as a whole can be viewed as an ongoing experiment in pluralism and liberalism, the results of which continue to vary from state to state.

In the wake of the 1989 revolutions many observers assumed that democracy, civil society, and market economics were so closely interrelated that the demise of single-party rule would herald the birth of all three pillars of a liberal order.[1] They disregarded a number of essential variables, including the legacies of communism, the social and cultural contexts in which the new institutions were supposed to function, the effectiveness of these institutions, and the new threats and challenges to democratic reform. The transformation process in the eastern half of Europe has involved fundamental shifts in public expectations, aspirations, responsibilities, and relationships with the state and with the emerging market system.

This introductory chapter provides an overall assessment of political development in the region, viewing the emergence of political parties and systems in a broader social and national context. It considers in turn the complex transition process, the persistent legacies of communism, the relationships between democracy and pluralism, the importance of constitutionalism and the separation of powers, authoritarian challenges to liberalism, nationalist threats to democracy, and the gradual emergence of a broad political spectrum. This overview enables a more informed assessment of the developing political structures in each of these twenty existing and aspiring East European states.

Eastern Europe's Transitions

The political earthquake that shook Eastern Europe in the fall of 1989 was a revolutionary event. It marked both the end of the one-party communist states imposed and maintained by an outside power (the Soviet Union), and the beginning of a comprehensive transformation of the region's political, economic, and social structures. This was the third time in a century that Eastern Europe had been convulsed by rapid systemic change. But unlike the national liberations of 1918 and the communist takeovers of 1945–1948, the 1989 revolutions proved remarkably peaceful. They developed without the threat of outside military intervention; they were generated and propelled by widespread public involvement; and they were directed by political actors who sought a smooth transition from monism to pluralism. In many respects (outside of Romania), these were "negotiated revolutions" whose leaders capitalized on profound social discontent to press for a new political arrangement, while in most instances avoiding mass arrests or purges of the outgoing regimes.

Any examination of political transition from communist authoritarianism to varieties of democratic pluralism cannot emphasize "objective" social and economic conditions alone, neglecting or underestimating more immediate and highly pertinent political and psychological elements. Several theorists of past transitions from authoritarian to democratic rule have stressed the role of long-term factors such as economic development or class conflict in bringing about revolutionary or systemic change.[2] But although such components evidently provide both parameters and constraints in a volatile revolutionary situation, they do not preordain either the form or the outcome of any process of transition.[3]

It is misleading to focus on the economic crisis in "real socialist" societies as the prime or sole determinant of the collapse of Communist Party rule. It can be argued that the centralized economies of Eastern Europe had been in a perpetual "crisis" for several years, beset by low industrial productivity, high energy consumption, continuous consumer shortages, and noncompetitiveness on world markets. But it would be more worthwhile to measure the impact of economic stagnation and material decline on the perceptions of broad sectors of the population.

Communist rulers largely had managed to cushion the working public from the full effects of economic failure by borrowing heavily from the West, preserving the Comecon trading network for poor-quality domestic products, increasing the money supply, or tolerating and encouraging the expansion of gray and black markets to meet public demands that the state sector could not fulfill. The ability of governments to protect the public from economic hardships was declining by the late 1980s. However, a full-blown crisis could still have been avoided for several years, especially in states not heavily indebted to Western creditors and where living standards remained relatively tolerable.

Thus, one cannot fully explain the revolutionary crisis by concentrating solely on economic conditions or on antagonisms between social classes, as Marxist and some post-Marxist writers have done.[4] Moreover, although Western sociologists and political scientists have fashioned exhaustive analyses of the causes and effects of "socialist" or "anti-colonial" revolutions, the literature on "anti-communist" or "post-socialist" revolutions is still in its formative stages. It is also riven by controversies between socioeconomic determinists in various guises and Kremlinologists primarily focusing on the Soviet role in the collapse of communist controls in Eastern Europe. Nonetheless, among the array of contributory conditions identified in this literature, several essentially political and psychological "subjective" factors clearly played a critical role in the breakout from monism in most states in the region.

First, there was an evident loss of regime confidence either that the political *status quo* could be preserved for much longer or that the use of force and repression could effectively prolong communist rule and not backfire against the government. In estimating costs and benefits, most East European leaders were not convinced that a violent crackdown would be supported by Moscow or effectively implemented by local military and police commanders, or that it would ensure prolonged social tranquility. After all, the effectiveness of martial law imposed in Poland in the early 1980s had proved short-lived, and it had failed to stimulate any meaningful economic recovery or acceptable political reforms.

Second, disputes and conflicts were evident within the leadership of the communist parties and governments regarding appropriate policy at a time of such unpredictable region-wide changes. Differences were evident between hard-line advocates of repression and reformists who calculated that some compromises with the opposition were essential to preserve social stability and improve their country's economic prospects. Government vacillation and compromises in turn encouraged opposition activists to press for more extensive concessions. Once a dialogue was initiated between the regime and local dissidents, prospects for a violent showdown receded. In addition, some sectors of the ruling elite—including government officials, local activists, satellite parties, and youth organizers—either declared their neutrality and withdrew support from the communist party leadership, or actively backed the democratic opposition, having concluded that revolutionary change was inevitable and retrenchment in orthodoxy unsustainable.

Third, as the communist authorities were seen to weaken and to waver, and as the tide of public protest swept the region, there was a visible decline in social acquiescence. Widening sectors of the intelligentsia and urban residents increasingly scorned government policy and rejected the implicit communist-era "social contract" by which independent activism had been forsaken in return for material security. Large public demonstrations became particularly notable in states that resisted political reform until fall 1989, including Czechoslovakia and the German Democratic Republic (GDR). These demonstrations were not only a method of expressing discontent but also an effective means of applying pressure on the incumbent governments. Their scale and intensity certainly aided the democratic activists during their "dialogue" with communist reformers.

Fourth, the strategies of opposition leaders proved highly effective in many states, in that violence was avoided and step-by-step compromises were arranged with the authorities.[5] The offer of negotiating a gradual transformation of the political system, and the discarding of violent or vengeful rhetoric, encouraged reformist officials to accede in order to salvage some of their positions, to gain a modicum of legitimacy, and to retain a measure of political influence for their liberalizing policies. Their abandonment of monopolistic communism in turn provoked rifts and splits within the ruling elite and helped accelerate the revolutionary process. The dissident counterelites were also able to organize a virtual alternative leadership and to mobilize credible and well-respected activists willing to fill vacant government positions. These stimuli for both stability and change helped promote a smooth and peaceful transition from totalitarian rule.

If a comparative approach to Eastern Europe's revolutionary transition from monism to pluralism is to be elaborated, an array of factors common to each state, and those peculiar to some of them, must be explored carefully. Oversimplified generalizations can be avoided if proper account is taken of economic conditions and popular perceptions of relative material circumstances; the extent and nature of political opposition and autonomous civic activity; and the factionalism within the governing circles in their approaches to political and economic reform. The interplay of various political forces must also be examined, from the inception of the regime–opposition dialogue, through the initial political compromises, to the remodeling of key governmental institutions. At each stage, the progress of democratization was contingent upon successfully negotiated bargains and workable compromises that could pacify public opinion and satisfy dissident demands without provoking a backlash by the retreating elite.

The breakout from communism was both a revolutionary event and part of a far-ranging transition. Indeed, it would be difficult to demarcate when the revolution or the transition was completed. Events were "revolutionary" because of the sweeping nature of the changes, entailing the wholesale transformation of key political and economic institutions, and because of the suddenness and speed of the communist collapse. They were "transitional" in that revolutionary developments were part of a process of transformation between two distinct political and economic systems. However, the transition could not be easily delineated, because it involved two simultaneous processes: a breakdown of existing structures and the emergence of new ones. In some instances, institutions such as parliaments and governments were merely revived, and were given a democratic substance. In other cases, new institutions were established, such as autonomous political parties or trade unions, as the machinery of pluralism.

To assess the degree of completion of each political transformation, one must examine the critical ingredients of the transition process: the surrender of power by the old regime at various political and administrative levels; the restructuring or rebuilding of key institutions; the democratization of the participatory process; and the expansion and consolidation of political pluralism. The transition to pluralism could not be readily mapped out in advance; the process was improvised and marked by compromises, slowdowns, and renewed bursts of activity. It also affected different political institutions with variable intensity, as political contestants attempted to benefit from the reforms either by propelling them forward or slowing down the process. Disputes revolved around the speed of transformation, the preservation of the broad coalitions that dislodged communist rule, and the division of powers and responsibilities among different governmental bodies.

It would be difficult to determine when a former communist system has become a stable and durable democracy. Much depends on the regularization of the formal features of democratic rule, including the periodic holding of free and fair, general and local elections; open competition between rival political parties; and the democratization and depoliticization of governmental and public institutions. Attention must also be paid to the extent of social participation, the degree of accountability, and the successful passage of important legislation. There may be unforeseen obstacles to democratic progress due to bureaucratic obstruction, nationalist manipulation, or persistent social disquiet. Parliament may be tied up in debates delaying the passage of vital legislation and obstructing institutional reform. In addition, the abrupt marketization of the economy can lead to major social disruption, impeding the development of specific democratic interest groups and embroiling the government principally in pacifying public unrest.

The disintegration of communist rule consisted of a combination of elite concessions, oppositionist pressures, and broad public support for change.[6] In the early stages, the revolutionary process was propelled primarily by dissident groups outside the ruling parties. Through pressure and persuasion, the dissidents forged provisional compacts with reformist communist elements in the pursuit of free, multiparty elections.[7] These largely peaceful revolutions ushered in a number of democratizing and liberalizing reforms throughout most of Eastern Europe. The most fundamental of these reforms included the termination of a single-party political monopoly; a respect for civil liberties and human rights; fundamental constitutional changes; increasing openness in the mass media; and the onset of judicial reform. Competitive elections were held on a regular basis. Parliaments and governments became genuine decision-making bodies, and political and organizational pluralism began to mushroom. Of course, the pace and scope of the democratic transformation varied among states.

Some analysts contend that a measure of "elite continuity" contributed to democratic development and national stability.[8] This effect has been evident in countries where a number of communist officials managed to or were allowed to adapt to democratic rule without major political losses, as was the case in Poland and Hungary. A degree of elite continuity prevented potentially disruptive conflicts, extraparliamentary opposition, and state repression. Accommodation, cooperation, and negotiated power-sharing among major elite groups, especially in the early stages of the post-communist transition, assisted in a smoother democratic transition. Elite division and fragmentation during the transition tended to undermine democratization and to perpetuate authoritarian habits.

During the past decade, new dividing lines have descended across the eastern part of the continent. Although not as impervious or stark as the defunct "Iron Curtain," they have nevertheless served to differentiate a number of subregions, including Central Europe, the Baltics, the post-Soviet region, and the Balkans, as areas of diversified progress toward democracy, pluralism, capitalism, stability, and security. The Central European and Baltic countries have moved faster than others in the enactment of political reforms, and all have held at least two multiparty national and local elections.

The first general elections were essentially plebiscites that resolved to legitimately break the communist stranglehold on power. They were won by broad-based national fronts or anti-communist coalitions of small parties or large movements. Their ideologies and programs were often blurred, and they invariably fissured soon after the assumption of power. These coalitions and their constituents were poorly organized and thus lacked durability, cohesion, and sustained programmatic competition. Their platforms consisted of a single overriding goal—to remove the communists from government. Subsequent ballots and the disintegration of the broad oppositionist movements in countries such as Lithuania, Poland, and the Czech Republic led to the emergence of more significant political formations. Nonetheless, most political parties and constituencies remain in flux.

The social base of political parties was shallow and shifting, which created additional problems for administrations seeking dependable public support and stable parties to mobilize and discipline voters and to implement reforms. State and party institutions generally possessed low levels of legitimacy in post-communist states precisely because of the communist legacy. Early elections became a mechanism for legitimizing the revamped institutions as well as for reducing the number of political parties formed during Leninism's demise. Many groups dropped out, or merged into larger coalitions to over-come the handicaps of limited electoral support and a shortage of funding. The elections were also a learning process for new political leaders, with regard to organizing, campaigning, and networking with the electorate.[9]

The early pro-democracy formations splintered into a number of small parties based on individual personalities and friendship networks rather than political programs. The proliferation of such political parties in governance was controlled by the establishment of stipulations that a minimum percent-age of the popular vote must be won in order for a party to gain seats in parliament. The organizational and programmatic consolidation of these small parties is still continuing in much of the region.

Sherman Garnett[10] makes a useful distinction among four categories of post-communist states: regimes with functioning democracies and robust civil societies; pluralist systems with weak democratic institutions and nascent civil societies; regimes that place order above democracy; and unstable regimes. The transition process between these categories is generally slow because of entrenched, conservative political interests, rudimentary civic cultures, and weak legislatures. Countries in the third and fourth categories are also char-acterized by bureaucratism, widespread corruption, a weak commercial sec-tor, the absence of an effective judicial system, the manipulation of populist and nationalist themes, cliquish politics, and the persistence of patronage net-works in which elements of the old *nomenklatura* continue to dominate.

During the past decade, most of the Central European and Baltic countries (Poland, Hungary, Czech Republic, Slovakia, Slovenia, Estonia, Latvia, and Lithuania) have displayed greater success in building stable pluralistic de-mocracies than the majority of post-Soviet and Southeast European states. In countries of Central Europe and the Baltic region, organized and broad-based alternative elites were present, and a wide spectrum of political parties emerged in which the influence of extremist groupings was effectively marginalized. Nevertheless, in the early stages of transition, many of the new ex-dissident leaders lacked political experience. A professional and effective class of poli-ticians clearly takes time to develop and mature. The reformist states of Cen-tral Europe and the Baltic area also proved more successful in developing an independent entrepreneurial middle class and establishing the institutional un-derpinnings of a private, non-state economy. This does not mean that democra-tization has been completed in Central and Baltic Europe. Further legal, political, and property reforms are necessary to bring these states into line with standards prevailing throughout Western Europe and to consolidate their development as viable contenders for European Union (EU) membership.

A decade after the unraveling of communist totalitarianism, several Balkan governments have either deliberately stalled the democratization process or unintentionally failed to capitalize on the opportunity to institutionalize lib-eral democracies. Furthermore, the anti-civilian wars in Croatia, Bosnia-Herzegovina, and Kosova have perpetuated the perception of ceaseless ethnic conflicts and intolerant nationalism as the inescapable destiny of the Balkan peoples.[11] Such images have undermined efforts to help transform the region and lay the groundwork for European integration. Although the ongoing turmoil in the Balkans is symptomatic of a deeply rooted political, economic, and social malaise, it is important to examine its context as well as the commonalities and differences among these states as they progress through complex transformations.

The Balkan states share a common history of communist rule, with all of its attendant legacies: political centralization, party control over state institutions and public bodies, police repression, centralized command economies, the outlawing of private initiatives, and the persistent atomization of society. However, three diverse communist systems operated in the Balkans, with different implications for post-communist reform: an essentially Stalinist and isolationist regime in Albania; orthodox communist regimes in the Soviet-bloc states of Romania and Bulgaria; and a more reformed communist system in Yugoslavia, that shared certain features with the Central European countries. In the most repressive systems (Albania and Romania), the opposition movements were weak, divided, disorganized, and without any significant social influence. Pervasive police controls, public fear, and widespread apathy prevented any large-scale manifestations of dissent and independent social activism. There was an absence of an alternative elite that could sow the seeds of a pluralistic civil society, and a dearth of large independent churches or other institutions that could nourish political and civic activism. In addition, the private economic sector was virtually nonexistent in Albania, Bulgaria, and Romania, and as a result there were no embryonic entrepreneurial interest groups that could help give impetus to the reform program. Power struggles within the ruling communist parties were largely between hard-liners and reformers rather than between intrasystem reformers and liberalizers favoring a multiparty system. Although a sizeable dissident movement functioned in several of Yugoslavia's constituent republics, no far-reaching political and economic liberalization emerged. Instead, reformist programs increasingly focused on questions of nationality, ethnicity, independence, and statehood—questions that diverted popular attention from the prospect of systemic transformation and that strengthened the hand of nationalist and authoritarian politicians in several republics.

In much of Southeastern Europe, the reform process has been obstructed by an entrenched post-communist political stratum, sometimes in alliance with populist or nationalist streams in the ex-dissident movement. Sectors of the old elite have managed to benefit directly from the limited reforms undertaken, preserving many of their offices, privileges, and resources. The development of a participatory civic society and the rule of law have been delayed by an assortment of authoritarian forces, many of which have manipulated populist, nationalist, welfarist, and statist themes to uphold their political positions. These negative trends have been particularly evident in several former Yugoslav republics, where the process of state building (or rebuilding) has taken precedence over political and economic reform, even though their points of departure in the late 1980s were comparable to those of the Central European states.

Democracy, Pluralism, and Capitalism

An enormous literature exists in political theory on the definition of democracy. Michael Saward considers "responsive rule" the prime determinant of democracy, measured in terms of the correspondence between acts of government and the wishes of citizens, and in the establishment and functioning of procedures designed to secure responsiveness.[12] In this context, the major indices of democratization include basic freedoms (speech, movement, assembly, and association); citizenship and participation to maximize responsive rule (the right to run for public office and to vote); appropriate administrative codes (governmental accountability and public notification); and adequate social rights (in health, security, and education). All such rights and freedoms must be guaranteed to each citizen regardless of the will of the majority or the minority, and they must be protected by the constitution and by a judicial system that is not part of the majoritarian decision-making process.

According to David Beetham, democracy is concerned with the making of collectively binding decisions about the rules and policies of a society.[13] It therefore consists of two main principles: popular control and political equality. Popular control involves the exertion of citizens' will over decisionmakers rather than over the entire decision-making process, and it requires a set of institutions and procedures designed to make that control effective. Political equality entails an equality of votes among electors and an equal right to stand for political office. In Beetham's analysis, popular control over the government rests on popular elections; the inclusiveness of parties, candidates, and voters; the fairness of elections and their independence from government control; the accountability of government to the parliament for the execution of policy; legal accountability of government to courts, ensuring that officials operate within the law; financial accountability of government to the legislature and the courts; guaranteed civil and political rights, including the open expression of dissent; and a vibrant civil society, involving a network of organizations through which people manage their own affairs and place checks on governmental powers.

Democracy is best measured as a series of values arranged in a continuum rather than as an absolute phenomenon that is either present or lacking. Among the criteria for measuring the degree of democracy in a particular state, one must include the following: presidential and legislative elections that are free, fair, and open; fair election laws; effective parliamentary power; multiple political parties; decentralized political power; the absence of political censorship; open public discussion; freedom of political organization, assembly, and demonstration; the nondiscriminatory rule of law, including an independent judiciary; and freedom from police persecution.[14] Formal democratic institutions are insufficient for the existence of a liberal democracy. Without an independent society arranged through various crosscutting interest groups, democracy may degenerate into authoritarianism. Hence the strength of a civic society can be measured by both "negative" and "positive" liberties. The former include such factors as freedom from government interference, and checks and balances against the accumulation of nonaccountable power.[15]

During the past decade, Eastern Europe has witnessed the emergence of an embryonic civil society in which the linkages within society and between society and state have developed slowly. The long process of rebuilding a civil society fractured and atomized by communism has been accompanied by both an autonomous political rebirth and widespread political fragmentation. This has been reflected in social diversification and organizational pluralism, with little solid party identification. Most political parties have had a limited social base and restricted regional structures. According to several public opinion polls, only a minority of respondents in each state during the first four years of the post-communist era identified themselves with a specific political party. Furthermore, there was little public trust in political parties—a reaction against the earlier enforced communist "partyism." But this did not mean that citizens lacked values and interests; it merely indicated their deep-rooted suspicion of party politics and fear of renewed party interference in their social lives.[16]

The relation between the political and the economic transformations in East European states must also be carefully considered. An intense debate has raged during the past decade on whether simultaneous political and economic reforms will be successful or will jeopardize one another's success. Some analysts have argued that democratic rule is not a necessary condition for creating a market economy and indeed may generate widespread opposition to the painful economic reforms being introduced. In their view, the consolidation of liberal democracy should be undertaken only after successful economic reforms have spawned a strong middle class.[17] However, this sequencing of economic and political reform is difficult to apply or justify in Eastern Europe because of such factors as public pressure, counterelite expectations, the ideologies of reformist parties, and the requirements of foreign governments, multinational institutions, and international lenders. The debate in the region has focused instead on the sequencing of structural economic reforms, and whether these should be gradual or radical. Whereas radical economic reformers are invariably political liberals, gradualists may be statists, socialists, or authoritarians who use the slowness of reform to preserve their power bases and economic interests. Although not all anti-communist opposition groups and dissident activists were initially free-marketeers and liberals, many increasingly have come to understand that economic freedoms, market forces, and structural reforms are essential for ensuring broader political liberties.

Long delays in overhauling and marketizing the economy may initially cushion the population and the regime against the rigors of a market economy. But in the long term, this regressive policy will simply drive the government further into debt and make the unavoidable reforms that much more painful and destabilizing in the future. Furthermore, where governing parties have unfairly dispensed privileges to a politically loyal elite, and where the legal system is unreformed or tied to party-state interests, corruption and mismanagement become endemic. Serious economic decline in conditions of political favoritism, organized corruption, and social revolt can rapidly propel a country toward authoritarian rule and provide opportunities for political factions determined to engineer ethnic and international conflicts.

In general, the higher the level of economic development, the greater the chance for sustainable democracy without a relapse into autocracy.[18] Moreover, there is a close correlation between democracy and a market economy. The former is barely possible without the latter, although the latter is conceivable without the former. In transitions from authoritarian systems, the creation of new political regimes is the major objective; post-communist democratization aims to establish both a productive economic system and a responsive political structure. In some instances, these two projects clash, and the pursuit of necessary but unpopular economic reforms can obstruct or derail the political transition.

Political Systems and the Separation of Powers

Eastern Europe has undergone a decade of transition from systems in which governments were unconstrained by their own laws, to constitutionalism and the rule of law.[19] Constitutionalism is a system in which a body of fundamental laws establishes the powers of government, institutionalizes the limits to its operations, and defines the prerogatives and responsibilities of officials. Throughout the region, parliaments in effect took on the task of constitutional assemblies, calling into question the impartiality and effectiveness of the constitution-making process. Andrew Arato argues that it is unwise to allow a legislature the authority to alter its own powers through constitutional changes and that a special constitutional convention instead should be called for the purpose of creating a new constitution.[20] In the eastern half of Europe no constitutional conventions were established, and transitional constitution making largely was subject to the vicissitudes of various domestic political struggles, including that between competing agendas of victorious parties after the first elections; to conflicts between old and emerging constitutions; and to imprecision of language. Moreover, there were delays in creating constitutions, as a result of intensive political struggle to control this process. Some analysts argue that a slower process of constitution making is preferable for conferring legitimacy, avoiding partisan pitfalls, and gradually establishing mechanisms for limiting government and countering potential abuses of power.

A more gradual approach also enables a clearer focus on creating provisions for establishing the structure of government.[21] In the new East European constitutions it has been particularly necessary to protect party and organizational pluralism, civil society, and marketization; to create legitimate governmental structures; to safeguard private property and reduce dependence on the state; and to guarantee the personal security necessary for democratic citizenship. A constitutional court or some other independent tribunal has also proved important to protect these rights.

The emerging democracies differ enormously in their form and structure. They include distinctions between presidential, prime ministerial, and parliamentary systems; federal and unitary structures; and majoritarian and consensualist procedures. According to Raymond Taras, there has tended to be a drift toward, rather than a decision in favor of, a particular type of political system. Whether a parliamentary or presidential system becomes dominant in any state depends on "relations between the first democratically elected president and the legislature, on the political ambitions of members of the new elite ensconced in different branches of government, and on the prevailing consensus about the desirability of strong leadership and the extent of checks and balances."[22]

Taras has argued that high degrees of elite continuity have been accompanied by centralized authoritarianism hiding behind a thin veneer of democratic form. Hence, both in order to eliminate the Leninist fusion of political power and to preclude new forms of political dominance, the separation of powers or the "division of governmental responsibilities" appears necessary for democratization to succeed. However, such a division in an embryonic democracy can also lead to fragmentation, paralysis, and permanent inter-institutional conflict (for example, between president and parliament). Fragmented parliaments and weak governments were characteristic of most East European states during their period of independence prior to World War II. This factor, together with a major economic downturn, provided an impetus for the emergence of authoritarian presidential systems during the 1930s.

In some cases, parliaments have become arenas for legitimate contests between opposing political parties. In other instances, the legislature has become a power center in its own right, challenging the executive for ultimate control over policymaking and often leading to political gridlock.[23] Disputes have also materialized on whether single-party or coalition cabinets are more effective. The former may exclude the views and inputs of important political forces with significant public support. The latter may lead to legislative gridlock, political paralysis, or ineffective policies as each party seeks to protect its special interest.

The rivalry between president and parliament has proved most destabilizing in the region. Institutional conflicts have been commonplace, particularly where a president elected in a direct popular ballot has represented one political formation and the majority of parliament (and the government) belongs to an alternative political tendency. But even in cases where the president is from the same party as the parliamentary majority, disputes over prerogatives and powers may occur. Where the president is both head of state and the chief executive, power may become monopolized and lead to the neglect or outright dismissal of constitutional limitations on the presidential office. Jakub Karpinski asserts that strong presidencies have proliferated in post-communist countries, as a legacy of the Leninist system; presidents replaced communist party secretaries-general as ultimate decisionmakers.[24] However, countries with longer or deeper traditions of parliamentary democracy, such as the Czech Republic and Estonia, have managed to restrict the role of their presidents.

An intensive debate has raged over the past decade as to which system is more appropriate in transitional political systems: a strong executive presidency like that in the United States or France, or a parliamentary system similar to that of Britain or Italy. The major difference between parliamentary and presidential systems is that in the former the head of government (premier) is dependent on the confidence of the parliament and its majority and can be dismissed together with his/her cabinet by a vote of no confidence, whereas in the latter the head of state (president) is elected for a fixed, constitutionally determined term and cannot be forced to resign under normal conditions.[25] In addition, in a dominant presidential system, the cabinet is accountable to a popularly elected president, who can dismiss the government.

Whereas presidents are popularly elected in presidential systems, premiers are selected by legislatures in parliamentary systems. In the former type of system there is a separation of executive and legislative powers, and in the latter there is a fusion of these powers. Presidential systems have a single executive; parliamentary systems have collegial executives based in the cabinet. Both systems have advantages and disadvantages. Presidentialism has executive stability but may foster executive-legislative stalemate or a "winner-take-all" government; parliamentarism has greater consensus building potential but may foster a frequent turnover of unstable governments. Parliamentary systems may remain particularly weak if political parties are fragile and the legislative process becomes fractured and disorderly.

Some observers in Eastern Europe have favored a powerful president who can issue decrees, appoint and dismiss the government, or even suspend parliament in order to push through an agenda of far-reaching economic reform. However, this allows for few guarantees against a presidential dictatorship and the possible reversal of both democratic and market reforms. Ambitious heads of state may try to undercut restrictions on their powers by creating presidential parties, playing various coalition parties or ministries against each other, balancing the government against the parliament, and exploiting legislative gridlock. In some cases, such as that of Belarus, the incumbent president has acted arbitrarily and undemocratically to dissolve parliament and impose personal rule.

Most states in Eastern Europe have established parliamentary forms of government in which the executive (prime minister and cabinet) is responsible to parliament, and governments are formed by coalitions of the majority parliamentary parties. The powers of the president have varied but are generally limited. Most countries have opted for direct presidential elections combined with cabinet governments headed by a prime minister: in other words, they have adopted neither the British nor the American system. Nevertheless, disputes have continued between proponents of a strong presidency and those favoring an accountable government with a parliamentary base.

Matthew Shugart argues that not all the systems of government that emerged in the region can be neatly identified as either purely presidential or parliamentary.[26] Many are mixed in complex ways, and one must look at the precise powers and prerogatives of each president, including their degree of veto power over legislation and government formation. Shugart concludes that the more poorly institutionalized and fragmented the party system, the greater the opportunities for the president to exploit any political divisions and increase his or her influence even where presidential powers have been restricted by constitutional stipulations.

The question of unitarianism versus federalism has also preoccupied several countries in the region, especially during the disintegration of Yugoslavia into its component federal and autonomous units. A unitary government is generally considered to be more effective in holding a country together. For this reason, suspicions have been voiced in states such as Romania, Slovakia, and Macedonia that support for federalism among the major ethnic minorities could lead to eventual calls for separatism. Nevertheless, even in unitary states, pressures for decentralization, regionalism, and local autonomy have continued throughout the 1990s and have been viewed as important for democratic development and local empowerment based largely on territory and residency rather than nationality or ethnic allegiance. Indeed, with the undermining of centralized communist controls, local politicians and parties have assumed more prominence, whether as reformist pro-democratic forces, as post-communist restorationists, or as populist nationalists with a separatist or anti-minority agenda.

The Communist Inheritance

Culturally, organizationally, ideologically, institutionally, economically, and socially, Marxism-Leninism has had a negative long-term impact on the evolution of liberal democracies in Eastern Europe. A political culture of dialogue, tolerance, liberalism, and compromise has shallow roots in much of the region. Communism fostered an anti-democratic political culture and public disassociation from politics. Atrophy, alienation, and public detachment from politics meant that people cased to believe in the efficacy of common actions and immersed themselves in their private lives. This undercut the pursuit of a participatory and politically influential civil society.

Communist rule significantly distorted political relations also by prescribing seemingly easy solutions to intricate problems. This legacy has infused governmental policy and permeated public debate in much of the region and resulted in turns toward simplistic populist, nationalist, and xenophobic solutions to complex structural and systemic problems. Political tolerance and compromise have too often been perceived as weakness and indecision, and strong and determined leaders are extolled even if their policy prescriptions lack substance and positive impact. The Leninist legacy has fostered various sources of radicalism, including ideological zeal, self-righteousness, intolerance, egalitarian populism, contempt for cultural elites, and a pervasive suspicion of foreign influences.[27]

Given the extreme repressiveness of the communist system in states such as Albania and Romania, the opposition movements there were weak, divided, and disorganized. Pervasive police controls, public fear, and widespread apathy thwarted any large-scale manifestations of dissent and independent social activism. There were no alternative elites to sow the seeds of a pluralistic civil society, and few large, independent churches to nourish civic activism. Moreover, a private economic sector and entrepreneurial class were virtually nonexistent in countries such as Albania, Bulgaria, and Romania. These facts seriously hampered the emergence of a strong reformist and internationalist lobby. The power struggles within the ruling communist parties in several Balkan and post-Soviet states were largely between dogmatists and reformers rather than between intrasystem reformers and liberalizers favoring a multiparty system.

To divert and control public attention, the region's new authoritarians have invariably identified ethnic, religious, cultural, or other minority groups as national traitors or alien enemies seeking to subvert both society and the state. With public attention riveted on scapegoats, several post-communist leaders have slowed down progress in civic acculturation, political participation, and the promulgation of liberal values. In such conditions, political life has frequently veered toward polarization, intolerance, and purposively engineered nationality conflicts. The decades of communist rule did not "freeze" ethnic relations or bury nationalist ideologies, as is commonly assumed. Political leaders often have exploited ethnic nationalism to replace the failing notions of class struggle and socialist internationalism. It was relatively easy for many communist functionaries schooled in collectivism and centralism to adopt overtly nationalist positions once the old system was defunct. Ethnic nationalism and state protection provided a political context for new alliances between former communists and ultranationalist anticommunists. Such concords helped deflect public attention from the burdens and necessities of political and economic reconstruction. Serbia and Croatia are the most pertinent examples of this process.

Leninism disfigured the Balkan societies by stifling the emergence of civil societies. It tended to buttress collectivist models of individual and group obligations to the state, rather than the principles of individual liberty and human rights protected by the government. When communist rule disintegrated, democratic institutions only slowly emerged in many of these societies, and public input into decisionmaking remained limited. Moreover, communist regimes poorly developed the principles of mediating and resolving intergroup disputes, including disputes based on distinctive ethnic and religious interests. Instead, cultural, ethnic, and political diversity was depicted as a threat to both nation and state.

Institutionally, under the old system, parliaments and other public bodies were formalistic structures, merely rubber-stamping the decisions of the communist leadership or acting as transmission belts for party policy. They provided a veneer of democratic legitimacy without having any real decision-making substance. Although the reinvigorated national institutions in the post-communist era gained genuine and popular democratic legitimacy, they also created some confusion and conflict between the different branches of government. This resulted in constitutional battles stemming from incessant competition for post-electoral authority.

Parliamentary development was obstructed also by the lack of a tradition of genuine constituency representation and of a competent and qualified network of parliamentary advisors enabling an efficient decision-making process. A similar situation prevailed in the administration, which lacked a publicly accountable bureaucracy and rational operating procedures. As a result, governments and parliaments, particularly in the early stages of democratization, were often reliant on the old communist apparatus and an array of official timeservers.[28]

In the economic arena, communist rule not only stifled development and modernization but it prohibited the emergence of an entrepreneurial middle class that could generate political liberalism and internationalization. It institutionalized the populace's dependence on the state for subsistence. Social groups and individuals were discouraged from taking any initiative, barred from organizing independently, and prevented from undertaking autonomous economic activities, which were condemned as "speculation" or "bourgeois deviations." The public viewed the state as protector and expected full employment and job security, cheap consumer prices for staples and basic commodities, and a comprehensive welfare system. When the statist system began to crumble and market relations were introduced and government spending was reduced, sizeable sectors of society were unprepared and failed to understand the necessity of such measures in order to rescue the ailing economies. As a result, public support increased, in the second round of national elections, for some of the communist successor parties that promised less severe economic policies and greater social welfare provisions.[29]

Socially, communist party rule had a negative impact on public perceptions of politics in general and political parties in particular. This popular disdain and suspicion limited public participation in the political process and hampered the development of party structures. Many citizens continued to view politics as an activity of the privileged elite on which public opinion had little impact. Much of the public had little familiarity with party competition, deal making, and political compromise in a democratic and pluralistic setting. To foster public trust in the reform program, some political leaders favored a far-reaching "lustration" process to eliminate and prohibit ex-communist functionaries from acquiring public office or purchasing privatized state companies. Pragmatists countered that a sweeping purge of this kind would upset the progress of reforms by provoking a political backlash and would prevent the emergence of a tolerant democratic state.

According to Jacques Rupnik, there are substantial differences between the Central European states on the one hand and many of the Balkan and post-Soviet countries on the other hand, in terms of their communist and oppositionist legacies.[30] The former moved swiftly toward institutional stability, the rule of law, a market economy, a stable party structure, and the development of civil society. Many of the latter have languished in "illiberal democracies" or "semi-authoritarian" systems and have engaged in gradual reforms and postponed far-reaching privatization.

The surprising success of neocommunist parties in Poland, Hungary, and Lithuania in the second series of national elections rekindled fears of counter-revolution throughout the region. These fears were exaggerated, due to ignorance of the complexities of transitional politics, and to a failure to anticipate the adaptability of former party members to post-communist realities. After losing its grip on power, the communist apparatus splintered into several interest groups. At least five fractions continued to operate throughout the 1990s either to protect their positions or to benefit from the reform process. In the economic realm, market reforms simulated the rapid metamorphosis of many well-connected communists into new capitalists. Access to assets and information gave many members of this "red bourgeoisie" a head start over entrepreneurs who had not been party members. Top-level managers began to focus on profit making, and benefited from the "insider" privatization process.

Beyond these new entrepreneurs, a larger category of the former *nomenklatura* remained ensconced as part of the bureaucratic strata. Thousands of mid-level party bureaucrats continued to occupy numerous government offices and in some cases resisted and slowed down the reform process, not out of ideological conviction but primarily to maintain their jobs in rapidly shifting economies. In some states, they backed socialist or social democratic parties, viewing them as guarantors of an expansive state bureaucracy. In other countries, as in parts of the former Yugoslavia, they supported pro-independence or nationalist forces that would provide them with employment in the new republican administrations.

Communists remained active also in the political arena. Some former officials displayed resilience, pragmatism, and adaptability to the new conditions and transformed themselves into an assortment of political actors.

Ex-communist activists can be divided into three main groups: orthodox dogmatists, social democrats, and populist nationalists. Orthodox Marxist-Leninists constitute only marginal elements in each state and have failed to mount any serious political challenges even among workers dismayed by rising unemployment. The more astute ex-communists switched to socialist and social democratic positions, seeking to fill the political vacuum to the left of the new liberal democrats. They calculated that a remodeled democratic left would gain credibility as a viable opposition and could maneuver itself into place to form future governments.

Most of these new center-left formations scored well in the second series of general elections, having inherited substantial financial assets and organizational networks. They proved skillful in presenting themselves as the protectors of vulnerable social categories, such as pensioners, manual workers, and farmers, exposed unfairly to the rigors of capitalism. However, once in power, most of these reborn democratic socialists did not attempt to reverse the course of economic reform. Some tried to maintain existing welfare programs, but others actually favored an acceleration of marketization and further cuts in state subsidies to unprofitable industries and welfare beneficiaries.

The most dangerous ex-communists have promoted nationalist and populist agendas. They have sought not only to stifle democratic and market reforms but also to replace class with ethnicity as a popular mobilizing device. Serbia, Croatia, and Bosnia-Herzegovina have been the prime examples of this process, although similar developments have been registered elsewhere. Nationalist demagogues represent the authoritarian tendency in post-communist politics, diverting the public agenda away from political and economic reforms and toward ethnic exclusivity and national protectionism.

Authoritarian Challenges

Several varieties of authoritarianism have emerged in the Balkans since the demise of the communist party-states.[31] As the former Marxist-Leninist parties discarded their traditional ideological positions, factions within them sought to retain or regain the most important levers of power and to benefit from the gradual dismantling of the centralized command economies. The ex-communists, the ex–anti-communists, and their various allies have adopted a flexible assortment of ideologies and programs so as to garner a sufficient measure of popular support to gain electoral office. They have attempted to manipulate public opinion to their advantage, rallying their constituents around two major clusters of issues: statist populism and ethnic nationalism.[32] (In some cases, even anti-communist politicians have veered toward authoritarian politics in order to impose a "new national order.")

In contrast to their communist predecessors, the statist populists have not presented a clear ideological message, and they lack a credible, long-term socioeconomic program. Instead, they have appealed to broad sectors of the population by offering simplistic remedies to complex economic and social problems. They have underscored the importance of the state in providing political continuity, strong leadership, public security, and a broad if leaky welfare umbrella.

They have not tried to revive classic Leninist parties with the intention of recommunizing their societies and reestablishing an absolute monopoly over political life but instead have exploited the transformation process to their advantage and have adopted strategies to undercut democratic, liberal, and reformist groupings. Serbia and Croatia in the 1990s exemplified this political strategy, regardless of whether their ruling regimes can be characterized as ethnic nationalist.

The new authoritarian leaders closely intertwined the ruling party with all government organs. This approach has been defined as "partitocracy" even though it falls short of a totalitarian one-party system. In some cases they used the strong presidential system specified in national constitutions to promote their powers, and disregarded parliamentary prerogatives, the division of powers, and constitutionalism. In other instances they benefited from political flux and constitutional and legal ambiguities to strengthen personal and party decisionmaking. One-party domination has been buttressed by the form of public administration prevalent in much of the region. In some states, instead of a merit system in the civil service, a "spoils system" developed, in which the election winners replaced virtually all government workers and administrators with party loyalists.

New authoritarian governments have ensured unequal political competition through their control of the most important public institutions and media outlets, especially state television and radio. They have retained most of the former communist party assets, communications networks, and organizational structures. They have deliberately slowed judicial reform and prevented the emergence of an independent judiciary. At the local level, especially in rural areas, the post-communist networks have remained particularly pervasive. Hence, the democratic forces have generally proved more successful in the larger and more cosmopolitan urban zones than in smaller towns and villages.

Statist populists in many cases established personal networks and broad patronage systems. Through them political loyalists benefited from the distribution of state assets and from quasi-privatization. The ruling parties maintained a system of intelligence gathering and police surveillance vis-à-vis the political opposition. Although not as pervasive or repressive as under communist rule, these practices nonetheless have hampered the development of a liberal democracy. In sum, the new autocrats calculated that formal democracy could coexist with informal authoritarianism. Instead of seeking to destroy all vestiges of political pluralism, the leader estimated that selective controls over the most important state and public institutions could preserve their positions of power within a quasi-democratic framework while diminishing the risks of their being publicly labeled as communists and dictators.

A further set of factors has assisted the nondemocratic elites: the political, ideological, and organizational fragmentation of the diverse democratic and liberal oppositionist movements. The broad anti-communist fronts formed during the collapse of Leninism in Romania, Bulgaria, and elsewhere, splintered as a result of personality clashes and policy differences. These movements found it difficult to gain sizeable constituencies, to construct stable political parties, and to build durable coalitions. This left open the political space to authoritarian, populist, and nationalist parties. The rebuilding of democratic coalitions broad enough to dislodge the state populists from power has proved difficult. Nevertheless, Romania, Bulgaria, and Croatia have succeeded in forming viable and electable alternatives in recent years. But, the danger remains that political power may continue to oscillate between liberal and anti-liberal alternatives in several unstable states.

Statist populists, often with a communist heritage, have been accused by the political opposition of dictatorial tendencies. Instructively, similar charges have been leveled against the anti-communist Democratic Party in Albania, which during its spell in government in the mid-1990s also upheld tight controls over the mass media, the judiciary, the security forces, and other public institutions, and built its own network of patronage, clientelism, and cronyism. The pervasiveness and persistence of such phenomena indicates that the political culture of centralism, political exclusivity, and authoritarianism have remained deeply embedded in the region among a broad spectrum of parties, including some ex-dissident circles. Moreover, populism, nationalism, statism, and authoritarianism have been reinforced by a generally poor economic performance.

Nationalist Threats

Ethnic-nationalist parties share several commonalities, including a focus on the ethnic community as the subject of unity, sovereignty, and statehood.[33] However, they display important ideological and programmatic differences. Whereas some organizations emerged as radical anti-communists, others were formed, financed, or supported by the failing communist parties to preserve their powers and privileges and to undercut the position of liberal and democratic competitors. In some cases, nationalist platforms have been adopted as temporary tactics to gain electoral support. In other instances, they became more enduring features of an organization's identity and program.

Important differences exist between civic nationalism and ethnicity-based nationalism. The former displays tolerance toward minorities and focuses on loyalty to the state; the latter views the ethnic group or nation as the supreme object of allegiance and remains suspicious of democratic institutions and unrestricted political pluralism. Among ethnic nationalists, the majority, or the "core nation," is considered the only permissible "state-forming" entity. It must predominate demographically, and its control of the state must be enshrined in the constitution. A great deal of debate has taken place over the past decade with regard to the relationship between individual and collective rights. Whereas in a consolidated democracy the legal protection of individual liberties can coexist with that of minorities, in transitional or quasi-authoritarian systems individual rights can camouflage majority rule that effectively deprives minorities of protection.[34]

In their approach toward ethnic minorities, nationalist movements may be assimilationist or segregationist. Assimilationism, in turn, maybe of two varieties—civic assimilationism, in which ethnic identity is subordinate to individual citizenship, or ethnic assimilationism, in which minorities are denied any collective rights and are pressured to integrate into the allegedly homogeneous, dominant *ethnos*. The former position is supported by moderate nationalist democrats and liberals, and the latter by ethnic nationalists and militant nationalists. "Ethnocratic" regimes may espouse democracy for one dominant nation; in effect, however, the denial of full citizenship rights to minorities dissipates any genuine democratic currents.

Ethnic segregationism is either egalitarian or hierarchical. In the former, different ethnic groups are hypothetically afforded the opportunity of "equal but separate" development. In practice, however, unless the state is organized along genuinely federalist lines, such theoretical equivalence does not translate into equality in access to political office or economic resources. This type of ethnic segregation may actually foster the benign neglect of minorities, and in its most extreme form, promote apartheid. In a hierarchically segregated system, minority disadvantages are consolidated, and subordinate minorities have to rely on their own resources without state assistance. They are also prevented from gaining autonomy or sovereignty, which would evidently undermine the integrity of the state. In some cases, the new constitutions adopted in post-communist states have singled out the majority ethnic group as the state-forming nation, with attendant privileges, whereas all other ethnicities are considered minorities and invariably confront discrimination.

Five major varieties of nationalism have emerged in Eastern Europe since the unraveling of communist rule. Aside from their stress on national unity and sovereignty, they have demonstrated significant ideological and programmatic differences. Each has had differing implications and a varied impact on domestic developments. The forms of nationalism are not exclusive or permanent in any specific state: some movements may become radicalized, but others may moderate their positions over time or disappear altogether.

The first variety of nationalism is evident in the independence-focused formations. The disintegration of the Yugoslav, Soviet, and Czechoslovak federations spawned the birth of various nationalist movements whose primary focus was on attaining state independence. The most successful parties were broad umbrella movements, such as DEMOS in Slovenia and *Rukh* in Ukraine, that mobilized the public along a wide political spectrum in the pursuit of sovereignty. With the achievement of statehood, many of these movements splintered into moderate and extremist elements. Most commonly, nationalist groups have attained importance in conditions of rapid change, competition over resources, and threats to national boundaries. Moreover, elites in newly independent states have tended to increase their controls over the state to secure or safeguard independence.[35] In some instances, this has led to restrictions on democratic development and citizens' participation. In such situations, large ethnic minorities are often perceived as a threat to independence, and repressive measures may be adopted against such minorities.

Newly independent states often develop a broad spectrum of nationalist movements that employ nationalist rhetoric during the state-building process. Moderates may reach for national slogans, rituals, and symbols to maintain public support in the face of competition from more radical nationalist formations. Conversely, moderates may tolerate militant elements within their movement, to prevent the emergence of a popular and viable nationalist competitor that might derail the democratization process. In the post-Soviet context, various pro-independence parties recognized a need to display their national-patriotic credentials in contradistinction to the remaining communist parties, which were widely perceived to be under Moscow's tutelage. At the same time, some communist officials sought to ride the wave of nationalist sentiment to new sources of power in an independent state.

Separatist movements need not be xenophobic or racist; indeed, their definition of citizenship and nationality may be inclusive beyond the majority ethnic group. However, the ethnic question may become an important element of conflict in a multiethnic republic seeking independence, as was the case in Croatia and the three Baltic states, where the loyalty and status of the Serbian and Russian populations, respectively, came into question and figured prominently in the domestic political debates. Nationalism can grow rapidly during wars of independence when certain minorities are considered hostile to state independence and territorial integrity. Even after independence is won and armed hostilities cease, the governing party may purposively manipulate ethnic and religious divisions and resentments to maintain its popularity and electoral success; the ruling Croatian Democratic Union is a case in point.

The second category of nationalists are the moderates. Key distinctions between moderate and militant nationalists are found in the degree of emphasis placed on ethnicity for full citizenship rights, and in the policies pursued toward minority groups. Moderate or democratic nationalists are tolerant of ethnic diversity, and they are often assimilationist rather than segregationist or discriminatory toward minorities. However, some democratic nationalist organizations may contain more radical wings, such as the anti-Semitic Csurka faction in the ruling Hungarian Democratic Forum. Moderate nationalists support parliamentarism and constitutionalism, but like civic liberals, they generally oppose the expansion of collective rights to ethnic, religious, and regional minorities, as this would evidently undermine the democratization of the state.

Moderate nationalists support parliamentarism, constitutionalism, elections, and the separation of government powers. However, they may oppose the institutionalization of collective minority rights, either on the grounds of civicism (in which citizenship is not defined by ethnicity and where individual rights prevail) or those of nationalism (the pursuit of national integrity and ethnic exclusivity). Many have voiced opposition to granting "special privileges" to minorities, together with the belief that group rights undermine the civic polity and the democratization process. Moderate nationalists may adopt more repressive policies where minority leaders persist in seeking political or territorial autonomy. In contrast, moderate nationalist organizations with a good deal of popular support have emerged in Hungary, Albania, and Slovenia—countries that contain small and largely dispersed ethnic minorities that have not campaigned for political autonomy. However, in both Hungary and Albania the moderate nationalists in positions of government also have been active in behalf of sizable groups of their majority coethnics (i.e., Hungarians and Albanians) resident in neighboring states, where they are minorities.

Third are the conservative nationalist parties. Such groupings, espousing a more pronounced degree of ethnic chauvinism, have emerged throughout the region.Their origins and programs differ. Some consist of former communists who have adopted nationalist positions; others, of former anti-communist dissidents who have become xenophobes. Both kinds of parties are active in some states. The ideological underpinnings of conservative nationalism may include elements of clerical radicalism, folk traditionalism, and ethnic populism.

Conservative nationalism often combines Christian (or Islamic) radicalism with ethnic populism. The bond between the majority ethnic nation and the majority Church (whether Catholic, Orthodox, or Muslim) is emphasized, denigrating the status of the nonreligious and of other denominations. Christian (or Islamic) values are stressed in formulating government programs, and anti-Semitism is often visible in attacks against secularism, liberalism, intellectualism, and allegedly destructive "alien influences." Xenophobic ethnic populists underscore the development of the "national community" above all other political and economic considerations, and oppose foreign involvement in the national culture and economy. Minority communities are invariably scapegoated for supporting outside interests and unfairly benefiting from the economic transformation. Anti-minority measures are therefore prescribed to protect the "national community." Proponents of clerical radicalism seek to influence state policy by stressing religious values in the formulation of governmental programs. This has been evident in their stance against family planning, which they view as a largely self-imposed form of "national genocide," and in their support of compulsory religious education in public schools. Additionally, such parties tend to advocate or tolerate the involvement of the clergy in all political institutions. Religious radicals may be described as anti-consumerist and anti-materialist in the sense that they view economic competition, capitalism, profit making, and material acquisition as essentially corrupt and inspired by foreigners.

Folk traditionalism idealistically depicts the values of the peasantry, the village, and the countryside, glorifying a mythical pristine ethnic-national community untainted by foreign, alien, and modernizing influences. Conservative proponents of such an ideology display elements of anti-urbanism, anti-intellectualism, anti-capitalism, anti-cosmopolitanism, and anti-Semitism in their strivings for "national purity." The major planks of folk traditionalists include state protection for the agricultural population; a return to the idealized "traditional" values of nation, family, and religion; and the resuscitation of a purportedly endangered national culture. In some instances, nationalist traditionalists call for the restoration of a constitutional monarchy and complain about the democratic chaos associated with republican or democratic constitutions.

Another major component of conservative nationalist ideology has been anti-communism. Spokesmen for this ideology have exacerbated public perceptions that ex-communists have benefited most from the political and economic reforms, and they have typically called for the expulsion of all officials of the former regime from positions of authority. They have adopted a strong "law-and-order" platform, allegedly to eliminate corruption and crime and to provide full security for the "national community." Conservative nationalists commonly exaggerate threats to "national survival," whether from internal or external sources.

Conservative nationalist formations have been the majority ruling parties in Croatia and Bosnia-Herzegovina and have constituted important components of the opposition movement in Serbia and Montenegro. In Romania and Slovakia they have formed governing coalitions with the ex-communists. In Hungary and Macedonia they have gained a respectable percentage of parliamentary seats. In Poland, Ukraine, Albania, Bulgaria, Slovenia, and the Czech Republic they have proved marginal players in national politics, although their influence could increase in states experiencing internal turmoil and perceiving an outside threat.

The fourth major category is socialist nationalists. In some countries, splinter groups from the ruling communist parties adopted nationalist elements. In others, the ruling *nomenklatura* transformed itself into a socialist-nationalist formation. The ideology and program of such groupings have remained flexible, with their objective being to preserve as much as possible the powers and privileges of the ruling elite through the exploitation of nationalist themes. They may pose as protectors of "national interests" against internal and external subversion, and when in government, they may urge repressive campaigns against minority populations. They support the preservation of a large, state-centered economy and are protectionist vis-à-vis foreign investment and ownership of "national resources," a platform they may share with the conservative nationalists. Economic nationalism may span all five categories of national-ism, with state protection being sought from "foreign takeovers" and the trau-matic effects of unregulated international markets and multinational corporate takeovers.

Socialist nationalists are usually open to alliances with a broad range of political parties, including communist dogmatists and radical nationalists. They can flexibly alter their platforms and appeal to different constituencies in order to compete for power. By taking aboard explicitly nationalist issues, including the protection of "national integrity," the combating of autonomist trends among ethnic minorities and regionalists, and defense against "foreign penetration," socialist nationalists can broaden their constituency and entice some former anti-communist dissidents to join their ranks. The ruling post-communist parties in Serbia, Romania, Slovakia, and Bulgaria have consti-tuted regimes that were socialist nationalist to varying degrees, with broadly developed patronage networks controlling a substantial sector of the national economy.

The fifth formation is the neofascists.[36] The most radical ultranationalist groupings share many features of conservative and socialist nationalism but also display additional ingredients. There is a strong emphasis on the leader-ship principle, a strict party hierarchy, intolerance of any political opposition, and open hostility toward ethnic and religious minorities. Neofascism is mili-tantly ethnic-nationalist, stressing the nation's supremacy over all minorities, foreigners, and neighboring states. Claims are often made on other nations' territories that are inhabited by coethnics or that at one time were part of the state issuing the claim.

Neofascists deliberately exacerbate anti-minority sentiments by scape-goating specific groups as agents of foreign subversion. They openly advo-cate violence against minorities and propound strict conformism on behalf of "national interests" or "racial purity." In some cases, they have created clandestine paramilitary detachments or have recruited existing urban gangs, including skinheads, to their cause. Neofascists exhibit a propensity for ritu-alistic mysticism glorifying their ethnic culture and history, and often main-tain contacts with fascist émigrés, who may provide funds and literature for their organizations. They seek to build a mass national movement along-side a vanguardist militant party leadership and are disdainful of parlia-mentary democracy and political pluralism. In particular, they appeal to alienated young people, the unemployed, pensioners, and frustrated na-tionalist intellectuals.

Neofascist activists exhibit admiration for militarism and tend to promote uniforms and uniformity among their membership. Neofascist groups have been established throughout the region, but they have had a limited impact on political developments. Nevertheless, their existence remains a cause for con-cern among minorities and resident foreigners at risk of racist attacks. The potential radicalization of the youth at a time of profound social change and economic dislocation needs to be carefully monitored. Neofascists have been most active and visible in Serbia, Croatia, Romania, and Hungary, where they have tried to resuscitate the wartime pro-Nazi regimes; but their influence thus far has been limited.

Ethnic politics has been manipulated by a range of political groups. Leaders looking for popular support have capitalized on nationalist sentiments and exploited minorities and foreigners as scapegoats. In some cases, astute politicians have tapped into millenarian strains in traditional folk culture and into powerful national mythologies. Intense political competition has tended to engender conflicts framed in nationalist terms in which ethnic tensions are deliberately heightened. Political extremists and criminal opportunists, especially in parts of the former Yugoslavia, have taken advantage of widespread public disorientation and have deflected mass fears and blame onto vulnerable minorities or ethnic neighbors. Radical nationalists have launched offensives on various "enemy" ethnic groups and their leaders. And in some instances, the post-communist authorities have relied on smaller ultranationalist parties to maintain workable governing coalitions. Although Serbia has been the most obvious example of this process, similar coalitions have been attempted by ex-communists in Romania and Bulgaria. The danger remains that even in opposition, authoritarian populists will continue to forge alliances with radical nationalists to disrupt the liberal project and to promote radical anti-minority programs. Such an approach may have resonance among sectors of the population experiencing serious economic decline and benefiting little from economic reforms.

The collapse of Tito's Yugoslavia and the emergence of five new states at the beginning of the 1990s sparked a variety of nationalist responses, which continued to be manifest throughout the decade. They ranged from the relatively benign pro-independence nationalism of the Slovenian government and the defensive nationalism of the Macedonian administration, to the radical and xenophobic racism exhibited by militant Serb and Croat militias in Bosnia-Herzegovina and the latter's nationalist patrons in Serbia and Croatia. Their policies led to forced expulsions and the mass murder of "rival" ethnic groups in order to create ethnically exclusive territories controlled by authoritarian and corrupt politicians posing as national saviors.

Radical nationalists strictly define the parameters of the community in such a way that ethnic boundaries correspond with political units. They exhibit a pronounced anti-liberal and ethnocentric bias, asserting the primacy and dominance of one ethnic group's culture, history, language, and religion, and denigrating others' as inferior. By focusing on "ethnic protection," nationalist leaders may exclude various categories of nonmembers as untrustworthy aliens. Xenophobic nationalists operate on the valid assumption that a perceived domestic or foreign threat helps unite a "people." This approach toward national unification, however, leads to discrimination against minorities and other nationalities and provokes hostility toward neighboring states.

Where wrenching economic reforms disadvantage sizable sectors of the population, radical forces prey on popular frustrations in order to unbalance vulnerable governments. Nationalists also employ virulent anti-communist and anti-liberalist rhetoric to attack their political opponents. The "communist," "liberal," or "internationalist" labels are commonly employed to imply that traitors, aliens, and hostile outside powers have gained control of the state and the nation's resources.

The activities of nationalist parties, amid popular perceptions of internal or external threat, can act as a catalyst for the emergence of authoritarian regimes espousing "national unity" and intolerance for political pluralism and democratic competition. Such a process can severely inhibit progress toward liberal democracy, the rule of law, free media, and the development of a participatory civic society. Xenophobic nationalism promotes authoritarianism as it fosters an intolerant political climate and justifies governmental controls over various public institutions on the pretext of defending endangered national interests. The proponents of a civic society based on a balance between individual and minority group rights, unrestricted political competition, open mass media, and legality may then face an uphill struggle.

The emergence of a pluralistic political spectrum has been obstructed in several East European countries by nationalist, ethnic, and regionalist politics. A nationalist-civicist spectrum often intersects with the traditional left-right continuum, confusing the programs of specific political parties. This phenomenon focuses political life around collective national questions rather than civic issues and has often sidetracked economic and political liberalization. Even where nationalists do not hold political office, they can play a destabilizing role within society by provoking conflicts with minorities and attacking the government for its alleged neglect of the country's "national interests." The long-term impact of nationalist movements is contingent upon a number of factors, including the extent of democratic consolidation, institution building, political competition, cross-party consensus building, economic stabilization, administrative decentralization, trans-ethnic citizenship, and legalized minority rights.

Parts of Eastern Europe, particularly the Balkans, have witnessed a recrudescence of authoritarian politics and ethnic-national conflicts promoted by nationalist politicians. Yugoslavia has proved a fertile case study of how the growth of nationalism can trigger an escalation of competition between two or more ethnic groups for political office and economic privilege. Nationalist politics in this context is interpreted as self-defense against discrimination, repression, expulsion, or even physical annihilation. Such fears and sentiments encourage nationalist leaders to seek a single, ethnically homogeneous state in which the presence of other ethnic groups is considered anomalous. The dominant ethnicity is defined as the sole "state-creating" nation on a particular territory, and this definition is codified in a new national constitution that is based on the right of national self-determination rather than on that of individual self-determination or the people's self-determination.

In analyzing nationalist parties in Eastern Europe, it is worthwhile to distinguish among power holders, power brokers, and power aspirants with limited public influence. In many states, nationalists have remained confined to the political fringes and in competition for the radical vote and the most "authentic" national program. A more significant danger in parts of the region has been the deliberate aggravation of ethnic relations by quasi-authoritarian parties and nonreformist governments. In some instances, even a democratically elected administration fearful of losing control over decisionmaking to challengers from the liberal or the authoritarian camp may rally around nationalist and xenophobic causes. An initially moderate regime can become radicalized or adopt certain anti-minority measures in what may be widely perceived as a form of "national defense" against pressures from neighboring states and against the militant stance of some minority leaders. This can precipitate a spiral of conflict that radicalizes both the majority and the minority populations. Additionally, the impact of small, ultranationalist parties in divided national parliaments may be disproportionate to their actual electoral representation and can inject radicalism into state policy.

Weak States, Crime, and Corruption

With the termination of monopolistic and centralized one-party rule, much of Eastern Europe experienced political fragmentation, institutional weakness, legal confusion, and official corruption. In some Balkan countries, such conditions persist, and the weak state structures and feeble leaders are incapable of implementing political reforms, economic restructuring, or modernization. In the late 1990s, Albania presented the most poignant example of these problems, during and after the collapse of the myriad "pyramid" schemes in the spring of 1997. The country's state structure was weakened, and the central and local governments only slowly regained control and restored public order. Equally worrisome was an evident symbiosis between politics and crime, with evidence of corruption surfacing among politicians and policemen, and with criminal gangs controlling substantial sectors of the economy. Criminal gangs possess no political affiliation or ideological loyalty. They are commonly opportunistic and gravitate toward those in power so as to bribe and bypass officialdom. This type of criminality is both a symptom and a cause of political paralysis.

Although strictly centralized command economies no longer exist in the region, the progress of systemic transformation, privatization, and marketization has been obstructed by special interest groups, many of which emerged from the communist apparatus. Sectors of the old elite have benefited directly from limited economic reform programs by conducting what has been labeled "*nomenklatura* privatization." In this process, state property was sold cheaply to newly formed companies controlled by well-connected members of the former communist parties. Although Central Europe and the Baltics did not escape this corrupt practice, in the Balkans and in many former Soviet republics it assumed more significant proportions. It has restricted market competition and the development of a genuine entrepreneurial stratum that could strengthen the democratization process and accelerate economic progress.

Fearful of a market reform program that could dislodge the old *nomenklatura* from its privileged positions, and seeking to benefit from the legal and regulatory confusion, statist populists have hampered market reform in virtually all of the Balkan states. Through their control over major media outlets, they have played on fears of far-reaching market reform, especially among vulnerable sectors of society, including unskilled manual workers, pensioners, and state employees. Substantial sectors of the population have exhibited fear of economic decline, confusion about their future material prospects, resentment toward the new rich, concerns about safety and security, and susceptibility to populist, socialist, and nationalist rhetoric. Hence, demands for economic security, personal safety, and political predictability, encouraged by the state media, have promoted electoral support for paternalism, welfarism, statism, and authoritarianism. Large sectors of the population still expect the state to look after their interests and provide them with lifelong job security and a reasonable standard of living. In this context, civic consciousness has remained poorly developed and the concepts of self-help and self-organization continue to be lacking.

The ill effects of socialist mismanagement, inefficiency in production, and industrial uncompetitiveness have been compounded by nepotism, patronage, and outright corruption. Indeed, a growing wave of officially tolerated or politically sponsored criminality has swept across the region. Not only has crime seriously undermined legality and terrorized a nervous public, but it has also destabilized the region's fragile economies and quasi-democratic political institutions. Eastern Europe has proved a bountiful land of opportunity for assorted criminal elements, organized gangsters, and corrupt officials. The varieties of organized criminal activity can be divided into three broad categories: domestic gangsterism, international criminal syndicates, and politically connected networks capitalizing on the disintegration of state-controlled economies. All three forms of criminality have prospered not only because the forces of law and order were unprepared to deal with them but also because well-connected politicians and security officials themselves have benefitted from "robber capitalism" and illicitly acquired funds.

In the domestic context, local gangs, which can easily bribe poorly paid or corrupt police officials, thrive on the new availability of weapons and other illicit goods and the fear or gullibility of large sectors of the population. Robbery, murder, drug smuggling, prostitution, and money laundering have been on the rise in recent years, and the police have appeared to be overwhelmed by the scale of the problem. Mobsters have filled the legal limbo between communism and an embryonic market economy. Domestic East European gangs are either linked with or remain in competition with well-organized international syndicates. These new "multinationals" focus primarily on smuggling weapons, drugs, stolen goods, and people. In many instances, the syndicates are better armed than the local police forces. Racketeers also smuggle East Europeans nationals and refugees from the developing world into the prosperous European Union for substantial profits.

Drug traffickers have endeavored to revive the traditional "Balkan route" between Asia and Western Europe since the lifting of United Nations sanctions against Yugoslavia. The route runs through Turkey, Bulgaria, and Yugoslavia into Central Europe. Heroin, hashish, and cocaine from Turkey, Pakistan, and the Middle East have once again flooded the European market, and analysts believe that many local couriers as well as East European officials have benefited from this lucrative trade. Meanwhile, customs officials lack the necessary equipment to detect drugs and are desperately looking for Western assistance, particularly those situated along the Black Sea coast and the Danube River.

As economic performance has stagnated or deteriorated, organized crime has escalated. Violent attacks are a common means of settling scores between mafia-like business groups. Such phenomena tend to destabilize the transition process. Albania has presented the most dramatic example of how illegitimate businesses in conditions of economic crisis can trigger political instability. The collapsing "pyramid" schemes not only left masses of Albanians destitute but also undermined the country's security and political stability, as a popular revolt spread through the country.

Links between corrupt officialdom and organized crime can be traced across much of Eastern Europe. When the system of centralized controls collapsed, the well-connected communist *apparatchik*s pounced on state resources and lined their pockets with public assets. They posed as "businessmen" while stripping their countries of scarce funds and resources. A process of "*nomenklatura* privatization" has plagued the region, in which property rights and assets were obtained by well-placed individuals linked with the old communist party networks. This phenomenon and the financial scandals often associated with it can seriously undermine the public's support for liberalization and market reform and may even discredit the government and legislature. Moreover, the illicit funding of political parties has been rampant in the region due to the paucity of governmental and public funding, which has expanded opportunities for corruption and invariably given illicit and untaxed businesses substantial influence and control over political life.

Leading political figures in a number of states have embezzled state funds or established semi-legal companies using public resources without any legal restraints. The stability of the Balkan states is as dependent on effectively combating organized criminality as it is on emphatically pursuing market reforms. Without an effective anti-syndicate campaign alongside economic progress, the rule of law, and regulated market competition, an increasingly pauperized and desperate public may become prone to social unrest, which in turn fuels political instability.

The Emergence of a Political Spectrum

Political parties are vehicles for the expression of group interests and coherent policy proposals that may form the core of government programs once the parties' candidates for office are elected.[37] Parties are the building blocks of a pluralistic democracy in that they are the chief political structures connecting national elites, local leaders, various interest groups, and the broader public. In ideal conditions, a handful of reasonably strong parties would emerge, spanning a broad political spectrum and representing the interests of various sectors of society. A stable party system, together with democratic institutions of government, free media, and a thriving civil society, can help keep extremists in check and can dampen the influence of authoritarian demagogues.

East European democracy and political pluralism are contingent upon the consolidation of stable and representative governments and a constitutional system in which ethnicity or some other narrow identity does not determine gradations of citizenship. Such conditions are necessary for managing and containing extremism and building a civic-oriented polity in which universalistic and not particularistic values predominate. A broadly based political spectrum is an essential component of this process.

Some parties, especially in the newly independent states that remained focused on the imperative of protecting statehood and maintaining territorial integrity, have organized around ethnic, regional, religious, class, or other collective identities. Other political organizations have rallied around new interests and programs in response to the ongoing social transformation. Parties are also extremely diversified internally, and some parties' left and right factions have more in common with similar wings in other parties than with each other. In many instances, party names and self-definitions are either generalized or do not accurately denote their ideological or programmatic positions and can therefore be misleading. Thus, instead of defining all political parties in Eastern Europe according to a "traditional" but simplistic left-right divide, this volume classifies parties principally according to what can be gleaned of their ideological and programmatic identity, which is often difficult to discern in a fluid and sometimes unclear political climate. It is worth remembering that a party's ideology, program, or strategy may change even when its name, leadership, and membership remain constant. There are of course many existing organizations that defy neat and accurate classification. The following major groupings are identified in this book: socialists and social democrats; liberals; Christian democrats; agrarians; greens; communists;

nationalists; neofascists; ethnic and religious parties; regionalists; and independents. In many cases, these categories may overlap, and some organizations can be included in more than one category. Nevertheless, such a division helps in identifying and classifying the various political formations present in the region.

Because of their relatively small size and modest influence, some political parties and movements that are essentially or solely monarchist, militarist, or imperialist are not examined in detail in this book. (Some larger, broader-based parties that may share those same sympathies are nonetheless included.) The book also generally excludes organizations that focus exclusively on single issues such as women's liberation, consumer advocacy, or homosexual rights, although such movements may play an important role in the development of civil societies in the future. I have chosen to concentrate on the most significant parties across the political spectrum—organizations that have gained parliamentary representation at the national, regional, or local level during the past decade, or those whose influence is discernible regardless of parliamentary representation.

Socialists and Social Democrats

During the past decade, many of the communist successor parties or leftist formations subordinate to the communists have restyled themselves as socialist or social democratic organizations and have endeavored to join the West European mainstream. In addition, a number of pre-communist leftist parties that were active before the communists seized power have been re-created in the region. Despite their espousal of programs similar to those of the post-communist socialists, the latter have remained wary of establishing any compacts or coalitions with them. Like the core members of other "historical" parties, many leftist activists belong to an older generation. Many spent years in exile in the West and inevitably lost touch with the social and structural changes in their native countries. They also control limited assets, usually benefit from a small base of public support, and have little media exposure.

The leftist parties have differed in their economic prescriptions, with some favoring greater state intervention and welfarism than others. Some socialist groups have taken aboard populist or nationalist issues and even allied themselves with more extreme parties, principally to garner public backing. Several parties have made a particular effort to mobilize support from the labor movements, which have faced enormous disruptions due to market reforms that negatively affected their working-class constituencies. Some have favored a mixed economy in which large sectors remain under state control, with more gradual structural reforms that cushion the population against unemployment and falling living standards.

However, the pro-market socialists, often with a younger leadership, find it difficult to combine a capitalist platform with a state protectionist agenda, especially as they want to become part of the pro-business European "modern" left. Indeed, the imperatives of European integration, and the strict criteria for membership in a united Europe, have propelled the social democrats to adopt liberal reform programs and largely to discard their socialist economic prescriptions, in practice if not in theory. Nevertheless, with an inevitable increase in economic inequality in the post-communist countries, some of the social democrats can be expected to adopt more traditional socialist positions in defense of the underprivileged sectors of society and to espouse a broader welfare agenda.

Liberals

Liberalism in Eastern Europe encompasses diverse ideologies, factions, and policy prescriptions, but the main division remains that between free-marketeers and social liberals. Liberals tend to disagree on the role of the state in the economic reform process. "Minimalist liberals" favor a slender governmental role, primarily in the creation of a legal framework for private property and the sale of state assets, and not in the establishment of overarching regulatory institutions or in persistent interference with market competition. A major obstacle to free-marketeers is the backward nature of the East European economies and the need for modernization along Western lines. But this in turn requires the creation of appropriate legal and political institutions—institutions that some think are likely to obstruct market competition.

Social liberals argue for a more active state role in providing collective goods not supplied by the market, especially during the difficult transition process, even though they view the state as less efficient than markets. They believe that the state should create the institutional infrastructure for capitalism and provide credits to key industries as well as export and import subsidies. Social liberals also favor using the state to redistribute resources to enhance equal opportunity, to help disadvantaged minorities through affirmative action, and to promote social goals such as family cohesion.

Liberals are also split on social and cultural questions between traditionalists and modernists. The former support political and economic individualism but are more conservative on social, moral, and life-style questions. The latter favor individual freedom and liberation from social norms and are more libertarian in their approach. Nevertheless, liberals are generally pragmatic, and many remain neutral on social and cultural issues that are outside the realm of government.

Liberals are characteristically pro-European and attempt to apply Western standards in such arenas as human rights and marketization. Liberal parties are often dominated by urban intellectuals and the most educated strata of society and usually maintain good contacts with Western governments and institutions. They are vehemently opposed to nationalism, authoritarianism, and clericalism. They are tolerant of ethnic and religious minorities but are hesitant to grant collective rights that may undermine individual equality and citizenship. Nationalist, populist, and communist critics have charged liberal formations with selling out the state and the country to foreigners and with being "cosmopolitan" —i.e., lacking in historical, cultural, and national consciousness.[38]

Christian Democrats

Christian democratic movements have emerged in most East European countries, often as resurrections of historic parties that had existed before communist party rule was imposed. Some have adopted traditional and nationalist postures; others have opted for relatively moderate, centrist positions similar to those of West European Christian democrats. However, the development of strong Christian democratic parties in the East has been slow and uneven for a number of reasons. After the collapse of communism, the clergy and laity of Catholic, Protestant, and Orthodox churches became less involved in politics. In addition, a number of former liberal defenders of the anti-communist churches began to advocate the separation of church and state and to criticize the attempts of some clerics to impose their social agendas (in family planning, education, anti-gay discrimination, or media censorship) on the political process. In the economic domain, some Christian democrats have allied themselves with liberal market reformers, and others have forged links with industrial and rural sectors and promoted a more protectionist and welfarist program.

Agrarians

Agrarian groupings in Eastern Europe can be similarly divided into "successor" and "historic" parties. The former began as communist-controlled front organizations created for the peasantry and collectivized farm workers. After the collapse of communist rule, they were transformed into democratic parties seeking to represent the interests of farmers, farm managers, and other sectors of rural society. The historic parties trace their heritage to the precommunist period and have sought to establish a distinctly rural constituency of private farmers. In general, the successor parties have proved more adept at attracting collective farm workers fearful of losing their jobs in any large-scale privatization process. The historic parties have greater appeal to private farmers and former landowners who were dispossessed by the communists when the latter seized power.

Agrarian parties have proved most successful in countries with an extensive farming sector, a tradition of organized rural politics, and government policies that have negatively affected the countryside. Agrarian parties have diverse ideological and programmatic profiles in seeking favorable governmental policies toward farmers. Some are conservative and pro-church; some are populist and protectionist; and others are statist and socialist, and seek greater governmental subsidies for the countryside. A few organizations have become stridently nationalist in orientation and have rallied against urban, intellectual, alien, and foreign influences. They have campaigned against foreign purchases of land and protested the drive for their nations' integration into the European Union, viewing this as a threat to traditional farming and national heritage.

Greens

Various "green" parties appeared early in the transition process. In several countries, environmentalist groups were established before the fall of communism, as dissident pressure movements against the incumbent regimes. A number of green groups participated in the mass movements that helped topple single-party rule. Green parties have displayed limited durability partly because of their single-issue focus (environmentalism and conservationism) and because other political parties have embraced ecological questions in their programs. Moreover, the green platform has had limited public resonance during difficult economic times, when citizens are focused on material survival. As a result, the green movement has remained small and largely marginal throughout the region, with a slender parliamentary representation.

Communists

After losing their monopoly on political power, the communist parties splintered into three main groups: orthodox dogmatists, social democrats, and populist nationalists. Orthodox Marxist-Leninists have constituted only marginal elements in each state and have been unable to gain any serious public support even where disaffected workers have faced rising unemployment. The more effective communists have switched to socialist and social democratic positions, seeking to fill the political vacuum to the left of the new liberal democrats. Some communist leaders, such as those in the Czech Republic, have revamped their parties as "democratic communists" or "Eurocommunists" and dispensed with much of their Leninist heritage. They have supported continuing state control over the most vital economic sectors and have voiced skepticism if not outright opposition to their countries' joining the North Atlantic Treaty Organization (NATO) and the European Union (EU). Some have underscored national protectionism against foreign "takeovers" and "alien influences" and have veered into the nationalist camp.

Nationalists

Sundry political groupings have adopted nationalist causes. The main point of divergence between moderate and radical nationalists is in the emphasis they place on ethnic identity, language, culture, and religion for determining "national" membership and citizenship rights, together with their policy toward minorities.[39] Moderate or democratic nationalists are more tolerant of ethnic diversity than are militants, and they are assimilationist rather than segregationist or discriminatory toward minorities loyal to the state. At one end of the spectrum, moderate nationalists merge into civic-oriented parties; at the other extreme, they assume an exclusionist ethnic-national ideology. Even a single formation may contain a moderate and a militant wing; in this case, either the party leadership veers between these two poles, or the organization fragments into distinct factions or separate structures.

Ultranationalists are inevitably authoritarians who are suspicious of pluralism and democratic procedure and favor a "strong hand" in guaranteeing "national interests," rooting out anti-national elements, and restricting the rights of minority groups. Nevertheless, they may function in a pluralistic setting, with the aim of gaining influence and power through electoral politics. Ideologically, militant nationalists operate according to a variety of often convoluted or even comical conspiracy theories revolving around nefarious foreign threats and traitorous domestic enemies. Ultranationalist ideologues conjure up appealing images of a glorious and unpolluted ethnic history that evidently needs to be re-created to maintain the continuity and integrity of the nation.

Neofascists

In addition to an invariably exclusionist agenda, neofascist groups embrace the "leadership principle," favor a strict hierarchical party structure, display intolerance toward political rivals, espouse violence as a legitimate form of political activity, and seek to establish a party-state with totalitarian ambitions to control political, public, and private life. Neofascists are radical, racist nationalists; they scapegoat ethnic, cultural, and religious minorities as traitors or agents of foreign subversion. They may also single out other groups for verbal or physical assault, including gays, foreigners, the homeless, or alternative youth movements.

Neofascist economic programs in the domestic arena are generally corporatist and statist, espousing close links between the state and large business, but they favor private ownership within "patriotic" limitations. As protectionists, neofascists are suspicious of foreign investors and international financial institutions, which they generally suspect of seeking control over strategic sectors of the national economy. Such positions are commonly couched in anti-Semitic terms, using the imagery of a global Jewish conspiracy. Like the ultranationalists and some militant religious groupings, the neofascists oppose "globalization," which they envisage as an attempt to subvert and destroy the identity of distinct nations. In essence, neofascists are revolutionary, promoting a major turnover in the elite, mobilization of the masses, and outright subjugation, expulsion, or elimination of allegedly threatening minorities. Small neofascist groups have sprung up throughout Eastern

Europe, but thus far they have had a limited impact on major political developments.

Ethnic Minority and Religious Parties

Ethnic minority– and religion-centered parties act as special interest groups that focus on issues of direct and often exclusive concern to a distinct segment of the population. As a result, they have limited prospects for interparty discourse and compromise across ethnic lines, especially with the majority group. This may be particularly evident where the government has adopted nationalist or populist positions or scapegoated minority leaders as separatists. Nevertheless, ethnic parties may enter into coalition governments with reformist forces that recognize the importance of minority rights and that seek minority representation in the administration to buttress their reform programs. There may also be instances where two or more ethnic parties representing different minority groups may cooperate in order to consolidate their efforts at gaining concessions from the government. Ethnic political formations tend to collectivize political life and invariably limit the political or ideological choices minority populations make. In an uncertain political climate, minorities tend not to vote as rightists, centrists, or leftists but for their ethnic leaders and representatives, who negotiate with the central or local authorities in the name of the ethnic collectivity.

In the post-communist states there has been a revival of community life among recognized ethnic groups as well as a reconstruction in ethnic terms, or "ethnogenesis," of cultural, religious, or regional groupings whose distinctiveness was not fully acknowledged by previous governments. In several cases, the latter process has evoked hostility from the "historic nations" that have long since achieved statehood and whose leaders have dismissed further ethnic redefinition of the state as artificial and potentially destructive of the state's unity and integrity. Nonetheless, new ethnic or regional identities continue to develop in a liberalized or fractured political climate, especially where they convey material or political rewards or enhance community self-defense against unwelcome outside interests or foreign threats.

Ethnic politics in post-communist Eastern Europe has revolved around five major tendencies. The precise form it takes in any state depends partially on historical traditions, on the policies and objectives of ethnic organizations, and on the comparative position of ethnic communities in the existing state structures. The first tendency, cultural revivalism, is noticeable among small or dispersed ethnic, religious, or regional minorities with limited experience of sovereignty or statehood, whose leaders demand the freedom and resources to rebuild their social, cultural, religious, and educational institutions, to redefine their history, to reinforce their identity, and to revive their dialect or language.

The second tendency, political autonomism, is characterized by a more

pronounced form of self-organization among minority populations that constituted majorities in previously existing states or that possess a history of
organized political involvement in a multiethnic state. Calls for political autonomy rather than territorial self-government are also more likely in ethnically mixed regions in which no single group predominates and where the
political system allows for the active participation of minorities in public life.

The third tendency, territorial self-determinism, is visible among reasonably large, well-organized, and territorially compact ethnic groups or sub-
groups that form a relative or absolute majority of the population in a particular
region. Ethnic leaders may seek to reorganize the administration of the state
from a unitary to a federal or confederal structure, in which specific regions
gain some degree of provincial autonomy or full republican status. Territorial
self-determination may also be demanded jointly by several ethnic groups in
mixed-population areas with a distinct regional history and a tradition of autonomy and resistance to a centralizing state.

The fourth tendency, separatism, is characteristic among ethnically and
territorially compact populations, usually with some history of statehood, that
oppose their continuing inclusion in the existing federal or unitary state or
that fear a loss of status in a newly centralized state and therefore campaign to
create their own independent state structures. And the fifth, irredentism, is
evident in separatist movements in one state that seek to join their territories
and populations with structures in another, nearby state, either as autonomous
regions or as integral administrative units. In some instances, such movements may be directly sponsored and assisted by the neighboring states in
order to expand their own borders.

These five variants of ethnic politics are not necessarily mutually exclusive or permanent; they can be envisaged as potential stages of development, particularly in instances where an ethnicity-based organization, due
to internal or external pressures, escalates its demands from cultural revivalism to full-scale territorial self-determination or even secession. Of course,
the programs and achievements of distinct ethnic communities depend on
several interrelated factors, including the response of the government and
other in-state communities to minority and majority demands as well as the
role of foreign governments in sponsoring or discouraging various autonomist movements.

Regionalists

Regionalist parties may be based around single, compact ethnic groups pushing for national-administrative and territorial autonomy within a wider state,
or they may be multiethnic groupings in which leaders call for political devolution and regional autonomy in a broad array of activities. Other regional
movements may involve political groups in different regions seeking broad
decentralization from the state or a stronger position from which to negotiate

with the central government. They may represent the interests of various subregional or cross-regional constituencies. With the loosening of central controls, administrative reorganization, and local government reform, local issues, interest groups, and even multiparty local coalitions are likely to play an increasingly important role in the political systems of several states.

Independents and Others

In several post-communist states the role of independents has proved significant in the absence of a coherent and consolidated political party structure and in the context of widespread popular suspicion about the motives and goals of political parties in general. In some cases, however, candidates and parliamentarians claiming to be independents have had close connections with a major party organization (including communists, socialists, and agrarians) but hoped to maximize their popular appeal by posing as "independents." (Likewise, some individuals have joined parties or stood on party lists for elections not because they were ideologically committed to a specific position but because they viewed the party as a useful vehicle for gaining office.) In addition, a number of "miscellaneous" parties have emerged that do not fit any neat classification. The few that are included in this volume are primarily formations that have either achieved parliamentary representation or that have had some public resonance in the region.

Coalition Politics

Another question worth considering in the political transformation of the eastern half of Europe is the role of coalition politics. Are multiparty or multimovement coalitions conducive to a political transformation, or do they obstruct and unnecessarily prolong the democratization process? To answer this important question, one must examine numerous variables before attempting any broader generalizations.

Eastern Europe has witnessed a high degree of coalition building, invariably followed by coalition collapse and various attempts at coalition reformulation. Indeed, most of the movements that brought down communism were broad popular coalitions encompassing a variety of groups and ideologies. Most parties and governments in the region today are coalitions of differing ideologies, policies, and personalities. In deciding what distinguishes each coalition, it may be useful to look at five variables: first, the breadth of the political spectrum in a working coalition; second, the degree of internal coalition cohesion; third, the objectives of specific coalitions; fourth, the external political environment in which political coalitions operate; and fifth, the impact of coalitions on domestic political developments.

Coalition movements and coalition governments may consist of a single broad front, party, or movement containing various interest groups and factions committed to a single policy platform; they may be coalitions of two or three distinct parties with some overlap in their programs and policies and with a relative balance in their influence and decisionmaking; or they may encompass a broader spectrum of political parties and interest groups, with one or two formations predominating.

Coalitions may be necessary to form a parliamentary majority and a working government. Alternatively, they may be forged principally to broaden the base of political and public support for the government, even though they may not be operationally or technically necessary. In multiethnic or multiregional states, minority or regionalist parties may be deliberately incorporated into the government in an effort to resolve ethnic disputes, regional demands, and minority grievances as well as to meet international criteria for human rights or for membership in various international institutions such as NATO or the EU. The formula for power-sharing among parties varies accordingly. Some small parties may obtain the key ministerial portfolios that most closely correspond to their policy priorities—for example, agriculture, environment, minority affairs, or culture. In other instances, parties simply obtain a proportional share of parliamentary seats in the cabinet, or control of a nominal ministry, in return for their participation in the coalition.

The effectiveness of a political coalition is measured in terms of its ability to implement a prescribed policy platform. Some coalitions are long-lasting and programmatically effective; some are durable but less effective; and some are effective only in the short term. Government cohesion and coalition longevity are products of both policy and personality. Clear rules of engagement and decisionmaking must be operational to minimize leadership conflicts and disruptive rifts. Alternatively, conflicts can be curtailed by focusing on the pursuit of policies that are less controversial. But this approach carries the risk that effectiveness will be less significant. In the "politics of the lowest common denominator," election platforms are trimmed down or abandoned to preserve unity, paralyzing a government simply in order to ensure its survival. Such a scenario can promote policy stagnation, wherein the durability of a coalition becomes a by-product of the intention to maintain power rather than a measure of policy success.

A multiparty coalition may have diverse objectives, especially in a fragile, post-communist context. In terms of the progress of democratization, some of these objectives may have a positive effect, and others may be negative. On the positive side, a coalition may be a means of preserving broad public support for normally unpopular or disruptive economic policies, such as price liberalization, cuts in state subsidization, wholesale industrial restructuring, or rapid privatization. The objectives here are to maintain sufficient political and social stability as well as policy continuity and sustainability to push such programs through, and to gain expertise by including specialized smaller formations.

On the negative side, coalition politics may be a means of upholding certain privileges of office among a circumscribed elite, or co-opting ambitious politicians into political office and thereby limiting genuine opposition. In the worst-case scenario, as was most glaringly evident in Serbia throughout the 1990s, coalitions may simply provide cover for ethnic nationalism, an anti-minority agenda, or even foreign aggression.

Governing coalitions are created by and in turn influence the domestic political environment. In the immediate post-communist settings, broad-based coalitions and united fronts of diverse groupings proved instrumental in dismantling much of the old system and avoiding political fracturing. In many cases, however, reformed elements of the ex-communist parties became power sharers or returned to office in the second series of national elections. Some communist successor parties were organizationally more successful than ex-dissident groupings, benefiting from persistent splits in the democratic coalitions and from the slow emergence of a genuine party spectrum.

Another important question is whether coalitions promote the development of political parties as incubators of specific platforms and structures, or conversely, whether long-term coalitions of extremely diverse political elements actually stifle democratization and political competition by prolonging the transition period and obstructing the development of a spectrum of parties. The failure of a broad and essentially democratic coalition, coinciding with the absence of credible democratic alternatives, may indeed create political space for the return of authoritarian post-communist or other autocratic forces. On the basis of these observations, coalition politics in Eastern Europe can be grouped into four broad categories, as described below.

Anti-communist Coalitions

These were visible in most countries before, during, and immediately after the fall of the one-party state. The overall objective of such coalitions was to oust the old-line communists and to launch a systemic political and economic transformation. In these early stages, specific political parties had still to crystallize, whether from the ex-dissident or the ex-communist structures. Democratic coalitions have also been formed in countries such as Slovakia and Croatia to defeat an essentially authoritarian regime that has superimposed itself on the skeleton of the old communist structure and thwarted political and economic reforms. Such coalitions invariably possess a limited life span because of internal fractures and a changing political environment.

Ex-communist Coalitions

In this scenario, post-communist parties, whether they are socialists, social democrats, or broader "national fronts," create governing coalitions with former front parties or with other, smaller party entities established by elements of the ex-*nomenklatura*. In many cases, these coalitions have included radical leftist, populist, or nationalist parties. Romania, Bulgaria, and Slovakia during the 1990s provided valuable examples of this process. The nationalists may be discarded if the more centrist post-communists gain sufficient strength, cohesion, and popular support. In order to understand and contextualize the democratic coalitions, it is important to consider the shape and impact of various post-communist coalitions.

Multiparty Coalitions

Multiparty coalitions are formed during or after the emergence of more coherent political parties, in countries that traditionally have had several stable political parties each of which has lacked a clear parliamentary majority to form a government. Such coalitions may deliberately exclude or include some post-communist formations, depending on such factors as the role of the communists in the democratization process, their current program and degree of commitment to democracy, their ongoing alliances, and the necessity of forming a broader coalition to obtain a governing majority. Useful examples from the past decade are the liberal socialist Hungarian government and the broad coalition administration in Slovenia. Of course, the size and popularity of each coalition partner vary, determining coalition structures that range from one strong party with a cluster of smaller formations to two or three relatively equal parties.

Cross-Ethnic Coalitions

In states containing sizable national minorities, multiethnic or multiregional coalition governments may be forged principally to prevent polarization and provide minority and regional representatives with a stake in implementing important political and economic reforms. In some cases, such administrations may themselves consist of an assemblage of smaller coalitions as majority and minority parties coalesce into larger blocs. Valuable examples of this process are the Romanian and Slovakian multiethnic governments. However, as in other coalition arrangements, there may be a misfit here between commitment to stability and commitment to reform. The incorporation of minority representatives in government may smooth over real or potential ethnic and regional divisions but at the same time make it difficult to implement far-reaching economic reform programs. The government could remain primarily concerned about keeping the coalition together rather than pursuing unpopular reforms that could impose severe social hardships. Conversely, in some countries, rapid and drastic reform may actually prove easier if minority representatives have a voice in government and actively support reform programs. They can more easily convince their ethnic constituents that government programs ultimately will be beneficial.

On balance, democratic coalitions have played a valuable role at critical periods of the post-communist transition, whether in launching democratic reforms or preventing the return to power of authoritarian elements. In the long term, however, coalitions may become a weak substitute for a broader political spectrum incorporating fewer, more distinct, policy-based, and con-stituency-strong political parties. Such parties could still form multiparty coalitions in order to pursue a common agenda, rather than simply for the purpose of surviving in power or blocking the emergence or victory of rival political coalitions.

Objectives of a Political Guidebook

The purpose of this book is to provide both a guide and an easily accessible directory to the political systems and political parties that have emerged in Eastern Europe in the first decade of transition from one-party communist rule. It provides an overview of each country by examining major political developments during the 1990s, including the structure of the political system, the relative strength and the particular roles of the most important political formations, and the key issues that each state has faced.

The eighteen recognized countries and the two aspiring states examined in this book are divided for convenience, and without political or national prejudice, into four geographic subregions: the Baltic (Belarus, Estonia, Latvia, Lithuania, Poland); the Danube (Czech Republic, Slovakia, Hungary, Serbia); the Adriatic (Kosova, Montenegro, Bosnia-Herzegovina, Croatia, Slovenia, Albania); and the Black Sea (Macedonia, Bulgaria, Romania, Moldova, Ukraine). The name of each political party, movement, and organization is given in English and in the official state language of the country in question.

The sources used to compile this directory, apart from newspapers and news agencies, are listed in the references. However, in many cases, information or confirmation was obtained during my visits to the region, or in discussions with regional political actors or analysts. The absence of a specific reference signals either that the data were obtained from unpublished sources or that the source was previously cited. Although the guidebook is as complete as possible, due to practical considerations it cannot be exhaustive. A number of political parties, movements, organizations, and other formations have not been included or are only briefly mentioned because data were sketchy, incomplete, contradictory, questionable, or not readily available at the time of research. Furthermore, in a highly fluid political climate, new associations and parties continue to form, and existing organizations frequently fracture, merge, or disappear. I apologize for any resultant omissions of individuals and organizations. Nevertheless, I believe that this volume provides the most comprehensive and documented assessment of Eastern Europe's political evolution since the fall of communism, during the first decade of a major political and structural transformation.

Notes

1. Paul Aligica, "The Institutionalists' Take on Transition," *Transition*, Vol. 3, No. 4, 7 March 1997.

2. See Barrington Moore, *Social Origins of Dictatorship and Democracy*, Boston: Beacon Press, 1965.

3. For a valuable discussion of transition issues see Adam Przeworski, "Some Problems in the Study of the Transition to Democracy," in Guillermo O'Donnell, Philippe Schmitter, and Lawrence Whitehead (Eds.), *Transition from Authoritarian Rule: Prospects for Democracy*, Baltimore: Johns Hopkins University Press, 1986 pp. 87ff.

4. Thoughtful theories of revolution can be found in: Krishan Kumar (Ed.), *Revolution: The Theory and Practice of a European Idea*, London: Weidenfeld and Nicolson, 1971; Crane Brinton, *The Anatomy of Revolution*, New York: Vintage Books, 1965; Peter Calvert, *Revolution*, London: Macmillan, 1970; and Hannah Arendt, *On Revolution*, Harmondsworth, UK: Penguin, 1973.

5. With regard to the collapse of communism and the role of the opposition see Janusz Bugajski and Maxine Pollack, *East European Fault Lines: Dissent, Opposition, and Social Activism*, Boulder: Westview Press, 1989.

6. For distinctions between elite-generated "transformations," opposition-led "replacements," and the combined "transplacement" of authoritarian systems see Samuel P. Huntington, *The Third Wave: Democratization in the Late 20th Century*, Norman & London: University of Oklahoma Press, 1992, p. 114.

7. See Anton Przeworski, "Democracy as a Contingent Outcome of Conflicts," in Jon Elster and Rune Slagstad (Eds.), *Constitutionalism and Democracy*, Cambridge: Cambridge University Press, 1988, pp. 62–63.

8. For example, check John Higley, Judith Kulberg, and Jan Pakulski, "The Persistence of Postcommunist Elites," *Journal of Democracy*, Vol. 7, No. 2, April 1996, pp. 132–147.

9. See Michael G. Roskin, "The Emerging Party Systems of Central and Eastern Europe," *East European Quarterly*, Vol. XXVII, No.1, March 1993, pp. 47–63; and Herbert Kitschelt, "The Formation of Party Systems in East Central Europe," *Politics and Society*, Vol. 20, No. 1, March 1992, pp. 7–50.

10. Sherman Garnett, "Europe's Post-Communist Democracies," *Strategic Survey*, 1996/1997, IISS: Oxford University Press, 1997, pp. 50–60.

11. An excellent discussion of perceptions and misperceptions about the Balkans is contained in Maria Todorova, *Imagining the Balkans*, New York: Oxford University Press, 1997.

12. Michael Saward, "Democratic Theory and Indices of Democratization," in David Beetham (Ed.), *Defining and Measuring Democracy*, London: Sage, 1994, pp. 6–24.

13. David Beetham, "Key Principles and Indices for a Democratic Audit," in David Beetham (Ed.), *Defining and Measuring Democracy*, London: Sage, 1994, pp. 25–43.

14. Raymond Duncan Gostil, "The Comparative Survey of Freedom: Experiences and Suggestions," in Alex Inkeles (Ed.), *On Measuring Democracy: Its Consequences and Concomitants*, New Brunswick, NJ: Transaction, 1991, pp. 21–46.

15. Consult Michael Ignatieff, "On Civil Society: Why Eastern Europe's Revolutions Could Succeed," *Foreign Affairs*, Vol. 74, No. 2, March/April 1995, pp. 128–136. See also Ghita Ionescu, "The Painful Return to Normality," in Geraint Parry and Michael Moran (Eds.), *Democracy and Democratization*, London: Routledge, 1994.

16. For a useful study of public attitudes toward politics see Richard Rose and Christian Haerpfer, "Mass Response to Transformation in Post-Communist Societies," *Europe-Asia Studies*, Vol. 46, No. 1, 1994, pp. 3–25.

17. For an excellent discussion of these issues see Beverly Crawford, "Post-Communist Political Economy: A Framework for the Analysis of Reform," in Beverly Crawford (Ed.), *Markets, States, and Democracy: The Political Economy of Post-Communist Transformation*, Boulder: Westview, 1995, pp. 3–42.

18. Ghia Nadia, "How Different Are Postcommunist Transitions," *Journal of Democracy*, Vol. 7, No. 4, October 1996, pp. 15–30.

19. For a valuable collection of essays on democratization in Eastern Europe in the context

of electoral laws, institution building, party building, and judicial reform consult John S. Micgiel (Ed.), *Perspectives on Political and Economic Transitions after Communism*, New York: Columbia University, Institute on East Central Europe, 1997.

20. Andrew Arato, "Dilemmas Arising From the Power to Create Constitutions in Eastern Europe," in Michael Rosenfeld (Ed.), *Constitutionalism, Identity, Difference, and Legitimacy: Theoretical Perspectives*, Durham, NC: Duke University Press, 1994, pp. 165–194.

21. Consult Stephen Holmes, "Conceptions of Democracy in the Draft Constitutions of Post-Communist Countries," in Beverly Crawford (Ed.), *Markets, States, and Democracy: The Political Economy of Post-Communist Transformation*, Boulder: Westview, 1995, pp. 71–81. Holmes examines the complex problem involved in simultaneously liberalizing, legitimizing, and strengthening state institutions.

22. Raymond Taras, "Separating Power: Keeping Presidents in Check," in Ray Taras (Ed.), *Postcommunist Presidents*, Cambridge: Cambridge University Press, 1997, p. 16.

23. Thomas F. Remington, "Introduction: Parliamentary Elections and the Transition from Communism," in Thomas F. Remington (Ed.), *Parliaments in Transition: The New Legislative Politics in the Former USSR and Eastern Europe*, Boulder: Westview, 1994, pp. 1–29.

24. Jakub Karpinski, "In the Wake of Presidential Elections, A Crisis of Authority," *Transition*, Vol. 2, No. 2, 26 January 1996, pp. 56–59.

25. See Arend Lijphart (Ed.), *Parliamentary Versus Presidential Government*, Oxford: Oxford University Press, 1992.

26. Consult Matthew Soberg Shugart, "Executive-Legislative Relations in Post-Communist Europe," *Transition*, Vol. 2, No. 25, 13 December 1996, pp. 6–11.

27. See Vladimir Tismaneanu, *Nationalism, Populism, and Other Threats to Liberal Democracy in Post-Communist Europe*, The Donald Treadgold Papers in Russian and Central Asian Studies, No. 20, January 1999, Henry M. Jackson School of International Studies, University of Washington.

28. A good discussion of bureaucratic and procedural problems in the early post-communist period can be found in Valerie Bunce and Maria Csanadi, "Uncertainty in the Transition: Postcommunism in Hungary," *East European Politics and Society*, Vol. 7, No. 2, Spring 1993, pp. 240–275.

29. For a valuable study of post-communist social democracy consult Linda J. Cook, Mitchell A. Orenstein, and Marilyn Rueschemeyer, *Left Parties and Social Policy in Postcommunist Europe*, Boulder: Westview, 1999.

30. Jacques Rupnik, "The Postcommunist Divide," *Journal of Democracy*, Vol. 10, No. 1, January 1999, pp. 57–62.

31. On the dangers of authoritarian rule and the conditions in which it may thrive see Daniel Chirot, *Modern Tyrants: The Power and Prevalence of Evil in our Age*, New York: Free Press, 1994.

32. For an analysis of the varieties of authoritarian nationalism see Janusz Bugajski, "The Many Faces of Nationalism," *Uncaptive Minds*, Vol. 8 Nos. 3–4 (30), Fall/Winter 1995–1996, pp. 7–30. Also consult Janusz Bugajski, "The Rise of Nationalism in Central and Eastern Europe: Kinds, Causes, Consequences, Countermeasures" (Symposium Report), *Uncaptive Minds*, Vol. 9, No. 3–4, Fall 1997, pp. 99–192.

33. For a brief discussion of East European nationalism see Todoritchka Gotovska-Popova, "Nationalism in Post-Communist Eastern Europe," *East European Quarterly*, Vol. XXVII, No. 2, June 1993, pp. 171–186. The author argues that unlike in Western Europe, in the East popular sovereignty and national independence historically did not coincide with individualism and civic values. In nationalist perceptions, personal freedom could only be attained by submitting to the collective will of the nation. Under communism this became submission to the party as the "vanguard" of the nation. The middle class, which could have promoted liberal values, had been dispossessed and eliminated.

34. For a useful discussion of these issues see Evelyn Farkas, "The Politics of Ethnicity and Stability: Collective Rights, Democracy, and Hungarian Minorities," in John S. Micgiel (Ed.), *State and Nation Building in East Central Europe: Contemporary Perspectives*, New York: Columbia University, Institute on East Central Europe, 1996, pp. 133–152.

35. Anton Steen, *Between Past and Future: Elites, Democracy and the State in Post-Communist Countries*, Aldershot, U.K.: Ashgate Publishers, 1997, p. 7.

36. For a useful analysis of neofascism see A. James Gregor, "Fascism at the End of the Twentieth Century," in *Society*, Vol. 34, No. 5, July–August 1997. For a valuable survey of neofascist groups in post-communist Eastern Europe see Paul Hockenes, *Free to Hate: The Rise of the Right in Post-Communist Eastern Europe*, New York: Routledge, 1993.

37. Jan Ake Dellenbrant, "Parties and Party Systems in Eastern Europe," in Stephen White, Judy Batt, and Paul G. Lewis (Eds.), *Developments in East European Politics*, Durham, NC: Duke University Press, 1993, pp. 147–162.

38. See Andrew Janos, "Continuity and Change in Eastern Europe: Strategies of Post-Communist Politics," in Beverly Crawford (Ed.), *Markets, States, and Democracy: The Political Economy of Post-Communist Transformation*, Boulder: Westview, 1995, pp. 150–174.

39. For a valuable analysis of nationalist politics see Sabrina P. Ramet, "Defining the Radical Right: The Values and Behaviors of Organized Intolerance," in Sabrina P. Ramet (Ed.), *The Radical Right in Central and Eastern Europe Since 1989*, University Park: Pennsylvania State University Press, 1999, pp. 3–27.

Political Parties of
Eastern Europe

Belarus

HISTORICAL OVERVIEW

Slavic tribes settled in the territories now known as Belarus around the seventh century AD and subsequently underwent a process of cultural and linguistic differentiation from their neighbors. Contrary to much of Russian and Soviet communist historiography, Belarus (*Belaia Rus,* or White Rus) claims a distinct national and ethnic history of several hundred years.[1] The Belarusian principalities of Polachak, Turau, and Navahradak were incorporated in the Grand Duchy of Lithuania, Rus, and Samogitia during the thirteenth century. The Duchy was a confederated state forged primarily through voluntary alliances and marriages in which the Belarusian territories maintained a significant degree of autonomy. There are no recorded instances of major battles between Belarusians and the non-Slavic Lithuanians, nor any significant ethnic oppression, but rather long periods of tolerance and cohabitation.

From the early fourteenth century onwards, the rulers of Moscow used Orthodoxy as a pretext for purportedly "reuniting" the Christian Slavic peoples. They claimed the Belarusian lands as part of their ecclesiastical and ethnic heritage, alleging an inheritance from the lands of Kievan Rus, a Christian principality that disintegrated in the twelfth century. Muscovite leaders also claimed that the three East Slavic peoples—Belarusians, Russians, and Ukrainians—sprang from an ancient Russian root, hence effectively denying the distinctiveness of a separate Belarusian nationality.

At the end of the fourteenth century, the Grand Duchy of Lithuania, Rus, and Samogitia was united through marriage with the Kingdom of Poland, a move that was politically and strategically beneficial for both sides. In 1569 the two entities forged a federation under the provisions of the Lublin Union but still leaving a significant degree of autonomy for the Grand Duchy. Nonetheless, over the next two centuries most of the Belarusian nobility and gentry were Polonized while much of the peasantry were pressured to convert to the Uniate Church, which maintained allegiance to the Vatican while preserving its traditional Orthodox liturgy. Because nationality and religion were so closely interwoven, this process was perceived as Polish colonization and acculturation. By the late eighteenth century, the Grand Duchy had been transformed into a unitary and more centralized Polish Commonwealth.

The partitions of the Commonwealth by Russia, Prussia, and Austria at the end of the eighteenth century initiated a process of Russification on the Belarusian territories as Moscow under the rule of Catherine II assumed full control over the region. Muscovite propaganda depicted the takeover of Belarus and Ukraine as a natural "merger" with the Great Russians. The name Belarus was banned from official use, the Uniate Church was liquidated, and Russian was made the sole official language. The Tsarist government claimed Belarus as a solely Russian province. When the Tsarist Empire collapsed in 1917, a Belarusian independence movement sprang up. A Belarusian National Committee, elected by a number of political parties and organizations, sought the creation of a democratic republican administration and a much looser link with Russia.

Bolshevik forces seized power in the Belarusian capital Minsk in November 1917 and excluded the autonomy of Belarus from their program. An All-Belarusian Congress was subsequently convened by independence activists who proclaimed a Belarusian Democratic Republic in March 1918 and refused to recognize Bolshevik authority. The move was condemned by Russia's communist leaders who in January 1919 established the Belarusian Soviet Socialist Republic. Meanwhile, Polish forces occupied western Belarus and fought a series of battles with the Soviet Red Army. After the conclusion of peace talks between Moscow and Warsaw, the Treaty of Riga was signed in March 1921, which divided Belarus between the Russian Soviet Federated Socialist Republic and independent Poland.

After a short period of "Belarusization," through the incorporation of nationally minded elites in the governing structure and the promotion of the Belarusian language and culture, the Soviet authorities launched a violent crackdown against all manifestations of Belarusian political and national autonomy. During the 1930s, hundreds of thousands of people were either sent to labor camps or more rapidly exterminated in mass executions. The rural areas were brought under strict central control through a program of forced collectivization. The country's intelligentsia was the main victim of Stalin's repression, and this policy was extended to western Belarus after the area was annexed from Poland and incorporated into the Soviet Union in September 1939. In inter-war Poland, a policy of Polonization was pursued by Warsaw from the mid-1920s onwards, and by the late 1930s many Belarusian cultural and political organizations were banned and Belarusian deputies lost their seats in the Polish parliament.

Belarus's losses during World War II (1941–1945) were staggering: an estimated 2.2 million people lost their lives as a consequence of the German invasion and occupation, the Nazi genocide, and the Soviet repression and mass deportations. Over two hundred cities were destroyed as was most of the country's industry and agriculture. A struggle for independence led by nationalist guerrillas was crushed by Moscow during the late 1940s and Stalinist totalitarianism was reimposed on the country. Moscow's purges eliminated all top Belarusian communists whose loyalty and absolute obedience to Moscow was suspect. The post-war denationalization campaign was intended to extinguish the Belarusian language as well as any independent political, cultural, religious, and economic activities.

POST-COMMUNIST DEVELOPMENTS

A major reason for the weakness of the Belarusian national movement was an "inability to displace hegemonic Russophile myths and anchor a new Belarusian identity firmly in a rival historiography."[2] Lacking a strong national identity and a prolonged history of independent statehood, and with its intelligentsia largely eliminated and replaced by Russian officials, Belarus became one of the most docile of Soviet republics.[3] The Communist Party of Belarus (CPB) served as a puppet of Moscow and acquiesced to all of its initiatives. Russification was an important component of Stalinism and Sovietization. Belarus's communist leaders resisted the reform program of Soviet Secretary General Mikhail Gorbachev in the late 1980s fearing that any resurgence of Belarusian identity would dislodge them from power.

Not until the Chernobyl nuclear power plant disaster in neighboring Ukraine in 1986, which predominantly affected the territory of Belarus, did growing sectors of the population seriously question the logic of Soviet rule. The discovery of mass graves in the forests of Kurapaty on the outskirts of the capital Minsk, where Stalin ordered the execution of hundreds of thousands of Belarusians by Soviet internal security forces, exacerbated opposition to the republic's subservience to Moscow's *dictat*. Nonetheless, Belarus failed to develop a reformist and market-oriented wing within the ruling party, which remained susceptible to demagogic and authoritarian pressures even after the demise of the Soviet Union.

By the close of 1986, growing numbers of intellectuals, cultural workers, and students were writing documents and arranging demonstrations calling for a national rebirth. Letters calling for the restoration of the Belarusian language were dispatched to Gorbachev, but the official reaction in Minsk was to harass the signatories. Hundreds of informal groups sprang up around the country, calling for a national "renewal" *(adradennie)*. Disclosures about the Soviet mass murders at Kurapaty in 1937–1941 further galvanized national activists around the country.

In June 1989, at a meeting held in Vilnius, Lithuania to avoid state repression, the Belarusian Popular Front (BPF) was established from a conglomerate of clubs, associations, and parties. Its leader was archaeologist Zyanon

Paznyak, who first discovered the graves at Kurapaty. The BPF announced itself as a movement and not a political party, initially calling for the restructuring of society, a renewal of the Belarusian nation on the principles of democracy and humanism, and greater Belarusian autonomy within the Soviet Union. Unlike in the three Baltic states, where even the local communists supported political independence by the early 1990s, the "Russified Party apparatus in Minsk was immobilized by its view of the republic as a province of Moscow."[4] Hence, attempts to create a political compromise between ex-communists and pro-independence forces ended in failure and politics remained highly polarized.

With public pressures mounting through rallies, demonstrations, and strikes, and the Soviet Union on the verge of disintegration, the regime in Minsk grudgingly conceded to the forces of national independence. In January 1990, a law was passed making Belarusian the official language of the republic and thereby replacing Russian. In March 1990, elections were held to the Belarus Supreme Council (parliament) and were open to opposition candidates. Although these were the first openly contested elections, no organized opposition to the Communist Party existed aside from the Belarusian Popular Front (BPF). The Communist Party controlled the media and limited BPF campaigning and influence. Most of the seats outside of the major cities and the Minsk region were uncontested. The BPF only won 34 seats of 365, with the remaining seats going to Communist Party members. Many of the representatives could not be identified according to party lines, although approximately 40 to 50 deputies were allied with or sympathetic to the BPF.[5]

Communist-appointed electoral committees were empowered to screen all parliamentary candidates. The Russified communist old guard won an overwhelming majority of seats due to their control of the media, state funds, industrial enterprises, and collective farms. The BPF faction in the legislature, together with agrarian and veterans' groups and some communists, established a Democratic Club in opposition to the conservative majority. It declared its main goals to be Belarusian independence and the creation of a political democracy and a market economy.

On 27 July 1990, the Supreme Council adopted a Declaration of Belarusian State Sovereignty under the authority of constitutional law. In a referendum on the preservation of the Soviet Union held on 17 March 1991, 83.3% of Belarusians eligible to vote took part and of that number 82.7% chose to stay in the Union whereas 16.1% favored separation and 16.7% abstained. During the coup attempt in Moscow on 19 August 1991, Mikalai Dzemyantsei, chairman of the Belarusian Supreme Council, announced his support for the pro-Soviet hard-line coup plotters. When the coup attempt collapsed, Dzemyantsei was forced to resign from office. Stanislau Shushkevich, his first deputy and a political outsider, replaced him. Shushkevich had entered politics only after the Chernobyl disaster and although he supported Belarusian sovereignty he was unable to mobilize the country to achieve democratic statehood until the Moscow coup attempt.

On 25 August 1991, the Shushkevich government proclaimed an independent Belarus, and four days later the Communist Party of Belarus was declared illegal and all of its assets were frozen. The authorities announced the "departization" of all government organs, state enterprises, and public institutions. Most party members, including Prime Minister Vyacheslau Kebich, resigned from the party the day before its dissolution and thereby remained in power. In September 1991, the chairmanship (presidency) of the Supreme Council was opened for election. Kebich and Shushkevich faced off for the position, but after consecutive rounds of voting, neither could attain a majority. Eventually, Kebich dropped out of the race and handed the position to Shushkevich. But Kebich remained the dominant force in the Supreme Council, blocking Shushkevich's relatively moderate economic reform program.

At an extraordinary session on 17–19 September 1991, the Supreme Council changed the name of the state from the Belarusian Soviet Socialist Republic to the Republic of Belarus. It also adopted as new state symbols the white-red-white flag of the 1918 Belarusian Democratic Republic and the coat-of-arms of the Grand Duchy of Lithuania, Rus, and Samogitia. Due to the Supreme Council's negligent economic policy and its emphasis on closer ties with Russia, the BPF began calling for early elections in the fall of 1992. Although the movement managed to garner enough signatures for a referendum on early parliamentary elections, the Supreme Council repeatedly defeated these attempts by raising technical problems and voting against the referendum. In July 1993, after refusing to sign the Collective Security Pact of the Moscow-led Commonwealth of Independent States (CIS), Shushkevich was faced with a no-confidence vote by the communist old guard in parliament. Although this attempt failed, it laid the ground for greater political and social upheaval.

In November 1993, Alyaksandr Lukashenka, head of the Supreme Soviet's anti-corruption committee, began to attack the credibility of both Shushkevich and Kebich, accusing them of abusing state funds for their personal use. Neither of the charges was proven but the reputation of both politicians suffered as a result. In January 1994, Lukashenka raised the charges again, this time forcing no-confidence votes against both Shushkevich and Kebich. Shushkevich failed to survive but Kebich remained in his post. Myacheslau Hryb, a member of the old communist *nomenklatura* and effectively a puppet of Kebich, replaced Shushkevich as chairman of the Supreme Council.

On 30 March 1994, the new Belarusian constitution was passed, creating the Office of President and declaring Belarus a presidential republic and delineating executive powers. The new constitution also created a smaller, 260-member unicameral parliament but it failed to create a full-time legislature. The BPF opposed the creation of an executive branch, fearing that such a powerful office had the potential for dictatorial tendencies so early in Belarus's democratization efforts. Elections for the post were held in June and July 1994 with Lukashenka winning the ballot by an overwhelming majority of over 80% of the vote in the second round. Kebich was favored at the beginning of the campaign with Lukashenka running as an outsider. Kebich's heavy-handed control of the media led to a decrease in public favor and tended to support Lukashenka's accusations of official corruption.

Lukashenka and Kebich ran on similar economic and foreign policy platforms but the issues of corruption and trust dominated their contest. Shushkevich's campaign emphasized the importance of Belarusian independence together with a slow pace of economic reforms. In the first round of the ballot, BPF leader Paznyak adopted a platform emphasizing Belarusian nationalism and dedication to far-reaching economic reforms. Paznyak and Shushkevich competed with one another by appealing to similar constituencies, whereas the high-profile struggle between Kebich (representing the status quo) and Lukashenka (emphasizing a dynamic anti-corruption crusade) dominated the second election campaign. On 21 July 1994, after he was elected, Lukashenka appointed Mikhail Chihir as the new prime minister.

During the presidential campaign, Lukashenka had supported a command economy and closer ties to Russia. Over time, he began to implement those policies and increase his hold over the country. In July 1994, he signed an agreement on economic and monetary union with Russia to complement the signing of the Commonwealth of Independent Sates (CIS) Defensive Security Pact, which had passed earlier in December 1993. On 25 February 1995, Lukashenka signed a comprehensive friendship treaty with Russia for joint defense, monetary, and economic policies and thereby pushed the previous agreements even further. On 14 May 1995, a referendum was passed by the electorate declaring Belarusian and Russian as the two official state languages, replacing the Belarusian flag with the Soviet era emblem, calling for full integration with Russia, and giving the president the right to dissolve parliament.

Also in May 1995, the International Monetary Fund (IMF) forced Lukashenka to restart the stalled privatization plan or risk losing financial loans. He eventually complied, but these reform efforts became linked to Russian reform policies that further complicated the process. In July 1995, Lukashenka halted the transfer of nuclear weapons to Russia as stipulated under the renegotiated Strategic Arms Reduction Treaty (START) and ended Belarusian compliance with the Conventional Forces in Europe (CFE) treaty. In response to growing international criticism, Lukashenka claimed that the eventual union of Belarus and Russia would ensure that the arms treaties were obsolete.

Lukashenka's policies emasculated the Supreme Council and created a virtual one-man dictatorship over the country. The President became both head of state and chief executive. Belarusian nationalism was systematically stifled and efforts to create a union with Russia were stepped up dramatically. Seven main opposition parties, initiators of the "round table," appealed to the national parliament to announce the impeachment of the President for his violation of the country's laws and constitution. However, Lukashenka largely controlled the parliamentary elections in May 1995 by dominating the media and limiting the amount of money candidates could spend on their campaigns.

The elections took several months to complete because of a consistently low voter turnout for numerous parliamentary seats. In the meantime, Lukashenka refused to recognize the legitimacy of the legislature and largely ruled by issuing presidential decrees.[6] He threatened to impose direct presidential rule if the elections failed to produce the required quorum for a working parliament. By December 1995, a sufficient number of seats were filled for parliament to make the general elections valid.

The new Supreme Council was composed mainly of Communists (42 seats), their Agrarian Party allies (33 seats), a forty-deputy bloc of Lukashenka loyalists (styling itself as "Accord"), and a 96-seat majority of purportedly unaffiliated or "independent" candidates. Opposition and democratic groups remained small and weak with the BPF proving unable to gain a single seat in the legislature.[7] The urban-based democratic parties were effectively routed, with estimates that the centrists had obtained fewer than thirty parliamentary seats. International election monitors declared that the parliamentary elections were "neither free nor fair" because of numerous irregularities. The struggle between President and parliament continued throughout the second half of the decade with Lukashenka constantly gaining ascendancy over government decision-making. For example, Lukashenka gained the power to appoint and dismiss local government officials.

Oppositionist politics was marked by dispute, fractiousness, and governmental obstruction. The Civic Accord Bloc (CAB) was an attempt to unite moderate democrats and economic reformers. Initially, it elicited a great deal of attention because it added a moderate element to the polarized political landscape. Joint documents were signed between the member parties and constituencies were divided up. The United Civic Party (UCP), however, was delayed in gaining registration and could not nominate candidates. Meanwhile, the Social Democratic Party of National Accord (SDPNA) suffered internal differences over a lack of a clear ideology and organizational structure. Party leaders could not control the situation and party members began to violate agreements with the United Democratic Party (UDP) over constituency distribution. These factors eventually led to the dissolution of the CAB.

On 27 September 1996, the Civic Action Caucus (CAC) was formed as a centrist movement dedicated to breaking the deadlock between the BPF and the communists in the Supreme Council. This caucus included the United Democratic Party, the Peasants Party, the Green World Party, and the United Civic Party, but it exerted little or no influence on Lukashenka's policies.

Lukashenka sought to pass a new version of the constitution by increasing his own powers and further limiting the Supreme Council and the constitutional court. This would have left him as the *de facto* sole authority in the country. The President wanted to submit his version of the constitution directly to the people through a national referendum. Sixty deputies of the parliament supported him while 135 were opposed. The Speaker of the Supreme Council, Syamyon Sharetsky, proposed an alternative constitution whereby the office of President would be dissolved. The two sides eventually agreed to hold a national referendum on 24 November 1996 with a total of seven questions. Two of the questions dealt with the alternative versions of the constitution. Lukashenka offered three other questions on the free sale and purchase of land, the continuation of the death penalty, and changing Belarusian Independence Day to the date Soviet forces liberated Belarus from the Nazis. The parliament offered two questions on banning special funding not included in the budget and on direct elections for local officials.

The constitutional court ruled that neither version of the constitution would be legally binding if approved by the public. Instead, the parliament would need to decide how to enforce the proposed constitution. Lukashenka opposed the ruling and demanded that the referendum result be legally binding. He dismissed Viktor Hanchar, chairman of the Electoral Commission, thus overstepping his constitutional powers. In response, Prime Minister Chihir and several cabinet members resigned while Lukashenka issued a decree making the results of the upcoming referendum legally binding. The new Prime Minister, Syarhei Linh, proved loyal to Lukashenka, who was seeking to curtail legislative powers and vastly expand those of the presidency.

The political crisis continued through late November 1996, when the Supreme Council Speaker Syamyon Sharetsky called for Lukashenka's impeachment. Impeachment proceedings were to begin, when Russian mediators stepped in and brokered a compromise between the executive and legislative branches. Both sides agreed to hold the joint referendum and have the questions on the constitution stand as non-binding suggestions to be enforced by a 100-member committee equally represented by the two sides. The compromise collapsed the day after it was reached, due to parliament's failure to approve it. Lukashenka then returned to his previous stance to make the referendum legally binding, and impeachment proceedings were delayed until after the referendum.[8]

Lukashenka's version of the constitution was supported by 70.5% of the voters, and all of his other proposals passed.[9] Only 7.9% of voters supported the parliament's version and neither of their other two propositions passed. In the last four hours of voting, turnout reportedly jumped from 59% to 84% of the 7.5 million eligible voters. These numbers were widely seen as inflated and the entire referendum was perceived as unfair. Lukashenka gave himself sweeping powers, as the controversial referendum allowed him to change the constitution and extend his presidency by two years, until 2001.

The 260-seat Supreme Council was abolished and a bicameral legislature was established consisting of a 110-seat Chamber of Representatives (the lower house) and a 64-seat Council of the Republic (upper house). Parliament became an ineffective and largely paralyzed body that was not even empowered to draw up a budget. The Prime Minister and his Cabinet of Ministers were appointed by the President as were the governors of Belarus's six regions *(oblasts)*. At the same time, Lukashenka was able to maintain his popularity and public mandate by blaming the parliament and government for corruption, incompetence, and economic decline, thereby deflecting attention and responsibility away from his office.

Regardless of domestic and international protests, Lukashenka began to implement the new constitution. The draft signed into law by the president on 28 November 1996 called for the dissolution of the Supreme Council and the creation of a 110-member House of Representatives. The parliament was dissolved and a new legislature was quickly chosen from former Supreme Council deputies who supported Lukashenka; they first convened on 28 November 1996. Through the referendum and its quick enforcement, Lukashenka further solidified his drive for one-man rule, styled as a "vertical presidency," and extended his term in office from five to seven years.

Meanwhile, the ousted parliament continued to meet and refused to recognize the authority of the new legislature. In addition, five of the eleven constitutional court justices resigned and were replaced by Lukashenka's personal appointees. Through these developments, the prospects for democracy in Belarus suffered a severe blow and Lukashenka began to govern by decree without regard for constitutional norms. The results of the referendum also accelerated the reintegration of Belarus into the Russian orbit and led to increasing friction with and isolation from the West.

During the following three years, between 1996 and 1999, the Belarusian political scene was dominated by the constitutional dispute between the opposition and the government over the legitimacy of the constitution. As an expression of protest, the BPF opposition did not recognize the constitution and held its meetings virtually illegally in private apartments. Western governments regarded the new parliament as illegitimate and called for new presidential elections, despite Lukashenka's efforts to gain legitimacy for his extension of the presidency. The U.S. State Department's annual human rights reports concluded that the rights of Belarus's citizens were sharply limited and nearly all the power was concentrated in Lukashenka's hands. The President had successfully suppressed the opposition movement and the media by harassing them and putting restrictions on freedom of association, movement, and religion.

The political opposition hoped that by organizing alternative presidential elections they would attract international attention and thus force the Belarusian authorities to hold fully democratic general elections. However, the regime warned that this attempt would be looked upon as a plot to seize power. To forestall such an eventuality, Lukashenka detained a number of opposition election organizers, jailed one of the two major presidential candidates, while the second had to announce his candidacy from exile.[10] Despite official harassment the opposition managed to organize nationwide presidential elections between 6 and 16 May 1999. Opposition leaders claimed that Lukashenka's term would have ended if he had not unconstitutionally extended it until 2001 through the illegal 1996 referendum. According to the

1994 constitution his term in office expired in July 1999. Lukashenka took repressive measures against the organizers of the parallel election and moved to suppress their efforts.

Viktor Hanchar, the head of the Central Electoral Commission, announced that the elections were invalid. He called for a second round of voting to take place within three months. Hanchar claimed that the reasons for their invalidity included various irregularities during the vote, the hostility of the authorities, the absence of conditions for free election campaigning, and violations of the electoral law by Paznyak, one of the presidential candidates. Analysts agreed that an election designed to help promote the democratic opposition actually significantly damaged it. This gave Lukashenka an additional pretext not to enter into a dialogue with a fractured opposition.[11]

As Belarus was a member of the Organization for Security and Cooperation in Europe (OSCE), this international body tried to mediate the dispute between the government and opposition. It stressed the OSCE membership obligations in which member countries were obliged to respect democratic principles. During its eighth session, which took place in Russia in July 1999, the assembly called on all political forces in Belarus to cooperate and to seek a way out of the crisis while respecting Belarus's commitments to the OSCE. The assembly also requested all of the OCSE governments to support the development of the democratic electoral process and to render any necessary assistance.

Another dimension of this conflict was the strategic game that Lukashenka played with Russia. During the disintegration of the USSR, Moscow made certain that the Belarusian government signed a bilateral agreement creating a "common economic, political, and social space" between the two countries and recognizing Russian control over the 30,000 Belarus-based strategic troops and technical facilities. This gave Moscow the opportunity it wanted to subvert the new country's independence. Cognizant of Russian objectives, Lukashenka sought to gain additional power and prestige by uniting the two countries into one unitary state. He probably calculated that he would take the position of a vice-president in the new union while the actual presidency would be a rotating position. The first step both countries took in the process was the establishment of a Union of Russia and Belarus on 2 April 1997.

Lukashenka also planned to strengthen trade links with Russia and to use Russia's Kaliningrad region on the Baltic Sea for shipping Belarusian goods. Russian interests focused on the possibility of prolonging Yeltsin's presidency. Some analysts suggested that the Russian-Belarusian Union might have served Yeltsin much like the creation of the Federal Republic of Yugoslavia (FRY) helped the Serbian leader Slobodan Milošević to remain as head of the united state of Serbia and Montenegro. According to the Russian constitution, Yeltsin was barred from running again for the presidential post.

Nevertheless, Moscow moved slowly in the actual unification process fearing that Belarus would simply become an expensive Russian dependency.

Only a handful of agreements were signed and all of them were largely declarative and symbolic. On several occasions, Lukashenka displayed his impatience with this slow progress and threatened that he would turn to the West. He also warned Russia that he would stop key Russian gas transits across Belarus to Europe. There were clearly numerous obstacles to the grand design of Slavic unification as envisaged by the Belarusian President.

The economic and fiscal problems of both Russia and Belarus were enormous. But while Russia was subsidized by generous amounts of money from various international organizations, Belarus remained basically self-isolated. Minsk calculated that reintegration with Russia would prove a valuable substitute for Western-supported economic reforms. However, because of Moscow's own dire predicament, Russia was able to "reward" Belarus mostly by forgiving Minsk's substantial gas debt.[12] On 25 December 1998, Russian President Boris Yeltsin and Belarusian President Alyaksandr Lukashenka finally signed a "historic" agreement toward the total merger of the two countries. The Presidents said they would move steadily to introduce a single currency and harmonize taxes.

In discussions with the OSCE, Lukashenka asserted that any change in Belarus's foreign policy was conditional on international acceptance of the new constitution adopted in 1996 as the basis of the state system. However, his strong desire for recognition may also have been the result of the insecurity of his own position. According to the old constitution, Lukashenka should have vacated his post on 20 July 1999.

Belarus remained in poor economic condition, diplomatically and economically isolated and with a bankrupt currency. Lukashenka's Soviet-style economy had clearly failed but his rule persisted. Even though the union with Belarus was generally popular in Russia, political leaders in Moscow held different perceptions of the unitary state than Minsk. While Lukashenka expected some rapid economic benefits, Russia looked at the Union more as a long-term project. In fact, Russia largely gained what it wanted through the existing Union, by reintegrating its air defenses, intelligence operations, and arms production. The election of President Vladimir Putin in March 2000 created new complications for Lukashenka in that the Belarusian President faced a younger Kremlin leadership that could simply seek to incorporate Belarus as a republic within the Russian Federation and thereby curtail Lukashenka's ambitions to head the Russian-Belarusian Union.

Since his election as President, Lukashenka has systematically imposed a "presidential dictatorship" and a personalized authoritarianism over Belarus. Paradoxically, unlike in Serbia, Croatia, and elsewhere, this was accomplished not through the manipulation of ethno-nationalist sentiments but through the traditions of Soviet totalitarianism and Belarusian subservience to Moscow. Integration with Russia was part of a broader objective to reconstitute a pan-Slavic state in which Belarus could play a galvanizing role. Lukashenka used populism and "socialist nostalgia" to gain public support and he "exploited the weak foundations of representative government, democratic processes, and legal norms into a general indictment of the parliamentary system."[13]

In addition, the country's democrats possessed little experience, resources, and public support outside the capital and a handful of other major cities. However, the absence of any sizeable ethnic minorities in Belarus, or calls for ethnic or territorial autonomy, prevented the fomenting of ultra-nationalism and inter-ethnic disputes by the government. Out of approximately 10.2 million citizens, 78% were Belarusians, 13% Russians, 4% Poles, 3% Ukrainians, and 1% Jews. Minsk did not in general employ xenophobia or nationalism to find scapegoats based on ethnicity. In essence, the Lukashenka regime could be defined as essentially "anti-nationalist," "pan-Slavic," and "Soviet restorationist" in its orientation and this provided a foundation for its statist-populist authoritarianism.

Lukashenka relied principally on the country's internal security organs to uphold his power and to deter or terrorize his opponents. The number of security force personnel rose to about 180,000 troops or double the size of Belarus's armed forces. Lukashenka also increased the number of administrative posts through the establishment of executive "vertical structures" from the center to local level, and centrally controlled the economy and financial system. This effectively overrode any alternative sources of authority. The Lukashenka regime engaged in systematic repression against any manifestations of political dissent and opposition. For example, it outlawed independent labor unions and abolished parliamentarians' immunity from prosecution among.

As a result of incessant official pressures, in August 1996 Zyanon Paznyak, the Chairman of the Belarusian Popular Front, and Sergei Naumchik, representative of the Belarusian Helsinki Human Rights Committee, obtained political asylum in the United States. The European Union charged that the human rights situation in Belarus was "inadmissible." The organization criticized Belarus for its failure to uphold freedom of the press and the right of citizens to demonstrate freely. The Strasbourg-based European Parliament complained that President Lukashenka had adopted an increasingly "dictatorial style of government," which raised serious questions about future EU relations with Belarus. In particular, the European Parliament accused Lukashenka of total disregard for the democratically elected legislature and of repressing any opposition to his regime.

In May 1997, Nikolai Statkevich, the leader of the Belarusian Social Democratic Party, was sentenced to jail for violating a presidential ban on organizing unsanctioned rallies. Statkevich was arrested the previous day after he persuaded about 5,000 participants in a trade union rally to join an opposition march against Lukashenka.

In November 1997, Belarusian authorities closed the nation's main opposition newspaper *Svaboda* (Freedom), marking one of the harshest crackdowns by the regime on the political opposition. Indeed, the Belarusian government consistently restricted the development of independent media. It maintained a tight monopoly over printing and broadcasting facilities and over media distribution outlets. Most television stations were state owned and controlled and private media were terminated when they fell afoul of the authorities. The U.S.-based Committee to Protect Journalists reported that the leaders of Belarus were among the world's top ten "enemies of the press." According to the report, President Lukashenka "bullies the press with Soviet-era tactics, tightening his stranglehold by shutting down independent media and publicly denouncing journalists."[14] Indeed, under Lukashenka the Belarusian media had far less freedom than they did during Gorbachev's *glasnost.*

In January 1998, thirty-four well-known Belarusian intellectuals signed the Belarusian Declaration of Freedom, a document created within the framework of Charter 97, a popular opposition political movement initiated in November 1997 with the goal of combating the dictatorship by peaceful means. In April 1998, the Belarusian authorities officially liquidated six political parties. Opposition politicians, journalists, and writers established a Belarusian Association of Prisoners of Conscience of the Lukashenka Regime. The association united people who had been imprisoned for political activities. It included poet Slavamir Adamovich, journalist Pavel Sheremet, and the Belarusian Popular Front (BPF) Deputy Chairman Yury Khadyka. The organization adopted a statement demanding that trials of current political prisoners be fully open.

In September 1998, a new pro-communist Popular Patriotic Union (PPU) announced that it would support President Lukashenka in the next presidential elections. Under the new Belarusian law, anyone found guilty of any offense, including even those of an administrative nature, was barred from running in local and national elections. This provision primarily affected the opposition since many opposition activists were fined or detained for taking part in protest actions. Lukashenka warned legislators that if such a provision were not included in the election law he would simply introduce it by decree.

Leading members of the Belarusian opposition responded that the new local election law was undemocratic. Barys Hyunter of the Belarusian Popular Front stressed that his organization would not participate in elections organized under the law passed by the "illegitimate Chamber of Representatives." Alyaksandr Dabravolsky of the United Civic Party (UCP) stated that the authorities were afraid of democratic elections and had done everything to ensure that opposition organizations did not participate in them.

In January 1999, Syamyon Sharetsky, speaker of the 1994 parliament, confirmed his intention to convene that body, despite a warning by the prosecutor's office. The officially disbanded 1994 parliamentary body scheduled presidential elections for 16 May 1999. The 43 deputies attending the session also approved a 19-member Central Electoral Commission headed by Viktor Hanchar, who chaired that body before the 1996 referendum. The authorities warned the opposition that their actions would be considered unconstitutional.

Despite the incessant pressure and harassment, Belarusian democrats continued to organize and mobilize in an oppressive political climate. On 12 January 1999, several Belarusian opposition parties elected their representatives to a Congress of Democratic Forces of Belarus (CDFB). The Belarusian Popular Front, the country's largest opposition organization, announced that it would send 100 of its activists to the congress. The Belarusian Popular Front, the Belarusian Social Democratic Party, and the United Civic Party decided to consolidate their efforts to hold presidential elections on 16 May 1999. In addition, representatives of more than 100 non-governmental organizations in the Vitebsk region proposed launching a nationwide social and political movement, called "For Belarus," with the aim of defending Belarusian sovereignty and "deposing the country's bankrupt leadership in a nonviolent way."

On 22 February 1999, the Belarusian opposition formed a Consultative and Coordination Council of Democratic Forces (CCCDF) to unify all democratic opposition organizations. This was a broad group of anti-Lukashenka parties including social democrats, liberals, nationalists, agrarians, and communists. On 15 March 1999 about 3,000 anti-government protesters marched in Minsk marking the fifth anniversary of the post-Soviet constitution and urging President Lukashenka not to exceed his term. In March 1999, OSCE proposed negotiations between Lukashenka and four opposition leaders: Syamyon Sharetsky, Chairman of the 1994 parliament, Viktor Hanchar, chairman of the Central Electoral Commission, and Zyanon Paznyak and Mikhail Chihir, candidates in the presidential elections.

In April 1999, Western governments criticized local elections in Belarus as an undemocratic attempt by its leaders to consolidate power. On 16 May 1999, several hundred voters were arrested on the presidential election day unrecognized by Lukashenka. The election turnout was reported at 53%, but there was no winner in the elections although some unofficial data showed that Zyanon Paznyak came first. In July 1999, Lukashenka declared that he planned to rule until November 2001, despite the fact that his presidential term had legitimately expired. That same month, Syamyon Sharetsky, speaker of the 1994 parliament, sought refuge in the OSCE office and later fled Belarus for Lithuania for fear of persecution.

On 19 September 1999, the 1994 "opposition parliament" appointed delegates to represent the opposition at the OSCE-mediated talks with the government. The delegates included Stanislau Bohdankevich and Anatoly Lyabedzka of the United Civic Party, Yury Belenky and Vintsuk Vyachorka of the Belarusian Popular Front, Sergei Kalyakin and Yelena Skrygan of the Belarusian Party of Communists, Nikolai Statkevich and Myacheslau Hryb of the Belarusian Social Democratic Party, Alyaksandr Bukhvostau and Leonid Lemesonok of the Belarusian Party of Labor, Stanislau Shushkevich and Aleh Trusau of the Belarusian Social Democratic *Hramada*, and Valentina Polevikova of the Women's Party *Nadzeya* (Hope).

During a march for freedom in Minsk on 17 October 1999, with over 20,000 participants, hundreds were arrested and injured after a police assault. The

International Helsinki Federation for Human Rights (IHF) declared that the state of human rights and democratic institutions in Belarus was worsening by the day. The Council of Europe urged the Lukashenka regime to cease the policy of mass harassment of the opposition, to release all political dissidents, and disclose details about recent abductions. Meanwhile, Belarusian opposition parties pledged to boycott the scheduled October 2000 elections for the "illegitimate parliament" that Lukashenka's supporters were organizing.

The parliamentary elections on 15 October 2000 were comfortably won by parties and "independents" supporting President Lukashenka. The Belarusian opposition and international organizations declared the ballot to be seriously flawed because of Lukashenka's tight media controls, harassment of opposition candidates, and close governmental supervision over the election process. Dozens of democratic candidates were disqualified from the elections and the vote counting was suspected to have been rigged by officials. By the close of 2000, the major opposition activists planned to field a joint candidate and participate in the presidential ballot scheduled for September 2001 in the hope of finally unseating Lukashenka. Belarusian democrats had evidently taken heart from the dramatic developments in Serbia in October 2000, when Milošević was ousted from power despite attempts to defraud the electorate.

POLITICAL PARTIES

Socialists and Social Democrats

Belarusian Patriotic Movement (BPM)
Belaruski Patryatychny Rukh (BPR)

The constituent assembly of the BPM was held on 8 October 1994 with the participation of some 300 delegates. Alyaksandr Lukashenka and his supporters created the movement after he won the presidential elections in June–July 1994. The party's first chairman was Anatoly Barankevich. Lukashenka ran on a platform of anti-corruption, economic reform, and close economic and military ties to Russia. The Movement sought to attract those undeclared members of the Supreme Council who were disenchanted with the collapse of the Soviet Union. Its core consisted primarily of retired military officers. In the May 1995 general elections, the BPM ran in a bloc named the National Movement of Belarus together with the Liberal Democratic Party and the Slavic Assembly. The BPM won one seat after the second round of the elections in June 1995.

Barankevich characterized the party as a "voluntary sociopolitical organization" with a course set toward a "socially just society." According to him, the party stood for a "renovated union of fraternal republics—made up voluntarily and based on respect for nations and all national distinctive features."

The BPM stood against Belarus's participation in NATO's Partnership for Peace program, and against full membership in NATO. In August 1996, the BPM picketed the U.S. embassy in Minsk with such slogans as "No to the CIA Provocation" and "Hands off the Belarusian People and their President." The action was authorized by the Minsk City Council.[15] A similar event was staged in April 1998, together with other leftist forces, and under similar slogans. According to Barankevich, the protest was provoked as a result of direct American interference in Belarusian affairs.[16]

The BPM signed the August roundtable agreement formulated by various political actors. It strongly supported the constitutional referendum and attacked the opposition forces as "anti-national." In a radio address in the wake of the referendum, Barankevich stated that the results were "the most convincing epilogue to the political spectacle which the opposition was unable to play out to the end." He accused the opposition of "ceaseless provocations," attacked the West for subversion, and characterized Stanislau Shushkevich as a "first-rate Russophobe."[17] In another address, Barankevich urged the expulsion of OSCE representatives from Belarus.

Belarusian Social Democratic Union (BSDU)
Belaruskaya Satsiyal Demakratychnaya Hramada (BSDH)

The party held its founding congress on 2–3 March 1991 and was registered in May of the same year. Parliamentarian Aleh Trusau became the BSDU chairman after the death of its first leader Mikhas Tkachou in October 1992. Its deputy chairmen were Mikalai Kryzhanouski and Ihar Charniauski. The party represented a revival of the Revolutionary Hramada Party (founded in 1902), which sought an independent Belarus but was outlawed after the formation of the Soviet republic in 1919.

The BSDU supported the creation of a humanitarian society with a "multi-structured economy," and stressed the freedom of the individual, social justice, solidarity, and the political independence of Belarus. It favored a strong state presence in a market economy. The party considered itself a part of the global social democratic movement and claimed a constituency of workers, peasants, students, military personnel, and rural and urban intelligentsia. By the spring of 1995, it was reported to have 1,500 members and 83 local organizations. It held 12 seats in the pre-1995 Supreme Council and was closely allied with the Belarusian Popular Front. The BSDU put forward 62 candidates for the May 1995 parliamentary elections; eight went into the second round, but only two were elected.

The Union also established a military section in March 1991, which became the organizational core of the pro-independence Belarusian Association of Servicemen (BAS). In June 1996, as a result of an internal split, the BSDU joined the Party of People's Concord (PPC) and formed the Belarusian Social Democratic Party (BSDP). The Ministry of Justice officially disbanded the BSDU and gave registration to the newly formed BSDP.[18] A faction of BSDU members, including the chairman Aleh Trusau, opposed the creation of the BSDP and recreated the BSDU in September 1997. The party was to retain its old symbols and function as it did before the merger with the PPC and sought to restore its legal rights. At the founding congress in February 1998, Stanislau Shushkevich was elected chairman of the restored party and Aleh Trusau and Anatol Astapenka became his deputies. According to Shushkevich, the party's main aim was the restoration of the 1994 constitution.[19] The subsequent BSDU chairman was Nikolai Statkevich.

Belarusian Social Democratic Party (BSDP)
Belaruskaya Satsiyal Demakratychnaya Partiya (BSDP)

In early 1996, the Belarusian Social Democratic Union (BSDU) united with the Party of People's Concord (PPC) to form the Belarusian Social Democratic Party (BSDP), with Nikolai Statkevich as leader. However, out of 2,000 registered BSDU members, only 300 joined the new party. In early 1997, the BSDP was active in organizing popular rallies. In June 1997, its leadership claimed 108 branches in over 90 localities throughout the country. The party cooperated closely with Social Democrats in Denmark and the Netherlands and prepared to join the Socialist International.[20] The party issued numerous warnings about the country's future and the creeping authoritarianism of the Lukashenka regime.

In the summer of 1997, around 600 BSDP members decided to re-establish the BSDU (*Hramada*) and created a committee for that purpose which included Aleh Trusau, the original leader of the BSDU, and Stanislau Shushkevich, former speaker of the parliament. Trusau, Shushkevich and their supporters established a committee in April 1998 for the revival of *Hramada*. Statkevich considered the committee as representing a "force making another attempt to split the Social Democrats."[21] The party was ordered to leave its office for allegedly failing to pay its rent; its representatives claimed the purpose of this measure was to stifle the opposition.

As the 13th Supreme Council resumed its work, the BSDP held its third national convention in August 1998. According to Myacheslau Hryb, BSDP members and non-party people planned to create a Social Democratic faction that would hold monthly meetings at the BSDP office. Hryb was also elected as its chairman. The BSDP intended to concentrate on economic and human rights issues in Belarus. In January 1999, the BSDP, with Statkevich as its leader, organized a demonstration in support of a sovereign Belarus. The leitmotiv of the demonstration was a protest against further integration with Russia. Stanislau Shushkevich became the BSDP chairman.

Belarusian Party of Labor (BPL)
Belaruskaya Partiya Pratsy (BPP)

Alyaksandr Bukhvostau became the leader of the Belarusian Party of Labor (BPL), which in the spring of 1995 claimed to have 560 members who were mostly labor union activists.[22] The party's stated aim was to construct a democratic society, to create a judicial state on the principles of individual freedoms, and to achieve "well-being, morality, social justice and concord." In June 1995, the BPL denounced the economic situation in the country and warned of spontaneous mass protests. At the third special party congress, the delegates defined the referendum of November 1996 as a *coup d'état*. They voiced support for the 1994 constitution and for the 13th Supreme Council, and the party favored early parliamentary and presidential elections. The BPL also advocated abolishing the presidency altogether. The congress elected the leader of the Radio electronic labor union Henadz Fyadynich as deputy chairman of the party and decided to establish a newspaper called *Workers' Solidarity*.[23] The BPL condemned the presidential decree "On Urgent Measures for Strengthening Labor and Executive Discipline" as authoritarian and unnecessary.

In March 1998, the party issued a statement condemning the political repression orchestrated by Lukashenka. Party leaders believed that the roots of Belarus' unfavorable situation stemmed from the November 1996 referendum that created a dictatorial regime. The party claimed that the only way out of the situation was to re-establish the provisions of the 1994 constitution, as well as the principle of a separation of powers, as in regular Western democracies.[24]

Socialist Party of Belarus (SPB)
Satsiyalistychnaya Partiya Belarusi (SPB)

The Socialist Party of Belarus (SPB) was founded after the 1994 presidential elections for those favoring the restoration of Soviet era policies. It was registered in September 1994 and won one seat in the May 1995 parliamentary elections. It called for the political union of all members of the Commonwealth of Independent States (CIS). The party was a strong supporter of the Kebich government and basically represented the interests of the higher *nomenklatura* class. Vyacheslau Kuznyatsou became the head of the party's political committee, the supreme body of the party. Membership of the SPB in 1996 was reported to be about 650 people. Kuznyatsou claimed that the party had among its members collective farmers, teachers, entrepreneurs, and business executives.[25] The SPB declared as its objective "the creation of a socialist-oriented society, the construction of a legal social democratic state, and the creation of conditions for a fitting and happy life for the entire population of Belarus."

At least two other social democratic formations were active during the 1990s, although both were small and uninfluential: the Social Democratic

Party of Belarus (SDPB) *(Satsiyal-Demakratychnaya Partiya Belarusi, SDPB)*, formed in March 1991 and chaired by Mikhas Tkachou; and the Republican Party, Labor and Justice (RPLJ), formed in June 1993 and chaired by Anatol Netsilkin.

Liberals

Party of National Accord (PNA)
Partiya Narodnay Zhody (PNZ)

The Party of National Accord (PNA) was inaugurated in April 1992 and registered in June of the same year with Henadz Karpenka as chairman. After June 1995, the party's chairman was Leonid Syachka. PNA membership in early 1995 was reported at 2,117 people with 52 local organizations. The PNA managed to gain eight seats in parliament after several rounds of elections between May and December 1995. The PNA refused to identify with either the Belarusian Popular Front (BPF) or with the Belarusian Patriotic Movement (BPM) but associated with similar democratic parties. It stood for market economic reforms, the construction of a "civilized judicial state," and improvements in living conditions. Primarily a party of technocrats, the PNA was courted by both governmental and oppositionist parties. It supported the acceleration of economic reforms and pressed for early general elections, backing the BPF's effort to hold a referendum on the elections. The PNA's constituency united the regional *nomenklatura* with the popular intelligentsia. It possessed a largely social democratic philosophy, but regarded itself as centrist and liberal and sought to achieve national accord and broad public support.

United Democratic Party of Belarus (UDPB)
Abyadnanaya Demakratichnaya Partiya Belarusi (ADPB)

The United Democratic Party of Belarus (UDPB) was formed on 4 November 1990 and was officially recognized in March 1991 as the earliest registered independent political party. Its leaders included Alyaksandr Dabravolsky, the chairman, Mikhail Plisko, and Stanislau Husak. By the end of 1995, UDPB membership reportedly stood at around 1,500 with 83 local party organizations. The UDPB was the first political party outside the Belarusian Communist Party. It formed when three pro-democratic reform parties merged: Communists for Perestroika (formed in March 1989), the Democratic Party of Belarus (formed in October 1989), and the Republican Party (formed in May 1990). The party's main support came from the technical and scientific intelligentsia, as well some working-class and peasant backers. The UDPB was more committed to democratic reform than nationalism, claiming that the revival of the Belarusian language was not a paramount concern.

The UDPB supported Stanislau Shushkevich during the June–July 1994 presidential elections. It was originally allied with the BPF but joined the Civic Accord Bloc due to its more centrist views prior to the May–December 1995 Supreme Council elections. The UDPB was ideologically liberal and it supported the priority of human rights and the interests of the individual over that of the state. It strongly favored a market economy and a limited role for the government. It nominated 82 candidates in the May–December 1995 elections and in October 1995 it became one of the co-founders of the United Civic Party (UCP). It took nine seats in the legislature created at the end of 1995. The party established its own institute in Minsk for the study of socio-economic trends.

United Civic Party (UCP)
Abyadnanaya Grazhdanskaya Partiya (AGP)

The United Civic Party (UCP) was a center-right group formed in October 1995 on the basis of a merger between the United Democratic Party and the Civic Party. The former chairman of the National Bank of Belarus, Stanislau Bahdankevich, ousted from this position by President Lukashenka, became the party's leader. Bahdankevich remained a fierce critic of the government's economic policies. The UCP was described as one of liberal-conservative orientation. Its main goals were outlined as the preservation of Belarusian sovereignty, the introduction of private ownership and a free market for land, and the privatization of state property. Within the party, two groups could be identified—those supporting radical actions and those believing in more gradual change.[26]

In January 1997, the UCP tabled an initiative for the opposition parties to establish a shadow cabinet named the Public Coalition Government of Democratic Forces–National Economic Council (NEC). According to Henadz Karpenka, one of the most popular and influential UCP leaders, the NEC would be tasked with an analysis of the political and economic situation within Belarus in order make prognoses and train politicians.[27] On 22 March 1997, the UCP held its third congress at which Bahdankevich was re-elected the party's chairman. Anatoly Lyabedzka was elected deputy chairman; Vasil Szhlydzikau and Alyaksandr Dabravolsky were re-elected deputy chairmen for another term. Bahdankevich called for a single leader for the entire democratic movement in Belarus and proposed Henadz Karpenka as the candidate.

The UCP's aims as declared at its third congress were the re-establishment of constitutional law, the preservation of Belarusian sovereignty, closer cooperation with all democratic forces, the implementation of market reforms, and the formulation of an action program in case Lukashenka was overthrown. Chairman Bahdankevich stressed the strengthening of the party's organization and membership composition. The party claimed 92 district and town organizations as of March 1997. UCP members included several well-known scientists, political analysts, journalists, and diplomats. It also maintained close links with the Union of Belarusian Entrepreneurs, headed by parliamentary deputy Viktor Karyakin, a lobbying group active in seeking to improve economic and business opportunities in the country.

The UCP remained vehemently opposed to President Lukashenka's authoritarian style and destructive policies. It was active in organizing rallies and protested against any negotiations with Lukashenka. The party did not recognize the results of the constitutional referendum of November 1996, which it viewed as a disguised *coup d'état*. It stated that it would not participate in any elections on Lukashenka's terms. The UCP protested against the consultations between the sacked 13th Supreme Council and the Belarusian government under European mediation, charging that Lukashenka's constitution was not recognized by the "entire civilized world."[28] In 1999, the UCP staged a campaign for new presidential elections that were outlawed and suppressed by the authorities.

Belarusian Republican Party (BRP)
Belaruskaya Respublikanskaya Partiya (BRP)

The Belarusian Republican Party (BRP) was created in March 1994. The party co-chairmen included Valery Artyshevsky and Vladzimir Ramanau. The party's reported membership in early 1995 was 350 with 30 local organizations. The BRP stood for the creation of a sovereign democratic state with clear divisions of power and it emphasized the well-being of Belarusians and the development of national culture. A separate Republican Party (RP) *(Respublikanskaya Partiya, RP)* was reportedly formed in March 1994, with Viktor Talmachou as chairman. The party supported far-reaching economic reforms, placing aside nationalism and Belarus' relations with Russia. It aimed for the regeneration of a strong democratic Belarus and the strict observance of human rights. In 1995, it was reported to have 2,500 members and 60 local organizations. Vladimir Belazov became the party's leader. Another essentially liberal and pro-market formation was the Belarusian National Party (BNP) *(Belaruskaya Narodnaya Partiya, BNP)* established in November 1994 with Viktor Tsyareshchanka as chairman. It supported the construction of a unitary democratic state along socio-judicial principles, the implementation of far-reaching market reforms, guaranteed rights and freedoms, and a measure of social security for all citizens. Anatoly Astapenko became the subsequent BNP chairman in the late 1990s.

Christian Democrats

Belarusian Popular Front (BPF)
Belaruski Narodni Front (BNF)

The Belarusian Popular Front's (BPF) organizational committee was created in October 1988 by such prominent Belarusian intellectuals as Zyanon

Paznyak, Vasil Bykau, and Mikhas Dubyanetsky. The first congress, at which the governing organization (the *Soim*) was formed, took place in Vilnius, Lithuania, in June 1989. The BPF was registered as a party in May 1993. According to its leadership, the party possessed 4,000 registered members in June 1997.[29] Its leaders included Zyanon Paznyak (chairman), Sergei Naumchik, Lyavon Barshchevsky (acting chairman), Valentin Golubev, Yury Khadyka (co-deputy chairman), Vladzimir Zablotsky (co-deputy chairman), and Vintsuk Viachorka (secretary). The BPF was created as a movement and not a political party and was open to all individuals and groups who espoused Belarusian democracy and independence, including political parties and labor unions.

The BPF was declared a party only in 1993 when a pending law would have prevented non–registered parties from participating in national elections. Thus, the BPF lost its position as a "force above politics" and was pressured to enter the existing political arena and to deal with other parties on an equal basis. The BPF originally supported some form of sovereignty for Belarus within the Soviet Union but increasingly espoused full national independence.

Following the fall of communism throughout Eastern Europe in 1989, opposition candidates from the BPF were allowed to run for the Belarusian Supreme Council or parliament. Nevertheless, the ruling party undercut the potential popularity of the BPF by denying the Front access to the media and pressurizing many of its founders to leave the movement for fear of losing their jobs or other "privileges." Moreover, because of the poorly formed Belarusian identity and the continuing grip of the communist *nomenklatura*, the Popular Front could marshal only limited public support and faced a great deal of public indifference in building a broad-based national organization.

The BPF won only 37 seats out of a total of 360 in the 1990 parliamentary elections. Although a minority group, it used the parliament as a means of addressing the nation.[30] It supported the downfall of the Communist Party and the declaration of Belarusian independence. It criticized the slow pace of economic reforms in the following years, twice gathering signatures for a referendum to hold early parliamentary elections. The leftist majority in the Supreme Council blocked both efforts. In sum, the BPF was a Christian democratic and quasi-nationalist grouping supporting strong market reforms and affiliated with the Christian Democrat International. It fielded 147 candidates in the May–December 1995 parliamentary elections, but won no seats. Zyanon Paznyak and Sergei Naumchik both left the country and attempted to bolster Western opposition to Lukashenka. In their absence, Lyavon Barshchevsky became the BPF's acting chairman and leader.

The Front opposed the presidential constitution of March 1994, believing a strong presidency so early in the country's independence would plant the seeds of authoritarianism and prevent the flowering of genuine democracy. It preferred a stronger parliamentary system answerable to the people. It also opposed the monetary union with Russia of April 1994 and the CIS (Commonwealth of Independent States) security pact. The BPF presidential candidate, Paznyak, won 13.9% of votes in the first round of Belarus's last relatively democratic presidential elections in June–July 1994. Largely because of its persistent resistance to closer ties with Russia, the Front failed to win a larger share of Supreme Council seats in the May–December 1995 elections.

The BPF was one of the staunchest critics of Lukashenka's constitution and the controversial referendum of November 1996. It never recognized the constitution and considered Lukashenka's actions and his regime illegal. At a session in September 1994, the BPF stressed the need to unify the country's pro-independence democratic forces and explained the victory of Lukashenka in the presidential elections as a result of the economic crisis, a lack of social consciousness, Lukashenka's populism, and the short duration of the election campaign. Paznyak emphasized the need for Belarus to orient its policy and economy towards the survival of the nation. According to the party's program, foreign policy should be directed towards Europe and Germany in particular.[31]

The fourth congress of the BPF took place on 9 April 1995. It decided to enter the upcoming parliamentary elections with the same slogans as it had in 1990, "Let's Vote for Belarus's Independence, Well-being, Peace, and Consolidation on the Basis of Statehood and Independence."[32] After the BPF's failure to win seats in the parliamentary ballot, several BPF officials resigned from their posts. Deputy chairman Yury Khadyka claimed the BPF's alienation from the consciousness of the masses as well as the isolation of the Front's parliamentary opposition from the BPF were the primary causes of the BPF's failure during the elections.

The BPF remained active in organizing meetings and rallies in protest against the regime. In August 1996, the Front took part in the roundtable negotiations among political parties concerning the referendum on the new constitution proposed by Lukashenka. The BPF representative, Yury Khadyka, together with UCP's Bahdankevich, suggested initiating impeachment procedures against Lukashenka.[33] In early 1997, the BPF leadership called for Lukashenka to be medically examined by an international commission after reports by some of his entourage that he had been making important decisions without consulting anyone. The BPF was also actively engaged in the Independent Labor Unions of Belarus, an organization that faced substantial state repression throughout the 1990s.

At the Front's fifth congress on 21 June 1997 in Minsk, Paznyak, who had been in exile in the U.S. for two years, received the votes of 98% of the delegates as chairman of the party.[34] In his address to the congress, Paznyak stressed the need for the BPF to become a Belarusian national liberation movement and that the movement itself should be a wider phenomenon than the BPF through the coordination of additional forces and activities. Khadyka, a deputy chairman and a potential alternative leader to Paznyak, criticized the latter for his attacks on the other opposition parties and movements, which were often insulting and rude. Khadyka feared that such criticism could lead to a split within the democratic opposition movement.[35]

In August 1997, the BPF organization in the city of Vitsebsk issued a joint manifesto with the local organizations of the Christian Democratic Party, the United Civic Party, and the Belarusian Social Democratic Party. The manifesto called for a new movement, "Belarus," that would strive to make the country a "democratic, independent, and equal member of the family of European countries."[36] In January 1998, the names of opposition leaders, including Paznyak, were mentioned in connection with the alleged plot against the government that critics believed had been fabricated by Lukashenka.

The BPF agreed with the United Civic Party (UCP) on a plan for joint action. The two parties also considered the possibility of holding parliamentary and presidential elections in 1999 in accordance with the 1994 constitution.[37] The BPF called for a boycott of any elections called by Lukashenka and vowed to abstain from parliamentary elections scheduled for the fall of 1998, claiming it would not participate in any "election performance" while the anti-democratic regime was preserved. On 1 November 1999, Vintsuk Vyachorka replaced Zyanon Paznyak as the new BPF leader.

Belarusian Christian Democratic Association (BCDA)
Belaruskaya Khrystsiyanska Demakratychnaya Zluchnasts (BKDZ)

The Belarusian Christian Democratic Association (BCDA) was formed in June 1991 as a continuation of the former Belarusian Christian Democratic Party in West Belarus, disbanded by the pre-war Polish authorities in the 1930s. The leadership of the party in 1991 included Pyatro Silka (chairman) and Mikhail Areskau. It viewed itself as a religious and nationalist party seeking a moral, spiritual, and national rebirth through the Church and aimed to unite representatives of all Christian denominations. Its leadership included Silka, I. Bohdanovich, M. Areskau, E. Sabila, and E. Yanushevich. In June 1992, the BCDA joined in a coalition with the Belarusian Peasant Party and the National Democratic Party. It held a congress of landless peasants and was opposed to the registration of the Party of Communists of Belarus. In August 1997, jointly with other democratic parties, including the UCP and BPF, the BCDA formed the Belarus democratic movement. Other Christian-oriented parties during the 1990s included the Christian Democratic Party (CDP), led by Nikolai Krukovsky, and the Christian Democratic Choice (CDC), led by Valery Soroka.

Agrarians

Belarusian Peasant Party (BPP)
Belaruskaya Syalyanskaya Partiya (BSP)

The Belarusian Peasant Party (BPP) was formed on 23 February 1991 as a successor to the pre-Soviet agrarian movement that supported peasant ownership of land. It was registered in April the same year. The central party council chairman was Yehen Luhin; the deputy chairmen were Mikhail Antanienka, Ivan Nikitchanka, and Alyaksandr Dubko, who also ran for president. The party became one of the largest in Belarus, with over 15,600 members and 94 local organizations by the mid-1990s.

The BPP allied itself with the BPF for democratic and economic reform, but presented its own presidential candidate in the 1994 elections, who won only 6% of first-round votes. The party's members held deputy positions in local councils and several seats in the Supreme Council before the 1995 parliamentary elections. But after the May–December 1995 ballot it only took one legislative seat. The party maintained ties with the Christian Democratic Union in its support for a moral, spiritual, national, political, and economic rebirth of Belarus. It sought a reorganization of the collective and state farms through comprehensive privatization.

Among the BPP's goals were defense of the political and economic interests of the peasantry, and a "self-conscious" Belarusian nation with the preservation of its language and culture. In September 1995, the BPP broke away from the BPF due to its extreme opposition to the communist faction in the movement and joined other centrist parties in the Civic Action Caucus. The party denounced the regime in Belarus as dictatorial. It participated in the National Economic Council–Public Coalition Government shadow cabinet organized by the UCP. The BPP was instrumental in the creation of the Belarusian Peasant Union (BPU) *(Belarusky Syalyansky Sayuz, BSS)*, founded in November 1989 and registered in August 1991. By the mid-1990s, its membership stood at several hundred, mostly peasants, with branches in a majority of Belarusian counties. Led by BPU president Kastus Yarmolenka, several BPU members served as deputies in local governments. The Union's chief goal was the expansion of private farming, an unrestricted market economy, and full national independence for Belarus.

Agrarian Union of Belarus (AUB)
Agrarny Sayuz Belarusi (ASB)

The Agrarian Union of Belarus (AUB) was formed in June 1992. Its leader, Syamyon Sharetsky, was the speaker of the 13th Supreme Council. Other leaders included Myacheslau Hiruts and Alyaksandr Dubko. It claimed over 8,000 members as of early 1995. The AUB advocated a conservative and gradual economic reform policy and a state-regulated market economy, including the development of various kinds of ownership and an interaction between economic competition and state regulation. It essentially represented the interests of collective and state farm officials and other leading representatives of the agrarian sector. It was formed in opposition to the restoration of peasant land ownership advocated by the market-oriented BPP.

The AUB was regarded as Lukashenka's strongest supporter in the Supreme Council. It nominated 120 candidates in the May–December 1995 parliamentary elections and won the majority of seats in the first round. It finished in second place during the December 1995 round of balloting by garnering a total of 33 seats. In its program, the party sought a reform of the social system on the principles of democratic socialism. It was considered a close ally of the Party of Communists of Belarus (PCB) in rural areas, being better able to attract agrarian voters due to its access to funds and transportation.[38]

After the constitutional referendum in November 1996, Sharetsky became one of the outspoken opponents of President Lukashenka, criticizing him in particular on the question of Belarusian sovereignty, which the Agrarians supported. At a session of the executive committee in March 1998, its members voiced their disagreement with Sharetsky's position and deprived him of the right to represent the party. Sharetsky characterized the processes within the party as an attempt to "fit the party under the president" and claimed that he could not be deprived of any rights within the party since he left it upon becoming the Supreme Council speaker.[39] Alyaksandr Pavol became acting chairman of the party.

Greens

Green Party of Belarus (GPB)
Belaruskaya Partiya Zyalyonykh (BPZ)

The Green Party of Belarus (GPB) was founded in December 1992 and registered in February 1993. The GPB leader was Mikalay Kartash and it was reported that the party had 540 members by mid-1995 and obtained one Supreme Council seat in the May–December 1995 elections. The GPB arose out of outrage and concern over the Chernobyl nuclear accident and thus aimed to provide citizens with a healthy living environment. The party possessed its strongest support in the Gomel region and other areas most affected by the Chernobyl disaster. The party was against the construction of any new nuclear plants in Belarus, advocating instead the use of other resources such as biogas. It also threatened a mass campaign for a referendum on this issue.[40] The GPB also helped to establish a Belarusian Ecological Union in 1989 with Boris Savitsky as chairman.

Belarusian Ecological Union (BEU)
Belarusky Ekalagichny Sayuz (BES)

The Belarusian Ecological Union (BEU) was established in the spring of 1989 and registered in July of the same year. It claimed a membership of several thousand activists among all strata of the population with chapters in various cities and towns. Its first president was Boris Savitsky, a member of the presidium of the Belarusian Supreme Council. Its vice presidents included Radzim Haretsy, Y. Pyatrayeu, and L. Tarasienka. More than twenty members of the Union were legislators at various administrative levels, including five in the Supreme Council after the May 1995 and October 2000 parliamentary elections. The BEU's chief plank was defense of the environment in cooperation with other parties and movements, including Green parties throughout Europe.

Belarusian Ecological Party (BEP)
Belaruskaya Ekalagichnaya Partiya (BEP)

The Belarusian Ecological Party (BEP) was founded in December 1993 and registered in April 1994. The chairman of the Central Council was Aleksey Mikulich. The party counted 600 members and 11 local organizations in early 1995 and it took one seat in the parliament formed at the end of 1995. The party's major goals were the defense of civil rights and freedoms and the organization of active public participation in the conservationist movement. Liudmila Yelizarova became the BEP leader in 1994.

Another ecological formation, the Green World Party (GWP) *(Partiya Zelyonyy Mir, PZM)*, was founded in April 1994. It was led by Aleh Hramyka, and claimed to be the largest environmentalist party, with around 1,000 members and 15 local organizations by early 1995. The party's objectives included the creation of a healthy living environment and a "maximum opportunity for individual development."

Communists

Popular Movement of Belarus (PMB)
Narodny Ruh Belarusi (NRB)

The Popular Movement of Belarus (PMB) was formed in 1992 as an alliance of pro-government groupings. Chief among them were the three communist parties listed below. It embraced the hard-line left and the pro-Slavic "right" in an effort to challenge the Belarusian Popular Front (BPF). It advocated closer ties with Russia and an avoidance of Western influence, especially capital and market reform. The PMB held most of the seats in the Supreme Council after the 1990 elections. It backed Kebich against Shushkevich in the 1994 presidential elections, blocked most economic reforms, and opposed the holding of any referenda for early parliamentary elections. PMB leaders throughout the 1990s claimed to have a constituency of some 500,000 people, consisting largely of the *nomenklatura*, pensioners, active and retired military personnel, the administrative apparatus, and the most russified Belarusian citizens. Its chairman was Syarhey Haydukevich and its presidential candidate was Vyacheslau Kebich.

Communist Party of Belarus (CPB)
Kamunistychnaya Partiya Belarusi (KPB)

The Communist Party of Belarus (CPB) was revived and re-legalized in February 1993. Its leaders included Viktor Chykin, Anatol Malafeyeu, first secretary of the party, and Anatol Laskevich. The CPB originated as a regional committee of the Russian Social Democratic Labor Party (formed in 1904). It was established as the ruling party of the Belarusian Soviet republic in 1920. It underwent many purges during the 1930s as a result of Stalin's machinations and thereafter became totally subservient to Moscow's control from the 1940s until the collapse of the Soviet Union in 1991.

Communist leaders in Minsk backed the August 1991 hard-line coup against Soviet Secretary General Mikhail Gorbachev, leading to their demise when the coup was unsuccessful. Many party leaders were ousted, rank-and-file members abandoned the organization by the thousands, and the party itself was outlawed and had its property confiscated on 25 August 1991. In order to preserve their positions, many communist leaders left the party and supported the BPF initiative to declare Belarus independent of the USSR.

On 3 February 1993, the Supreme Council lifted the ban on the party but CPB property remained state-owned. Eighty percent of the Supreme Council elected in 1990 was composed of former party members. However, few of these members chose to rejoin the party. The party's new leaders backed the ouster of Shushkevich during Lukashenka's takeover. The CPB and the Party of Communists of Belarus (PCB) were considered part of a united communist party, but members of the two internal factions (old guardists grouped around former First Secretary Malafeyeu, and new activists) were in conflict over the issue of party leadership and political allegiance. Members of both factions were originally members of the Soviet-era Communist Party before it was banned.

The CPB was re-formed by some former members who disagreed with the PCB leadership on several issues. A split occurred, with the CPB headed by Chykin and Yefrem Sokolov establishing itself as a separate party. Unlike the PCB, the CPB was pro-Lukashenka and frequently expressed its support for him. It participated in a union of the communist parties of the Commonwealth of Independent States. Chykin voiced support for the restoration of the Soviet Union even if it only consisted of two states. Sokolov became the party's subsequent leader. Several other pro-unification groups joined the party, including the Movement for Social Progress and Justice (MSPJ), a grouping formed in October 1993, led by the self-styled Bolshevik Chykin, professing a Stalinist and Russia-oriented agenda. It staged a number of anti-NATO rallies and was believed to benefit from governmental financial support. An associate party of the MSPJ, the Republican Party for Labor and Justice (RPLJ), gained one seat in the May–December 1995 national elections. Chykin claimed in October 1997 that the party had up to 7,000 members and had restored its *oblast*-level and most of its *rayon*-level cells.[41]

Party of Communists of Belarus (PCB)
Partiya Kamunistau Belarusi (PKB)

The Party of Communists of Belarus (PCB) was formed on 7 December 1991 to replace the banned Communist Party of Belarus (CPB). After the banning of the Communist Party during 1991, Belarusian communists regrouped and formed the PCB. However, they lost all of the assets of the former CPB as party funds were confiscated by the state or stolen by former members for their own use. The party re-emerged on the public scene during the summer of 1992 and espoused the traditional Leninist slogans: to unite all workers, to liberate workers from all forms of exploitation, and to build a classless society based on social justice.

Most of the party's supporters resided in rural areas. In February 1993, the country's Supreme Council formally lifted the suspension on communist party activities but its organizers failed to reclaim their property from the state. The party supported a state-controlled economy, as well as close economic and political ties with Russia, and wanted a restoration of the Soviet Union or the formation of a "Slavic Union." It demanded that both Belarusian and Russian be the country's official languages. The PCB's chairmen were Vasil Navikau, who ran in the first round of the presidential elections in 1994, and Sergey Kalyakin, who led the communist bloc in the Supreme Council. In the May–December 1995 parliamentary elections, the communists gained 42 seats, thus becoming the largest party in the legislature. By 1997, the party claimed about 15,000 members.

The PCB did not view any threat to Belarusian sovereignty from the unification treaty with Russia, but believed it should include a provision enabling each side to veto the decisions of supranational institutions. The leader of the PCB parliamentary group, Sergey Kalyakin, was against a joint legislature, but spoke favorably about a joint command of the armed forces. He also emphasized that by integration he did not mean Belarus' incorporation into the Russian Federation or the re-creation of the USSR.[42] However, the Communist faction in parliament proposed, in March 1996, to declare the dissolution of the USSR as a criminal act. They also voiced support for Lukashenka's steps towards integration with Russia.

In August 1996, Kalyakin joined the opposition against President Lukashenka by signing the appeal of seven leading parties criticizing his policies. This led to protests within the ranks of the PCB, as the supporters of Lukashenka denounced the document, which was also initialed by the BPF. The PCB was opposed to President Lukashenka's constitution proposed in 1996, and at a session in October of that year issued a statement claiming that Belarus was "on the brink of ruin." It characterized the proposed constitution as "pro-bourgeois and anti-democratic."[43] The fourth congress of the PCB, which took place in January 1997, condemned the November 1996 constitutional referendum as a state coup, and decided to enter into opposition against the government.

Nationalists

Liberal Democratic Party of Belarus (LDPB)
Liberalna Demakratychnaya Partiya Belarusi (LDPB)

The Liberal Democratic Party of Belarus (LDPB) was organized in February 1994 as a rightist pan-Slavic movement advocating close links with Russia and the recreation of Russia's imperial territory. The chairman of the party was Sergey Haydukevich and its membership in 1995 stood at around 500. The party was associated with Vladimir Zhirinovsky's Liberal Democratic Party in Russia and it initially viewed both the CIS and the USSR as legal structures and strongly opposed the independence of Belarus. It successfully petitioned President Lukashenka to withdraw school history books written after independence on the grounds that they contained "nationalist excesses." At the same time, the party claimed to support individual freedoms, democratic government, and liberal social policies. The LDPB was also strongly opposed to NATO expansion.

The party was supportive of President Lukashenka and expressed a readiness to cooperate with him.[44] It also initiated several pro-government and pro-Lukashenka rallies. However, in early 1997 the LDPB stated that the new bicameral legislature installed as a consequence of the constitutional referendum was illegitimate and should have been considered an interim measure. The party also called for the dissolution of the National Assembly and expressed deep concern with the political situation in the country. It even claimed that integration with Russia might be illegitimate if it were conducted without the participation of a legally elected parliament.

In December 1997, the party decided to close its newspaper *Pravda Haydukevicha* (Haydukevich's Truth) and open a new one, *Liberalnaya Hazeta* (Liberal Gazette).[45] The LDPB developed ties with Iraq and sent delegations there on several occasions. In July 1998, the Vitebsk regional organization of the LDPB, together with the Communist Party of Belarus, the Belarusian Patriotic Party, and the Slavic Assembly White Russia formed a pro-presidential bloc of parties to "insure stability in the nation's leadership and its course toward integration within the framework of the CIS."[46] During the 1990s, the CIS was increasingly viewed by pro-Russian nationalists as a useful tool for restitching together Moscow's imperial territories, but not under a communist system of rule.

Slavic Assembly White Russia (SAWR)
Slavyansky Sabor Belaia Rus (SSBR)

The Slavic Assembly White Russia (SAWR) was formed in June 1992 as a non-communist party dedicated to pan-Slavism and the union of Belarus, Ukraine, and Russia. It aimed to defend Slavic interests on the basis of their political and territorial unification and it emphasized the traditional values of Slavic civilization while voicing virulent anti-Western sentiments. The party's chairman was Mikalay Syarheyeu. In early 1995, SAWR membership was reported at 1,000, with around 20 local organizations. The party was one of the most outspoken supporters of the constitutional referendum and the unification treaty with Russia. As a result, Belarusian oppositionists dubbed it Russia's "fifth column" in the country.

National Democratic Party of Belarus (NDPB)
Natsyianalnaya Demakratychnaya Partiya Belarusi (NDPB)

The National Democratic Party of Belarus (NDPB) was founded on 24 June 1990 and registered in June 1991. It defined itself as a right-wing party supporting political and pro-market economic reforms and was open to Belarusian-speakers committed to cultural independence and the cultivation of a "national renaissance." The party's first co-presidents included Viktor Naumenko, Anatol Astapenka, and M. Yermalovich. The party counted around 500 members and 15 local organizations during the mid-to-late 1990s.

Belarusian Nationalist Party (BNP)
Belaruskaya Natsianalistychnaya Partiya (BNP)

While strongly pro-Russian groups constituted one stream in the country's nationalist politics, vehemently pro-Belarusian organizations were also active. They included the Belarusian National Party (BNP), which was formed in September 1994 with Supreme Council member Anatol Astapenka as its chairman. The party's stated goals were "national rebirth, the achievement of complete independence for Belarus, and the creation of a judicial democratic state."

Belarusian nationalists, including the Christian democratic–oriented Belarusian Popular Front (BPF), have been subject to government harassment and intimidation as well as frequent attacks in the state-controlled media.

Ethnic Minority and Religious Parties

Polish Democratic Union (PDU)
Polskaye Demakratychnaye Zhurtavanne (PDZ)

Several of the country's major ethnic minorities created their own cultural and political groupings during the 1990s. One of the most significant was the Polish Democratic Union (PDU), led by Viktor Tarasevich, which campaigned for the interests of the Polish minority while supporting Belarusian "national rebirth." The PDU stood in opposition to President Lukashenka and his policy of unification with Russia and it cooperated closely with the Belarusian Popular Front (BPF) on behalf of Belarusian independence.

Other ethnic minority organizations were established among the country's sizeable Ukrainian population.

Regionalists

All-Belarusian Party for Unity and Accord (ABPUA)
Belaruskaya Partiya Usebelaruskaga Adzinstva i Zhody (BPUAZ)

This inter-regional party did not represent the specific political or ethnic interests of any distinct Belarusian region but rather the interests of the regional *nomenklatura* and commercial structures in relation to the central government in Minsk. It focused on the problem of economic and political development of several of the country's regions. The ABPUA was formed in June 1994 and its leader was Dimitry Bukalau. It nominated 23 candidates during the May–December 1995 general elections and claimed to be the strongest party in the Mogilev region. It obtained two seats in the national parliament.

Independents and Others

Belarusian Women's Party "Hope" (BWP)
Belaruskaya Partiya Zhanchyn "Nadzeya" (BPZ)

The Belarusian Women's Party "Hope" (BWP) was founded on 28 April 1994. Its first president was Valentina Polevikova, who also chaired the executive committee of the Labor Union Federation of Belarus and headed its informational-analytical center. The priorities of the Women's Party revolved around the protection of the family, motherhood, and childhood. It declared itself a party of "civil progress and democratic reforms, social justice and global human values, and of economic and political freedom."[47]

BWP membership included representatives and leaders of local labor unions and various other women's movements. The party claimed a membership of around 5,500 people, and had 39 offices throughout the country, as well as four regional branches. The main goal of the party was to engage female activists in the country's sociopolitical and economic life. Because of its independent stance, the party found itself in opposition to the Belarusian President and government. It participated in the "roundtable" initiative of major political forces against Lukashenka's policies in 1996. The party also maintained close contacts with women's organizations throughout the world. In an opinion poll in May 1997, the BWP ranked highest among all political parties, receiving an 8% rating, although it had not captured any parliamentary seats in the May–December 1995 ballot.[48]

Beer Lovers' Party (BLP)
Partiya Amatarau Piva (PAP)

The Beer Lovers' Party (BLP) was formed in August 1993 and led by Vadim Chernyshov. In order to attract attention, the party had campaigned for the high quality of beer, but its principal goal appeared to be the strengthening of Belarusian sovereignty and neutrality. It promoted liberal economic policies and reforms and campaigned for the inviolability of individual and private property. The BLP claimed a membership of around 600 people.

Several other small, single-issue or ideologically neutral parties emerged during the 1990s, including the Belarusian Humanitarian Party (BHP) (*Belaruskaya Humanitarnaya Partiya, BHP*). The BHP grew out of the League of Human Rights organization in February 1994. Its chairman was Yawhen Novikaw and it claimed to unite the major intellectual forces in society. The party's stated goals were the "humanization" of society and the protection of human rights. It was reported to have around 2,000 members in early 1995. The Belarusian Social and Sports Party (BSSP) was created in November 1994 and chaired by Uladzimir Alyaksandrovich. Its goals were the creation of a democratic, economically strong, and humane state. It aimed at the "perfection of social norms" and improvements in physical education, as well as the country's dilapidated health care system. The BSSP managed to take one parliamentary seat, following the prolonged 1995 elections, and one seat in the October 2000 ballot.

POLITICAL DATA

Name of State: Republic of Belarus *(Respublika Bylarus')*
Form of Government: Republican, with directly elected president and parliament
Structure of Legislature: National Assembly *(Natsionalnoye sobranie)*
Size of Territory: 80,200 square miles
Size of Population: 10,366,719 (July 2000 estimate)

Composition of Population: (1989)

Ethnic Group	Number	% of Population
Belarusians	7,904,600	77.9
Russians	1,342,100	13.2
Poles	417,700	4.1
Ukrainians	291,000	2.9
Jews	112,000	1.1
Others	84,400	0.8
Total	1,015,800	100.0

Source: See the United Nations Human Rights Website, www.unhchr.ch/tbs/doc.nsf/.

ELECTION RESULTS

Presidential Election, 9 September 2001*

Turnout: 83.86%

Candidate	Votes	% of Vote
Alyaksandr Lukashenka	4,666,680	75.65
Uladzimir Hancharyk	965,261	15.65
Syarhey Haydukevich	153,199	2.48
Invalid	138,706	2.20
Total	5,923,846	95.98

Source: British Broadcasting Corporation, BBC Monitoring Kiev Unit, 14 September 2001.

*The election results were contested as fraudulent by the Belarusian opposition, as well as by monitors from various international organizations, including the Organization for Security and Cooperation in Europe (OSCE).

Presidential Election, 23 June and 10 July 1994*

First Round, 23 June 1994
Turnout: 80%

Candidate	Votes	% of Vote
Alyaksandr Lukashenka	n/a	44.82
Vyacheslau Kebich	n/a	17.33
Zyanon Paznyak	n/a	12.82
Stanislau Shushkevich	n/a	9.91
Alyaksandr Dubko	n/a	5.98
Vasil Navikau	n/a	4.29
Total	n/a	95.15

Second Round, 10 July 1994
Turnout: 70%

Candidate	Votes	% of Vote
Alyaksandr Lukashenka	n/a	80.1
Vyacheslau Kebich	n/a	19.9
Total	n/a	100.0

Source: http://www.agora.stm.it/elections/election/belarus.htm.

*Unfortunately, data on elections are incomplete despite numerous attempts to elicit information from the Belarusian administration and other official sources. One must conclude either that accurate data gathering, recording, and publication is difficult in

Parliamentary Elections, 15 and 29 October 2000

Turnout:*

Party/Coalition	Votes	% of Vote	Seats
Unaffiliated	—	—	81
Communist Party of Belarus	—	—	6
Agrarian Union of Belarus	—	—	5
Republican Party for Labor and Justice	—	—	2
Liberal Democratic Party	—	—	1
Social-Democratic Party of National Accord	—	—	1
Social and Sports Party	—	—	1
Total	—	—	97

Source: Elections in Belarus, http://www.agora.stm.it/elections/election/belarus.htm.
*The Central Election Bureau of Belarus reported the election turnout at 60.6 percent, however, opposition leaders stated that turnout was at 45 percent. (Radio Free Europe/Radio Liberty, 16 October 2000)

Parliamentary Elections, 14 and 28 May 1995, and 10 December 1995

First Round: 64.7%
Second Round: 56.6%

Party/Coalition	First Round*	Second Round	Percent- age	Total
Unaffiliated	9	44	44.0	53
Agrarian Party	5	25	25.0	30
Communist Party	3	24	23.0	27
Party of National Accord	1	2	2.0	3
Social Democratic Union	—	1	1.0	1
Green Party	—	1	1.0	1
Belarusian Party of Labor and Justice	—	1	1.0	1
Belarusian Peasant Party	—	1	1.0	1
Socialist Party of Belarus	—	1	1.0	1
Belarusian Patriotic Movement	—	1	1.0	1
Belarusian Popular Front	—	—	—	—
Total	18	101	100.0	119

Sources: Organization for Security and Cooperation in Europe, Report on Parliamentary Elections in Belarus: 14 and 28 May 1995, p. 7; and Deutsche Presse-Agentur, 11 December 1995.

*As complete results for this election were not available, only the number of seats won in each round, together with the percentage of seats won and the total number of seats are provided. A minimum of 174 out of 260 candidates are needed for a legal quorum as stipulated by Belarusian law. Due to the inability to fulfill this requirement, a third round of voting occurred on 10 December 1995. This data reflects preliminary results only, with an additional twenty seats subsequently filled in run-off elections for which data is simply not available.

Final Round, 10 December 1995

Turnout: 52.4%

Party/Coalition	Votes	% of Vote	Seats
Unaffiliated Candidates	n/a	n/a	95
Communist Party	n/a	n/a	42
Belarusian Popular Front	n/a	n/a	—
Agrarian Union of Belarus	n/a	n/a	33
United Democratic Party	n/a	n/a	9
Party of National Accord	n/a	n/a	8
Social Democratic Union	n/a	n/a	2
All-Belarusian Party	n/a	n/a	2
Belarusian Patriotic Movement	n/a	n/a	1
Green Party	n/a	n/a	1
Belarusian Party of Labor and Justice	n/a	n/a	1
Belarusian Peasant Party	n/a	n/a	1
Belarusian National Party	n/a	n/a	1
Social and Sports Party	n/a	n/a	1
Belarusian Ecological Party	n/a	n/a	1
Total	n/a	n/a	198 of 260

Source: Fifty-nine additional seats were filled in the 10 December 1995 round, bringing the total number of parlimentary mandates to 198, and thus meeting the two-thirds quorum needed for parliament to be activated. However, as no official results could be obtained for the 1995 election, personal information obtained from organizations in neighboring countries was used to compile the final round of data.

NOTES

1. For a valuable recent history of Belarus see Jan Zaprudnik, *Belarus: At a Crossroads in History*, Boulder: Westview Press, 1993. Also consult Richard S. Clem, "Belorussians," in Graham Smith (Ed.), *The Nationalities Question in the Soviet Union*, London: Longman, 1993; Oscar Halecki, *Borderlands of Western Civilization: A History of East Central Europe*, New York: Ronald Press,1952; Edward C. Thaden, *Russia's Western Borderland, 1710–1870*, Princeton: Princeton University Press, 1984; and Marceli Kosman, *Historia Bialorusi*, Wroclaw-Warsaw: Wydawnictwo Ossolinskich, 1979.

2. Graham Smith, Vivien Law, Andrew Wilson, Annette Bohr, and Edward Allworth, *Nation-Building in the Post-Soviet Borderlands: The Politics of National Identities*, Cambridge: Cambridge University Press, 1998, p. 23. See also Andrew Wilson, "Myths of National History in Belarus and Ukraine," in George Schopflin and Geoffrey Hosking (Eds.), *Myths and Nationhood*, London: Hurst, 1997, pp. 182–197.

3. See Ivan S. Lubachko, *Belorussia under Soviet Rule, 1917–1957*, Lexington: University of Kentucky Press, 1972.

4. Zaprudnik, *op. cit.*,1993, p. 137.

5. For more data on the Belarusian elections see Commission on Security and Cooperation in Europe, *Report on the Belarusian Presidential Elections*, July 1994; OSCE Parliamentary Assembly, "Report on Parliamentary Elections in Belarus," June 1995; European Institute for the Media, "The May 1995 Belarusian Parliamentary Elections," 1 July 1995; "Results of Second Round Parliamentary Elections," 8 June 1995; *FBIS*, "Reportage of 10 December Parliamentary Elections," 11 December 1995; *IFES Pre-Election Technical Assessment* by Linda Edgeworth, Richard Messick, Jan Zaprudnik, December 1993.

6. Read Ustina Markus, "A New Parliament, Despite the President," *Transition*, Vol. 2, No. 1, 12 January 1996, pp. 62–63.

7. See Linda Edgeworth, Richard Messick, and Jan Zaprudnik, "IFES Pre-Election Technical Assessment," Washington, D.C., December 1993; and Bogdan Szajkowski, *Political Parties of Eastern Europe, Russia and the Successor States*, Essex, U.K.: Longman Information and Reference, 1994. Also consult the British Helsinki Human Rights Group report on the "Belarusian Parliamentary Elections and Referendum, 14 and 28 May 1995," Oxford, England.

8. For more details on Lukashenka's political maneuverings see "Belarus: Popular Front Urges Parliament to Impeach President," 4 September 1996, *FBIS*; "Belarus: Lukashenka Interviewed on Eve of Referendum," 11 November 1996, *FBIS*; "Belarus: Parliament Speaker Explains Refusal to Meet with Lukashenka," 20 November 1996, *FBIS*; "Belarus: Lukashenka Under Pressure From All Sides," 20 November 1996, *FBIS*; "Belarus: Lukashenka Aide Views Current Conflict," 20 November 1996; Gordon, Michael, "President of Belarus Wins Referendum on Expanding His Power," *New York Times*, 26 November 1996; Belarusian Embassy Press Release, "New Parliament Formed in Belarus," 28 November 1996; Belarusian Embassy Press Release, "Belarus President on the Constitution," 29 November 1996.

9. See Ustina Markus, "Belarus Chooses Dictatorship," *Transition*, Vol. 3, No. 2, 7 February 1997, pp. 26–28; and Alexander Lukashuk, "Going Backward Fast," *Transition*, Vol. 5, No. 5, May 1998, pp. 48–53.

10. *Central and Eastern Europe,* Radio Free Europe/Radio Liberty Newsline, 4 March 1999.

11. *Central and Eastern Europe,* Radio Free Europe/Radio Liberty Newsline, 20 May 1999.

12. "Alexander Lukashenka, Europe's Odd Man Out," *Economist*, 25 July 1998.

13. Kathleen J. Mihalisko, "Belarus: Retreat to Authoritarianism," in Karen Dawisha and Bruce Parrott (Eds.), *Democratic Changes and Authoritarian Reactions in Russia, Ukraine, Belarus, and Moldova*, Cambridge: Cambridge University Press, 1997, p. 225.

14. For a useful survey of media repression in Belarus see Ustina Markus, "Belarus Maintains Strong Control Over Most Media," *Transitions*, Open Media Research Institute (OMRI), Vol. 1, No. 18, 6 October 1995, pp. 19–21; and Ustina Markus, "Belarusian Media Struggle Under Authoritarian Rule," *Transitions*, OMRI, Vol. 2. No. 21, 18 October 1996, pp. 57–59.

15. *Radio Minsk Network*, 11 August 1996, in *FBIS-SOV-96–156*, 11 August 1996.

16. *ITAR-TASS*, Moscow, 10 April 1998, in *FBIS-SOV-98–100*, 10 April 1998.

17. Radio address by Anatol Barankevich, *Radio Minsk Network*, 5 December 1996, in *FBIS-SOV-96–236*, 5 December 1996. See also *Radio Minsk Network*, 15 July 1997, in *FBIS-SOV-97–196*, 15 July 1997.

18. *Radio Minsk Network*, 7 September 1997, in *FBIS-SOV-97–251*, 8 September 1997.

19. *Belapan*, Minsk, 16 February 1998, in *FBIS-SOV-98–047*, 16 February 1998.

20. *Belapan*, Minsk, 30 June 1997, in *FBIS-SOV-97–181*, 30 June 1997.

21. *Belapan*, Minsk, 4 August 1997, in *FBIS-SOV-97–216*, 4 August 1997.

22. Data for most parties is given by the Ministry of Justice information in the report by *Belapan*, Minsk, 7 March 1995, in *FBIS-SOV-95–061–S*, 7 March 1995.

23. See *Belapan*, Minsk, 28 May 1997, in *FBIS-SOV-97–148*, 28 May 1997 and *Belapan*, Minsk, 7 October 1997, in *FBIS-SOV-7–280*, 7 October 1997.

24. *Belapan*, Minsk, 3 March 1998, in *FBIS-SOV-98–064*.

25. Yuras Karmanaw, "Vyachaslaw Kuznyatsow: The Socialist Party Has Been Created in Empty Place of the Golden Mean," *Zvyazda*, Minsk, 20 September 1994, p. 1, in *FBIS-SOV-94–186*, 20 September 1994. Also consult *Belapan*, Minsk, 16 September 1994, in *FBIS-SOV-94–181*, 16 September 1994.

26. *Belapan*, Minsk, 19 October 1997, in *FBIS-SOV-97–292*, 19 October 1997.

27. See *Belapan*, Minsk, 11 January 1997, in *FBIS-SOV-97–008*, 11 January 1997; and *Belapan*, Minsk, 23 March 1997, in *FBIS-SOV-97–082*, 23 March 1997.

28. *Belapan*, Minsk, 8 July 1997, in *FBIS-SOV-97–189*, 8 July 1997.

29. Valer Kalinowski, "Zyanon Paznyak Remains BNF Leader," *Zvyazda*, Minsk, 24 June 1997, p. 7, in *FBIS-SOV-97–177*, 26 June 1997.

30. Introduction, BPF website, http://pages.prodigy.net/dr_fission/bpf/bpfjntro.htm.

31. Vera Chuyko, "Popular Front Advocates the Idea of a Bloc of Independent Democratic Forces," *Svaboda*, Minsk, 13–19 September 1994, p. 4, in *FBIS-SOV-94–183*, 21 September 1994.

32. *Belapan*, Minsk, 19 April 1995, in *FBIS-SOV-95–076*, 19 April 1995.

33. Tatsyana Kalinowskaya, "Agreement Was Reached Quickly," *Zvyazda*, Minsk, 22 August 1996, pp. 1–2, in *FBIS-SOV-96–168*. See also *Interfax*, Moscow, 26 March 1997, in *FBIS-SOV-97–085*.

34. Valer Kalinowski, "Zyanon Paznyak Remains BNF Leader," *Zvyazda*, Minsk, 24 June 1997, p. 7, in *FBIS-SOV-97–177*, 26 June 1997.

35. *Belapan*, Minsk, 23 March 1997, in *FBIS-SOV-97–082*, 23 March 1997.

36. *Belapan*, Minsk, 26 August 1997, in *FBIS-SOV-97–238*.

37. *Belapan*, Minsk, 14 March 1998, in *FBIS-SOV-98–073*; and *Interfax*, Moscow, 11 April 1998, in *FBIS-SOV-98–101*.

38. Syarhey Astrawtsow, "The Collective Farm Meeting Instead of Legislature?" *Svaboda*, Minsk, 3 June 1995, p. 2, in *FBIS-SOV-95–109*, 3 June 1995.

39. Vadim Sekhovich, "Information Department of the BDG," *Belorusskaya Delovaya Gazeta*, Minsk, 2 April 1998, Internet edition, http://bdg.press.net.by/1998/98_04_02.455/sharik.htm.

40. *Belapan*, Minsk, 26 March 1997, in *FBIS-SOV-97–005*, 26 March 1997.

41. Yuriy Dudzinaw, "Viktor Chykin Is Getting Ready for Congress and Asserts that the CPB Has Been Reborn," *Narodnaya Gazeta*, Minsk, 1 October 1997, pp. 1, 4, in *FBIS-SOV-97–281*, 8 October 1997.

42. See *Interfax*, Moscow, in English, 11 March 1996, in *FBIS-SOV-96–049*, 11 March 1996, and *Radio Minsk Network*, 15 March 1996, in *FBIS-SOV-96–052*, 15 March 1996.

43. *Belapan*, Minsk, 7 October 1996, in *FBIS-SOV-96–196*, 7 October 1996.

44. See *Radio Minsk Network*, 14 August 1996, in *FBIS-SOV-96–159*, 14 August 1996; *Belapan*, Minsk, 24 March 1997, in *FBIS-SOV-97–083*, 24 March 1997; and *Belapan*, Minsk, 23 April 1997, in *FBIS-SOV-97–113*, 23 April 1997.

45. *Belapan*, Minsk, 5 December 1997, in *FBIS-SOV-97–339*, 5 December 1997.

46. *Belapan*, Minsk, 6 July 1998, in *FBIS-SOV-98–188*, 7 July 1998.

47. Mission Statement of the Party "*Nadzeya*," "Nadzeya" website, www.ruf.rice.edu/~sergei/

family/mom/hope.html#mission. See also the program and history of the party "*Nadzeya*," on the "Nadzeya" website, www.ruf.rice.edu/~sergei/family/mom/hope.html#program.

48. Yuriy Dudyinov, "Political Parties Still Need to Win the Confidence of People," *Narodnaya Gazeta*, Minsk, 16 May 1997, on "Nadzeya" website, www.ruf.rice.edu/~sergei/family/mom/ratings.html.

Estonia

HISTORICAL OVERVIEW

Historians assert that the ancestors of the modern-day Estonians, a Finno-Ugric speaking people, settled along the shores of the Baltic Sea around 3500 BC. By approximately 1000 AD, the Estonian areas on the northeastern shores of the Baltic had evolved into an important transit route for the Viking penetrations to Russia and Byzantium. A major trading center was built on the site of the future Estonian capital of Tallinn. At that time, Estonian social-political units were organized into eight major and several minor federations for the defense of villages and for raiding non-Estonian neighbors.[1] However, there was no countrywide leadership or unified political structure in the Estonian territories.

Christianity was introduced slowly into Estonia during the twelfth and thirteenth centuries primarily by German, Danish, and Swedish invaders. Conquest by German knights was justified as Christianization after the Pope had declared the Baltic region the "Land of Mary." The German "Order of the Knights of Christ" or the "Swordbrothers" subdued the Latvian territories south of Estonia in the early thirteenth century and subsequently moved into southern Estonia. Meanwhile, the Danes invaded the territory from the north and founded the present-day capital of Tallinn. Estonia was effectively partitioned between German and Danish rulers partly as a result of the invaders' demographic strength and technological superiority. The entire country fell under German control in 1346 after the Danish king was forced to sell his Estonian possessions.

For the next two hundred years, German settlers remained a small upper class of some 5% of the population, but they controlled the region's political structures, feudal estates, and religious orders. During the early part of the sixteenth century, Lutheranism spread to Estonia from Germany and soon became the predominant religion. As German rule collapsed in the mid-1500s, Estonia was subject to various invasions and incursions by Swedish, Russian,

Danish, and Polish troops. By the end of the century, Sweden controlled the northern portion of the country, the Polish-Lithuanian Commonwealth dominated the south, and Denmark captured the island of Saaremaa. By 1645 Sweden had gained control over the entire Estonian territory.

Swedish rule continued until the beginning of the eighteenth century and was considered to be the most enlightened foreign occupation in Estonian history. A university was founded in the city of Tartu and serfdom was legally abolished. The Great Northern War (1700–1721) ended Swedish rule in the Baltic region as the Russians under Peter the Great gradually conquered Estonia, or what was then known as the provinces of Estland and northern Livland. Tsarist Russian rule in Estonia lasted for about two hundred years, and in the initial period Estonia was left with considerable local autonomy.

For the most part, Moscow supported the Baltic German aristocracy, who controlled the predominant share of the country's land and economic resources and many of whom became officials, generals, and ministers for the Muscovite occupation. With the final emancipation of the Estonian peasantry from feudal serfdom in the early 1880s, agriculture became increasingly commercial. As the Russians sought to create a unitary, monolingual, and monoreligious state, Baltic autonomy came under increasing attrition.

Estonia's struggle for autonomy and independence markedly increased during the 1800s as the Russification process intensified. Cultural, educational, and literary groups sprang up to challenge Muscovite hegemony and to promote the use of the Estonian language. The national movements sought to achieve equality for the Estonian language and culture within the Russian domain. In the 1870s, a new orthography patterned on the Finnish was widely accepted and the northern Estonian dialect was enshrined as the national language. The first Estonian daily newspaper was founded in 1891. Meanwhile, Russification of the Baltic provinces intensified from the 1880s onwards to forestall any prospects for Germanization, and the Baltic Germans lost much of their power and influence.

Following the Russian revolution of 1905, there was an upsurge of Estonian national activity; political parties were organized and various cultural societies sprang up. An All-Estonian Congress was established to demand autonomy for Estonia within the Russian Empire, and a more radical Congress of People's Representatives called for the overthrow of the tsarist regime. But Moscow thwarted efforts to transform the autocratic tsarist system into a constitutional monarchy, and it outlawed movements for Estonian autonomy.

During World War I, about 100,000 Estonians were mobilized in the Russian army, but the tsarist military soon collapsed, thus placing Estonian independence firmly on the agenda. Moscow's offer of autonomy in 1917 to Tallinn was simply too little and too late. A representative assembly, the *Maapäev*, was elected in Estonia and preparations were made for holding general elections. Before it was disbanded by invading Bolshevik forces, on 28 November 1917 the *Maapäev* declared itself the supreme authority in the country, whereby it alone possessed the authority to decide on Estonia's status.

When the German army overran Estonia near the close of World War I, a three-person National Salvation Committee empowered by the *Maapäev* proclaimed Estonia an independent state on 24 February 1918. Following Germany's collapse in November 1918, an independent provisional government was established in Tallinn. Meanwhile, Lenin's Bolsheviks captured the city of Narva and declared the creation of an Estonian Workers' Commune. A war for independence ensued between Estonian and Russian Bolshevik forces, with the Estonians emerging victorious by the close of 1919. In February 1920, the Tartu Peace Treaty was signed between Estonia and Soviet Russia, which signified *de jure* recognition by Moscow of the country's independence. But the border question was not fully resolved. Although Estonia received additional territories in the Narva and Setu areas, these territories were later contested and annexed by Russia after the 1940 occupation.

Similarly to its two neighboring Baltic states, Estonia briefly enjoyed independence between 1920 and 1940. The period of independence was characterized by a period of intense state-building and economic development.[2] Estonia, like its neighbors, emerged as a small but economically successful agrarian country with an emphasis on self-education, cultural pluralism, and cooperative agriculture. A land reform program in 1919 ended German landlord domination and created a large class of small independent farmers.

From 1920 to 1934, the country remained a parliamentary democracy with an ultra-democratic structure in which governments were replaced on average every eight months. Estonia had 17 cabinets during its first fourteen years of independence, amid growing fears of political instability. A strong presidential constitution was introduced in October 1933, after the caretaker Prime Minister Konstantin Päts led a "palace coup" with overwhelming public support and was subsequently elected unopposed as Estonia's President. Between 1934 and 1940, Estonia had a conservative authoritarian regime, partly as a reaction to threats from the extreme right and partly in response to widespread disenchantment with an often unwieldy parliamentarism and frequent turnover of governments. The new President, with the support of business, agrarian, and military elites, declared a state of martial law, prohibited all political parties, deactivated the parliament, and postponed any subsequent general elections. At the same time, he cracked down on nascent fascist groupings, largely maintained a free market, and gradually began to reintroduce some democratic elements.

With the outbreak of World War II in September 1939, Estonia was pressured by Moscow to sign a defense pact with the Soviet Union. At that time, the Estonian government was unaware of the secret protocols of the Molotov-Ribbentrop Pact, concluded in August 1939, which delineated future spheres of control in Eastern Europe between Russia and Germany. After accusing Tallinn of violating the defense treaty, Russian forces occupied Estonia in June 1940 without any significant resistance and installed a puppet government and a pliant parliament. On 6 August 1940, Estonia was formally annexed by the Soviet Union. A rapid process of Sovietization was initiated that sought to eliminate all vestiges of independence and democracy. Approximately 10,000 Estonians were arrested and deported to slave labor camps in the Soviet *gulag*. About 33,000 people were conscripted into the Red Army. Total Estonian losses during the wartime occupation amounted to 60,000, or 6% of the population.

In July 1941 German forces occupied Estonia and thwarted any hopes for independence. About 5,000 Estonian citizens, including the country's Jews, were rapidly murdered or sent to death camps. Thousands more Estonians perished in the German army, into which about 70,000 had been conscripted. In September and October 1944 Soviet forces reoccupied Estonia after German resistance crumbled. The provisional independent Estonian government had been in partial control of Tallinn when Russian troops entered the city, arrested its members, and installed their own, communist administration. About 60,000 people fled the country, while a further 30,000 Estonians were deported to Soviet labor camps. Estonia lost about 5% of its territory as Russia directly annexed the right bank of the Narva River and most of the southeastern Petseri (Pechery in Russian) district. In sum, the country lost 30% of its pre-1939 population by the end of the war.

The early post-war years were marked by intensive Sovietization, Russification, and colonization of the Estonian Soviet Republic. Communist loyalists imported from Russia were implanted in the government, because local communists were distrusted by Moscow. A guerrilla resistance movement, the "forest brethren," with about 15,000 active participants and thousands more sympathizers, was brutally crushed through forced collectivization in the countryside and the deportation of thousands of Estonian farmers to Russia. High-speed industrialization brought in thousands of Russian colonists with the aim of dramatically reducing the ethnic Estonian proportion of the population. The share of Estonians dropped from 94% in early 1945 to about 72% by 1953, and to 64.7% by 1989. The decline was compounded by a low birth rate among ethnic Estonians.

Political purges and intense repression of Estonian culture and education was designed to thoroughly russify the population and to eliminate any autonomous spheres of public life. Leading positions in the country were occupied by Russified and Sovietized Estonians, who were imported into the country, and periodic purges of the Communist Party were conducted to root out any dissenters and to maintain a state of constant political terror. After Stalin's death in 1953, a partial thaw was visible throughout the USSR and several local Estonian communists replaced the Russian implants in the republican administration. However, there was no extensive liberalization, and under Leonid Brezhnev's regime, between 1968 and 1980, the country sank into bureaucratic stupor and economic stagnation. However, a number of dissident organizations remained active in clandestine conditions. They included the Estonian Democratic Movement, the Estonian Patriots, and the Estonian National Front. But their influence remained limited under highly repressive conditions.

Estonia's drive for statehood and democratic rule began in the late 1980s with the birth and growth of various independent ecological, cultural, informational, student, and political groupings. These were either protest movements against specific aspects of Soviet policy, such as environmental devastation and censorship, or elements of national rebirth in which Estonian history, culture, and language were rediscovered. For example, in 1987 an ecological movement was formed to protest highly polluting phosphate mining, and a group was formed calling for the commemoration and condemnation of the Molotov-Ribbentrop Pact. By early 1988, public protests and rallies had become more commonplace and less likely to be violently dispersed by the police. Demands rapidly began to escalate from mere autonomy within the Soviet Union to full-scale national independence.

During 1988, the press and cultural organizations increasingly disengaged themselves from Soviet censorship, and even the Estonian Communist Party (ECP) began to call for republican sovereignty in the economic and administrative arenas. For instance, on 23 June 1988 the Estonian Supreme Soviet (parliament) legalized the Estonian national flag, and on 9 September 1988 the ECP supported demands for making Estonian the republic's official language. The reformist Vaino Väljas was appointed as the new ECP leader, and pressures began to build for a new relationship with Moscow to test the bounds of the reforms being pursued by Soviet Secretary-General Mikhail Gorbachev. Despite its initial popularity, the ECP was overtaken by events and quickly lost control over the political process.

Outside of the local Communist Party, a Popular Front of Estonia (PFE) *(Eesti Rahvarinne, ER)* was established, which by June 1988 claimed 40,000 members. The PFE was an umbrella organization that included human rights groups, religious organizations, environmental movements, heritage groupings, nascent political parties, and even some fractions of the Communist Party. It involved various intellectual and cultural figures as well as young politicians who would later rise to prominence in an independent Estonia. As the communist organizations crumbled, the PFE lodged increasingly far-reaching demands and staged a number of large-scale public rallies, including the Song of Estonia demonstration on 11 September 1988, which brought out over 250,000 people from all over the country—about 20% of the Estonian population.

On 16 November 1988, the Supreme Soviet of the Estonian Republic adopted a "Declaration on the Sovereignty of the Estonian SSR," its first major step toward independence. Moscow declared this move unconstitutional but was not prepared to use force to overturn the Estonian government. By the time the Kremlin formally accepted economic autonomy for the Baltic states, in January 1989, public opinion was rapidly shifting toward independence. The autonomy offered by Gorbachev in early 1991, couched in a new Union Treaty, was considered to be a fake and a desperate attempt to keep the USSR together.

During 1989 political changes began to accelerate. Pro-independence organizations led by the Estonian National Independence Party (ENIP), the National Heritage Society (NHS), the Estonian Conservative People's Party (ECPP), and the Estonian Christian Democratic Party (ECDP), established local citizens committees and the Estonian Congress as a parallel national parliament untainted by any compromises with communism. The Congress emerged partly in opposition to the PFE, as its initiators feared that the Front would make too many concessions to Moscow and the communist authorities in Tallinn. Elections were held to the Congress on 24 February 1990, with over 90% of the population participating, and an Estonian Committee was subsequently established. The Congress was not only important for placing the statehood issue firmly on the agenda and mobilizing Estonian citizens, but it also permitted Estonian citizens living abroad to participate directly in the country's internal political developments.

Faced with this radical challenge of an alternative national parliament, the PFE, which included liberals, social democrats, agrarians, and independents, declared a new program in support of national independence. In order not to be marginalized, some centrist and reform communist leaders formed the Free Estonia (FE) *(Vaba Eesti)* group in January 1990. The FE was led by Prime Minister Indrek Toome, and it supported Estonian statehood. In fact, the Communist Party began to split on the issue of independence, with the larger faction backing statehood and a minority grouping maintaining a pro-Moscow stance. Elections to the Estonian Supreme Soviet were held on 18 March 1990, and in a display of broadening pluralism, 31 parties competed in the ballot. On 25 March 1990, the Supreme Council (parliament) convened and proclaimed the state authority of the USSR in Estonia unlawful. As political developments accelerated, the ruling communists were rapidly outflanked by a number of independent groupings, including environmentalists, the PFE, and an informal citizens' committee movement.[3]

POST-COMMUNIST DEVELOPMENTS

The collapse of communist rule in Estonia can be traced to 8 May 1990 when the Estonian Supreme Council restored the name "Republic of Estonia" and the country's state symbols while eliminating those of the USSR. At the same time, parliament installed Edgar Savisaar, the Popular Front of Estonia (PFE) leader, as Prime Minister, while Arnold Rüütel, a leading ex-communist, was re-elected as Chairman of the Supreme Council and transformed himself into a proponent of Estonian independence. Moscow denounced Tallinn's decision on independence and tried but failed to fabricate a coup by Russian colonists and security officers. As a result, the Estonian government established a Home Guard of volunteers, which became the embryo of the future Estonian army. After this point, Moscow rapidly lost control of events, as Tallinn vetoed Soviet laws that violated the rights of the republic.

On 3 March 1991, Estonia held an independence referendum despite the protests of the Kremlin and opposition from local Soviet representatives and Russian minority leaders; 77.8% of the population voted positively and only 17.7% negatively. The latter were primarily Russians who had settled in Estonia during the period of Soviet occupation. For the next few months, Estonia had to resist threats of economic sanctions and military provocations from Russia. Tallinn also boycotted Gorbachev's all-Union referendum on the future of the USSR. In the midst of the failed hard-line coup in Moscow, on 20 August 1991, the Estonian Supreme Council adopted a "Resolution on the National Independence of Estonia." The declaration stressed the continuity of the independence declared in 1918. Within a week, about forty states had recognized Estonia's independence; and within the next two years, the country was admitted to the United Nations, the Organization for Security and Cooperation in Europe (OSCE), and the Council of Europe.

At the end of August 1991, the Soviet Communist Party was declared illegal. The pro-independence Estonian Communist Party continued to operate even while it continued to disintegrate. Meanwhile, a national Constituent Assembly was formed, with thirty members elected by the Supreme Council and thirty by the Estonian National Independence Party (ENIP)–sponsored Estonian Congress. Centrists occupied about twenty seats, twenty were taken by national radicals, and thirteen by moderates and reform communists. Seven representatives of the Russian minority were also included in the Assembly.

The Assembly was empowered to draft a new Estonian constitution and began its deliberations in September 1991. The constitution allowed for the first presidential elections to be direct, but subsequent ballots were limited to parliament, in which a two-thirds majority votes for a presidency for a five-year term. It also created a balance between executive and legislative powers, although the parliament *(Riigikogu)* upheld its overall political supremacy and was empowered to appoint the Prime Minister and other leading state officials, to declare states of emergency, and to make international treaties. The unicameral *Riigikogu* was to consist of 101 members elected for a four-year term. On 28 June 1992, 66.3% of eligible Estonian voters went to the polls and 91.2% approved the new constitution.

Estonia's political spectrum began to crystallize after the achievement of independence. Both the PFE and the Estonian Congress were essentially pluralistic formations that subsequently split into a diversity of political parties. Various centrist and moderate parties emerged from the PFE, while the more radical nationalist forces sought to consolidate and create a viable electoral bloc in opposition to the centrists and ex-communists tied to Prime Minister

Savisaar. Between the end of 1990 and the beginning of 1992, the premier lost the support of most ethnic Estonians in parliament. In January 1992, Savisaar resigned despite surviving a confidence vote in parliament and new elections were scheduled.

The general elections on 20 September 1992 and the creation of a new parliament *(Riigikogu)* marked the end of both the Supreme Council inherited from the Soviet period and of the Estonian Congress established during the drive for independence. Seventeen parties or electoral alliances contested the ballot, 67.8% of voters participated, and nine parties succeeded in gaining parliamentary seats. The Estonian Communist Party failed to win a single seat in the 101-seat legislature. In the September 1992 presidential elections, the writer and former Foreign Minister Lennart Meri was elected head of state. Throughout his tenure, Meri played a very active and constructive role in the political reform process. Between September 1992 and March 1995, Estonia was governed by a right-of-center coalition that supported two different Prime Ministers.

President Meri nominated Mart Laar, the head of the "Fatherland" or "Pro Patria" *(Isamaa)* electoral alliance with 28.7% of parliamentary seats, as Prime Minister. On 21 October 1992, Laar formed a three-party, right-of-center coalition government, consisting of the Estonian National Independence Party (ENIP), the Rural Center Party (RCP), and the Estonian Social Democratic Party (ESDP). The Laar cabinet remained in office until 28 September 1994, but resigned after a vote of no confidence in parliament following a controversial arms deal with Israel and disclosures about secret sales of surplus Russian rubles to Chechnya.

On 4 November 1994, Andres Tarand of the Moderates formed a new government consisting of the same parties as in the previous coalition. New parliamentary elections were held on 5 March 1995, and fourteen parties gained seats, with a total of 90 deputies.[4] The ruling coalition had lost over half their vote and two-thirds of their parliamentary seats. Estonia maintained a mixed electoral system, which tended to favor proportional representation. The leader of the largest party in the victorious electoral coalition, Tiit Vähi of the Estonian Coalition Party, was selected as Prime Minister. The Coalition Party, with 41 deputies, possessed by far the largest number of parliamentary seats.

Vähi formed a three-party, center-left coalition with the Rural People's Party (RPP) and the Estonian Center Party, which held 16 seats. The three coalition partners combined 46.8% of the vote, and the government was sworn in on 17 April 1995. Although left of center, the coalition pursued a market reform program while benefiting from the backlash against inevitable hardships stemming from the initial dismantling of the state-controlled economic system. But the new administration only lasted six months, falling on 11 October 1995 following a wire-tapping scandal involving Edgar Savisaar, the interior minister and leader of the Center Party. Vähi formed a new government, this time with the Estonian Reform Party (ERP), which held19 seats in parliament. The new government took office on 6 November 1995.

Despite this frequent turnover of governments, fragile inter-party coalitions, the weak popular base of all political parties, and a fragmented parliament during the first few years of independence, the political process worked smoothly and constitutionally. In addition, the May 1994 law on political parties was intended to limit their number by requiring a minimum membership of 1,000 citizens for registration and the right to run in national elections. Moreover, any registered party unable to obtain parliamentary representation in two consecutive elections would be disbanded. As a result of these rulings, political mergers became more frequent, such as the unification of Pro Patria with the ENIP to form the Pro Patria Union (PPU) in December 1995. As in other post-communist states, parties were established by political elites rather than being created by mass mobilization with broad, countrywide networks.[5]

In August–September 1996 Lennart Meri was re-elected as the country's President in an indirect election in a specially formed Electoral College, after parliament was unable to vote a sufficient two-thirds majority for any candidate. According to the Estonian constitution, the President was elected by the *Riigikogu* and he could not maintain a party affiliation. President Meri was formerly with the Pro Patria organization. Meri's nearest challenger was Arnold Rüütel, the deputy speaker of the parliament. Also in late 1996, the governing coalition collapsed. It had consisted of a shaky coalition between the Coalition Party and the Rural Union led by Prime Minister Tiit Vähi and the Reform Party led by Foreign Minister Siim Kallas.[6] The disintegration of the government was precipitated by the signing of a cooperation agreement between Vähi and the oppositionist Center Party, about which the Reform Party had not been informed.

From the summer of 1996 into mid-November the same year, the governing coalition of the Coalition Party, the Rural Union, and the Estonian Reform Party was threatening to break apart. The senior Coalition Party repeatedly sought to circumvent the Reform Party by aligning itself with its former coalition partner, the Estonian Center Party. Prime Minister Vähi denied that serious problems existed in the coalition government and was proved correct for over three months, as the government remained intact. On 20 November 1996, however, six ministers from the Reform Party resigned from—the entire contingent of that party in the cabinet. These ministers based their resignations on a cooperation deal that the Prime Minister (a leading member of the Coalition Party) had signed with the Center Party and on allegations that the Reform Party proposed closer relations with Russia, at the expense of Estonian ties with the West.

By law the government did not have to be dissolved if a coalition collapsed, and neither were early elections necessary for the creation of a new minority government. During the 1996 crisis, opposition parties called for early elections, citing persistent problems within the governing coalition and its constituent parties. However, the Coalition Party formed a new government, and parliamentary elections did not take place. On 17 November 1998, Estonian lawmakers voted 66 to 5 with five abstentions, to disallow electoral alliances in future ballots. Eighteen deputies, mostly from the ruling coalition, did not take part in the vote. Observers believed that as a result of the ban, only six to eight political parties would win seats in the next parliament, compared with 12 in the previous legislature.

The Estonian Center Party won the 7 March 1999 elections with 23.41% of the vote and 28 seats. The Pro Patria Union won 16.09% and 18 seats; the Reform Party, 15.92% and 18 seats; the Moderates, 15.21% and 17 seats; the Coalition Party (in coalition with two other parties), 7.58% and 7 seats; the Country People's Party, 7.27% and 7 seats; and the United People's Party, 6.13% and 6 seats. Turnout stood at 57.43%. A right-of-center alliance consisting of the Reform Party, Moderates, and the Pro Patria Union, which had a combined total of 53 seats, formed the next government.

Mart Laar of Pro Patria, Siim Kallas of the Reform Party, and Andres Tarand of the Moderates informed President Lennart Meri on 8 March 1999 that they were ready to form a new cabinet. Although the left-leaning Estonian Center Party actually gained the majority of seats, the rightist alliance had a combined total of 53 seats in the 101-strong parliament.[7] Mart Siimann, outgoing premier and leader of the Coalition Party, which foiled pre-election expectations by winning some 7% of the vote and seven parliamentary seats, expressed his party's support for the rightist alliance. Meri was required to nominate a Prime Minister within two weeks of the election, according to the constitution, and was not obliged to name a candidate from the party that won the most votes.

On 17 March 1999, the Reform Party, the Moderates, and the Pro Patria Union signed a coalition agreement naming Mart Laar, chairman of the Pro Patria Union, as their candidate for Prime Minister. The three parties pledged to continue pursuing the country's foreign-policy goals of admission to the European Union (EU) and North Atlantic Treaty Organization (NATO) as well as a "stable and reliable" monetary policy. Beginning in January 2000, the 26% corporate tax was abolished, as called for by the Reform Party's platform. Another goal of the alliance was to gradually increase defense spending to 2% of Gross Domestic Product (GDP) by 2003.

The former ruling Coalition Party announced that it would become a "constructive opposition," joining with the Center Party, the Rural People's Party, and the United People's Party. Earlier, some members of the rightist alliance had hinted at the possible inclusion of the Coalition Party in the ruling coalition. At its first session on 18 March 1999, the new parliament re-elected Toomas Savi of the Reform Party as its speaker. In the secret ballot, 55 out of the 101 lawmakers voted in favor of Savi's re-election. Also on 18 March 1999, the outgoing government of Mart Siimann resigned but continued to perform its functions until the new cabinet was formed.

Lawmakers on 22 March 1999 voted strictly along party lines to endorse Mart Laar of the Pro Patria Union as Prime Minister. The vote was 53 to 48, accurately reflecting the constellation of parliamentary forces. In September 1999, opposition groups endorsed the Center Party's call for direct presidential elections in the future. All factions not belonging to the ruling coalition supported a bill calling for a referendum on changing the presidential election system. Under the existing system, parliament elected the president; in the event that it was unable to gain a two-thirds majority an electoral college was convened. The ruling coalition was hesitant about supporting the opposition bill, although many prominent members, such as Foreign Minister Toomas Hendrik Ilves, lodged similar proposals in the past.

On 17 October 1999, Estonia held local elections, a useful barometer of party support, in which even non-citizens could participate. Turnout at the ballot was 49.4% of eligible voters, down from 52.1% in the 1996 local elections. Among citizens turnout was 50.9%, while 43% of non-citizen voters cast ballots. The lowest turnout was in the city of Tartu, where only 38.4% voted. Voter participation in Tallinn was 48.4%.[8] The Center Party gained a majority of seats in Tallinn, winning 21 of the 64 seats to the City Council. The Pro Patria Union came in second, with 14. No single party gained the 33 seats needed to form a majority city administration.

The ruling coalition of Pro Patria, the Reform Party, and the Moderates, which together won 28 seats to the Tallinn City Council, signed a preliminary agreement with the Peoples' Trust, a Russian electoral union. The four seats won by the Peoples' Trust ensured a ruling majority in the Estonian capital's 64-seat city council. The three-year agreement called for the post of mayor to be given to a Pro Patria Union member, while the position of deputy mayor would go to a member of the Peoples' Trust. The unlikely coalition of nationalist Estonian parties and ethnic Russian organizations was evidently based on their common interest in combating corruption in the local city administration. Nationally, the Center Party was the most successful party, especially in the cities and the industrial northeast. The three parties belonging to the ruling coalition formed 13 out of the country's 15 municipal councils.

Despite the numerous changes in governments, Estonia did not repeat the inter-war pattern of a rapid succession of weak governments, but embarked on a prolonged process of party consolidation and democratic institution building. Indeed, it appeared that by the late 1990s a handful of stable and relatively large parties were beginning to emerge. As in other East European states, parties did not originate as mass organizations but as small groupings with a core leadership based largely on personal and political ties and often with similar programs. It took several years for political parties to gain public confidence, internal stability, organizational competence, programmatic clarity, and a constituency base.

Overall, Estonia seemed to be the most forward-looking of the Baltic states, especially in terms of its economic and political transition. The country's inter-war experience with liberal democracy, although flawed and short-lived, provided the country with a base on which to build a more modern and better functioning democratic state. Estonia was successful in instituting the "rule of law" and creating the political, economic, and social institutions necessary for a strong democracy and free market.

One of the most significant problems that faced the Estonian government since the country's independence has been the large and vocal resident Russian minority. According to census statistics at the beginning of the decade, out of a population of some 1.5 million, 600,000 were non-Estonians, among which were 125,000 non-Russians. Of the 475,000 Russians, almost 100,000 were pre-occupation Estonian citizens by parentage or birth. The remaining 375,000 were widely considered to be "colonists" who had been settled in Estonia since World War II under instructions from Moscow. By 1995, the Estonian Statistical Office estimated that out of a total population of 1,491,000, Estonians numbered 956,000 and non-Estonians 535,000; hence the ethnic Estonian share of the population had risen to just over 64%.[9]

As in Latvia, certain cities in Estonia were overwhelmingly ethnically Russian at the time Estonia broke away from the Soviet Union. Most of the post-war settlers had converged on Estonia's urban and industrial areas, especially in the northeastern corner of the country. Regions in eastern Estonia and the major metropolitan area of Narva were predominantly Russian-speaking: Narva was over 90% Russian. Tallinn did not have a Russian-speaking majority. During the 1990s, the ethnic Estonian proportion of the population began to rise. It increased to 64.6% in 1996, largely because of the departure of Russians, Ukrainians, and Belarusians.

The existence of a large resident Russian community created a variety of problems. In response to Estonia's drive for independence, Russian "colonists" formed several counter-state organizations that complained about the "Estonianization of Soviet Estonia." The most significant was the International Movement of Workers in the Estonian Soviet Socialist Republic (Intermovement), which was sponsored by Moscow to defend the privileged position of Russian ethnics in political, administrative, and economic life, and to undermine Estonia's bid for independence. It had only limited support among Russian ethnics, and so that the planned general strike in August 1989, as well as other protest actions, generated no significant support.

For ordinary Russians, the question of Estonian citizenship became the most salient issue, both domestically and internationally, as its potential denial threatened to marginalize the minority population both politically and economically. Estonian parties were split on the issue of citizenship, with national radicals demanding that all settlers in the country since the end of World War II be excluded, while moderates opposed such comprehensive discrimination and approved citizenship rights for residents who could pass some minimum language requirements.

Estonian political activists sought to fully reinstate the country's 1938 citizenship law, according to which all individuals who were citizens in June 1940 and their descendants, regardless of ethnic background, were automatically considered citizens. Aspiring citizens would need to go through a three-year naturalization procedure including the demonstration of a modest level of competence in Estonian.[10] But these requirements were far from discriminatory, as ordinary Russians had the right to use their own language in public places and there was state support for national minority education in the native language.

On 26 February 1992, Estonia passed a new citizenship law that confirmed the 1938 legislation. It denied automatic citizenship and national-level voting rights to Russians who had settled in Estonia since the country's occupation and annexation by the Soviet Union. The law also required all prospective citizens, except those exempted by marriage or national service, to possess two years of residence, to pass an elementary language test, to demonstrate their ability to support themselves, and to declare that they supported the Estonian constitution. Backers of the law argued that Estonia's residency stipulations were actually more liberal than those of most West European democracies. If all non-Estonians had registered for citizenship by March 1990, then the question would no longer have been a political issue. However, only 30,000 migrants actually registered by that date, thus creating tensions with the remainder of residents.

Critics of the citizenship law and the requirements for voting argued that it effectively disenfranchised about half a million Estonian residents.[11] As a consequence, the ethnic Estonian share of the electorate went up from about 65% in 1990 to over 90% in 1992; hence, the first post-independence parliament was completely Estonian. Although such a policy largely took the ethnic question outside the realm of party politics, it seemed to simply defer challenges stemming from ethnic rivalries, as greater numbers of Russians acquired citizenship and voting rights over the following years.

Despite claims by some spokesmen linked with the communist-sponsored Intermovement (short for International Movement), Russians were not relegated to the category of stateless persons, as Russia itself adopted an extraterritorial definition of citizenship that included the Russian *diaspora* in all former Soviet republics. This in turn was used by radical nationalists in Estonia not only to press for Russian exclusion from citizenship but also for Russian emigration.[12] A new citizenship law was passed in January 1995, raising the residency requirements to six years but only for new immigrants. Russian minority leaders criticized the law for not making citizenship easier. Nevertheless, by November 1995 an estimated 25% of non-Estonians had already acquired citizenship, half of the total by descent and half by naturalization, and the rate of acquiring citizenship was increasing.[13]

On 1 July 1997, parliament passed amendments to the law on aliens, granting the right to apply for permanent residence permits to non-citizens. Under the amended law, aliens who applied for temporary residence permits before

12 July 1995 would be eligible to request permanent residency. The amendment was to apply to some 200,000 aliens, mostly from Russia and other CIS (Commonwealth of Independent States) countries. By early 1997, approximately 120,000 Russians had become Estonian citizens, a similar number had opted for Russian Federation citizenship, and about 200,000 remained essentially stateless.

Lawmakers on 19 November 1997 also passed amendments to the language law, requiring parliamentary deputies and local government officials to prove knowledge of the Estonian language if they did not have at least elementary schooling in Estonia. All six ethnic Russian deputies voted against the amendments, claiming that they contradicted the constitution and international conventions. President Meri subsequently refused to promulgate amendments to the language law adopted by parliament. He argued that under the amendments, the executive branch was given too much power to decide whether deputies had sufficient knowledge of the Estonian language.

On 24 November 1997, amendments to the state language law that provided for language proficiency requirements for officials passed in the first reading. Under the amendments, civil servants and those who needed to communicate with the public through their work had to speak Estonian sufficiently well to be able to carry out their duties. The bill specified that the government was authorized to define language proficiency levels. Those who completed secondary school with instruction in Estonian would not be required to take a test. A similar bill passed by the parliament in 1996 was deemed unconstitutional by the Constitutional Court because that legislation delegated to the government the authority to establish language proficiency requirements for elected officials. The court ruled that such requirements could be established only by law, not by delegating such authority to the executive.

On 8 December 1997, Estonian lawmakers voted to pass amendments to the citizenship law that would facilitate the granting of citizenship to stateless children. Votes against the amendments came from the more nationalist Pro Patria Union, the People's Party, the Reform Party, and the Rural People's Party. According to the amendments, stateless children under 15 who were born after 26 February 1992 (when the country's 1938 citizenship law was reinstated) were eligible to gain citizenship. The children's parents needed to apply on their behalf, had to be stateless themselves, and must have lived in Estonia for at least five years. Those opposed to the bill had argued in favor of the applicants having to pass a language proficiency test.

Lawmakers on 9 February 1998 passed amendments to the state language law and tax law, requiring those working in the services sector to be proficient in the Estonian language. The vote was 35 to six with one abstention. President Meri on 13 February 1998 promulgated amendments to the state language law and tax law, requiring those working in the services sector to be proficient in the Estonian language. Final amendments to the language law were made on 14 June 2000, which the OSCE declared were in total compliance with international norms. The amendments replaced controversial provisions and stipulated that knowledge of Estonian was required only in public sector employment considered vital, and not in the private sector. The Russian Party in Estonia had appealed to the President not to promulgate any amendments, while the United People's Party, the largest party of Russian-speakers in Estonia, issued a statement urging the EU and the OSCE to pressure Tallinn to revoke the legislation.

On 18 December 1998, parliament promulgated amendments to the citizenship law that facilitated the granting of citizenship to stateless children born in the country to stateless parents. On 31 December 1998, President Meri signed legislation that imposed language requirements on members of the parliament and local governments. Russia criticized that legislation, as did the OSCE High Commissioner on National Minorities Max van der Stoel in a letter addressed to Meri. Van der Stoel asserted that the draft law on the state language "over-regulated" the use of foreign languages in the private sphere. On 27 July 1999, the Estonian government issued regulations on implementing the language law, passed in February. Under the law's provisions, stricter language requirements would be needed in the public sector. The government examined all the ramifications before implementing those parts of the law dealing with the private sector.

Estonia's law on voting rights in local elections was not tied to citizenship. All those who had resided in one locality for at least five years were allowed to vote in local elections regardless of citizenship status. This was perceived as a first step in the process of integrating Russians into Estonian politics. As a result of this relatively liberal voting rights law (in Latvia and Lithuania, one had to be a citizen to vote in any election), high voter turnout in predominantly Russian regions resulted in the formation of local governments in Tallinn and Narva that included ethnic Russian or leftist parties.[14] These organizations actively sought greater political, social, and economic integration of the Russian minority into Estonian society. Eventually a center-right coalition emerged in Tallinn that was not dominated by Russian or leftist parties.

At the same time, Estonia's constitution stipulated that only Estonian citizens possessed the right to form or become members of political parties, thus excluding many Russians from becoming active in the political process. Furthermore, the elevation of Estonian as the state language was accompanied by language requirements for all citizenship applicants. According to the 1989 Soviet census, only 13% of Russians in Estonia actually knew the Estonian language; hence, only this number could automatically qualify. The remainder also faced discrimination in professional occupations because of their poor grasp of Estonian.

Regional disparities in employment and wealth, with the "Russian" regions having both higher rates of unemployment and lower standards of living, exacerbated the problems associated with the non-citizen Russian population. Despite the high growth of the Estonian economy and an official national unemployment rate of only 1.9%, among ethnic Russians unemployment was several times higher. This relatively high jobless rate reflected the predominance of ethnic Russians in industrial occupations that were undergoing rapid transitions and thus experiencing significant employment losses. Russian ethnics also lost their privileged position vis-à-vis the state because of strict language and citizenship laws that *de facto* barred them from employment within the government apparatus.

Despite these political, social, and economic cleavages, many non-Estonians developed a positive attitude toward the independent Estonian state and increasing numbers viewed themselves culturally as more Estonian than Russian and sought to assimilate into the predominant culture. Moreover, most Russians calculated that it was better to live as a potential "underclass" in Estonia than to return to a turbulent and economically uncertain Russia. In January 1996, the government decided to grant alien passports to the approximately 300,000 residents who carried Soviet passports. Tallinn also decided to issue alien residence permits to about 10,000 ex–Red Army personnel, as their denial was widely seen as discriminatory by prevailing international standards.

Estonia's domestic issues negatively influenced the country's relations with Russia. The standards of living as well as the political rights of the ethnic Russians in Estonia have been watched closely by the Russian government, which on occasion has accused Tallinn of engaging in a policy of "apartheid" and "ethnic cleansing." While relations have not focused solely on these issues, the Russian government kept close tabs on ethnic Russians in Estonia and throughout the former Soviet Union. Where the official border between the two countries should be demarcated was another frequently discussed issue.[15] Some progress on the border question was made in early November 1996, and on 5 March 1998, the Estonian Foreign Minister Raul Mälk and the head of Russia's border negotiations committee, Ludvig Chizhov, initialed a border treaty between their countries, some seven years after talks were launched. Under the agreement, the two countries were to exchange small parcels of land totaling some 30 square kilometers. However, no precise date was specified for the signing of the treaty.

The Estonian government continually stressed that its position on the frontier question was based on the principle of the internationally recognized legal continuity of the Republic of Estonia founded on 24 February 1918 and that negotiations between Estonia and Russia must proceed from that point. Although by 1995 Tallinn was no longer seeking the return of approximately 2,000 square kilometers of land that Russia had annexed after World War II, it wanted acknowledgement that the incorporation of Estonia in the USSR and the changing of its borders in the 1940s had been an illegal act and that the 1920 Tartu Treaty remained valid.

Estonia's reaction to its strained relations with Russia has been to seek security guarantees from existing regional security structures while seeking to create new alliances. Estonia's vocal and determined pursuit of North Atlantic Treaty Organization (NATO) membership has been widely discussed internationally. However, despite the country's pledge to spend over 2% of its GDP on defense to bring its newly created army up to date, and to do whatever else was necessary to gain membership, by 2000 an imminent invitation to join NATO seemed unlikely. Nevertheless, Estonia, Latvia, and Lithuania continued to press for admittance. A greater sense of security was evident after August 1994 with the final withdrawal of ex-Soviet troops from Estonia, but Tallinn still felt vulnerable to Russian pressures and unpredictabilities.

NATO created the "Partnership for Peace" (PfP) program in 1994 to further the orientation of formerly communist countries toward the democratic states of Western Europe and North America and to help strengthen their national defense structures. Through PfP, Estonia increased its participation in military exercises with NATO members. Estonia, Latvia, and Lithuania pledged to strengthen their individual national armies by substantially increasing their size and their annual budget allocations.

Further integration with Western Europe in the economic, political, and social realms remained the highest priority of the Estonian government. The country gained the ability to engage in free trade with the European Union (EU) in 1994 and became an associate member of the Union on 12 June 1995. By the late 1990s, less than a third of Estonia's trade was with CIS countries, while over 60% of its trade was with the rest of the world. Further economic and trade integration with the Scandinavian countries, particularly Finland, was assured, and the Baltic Free Trade Zone, established in 1994, increased trade among Lithuania, Latvia, and Estonia. The Estonian government worked diligently to bring its laws and procedures into line with those of the EU, and in 1999 the country was included among six former communist countries for EU accession talks. Observers believed that Estonia would be ready for full membership by 2003.

The Estonian economy improved due to early and far-reaching structural changes in its monetary and fiscal policies. It was the first ex-Soviet republic to introduce its own currency (in June 1992), the kroon, which was pegged to the German mark; and the exchange rate remained stable. Monetary policy was controlled by a "currency board," which was separate from the Central Bank, and the kroon was fully backed by foreign exchange. Central Bank Governor Vahur Kraft claimed in October 1999 that the Estonian economy had overcome the crisis that gripped the region following Russia's financial collapse in August 1998.

The economy registered consistent annual growth and the government was determined to maintain a balanced budget. Estonia's strong ties with Finland were an important factor in its growth. The two countries shared cultural and linguistic similarities. Some analysts argued that Estonia's dramatic economic growth was in large part due to high levels of Finnish investment, both from government and private sources. Finland's membership in the EU promised continued economic benefits. Estonia and Finland instituted visa-free travel that further strengthened their economic and social ties. Estonia also established visa-free travel to the Schengen states. The Schengen Treaty adopted by the European Union allows for the free movement of EU citizens across the borders of member states. The treaty went into effect in July 1995.

POLITICAL PARTIES

Socialists and Social Democrats

Estonian Social Democratic Party (ESDP)
Eesti Sotsiaaldemokraatlik Partei (ESDP)

The Estonian Social Democratic Party (ESDP) was established on 8 September 1990 at its "amalgamation congress" and registered on 8 September 1990. It had emerged partly from a section of the Popular Front of Estonia (PFE), which had played a major role between 1998 and 1991 in mobilizing support for Estonian independence. It included the defunct Estonian Democratic Labor Party (EDLP), the Russian Social Democratic Party of Estonia (RSDPE), which broke away from the pro-Moscow Intermovement, and the Estonian Social Democratic Independence Party (ESDIP). In fact, the ESDP was the first political grouping that was able to bridge the ethnic gap between Estonians and Russians. The ESDP also merged with the émigré Estonian Socialist Party (ESP) at its founding congress and claimed several hundred members.

With an initial membership of only 300 people, the ESDP was chaired by Tiit Toomsalu and closely resembled other European social democratic parties. Its platform included an appreciation of "nature and culture, where everyone has freedom of self-determination and the less fortunate are not forgotten."[16] It was a strong supporter of parliamentary government and stated in its platform that the opposition should play a role in introducing alternative ideas and pointing out the weaknesses of the government. The ESDP became the dominant member of a coalition called the Moderates, in which the Estonian Rural Center Party (ERCP) formed the smaller party. The ESDP was one of the three-party coalitions that composed the first post-communist administration between 1992 and 1995. Andres Tarand, Prime Minister following the collapse of the government led by Mart Laar, was a member of this party. In 1996, the ESDP formed an electoral and political bloc with the Estonian Rural Center Party styled as the "Moderates."

In September 1998, the ESDP was close to being declared bankrupt, facing a debt to the state of some 8 million kroons ($533,000). The debt accumulated as a result of a dispute between the ESDP and the government over a building occupied by the party that was declared state property, along with all other assets of the former Communist Party. The ESDP continued to occupy the building and to garner income from leased office space. Following court sessions in late 1998 and calls for the party to be declared insolvent, Toomsalu claimed that the case was politically motivated and aimed at the liquidation of the country's only significant leftist party.[17]

People's Party Moderates (PPM)
Rahvapartei Mõõdukad (RM)

The People's Party (PP) was created when the Estonian Social Democratic Party (ESDP) merged with the Estonian Rural Center Party in 1996. It was chaired by Andres Tarand. On 30 May 1999, the People's Party, led by Toomas Hendrik Ilves, merged with another center-leftist formation styled as the Moderates. During the March 1999 general elections, the two parties ran on one list under the Moderate label. The new party retained the Moderate name, and the merger became legalized in early 2000. Following the local elections in 1999, the party formally changed its name to the People's Party Moderates (PPM). The new party remained a member of the Socialist International and was described as "right-wing socialist."[18]

    Some members of the PPM announced that they would split, arguing that the merger with the Moderates had changed the political direction of the party. Most of the departed members joined the Pro Patria Union, which was also a member of the three-party ruling coalition. Estonia's other leftist parties included the Pensioners' and Families' League Faction (PFLF), the Progressive Party Faction (PPF), the Russian Faction (RF), the Estonian Democratic Labor Party (EDLP), the Party for Legal Justice (PLJ), and the Estonian United People's Party (EUPP).

Liberals

Estonian Coalition Party (ECP)
Eesti Koonderakond (EK)

With a membership of only a few hundred people and chaired by Andrus Öövel, the Estonian Coalition Party was established on 9 December 1991 and registered on 30 January 1992. Its chief architect was Tiit Nuudi, personal advisor to Arnold Rüütel. It became the senior party in the first post-independence coalition government, which comprised the Coalition Party and the Rural Union (RU). It styled itself as a pragmatic pro-market and centrist formation and consisted of two main constituencies, former managers of smaller state enterprises who favored economic reconstruction and ex-communists from the Free Estonia (Vaba Eesti) movement. Prime Minister Tiit Vähi was also the chairman of the party, and he formed a government around the Coalition Party in January 1992, following the collapse of the Savisaar cabinet. The Vähi government was instrumental in liberalizing prices, introducing an Estonian currency, the kroon, and laying the foundations for a market economy.

During the parliamentary elections on 20 September 1992, the Coalition Party emerged as the most successful opposition party, as part of the Secure Home *(Kindel Kodu)* coalition. It also performed well at the October 1993 local elections and gained control over the Tallinn city council. The Coalition Party won twice as large a percentage of the 1995 parliamentary vote as the next highest contender, its former coalition partner, the Estonian Reform Party (ERP). The Coalition Party also scored well in the local elections held in October 1996 despite the fact that parties holding power had never won subsequent elections: "The winners have always come from the ranks of the opposition," remarked Prime Minister Vähi after the local ballot.

The party viewed the results as strengthening the Coalition Party's position as a senior member of the government. After the March 1995 elections, Vähi created a new coalition government comprising the Coalition Party, the Rural Union, and the Estonian Center Party. Vähi stated that the goals of the government were to further the reforms undertaken by the preceding administration, to seek full membership in the European Union, and to improve relations with the Russian Federation. The government lasted only until October 1995 because of the scandals surrounding Edgar Savisaar, Minister of the Interior.

President Meri asked Vähi to form a new government, and Vähi chose a coalition of the Coalition Party, the Rural Union, and the Estonian Reform Party, led by Siim Kallas, former head of the Bank of Estonia. This coalition lasted until November 1996, when after months of rumors that there were irreconcilable differences within the coalition, six ministers representing the ERP resigned and the government fell. Soon after, however, the Coalition Party and Rural Union formed a minority government. The Estonian Coalition Party was principally a center-left and pro-liberal party rather than a socialist or social democratic formation. In September 1997, Tiit Vähi, the chairman of the ruling Coalition Party and former Prime Minister, announced that he was quitting politics. He submitted his resignation as party chairman and parliamentary deputy but remained a member of the Coalition Party.

At a party congress in September 1998, the Coalition Party elected Prime Minister Mart Siimann as its chairman. At a subsequent party congress on 2 May 1999, the party chose former Defense Minister Andrus Öövel as its chairman. Öövel, who was the only candidate for the post, declared his major task was to stop infighting within the party. With declining public support, the former ruling Coalition Party won only seven parliamentary seats and 7.6% of the popular vote in the March 1999 general elections.

Estonian Center Party (ECP)
Eesti Keskerakond (EK)

The Estonian Center Party was established on 4 September 1991, initially as the People's Center Party. It changed its name in October 1991 and was registered on 9 April 1992. Its founding members consisted of 202 activists, many of whom were leading reformist figures. This number rose to over 1,400 by the mid-1990s. The party was chaired by former Prime Minister Edgar Savisaar, who was prominent in the pro-independence Popular Front of Estonia (PFE). It initially defined its strategy as steering a middle course between reform communism and national independence. The party stood for the September 1992 elections and was asked to join a coalition government with the Coalition Party, forming a center-left majority government. Although the Center Party came in third in total vote's cast in the March 1995 general elections, it played an important if sometimes controversial role as an ally of the ruling Coalition Party.

The Center Party was asked to join the coalition government as a junior partner in late March 1995. The stated priorities of the government were to obtain a full membership in the European Union and to improve relations with the Russian Federation. This government lasted only until October 1995, when it was discovered that Edgar Savisaar, then Minister of the Interior, had secretly made tapes of negotiations to form a new government after the 1995 elections. Vähi dismissed him, but Savisaar refused to step down, thus provoking the rest of the government to offer its resignation. The next administration, also formed by Vähi, did not include the Center Party.

Seven members of the Center Party broke away to form a parliamentary faction called the Progressive Party (PP) in 1996. Their policies were not significantly different from the Center Party's, but the Progressive Party refused to join any government that included its former partners. Thus, the PP faction rejected Tiit Vähi's offer to join his minority government after the Reform Party ministers all resigned in November 1996. A cooperation agreement signed by the Coalition Party and members of the Center Party proved to be the breaking point for ministers from the junior coalition member, the Estonian Reform Party (ERP). Six ERP ministers resigned from the coalition government in November 1996, soon after the cooperation agreement became public.

One of the primary allegations made by the ERP ministers was that any coalition that included the Center Party would undoubtedly move Estonia's foreign policy focus eastward, toward the Russian Federation and the rest of the CIS (Commonwealth of Independent States). A public opinion poll taken shortly before the October 1996 local elections showed that 20% of the non-Estonian population supported the Center Party. This sector of society evidently felt that having the Center Party in the government could balance Estonia's interests in the East with its interests in the West. Under Savisaar, the ECP both lost and won in two elections by winning most of the seats in the Riigikogu and by Savisaar's exclusion from the Riigikogu and Tallinn City Council. The party frequently voted with the Estonian People's Union, the Coalition Party, and the United People's Party.

Estonian Liberal Democratic Party (ELDP)
Eesti Liberaaldemokraatlik Partei (ELP)

The Estonian Liberal Democratic Party (ELDP) was founded on 9 March 1990 through a merger of two groups that emerged from the Popular Front of Estonia: the Liberal People's Party (LPP) and the Free Democratic Party (FDP). The former had social democratic leanings, while the latter primarily consisted of humanistic intellectuals and cultural figures. The ELDP favored a "humanistic and social approach" to the introduction of a market economy in contrast to some of the free marketeers, and was viewed as "social liberal." The party was subject to internal fissures particularly with regard to its cooperation with other organizations. In October 1990, the ELDP was granted observer status at the Liberal International, becoming the first East European party to be admitted to the organization. The ELDP merged with the Reform Party during 1994 to form the Estonian Reform Party (ERP).

Estonian Reform Party (ERP)
Eesti Reformierakond (ER)

The Estonian Reform Party (ERP) was established on 18 November 1994 with 710 members, and was chaired by Siim Kallas. It formed the junior partner of the incoming government, but its ministers resigned from their posts in mid-November 1996, after a little over a year in government. The party was considered right-of-center and maintained contacts with the German Free Democrats, the Swedish Liberal Folk Party, the Finnish Swedish Folk Party, and Latvia's Way. The ERP was formed through a merger between the small Reform Party and the Estonian Liberal Democratic Party, which broke off from the Estonian Popular Front in 1990. Its founder, Siim Kallas, was the former president of the Bank of Estonia and one of the individuals who was instrumental in making the introduction of the Estonian kroon a success.

When the ERP became the junior coalition partner in the Coalition Party–Rural Union–led government, Kallas was appointed as the country's foreign minister. This was largely due to the fact that the public viewed him as remaining outside of the political battles that had undermined the previous government. Additionally, many believed that Kallas would prove as responsible and efficient in his new post as he had been in his Bank of Estonia position. The ERP left the Coalition Party-led administration at the end of 1996 over a cooperation agreement that the Coalition Party concluded with the Center Party. At the ERP congress in Tallinn on 15 May 1999, Kallas was re-elected party head.

Estonian Republican Coalition Party (ERCP)
Eesti Vabariiklaste Koonderakond (EVK)

The Estonian Republican Coalition Party (ERCP) emerged in September 1990 through the combination of three groupings: young intellectuals, industrial managers who supported Estonian independence, and free market conservatives. The party became a keen supporter of a capitalist economy and was involved in the governing Isamaa coalition between the fall of 1992 and the summer of 1994 under the premiership of Mart Laar. After that, its fortunes sagged and it virtually vanished from the political scene.

Progressive Party (PP)
Arengupartei (AP)

Established on 25 May 1996, this coalition at its inception numbered approximately 200 people. The Progressive Party (PP) was liberal and centrist in its orientation. It began when several dissatisfied parliamentary deputies left the Estonian Center Party and created the Liberal Centrist faction in the Riigikogu. In April 1996, members from the Centrist faction and four former Center Party members joined to form the small New Democratic Union (NDU). The NDU became the Progressive Party faction in May 1996. Members of the PP claimed that the return of Edgar Savisaar to public life and to leadership of the party, after the political scandal during the fall of 1995, was the primary reason for their having left the ECP in protest.[19] Andra Veidemann became the party's leader. The PP was not officially a member of the government coalition, but Veidemann became a minister without portfolio.[20] During the late 1990s, the Progressive Party was deregistered because of a lack of members and Veideman's defection from the organization.

People's Party (PP)
Rahvaerakond (RE)

The People's Party was created from the merger of an agrarian party, the Estonian Farmers Union (EFU), and the Right-Wingers (Parempoolsed) organization.[21] At the time of its formation, the attitude of the People's Party toward the government was unclear. One week before joining the party, the EFU stated it would support neither the government nor the opposition. The People's Party ran on a joint list with the Moderates for the March 1999 elections, but at the time no decision was made as to whether the two parties would merge. Foreign Minister Ilves was elected People's Party chairman on 5 April 1998.

In October 1998, Indrek Kannik, secretary-general of the People's Party, announced that his party was officially breaking the cooperation agreement with the ruling coalition. This move came after party leader Ilves submitted his resignation as foreign minister. Unofficially, however, the party had broken the agreement shortly after it was signed in April. That same month, the People's Party called for the resignation of environment minister Villu Reiljan on corruption charges, which in turn prompted demands by the rural parties that Ilves should step down as foreign minister. The PP joined the Moderates *(Mõõdukad)* coalition before the elections in March 1999, and the two parties (the PP and the PPM) officially merged in April 2000 to create a single People's Party.[22]

Estonian Entrepreneurs' Party (EEP)
Eesti Ettevõtjate Erakond (EEE)

The Estonian Entrepreneurs' Party (EEP) was founded on 2 March 1990 and led by the well-known reform communist, Tiit Made, who was a driving force for the economic autonomy of Estonia in the late 1990s. The party involved several interest groups, including the Union of Private Enterprises and Cooperatives *(Eesti Kooperatiivide ja Eraettevõtete Assosiatsiooni Liit)* and the Small Business Association *(Eesti Vaikeettevotete Assosiatsioon)*. The party managed to gain only 2.3% of the vote at the September 1992 parliamentary elections and subsequently joined the Estonian Center Party and gained a seat in parliament.

Other liberal parties included the Estonian Democratic Union (EDU) *(Eesti Demokraatik Liit, EDL)* which was established on 17 November 1990, registered as an association on 7 March 1991, and as a party on 1 February 1994. Its chairman was Miina Hinta, and it remained a small party of the political center.

Estonian Blue Party (EBP)
Eesti Sinine Erakond (SE)

The Estonian Blue Party (EBP) was formed on 29 November 1994 and registered on 8 December 1994. There were 73 founding members and 207 at the party's registration. The party was led by Aleksander Einseln and by its chairman Jaan Laas, and it was consistently centrist in its orientation. The EBP strongly supported the increased demographic growth of the Estonian nation while insisting that the equality and welfare of all individuals be upheld. In the March 1999 general elections, it barely garnered 1.6% of the popular vote, and it subsequently virtually disappeared from political life. Critics accused Einseln of moving the EBP toward more populist positions.

Christian Democrats

Estonian Christian Democratic Union (ECDU)
Eesti Kristlik Demokraatlik Liit (EKDL)

The Estonian Christian Democratic Union (ECDU) was established on 17 December 1988 and was originally known as the Estonian Christian Union. Its more prominent members included Mart Laar, Illar Hallaste, and Trivimi Velliste, all former members of the governing body of the National Heritage

Society. The party initially included members from a diversity of religious traditions, including Lutheran, Catholic, Orthodox, Methodist, and Baptist. However, it eventually evolved into a primarily Lutheran political organ, which sought to give the Lutheran Church a pre-eminent position in Estonian society. It also supported the creation of a "social market economy" in which the poorer segments of society would be adequately protected by the state. A separate organization, the Estonian Christian Democratic Association (ECDA) *(Eesti Kristlik Ühendus, EKU),* was created to focus on social work rather than on explicitly political activities. The ECDU itself changed its name in 1988 to the Estonian Christian Democratic Party (ECDP) and gained membership in the Christian Democratic International in 1990. That same year the party created a Youth Organization with Tõnu Koiv as chairman.

Estonian Christian Democratic Party (ECDP)
Eesti Kristlik Demokraatlik Erakond (EKDE)

The Estonian Christian Democratic Party (ECDP) was founded on 23 July 1988 as the earliest non-communist political formation. Its initial phase combined a number of young Christian activists, mostly students from the Technical Training College in Tallinn, none of whom were clergymen. It had close links with the National Heritage Society, which campaigned in the late 1980s and early 1990s for the restoration of historical and cultural monuments and supported Estonian independence. The ECDP was criticized by other Christian democratic parties for being too far removed from any major Church and therefore lacking both influence and authority. Other Christian political movements included the Estonian Christian People's Party (ECPP) *(Eesti Kristlik Rahvapartei, EKRP),* which was chaired by Aldo Vinkel.

Agrarians

Estonian Rural Center Party (ERCP)
Eesti Maa Keskerakond (EMK)

The Estonian Rural Center Party (ERCP) was established on 7 April 1990 by the future minister of agriculture Jan Leetsaar and by Ivar Raig, an economist, chairman of the rural section of the Popular Front of Estonia (PFE), and a member of the Council of Estonia. The party was especially active in central Estonia, traditionally a region of wealthy farmers. The main part of the ERCP platform called for the restoration of private farming, which was viewed as key to economic development. With private agriculture restored during the early 1990s, nearly half of the party's members consisted of private farmers. The ERCP formed the Moderates coalition with the Estonian Social Democrats, which won 9.7% of the popular vote and 12 parliamentary seats in the

September 1992 elections. In the March 1995 elections, the Moderates slipped to 6% of the vote and captured only six seats, but rebounded in the March 1999 elections to gain 15% of the vote and 17 seats.

Estonian Rural Union (ERU)
Eesti Maaliit (EM)

The Estonian Rural Union (ERU) was established on 29 September 1994 and registered on 28 October 1994. The number of founding members stood at 540, with Arvo Sirendi as chairman. It included both reform communists and former members of the pre–World War II Rural Union. As the majority of rural inhabitants were ethnic Estonians, the party became moderately nationalistic and sought to address the specific needs of the rural population in agriculture, material well-being in the midst of the economic transition, and the preservation and development of the "unique" Estonian culture and its traditions. The ERU wanted the collective farms returned to their original owners with the remainder of holdings used as voluntary cooperative farms.

The Estonian Rural Union joined with the Estonian Coalition Party in 1995 to form an electoral union. It thereby managed to win the largest number of votes (32%) in the March elections of that year and picked up 41 parliamentary seats. The ERU subsequently merged with the Estonian People's Party but failed to establish a cooperative relationship with a rival parliamentary agrarian party, the Estonian Rural Center Party, which was part of the Moderates coalition.

Estonian Rural People's Party (ERPP)
Eesti Maarahva Erakond (EME)

Another significant agrarian organization was the left-leaning Estonian Rural People's Party (ERPP). It was chaired by Arnold Rüütel, a prominent reform communist who served as chairman of the Supreme Council until he chose to run for the Estonian presidency against Lennart Meri in the September–October 1992 elections. The ERPP was formed after a merger between the Rural League and the Families' and Pensioners' Party. It managed to gain 7.3% of the popular vote in the March 1999 elections and garnered seven parliamentary seats.

Estonian Foresters' Party (EFP)
Eesti Metsnike Erakond (EME)

The Estonian Foresters' Party (EFP) was founded on 10 September 1994 and registered on 28 October 1994. It had 728 founding members and was chaired by Vello-Tavio Denks. It was a rural-based party that supported a free market economy to the extent that it did not harm the "traditional and dignified life of the rural people."[23] Despite the party's clear interest in individual economic autonomy, it viewed the state as having a central role in the regulation of the economy and in the preservation of Estonia's heritage, resources, and culture. The party also viewed the natural environment of Estonia as having both marketable and spiritual value. Its party platform for the March 1995 parliamentary elections ended with the words "Estonia is a country of forests. The forests will save Estonia." By the late 1990s the Foresters' Party became obsolete, with dwindling public support.

Estonian Farmers' Party (EFP)
Eesti Talurahva Erakond (ETE)

The Estonian Farmers' Party (EFP) was launched on 5 November 1994 and registered on 30 November 1994. Its founding members numbered 219 and it was chaired by Jaak-Hans Kuks. The Farmers' Party was considered a conservative quasi-nationalist group that was wary of outside influence and intervention in Estonia. The party strongly supported the rights and "spirit of the Estonian nation." The EFP joined the new Estonian People's Party (EPP) in 1996, which in turn merged into the People's Party Moderates (PPM).

Several other small, rural-based parties were formed in the early 1990s, including the Estonian People's Union (EPU) *(Eestimaa Rahvaliit)*; the Farmers' Assembly (FA) *(Põllumeeste Kogu, PK)*, chaired by Eldur Pardel but gained little national influence.

Greens

Estonian Green Party (EGP)
Eesti Roheline Partei (ERP)

The environmentalist campaign, the Estonian Green Movement (EGM) *(Eesti Roheline Liikumine, ERL)*, was established in May 1988 by the television journalist Juhan Aare. Ecological activists were successful in the late 1980s in mobilizing public protests against Moscow's plans for a new phosphate mining project near the town of Maardu. The project was eventually cancelled and the experience helped to propel forward Estonia's embryonic civic society. During the summer of 1989, the Movement was beset by internal conflicts and left-right divisions, and two separate Green parties with the same name emerged in Estonia. The Estonian Green Party (EGP) was founded on 19 August 1989, composed of right-of-center elements critical of the EGM's conciliatory policies toward Moscow and the Movement's refusal to call for outright national independence. As it developed, the EGP largely abandoned environmentalist issues.

Estonian Greens (EG)
Eesti Rohelised (ER)

The rival Estonian Green Party *(Eesti Roheline Erakond, ERE)*, was established in May 1990 under the leadership of Vello Pohlaa and was largely the political voice of the Estonian Green Movement (EGM). After two years of conflict and fragmentation, a new party, the Estonian Greens (EG) *(Eesti Rohelised)*, was created in December 1991. It constituted a merger between like-minded people in various Green organizations. Only one Green representative, Rein Järlik, was elected to parliament following the September 1992 general elections. The party's support then stood at about 3% of the electorate, but it declined during the latter part of the decade.

Communists

Estonian Democratic Workers' Party (EDWP)
Eesti Demokraatlik Tööpartei (EDT)

This majority wing of the former Estonian Communist Party (ECP) was officially registered as a political party in June 1991, even prior to the banning of the Soviet Communist Party in Estonia. It styled itself as the Independent Communist Party (ICP). The ICP favored democratic and market reforms and sought to distance itself completely from its servile pro-Soviet past. A proposal to eliminate the ICP after Estonia regained its independence was rejected by parliament. The ICP contested the September 1992 general elections as part of the Leftist Alternative (LA) *(Vasak Võimalus, VV)* but failed to win any seats in parliament. On 28 November 1992, the party renamed itself the Estonian Democratic Workers' Party (EDWP), but it failed to gain any significant public support.

Estonian Social Democratic Labor Party (ESDLP)
Eesti Sotsiaaldemokraatiik Tööpartei (ESDTP)

The Estonian Social Democratic Labor Party (ESDLP) was established on 28 November 1992 and registered on 4 May 1993 with a membership of 1,100. It was chaired by Tiit Toomsalu. The party was founded by reform-minded and well-known communists but did not win enough votes to gain seats in the *Riigikogu* in either the 1992 or the 1995 parliamentary elections. The Estonian Communist Party had tried to reform itself after the failed August 1991 coup in Moscow, but by November 1992 it had become increasingly clear that the party would be unable to muster the support needed to enter parliament without making a more public break with its past and changing its name.

The party's precursor was the Free Estonia (FE) *(Vaba Eesti, VE)* movement, which emerged in early 1990 and sought to depict itself as a modern social democratic formation under the leadership of former Prime Minister Indrek Toome. It contested the last Supreme Soviet elections in 1990 on a separate list and gained about one quarter of parliamentary seats. The ESDLP adopted a more traditional social democratic platform and became part of the electoral union "Justice" during the March 1995 parliamentary elections. After the parliamentary vote to ban electoral alliances in November 1998, the Social Democratic Labor Party, the United People's Party, and the Russian Unitary Party merged to form a new organization.

Party for Legal Justice (PLJ)
Õigusliku Tasakaalu Erakond (OTE)

The Party for Legal Justice (PLJ) was founded on 25 October 1994 and registered on 6 December 1994. It had eleven founding members and 220 at the time of registration. It was chaired by Peeter Tedr. The PLJ was a far-left party that failed to gain any representation in the *Riigikogu* on its own. Its platform advocated both stronger local government and greater focus on the responsibility of the state to ensure the welfare of every permanent resident of Estonia, both citizen and non-citizen. Citizenship was not discussed directly, but the party's 1995 parliamentary election platform made clear that an extensive legal system had to be created to enforce laws and bring justice "for all people." The PLJ was part of the electoral union "Justice" during the March 1995 election campaign but subsequently ceased to exist.

Nationalists

Popular Front of Estonia (PFE)
Eesti Rahvarinne (ER)

The Popular Front of Estonia (PFE) was established on 13 April 1988 when an initiative group was formed under the name of the Popular Front for the Support of Perestroika. By June 1988, the PFE claimed about 40,000 members and was an umbrella organization for democratic and pro-sovereignty forces that included human rights groups, religious organizations, environmental movements, heritage groupings, nascent political parties, and even some fractions of the Communist Party. In fact, five out of seven members of the initial executive committee were Communist Party members, including Edgar Savisaar, the former head of the State Planning Commission (Gosplan). The PFE involved various intellectual and cultural figures as well as young politicians who would later rise to prominence in an independent Estonia. As the communist organizations crumbled, the PFE lodged increasingly more extensive demands and staged a number of large-scale public rallies, including the Song of Estonia demonstration on 11 September 1988, which brought out over 250,000 people from all over the country–about 20% of the Estonian population. The PFE disintegrated into competing political formations after the September 1992 elections, in which it gained 12.3% of the vote and 15 parliamentary seats.

Pro Patria Union (PPU)
Isamaaliit (EI)

The Pro Patria Union (PPU) was established on 21 November 1992, with a membership of 800 people and was chaired by Mart Laar. A coalition of four national conservative parties, it became an official party itself after the September 1992 parliamentary elections. Pro Patria (Fatherland) was one of the most radical nationalist parties in the Estonian political spectrum. This was mainly due to its core belief in the continuation and strengthening of a "truly Estonian" nation-state and its emphasis on ethnic exclusivity and citizenship based on ethnicity. The party received the largest share of the vote in the September 1992 parliamentary elections, as the Fatherland coalition garnered 22% of the vote and captured 29 seats. But it subsequently saw its influence decline in the March 1995 elections despite forming an electoral coalition with another conservative party-the Estonian National Independence Party (ENIP).

The coalition government created after the 1992 elections consisted of the Pro Patria Union, ENIP, and the Moderates. Mart Laar was Prime Minister from 1992 until the government fell in 1994, when Andres Tarand, also of the Moderates, assumed the position. The more radical PPU members left the party due to the PPU's "moderate" stance on issues such as citizenship; they formed the Right-Wingers, which subsequently merged to form the People's Party. This group, however, rejoined the Pro Patria Union after the Moderates merger with the People's Party. After defeating Toivo Jürgenson, a former minister of the economy, Mart Laar continued as the party's chairman. In December 1995, the PPU merged with the Estonian National Independence Party.[24] Laar resigned from the post of party chairman after the 1995 general election, but he was still considered the most influential member of the party.[25] Toivo Jürgenson became the new party chairman.

Estonian National Independence Party (ENIP)
Eesti Rahvusliku Sõltumatuse Partei (ERSP)

The Estonian National Independence Party (ENIP) was established illegally on 20 August 1988 and registered on 10 May 1989. It was the first party to be created that openly opposed communist and Soviet rule in Estonia. It grew out of the movement in the late 1980s for disclosing the truth about the Molotov-Ribbentrop Pact. The ENIP had an initial membership of about 1,200 people and was chaired by Tunne Kelam, with a core of leading political dissidents. It worked closely with the Estonian Heritage Society (EHS) in creating "citizens' committees" in the late 1980s that pressed for full state independence.

From the outset, the ENIP was more radical than the Popular Front of Estonia (PFE), with which it was regularly in competition. The party's radicalism (or "high principles") was highlighted by the fact that it did not participate in the elections to the Supreme Council, but rather chose to support the alternative Estonian Congress *(Eesti Kongress)*, which sought more independence for Estonia and tried to register Estonian citizens based on the definition of "citizen" in the pre-war constitution. ENIP's support base was limited to ethnic Estonians, and it was surpassed by the PFE as the latter's demands became more strident—especially after the PFE included in its electoral platform the right of the Estonian people to proclaim the country's independence from the Soviet Union. The ENIP played an important part in the creation of the new national constitution by supplying 13 of the 30 members allocated to the Council of Estonia in the 60-member Constitutional Assembly.

The ENIP spoke out for comprehensive "de-Sovietization" and the wholesale purge of all former communist functionaries from public life. The ENIP also supported "de-Russification" and opposed granting citizenship rights to ethnic Russians who settled in Estonia after World War II. It argued that as a "restored state," and not the legal successor of the Estonian Soviet Socialist Republic, Estonia should only admit pre-Soviet citizens and their descendants to citizenship.

In the September 1992 general elections, the ENIP was one of the few formations with a national organization. It polled 8.7% of the vote and won ten parliamentary seats. The party ran on a combined ticket with Pro Patria in the March 1995 parliamentary elections and won 7.9% of the total vote, giving it eight seats in the *Riigikogu*. Like Pro Patria, the ENIP believed strongly in the Republic of Estonia as a nation comprising primarily Estonian citizens. It was therefore considered a nationalist formation and subsequently merged with Pro Patria. The party was beset by fractionalism and internal division that resulted in several splits throughout the 1990s.

Estonian Home (EH)
Eesti Kodu (EK)

The Estonian Home (EH) was established on 24 April 1994 and registered on 6 December 1994. It had a small founding membership of some 200 people and was chaired by Kalju Põldvere. This minor party was primarily interested in increasing democratic participation and punishing those who committed crimes against the Estonian people and the Estonian nation throughout the communist era. It believed strongly in the First Republic of Estonia as "the highest form of identity for the Estonian people."[26] Following from this, it advocated in 1995 the "decolonization" of Estonia and the treatment of non-Estonians as "guest workers" without the right to own land.

The party wanted to increase Estonia's integration with Europe, although at a slower pace than the incumbent governments. The EH also wanted the Estonian government to build a relationship with Russia based on the 1920 Tartu Peace Treaty and not any of the later treaties that the Russian government was advocating. In other words, subsequent Soviet-Estonian treaties would not be formally recognized, particularly the "treaty" that incorporated Estonia into the Soviet Union. The Estonian Home, like most other Estonian parties, viewed this "agreement" as a farce that simply covered up the forced annexation and colonization of Estonia by the Soviet Union. The EH disappeared from the political scene during the late 1990s because it could not compete with other nationalist formations.

Estonian Future Party (EFP)
Tulevikupartei (TP)

The Estonian Future Party was formed on 19 August 1993 and registered on 4 November 1993. It was created by former ENIP executive board member Arvo Kiir. Its membership reached approximately 1,000 people and the party was subsequently led by Jaanus Raidal. The Future Party was widely considered nationalist and isolationist. It advocated strengthening local government and limiting Estonia's participation in international institutions and initiatives. For example, the party supported "cooperation with Europe" but did not want to join the European Union because the Union's policies include the free movement of labor and capital.[27] The Future Party's leaders proclaimed the goal of national unity, hoping to benefit from public dissatisfaction with the major existing parties and political discords.

Estonian Conservative People's Party (ECPP)
Eesti Konservatiivne Rahvaerakond (EKR)

The Estonian Conservative People's Party (ECPP) was founded on 6 January 1990 by Enn Tarto, a prominent anti-communist dissident and rector of the Estonian Institute of Human Rights. The party held its founding congress the following June. The ECPP rejected the clericalism of most of the Christian democratic formations and sought a strict separation of the state from any church as well as the protection of all religious minorities. The ECPP included Catholics and Orthodox Church members as well as conservative intellectuals who favored a pro-independence nationalism. Its leaders stressed the legal continuity of the Estonian state and the illegality of communist rule, and maintained close contacts with the Estonian government-in-exile. It was one of the first parties to call for a restoration of an independent Estonian army and border guards. In its economic program, the ECPP displayed isolationist views, opposing any foreign ownership of Estonian resources or companies and eschewing any special cooperative relationships with the other Baltic or Nordic countries. It sought to create a neutral Estonia outside of any military alliances and modeled on Switzerland. The ECPP did not have any lasting impact on the country's politics and was disbanded in the mid-1990s.

Republican and Conservative People's Party–Right-Wingers (RCPP-RW)
Vavariiklaste ja Konservatiivne Rahvaerakond–Parampoolsed (VKR)

The Republican and Conservative People's Party–Right-Wingers (RCPP-RW) was established on 10 September 1994 and registered on 28 October 1994. It was chaired by Kristjan-Olari Leping with a founding membership of 217 people. The party was wary of a strong, centralized government and declared that individuals and local communities were the "repositories of freedom" in Estonia: "the state is there for the people, not the people for the state."[28] The party also felt that the continued existence of the Republic of Estonia was critical for the further development of the "unique Estonian culture." The RCPP-RW received more votes than had been expected in the local elections in October 1996, most notably winning 10 seats in Tallinn. The party declared that it would eventually join the Pro Patria Union.[29] The RCPP-RW first merged into the People's Party together with the Farmer's Union, and then into the Moderates.

Estonian National Progress Party (ENPP)
Eesti Rahvuslik Eduerakond (ERE)

The Estonian National Progress Party (ENPP) was formed on 27 November 1993, being largely the creation of Ants Erm and Toivo Uustalo–former Estonian National Independence Party (ENIP) members. The party took a hard-line stance on the national question, declaring that Estonia should only include ethnic Estonian citizens and that the Russian minority should be encouraged to leave the country. It promoted Estonian language and culture and supported state measures to encourage a growth in the Estonian birth rate, and spoke out for the "moral regeneration of the nation." The latter was invariably considered a catchphrase for an anti-Russian stance. The ENPP took part in the March 1995 general elections as part of the radical rightist Better Estonia alliance, gaining 3.6% of the vote and no parliamentary seats. It subsequently vanished from political life.

Estonian Citizen (EC)
Eesti Kodanik (EK)

The Estonian Citizen (EC) was created by U.S. army veteran Jüri Toomepuu as a collection of independent activists. The organization was vehemently nationalist, anti-communist, anti-Russian, anti-establishment, militaristic, and populist. It polled 6.9% of the popular vote and gained eight parliamentary seats in the September 1992 elections. Its populist propensities indicated that it could swing easily from a pro-market to an anti-capitalist economic program. The EC claimed to have an armed volunteer force that rejected the legitimacy of the new Estonian government in favor of the Estonian "government-in-exile" based in Sweden. Toomepuu was the defense minister in the émigré organization. The EC considered the country's citizenship law too liberal and accommodating to the Russian population and sought to severely restrict naturalization. EC joined the Better Estonia coalition for the March 1995 elections, but the coalition mustered only 3.6% of the popular vote. Like many other nationalist groupings the EC disappeared from public life in the late 1990s.

Estonian National Protection Party (ENPP)
Eesti Rahvusliku Kaitse Erakond (ERKE))

The Estonian National Protection Party (ENPP) was created on 12 November 1994 and registered on 8 December 1994. Its founding membership consisted of a mere few dozen people and it was chaired by Asso Kommer. The party's main concerns were "freedom, justice, and law."[30] It wanted to dramatically enhance grassroots democracy and to make all levels of government more accountable to the citizens of Estonia. Its economic platform supported a stable currency that was fully backed by the Bank of Estonia and protected from political interference. The party maintained that Estonians must fully commit themselves to the defense of the country from both "eastern and western threats," thus displaying its protectionist and isolationist approach to foreign policy. The ENPP failed to garner any significant public support.

Ethnic Minority and Religious Parties

Our Home Is Estonia (OHE)
Meie Kodu on Eestimaa (MKE)

Chaired by Viktor Andrejev, the Our Home Is Estonia (OHE) coalition consisted of the Estonian United People's Party (EUPP) and the Russian Party in Estonia (RPE). Three political parties that sought to represent Russian speakers in Estonia—the United People's Party (UPP), the Russian Christian Union (RCU), and the Russian Unity Party (RUP)—formed a common bloc for the March 1995 parliamentary elections. The new group was called "Our Home Is Estonia."

Russian minority activists, with Moscow's support, first established an International Movement of Workers in the Estonian SSR (Intermovement) in July 1988, in opposition to growing demands for Estonian independence, as well as a Joint Council of Work Collectives. They staged several demonstrations and were supported by hard-line elements within the Soviet bureaucracy and security services. Intermovement claimed to have about 200,000 supporters, and when Estonian independence appeared inevitable, it demanded the creation of an autonomous Russian republic in northeastern Estonia with its capital in Narva. Some militants even demanded the secession of this heavily Russified region and its attachment to Russia. However, Intermovement's support base dissipated—particularly after the disintegration of the Soviet Union in 1990–1991—and there was little support for Russian autonomy or secession.

Various moderate minority organizations and non-communist groupings emerged in the 1990s, primarily seeking to protect ethnic and linguistic rights within the emerging independent Estonian state and distancing themselves from their pro-Soviet past. They included the Forum of Estonia's Nationalities (FEN), which brought together the representatives of seventeen minorities, including Russians, Armenians, and Jews. In the March 1995 parliamentary elections, the "Our Home Is Estonia" coalition gained 5.7% of the national vote and six parliamentary seats. This was the first occasion at which Russian parties had run slates of candidates in an Estonian general election. Subsequent to the ballot, in late 1996, the OHE began to splinter between more pragmatic and nationalist factions. This put into doubt whether the Russian community could grow into a unified constituency, especially as the number of Russian voters was increasing through naturalization, and given the increasing social diversification.

Estonian United People's Party (EUPP)
Eestimaa Ühendatud Rahvapartei (EÜRP)

The Estonian United People's Party (EUPP) was established on 8 October 1994 and registered on 8 December 1994. It had 103 founding members and 214 at the time of registration. It was chaired by Viktor Andrejev. The EUPP grew out of the non-communist Russian Democratic Movement (RDM) and became one of the principal parties supported by ethnic minorities, primarily the Russian population. It strongly backed the extension of citizenship to all those who legally resided in Estonia at the time of the country's independence from the Soviet Union.[31] Additionally, the party wanted to normalize relations with Russia. The EUPP viewed Estonia as ideally poised to have strong ties with both the East and the West. The party held that in a civil society the rights and interests of persons were more important than those of any group. This meant that no segment of the society should benefit from preferential relations with the state or with regard to the country's laws; "every one should have an equal opportunity to participate in the economy; and all groups [should be] extensively represented in the state and in the function of its agencies." The EUPP performed well in the 1996 local elections, and won six seats to parliament in the March 1999 general elections with 6.1% of the popular vote.

Russian Party in Estonia (RPE)
Vene Erakond Eestis (VEE)

The Russian Party in Estonia (RPE) was established on 1 October 1994 and registered on 12 December 1994. It had 37 founding members, and 204 at its registration, and was chaired by Sergei Kuznetsov. The Russian Party in Estonia was the legal successor to the Russian National Union (RNU) established in 1920. At that time, the RNU played an important role in Estonian politics, protecting and representing the interests of the Russian minority in national and local governments.[32] The RPE opposed the assimilation of the Russian population into ethnic Estonian society. However, it did support the inclusion of Russian minority representatives in the Estonian parliament as well as cultural and other public agencies. The party's platform stressed equality in the pursuit of economic, political, cultural, intellectual, and religious fulfillment. At the local level, the Russian Party scored well in elections in areas where there were large communities of ethnic Russians, especially as non-citizen ethnic minorities generally exhibited high voter turnout levels for local elections.[33] The RPE failed to garner any seats in the March 1999 parliamentary ballot.

On 22 June 1998, the Russian Citizens' League (RCL) became the first organization of its kind to be registered in Estonia. The league was set up in early March 1998 after leading members had split from the unofficial Tallinn Union of Russian Citizens. The chairman of the new organization, Vladimir Lebedev, claimed that the league was apolitical but would be active in the social, economic, and humanitarian fields.

Other significant minority organizations included the Russian Christian Union (RCU) which was established on 24 May 1996 and was chaired by Boris Pilar. All members of the Russian Christian Union were citizens of Estonia who felt that the administration had not done enough for the Russian minority, including both citizens and non-citizens.[34] The RCU had little evident impact on national politics.

Regionalists

Northern Estonia Citizens' Party (NECP),
Põhja-Eesti Kodanike Erakond (PEKE), and
Southern Estonia Citizens' Party (SECP),
Lõuna-Eesti Kodanike Erakond (LEKE)

The Northern and Southern Estonia Citizens' Parties were regionalist organizations and staunchly nationalistic. They placed a great deal of stress on returning ethnic Russians to the Russian Federation. The Northern Estonia Citizens' Party (NECP) was chaired by Karli Eskusson and registered on 30 November 1994. The Southern Estonia Citizens' Party (SECP) was registered on 30 November 1994 and chaired by Alar Sepp. Their platforms and objectives were essentially identical. The two coalitions sought the introduction of stricter citizenship laws than those currently in place, although much of the international community generally viewed the Estonian laws as being too strict. The two organizations wanted to encourage an increase in the ethnic Estonian birth rate and to take other measures to insure the continued cultural, political, and economic hegemony of ethnic Estonians as automatic citizens of the republic. The NECP and SECP also campaigned for a regeneration of decaying rural regions, particularly in the northeast and southeast parts of the country, through greater government investment. In the September 1992 elections, the coalition received 6.8% of the total vote, garnering 8 seats in the *Riigikogu*. However, in March 1995, despite having joined with the Entrepreneurs' Party, the coalition won only 3.6% of the total vote, thus failing to gain entry into parliament.

Independents and Others

Estonian Democratic Justice Union (EDJU)
Eesti Demokraatlik Õigusliit (EDÕ)

The Estonian Democratic Justice Union (EDJU) was established in December 1991, largely as a pressure group to protect the interests of marginalized sectors of society such as pensioners, invalids, and veterans.[35] The Union obtained two parliamentary representatives after the September 1992 ballot, Raoul Üksvärav and Edgar Spriit. It also cooperated with other single-issue pressure groups including the Estonian Pensioners' Union (EPU) *(Eesti Pensionäride Liit, EPL)* and the Estonian Union of Handicapped Societies (EUHS) *(Eesti Invaühingute Liit, EIL)*. In 1994, the EDJU changed its name to the Association of Pensioners and Families (APF) *(Eesti Pensionäride ja Perede Liit, EPPL)*.

Independent Royalists (IR)
Sõltumatud Kuningriiklased (SK)

Established on 27 September 1989 and registered on 14 October 1993, the Independent Royalists (IR) claimed a membership of approximately 400 people, led by Kalle Kulbok. The IR was largely a vociferous protest party and it remained very small and with little public influence. IR activists focused on ridiculing and satirizing politicians from the major parties. One of their most publicized campaigns was against the introduction of a religious service in the national parliament. Some of the party's members were genuine monarchists who believed that a constitutional monarchy would help restore national unity and Estonian traditions. For the March 1995 general elections, the party formed an electoral coalition with the Estonian Greens, but it failed to win any seats as the coalition received only 0.8% of the total national vote. The IR became obsolete by the late 1990s.

POLITICAL DATA

Name of State: Republic of Estonia *(Eesti Vabariik)*
Form of Government: Parliamentary democracy
Structure of Legislature: Unicameral parliament *(Riigikogu)*, 101 members
Size of Territory: 17,462 square miles
Size of Population: 1,506,927

Composition of Population:

Ethnic Group	Number	% of Population
Estonians	946,646	65.1
Russians	409,111	28.1
Ukrainians	36,929	2.5
Belarusians	21,589	1.5
Finns	13,317	1.0
Tatars	3,271	0.2
Latvians	2,691	0.2
Jews	2,423	0.2
Others	17,867	1.2
Total	1,453,844	100.0

Sources: Official population estimates for 1994 can be found in *Europa 1995 World Book.* Also see United Nations, "International Convention on the Elimination of All Forms of Racial Discrimination, Fourth periodic report of states parties due in 1998," at http://www.unhchr.ch/tbs/doc.nsf.

ELECTION RESULTS

Presidential Election, 27 and 28 August 2001

First Round (Indirect), 27 August 2001

Candidate	Votes	% of Vote
Peeter Kreitzberg	40	44.0
Andres Tarand	38	42.0
Blank ballots	13	14.0
Unaccounted for	10	—
Total	101	100.0

Note: A candidate needed 68 votes to win.

Second Round (Indirect), 28 August 2001

Candidate	Votes	% of Vote
Peeter Kreitzberg	36	40.0
Peeter Tulviste	35	39.0
Blank ballots	19	21.0
Unaccounted for	11	—
Total	101	100.0

Third Round (Indirect), 28 August 2001

Candidate	Votes	% of Vote
Peeter Kreitzberg	33	36.7
Peeter Tulviste	33	36.7
Blank ballots	24	26.6
Unaccounted for	11	—
Total	101	100.0

Source: Radio Free Europe/Radio Liberty, Newsline, 2001.
Note: No candidate received the 68 votes needed to win.

Presidential Election, 21 September 2001

First Round (Indirect)

Candidate	Votes	% of Vote
Arnold Rüütel	114	31.0
Toomas Savi	90	25.0
Peeter Tulviste	89	24.0
Peeter Kreitzberg	72	20.0
Unaccounted for	2	—
Total	367	100.0

Second Round (Indirect)

Candidate	Votes	% of Vote
Arnold Rüütel	186	51.0
Toomas Savi	155	42.0
Unmarked	23	6.0
Invalid	2	1.0
Absent	1	—
Total	367	100.0

Source: Baltic News Service, 2001.
Note: The president is elected by parliament. However, should no candidate receive the necessary 68 votes to win in the first round, a second round is automatically held the next day. Should no candidate receive 68 votes in the second round, a third round of voting is scheduled. Should the third parliamentary round fail to elect a president, the vote shifts to an electoral college, which consists of the members of parliament and the local government representatives. A simple majority of votes is required to win the presidency.

Arnold Rüütel was elected president by a 367-seat electoral assembly consisting of the 101 members of parliament and 266 local government representatives.

Presidential Election, 20 September 1996

First Round (Indirect), 20 September 1996

Candidate	Votes	% of Vote
Lennart Meri	139	37.0
Arnold Rüütel	85	23.0
Tunne-Kelam	76	20.0
Enn Tõugu	47	13.0
Siiri Oviir	25	7.0
Total	372	100.0

Second Round (Indirect), 20 September 1996

Candidate	Votes	% of Vote
Lennart Meri	196	61.0
Arnold Rüütel	126	39.0
Total	322	100.0

Presidential Election, August–September 1996

First Round (Indirect), 26 August 1996

Candidate	Votes	% of Vote
Lennart Meri	45	57.0
Arnold Rüütel	34	43.0
Total	79	100.0

Note: Neither candidate received the required two-thirds majority.

Second Round (Indirect), 27 August 1996

Candidate	Votes	% of Vote
Lennart Meri	49	59.0
Arnold Rüütel	34	41.0
Total	83	100.0

Note: Neither candidate received the required two-thirds majority.

Third Round (Indirect), 27 August 1996

Candidate	Votes	% of Vote
Lennart Meri	52	62.0
Arnold Rüütel	32	38.0
Total	84	100.0

Note: Neither candidate received the required two-thirds majority in any of the rounds.

Presidential Election, September–October 1992

First Round, 20 September 1992

Turnout: 68%

Candidate	Votes	% of Vote
Arnold Rüütel	195,743	41.77
Lennart Meri	138,317	29.52
Rein Taagepera	109,631	23.40
Lagle Parek	19,837	4.23
Invalid votes	5,077	1.08
Total	468,605	100.00

Sources: Vabariigi Valimiskomisjon (Estonian National Electoral Committee), and http://www.rk.ee/VVK/president/vpv192.html; and http://www.vvk.ee/english/overview.html.

Second Round (Indirect), 5 October 1992

Candidate	Votes	% of Vote
Lennart Meri	59	66.0
Arnold Rüütel	31	34.0
Total	90	100.0

Parliamentary Elections, 7 March 1999

Turnout: 57.43%

Party/Coalition	Votes	% of Vote	Seats
Estonian Center Party	113,378	23.4	28
Pro Patria Union	77,917	16.1	18
Estonian Reform Party	77,088	15.9	18
Moderates	73,630	15.2	17
Estonian Coalition Party	36,692	7.6	7
Estonian Rural People's Party	35,204	7.3	7
Estonian United People's Party	29,682	6.1	6
Estonian Christian People's Party	11,745	2.4	—
Russian Party in Estonia	9,825	2.0	—
Estonian Blue Party	7,745	1.6	—
Farmers' Assembly	2,421	0.5	—
Progressive Party	1,854	0.4	—
Independent candidates	7,058	1.5	—
Total	484,239	100.0	101

Sources: http://www.agora.stm.it/elections/election/estonia.htm and http://www.riik.ee.government/valitsus.html and http://www2.essex.ac.uk/elect/electer/est_er_nl.htm.

Parliamentary Elections, 5 March 1995

Turnout: 68.92%

Party/Coalition	Votes	% of Vote	Seats
Coalition Party and Rural Union	174,248	32.2	41
Estonian Reform Party	87,531	16.2	19
Estonian Center Party	76,634	14.2	16
Pro Patria Union and Estonian National Independence Party	42,493	7.9	8
Moderates (Estonian Social Democrats and Estonian Rural Center Party)	32,381	6.0	6
Our Home Is Estonia (United People's Party, Russian Party, and Estonian Russian People's Party)	31,763	5.9	6
Right-Wingers	27,053	5.0	5
Better Estonia and Estonian Citizen	19,529	3.6	—
Future of Estonia Party	13,907	2.6	—
Justice	12,248	2.3	—
Others	22,912	4.1	—
Total	540,699	100.0	101

Sources: Riigikogu Postimees, Tartu, 21 March 1995, pp. 1–15, and Postimehe Valimisteatmik, Tartu, 1995, pp. 31–60.

Parliamentary Elections, 20 September 1992

Turnout: 67.84%

Party/Coalition	Votes	% of Vote	Seats
Pro Patria Coalition	100,828	22.0	29
Secure Home (including Estonian Coalition Party)	62,329	13.6	17
Estonian Popular Front	56,124	12.3	15
Moderates (Estonian Social Democrats and Estonian Rural Center Party)	44,577	9.7	12
Estonian National Independence Party	40,260	8.8	10
Independent Royalists	32,638	7.1	8
Estonian Citizen	31,553	6.9	8
Greens	12,009	2.6	1
Estonian Entrepreneurial Party	10,946	2.4	1
Union of Estonian Pensioners	17,011	3.7	—
Farmer's Union	13,356	2.9	—
Left Alternative	7,374	1.6	—
Others	29,242	6.4	—
Total	458,247	100.0	101

Source: Vabariigi Presidendi ja Riigikogu Valimised 1992: Dokumente ja materjale, Tallinn: Eesti Vabariigi Valimiskomisjon, 1992, pp. 138–139.

NOTES

1. For valuable recent histories of Estonia see Rein Taagepera, *Estonia: Return to Independence*, Boulder: Westview Press, 1993; Toivo U. Raun, *Estonia and the Estonians*, Stanford: Hoover, 1987; Romuald J. Misiunas; Rein Taagepera, *The Baltic States: Years of Dependence, 1940–1980*, London: Hurst, 1983; David Kirby, *The Baltic World, 1772–1993: Europe's Northern Periphery in an Age of Change*, London: Longman, 1995; Dietrich A. Loeber et al. (Eds.), *Regional Identity Under Soviet Rule: The Case of the Baltic States*, Hackettstown, New Jersey: Association for the Advancement of Baltic Studies, 1990; and V. Stanley Vardys and Romuald J. Misiunas (Eds.), *The Baltic States in Peace and War 1917–1945*, University Park: Pennsylvania State University Press, 1981.

2. Consult Graham Smith (Ed.), *The Baltic States: The National Self-Determination of Estonia, Latvia, and Lithuania*, New York: St. Martin's Press, 1996.

3. For an excellent analysis of political developments in Estonia in the early 1990s see David Arter, *Parties and Democracy in Post-Soviet Republics*, Aldershot, UK: Dartmouth Publishing Company Limited, 1996, pp. 123–254.

4. "Information on Party Platforms for the 1995 General Elections," Ministry of Foreign Affairs, Republic of Estonia.

5. Consult Anton Steen, *Between Past and Future: Elites, Democracy, and the State in Post-Communist Countries: A Comparison of Estonia, Latvia, and Lithuania*, Aldershot, UK: Ashgate Publishers, 1997, p. 169.

6. See John That, "Estonia Proves Itself," *Transition*, Vol. 3, No. 2, 7 February 1997, pp. 24–25.

7. See Radio Free Europe / Radio Liberty (RFE/RL) *Newsline*, 8 March 1999.

8. Information from Radio Free Europe / Radio Liberty (RFE/RL) *Newsline*, 18 October 1999.

9. See Toivo U. Raun, "Estonia: Independence Redefined," in Ian Bremmer and Ray Taras, (Eds.), *New States, New Politics: Building the Post-Soviet Nations*, Cambridge, UK; Cambridge University Press, 1997, p. 406.

10. Toivo U. Raun, "Democratization and Political Development in Estonia, 1987–1996," in Karen Dawisha and Bruce Parrott (Eds.), *The Consolidation of Democracy in East-Central Europe*, Cambridge: Cambridge University Press, 1997, p. 348.

11. Check Vello Pettai, "Political Stability through Disenfranchisement," *Transition*, Open Media Research Institute, Vol. 3, No. 6, 4 April 1997, pp. 21–23.

12. See Graham Smith, Aadne Aasland, and Richard Mole, "Statehood, Ethnic Relations and Citizenship," in Smith (Ed.), *The Baltic States*, pp. 181–205.

13. Raun, pp. 362–363.

14. See Ole Norgaard, *The Baltic States After Independence*, Cheltenham, UK: Edward Elgar, 1996, p. 187.

15. See Press Release, 5 November 1996, Estonian Ministry of Foreign Affairs web site: http://www.vm.ee/pressrel/1996/9611052pr.html. Also consult Saulius Girnius, "Relations With Russia Turn Bitter," *Transition*, Open Media Research Institute, Vol. 2, No. 11, 31 May 1996, pp. 42–45.

16. Taken from the "Estonian Social Democratic Party Platform for the 1995 National Elections," http://www.vm.ee/elections/rk1995/sonplat/95esvene.html.

17. Radio Free Europe/ Radio Liberty (RFE/RL) *Newsline*, 3 September 1998.

18. See www.ce-review.org/00/13/amber13.html.

19. Baltics Online, http://www.viabalt.ee/news/ETA/960408/3.html.

20. See http://www.europeanforum.bot-consult.se/cup/estonia/index.htm.

21. See www.ce-review.org/00/13/amber /13.html.

22. See www.ce-review.org/00/13/amber /13.html.

23. Taken from the "Forest Party Platform for the 1995 National Elections," http://www.vm.ee/ elections/rk1995/sonplat/95esvene.html.

24. *Europa World Book*, 1996, p. 1159.

25. See http://www.europeanforum.bot-consult.se/cup/estonia/index.htm.

26. Taken from the "Estonian Home Platform for the 1995 National Elections," http://www.vm.ee/elections/rk1995/sonplat/95esvene.html.

27. Taken from the "Future Estonia Party Platform for the 1995 National Elections," http://www.vm.ee/elections/rk1995/sonplat/95esvene.html.

28. Taken from the "Republican and Conservative People's Party Platform for the 1995 National Elections," http://www.vm.ee/elections/rk1995/sonplat/95esvene.html.

29. Member of Parliament, Mart Nutt, *Latnet*, 18 October 1996, gopher://namejs.latnet.lv

30. Taken from the "Estonian National Protection Party Platform for the 1995 National Elections," http://www.vm.ee/elections/rk1995/sonplat/95esvene.html.

31. Taken from the "Estonian United People's Party Platform for the 1995 National Elections," http://www.vm.ee/elections/rk1995/sonplat/95esvene.html.

32. See "The Russian Party in Estonia Platform for the 1995 National Elections," http://www.vm.ee/elections/rk1995/sonplat/95esvene.html.

33. "1996 Local Government Elections Held," *Estonian Review*, Vol. 6, No. 42, 14–20 October 1996, Estonian Foreign Ministry, http://www.vm.ee/ring/1996/96101420.html.

34. *BBC Summary of World Broadcasts*, 27 May 1996 on NEXIS.

35. David Arter, 1996, pp. 180–181.

Latvia

HISTORICAL OVERVIEW

Proto-Baltic peoples settled in the Baltic littoral around 2000 BC. Their language was a branch of Indo-European. The Balts merged with or displaced the Finno-Ugric peoples who inhabited these territories prior to the Balts' arrival.[1] The ancestors of the present-day Latvians consisted of several tribal groupings, including the Couronians in the western regions, the Semigallians in the south-central area, and the Letgallians and Selians in the eastern regions. The Livs, a Finno-Ugric–speaking people, also inhabited the area around the Gulf of Riga. The medieval state of Livonia, which took its name from them, included the territories of all five groups. The five tribal groupings lacked a single political authority, being divided into regional chieftainships. The Latvian territories were situated along major trade routes between Scandinavia and Central-Eastern Europe, and the navigable Daugava River became an important commercial artery, particularly during the Viking period, in the second half of the first millennium ad.

German influences from the Holy Roman Empire were felt in the region from the twelfth century onwards. Merchants were accompanied by clerics who sought to convert the non-Christian Baltic tribes. In 1199, a Baltic crusade was proclaimed by Pope Innocent III to be enforced by Saxon soldiers under the control of Bishop Albert of Buxhovden. Albert forcibly pacified and converted the Livs and began to build the city of Riga, close to the mouth of the Daugava. In 1202, Albert transformed his military contingent into an order of knights known as the Swordbrothers or the Militia of Christ, which pursued territorial acquisition in the construction of the state of Livonia. By 1230 most of the Latvian areas were firmly under German control, except the Semigallian region, which was not taken until 1290.

The Swordbrothers were merged into the Livonian Order and established the German-controlled Livonian Confederation, which included Estonia and the Latvian-populated territories of Courland, Livland, Latgale, and

Semigallia. The city of Riga became a member of the prosperous trading organization the Hanseatic League. Nationality divisions in Livonia closely mirrored class distinctions over the next five centuries. The upper classes, including the landowning nobility, wealthy merchants, and the clergy, were predominantly German, while the peasants were primarily Latvians. Professional occupations were only open to Latvians if they mastered German and assimilated into Germanic culture. At the same time, the merger of five distinct regions in Livonia contributed to producing a more coherent Latvian identity.

Livonia became increasingly secularized during the fourteenth and fifteenth centuries as the power of local bishops waned. Lutheran ideas spread from Germany to Livonia in the 1520s and Riga became an important center of the Protestant Reformation. By the mid-1550s, Lutheranism had become the dominant religion in Livonia among the ruling elites, while the peasantry followed the example of the large landowners.

Livonia remained a decentralized and weak state in a strategic location that ensured that it was a prime target for neighboring expansionist powers. Russian forces launched attacks on Livonia in 1558 and captured several cities in the north of the territory. Meanwhile, Danish contingents seized control of Courland. The elites of northern Livonia (Estonia) obtained Swedish protection, while the territories that had not been occupied by Russia asked for protection from the Polish-Lithuanian Commonwealth.

In 1561, the Livonian nobility swore loyalty to the Polish king, Zygmunt II Augustus. Only the city of Riga remained independent, and the Livonian Confederation ceased to exist. Most of the Latvian territories remained under Polish control from 1561 until 1629. These consisted of two main regions: the Inflanty province in the east and the Duchy of Courland and Semigallia in the west. During a new round of warfare between Sweden and Poland, in 1621, Swedish armies captured Riga, and shortly afterwards Polish control over most of Inflanty ended. For the remainder of the seventeenth century, three Latvian regions existed: Livland, controlled by Sweden; a Polish Livonia; and the semi-independent Duchy of Courland and Semigallia.

During the eighteenth century, the entire Baltic littoral fell under Russian control. The Swedish-held Latvian territories were incorporated by Tsar Peter the Great after a victorious Great Northern War. Tsarina Catherine II acquired Latgale during the First Partition of Poland by Austria, Prussia, and Russia, in 1772. The Third Partition of Poland, in 1795, gave Russia the Duchy of Courland. The Latvian peasantry was freed from serfdom in 1861 and allowed to settle anywhere in the province. But the land of migrant peasants often reverted to the nobility, and migrants had to enter contracts to perform labor service on landowners' estates. Although a sizeable Latvian smallholder class developed, the number of landless peasants swelled, and agricultural laborers remained impoverished.

The impetus for Latvian liberation during the second half of the nineteenth century was provided by the Young Latvians movement based at Tartu University. The students engaged in meetings and publishing and called for the Latvian peasant population to be freed from the German nobility and clergy. They claimed that the reforms enacted had failed to bring freedom to the Latvian population. The Young Latvians also sought to replace the dominant German influences with a purely Latvian culture and to revive and codify the Latvian language.[2] Their spiritual mentor was Atis Kronvalds, whose famous essay *Nationale Bestrebungen*, published in 1872, became the primary manifesto of Latvian nationalism. Riga became the second center of the Latvian national awakening. The Riga Latvian Association was formed in 1868, organizing song festivals and conferences on Latvian folklore and publishing newspapers.

To counter the Latvian revival, from 1885 onward the Russian authorities introduced a series of decrees aimed at more effectively Russifying the province. For example, German and Latvian were to be replaced with Russian in the legal and educational systems. Such measures increased local resistance to the Tsarist autocracy. During the 1905 Revolution, throughout the Russian Empire, various opposition groups became active, and a Peasants' Congress was established in Riga. The Congress resolved to break off all relations with the government in St. Petersburg, to ignore its laws, and to refuse to pay taxes. It also organized a people's militia and elected local committees of popular self-government independent of Russia. All these movements were crushed by Tsarist forces, and hundreds of Latvian activists were executed, thousands were exiled to Siberia, and more than five thousand fled westward.

At the onset of World War I in August 1914, German troops defeated the Tsarist armies. By the fall of 1915 the Germans occupied the whole of Courland south of the Daugava River; about 15,000 Latvian soldiers perished in battle, mostly in the Russian Imperial Army. During the course of the war, the cause of Latvian independence gained increasing support. The first Latvian National Assembly met in mid-November 1917 and proclaimed itself a provisional national government. It demanded autonomy for Latvia within any Russian state, and that Latvia's future status be determined by a constitutional assembly elected by the Latvian people.

As Russian forces withdrew from the region, on 18 November 1918 representatives from all the major political parties formed a new National Council and promptly proclaimed an independent Republic of Latvia. Kārlis Ulmanis, the leader of the Agrarian Union, was elected President, and Jānis Čakste became Prime Minister of the new Latvian provisional government. However, this administration had limited powers to enforce its authority, because Latvia was under German occupation. With Germany suffering defeats through the summer and fall of 1918, Russian forces under the Bolshevik regime reoccupied the eastern parts of Latvia, captured Riga in January 1919, and installed a Soviet Latvian government headed by Peteris Stučka.

With no significant armed forces of its own, the Latvian government appealed to Germany and other Western powers for help. A volunteer force was quickly assembled, commanded by German officers who had little regard for Latvian independence. German forces captured Riga from the Russians on 23 May 1919 and brought down the Stučka regime. But as they pushed further north, the Germans were defeated by a combination of Latvian and Estonian nationalist units. Under pressure from the Western Allies, Berlin ordered the evacuation of German troops from the three Baltic states during the summer of 1919. The remaining Bolshevik forces were pushed out of eastern Latvia by January 1920, after the Latvian government obtained military assistance from Poland. The victorious Ulmanis government signed a peace treaty with Soviet Russia on 11 August 1920, and Latvia's independence was recognized by Moscow. About 7,100 Latvians soldiers died in the country's independence war, and about 60,000 people were left outside Latvia's borders as a result of the territorial settlement with Russia.

Following the convocation of a Constitutional Convention on 1 May 1920, Jānis Čakste was elected President, and Ulmanis, Prime Minister. A national constitution was passed on 15 February 1922. One of the major achievements of the new government was the creation of numerous smallholder farms through the redistributive land reform process. This also helped to legitimize the new administration and produced a conservative-nationalist sector of society that staunchly opposed the more vocal minorities, particularly the Germans. This rural sector also tended to support the authoritarian government that took over the country in the 1930s.

Between 1922 and 1934 Latvia held four parliamentary elections and was governed by thirteen different cabinets. Although the authorities were successful in building a state structure, incessant political fragmentation created public dissatisfaction with the evident paralysis of parliamentary government. On 15 May 1934, Prime Minister Kārlis Ulmanis assumed absolute power in a bloodless coup and proceeded to fuse the offices of President and Premier– a process that was completed by 1936.

Contrary to communist claims, the presidential dictatorship was not a fascist regime and actually combated the Latvian Nazi-type paramilitary groupings that were active through the 1930s. Indeed, the threat of a fascist coup strengthened the case for strong presidential rule. This threat was exacerbated by severe financial crisis in the early 1930s precipitated by the global depression. Although communist and fascist parties were banned, parliament was dissolved, a presidential government was appointed, and labor unions were placed under corporate control, limited freedoms were afforded to the press, the courts remained independent, municipal self-governments were supported, and a restricted free market was allowed to operate.

Under the terms of the Nazi-Soviet Pact of August 1939, Latvia was to revert to Soviet control in the wake of Hitler's war against Poland. On 16–17 June 1940, Red Army troops poured into Latvia, after months of pressure from Moscow for the establishment of Soviet bases on Latvian territory. The government in Riga was unable to resist Soviet occupation. A communist regime was implanted in the country, and rigged elections were held, to legitimize the forcible annexation of Latvia as a Soviet republic on 5 August 1940. Opposition parties were banned, many pre-war institutions were disbanded, and police, army officers, and civil servants were dismissed. In a wave of deportations, over 35,000 Latvians were arrested and sent to prisons and Siberian labor camps or were summarily executed. They included opposition activists, intellectuals, and prominent public and religious figures.

Following the German invasion of the Soviet Union in June 1941, an insurrection against Soviet rule broke out in Latvia. About 60,000 resistance fighters took part in the rebellion. They managed to expel the Red Army from Riga on 28 June 1941 and announced the formation of an independent Latvian government. However, Soviet forces retook the capital within the day and eliminated the new government. German armies recaptured Riga on 1 July 1941 and quashed any opportunities for Latvia's independence. Under Hitlerite occupation, over 30,000 Jews were murdered, as Berlin planned to depopulate the Baltic area and move in thousands of German settlers.

At the close of World War II, with the defeat of Nazi Germany, Soviet forces regained control of the country. Approximately 150,000 Latvians fled westward from the advancing Red Army. As a result of the war and Soviet conquest, the country's population dropped from about 2 million to approximately 1.4 million. Stalin implanted a loyal and subservient Latvian communist regime, and an estimated 70,000 persons were executed or deported to the Soviet Union soon after the takeover; a further 43,000 followed during the forced collectivization of the countryside. A substantial armed resistance movement continued to operate until 1952, and over 40,000 guerrillas battled Soviet occupation. While the Russians controlled all major cities, much of the countryside remained under partisan control. Soviet forces systematically destroyed their rural support base through repressive attacks, wholesale deportations of peasants, arbitrary executions, confiscation of property, and comprehensive agricultural collectivization.

Moscow steadily created a loyalist communist party after purging all suspect Latvian elements, and imposed a harsh Stalinist dictatorship, in which all independent institutions, organizations, and activities were prohibited. About half a million Russians, Belarusians, and Ukrainians were settled in Latvia during the first post-war decade further undercutting the proportion of Latvians. By 1955, the number of Russian-speaking residents reached about 38%, and the use of the Latvian language in public life steadily declined.

Following Stalin's death in March 1953, a partial cultural thaw was evident in the country, and about 30,000 Latvian deportees were allowed to return. But in order to thwart Latvian ambitions toward autonomy, a crackdown was staged by Moscow in 1958–1959. Numerous ethnic Latvians were purged from the communist party and the country's administration and charged with "bourgeois-nationalist deviations." This was accompanied by an accelerated policy of Russification. With the ongoing industrialization drive, large numbers of Russian workers settled in the republic, and the non-Latvian share of the population increased to 43.2% by 1970. In Riga itself the Latvian proportion decreased from 44.6% in 1959 to 36.5% in 1989.

During the 1970s, dissent against Soviet and communist rule steadily developed. Various independent groups came into existence, including the Latvian Independence Movement, the Democratic Youth Committee, and the Latvian Christian Democratic Organization. They issued joint statements to the Latvian and foreign governments, protesting human rights repression in the country. The Organization for Latvia's Independence became active in the late 1970s and through the 1980s, organizing protest actions and public petitions. Although these were small groupings, they began to have an impact on Latvian society by testing and extending the limits of the possible. But they faced frequent arrest and repression for their dissent. Other organizations were formed during the 1980s, including the Environmental Protection Club in 1987 and the human rights group "Helsinki '86" which supported the restoration of Latvia's national independence.

According to Smith, there were three stages in the development of pro-independence politics: a period of national reawakening (1986–1988), the emergence of nationalist movements in the form of popular fronts (1988–1990), and formal republic support for secession from the Soviet Union and outright state independence (1990–1991).[3] The Latvian Popular Front (LPF), similarly to that of its two Baltic neighbors, was initially formed in May 1988, in response to Soviet Secretary General Mikhail Gorbachev's call for reform in the USSR. But it rapidly developed into a nationalist movement committed to the cause of Latvian independence and evaded communist party influence. Within a few months of its inception, it claimed a membership of some 110,000 people.

Initially focusing on single-issue campaigns, such as protests against environmental pollution, the LPF developed into a well-organized movement for national emancipation. The LPF registered its first success in protesting against plans to construct a hydroelectric power plant on the Daugava River. Environmental issues played an important role in eventually dislodging the conservative communist leadership from power and providing the organizational capacity and practical experience for pursuing more far-reaching demands, including greater economic, cultural, political, and national autonomy.

The LPF became an umbrella organization that included numerous groupings such as heritage societies, ecological movements, religious organizations, human rights groups, nationalist movements, and communist reformers. The Front's inception coincided with the replacement of the conservative communist leadership. Boris Pugo, the party first secretary, was replaced by Jānis Vagris. The reformer Anatolijs Gorbunovs was appointed chairman of the Presidium of the Latvian Supreme Soviet amid increasing calls for reform within the political establishment.[4] A series of important symbolic measures were taken in restoring Latvian self-determination. These included making Latvian the republic's state language, reintroducing the national flag and national anthem, and formalizing republic-based citizenship.

The Latvian Communist Party (LCP), over half of whose members were ethnic Russians, became increasingly torn over the question of relations with Moscow, especially after the accession of Gorbachev. Reformist elements gained ascendancy in the late 1980s and acted increasingly independently of the center. However, reform communists began to lose the initiative from about 1987 onward, when the LPF and other independent groups were able to organize large-scale public protests against such issues as environmental pollution and increasingly to voice demands for national independence. The first congress of the Popular Front took place on 8–9 October 1988, elected Dainis Ivāns as president, and announced a platform for national sovereignty. Congress participants included political dissidents, intellectuals, religious activists, nationalists, and reform communists.

On 23 August 1989 there occurred an unprecedented show of solidarity among the three Baltic peoples, when the Latvian, Estonian, and Lithuanian Popular Fronts organized up to two million people to form a human chain stretching across the three territories, in condemnation of the Molotov-Ribbentrop Pact. This action gained extensive international publicity for the peaceful revolution in the Baltic states. In late 1989, the Latvian Supreme Soviet officially declared the incorporation of Latvia into the USSR a criminal act, hence legitimizing the struggle for national independence. At the same time, Latvia's nationalist movement split into two major trends: an ethno-exclusivist stream that sought to diminish the position of the Russian minority by basing citizenship on ethnicity, and a civic nationalist tendency that sought to integrate the large minority population.

"Citizens' committees" were formed throughout the country whose leaders voiced frustration with the allegedly accomodationist position of the LPF on the issue of independence. The committees, which benefited from substantial public support, did not want to negotiate with Moscow or to include communists in their ranks, and they organized an alternative Citizens' Congress on 30 April 1990. By the beginning of 1990, the Citizens' Movement had gathered about 900,000 signatures in support of Latvian independence, considering this an informal referendum on the issue.

Some nationalist activists injected more radical proposals on the future status of the Russian minority and came into conflict with the LPF's moderate nationalists. An even more adamant position on national independence was taken by the newly formed Latvian National Independence Movement that had initially cooperated with the LPF. A number of other independent political parties were also established at this time. To avoid being sidelined, the LPF abandoned its idea of sovereignty within the Soviet Union, and on 31 May 1989 it came out for full Latvian independence.

POST-COMMUNIST DEVELOPMENTS

The beginning of Latvia's post-communist era can be traced to 4 May 1990, when the republic's Supreme Soviet (which was renamed the Supreme Council) formally declared null and void the Soviet annexation of Latvia and announced its intention of restoring the country's independence, although it did not specify a timetable. In elections to the Supreme Council on 18 March 1990, the LPF and the Latvian National Independence Movement (LNIP) gained 134 out of 170 seats and thus accelerated the momentum for state independence.

During this period, the ruling Latvian Communist Party (LCP) fractured into pro-Moscow and pro-independence wings. A majority of the LCP remained loyal to Moscow, at least for the time being. As the party disintegrated, Moscow's leverage in Latvia dramatically diminished and short of military intervention it could not reverse the thrust toward statehood. The Kremlin declared the moves toward independence illegal. It tried to apply pressures on the Latvian administration and was evidently preparing some provocations in the republic, but this merely served to stiffen public resistance.

The impasse between Moscow and Riga continued through 1990, amid growing turmoil throughout the Soviet Union. In July 1990, the three Baltic governments refused to participate in Gorbachev's initiative to create a new Union treaty and instead pursued the creation of a common Baltic market in which the Kremlin would play no role. Soviet special forces staged several provocative incidents in Riga, seizing the national press building and the Internal Affairs Ministry, where four people were shot dead on 20 January 1991. Tens of thousands of Latvians poured onto the streets and built barricades against any potential military crackdown. Moscow backed down, realizing that only large-scale bloodshed with potentially even more damaging consequences could stifle the drive toward Latvia's independence.

On 3 March 1991, 87.5% of eligible Latvian citizens participated in a referendum on national independence; 73.6% voted in favor and 24.8% against. A high proportion of non-Latvians evidently also favored secession from the USSR. On 17 March 1991, the Latvian authorities announced that they would not participate in the all-Union referendum that Gorbachev had devised to keep the Soviet Union together. The stalemate between Riga and Moscow was finally broken on 19 August 1991 when the failed coup attempt by hardliners in the Russian capital effectively terminated Kremlin rule in Latvia. The pro-independence communists, led by Ivars Ķezbers, who had renamed themselves the Latvian Democratic Labor Party (LDLP), condemned the coup plotters. Three persons were killed in Riga as Soviet special forces tried to stage their own coup in the Latvian capital.

As the Moscow coup unraveled, the Latvian Supreme Council on 21 August 1991 announced that Latvia was now an independent, sovereign republic operating according to the 1922 Latvian constitution. On 24 August 1991, Boris Yeltsin, as the new leader of the Russian Federation, promptly recognized Latvian independence. At the same time, the Latvian government declared the Communist Party to be unconstitutional and began to confiscate the party's property. Alfrēds Rubiks, the orthodox Latvian leader of the pro-Moscow communists, was arrested and charged with conspiracy to seize power from the democratically elected government.

Between March 1990 (the Supreme Council elections) and June 1993 (the first parliamentary elections in an independent Latvia), two individuals dominated Latvian politics: president of the Supreme Council and transitional head of state Anatolijs Gorbunovs, and Prime Minister Ivars Godmanis. The Council and the government had an extensive agenda in revoking Soviet-era laws, revising and passing new legislation, establishing the basis for a market economy, creating a civil service and a diplomatic corps, and forming a national defense force. The new elite was a conglomerate of former communists and democratic activists committed to state-building and political pluralism. But the administration that oversaw the dawn of statehood rapidly lost much of its popular support, largely because of declining economic conditions following the collapse of the Soviet market.

The first post-Soviet parliamentary elections were held on 5–6 June 1993. The absence of a full citizenship law and the definition of the "political community" as citizens at the time of elections meant that large numbers of ethnic Russian were excluded from the ballot. Yet 89% of eligible voters participated in the elections, while 23 parties and coalitions canvassed for the 100 parliamentary seats. Only seven parties managed to pass the threshold of 4% to gain parliamentary representation. The electoral coalition Latvia's Way (LW) won the largest number of seats and 32.4% of the vote; the Latvian National Independence Movement (LNIP), 13.4%; Harmony for Latvia–Economic Revival Party (HL-ERR), 12%; the Agrarian Union (AU), 10.6%; the Equal Rights Movement (ERM), 5.7%; For Fatherland and Freedom (FFF), 5.4%; the Democratic Center (DC), 4.7%; and the Latvian Christian Democratic Union (LCDU), 5%. The Latvian Popular Front only received 2.6% of the popular vote and was therefore excluded from the *Saeima* (parliament).

The new parliament elected Gorbunovs as *Saeima* speaker and Guntis Ulmanis, a deputy from the Agrarian Union, was elected Latvian President. Ulmanis was the grandnephew of Kārlis Ulmanis, the last inter-war Latvian President. Valdis Birkavs of Latvia's Way was appointed Prime Minister. His center-right cabinet of thirteen ministers included three people from the Latvian *diaspora*. The Birkavs government survived until July 1994, when three Agrarian Union ministers resigned from the cabinet in protest against insufficient state protection for Latvian farmers. The administration collapsed for a number of reasons, primarily over protests about the newly passed citizenship law, because of its agreement with Moscow over welfare payments to retired

Russian military officers in Latvia, and due to the treaty signed with Russia, which nationalist forces considered to be too accommodating to the Kremlin.

On 15 September 1994, the centrist Latvia's Way formed a new cabinet under the premiership of Māris Gailis. Meanwhile, rightist forces performed well in the local elections on 29 May 1994, especially in the urban areas. Because they lacked citizenship, many Russian ethnics did not participate in the balloting. The three largest winners were the LNIP, For Fatherland and Freedom, and a new center-left party called *Saimnieks*. Their control over the Riga City Council was significant, as about one third of the country's population (856,000 people) resided in the capital.

On 30 September–1 October 1995, Latvia held its second parliamentary elections, with inconclusive results. Nineteen political parties and coalitions took part in the balloting, and despite a higher, 5% threshold for parliament, only nine parties gained seats. Both the left and right of the political spectrum improved their positions at the cost of the centrist parties. No party obtained a majority or a sufficient number of seats to form a government. Of the four biggest winners, *Saimnieks* gained 18 seats; Latvia's Way, 17 seats; the National Movement for Latvia–Siegerist's Party, 16 seats; and For Fatherland and Freedom, 14 seats.

Of the remaining parties, For Fatherland and Freedom won 9 seats; the coalition of Greens and the Latvian National Independence Movement, 8 seats; the Agrarian Union, 7 seats; the Socialist Party, 8 seats; and the Harmony Party, 6 seats. Because of this fragmentation, it was late December 1995 before a new government was finally formed. Andris Šķēle, a former deputy minister of agriculture, became Prime Minister. His cabinet included ministers from both major "blocs," the left and the right, and included *Saimnieks*, For Fatherland and Freedom, Latvia's Way, the Latvian National Independence Movement, the Unity Party, and the Agrarian Union.

On 28 July 1997, Premier Šķēle submitted his resignation but rejected criticism that he had impaired parliamentary democracy. Although he was not a popular figure, Šķēle was able to implement necessary austerity measures on several occasions when Latvia faced financial crisis. Šķēle had increasingly come into conflict with the seven parties that formed the ruling coalition. Five ministers in the government were forced to resign, four of them amid allegations of violating the anti-corruption law. President Ulmanis named Economics Minister Guntars Krasts as Prime Minister. Krasts was a member of the right-of-center For Fatherland and Freedom party. Unlike the previous government, the new coalition did not include the National Reform Party or the Green Party.

The new provisional administration was voted into power by parliament on 7 August 1997. The Krasts government was supported by 73 deputies in the 100-seat parliament, and his coalition held 67 seats. Krasts asserted that he would stick to the strict monetary and budget policies of the previous premier, regardless of the risk of short-term unpopularity. Public support for the new authorities quickly evaporated and new general elections were scheduled.

The People's Party won the parliamentary elections on 3 October 1998, while Latvia's Way came a close second, but the PP proved unable to form a coalition government. On 2 November 1998, Latvia's Way, the For Fatherland and Freedom party, and The New Party signed an agreement on forming a coalition government and supporting the prime ministerial candidate of Latvia's Way, the transport minister Vilis Krištopans. President Ulmanis subsequently named Krištopans as Prime Minister. The People's Party was left out of the new coalition government, which held 46 seats in the 100-member parliament.

In Latvia's parliamentary system of government, the legislature elected the country's president; and on 17 June 1998, Vaira Vīķe-Freiberga was elected by parliament. She received 53 votes in support of her candidacy from For Fatherland and Freedom, a member of the governing coalition, as well as from the Social Democratic Workers' Party and the People's Party. Foreign Minister Valdis Birkavs of Latvia's Way gained 20 votes, while Economic Minister Ingrīda Ūdre of The New Party won nine votes. Vīķe-Freiberga was able to run for President after she received confirmation the day before the elections that she no longer possessed Canadian citizenship. The incumbent President Guntis Ulmanis was prohibited from running for a third term.

Prime Minister Vilis Krištopans resigned on 5 July 1999, claiming that there was an "atmosphere of distrust" in his government. Krištopans made it clear that the catalyst for his decision was the signing of a cooperation agreement between For Fatherland and Freedom, a member of the governing coalition, and the opposition People's Party. Former Prime Minister and leader of the People's Party Andris Šķēle was asked on 12 July 1999 by President Vīķe-Freiberga to form the next government. The New Party, the junior member of Krištopans's government, expressed its willingness to cooperate and join the new government, but did not become a member of the coalition. On 16 July 1999, the Latvian parliament approved the new cabinet by a 60 to 37 vote. Comprising the three largest parties in the parliament—the People's Party, Latvia's Way, and For Fatherland and Freedom—the new government controlled 62 out of 100 legislative seats. Although all three non-coalition parties voted against confirming Šķēle's cabinet, several ministers retained their portfolios.

After gaining independence from the Soviet Union, the Latvian government and the country in general faced challenges similar to those faced by Estonia and Lithuania.[5] As in Estonia, one of the most pressing domestic and foreign affairs issues in Latvia was how to deal with the presence of a large Russian minority, many of whom moved into Latvia after the country was forcibly incorporated as a republic of the Soviet Union. Out of a total population of 2.68 million (according to the 1989 census), the ethnic Latvian share in 1989 amounted to 51.8%, as compared to 75.5% in 1939. The

Russian minority had reached 34%. Echoing practices throughout the Soviet Union, few members of the Russian populace learned Latvian or integrated themselves into the indigenous community in other ways.

During Latvia's drive toward independence, Russian communists with direct backing from Moscow created the International Front (Interfront) movement in support of preserving the Soviet Union. Interfront was particularly active in the larger cities with sizeable Russian working-class concentrations and tried to mobilize Russian workers in the all-Union factories. Nevertheless, opinion polls indicated that by 1990 nearly two-fifths of Russian-speakers actually favored Latvia's statehood, believing that this would guarantee higher living standards and integration with the prosperous West. This position was subsequently confirmed in the Latvian referendum on independence. Only a small minority of Russians were actively involved in Interfront or other anti-independence movements.[6]

The failure of the Russian community to integrate itself during the time when Latvia was a Soviet republic resulted in newly independent Latvia's denying automatic citizenship to ethnic Russians. However, ethnic Russians who could demonstrate that they or their direct ancestors resided in Latvia prior to the Soviet takeover in 1940 were given automatic Latvian citizenship.[7] Russian fears were exacerbated by ethno-nationalist Latvian parties that sought to place severe restrictions on the minority, to exclude them from acquiring citizenship, and to encourage them to leave the country. By contrast, the LPF adopted a more conciliatory approach, considering all residents, regardless of nationality, full-fledged Latvian citizens.

Initial attempts at creating citizenship laws proved exclusionary towards Russians and other non-Latvian ethnic groups. The Latvian Citizens' Congress stressed that citizenship should be based on ethnic purity. It wanted the government to reinstate the pre-war citizenship legislation with stringent regulations on the naturalization of immigrants. Some nationalists supported the introduction of quotas for citizenship, whereby a priority list would be assembled, favoring ethnic Latvians and their spouses and clearly discriminating against ethnic Russians. Such voices contributed to further polarizing ethnic relations in the country.

The 1989 language law had envisioned a transitional period of three years during which the non–Latvian-speaking employees of state institutions would be required to learn Latvian. This law was strengthened after independence, and comprehensive implementation began. The March 1992 language law acknowledged the right of minorities to use their mother tongue, but it guaranteed a state education only in Latvian. The legislation also made knowledge of Latvian a prerequisite for many government posts. Enforcement of this legislation led to exaggerated charges by Russian leaders of human rights violations by the Latvian authorities.

On 9 December 1999, the Latvian parliament approved a new language law by a vote of 52 to 26. The legislature originally passed the law on 8 July 1999, but a week later President Vīķe-Freiberga returned it for revision in "conformity with European norms."[8] The president claimed that the new law fully complied with our international legal obligations. OSCE High Commissioner on National Minorities Max van der Stoel also asserted that the revised law was "essentially in conformity" with international norms. The law regulated language use in the public sphere and in areas of the private sector where public safety and health were concerned. The law also required public events and meetings of state-controlled companies to be in Latvian or translated into Latvian. On 20 December 1999, President Vīķe-Freiberga signed the new language law, which was to take effect on 1 September 2000.

Regarding the question of citizenship, temporary regulations were introduced before the August 1991 declaration of independence according to which all people who had been citizens before 17 June 1940 and their descendants automatically became citizens of the "renewed" state. Meanwhile, all those who had arrived in Latvia after that date needed to be screened before citizenship rights could be granted. By mid-1993, 98.4% of Latvians and 39% of Russians had obtained citizenship.[9] International pressure helped to ease the requirements for knowledge of the Latvian language and the length of residency.

In public debates on the new citizenship law, two basic positions emerged: the "zero option," to grant all residents citizenship immediately; and the "quota option," whereby naturalization would proceed according to annual quotas linked to total population growth and to minimum residency requirements. A new citizenship law was initially passed by parliament on 28 July 1994. In the face of Western criticisms over an initial draft and with a direct appeal from President Ulmanis, the law abandoned the proposed quota system. The residency stipulation was reduced from sixteen to ten years thus including a substantial portion of the Russian minority. It permitted from 1996 onward the start of a naturalization process for all non-citizens born in Latvia, which would include a language and history test and an oath of allegiance. After the year 2000, a three-year residency requirement would apply.

Critics charged that stringent citizenship requirements in effect disenfranchised a substantial portion of the country's residents. After independence, the Latvian share of the electorate rose to about 75%, while more than 60% of ethnic Russians were unable to vote in national elections. The significance of ethnic politics is likely to increase as a growing number of Russians gain Latvian citizenship, assuming that they will maintain a measure of political coherence.[10]

The law provoked substantial resentment among Latvians who objected to citizenship being extended to Russian "colonists." But the legislation was approved by the Council of Europe, despite Moscow's objections to some of its stipulations. Regardless of general international approval of the 1994 citizenship law, the Russian Federation and active members of the Russian community in Latvia alleged that the Latvian government was committing human rights abuses. Moscow periodically exploited the citizenship issue for the Russian diaspora as a means of applying pressure on all three Baltic states. Furthermore, delays and disputes over passage of the citizenship law and other legislation also hindered the passage of a new Latvian constitution. Indeed, Russian deputies in the Supreme Council deliberately made it difficult to generate stable alliances of deputies behind particular reforms.[11]

The Latvian parliament on 22 June 1998 approved an amendment to the citizenship law in the third and final reading, whereby citizenship would be granted to all children born to non-citizens after 21 August 1991 if their parents requested it. In an emergency parliamentary session called by the opposition Democratic Party *Saimnieks*, lawmakers voted by 54 to 14 to adopt the amendment. The parliament also voted to abolish the so-called "naturalization windows," which placed quotas on granting citizenship, and to simplify language tests for people over 65. The OSCE had strongly recommended that the parliament adopt those changes.

Latvia's population diminished during the early 1990s, from a total of 2.66 million in 1989 to 2.52 million in 1995. This was the result of several factors: fewer births, declining life expectancy, and higher infant mortality. The ethnic balance only slowly changed: the Latvian proportion grew from 52% in 1989 to 53.5% in 1993 and 54.1% in 1994. Riga and most other major cities still had non-Latvian majorities. Meanwhile, the country's new political leadership was almost exclusively Latvian.[12]

By the mid-1990s, approximately two thirds of the 724,000 stateless individuals were ethnically Russian. additionally, approximately half of the Russian community had obtained voting rights because they registered as citizens.[13] The Equality Party (EP) and Latvia's Russian Citizens' Party (LRCP) continued to protest against the government's policies on citizenship because of the high number of Russian residents without a political voice. Unfortunately, this issue also became a sore spot in Russian-Latvian relations, exacerbating other problems between the two countries. The *Saeima* passed a controversial language bill in July 1999, which was criticized by the Organization for Security and Cooperation in Europe (OSCE) and European Union (EU) because of language restrictions concerning the private sector and public gatherings. OSCE High Commissioner for National Minorities Max van der Stoel denounced the law, claiming that it violated human rights. The bill was widely supported among Latvians and was promoted by several parties including For Fatherland and Freedom, Latvia's Way, the LSDWP, and the People's Party.[14]

Economic problems have contributed to the Russian minority's allegations of discrimination, as they have witnessed their once privileged economic, social, and political positions significantly decline. However, profound changes in living standards occurred throughout the country, most notably in the growing gap between the very rich and the poor. The lifestyle of the small wealthy minority that benefited most from the economic transition contrasted sharply with the lifestyles of those who were negatively affected by structural economic changes.[15]

Reforms in the economic sector, in particular in the banking system, taxation, and the state treasury, brought mixed results. International organizations such as the International Monetary Fund (IMF), the World Bank, the World Trade Organization (WTO), and the EU remained confident that Latvia's economic environment was gradually improving and conditions were stabilizing. Latvia went through a "banking crisis" in 1994 that some dubbed a rite of passage for East European countries in transition, and its banks have since stabilized.[16] Tax collection steadily improved as the state bureaucracy became more institutionalized and efficient. The Latvian *lats* was introduced in 1993 to replace the transitional Latvian ruble, which was used from 1991 to 1993 to replace the Soviet ruble.

Privatization started slowly in Latvia because appropriate policies were not implemented until after the first parliamentary elections in 1993. The Latvian Privatization Agency was subsequently created to privatize large companies, while the privatization of smaller entities was put in the purview of local governments. Vouchers also became part of the privatization process, most specifically in the privatization of flats and farms.

A critical problem for the government was the escalation of organized crime—a region-wide trend. Crime curtailed governmental abilities to implement economic and political reforms, because of the resources, corruption, and violence involved in illicit activities. The Baltic Assembly initiated several projects to support its three member countries in combating the harmful effects of organized crime.

In foreign affairs, integration with Western Europe, economically, politically, and militarily, remained the highest priority for the Latvian government. The country gained the ability to engage in free trade with the EU in July 1994 and became an associate member of the EU in June 1995. In 1995, nearly one half of Latvia's trade was with the EU, followed by 32.4% with CIS countries and 14.7% with Germany.[17] Further economic and trade integration with the Scandinavian countries was enhanced when the Baltic Free Trade Zone was established in 1994 and measures were taken to boost trade between Latvia, Lithuania, and Estonia. Similarly to other aspirant states, the Latvian government was burdened with passing a vast array of laws and procedures to bring the country in line with those of the European Union.

Entrance into the North Atlantic Treaty Organization (NATO) has not proved as steady or assured a process as entrance into the EU. Historic questions of the "defensibility" of the Baltics, and fears in the West that admitting the Baltic states would be seen by Russia as an aggressive gesture, have seriously hampered Latvia in securing guarantees of future membership. The West has sought to create an alternative security arrangement for the region without abandoning the prospect of Baltic membership in NATO, most notably through the Partnership for Peace (PfP) program and various bilateral initiatives. Nonetheless, Latvia, Lithuania, and Estonia remained adamant that their security interests could best be served by eventual membership in NATO.

The main reason behind Latvian desires to join NATO was the lingering threat of Russian irredentism through Moscow's strategic and historical claims to Baltic territory. The substantial Russian minority in Latvia offered Russian politicians and officials an opportunity to place pressures on the Latvian authorities when it suited their foreign policy goals. An extreme example of this was the response of the Russian *Duma* (parliament) to a statement by the Latvian *Saiema* declaring that Latvia was forcibly annexed by the Soviet Union in 1940 and in 1945, and requesting official recognition of this by the Russian Federation.[18] The *Duma* responded by declaring that the Russian Federation did not recognize the illegal secession of the Latvian Republic from the Soviet Union in 1991.

Although the Russian army withdrew from Latvia in August 1994 and relations remained reasonably cordial between the Latvian and Russian governments, Riga did have real if sometimes exaggerated fears concerning future contacts with Moscow, primarily because of the latter's economic, political, and social instability. Relations with Russia worsened after December 1997, when Russia demanded a change to the citizenship law. After the *Saeima* passed the amendments to the citizenship law in July 1999, relations with Moscow improved slightly.[19]

Ties with Estonia and Lithuania have steadily developed. The Baltic states have regularly cooperated or supported each other on matters relating to EU and NATO membership and in dealing with Moscow. A free trade zone was established with the European Union in 1995, but Latvia was not accepted as one of the "fast-track" countries at the 1997 Luxembourg summit. The European Commission had concluded that Latvia was not a fully functioning market economy, and had a lingering problem associated with the Russian minority. The maintenance of the death penalty was also a problem for gaining accession to the Union and it was finally abolished in July 1999.[20]

Due to its domination by various regional powers over the past four centuries, Latvia has had limited experience with self-government. Despite this drawback, the country has made significant progress in creating a democratic society and a market-based economy. It will continue to seek more intensive integration with European and international institutions while dealing with its complicated communist legacy. On the whole, the political scene in Latvia seemed stable, despite frequent changeover of government and periodic problems among the many parties that comprised the governing coalitions. The country had nine administrations in its first decade of independence and critics claimed that petty rivalries and special business interests played too prominent a role in state affairs. The political system of Latvia was decidedly "statist" and the president played an important, if not institutionally direct, role in both domestic and foreign policy decisions.

Many analysts have commented that the conventional political spectrum of left–center–right was not applicable to the post-communist countries of Eastern Europe, including Latvia. For example, nationalistic parties, could be close ideologically to traditional conservative parties, or their platforms might resemble those of leftist parties. The coalition between the Latvian National Independence Movement and the Green Party was a poignant example of this phenomenon. One important characteristic of almost all ethnic Latvian parties was their unflinching support for the preservation of the Latvian state and nation. The degree to which a party felt that the Latvian nation must be culturally Latvian depended on specific ideological orientations. Rightist parties tended to stress the "purity" or "purification" of the Latvian *tauta* ("people" or "nation").

Additionally, rightist parties have been concerned with making absolute breaks with Latvia's Soviet past. Although they have sought to increase the democratic participation of the electorate, they also wanted to keep that electorate almost wholly ethnically Latvian. Parties on the "left" have experienced a more difficult time unifying themselves around particular themes because of the communist legacy and public perceptions regarding socialism. Almost all leftist parties have had to defend themselves against allegations that they wanted to return to pre-independence politics (in other words, to authoritarian communism).

Furthermore, there were persistent allegations that the ranks of leftist parties were composed almost solely of former communists and non-Latvians. These charges had an element of truth, but the communist past needed to be placed in perspective. The Communist Party was a vehicle for political, educational, social, and economic status, especially for the Russian minority. Therefore, many ethnic Latvian communists chose to leave the CPSU much earlier than their Russian counterparts, some of the latter ended up in the anti-independence Interfront movement. Most of the parties that emerged on the "left" adopted a social democratic program similar to those of their colleagues in Western Europe. But leftist parties also have been much less cohesive than rightist organizations, and this has created serious obstacles to the formation of viable socialist or social democratic coalitions.

Across the political spectrum, the term "party" has carried negative connotations in the country. During the inter-war period, the political scene was inundated by parties (as in Weimar Germany) and parliamentary instability was the rule. The Soviet Union's Communist Party, the major power in Latvian politics during the 1945–1990 period, was dominated by ethnic Russians, furthering the general feeling among ethnic Latvians that their country was under foreign occupation. In addition, most Latvians have not displayed a strong interest in working for specific parties, tending to view them primarily as vehicles for individuals seeking election to office.

Latvian parties have not fully developed as political entities in the Western tradition. They often have been organized around individuals or small groups, and none have had a large membership (except the Siegerist Party, whose statistics remain highly contested). Latvian parties have mainly served to institutionalize the new elites, who largely have determined the country's economic, political, and social agendas. The combination of the profusion of parties across the political spectrum; the pervasiveness of parties built around personalities rather than ideology; and the relative inexperience of the parties and the political system itself, made it difficult for the electorate to discriminate between distinct organizations and make well-informed political choices.

For much of the 1990s, Latvia's political landscape remained fragmented, with over forty officially registered political formations. Latvia's Way became the dominant party, but then its preeminent position steadily faded. On the whole, political parties did not possess well-defined structures or ideological foundations, and politics took place mainly on the basis of personalities. A change in the electoral law in 1997 resulted in the proscribing of coalition lists in parliamentary elections. Only fully registered unions were allowed and this led to the creation of two *pro forma* unions.[21]

In order to consolidate the number of political parties, parliament tried to pass more restrictive legislation on party registration. On 23 October 1999, President Vīķe-Freiberga returned to the parliament proposed amendments to the law on public organizations that would have raised the required minimum number of members for a party from 200 to 1,000. The President claimed that the amendments would have curtailed the legal rights of citizens by imposing groundless restrictions. The parliament had adopted the amendments on 21 October 1999, despite objections by Latvia's Way, the only ruling coalition party that had fewer than 1,000 members.

Another major issue in Latvian politics has been the balance between presidential and parliamentary powers. The young country's two presidents favored direct presidential elections in order to give the office a wider popular mandate, but this was opposed by a number of parties. Under the existing law, the head of state was elected by the parliament, while a direct popular vote would have increased the president's responsibilities.

Regional differences in political party support have not been dramatic. Divergences stemmed from traditional cleavages between rural and urban populations, between different ethnic groups, between citizens and non-citizens, and between Lutherans (the majority of the population) and Catholics (from the Latgale region in southeast Latvia, in particular). This last cleavage, though encompassing religious tradition, derived from significant differences in historical experience and economic development. The Latgale region was ruled by Poland for several centuries, and hence was largely Catholic and more Slavicized than other regions in Latvia.

Latvia was the only one of the three Baltic states that did not allow non-citizens to vote in local elections. All those who had resided in the same locality for over five years could vote in Estonia's local elections; and the vast majority of Lithuania's inhabitants, whether ethnic Lithuanian or not, became citizens and could vote. The prohibition on non-citizens from voting was primarily due to fears about the large size of the minority community, which was mainly concentrated in the cities and in the southeastern region of the country. If all residents were permitted to vote, there was a possibility that non-citizens or non-Latvians would gain power. In such a scenario, issues such as the demarcation of borders with Russia and restrictions on the promotion of Latvian culture and language at the local level could come to the forefront.

The international community hoped that Latvia would be able to better integrate its minority populations into its public institutions. The Latvian government's treatment of ethnic minorities did win international praise at the end of the 1990s, but it continued to be criticized by Russian authorities. The integration of ethnic minorities into Latvian political and civic society will remain one of the most pressing challenges facing the country over the next decade.

POLITICAL PARTIES

Socialists and Social Democrats

Latvian Social Democratic Alliance (LSDA)
Latvijas Sociāldemokrātu Apvienība (LSDA)

The Latvian Social Democratic Alliance (LSDA) was the main leftist coalition, which originally emerged in 1990 and included the Latvian Democratic Labor Party (LDLP). For the *Saeima* elections in September–October 1995, the LDLP formed a coalition styled as Labor and Justice with the Latvian Social Democratic Workers' Party (LSDWP). Before the seventh *Saeima* elections in 1998, the Labor and Justice coalition became the Latvian Social Democratic Alliance (LSDA). The Alliance won 14 seats in the October 1998 parliamentary elections. The LSDA stressed that it was a social democratic grouping in the West European mold. It was, however, more left oriented than many of its contemporary European social democratic counterparts. The LSDA program was purportedly a "synthesis of the best social democratic teachings in Europe and Australia."[22] In 1999, the coalition government struck a deal with the smaller Latvian Social Democratic Party (LSDP) *(Latvijas Sociāldemokrātu Partija)*. Although not formally part of the government, the LSDP promised to support certain government initiatives in the *Saeima* in exchange for the agricultural ministry portfolio and some other, smaller concessions.[23]

Like all leftist formations in post-independence Latvia, the LSDA experienced problems in garnering political legitimacy and overcoming severe political fragmentation.[24] Moreover, the left was associated among many Latvian ethnics with defending the interests of the large Russian minority and therefore in undermining the country's national interests. Many Latvians viewed the leftist parties as willing to compromise on the language and citizenship questions to the advantage of Russian-speakers; hence, these organizations had limited appeal among Latvian voters. In addition, leftists' criticisms of wrenching economic reform programs were depicted by their rivals as supporting a return to the "command economy" of Soviet times.

Latvian Democratic Labor Party (LDLP)
Latvijas Demokrātiskā Darba Partija (LDDP)

The Latvian Democratic Labor Party (LDLP) was the reformist wing that broke away from the Latvian Communist Party in 1990, but it was considered to have a somewhat tainted past. It was led by ex–KGB major Juris Bojārs, who was banned from running in the June 1993 and October–November 1995 parliamentary elections because of his Soviet past, as well as by the reform communist Ivars Ķezbers. It claimed to have over 1,000 members in 1995. The LDLP was part of the Labor and Justice coalition in the October 1995 parliamentary elections. After the balloting, the party changed its name to the Latvian Social Democratic Party (LSDP), and in May 1999 the LSDP merged with the Latvian Social Democratic Workers' Party (LSDWP).

Latvian Social Democratic Workers' Party (LSDWP)
Latvijas Sociāldemokrātiskā Stradnieku Partija (LSDSP)

The Latvian Social Democratic Workers' Party (LSDWP) renewed its status in 1989, having been originally founded in 1904. It therefore claimed to be descended from Latvia's oldest political party. Its membership remained small. The party was a traditional, social democratic formation and cooperated with several labor unions, but not with either the far left or far right. After a change in the country's electoral laws, the party merged with the LDLP. The merger became official in May 1998, but both parties still maintained a high degree of independent organizational structure. The LSDWP-LSDA leftist coalition gained 14 seats in the October 1998 parliamentary elections, with 12.88% of the popular vote.

National Harmony Party (NHP)
Tautas Saskaņas Partija (TSP)

The National Harmony Party (NHP), or the Concord Party, was created in February 1994 as a result of the breakup of the coalition Harmony for Latvia–Economic Rebirth (HFL-ER) (Saskaņa Latvijai–Ekonomiska

Ardzimšana, SL-EA) in February 1994. The HFL-ER emerged as the largest organized anti-nationalist force. Its inheritor, the NHP, chaired by Jānis Jurkāns, claimed 400 members in 1995. The HFL-ER coalition won 13 seats in the June 1993 legislative ballot. Subsequently, the NHP inherited five seats in the parliament and ran on a separate list for the September–October 1995 parliamentary elections when it captured 5.6% of the vote and obtained six parliamentary seats. It also gained 16 seats in the October 1998 general elections. The party, which was essentially ex-communist and defined itself as a left-wing liberal formation, primarily sought the support of ethnic Russians, as it advocated a conciliatory policy towards this section of society and focused on the issue of citizenship and the so-called "zero option" for granting citizenship, seeking to integrate the Slavic peoples in the Latvian state. Observers believed that most of the party's support came from the traditional Slavic population rather than from the post-1940 immigrants. The party also canvassed for closer Latvian cooperation with Russia.[25] After 1998, the NHP participated in the coalition For Equal Rights in a United Latvia.

Democratic Party "Master" (DPM)
Demokrātiskā Partija "Saimnieks" (DPS)

The Democratic Party "Master" (DPM) initially emerged during the 1994 local elections but was formally established in April 1995 by a merger of the Democratic Party (formerly the Democratic Center Party) and a parliamentary group that called itself *Saimnieks*.[26] The DPM was led by Ziedonis Čevers, a former Interior Minister, and Juris Celmiņš, the former head of the *Saimnieks* faction. *Saimnieks* has no direct translation in English; however, the connotation of the word is "master" or "lord of the estate." Almost up until the time of the initial creation of the Latvian state in 1920, most Latvians were peasants who were formally or informally tied to large estates. The *Saimnieks* was the individual who provided for and took care of peasants on the estate while managing many of the daily operational tasks that the real owners of the estate felt were beneath them.

The DPM claimed approximately 760 members in 1995 and had five members in the *Saeima,* one of whom was Ziedonis Čevers. The DPM program consisted of a moderate form of statism and welfarism to protect the poorer sections of society from the consequences of market reform. The party was known for its fairly broad left-of-center ideological base, and most of its policies were focused on the country's economic situation. The DPM often featured in the news because of its high-profile members. For example, Ilga Kreituse, the speaker of the sixth *Saeima*, resigned her post because of the expulsion of her husband, former finance minister Aivars Kreituss, from the faction. Kreituse had been involved in campaigning for the presidency earlier in the year. additionally, faction member Valdis Krisbergs was suspended for his alleged involvement in a corruption scandal associated with an investment firm.

The DPM was included in the Labor and Justice coalition formed in 1995, together with the Latvian Democratic Labor Party (LDLP), the Latvian Social Democratic Workers' Party (LSDWP), and the Party of Cheated Persons/ Justice Party (PCP/JP). The DPM left the government coalition in April 1998 after its economics minister was dismissed. Its leaders called for a resolution of the citizenship issue and for an emergency session of parliament. This led to a change of the law in July 1998. The DPM subsequently lost all its parliamentary seats in the October 1998 elections, after receiving only 1.6% of the popular vote.[27]

Ziedonis Čevers resigned as DPM chairman after the general elections, claiming responsibility for the party's poor showing. At an extraordinary congress on 28 November 1998, the party elected Andris Ameriks as its new chairman. Čevers told the congress he would not accept any elective post in the party. Ameriks did not rule out the possibility that *Saimnieks* might join forces with another political group in the future "while preserving its identity."

Union of Economists (UOE)
Ekonomistu Savienība (ES)

The Union of Economists (UOE) was established in March 1994 as a "moderate left" formation resulting from the split in the Harmony For Latvia movement. The UOE placed less stress than its former partners on the position of the Slavic population and generally supported the program of economic development. However, it criticized the ruling Latvia's Way for its allegedly "extremist liberalism" and called for greater central guidance of the economic reform process. In 1995, the UOE had 300 members, and five deputies in the parliament, inherited from the Harmony coalition.

Latvian Unity Party (LUP)
Latvijas Vienības Partija (LVP)

The Latvian Unity Party (LUP) was established in December 1992 but was not represented in the 1993 parliament. The history of the party and its members were viewed with suspicion. In fact, it was a leftist party made up mainly of old communists and chaired by Alberts Kauls, a former collective farm director and supporter of the pro-Moscow wing of the Latvian Communist Party. Because of his notorious past, Kauls was excluded by law from becoming a candidate in the September–October 1995 general elections. The party gained five parliamentary seats in the 1995 ballot, after which its members defected to other parties or factions. In the October 1998 general elections, the party failed to win any parliamentary seats.

Latvian Socialist Party (LSP)
Latvijas Sociālistiskā Partija (LSP)

Formerly known as the Equality Party (EP) *(Līdztiesība Partija, LP)*, the Latvian Socialist Party (LSP) represented the Latvian Slavic population in the June 1993 elections and won six seats to parliament. The EP became the basis for the Latvian Socialist Party, formed in January 1994, and claiming to have about 1,000 members in 1995. It was chaired by Sergejs Dīmanis. The party advocated increasing the numbers of non–ethnic Latvians awarded citizenship. It proposed Alfrēds Rubiks for the presidency in 1995, a move that was seen as a slap in the face to many Latvians because Rubiks had been the leader of the pro-Moscow wing of the LCP during the 1991 attempted coup in Russia. Rubiks was subsequently convicted of crimes against the Latvian state because of his role in the repressive events of August 1991 and his support for the hard-line coup plotters in Moscow. The party believed in widening the definition of who could be elected to the legislature to include those who were active in the former Latvian Communist Party.

Democratic Party (DP)
Demokrātiku Partija (DP)

Founded after the June 1993 parliamentary elections, the Democratic Party (DP) claimed to have 2,378 members by 1995. It was known popularly as the Family Party and was led by Marģers Martinsons. Its program focused on the protection of the "Latvian family" from the ravages of economic reform. The DP failed to win any parliamentary seats in the October 1998 elections. Other leftist organizations included the Party of Cheated Persons (PCP), also known as the Justice Party (JP), founded in February 1994 and claiming 352 members by 1995. It ran in the September–October 1995 parliamentary elections in the Labor and Justice coalition, avowedly representing the interests of poorer sectors of society traumatized by the fast-paced market reforms.

Liberals

Latvia's Way (LW)
Latvijas Ceļš (LC)

Latvia's Way (LW) was established by intellectuals grouped in the informal Club 21 and included politicians, businessmen, and cultural figures. The Club was a useful meeting place for Latvian activists from across the political spectrum. Chaired by Andrejs Panteļējevs, the LW grew into an electoral coalition and was officially announced in February 1993. It comprised prominent Supreme Council members such as Anatolijs Gorbunovs, Latvian Popular Front activists, and individuals of the Latvian diaspora in the West, including the chairman of the World Federation of Free Latvians, Gunārs Meierovics. It was formally registered in October 1993 and claimed 387 members in 1995. Latvia's Way obtained 36 seats in the June 1993 parliamentary elections and formed a coalition government with the Agrarian Union led by Prime Minister Valdis Birkavs that lasted until July 1994. It subsequently formed a governing coalition with the small Economists' Party under the premiership of Māris Gailis. It was the only party that could gain a plurality in the parliament if not an absolute majority.

In the October 1998 elections, Latvia's Way won 18% of the vote, which brought it 21 parliamentary seats. The party aimed to garner support primarily from voters of the emerging middle class. LW was considered a centrist party and a promoter of liberal economic policies resembling the German *Soziale Marktwirtschaft* system. It also depicted an image of permanence, pragmatism, and experience, contrasting itself with the purportedly unpredictable leftist and rightist forces.

Latvian Liberal Party (LLP)
Latviešu Liberāla Partija (LLP)

The Latvian Liberal Party (LLP) was founded in January 1990 by pro-business and liberal members of the Latvian Popular Front. The LLP did not manage to surpass the 4% barrier in the June 1993 parliamentary elections. It claimed only 300 members by 1995 and did not develop any notable constituency. It only received 0.2% of the popular vote in the September–October 1995 parliamentary elections and failed to gain any seats. Although it espoused a strong free market ideology, it did not represent a strong political force.

Political Union of Economists (PUE)
Tastsaimnieku Politiska Apvienība (TPA)

The Political Union of Economists (PUE) was founded in February 1994 and inherited five seats in parliament in 1994. It was chaired by Edvīns Ķide and had 300 members in 1995. The party adopted a vehemently pro-market and pro-business position.

Several other moderate, centrist, and pro-market formations emerged during the course of the decade. Leaders of the Democratic Center Party (DCP) *(Demokrātiskā Centra Partija, DCP)* declared the party to be a modern version of the successful moderate organization active before World War II. The Democratic Center Movement (DCM) was a former moderate wing of the Latvian Popular Front led by several original founders of the Front, including Jānis Skapars and former foreign minister Jānis Jurkāns.

Christian Democrats

Latvian Christian Democratic Union (LCDU)
Latvijas Kristīgo Demokrātu Savienība (LKDS)

Founded in March 1991 and chaired by Tālavs Jundzis, the Latvian Christian Democratic Union (LCDU) followed in the tradition of West European Christian Democratic parties. It had 650 members in 1991 and obtained six seats in the June 1993 *Saeima* elections. The Latvian Agrarian Union (LAU) *(Latvijas Zemnieku Savienība, LZS)*, the Latvian Christian Democratic Union (LCDU) *(Latvijas Kristīgo Demokrātu Savienība, LKDS)*, and the Latgale Democratic Party (LDP) *(Latgales Demokrātiskā Partija, LDP)* formed an electoral coalition in April 1995. The coalition took eight seats in the *Saeima* following the September–October 1998 elections. The LCDU, which could be described as a center-right party, entered into a coalition with the Labor Party and the Green Party for the October 1998 elections but failed to garner any legislative seats.

The New Party (TNP)
Jaunā Partija (JP)

Founded in 1998, The New Party (NP) was part of the government coalition formed after the October 1998 general elections, until Prime Minister Krištopans resigned in July 1999. The TNP performed well in the 1998 ballot, largely due to the popularity of some of its members, including the former Popular Front leader and popular composer Raimonds Pauls. The TNP describes itself as a center-left formation and was relatively rich because of its business origins and its close links to Scandinavian corporations.[28] The TNP nominated party leader Pauls as its candidate for national President in the June 1999 elections.

Agrarians

Latvian Agrarian Union (LAU)
Latvijas Zemnieku Savienība (LZS)

Originally established in 1917 but disbanded by pre-war President Kārlis Ulmanis in 1934, the Latvian Agrarian Union (LAU) was resuscitated in April 1991. The post-independence LAU considered itself the successor of the inter-war Latvian Agrarian Union, the party of Kārlis Ulmanis, which dominated Latvian politics before the onset of authoritarian presidential rule before World War II. Chaired by Laimonis Strujevičs, it claimed 3,800 members in the early 1990s and focused its work primarily among rural residents, who constituted approximately one third of Latvia's total population.

The LAU was considered a center-right conservative party and became a strong advocate of agricultural protectionism.

The LAU obtained 12 seats in the June 1993 parliamentary elections and entered the coalition government, which it subsequently brought down in July 1994 after its ministers resigned from the cabinet. For the September–October 1995 parliamentary elections, the LAU established a coalition with the Latvian Christian Democratic Union (LCDU) and the regionalist Letgallian Democratic Party (LDP). The LAU took 6.1% of the vote and seven legislative seats. Although the LAU's program resembled that of the centrist-liberal Latvia's Way, its focus on agrarian protectionism precluded close cooperation with its larger competitor and former government partner. The LAU did not pass the threshold in the October 1998 elections and lost all of its parliamentary seats.

Greens

Latvian Green Party (LGP)
Latvijas Zaļā Partija (LZP)

Established in January 1990 and chaired by Indulis Emsis, the Latvian Green Party (LGP) claimed 228 members in 1995. In its early years, it had to compete with the Latvian Popular Front for voters even though the link between ecological politics and the movement for national emancipation remained strong. Subsequently, the LGP experienced difficulties in retaining the loyalty of environmentalist voters. In June 1993, the party received only 1.2% of the popular vote and it failed to gain any parliamentary seats. The center-right Green Party entered into a coalition with several small formations, including the Labor Party (LP) (*Darba Partija, DP*) and the Christian Democratic Union (CDU) *(Kristīgo Demokrātu Savienība, KDS)*, for the October 1998 elections, but failed to win any seats. An Environmental Club was also active throughout the 1990s.

In Latvia, the green movement was closely linked with nationalist causes, such as strict criteria for citizenship for the Russian population and the speedy removal of all Russian troops. It also had deep connections with the land, traditional values, and with Latvia's cultural heritage.

Nationalists

Latvian Popular Front (LPF)
Latvijas Tautas Fronte (LTF)

The first congress of the pro-independence Latvian Popular Front (LPF) took place on 8–9 October 1988, with some 1,000 delegates present and representing over 110,000 members organized in 2,300 local chapters; 88% of the congress delegates were ethnic Latvians. Front leaders included reform communists, former anti-communist dissidents, activist intellectuals, religious leaders, environmentalists, and assorted nationalists. At its height the LPF claimed to have over 200,000 members. In elections to the Supreme Council on 18 March 1990, the LPF and the Latvian National Independence Movement gained 134 out of 170 seats and 68.2% of the popular vote and thus accelerated the momentum for state independence.

However, the umbrella-like structure of the LPF was both advantageous and restrictive. Although it was a large movement, it could not satisfy the demands of all members, and critics charged it was too willing to make compromises with Moscow over the question of regaining full national independence. The LPF initially supported the concept of Latvian sovereignty within the USSR but eventually declared itself for full national independence. It experienced an internal conflict between reform communists who supported a gradualist approach toward sovereignty and Latvian nationalists of various tendencies who urged it to adopt a more radical position. Analysts believed that the Front remained essentially moderate primarily because of its early fears of a Russian military intervention. Once this threat receded, it adopted a harder position on national questions.

At its fifth congress in November 1992, the LPF lost several factions; its parliamentary representation was reduced to 53 deputies out of the original 132 elected on the Front ticket. Because the LPF did not formally register as a political party until 1994, under chairman Uldis Augustkalns, it lost many activists to political formations registered prior to the June 1993 parliamentary elections. The Front only received 2.5% of the total vote and failed to win any parliamentary seats. By 1995, the LPF claimed a membership of 2,025, but it was unable to promote itself as a distinct political force. It increasingly adopted a nationalist and anti-communist position after its November 1991 congress, claiming that Latvian politics had been hijacked by members of the former *nomenklatura* in league with criminal elements. But its stance became largely irrelevant by the mid-1990s or had been more effectively presented by other nationalist political forces, and the LPF was dissolved.

Latvian National Independence Movement (LNIM)
Latvijas Nacionālas Neatkarības Kustība (LNNK)

Led by Eduards Berklāvs and Andrejs Krastņš, the Latvian National Independence Movement (LNIM) was founded on 18 June 1988.[29] It held its first congress on 18–19 February 1989. Although it was smaller than the Latvian Popular Front, its insistence on full national independence kept the issue at the center of the political stage. During the period between 1988–1991, the LNIM focused on the issues of national sovereignty and statehood. It formed a coalition with the Green Party because the association between environmental protection and Latvian nationalism was strong from the outset. The

Movement was formally registered as a party only in July 1994. It obtained 15 seats in parliament in the June 1993 elections and claimed approximately 2,130 members by 1995.[30] The LNIM merged with For Fatherland and Freedom in June 1997.[31]

At a joint congress on 21 June 1997, the LNIM and For Fatherland and Freedom voted to establish a new political formation called Fatherland and Freedom–LNIM. For Fatherland and Freedom leader Māris Grīnblats stated that the new party's program would be based on "national values, the inviolability of the fundamental principles of the constitution, passage of a tough citizenship law, the promotion of the repatriation of aliens, and the preservation of the purity of the Latvian language." The new party inherited 17 parliamentary seats and thereby became the second largest formation in the legislature.

For Fatherland and Freedom (FFF)
Tēvzemei un Brīvībai (TVB)

Chaired by Māris Grīnblats, For Fatherland and Freedom (FFF) was formally registered as a party in January 1995. However, the movement actually began during the so-called Third Awakening,[32] denoting a direct link with pre-war Latvian politics. The founders of FFF were closely linked to the "Congress Movement" in the late 1980s, a group that sought to create an alternative government to the republican administration in Riga. It originally consisted of two political formations, the 18th November Union and Fatherland. The two groups merged in 1993 for the June general elections, when they took four parliamentary seats. FFF had only 670 members in 1995.

For Fatherland and Freedom was largely an ethno-populist party that focused on "the consequences of the Soviet occupation." It was staunchly anti-Russian and supported the repatriation of the majority of the Russian "colonists." It also opposed land ownership reforms, especially those that would give foreigners the right to own land in Latvia. The party began to create an all-Baltic conservative movement, the Baltic Democratic Union, of which Estonia's Isamaaliit Party and For Fatherland and Freedom were the founding members. The party merged with the LNIM on 21 June 1997.

National Movement for Latvia–Siegerist's Party (NML-SP)
Tautas Kustība Latvijai–Zīgerista Partija (TKL-ZP)

The National Movement for Latvia–Siegerist's Party (NML-SP) was formally registered in November 1994 by four defectors or expellees from the Latvian National Independence Movement (LNIM) faction in the *Saeima*. It claimed to have over 12,000 members, but the numbers could not be independently verified. The NML-SP was a controversial party led by a German extremist named Joachim Siegerist, who claimed to have Latvian ancestry but failed to learn the Latvian language despite repeatedly promising to do so. By law, the language in parliament was Latvian and Siegerist openly disregarded the legislation. Siegerist's deputy was the Latvian historian Odisejs Kostanda. In June 1993, Siegerist ran an avidly populist campaign that sought to gain the votes of those most adversely affected by the economic, political, and social transformation, such as elderly, relatively undereducated, rural, and non-Latvian voters. Like For Fatherland and Freedom, the NML-SP opposed allowing foreigners to own land in Latvia.

Although the party informally continued to bear his name, Siegerist was expelled from the *Saeima* in 1993 for frequent unexcused absences from parliamentary debates. The NML-SP scored surprisingly well in the September–October 1995 parliamentary elections, garnering 15% of the national vote and 16 deputies. However, it subsequently underwent a significant decline in its popularity. After the party won less than 2% of the vote in the October 1998 general elections, Siegerist announced that he would step down as party leader on 4 October 1998, saying that he took full responsibility for the party's failure to gain entry into parliament.[33]

Christian People's Party (CPP)
Latvijas Kristīgo Demokrātu (LKD)

Formerly known as the Latvian Popular Front, the Christian People's Party (CPP) was established in July 1988 with the Latvian National Independence Movement. Its membership at the congress of the Latvian Popular Front on 1 October 1988 was reported to be approximately 110,000 people, organized in 2,300 local chapters. The party was chaired by Uldis Augustkalns, and its members included Communist Party members, environmentalists, dissidents, radical independence seekers, members of religious groups, and intellectuals. But the Popular Front did not become a formal party until 1994, and it lost many of its members. It garnered only 2.6% of the vote in the June 1993 elections. The CPP had 2,025 members in 1995 and was widely viewed as ultra-nationalistic.[34] The Christian People's Party merged with the Christian Democrats to form the Christian Democratic Union (LCDU) in 1997.[35]

People's Party (PP)
Tautas Partija (TP)

The People's Party (PP) was established on 2 May 1998 under the chairmanship of Andris Šķēle. Its membership numbered 1,860 in January 1999. The party's motto was a "family of three," meaning that it encouraged three children per family, to increase the Latvian population. The party's goal was also to achieve a European standard of living for the Latvian people. The PP claimed its chief objectives were to strengthen Latvia's independence and to provide an alternative to existing parties. The party sought close cooperation with the two other Baltic states, and membership in NATO, the EU, and the WTO.[36]

Latvian National Conservative Party (LNCP)
Latvijas Nacionāli Konservatīvā Partija (LNKP)

The Latvian National Conservative Party (LNCP) was chaired by Māris Grīnblats. The party came into being as a result of a merger between For Fatherland and Freedom and the Latvian National Independence Movement, and was formally registered in January 1995. The party, whether inside or outside government, was staunchly anti-Russian and nationalistic in its stance. The LNCP opposed changes in the pre–World War II citizenship law.

Another Latvian nationalist organization was the Our Land and Anti-Communist Union (OLACU) *(Mūsu Zeme un Pretkomunistu Apvienība, MZPA)*, chaired by M. Dambekalne. It accused the *Saeima* of having violated the 1922 Latvian constitution and thus of having carried out a *coup d'état* in passing the 1994 citizenship law without a national referendum. It failed to win any seats in the September–October 1995 general elections.

A number of smaller nationalist parties that were also unable to win any parliamentary seats included the Latvian National Democratic Party (LNDP) *(Latvijas Nacionāli Demokrātiskā Partija, LNDP)*, the Latvian Independence Party (LIP), and the Political Union of the Unprotected (PUU).

Ethnic Minority and Religious Parties

Latvia's Russian Citizens' Party (LRCP)
Latvijas Krievu Pilsoņu Partija (LKPP)

Led by V. Sorochin and V. Ivanov and founded in January 1995 as an alternative to the Latvian Socialist Party, the Latvia's Russian Citizens' Party (LRCP) was an advocate of the Russian-speaking population. It claimed approximately 700 members at the time it was created and sought a more representative voice for the country's largest minority. The party's parliamentary faction Nation and Justice *(Tautai un Taisnībai)* was established in 1996. The LRCP initially favored the creation of a "two-community state," with two official languages and the right to dual (Latvian and Russian) citizenship. On the other hand, it declared its loyalty to the Latvian state and increasingly promoted a "Latvian unity" that was not based on ethnic criteria. Its program thus differed markedly from the Russian-based Internationalist Front of the Workers of the Latvian SSR (Interfront) that was established in January 1989 in open opposition to Latvian statehood. Interfront had depicted itself as the defender of the Russian-speaking community and was backed by hard-liners in Moscow, but it lost its influence during the early 1990s.

A Russian nationalist grouping, Russian National Unity (RNU), also became

Presidential Election (Indirect), 6–7 July 1993

First Round, 6 July 1993

Candidate	Votes	% of Vote
Gunārs Meierovics	35	57.0
Aivars Jerumanis	14	23.0
Guntis Ulmanis	12	20.0
Total	61	100.0

(No candidate obtained the 51 votes needed to capture the presidency.)

Second Round, 7 July 1993

Candidate	Votes	% of Vote
Guntis Ulmanis	53	67.0
Aivars Jerumanis	26	33.0
Total	79	100.0

Parliamentary Elections, 3 October 1998

Turnout: 71.89%

Party/Coalition	Votes	% of Vote	Seats
People's Party	203,585	21.30	24
Latvia's Way	173,420	18.15	21
For Fatherland and Freedom	140,773	14.73	17
National Harmony Party	135,700	14.20	16
Latvian Social Democratic Workers' Party/Latvian Social Democratic Alliance	123,056	12.88	14
The New Party	70,214	7.35	8
Latvian Agrarian Union	23,732	2.48	—
Labor Party/Christian Democratic Union/Latvian Green Party	22,018	2.30	—
National Movement for Latvia–Siegerist's Party	16,647	1.74	—
Democratic Party "Master"	15,410	1.61	—
Total	955,581	100.00	100

Sources: http://www.agora.stm.it/elections/election/latvia.htm; http://www.mk.gov.lv/eng/cabinbetofministers/structure/welcome.htm; http://www2.essex.ac.uk/elect/electer/latvia_er_nl.htm.

Parliamentary Elections, 30 September–1 October 1995

Turnout: 72.65%

Party/Coalition	Votes	% of Vote	Seats
Democratic Party "Master"	144,573	15.3	18
National Movement for Latvia	141,945	15.0	16
Latvia's Way	138,132	14.6	17
For Fatherland and Freedom	109,574	11.6	14
Latvian Unity Party	68,281	7.2	8
Latvian National Independence Movement/Greens	58,140	6.1	8
Latvian Agrarian Union	57,857	6.1	7
Socialist Party	53,288	5.6	6
National Harmony Party	52,899	5.6	6
Labor and Justice Coalition	43,539	4.6	—
Political Union of Economists	14,231	1.5	—
Union of Latvian Farmers	12,741	1.3	—
Russian Citizens' Party	11,871	1.2	—
Popular Front	11,007	1.1	—
Independence Party	9,469	1.0	—
Our Land and Anti-Communist League	4,978	0.5	—
Democratic Party	2,507	0.2	—
Liberal Party	2,122	0.2	—
National Democratic Party	1,336	0.1	—
Total	951,007	100.0	100

Source: The Baltic Observer, 5–11 October 1995, p. 1.

Parliamentary Elections, 5–6 June 1993

Turnout: 91.18%

Party/Coalition	Votes	% of Vote	Seats
Latvia's Way	362,479	32.30	36
Latvian National Independence Movement	149,455	13.40	15
Harmony for Latvia–Economic Rebirth	124,282	12.00	13
Latvian Agrarian Union	119,134	10.60	12
For Equal Rights in a United Latvia	64,495	5.80	7
For Fatherland and Freedom	59,994	5.40	6
Christian Democratic Party	56,136	5.00	6
Democratic Center Party	53,303	4.80	5
Latvian Popular Front	29,349	2.60	—

Green Party	13,387	1.20	—
Russian National Democratic List	13,008	1.20	—
Democratic Labor Party	10,512	0.90	—
Latvia's Luck	9,842	0.80	—
Our Land	9,274	0.80	—
Economic Activity League	8,400	0.70	—
Social Democratic Workers' Party	7,432	0.60	—
Anti-Communist Union	5,969	0.50	—
Republican Platform	5,071	0.40	—
Conservatives' and Farmers' Party	2,800	0.30	—
Independence Union	1,966	0.20	—
Latvian Liberal Party	1,517	0.20	—
Latvian Unity Party	1,017	0.10	—
Liberal Alliance	523	0.05	—
Total	1,118,316	100.00	100

Sources: The Baltic Observer, 11–17 June 1993; and *Diena*, Riga, 8 June 1993.

NOTES

1. Useful recent histories of Latvia can be found in Andrejs Plakans, *The Latvians: A Short History*, Stanford: Hoover Press, 1995; Marijas Gimbutas, *The Balts*, London: Thames and Hudson, 1963; Arnold Spekke, *History of Latvia: An Outline*, Stockholm: M. Goppers, 1957; David Kirby, *The Baltic World, 1772–1993: Europe's Northern Periphery in an Age of Change*, London: Longman, 1995; Walter C. Clemens, Jr., *Baltic Independence and Russian Empire*, New York: St. Martin's Press, 1991; George von Rauch, *The Baltic States: The Years of Independence, Estonia, Latvia, Lithuania, 1917–1940*, Berkeley and Los Angeles: University of California Press, 1974; and John Hiden and Patrick Salmon, *The Baltic Nations and Europe: Estonia, Latvia and Lithuania in the Twentieth Century*, London: Longman, 1996.

2. James D. White, "Nationalism and Socialism in Historical Perspective," in Graham Smith (Ed.), *The Baltic States: The National Self-Determination of Estonia, Latvia, and Lithuania*, New York: St. Martin's Press, 1996, pp. 21–22.

3. Graham Smith, "The Resurgence of Nationalism," in Graham Smith (Ed.), *The Baltic States: The National Self-Determination of Estonia, Latvia, and Lithuania*, New York: St. Martin's Press, 1996, pp. 121–143.

4. A valuable summary of Latvia's drive for independence can be found in Nils Muižnieks, "Latvia: Restoring a State, Rebuilding a Nation," in Ian Bremmer and Ray Taras (Eds.), *New States, New Politics: Building the Post-Soviet Nations*, Cambridge, UK: Cambridge University Press, 1997, pp. 376–403.

5. For background see Jill Bender, *Baseline Assessment of the Latvian Parliament*, National Democratic Institute for International Affairs, Washington, D.C., Department of State, 1995; Ole Norgaard, Dan Hindsgaul, Lars Johannsen, and Helle Willumsen, *Reconstructing Democracy in the Baltic States after Independence*, Cheltenham, UK: Edward Elgar, 1996; Andrejs Plakans, "Democratization and Political Participation in Post-Communist Societies: The Case of Latvia," in Karen Dawisha and Bruce Parrott (Eds.), *Authoritarianism and Democratization in Post-Communist Societies*, Cambridge, UK: Cambridge University Press, 1996; and Jan Arveds Trapans, "Continuities and Discontinuities," in *The Latvians*, XXX; pp. 184–203; Jan Arveds Trapans, "The Sources of Latvia's Popular Movement," in *Toward Independence: The Baltic Popular Movements*, Boulder, CO: Westview Press, 1991.

6. For useful analysis of the position of the Russian minority see Anatol Lieven, *The Baltic Revolution: Estonia, Latvia, Lithuania, and the Path to Independence*, New Haven: Yale University Press, 1993, pp. 174–213.

7. Juris Dreifelds, *Latvia in Transition*, Cambridge, UK: Cambridge University Press, 1996, p. 173.

8. See Radio Free Europe/Radio Liberty (RFE/RL) *Newsline*, 15 July 1999.

9. Andrejs Plakans, *The Latvians*, p. 190.

10. Check Vello Pettai, "Political Stability through Disenfranchisement," *Transition*, Open Media Research Institute, Vol. 3, No. 6, 4 April 1997, pp. 21–23.

11. David Arter, *Parties and Democracy in the Post-Soviet Republics: The Case of Estonia*, Aldershot, UK: Dartmouth Publishing Company, 1996, p. 58.

12. See Andrejs Plakans, "Democratization and Political Participation in Postcommunist Societies: The Case of Latvia," in Karen Dawisha and Bruce Parrott (Eds.), *The Consolidation of Democracy in East-Central Europe*, Cambridge, UK: Cambridge University Press, 1997, pp. 245–289.

13. Ole Norgaard with Dan Hindsgaul, Lars Johannsen, and Helle Willumsen, *The Baltic States after Independence*, Cheltenham, UK: Edward Elgar, 1996; p. 103.

14. http://www.europeanforum.bot-consult.se/cup/latvia/.

15. See UNDP Country Report on Latvia, United Nations, 1995, for more detailed analysis of the growing disparity between rich and poor in Latvia.

16. *EUROPA World Book*, 1996, p. 1932.

17. Louis Berger International, Inc. for the USTDA, *Opportunities for Investment in the Republic of Latvia's Pulp and Paper, Harbor Development and Electricity Generation Sectors*, September 1996, p. 8.

18. Republic of Latvia, Saeima, "Declaration on the Occupation of Latvia," 22 August 1996.

19. http://www.europeanforum.bot-consult.se/cup/latvia/.

20. http://www.europeanforum.bot-consult.se/cup/latvia/.

21. See http://www.europeanforum.bot-consult.se/cup/latvia/.

22. See http://www.mfa.gov.lv/ENG/LATVIA/polpart.htm.

23. "Latvia: Review 1999," *Europe Review World of Information*, 11 November 1999.

24. Andrejs Plakans, in Dawisha and Parrott (Eds.), 1997, p. 276.

25. See http://www.mfa.gov.lv/ENG/LATVIA/polpart.htm.

26. In articles written in English, the Latvian name and not a translation, is preferred (*LETA*, 3 September 1996).

27. See http://www.europeanforum.bot-consult.se/cup/latvia/.

28. See http://www.mfa.gov.lv/ENG/LATVIA/polpart.htm.

29. Jan Arveds Trapans, "Latvia's Popular Front," in *Baltic Popular Movements*, Boulder, CO: Westview Press, 1991, p. 29.

30. Andrejs Plakans, in Dawisha and Parrott (Eds.), 1997, p. 33.

31. Consult the party homepage in Latvian: http://www.saeima.lv/LapasEnglish/7thSaeima_Visa.htm.

32. The "Third Awakening" refers to the rebirth of independent Latvian political life in the late 1980s. In this context the "First Awakening" refers to the original Livonian state, and the "Second Awakening" to the independent Latvian state between the two world wars.

33. See http://www.rferl.org/newsline/1998/10/061098.html.

34. Juris Dreifelds, *Latvia in Transition*, Cambridge, UK: Cambridge University Press, 1996, p. 148.

35. See http://www.europeanforum.bot-consult.se/cup/latvia/.

36. See www.tautaspartija.lv/english.htm.

Lithuania

HISTORICAL OVERVIEW

The Lithuanians are part of the Baltic group of Indo-Europeans. Their ancestors, the Samogitians and Aukštaičai, inhabited the territories of present- day Lithuania before the tenth century AD. The first Lithuanian state can be traced back to the rule of King Mindaugas, a chieftain who in 1236 managed to unite several disparate tribes into a single entity. Under his rule, the Lithuanians successfully withstood periodic incursions by German Teutonic Knights. In order to protect his kingdom against a German-led Crusade, Mindaugas accepted Christianity and received a crown from Pope Innocent IV in 1251. After his assassination ten years later, the Lithuanians reverted to their traditional, pre-Christian beliefs.

One of Mindaugas's successors, Gediminas (1316–1341), became the real founder of the Lithuanian state after extending his control over several nearby principalities. The town of Vilnius became his permanent residence. His son Algirdas (1341–1377) expanded the country's territory southward into Ukraine and toward the shores of the Black Sea, and eastward toward Moscow. Despite these conquests, many local Russian princes welcomed the Lithuanians as liberators from Tartar rule and as protectors against German expansion. Lithuanian rulers left largely untouched the political, administrative, and religious organizations in most of the principalities that recognized their supremacy. Some regions of present-day Belarus, western Ukraine, and western Russia became a part of Lithuania at this time.

During the thirteenth and fourteenth centuries, the Grand Duchy of Lithuania was a multinational state. It was dominated by Lithuanian nobles, even though Lithuanians constituted a minority of the population. Lithuanian rulers invited foreigners to help build the state and to develop its economy and trade, and the rulers proved highly tolerant of diverse Catholic, Orthodox, and Jewish populations.[1] Gediminas's son Algirdas assumed the title of Great Prince. Algirdas's son Jogaila sought alliances against the growing threat from the German Teutonic Order in the Baltic region.

The Lithuanian-Polish union originated in 1385 when Jogaila (Jagiełło in Polish), the Grand Duke of Lithuania, married Poland's Queen Jadwiga and was crowned King of Poland. In 1410, a joint Polish-Lithuanian army decisively defeated the Teutonic knights at the battle of Grunwald (Tanenberg); subsequently the German threat to the Union subsided. The Lithuanian-Polish Union brought with it the Christianization of the Lithuanian population and the gradual Polonization of the Lithuanian nobility. But it also brought Lithuania within the influence of dynamic West European traditions. In 1569 the bi-state Union was officially transformed into a Commonwealth in which nobles elected a joint sovereign, although separate administrations, laws, and armies were maintained. Polish became the official language of the new state, and Poles increasingly considered Lithuania to be merely a region of the Polish Commonwealth. The 1569 Union of Lublin further tightened links between the two entities and effectively increased Polish domination.

The Lithuanian-Polish Commonwealth was destroyed in the late eighteenth century with the partition of the state by neighboring Russia, Prussia, and Austria. The Lithuanian territories gained by Russia were initially divided into two administrative units—the provinces of Vilnius and Slonim—then merged into one Lithuanian province, and subsequently were re-divided into three—Vilnius, Kaunas, and Grodno. The province of Suwalki with a Lithuanian majority was attached to the Duchy of Warsaw, while a large Lithuanian population inhabited the northern part of German-controlled East Prussia, along the Baltic Sea.

Lithuanian national consciousness developed during the Tsarist Russian occupation in the nineteenth century. Many young activists and student societies were inspired by the founding of the independent newspaper *Aušra* (Dawn) in March 1883. Its editor, Jonas Basanavičius, endeavored to reinvigorate the Lithuanian language, culture, and educational system. Lithuanians participated in the 1830–1831and the 1863 Polish uprisings against Russian rule. St. Petersburg subsequently decided to drive a wedge between the two peoples through various economic and cultural enticements to the Lithuanians. The Lithuanian cultural and national revival was subsequently thwarted by Russian censorship and repression and a growing wave of Russification, whereby the local government and educational systems were remodeled on the Russian pattern. Not surprisingly, *Aušra's* successor, *Varpas* (The Bell), adopted a more combative stance against Russia's autocratic authorities, during the early 1900s.

The abolition of serfdom in 1861 provided a further impetus to the Lithuanian renaissance as peasants acquired land and emancipated themselves from their Polish and Russian landlords. They provided a solid base for future calls for the restoration of national independence. Lithuania's national movement, consisting of prominent intellectuals, professionals, and cultural figures, established its base in Vilnius, the ancient capital of the Grand Duchy of Lithuania. They helped to develop a thriving press and literature, and gained increasing influence among the public.

During and after the Russian Revolution of 1905, Lithuanian political groups also became more active. The Vilnius Diet of November 1905 assembled representatives of all social groups and issued demands for an autonomous Lithuania within its ethnic boundaries together with a democratically elected parliament in Vilnius. Indeed, Lithuania became the first captive nation to demand autonomy from Moscow. The nationalist movement became evident in the emergence of numerous educational, scientific, literary, and artistic societies, as well as the creation of Lithuanian schools, businesses, and agricultural cooperatives. Political parties were generally divided into two blocs: the "conservatives" and the "radicals." Although both movements wanted to re-establish an independent Lithuanian state, the latter also sought to introduce far-reaching social and economic reforms.

Lithuania did not formally participate in World War I, but its servicemen fought on several fronts for different armies. German troops pushed Russian forces out of Lithuania in the spring of 1915 and captured Vilnius on 19 September 1915. The collapse of the Tsarist regime in Russia during the March 1917 Revolution afforded a unique opportunity for Lithuanian self-assertion. A Lithuanian National Council was formed, and on 9 June 1917 it convened a Lithuanian *Seimas* (Congress), but its activities were disrupted by the civil war throughout the Russian Empire. Lithuanian activists gathered for a major national conference from 18 to 22 September 1917 and elected a twenty-member Council of Lithuania (*Lietuvos Taryba*) that was empowered to act as the executive authority of the Lithuanian people. Antanas Smetona became the Council's chairman.

Even though the Council possessed no real administrative powers, because the country was occupied by Germany, on 16 February 1918 the Council proclaimed the restoration of Lithuania's independence. Augustinas Voldemaras was selected to be Prime Minister, a Cabinet of Ministers was elected, and the Council itself adopted a provisional constitution in which it would now function as the country's legislature. This arrangement remained in force until the convocation of the Constituent Assembly in May 1920.

The Bolshevik regime in Russia opposed the loss of any Tsarist territories and mounted a military campaign to regain control of the Baltic provinces. On 13 November 1918, Lenin annulled the Treaty of Brest-Litovsk, whereby Russia had surrendered its claims to Lithuania as part of a peace treaty with Germany. On 16 December 1918, Russia sought to re-annex Lithuania by establishing a Lithuanian Communist regime on captured Lithuanian territory and declaring a Lithuanian Soviet Republic. This republic was subsequently merged with the neighboring Belarusian Soviet Republic to form a single Soviet republic called "Litbel." The legitimate Lithuanian authorities responded by ordering the creation of a Lithuanian army. When Bolshevik forces occupied Vilnius on 5 January 1919, the Lithuanian government relocated to Kaunas.

The embryonic Lithuanian army pushed Red Army forces out of the country while the Bolsheviks were preoccupied with their war with Poland. On 19 April 1920, Polish forces entered and occupied Vilnius and claimed the city as their national heritage. A military conflict with Poland ensued in which the Lithuanians in effect lost Vilnius in October 1920, in addition to a third of their ethnic territories. Kaunas became the country's "provisional" capital. Virtually all diplomatic, economic, and cultural ties with Poland were ruptured throughout the entire inter-war period. However, Lithuania was able to gain control over the port of Klaipėda from Germany; this became the country's chief outlet to the Baltic Sea.

On 4 April 1919, Antanas Smetona became Lithuania's first president, and between 1920 and 1923 the institutional foundations for a democratic state were established. The major political divide in inter-war Lithuania was between Christian Democrats and Populists. It centered on such issues as the "ethnic purity" of the new state and the position of the Catholic Church in state affairs and in the educational system. The Christian Democrats favored a pronounced clerical role in the Lithuanian government, while the Populists opposed Church interference.

In response to intensifying political conflicts between leftist and rightist factions, and amid fears by conservative leaders over the perceived threat to national independence, a coup d'état was staged on 17 December 1926. It was led by military and political leaders who promptly dissolved the parliament and introduced martial law. The coup leaders selected Antanas Smetona as the new head of state. After a new, compliant legislature was installed, Smetona was elected President with invigorated executive powers, and Augustinas Voldemaras became Lithuania's Prime Minister.

Lithuania's presidential republic lasted until World War II. Although it was authoritarian and restrictive, the regime was not fascistic and did not engage in mass repression. It opposed the restoration of a strong parliamentary system, arguing that this simply fostered weak coalition governments and left the country vulnerable to unrest, instability, and foreign interference. Special regulations were introduced granting wide-ranging powers to military commandants and curtailing a range of civil liberties. A new constitution was promulgated in May 1928, which institutionalized strong presidential powers. The President could dissolve the government, appoint officials, and promulgate laws, and he also served as commander in chief of the armed forces. However, the authoritarian government was largely secular and came into conflict with the conservative Catholic Church, which consistently criticized presidential rule.

With the signing of the Molotov-Ribbentrop Pact on 23 August 1939, Nazi Germany and the Soviet Union conspired to divide up Eastern Europe into respective "spheres of influence." According to their "non-aggression pact," Lithuania was to fall into the German zone. However, shortly after the outbreak of World War II, in September 1939, Lithuania was transferred to the Soviet sphere in return for additional Polish territories that reverted to Germany. Despite Stalin's promises to respect Lithuanian neutrality during the war, the country was cajoled into granting access to Soviet military units.

Following an ultimatum to replace the government with a more compliant, pro-Moscow regime, Soviet troops occupied Lithuania on 15 June 1940. President Smetona fled the country, and a puppet regime was established that voted to incorporate Lithuania into the USSR on 3 August 1940.[2]

As German armies invaded the Soviet Union in June 1940, Lithuania fell under Nazi control. A new puppet administration was established and independence was again thwarted. German units with some Lithuanian collaborators murdered over 80% of the country's Jewish population, or about 140,000 people. Many Lithuanian ethnics were recruited into German armies or made to perform forced labor for the Third Reich economy.

With the defeat of Germany at the close of World War II, in late 1944, Soviet forces reoccupied the country and reinstalled a compliant communist regime that declared Lithuania a constituent republic of the USSR. The political opposition was outlawed, imprisoned, exiled, or eliminated, and fraudulent elections were held in the country under close Soviet supervision. Armed resistance by Lithuanian partisans organized in the Lithuanian Freedom Army continued until 1953. Over 30,000 guerrillas perished. In addition, Stalin's special forces deported, in the aftermath of World War II, over 175,000 Lithuanians to slave labor camps and prisons inside the Soviet Union. Unlike in Latvia or Estonia, there were no major party purges, as Lithuania's communist leader, Antanas Sniečkus, was a strong, autocratic figure who maintained the confidence of Stalin. After Stalin's death in 1953, a partial thaw was visible in Lithuania as Soviet authorities allowed a limited cultural revival. But any overt opposition to communist rule or Soviet overlordship was not tolerated, and offenders were persecuted and imprisoned.

Throughout the 1970s, dissent in Lithuania was manifested through a number of underground publications including the widely circulated *Chronicles of the Catholic Church in Lithuania.* Soviet authorities were unable to stamp out the publication or arrest all of its activists. A civil rights movement, the Lithuanian Helsinki Watch Group, was established in 1976. It protested against Moscow's persistent violations of the Soviet constitution and the UN Declaration on Human Rights, and spoke out for individual and group rights. In 1980 the Committee for the Defense of the Rights of Catholics was established. Several groups calling for outright national independence were also active, including the Lithuanian Freedom League (LFL) *(Lietuvos Laisvės Lyga, LLL).* A certain degree of coordination and cooperation was also visible between dissident groups in the three Baltic republics, especially in the commemoration of important national anniversaries such as the signing of the Molotov-Ribbentrop Pact.

Lithuanian activists were at the forefront of the campaign for systemic reform after the accession of Mikhail Gorbachev to the Communist Party leadership in Moscow. On 3 June 1988, intellectuals in Vilnius organized the Lithuanian Movement for Perestroika (LMP) *(Lietuvos Persitvarkymo Sąjūdis, LPS),* popularly known as *Sąjūdis* (Movement). It initially focused attention primarily on environmental issues, including calls to halt the building of a fourth reactor at the Ignalina nuclear power plant, and to protect the Lithuanian language and culture. Public support for the movement rapidly grew. In addition to intellectuals and anti-Soviet dissidents, *Sajūdis* included a number of reform communists such as Kazimiera Prunskienė and Romualdas Ozolas.[3]

Other independent organizations were created at this time, with several becoming increasingly outspoken on the question of national independence. For example, the Lithuanian Freedom League (LFL), created clandestinely in 1978, demanded outright statehood for the country and the restoration of its pre-Soviet status. *Sajūdis* and other independent groupings sponsored mass rallies and demonstrations throughout 1988 and 1989 and mobilized hundreds of thousands of citizens.

To avoid being completely overtaken by events, reformist elements gained control within the Lithuanian Communist Party (LCP) and installed Algirdas Brazauskas as the new First Secretary, to replace the dogmatist Ringaudas Songaila. As controls from Moscow weakened and the Lithuanian independence movement gained prominence and influence, the Lithuanian Communist Party formally separated from its Soviet counterpart. In December 1989, Brazauskas and over 80% of the LCP membership established a separate Lithuanian Communist Party and opened the path for a multiparty system in the country. Vilnius also implemented various *Sajūdis* proposals, including the reinstatement of Lithuanian as the national language, allowing the Catholic Church to function freely, and giving Vilnius control over the Lithuanian economy. But despite these measures, *Sajūdis* candidates won a majority of seats in elections to the All-Union Congress of People's Deputies in March 1989.

POST-COMMUNIST DEVELOPMENTS

The Communist era effectively expired in Lithuania during 1990–1991. In elections on 24 February 1990, and in runoffs on 4 and 10 March 1990, *Sajūdis* won 80% of the seats in the new Lithuanian Supreme Council. Communist reformers were effectively sidelined by *Sajūdis*, which was now at the height of its power and popularity. The movement promptly elected Vytautas Landsbergis, the Chairman of *Sajūdis*, as chairman of the Council—in essence, chief of state. Kazimiera Prunskienė was chosen as Prime Minister.

Under Landsbergis's leadership, on 11 March 1990 the newly elected government declared the restoration of Lithuania's statehood as it had existed under the 1938 constitution. Like Estonia and Latvia, Lithuania ignored as irrelevant the provisions of the Soviet constitution for republican secession, arguing that acceptance would have legitimized fifty years of Soviet occupation. Vilnius's move toward independence sparked a chain of events that eventually led to the dissolution of the Soviet Union.

In reaction to Vilnius's declaration, Moscow declared the move illegal and responded with a variety of repressive measures. From April until June 1990, an economic blockade was imposed on Lithuania; in response, on 23 June 1990, Vilnius agreed to embargo its implementation of independence. A violent attack on Lithuanian television headquarters by KGB units and Soviet troops on 12 January 1991 claimed the lives of 14 unarmed protestors. However, because of indecision, confusion, and growing international criticism, Gorbachev did not order a full-scale attack on the Lithuanian government. In addition, Moscow no longer possessed a loyal or effective party network in Lithuania that it could easily mobilize. On 13 January 1991, the *Sajūdis*-controlled legislature selected Gediminas Vagnorius as Prime Minister. Attempts by Moscow to coerce Vilnius into submission through provocative actions failed to achieve their target. Following the failed August 1991 putsch by hard-liners in Moscow, Lithuania reinstated its independence proclamation, and the country was finally recognized as an independent state.

The Lithuanian leadership proceeded to establish the foundations of a pluralistic democracy. For example, a law on political parties passed on 25 September 1991 enabled Lithuanians to establish parties if they gathered at least 400 signatures and possessed a party program; parties with a foreign affiliation were declared illegal. Meanwhile, *Sajūdis* fractured into a number of factions and proved unable to reach political consensus at a time of major economic hardship for the populace, when Lithuania's traditional market with the former USSR was disrupted. In May 1992, a referendum was held to create a new constitution and to strengthen the powers of the presidency. Out of 57.5% of participating voters, 70% came out in favor of the constitution, but the referendum failed because it did not win the required support of an absolute majority of eligible voters. On 14 July 1992, premier Vagnorius resigned and was replaced by Aleksandras Abišala; he in turn was replaced by Bronislovas Lubys on 2 December 1992.

The country's electoral law was passed by the Supreme Council in the summer of 1992. The law established a mixed majoritarian-proportional system of national elections: 71 members of the *Seimas* were to be elected directly, in single-mandate electoral districts, and 70 parliamentary seats were to be filled on a proportional basis. All parties needed 4% of the vote to gain parliamentary seats, except parties representing ethnic minorities. In June 1996, the electoral law was changed. All parties were to take part in a distribution of seats under a proportional system if they received 5% of the vote. Moreover, electoral coalitions needed to receive 7% of the vote. Results in single-mandate electoral districts were lawful if no less than 40% of all eligible voters took part in the elections.[4]

In Lithuania's first post-Soviet parliamentary elections, held on 25 October 1992 and 9 November 1992, 75.2% of the electorate participated. Seventeen parties competed for seats, and the ex-communist Lithuanian Democratic Labor Party (LDLP) gained an overwhelming victory, with 73 out of 141 seats, followed by the *Sąjūdis* coalition with 30, the Christian Democrats with 18, and the Social Democrats with 8. The remainder of the seats were dispersed among smaller parties and non-party candidates. As an ethnic party, requiring 2% of the vote for parliamentary representation, the Union of Poles received four seats in the legislature. No Russian minority parties gained any deputies; it appeared that the Russian population largely voted for the LDLP.[5]

The ex-communists were successful partly because of the fragmentation of *Sąjūdis* and the movement's inability or unwillingness to create a national party structure, and partly because of harsh economic conditions and a steep decline in living standards that were attributed to the incumbent government. The LDLP possessed a well-organized party structure and sufficient funds to run an effective election campaign.[6] It was successful across the country, but especially so in rural areas and the southeast region, where large Russian and Polish minorities live.

On 2 October 1992, a referendum on a new Lithuanian constitution was approved by 85% of those voting, but with a turnout of only 53%. The document formally established a parliamentary democracy with a unicameral legislature, and a presidency with enhanced powers especially in the international affairs arena. The constitution granted the President the veto right and the prerogative to appoint and dismiss many of the highest state officials such as the State Controller, the chairman of the Bank of Lithuania, the chief of the armed forces, the head of the Security Service, and high court judges. The highest authority of the executive power was the government. The Prime Minister was appointed or dismissed by the President, with the approval of the *Seimas*. Ministers were appointed by the President following the nomination by the Prime Minister.

The highest legislative power in Lithuania was the *Seimas*. Besides its legislative work, the *Seimas* called presidential elections, approved or rejected the candidacy of the Prime Minister, ministers, and judges of the Constitutional and Supreme Court, and reviewed the government program and the state budget.[7] Local governments, a fundamental component of the territorial division of power, were elected for three years. The main power was concentrated in the hands of the local mayor, who was a local "president," head of government, and head of parliament.[8] The President was directly elected by citizens for a five-year term (with a limit of two consecutive terms) on the basis of universal, equal, and direct suffrage and by secret ballot.[9] For the period of his or her presidency, the person has to forgo any party membership.

In the first direct presidential elections, on 14 February 1993, the LDLP leader Brazauskas won 60% of the vote, while his *Sąjūdis*-sponsored rival Stasys Lozoraitis only gained 40%; the turnout reached 78.6%. On 26 February 1993, Adolfas Šleževičius replaced Bronislovas Lubys as Prime Minister. The retiring head of state, President Landsbergis, calculating that his popularity had waned in the country, did not compete in the presidential elections and subsequently formed his own party, the Conservative Party. Following allegations of corruption and insider trading on government contracts, Šleževičius was replaced on 8 February 1996 by Mindaugas Stankevičius.[10]

Throughout the 1990s, Lithuania experienced political fluctuations between center-right and center-left governments but successfully avoided extremist policies. Indeed, both the post-communists and the post-dissidents have been committed to political pluralism, market reform, and full integration into the major trans-Atlantic institutions. As Lithuania's economic difficulties persisted in the wake of the October–November 1996 elections, voters grew disenchanted with the leftist government, and the administration lost a vote of no-confidence in the summer of 1996. The swing to the right was first reflected in the municipal elections in the spring of 1995, when the rightist parties garnered more than half of the total seats. The Homeland Union gained 29.1% of the vote, the Christian Democrats 16.9%, and the Labor Party 19.9%.

This trend continued during the parliamentary elections on 20 October 1996, when the Homeland Union was returned to power with a convincing majority. The Union obtained 70 seats; the Christian Democrats, 16 seats; the Democratic Labor Party, 12 seats; the Center Union, 13 seats; and the Social Democratic Party, 12 seats. Only five parties gained enough mandates to form parliamentary factions (a faction needed at least three deputies). These were the Conservatives, the Christian Democrats, the Social Democrats, the Center Party, and the Labor Democrats.

LDLP support plummeted in the parliamentary ballot from 43% in 1992 to about 11% in 1996. The party lost much of its vote because of persistent reports about corruption and financial scandals associated with the party leadership. The party also bore the brunt of frustration with declining economic conditions. In accordance with the proportional electoral system, only five parties gained the 5% threshold, which allowed them to be represented in the parliament. Eight other parties obtained one to three representatives elected through single-mandate ratings. The voter turnout was 53% in the first round, compared to 75% in the first round of the 1992 parliamentary elections. Some observers noted a disquieting trend of voter apathy or disenchantment with the country's political leaders because of economic decline and perceptions of rampant corruption.[11] Several former *Sajūdis* officials resumed duties in the newly formed rightist government. Gediminas Vagnorius became the new Prime Minister, and Landsbergis, the new *Seimas* chairman.

On 4 January 1998, Valdas Adamkus narrowly defeated Artūras Paulauskas in the runoff for the Lithuanian presidency: 1,921,806 votes were cast, of which Adamkus received 50.37% and Paulauskas 49.6%. Only 14,000 votes separated the two candidates. The former head of state and chairman of the Supreme Council Landsbergis was eliminated in the first round of the ballot. Paulauskas subsequently announced that he would establish a center-left political party. Meanwhile, President Adamkus signed a decree asking parliament for a vote to keep Prime Minister Gediminas Vagnorius in office. Under the Lithuanian constitution, a newly elected President possessed the right to ask the legislature whether it had confidence in the head of government. Lawmakers on 10 March 1998 voted by 92 to 19 with nine abstentions to keep Vagnorius in office. The premier asserted that the main objective of his administration was entry to the European Union (EU) and the launching of an administrative reform program. A streamlined cabinet was then installed.

On 30 April 1999, Prime Minister Vagnorius announced his resignation, largely because of ongoing conflicts between the government and the President. On 11 May 1999, President Adamkus nominated Vilnius Mayor Rolandas Paksas, a member of the ruling Conservative Party, for Prime Minister. The parliament on 18 May 1999 voted by 105 to 1, with 12 abstentions, to confirm Paksas as premier. Paksas told deputies that he would continue with the tight fiscal policy of his predecessor, noting that stable economic growth would be the cabinet's main task. Of the 14 new cabinet ministers, seven were from the previous government, including the ministers of foreign affairs and defense, who were Christian Democrats. On 10 June 1999, parliament approved the new government by 80 to 18 votes, with 22 abstentions. Broad support came from the former ruling coalition of Conservatives and Christian Democrats, while the Centrists abstained. The leftist opposition mainly voted against the new government.

At the end of October 1999, President Adamkus called for early parliamentary elections after accepting the resignation of Prime Minister Rolandas Paksas, who had refused to sign a business contract with the American Williams corporation that Adamkus had favored. Adamkus feared continuing political instability and fragmentation. On 29 October 1999, Adamkus named first deputy parliamentary speaker Andrius Kubilius as Prime Minister after acting premier Irena Degutienė declined to take over the premiership on a permanent basis. Kubilius was initially elected to the parliament in 1992, and he became first deputy speaker when the Conservative Party won the majority of seats in 1996. By a vote of 82 to 20, with 18 abstentions, the parliament approved Kubilius as Prime Minister. He became Lithuania's tenth premier since the restoration of national independence.

New parliamentary elections were held on 8 October 2000. For the first time since Lithuania gained its independence, the elections failed to return a majority party. The Algirdas Brazauskas Social Democratic Coalition received a plurality of the vote, and gained 51 seats in the 141-seat *Seimas*. The coalition consisted of the socialist Lithuanian Democratic Labor Party (LDLP), the Lithuanian Social Democratic Party (LSDP), the New Democratic Party (NDP), and the ethnic minority party, the Union of Russians in Lithuania (URL).

Although the Social Democratic Coalition won a plurality of votes, President Adamkus ignored this fact and instead looked to the New Policy bloc to form the government. New Policy, an informal alliance of parties ranging from center-left to center-right, was comprised of the social-liberal New Union–

Social Liberals (NU-SL), the liberal Lithuanian Liberal Union (LLU), the liberal Center Union of Lithuania (CUL), and the Modern Christian-Democratic Union (MCDU). The NU-SL and the LLU finished behind the Social Democratic Coalition in the voting, receiving 28 and 33 seats respectively. The New Policy bloc was able to form a government and a legislative majority with its 66 seats and the support of two other parties, the Lithuanian Peasants' Party (LPP) and the Lithuanian Poles' Electoral Action (LPEA).

The leader of the Liberal Union, Rolandas Paksas, became the country's new Prime Minister, and the New Alliance leader Artūras Paulauskas was selected as parliamentary speaker. As with previous governments, the new coalition expressed its adherence to Lithuania's main foreign policy priorities: NATO and EU membership.

Out of the three Baltic states, Lithuania was the first to shake off Soviet rule; but it was also the first country in Eastern Europe to vote the former communists, who had turned into social democrats, back into power. Lithuania successfully established and consolidated its democratic institutions, slowly developed its civil society, but generally lagged behind Latvia and Estonia in the creation of a prosperous market economy. Political parties and other characteristics of a democratic system functioned and evolved throughout the decade.

The three Baltic states—Lithuania, Latvia, and Estonia—often have been viewed as a natural grouping. However, this appearance has been largely externally created rather than being the result of a shared recent history. Although Lithuanians are Balts and their language is closely related to Latvian, the history of the Lithuanian people for the past six hundred to seven hundred years has differed greatly from that of Latvia and Estonia, in important respects. The Lithuanians were the only Baltic nation that could claim a historic state before the immediate post–World War I era, when all three Baltic countries gained their independence from Russia. The Lithuanian Kingdom, and subsequently, the Commonwealth of Poland and Lithuania, were vast and powerful entities that remained intact until partition in the late eighteenth century. While the ancestors of today's Latvians and the Estonians were being alternately ruled by Swedes, Germans, and Russians, the Lithuanians, especially the nobility, were integrated into Polish culture.

The repercussions of Estonian and Latvian interactions with northern European groups, and the experiences of both nations with Russia, differed significantly from those of the Lithuanians and the Central European Poles. The northern Europeans brought Protestantism, industrialization, trade, immigrants, and settlers to Latvia and Estonia, while the Poles reinforced Lithuania's ardent Catholicism and its feudal agricultural system. As a result of these historical circumstances, over the centuries Lithuania remained much more agriculture-based than the other two Baltic countries, as well as more ethnically homogeneous.

The high percentage of the resident population that remained ethnically Lithuanian set the country apart from both Latvia and Estonia. Ethnic Latvians and Estonians comprised smaller majorities of their respective countries' populations, and this created numerous disputes in the arenas of citizenship, relations with Russia, and the democratic process. Lithuania, being over 80% ethnically Lithuanian, largely escaped these problems. It could afford the luxury of passing the most liberal citizenship law without fear of an indigenous nationalist backlash. Lithuania's election laws also ensured that the larger ethnic minorities, especially the Poles, obtained parliamentary representation. Furthermore, the country's language law stipulated that if more than a third of a locality consisted of non–Lithuanian-speakers, then public institutions had to conduct their affairs in the language of the minority population. This helped to assuage any fear and resentment of Lithuanian independence.

Lithuania's citizenship law, adopted on 3 November 1989, provided automatic citizenship, within a two-year period, to all who were living and working in the country on a continual basis at the time of independence from the Soviet Union: this was called the "zero option." The law helped to counter the fears of disenfranchisement among the two largest minorities: Russians (8.4% of the population) and Poles (7%). Former communist activists among the minorities, at the urging of Moscow, had established an anti-independence movement known as *Edinstvo* (Unity), or the International Front Movement, but it failed to gain any significant public support.

Some Lithuanian ultra-nationalist groups sought to restrict the number of minority residents eligible for citizenship, but the authorities opposed holding a referendum on the question, fearing that it would unnecessarily provoke inter-ethnic antagonisms and could provide Moscow with a pretext for intervention. As a consequence of their participation in the democratic political system, the minorities themselves were much more likely to support the former communists or other leftist parties in national and local elections. This was largely due to fears that the centrist and rightist forces were more nationalistic and potentially chauvinistic. Such factors, coupled with deteriorating living standards at the time of the 1990 and 1992 legislative elections, largely explained the LDLP's return to power in 1992. However, unlike Estonia and Latvia, Lithuania possessed no significant non-citizen population and could focus more attention on ideological rather than ethnic issues.[12]

Religion figured as another arena of difference between Lithuania and its two Baltic neighbors. The relationships between Lithuanians and the Catholic Church and between the Lithuanian state and the Catholic Church leadership have left important legacies. Since its conversion to Catholicism in the fourteenth century, as the last European country to undergo this process, Lithuania has been fiercely loyal to the Catholic Church. Lithuanians resisted Russian attempts to convert them to Orthodoxy and later Soviet attempts to extinguish religion altogether, as well as the sustained campaign to eradicate the social, political, and economic prominence of the Church in Lithuania.

It was not surprising that Catholicism played a central role in Lithuania's fight for independence from the Soviet Union, and subsequently assumed an important role in many areas of public and private life. Nevertheless, Church-state relations have also been a source of dispute in the country, probably more so than in the other Baltic states, between secularists and parties with clerical connections seeking to inject the Church's social program into government policy. The precise role of the Catholic Church has not been well defined, and a number of pro-Western groups in Lithuanian society remain wary of the Church exerting too much influence over the state, its institutions, and its policies.

As in other formerly centralized post-communist states, relations between central and local governments have become a source of debate and even conflict in Lithuania.[13] The territorial reorganization plan adopted by parliament on 19 July 1994 established 56 local governments at the lowest tier and ten regional governing bodies. Although in theory the local authorities were to gain more independence, in practice the central government appropriated greater powers by appointing governors and taking away several decision-making responsibilities from the municipalities. Issues of central-regional relations will evidently remain a source of friction and rivalry for the foreseeable future.

Other problematic issues facing the country included the nature and the scope of the Lithuanian welfare state. Most parties, except for a few small liberal parties in the center, favored the continuation or even the expansion of the welfare state. Whether the creation of a West European type of welfare system could be financially viable remained debatable. Parliamentary disputes often focused on what aspects of the state system were compatible with the development of democratic pluralism and a productive market economy, and how all sectors of the public could be shielded from pauperization.

In the international realm, Lithuania shared with Latvia and Estonia a strong desire for integration into such organizations as the EU, the WTO, NATO, and the OECD. Lithuania, more than Latvia or Estonia, also endeavored to maintain a relatively cordial relationship with Russia and the other CIS (Commonwealth of Independent States) member countries. This approach was favored by the fact that the Russian minority population was not perceived as threatening to Lithuanian independence or the country's political stability.

Nonetheless, several problem areas with Moscow remained. Besides disagreement over some border demarcations, the area of Kaliningrad, which remained a Russian outpost on the Baltic Sea, presented Lithuania with a unique problem in its relations with Moscow. Kaliningrad could only be accessed over land across Lithuania or Poland, and throughout the Soviet era, transport between Kaliningrad and the rest of Russia was by train through southern Lithuania. Since Lithuania's independence, the Russian Federation's transportation system through Lithuania has been a particularly contentious issue because of the strong Russian military presence in Kaliningrad.

The Lithuanian government ideally wanted to see a demilitarized Kaliningrad, and it supported a decrease in armaments and military forces in the enclave. Vilnius also wanted to circumscribe or control transit across its territory to Kaliningrad. Some Lithuanian activists wanted Kaliningrad to become a fourth independent Baltic republic that would have some opportunity for economic development and European integration. This would also remove the possibility of a future Russian government using the territory to apply pressure on any of the Baltic states. Moscow viewed proposals for Kaliningrad's independence as a provocation and a threat to Russia's territorial integrity. Clearly, problems related to Kaliningrad were unlikely to be resolved for the foreseeable future.[14]

In the mid-1990s, Lithuania's main trading partners were still Russia and other former Soviet republics. Nevertheless, Vilnius's objective was to diversify its trading relations and to develop stronger links with the European Union in preparation for future integration. Lithuania's currency, the *litas*, remained weak due to inflation, a serious bank crisis, and a sluggish economy. A national banking crisis affected all three Baltic states early in 1995. The crisis, which depleted the deposits of many average citizens in Lithuania, forced Prime Minister Šleževičius to resign and his government to fall in a vote of no confidence. Since that time, regulation of the banking sector has improved, as has the country's experience with Western banking methods.

Within the Baltic region, Lithuania has developed close ties with both Latvia and Estonia, through such mechanisms as the Baltic Free Trade Zone and the Baltic Assembly, although some vexing border demarcation questions have posed some problems between Latvia and Lithuania. Recently discovered offshore oil reserves have been claimed by both countries, and there has been an ongoing dispute over the issue. Unfortunately, although negotiations have been almost constant, Latvia initiated preparations with a major oil company to begin drilling without Vilnius's approval. All levels of government in both countries have been involved in trying to find a mutually agreeable solution to a problem that neither country would like to see compromise their overall positive relationship.

Lithuania has not been as successful as Estonia or Latvia in making a rapid transition to a market-based economy. Because of its slower pace of reform, however, the social dislocations experienced in other countries are less pronounced in Lithuania. Unfortunately, the benefits gained from more rapid reform have also been less evident. Lithuania's trade, industry, technology, and agricultural sectors required modernization if the country was to further integrate with Western and Central Europe. Modernization and a further deepening of relationships with both Europe and the CIS would make Lithuania stand out as a genuine economic and social "crossroads" between the West and the East—a position that could help improve political and economic conditions in the country. In order to position itself more firmly for EU and NATO integration, Lithuania developed cordial ties with Poland, seeing the country as a gateway to "the West." Warsaw in turn became the chief proponent of Lithuania's inclusion in NATO, viewing such a prospect as helping to secure and stabilize Poland's eastern borders.

POLITICAL PARTIES

Socialists and Social Democrats

Lithuanian Democratic Labor Party (LDLP)
Lietuvos Demokratinė Darbo Partija (LDDP)

The Lithuanian Democratic Labor Party (LDLP) was established on 19 December 1990 as a reformist and pro-independence successor to the Lithuanian Communist Party (LCP). LDLP membership was estimated at about 8,000 in the mid-1990s. The party's chairmen during the 1990s included Adolfas Šleževičius and Česlovas Juršėnas. The LDLP was one of the most well-organized parties in Lithuania, with local branches operating throughout the country. President Algirdas Brazauskas was also a former chairman of the party, but as the country's President he could not hold a party post or be active in party affairs. The LDLP held power between 1992 and 1996, after an overwhelming victory in the October 1992 election. In fact, the LDLP was the first former Communist Party to return to power in Eastern Europe after the collapse of the communist systems.

Unlike the communist parties in Estonia and Lithuania, the Lithuanian Communist Party (LCP) was largely composed of ethnic Lithuanians and therefore could more closely associate itself with national issues. As a result, as political groups within Lithuania became more radicalized, the LCP was pushed into adopting more fervent pro-independence positions. The party broke from the All-Union Communist Party of the Soviet Union (CPSU) in late 1989—the first republican formation in the Soviet Union to do so. During the following year, many within the party viewed the LCP as a counterbalance to the more nationalist forces or factions within *Sajūdis* and other smaller parties, claiming that they were intent on steering the country toward democracy as well as statehood.

Late in 1990, the party changed its name to the Lithuanian Democratic Labor Party to better reflect the severance of its ties with the communist past, and its desire to become a more mainstream social democratic party. In addition, chairman Brazauskas transferred all the resources of the former CPSU to the LDLP, thus transforming it into one of the largest and best-organized political parties in the Baltic region.

According to its own documents, the LDLP was a parliamentary, social democratic political party that purportedly grounded its activities on the principles of the Socialist International, although it was not a member of the organization. The party focused on the "consistent construction" of a democratic Lithuanian state, maintaining the principles of "common human values."[15] During the late 1990s, there was growing speculation that the LDLP might split, creating a more leftist organization and leaving others to join the Social Democrats or one of the other center-left parties. Until that time, however, the LDLP had to adjust to its decreased role in the *Seimas*. In party documents from the period immediately following the October–November 1996 elections, when the LDLP was voted out of power, party leaders voiced their desire to become a strong and constructive opposition.

After losing the 1996 elections, the party focused its platform on economic growth through privatization, an open economy, and increased exports. The LDLP was in favor of agricultural subsidies, while claiming that small and medium-sized businesses should be under cooperative ownership. The party wanted Lithuania to take a "middle position" between Russia and the West but was supportive of the country's membership in NATO and the European Union.[16] In the October 2000 general elections, the LDLP formed a broader Social Democratic coalition led by Brazauskas. Although the elections demonstrated a swing to the left among voters, the coalition only gained a total of 51 parliamentary seats—short of the 71 needed to obtain a legislative majority. The LDLP and its smaller partners became the major opposition party after the Liberal Union assembled its centrist coalition government.

Lithuanian Social Democratic Party (LSDP)
Lietuvos Socialdemokratų Partija (LSDP)

The Lithuanian Social Democratic Party (LSDP) was originally established in 1896 and restored on 17 January 1990. It claimed a membership of some 1,500 people and was chaired by Aloyzas Sakalas until 1999, when Vytenis Andriukaitis took over. The LSDP resembled social democratic parties in other former communist states and in the West European countries that had not been tainted by a communist association. It waged a constant struggle for survival against the LDLP. Many members of both organizations wanted the two parties to merge at some future point. The LSDP leadership made it clear, however, that it wanted the two organizations to remain separate for the foreseeable future. This was evident in the vote of no confidence in the LDLP government lodged by the LSDP in 1994.

The LSDP was more centrist than the LDLP and the Lithuanian Socialist Party. It increased its representation in the *Seimas* from 8 to 12 deputies after the October–November 1996 elections. The party had been fairly open about its willingness to join with other center-left parties in the *Seimas*, but it won enough seats to enable it to have its own faction. On 18 December 1999, a moderate centrist wing of the party, led by deputy parliamentary speaker Rimantas Dagys, broke away to form the Social Democracy 2000 Party.

Several smaller socialist and social democratic parties were also established in Lithuania during the 1990s. They included the Lithuanian Party of the Economy (LPE) *(Lietuvos Ūkio Partija, LUP)*, chaired by Klemensas Šeputis and registered on 22 January 1996, which believed in the resurrection of a "welfare state" in Lithuania. The LPE remained a small party that considered Lithuania to be best served by the joint efforts of a spectrum of political parties in the *Seimas*.[17] The Lithuanian Socialist Party (LSP) *(Lietuvos Socialistų Partija, LSP)* was chaired by Albinas Visockas and registered on 11 September 1995.

Liberals

Homeland Union–Lithuanian Conservatives (HU-LC)
Tėvynės Sąjunga–Lietuvos Konservatoriai (TS-LK)

Homeland Union–Lithuanian Conservatives (HU-LC) was established on 1 May 1993 and was chaired by former *Sąjūdis* leader and Lithuanian President Vytautas Landsbergis. Its membership stood at about 16,000 people. It grew out of the more conservative wing of the Lithuanian reform movement and assumed a variety of names before settling on HU-LC in May 1993. Its crushing loss to the ex-communist LDLP in the October–November 1992 parliamentary elections surprised many observers, but it was widely believed that economic hardships were the driving force behind the public's desire to slow the rapid reforms initiated by this liberal nationalist party. The *Sąjūdis* coalition garnered only 20.52% of the national vote and mustered a mere 30 parliamentary seats.

Remaining as one of the strongest parties in Lithuania and possessing a nationwide grassroots structure, the HU-LC staged a resounding victory over the LDLP in the October–November 1996 *Seimas* elections, despite the lackluster 55% voter turnout.[18] The Homeland Union could be considered a classic "liberal conservative" party in its economic agenda, believing in strict monetary and fiscal policies. At various times, the party forged coalitions or alliances with the Christian Democratic Party, the Democratic Party, the Lithuanian National Union, and the Union of Political Prisoners and Deportees. It obtained associate membership in the European Democratic Union and sought full membership in that organization. In local elections in 1995, the HU-LC ran a very effective campaign and won almost 30% of the total votes cast; and most of the 36 mayors in Lithuania were members of the party.[19] For many citizens, living conditions had not improved as greatly as they had anticipated under the LDLP cabinet, so the opposition was voted back into power.

Before the October–November 1996 elections, the party ran a populist campaign with promises of public sector tax cuts, pay increases, and higher pensions. It became a strong advocate of crime-fighting and anti-corruption measures. The party also favored Lithuania joining the EU and NATO as soon as feasible, while at the same time claiming that it was acting as a guardian of the country's sovereignty.[20] The Homeland Union gained 70 seats in the fall 1996 parliamentary ballot, with nearly 30% of the popular vote, and thereby gained a majority in the *Seimas*.

A breakaway faction of the HU-LC, the Homeland People's Party, was formed on 18 December 1999 by parliamentarians Laima Andrikienė and Vidmantas Žiemelis. Both deputies were expelled by the Conservative Party for "acting against the Conservatives and the coalition government." In the October 2000 parliamentary elections, the Conservatives suffered a major reversal as the electorate swung toward the centrist and leftist parties. It obtained only nine parliamentary deputies through the system of partial proportional representation.

Independence Party (IP)
Nepriklausomybės Partija (NP)

Established on 19 November 1990 and originally called the March 11 Party, the Independence Party (IP) claimed a membership of some 400 people. It was chaired by Valentinas Sapalas. The IP gained a multi-ethnic base that included many former members of *Sajūdis*.[21] The party positioned itself slightly to the right of the CDU in the Lithuanian political spectrum. It ran with the Lithuanian National Union (LNU) in the October–November 1992 elections and won one seat in the *Seimas*. In the October–November 1996 ballot, the IP failed to win any seats in the parliament.

Lithuanian Liberal Union (LLU)
Lietuvos Liberalų Sąjunga (LLS)

The Lithuanian Liberal Union (LLU) was established on 11 March 1990 under its chairman Eugenijus Gentvilas, with an initial membership of under 1,000 people. The LLU was one of the few small centrist parties that supported a much smaller role for the state in the Lithuanian economy and in society at large. The LLU held that "respect for freedom of personal autonomy, a person's economic activity and private possessions, the right to live according to one's beliefs, initiative, expediency, and responsibility are the main ideas of liberalism."[22] Its members were generally younger and much more highly educated than those of many other parties.[23] The party won one seat in the fall 1996 *Seimas* elections.[24] It also won 2.69% of the vote in the 1995 local elections, giving the party 40 positions in local governments across the country.

The party continued to grow throughout the late 1990s. It stressed a dynamic pro-market approach to government policy and strongly favored Lithuania's European Union and NATO integration. On the eve of general elections in October 2000, the LLU was led by Rolandas Paksas, who benefited from considerable public popularity. The LLU gained 33 parliamentary seats with 17.3% of the popular vote and looked set to establish a new centrist coalition government with Paksas as the new Prime Minister. After the ballot, the LLU reaffirmed its commitment to work together with the New Union (NU); between them the two parties captured 61 legislative seats.

New Democracy–Women's Party (ND-WP)
Naujoji Demokratija–Moterų Partija (ND-MP)

Established on 20 April 1995, the New Democracy–Women's Party (ND-WP) was founded and led by former Prime Minister Kazimiera Prunskienė. The party was an outgrowth of the Lithuanian Women's Association, which was formed in 1992. It asserted a membership of some 1,000 people and sought to represent women and their views in the national legislature. The party was generally centrist and sought to incorporate the diverse views of women in Lithuanian society. The party narrowly missed entering parliament on its percentage of the total votes, but Prunskienė herself won a seat in the *Seimas* through the first round of first-past-the-post voting. The party proposed "to unite its members to participate in politics and to solve urgent community problems." Its purpose was to "develop women's self-expression, patriotism and responsibility for the Republic's affairs." The party endeavored to create conditions encouraging women's participation in politics and in the country's governance. The ND-WP cooperated in parliament with the Lithuanian Center Union (LCU), the Lithuanian Social Democratic Party (LSDP), and the Lithuanian Peasants' Party (LPP) to increase the position of its one *Seimas* representative, Prunskienė. In the parliamentary election of 20 October 1996, the LWP obtained only 3.6% of the vote and gained one *Seimas* seat.

Lithuanian Democratic Party (LDP)
Lietuvos Demokratų Partija (LDP)

The Lithuanian Democratic Party (LDP) was originally established in 1902 and restored on 29 December 1989. It claimed a membership of about 2,000 people and was chaired by Saulius Pečeliūnas. The LDP formed electoral coalitions with the Lithuanian Christian Democratic Party (LCDP) in the October–November 1992 parliamentary elections and during the 1995 local elections. The LDP established an electoral coalition with the National Union for the *Seimas* elections on 20 October 1996 and won three seats, one less than its former parliamentary representation. The LDP was politically and economically centrist and sought to develop Lithuania's civil society, its welfare state, and its national identity, and to make "intellectual culture" a priority. The LDP promoted the creation of a broad middle class in the country as a foundation of a democratic and capitalist system. On international issues, it believed that Lithuania's security interests were best served by entry into NATO, and the country's economic and political interests, by membership in the European Union. Additionally, it wanted to demilitarize Russia's Kaliningrad *oblast*, which borders Lithuania.[25]

Lithuanian Center Union (LCU)
Lietuvos Centro Sąjunga (LCS)

The Lithuanian Center Union (LCU) was founded on 27 October 1993, claimed a membership of about 1,000 people, and was chaired by Romualdas Ozolas. While the Center Union was not a particularly strong party by itself, it seemed to be one of the primary choices for a coalition partner for both moderate-left and moderate-right parties. The stated goal of the party before the October 1996 elections was to gain 5% of the vote, as the party was only represented by two deputies in the previous *Seimas*.[26] It actually gained 8.2% of the ballots, thus increasing the number of its parliamentary deputies to 13. Prior to the October 1996 general elections, the LCU agreed with the Lithuanian National Union (LNU) "to coordinate actions with the bloc of centrist forces."[27] The party believed that "as a means of political action and a structure for implementing policies, centrism manifested itself through the reconciliation and balance of societal interests, through peace, and through the stability of the state."[28] The LCU won just under 5% of the vote in the 1995 local elections, giving the party 74 seats overall in local government organs. It also performed poorly in the October 2000 parliamentary elections, although it was a coalition partner with the Liberal Union and the New Union, which together won a majority in parliament. The LCU obtained a mere 2.9% of the vote and was only able to claim two parliamentary seats.

New Union–Social Liberals (NU-SL)
Naujoji Sąjunga–Socialliberalai (NS-SL)

New Union–Social Liberals (NU-SL) was founded by former presidential candidate Artūras Paulauskas, and was seen by many observers and critics as essentially serving his personal interests. The party styled itself as a "social liberal" formation that sought better economic protection for all sectors of Lithuanian society. For example, the NU-SL initiated a petition in order to redirect funds from defense to education, although the party was staunchly pro-NATO and in favor of an increase in defense spending. Despite its critics, the NU-SL gained in stature throughout 2000 and looked poised to enter a new coalition government following the general elections in October, in which the party gained 28 parliamentary seats. Paulauskas was slated to be the next parliamentary chairman.

Among other minor liberal parties, it is useful to note the Lithuanian Party of Justice (LPJ) *(Lietuvos Teisingumo Partija, LTP)*, chaired by Bronius Simanavičius and established on 11 September 1995; the Lithuanian Party of Humanists (LPH) *(Lietuvos Humanistų Partija, LHP)*, chaired by Leopoldas Tarakevičius and registered on 1 June 1990; and the National Progressive Party (NPP) *(Tautos Pažangos Partija, TPP)*, chaired by Egidijus Klumbys and registered on 21 June 1994.

Christian Democrats

Lithuanian Christian Democratic Party (LCDP)
Lietuvos Krikščionių Demokratų Partija (LKDP)

The Lithuanian Christian Democratic Party (LCDP) was originally established in 1904 and restored on 22 March 1990. After the party was outlawed in 1941, following the Soviet annexation of Lithuania, the LCDP functioned in exile until its restoration. By 1995, it claimed a membership of some 8,500 people; this climbed to 10,000 by the close of the decade. It was chaired by Algirdas Saudargas. The LCDP was center-rightist, much like Christian democratic parties in other countries. In the early 1990s, the party coordinated many of its activities with the Independence Party and with the local Catholic Church.

The party was very religiously focused and believed that Lithuanian society should move towards transforming the country into a more Christian nation-state. Many priests openly supported the LCDP and urged their congregations to vote for the party. Despite the fact that the overwhelming majority of Lithuanians were Catholic and displayed a great deal of respect for the Church, LCDP policies aimed at making Lithuanian society more religious invariably failed to have the desired effect. In the October 1996 general elections, LCDP representation almost doubled in parliament from 9 to 16 deputies. The party became one of the five major parties in the *Seimas* that was able to form a party faction. It was the second highest vote recipient, although its 16 seats distantly trailed the 70 seats of the Conservatives. The LCDP was a strong supporter of the protection of small and medium-sized businesses and of a severe crackdown on crime.[29]

A split was evident in the party between traditionalist and pro-clerical "conservatives" and a more "progressive" faction that favored a clearer separation of Church and state. The latter believed that the Catholic Church in Lithuania was too rigid and dogmatic, and supported a lesser role for religious organizations in social and secular issues such as abortion or family planning. The Catholic Church was also in conflict with the Labor government during the early 1990s over the possession and return of Church property that was confiscated by the communists after World War II.

Other Christian Democratic formations active during the 1990s included the Christian Democratic Union (CDU) and the Modern Christian Democrats (MCD).

Agrarians

Lithuanian Peasants' Party (LPP)
Lietuvos Valstiečių Partija (LVP)

Chaired by Ramūnas Karbauskis, the Lithuanian Peasants' Party (LPP) was registered on 10 October 1990. It was largely a rural appendage of the LDLP and claimed a membership of some 400 people. Its leaders belonged to the old communist cells active on state and collective farms during the Soviet era. It was unable to attract the votes of young people or of the growing number of private farmers. The LPP was one of the smaller parties that gained one seat in the 1996 *Seimas*, together with seven other formations, through a single-member district. The party obtained approximately 1.2% of the proportional vote. In the 19 March 2000 local elections, the party took advantage of rural discontent and came in second place, winning 109 seats in municipal governments. After the elections, Karbauskis asserted that if the party was equally successful in the parliamentary elections, it would work to distance the country from the European Union (EU) and the World Trade Organization (WTO), which he viewed as fundamentally disadvantageous to Lithuanian agriculture.[30] However, the LPP only managed to pick up 4.1% of the vote in the October 2000 ballot and four deputies and was discredited for its essentially anti-integrationist stance in international issues.

Greens

Lithuanian Green Party (LGP)
Lietuvos Žaliųjų Partija (LZP)

The Lithuanian Green Party (LGP) was established in 1989 and chaired by R. Astrauskas. Even though the LGP had only a small core group of members, it enjoyed widespread sympathy largely because of its early support of *Sajūdis* and its campaigns on behalf of Lithuanian independence. Its post-independence agenda included improving the country's environment and its human rights record, but it failed to build any large-scale public backing and proved unable to secure any parliamentary representation.

Nationalists

Lithuanian Restructuring Movement (LRM)
Lietuvos Persitvarkymo Sajūdis (LPS)

Founded in October 1988, the Lithuanian Restructuring Movement (LRM), popularly known as *Sajūdis,* was an umbrella organization that was instrumental in creating mass support for Lithuanian independence from the Soviet Union.

Many of the unaffiliated individuals elected to the Supreme Council in 1990 were involved with *Sajūdis*. As a movement, *Sajūdis* consisted of many different groups, including the Lithuanian Greens, the Citizens' Charter of the Republic of Lithuania, the Union of Political Prisoners, the Lithuanian Workers' Union, and the Farmers' Movement of Lithuania. Its leaders were predominantly intellectuals from the arts, humanities, and scientific communities, and some junior members of the Communist Party. Indeed, 17 of the 36 founders of the *Sajūdis* Initiative Group were Communist Party representatives. The overwhelming majority if its leadership and its congress delegates were ethnic Lithuanians. The organization was the driving force behind the early protests against the Soviet Union, propelling many Lithuanian Communist Party reformers toward the cause of Lithuanian statehood.

By the time of its second congress, on 22–24 October 1988, *Sajūdis* had been radicalized by avid independence activists from Kaunas, including future Defense Minister Audrius Butkevičius, future Foreign Minister Algirdas Saudargas, and future Prime Minister Aleksandras Abišala.[31] *Sajūdis* won an overwhelming victory in elections to the Congress of People's Deputies in March 1989, gaining 36 out of 42 seats. Subsequently, one of the movement's leaders, Vytautas Landsbergis, was elected chairman of the Lithuanian Supreme Council (parliament)—in effect, the country's President. The movement began to split into rival factions and the effectiveness and influence of the organization began to seriously suffer by the time of its third congress in December 1991. Landsbergis attempted to transform the movement into a more disciplined political party but failed to elicit any significant support, and instead was attacked for allegedly pursuing personal ambitions.

As a result of factionalism and personal rivalries within the movement, *Sajūdis* steadily declined in membership and influence, and in the October–November 1992 parliamentary elections it won only 30 seats. Its disintegration accelerated after the new legislature was convened, with the Kaunas wing breaking off to create the National Progress Faction and Landsbergis subsequently establishing his own political party, the Homeland Union–Lithuanian Conservatives (HU-LC).

Lithuanian National Union (LNU)
Lietuviu Tautininkų Sajunga (LTS)

The Lithuanian National Union (LNU) was originally established in 1924 and subsequently restored on 23 February 1990. Its membership reached 3,000 people, and it was chaired by Rimantas Smetona. The Lithuanian National Union formed the presiding government from 1926 until 1940, at which time the country was annexed by the Soviet Union. The party was restored when ten members of the LNU formed a faction in the Lithuanian Supreme Council that lasted until the 1992 parliamentary elections. For this ballot, the LNU formed the electoral coalition National Union List of Lithuania together with the Independence Party. The LNU was center-rightist, fairly nationalistic, and believed in a strong role for the state. Its membership primarily included farmers, business owners, and entrepreneurs. For the parliamentary elections in October–November 1996, the LNU joined with the Democratic Party in an electoral union, but ended up winning only one seat. It had gained four deputies in the previous election to the *Seimas*.

Lithuanian Nationalist Party "Young Lithuania" (LNP-YL)
Lietuvių Nacionalinė Partija "Jaunoji Lietuva" (LNP-JL)

The Lithuanian Nationalist Party "Young Lithuania" (LNP-YL) was formed before the national elections in October 1992 but only registered on 7 September 1994. It was chaired by Stanislovas Buškevičius. "Young Lithuania" supported the parliamentary candidacy of Kazys Bobelis, former leader of the ultra-nationalist émigré organization the Committee for the Liberation of Lithuania. It gained only one seat in the parliamentary elections of 20 October 1996.

Several other nationalist or ultra-nationalist groups have been formed in Lithuania during the past decade. They include the Lithuanian Freedom League (LFL) *(Lietuvos Laisvės Lyga, LLL)*, chaired by Antanas Terleckas, which was founded in 1988 and registered on 8 November 1995; the LFL claimed a membership of 400.[32] During the drive for national independence, it proved more radical than *Sajūdis*. It advocated a boycott of the 1990 Soviet parliamentary elections, claiming that normal elections could occur only in a free and independent Lithuania.

Other nationalist groups include the Republican Party (RP) *(Lietuvos Respublikonų Partija, LRP)*, chaired by Kazimieras Petraitis and registered on 6 January 1991; the Lithuanian Freedom Union (LFU) *(Lietuvos Laisvės Sajunga, LLS)*, chaired by Vytautas Šustauskas and registered on 13 September 1994; and the Lithuanian Party of Forefathers' Rebirth (LPFR) *(Lietuvos Protėvių Atgimino Partija, LPAP)*, chaired by J. Ramanauskas and registered on 1 June 1993. A small number of marginal neofascist or neo-Nazi parties have also appeared in Lithuania over the past decade, but they have exerted no discernable political or public influence and have been outlawed by the government. They include the Lithuanian National Social Union (LNSU), led by Mindaugas Murza, which was refused official registration by the Justice Ministry.

Ethnic Minority and Religious Parties

Lithuanian Poles' Electoral Action (LPEA)
Lietuvos Lenkų Rinkimų Akcija (LLRA)

Lithuanian Poles' Electoral Action (LPEA) was officially registered on 21 October 1994. It was chaired by Jan Šenkevič, with a membership of 1,000 people. Formerly known as the Lithuanian Polish Union (LPU), the LPEA won only 2.8% of the vote in the October–November 1996 general elections, gaining one seat in the *Seimas* due to its status as an ethnic minority party. Many Polish activists initially opposed Lithuanian independence, and some who were communist functionaries supported the Moscow coup attempt in August 1991. As a result, President Landsbergis removed Polish officials from office in two municipalities and replaced them with presidential appointees before the next scheduled municipal elections. A pro-Soviet grouping declared a Polish Autonomous Region of Lithuania in the southeastern part of the country, evidently with OMON (Soviet paramilitary police) commander Bolesław Makutinowicz as their leader. But the initiative fizzled soon after Lithuania achieved independence, as it had little public backing and little support from Moscow.

However, not all Polish activists concurred with the pro-Soviet organizations. For example, the prominent politician Czesław Okińczyc joined *Sajūdis* soon after it was founded, and was elected to the Lithuanian parliament in 1990, while the Polish publisher Romuald Mieczkowski (editor of *Znad Wilii*) also supported Lithuania's independence. Mieczkowski's wife, Wanda Mieczkowska, became an official in the Women's Party established by former Prime Minister Kazimiera Prunskienė.

The Polish Union obtained four seats in the *Seimas* in the October–November 1992 parliamentary elections but subsequently came into conflict with the Labor government because it was not registered as a political party. The LPEA was subsequently founded to take part in the municipal elections in 1995. It won 69 seats in the Vilnius and Šalčininkai regions, where indigenous Poles constituted a substantial segment of the population. The Polish community has been divided on how hard it should canvass for the establishment of a Polish university and other educational institutions without undermining or challenging Lithuania's political and territorial integrity.[33]

Union of Russians in Lithuania (URL)
Lietuvos Rusų Sąjunga (LRS)

The Union of Russians in Lithuania (URL) was registered on 28 December 1995. It was chaired by Sergejus Dmitrijevas and claimed a membership of 400. The party received only 1.63% of the total vote in the October–November 1996 general elections. It was not represented in the *Seimas*, despite stipulations that ethnic minority parties did not need to overcome the 5% barrier for parliamentary seats. Opinion polls and election results indicated that the Russian minority was more favorably disposed toward the social democratic options and supported the ex-communist LDLP in local and national elections. Initial Russian and Polish minority support for the anti-independence *Edinstvo* organization, or the International Front Movement sponsored by Moscow hardliners, ebbed away after the breakup of the Soviet Union in August 1991.

An Alliance of Ethnic Minorities (AEM) *(Lietuvos Tautinių Mažumų Aljansas, LTMA)* was also formed in the country during 1996 and was chaired by R. Litvinovič. Its aim was to bring together Lithuania's larger minorities into one electoral bloc. The AEM received 2.44% of the vote in the October–November 1996 parliamentary elections and failed to obtain any legislative seats.

Independents and Others

Union of Political Prisoners and Deportees (UPPD)
Lietuvos Politinių Kalinių ir Tremtinių Sąjunga (LPKTS)

The Union of Political Prisoners and Deportees (UPPD) was registered on 25 June 1991 and chaired by Balys Gajauskas. The UPPD's representation in the *Seimas* dropped dramatically from five deputies to one deputy following the October–November 1996 general elections.

A similar organization, the Lithuanian Party of Political Prisoners (LPPP) *(Lietuvos Politinių Kalinių Partija, LPKP)* was registered on 8 March 1995 and chaired by Zigmas Medineckas. It adopted a rightist and nationalist profile but failed to win enough votes to gain entrance to the *Seimas* after the October–November 1996 elections, although under its prior name, the Union of Political Prisoners of Lithuania (UPPL), it held one seat in the previous parliament. In the 1995 local elections, the party won 56 seats nationwide, or approximately 3.75% of the total vote.

Other miscellaneous political organizations included the Lithuanian Union of Social Justice (LUSJ) *(Lietuvos Socialinio Teisingumo Partija, LSTP)*, registered on 29 April 1996 with a membership of 1,000 and chaired by Kazimieras Jočius. The LUSJ was specifically created to mobilize voters who lost money during Lithuania's severe 1995 banking crisis.[34]

POLITICAL DATA

Name of State: Republic of Lithuania *(Lietuvos Respublika)*
Form of Government: Democratic republic
Structure of Legislature: Unicameral parliament or *Seimas* (141 seats, 71 members are directly elected by proportional representation). President is directly elected by popular vote.

Size of Territory: 25,212 square miles
Size of Population: 3,610,535 (July 2001 estimate)

Composition of Population:

Ethnic Group	Number	% of Population
Lithuanians	3,022,400	81.1
Russians	310,900	8.5
Poles	259,200	7.0

Belarusians	55,900	1.5
Ukrainians	37,700	1.0
Jews	5,900	0.1
Total	3,717,7000	100.0

Sources: Most data from *Europa Worldbook* 1996. For all governments since 1990 see the Government of the Republic of Lithuania: Former Government, http://www.lrvk.lt/anglu/a-vyriaus/a-vyrsen.html.

ELECTION RESULTS

Presidential Election, 21 December 1997–4 January 1998

First Round (Direct), 21 December 1997

Turnout: 71.45%

Candidate	Votes	% of Vote
Artūras Paulauskas	838,819	45.28
Valdas Adamkus	516,798	27.90
Vytautas Landsbergis	294,881	15.92
Vytenis Povilas Andriukaitis	105,916	5.72
Kazys Bobelis	73,287	3.96
Rolandas Pavilionis	16,070	0.87
Rimantas Smetona	6,697	0.36
Total	1,852,468	100.00

Source: See http://www.lrs.lt/n/rinkimai/pr97/rez/reza_6_1.htm.

Second Round (Direct), 4 January 1998

Turnout: 73.66%

Candidate	Votes	% of Vote
Valdas Adamkus	968,031	50.37
Artūras Paulauskas	953,775	49.63
Total	1,921,806	100.00

Presidential Election, 14 February 1993

Turnout: N/A

Candidate	Votes	% of Vote
Algirdas Brazauskas	1,212,075	60.0
Stasys Lozoraitis	772,922	40.0
Total	1,984,997	100.0

Source: Statistical Yearbook of Lithuania, 1994–1995, Vilnius: Methodical Publishing Center, 1995, p. 67.

Parliamentary Elections, 8 October 2000

Turnout: 58.63%

Party/Coalition	% of List Seats	% of SM* Seats	Total Seats
Algirdas Brazauskas Social Democratic Coalition	40.0	32.39	51
New Union–Social Liberals	24.29	15.49	28
Lithuanian Liberal Union	21.43	25.35	33
Homeland Union-Lithuanian Conservatives	11.43	1.41	9
Christian Democratic Union	—	1.41	1
Lithuanian Peasants' Party	—	5.63	4
Lithuanian Christian Democratic Party	—	2.82	2
Lithuanian Center Union	—	2.82	2
Moderate Conservative Union	—	1.41	1
Lithuanian Poles' Electoral Action	—	2.82	2
Lithuanian Freedom Union	—	1.41	1
"Young Lithuania," New Nationalists and Political Prisoners' Union Bloc	—	1.41	1
Lithuanian Social Democracy 2000 Party/Modern Christian-Democratic Union	2.86	1.41	3
Independents	—	4.23	3
Total	100.01	100.01	141

Sources: University of Essex, *Political Transformation and the Electoral Process in Post-Communist Europe* at http://www2.essex.ac.uk/elections; and Elections to the Seimas of the Republic of Lithuania at http://www.lrs.lt/n/rinkimai/20001008/rda.htm.
    *SM stands for Single Member.

Parliamentary Elections, 20 October and 10 November 1996

Turnout: 52.92% (first round), 38.16% (second round)

Party/Coalition	% of List Seats	% of SM* Seats	Total Seats
Homeland Union-Lithuanian Conservatives	47.14	55.22	70
Christian Democratic Party	15.71	7.46	16
Lithuanian Center Union	12.86	5.97	13
Lithuanian Democratic Labor Party	14.29	2.99	12
Lithuanian Social Democratic Party	10.00	7.46	12
Lithuanian National Union/Lithuanian Democratic Party Coalition	—	4.48	3
Lithuanian Nationalist Party "Young" Lithuania	—	1.49	1
Christian Democratic Union	—	1.49	1

Lithuanian Poles Electoral Action	—	1.49	1
Lithuanian Women's Party	—	1.49	1
Union of Political Prisoners and Deportees	—	1.49	1
Lithuanian Liberal Union	—	1.49	1
Lithuanian Peasants' Party	—	1.49	1
Independents	—	5.97	4
Other parties	—	.02	—
Total	100.00	100.00	137

Sources: University of Essex, *Political Transformation and the Electoral Process in Post-Communist Europe* at http://www2.essex.ac.uk/elections. See also the Kaunas University of Technology, Department of Public Administration at http://vingis.sc-uni.ktu.lt/rinkimai/iiround.htm; and the Lithuanian Seimas: Lietuvos Respublikos Seimo Rinkimai '96 at http://rc.lrs.lt/n/rinkimai/seim96/rsnl.htm.

Parliamentary Elections Results, 25 October and 9 November 1992

Turnout: 75.25% (first round), 64.76% (second round)

Party/Coalition	% of List Leats	% of SM* Seats	Total Seats
Lithuanian Democratic Labor Party	51.43	52.11	73
Sajūdis Coalition	24.29	18.31	30
Christian Democrats (Lithuanian Christian Democratic Party, Union of Political Prisoners, and Seportees and Lithuanian Democratic Party)	14.29	11.27	18
Lithuanian Social Democratic Party	7.14	4.23	8
"Young Lithuania" for United Lithuania	—	1.41	1
Forum of Lithuanian Future (Alliance of Christian Democratic Union of Lithuanian Youth)	—	1.41	1
Center Movement	—	2.82	2
Polish Union	2.86	2.82	4
Lithuanian National Union List (National Union Party and Independent Party)	—	5.63	4
Total	100.1	100.1	141

Sources: University of Essex, *Political Transformation and the Electoral Process in Post-Communist Europe* at http://www2.essex.ac.uk/elections; and *Statistical Yearbook of Lithuania, 1994-1995*, Vilnius: Methodological Publishing Center, 1995, p. 6.

Due to the combined system of list and single member votes and the distribution of corresponding seats, only the percentage of list seats, percentage of single member seats, and total number of seats are provided by party. For a full breakdown of the election results, including the number of votes for the list seats, as well as the single member votes, please consult the University of Essex, *Political Transformation and the Electoral Process in Post-Communist Europe* at http://www2.essex.ac.uk/elections.

NOTES

1. For histories and analyses of Lithuania consult: Edvardas Tuskenis (Ed.), *Lithuania in European Politics: The Years of the First Republic, 1918–1940*, New York: St. Martin's Press, 1997; Walter C. Clemens, Jr., *Baltic Independence and Russian Empire*, New York: St. Martin's Press, 1991; Alfred Erich Senn, *The Emergence of Modern Lithuania*, New York: Columbia University Press, 1959; V. Stanley Vardys, *The Catholic Church, Dissent and Nationality in Soviet Lithuania*, New York: Columbia University Press, 1978; John Hiden and Patrick Salmon, *The Baltic Nations and Europe: Estonia, Latvia and Lithuania in the Twentieth Century*, London: Longman, 1996; and David Kirby, *The Baltic World, 1772–1993: Europe's Northern Periphery in an Age of Change*, London: Longman, 1995.

2. A useful summary of Lithuania's twentieth-century history can be found in Graham Smith (Ed.), *The Baltic States: The National Self-Determination of Estonia, Latvia, and Lithuania*, New York: St. Martin's Press, 1996.

3. For a valuable summary of the drive toward Lithuanian independence see Richard J. Krickus, "Democratization in Lithuania," in Karen Dawisha and Bruce Parrott (Eds.), *The Consolidation of Democracy in East-Central Europe*, Cambridge, UK: Cambridge University Press, 1997, pp. 290–333.

4. See the Kaunas University of Technology, Department of Public Administration, http://vingis.sc—uni.ktu.lt/rinkimai/introd.htm.

5. See David Arter, *Parties and Democracy in the Post-Soviet Republics: The Case of Estonia*, Aldershot, UK: Dartmouth Publishing Company, 1996, p. 53.

6. For a valuable summary of the immediate post-independence period see Alfred Erich Senn, "Lithuania: Rights and Responsibilities of Independence," in Ian Bremmer and Ray Taras (Eds.), *New States, New Politics: Building the Post-Soviet Nations*, Cambridge, UK: Cambridge University Press, 1997, pp. 353–375.

7. See the Minister of Foreign Affairs of Lithuania, *Basic Facts about Lithuania*, http://www.urm.lt/about/.

8. See the United Nations Development Program, *Lithuanian Human Development Report, 1997*, Chapter 7, "The Transformation of Social Relations and Institutions: from Totalitarianism to a Democratic and Pluralistic Society," at http://www.undp.lt/HDR/1997/chapter7/ch7_.htm.

9. See the Law on Presidential Elections (as amended 19 September 1996), http://rc.lrs.lt/cgi—bin/preps2?Condition1=39566&Condition2=.

10. For some background and analysis see Saulius Girnius, "The Political Pendulum Swings Back in Lithuania," *Transition*, Open Media Research Institute, Vol. 3, No. 2, 7 February 1997, pp. 20–21.

11. Consult the United Nations Development Program, *Lithuanian Human Development Report, 1997*, Chapter 7, "The Transformation of Social Relations and Institutions: from Totalitarianism to a Democratic and Pluralistic Society," at http://www.undp.lt/HDR/1997/chapter7/ch7_.htm.

12. See Vello Pettai, "Political Stability through Disenfranchisement," *Transition*, Open Media Research Institute, Vol. 3, No. 6, 4 April 1997, pp. 21–23.

13. Consult Saulius Girnius, "Central and Local Governments Battle for Control," *Transition*, Open Media Research Institute, Vol. 1, No. 24, 29 December 1995, pp. 55–57.

14. See http//www.europeanforum.bot—consult.se/cup/lithuania/develop.htm.

15. *"On the Way to Social Democracy,"* Vilnius, Lithuania: LDDP, International Commission, 10 December 1994.

16. See http//www.europeanforum.bot—consult.se/cup/lithuania/parties.htm.

17. "Lithuanian Party of the Economy: Program for the *Seimas* elections 1996," at http://rc.lrs.lt/rinkimai/IMG/g71.gif.

18. Patrick Lannin, "Landsbergis Savors Win in Lithuania," *Washington Times*, 22 October 1996, A12.

19. "Local Elections," Embassy of Lithuania, Washington, D.C., 26 March 1995.

20. See http//www.europeanforum.bot—consult.se/cup/lithuania/parties.htm.

21. Lithuanian Information Center, "Political Parties of Lithuania," Brooklyn, New York, 1991.

22. "Lithuanian Liberal Union Party Platform," http://vignis.sc—uni.ktu.lt/rinkimai/llsprogr.htm.

23. International Republican Institute (IRI), "IRI Briefing Paper on Political Party Development in the Republic of Lithuania," New York, 1991.

24. Lithuanian Seimas home page at http://rc.lrs.lt/rinkimai/IMG/g71.gif.

25. See http//www.europeanforum.bot—consult.se/cup/lithuania/parties.htm.

26. http://www.agora.stm.it/elections/election/lithuania.htm.

27. "Lithuanian Centrist Union does not rule out any coalition but only after parliamentary elections," BNS, 17 October 1996 on LATNET.

28. "The New Lithuania: The Political Platform of the Centre Union," *Vrublevskio* 6, Vilnius, Lithuania, 1995.

29. See http//www.europeanforum.bot—consult.se/cup/lithuania/parties.htm.

30. See http://www.ce—review.org/00/12/amber12.html.

31. Consult Anatol Lieven, *The Baltic Revolution: Estonia, Latvia, Lithuania, and the Path to Independence*, New Haven: Yale University Press, 1993, p. 226.

32. "Lithuania's Political Parties, 1988–1996," at http://vignis.sc—uni.ktu.lt.

33. See Krickus, "Democratization in Lithuania," p. 321.

34. "Peculiarities of the Seimas Elections 1996 Campaign," Algis Junevičius, Kaunas University of Technology.

Poland

HISTORICAL OVERVIEW

Slavic tribes permanently settled in the present-day Polish territories during the sixth century AD. The large Polian tribe based in the sprawling flatlands became the core of the emerging Polish nation, absorbing the Pomorzans, Mazovians, Kujavians, Silesians, and Wislans. Their territory in the region of Gniezno and Poznań became the nucleus of the future Polish state. The first recorded Polian dynasty was that of the Popielides. It was followed by the Piasts who dominated the Polish region for several hundred years. In 966, the Piast king Mieszko I, together with other Polish tribal leaders, adopted Christianity, largely to deprive German invaders of the pretext for conducting a crusade against the Poles. Mieszko rapidly organized the state and inflicted several defeats on the neighboring Germans.[1]

Under the reign of Bolesław the Brave in the early part of the eleventh century, Poland grew into one of the most powerful states in Central-Eastern Europe. Its territories included parts of Moravia and Slovakia, and extended westward as far as the river Elbe. During wars with the Germans, Polish armies reached as far as Bavaria. The Papal See in Rome granted permission for an independent Polish ecclesiastical organization to be established with its seat in Gniezno, thus establishing a close connection between Poland and the Vatican that was to endure throughout Polish history. Catholicism and allegiance to Rome also became a factor of national unity.

The Polish kingdom declined after Bolesław's death in 1025 but was restored at the beginning of the thirteenth century by Kazimierz I and Bolesław II. Polish kings attempted to restore their control along the Baltic Sea coastline and to push back German encroachments. But the Piast dynasty suffered from the principle that each member of the royal family had to gain his own province. This effectively fractured the state into smaller principalities, fostered regional particularisms, created internecine rivalries, and left the country vulnerable to foreign pressures and invasions. In 1241, Polish forces were defeated by Mongol armies at the battle of Legnica, but Mongol pressure on Eastern Europe was subsequently relieved.

A major new menace emerged during the thirteenth century with the settlement of the German Order of the Cross in the Prussian areas along the Baltic coast. On the pretext of combating paganism, the German knights exterminated the indigenous Prussians and pursued the creation of a new German state, linked with Germany proper through the conquest of Polish Pomorze (Pomerania).

Under King Kazimierz the Great (1333–1370) Poland restored its control over lands captured by Ruthenian princes and extended its domains into ethnic Ukrainian territories. Kazimierz succeeded in economically developing and politically consolidating the Polish state. In 1385, a state union was achieved between Poland and Lithuania through the marriage of Poland's Queen Jadwiga with Lithuania's Grand Duke Władysław Jagiełło. The union created a new dynasty and the largest and most powerful state in Eastern Europe. It included all or most of present-day Poland, Lithuania, Latvia, Belarus, Ukraine, and parts of Russia, while the principality of Moldova became a vassal of Poland.

In 1410, the German knights were defeated by Polish, Lithuanian, and Ruthenian forces at the battle of Grunwald. Although the Order of the Cross was not completely destroyed, it ceased to be a menace to the Polish-Lithuanian Commonwealth. Meanwhile, the Jagiellonians pursued various domestic reforms that expanded the powers of the gentry and placed some constitutional limits on royal prerogatives vis-à-vis the magnates in the Senate (upper house of parliament) and the gentry in the *Sejm* (lower house).

In 1569, Poland and the Grand Duchy of Lithuania were more closely tied through the Union of Lublin. Ukrainian nobles also tightened their links with the Polish crown. Throughout the sixteenth and seventeenth centuries, Poland faced increasingly powerful rivals on all of its frontiers. Russia under Tsar Ivan the Terrible and his successors grew into a formidable power and threatened Polish interests throughout the eastern territories. German pressure along the Baltic coast and in Pomerania continued to intensify. Swedish ambitions towards Latvia and the Baltic hinterlands culminated in an invasion of Poland in 1655. Meanwhile, the Ottoman Turks were gradually extending their domains from the south and threatening Polish-controlled lands. In addition, a large-scale Cossack revolt in Ukraine in 1648, against the abuses Polish magnates toward Ukrainian peasants, presented a serious internal challenge to the Commonwealth's stability. This period in Polish history came to be known as the "Flood," as invading armies poured over the country's extensive borders from almost all directions.

Although Poland withstood the onslaught and King Jan Sobieski won a major victory over the Turks at Vienna in 1683, the country was severely weakened and lost territories in the north and east. Poland became further fractured during the eighteenth century because of the extensive liberties afforded to the gentry class, who were able to suspend the parliament through individual vetoes on its decisions *(liberum veto)*. The parliamentary system degenerated, financial resources for the armed forces were blocked, Polish towns declined, and the executive power was significantly weakened.

At the end of the eighteenth century, Poland was partitioned in three stages among its three absolutist and imperialist neighbors—Tsarist Russia, Prussia-Germany, and Habsburg Austria. By 1795, Poland had ceased to exist and all of its lands were under foreign control. A series of bloody uprisings against Russian, German, and Austrian rule during the nineteenth century failed to recreate the Polish state, even though a semi-autonomous Duchy of Warsaw was established by Napoleon's French forces, which was later formalized as the Kingdom of Poland at the Congress of Vienna in 1815. Many prominent Poles emigrated from the country but continued to campaign for Poland's restoration as an independent state.

Throughout the latter part of the nineteenth century, Polish leaders and intellectuals pursued a program of "organic work" whereby national culture, language, and education were promoted in preparation for more favorable circumstances when Poland could regain its independence. Armed uprisings were generally avoided because of the brutal and repressive pacification campaigns conducted by the Russian and German authorities. The strengthening of Polish identity during a century of foreign occupation also enabled Poles to resist the mounting campaign of Germanization and Russification in the late 1800s.

Austrian-controlled Galicia gained a limited measure of autonomy, and it was in this province that Poland's new independence movements were created. Poland's liberationist groups were broadly divided into three camps: the leftist or socialist orientation, led by Józef Piłsudski, which viewed Russia as the chief enemy; a more ethno-nationalist tendency, led by Roman Dmowski, that was principally anti-German; and a peasant movement, led by Wincenty Witos, with a focus on extensive social and economic reform. Cognizant of the coming war, Piłsudski began to organize detachments of young soldiers that grew into the Polish Legions in preparation for the struggle for national independence.

Poland regained its independence on 11 November 1918, at the close of World War I, following military defeat or internal upheaval among all three partitioning powers. A Polish government of National Unity was formed combining the spectrum of political forces, a *Sejm* was convened in Warsaw, and Piłsudski was proclaimed the head of state. The boundaries of the new Polish Republic were established in the wake of a full-scale war with Bolshevik Russia and protracted conflicts with the German and Lithuanian states. After defeating and pushing back invading Bolshevik forces in August 1920, Poland signed the Treaty of Riga on 18 March 1921, thereby regaining about half of its pre-partition territory. Poland captured the Vilnius province from a newly independent Lithuania; this remained a source of conflict throughout the inter-war period. Plebiscites were also held in the German-disputed areas of Upper Silesia and East Prussia, from which Warsaw managed to secure several territorial gains.

A substantial ethnic minority was left within the Polish state, constituting over 30% of the country's total population, including Ukrainians, Jews, Belarusians, and Germans. The new Polish state was constructed along centralist rather than federalist lines. This resulted in conflicts between the government and minority leaders aspiring to greater autonomy. Warsaw embarked on a program of assimilation and Polonization, and occasional local revolts led to repressive "pacification" campaigns. Under the League of Nations' provisions, Poland was required to sign a minority treaty guaranteeing all ethnic groups equal treatment and non-discrimination, but it periodically violated that treaty. Warsaw charged that the treaty was manipulated by foreign governments, particularly by Germany, to undermine Polish stability, to stimulate revanchist and irredentist sentiments, and to discredit Warsaw in the eyes of the international community. As a result, demands for minority rights were often viewed with suspicion by Polish officials. Warsaw unilaterally abrogated the minority treaty in the mid-1930s, further aggravating an already deteriorating inter-ethnic situation.

The Ukrainian population was the largest and in many respects the most problematic in inter-war Poland, exceeding 5.6 million by the early 1930s. Ukrainians were mainly concentrated in southeastern Poland, in the provinces of Galicia and Wołyń, and the overwhelming majority were farmers or peasants. The population was well organized into a spectrum of political parties, most of which demanded autonomy and eventual Ukrainian independence. The more moderate parties elected deputies to the Polish parliament, although there were periodic boycotts of its proceedings.

Radicalization among some sectors of the population, and the creation of an openly separatist political and military Ukrainian organization in the late 1920s, led to further ethnic polarization and government persecution. Toward the end of the 1930s, more hard-line forces gained ascendance in the Polish government, and they opposed granting any concessions to Ukrainians or other minorities. Moreover, Poland was facing increasing threats from both Nazi Germany and the Soviet Union, and the government expected minority leaders to place loyalty to the republic above all other considerations.

Inter-war Poland contained the largest Jewish population in Europe, numbering about 2.85 million by the early 1920s. The vast majority lived in urban areas and larger villages, and spanned a range of professions. The new Polish government sought to assimilate Jews into Polish society and applied restrictive policies on Jewish self-government, educational activities, and social welfare programs. Official policy also discriminated against Jewish businesses, civil servants, and professionals in favor of ethnic Poles. Jewish economic and social life suffered correspondingly. Some extremist anti-Semitic organizations also became active, although Poland did not descend into a fascist-type dictatorship. A range of Jewish political parties continued to function and participated in the Polish parliament.

The Belarusian population numbered some 2.2 million by the early 1930s, mostly concentrated in Poland's northeastern provinces. The majority were peasants and small farmers and among the poorest sectors of Polish society. Belarusians lacked the well-developed social, political, and economic self-help organizations evident among Ukrainians, Jews, and Germans, and they too were exposed to campaigns of Polonization and assimilation. Polish pressures in turn spurred autonomist and separatist movements. Concessions offered by Warsaw failed to satisfy Belarusian leaders, many of whom looked toward union with Soviet Belarus even though few were committed communists.

Poland's German population declined to some 1.1 million people following a large-scale emigration from the former German-inhabited regions. Germans were distributed around the country, although the majority resided in Upper Silesia, Posnania, and Pomerania. Most were engaged in industrial and commercial activities or were medium-sized farmers. Although the Warsaw government permitted German educational, cultural, social, and economic institutions to operate, various restrictions were imposed and a policy of assimilation was pursued in some regions. With Hitler's rise to power in Germany during the 1930s, the Polish authorities increasingly feared that the German minority sympathized with German irredentist designs and could be used as a fifth column to undermine Polish independence.

Poland's first independent constitution of 17 March 1921 was a broadly democratic document that focused much authority in the parliament. As a result of frequent changes in government and often fractious politics that paralyzed decisionmaking, Marshal Piłsudski staged a coup d'état on 12 May 1926 and installed a more authoritarian regime. A new constitution was passed on 23 April 1935 that vested substantial powers in the presidency: for example, the President gained the right to dissolve parliament and to veto legislation. Piłsudski died in May 1935 and Poland faced increasing pressures from its two aggressive neighbors, Nazi Germany and the Soviet Union, which culminated in a joint invasion and partition of the country in September 1939. The Polish government fled into exile in France and then Britain, and an underground administration and resistance movement were formed that were loyal to the exiled government. Over one million Poles were deported by Stalin's security forces into the USSR. The Nazis pursued a systematic policy of exterminating the Polish intelligentsia and national leadership.

Poland was devastated by World War II and sustained substantial population and territorial losses. The country was deprived of about one third of its pre-war territory, which was incorporated into the Soviet Union, while gaining areas in the north and west from Germany. In sum, Poland's post-war territory was about 20% smaller than in 1939. The country's population dropped from 34.8 million in 1939 to about 25.5 million by 1951. Approximately 6 million Polish citizens perished during the war, half of whom were Jews. The country became ethnically homogenized, with over 95% registered as ethnic Poles in the late 1940s. The Jewish population was exterminated by the Nazis; an estimated 80,000 survived the war in Poland and another 150,000 returned from exile in the USSR. Thousands more Jews emigrated from the country after the war, and less than 30,000 were left by the end of the 1950s. A further exodus during a communist-sponsored anti-Semitic campaign in the late 1960s left fewer than 5,000 Jews in the country.

About 6 million Germans fled at the close of the war or were deported by the Polish and Soviet authorities; in official estimates less than 10,000 remained in the country by the early 1950s, although the figure was considered conservative. The loss of Poland's eastern territories removed large numbers of Ukrainians and Belarusians. About 200,000 Ukrainians and 160,000 Belarusians were registered by the authorities in the early 1950s. Over 150,000 Ukrainians and Ruthenians were forcibly deported from southeastern Poland on charges of collaboration with anti-communist guerrillas. They were settled in over a dozen vojvodships (administrative divisions) and prohibited from returning to their ancestral lands. In addition, hundreds of thousands of Poles were resettled in the western territories that were reclaimed from defeated Germany.

The communist takeover in Poland at the close of World War II followed a pattern familiar throughout Eastern Europe. A Soviet-sponsored puppet communist party led by Bolesław Bierut, and with extremely limited public support, seized power through intimidation, forged elections, and the elimination of political opponents. During the late 1940s a harsh Stalinist system was imposed on the country and thousands of political activists perished. A certain degree of liberalization beginning in the late 1950s injected some national elements into communist rule but failed to legitimize the system of government.

The attempted collectivization of Polish agriculture met with substantial peasant resistance and was abandoned during the 1950s. For most of the postwar period, the Catholic Church under the leadership of Cardinal Stefan Wyszyński maintained its independence from the regime. Periodic workers' and students' revolts were brutally suppressed by the government of Władysław Gomułka; hundreds of workers perished in the Baltic seaports of Gdańsk and Gdynia in December 1970. Further protests in 1976, during the rule of communist leader Edward Gierek, led to the creation of a Workers' Defense Committee through which intellectuals provided direct assistance to repressed and imprisoned workers. In 1977, a movement for the defense of human and civil rights was also established to monitor the government's compliance with the international Helsinki accords.

The worker-intellectual compact led to the birth of the independent free trade union Solidarity *(Solidarność)* on 31 August 1980, following a wave of strikes protesting economic conditions and police repression. The union was led by Lech Wałęsa and increasingly lodged political demands that were unacceptable to the communist regime. On 13 December 1981, General

Wojciech Jaruzelski imposed martial law in the country and outlawed all in-dependent organizations. Several dozen workers and protestors were killed by the communist security forces before martial law was finally lifted in 1983.

During the spring and summer of 1988, a new series of workers' strikes served warning to Warsaw of impending social revolt as economic conditions deteriorated and official reforms proved inconsequential. In the fall of 1988, the government began to make overtures to the opposition in order to avert a spiral of instability. Jaruzelski's regime agreed to an "anti-crisis pact" with members of the moderate Solidarity opposition. Roundtable negotiations be-tween communist officials and Solidarity representatives began in February 1989 and ended in April 1989 with the signing of various agreements on labor union pluralism, the reinstatement of Solidarity, semi-democratic parliamentary elections, and economic reforms.[2]

POST-COMMUNIST DEVELOPMENTS

Poland established the first non-communist government in the Warsaw Pact on the basis of a historic roundtable agreement in April 1989 between the communist government and the opposition movement led by Solidarity. Wałęsa's "Citizens' Committee" fielded candidates for the June parliamen-tary elections with a pledge that opposition deputies would change the consti-tution, eliminate the communist monopoly, and push for fully democratic elections. In the June 1989 ballot, Solidarity candidates easily won the 35% (or 161 out of 460) of lower house *(Sejm)* parliamentary seats that they had been allowed to contest. The union also won 99 out of 100 seats in the new upper house, or Senate, where Solidarity could contest all seats. The ruling Polish United Workers' Party (PUWP) had reserved for itself 38% of the seats in the *Sejm*, with the remaining 27% for its two allied parties.

Parliament narrowly elected Jaruzelski as President, largely to avert a full-scale confrontation with Moscow over Poland's continuing allegiance to the Warsaw Pact. The President was afforded special powers in national security, defense, and foreign affairs. Jaruzelski nominated former Interior Minister Czesław Kiszczak for premier, but the nominee failed to form a new government as the two former satellite parties defected from the communists. The Solidarity caucus declined offers of cabinet posts in a communist-led coalition.

Despite limited time and resources, Solidarity successfully transformed itself from an illegal underground movement into an election coalition and a potential government. Disputes were evident over the role of Solidarity as a labor movement, a social organization, or a political coalition. Differ-ences emerged over whether the "Citizens' Committee" should remain non-partisan to provide stability during Poland's political transformation or whether the formation of distinct political parties advanced pluralism. Wałęsa favored the latter approach.

Several stages in the evolution of Poland's pluralistic party system can be identified.[3] The first commenced with the destruction of the hegemonistic communist party system between May 1988 and January 1990. The second phase was the breakup of the dominant Solidarity movement, leading to a fragmented party system for the October 1991 parliamentary elections. This was followed by a considerable realignment prior to the September 1993 elections that inaugurated the third phase of party consolidation across the political spectrum.

In August 1989, Wałęsa proposed that Solidarity form a government with the two parties formerly allied with the communists, the United Peasants' Party (UPP) and the Democratic Party (DP). During protracted maneuvers to form a new administration, Soviet and Polish leaders understood that only a Solidarity-led cabinet could assure political stability and public calm, and that the PUWP was in no position to tackle the country's dire economic problems. A new coalition government was formed in September 1989. The communists were allowed to maintain control over the defense and interior ministries in order to assuage Moscow. Opposition activist Tadeusz Mazowiecki was confirmed as Prime Minister. Mazowiecki launched a radical "shock therapy" economic reform program designed by Finance Minister Leszek Balcerowicz to rapidly create a market economy.

In September 1990, following intensive political pressure, Jaruzelski stepped down as head of state. Wałęsa won the direct presidential elections in November and December 1990 after two rounds of voting, receiving 74% of the total. Prior to the ballot, the Solidarity movement had split into two major wings, the pro-Wałęsa Center Alliance and the pro-Mazowiecki Democratic Action, later renamed the Democratic Union. Mazowiecki only received 18% of the vote in the first round of the presidential elections, losing to unknown populist Stanisław Tymiński, who played on public impatience with falling living standards and rising unemployment and who eventually finished second to Wałęsa. Shortly after the elections, Mazowiecki resigned as Prime Minister, claiming a lack of public confidence in his government. Wałęsa nominated Jan Krzysztof Bielecki as Prime Minister, and the premier formed a "government of experts."

The first fully free parliamentary elections, in October 1991, held under a proportional representation system, produced an extremely fragmented parliament, with 29 parties taking seats in the *Sejm*. Only 43% of voters had participated in the elections, and no party had scored more than 12% of the vote; 11 parties or coalitions obtained only one seat each in the legislature. Most of the parties entering parliament were small and based around personalities rather than policies and constituencies. After six weeks of negotiations, a coalition government was formed in December 1991 under the premiership of Jan Olszewski. But the coalition proved weak, and broke up after only six months.

The Olszewski government asked for emergency powers in February 1992 because of growing frustrations over relations between president and government. The cabinet also came into conflict with the ex-communist bloc and with several post-Solidarity parties when it launched a controversial campaign of revelations about communist collaborators. Olszewski removed Wałęsa's appointee for the Minister of Defense and precipitated a showdown between the ministry and the President's National Security Bureau. The Olszewski government fell in June 1992, with a vote of no-confidence in the *Sejm*.

A short-lived candidacy by Waldemar Pawlak for prime minister in June 1992 was followed in July 1992 by the formation of a seven-party coalition under Prime Minister Hanna Suchocka, the first woman to be elected premier in Polish history. This broad coalition included liberals, social democrats, and Christian democrats. The Suchocka administration survived until it lost a parliamentary vote of no-confidence by a single vote on 28 May 1993. President Wałęsa dissolved parliament and called new elections.

The new electoral law introduced a threshold for parliamentary entry: a party needed to obtain 5% of the vote, and a coalition had to gain 8%. This limited the number of parties entering the *Sejm* but created a skewed party configuration that favored the more united leftist bloc against a fractured post-Solidarity movement. The parliamentary ballot on 19 September 1993 brought former communists and communist-allied parties to power, as the public had become disillusioned with the post-Solidarity government and expected a leftist administration to help cushion them against rapid economic reform. The ex-communists themselves had avoided the bitter frictions that characterized the Solidarity movement and had maintained their substantial assets and organizational networks to mount a credible election campaign. While the ex-communists pursued a market reform program, some sections of the Solidarity coalition adopted a more welfarist and statist economic agenda. The center-right parties failed to forge sufficient political unity, despite calls for a broad Christian democratic bloc, thus exaggerating the margin of victory for the leftist parties.

The Democratic Left Alliance (DLA) won 20.4% of the vote and gained 171 seats in the 460-seat *Sejm*. It formed a majority coalition with the Polish Peasant Party (PPP), which won 15.4% of the vote and 132 seats. The two parties came close to having a two-thirds majority in the legislature enabling them to change constitutional laws. The leftist government, first under Waldemar Pawlak of the PPP (October 1993), then under Józef Oleksy of the DLA (March 1995), and finally under Włodzimierz Cimoszewicz (February 1996), found itself at odds with President Wałęsa over numerous issues. For the most part, the DLA-PPP governments upheld the main tenets of structural economic reform and pursued a pro-Western foreign policy.

The early 1990s were marked by persistent battles between the President and the parliament, as Poland had inherited a semi-presidential system in which the powers of the executive were not strictly defined or circumscribed.

In December 1992, a "Little Constitution" was passed, giving the President substantial powers in a complex process of nominating governments. Wałęsa used the numerous constitutional ambiguities to extend his prerogatives and the powers of the executive branch while keeping the leftist government off balance. For example, the President retained powers over the government through his appointment of three key ministries: defense, interior, and foreign affairs. He also retained veto powers and the right to dissolve parliament, thus often creating a political stalemate between the executive and the legislature.

However, the "Little Constitution" was only a temporary replacement for the 1952 communist document. It was supposed to ensure political stability, but in fact, it laid out an unclear framework for legislative-executive relations that led to conflicts between these two branches of government. The early elections of 1993, which brought the Democratic Left Alliance (DLA) coalition into power, offered an opportunity to work on a new full constitution. The parliamentary constitutional committee, chaired by DLA politicians, began work on the draft of the constitution in 1994. After years of acrimonious debate, on 2 April 1997, both the *Sejm* and the Senate approved a new constitution with the votes of the DLA, the Polish Peasant Party (PPP), Freedom Union (FU), and the Union of Labor (UL), despite the objections of the Non-Party Bloc for the Support of Reforms (NBSR), the Confederation for an Independent Poland (CIP), Solidarity, and a few representatives from the PPP. On 25 May 1997, the Polish electorate voted in a referendum, with 52.71% approving the new constitution that limited presidential powers, and 45.09% against. On July 15, 1997, the Supreme Court confirmed the validity of the referendum results. The new constitution of the Polish Third Republic went into effect on 17 October 1997.[4]

Presidential elections were held on 5 and 19 November 1995. The social democrat leader and former communist official Aleksander Kwaśniewski defeated the incumbent Wałęsa by 51.7% to 48.3% in the second round of the ballot. The voting preferences of the public indicated that they did not automatically transfer their support to the presidential candidates their parties had backed. Parties evidently maintained only limited influence over their supporters.[5] Kwaśniewski was inaugurated on 23 December 1995, but his swearing in was overshadowed by a government scandal over alleged contacts between the Soviet KGB and Polish Prime Minister Oleksy. Oleksy rejected the charges but subsequently resigned. President Kwaśniewski appointed deputy parliamentary speaker Włodzimierz Cimoszewicz of the DLA to be Prime Minister in February 1996.

Parliamentary elections were held on 21 September 1997. In the preceding months, approval ratings for the governing DLA-PPP coalition had dipped into single digits. The Solidarity Electoral Action (SEA) alliance, composed of three dozen centrist and rightist parties associated with the Solidarity labor union, presented itself as the noncommunist alternative to the ruling parties.

Under the leadership of Solidarity president Marian Krzaklewski, it took the center-right several years to regroup after their stunning loss in the 1993 general elections. In the vote, the SEA won the largest share with 33.8%, thus gaining 201 parliamentary deputies. The DLA obtained 27.1% and 164 seats, the Freedom Union (FU) 13.4% and 60 deputies, the Polish Peasant Party (PPP) garnered 7.3% of the vote and 27 deputies, and Movement for Reconstruction of Poland (MRP) 5.6% and six deputies. Two seats were also given to representatives of the German minority. The SEA gained a majority in the Senate race, obtaining 51 seats, while the DLA obtained 28 senators, the FU eight, the MRP five, and the PPP three; five senators were independent.[6]

Subsequently, the SEA entered into a coalition with the FU; together they held 261 out of 460 seats in the *Sejm*. Under a coalition agreement, the SEA headed most of the ministries, but the FU held the important posts of foreign affairs, defense, finance, and justice. On 15 October 1997, the SEA named Jerzy Buzek as prime minister, and the center-right cabinet was sworn in on 31 October 1997. In the local elections of October 1998, the first since a major administrative reorganization of the country, the SEA won the largest number of seats and the opposition DLA came in second. The FU performed poorly in the vote.[7]

Rifts became evident within the governing coalition over the pace of structural reform. The FU Finance Minister, Balcerowicz, periodically attacked the authorities for slow reforms, especially in privatizing the state sector. Disputes over cabinet seats amidst ministerial scandals contributed to a drop in government popularity. Political conflicts inside the administration between liberals and protectionists led to the departure of the FU from the coalition on 7 June 2000. Although the Buzek government survived, it remained weak and unpopular.

Support for the administration was low in public opinion polls, largely due to discontent over the ambitious reform programs in heath care, social security, education, the mining sector, and the pension system. Critics charged that too many reforms provoked numerous simultaneous social conflicts. Meanwhile, support for the opposition Social Democrats was steadily climbing, and their candidate, Kwaśniewski, regained the country's presidency in elections on 8 October 2000. Kwaśniewski gained 53.9% of the popular vote in the first round, easily beating the nearest challengers from the Solidarity coalition, including its leader Marian Krzaklewski.

Poland was not burdened with onerous minority questions during its systemic transformation. The country's ethnic minorities totaled fewer than 3% of the population. Shortly after the accession of the first post-communist government in August 1989, minority affairs were removed from the jurisdiction of the Interior Ministry and placed under the control of the Ministry of Culture. Other institutions were established to protect minority rights, including a Commission for National and Ethnic Minorities in the *Sejm*. The Commission included representatives of ten ethnic organizations and deputies whose constituencies included sizable minority groups. Commission members pressed for an increase in state funds for minority organizations and their cultural and educational activities. They also sought to amend the Polish constitution in order to strengthen the defense of minority rights and to create the office of ombudsman for national minorities. In July 1991, the *Sejm* Commission for National and Ethnic Minorities recommended guarantees for minority representation in parliament, but its proposals were not ratified. In July 1992, the Extraordinary Commission for Electoral Affairs formulated an electoral law that lowered the number of signatures required by minority candidates for registration, eliminated the need for minority parties to acquire a minimum 5% of the vote, and established single minority districts. This move specifically addressed the problems faced by minority populations such as Ukrainians, who were spread throughout the country and not consolidated in easily demarcated electoral districts.[8]

The question of Silesian regionalism gained more prominence in Polish politics, and a Silesian movement elected two deputies to the lower house of parliament in the October 1991 elections. Some Polish Silesian organizations pressed for administrative decentralization and greater autonomy in economic, cultural, and political affairs, claiming discrimination by Warsaw. They calculated that Silesian autonomy would result in a substantial inflow of German capital into the region. By contrast, many local Polish activists feared that autonomist movements could be manipulated by radical German organizations.

The Charter of Rights and Liberties, signed by President Wałęsa in November 1992, stated that all citizens were equal before the law and that no individual would be discriminated against because of his or her membership in an ethnic group.[9] The Polish authorities recognized the right of all minorities to their distinct identity, culture, language, and social and political representation. Warsaw took several steps to improve opportunities for ethnic groups to establish independent organizations, gain education in their mother tongue, engage in cultural and artistic pursuits, and to obtain political representation at local and national levels. Conversely, there was a visible ethnic revival, particularly among members of the younger generation and among minorities emboldened by the achievement of national independence by Ukraine, Belarus, and Lithuania.

POLITICAL PARTIES

Socialists and Social Democrats

Democratic Left Alliance (DLA)
Sojusz Lewicy Demokratycznej (SLD)

Formed on 26 July 1991, the Democratic Left Alliance (DLA) served initially as an electoral committee that combined an assortment of left-wing forces.

DLA members included political parties, civic organizations, and labor unions. Social Democracy of the Republic of Poland (SDRP) took the leading role in the Alliance. Other significant members were the All-Polish Accord of Trade Unions (AATU) and the Polish Socialist Party (PSP). In the October 1991 parliamentary elections the DLA won a total of 12% of the vote. On 7 July 1993, before the early general elections, leaders of 28 leftist parties and organizations again signed an accord, which formed the DLA coalition and inaugurated the DLA's parliamentary club. In that election held in September 1993, support for the DLA rose to 20.4% of the total vote. The DLA formed the governing coalition, together with the Polish Peasant Party (PPP). In the September 1997 parliamentary election, the Alliance repeated its success, gaining 27.1% of the popular vote but were defeated by the Solidarity coalition. On 26 April 1999, representatives of the DLA's member organizations created a political party under the DLA name that was headed by Leszek Miller.

Social Democracy of the Republic of Poland (SDRP)
Socjaldemokracja Rzeczpospolitej Polskiej (SdRP)

Social Democracy of the Republic of Poland (SDRP) was created as the successor to the Polish United Workers' Party (PUWP), which had dominated the country between 1948 and 1989.[10] Following the June 1989 elections, the PUWP suffered a major identity crisis with a major outflow of members and severe personality conflicts. Several party factions tried to emerge out of the splintering PUWP. Initially, a leftist party, the Polish Social Democratic Union (PSDU) *(Polska Unia Socjaldemokratyczna),* emerged from the defunct PUWP. The party was led by Tadeusz Fiszbach, former first secretary of the Gdansk PUWP Committee, together with 25 parliamentary deputies. The party failed to attract any significant followers and it quickly disappeared. Meanwhile, a former PUWP satellite, the Democratic Party (DP), also lacking any social base, departed from the political scene after contesting the October 1991 parliamentary elections. SDRP emerged as the only viable successor to the PUWP.

The eleventh and last congress of the PUWP on 27 January 1990 was postponed while its delegates took part in the founding congress of Social Democracy of the Republic of Poland (SDRP) on the following day. In a process described as a congressional transfer, SDRP was acknowledged as the successor to the PUWP on 28 January 1990 and elected Aleksander Kwaśniewski as its chairman. The resumed PUWP congress announced the party's dissolution and transferred all of its property to SDRP.

SDRP faced attempts to confiscate its assets based on the claim that they had been illegally accumulated. Some SDRP buildings were taken over by local authorities and citizens' committees, and the *Sejm* created a government commission to deal with PUWP assets. The post-communist origins of SDRP also led to accusations by opponents that it had essentially remained the same party painted in different colors. This was denied by SDRP leader Kwaśniewski, who emphasized that the party was formed by pro-reform groups that had been active within the PUWP.

The SDRP founding declaration formulated its social democratic orientation. It recognized the will of the people expressed through democratic elections as the only source of power, and associated the future of Poland with democratic socialism. It supported a parliamentary democracy, a multi-party political system, and local self-government. Emphasis was placed on tolerance, the separation of church and state, and the state's neutrality with respect to citizens' religious beliefs. In the economic sphere, the SDRP underscored "social justice" and supported a market economy with "elements of interventionism and the social responsibility of the state." It denounced treating unemployment as an element of the market mechanism, and called for the constitutional protection of natural resources and the environment, for the equality of women, and for decreasing the difference in the standard of living between rural and urban areas. It also aspired toward creating a united left bloc.[11]

In March 1990, party membership was estimated at 47,000, and the number grew to 65,000 by February 1994.[12] For the 1990 presidential elections, the SDRP supported the candidacy of nonpartisan Włodzimierz Cimoszewicz (who became Poland's Prime Minister in 1996–1997) as part of its campaign for a unified left. Cimoszewicz won 9.21% of votes in the first round. On 26 July 1991, the national election committee of the Democratic Left Alliance (DLA) was formed, which included the SDRP and 14 small leftist organizations, trade unions, and political parties. In the October 1991 parliamentary elections, the DLA won over 11% of the vote—only 0.3% behind the liberal Democratic Union (DU)—and obtained 60 seats in the *Sejm* and four in the Senate.

Within the DLA coalition, the SDRP achieved significant success in the parliamentary elections on 19 September 1993. The DLA received 20.4 % of the vote and 171 seats in the *Sejm*, 37 in the Senate, and formed a coalition government with the Polish Peasant Party (PPP), led by Waldemar Pawlak. The Pawlak government survived until February 1995, when the premier had to step down after a threat by President Wałęsa to dissolve the parliament. The PPP agreed to the candidacy of Józef Oleksy, the speaker of the *Sejm* and vice chairman of SDRP, for the post of prime minister, in exchange for the election of the PPP's Józef Zych as the new parliamentary speaker. The DLA and the PPP formally confirmed their coalition agreement in October 1993.[13]

On 25 November 1995, after winning the presidential elections, SDRP Chairman Kwaśniewski gave up the party leadership and claimed that he would never join any other party. At the fifth SDRP convention, on 27 January 1996, Józef Oleksy was elected the new party chairman, receiving 308 out of 325 votes, only days after he had resigned from the post of prime minister, which he had occupied since March 1995. Oleksy stressed the need for the party to be more active at the grassroots level and confirmed the SDRP's continued commitment to the coalition with the PPP. Oleksy was succeeded as Prime

Minister by the nonpartisan deputy Sejm speaker, Włodzimierz Cimoszewicz. In the local elections in June 1996, the DLA won in 75 out of 142 cities. SDRP participated in drafting the new national constitution, and the DLA coalition voted in support of it in February 1997.

In the September 1997 parliamentary elections, the DLA ended up second, with 27.1% of the vote, almost 7% behind the Solidarity Electoral Action (SEA) and nearly 14% ahead of the third-place FU. The SEA and the FU gained 201 and 60 seats respectively and formed a coalition government headed by Jerzy Buzek of the SEA. Since the DLA received only 164 seats, SDRP, the backbone of the leftist coalition, became an opposition party. SDRP's image had been damaged by Warsaw's inability to deal effectively with the heavy floods that had affected southwestern Poland in the summer of 1997. Party leaders pointed to improvements in many social spheres, such as the condition of public sector employees and pensioners, as well as to the foundation laid for economic growth, as the fulfillment of their 1993 pre-election promises.[14] The party's revamped election program set the goals of economic growth, the lowering of personal and corporate taxes, an active industrial policy, privatization, and preparation for entry into the North Atlantic Treaty Organization (NATO) and the European Union (EU).[15]

At the third SDRP congress, on 6 December 1997, Leszek Miller, leader of the DLA parliamentary club, was elected chairman.[16] Krzysztof Janik replaced Jerzy Szmajdziński as secretary-general, while Szmajdziński was elected deputy chairman. The congress concluded that the party's most important tasks were to improve its infrastructure, strengthen regional and local party structures, and create conditions for the equality of women in social life.[17]

On 8 October 2000, Aleksander Kwaśniewski was re-elected to the presidency by a wide margin, gaining 53.9% of the vote. Andrzej Olechowski, an independent, came in second, with 17.3%, and Marian Krzaklewski, of the Solidarity Electoral Action (SEA), came in third, with 15.6%. Kwaśniewski was a prime example in Central Europe of a former Communist Party official active in the official youth movement who genuinely transformed himself into a democratic leader. He garnered substantial support both at home and abroad for his commitment to far-reaching structural reform, NATO membership, and Poland's inclusion in the European Union. Despite government cuts in social programs as a means of controlling the state budget and furthering the development of a free-market economy, Kwaśniewski retained broad popularity in Poland throughout his first term in office.

Union of Labor (UL)
Unia Pracy (UP)

Economist Ryszard Bugaj founded the Union of Labor (UL) in October 1992, following a merger between Labor Solidarity and the Democratic Social Movement organized outside parliament by Zbigniew Bujak, a former Soli-

darity underground activist. The UL became a social democratic party with
roots in the Solidarity labor movement, drawing upon the pro-independence,
anti-communist, and cooperative traditions of the Polish left. The party also
remained open to former members of the communist party. The UL depicted
itself as a party of the new left wing, indeed the only substantial and consistently leftist party on the Polish political scene.[18] It refused to recognize the
post-communist social democrats as genuinely left-wing and instead accused
them of "crypto-liberalism."

In the initial post-communist period, the party's program focused on curbing recession, fighting poverty, and limiting social inequalities through income redistribution. The Union supported a mixed, social market economy
close to the German or Scandinavian model, with considerable space for a
state economic sector. In the party's view, privatization needed to be carried
out according to commercial principles, "on honest financial terms." The Union
also gave consistent support for a civic state ruled by law.

In the general elections of 19 September 1993, the Labor Union won 7.3%
of the vote and obtained 41 *Sejm* seats. It remained in opposition and refused
to join the PPP-DLA coalition. However, it supported the coalition on occasion—for example, to overrule presidential vetoes.[19] The UL congress in May
1995 expressed support for the candidacy of Tadeusz Zieliński for the Polish
presidency.[20] Some UL members, however, supported the former Labor Minister Jacek Kuroń. In some cities, such as Wrocław, Kraków, Bydgoszcz, and
Białystok, they refused to withdraw from the Social Committee in Support of
Jacek Kuroń for President. The possibility of a split in the party became apparent. Karol Modzelewski, a UL honorary chairman, left the party after it
decided to support Zieliński. In June 1995, the party's National Council decided that the Union would be involved in Zieliński's presidential campaign.
Individual party members were allowed to support Kuroń. In addition, while
ruling out any alliances with the Social Democrats, the Council decided that
other coalitions might be formed.[21]

After 1995 the Union steadily lost popular support, resulting in a failure to
gain any seats after the September 1997 elections, when it only captured 4.4%
of the vote. The UL expressed willingness to cooperate with the new President on matters of importance to the state such as foreign policy and internal
security. According to UL spokesmen, the ruling Social Democrats, while
presenting themselves as leftist, were actually continuing the policies of liberal capitalism. The UL intended to defend the interests of working people by
establishing a "social market economy." Ryszard Bugaj proposed the idea of
creating a social-liberal bloc, independent of the DLA, with Jacek Kuroń as
its head.[22] The party also decided to exclude Wojciech Lamentowicz from the
party due to his active support of Kwaśniewski in the presidential campaign.

In a UL National Council resolution in February 1996, the party reaffirmed
its commitment to develop alone on the political stage and its reluctance to
join either the post-communist or the post-Solidarity camp. The resolution

addressed the issue of waning UL support, attributing this to the failure of the party to project a positive and distinct image. It planned to develop an "alternative project" for resolving socioeconomic problems.[23] Some overtures were also made for collaboration with the post-communist All-Polish Accord of Trade Unions (AATU).[24]

For the parliamentary elections of September 1997, the UL campaigned under the slogan "You deserve more." It fielded 700 candidates, among them Ryszard Bugaj, Artur Smołko, Zbigniew Bujak, Tomasz Nałęcz, and Aleksander Małachowski. Agreements were signed with several labor unions, under which their representatives could run on UL lists. An agreement was also arranged with members of the Belarusian Union.[25] The UL excluded the possibility of a coalition with either the Movement for the Reconstruction of Poland (MRP) or with the Union of Real Politics (URP), claiming that their programs contained many populist and unrealistic elements at a time when ideology should be left out of government programs.

In September 1997, the UL failed to reach the 5% barrier and did not enter the *Sejm*. This defeat prompted the resignation of Bugaj from the chairmanship, as he accepted responsibility for the debacle. However, he did not resign from the party or abandon political activity altogether, expressing an interest in dealing with programmatic issues. At the sixth congress of the party, held on 28 February 1998, Marek Pol was elected chairman. His deputies included Izabela Jaruga-Nowacka, Józef Pinior, and Tomasz Nałęcz. Aleksander Małachowski became the chairman of the UL national council. At the same time, 30 UL members, eaded by Zbigniew Bujak, left the Union and joined the FU in protest against allegedly closer cooperation by UL leaders with the ex-communists.

On 27 June 1998, the UL formed a coalition with the PPP and the National Party of Senior Citizens and Pensioners (NPSCP), called the Social Alliance, to run together in the local elections of October 1998. According to UL chairman Pol, the coalition would remain oriented toward social issues and represent people who suffered as a result of Poland's far-reaching economic reforms.[26] Another social democratic formation, the historical Polish Socialist Party (PSP), proved unable to capture any significant support after it became active again in Poland, especially after the death of two of its chief activists, Edward Lipiński and Jan Józef Lipski.

National Party of Senior Citizens and Pensioners (NPSCP)
Krajowa Partia Emerytów i Rencistów (KPEiR)

The National Party of Senior Citizens and Pensioners (NPSCP) was founded in June 1994 after a merger of several organizations from Bydgoszcz, Łódź, Konin, Słupsk, and Warsaw. Initially only pensioners and people nearing retirement were admitted, but in early 1996 all adults became eligible. In April 1997, the party had 44 regional offices, with a membership of 23,000.[27] The NPSCP expressed its desire to be a centrist party. Its political priorities included a defense of "national interests" and economic growth, to improve the living conditions of older people, pensioners, the unemployed, the homeless, and single parents. According to the party's deputy chairman, Lucjan Patyk, the platform was for those persons treated like second-class citizens.[28] The party also expressed its support for Poland's integration into the EU and NATO.

NPSCP supporters were almost exclusively people over 50 years of age who believed that the party could stand up for their interests. Younger people demonstrated almost no interest in joining. The election lists for the September 1997 parliamentary elections included scientists, physicians, and lawyers. Polls conducted by the Public Opinion Research Center (CBOS) in 1996–1997 showed limited support for the party countrywide, ranging from 3% in December 1996 to 6% in January 1997.[29] In the elections the party won only 2.7% of the vote, thus failing to obtain *Sejm* seats. In June 1998, the NPSCP entered into an alliance with the PPP and the UL in preparation for the October 1998 local elections.

All-Polish Accord of Trade Unions (AATU)
Ogólnopolskie Porozumienie Związków Zawodowych (OPZZ)

The All-Polish Accord of Trade Unions (AATU) was founded on 24 November 1984, after all existing union organizations had been disbanded by communist leader General Wojciech Jaruzelski under martial law in 1982. It grouped together 126 union federations and 9 national unions. Alfred Miodowicz was elected as the leader. Created under administrative pressure, the AATU became a part of the communist system not much different from the pre-1980 period, and it took the place of Solidarity along with its members and property.[30] As of the end of 1996, the union claimed a membership of 3.2 million; as part of the DLA it had 42 deputies in the *Sejm* elected in 1997.

Despite being a labor organization, the AATU played a significant role in the Polish political scene. In the late 1980s, the leadership of the AATU demonstrated independence from the PUWP and their opposition to government policies. AATU representatives took part in the national roundtable negotiations, attempting to emphasize their independence from the government. In the elections of June 1989, the AATU participated as a member of the government coalition and received 11 mandates. After Miodowicz resigned in July 1989 from the PUWP politburo, relations between the party and the AATU worsened. The AATU initially supported the government of Tadeusz Mazowiecki, but disagreements appeared after the implementation of tough economic reforms. The AATU was critical of the social and economic situation and presented 12 demands, mainly regarding issues of salaries and indexation. In the 1990 presidential elections, the AATU supported Mazowiecki while not voicing any support in the second round. In June 1990, at the second AATU congress, a programmatic declaration voiced support for a transition to a market economy, with the state retaining influence over the economy to "enable the realization of the appropriate policy in the social sphere."[31]

In December 1991, Ewa Spychalska became the AATU chairwoman. Spychalska was replaced by Józef Wiaderny in September 1996, after she was appointed ambassador to Belarus. Wiaderny won 137 out of 187 votes in the union council, defeating Stanisław Wiśniewski. Wiaderny emphasized the need for the union to become more professional while obtaining a stronger position within the DLA and striking a balance between business and working circles.[32] Wiaderny was re-elected to the post of chairman at the fourth congress, on 29–30 May 1998, by nearly 85% of the votes.

In July 1993, the AATU was one of the signatories of the SDRP-led DLA coalition agreement. The success of the DLA in the September 1993 parliamentary elections provided the AATU with over 60 seats in the *Sejm*. In February 1996, relations between the AATU and SDRP underwent a crisis, as the Accord complained about being disregarded as a partner and demanded that SDRP enter a cooperation agreement concerning economic, informational, and propaganda policies, so that the DLA would not be represented solely by SDRP.

The AATU also felt offended for not being invited to participate in government coalition talks. AATU chairwoman, Spychalska suspended her duties as the deputy chairwoman of the DLA parliamentary club until the agreement was signed.[33] In a meeting with President Kwaśniewski in April 1996, AATU representatives complained about social conditions in the country and criticized the President for making promises he could not fulfill. They also expressed concerns about Poland's accession to the EU and NATO, claiming that Poland would be treated as a second-class member and fearing that the country's agricultural sector would be destroyed.[34]

After the September 1997 parliamentary elections, the AATU, as part of the DLA, found itself in the political opposition. In March 1998, it entered into a dispute with the Solidarity coalition government of Jerzy Buzek regarding Warsaw's failure to negotiate with the AATU on its social and welfare policy demands. AATU spokesman Marek Opaśnik organized protests in April 1998 with the participation of the UL and SDRP. The participants accused the government of breaking the law by not consulting the trade unions about draft laws. The unionists threatened withdrawal from the Trilateral Commission (of government, employers, and union representatives) and complained to the International Labor Organization that their demands for talks with the government had not been met.

Liberals

Freedom Union (FU)
Unia Wolności (UW)

The Freedom Union (FU) was established on 23 April 1994, with the unification of the Democratic Union (DU) *(Unia Demokratyczna)*, led by former

Prime Minister Tadeusz Mazowiecki, and the Liberal Democratic Congress (LDC) *(Kongres Liberałów Demokratycznych)*, with Krzysztof Bielecki as its leader. Both organizations were splinters of the Solidarity labor movement that supported fast-paced market reform and the construction of a capitalist economy. The LDC was more fervently *laissez-faire* than the DU. In March 1998, the FU claimed a membership of over 11,000. It was one of the country's biggest political parties.[35]

The DU was established in December 1990 and grew out of the Citizens' Movement for Democratic Action (CMDA) *(Ruch Obywatelski Akcji Demokratycznej)* created by prominent Solidarity activists and intellectuals, including Bronisław Geremek, Jacek Kuroń, and adam Michnik. It also absorbed the Forum of the Democratic Right (FDR), which included moderate conservatives such as Aleksander Hall and Jerzy Turowicz. The DU rallied together several groups supporting Tadeusz Mazowiecki as candidate in the presidential elections of November–December 1990. The Gdansk-based LDC had existed since October 1990. The first FU chairman was Mazowiecki, and the deputy chairman, Donald Tusk.

The FU consisted of several political strands, including liberals, social democrats, and Christian democrats. The liberal wing of the party, led by Jan Maria Rokita, suggested that the party leadership be handed to someone not associated with any of the party's factions. He favored Leszek Balcerowicz, the former deputy prime minister of the first two post-communists governments, as an ideal candidate. While Mazowiecki took the chairman's post, party leaders tried to convince Balcerowicz to join the party and become its leader. The left wing of the party was the strongest supporter of this idea and expected Balcerowicz to change the FU's public image into a more dynamic one. The right wing claimed that under his leadership the Union would tilt toward social liberalism, and that only Mazowiecki could guarantee the stability of the party and maintain a credible opposition to the governing coalition.[36]

The Freedom Union was basically a pragmatic centrist party, grouping people of different ideological backgrounds. The FU tried to cover the entire political center and thus tended to suffer from internal structural problems.[37] The Union's objective was to strengthen Poland's democratic system and lead the country towards integration with NATO and the EU. It supported comprehensive privatization, but also wanted to ensure a broad social welfare umbrella. The Union preferred an active social policy, seeking to curb unemployment through the stimulation of private enterprise, and it supported a reform of the social insurance system. The other important goals of the Union included the development of citizens' activism, administrative decentralization, and local self-government.

In the October 1991 parliamentary elections, the DU gained the largest percentage of votes, with 12.3%, and captured 62 seats in the *Sejm*, while the LDC attained 7.4% and 37 seats. The two parties participated in the broad coalition government of Hanna Suchocka. In the September 1993 elections following the downfall of the Suchocka government, the DU received a modest 10.6% of the votes, coming in third behind the DLA with 20.4% of the vote and the PPP with 15.4%. The DU gained 74 seats in the *Sejm*. The LDC, receiving just 4%, did not obtain the minimum necessary for representation in parliament. The two parties united to form the FU in April 1994. Following the local elections on 19 June 1994, the FU governed or co-governed in many districts, especially in the larger cities.

In 1994, the social liberal Democratic Forum (DF) emerged within the FU; the faction was established by Władysław Frasyniuk and Zofia Kuratowska. A center-right fraction also emerged despite the fact that the party's statutes prohibited internal factions. In December 1994, the Union's presidium appealed to the FU council not to acknowledge the DF. Bronisław Geremek and Jan Lityński voted against this decision. It became clear that two wings of the party, the social liberal and the center right, were in confrontation: the Union's center seemed too weak to prevent it.[38]

The FU took a critical position toward the government of Waldemar Pawlak, especially its economic policy. The Union insisted on implementing a plan for keeping inflation at a level of some 17%, as well as on reforming the insurance system, health service, and the pension and educational systems.[39] When Prime Minister Józef Oleksy was involved in spying allegations, the Union's national council demanded his immediate resignation and called for the formation of a new government.[40]

On 1–2 April 1995, the Union held its second national congress. Balcerowicz was elected as the new leader, replacing Mazowiecki. The congress also named Jacek Kuroń, the former minister of labor and social policy, as the party's presidential candidate. Observers from the right of the political spectrum noted that the Union had moved leftward at its congress.[41] According to Jan Maria Rokita, a Union deputy, the selection of Kuroń antagonized party voters; opinion polls indicated that only 40% of voters favored Kuroń's candidacy, while 20% were against him.[42]

In the first round of presidential elections in November 1995, the Union supported Kuroń. In the second round, the party's national council appealed for support for Wałęsa. The council stressed that Kwaśniewski's presidency would jeopardize political change in Poland and that the continuation of reform could only be guaranteed by Wałęsa. After the elections, the possibility of confrontation within the party increased. Chairman Balcerowicz accused Rokita of hurting Kuroń's campaign, while the right wing of the party declared that Rokita's removal from the national council presidium would be followed by their resignations. Balcerowicz stressed the need to maintain party discipline. He also opted for the Union's accession to the International Organization of Christian Democratic and Conservative Parties. The FU's left wing, represented by Frasyniuk, Kuratowska, and Krzysztof Dołowy, were opposed to this proposal.[43]

The Union's national council expelled Rokita from the presidium for disloyalty to the party and for not making an unequivocal declaration of support for Kuroń during the 1995 presidential elections. After the elections, the Gdansk FU group, together with five other post-Solidarity parties, decided to form a bloc to stand in the September 1997 parliamentary elections. The group also included Gdansk activists of the Center Accord, the Christian National Union, the Conservative Party, the Non-Party Bloc for the Support of Reforms, and Solidarity.[44]

The FU assumed a supportive position with respect to the new constitution adopted on 22 March 1997, and urged all the post-Solidarity political groupings to back it. It called for approval of the constitution in the May 1997 national referendum. In presenting the party's economic platform before the September 1997 parliamentary elections, FU Chairman Balcerowicz claimed that liberalization of the economy was a key to faster development. He stressed the reduction of taxes, particularly those that prevented the creation of legal workplaces, and the party's commitment to a liquidation of monopolies in the telecommunications, power, and gas sectors.[45]

In preparing for the September 1997 elections, the FU called upon the post-Solidarity political groupings not to engage in mutual attacks that would play into the hands of the post-communist left. FU leaders asserted that the Solidarity-led SEA was its main coalition partner, but cooperation with the Union of Labor was not ruled out. Cooperation with the PPP was said to be impossible, since it had participated in a government that had discredited itself according to the FU.[46]

In the general elections, the FU finished third, with 13.4% of votes, and gained 60 seats in the *Sejm*. Immediately after the elections, Union leadership became determined to form a coalition with the SEA. After difficult negotiations, a coalition agreement was signed on 20 October 1997 by Balcerowicz, SEA chairman Marian Krzaklewski, and new Prime Minister Jerzy Buzek. The coalition agreement contained 30 items concerning social, economic, and state issues. It stressed that increases in living standards should accompany economic growth. adherence to the principles of Christian civilization and patriotic upbringing of the younger generations was also agreed to.[47] On 28 February 1998, at the fourth FU congress, Balcerowicz was re-elected party chairman. In May 1998, the FU threatened to break the coalition as a result of the SEA's failure to consult on personnel decisions. Relations between the coalition partners remained strained until the resignation of all FU ministers from the Buzek cabinet in June 2000.

Liberal Conservative Movement of the One Hundred (LCMOH)
Liberalno-Konserwatywny Ruch Stu (LKRS)

The Liberal Conservative Movement of the One Hundred (LCMOH) was begun as the Committee of One Hundred (*Komitet Stu*), on 8 April 1995, by one hundred personalities from Polish politics, arts, and sciences. It was registered as a party on 24 November 1995. Czesław Bielecki, architect and publicist, and Andrzej Olechowski, economist and former minister of finance and foreign affairs, became the movement's leaders. LCMOH placed itself on the liberal conservative side of the political scene. Its long-term goals included reinforcing private ownership and the free market, increasing individual independence, improving the effectiveness of the state, and enhancing Poland's international position, while developing national culture and preserving the nation's heritage. As its most important task, LCMOH stressed increased private ownership, lowering taxes, making government accessible, and increasing local activities.[48]

The movement was one of the signatories of the SEA declaration in June 1996. In November 1996, Czesław Bielecki became a member of the SEA's provisional coordinating team. For the September 1997 elections, the LCMOH placed 40 candidates on the SEA electoral lists. Andrzej Olechowski left the party in August 1997, in protest against its joining the SEA, but he returned in December and resumed the party leadership alongside Bielecki. In January 1997, he resigned as chairman of the Movement's political council.

Christian Democrats

Solidarity Electoral Action (SEA)
Akcja Wyborcza Solidarność (AWS)

The origins of Solidarity Electoral Action (SEA) can be traced to the birth of the Independent Self-Governing Trade Union Solidarity (ISGTUS) *(Niepodległy Samorządny Związek Zawodowy Solidarność)*. The Union originated in 1980 as a result of workers' discontent with social conditions, which led to a series of strikes and the Union's recognition in the Gdansk Agreement of 31 August 1980. Solidarity was established at a conference of independent labor groups that was held in Gdansk on 17–18 September 1980 and chaired by Lech Wałęsa, who was to become the organization's undisputed leader. It was officially registered on 24 October 1980. In 1981, it had an estimated membership of 10 million workers—about half of the Polish labor force.

Solidarity was banned after the imposition of martial law by General Wojciech Jaruzelski on 13 December 1981. Several thousand of its leaders, members, and sympathizers were imprisoned.[49] A Provisional Coordinating Committee was formed to organize the underground functioning of the union, and it was able to continue its activity as a clandestine opposition, issuing appeals for strikes and demonstrations. In October 1987, the National Executive Commission (NEC) *(Krajowa Komisja Wykonawcza, KKW)* was created. It was comprised of all of the underground members of Solidarity and was chaired by Wałęsa. Its main purpose was to prepare for the union's re-legalization.

On 6 February 1989, crucial roundtable negotiations were initiated between Solidarity and the communist government. The negotiations lasted for two months and led to an agreement on partial non-communist representation in parliament, allowing for 35% of the *Sejm* deputies and all of the Senate deputies to be chosen in free elections. In the balloting held in June 1989, Solidarity-supported candidates won all the seats subject to free elections in the *Sejm* and almost all the Senate seats.

The first multiparty government was created in August 1989, and Tadeusz Mazowiecki, Wałęsa's advisor since the events of August 1980, was appointed prime minister. A critical situation developed within Solidarity when Wałęsa called for early presidential elections, intending to replace Jaruzelski. He pointed out that since the PUWP had ceased to exist, the roundtable accords were void. An informal split followed within Solidarity between those supporting the candidacy of Mazowiecki and those in favor of Wałęsa. Jarosław Kaczyński, an underground Solidarity activist during the 1980s and chief editor of the *Solidarity Weekly (Tygodnik Solidarność)* from 1989 to 1991, formed the Center Democratic Accord (CDA) (*Porozumienie Demokratyczne Centrum*) in support of Wałęsa's candidacy. Wałęsa admitted that he wanted to split Solidarity in two, in an attempt to prevent it from becoming a leftist party.

Two other organizations originated on the initiative of Solidarity members: the Democratic Right Forum (DRF) and the Citizens' Movement for Democratic Action (CMDA) *(Ruch Obywatelski Akcji Demokratycznej)*, which supported the candidacy of Mazowiecki. They formed an electoral alliance called the Democratic Union. After the elections, they united into a party with the same name; it later joined the Liberal Democratic Congress (LDC) to form the Freedom Union (FU). In the presidential elections of November–December 1990, Wałęsa was elected President, receiving 39.96% of votes in the first round and 74.75% in the second. In the October 1991 parliamentary elections, Solidarity only received 5.8% of the vote and gained 27 seats in the *Sejm* and 12 in the Senate. The *Sejm* was characterized by a broad dispersal of seats among parties, thus preventing any single group from acquiring significant influence.

In the September 1993 elections, following the dissolution of parliament after a no-confidence vote in the Suchocka government, Solidarity received 4.9% of the vote, thus failing to attain the minimum 5% necessary to gain representation in the *Sejm*. It had only nine seats in the Senate. Because of its election failure and due to the shock produced by the victory of the post-communist left and the presidential victory of Aleksander Kwaśniewski, an initiative was launched for rightist parties to unite into a broader bloc. The initiators believed that only Solidarity could serve as the unifying factor.[50] On 8 June 1996, a meeting of leaders of over 20 political groups took place in Warsaw organized by Solidarity Łódź region leader, Janusz Tomaszewski. The participants signed a declaration establishing the Solidarity Electoral

Action. The signatories expressed hope that SEA would be joined by the Movement for the Reconstruction of Poland (MRP), while rejecting possible cooperation with the FU.

Within the SEA, Solidarity Chairman Krzaklewski played the most prominent role, both in formulating the broad political platform that allowed cohabitation of diverse rightist parties, and in settling disputes among them. Unlike the All-Polish Accord of Trade Unions, which was described as a vassal of SDRP, Solidarity was compared to a feudal lord with numerous vassals forged into an effective election machine but made almost unrecognizable by an overlay of several dozen allied parties with which it formed the SEA bloc.[51]

The program adopted at Solidarity's seventh national congress identified its principal goals as the distribution of wealth through general enfranchisement, increasing real wages, protection against poverty, reducing unemployment, providing universal access to medicine, education, and culture, and securing social benefits. It paid particular attention to the protection of employee rights, including their participation in the privatization of state enterprises. Another important aspect of the program was the commitment to build social relations based on Catholic teachings.[52]

The SEA performed well in the September 1997 elections, receiving 33.8% of the vote, almost 7% ahead of the DLA, and gained 201 seats in the *Sejm* and 51 seats in the Senate. A ruling coalition was negotiated between the SEA and the Freedom Union, which led to the formation of the government of Jerzy Buzek, a prominent Solidarity activist. But by early 1999, public support for the SEA had slipped significantly as a result of a number of socially costly but economically necessary reform programs, including a restructuring of the health care system. As a result, the DLA opposition steadily gained in popularity, particularly among pensioners, employees of state-owned companies, housewives, skilled workers, farmers, and unskilled workers.[53] Some SEA leaders planned to transform the movement into a Christian democratic party along the lines of the German CDU, although such an ideological consolidation would likely result in a shrinkage of support and influence and a fragmentation of the broad-based coalition.

Christian National Union (CNU)
Zjednoczenie Chrzescijańsko-Narodowe (ZChN)

The Christian National Union (CNU) was founded in October 1989 by national-focused, right-of-center political activists from twenty regional centers. Led by Wiesław Chrzanowski and Antoni Macierewicz, the CNU cast itself as a Catholic-oriented traditionalist party that sought to recreate a fully independent Poland on the principles of "Catholic ethics" and a "Christian state." The Union wanted to guarantee strong Church influence in political and social life and declared a prolonged struggle against all leftist formations, including the post-communist and post-Solidarity socialists. Its program stressed Polish national unity and opposed any political or legal measures that encouraged regional separatism. In the field of culture, the CNU sought to develop a strong "national culture" and an education system free of "communist and materialist influences."

The CNU claimed a membership of 4,000 in 1990 and around 6,000 by 1994. It had an organizational base in 22 provinces, with particularly strong support in Białystok, the southern regions of Tarnów and Nowy Sącz, and in Łódź. CNU supporters generally advocated moderate pro-social solutions and were critical of the DLA-PPP government. They were also the most devout Catholics and supporters of the Church's social teachings.[54] In the 1990 presidential elections, the CNU supported the candidacy of Lech Wałęsa.

In the general elections of October 1991, the CNU entered the Catholic Action Coalition with several smaller groupings, scoring 8.73% of the popular vote and finishing third in an extremely fractured election. The Union obtained 49 deputies in the 460-seat lower house, and nine out of 100 senators. While several Christian democratic groups disassociated themselves from the CNU because of its allegedly extremist orientation, the Union was unofficially supported by many Catholic priests, some of whom reportedly instructed parishioners on how to cast their ballots on election days. The Union was a major supporter of anti-abortion legislation and of the 1992 lustration initiative to root out former communist collaborators.

After the fall of Jan Olszewski's government in June 1992, a group loyal to the ousted Prime Minister established the Movement for the Republic (MFR) *(Ruch dla Rzeczypospolitej)*, which retained 16 seats in the *Sejm* and adopted a quasi-nationalist, ultra-Catholic position. Macierewicz, a founder of the CNU, created a separate party, the Christian National Movement–Catholic Action (CNM-CA), while another Olszewski supporter, Jan Parys, created the Third Republic Movement (TRM). The CNU subsequently entered the governing coalition under premier Hanna Suchocka but continued to criticize its centrist and leftist partners for a failure to promote the desired Catholic renaissance and to oust former communist officials from all public posts. Leaders of various nationalist groupings purportedly hoped to build a larger "Christian coalition" in preparation for the September 1993 elections. The task proved difficult, as Poland's Catholic and nationalist-oriented forces remained more splintered than the center, the left, and the capitalist right.[55]

In the September 1993 elections, the CNU ran as a part of the Fatherland Catholic Electoral Committee, together with the Conservative Party and the Christian Peasant Alliance. The coalition failed to achieve the 8% minimum required to enter the *Sejm*, and the CNU found itself outside parliament. In October 1994, Wiesław Chrzanowski resigned as chairman of the party because of his age and stated that he would not be a candidate for the presidential elections. His post was assumed by Ryszard Czarnecki, who was elected at the fourth CNU congress in March 1995. Czarnecki focused his efforts on uniting different factions within the party, notably his own liberal wing and the nationalist faction led by Marek Jurek. In May 1995, the Union entered the Alliance for Poland (AFP), a rightist coalition, with the Center Accord (CA), later joined by Romuald Szeremietiew's MFR, the Peasant Accord (PA), and the Conservative Party (CP).

After the congress, the party leadership included a significant number of supporters of Wałęsa's candidacy, and its chief council assembled representatives of all party factions. In May 1995, Jurek was appointed by Wałęsa to head the National Radio and Television Council, in a move that was characterized as an attempt by Wałęsa to tip the balance within CNU to his advantage. The Union was undecided on whether to support adam Strzembosz, Wałęsa's rival for the presidency.[56] Eventually, Czarnecki and his followers supported Hanna Gronkiewicz-Waltz. At the fifth extraordinary congress, Czarnecki submitted his resignation after being accused of allowing the party to be pushed to the political margins. Czarnecki was replaced by Marian Piłka, who was re-elected chairman in February 1998.

The CNU was one of the parties that formed the Solidarity Electoral Action (SEA) in June 1996, and Marian Piłka became one of the deputy chairmen of the bloc. CNU ran in the September 1997 parliamentary elections as a part of the SEA. After the ballot, the Union assumed an aggressive stance towards the DLA, claiming that it should be isolated as an extremist party that builds its identity on the basis of conflict with Polish national traditions and on a struggle with the Catholic Church. The CNU was also critical of the coalition negotiations between the SEA and the FU.

Conservative Peasant Party (CPP)
Stronnictwo Konserwatywno-Ludowe (SKL)

The Conservative Peasant Party (CPP) was established on 12 January 1997, the result of the unification of Aleksander Hall's Conservative Party (CP) (Partia Konserwatywna) and Artur Balazs's Christian Peasant Alliance (CPA), as well as, represented by other rightist groups, including the Freedom Union— Jan Maria Rokita, Bronisław Komorowski, Wojciech Arkuszewski, Zdobysław Milewski, Andrzej Machowski, and Piotr Bruczkowski.[57] The CP had been established by Hall, who had left the Democratic Union to form a moderate conservative organization devoid of extremism. The CPP declared itself in favor of building a broad camp of the "contemporary right" and to create a viable alternative to the leftist formations. In its program, the CPP declared itself in support of such values as family, religion, and patriotism, and aspired to be a party functioning as a public service, deeply ideological but ready to make political compromises.[58] The CPP acknowledged its association with the Solidarity heritage from the 1980s and it participated in the Solidarity Electoral Action (SEA).[59]

The Conservative Party evolved when Hall's right-wing faction of the

Democratic Union left the DU in the fall of 1992 to establish a Christian democratic party that would counterbalance the CNU. For the September 1993 elections, the Conservative Party entered the Fatherland *(Ojczyzna)* alliance with the CNU and the CPA, but the coalition failed to gain the required 8% of the vote. A split occurred in the party after Kazimierz Michał Ujazdowski's Conservative Coalition withdrew its support. The CP's program emphasized a liberal economic policy, Christian values, and a pro-Western foreign policy. For the October 1991 parliamentary elections, the Christian Peasant Alliance had been a part of the Peasant Accord, which had evolved out of the Polish Peasant Party–Solidarity but later became a separate political party under the leadership of Artur Balazs. It held ten seats in the *Sejm* until the general elections of September 1993.

The supreme authority of the newly formed CPP elected Jacek Janiszewski as the national presidium chairman and Aleksander Hall as chairman of the political council, with Jan Maria Rokita and Mirosław Styczeń as deputies. Bronisław Komorowski was elected general secretary.[60] Hall sought to establish a conservative political segment within the SEA, apart from the labor union core, in order to create a program that would not only be radically anti-communist but also supportive of the middle class. Janiszewski affirmed the CPP's dedication to the interests of farmers, claiming that his party had always maintained that the interests of rural communities would be better protected by one strong political representation. The CPP was active within SEA, and after the latter's victory in the September 1997 elections, Hall proposed Rokita for the post of prime minister.

Non-Party Bloc for the Support of Reforms (NBSR)
Bezpartyjny Blok Wspierania Reform (BBWR)

The Non-Party Bloc for the Support of Reforms (NBSR) was founded in June 1993 with the support of Wałęsa and took the same initials as a group of Marshal Józef Piłsudski's supporters in 1928. According to one view, the idea was to make Wałęsa into a Piłsudski of the 1990s and to create a strong support base for him.[61] The Bloc was also intended to attract voters disenchanted with party politics.[62] However, it garnered only 5.4% of votes and 16 seats in the *Sejm* following the September 1993 elections. Andrzej Olechowski was the Bloc's unofficial leader and was succeeded by Jacek Lipiński after being appointed minister of foreign affairs in the Pawlak government. Among the questions confronting the NBSR was whether to remain a movement or to become a political party. It also needed to redefine its relations with President Wałęsa, who toned down his association with the Bloc after the unsuccessful election results. According to Zbigniew Religa, a prominent NBSR member, the Bloc would part company with Wałęsa if he ran with a different program.

The NBSR emphasized its differences with other parties in three aspects of its platform: support for a strong presidential system of government, a maxi-

The October 1991 parliamentary elections gave the PPP 8.7% of votes and 49 *Sejm* seats.

In the September 1993 elections, the PPP finished in second place, with 15.4% of the vote and 132 parliamentary seats. It formed a coalition with the DLA that led to the establishment of the government of Waldemar Pawlak, which lasted until March 1995, when under pressure from President Wałęsa and in agreement with the PPP's coalition partner, Pawlak stepped down and SDRP chairman Józef Oleksy formed a new government.

PPP influence in the countryside diminished significantly months before the September 1997 elections. According to a poll in July 1997, the SEA and the DLA each benefited from 24% support in rural areas, while the PPP had only 20%.[69] The DLA-PPP coalition lasted until the September 1997 elections, when it gained only 7.3% of the votes and 27 *Sejm* seats and subsequently went into opposition.

On 11 October 1997, both Pawlak and Zych were dismissed by the party's supreme council from their positions as party chairman and supreme council chairman respectively. Jarosław Kalinowski was elected as the new party chairman. He claimed that the PPP had been damaged by its participation in the coalition government with the DLA and he promised to rebuild the party's image in the countryside. On 27 June 1998, in preparation for the local government elections in October 1998, the PPP joined the Union of Labor (UL) and the National Pensioners' Party in a coalition called the Social Alliance. It was presented as a working people's alternative to the "next varieties of post-Solidarity and post-communist liberalism."[70]

Mikołajczyk–Polish Peasant Party (M-PPP)
Polskie Stronnictwo Ludowe–Mikołajczykowskie (PSL-M)

The Mikołajczyk–Polish Peasant Party (M-PPP) was organized on the initiative of Henryk Bak and Mieczysław Wardziński in June 1988. At the end of July 1989, the M-PPP united with the Independent Peasant Movement Solidarity. In April 1990, as a result of the conflict around unification with the PPP "Rebirth," Bak's supporters refused to take part in the unification congress and excluded its participants from their party. Bak became the chairman of the executive committee and Mieczysław Wardziński was elected chairman of the supreme council. The party claimed to be the heir to the ideals of the PPP led by Stanisław Mikołajczyk in the post–World War II years. It sued the PPP, led at that time by Roman Bartoszcze, for the right to use the party name, but while waiting for the court's decision it added to its name the adjective *Mikołajczykowskie*. Its statute was founded on that of the PPP of 1947. The party was registered in September 1990.

Peasant Alliance (PA)
Porozumienie Ludowe (PL)

The Peasant Alliance (PA) formed in 1991 when the Solidarity Polish Peasant Party (S-PPP) and the Rural Solidarity peasant union decided to run together in the October parliamentary elections. The leader of the party was Gabriel Janowski. After the elections, a faction of the S-PPP left to form the Christian Peasant Alliance (CPA), which later formed the Conservative Peasant Party (CPP). The Alliance gained 28 seats in the 1991 *Sejm*. It participated in the Olszewski and Suchocka government coalitions. The PA withdrew from the latter in April 1993 in protest of the government's agricultural policies. The party emphasized its anti-communism and its support for national and Christian values. It supported anti-abortion legislation and the lustration initiative. Its program included protectionism, cheap credit, price support for agriculture, and improved social benefits for farmers. Several smaller agrarian political groups were also formed in Poland, including the radical Farmers' Self-Defense (FSD) led by Andrzej Lepper, which supported violent protest actions allegedly in defense of peasants' interests and against an assortment of scapegoats, including liberals, bankers, and foreigners.

Greens

Polish Green Party (PGP)
Polska Partia Zielonych (PPZ)

The burst of political activity in the late 1980s and the early 1990s included the establishment of over 2,000 organizations with environmental agendas. The diverse groups that appeared during this period lacked cohesion and common goals and this deprived the movement of political influence.[71] The three main representatives of the Polish ecological movement were the Polish Green Party (PGP), the Polish Ecological Party of Greens (PEPG) *(Polska Partia Ekologiczna Zielonych)*, and the All-Poland Union of Greens (APUG) *(Ogólnopolski Związek Ruchów Zielonych)*. The PGP was set up on 10 December 1988 and claimed a membership of 4,000 supporters. The party launched the idea of an ecological green table, which would be a forum for all ecological organizations. Its priorities were the protection of the natural environment and changing ecological attitudes in society. In the October 1991 parliamentary elections, the PGP received a total of 71,043 votes, which did not guarantee any seats in parliament. No environmental group or party was represented in the Polish legislative branch during that term. In 1995, the PGP supported the candidacy of Aleksander Kwaśniewski for president. In September 1997, members of the PGP took part in the parliamentary elections on the Democratic Left Alliance (DLA) electoral list. The All-Poland Union of Greens, established in 1993, included thirteen local organizations and claimed a membership of some eight thousand people.

Nationalists

Confederation for Independent Poland (CIP)
Konfederacja Polski Niepodległej (KPN)

The Confederation for Independent Poland (CIP) was established in September 1979 as a political party challenging the communist monopoly of power and calling for an independent Poland. It was officially registered in August 1990. Its leader, Leszek Moczulski, served several prison sentences because of his oppositionist beliefs but was released shortly after the creation of the Solidarity free trade union in the summer of 1980. The CIP adopted a more militant position than the dissident movement linked with the Workers' Defense Committee and argued that Solidarity's agenda was too moderate in calling for independence and an end to Soviet domination. It obtained a following in several industrial centers, particularly in Szczecin, Łódź, and Upper Silesia, before the declaration of martial law by General Jaruzelski in December 1981. The Confederation continued to operate underground during martial law and throughout the 1980s, emerging as a distinct political formation in 1989.

The CIP traced its heritage to the "independence" tradition of Marshal Józef Piłsudski, who was instrumental in the formation of an independent Polish state after World War I. It criticized the various Solidarity splinter groups for their compromising approach toward the former communists. The CIP supported the creation of a market economy but expressed reservations about foreign investment and alien influences in Polish affairs. Although it considered its position to be both patriotic and pragmatic, it was criticized for its tendencies toward demagogy and populism and for calling for severe retribution against the deposed communist leadership and its accomplices.

The Confederation underwent various splits and fractures, and several of Moczulski's associates established their own parties and movements while continuing to draw upon the "independence" tradition. The CIP maintained a respectable support base in several Polish cities. It competed separately from Solidarity for the June 1989 elections, but failed to capture any parliamentary seats. Moczulski ran in the presidential elections in November 1990, having gathered the required 100,000 signatures for inclusion on the ballot. However, he finished in last place, garnering only 2.5% of the popular vote. In the May 1990 local elections, the CIP barely gained 0.1% of the available seats in local and municipal councils. The Confederation worked hard on expanding its national structures, and in the October 1991 general elections it gained 7.5% of the popular vote and obtained 48 *Sejm* seats, becoming the fourth largest party in parliament.

The CIP remained at odds with the governing coalition of Prime Minister Suchocka, and together with the ex-communist Democratic Left, the Peasant Party, the Center Alliance, and the quasi-nationalist Movement for the Republic (MFR), it successfully pressed for a vote of no-confidence in May 1993 and brought down Poland's fifth post-communist government. The CIP gained support among citizens dissatisfied with the effects of economic reform and the failure to purge the old communist structures. Like many nationalist organizations, the CIP proved difficult to pigeonhole programmatically. It adopted secular positions vis-à-vis the Catholic Church, voiced some support for preserving the welfare state, and did not adopt any overt racist or xenophobic positions. On the other hand, its chief focus was on increasing and preserving Poland's independence, guarding against unwelcome Russian influence, building an "Eastern Confederation" with Ukraine and Belarus, and defending the rights of Polish minorities in neighboring states.[72]

The CIP branded itself as an independence-minded party of the broadly defined "left wing." Many of its slogans, especially the economic ones, contained strong anti-communist rhetoric. Political opponents criticized the party's centralized, semi-democratic character. The CIP aimed at a model of a "social market economy" with various forms of ownership and a prevalence of private ownership and the guarded admission of foreign capital. The party believed that cheap credits and low taxes would accelerate the emergence of small private businesses. It also wanted a reduction in taxes, systematic wage increases, and full employment. At the CIP's third congress on 4 March 1989, Moczulski was elected chairman, and Krzysztof Król and Adam Słomka, deputy chairmen, of the CIP political council.

In the elections of 19 September 1993, the CIP won 5.8% of the votes and 22 seats in parliament. In public opinion polls held in December 1994, the Confederation benefited from about 4% of public support, and in January 1995, about 5%. In June 1995, it joined the St. Catherine's Covenant, composed of several minor rightist groupings, among them the Movement for the Republic, the Christian Democratic Party, the Movement for the Third Republic, and the Peasant Agreement. The Covenant held presidential primaries. Among others taking part were adam Strzembosz, Hanna Gronkiewicz-Waltz, Henryk Bąk, Jan Parys, Jan Olszewski, Wojciech Ziembiński, and Leszek Moczulski.[73] Moczulski's decision to run in the primaries was reached at the CIP's fifth congress in May 1995. The congress was held under the motto of integrating the anti-communist forces. In 1995, the membership of the CIP was 15,000.

On November 1995, after the first round of presidential elections, Moczulski appealed for public support for Wałęsa's candidacy. In early 1996, the party underwent an internal crisis, prompted by discontent with Moczulski's leadership. At an extraordinary CIP congress in mid-February, Moczulski and the leader of the party's parliamentary club, Krzysztof Król, lost votes in the political council and threatened to leave the Confederation and organize a new political formation.[74] On 16 March 1996, at an extraordinary session of the fifth CIP congress, adam Słomka was elected party chairman, while Moczulski was given the post of honorary chairman. He was accused of usurping decisionmaking in the party. Moczulski responded by calling a meeting of the old political council, which excluded the organizers of the congress, adam Słomka, Janusz Koza, and Maciej Popenda, from the party. Moczulski claimed that the congress was called illegally, alleging that the required minimal support for its organization, one fifth of active CIP members, had not been achieved.[75] Słomka did not recognize his expulsion and continued to consider himself the party leader while proclaiming a wish to build a "modern" party that would eliminate "one-person leadership."

On 24 April 1996, Moczulski excluded 10 deputies out of the 16 who had formed the CIP parliamentary club, and created instead a six-member CIP circle, together with his supporters—Grzegorz Cygonik, Krzysztof Kamiński, Krzysztof Król, Andrzej Ostoj-Owsiany, and Dariusz Wójcik.[76] Słomka and 10 other CIP deputies joined with 10 deputies from the Non-Party Bloc in Support of Reform to form the Federated Parliamentary Club. In December 1996, the Court of Appeals confirmed the legality of the fifth congress, where the decision to replace Moczulski and elect Słomka was taken. After rejecting once again the proposition to become honorary chairman, Moczulski, Król, and Wójcik were excluded from the party by the political council.[77]

In June 1996, both Moczulski's and Słomka's factions joined Solidarity Electoral Action (SEA), with Słomka becoming one of the deputy chairmen. Słomka's CIP became known as the CIP-Patriotic Camp. He threatened to leave the SEA if it were joined by the Freedom Union, while Moczulski stated that the SEA and the FU running separately would constitute suicide for the right.[78] Moczulski's CIP proposed in January 1997 that three programmatic blocs be formed within the SEA—national-independence, Christian-democratic, and democratic-liberal—so that voters could decide which program would receive more support.[79] In June 1997, deputy chairman Król accused the DLA and the FU of discriminating against the Catholic Church. In July 1997, Moczulski's CIP left the SEA, claiming that none of its members had been listed on the SEA's slate. He also announced the creation of a new rightist alliance that "would not act under the diktat of trade unions." Later, the Polish Right-Wing Alliance led by Moczulski's CIP asserted that it was ready to cooperate with the SEA, but the latter excluded the possibility of Moczulski's return.[80]

Słomka's CIP aggressively attacked the left, accusing the DLA of promoting the interests of the main centers of capital in the West, and claiming the DLA privatization program had given around 30 billion dollars to foreign management. The CIP staunchly opposed the new constitution and questioned the validity of the constitutional referendum that took place in May 1997. CIP deputies abstained during the SEA parliamentary group vote approving Jerzy

Buzek as Prime Minister. In February 1998, CIP leaders criticized the work of the new cabinet, charging it with carrying out the program of the Freedom Union and claiming that the SEA was departing from its pre-election promises. It also called for the replacement of three ministers.[81]

The CIP ran into conflict with the SEA due to disagreements on Poland's administrative reform. It voted against the division of the country into 12 voivodships. As a result, seven CIP deputies, including Słomka, were ejected from the SEA parliamentary club.[82] On 16 July 1998, Słomka resigned as deputy chairman of the SEA, in protest over the agreement reached by the SEA and leftist parties on a 16-voivodship structure. On 28 July 1998, the CIP created the Patriotic Movement–Homeland bloc, together with the Movement for the Reconstruction of Poland, the Bloc for Poland, and the National Alliance of Pensioners and Senior Citizens of the Republic of Poland, to run together in the October 1997 local elections, and to present an alternative to the SEA.

Movement for the Republic (MfR)
Ruch dla Rzeczypospolitej (RdR)

Jan Olszewski founded the Movement for the Republic (MFR) in the summer of 1992 after his Christian democratic faction left the Center Democratic Accord (CDA). The MfR was joined by the small Polish Independence Party, a Piłsudskiite formation that advocated a free market, Christian social teachings, the regionalization of Poland along historical borders, and the cooperation with the former Soviet states, Germany, the EU, and NATO. The MfR was led by Romuald Szeremietiew, formerly defense minister in Olszewski's government. Before the September 1993 parliamentary elections, the MfR sought alliances with other small rightist parties, including the Christian Democratic Labor Party (CDLP) and the CDA. In the elections the MfR ran together with Antoni Macierewicz's Polish Action and Kornel Morawiecki's Freedom Party in a Coalition for the Republic (CfR). They won 2.7% of the vote but failed to get seats in the *Sejm*.

The MfR sought to unite patriotic and pro-independence forces against the perceived communist threat, advocating lustration, decommunization, and an interventionist economic policy. In December 1993, a split occurred in the party after Szeremietiew was elected chairman at the second MfR congress. In March 1994, an alternative extraordinary congress elected Stanisław Węglowski as party chairman, and Olszewski as honorary leader. The party in August 1994 had about 3,000 members; Węglowski claimed support among the majority, while asserting that Szeremietiew's faction was backed by the majority of regional chairmen.[83] Węglowski's MfR signed a declaration of cooperation with Roman Bartoszcze's Christian-Peasant Alliance and with Łukasz Czuma's Party of Christian Democracy.

Szeremetiew's MfR named Zbigniew Farmus, Romuald Kukołowicz, and

Lech Jeczmyk as deputy chairmen. In the program, the party declared its basic values as "faith, nation, state, independence, self-government, family, and the right to life, freedom, and property." It advocated policies to protect the family unit against the harmful effects of "civilization." It advocated reprivatization and the return of confiscated property to former owners, the liberalization of tax policy, the implementation of anti-monopoly measures, and protection of Polish producers. Its foreign policy priorities were the creation of conditions for successful industrial development and the security of the nation. Accession to the EU needed to take place after assuring the development of Polish agriculture and industry. The MfR advocated a "Europe of Fatherlands" in order to preserve national identities, and it opposed the creation of a supranational state.[84]

Szeremietiew's MfR participated in the Alliance for Poland (AfP) together with the Christian National Union and the CDA. In September 1994, disagreements appeared between the MfR and other members over the Alliance.[85] In 1995, the party entered the rightist Patriotic Camp (PC) *(Obóz Patriotyczny)*, in which the CIP and the Non-Party Bloc in Support of Reforms also participated. The PC declared its wish to become a federated political party and promised to bring President Kwaśniewski before the state tribunal in the event of its electoral victory. In June 1996, it entered the Solidarity Electoral Action. Within the SEA, the MfR was active in promoting rightist initiatives, such as the creation in September 1996 of a team of 22 SEA parties to counterbalance the influence of Solidarity, and the establishment of the SEA Right Accord in January 1997 to give the Alliance a rightist program.[86] The MfR received one seat as part of the SEA parliamentary club following the September 1997 elections.

National Democratic Party (NDP)
Stronnictwo Narodowo-Demokratyczne (SND)

The National Democratic Party (NDP) was founded in 1991 with the help of the National Party in exile, headquartered in London. It considered itself the only legitimate continuation of the National Democratic *(Endecja)* movement, the ultra-nationalist trend established and led by the pre-war chauvinist Roman Dmowski, and was renowned for its extreme nationalist positions, consisting of anti-German, anti-Semitic, pro-Church, and latent pan-Slavic tendencies. Despite this, the NDP in Poland was not viewed as a militant nationalist organization but was perceived as being closer to the Christian Democratic Union. The party leaders, Jan Zamoyski, Napoleon Siemiaszko, Jan Engelgard, Krzysztof Majek, Bogusław Kowalski, and Witold Staniszkis, considered the party's ideology similar to that of the right wing of the Conservative Party in Great Britain and the Gaullist movement in France.

The NDP supported a free market economy and foreign investment, as long as this would be used to stimulate domestic capital. They also opposed the "Americanization" and commercialization of Polish culture, and believed the state should play a "productive" role in the economy. Like other ultranationalist groups, the NDP often portrayed consumerism and materialism imported from the West as grievous threats to Polish culture and tradition. They also played upon the government's inability or unwillingness to purge former communists from prominent positions. The party's goals included propagating a strong national ideology and Christian values among Poland's young people. The NDP published the monthly *Nowe Horyzonty* (New Horizons).

National Party (NP)
Stronnictwo Narodowe (SN)

The National Party (NP) was originally founded in 1928 and reactivated in 1989. The NP emphasized the beliefs that Poles were able to improve the country by themselves and that the national interest of Poles should have a preferred position over that of foreigners. The NP believed that the national economic system should be under government control; that privileges for foreign capital should be reduced; and that there should be a strong executive branch within a parliamentary democracy. NP leaders believed the state should be responsible for a cultural program that would promote moral values, require the media to be owned by Poles, and allow the Catholic Church to fully participate in the social and cultural life of the nation. NP leaders aimed to unify all nationalist movements. The leadership of this 4,000-member party included Leon Mirecki, Maciej Giertych, Józef Wiecławek, Stefan Jarzębski, and Bogusław Jeżnach. The NP published *Tygodnik Narodowy* (National Weekly) and the biweekly *Przegląd Narodowy* (National Review).[87]

Movement for the Reconstruction of Poland (MRP)
Ruch Odbudowy Polski (ROP)

The Movement for the Reconstruction of Poland (MRP) originated as a result of former Prime Minister Jan Olszewski's presidential campaign in November 1995. The election committee became the foundation of the Movement. Its two founding documents were the "Contract with Poland" of 3 May 1996 and the "Independence Charter" of 11 November 1997. The Movement characterized itself as a nationwide center-right party guided by the principles of Catholic social science and Polish national interest.[88] The "Contract with Poland" was proclaimed as a "program of moral and civilizational reconstruction of the country." At the congress held on 16 December 1995, Olszewski said that he was ready to reach agreement with other rightist forces. Participants called upon the *Sejm* to declare the Polish United Workers' Party (PUWP) a criminal organization. A resolution called for a Poland based upon the social teachings of the Church and stated that the MRP would strongly oppose liberalization of the anti-abortion law.[89]

The "Contract" listed among its goals a decrease in taxes, the restraint of inflation, and a just distribution of national income. It placed emphasis on caring for pensioners and the disabled, reducing unemployment, increasing funding for education, and promoting local government. It sought limits on land purchase by foreigners and supported Polish industry. Particular attention was given to harmonious cooperation between Church and state, and a commitment was made to ratify the Concordat with the Vatican.

Friction arose within the party between its radical wing, represented by Antoni Macierewicz and Zygmunt Wrodzak, and the moderates, such as Zbigniew Romaszewski, Wojciech Włodarczyk, and Andrzej Kieryło. The radicals were accused of creating a negative party image with anti-Semitic undertones, and were blamed for the drop in party popularity from 16% in June 1996 to 8% in November 1996.[90] The MRP maintained close ties with Solidarity and strongly opposed the new constitution adopted by the *Sejm* in March 1997, and together with the SEA it attempted to change the referendum law, so that a minimum 50% turnout would be required for a referendum to be valid.

The MRP received 5.6% of the vote in the September 1997 parliamentary elections and obtained six seats in the *Sejm*. Its poor performance led to accusations by the party leadership of incompetence. The result was the exclusion, on 2 October 1997, of Antoni Macierewicz, the main council chairman, from the party because of his attacks on Olszewski. On 11 October 1997, the MRP's supreme council suspended the party board chaired by Olszewski and reversed the decision to expel Macierewicz. The latter's supporters held an MRP congress in December 1997, which Olszewski declared illegal, and formed a new party, later known as the Catholic National Movement (CNM). Olszewski was reelected MRP leader at the second congress, on 22 February 1998. Olszewski reiterated the party's commitment to the traditions of independence, Polish national interests, and the social teachings of the Church.

Neofascists

Polish National Commonwealth–Polish National Party (PNC-PNP)
Polska Wspólnota Narodowa–Polskie Stronnictwo Narodowe (PWN-PSN)

An ultranationalist party originally founded in 1955, the Polish National Commonwealth—Polish National Party (PNC-PNP) was reactivated in December 1990 by the eccentric racist and extreme anti-Semite Bolesław Tejkowski. Claiming 4,000 members, the party declared that it was neither a leftist nor a rightist organization but a nationalist movement and a centrist party encompassing "all Polish national forces" in the tradition of the pre-World War II National Democrat leader Roman Dmowski. The party's stated goals were to achieve full political and economic independence for Poland, as well as to facilitate the "moral rebirth" of the nation. It desired to build a state with a "national structure," rather than a communist, socialist, capitalist, or liberal system. The party advocated that authority should only be held by Poles who understood the interests of the Polish nation and that property should only be owned by Poles without dual citizenship. The party believed that foreign investment should exclude property ownership and benefit from limited profit margins, and that foreign influence over Polish affairs should be eliminated.

The PNC-PNP was against the concept of a "Europe without borders," preferring instead a model of cooperation between separate nations, in which collaboration between Slavic countries was a primary goal, thus displaying its pan-Slavic leanings. Its cultural program attempted to keep Polish culture "clean" and separate from other national cultures. The party published the monthly *Myśl Narodowa Polska* (Polish National Thought). In March 1993, Tejkowski was brought to trial for defaming the government, the Catholic Church, and the country's Jewish community. The court ordered Tejkowski to be detained again in July 1993 after he refused to undergo psychiatric examination to determine his fitness to stand trial.[91]

Several other small Polish ultranationalist organizations also operated in Poland, including the National Organization of the Republic, the Party of Working Legionnaires, the Party of Loyalty to the Republic—Congress of National Solidarity; and the Universal Party of Slavs and Allied Nations (UPSAN).

Polish National Front (PNF)
Narodowy Front Polski (NFP)

The Polish National Front (PNF), initially led by Wojciech Podjacki and then by the racist Janusz Bryczkowski, openly sought to build a "Great Poland," a reference to fifteenth-century Poland, which stretched from the Baltic Sea to the Black Sea. Its leaders advocated a large, modern army and believed only Polish capital should have a preferential position in the country. In this protectionist agenda, foreign capital would be limited to a necessary minimum and would remain under government supervision. The party believed the state had an obligation to protect Polish cultural traditions and to develop national culture above all other considerations. The PNF was believed to have ties with Poland's nascent skinhead movement and to have provoked attacks on Roma (Gypsy) communities by calling on citizens to expel all of Poland's Roma population.

National Rebirth of Poland (NRP)
Narodowe Odrodzenie Polski (NOP)

The National Rebirth of Poland (NRP), an ultranationalist organization, was founded in Warsaw in 1981. It was reportedly co-sponsored by the Confederation for an Independent Poland and the Polish National Front. In

1989, it merged with the *Szczerbiec* (The Jagged Sword) political group in Katowice, Upper Silesia. The strongest branches functioned in Warsaw and Katowice. The NRP viewed itself as developing the traditions of Roman Dmowski, although more in line with the coalitionist Great Polish Camp (founded in 1926) than the original National Party. The party advocated a "democratic national state," denied the existence of a German minority in Poland, and viewed the progressive unification of Europe and the creation of a joint European government as the greatest threat to individual nations and national movements. It opposed the concentration of property either in the hands of the state or of "anonymous capital." It also rejected what it called a system of "false democracy," which allegedly led to moral relativism and put the nation's destiny into the hands of a corrupted political class.[92]

National Movement (NM)
Ruch Narodowy (RN)

The National Movement (NM), led by Mariusz Urban, purported to defend Europe as a "Christian civilization," and promoted Catholic ethics as the priority in individual and social life. However, it also expressed reservations about the direct participation by the Catholic Church in formulating government policy. It demanded reparations from Germany and Russia for war damages and population losses; the defense of "Polish character"; the recovery of the Eastern territories lost to the Soviet Union during World War II; and the acceptance of full Polish minority rights in the Zaolzie area of the Czech Republic. The NM not only desired to prohibit the sale of land to foreigners but also to nationalize land previously sold to aliens. It demanded an official condemnation of the participation of Jews in the communist regime as well as a concerted defense against alleged "Jewish demands." The party proposed to create a "classic" Polish model for culture that would serve as an alternative to the existing "commercial subculture." The NM published the yearly *Ruch Narodowy* (National Movement).

Polish League (PL)
Liga Polska (LP)

The Polish League (PL) was a radical nationalist party with anti-Semitic undertones. It declared as its main task a war against anti-Polonism created by the mass media of various kinds inside the country and abroad. It declared its principal values to be "family, religion, fatherland, and nation," and saw grievous threats to the Polish nation from all sides: communist, leftist, liberal, Masonic, and sectarian.

In sum, ultranationalist and fascistic groups in Poland have only attracted a small, hard-core following: one of their key problems is "the lack of a persuasive target against which to mobilize constituents."[93]

Ethnic Minority and Religious Parties

National Minorities Council (NMC)
Rada Mniejszości Narodowych (RMN)

During the initial Solidarity era in the early 1980s, there was some resurgence of minority activism as central controls were loosened and the communist party lost its grip over public life. Several minorities sought to have their sociocultural associations transformed into politically representative bodies, demanded parliamentary seats, petitioned for greater access to the mass media, and claimed larger state funds for their publishing ventures. This trend was reversed after the December 1981 martial law crackdown, when attempts to form independent minority organizations were thwarted by the Jaruzelski regime. With the unraveling of communist rule in 1989 and the election of the Solidarity coalition, restrictions on minority activities began to evaporate. A representative of the Ukrainian minority was elected on the Solidarity ticket and a Belarusian also gained a seat in parliament during the first multiparty elections in June 1989.

Attempts were made during 1990 to politically integrate various minority groupings and create a nationwide representation. In March 1991, leaders of ten organizations, including Belarusians, Lithuanians, and Ukrainians, established a National Minorities Council (NMC). Its objectives revolved around speeding up legislation on minority rights, including the introduction of appropriate constitutional stipulations. Although the Council ceased to function after a few months, the inter-minority contacts it established contributed to forging various electoral coalitions for the October 1991 ballot, including the Orthodox Electoral Committee and the Minority Electoral Bloc. The Bloc put forward 60 candidates in 16 electoral districts and 10 candidates for the national list. However, the coalition only received 29,428 votes and failed to elect a *Sejm* deputy. Loose electoral coalitions and inter-minority lobbying groups were likely to continue in pursuit of the interests of various ethnic and religious minorities.[94]

Union of German Sociocultural Associations in Poland (UGSCAP)
Związek Niemieckich Stowarzyszeń Społeczno-Kulturalnych w Polsce (ZNSSKP)

After the democratic breakthrough in 1989, Warsaw allowed German associations to operate in the country, especially in the cultural, educational, and economic domains. But the size and activities of the German population continued to generate disputes: Polish sources estimated about 200,000 ethnic Germans, while German calculations ranged from 400,000 to 500,000. Poles suspected that many non-Germans claimed German heritage in order to benefit from Bonn's liberal immigration policies.

The Union emerged from the Central Council of German Associations in September 1991, to coordinate the activities of German societies in various regions of Poland: the majority of voivodship-based associations subsequently entered the Union. Estimated membership by the close of 1991 exceeded 220,000 people. As an umbrella organization, the UGSCAP attempted to combine the efforts of various German associations, societies, and groupings (including the German Friendship Circles) into a cohesive program. Its principal aim was to maintain German national identity and to develop the main regions inhabited by Germans, such as Silesia, Mazuria, and Warmia.

The Union lobbied for dual citizenship for both Germans and Poles, the free movement of people, and the easy transfer of capital. Its leaders rejected all attempts to involve the minority in political disputes and to misuse it to fan the flames of nationalism. Union leaders demanded constitutional stipulations guaranteeing minority rights and the use of German in all administrative affairs in regions with a substantial minority population. It encouraged increased Polish-German cooperation in all areas of social, political, and economic life, in the context of building a "Common European Home." A closely linked organization, the Chief Council of Germans in Upper Silesia (CCGUS), sought to transform Upper Silesia into a "modern Euroregion."[95] In the parliamentary elections in September 1997, only one of the German minority parties—the Sociocultural Association of the German Minority in Silesian Opole (SCAGMSO)—gained enough votes to seat deputies in parliament. German representatives received a total of 51,027 votes, ensuring two seats in the *Sejm*, held by Henryk Kroll and Helmut Paździor.[96]

German Friendship Circles (GFC)
Kola Przyjaźni Niemieckiej (KPN)

The German Friendship Circles (GFC) were founded by Jan and Henryk Kroll at the end of 1988 as small support groups for Germans who faced discrimination in communist Poland, and as the basis of an influential minority organization. After January 1990, this organizational network grew rapidly and established circles throughout Upper Silesia, boasting a membership of over 300,000 people by early 1991. The Circles championed the rights of Germans in Silesia and supported the development of German learning, culture, and art, the submission of recommendations to official institutions to improve living conditions among Germans, German language instruction in all Silesian schools, regional business promotion in Silesia, and the recognition of rights to cultural autonomy. As a result of these objectives, the GFC hoped to curb German emigration from Silesia. The Circles established cordial relations with other ethnic groups and backed the German-Polish Treaty of 1990, rejecting all attempts by either country to involve the minority in political disputes.

Sociocultural Association of the German Minority in Silesian Opole (SCAGMSO)

Towarzystwo Społeczno-Kulturalne Mniejszości Niemeckiej na Śląsku Opolskim (TSKMNSO)

This sociocultural organization for Germans was registered in January 1990 in Opole, a region with a substantial German minority population. Like-minded bodies were established in two other German-inhabited areas: the Sociocultural Association of People of German Origin in the Katowice voivodship (SCAPGOKV) and the Sociocultural Association of People of German Origin in the Częstochowa *voivodship* (SCAPGOCV). Other smaller organizations were established in Gdansk, Toruń, and Olsztyn. The Associations maintained connections with the German Union of Expellees, a relationship that provoked dispute within the German minority. Association activities focused on developing German education, culture, and art. Its leaders declared support for the political integration of Poles and Germans and the eradication of 45 years of distrust.

Due to schisms within the Solidarity movement, SCAGMSO became the strongest political grouping in the Opole voivodship. In the local elections of May 1990, deputies representing the German minority gained 380 seats on local councils in 35 out of 61 townships, with an absolute majority in 26 townships. For the parliamentary elections of October 1991, two German election committees were established, one based in Opole and one in Katowice. From Opole, seven German deputies were elected to the *Sejm*, receiving a total of 133,000 votes, and one deputy to the Senate (upper house), Gerhard Bartodziej, who obtained 82,000 votes. German deputies established a German minority parliamentary club under the leadership of Henryk Kroll.[97]

National Offensive (NO)
Narodowa Ofensywa (NO)

A self-defined national-radical party that was founded in 1988 in Augsburg, Germany, National Offensive (NO) "struggled" for the "national interests" of all Germans. It endeavored to create a pan-European nationalist movement, as well as to further German national identity in Silesia through publishing ventures, the teaching of German, and by preaching their neo-Nazi ideology to young Silesians. The NO organized "patriotic discos" for young Germans in Silesia. Its platform was deliberately patterned after that of the National Socialist German Workers Party (Nazis), particularly in attitudes toward Jews and other nationalities. According to party leader Michael Świerzek, NO membership was approximately 500. NO also maintained an outpost in the Kaliningrad region of Russia, on Poland's northern border.

The party aimed to create a Greater Germany that would stretch from the Meuse to the Niemen. In the summer of 1992, it was reported to be operating out of the town of Dziewkowice, where it created an Opole branch earlier in the year. However, the NO did not establish a broad base of support and was condemned by moderate German leaders. Gunter Boschuetz, head of the NO in North Rhine Westphalia, who organized a congress of the Silesian-based National Offensive attended by 30 Silesian representatives and 20 German representatives, was expelled from Poland in December 1992. The Polish Senator from this region, Dorota Simonides, stated that all legal means would be used to rid the area of NO activists. But at a February 1993 briefing of the *Sejm* Committee on Ethnic Minorities, Provincial Governor of Opole Ryszard Zembaczyński admitted that the decision to deport groups of neo-Nazis had little practical effect.[98]

Union of Ukrainians in Poland (UUP)
Związek Ukrainców w Polsce (ZUP)

The Ukrainian population began to organize independent associations in order to promote their distinct culture and language. These activities were further spurred by neighboring Ukraine's achievement of independence. Although the new Polish government was well disposed toward a rejuvenation of religious, educational, and cultural activities, inter-communal enmities were also evident. For example, some Ukrainian activists called for the return of land and property seized by the Polish state in the 1940s. Frictions also surfaced over the previous confiscation of Ukrainian Uniate and Orthodox Church properties by Poland's Catholic Church.

The Union of Ukrainians in Poland (UUP), formerly known as the Ukrainian Sociocultural Association, transformed itself into a Union in February 1990. The UUP consisted of a network of local chapters chaired by Ukrainian professionals and presided over by a chief council and a general assembly. About 10,000 Ukrainians belonged to this organization, grouped in 180 local circles and 11 regional branches. The Union dedicated itself to changing the poor image of Ukrainians in Polish society and strengthening their national identity. Its general goals included defending minority rights in culture, education, language, and religion. The Union promoted the development of a Ukrainian intelligentsia, the production of accurate history books on Polish-Ukrainian relations, the fostering of contacts with Ukraine and with the Ukrainian diaspora, and the formation of distinct economic institutions.

More controversial demands included the official condemnation of the post–World War II deportations; "moral and material" compensation for property confiscated by communist decrees in 1947, 1949, and 1958; the regulation of the legal and property status of the Uniate and the Polish Autocephalous Orthodox churches; the passage of a minorities law; and guaranteed Ukrainian representation in the Polish parliament. The activities of the Union won approval among officials in Warsaw, who argued that they would help in forging cooperative links with Ukraine. However, UUP leaders expressed some concern over the activities of Polish nationalist groupings as well as some societies consisting of former residents and offspring from Poland's pre-war eastern territory.

By the beginning of 1992, an estimated 1,500 children and youth were enrolled in Ukrainian classes at 46 learning centers in Poland. Ukrainian elementary and secondary schools existed in the Suwałki, Koszalin, and Olsztyn voivodships; 30 cultural centers and 40 artistic associations were functioning; and three newspapers, *Nasze Slowo* (Our Word), *Zustriczi* (Meetings), and *Nad Buhom i Narwoju* (By the Rivers Bug and Narew) were published in Ukrainian. More contentious issues also materialized, including calls for the return of Ukrainians to the Bieszczady mountains, from where many persons had been deported after World War II on charges of collaboration with anticommunist guerrillas, and the return of property seized by the state in the late 1940s. The latter included over 250 churches confiscated from the Greek Catholic (Uniate) Church in 1947.

Frictions with the local Polish population were aggravated during the prolonged dispute over the Carmelite Cathedral of St. Theresa in Przemyśl during the spring and summer of 1991. The dispute was largely resolved by Pope John Paul II during his visit to the city in 1991, when the Ukrainian Uniates received an alternative place of worship. The Pope reactivated the Uniate diocese in western Ukraine and the Przemyśl region. In sum, the Uniates had 60 parishes, two monasteries, and three nunneries in the country. A substantial portion of Ukrainians also belonged to the Autocephalous Orthodox Church, with dioceses in Przemyśl-Nowy Sącz and Chełm-Lublin.

At the August 1992 World Forum of Ukrainians, Jerzy Rejt, UUP chairman, stated that more financial aid from the state was needed to promote Ukrainian culture, but stressed that the most important priority for the Ukrainians was the passage of a national minorities law. Ukrainian leaders became politically active during the collapse of communist rule, when Włodzimierz Mokry was elected to parliament in the June 1989 ballot on the Solidarity electoral list. In the May 1990 local elections, 70 Ukrainian representatives were elected to various local councils. Before the general elections of October 1991, Ukrainian leaders entered the Minority Electoral Bloc, which received 26,962 votes but failed to elect a parliamentary deputy. Some entered alternative election coalitions, including Mokry, who was re-elected from the Solidarity list.[99]

Association of Lithuanians in Poland (ALP)
Stowarzyszenie Litwinów w Polsce (SLP)

The approximately 15,000 Lithuanians in Poland's northeastern regions became active in developing their educational and cultural life, but did not push for political or territorial autonomy. Formerly the Lithuanian Sociocultural Association, the Association of Lithuanians in Poland (ALP) was established in March 1992 and claimed a membership of 2,500. It was led by Eugeniusz Pietruszkiewicz.

The ALP called for guaranteed Lithuanian representation in parliament, for the nomination of a Lithuanian as deputy governor in the Suwałki voivodship and as governor in the Sejny district, for bilingualism in administrative work in the Sejny and Punsk districts, for Lithuanian language instruction in Polish schools, and for Lithuanian church services. The party financed the biweekly, Lithuanian-language *Aušra* (Dawn), and the House of Lithuanian Culture in Punsk. In the local elections of May 1990, Lithuanian representatives gained 16 seats to local councils in the Punsk district. Ten candidates stood for the October 1991 parliamentary elections in the National Minorities bloc but failed to gain any *Sejm* seats. As a result of ALP involvement, an increasing number of pupils enrolled in the six elementary schools and one lyceum that provided lessons in Lithuanian.[100]

The Lithuanian Society of Saint Casimir (LSSC) *(Litewskie Towarzystwo Św. Kazimierza)*, headed by Olgierd Skrzypka, was created in 1990, continuing the tradition of an identically named organization that existed prior to World War II. Its key principle was the combination of religious work with the strengthening of Lithuanian identity among this compact ethnic minority. It endeavored to teach the Lithuanian language and propagate the nation's culture and customs, particularly through establishing libraries and aiding Lithuanian artistic groups. By creating a Center for Lithuanian Culture in the Suwałki region, the organization also endeavored to build better relations between Poles and Lithuanians.

Citizens' Circle of Lemkos "Hospodar" (CCL)
Obywatelski Krąg Lemków "Hospodar" (OKL)

Paweł Stefanowski, Michał Kiec, and Zenobia Czerhoniak became the leaders of the Ruthenian political group Citizens' Circle of Lemkos "Hospodar" (CCL), founded in 1990. The majority of Lemko Ruthenians lived in the western and northern areas of the country, to which many had been deported by communist authorities in the 1940s, and where the movement claimed some 10,000 supporters. The Lemko Circle stressed Ruthenian civil rights rather than their ethnic or regional specificity, while asserting their loyalty to the Polish republic. They wanted to educate Poles about Lemko-Ruthenian history, including their forced deportations and colonization of deserted farms after World War II. The group encouraged the formation of a Polish-Lemko roundtable that would stimulate the economic recovery of traditional Lemko territories in southeastern Poland. Lemko representatives endeavored to cooperate with the state and with various social organizations in order to improve conditions in the Lemko region so that the indigenous population could return to the area. The CCL believed in the necessity of protecting Ruthenian monuments and in the value of education in the mother tongue. Among its goals was to establish a Center of Lemko Culture, a Museum of Lemko Culture, and a Foundation of Lemko Culture.

Lemko Association (LA)
Stowarzyszenie Łemków (SL)

The Lemko Association (LA) was created in 1989 in the Legnica voivodship in southwestern Poland. The chairman of the LA's chief council was Andrzej Kapoza, and the party claimed nearly 400 members in 13 local circles. It financed the quarterly publication *Besida* and tried to promote Ruthenian cultural activities. LA spokesmen estimated the Ruthenian population in Poland to be somewhere between 60,000 and 80,000 on the basis of their native language and their place of residence before the deportations during the 1940s. They also claimed that the Lemkos formed part of the Carpatho-Ruthene nation and not a subdivision of the Ukrainian nation.

Lemko Union (LU)
Zjednoczenie Łemków (ZL)

The Lemko Union (LU) was formed in 1989 and registered in Nowy Sącz in southeastern Poland. Wacław Szlanta was elected chairman of the chief council. The Union claimed about 500 members in 27 local circles in six voivodships. The LU received some funding from local authorities to organize Ruthenian cultural events. LU leaders estimated the Lemko population to number approximately 100,000 people, including those who were deported to the Soviet Union after World War II. The Union supported the main Ukrainian organizations in Poland and evidently considered Lemko Ruthenians to be a branch of the Ukrainian nation.

Belarusian Democratic Union (BDU)
Białoruskie Zjednoczenie Demokratyczne (BZD)

The Belarusian Democratic Union (BDU) was the first official national minority party in Poland. It was founded in February 1990 by Sokrat Janowicz, a Belarusian poet, Eugeniusz Minorowicz, and Piotr Juszczuk, and possessed a membership of some 1,500 people. The importance of this party did not extend far beyond the Białystok voivodship and nearby areas inhabited by Belarusians. The BDU's primary goals were to reinforce Belarusian ethnic identity in Poland, to prevent any further depopulation and acculturation of the minority, and to counteract the economic degradation of the region. This goal extended to the belief that foreign capital should be restricted in order to prevent the "colonization" of Poland. Together with the Hromada Social Committee, the BDU campaigned for the official use of the Belarusian language in the local administration, the return of original Belarusian place-names, the development of research on the history and culture of the Białystok region, and broader investment in resuscitating the area's economy, particularly its agriculture. The Union complained about the shortage of Belarusian elementary and secondary schools and pressed for the introduction of bilingual schooling. In 1991, the Belarusian language was taught in only 45 schools.

The BDU has fielded candidates in Poland's local and national elections. Seventy-three Belarusian deputies were elected to district councils in the May 1990 ballot, constituting 10.5% of all mandates in the Białystok voivodship. Clear majorities were obtained in four districts, and a Belarusian inter-district union was subsequently formed to help coordinate economic development in the region. Two electoral blocs were formed for the October 1991 ballot: the Belarusian Electoral Committee and the Orthodox Electoral Committee. The latter elected Eugeniusz Czykwin as a deputy to the *Sejm*, with the strong support of the Orthodox Church. The BDU backed the former bloc, which failed to win any seats, principally because of a lack of campaign funds. They also pursued cross-border contacts with Belarus, without advocating secession from Poland. One consistent source of tension was religious issues, as Poles were primarily Roman Catholic and Belarusians mostly Orthodox. Disputes have focused on such questions as the use of churches for Orthodox services, the language employed during masses, the allegedly missionary attitude of the Polish clergy, and accusations of Polish discrimination against Belarusians in local education and employment.[101]

Other Eastern minority organizations in Poland included the Belarusian Farmers' Society (BFS) *(Białoruskie Stowarzyszenie Rolników)*, the Ukrainian Christian Brotherhood of Saint Volodimir, the Union of Independent Ukrainian Youth, the Ukrainian Teachers' Society, the Belarusian Students' Association, the Association of Belarusian Journalists, the Belarusian Youth Association, the Brotherhood of Orthodox Youth, and the Belarusian Literary Society.

Cultural-Social Society of Czechs and Slovaks in Poland (CSSCSP) Towarzystwo Społeczno-Kulturalne Czechów i Słowaków w Polsce (TSKCiSwP)

The leaders of the Cultural-Social Society of Czechs and Slovaks in Poland (CSSCSP) included Eugeniusz Misiniec and Lubomir Molitoris. Although accused by Catholic priests of embracing Slovak nationalism, leaders of this 3,200-member organization stated that they harbored no intention to promote secessionist movements or border revisions. The society advocated the passage of a Polish law on ethnic minorities, increased Slovak language instruction in schools, and Slovak church services. The monthly *Zivot* (Life) was financially supported by CSSCSP.[102]

Sociocultural Society of Jews in Poland (SCSJP)
Towarzystwo Społeczno-Kulturalne Żydów w Polsce (TSKŻwP)

The Sociocultural Society of Jews in Poland (SCSJP) was officially formed by the communist authorities in 1956 to supervise and control the Jewish population. At the time of the democratic changes in 1989, its membership was approximately 2,000, and it operated 15 local branches in Poland. The society produced the *Folks-Sztyme*, a publication in both the Polish and Yiddish languages, and was connected with the biweekly *Słowo Żydowskie* (Jewish Word). In 1991, the heads of the SCSJP, the Jewish Religious Union, and the Jewish Historical Institute established a Coordinating Commission for Polish Jewry (CCPJ), which officially represented the interests of the remaining Polish Jews.[103]

Podhale Sociocultural Association of Gypsies in Nowy Targ (PSCAGNT)
Podhalanskie Stowarzyszenie Społeczno-Kulturalne Cyganów w Nowym Targu (PSSKCwNT)

The Podhale Sociocultural Association of Gypsies in Nowy Targ (PSCAGNT), a Romani (Gypsy) organization, was initially established in the Nowy Targ voivodship of southeastern Poland in 1970. Its membership remained small but it claimed to represent the interests of about 3,000 local Gypsies. Similar organizations have been formed in a number of neighboring voivodships to cultivate Romani culture and defend Gypsy interests vis-à-vis the local administration.

   Other minority-based organizations included the Gypsy Cultural-Educational Society, the Association of Romas in Poland, the Association of the Children of the Holocaust, the Greek Association in Poland, the Bulgarian Cultural Educational Society of Chrysto Bolew, and the Armenian Cultural Society.

Regionalists

Kaszubian Pomeranian Union (KPU)
Kaszubski Związek Pomorski (KZP)

The Kaszubian Pomeranian Union (KPU) was founded by Lech Bądkowski, co-creator of the Gdansk Agreement, which gave birth to Solidarity in August 1980. Józef Borzyszkowski became the Union's president. Historically, the Kaszubian population in northwestern Poland was significantly more resistant to Germanization than its Silesian counterparts. Few Kaszubs migrated to Germany, because they considered themselves part of the Polish nation. In addition, almost all of the Kaszubian intelligentsia remained in close cooperation with Catholic priests. The

KPU endeavored to introduce Kaszub ethnicity into geography handbooks and history textbooks, and worked to promote ethnic awareness in Polish schools. One of its achievements was the rescue of the Kaszubian People's University. Overall, the Union supported the building of a Polish homeland that would respect all ethnic groups.[104]

Mazurian Association (MA)
Stowarzyszenie Mazurskie (SM)

The Mazurian Association (MA), a regionalist organization, was set up in 1990 to cover three voivodships in northeastern Poland: Olsztyń, Elbląg, and Suwałki. It claimed to represent about 8,000 people who declared themselves to be Mazurian or Mazuro-Germans. The MA was composed of a chief council, whose chairman was Tadeusz Zygfryd Willan, and a membership of some 1,200 people. Among its activities, the MA financed the monthly *Mazurska Poczta Bociania* (Mazurian Stork Mail), and supervised the *Chata Mazurska* (Mazurian Cottage) Museum in the town of Sadry, and small village libraries throughout the Mazury region. The MA endeavored to cooperate with the local authorities, the ministry of culture, and the Polish mass media to promote Mazurian identity.

Movement for Silesian Autonomy (MSA)
Ruch na Rzecz Autonomii Śląska (RRAS)

The Movement for Silesian Autonomy (MSA) was led by Paweł Andrzej Musioł, Rudolf Kołodziejczyk, and Ryszard Klinger. The MSA set out to nurture a consciousness among Silesians that was favorably disposed toward autonomy. The Movement advocated a division of authority between the central and regional administrations by creating an autonomous Silesian region with its own legislative and executive prerogatives, similar to those of Silesia before World War II. Furthermore, the MSA wished to halt the increasingly devastating environmental degradation of Silesia's natural resources. Members also upheld the necessity of good economic and cultural contact among Silesians; the importance of integrating all Silesians into one political unit, regardless of their ethnic heritage; and the desire to prevent the Germanization of Silesia. In the October 1991 general elections, the MSA managed to gain two seats in the lower house of parliament, indicating that a potential base of social support existed for its program of devolution and autonomy.[105]

Upper Silesian Union (USU)
Związek Górnośląski (ZG)

The Upper Silesian Union (USU) appeared to be the strongest regional movement in Upper Silesia, with many members holding key positions in the local administration. Leaders Jerzy Wuttke and Jan Rzymelka estimated its membership to be several thousand strong. Party membership remained contingent upon supporting "Upper Silesian values" and considering the region a "small motherland." The Union advocated that Poland become a state of self-governing regions, with Silesia expanding its current frontiers to assume its traditional historical borders, presumably including parts of Czech Moravia. The USU co-owned the *Trybuna Śląska* (Silesian Tribune) , the most widely sold newspaper in Silesia.[106]

Polish Western Union–Movement of Polish Silesia (PWU-MPS)
Polski Związek Zachodni–Ruch Polskiego Śląska (PZZ-RPS)

The Polish Western Union–Movement of Polish Silesia (PWU-MPS), reactivated in 1991, previously operated in the Prussian sector of nineteenth-century partitioned Poland. It staunchly opposed Silesian autonomy and separatism, fully respected Polish claims to these territories, and advocated strong public and minority allegiance to the Polish state. The Union obtained four seats in the lower house in the October 1991 parliamentary elections, gaining 0.23% of the popular vote.

Alliance of Upper Silesian Societies and Associations (AUSSA)
Porozumienie Górnośląskich Stowarzyszeń i Towarzystw (PGSiT)

The Alliance of Upper Silesian Societies and Associations (AUSSA) united seven Silesian organizations, including the Movement for Silesian Autonomy. It was formed in order to provide a defense of the region's "vital interests," and its spokesmen believed that Upper Silesia should eventually govern itself through the elected authorities of the Katowice, Opole, and Bielsko Biała voivodships. Edward Poloczek was elected chairman of the Alliance.[107] Other regionalist groups included the Union of *Gminas* (districts) of Upper Silesia, the Union of the *Gmina* of Zagłębie, the Union of Wielkopolans in Poznań, the Association of Upper Silesians in Opole, the Union of the Upper Silesian Communes, and Upper Silesian Christian Democracy.[108]

Independents and Others

Polish Beer Lovers' Party (PBLP)
Polska Partia Przyjaciół Piwa (PPPP)

Registered as a political party in December 1990, the Polish Beer Lovers' Party (PBLP) may have started as a prank. However, in time its members developed a serious platform, which included freedom of association and expression, intellectual tolerance, and a higher standard of living. The party's humorous name probably helped it win votes from a politically disenchanted populace in the October 1991 parliamentary elections, in which the PBLP captured sixteen *Sejm* seats with 3.27% of the vote. In early 1992, following a split within the PBLP into the "Big Beer" and "Little Beer" parties, the former assumed the name the Polish Economic Program (PEP), with Janusz Rewiński as its leader. Losing its image of quirkiness, the PEP became associated with the Democratic Union (DU) and the Liberal Democratic Congress (LDC) in the Little Coalition of liberal pro-market parties, and it supported the candidacy of Hanna Suchocka for prime minister in 1993. Since that time, the "beer lovers" have virtually disappeared from the political scene.[109]

POLITICAL DATA

Name of State: Republic of Poland *(Rzeczpospolita Polska)*
Form of Government: Directly elected president and bicameral parliament
Legislature: Bicameral National Assembly *(Zgromadzenie Narodowe)*, consisting of the 100-seat upper house (Senate) and the 460-seat lower house *(Sejm)*
Size of Territory: 120,727 square miles
Size of Population: 38,608,929 (July 1999 estimate)

Composition of Population:

Ethnic Group	Number	% of Population
Poles	37,605,108	97.88
Ukrainians	300,000	0.78
Germans	200,000	0.52
Belarusians	200,000	0.52
Roma	25,000	0.07
Lithuanians	15,000	0.04
Jews	15,000	0.04
Ruthenians	15,000	0.04
Slovaks	12,500	0.03
Czechs	7,500	0.02
Others	23,000	0.07
Total	38,418,108	100.00

Sources: Population data from 1999 CIA World Factbook, http://www.odci.gov/cia/publications/factbook/pl.htm.

ELECTION RESULTS

Presidential Election, 8 October 2000

Turnout: 61.1%

Candidates	Votes	% of Vote
Aleksander Kwaśniewski	9,485,224	53.9
Andrzej Olechowski	3,044,141	17.3
Marian Krzaklewski	2,739,621	15.6
Jarosław Kalinowski	1,047,949	6.0
Andrzej Lepper	537,570	3.1
Janusz Korwin-Mikke	252,499	1.4
Lech Wałęsa	178,590	1.0
Jan Łopuszański	139,682	0.8
Dariusz Grabowski	89,002	0.5
Piotr Ikonowicz	38,672	0.2
Tadeusz Wilecki	28,805	0.2
Bogdan Pawłowski	17,164	0.1
Total	17,598,919	100.1

Sources: http://www.agora.stm.it/elections/election/poland.htm; http://www.cspp.strath.ac.uk//polelec.html.

Presidential Election, 5 and 19 November 1995

First Round, 5 November 1995

Turnout: 64.79%

Candidates	Votes	% of Vote
Aleksander Kwaśniewski	6,275,670	35.11
Lech Wałęsa	5,917,328	33.11
Jacek Kuroń	1,646,946	9.22
Jan Olszewski	1,225,453	6.86
Waldemar Pawlak	770,419	4.31
Tadeusz Zieliński	631,432	3.53
Hanna Gronkiewicz-Waltz	492,628	2.76
Janusz Korwin-Mikke	428,969	2.40
Andrzej Lepper	235,797	1.32
Jan Pietrzak	201,033	1.12
Tadeusz Koźluk	27,259	0.15
Kazimierz Piotrowicz	12,591	0.07
Leszek Bubel	8,825	0.04
Total	17,872,350	100.00

Source: Elections in Poland at http://www.agora.stm.it/elections/election/poland.htm.

Second Round, 19 November 1995

Turnout: 68.23%

Candidates	Votes	% of Vote
Aleksander Kwaśniewski	9,704,439	51.72
Lech Wałęsa	9,058,176	48.28
Total	18,762,615	100.00

Presidential Election, November–December 1990

First Round, 25 November 1990

Turnout: 61%

Candidates	Votes	% of Vote
Lech Wałęsa	6,569,889	39.96
Stanisław Tymiński	3,797,605	23.10
Tadeusz Mazowiecki	2,973,264	18.08
Włodzimierz Cimoszewicz	1,514,025	9.21
Roman Bartoszcze	1,176,175	7.15
Leszek Moczulski	411,516	1.49
Total	16,422,474	100.00

Second Round, 9 December 1990

Turnout: 54%

Candidates	Votes	% of Vote
Lech Wałęsa	10,622,696	74.25
Stanisław Tymiński	3,683,098	25.75
Total	14,305,794	100.00

Parliamentary Elections, Sejm and Senate, 23 September 2001

Voter Turnout: 46.29%

Party/Coalition	Votes	% of Vote	Seats
Coalition SLD-UP:	5,342,519	41.04	216
Alliance of Democratic Left			
Union of Labor			
Civic Platform	1,651,099	12.68	65
Self-Defense	1,327,624	10.20	53
Law and Justice	1,236,787	9.50	44
Polish Peasant Party	1,168,659	8.98	42
League of Polish Families	1,025,148	7.87	38
Solidarity Electoral Action of the Right	729,207	5.60	—

Freedom Union	404,074	3.10	—
German Ethnic Minority	47,230	0.36	2
Other Parties	85,582	0.67	—
Total	13,017,929	100.00	460

Senate:

Party/Coalition	Seats
Coalition SLD-UP:	75
Alliance of Democratic Left	
Union of Labor	
Bloc Senate 2001:	15
Civic Platform	
Freedom Union	
Law and Justice	
Solidarity Electoral Action	
of the Right	
Polish Peasant Party	4
Self-Defense	2
League of Polish Families	2
Independents	2
Total	100

Source: Polish Central Election Commission, 2001.

Parliamentary Elections, Sejm and Senate, 21 September 1997

Voter Turnout: 47.93%

Party/Coalition	% of Vote	Seats in Sejm	Seats in Senate
Solidarity Electoral Action	33.8	201	51
Democratic Left Alliance	27.1	164	28
Freedom Union	13.4	60	8
Polish People's Party	7.3	27	3
Movement for the Reconstruction of Poland	5.6	6	5
Union of Labor	4.4	—	—
National Party of Senior Citizens and Pensioners	2.7	—	—
Union of Right of the Republic of Poland	2.3	—	—
National Alliance of Senior Citizens and Pensioners	1.5	—	—
Sociocultural Association of the German Minority in Silesia Opole	—	2	—
Independents	—	—	5
Total	100.0	460	100

22. Igor Zalewski and Piotr Zaremba, "Will Heads Roll After the Elections?" *Życie Warszawy*, Warsaw, 2 December 1995.

23. "The Union of Labor advocates Social Justice; Neither With the Right nor With the SLD," *Gazeta Wyborcza*, Warsaw, 26 February 1996.

24. "OPZZ Met With Union of Labor: Anything May Happen," *Rzeczpospolita*, Warsaw 20 March 1996.

25. Report by DOM, "Labor with Union of Labor: Similar Views, Not a Certificate of Loyalty," *Gazeta Wyborcza*, Warsaw, 13 August 1997.

26. "Alliance of Those Who Failed: A New Political Tree," *Gazeta Wyborcza*, 29 June 1998, p.3, in *FBIS-EEU*, 29 June 1998.

27. Article by B.I.W. and R.W., "An Electoral Alternative for Senior Citizens and Pensioners: Politically Homeless," *Rzeczpospolita*, Warsaw, 15 April 1997.

28. Report by B.I.W., "The Party of Senior Citizens Is Getting Ready for Elections: To Second-Category Citizens," *Rzeczpospolita*, Warsaw, 16 April 1997.

29. "Identity of Parties," *Gazeta Wyborcza*, Warsaw, 17 April 1997.

30. Małgorzata Dehnel-Szyc and Jadwiga Stachura, *Gry Polityczne: Orientacje na Dziś*, Warsaw: Oficyna Wydawnicza Volumen, 1991, p. 67.

31. Program, OPZZ website, www.opzz.org.pl/opzz/program/index.htm.

32. Małgorzata Ilka, "Better than Wachowski," interview with Józef Wiaderny, *Życie Warszawy*, Warsaw, 27 September 1996.

33. Report by SAR, "The SLD: The OPZZ Wants Partnership Relations With the SDRP," *Życie Warszawy*, Warsaw, 8 February 1996.

34. Agata Nowakowska and Natalia Skipietrow, "The OPZZ Fears the EU and NATO: They Will Buy Wrocław, Poznań, Gdańsk," *Gazeta Wyborcza*, Warsaw, 19 April 1996.

35. Bogdan Turek, "Poland: Balcerowicz Re-elected Head of Co-ruling Party," *RFE/RL*, 2 March 1998, www.rferl.org/nca/features/1997/03/F.RU.980302143531.html.

36. Małgorzata Subotic, "After Balcerowicz Has Joined the Freedom Union: Unexpected Change of Supporters," *Rzeczpospolita*, Warsaw, 21 February 1995.

37. See Major Political Parties in Poland, European Forum website at http://www.europeanforum.bot-consult.se/cup/poland/parties.htm.

38. Dominika Wielowieyska, "Will the Conflict Over the Democratic Forum Cause UW to Split? The Union Left and Right," *Gazeta Wyborcza*, Warsaw, 2 December 1994.

39. "Freedom Union Critical of Government's Economic Policies," *Rzeczpospolita*, Warsaw, 18 January 1995.

40. Text of the resolution in *Gazeta Wyborcza*, Warsaw, 22 January 1996.

41. "Freedom Union's New Direction," FBIS Media Note, *FBIS-EEU*, 20 April 1995, p. 16.

42. "A Symbolic Dispute Over Poland," *Czas Krakowski*, Krakow, 2 August 1995.

43. Igor Zalewski and Piotr Zaremba, "Will Heads Roll After the Elections?" *Życie Warszawy*, Warsaw, 2 December 1995.

44. Jaroslaw Popek, "Alliance of Six Groups: Beginning of a Parliamentary Coalition," *Gazeta Wyborcza*, Warsaw, 21 November 1995, p. 5.

45. "Promises of Freedom Union: Balcerowicz for the Second Time," *Gazeta Wyborcza*, Warsaw, 10 September 1997.

46. "Freedom Union on the Anniversary of August 1980: How To Deprive the SLD-PSL Coalition of Power," *Gazeta Wyborcza*, Warsaw, 1 September 1997.

47. Bogdan Turek, "Poland: Center-Right Parties Initial Coalition Agreement," *RFE/RL*, 21 October 1997, www.rferl.org/nca/features/1997/10/F.RU.971021152307.html.

48. English Summary, Ruch STU website, www.ruch100.ipl.net/summa.htm.

49. "History and Political Changes," Solidarity website, www.solidarnosc.org.pl/about/00000001.html.

50. See, for example Akcja Wyborcza Solidarnosc in Polish, AWS website, www.solidarnosc.org.

51. Wiesław Władyka and Mariusz Janicki, "For the Lack of a Locomotive," *Polityka*, Warsaw, 14 March 1998, pp. 20–21.

52. Solidarity Program Resolution, Solidarity website, www.solidarnosc.org.pl/doc/.

53. Eliza Olczyk, "Rzeczpospolita Poll: AWS Down, SLD Up: Price Hikes Negatively Affect Popularity of Those in Power," *Rzeczpospolita*, Warsaw, 23 December 1997.

54. Tomasz Żukowski, "Spectators on the Political Scene," *Gazeta Wyborcza*, Warsaw, 12 June 1996.

55. *Partie Polityczne w Polsce*, Warsaw: Polish Information Agency, October 1991; David McQuaid, "The Parliamentary Elections: A Postmortem," RFE/RL, *Report on Eastern Europe*, Vol. 2, No. 45, 8 November 1991; and Marcin Dominik Zdort, "The Competitive Ticket of Death," *Rzeczpospolita*, Warsaw, 6 June 1993, in *FBIS-EEU-93–129*, 8 July 1993.

56. Piotr Zaremba, "The President's Stratagem," *Życie Warszawy*, Warsaw, 10 May 1995.

57. Edyta Karczmarska and Małgorzata Tańska, "Six Deputies Split With the Freedom Union: A New Party Is Coming into Being," *Życie Warszawy*, Warsaw, 9 January 1997.

58. "Deklaracja Ideowa Stronnictwa," SKL website, www.skl.sos.com.pl/declaracja.htm.

59. Stronnictwo Konserwatywno-Ludowe website, www.skl.sos.com.pl/ludzie.htm.

60. Władze Stronnictwa Konserwatywno-Ludowego, SKL website, www.skl.sos.com.pl/wladze.htm.

61. Krzysztof Burnetko, "BBWR Crossroads," *Tygodnik Powszechny*, Kraków, 5 June 1994, p. 3.

62. See Congressional Research Service Report, "Poland after the September 1993 Elections," by Julie Kim.

63. Mariusz Janicki, "Armchairs, Chairs, Couches: In Poland, 300 Political Parties Exist," *Polityka*, Warsaw, 30 March 1996, No. 13, pp. 3–4.

64. "The AWS Club: Dominance of Unionists and National Catholics: A Political Map of the AWS," *Rzeczpospolita*, Warsaw, 27–28 September 1997.

65. Declaration of the UPR, UPR website, www.upr.org.pl/English/dekl-ang.html.

66. See Program of the UPR, UPR website, www.upr.org.pl/English/prog-ang.html.

67. "Ideological Declaration of the Polish People Party," 18 February 1995, on PSL website, www.psl.org.pl/anglia/psl-ide.html.

68. "Program of the PSL," PSL website, www.psl.org.pl.

69. "Fight for Votes in Rural Areas, *Rzeczpospolita*, Warsaw 14 July 1997.

70. "Alliance of Those Who Failed: A New Political Tree," *Gazeta Wyborcza*, Warsaw, 29 June 1998.

71. See "Poland Environmental Groups," Library of Congress, http://lcweb2.loc.gov/cgi-bin/query; Mariusz Janicki, "Po Denominacji," *Polityka*, Warsaw, No. 4, 1998; and "Polish Green Party," http://utopia.knoware.nl/users/otherhaar/greens/europe/poland.htm.

72. See Louisa Vinton, "From the Margins to the Mainstream: The Confederation for an Independent Poland," *RFE/RL, Report on Eastern Report*, Vol. 2, No. 46, 15 November 1991.

73. Igor Zalewski, "The Right: Hearings of Candidates for the Presidency; Krzaklewski's Tour," *Życie Warszawy*, Warsaw, 21 June 1995.

74. Article by POZ, "KPN: Nadzwyczajny Kongres," *Życie Warszawy*, Warsaw, 12 February 1996, in the electronic edition, www.zw.com.pl/1996/960212/File14s.html.

75. See Piotr Smilowicz, "KPN: Nadzwyczajny Kongres: Moczulski tylko honorowym szefem?" *Życie Warszawy*, Warsaw, 18 March 1996, in the electronic edition, www.zw.com.pl/1996/960318/File16s.html; article by PS, "Konfederacja Wewnątrz Konfederacji?" *Życie Warszawy*, Warsaw, 19 March, 1996, in the electronic edition, www.zw.com.pl/1996/960319/File11s.html; and the article by EK, "KPN: Zapowiedź Zjednoczenia Frakcji," *Życie Warszawy*, Warsaw, 8 May 1996, in the electronic edition, www.zw.com.pl/1996/960508/File24s.html.

76. Article by PS, "Koło czy klub KPN?" *Życie Warszawy*, Warsaw, 25 April 1996, in the electronic edition, www.zw.com.pl/1996/960425/File9s.html.

77. Article by EK, "KPN: Leszek Moczulski Wykluczony," *Życie Warszawy*, Warsaw, 16 December 1996, in the electronic edition, www.zw.com.pl/1996/961216/File11s.html.

78. Article by ROS, "KPN Słomki liczy na 40 miejsc w Sejmie," *Życie Warszawy*, Warsaw, 9 September 1996, in the electronic edition, www.zw.com.pl/1996/960909/File14s.html.

79. Article by DBB, "Akcja Wyborcza Solidarność: Konfederaci proponuja cztery bloki programowe," *Życie Warszawy*, Warsaw, 6 January 1997, in the electronic edition, www.zw.com.pl/1997/970106/File9s.html.

80. Report by LP, "Winning Over KPN Politicians," *Życie Warszawy*, Warsaw, 5 August 1997.

81. Report by PAP, "KPN-OP: Three Ministers Must Go; We Will Be Standing Guard Over AWS Program," *Rzeczpospolita*, Warsaw, 2 February 1998.

82. Marcin Dominik Zdort, "Farewell to the Action," *Rzeczpospolita*, Warsaw, 8 June 1998.

83. E.Cz. and M.J., "Movement for the Republic: The Split Continues," *Rzeczpospolita*, Warsaw, 9 August 1994.

84. Założenia Programowe, Ruch dla Rzeczypospolitej-Obóz Patriotyczny website, www.elender.hu/rdr-op/zasady.htm.

85. M.D.Z., "New Alliances on the Right," *Rzeczpospolita*, Warsaw, 21 September 1994.

86. Article by WZ, "A Team of 22 Parties: A Counterbalance to Solidarity," *Gazeta Wyborcza*, Warsaw, 6 September 1996.

87. See Stronnictwo Narodowe website at http://www.geocities.com/CapitolHill/8631.

88. "Geneza Ruchu odbudowy Polski," ROP website, www.rop-jo.com/historia.html.

89. "ROP Congress: To Prevent Thieves from Governing the Country," *Gazeta Polska*, Warsaw, 27 December 1995.

90. Wojciech Załuska, "ROP Fights for Its Face: There Is a Dispute of Two Orientations Going On in Jan Olszewski's Party," *Gazeta Wyborcza*, Warsaw, 27 November 1996.

91. See *Country Reports on Human Rights Practices for 1992*, U.S. Department of State, February 1993.

92. "Narodowe Odrodzenie Polski: Historia," on the NOP webpage, www.ikp.pl/~nop/historia.htm.

93. David Ost, "The Radical Right in Poland: Rationality of the Irrational," in Sabrina P. Ramet (Ed.), *The Radical Right in Central and Eastern Europe Since 1989*, University Park: Pennsylvania State University Press, 1999, pp. 86–107.

94. Sławomir Łódzinski, "Social Political Activism and Cultural-Educational Activities among National Minorities in Poland in the Period 1989–1992," *Sejm,* Chancellery, International Affairs Section, Report No. 29, Warsaw, November 1992.

95. *Dziennik Bałtycki*, Gdańsk, 12 October 1990, in *JPRS-EER-0–157*, 26 November 1990; *Trybuna*, Warsaw, 16 October 1990, in *FBIS-EEU-90–203*, 19 October 1990; Halina Kowalik, "Short Cut," *Prawo i Życie*, Warsaw, 4 May 1991; and Barbara Cieszewska, "Upper Silesia Together or Separately," *Rzeczpospolita*, Warsaw, 5 September 1991.

96. Elections in Central and Eastern Europe: Results and Legislation, University of Essex, http://www2.essex.ac.uk/elect/electer/pl_er_nl.htm.

97. For information on the German minority see Thomas Kleine-Brockhoff, "The Creeping Anschluss," *Die Zeit*, 5 October 1990; Daniel Tresenberg, "Who Wants Autonomy?" *Panorama*, Warsaw, 14 April 1991; Włodzimierz Kalicki, "The Closet Germans: A Holiday Issue Report on the German Minority in Poland," *Gazeta Wyborcza*, Warsaw, 21 September 1991; and Boleslaw Wierzbianski, "On Polish and German Minorities," in *Polish Review*, Vol. 37, No. 4, 1992.

98. See Mirosław Pęczak, "At the Unity Tavern: The Platform of National Offensive Is Modeled on the Program of the NSDAP," *Polityka*, Warsaw, 31 October 1992, in *JPRS-EER-92–161*, 20 November 1992; Eva Wilk and Jerzy Ziółkowski, "Strong Men from a Woman's Field," *Spotkania*, Warsaw, No. 45, 5–11 November 1992, in *JPRS-EER-93–002*, 7 January 1993.

99. See *Gazeta i Nowoczesność*, Warsaw, 7 June 1990, in *JPRS-EER-90–119*, 20 August 1990; McQuaid, "The Growing Assertiveness of Minorities"; Grzegorz Polak, "Dispute Over the Cathedral," *Gazeta Wyborcza*, Warsaw, 6 March 1991.

100. *Warsaw Domestic Service*, 1 March 1990, in *FBIS-EEU-90–042*, 2 March 1990; see Ryszard Walicki, "National Minorities in Poland in 1992 in the Light of Empirical Studies," Bureau of Studies and Expertise, Sejm Chancellery, No. 12, Warsaw, March 1993.

101. See *Trybuna*, Warsaw, 25 October 1990, in *JPRS-EER-91–001*, 2 January 1991; Agnieszka Magdziak-Miszewska, "Understanding Belarus," *Życie Warszawy*, Warsaw, 16 October 1990; and Stanisław Brzeg-Wielunski, "The Belarusian Democratic Union," *Ład*, Warsaw, 7 October 1990.

102. *Smena*, Bratislava, 23 July 1990, in *FBIS-EEU-90–143*, 25 July 1990. Also see "A Panorama of Nationalities," *Rzeczpospolita*, Warsaw, 12 March 1991, in *JPRS-EER-91–055*, 29 April 1991.

103. Consult Charles Hoffman, *Gray Dawn: The Jews of Eastern Europe in the Post-Communist Era*, New York: Harper Collins, 1992, pp. 243–314.

104. Information on Polish regional organizations is taken partly from *Prawo i Życie*, Warsaw, 23 June 1990, in *JPRS-EEU-90–124*, 30 September 1990.

105. For more information see *Radio Warsaw*, 22 July 1991, in *FBIS-EEU-91–141*, 23 July 1991; *Trybuna Robotnicza*, Warsaw, 18 June 1990, in *JPRS-EER-90–109*, 24 July 1990; and *Wspólnota*, Warsaw, 6 June 1992; "Weekly Review," RFE/RL *Research Report*, Vol. 1, No. 7, 14 February 1992.

106. Ciszewska, "Upper Silesia Together or Separately"; Kowalik, "Short Cut"; see also Andrzej Bęben, "Will There Be a Silesia?" *Sztandar Młodych*, Warsaw, 5 September 1991.

107. *Prawo i Życie*, Warsaw 31 October 1992, in *JPRS-EER-92–61*, 20 November 1992.

108. See Stanislaw Bubin, *Prawo i Życie*, 31 October 1992.

109. See Poland, "Beer Lovers Party," Library of Congress, at http://lcweb2.loc.gov/cgi-bin/query/r?frd/cstdy:@field(DOCID+p10210.

Czech Republic

HISTORICAL OVERVIEW

The Czech territories were inhabited by an assortment of tribal groups before the establishment of permanent Slav settlements in the fifth century AD. The ancestors of the Czechs lived in present-day Bohemia and Moravia. In the sixth century AD the area was overrun by Avars, who established an empire between the rivers Elbe and Dnieper. A loose and short-lived Slavic empire emerged in the seventh century AD that is believed to have been centered in Bohemia. It disappeared after the death of its ruler, Samo, in 658 AD.[1]

The eastern Moravian territories witnessed the creation of the first durable and coherent Slavic state after the Czech tribes of Moravia helped Charlemagne, the Holy Roman Emperor, destroy the Avar Empire. Early in the ninth century AD, the Slavic chief Mojmír created the Moravian Kingdom. His successors expanded the Kingdom to include Bohemia, Slovakia, southern Poland, and western Hungary, and this entity became known as the Great Moravian Empire.

Roman Christianity came to the Czech lands through incursions by Germanic settlers and missionaries. Mojmír was baptized but his successor Rastislav initially turned to Byzantium for fear of German domination. The Orthodox Slavic monks Cyril and Methodius visited Moravia to spread the Eastern rite liturgy in the newly devised Slavic alphabet. However, Rastislav's successor, Svätopluk, chose to ally the kingdom with German clerics. After the death of Methodius in 885, the Great Moravian Empire entered the sphere of Roman Catholic influence.

With the arrival of Hungarian tribes in Central Europe in 896 AD, the Moravian empire disintegrated. The Bohemian Czechs broke away from Moravia and formed an alliance with the Franks. The Bohemian Kingdom emerged in the tenth century when Czech tribes, under the Premyslid chiefs, established a more centralized political system. The Kingdom would play an important role in forging Czech identity. Following conflicts with Hungary and Poland, the Bohemian Kingdom acquired Moravia in 1029; but for the next five centuries Moravia's ties with Bohemia were periodically severed because of subordination to either Hungary or the Holy Roman Empire.

In the thirteenth century, the Bohemian rulers acquired through marriage upper and lower Austria and a part of Styria; the rest of the region, up to the current Slovenian border, was also conquered. But the Austrian Habsburg dynasty began to reassert its authority and all of Bohemia's Austrian possessions were lost by 1276. Large-scale German migration into the Czech lands took place during the course of the thirteenth century and proved a source of major conflict throughout Czech history.

The reign of Charles IV in Bohemia (1342–1378) was considered the golden age of Czech history. The powers of the Czech nobility were curtailed; Bohemia gained the territories of Brandenburg, Lusatia, and Silesia; and the capital, Prague, became a major imperial center. The Hussite movement swept Bohemia at the end of the fourteenth and beginning of the fifteenth centuries. It constituted both a national Czech movement against German imperialism and a religious assertion against papal authority and church corruption and wealth. It was led by the Czech Jan Hus, a reformist preacher who promulgated the anti-Vatican teachings of Englishman John Wycliffe, and it precipitated the Protestant Reformation.

Hussitism gained a stronghold in Bohemia, but Hus's followers were persecuted by the clergy and Hus himself was condemned as a heretic and burned at the stake in 1415. His death sparked decades of religious warfare between Catholic and Hussite Czechs with the intervention of German and Hungarian Catholics. In 1490, the Polish-Lithuanian Jagiellonian kings gained control over Bohemia, but the Czechs maintained a high degree of independence. However, in the early part of the sixteenth century, Bohemia fell under almost three centuries of Habsburg rule when its nobles elected Austrian Archduke Ferdinand as king. Conflicts quickly materialized as Vienna pursued a policy of centralization and a struggle ensued for the preservation of Czech national identity. The Czechs lost a major part of their native aristocracy, the Czech Reformed Church (Hussite) was persecuted during the Counter-Reformation, and the use of the Czech language was undermined. Periodic revolts by the Czech nobility were crushed by the Habsburgs. The most decisive Czech defeat occurred in November 1620 at the Battle of White Mountain.

During the seventeenth century, all Czech lands were declared the hereditary property of the Habsburgs and large-scale German immigration into Bohemia strengthened Vienna's controls. In 1648, the Treaty of Westphalia confirmed the incorporation of the Bohemian Kingdom into the Habsburg imperial system. Vienna's control was challenged by a resurgent Prussia, which in the 1740s seized the highly industrialized Silesian territories in the northern part of the Czech lands. The remainder of Bohemia was merged into the Habsburg's Austrian provinces and the separate administrative status of Moravia was abolished in the eighteenth century.

A Czech national revival took place during the nineteenth century. For example, *Matice Česká* (Czech Motherland) was established by Czech intellectuals in the 1830s to publish scholarly books and to develop Slavic learning and culture. Among the most notable figures were František Palacký, the leading Czech historian. Palacký proposed the federalization of the Austro-Hungarian empire as a buffer against both German and Russian expansionism. During the national revolutions of 1848, Czech intellectuals made increasingly bolder political demands for self-government but were rejected by Vienna.

New activists came to the fore at the turn of the twentieth century, including Tomáš Masaryk, who campaigned for national autonomy, universal suffrage, and parliamentary democracy. He also advocated the idea of a "Czechoslovak" entity as contacts between Czech and Slovak intellectuals intensified. During World War I, the idea of a fully independent Czechoslovak state emerged. In 1916, together with the Czech Eduard Beneš and the Slovak Milan Štefánik, Masaryk created the Czechoslovak National Council (CNC). With the collapse of the Habsburg empire in 1918, the CNC was recognized as the supreme organ of an emerging Czechoslovak government. Czechoslovak independence was formally proclaimed on 28 October 1918, and Czech troops reoccupied the Sudetenland region, which had been seized by German forces during the war.

The new state encompassed the historic Bohemian Kingdom (Bohemia, Moravia, and Silesia), together with Slovakia and Ruthenia, which were taken from Hungary. Czechoslovakia developed into a parliamentary democracy held together by the authority of President Masaryk. Although the country had a fairly liberal minorities policy, there was significant disquiet in Slovakia, which was denied autonomy under the 1920 constitution. However, the most destructive opposition was among the German population in the Sudetenland, which increasingly supported the expansionist pan-German policies of the Nazis. Under intensive pressure from Berlin and with Western acquiescence, Prague surrendered the Sudetenland to Germany in October 1938. In March 1939, German forces occupied all of Bohemia and Moravia and declared these territories a German protectorate. Meanwhile, Slovakia declared its independence, and Ruthenia was taken by Hungary.

Soviet forces overran the country at the close of World War II. Local national committees took over the administration and expelled the bulk of the German population—over two and a half million fled to Germany and Austria. While the Soviet Union annexed Ruthenia and incorporated it into the Ukrainian Soviet Socialist Republic, the rest of pre-war Czechoslovakia was reconstituted. An initial democratically elected multi-party government under President Beneš was overthrown in a communist *coup d'état* in February 1948. The country was declared a "people's democracy," and the Communist Party, under Russian supervision, proceeded to establish a totalitarian Stalinist system.

The 1960 constitution proclaimed the creation of Czechoslovak Socialist Republic. But a reformist movement sprang up in the mid-1960s, including intellectuals, students, and members of the ruling party, that culminated in the "Prague Spring" of 1968. It was embodied in the figure of Alexander Dubček, who became first-secretary of the Communist Party in January 1968 and supported far-reaching political, economic, and cultural reforms. The "Prague Spring" movement was crushed in August 1968 by a Warsaw Pact military invasion led by the Red Army. Moscow feared that the Czechoslovak reforms could dislodge communist rule and spread throughout its satellites in Eastern Europe. Dubček was removed from power in April 1969 and a program of "normalization" was imposed that restored the communist dictatorship under party chief Gustav Husák. Throughout the 1970s Czechoslovakia remained one of the most conservative communist bastions in the region.

After the late 1970s, the main source of opposition to the communist regime came from a circle of dissidents linked with the Charter 77 declaration and the Committee for the Defense of the Unjustly Prosecuted (*Výbor na Obranu Nespravedlivě Stíhaných*, VONS). Charter 77 and VONS were not organized as mass movements or political parties but as informal pressure groups monitoring the regime's human rights record and pushing for concrete reforms.[2] Both groups consisted primarily of dissatisfied intellectuals and former Prague Spring activists who were regularly harassed by the government. However, they were not perceived as a major threat as long as their operations were confined to a narrow circle of intellectuals under constant police surveillance.

Charter 77 spanned a diversity of political and ideological currents, including dissident Marxists, socialists, liberals, Christians, independents, and humanists. Although its signatories barely exceeded 1,000, mostly concentrated in the Czech Republic, thousands more sympathized with the initiative or actively circulated its documents. But the Charter was primarily intellectual and reformist, and not broad-based or politically revolutionary. It was loosely structured, with no explicit political ambitions. By early 1989, several closely linked groups adopted more overtly political stances, including the Democratic Initiative and the Movement for Civic Liberty, whose leaders openly spoke out for a multi-party system.

During the 1980s, several new independent groups were formed outside the traditional dissident community and focused their attention on a variety of pressing issues. The Independent Peace Association denounced the 1968 Soviet invasion and demanded a full disclosure of the events surrounding the intervention. The Social Defense Initiative Group was formed to provide legal and financial assistance to persecuted political activists; the Brontosaurus ecology group was created to press for environmental protection; and an alternative student organization mobilized individuals dissatisfied with the state-controlled student union. In addition, independent *samizdat* publishing became widespread to evade stifling official censorship.

By the fall of 1989, Czechoslovakia had become increasingly isolated in the Soviet bloc as each of its neighbors had embarked upon the dismantling of communist rule. The regime in Prague had harangued both Warsaw and Budapest for their tolerant approach toward the opposition, but the surge of public protests in the German Democratic Republic and the resignation of the Erich Honecker regime took the Czechoslovak government by surprise. As the pace of change quickened in the region and Moscow gave no indication of intervening, the Prague communists found themselves stranded and perceived as the last anachronistic outpost of Leninism in Central Europe. Furthermore, their basis of legitimacy, as the pro-Soviet loyalists who had quashed the 1968 Prague Spring reforms, had worn threadbare. In refusing to salvage the hard-line administration by political or military means, Moscow had given notice that it would distance itself from the regime it installed in 1968. By resisting meaningful reform, the governing elite had displayed their inability to adjust to new realities and heightened public demands for their replacement.

Although the Czech and Slovak population had been largely shielded from the rapid economic decline visible in Poland, the implicit "contract" between state and society gradually unraveled during the 1980s. The authorities were no longer able to ensure a reasonable standard of living, stable prices, and full employment. Broader sectors of the populace were willing to engage in public activities that explicitly challenged the political stalemate. A growing number of students, intellectuals, and urban youths became involved in political or cultural activities not sanctioned by the government, and some engaged in protest actions against official policies.

The hard-line Czechoslovak regime, even after the leadership changes in 1987 that brought Miloš Jakeš to the post of Communist Party first-secretary, had only initiated cosmetic reforms since the accession of Mikhail Gorbachev to the Soviet leadership. Indeed, the Kremlin's calls for *glasnost* (openness) and *perestroika* (restructuring) were barely heeded in Prague. Communist leaders considered such policies to be unnecessary and disruptive. Even the notion of "reform" implicitly undermined their own mandate, founded on the elimination of "reform socialist" currents in Czechoslovakia twenty years earlier. They calculated that Gorbachev's policies would be short-lived and that the Soviet leader would be ousted by more reliable, Brezhnevite forces once the reforms began to threaten the communist monopoly of power. Unlike its counterparts in Poland and Hungary, the Czechoslovak Communist Party contained no significant group of reformers in prominent positions willing to seek agreements with opposition leaders.

The regime faced mounting socio-economic problems and accelerating public opposition.[3] Massive repression was not a viable option, especially as international conditions had radically altered since the mid-1980s. Moscow was no longer the guarantor of communist rule in the region as the "Brezhnev doctrine" had been abandoned by Gorbachev. Soviet non-intervention in Poland, Hungary, and East Germany during 1988–1989 both undermined the Prague regime and emboldened the opposition movement.

Public demonstrations increased significantly in Czechoslovakia from mid-1988 onward.[4] On 21 August 1988, an estimated 10,000 people marched through the center of Prague chanting pro-freedom slogans in a commemoration of the twentieth anniversary of the Soviet invasion. On 15 January 1989, a "Palach Week" was arranged by dissident circles in commemoration of the young Czech who had immolated himself twenty years earlier in protest against the Soviet invasion. Police units attacked thousands of demonstrators in Prague, and several organizers were arrested, including the prominent dissident playwright Václav Havel, who was sentenced to nine months in jail. The authorities were especially perturbed that many of the protestors were not well-known dissidents and did not belong to the activist intellectual circles. Many were younger people with little experience of imprisonment and bureaucratic persecution.

Protest actions accelerated during the course of 1989. The arrest of Havel stimulated a public petition demanding his release and led to increasing protests among artists, scientists, and academics. An open letter to the government was signed by 200 intellectuals demanding a dialogue with state and party officials as a first step toward a pluralistic democracy. These moves led to a major petition, known as the "Several Sentences" declaration, that began to circulate in Prague in June 1989. By September 1989, over 40,000 signatures had been collected. The petition called for the release of all political prisoners and official respect for a wide spectrum of human and civil rights as enshrined in international conventions.

By November 1989, tensions were visibly mounting. The opposition was unsure whether the regime would react with repression or compromise, and growing sectors of the population were evincing restlessness over the slow pace of reform. The revolutionary events of November 1989 were sparked by another substantial public demonstration in the streets of Prague. On 17 November 1989, a march was organized by young people in memory of the fiftieth anniversary of the murder of Jan Opletal, a Czech student killed by the Nazis. About 15,000 people calling for free elections marched through the streets of Prague, gathering support from onlookers. When police attacked the peaceful demonstrators, it was unclear whether the Jakeš regime simply wanted to forestall further protests through a violent confrontation or whether some party leaders sought to unseat Jakeš and other hard-liners by staging a provocation.

Police actions spurred popular outrage and further protests, marking the beginning of the first stage of Czechoslovakia's political transition. Within a six-week period, the communist monopoly over the key political institutions rapidly and peacefully unraveled, even though some reformists were able to maintain their positions. Opposition leaders did not set out to overthrow the government but were determined to extract maximum advantage from growing public protests by pressing for durable political reforms. The Civic Forum (CF) *(Občanské Fórum, OF)* was established on 18 November 1989 to coincide with a planned demonstration of some 200,000 people in Prague.

Within days of its inception, local branches of the CF sprang up all over Prague and other major Czech cities. They were established as autonomous cells, with little or no central direction or control.

The Civic Forum brought together various activists from the counterelite and quickly grew into a national umbrella movement of opposition to the regime. It encompassed five main groups: Chartists, Prague Spring reformers, students and independents, pro-market economists, and disillusioned party officials. Some Prague Spring reformers became active, including the purged reformist Communist Party leader Aleksander Dubček. Hoping to revive the socialist ideals of 1968, they lent support to CF while forming a distinct *Obroda* (Renewal) group within the broad coalition. Thousands of students and young people joined the CF, some of whom had been active in the Independent Peace Association. Personalities in the semi-official cultural, artistic, and scientific circles demonstrated against the regime. Indeed, artists, actors, and journalists became a vital conduit of accurate and timely information for the general public during the early stages of the revolution.

As the authorities surrendered ground to the opposition, a number of anti-socialist and pro-market economists or "technocrats" also became vocal. They had not been part of the pre-1989 dissident movement, although a few had persistently propagated their free-market ideas through *samizdat* (underground) materials. Economists such as Václav Klaus gained increasing influence within the CF and their economic prescriptions were often more valued than those of the Prague Spring socialists. A number of former Party officials and administrators also defected to the Forum, including Prime Minister Marián Čalfa, and their reformist credentials made them credible partners for the CF. In addition, leaders of the former satellite parties abandoned the regime and directly assisted the opposition.

The communist leadership was overtaken by events and found itself constantly on the defensive.[5] Having eschewed the use of further police violence to pacify opposition, unable to muster military support for a crackdown, and with visible rifts appearing in the highest party echelons, on 24 November 1989, Jakeš resigned as party chief, together with the entire communist presidium. The resignations failed to stem the protests, and on the next day an estimated 750,000 citizens gathered in Prague to demand wholesale government changes and the introduction of a multi-party democracy.

A major breakthrough was achieved by the opposition on 27 November 1989. As a general strike erupted in several major cities, formal talks were initiated between the CF and the government. The initially moderate position of the Forum encouraged communist leaders, including Prime Minister Ladislav Adamec, to enter into a dialogue with the opposition. As talks began, the Federal Assembly removed the clause in the constitution guaranteeing the communist party a "leading role" in the state and in society. On 3 December 1989, a new government was formed that contained five non-communist ministers.

POST-COMMUNIST DEVELOPMENTS

Following intensive roundtable negotiations among the Civic Forum (CF), communist leaders, and former satellite parties, a "government of national understanding" took office. Although the reform-communist Marián Čalfa was nominated as prime minister, the majority of ministers were non-communists. Husák resigned as Czechoslovakia's president and opposition leaders demanded a non-communist head of state. Extensive parliamentary changes accompanied the government shake-up. A reorganized Federal Assembly was installed with the nomination of 120 non-communist deputies. Similar steps were taken in the Czech republican assembly where democratic deputies were co-opted pending new elections. On 28 December 1989, Dubček was sworn in as chairman of the Federal Assembly, and a day later Václav Havel was elected president of the country by the same body.

Following Havel's inauguration, the momentum of political transformation moved away from the streets and work enterprises to various parliamentary, political, and public institutions. Between January and June 1990, the groundwork was laid for multi-party general elections. But the pace of political and economic reform, and the compromises arranged between political leaders, exposed the Civic Forum to criticism that it was deliberately slowing down the transition and prolonging the existence of a semi-democratized state. Moreover, the preservation of the mass coalition movement led to charges of obstructing the development of political pluralism.[6]

Changes in the Federal Assembly went into effect on 30 January 1990, when 120 Czech and Slovak non-communists were co-opted to replace Leninist deputies. Although this was a technically unconstitutional step, it was considered essential to uphold the pace of reform and disassemble the communist monopoly. Communist Party members were left with only 40% of parliamentary seats following the turnover. In the federal "government of national understanding" the communists retained only three out of 23 ministries: the rest were CF or Slovak democrats and a handful of representatives from the Socialist and People's parties. This transitional federal administration endured until 29 June 1990; its main task was to lay the legal foundations for free elections and a multi-party system.

In early 1990, the supervisory role of the Communist Party was lifted from public organizations. Party cells were banned in all work enterprises and farms and Marxism-Leninism was invalidated as the state ideology or the basis for educational and cultural policy. The mass media, educational and cultural institutions, the trade unions, and other public bodies were de-politicized. Censorship and other restrictions were lifted; independent newspapers could appear freely, although television and radio remained under overall government control. Numerous new independent organizations sprang up, including labor unions, youth groups, and civic associations. The confiscation of communist property began early in 1990, generating disputes among former owners, government officials, and new entrepreneurs.

Important legal changes were enacted early on as the authorities moved to strengthen the rule of law guaranteeing individual rights. These were subsequently enshrined in the Bill on Fundamental Rights and Liberties, passed in January 1991, which codified freedom of speech, association, assembly, petition, and the press. The judiciary was de-politicized, the most blatant collaborators of the Husák regime went into early retirement, and judges' salaries were raised to help build an independent justice system. A Constitutional Court was established, as well as administrative courts at which ordinary citizens would have recourse to appeal against official rulings. Religious freedoms were restored, and the state renounced the right to license priests and reached agreement with the Vatican on filling vacant Catholic bishoprics. Legal restrictions on travel were rescinded, university autonomy was increased, and former political prisoners were rehabilitated.

The Czech Republic's ethnic minorities began to organize soon after the "velvet revolution" and established various associations to protect their interests. However, because of their comparatively small numbers and the restrictive election law stipulations, they were unable to gain more than a handful of seats in the republican parliament. To improve their political position, Polish and German organizations entered the multi-ethnic Coexistence coalition based in Bratislava, coordinated by leaders of the large Hungarian population in Slovakia. Although minority representatives welcomed the collapse of communist rule and the process of democratization, they were concerned over the shortage of state funds for their publishing, cultural, and educational ventures, and demanded the return of property confiscated either by the post–World War II coalition government or by the communist regime.

While discrimination on the basis of race, religion, or ethnicity was forbidden under the Charter of Fundamental Rights and Liberties, and under additional federal and republican legislation, it still permeated various facets of life, particularly against the Romani minority.[7] Indeed, liberalization in Czechoslovakia may have given vent to previously hidden anti-Gypsy prejudices. According to some reports, with the decline of central government supervision, discrimination against Roma actually increased in housing, employment, and in access to public and private services, particularly at local levels. In addition, anti-Gypsy violence mushroomed after 1989 as ultra-nationalist and racist groups were able to operate more freely. In conditions where Gypsies were widely scapegoated as criminals and where police displayed indifference to anti-Romani manifestations, skinhead gangs targeted Romas for random violence. Romani leaders in turn criticized the legal system and the security forces for failing to protect Romani communities and blamed much of the national media for perpetuating negative Gypsy stereotypes.

In the security realm, political activities were banned in the military and the police forces; the army's role in internal security was drastically curtailed; cuts were initiated in the military; and military service was reduced from 24 to 18 months, with the option of civilian service. The police forces were de-politicized, and the secret police department dealing with anti-dissident activities was abolished, although some of its strictly security functions were transferred to other units. Screening was launched in the Interior Ministry to force out the most compromised communist collaborators. But the pace of transforming the security forces was criticized by some activists who demanded a more thorough purge. The authorities contended that more rapid replacements would have seriously weakened the country's security posture.

Although de-communization proceeded in key institutions at the central level, the situation at lower administrative rungs remained less clear-cut. Communist activists and bureaucrats adjusted to political developments in several ways. While the CCP lost over one-third of its membership in the first quarter of 1990, most of its local structures remained intact because officials were determined to preserve much of their power base in small towns. The party retained its name, carried through a series of purges of discredited leaders, conducted some internal democratization, brought in a younger and more competent leadership, and canvassed as the most viable left-of-center party in the general elections. Some communists entered new parties. Others adjusted to the rebirth of capitalism by establishing private businesses, often with funds and assets that they had acquired through their political connections. These "*nomenklatura* businesses" became a prominent object of attack by critics of the government's avowedly soft-line approach to discredited officialdom.

Civic Forum leaders were lambasted for allowing the Communist Party to maintain much of its assets. They defended themselves by arguing that a gradual replacement of party officials prevented major upheaval. CF organizers maintained that any major purges of the bureaucracy could destabilize the reforms and lead to charges of replicating communist-like methods. However, as a result of pressure from newly formed rightist parties, various measures were introduced to screen and dismiss former communist collaborators. This "lustration" issue soon preoccupied all political activists and proved a major point of confrontation.[8]

In January 1991, the Federal Assembly adopted a resolution requiring all federal officials to be vetted for their prior links with the secret police. There were suspicions that police personnel were deliberately fabricating their files to discredit prominent anti-communist opponents. In October 1991, a law on the screening of all former party officials, the secret police, and top managers in state-owned industry was adopted by the Federal Assembly. Those deemed to have cooperated with the police or who held high positions in the communist apparatus were investigated and barred from serving in important positions for five years. The law was criticized for introducing the principle of collective guilt, for not distinguishing between willing collaborators and blackmailed citizens, and for relying on unreliable police files.

The CF itself was accused by rivals of filling key positions in the new administration from a narrow circle of colleagues who derived their mandate from the early days of the "velvet revolution."[9] President Havel was attacked by political opponents for establishing a "college of advisers" consisting of dissident compatriots who lacked suitable political or economic experience. Havel responded that he needed a reliable and close-knit team to counter the obstructive government bureaucracy, while dismissing charges that they formed a virtual shadow government.[10]

In the months leading to the first general elections of 8–9 June 1990, the process of political differentiation and polarization within the Civic Forum gathered pace. An important strategic division emerged over both economic and political issues. One prominent wing continued to support the idea of a "social market economy" in which economic reform would be accomplished gradually to cushion against possible social unrest. By contrast, rightist marketeers considered any delay in instituting a fully-fledged market economy as ultimately more damaging. This division also mirrored the contrast between "coalitionists," who sought to preserve the CF movement as a broad umbrella during the transformation process, and the "partisans," who calculated that the government should encourage the creation of distinctive political parties.

While the CF "coalitionists" were largely liberals, the "partisans" considered themselves as conservatives. These divisions soon began to crystallize into separate political groups within the Forum. The CF "coalitionists" established a Liberal Club in both the Federal Assembly and the Czech parliament and formed a circle of advisers around President Havel. In October 1990, the liberals founded an Interparliamentary Civic Association, seeking to maintain the CF as a supra-political and non-partisan movement. This was superseded in December 1990 by the Liberal Club of the Civic Forum, containing 90 parliamentarians in the Federal Assembly who were determined to prevent the CF from turning into a rightist party. The "partisans" established an Interparliamentary Club of the Democratic Right. This linked federal and republican parliamentarians with the Forum's local centers that supported fast-paced market reforms and the creation of a distinct conservative party. This organization captured the support of the major regional Forum groupings in Prague and Brno, the two largest Czech cities.

The conflicts between the two main wings of the Forum extended beyond ideological and policy issues; they centered on differing approaches toward democratization and pluralism. The "coalitionists" were determined to preserve the original movement as a broad association spanning a range of political trends and ideologies. Their critics charged that this was utopianism and would retard the emergence of a healthy spectrum of parties. The "partisans" argued that the obstruction of a multi-party system would hinder the public's ability to distinguish and choose between contrasting platforms. The coalition may have been invaluable during the pre-election period, but it had evidently outlived its usefulness once the new non-communist parliament was installed.

The "partisans" also charged that the CF had become too elitist, intellectual, and Prague-centered, neglecting the provinces and rural areas, and allowing little opportunity for local activists to influence the leadership.[11] Indeed, the Forum's organizational structure remained weak and decentralized, and its undetermined political profile resulted in a steady erosion of public support. Critics of the "coalitionists" also questioned the purportedly biased support they received from government leaders, including Havel himself, and the unfair advantage this conferred during election campaigns.

Defenders of the Forum's "movement" status argued that the CF's perceived weakness was in fact its strength. A loose structure and informal membership allowed for the flexibility needed to mobilize large numbers of citizens. It also prevented political fracturing that could have benefited the communists. According to the "coalitionists," many people remained suspicious of politics and parties, hence a broad non-partisan movement was better able to mobilize civic action.[12] They also argued that parties could not establish a firm foothold in a society that lacked strong interest groups and distinct constituencies. The "coalitionists" distrusted political parties and feared that they would create new centers of political exclusivity without increasing public involvement. A temporary compromise was reached between the two wings before the first general elections: they would remain together but contain a number of crystallizing political organizations.

A federal law passed in January 1990 allowed all citizens the right to form political parties, whereby 10,000 signatures were needed for registering a new party. During the first few weeks of the decree, over 90 parties emerged, ranging from reform communists to nationalists, although most parties had almost identical general principles: a commitment to democracy and a market economy.[13] The process of programmatic specification and differentiation became more pronounced after the national elections. While numerous small parties either disappeared or merged, a clearer political spectrum began to take shape. Four main political clusters emerged during the transition process: communist inheritors, former satellites, post-coalition parties, and independent formations.

In October 1990, the federal and finance minister Václav Klaus was elected CF chairman at a national congress in which the majority of delegates backed a tighter CF structure; Klaus was the undisputed leader of the "partisan" forces. Another CF congress in January 1991 determined that the movement should transform itself into distinct political formations with coherent internal structures.[14] This was a significant victory for those who perceived the loose movement as an impediment to stable government. Klaus himself asserted that the Forum had obstructed the development of parliamentary democracy and the emergence of a spectrum of strong parties with clearly defined positions, supporters, organizations, parliamentary deputies, and government representatives.[15]

The new election law, passed in February 1990, providing for the first free elections in Czechoslovakia in 44 years, was an important step in framing the structure of the new parliament and determining the degree of political stability.[16] Restrictions were placed on parliamentary fragmentation: in order to qualify for parliamentary seats under the system of proportional representation a party needed to gain at least 5% of the total vote. Only 23 political parties, movements, and coalitions competed in the elections, as several dozen groups failed to qualify for the balloting.

The first multi-party general elections in June 1990 were more in the nature of a public plebiscite against communism than an open competition between distinct parties. The maintenance of the CF coalition guaranteed a sweeping election victory, particularly as most of the best-known national personalities ran on the coalition ticket.[17] The CF/Public Against Violence (PAV) alliance gained 170 out of 300 seats in the Federal Assembly. The communists in both republics managed to score 47 seats; the Christian and Democratic Union obtained 40 seats; and the remainder were divided between regionalist, nationalist, and ethnic-based organizations. In the Czech National Council, the CF gained 127 out of 200 seats, the Communists 32, the Association for Moravia and Silesia 22, and the Christian Democratic Union 19.[18]

The federal government, inaugurated on 29 June 1990, was built around the CF/PAV alliance, which received the key ministries. The communists were denied any posts, and their leaders appeared content to operate as the strongest opposition party, calculating that the ruling coalition would splinter and lose support once it implemented painful economic reforms.[19] The new Czech administration was also dominated by the Forum. The biggest losers in the elections at the federal level were the Christian Democrats, Social Democrats, former communist satellite parties (Socialists, Peoples', Democrats), and smaller groups that decided to stand outside the umbrella movements.

Following the national elections, progress was registered in decentralizing the government structure, by placing greater powers in the Czech and Slovak National Councils and devolving various responsibilities to local governments.[20] Under the old system, a structure of national committees at all administrative tiers executed orders from the next highest level and ensured centralized decision-making. Local government was, in practice, an arm of central government. Following the June 1990 elections, the powers of the republican governments and the local administrations were strengthened. Several federal ministries were abolished and their responsibilities devolved to the republics. Local government was buttressed by limiting the size of district national committees and abolishing the regional tier altogether. Municipal and local-level committees were given greater autonomy in tax collection than the federal or republican administrations. Some activists demanded a more far-ranging devolution of power to Bohemia, Moravia, Silesia, and Prague; but these proposals were not adopted by the Czech authorities.

The first multi-party local elections, on 24–25 November 1990, proved less constrained by coalition politics than the general elections.[21] However, the results were not fully representative of the influence of political forces at the central level, as many parties possessed only a skeletal local structure and did not compete in all electoral districts. Personal knowledge of the candidates proved a more important criterion for many voters than political party affiliation. Although the CF remained the strongest force, its vote total decreased from 49.5% in June to 35.8% in November. The Communists finished second with 17.2%, up from 13.2% in June. The People's Party improved from 8.4% to 11.5%, while the Association for Moravia and Silesia gained only 4.2% of the vote, down from 10% in June, although it was on the ballot only in the Moravian counties. The Social Democrats slightly improved their total, from 4.1% to 5%, as did the Socialists, up from 2.7% to 3.2%.

The local elections demonstrated that the umbrella coalitions were losing their cohesiveness and popularity. But while the process of political pluralization was developing, most of the newly formed parties maintained only an embryonic organizational structure, a limited and fluid social base, and insufficiently distinctive platforms. Two major groupings crystallized within the CF: the Civic Movement (CM) and the Civic Democratic Party (CDP). The CM consisted of the "coalitionist" stream, which was most clearly linked with a "center-left" or "liberal-left" position. The Movement was led by Federal Foreign Minister Jiří Dienstbier and included most of Havel's circle of advisers and a broad group of intellectuals. The CM favored a slower approach to market reform than its CF rivals and supported the preservation of an extensive welfare umbrella. It retained a loose and decentralized organizational structure, which clearly handicapped its election performance.

The Civic Democratic Party (CDP), led by Václav Klaus, emerged as the strongest pro-market, right-of-center party, with substantial support among young professionals and new entrepreneurs. It also backed more stringent measures against former communist officials and collaborators, thus endearing Klaus to large sectors of the population. The CDP defined itself as a radical conservative movement. It acquired majority support in the Civic Forum and established robust party branches throughout the Czech republic. The two main wings of the CF agreed to continue cooperating closely in parliament to fulfill the Forum's election program, while constructing their separate party structures. A deal was struck to divide up assets fairly between the new parties, and both were to desist from using the CF name. A provisional joint coordinating committee continued to represent the CF as a whole, giving a facade of unity until the second general elections.

The CF also embraced an assortment of miscellaneous political trends and movements. On the left, the *Obroda* Club for Socialist Restructuring was composed of former Prague Spring reformers, while the Left Alternative consisted of various independent leftists. Both groups were eventually expelled from the Forum because of mounting conservative opposition within the movement. On the right, the Democratic Initiative, founded in 1987, broke away from the CF a few days after the general elections and renamed itself the Liberal Democratic Party (LDP). The Civic Democratic Alliance (CDA) was ideologically close to the

CDP but did not merge with the larger party, as a result of personality disputes between the leaders. A plethora of independent parties were also founded or revived.[22] They cooperated with the CF in the initial stages of the revolution but decided to separate even before the formal split in the coalition.

The 1992 general election law was designed to buttress the growth of stronger parties. The 5% vote minimum for obtaining parliamentary seats was supplemented by stipulations that coalitions of two or more parties had to gain 7% of the vote and a four-plus coalition needed 10% to qualify. The objective was to counter unrestricted political fragmentation by excluding smaller parties and to create distinct parties through durable mergers. In the elections of June 1992, a total of 36 parties, movements, and coalitions competed for the Federal Assembly, and 19, for the Czech National Council. Right-of-center parties scored victories in the Czech Republic, and the biggest losses were sustained by centrist and federalist forces.[23] The CDP gained 29.73% of the vote, obtaining 76 seats out of 200 in the Czech National Council; the Left Bloc (including the Communist Party) won 14% of the vote with 35 seats, and the Republicans obtained 14 seats, the Soviet Democrats and Liberals captured 16 seats, and the Christian Democrats 15. The Association for Moravia and Silesia gained a total of 5.87% and took 14 seats—in southern Moravia they registered 16.2% of the vote, and in northern Moravia, 12.6%.

At the federal level, a transitional government was installed because there was no agreement between the most successful Czech and Slovak parties on preserving the federation. In the Czech chamber of the Federal House of the People, the CDP won comfortably with 33.9% of the vote, followed by the Left Bloc (a coalition of reform communists) with 14.27%. Social Democrats gained 7.67%, and the Republicans registered a modest 6.48%. The Civic Movement only managed a disappointing 4.39% of the vote for the Federal Assembly, and the Civic Democratic Alliance achieved 4.98%; both failed to gain seats in parliament. The remaining centrist forces scored somewhat better: the Liberal and Social Union obtained 5.84%, and the People's Party, 5.98%.

Following the June 1992 elections, only a caretaker federal government was set up to administer the division of the country. The federal cabinet was reduced and Havel himself failed to be re-elected as Czechoslovak president, due to opposition by Slovak deputies. In an agreement between the Czech and Slovak Prime Ministers, Václav Klaus and Vladimír Mečiar, republican governments were to decide on the federal split and establish the legal foundations for Czech and Slovak statehood. A timetable of separation was agreed upon, and in September 1992, the federal cabinet approved a bill on dissolving the federation.

Paradoxically, Slovak demands for sovereignty or independence, and delays in signing binding constitutional agreements, spurred calls for an independent Czech state. In particular, conservatives, free-marketeers, and some nationalists in Prague underscored the numerous advantages of a clean break, such as a more streamlined administration, budget savings, and improved chances for the Czech Republic to join the European Union. Preparations were undertaken to pass a Czech constitution and to reorganize the republic into several self-governing regions to pacify Moravian-Silesian demands for greater autonomy. In October 1992, the federal government approved the draft of a constitutional act on terminating the federation. In November 1992, the Federal Assembly voted to disband the Czech and Slovak federation, phase out all federal institutions, and give the two republics equal successor status.[24]

The Czech Republic gained independence on 1 January 1993, and during its first year of statehood achieved a high measure of political stability. Part of Prague's success rested on shedding time-consuming disputes with Bratislava over the division of federal powers. Instead, both government and parliament could focus on constitutional and economic reforms within a more coherent political entity. In January 1993, the Czech parliament elected Havel as the first president of the Czech Republic. In June 1993, a Constitutional Court was established and decisions were made on the creation of an upper house or senate with 81 members. The 200-member Czech National Council became the Chamber of Deputies. There were no complications in dividing up party representation, as the party system was from the outset republic-centered rather than federal.[25] The question of administrative reorganization generated some controversy. While some parties favored giving federal status to Moravia-Silesia, premier Klaus believed that federalizing the Czech lands would lead to divisions reminiscent of the disputes with Slovakia.

The Czech law on citizenship passed in December 1992 laid down a range of stipulations for acquiring Czech citizenship. Most of the articles appeared to be non-controversial. Persons who were citizens of Czechoslovakia prior to 31 December 1992 automatically became citizens of the new Czech Republic. However, some of the stipulations seemed restrictive and lent themselves to potential discrimination. In particular, the condition that Czech citizenship would be granted to those who had not been convicted of a crime in the previous five years could be used to disqualify a substantial number of residents. Knowledge of the Czech language was also required: this clause could be used to disqualify a segment of the Romani population originally from Slovakia from gaining full citizenship.

The Czech constitution was adopted in December 1992. It proved to be a broadly liberal document defining the Czech Republic as "a sovereign, unified, and democratic, law-observing state based on respect for the rights and freedoms of the individual and citizen."[26] It reconfirmed that the Charter of Fundamental Rights and Liberties passed by the defunct Federal Assembly in January 1991 was an essential part of the country's constitutional order. The constitution provided few details about minority rights but simply stated that minorities would be protected by the majority in decision-making. Although the constitution placed no special emphasis on Czech ethnic identity and considered the individual and not the group the basic subject, its lack of specificity on the position of minorities and their parliamentary representation left the question open to legal interpretations.

The Czech National Council in the Czechoslovak Federation was transformed into the new sovereign parliament of the Czech Republic. The division of Czechoslovakia also assisted the movement toward the consolidation of a pluralist party system in the Czech Republic between 1992 and 1996. The number of parliamentary parties shrank and only six parties remained in parliament. The CDP, the CDA, and the Christian Democrats held 105 out of 200 parliamentary seats and created a stable ruling coalition. The Social Democrats remained weak with only 16 seats. The unreformed Communists and nationalist Republicans were also represented but they proved inimical to the democratic system and were excluded from any coalition discussions.[27] The Czech Republic had one of the few coalition governments in the 1990s that survived its full four-year term even though it only held a slim parliamentary majority.

With only a weak leftist opposition to the ruling right-of-center government, the coalition could pursue its political program practically unchallenged. There was minimal consultation with the opposition and the work of the parliament was curtailed. Indeed, according to critics the legislature became largely an appendage of the government. Prime Minister Klaus limited political discussion inside the coalition, thus fueling disputes among the coalition members. Klaus also did not accept a serious discussion on political programs inside his party and thereby hindered innovation and the emergence of new personalities.

The government coalition also shunned the common policy initiatives of the Visegrad group of Central European states, which could have been a strategic partnership in the transformation process. Instead, the Czech government saw cooperation with Hungary and Poland as potentially delaying the Czech drive toward Europe. On the other hand, Klaus's criticisms of the European Union contributed to a decline in positive Western perceptions of the new state.[28]

The most important economic policy introduced by the first Czech government was "coupon privatization." The concept was supposed to quickly privatize post-communist enterprises. The vouchers were to become fully fledged shares traded on the stock market. About six million citizens purchased the vouchers, and 400 investment funds were created. Since foreign investment was excluded from the process, a great deal of state property was transferred into Czech hands.[29] As problems in the process multiplied, "coupon privatization" was strongly criticized. The fast-paced program did not allow enough time to develop a legal framework for the new stock market. The government did not introduce laws to regulate the activities of investment funds, and there were no clear rules for the functioning of capital markets, thus fostering a great deal of chaos and abuse.

Increasing economic and political problems were reflected by the time of the June 1996 parliamentary elections, when the right-of-center coalition, consisting of the CDP, the CDA, and the Christian Democrats, won only 99 out of 200 seats, and lost their parliamentary majority. The Czech Social Democratic Party (CSDP), led by Miloš Zeman, received 26.44% of the vote and 61 parliamentary seats, but was unable to find any willing coalition partner. The CSDP quadrupled its support since the 1992 ballot, largely because of dissatisfaction with economic conditions—especially in the depressed districts of northern and southern Moravia and northern Bohemia.[30] The two extremist parties, the nationalist Republicans and the Communists, gained 8% and 10% of the vote respectively, but their support base remained unchanged.

Eventually, a minority government was formed by Prime Minister Václav Klaus, but it remained dependent on the approval of the opposition parties, particularly the CSDP. The CDM-led coalition signed an agreement on 27 June 1996 providing for the composition and principles of operation of the minority government.[31] The agreement was the result of four weeks of negotiations and included three parties: the CDP, the CDA, and the Christian and Democratic Union–Czechoslovak People's Party (CDU-CPP).[32] The Social Democrats agreed to support the minority government; in exchange, they were given important leadership positions in parliamentary committees, and party chairman Zeman was elected chairman of the lower house.

The 1992 Czech constitution had also established a Senate or upper house of parliament. However, the lack of legal clarity, as well as political wrangling over electoral procedure, postponed the elections until November 1996. The government coalition won 52 of the 81 Senate seats and thereby strengthened its position. Following the 1996 ballots, economic problems deteriorated as macroeconomic indicators worsened. The unstable political climate, exacerbated by the minority government, contributed to a weakening of the currency on financial markets, and in May 1997 there was a monetary crisis and the value of the crown plummeted. This was perceived as a serious failure by Klaus, whose main political achievement had been keeping the crown the most stable currency in Eastern Europe. Social problems also began to escalate, and the number of strikes and industrial protests increased.

Economic problems undermined the authority of the government as the restructuring of enterprises was postponed and ownership rules and business regulations were delayed. In addition, several party scandals shook the political scene. The gravest scandal concerned a large donation to the CDP from the former tennis player Milan Šrejber, who had allegedly received a privatized metal business at a discount price in exchange for his party contribution. In October 1997, Foreign Minister and cofounder of the CDP Josef Zieleniec resigned, claiming that Klaus knew about Šrejber's donation. In November 1997, the media charged that the party had a secret bank account in Switzerland. Finance Minister Ivan Pilip and former Interior Minister Jan Ruml openly called for Klaus's resignation. At the same time, the CDA and the Christian Democrats decided to abandon the coalition.

In November 1997, Klaus was forced to resign as the coalition collapsed.

He was nevertheless re-elected as the CDP chairman at an extraordinary party congress. The lower house was dissolved by agreement of the major parties under a one-off constitutional amendment after the fall of the center-right government. In January 1998, a new temporary administration was appointed and led by former National Bank Chairman and new Prime Minister Josef Tosovský. His government won parliamentary endorsement in exchange for a promise of early elections.

Klaus and the majority of the CDP distanced themselves from the government. However, four members of the party accepted nominations to the Tosovský cabinet. The CDP leadership asked them to reject these posts or leave the party, but the four decided to take their ministerial positions and resigned from the CDP to form their own organization, the Freedom Union (FU). The main task of the new cabinet was to prepare the country for the 1998 extraordinary elections. Among its ministers were members of the FU, the CDA, the Christian Democrats, and some independent "technocrats." The Social Democrats agreed to support the coalition, provided that it agreed to hold new elections in June 1998.

During the June 1998 election campaign, the FU tried to consolidate the right by bringing young intellectuals without a questionable political past into its leadership. The FU hoped to become the main rightist party, completely overshadowing the weakened CDP. In 1998, new financial scandals were disclosed and CDA leader Jiří Skalický resigned and several party members joined the Freedom Union. But according to opinion polls, the FU fell well under the 5% parliamentary barrier, and thus it did not participate in the elections. The Social Democrats organized a large campaign attacking the right-wing parties and offering a leftist alternative. The CDP ran a strong campaign warning about the return of leftist socialism. The Social Democrats received 32% of the vote and became the strongest parliamentary party, with 74 seats. However, the CDP succeeded in winning 63 seats.

The rightist parties between them obtained 102 seats, which would have been enough for a parliamentary majority. Nevertheless, the Freedom Union and the Christian Democrats refused to let Klaus dominate the new government and rejected a coalition. The FU and CDU also refused inclusion in a coalition with the Social Democrats, and none of these parties were willing to build a coalition with the Communist Party. Meanwhile, the nationalist Republicans failed to win any parliamentary seats and garnered only 3.9% of the votes; hence the number of radical parliamentary deputies declined from 41 to 24.[33]

On 9 July 1998, the CSDP and the CDP signed an accord in which the CDP agreed not to topple a CSDP-led minority government until the expiration of its four-year term. In return, the CDP received the main parliamentary posts and the CSDP's agreement to consult it on all important governmental decisions. On 17 July 1998, President Havel named the CSDP leader Miloš Zeman as prime minister. His minority government was formed on

22 July 1998.[34] The cabinet consisted of fourteen ministers and four deputy ministers. In August 1998, the new government was approved by parliament.

Despite its pledges, the administration could not reverse the economic decline and in 1998 GDP growth was negative while inflation reached 10.7%, real income dropped by 1.8%, and unemployment rose to 7.5%. Prague launched a new program to combat corruption but it did not bring any substantial results and was widely criticized by the public. There were also escalating problems with the Roma population that further dented Prague's image internationally. Human rights organizations repeatedly criticized the Czech government for tolerating racism in society. In July 1999, the administration approved new legal measures to counter extremist groups while fostering racial tolerance in the state education system.[35] One notable success was registered by the minority government in March 1999 when the Czech Republic entered NATO alongside Poland and Hungary.

According to opinion polls in June 1999, the CDP was the most popular party, with a 23.9% approval rating; the CSDP received 18%, the Communist Party, 15.7%, and the Freedom Union and the Christian Democrats, 11.6% each.[36] The poll reflected pronounced discontent in Czech society. The Social Democrats rapidly lost their broad support, especially as the government had to introduce various unpopular measures, such as raising the price of rents and energy. Another reason was the confusing behavior of Prime Minister Zeman, who repeatedly accused several public figures of corruption and abuse of power but failed to produce any evidence. At the same time, Zeman had a poor relationship with the media, in which he was regularly criticized. Increasing public support for the Communists was more in the nature of a protest than due to any lingering nostalgia for a return to the previous system.[37]

The Social Democrat–CDP accord was extended in January 2000 with some amendments, but this "opposition agreement" created political turmoil. Personal animosities between party leaders prevented the formation of a stable government. The only durable solution was the creation of a new majority government, but this was problematic without new general elections. There were various possibilities to replace the minority government, including a left-right coalition (CSDP and CDP), a center-right coalition (Christian Democrats, Freedom Union, CDP), or a grand coalition (all the major parties excluding Communists), but there was too much hostility between the major parties to make this a reality. Most leaders did not favor early elections, as this would have further obstructed the legislative process and delayed EU entry.

Throughout 2000, support for the Social Democrats continued to erode. They failed to win elections to any of the 13 regional assemblies that took place on 12 November 2000. The CSDP only received 14.7% support, while the oppositionist Civic Democratic Party (CDP) received 23.8%, a liberal four-party coalition, 22.9%, and the Communists, 21%. The CDP won in six regions and tied in another with the liberal coalition, which won outright in five regions. The coalition of four small liberal parties, composed of the Christian and Democratic Union–Czechoslovak Party (CDU-CP), the Freedom Union (FU), the Civic Democratic Alliance (CDA), and the Democratic Union (DU), also took 17 out of the 26 open Senate seats in a new round of voting on 12 and 19 November 2000. With a total of 39 seats, the coalition became the strongest force in the upper house. The Civic Democratic Party (CDP), gain-ing 8 seats, and the Social Democrats, with one additional seat, were stripped of their majority in the Senate, and their plans to reduce the powers of President Havel by reforming the constitution were curtailed.

President Havel remained critical of the government on numerous issues, from foreign policy to the spread of corruption. He asserted that the Czechs needed a majority government, not the "unnatural" agreement between the CSDP and the CDP. He was embarrassed by government criticisms of the NATO operation in Serbia in the spring of 1999 and by lukewarm support for EU accession. On at least one occasion Havel threatened to resign in reaction to proposed constitutional amendments that would have further limited presi-dential powers; these measures were rejected by parliament.

POLITICAL PARTIES

Socialists and Social Democrats

Czech Social Democratic Party (CSDP)
Česká Strana Socialna Demokratická (CSSD)

Being the oldest Czech party, the CSDP was originally founded in April 1878 as the Czechoslovak Social Democratic Party within the Austrian Social Demo-cratic Party. It was dissolved in 1938 after the German annexation, restored in 1945 as the Czechoslovak Social Democratic Party, and forcibly merged with the Communist Party of Czechoslovakia on 27 June 1948. After a brief period of activity during the 1968 "Prague Spring" reform movement, the party re-sumed its activities on 19 November 1989.

Although it had the potential to grow into a major political force and re-coup its confiscated property, similarly to other left-wing parties it suffered from a major handicap—the communists had largely discredited "socialism." It had an additional problem, in that two social democratic groups were formed in the Czech lands, one by the former Charter 77 dissident Rudolf Battek, the other by the returned exiles Slavomír Klaban and Jiří Horák. There was a great deal of rancor in the Czech party whether to run within or outside the Civic Forum (CF) in the first multi-party general elections in June 1990.

The Klaban-Horák group decided to stand separately; Battek's Club of Social Democrats stayed under the CF umbrella. The CSDP failed to gain any seats in either the republican or federal parliament. Battek was subsequently expelled from the CSDP, and Horák was elected its chairman. Leaders of the two wings set up a coordinating committee and the two eventually merged as one federal party. Former CF social democrats also joined the party after the Forum fractured and its successor, the Civic Democratic Movement, disappeared from the political scene.

The party's membership grew to about 18,000 people by the late 1990s. In 1993, Miloš Zeman was elected chairman. A younger and more dynamic group of activists became involved in the party in the mid-1990s, including its vice chairperson Petra Buzková. CSDP influence began to climb, especially among sectors of society that had not greatly benefited from the reforms and wanted to counterbalance the strongly market-oriented government. Others supported the CSDP in reaction to the corruption and financial scandals in the last year of the Klaus government. In the June 1992 elections, the CSDP obtained 16 seats in the Chamber of Deputies of the Czech Republic. CSDP popularity steadily climbed and in the June 1996 elections the party nearly quadrupled its number of seats in the Czech parliament to 61 and became the second strongest formation. Receiving 25 seats in the Senate elections, the CSDP maintained its position as the chief rival to the ruling CDP. It benefited from public frustration with falling living standards among sectors of the population that had failed to adjust to a market economy.

In December 1996, Jozef Wagner and Tomáš Teplík, who had voted in favor of the 1997 budget, were expelled from the party. This move, and the undemocratic means by which it was carried out, damaged the reputation of the party. Moreover, it underscored divisions between the moderate wing led by Karel Machovec and a more leftist faction. On 17 March 1997, Miloš Zeman was re-elected as CSDP chairman.

During the wave of political scandals that swept the country in 1997–1998 the CSDP was faced with the so-called Bamberg affair. This involved allegations that Zeman met with the Czech-Swiss businessman Jan Vizek in Bamberg, Germany and agreed to offer him influence in a CSDP-led government in return for cash contributions to the party. Zeman claimed the affair was staged with forged documents and the false testimony of Machovec, who publicly stated he wanted to discredit Zeman.[39] What harmed the CSDP most was the unwillingness of the party leadership to explain the affair in a satisfactory way.[40] Despite the release of a report by the Czech Security and Information Service (CSIS) that cleared the party chairman, several questions surrounding the affair remained unanswered. Furthermore, Zeman was frequently criticized for being populist and authoritarian. The younger generation of activists demonstrated greater potential, with public opinion surveys showing a high approval rating for leaders such as Stanislav Gross and Petra Buzková.

The Social Democrat program was based on the search for a "balance" between capitalism and state control. Unlike other East European social democratic parties, the CSDP did not emerge from the former communist party and it vehemently rejected any cooperation with the communists, at least in central government institutions. The party platform also focused on a crackdown on financial crime; increased support for housing, pensions, and social benefits; and economic growth over inflation control. The CSDP railed against the corruption evident during the economic transition and the inadequacy of the social safety net. While supportive of NATO membership, the Social Democrats remained opposed to the presence of foreign troops on Czech territory. The party also was in favor of EU membership.

In the June 1998 elections, the CSDP gained 74 seats in the Chamber of Deputies but failed to form a coalition with any of the center-right parties. Eventually, the party was compelled to form a minority government tolerated by the Civic Democratic Movement, the largest opposition party, in return for the latter's input in decision-making.[41] The party also had 20 seats in the Senate. In 1999, Zeman claimed that he would not run for party chairman at the next party congress scheduled for 2001, and recommended Vladimír Spidla to succeed him.[42] The party's popularity continued to drop in 2000 as it lost its majority in the Senate and performed poorly in the November local elections, failing to win seats in any of the country's 13 regional assemblies.

Liberal National Socialist Party (LNSP)
Liberální Strana Národne Sociální (LSNS)

The Liberal National Socialist Party (LNSP) originated in March 1897 as the Czech National Socialist Party and changed its name several times. The party strongly influenced Czech politics between 1918 and 1938. Among its prominent members was the Foreign Minister and later President Eduard Beneš. In the fall of 1938, the party was dissolved. It was resurrected in 1945 as one of the parties of the National Front under the name of the Czechoslovak National Socialist Party and subsequently the Czechoslovak Socialist Party. It shared power with the Czechoslovak Communist Party until the 1989 "velvet revolution."

The Czech satellite parties distanced themselves from their communist mentors during the "velvet revolution" in November 1989 and revived their image as autonomous political forces.[43] The Czechoslovak Socialist Party regained a measure of popularity when it openly sided with the Civic Forum. It participated in preliminary meetings that helped establish the CF, and it allowed its publishing house to be used by opposition figures in addressing vast crowds in Prague's Wenceslas Square. The Socialists formed their own youth wing, merged with the exiled National Socialist Party in March 1990, and stressed their social democratic program. But the party found it difficult to recapture its pre-war strength or to enter into any coalition with like-minded parties, largely because of its prior collaboration with the communists.

In March 1990, the LNSP joined forces with the Czechoslovak People's Social Party. In the June 1992 general elections, this bloc became a part of the election coalition called the Liberal Social Union. At its 1993 congress it changed its name from the Czechoslovak Socialist Party to the Liberal People's

Social Party. This was also accomplished to dissociate the party from its pro-communist heritage. In the same year, the party formed its own deputy club in parliament, numbering five deputies. In December 1995, the LNSP joined with the Free Democrats to form the FD-LNSP. The LNSP presented itself as a centrist party of the middle social class and one of "constructive opposition" but proved unable to garner any parliamentary seats.[44]

Pensioners for Secure Living (PSL)
Důchodci za Životní Jistoty (DZJ)

The Pensioners for Secure Living (PSL) was founded by retired labor union members as the Pensioners' Movement for Secure Living in March 1990, and it became a political party in 1994. According to its own sources, the party had about 55,000 members. It failed to clear the 5% threshold for parliament in both the 1992 and 1996 elections, but it considered a success the fact that 20% of the more than two million pensioners voted for the PSL. In the 1994 local elections, the party managed to elect two town mayors. The party agenda focused on the need for higher pensions, claiming that retirement pay should be raised from 45% to 60% of an average monthly salary. The PSL also demanded that the state provide low-budget housing, education, and health care. Eduard Kremlička took over the post of party chairman from Josef Koníček in late 1995. Although the PSL was touted as a possible coalition member in a CSDP-led government, the party gained only 3% of the popular vote in the June 1998 elections.[45]

Democratic Left Party (DLP)
Strana Demokratické Levice (SDL)

The constituent committee of the Democratic Left Party (DLP) was established by communist reformers following a split at the congress of the Communist Party of Bohemia and Moravia (CPBM) in June 1993. Chairman Josef Meél led the party, and Jiří Svoboda was vice chairman. After 1992, it had one representative in the Left Bloc and deputies' club. The party was reasonably successful in the 1994 local elections. In the May–June 1996 parliamentary elections, the DLP failed to win any parliamentary seats, with a mere 0.13% of the vote.[46] In June 1997, the party joined with the Left Bloc to create the Party of Democratic Socialism (PDS).

Left Bloc (LB)
Levý Blok (LB)

The Left Bloc (LB) originated in 1992 from a pragmatic faction of the Communist Party of Bohemia and Moravia that split away from the CPBM. Its membership included 21 parliamentary deputies led by Chairman Jaroslav

Ortman. In the June 1992 elections, the Left Bloc gained 14.05% of the vote and captured 35 parliamentary seats. It presented itself as a modern left-wing party but failed to gain seats in the May–June 1996 parliamentary and Senate elections. The Bloc proved more successful in the 1994 local elections. In June 1997, the LB joined with the DLP to create the Party of Democratic Socialism (PDS).

Party of Democratic Socialism (PDS)
Strana Demokratického Socialismu (SDS)

The Party of Democratic Socialism (PDS) was the product of a fusion between the LB and the DLP in June 1997. The merger was intended to halt the divisions within the left-oriented parties. After 1999 the party was led by Chairman Jiří Hudeček. The PDS platform was based on democratic socialist principles, and the party was connected to the Socialist International. The PDS accepted the principles of a market economy with strong state regulation. It supported the integration of the Czech Republic into the European Union, but questioned Czech entry into NATO without a referendum. In fact, party leaders sought Czech security in the structures of the West European Union rather than NATO, although this body could not provide any credible security guarantees. The party protested against NATO air strikes against Yugoslavia in the spring of 1999 and the Czech government's support for this NATO action.[47]

Liberals

Civic Democratic Party (CDP)
Občanská Demokratická Strana (ODS)

On 16 February 1991, the Civic Forum split into the Civic Democratic Party (CDP) and the Civic Movement (CM). At its constituent congress in Plzeň in April 1991, the CDP elected Václav Klaus as its chairman. Civic Democratic Party leaders presented themselves as center-right and conservative. In coalition with the Civic Democratic Alliance (CDA) and the Christian and Democratic Union–Czechoslovak People's Party (CDU-CPP), the CDP became the strongest party after the June 1992 general elections. It captured 76 seats in the Chamber of Deputies and earned nine government ministerial positions. Klaus became prime minister. With 29.73% of the popular vote, the CDP entered into coalition with the CDU-CPP and the CDA. At its congress on 11 November 1995, the CDP re-elected Klaus as the party chairman. Klaus's *laissez-faire* policies were credited in the early 1990s for speedy economic liberalization and privatization.

The June 1996 general elections ended with an unexpected setback for the ruling coalition, which lost its majority in parliament. The CDP again formed a coalition with the CDU-CPP and the CDA. In the Senate elections in November 1996, the party won 32 of 81 seats but failed to obtain a relative majority. Regardless of these setbacks, at the party's national congress on 8 November 1996 Klaus was again re-elected chairman of his party. Despite the party financing scandal, which erupted in November 1997, Klaus was elected chairman in December 1997, with 227 votes to Jan Ruml's 72 votes.

The CDP was a liberal conservative party and modeled itself after the British Conservative Party. It became the primary representative of the emerging middle class and was committed to reducing the role of the state in the economy. The CDP strongly supported privatization and the rights of the individual. After the departure of several liberal personalities during 1998, the party remained dominated by the "Euro-skeptic" Klaus.[48] Despite the strong conservative rhetoric of its leader, the CDP's 1996 electoral program seemed to be tailored to appeal to more welfare-oriented voters. The party strongly supported the entry of the Czech Republic into NATO, and it sought the country's speedy acceptance into the EU. Key points in the party's platform included legislation mandating balanced budgets, a flat income tax on firms and citizens of approximately 20%, and the full privatization of banks and most state-held firms.[49]

In the June 1998 elections for the Chamber of Deputies, the CDP won under 28% of the vote, and the Social Democrats formed the new government. The poor result was mainly caused by the country's declining economic performance and by financial scandals inside the CDP. After the election, the CDP and the Social Democrats signed an agreement in which the CDP pledged not to topple the CSDP-led minority government. In return, the CDP occupied the chairmanship of both parliamentary chambers. In early 2000, the CDP held 63 seats in the Chamber of Deputies and 26 seats in the Senate, but no ministerial positions.

Civic Democratic Alliance (CDA)
Občanská Demokratická Aliance (ODA)

Founded on 17 December 1989, the Civic Democratic Alliance (CDA) was a part of the Civic Forum until the latter's division. The first national conference of the CDA was held in Prague on 20 October 1990, and soon after, the CDP claimed a membership of some 2,800 people. Until the June 1996 elections, the Alliance was a member of the government coalition, with three ministers and fourteen seats in parliament. In the 1996 general elections, the CDA won thirteen parliamentary seats and obtained four cabinet ministerial posts. In the Senate elections in November 1996, the CDA won seven seats; however, because it did not pay the election deposit, it was left off the June 1998 ballot. Hence, it did not have any seats in the Chamber of Deputies (although it still had five senators); it also failed to secure any cabinet ministers after 1998.

On 23 March 1997, Michael Žantovský was elected chairman of the Alliance, replacing Jan Kalvoda, who resigned for having used the title of "Doctor of Law" wrongfully. In November 1997, Jiří Skálický, who was also minister of the environment and deputy prime minister, was elected party chairman, but he resigned in February 1998 over secret party donations. Following the scandal, several CDA members left the party to join the newly formed Freedom Union (FU). In early 2000, Daniel Kroupa chaired the CDA. The party was increasingly split between a moderate pragmatic wing and a rightist fraction. In April 1998, the latter stream created the Conservative Contract Party (CCP) *(Strana Konzervativní Smlouvy, SKS)*, which decimated the party membership. The Conservative Party did not participate in the June 1998 elections.

The CDA was basically conservative in its political orientation and liberal in its economic program. It supported the de-communization of society and the implementation of the "lustration law" which banned the former communist *nomenklatura* from serving in public posts. The party advocated a less powerful central government and stronger regional units. In the economic sphere, the CDA backed faster privatization, a strong central bank, lower taxes, government spending cuts, decentralization, and tax exemptions for non-profit and charitable organizations. Socially, the party supported social insurance and aid for the "truly needy," and it had a strong "law-and-order" platform. Czech membership in the EU and NATO were also long-term party goals.[50]

Freedom Union (FU)
Unie Svobody (US)

The Freedom Union (FU) was formed in January 1998 when a number of CDP members left the party in protest against its continuing support for Václav Klaus. The main impulse for the formation of the FU was the position of several members of the CDP leadership toward the party financing scandal. The former Interior Minister Jan Ruml and Finance Minister Ivan Pilip called for Klaus's resignation. Ruml and Pilip were subsequently called "putschists" by their former party colleagues. Although Klaus stepped down from the office of prime minister, he kept his position within the party. At a special party congress in December 1997, Klaus was confirmed as party chairman. His opponent, Jan Ruml, received less than a quarter of the vote.

The "anti-Klaus" wing of the CDP wrote a platform that promised support for the new Tošovský government. However, the party leadership opposed any cooperation with the administration. It was this relationship to the new cabinet that precipitated the final breakdown of dialogue within the party. Followers of the platform, who had strong support within the CDP faction in parliament, accepted Tošovský's offer to participate in the new government. The party leadership gave Ivan Pilip, Michal Lobkowicz, Stanislav Volák, and Jan Černý an ultimatum to either resign from their ministerial posts or leave the party. The ministers refused to resign.

By the end of the year, the situation was so untenable that the "anti-Klaus" platform openly talked about leaving the party. In January 1998, the signatories of the platform approved a new formation—the Freedom Union. Almost half of the CDP parliamentary delegates left the party to join the FU together with several former CDP members. The Union thereby became a parliamentary party before participating in its first elections. Whereas in the lower house their position was relatively strong, in the Senate, Klaus's followers held an overwhelming majority, as only three CDP senators became FU members. According to opinion polls, public support for the FU rapidly rose to 20% as the disintegration of the CDP signaled an opportune space for a new rightist party.

The FU, which drew sympathizers from the CDP, subsequently lost its initial dynamism. Under the pressure of approaching elections, the FU needed to build up its structure, make a program, and prepare its leaders for an election campaign. However, most of its energy was used up in resolving problems within the party, which gave the public the impression that the Union was an introverted organization.

The Freedom Union was first chaired by Vladimír Mlynár. Following the 1998 elections, the FU obtained 19 seats in the Chamber of Deputies and one seat in the Senate. Party members participated in the Tošovský government in 1998, but the FU had no ministers in the cabinet of Prime Minister Zeman. The FU platform included calls for privatization and market reforms without corruption, a reduction in tax rates and interest rates, and new legislation to strengthen capital market oversight. The FU's program contained many of the same principles as the CDP's but placed a stronger emphasis on cleaning up the capital markets and made no suggestion of adopting a flat tax. Jan Ruml headed the party in early 2000.

Free Democrats (FD)
Svobodní Demokraté (SD)

The Free Democrats (FD) originated as the Civic Movement (CM). It was created during the breakup of the Civic Forum at its extraordinary congress on 23 February 1991. The constituent congress of the new party took place on 26–27 April 1991 in Prague, and Jiří Dienstbier, member of Charter 77 and Czechoslovakia's first foreign minister after the revolution, was elected chairman. In the June 1992 general elections the party was not able to exceed the necessary 5% threshold and consequently was not represented in parliament. The change of name to Free Democrats and the new character of the party were approved by delegates to a party congress in September 1993. In December 1995, the party joined with the Liberal People's Social Party to form the Free Democrats–Liberal National Socialist Party (FD-LNSP). The party emphasized the values of freedom, democracy, and justice.

Free Democrats–Liberal National Socialist Party (FD-LNSP)
Svobodní Demokraté–Liberální Strana Národne Sociální (SD-LSNS)

The Free Democrats–Liberal National Socialist Party (FD-LNSP) was established in December 1995 through the fusion of the Free Democrats and the Liberal People's Social Party. The party claimed about 8,000 members. After 1995, the party was chaired by Vavrinec Bodenlos. He resigned from his post after the party's defeat in the May–June 1996 parliamentary elections and he was replaced by Jiří Dienstbier, who became chairman at the 22 June 1996 meeting of the party's central council. The merger of the two parties in 1995 solved their financial problems while allowing them to retain their identities. The result of the fusion was the emergence of a social liberal party in the Czech political spectrum. On the one hand, the party claimed to have played a role in the creation of a democratic Czechoslovakia in 1918. On the other hand, the FD-LNSP viewed itself as the direct successor of the more recently founded Civic Forum, which had helped to mobilize the "velvet revolution." In any case, party leaders considered themselves an important factor in reintroducing democracy into Czech society.

The party emphasized the liberal ideas of freedom and justice. Its platform called for a market economy and the Czech Republic's membership in the EU and NATO. Its leaders also were close to one of the junior members of the coalition, the Christian and Democratic Union–Czech People's Party. In April 1996, the Czech electoral commission ruled that the FD-LNSP was not a party but a coalition of parties and thus had to garner at least 7% of votes in general elections in order to gain seats in the Chamber of Deputies. The Czech Constitutional Court subsequently, ruled that it could compete as a party, but the FD-LNSP failed to exceed the 5% minimum required to achieve representation. The defeat was attributed to various party scandals: Bodenlos received a suspended prison sentence in 1992 for threatening his neighbor with an axe, while Rudolf Baránek, chairman of the Czech Association of Entrepreneurs, had posted signs in a hotel he owned in Breclav banning Roma from the premises. The party also failed to get its co-chairman, Jiří Dienstbier, elected to the Senate.[51] Dienstbier succeeded Elizabeth Rehn as UN special reporter for human rights in the former Yugoslavia in March 1998. Another prominent party member, Martin Bursik, became a non-affiliated environment minister in the Tošovský government.

Czech People's Social Party (CPSP)
Ceská Strana Národne Sociální (CSNS)

In September 1997, the FD-LNSP, which was formed in December 1995, changed its name to CPSP. It tried to follow in the footsteps of the Civic Movement (CM), which itself originated as part of the Civic Forum (CF).

In June 1997, the party had close to 6,000 members. In the June 1998 parliamentary elections, the CPSP put forward its own candidates, among them representatives of the Association of Businessmen, Tradesmen and Farmers, but it did not clear the 5% hurdle for seats. Jan Sula was the party chairman.

Liberal Social Union (LSU)
Liberálne Sociální Unie (LSU)

The Liberal Social Union (LSU) registered in December 1991 as a movement chaired by František Trnka. It became a pre-election coalition of the Green Party, the Czechoslovak Socialist Party, the Agricultural Party, and the Agricultural Union. However, the individual parties gradually drifted apart, and by the end of 1993 all collective members had seceded from the LSU. At its 1994 congress, the Liberal Social Union declared itself a political party with individual membership. In the May–June 1996 general elections, it became part of the Bohemian-Moravian Union of the Center, but it failed to obtain any parliamentary seats.

Party of Businessmen and Tradesmen (PBT)
Strana Podnikatelů a Obchodníků (SPO)

Formerly known as the Popular Democratic Party, which ran on a coalition ticket with the Republican Party in the first multi-party elections of June 1990, this initially nationalist organization was led by Jaroslav Samek. Other prominent party members include Milan Kašpar, Petr Ryška, Ivan Vlk, and Josef Rejsek. At the end of June 1990, the Party of Businessmen and Tradesmen, under its former name, severed all relations with the nationalistic Republican Party. On 15 June 1995, its leaders registered the party under the PBT name. The PBT described itself as a "party of the middle class" that sought to create legislative conditions for small and medium-sized businesses and for trade to flourish. Despite its attempts to appeal to the new middle class, the PBT made little headway in capturing electoral support. According to its program, a primary objective of the party was "to eliminate the deleterious effect of tax regulations and high interest rates on credit, and faulty laws that hinder initiative instead of supporting it."[52] It was not represented in parliament following the 1992 or the 1996 elections.

A parallel organization, the Party of Czechoslovak Businessmen, Tradesmen and Farmers (PCBTF) *(Strana Československých Podnikatelů, Zivnostníků a Rolníků, SCSPZR),* was established as a political party at the general assembly of the Association of Entrepreneurs of the Czech Republic on 15 January 1992. It was chaired by Rudolf Baránek as a self-proclaimed right-wing political formation. It did not succeed in gaining any seats to parliament in the 1992 or 1996 elections.

Democratic Union (DU)
Demokratická Unie (DEU)

The Democratic Union registered as a political party in March 1994 and convened a constituent assembly in June 1994. In May 1997, the party had close to 1,500 members. It positioned itself as a center-right party, and its platform emphasized moral values in politics and advocated strict laws in economic transactions to prevent corruption.[53] Failing to clear the 5% hurdle in the May–June 1996 parliamentary elections (gaining only 2.8% of the vote), the DU contested the election law in the Constitutional Court, but its case was rejected. In November 1996, however, Pavel Heřman, who campaigned as an independent for the DU, won a seat in the Senate. After June 1996, the party was chaired by Ratibor Majzlík. Majzlík's predecessor, Alena Hromádková, became honorary chair.[54]

Right Bloc (RB)
Pravý Blok (PB)

The Right Bloc (RB) was registered as a party in March 1996 and held its constituent assembly on 29 June 1996. The sixty-three delegates elected Přemysl Vachaloský as chairman. At the time of its inception, the party counted about 100 members. In the May–June 1996 general elections, the RB campaigned independently, but was not on the ballot, as it had failed to pay the election deposit. In November 1996, Vachaloský resigned and Jan Votoček took his place. Jaroslav Andal became honorary chairman. The RB considered the integration of the country's rightist parties as the most important political task in order to counter the influence of the left.[55]

A similar grouping, the Czech Right (CR) *(Ceská Pravice, CP)*, was registered as a party in January 1994. It was a moderate nationalist and conservative party created in opposition to the post-communist formations. In the May–June 1996 general election campaign, the CR adopted a staunchly nationalistic platform. Furthermore, the party advocated classical conservative values such as justice and family.[56] But the CR acquired little public influence and failed to obtain any parliamentary seats.

Citizens' Coalition–Political Club (CC-PC)
Občanská Koalice–Politický Klub (OK-PK)

Citizens' Coalition–Political Club (CC-PC) was founded in October 1997 and registered as a party in February 1998. It had about 1,500 members. On its coalition slate there were also candidates from small organizations such as the Group of Non-Political Subjects and the Masaryk Democratic Party. Former CSDP deputy Jozef Wagner, musician and businessman Michael Kocáb, and former dissident Rudolf Battek took part in the congress at which the CC-PC was founded. The party brought together a number of former Civic Forum members, describing the Forum as its heritage. Wagner became the party chairman. In July 1999, a group of 200 Czech intellectuals created a new organization that purportedly aimed to build more robust civic institutions. The group, called Impuls '99, invoked memories of the dissident Charter 77. Among the initiators of Impuls '99 were Jiří Pehe and sociologist Tomas Halik. The movement did not plan to become a political party.[57]

Christian Democrats

Christian Democratic Party (CDP)
Kresťanskodemokratická Strana (KDS)

The Christian Democratic Party (CDP) originated in the mid-1980s as an unofficial ecumenical Christian group. It was formally established as an autonomous Christian democratic political club on 15 November 1989 and as a political party on 3 December 1989. Its inaugural congress was held on 24 March 1990. The first president was the former Charter 77 activist Václav Benda, who initiated the policy of eliminating the pre-1989 communist presence in public institutions and preventing their return to office through the lustration law. The party decided to stand in the elections outside of the CF. It initially opposed entering a coalition with the ideologically close Peoples' Party because of the latter's previous communist connections. The CDP did form a coalition, the Christian and Democratic Union, with the Slovak Christian Democratic Movement on the eve of the June 1990 general elections, but the Union collapsed soon after the balloting.

The CDP entered the June 1992 parliamentary elections in coalition with the Civic Democratic Party and obtained ten seats. It became a member of the government coalition and had two ministers in the cabinet before the June 1996 elections. In November 1995, Ivan Pilip was re-elected president of the party. At its November 1996 congress, the CDP decided to merge with the Civic Democratic Party. The party believed that Christian values should be present in political and social life. It was not a hierarchical Church-like movement but rather favored the democratic process, especially at the local level. Economically, the party had little objection to state participation in areas such as health, science, and education. However, it favored low taxes, particularly as the average CDP voter was a medium-sized businessman. The CDP supported the rapid accession of the Czech Republic to membership in NATO and the EU.[58]

Christian and Democratic Union–Czechoslovak
People's Party (CDU-CPP)
Kresťanská a Demokratická Unie–Československá
Strana Lidová (KDU-CSL)

The Christian and Democratic Union–Czechoslovak People's Party (CDU-CPP) originated as the Czechoslovak Peoples' Party in September 1918 through the merger of several Czech Catholic groupings. Dissolved in 1938, it was restored in 1945 as a part of the National Front. After World War II it was the only non-socialist party in parliament. The communist coup of 1948 left the party intact but emasculated. In November 1989, it rebuilt its tradition as a non-socialist group based on "Christian foundations." The standing of the party improved in November 1989 when a new party leadership offered its support to the Civic Forum, broke relations with the communists, and began to publish uncensored information. It managed to increase its membership but was rocked by scandal on the eve of the general elections in June 1990 when chairman Josef Bartončík was accused of collaboration with the secret police. Party leaders accused the communists of orchestrating the revelations to undercut the party's position in the elections. The People's Party reasserted its "Christian values" as a centrist and moderate force and tried to gain the support of religious believers. Its poor showing in the elections indicated that it was less than successful in regaining an independent image among voters.

In 1992, the People's Party joined the Christian Democratic Union and changed its name to the Christian and Democratic Union–Czechoslovak People's Party. In June 1992, the bloc obtained 15 seats in the Chamber of Deputies of the Czech parliament and received four ministers in the government. At the party's congress in Brno on 30 September 1995, Josef Lux was confirmed as chairman. But he resigned for health reasons in 1998. In the June 1996 elections, the CDU-CPP obtained 18 seats in the Chamber of Deputies and four ministerial posts in the government. The party was seen as a major victor in the November 1996 elections to the newly established Senate. Although it only registered in third place with 13 seats, it successfully challenged the dominance of its senior coalition partner, the CDP. Party members participated in both the Klaus and Tošovský governments.

After the June 1998 elections, the Union held 20 seats in the Chamber of Deputies and 13 seats in the Senate following the November 1998 Senate elections. Since it rejected a coalition with the Social Democrats, the party did not obtain any ministers in the Zeman cabinet. In May 1999, the CDU-CPP congress elected Jan Kasal as the new party chairman. According to its own sources, the party had 60,000 members.[59] The organization viewed itself as the "social conscience" of the governing coalition. It incorporated the more conservative elements of Czech society and described itself as a Christian-conservative party that stood for traditional family values, law and order, better pensions and access to housing, and the restitution of church property. It campaigned for what it called a "social-market" economy that would include easier access to housing, faster economic growth by strengthening the micro-economy, and a gradual lowering of income tax. Concerning international relations, the party favored Czech membership in the EU and NATO. The traditional electorate of the party came from rural areas. Defense Minister Miloslav Výborný was a party member, as was Josef Lux, the Minister of Agriculture.[60]

Agrarians

Agricultural Party (AP)
Zemědelská Strana (ZS)

The preparatory committee of the Agricultural Party (AP) was established on 1–2 December 1989 at the congress of agricultural cooperatives. The AP was the strongest member of the Liberal Social Union. In 1993, the party seceded from the Union, and its chairman, Jiří Vackar, intended to combine it with one of the centrist parties. However, the March 1994 congress decided that members of the AP would become individual members of the Liberal Social Union, and the party became extinct.

A rival agrarian organization, the Czechoslovak Agrarian Party (CAP), was established in early 1990 and was believed to have had close ties to members of the former communist apparatus seeking to preserve state farms and cooperatives as well as state subsidies to cooperative farms.

Several other agrarian lobbies were formed during the 1990s, including the Party of Free Peasants (PFP) and the Party of the Czech Countryside (PCC). However, no sizeable agricultural or peasant parties emerged in the Czech lands, especially as the rural population generally voted for either communist or Christian democratic parties.

Greens

Green Party (GP)
Strana Zelených (SZ)

The Green Party (GP) was founded on 9 December 1989 and held its constituent congress on 17 February 1990. It adhered to the principles of the "green international" and became the largest of the new environmentalist groupings. Although party membership dramatically increased in the first few months of 1990, the Greens' performance in the June 1990 elections proved disappointing. Several other parties had taken aboard much of the Green Party's platform, thus undercutting its appeal, and its leaders were not well known. A smaller Party of the Green Alternative (PGA) was also established in the early 1990s.

Calculating that it would not make a major parliamentary breakthrough with a primarily environmentalist program, in the fall of 1991 the Green Party helped to form the Liberal and Social Union (LSU) in coalition with Socialists and Agrarians. In June 1992, the GP participated in the general elections as part of the LSU coalition, which won 6.5% of the vote and 16 seats in parliament. In 1993, the GP left the LSU, and party chairman Jaroslav Vlček vacated the Liberal Social Union's deputy club. On 7 October 1995, Emil Zeman replaced Vlček as party chairman. The GP did not pay the election deposit in June 1996 and was therefore excluded from the ballot.

After the June 1998 elections, the GP had 142 local government representatives but no seats in parliament. In March 1999, the party congress in Brno elected Jiří Čejka as the new chairman and claimed to have about 1,800 members. The GP platform was based on providing "sustainable development." Besides the protection and reasonable use of natural resources, the party advocated the "social and cultural relief" of people's needs and indicated a social democratic orientation.[61] The GP also became a member of the oppositionist but marginal Realist Bloc.[62]

Communists

Communist Party of Bohemia and Moravia (CPBM)
Komunistická Strana Čech a Moravy (KSCM)

Shortly after the "velvet revolution," the Czechoslovak Communist Party (CCP) began to reorganize and recast itself as a democratic left-wing grouping.[63] At an emergency session in November 1989, the hard-line leadership was replaced by a new presidium and secretariat. By October 1990, the party lost 750,000 out of 1,700,000 members but it still had more members, assets, funds, and organizational networks than any other political grouping. The federalization of the party was completed in March 1990 when a Communist Party of Bohemia and Moravia was established in addition to the Communist Party of Slovakia: they became independent of each other.[64]

While the core of the CCP remained intact, there were several reformist and orthodox splinters established their own organizations in the aftermath of the revolution. Reformist offshoots included the Czechoslovak Democratic Forum (CDF) and the Independent Left (IL) which advocated "democratic socialism" and a "social market economy," respectively. The unrepentant Marxist-Leninists were left with a narrow and shrinking support base. The major post-communist parties adopted a wait-and-see approach toward the political changes, recasting themselves as social democrats and defenders of various underprivileged groups, including workers, farm laborers, and pensioners. They hoped to benefit from the fragmentation of the Civic Forum and their own long-term revival as the only credible leftist force given the disarray among various socialist groupings.

The constituent congress of the CPBM in Olomouc on 13–14 October 1990 determined its socialist orientation. It was the strongest party in the Left Bloc (LB) election coalition. However, at its congress in June 1993, the party's major factions quarreled, with the orthodox wing opposing any change in the party's name. The more pragmatic group, represented by a majority of communist deputies, founded the LB, and the more radical group established the Democratic Left Party (DLP). The CPBM was represented in parliament by nine deputies after the June 1992 elections. It garnered 22 seats in the June 1996 general elections, but only two seats in the 81-seat Senate elected in

November 1996. By the end of that year, the party held only ten seats in the 200-member parliament and commanded about 9% support in public opinion polls. According to polling agencies in June 1999, the party received additional support from voters who became discontented with the Zeman government.

After the June 1998 elections, the CPBM held 24 seats in the Chamber of Deputies and three seats in the Senate. Since all major parties rejected a coalition with the communists, the party did not participate in any government. According to its own sources, the party had 160,000 members and was led by its Chairman, Miroslav Grebenčík. Unlike other reformed communist parties in the former Soviet bloc, the Czech Communist Party had in many respects become more militant since it was dethroned. It admitted to committing many mistakes in the past but pledged itself to building a future "state of peasants and workers." In reality, its electorate consisted primarily of peasants and pensioners. The party retained a core support of around 10% of the electorate but remained isolated at the far left of the political spectrum. Key points in the party platform included the strengthening of state control over banks, the protection of domestic markets from foreign competition, and the ending of energy and housing price deregulations. The CPBM denounced both EU and NATO membership.[65]

One remnant of the former ruling party created the Party of Czechoslovak Communists (PCC) *(Strana Československých Komunistů, SCK)*, but it failed to garner seats in the June 1992 general elections. The party was led by Miroslav Štepán, the communist leader before 1989. The PCC remained loyal to Marxist-Leninist precepts and was unable to craft alliances with other parties. It dropped out of the May–June 1996 elections, having refused to pay the required election deposit.[66]

Nationalists

Association for the Republic–Republican Party of Czechoslovakia (AR-RPC)
Sdruzení Pro Republiku–Republikánská Strana Československa (SPR-RSC)

Ultranationalist parties also became visible in the Czech lands, although with limited public backing. The strongest organization, the Association for the Republic–Republican Party, was openly xenophobic and pro-federalist. It was officially founded on 26 December 1989 and was headed by a charismatic, young radical, Miroslav Sládek. Its constituent congress took place on 24 February 1990. The party failed to gain any parliamentary seats in the June 1990 elections. However, after 1991, its popularity steadily grew. A June 1991 public opinion poll showed the Republicans as the fifth most popular party in the Czech Republic, benefiting from about 5% of public support. Pre-election evaluations for the

June 1992 ballot indicated that public support for the Republicans might have been more widespread than indicated by its results at the polls. In the June 1992 general elections, the party won 14 out of 200 seats in the Czech National Council and registered 6.48% of the vote for the Czech Chamber of the Federal House of the People. Five of the party's deputies subsequently left the party.

The AR-RPC proved particularly successful in regions suffering from high unemployment and social unrest. While it won 10.6% of the vote in northern Bohemia, in Prague it took only 3%. Post-election assessments indicated that 73% of its supporters were under thirty years of age. In June 1996, the Republicans won 8% of the vote and took 18 seats in the Chamber of Deputies but no seats in the Senate elections. In parliament, the party was effectively sidelined, as no other political group was willing to cooperate with it.[67] In the run-up to the June 1998 elections, the AR-RPC came under criticism for using campaign posters when the other parties had pledged not to use large billboards. The posters read "Republicans reject NATO" and "Republicans against advantages for Gypsies." In January 1998, Sládek was acquitted of spreading racial hatred after spending 17 days in custody on remand. That accusation contributed to the party's election defeat in June 1998.

The party platform was nationalistic and racist, attracting young, unemployed, and less-educated voters. Most of the party's support came from Czech skinheads who were believed responsible for several racially motivated attacks on Gypsies and Vietnamese workers. The party supported free education, lowering the retirement age, the protection of Czech products through import tariffs, strong police, and the death penalty. It advocated the expulsion of Vietnamese and Cuban guest workers from the country and called for the withdrawal of "unjustified benefits for Roma," who were allegedly responsible for much of the crime plaguing the country. The Republicans exploited the Gypsy issue to garner public sympathy, as did several other marginal nationalist groupings. For example, the chairman of the Club of Committed Non–Party Members (CCNPM) from West Bohemia, Jiří Hájek, disclosed that plans were being drawn up to establish home guards to protect citizens from alleged abuses perpetrated by Roma, since citizens evidently did not feel secure enough with current police protection.

Links were believed to exist between the AR-RPC and a number of unofficial neo-fascist groupings such as the White League (*Bílá Liga*) and various skinhead and vigilante gangs.[68] Party leaders demanded the reevaluation of all communist laws and the removal of all former communists from governmental positions, and vehemently supported the far-reaching privatization of state-owned property. The Republicans did not issue comprehensive political and economic programs but instead relied upon public discontent with particular social issues. In November 1990, on the first anniversary of the "velvet revolution," the party staged a nationalist demonstration near Wenceslas Square in central Prague, where U.S. President George Bush and President Havel were addressing the crowds gathered in celebration.

With regard to foreign policy, the party rejected NATO membership for the Czech Republic and advocated neutrality. The party also did not seek any reconciliation with Germany. Sládek's anti-German campaign culminated in early 1997—when parliament was negotiating the Czech-German declaration—in his statement at a protest demonstration that "we can only regret having killed so few Germans in the war," as demonstrators burned the German flag. Parliament revoked Sládek's immunity and brought charges against him for inciting national and racial hatred.

The AR-RPC warned against allowing extensive foreign, especially German, investment in the country, arguing that it would make Czechs feel like guests in their own state. It also demanded the return of Subcarpathian Ruthenia, a former Czechoslovak region that was annexed by the Soviet Union in 1945 and that is today part of independent Ukraine. The party claimed that Moscow's annexation of Ruthenia was contrary to international law and that most Ruthenians wished to rejoin Czechoslovakia. The party planned a World Ruthenian Congress, purportedly to enable Ruthenian delegates freely to decide to which state they would prefer to belong. On several occasions, Sládek reportedly traveled to Mukachevo, in Ukrainian Ruthenia, where he publicly hoisted the Czechoslovak flag.

Sládek was not able to vote in the 1998 presidential election, in which he was a candidate, because he was in custody for attempting to evade a court trial. When Havel was elected president by a margin of only one vote, the Republicans appealed to the constitutional court.

Party activities consisted mainly of protest demonstrations. Apart from Sládek the most active party members were Jan Vík and delegate Josef Krejsa. Krejsa was also editor-in-chief of the weekly *Republican Front,* which was condemned for its openly racist views. The undemocratic practices of the party leadership were made public when the former vice chairman Pavel Mozga accused Sládek of wasting party finances. In a letter to the Interior Minister, he wrote that no one was allowed to know about party finances apart from Sládek and that any reference to them resulted in expulsion from the party.

Since the Republicans received only 3.9% of votes in the June 1998 elections, they obtained no parliamentary seats. Nevertheless, the party claimed a membership of 55,000 people. A closely linked grouping, the Association of Pensioners in the Czech Republic (APCR) *(Sdružení Důchodců CR, SDCR),* was founded in 1994 and led by Jan Vík.

Club of Committed Non–Party Members (CCNPM)
Klub Angažovaných Nestraníků (KAN)

The Club of Committed Non–Party Members (CCNPM), led by chairman Emil Dejmek, was established as an independent political movement seeking to create a platform for citizens of right-wing orientation who refused involvement in political parties. It developed a conservative political program and endeavored to unify several small nationalist groups. In November 1995, the party rejected a merger with the Christian Democrats. It has never been represented in the Czech parliament.[69]

Ethnic Minority and Religious Parties

Union of Slovaks (US)
Sdruzení Slováku (SS)

As the breakup of the Czechoslovak federation gathered pace, Slovak activists in the Czech Republic established a handful of independent organizations to represent what had now become a minority population. The US was chaired by former dissident and Federal Assembly Deputy Ján Mlynárik, who claimed that the organization was formed in order to eliminate the perception that Slovak leaders in Bratislava spoke for the Slovak population in the Czech Republic. The goal of the US was to promote cultural and educational activities and to be active in the political arena either through citizens' initiatives or by placing independent candidates on the slates of various parties, including the CDP and various Christian democratic organizations. In March 1993, Mlynárik made a point of disassociating the US from the recently formed Community of Slovaks (CS), which he claimed maintained links with the quasi-nationalist Slovak government. The CS considered itself a non-political organization representing Slovaks who either permanently or temporarily resided in the Czech Republic.[70]

Slovak citizens were given until 31 December 1993 to proclaim themselves as Czech citizens. They needed to prove permanent residence in the Czech Republic for two years, their release from Slovak citizenship, and the absence of a criminal conviction during the previous five years. According to the law, an individual had to renounce citizenship of all other states, as dual citizenship was not permissible. Of the 309,000 Slovaks declared in the 1991 census, only 160,000 held Slovak citizenship; 46,000 applied for Czech citizenship in 1992 and another 63,000 in early 1993. The Slovaks constituted a new ethnic minority in the Czech Republic, whereas under the federal system they had been defined as one of Czechoslovakia's two constituent nations. Although Slovaks did not suffer from any evident forms of discrimination and had been well assimilated in the new Czech state, some local spokesmen argued that the minority should be provided with all the group rights contained in international human rights agreements.

Community of Slovaks (CS)
Společnost Slováku (SS)

The Community of Slovaks (CS) held its first congress in Prague in February 1993, at which Jaroslav Škorík was elected president. The Community declared itself a non-political organization open to all Slovaks and to "friends of Slovakia" resident in the Czech lands. Although it began with a small membership of under 200, it opened branches throughout the country and expanded its numbers.

Several other Slovak groupings sprang up in the first half of 1993, including the Democratic Alliance of Slovaks (DAS), which aspired to become a political party; the apolitical Association of Slovaks; and the Club of Slovak Culture, originally founded in 1969 as a Prague-based branch of the Slovak Heritage Foundation. In March 1993, leaders of most of these groups met and nominated several representatives to the Council for Nationalities. They also put forward proposals for ensuring regular Slovak-language broadcasts on Czech radio and the creation of a Slovak magazine *Džavot* (Babble), funded primarily by the CS.[71]

Romani Civic Initiative (RCI)
Rómská Občanská lniciatíva (ROI)

Emil Scuka chaired this Romani association, which was founded in Prague in November 1989, initially in coalition with the Civic Forum. It proclaimed no specific ideology but combined like-minded citizens on the basis of their beliefs in the principles of "equality, freedom, and humanity." RCI leaders disputed official population statistics, claiming that over 300,000 Roma lived in the Czech Republic, with a further 500,000 in Slovakia. These figures were dismissed by many observers as vastly inflated. The RCI demanded that the Roma be defined as a nationality in Czechoslovakia's new constitution and census. The Initiative also wanted the Romani nationality to be explicitly named in the provisions of the Charter of Fundamental Rights and Liberties that prohibited ethnic discrimination. The RCI campaigned for full cultural and social freedoms for the Romani minority and the elevation of its language to the same position in schools as Hungarian in Slovakia and the languages of other minority nationalities in the Czech Republic, such as German.

By the close of 1992, over 30 Romani cultural organizations were registered with the Czech and Slovak Ministries of Culture, together with a Museum of Romani Culture in Brno and several cultural clubs for young Roma. The first Gypsy journal, *Lacho Lar* (Good Word), was launched under the editorship of Vincent Danihel to help improve knowledge of the Romani language and prepare the ground for issuing Romani school textbooks. RCI leaders supported the launching of a works program to induce Roma to build single-family houses in Gypsy settlements to replace all currently unsuitable residences except one, which would be left as an open-air museum.

Representatives of the RCI also lodged protests against the use of the word "Gypsy" when describing the perpetrator of a criminal act, since a different procedure was followed in the case of criminals of other nationalities. Because of its link to high unemployment, the low level of education (only 1%

of Roma were skilled workers or benefited from higher education) was considered the chief cause of criminality among Gypsies. Romani deputies attacked the collection of data on "Romani criminality" as a violation of the Charter of Fundamental Rights and Liberties. They pointed out that the Gypsy population was highly differentiated and possessed its own cadre of qualified professionals.

The RCI was formally reconstituted as a political party in March 1990, at its founding congress in Prague. It has participated in elections at the federal level alongside the Democratic Union of Roma in Slovakia. Eight deputies subsequently represented the RCI in various legislative bodies in Czechoslovakia. In addition, several Roma were selected as candidates on the Civic Forum and Communist Party candidate lists after the June 1990 elections.

Romani National Congress (RNC)
Romský Národní Kongres (RNK)

This small grouping, chaired by Vladimír Olah, was created in February 1991. It claimed to be an amalgam of fifteen social organizations and initiatives, including the Movement of Romani Activists, the Association of Romani Youth, the Romani Democratic Union, the Association of Slovak Roma, the Independent Organization of Roma, and the Christian Democratic Association *Romani Matica*. The RNC considered itself to be a left-of-center organization; it demanded that the Romani nationality be anchored in the constitution and that Roma be represented in all offices and ministries.

Polish Council (PC)
Rada Poláku (RP)

The Polish Council (PC), chaired by Tadeusz Wantuła, was founded in March 1990 to replace the Polish Cultural Union. The latter was considered a mouthpiece of the communist regime rather than a representative of Polish interests in Czechoslovakia. The PC was a nine-person council that oversaw and coordinated the activities of the six Polish minority organizations in Czechoslovakia. It demanded an end to alleged discrimination against Poles living in the Tesin Silesian region and called for the observance of human rights in accordance with the Helsinki Accords. Although ethnic Polish leaders in the Czech Republic complained about Prague's patronizing and bureaucratic attitudes and the government's apparent failure to restore property seized by the communist regime after World War II, the Polish community received state funding for its cultural and organizational development. The PC unsuccessfully attempted to gain parliamentary representation in the June 1990 elections; however, one of its leaders was elected on the ticket of the Bratislava-based multi-ethnic Coexistence coalition. In June 1992, the PC received one seat in the Czech National Council and two seats in the Federal Assembly.[72]

Union of German Cultural Associations (UGCA)
Svaz Nemeckých Kulturních Organizací (SNKO)

The Union of German Cultural Associations (UGCA) was founded in October 1990 with the merger of two organizations—the formerly communist-controlled Cultural Association of Czechoslovak Citizens of German Nationality and the Union of Germans in Czechoslovakia. Its leader was Walter Piverka, a Czech parliamentary deputy elected on the Civic Forum ticket. The UGCA called for the safeguarding of social and cultural rights for the German minority. Although it claimed over 8,000 members, it did not possess a large enough social base to have an impact on Czech politics. Although the German minority figured in Prague's disputes with German expellee organizations, its status did not upset the signing of a comprehensive treaty between the two states. The voting system prevented the UGCA from running on a separate ticket in the national elections, persuading it to collaborate with Coexistence. As a result, the organization only won one seat in the Czech National Council.[73]

German Landowners' Assembly (GLA)
Zemské Shromáždení Nemcù (ZSN)

This organization of Germans in Bohemia, Moravia, and Silesia, commonly known by its German name as *Deutsche Ländsmannschaft*, was created in November 1992 as a nonparty grouping that condemned any form of dictatorship or revanchism. Its 300 delegates approved new statutes and elected the GLA's central bodies. The new president stated that the group was not intended to be a fifth column for German revisionists, but wanted to build upon the amicable relations that used to exist among Germans, Moravians, Czechs, and Silesians. It disassociated itself from the more radical Society of Sudeten Germans, which demanded the return of all land and property to Germans expelled from Czechoslovakia at the close of World War II.

In January 1997, after several years of complex negotiations, a Czech-German Declaration was signed. Czech-German relations remained tense because of the trauma of the three million Germans who were deported from Czechoslovakia after World War II. The "resettlement" of Sudeten Germans had been approved by the international community at the Yalta Conference in 1944, and the Czechs did not consider this act illegal. The descendents of expelled Sudeten Germans, who lived mostly in Bavaria, demanded the return of their parents' property in the Czech Republic. The Czech government refused. The German government refused, in turn, to pay compensation to the Czech victims of Nazism until the issue of the Sudeten Germans was resolved. In the Czech-German Declaration, the German side acknowledged Germany's responsibility for the occupation of Czechoslovakia.[74] The Czech side regretted the forcible expulsion and resettlement of Sudeten Germans. Both sides stated that they would not "burden their relations with political and legal issues which stem from the past." The declaration also set up a German-Czech Future Fund, to which both sides made contributions. The fund was to be used to finance projects such as youth encounters, care of the elderly, preservation and restoration of monuments, the promotion of minorities, and the German-Czech Commission of Historians.

Council of Jewish Communities in the Czech Lands (CJCCL)
Rada Židovských Obcí Českých Zemí (RZOCZ)

The Council of Jewish Communities in the Czech Lands (CJCCL) was originally formed by the communist authorities to help supervise the remnants of Jewish cultural and religious life in Bohemia and Moravia. Its leadership was directly appointed by the Ministry of Culture and was expected to apply all government policies toward the dwindling Jewish community. Following the "velvet revolution," several Council leaders resigned, and in December 1989 an advisory group of young people was formed to help manage Jewish community affairs. Desider Galsky, an older community leader, was appointed chairman, but died in late 1990.

In addition, the Association of Friends of Jewish Culture was formed to preserve Czech Jewish heritage. Some non-Jews became members under the chairmanship of Bedřich Nossek, the director of the State Jewish Museum.[75]

Other minority organizations were created during the 1990s, including the Society of Friends of Subcarpathian Ruthenia and the Union of Hungarians (UH) *(Svaz Mădarù, SM)*. The latter was founded in February 1990 and represents the country's approximately 23,000 ethnic Hungarians.

Regionalists

Movement for Self-Governing Democracy–Society for Moravia and Silesia (MSGD-SMS)
Hnutí za Samosprávnou Demokracii–Společnost pro Moravu a Slezsko (HSD-SMS)

The Association for Moravia and Silesia was established on the platform of regional autonomy for distinct regions within the Czech republic. It scored well in the national elections but then began to splinter because of differing approaches toward federalism and devolution. Some groups sought a German-type *länder* status for Moravia and Silesia within the Czech Republic; others wanted quasi-republican status within the Czechoslovak federation.[76] Cleavages were also evident on whether to keep the Association together as a civic movement or transform it into a political party. The Association finally split into two groups in the spring of 1991, stressing two different approaches: radical republicanism within the Czechoslovak federation, and regional autonomy within the Czech republic.

Originally known as the Movement for Self-Governing Democracy–Society for Moravia and Silesia and headed by chairman Jan Krýcer, this organization was established as an umbrella movement for a number of Moravian political groups. It advocated replacing the dual federation with a tripartite system in which Moravia and Silesia would figure as the third federal republic, alongside Bohemia and Slovakia. The MSGD-SMS demanded full autonomy for Moravia and Silesia as a prerequisite for efficient regional self-government and fair distribution of state funds. In January 1990, the Movement left the Civic Forum coalition. Its leaders contended that CF representatives opposed the principal goal of "genuine self-government in Moravia and Silesia." It also drafted resolutions charging the Czech government with having discriminated against Moravian and Silesian districts in the federal budget.

The MSGD-SMS proved surprisingly successful in the June 1990 general elections, gaining about 6% of the overall federal vote, 10% in the Czech Republic, and about 25% of the region's vote. As a result, it acquired 16 seats in the Federal Assembly and 22 seats in the Czech National Council. It won 4.2% of the overall vote in the November 1990 local elections, and took almost half of the seats in the Brno city council. It based its election campaign entirely on the promotion of a "Moravian and Silesian identity." Bohumil Tichý, a member of the MSGD-SMS Central Committee, believed that the Movement's relative success was due to its "civic structure" and its program. The Movement emphasized "the formulation of principles for just distribution," especially in the state budget, as a key to Moravian economic independence. Movement leaders believed that Moravia had been the victim of discrimination by "totalitarian centralism."

Moravian leaders reacted with disappointment to the four-land arrangement models drafted by a Czech government commission in 1991. They argued that if the federation were restructured into three parts, tensions between Prague and Bratislava would be eliminated, as Moravia would act as a buffer between Slovaks and Czechs. In 1991, Moravian leaders criticized Prague's economic reforms, claiming that they discriminated against the region. The MSGD-SMS pointed out that although the region's inhabitants accounted for 39.2% of the Czech population, they received only 25.5% of industrial subsidies, 35% of contributions for the operation of non-profit establishments, and 34.8% of subsidies for housing, modernization, and heating.

MSGD-SMS notables met at a special session in August 1991 to discuss the actions of an independently formed "executive committee," which passed a vote of no confidence in the current leadership. Ivan Tužinský, deputy chairman of MSGD-SMS, claimed that the self-appointed "executive committee" was acting contrary to the movement's statutes. Krýcer refuted charges of collaboration with the Petr Pithart government. He emphasized the need to use available legislative options for achieving autonomy, asserting that the idea of a union republic had not been discarded. A Moravian-Silesian Council was formed in late 1991, encompassing a broad spectrum of thirteen political parties and movements active in the region. It called for autonomous and equal status for the region in the Czechoslovak federation. A draft treaty presented by the Council at a joint meeting of the Czech and Slovak National Councils stressed that the question of autonomy and power sharing could be solved by entrusting authority to three regional entities.

By early 1992, support for the party in Moravia-Silesia stabilized at about 5%. In the June 1992 elections, the MSGD-SMS won 14 seats out of 200 in the Czech National Council. Although the Czech government promised to re-evaluate the republic's constitutional setup and address some of the Movement's concerns, no significant progress was registered.

In an important move, three-quarters of the 242 delegates to the MSGD-SMS's third congress in January 1993 rejected the nationalist and separatist tendencies of the Moravian National Party (MNS) and distanced themselves from radical forces within the party. Instead, they declared their allegiance to the principles of liberalism and the goals of a self-governing democracy achieved only through parliamentary means. Most of the Movement delegates agreed that the transformation of the Movement into a fully fledged political party was premature.[77] While some members left to join mainstream political forces, the main group transformed itself into the Bohemian-Moravian Center Party (BMCP).

Czech-Moravian Center Union (CMCU)
Českomoravská Unie Stredu (CMUS)

The Czech- Moravian Center Union (CMCU) was established on 1 April 1990 by a resolution of the delegates of the first Kroměříž congress of the Society for Moravia and Silesia. The party was first christened as the Movement for Self-Governing Democracy–Society for Moravia and Silesia (MSGD-SMS). Its primary target was the self-government of Moravia and Silesia within the Czech state. In the June 1992 elections, the party obtained 14 seats and its program expanded. This resulted in the secession of several radical "Moravianists" and representatives of the Moravian National Party (MNP) from its parliamentary deputy club. In January 1994, the party adopted the CMCU name, but it failed to gain any seats in June 1996 or the June 1998 general elections.

Moravian National Party (MNP)
Moravská Národní Strana (MNS)

Founded in Brno, the Moravian capital, in the early part of 1990, the MNP became a political party under the chairmanship of Ivan Dzimal. Unlike the Movement for Self-Governing Democracy, the MNP did not claim that the Moravians were a constituent part of the Czech nation. It advocated an administrative arrangement for the Czech Republic based on a tripartite "national" structure composed of Bohemia, Moravia, and Silesia. It consistently complained against Prague-centric policies that allegedly resulted in the economic and cultural exploitation of Moravia. In March 1991, the MNP protested against the national census, alleging that it discriminated against the Moravian and Silesian nationalities. The significance of this group remained restricted, although it had some potential for growth. In December 1992, Dzimal attacked the new Czech constitution for aiming to break up Moravian integrity and suppress its national identity. The MNP demanded the recreation of the medieval Greater Moravia in its original borders and with its own executive and legislative bodies.[78]

Another radical organization was also formed, the Moravian National Party–Movement for Moravian-Silesian Unification (MNP-MMSU) *(Moravská Národní Strana–Hnutí Slezsksomoravského Sjednocení, MNS-HSMS)*.

Moravian-Silesian Citizens' Assembly (MSCA)
Občanské Shromázdení Moravy a Slezska (OSMS)

A preparatory committee of 24 members, chaired by author Jaromír Tomeček and including several federal and Czech parliamentary deputies, was formed in November 1990 in accordance with the "Moravian Declaration." It traced its roots to the Moravian margraviate as a state unit that was not always part of the Bohemian crown lands. The committee endeavored to establish an assembly that would unite "representatives from the various streams of social, political, cultural, religious, economic, and administrative life." In March 1993, the MSCA formally approved the creation of a five-member Moravian-Silesian government headed by Václav Kobliha, a former militant leader of the Republican Party. The government was to be responsible for working out a program focusing on economic and social issues in Moravia-Silesia. It sought to preserve a single Moravian-Silesian Land either as an equal unit with Bohemia in a Czech federation or as a sovereign political entity. The creation of the unconstitutional Moravian-Silesian government led to the initiation of criminal proceedings by the Czech prosecutor general in the spring of 1993.[79]

Bohemian-Moravian Union of the Center (BMUC)
Českomoravská Unie Stredu (CMUS)

This party, chaired by Jan Jelga, is the product of a merger in February 1996 of several small parties, the Bohemian-Moravian Center Party (BMCP), the Liberal Social Union (LSU), the Agricultural Party (AP), and the Christian Social Union (CSU). In 1989, when several Brno-based parties began campaigning on the basis of Moravian independence, the BMUC adopted a non-extremist policy, primarily advocating more influence for Moravians in deciding their own affairs. The BMUC was mostly a party of farmers, supporting both the small producers and the larger cooperatives, and promoting technological modernization. The party did not agree with the Czech federalists but preferred to divide the country into three provinces—Moravia, Bohemia, and Prague. BMUC adopted a liberal economic policy, claiming that Czech agriculture was the most decentralized economic sector in Central Europe. It therefore favored EU membership and did not fear the impact of the EU's agricultural policy. The BMUC supported gradual cooperation with NATO, preferring a Central European defense strategy. It became one of the few parties to assert its Central European identity over a broader internationalism. It failed to win any seats to the Chamber of Deputies or to the Senate in general elections.[80]

Moravian Democratic Party (MDP)
Moravská Demokratická Strana (MDS)

The Moravian Democratic Party (MDP) was created on 5 April 1997 through a merger of the Moravian National Party (MNP) and the Bohemian-Moravian Union of the Center (BMUC). The delegates at the merger elected Ivan Dzimal (the former MNS chairman) as the new party leader. The party's chief objective was to win parliamentary seats, given the departure of Moravian deputies from parliament after the previous elections. The MDP advocated the creation of a Czech-Moravian federation and further decentralization. The party's platform included leftist ideas of a "social state" and a state-linked economy. The MDP also stood for some national conservative ideas such as the protection of Moravian traditions, and family relief.[81] In February 1998 the party claimed about 2,500 members.[82]

Another Moravian organization, the Radical Moravian National Party (RMNP) *(Radikální Moravská Nacionální Strana, RMNS),* was an illegal and unregistered militant group seeking full Moravian sovereignty and independence. Prague accused the RMNP of being a front organization for unrepentant local communists wishing to cling to their privileges and seeking to stage a political provocation to undermine the progress of democratic reforms.[83]

Independents and Others

Independents (I)
Nezávislí (N)

The Independents (I) was a political movement founded through a merger of the Association of Independent Candidates and the Union of European Cooperation. The constituent congress took place in June 1995. According to its statutes, the main goals of the party were equal rights for all citizens and special protection for minorities.[84] In February 1998, the Independents claimed about 2,000 members. After June 1995 the chairman of the party was Jiří Mrázek. In the June 1996 elections, the organization put forward its own candidates. After the June 1998 elections, the Independents remained a non-parliamentary party.

Another non-affiliated movement, the Nationwide Caucus of Citizens (NCC) *(Celostátní Aktiv Občanù, CAO)*, originated in 1988 and was officially registered as a party in March 1990. It had nearly 2,000 members. In 1990, the NCC campaigned as part of the coalition Alliance of Farmers and the Countryside (AFC) *(Spojenectví Zemědelcù a Venkova, SZV)*. In May–June 1996 it put up its own candidates, but it was unable to pay the election deposit and thus was excluded from the ballot. The chairman was Milan Žezula. Several other independent political pressure groups were formed in the Czech lands, including the Confederation of Political Prisoners (CPP) *(Konfederace Politických Vezni, KPV)*, chaired by Stanislav Drobný.

POLITICAL DATA

Name of the State: Czech Republic *(Česká Republika)*
Form of Government: Parliamentary democracy
Structure of Legislature: Bicameral parliament consisting of Senate (81 seats; members elected by popular vote) and Chamber of Deputies *(Poslanecká Sněmovna)* (200 seats; members elected by popular vote)
Size of Territory: 30,464 square miles
Size of Population: 10,321,120 (July 1996)

Composition of Population (1991):

Ethnic Group	Number	% of Population
Czechs	8,372,868	81.30
Moravians	1,359,432	13.20
Slovaks	308,962	3.00
Poles	60,000	0.58
Germans	60,000	0.58
Roma (Gypsies)	50,000	0.49
Silesians	46,000	0.45
Hungarians	23,000	0.22
Jews	5,000	0.05
Others	13,000	0.13
Total Population	10,298,262	100.00

Sources: http:www.odci.gov/cia/publications/factbook/geos/ez.htm#Govt. For 1991 census figures see *Basic Information on Population, Government System and Historical Development, 1918–1992*, Czechoslovak News Agency, March 1992.

ELECTION RESULTS

Presidential Election (Indirect), 20 January 1998

Candidate	First Round Votes	Second Round Votes
Václav Havel	91 of 200 in lower house	99 of 200 in lower house
	39 of 81 in upper house	47 of 81 in upper house
Stanislav Fisher	26	Ineligible
Miroslav Sládek	22	Ineligible

Sources: See "Havel Re-elected Czech President," RFE/RL Vol. 2, No. 13, Part II, 21 January 1998; and "Czech President Election Response: Havel's Non-Election in First Round Assessed Differently," *Financial Times Information*, 21 January 1998.

Presidential Election (Indirect), 26 January 1993

Candidate	Votes	% of Vote
Václav Havel	109	54.4
Marie Stiborova	49	24.5
Miroslav Sládek	14	7.0
Unaccounted for	28	14.0
Total	200	100.0

Source: See Ján Obrman, "Havel Elected Czech President," RFE/RL Archive, No. 17, 27 January 1993.

Senate Elections, 12 and 19 November 2000

Turnout: 21.6%

Parties	Seats Won	Total Seats
[Liberal] Coalition of Four	17	39
Civic Democratic Party	8	22
Czech Social Democratic Party	1	15
Communist Party of Bohemia and Moravia	—	3
Nonpartisans	1	2
Total	27	81

Source: Elections in the Czech Republic, http://www.agora.stm.it/elections/election/czech.htm.

Senate Elections, 13–14 and 20–21 November 1998*

Turnout: 41.02% (First Round), 20.33% (Second Round)

Party/Coalition	First Round	Votes %	Second Round	Votes %	Seats
Civic Democratic Party	252,727	26.27	200,978	37.42	26
Czech Social Democratic Party	197,236	20.50	112,116	20.87	22
Christian and Democratic Union/ Czechoslovak People's Party	88,475	9.20	52,199	9.72	13
Civic Democratic Alliance	59,627	6.19	52,857	9.84	6
Communist Party of Bohemia and Moravia	165,139	17.16	31,097	5.79	4
Freedom Union	32,153	3.34	20,059	3.73	3
Independent	137,707	14.32	67,786	12.63	7
Others	29,047	3.02	—	—	—
Total	962,111	100.00	537,092	100.00	81

*The November 1998 election marked the first time in which a Senate election was held to decide one-third (27) of the body's members. Previously, all 81 members of the Senate were up for election in each general poll.

Parliamentary Elections, 19–20 June 1998

Turnout: 73.86%

Party/Coalition	Votes	% of Vote	Seats
Czech Social Democratic Party	1,928,660	32.31	74
Civic Democratic Party	1,656,011	27.74	63
Communist Party of Bohemia and Moravia	658,550	11.03	24
Christian and Democratic Union/ Czechoslovak People's Party	537,013	9.00	20
Freedom Union	513,596	8.60	19
Civic Democratic Alliance	—	—	—
Association for the Republic/ Czechoslovak Republican Party	232,965	3.90	—
Pensioners for Secure Living	182,900	3.06	—
Democratic Union	86,431	1.45	—
Others	173,379	2.91	—
Total	5,969,505	100.00	200

Sources: http://www.volby.cz and http://www2.essex.ac.uk/elect/czech_index.htm.

Senate Elections, 15–16 and 22–23 November 1996

Turnout: 34.92% (First Round), 30.59% (Second Round)

Party/Coalition	First Round		Second Round		
	Votes	% of Vote	Votes	% of Vote	Seats
Civic Democratic Party	1,006,036	36.47	1,134,044	49.14	32
Czech Social Democratic Party	559,304	20.28	733,713	31.80	25
Christian and Democratic Union/Czechoslovak People's Party	274,316	9.94	247,819	10.73	13
Civic Democratic Alliance	222,319	8.07	119,730	5.18	7
Communist Party of Bohemia and Moravia	393,494	14.27	45,304	1.95	2
Democratic Union	24,454	0.88	14,656	0.69	1
Independent	117,641	4.27	11,993	0.51	1
Others	160,561	5.82	—	—	—
Total	2,758,125	100.00	2,307,259	100.00	81

Source: University of Essex, *Political Transformation and the Electoral Process in Post-Communist Europe* at http://www2.essex.ac.uk/elections/.

Parliamentary Elections, 31 May–1 June 1996

Turnout: 76.41%

Party/Coalition	Votes	% of Vote	Seats
Civic Democratic Party	1,794,560	29.62	68
Czech Social Democratic Party	1,602,250	26.44	61
Communist Party of Bohemia and Moravia	626,136	10.33	22
Christian and Democratic Union/ Czechoslovak People's Party	489,349	8.08	18
Association for the Republic/ Republican Party of Czechoslovakia	485,072	8.01	18
Civic Democratic Alliance	385,369	6.36	13
Bohemian-Moravian Union of the Center Union	27,490	0.45	—
Others	648,989	10.71	—
Total	6,059,215	100.00	200

Sources: "Czech Parliamentary Election Results," *Czech the News: Newsletter of the Embassy of the Czech Republic*, Washington D.C., June 1996, p. 2; and "Czech Republic: Official Results of Parliamentary Elections," *Hospodárske Noviny*, Prague, 4 June 1996, p. 3; and http://www2.essex.ac.uk/elect/czech_index.htm.

Parliamentary Elections, Czech National Council, 5–6 June 1992

Turnout: 85.1%

Party/Coalition	Votes	% of Vote	Seats
Civic Democratic Party	1,924,483	29.73	76
Left Bloc	909,490	14.05	35
Czech Social Democratic Party	422,736	6.53	16
Liberal Social Union	421,988	6.52	16
Christian and Democratic Union	406,341	6.28	15
Republican Association	387,026	5.98	14
Civic Democratic Alliance	383,705	5.93	14
Moravia-Silesia Movement	380,088	5.87	14
Others	1,237,393	19.11	—
Total	6,473,250	100.00	200

Source: http://www.strath.ac.uk/Departments/CSPP/crelec.htm.

Parliamentary Elections, Czech National Council, 8–9 June 1990

Turnout: 96.7%

Party/Coalition	Votes	% of Vote	Seats
Civic Forum	3,569,201	49.50	127
Communist Party of Czechoslovakia	954,690	13.24	32
Movement for Self-Governing Democracy/Society for Moravia and Silesia	723,609	10.03	22
Christian and Democratic Union	607,134	8.42	19
Others	1,356,413	18.81	—
Total	7,211,047	100.00	200

Sources: http://www.strath.ac.uk/Departments/CSPP/crelec.html; "New Czech Republic Government Announced," *Prague Domestic Service*, 29 June 1990; "Parties Percentage in Assembly," *Prague Domestic Service*, 10 June 1990; and "Assembly, Czech Council Seats," *CTK*, Prague, 10 June 1990. See also "New Czech Republic Government," *Prague Domestic Service*, 29 June 1990.

Federal Czechoslovak Elections, 5–6 June 1992

Turnout: 83%

Chamber of the People (Czech Republic)

Party/Coalition	Votes	% of Vote	Seats
Civic Democratic Party	2,200,937	33.90	48
Left Bloc	926,228	14.27	19
Czech Social Democrats	489,030	7.67	10
Republican Association	420,848	6.48	8
Christian Democratic Union	388,122	5.98	7
Liberal Social Union	378,962	5.84	7
Others	1,688,956	25.86	—
Total	6,493,083	100.00	99

Chamber of Nations (Czech Republic)

Party/Coalition	Votes	% of Vote	Seats
Civic Democratic Party	2,168,421	33.43	37
Left Bloc	939,197	14.48	15
Czech Social Democrats	440,806	6.80	6
Republican Association	413,459	6.37	6
Christian Democratic Union	394,296	6.08	6
Liberal Social Union	383,182	6.06	5
Others	1,736,378	26.78	—
Total	6,485,739	100.00	75

Federal Czechoslovak Elections, 8–9 June 1990

Turnout: 95.39%

Chamber of the People (Czech Republic)

Party/Coalition	Votes	% of Vote	Seats
Civic Forum	3,851,172	53.15	68
Communist Party of Czechoslovakia	976,996	13.48	15
Christian and Democratic Union	629,359	8.69	9
Movement for Self-Governing Democracy Society for Moravia and Silesia	572,015	7.89	9
Others	1,215,908	16.79	—
Total	7,245,450	100.00	101

Source: University of Essex, Political Transformation and the Electoral Process in Post Communist Europe at http://www2.essex.ac.uk/elections/.

Chamber of Nations (Czech Republic)

Party/Coalition	Votes	% of Vote	Seats
Civic Forum	3,613,513	49.96	50
Communist Party of Czechoslovakia	997,919	13.80	12
Movement for Self-Governing Democracy Society for Moravia and Silesia	658,477	9.10	7
Christian and Democratic Union	633,053	8.75	6
Others	1,329,163	18.39	—
Total	7,232,125	100.00	75

NOTES

1. For recent accounts of Czech history consult Victor S. Mamatey and Radomír Luza (Eds.), *A History of the Czechoslovak Republic, 1918–1948*, Princeton: Princeton University Press, 1973; Josef Korbel, *Twentieth-Century Czechoslovakia: The Meanings of Its History*, New York: Columbia University Press, 1977; Derek Sayer, *The Coasts of Bohemia: A Czech History*, Princeton: Princeton University Press, 1988; Gordon H. Skilling, *Czechoslovakia's Interrupted Revolution*, Princeton: Princeton University Press, 1976; Vladimir Kusin, *From Dubček to Charter 77: A Study of "Normalization" in Czechoslovakia, 1968–1978*, New York: St. Martin's Press, 1978; and Ihor Gawdiak (Ed.), *Czechoslovakia: A Country Study*, Federal Research Division, Library of Congress, 1989.

2. See Janusz Bugajski, *Czechoslovakia: Charter 77's Decade of Dissent*, Washington, D.C.: Center for Strategic and International Studies, 1997.

3. Stephen R. Bowers, "The East European Revolution," *East European Quarterly*, Vol. XXV, No. 2, June 1991, pp. 129–143.

4. Details on the various demonstrations prior to the "velvet revolution" can be found in Bernard Wheaton and Zdenek Kavan, *The Velvet Revolution: Czechoslovakia, 1988–1991*, Boulder: Westview, 1992, pp. 3–36.

5. For useful summaries and analyses of these dramatic events consult Tony R. Judt, "Metamorphosis: The Democratic Revolution in Czechoslovakia," in Ivo Banac (Ed.), *Eastern Europe in Revolution*, Ithaca, N.Y.: Cornell University Press, 1992, pp. 96–117.

6. Andras Korosenyi, "Revival of the Past or New Beginning? The Nature of Post-Communist Politics," *Political Quarterly*, Vol. 62, No. 1, January–March 1991, pp. 52–74.

7. Consult *Struggling for Ethnic Identity: Czechoslovakia's Endangered Gypsies*, Helsinki Watch, New York, 1992.

8. Jiří Pehe, "Parliament Passes Controversial Law on Vetting Officials," Radio Free Europe/Radio Liberty Research Institute, *Report on Eastern Europe*, Vol. 2, No. 43, 25 October 1991.

9. See Karel Filka, "After the Elections," *Lidová Demokracie*, Prague, 15 June 1990.

10. Consult Tim D. Whipple, "Introduction, After the Velvet Revolution: The First Six Months," in Tim D. Whipple (Ed.), *After the Velvet Revolution: Václav Havel and the New Leaders of Czechoslovakia Speak Out*, New York: Freedom House, 1991.

11. Jiří Pehe, "The Civic Forum Before the Election Campaign Begins," Radio Free Europe, *Report on Eastern Europe*, Vol. 1, No. 14, 6 April 1990.

12. For a succinct justification of the "movement" approach see Fedor Gal, "The Future of Public Against Violence," in Tim D. Whipple (Ed.), *op. cit.*, pp. 234–236.

13. Jiří Pehe, "The Political Spectrum," Radio Free Europe, *Report on Eastern Europe*, Vol. 1, No. 10, 9 March 1990.

14. Jiří Pehe, "The Civic Forum Becomes a Political Party," Radio Free Europe/Radio Liberty Research Institute, *Report on Eastern Europe*, Vol. 2, No. 5, 1 February 1991.

15. Jiří Pehe, "Czechoslovakia's Changing Political Spectrum," Radio Free Europe/Radio Liberty, *Research Report*, Vol. 1, No. 5, 31 January 1992.

16. See Jiří Pehe, "The Electoral Law," Radio Free Europe, *Report on Eastern Europe*, Vol. 1, No. 11, 16 March 1990.

17. Ján Obrman, "The Main Contenders in the Election," Radio Free Europe, *Report on Eastern Europe*, Vol. 1, No. 23, 8 June 1990.

18. For details check Jan Obrman, "Civic Forum Surges to Impressive Victory in Elections," Radio Free Europe, *Report on Eastern Europe*, Vol. 1, No. 25, 22 June 1990.

19. Peter Martin, "The New Governments," Radio Free Europe, *Report on Eastern Europe*, Vol. 1, No. 30, 27 July 1990.

20. Ján Obrman, "Decentralizing the Government," Radio Free Europe, *Report on Eastern Europe*, Vol. 1, No. 31, 3 August 1990.

21. Check Jiří Pehe, "The Local Government Elections," Radio Free Europe, *Report on Eastern Europe*, Vol. 1, No. 50, 14 December 1990.

22. For useful summaries of the new parties consult *Lidové Noviny*, Prague, July 1991 issues.

23. Ján Obrman, "The Czechoslovak Elections," RFE/RL, *Research Report*, Vol. 1, No. 26, 26 June 1992.

24. For details on the federal split see Jirí Pehe, "Czechs and Slovaks Prepare to Part," RFE/RL, *Research Report*, Vol. 1, No. 37, 18 September 1992; Ján Obrman, "Czechoslovakia's New Government," RFE/RL, *Research Report*, Vol. 1, No. 29, 17 July 1992; *Hospodárske Noviny*, Prague, 10 September 1992; Jiří Pehe, "Czechs and Slovaks Refine Postdivorce Relations," RFE/RL, *Report on Eastern Europe*, Vol. 2, No. 45, 13 November 1992.

25. For a valuable analysis of the post-independence political system see David M. Olson, "Democratization and Political Participation: The Experience of the Czech Republic," in Karen Dawisha and Bruce Parrott (Eds.), *The Consolidation of Democracy in East-Central Europe*, Cambridge: Cambridge University Press, 1997, pp. 150–196.

26. See the *Constitution of the Czech Republic*, 16 December 1992, adopted by the Czech National Council, Prague.

27. S. Saxonberg, "A New Phase in Czech Politics," *Journal of Democracy*, No. 1, January 1999, pp. 99–100.

28. Jiří Pehe, "The Disappointments of Democracy," *Transitions*, Vol. 5, No. 5, May 1998. Also see http://www.ijt.cz/transitions/thedisa1.htm.

29. Radio Prague's History Online Virtual Exhibit: The Czech Republic Today, at http://www.radio.cz/history/history16.html.

30. Jiří Pehe, "Elections Result in Surprise Stalemate," *Transitions*, Vol. 2, No. 13, 28 June 1996, pp. 36–37.

31. See http://www.czech.cz/washington/newslet/cbz7896.htm, and "Daily Publishes Coalition Agreement," *Pravo*, Prague, 28 July 1996, p. 3.

32. "Government Coalition Agreement Signed," *Czech the News: Newsletter of the Embassy of the Czech Republic*, Vol. IV, No. 7–8, July/August 1996, p. 2.

33. After the June 1998 elections, only 24 communists remained in parliament. See: IPU, "Czech Republic: Last Elections," at: http://www.ipu.org/parline-e/reports/2083_E.htm.

34. See "The Inter-Parliamentary Union: Czech Republic: Last Elections," at http://www.ipu.org/parline-e/reports/2083_E.htm.

35. See *Radio Prague*, 29 July 1999 at: http://www.radio.cz/news/english.html.

36. See the results of the regular STEM (*Stredisko empirickych vyzkumu*, the Center for Empirical Research) opinion poll from 1–7 June 1999 at: http://www.cssd/cz/aktuality/a_130.htm.

37. P. Newman, "From the Weeklies," at the web page of *Radio Prague* on 29 July 1999, http://www.radio.cz/english/weekly.

38. Election results for both the regional councils and Senate November elections can be found at the Czech Central Election Commission, http://www.volby.cz/en/volbyen.htm.

39. Larsen, "Havel calls CSSD Scandal a Setup," *Prague Post*, 10 June 1998, available on http://www.centraleurope.com/ceo/media/praguepost/ppost.html.

40. Jiří Pehe, "The Disappointments of Democracy," in *Transitions*, Vol. 5, No. 5, May 1998.

41. "Daily Provides Data on Political Party Membership," *FBIS-EEU-97–282 Daily Report*, 9 October 1997, *Lidové Noviny*, Prague, 9 October 1997, p. 2. See http://www.prague.org/gov-cr/pol.html; http://www.centraleurope.com/ceo/czech/politics/czcssd.html; and http://www.ceskenoviny.cz/volby_CSSD.html.

42. See http://www.rferl.org/newsline/2000/03/3–cee/cee-140300.html.

43. For useful background consult Jiří Pehe, "Former Satellite Parties Seek Their Own Identity," Radio Free Europe, *Report on Eastern Europe*, Vol. 1, No. 15, 13 April 1990.

44. "Czech Republic: Bodenlos Resigns as Joint SD-LSNS Chairman," *Mlada Fronta Dnes*, Prague, 24 June 1996, p. 2, *FBIS-EEU-96–124*, 26 June 1996, p. 4. Also see http://www.prague.org/gov-cr/pol.html; and http://www.centraleurope.com/ceo/czech/politics/czlsns.html.

45. See party profile in http://www.ceskenoviny.cz/volby_DZJ.html.

46. See http://www.prague.org/gov-cr/pol.html.

47. See Party of Democratic Socialism: http://www.sds.cz/docs/sjezd/polprohl.htm.

48. See "Czech Right Wing Parties Viewed," *Mlada Fronta Dnes*, Prague, *FBIS-EEU-1999–0629*, 24 June 1999.

49. See "Daily Provides Data on Political Party Membership," *FBIS-EEU-97–282 Daily*

Report, 9 October 1997, Prague, *Lidové Noviny,* 9 October 1997 p. 2; "Czech Republic: Klaus Appointed PM to Form New Government," *FBIS-EEU-96–128,* 2 July 1996; http://www.prague.org/gov-cr/pol.html; http://www.centraleurope.com/ceo/czech/politics/czods.html; http://www.czech.cz/washington/newslet/co5–0197.htm; and "Czech Election: A Guide to Parties," http://www.ceskenoviny.cz/volby_ODS.html.

50. See http://www.prague.org/gov-cr/pol.html; http://www.centraleurope.com/ceo/czech/politics/czoda.html; http://www.oda.cz/en/Intpres2.htm; and www.ceskenoviny.cz/volby_ODA.html.

51. See http://www.prague.org/gov-cr/pol.html; and http://www.centraleurope.com/ceo/czech/politics/czlsns.html.

52. See "Party Founded to Represent Small Business," *Lidové Noviny,* Prague, 15 February 1995, p. 3.

53. See http://www.deu.cz/historie.html.

54. See http://www.prague.org/gov/pol.html.

55. "Right Bloc Holds Assembly, Elects Chairman," *Hospodárske Noviny,* Prague, 1 July 1996, p. 3.

56. See http://www.ceskapravice.cz/cp_fr.htm.

57. See R.A. Greene, "Forum Calls for a Change," *Prague Post,* 28 July 1999; and D. Hill and I. Navazelskis, "Czech Republic: New Group Strives For Civil Society," *Radio Free Europe,* 29 July 1999; and http://www.rferl.org/nca/features/1999/07/F.RU.990729133421.html.

58. See http://www.centraleurope.com/ceo/czech/politics/czkds.html; and *FBIS-EEU-95–223,* 20 November 1995; and "Chairman of Christian Democrats Reelected," *Radio Zurnal Radio Network,* Prague, 19 November 1995.

59. See http://www.kdu.cz/English/default.htm.

60. See http://www.prague.org/gov-cr/pol.html; http://www.centraleurope.com/ceo/czech/politics/czkdu.html; and "People Party and Communists Are in the Lead," *Lidové Noviny,* Prague, 16 April 1996; "Christian Democratic Union–Czechoslovak People's Party Congress," *Lidové Noviny,* Prague, 20 October 1995, p. 3; and www.cesknoviny.cz/volby_KDU.html.

61. See http://freeweb.bohemia.net/zeleni.

62. See http://www.prague.org/gov-cr/pol.html; and "Emil Zeman Elected Green Party Chairman," *Lidové Noviny,* Prague, 9 October 1995, p. 3. See also http://www.ceskenoviny.cz/volby/profil_strany.htm.

63. For a useful account see Peter Martin, "New Challenges for the Czechoslovak Communist Party," Radio Free Europe, *Report on Eastern Europe,* Vol. 1, No. 18, 4 May 1990.

64. Jiří Pehe, "Changes in the Communist Party," Radio Free Europe, *Report on Eastern Europe,* Vol. 1, No. 48, 30 November 1990.

65. See http://www.prague.org/gov-cr/pol.html; and http://www.centraleurope.com/ceo/czech/politics/czkdu.html.

66. See "The Stepanites Have Quit the Elections," *Lidové Noviny,* Prague, 17 April 1996, *FBIS-EEU-96–077,* 19 April 1996.

67. See http://www.prague.org/gov-cr/pol.html; and http://www.centraleurope.com/ceo/czech/politics/czspr.html.

68. Check Jiří Pehe, "The Emergence of Right-Wing Extremism," RFE/RL, *Report on Eastern Europe,* Vol. 2, No. 26, 28 June 1991; Jiří Pehe, "Czechoslovakia's Changing Political Spectrum," RFE/RL, *Report on Eastern Europe,* Vol. 1, No. 5, 31 January 1992; and Ján Obrman, "The Czechoslovak Elections: Party Profile," at http://www.ceskenoviny.cz/volby_SPR-RSC.html.

69. See "KAN Rejects Merger with ODS, Elects Executive," *Mlada Fronta Dnes,* Prague, 20 November 1995, p. 2.

70. See the interview with Ján Mlynárik, "We Are Not a Fifth Column," *Lidové Noviny,* Prague, 9 March 1993; and Vladimír Skalicky, "A Slovak Minority Exists," *Lidové Noviny,* Prague, 23 March 1993.

71. Jiří Pehe, "Slovaks in the Czech Republic: A New Minority," RFE/RL, *Research Report,* Vol. 2, No. 23, 4 June 1993.

72. *PAP,* Warsaw, 4 March 1990, in *FBIS-EEU-90–046,* 8 March 1990; and Vladimír V. Kusin, "Media in Transition," RFE/RL, *Report on Eastern Europe,* Vol. 1, No. 18, 3 May 1991.

73. *Národná Obroda*, Bratislava, 22 October 1990, in *FBIS-EEU-90–207*, 25 October 1990; Ján Obrman, "Minorities Not a Major Issue Yet"; and Jiří Pehe, "Czechoslovakia: Parties Register For Elections," RFE/RL, *Report on Eastern Europe*, Vol. 1, No. 18, 1 May 1992.

74. Consult the Czech-German Declaration on Mutual Relations and Their Future Development, signed on 21 January 1997. See at: http://www.library.byu.edu/~rdh/eurodocs/germ/czecheng.html.

75. See Charles Hoffman, *Grey Dawn: The Jews of Eastern Europe in the Post-Communist Era*, New York: Harper Collins, 1992, pp. 13–53.

76. See Jiří Pehe, "Postelection Changes in the Political Parties," Radio Free Europe, *Report on Eastern Europe*, Vol. 1, No. 31, 3 August 1990. For a Moravian criticism of the Prague-centered structure see Ján Trefulka, "I See What I See," *Lidové Noviny*, 25 July 1990.

77. For more information on the Moravian movements see the interview with Bohumil Tichy, member of MSGD-SMS Central Committees, in *Rude Pravo*, Prague, 23 June 1990, *FBIS-EEU-90–126*, 29 June 1990; interview with Boleslav Barta, MSDMS Chairman, in *Zemedelské Noviny*, Prague, 28 December 1990, *FBIS-EEU-91–002*, 3 January 1991; interview with Ján Krycer, *Ceske a Moravskoslezské Zemedelské Noviny*, Prague, 1 July 1991, *FBIS-EEU-91–131*, 9 July 1991; interview with Ján Krycer, *Lidové Noviny*, Prague, 23 July 1991, *FBIS-EEU-91–143*, 25 July 1991; Ján Obrman, "The Issue of Autonomy for Moravia and Silesia," RFE/RL, *Report on Eastern Europe*, Vol. 2, No. 15, 12 April 1991; Ján Obrman, "The Czechoslovak Elections: A Guide to the Parties," RFE/RL, *Report on Eastern Europe*, Vol. 1, No. 22, 29 May 1992.

78. Ján Obrman, "Slovak Politician Accused of Secret Police Ties," RFE/RL, *Report on Eastern Europe*, Vol. 1, No. 15, 10 April 1992; interview with Ján Krycer in *Lidové Noviny*, Prague, 23 July 1991, *FBIS-EEU-91–143*, 25 July 1991; and the interview with MNP member Alena Obcaciková by Monika Voleková, "Moravian Disquiet, Discontent," *Slovensky Národ*, Bratislava, 16 March 1993.

79. "A New Parliament Is Being Established," *Rude Pravo*, Prague, 14 November 1990, in *FBIS-EEU-90–224*, 20 November 1990.

80. See http://www.prague.org/gov-cz/pol.html; and http://www.centraleurope.com/ceo/czch/pol.

81. See the party program from April 1999 in http://www.mujweb.cz/www/mods.

82. "Czech Republic: Moravian Democratic Party Formed After MNS-CMUS Congress," *FBIS-EEU-97–098 Daily Report*, 8 April 1997, *Mlada Fronta Dnes*, Prague, 7 April 1997, p. 2.

83. Ján Obrman, "Minorities Not a Major Issue Yet," RFE/RL, *Report on Eastern Europe*, Vol. 2, No. 50, 13 December 1991.

84. See the party's statutes from April 1998 at http://www.geocities.com/CapitolHill/Senate/8122/0715stan.htm.

Slovakia

HISTORICAL OVERVIEW

The area of present-day Slovakia was first settled by Celtic tribes between the sixth and second centuries BC. The region became a source of dispute between German tribes and Roman forces, which established themselves along the southern shores of the Danube.[1] Major migrations from the east began in the fourth century AD, with the arrival of Huns, Goths, and other nomadic pastoral tribes. Slavic tribes settled in the region between the sixth and eighth centuries AD, but the area fell under the control of Avars, who created a rudimentary state structure. A short-lived Slavic Kingdom of Samo, basically a defensive alliance of Slavic tribes with its core south of the Alps, held sway in western parts of Slovakia in the early part of the seventh century AD.

Avar power was finally broken by the Frankish Kingdom at the close of the eighth century AD, and two Slavic principalities emerged on both sides of the Morava river (Morava and Nitra), which made up the core of the Great Moravian Empire. This state, beginning with the rule of Mojmír I (833–846), encompassed present-day western and central Slovakia and was later claimed by Slovak activists as the genesis of their nation. During the reign of Rastislav in the middle of the ninth century AD, Great Moravia underwent a process of expansion to include parts of eastern Slovakia, and an independent ecclesiastical province was created on the territory. Its ruler Svätopluk (870–894) eliminated Frankish influence, consolidated the state structure, further extended Moravian lands, and obtained papal protection for his Christianizing endeavors. But the Empire disintegrated shortly after his death, when Hungarian forces penetrated the central European region.

The Magyar rulers created a state that included the Slovak territories for over one thousand years. During this millennium the Slovaks developed and preserved their distinct identity. In the tenth and eleventh centuries, Slovak acquired the status of an independent Slavic language, as the Magyar system allowed for the growth of Slovak national consciousness. Slovak territories were subject to Turkish raids during the Ottoman occupation of the Hungarian plain in the sixteenth century, and these continued into the mid-1600s, until the Turks were driven out of Hungary.

Hungary and the Slovak lands fell under Austrian Habsburg control during the sixteenth century. During the eighteenth century, Vienna pursued a policy of royal absolutism in which local autonomy was stifled and Hungary was directly subordinate to the crown. The Slovak language and literary life continued to evolve, largely due to the activities of the Catholic Church. Slovakia was also impacted by the religious conflicts stemming from the Reformation and Counter-Reformation.

Slovakia was affected by the spread of nationalism throughout Europe during the eighteenth and nineteenth centuries. In 1792, Anton Bernolák codified the Slovak language, and a number of Slovak publications began to appear, in a veritable cultural and national revival. At the same time, the Slovak population was subject to the increasing pressures of Magyarization or assimilation into the Hungarian-dominated cultural and political system. Hungarian rulers were particularly concerned that demographic changes after the Turkish occupation had diminished Magyar numbers and increased those of Slavic and other minorities. Until the late eighteenth century, relations between Hungarian rulers and the Slovak masses were non-confrontational, but this began to change with the growth of nationalist sentiments on both sides of the ethnic divide.

During the 1848 national revolutions that swept the Habsburg Empire, the emerging Slovak leadership was unable to gain any concessions from Budapest for local autonomy. Hungary itself was engaged in a war of national liberation from Austria. As a result of their failure, Slovak leaders created the Slovak National Council, the first modern Slovak political institution, which pushed for greater national sovereignty. In September 1848, the Council declared Slovakia's separation from Hungary and called upon the Slovak nation to stage an uprising. The revolt was crushed by Hungarian troops. During a second revolt later in the year, Slovak leaders appealed to the Austrian emperor, requesting the creation of an autonomous Slovak territory directly subordinate to Vienna. But after the defeat of Hungarian forces by Austrian and Russian troops, Slovak demands were ignored by Vienna and the territory remained under Hungarian rule. The Austro-Hungarian Compromise (*Ausgleich*) of May 1867 disappointed Slovak leaders as well as other nations, as it forced them to deal directly with Budapest, without recourse to Vienna.

In the second half of the nineteenth century, the Slovak revival blossomed. In 1849, the *Matica Slovenská* (Slovak Cultural Institute) was created. It assembled some of the finest Slovak intellectuals and political activists, who wrote the Memorandum of the Slovak Nation as the basis for a future national constitution. The new institute united various Slovak groupings, regardless of region, dialect, and religion, around a common national program. By the close of the century, some Slovaks also began to look for support among the Czechs, and the idea of molding a joint Czech-Slovak state was first voiced. Among prominent leaders active at this time was Andrej Hlinka, a Catholic priest who became a leading member of the newly formed Slovak National Party and who vehemently attacked Hungarian rule.

At the close of World War I, with Austria-Hungary defeated, most Slovak leaders, including Hlinka and Milan Rastislav Štefánik, opted for a political union between the newly liberated Czechs and Slovaks. This culminated in the signing of the Martin Declaration on 24 May 1918 and the creation of a joint state that won international recognition. But instead of the decentralized, binational state envisaged by Slovak leaders, the new Czechoslovakia became a centralized, unitary republic dominated by Prague. Slovakia only gained rudimentary political institutions and its leaders were unprepared to resist creeping Czech control. Although Czechoslovakia was a democratic parliamentary republic throughout the inter-war period, Slovaks were underrepresented in the state structure and all decision-making powers were concentrated in Prague. Slovak grievances and nationalist sentiments were further raised in reaction to the new ideology of Czechoslovakism fostered by Prague.

With increasing Nazi pressures on the Czechoslovak state, in October 1938 Prague was forced to cede the German-inhabited Sudetenland to Germany. In the meantime, Slovak parties, sensing that the break-up of Czechoslovakia could be imminent, produced the Žilina Agreement on 5–6 October 1938, demanding Slovak autonomy. The semi-federated Czechoslovak state, consisting of a truncated Bohemia, Moravia, Slovakia, and Ruthenia, lasted only a few months. While German forces occupied the Czech Lands, Berlin's ally, Hungary, gained the southern portion of Slovakia in accordance with the Vienna Award of 2 November 1938. With Berlin's agreement, an independent Slovak state was declared on 14 March 1939 under the leadership of the Catholic priest and People's Party activist Jozef Tiso, who became its president.

The wartime Slovak Republic was essentially a client state of Nazi Germany, and the Bratislava government exercised a measure of autonomy. Its apologists argued that in order to survive, the Slovaks had to acquiesce to German demands, while its critics charged that the national leadership sacrificed too many principles for a relatively peaceful wartime interlude. In particular, the Tiso government collaborated in the expulsion of about 60,000 Slovak Jews to Nazi death camps and employed anti-Semitism in its own campaigns to stifle any political dissent. However, although it had a one-party system, Slovakia did not descend into a fascist dictatorship, despite the proclivities of some of its leaders, such as Prime Minister Vojtech Tuka.

A Slovak uprising was staged in September 1944 by a combined force of democrats and communists. While the former were sponsored by the Czechoslovak government-in-exile under Prime Minister Eduard Beneš, the latter received direct support from the Soviet Union. The Slovak Republic collapsed and the Red Army overran the country during 1945. Slovakia was subsequently reincorporated into a recreated Czechoslovakia. The new state lost the province of Ruthenia but Slovakia recovered the territories that were awarded to Hungary during the war. In the immediate post-war years, a coalition administration was formed but in February 1948 the Communist Party, with Soviet support, staged a coup and imposed a Stalinist system. Promises of Slovak autonomy were not fulfilled and Czechoslovakia became a highly centralized communist state in which all political opposition was extinguished and the Party controlled all aspects of economic, cultural, and social life. The Catholic Church was especially harassed because of its association with the wartime regime. In 1960, the country was renamed the Czechoslovak Socialist Republic, and the powers of Slovak national organs were further curtailed as the territory was divided into three administrative regions.

During the "Prague Spring" of 1968 several reformist groupings sprang up in the Slovak republic, including dissident intellectual clubs and Slovak national organizations demanding greater recognition of national issues. In response to their pressures, in July 1968 the country was turned into a federal state consisting of two republics (Czech Lands and Slovakia) by the reformist administration headed by Communist Party leader and Slovak national Aleksander Dubček. After the Soviet-led Warsaw Pact invasion of Czechoslovakia in August 1968, the federal structure was maintained but the powers of the republican governments were severely restricted under the reinvigorated communist monopoly styled as "normalization" that was implemented after August 1969.

Throughout the 1970s and 1980s, small groups of dissidents were active in Slovakia, although not on the scale of Charter 77 and other formations in the Czech republic. Some turned to single issues as a form of pressure on the regime. For example, the Guardians of Nature were at the forefront of the environmental protection campaign and condemned state neglect of Slovakia's ecology. Catholic activists such as Ján Korec created a "secret church" and demanded greater freedom to practice their faith. In addition, several writers and philosophers gained prominence including Milan Šimečka and Miroslav Kusý.

However, the influence and impact of these movements were extremely limited, thus contributing to the organizational unpreparedness of the Slovak opposition when communist rule collapsed. Greater mobilization was evident during the trial of the "Bratislava Five" in the summer of 1989, when the persecution of five well-known dissidents stirred public protests and led to the birth of the oppositionist movement Public Against Violence (PAV). PAV consisted of intellectuals, reformers, and young people who sensed that the days of communist rule were numbered.

POST-COMMUNIST DEVELOPMENTS

During the Czechoslovak "Velvet Revolution" in November 1989 and the rapid collapse of Communist Party rule, pressures began to increase in Slovakia for extensive political and economic autonomy. Several newly formed Slovak parties placed demands for sovereignty on the national agenda, even though they differed on the content and timetable for Slovak autonomy. Although the new federal Czechoslovak government was supportive of administrative decentralization and the devolution of most ministerial powers to the two republics, relations between Bratislava and Prague were strained by increasing demands from separatist groups and disagreements over the content of newly framed republican and federal constitutions.

Czechoslovakia's transition toward a pluralist polity was accompanied by a structural and administrative division between the Czech and Slovak republics that affected political developments in both emerging states. Although the federal structure was one of the few reforms that survived the Soviet invasion and the post-1968 "normalization," in practice there was little decentralization of executive or legislative powers as envisaged in the 1969 constitution. Following the "Velvet Revolution," the federal authorities failed to regulate relations between the two republics and to satisfy growing Slovak aspirations for autonomy.

Leaders of the broad Slovak democratic movement, Public Against Violence (PAV), and its Czech counterpart, the Civic Forum (CF), as well as President Václav Havel, believed that democratization and decentralization would prove sufficient to keep the federation together. This lack of foresight allowed autonomist and separatist forces to gain ground in Slovakia.[2] Moreover, the lifting of centralist communist controls and the national reawakening in Slovakia sparked a competition between the new Slovak parties, primarily focused on the issue of sovereignty. The PAV split into a pro-federal and a pro-sovereignty wing that gained broad public support and promoted an increasingly separatist platform.

After prolonged dispute, in April 1990 the Federal Assembly adopted a new name for the state, to provide equal recognition to both component nations: the Czech and Slovak Federal Republic. The first democratically elected central government set out to reorganize the federal structure. In June 1990, several federal ministries were merged or abolished, or their powers were transferred to republican ministries, and a series of meetings between Czech and Slovak leaders registered some progress in decentralizing the state. In the June 1990 general elections, the Czech Civic Forum and the Slovak PAV were the clear winners. For the Federal Assembly, the PAV took 32.5% of the vote and 19 out of 51 Slovak seats in the Chamber of People, and 37.3% of the vote and 33 out of 75 Slovak seats in the Chamber of Nations. The PAV also won 29.3% of the vote and 48 out of 150 seats in the Slovak National Council. The Christian Democrats came in second, followed by the Communist Party of Slovakia, the Slovak National Party, and a Hungarian Coalition. Vladimír Mečiar was named Slovakia's first democratic Prime Minister: a position he held for nearly a year before being replaced.

The streamlined Federal Assembly and the two National Councils became increasingly splintered. From the six parties and movements elected in June 1990, a total of twenty emerged by the close of 1991. In numerous instances, this complicated the process of decision-making and legislative work. The federal and Czech governments escaped any major reorganization or realignment, as a working consensus was maintained between the various CF factions. By contrast, political differentiation in Slovakia led to the fall of one government and mounting polarization over nationalist versus federalist issues.

In October 1990, it was agreed to limit federal powers to defense, border controls, currency, taxes, prices, and foreign policy. This led to a constitutional amendment passed in December 1990.[3] However, by this time Slovak moves toward sovereignty were already far advanced. Premier Mečiar adopted an increasingly "anti-unitarian position," being cognizant of the populist appeal of Slovak autonomy and the strident competition from other politicians.[4] Mečiar's outspoken position led to attacks on his motives from Slovak and Czech federalists, culminating in his ouster in April 1991 and appeals by the PAV to keep the federation together.[5]

Mečiar was accused by his former colleagues of pandering to nationalist feelings. But his removal from office served to exacerbate tensions and divisions in the PAV and raised Mečiar's popularity in Slovakia as a purported victim of a Prague-engineered coup. The new government of Christian Democratic Movement (CDM) leader Ján Čarnogurský, which pledged to work on a new federal constitution, rapidly lost support in the Slovak National Council, where anti-federalists gained a majority of votes. In September and November 1991, attempts were made to pass a Declaration of Slovak Sovereignty, but the initiative narrowly failed in the National Council.[6] Meanwhile, Mečiar's newly established Movement for a Democratic Slovakia (MDS) issued an "Initiative for a Sovereign Slovakia." It called for the passage of a "full" Slovak constitution not derived from the federal document and for Slovak laws to take precedence over federal legislation.

Both the MDS and the CDM affirmed that the adoption of a new federal constitution should be preceded by a state treaty between the two republics. This was opposed by Czech politicians and pro-federalists in Slovakia who argued that the republics did not have the sovereignty essential in international law to sign such documents; the forging of a state treaty required the prior dissolution of the federation.[7] The content and timing of such a treaty also became a source of dispute; for example, whether it should precede or follow the adoption of new constitutions. Czech leaders wanted constitutional agreements to be preceded by a political declaration stating the intention of the two nations to coexist in a common state.

A number of high-level meetings in late 1991 and early 1992 failed to determine the structure of relations between the two republics. Slovak leaders objected to the formulation that republics could only conclude international treaties consented to by the "common state." A tentative compromise was reached specifying that a joint inter-republican document would take the form of an "intra-state" and not an "inter-state" treaty. But a full agreement was again delayed by Slovak insistence that the two National Councils ratify the new Federal Constitution. Czech leaders argued that this would undermine the authority of the Federal Assembly. Slovak politicians also continued to demand that the Slovak constitution be adopted before the federal document. Although the Czech side proved willing to make various compromises—for instance, agreeing that the federal constitution could be ratified by the republican parliaments—Bratislava gave conflicting signals on its willingness to reach a final agreement and sign a constitutional treaty.

Czechoslovak President Havel also became involved in the dispute, although his intervention may simply have added fuel to the flames. Havel was concerned that the Czech-Slovak conflict was harmful to political and economic reform, and he dismissed the notion of a "confederation" as a smokescreen for separation.[8] In November 1991, Havel issued several proposals to break the constitutional deadlock. For example, he proposed an amendment to the constitutional law, giving the president powers to declare a referendum on preserving the federation, and a constitutional bill defining circumstances under which the Federal Assembly could be dissolved and new elections called. The proposals were rejected by the federal parliament and were blocked by Slovak deputies who attacked Havel for seeking extraordinary powers and a "presidential regime." Havel subsequently appealed directly to the public to support his initiatives and apply pressure on parliament. His moves were opposed by most Slovak, and even some Czech, politicians as extra-constitutional and his political influence subsequently declined.[9] Slovak nationalists opposed Havel's calls for a referendum on the future of the federation. They feared that if confronted with a simple choice, the majority of Slovaks would choose to remain in the federation.

Czech leaders grew impatient with persistent Slovak demands that hindered legislative work, introduced vitriol into the political debate, and slowed down progress toward a market economy and European integration. Paradoxically, demands by the major Slovak parties for sovereignty, and delays in signing binding constitutional agreements, spurred calls for an independent Czech state. Right-wing conservatives and Czech nationalists stressed the numerous advantages of separation, including a more streamlined administration, budget savings, and improved chances for the Czech republic to accelerate its integration into the European Community (EC).[10] At the same time, preparations were undertaken to pass a separate Czech constitution specifying a weakened presidency and a stronger government, and to reorganize the republic into several self-governing lands to pacify Moravian-Silesian demands for greater autonomy.

The election law for the 5 June 1992 ballot was partly designed to buttress the growth of stronger parties. The 5% vote minimum for obtaining parliamentary seats was supplemented by stipulations that coalitions of two or more parties had to gain 7% of the vote, and a four-plus coalition needed 10% to qualify. The objectives were to counter unrestricted political fragmentation by excluding smaller parties and to build distinct parties through durable mergers. A total of 36 parties, movements, and coalitions competed for the Federal Assembly, 19 for the Czech National Council and 23 for the Slovak National Council.[11] Right-of-center parties scored victories in the Czech republic, and left-of-center and pro-independence parties won in Slovakia. Centrist and federalist forces sustained the biggest losses.[12]

The 1992 elections propelled forward the process of federal dissolution. Parties advocating Slovak sovereignty or independence gained a comfortable majority in the Slovak National Council. Of the 150 available seats, the MDS captured 74, the ex-communist Party of the Democratic Left (PDL) won 29 mandates, the Slovak National Party (SNP) 15, and the CDM 18, while the Hungarian Coalition captured 14 seats.[13] The liberal offshoot of the PAV, the Civic Democratic Union, failed to gain a single parliamentary seat. Ironically, even though public opinion polls in Slovakia indicated that the majority of citizens favored maintaining the federation, the most popular politician was the reinstalled Prime Minister Mečiar, who skillfully manipulated the issue of national independence during the election campaign.

At the federal level, a transitory government was formed, as there was no agreement between the most successful Czech and Slovak parties on preserving the federal arrangement. In the Slovak chamber of the House of the People, the pro-sovereignty Movement for a Democratic Slovakia easily won with 33.53% of the vote; the PDL scored 14.44%; the Slovak National Party obtained 9.39%; and Coexistence gained 7.37%. The centrist and federalist groups faced a disastrous result: the Civic Democratic Union captured only 3.96% of the vote, the Democratic Party 3.95%, the Social Democrats 4.86%, and the Christian Democratic Movement dropped to 8.96%. Results in elections to the Czech and Slovak National Councils mirrored those in elections to the Federal Assembly. The MDS found itself in a strong position to form a new government, as the opposition proved weak and disunited.

Following the 1992 elections, a caretaker federal government was set up to administer the division of the country. The federal cabinet was reduced. Havel failed to be re-elected as Czechoslovak president, due to opposition by Slovak deputies. In an agreement between Mečiar and Czech premier Václav Klaus, republican governments were to decide on the federal split and establish the legal foundations for Czech and Slovak statehood. A timetable of separation was quickly agreed upon. In July 1992, the Slovak government declared sovereignty, and in October 1992, it ratified the country's new constitution.[14] The federal government approved the draft of a constitutional act on terminating the federation, and Mečiar and Klaus signed various agreements defining relations between the two republics following the dissolution; these included stipulations on a customs union and a common currency.[15]

Mečiar's talks with Klaus failed to resolve the federal question. Mečiar wanted the federation loosened to such a degree that it would no longer resemble a common state. This was unacceptable to Klaus, who declared that he preferred a complete split to an unworkable confederation. Mečiar proposed that two republican entities under international law agree to coordinate mutual defense, foreign policy, and the country's currency. Klaus considered such an arrangement worse than separation, as it would prove constitutionally confusing. It appeared that Mečiar was banking on further political and economic concessions from Prague in return for preserving close ties between the two republics. When Klaus moved quickly to end the stalemate, the Slovak side was caught by surprise. When Mečiar proposed the creation of a new Czech-Slovak Union, the notion was rejected by Prague, which suspected that Bratislava wanted to assure itself of continuing material support, fearing the economic impact of a full division.[16] Instead, the Czech side pushed strenuously for separation and the forging of international treaties between two new independent states.

In November 1992, the Federal Assembly voted to disband the Czech and Slovak Federation, phase out all federal institutions, and give the two republics equal successor status. More than 30 agreements were concluded, regularizing relations between the two republics and equitably dividing federal assets. Nonetheless, some disputes persisted, particularly in apportioning federal property between Prague and Bratislava and in restructuring trade relations. On 1 January 1993, Slovakia formally achieved statehood, and a few weeks later Michal Kováč, the MDS candidate, was elected Slovakia's president by the National Council. Slovakia did not hold a referendum on separation. The dissolution of Czechoslovakia was primarily an elite arrangement in which public opinion was barely consulted.[17]

Some Czech officials and foreign observers claimed that an independent Slovakia would be politically unstable and could veer toward some form of authoritarianism and economic protectionism. These views were not shared by the major Slovak parties. Czech premier Klaus underscored that the division of the state would mean a chance for Slovakia to develop a "normal political spectrum."[18] But while there was general confidence that the Czech transition to democracy and capitalism would prove successful, significant concern remained that Slovakia's transition would take much longer to complete and could be exploited by nationalist and statist forces.

After the fall of communism, ethnic minorities gained increasing importance in Czechoslovakia. In the first post-communist census, held in March 1991, there was an opportunity to declare oneself of an ethnic minority unrecognized by the previous regimes, including Romani, Moravian, or Ruthenian. The Charter of Fundamental Rights and Liberties, adopted by the Federal Assembly in January 1991, formed a new legal basis for the treatment of ethnic minorities. This document outlined the basic human, civil, and political rights of Czechoslovak citizens and was to serve as a foundation for the future federal and republican constitutions. In a special section that addressed minority rights, the Charter provided everyone the opportunity to decide on their nationality, prohibited anti-minority discrimination, and permitted all minorities to form their own associations. It also stated that under certain conditions minorities would have the right to be educated in their own language and to use it in dealings with officialdom.

The position of the Hungarian minority proved the most contentious nationality issue in Slovakia after the democratic changes. Hungarian activists began to organize openly and to campaign for collective rights. Whereas some leaders calculated that demands for minority rights should not take precedence over the wider democratization process, others viewed the nationality problem as paramount and were accused of radicalism and separatism. The largest minority organization, Coexistence, styled itself as a multi-ethnic and not simply a Hungarian movement and denied that it was seeking secession from Slovakia. This organization gained seats in the Slovak National Council and campaigned for the expansion of minority educational, media, and publishing activities.

Hungarian groups claimed that the position of minorities was under threat from rising Slovak nationalism and increasing disengagement by Prague. They claimed that Bratislava would apply various restrictions and discriminatory measures. Hungarian organizations also expressed concern over the incitement of ethnic conflict by ultranationalist Slovak forces, some of which staged anti-Magyar demonstrations and even called for the wholesale expulsion of the Hungarian minority. Conversely, radical Slovak groups accused Budapest of assisting Hungarian organizations in search of territorial gains, a charge that was strenuously denied by the Hungarian government.

Hungarian spokesmen contended that the Charter may have inadvertently reduced the existing rights of minorities by defining the state as the "national state of Czechs and Slovaks" and abrogating earlier constitutional laws relating to minorities. In protest, Hungarian deputies walked out of the Federal Assembly for the duration of the final vote on the Charter. Hungarian leaders also objected to laws adopted by the Federal Assembly relating to compensation payments for property expropriated after World War II. The compensation act and the land act passed in 1991 referred only to property confiscated after February 1948, the date of the communist takeover. No compensation was offered for losses sustained by Hungarians between 1945 and 1948, a period when anti-Magyar decrees deprived the minority of property and citizenship rights.

The Slovak constitution, ratified in September 1992, guaranteed basic rights and liberties regardless of language and national or social origin, and the right to affiliate with a nation or ethnic group without pressure to assimilate. The constitution formally secured the right of minorities to develop their culture, to disseminate and receive information in the mother tongue, to establish educational and cultural institutions, and allowed for the functioning of national minority associations. The language question was dealt with by reinforcing

the need to master the "state language" while guaranteeing the right to education in the mother tongue and the right to use that language in dealings with
officialdom. Minorities were assured the right to participate in solving problems pertaining to their status, as long as they exercised that right in a manner
that did not jeopardize Slovak sovereignty.

Hungarian members of the Slovak National Council unanimously rejected the constitution, arguing that it failed to guarantee the identity and
self-government of minorities or allow for the creation of territorial "self-
administrative" entities. Magyar deputies strongly objected to the constitutional definition of the new country as the "national state of Slovaks," claiming
that there were no explicit guarantees for the preservation and safeguarding
of minority identities. Specifically, they pointed out that only "national organizations" could be formed by ethnic minorities, thus opening up the possibility of dissolving Hungarian political parties. Moreover, the constitution
declared that the rights of minorities could not endanger Slovak sovereignty
and territorial integrity, a provision that was potentially open to abuse. Hungarian deputies proposed a constitutional amendment guaranteeing the right
to develop one's national, ethnic, linguistic, or cultural identity, while banning any activities that lead to assimilation.[19]

Magyar leaders claimed that the constitution failed to stipulate the rights
of minorities to establish and maintain schools in their mother tongue. The
constitution also offered no legal guarantees for the use of minority languages
in dealing with the authorities. The language issue was further defined by the
controversial language law passed by the Slovak National Council in October
1990. It declared Slovak the official language, and stated that if members of
an ethnic minority constituted 20% of the population in an administrative
area, they were entitled to formally use their language. But there was no stipulation requiring state officials to be proficient in minority languages or to
employ them if they were. The application of the law also resulted in Hungarian names no longer being recorded in birth registers, invalidated any moves
toward restoring Hungarian appellations for municipalities, and abolished
bilingual street signs. It also permitted officials to refuse to conduct marriage
and funeral services in Hungarian.[20] After Slovakia became a member of the
Council of Europe in June 1993, Bratislava came under international pressure
to alter some of its minority rights legislation. Indeed, in July 1993, in an
effort to defuse domestic and international criticism, parliament passed a law
again allowing minorities to register their names in their mother tongue.

Although the version of the language law that was finally passed in 1990
was not as radical as what some Slovak national parties had proposed, it was
depicted by Hungarian leaders as an impediment to minority rights. The Hungarian political movement Coexistence criticized the language law for not
ensuring the rights of national communities to use their native language in
official matters, for eliminating bilingual signs, and for disregarding referendums in which locals voted to replace the original township names.[21]

Hungarian activists complained that Slovakia's educational system had failed to reverse the assimilationist pressures evident since the 1950s. They argued that the steady reduction in the number of schools meant that many pupils were unable to attend Magyar-language schools, thus Hungarian students' performances were lower than they would have been, had instruction been in their native tongue. After 1989, the federal and republican governments rejected the principle of educational autonomy, leaving no firm legal safeguards for national minorities in receiving education in the mother tongue. To counter such criticisms, Slovak officials asserted that Hungarian schools accounted for over 8% of all teaching facilities in the country, while 12 of the 135 senior high schools were Hungarian. In addition, the state evidently supported the publication of 25 Magyar magazines, as well as two theaters and several publishing houses.[22]

Since the onset of decommunization, several Slovak nationalist groups have not only campaigned for Slovak independence but have remonstrated against the republic's minorities, particularly Hungarians, who have been scapegoated for alleged subversion, and the Roma, the perennial stereotypes of criminality and disorder. Although Jews barely numbered in the hundreds, mostly resident in Bratislava, anti-Semitism also resurfaced as ultranationalists sought to rehabilitate Jozef Tiso and other leaders of the wartime Nazi-puppet regime. The Slovak government was criticized for failing to protect the Romani population from acts of violence perpetrated by racist radicals or from persistent discrimination in employment, education, and housing. Nonetheless, Roma have been able to establish their own political organizations and to participate in local and legislative elections. Because they remained embryonic and splintered, Romani parties proved unable to pass the threshold for parliamentary representation.

The Slovak citizenship law passed in January 1993 did not stir significant controversy, although some of its stipulations for acquiring "state citizenship" could have precipitated bureaucratic discrimination against minority groups. For instance, in applying for citizenship, an individual needed to prove mastery of the Slovak language and the absence of a criminal record during the previous five years. The former provision could theoretically be used to disenfranchise older Hungarian residents, whose knowledge of Slovak was often rudimentary, while the latter stipulation could discriminate against Romani residents, particularly if the onus were on the individual to prove his or her innocence.[23]

Political developments in Slovakia quickly became impregnated with the national issue, as a spectrum of parties took aboard the question of Slovakia's position in the federation. While pluralism evolved steadily in both republics, in Slovakia party platforms focused on a narrower set of problems, often to the neglect of socioeconomic concerns. A general division emerged between federalists and autonomists, which widened after the first national elections. Furthermore, while the federalists were supportive of marketization, the autonomists favored the retention of a large state sector and restrictions on privatization, as they feared massive unemployment in Slovakia.

The PAV itself fractured on these issues in March 1991, when the larger wing, the Movement for a Democratic Slovakia (MDS), formally broke away from the coalition. Its popular leader, Mečiar, attacked Prague for its alleged centralism and its radical approach to economic reform that would unduly hurt the Slovak economy. He increasingly spoke out for the republic's political autonomy and was charged by critics of populist and separatist inclinations. The smaller PAV wing, the Civic Democratic Union, led by Fedor Gál, became increasingly isolated and marginalized. Its leaders became dismayed at the growth of separatist, statist, and protectionist sentiments in Slovakia.

Slovakia's Christian Democratic Movement (CDM) initially grew into the second strongest political force and its chairman, Ján Čarnogurský, was able to capture much of the Catholic vote in the republic. The Movement was pro-market and supported a looser federation, but increasingly swung toward an autonomist or confederalist position in order to keep pace with rival parties. In March 1992, a more nationalistic Slovak Christian Democratic Movement (SCDM), led by Ján Klepáč, broke off from the CDM. The party also advocated continuing state intervention in the economy. The split led to further erosion of support for Čarnogurský's gradualist approach toward Slovak sovereignty.

The nationalist Slovak National Party and the ex-communist Party of the Democratic Left staunchly supported Slovak autonomy and appeared to differ little in their economic prescriptions. Although the Social Democratic Party in Slovakia (SDPS) gained Dubček as its chairman in March 1992, it was unable to compete with the major Slovak parties. Slovakia's Hungarian minority formed several parties, with a division between the Independent Hungarian Initiative, allied with the federalist PAV, and the more militant Coexistence union, which also garnered support among the Polish, Ukrainian, and Ruthenian minorities and pressed for more extensive minority rights. The minority parties had a ceiling of support in the republic corresponding to ethnic minority numbers, and they grew increasingly dismayed at the growth of Slovak nationalism. They argued that Czechoslovakia's termination could leave them vulnerable to discrimination and persecution.

In 1993, when Czechoslovakia broke up into two independent states, both Slovakia and the Czech Republic were considered front runners for early North Atlantic Treaty Organization (NATO) and European Union (EU) membership. But while the Czech Republic registered consistent progress toward meeting the criteria for inclusion in Europe's security and economic structures, Slovakia failed to secure a place in the first round of enlargement at NATO's Madrid summit in July 1997. Slovakia's divorce from Prague was peaceful and largely conflict-free. The newly independent country possessed reasonable economic potential, relatively open access to the West, a well-educated population, and a new elite committed to democratic values. But political developments in the wake of independence proved disappointing and Slovakia faced isolation. The country was governed by a quasi-authoritarian and personalistic regime dominated by Prime Minister Mečiar.

The elections of 30 September–1 October 1994 were the first in independent Slovakia. They were scheduled early, an attempt to solve the political crisis that arose after the no-confidence vote of the government headed by Prime Minister Mečiar in March 1994.[24] The MDS government had collapsed following the defection of 15 parliamentary deputies and the unstable coalition with the SNP. A five-party, center-right coalition government under Prime Minister Jozef Moravčík governed for only eight months during 1994 but made a bold start in implementing market reforms. However, the coalition was unable to survive because one of the largest coalition parties, the PDL, insisted on holding elections early instead of in June 1996 as originally scheduled.[25]

In the general elections in September 1994, the MDS, in an electoral bloc with the small Peasant Party of Slovakia (PPS), gained 34.96% of the vote and captured 61 parliamentary seats. The leftist Common Choice coalition, consisting of the PDL, the SDPS, the Green Party of Slovakia (GPS), and the Movement of Farmers of the Slovak Republic (MFSR), garnered 10.41% of the vote, and 18 seats. Other opposition organizations performed poorly, and Mečiar once again became prime minister in December 1994. According to public opinion surveys, Slovaks generally exhibited low levels of identification with any political party, and few were willing to join any organization, partly as a reaction to decades of communist coercion.[26]

The MDS formed a governing coalition with the nationalist Slovak National Party (SNP) and the neocommunist Association of Slovak Workers (ASW) (the two parties had gathered 22 seats between them). Twelve posts in the eighteen-member cabinet were assigned to the MDS. The democratic opposition remained comparatively weak and divided into competing parties with little access to the major mass media outlets and with restricted impact on public opinion. Critics charged that Prime Minister Mečiar sought to concentrate power in his office and to eliminate rival sources of authority. Mečiar employed a mixture of political favoritism, patronage, nationalism, populism, and even sheer intimidation and human rights violations. The MDS dispensed privileges and offices to loyalist politicians, managers, and directors in a broad range of public and private institutions, including economic enterprises, business ventures, media outlets, cultural bodies, and local administrations. As a result, Mečiar established a network of patronage, which remained dependent on his keeping office and buttressing his personal and party controls over the state. Such a system did not favor democratization and competitive pluralism.

Mečiar also constructed a personality cult in which he was glorified by the state-controlled media as the "father of the nation."[27] According to the official media, his autocratic style had purportedly ensured Slovak independence and the protection of the country from hostile alien influences. Such assertions ignored the fact that Mečiar was once a strong supporter of Czechoslovak federalism. The prime minister constructed a highly personalistic system of rule in which his decisions were virtual decrees that could not be challenged. Analysts believed that this strict hierarchy and Mečiar's popularity kept the MDS together: without their charismatic leader, the Movement would disintegrate into rival factions and interest groups.

The network of patronage and clientage also penetrated the privatization process. State firms were reportedly sold off at rock bottom prices to MDS supporters and other figures loyal to Mečiar. This capitalist *nomenklatura* stood accused of nepotism, corruption, and unfair competition with genuine entrepreneurs. The Mečiar *nomenklatura* also managed to occupy the most important administrative bodies, cultural and educational institutions, and local government offices. Job discrimination became rampant, as political loyalty and personal favoritism invariably counted for more than merit or ability.

Mečiar also deliberately polarized Slovak society in order to enhance his influence. In a classic strategy of "divide and rule," the population was fragmented into "good" and "bad" Slovaks: those who supported the government's policies were favored and those who publicly opposed policies were branded as traitors. Such divisive politics exploited ethnic, regional, class, urban-rural, and other cleavages in order to undermine any coherent opposition to Bratislava's policies. The country was fractured through emotionally loaded symbols that shifted public attention away from mounting economic problems and growing international criticism and isolation.

A key reason for the success of "Mečiarism" was the relative failure of the fractured political opposition throughout most of the 1990s. The opposition lacked a charismatic and popular personality who could mobilize the citizenry. Moreover, Mečiar's simplistic populist messages were easily understood by the public, whereas the more sophisticated programs of opposition candidates had limited resonance outside intellectual and urban circles. The governing party retained a monopoly over the main media outlets, especially state television and radio. Critics were denied access while Mečiar used media channels as pulpits to enhance his prestige and denigrate the opposition. The reformist parties possessed their own newspapers and other outlets; but outside the capital Bratislava and a few major cities, these had only a limited impact on the electorate. The MDS also refused to involve the opposition in important parliamentary committees, and it often disregarded constitutional provisions and relegated parliament to a marginal role in decisionmaking.

A major conflict took place between Prime Minister Mečiar and the country's President, Michal Kováč, who assumed office in March 1993 and took the role of spokesman for the political opposition. After gaining office in November 1994, Mečiar consistently sought to limit the power and influence of the presidency and to force Kováč to resign. Observers believed that Mečiar sought revenge for Kováč's support of his ouster in March 1994. However, the MDS lacked the parliamentary majority necessary to secure the president's removal, having only 80 seats in the governing coalition instead of 90. Mečiar thus sought to cut back presidential powers through various laws, and to discredit and isolate Kováč through a campaign of vilification in the media.

Kováč's popularity was limited, particularly as he was not directly elected by citizens but by parliament, and unlike Mečiar, he did not benefit from a broad political power base. Throughout the MDS period in government the country remained divided between pro-Kováč and pro-Mečiar sentiments. A referendum on the direct election of the president in July 1997 was foiled on a technicality by the government; the result could have increased Kováč's authority in the country. The MDS also passed a non-binding vote of no confidence in the president in May 1995, in a move to further undermine his authority and legitimacy.

The Mečiar regime was not a classic one-party structure but rather a personality-centered system based on patronage and political loyalty. The MDS itself was not an ideology-based party but an eclectic interest group dispensing favors and privileges to its supporters and exploiting public fears about a potential loss of Slovak identity and statehood. It periodically employed nationalism and xenophobia to heighten the sense of danger and threat in order to boost the government's popularity. The MDS maintained a coalition with the ultranationalist Slovak National Party, which avidly attacked Hungarians, Czechs, Jews, and Romas (Gypsies) for allegedly conspiring against the state.

The Hungarian population in particular became an easy target for such propaganda campaigns. Magyar leaders claimed that their minority's position, especially in the realm of education and language use, actually deteriorated since the signing of the Slovak-Hungarian Basic Treaty an agreement on borders and the protection of ethnic minorities that was signed on 19 March 1995 and was hailed as a major international achievement. For example, in September 1997 the Slovak constitutional court upheld a controversial law declaring Slovak the country's only official language. The language law had been passed in November 1995 and had replaced one that permitted the official use of other languages in communities with large ethnic minorities.

Bratislava delayed setting up joint implementation committees for the Basic Treaty, primarily because the MDS objected to having Hungarian representatives officially monitoring the condition of minority rights. The Hungarian government persistently complained about Slovak failures to honor the treaty and asserted that the position of the minority had steadily declined. Relations between Bratislava and Budapest were further strained in September 1997, when it was revealed that Mečiar had proposed resettling Magyars in Hungary. His comments were assailed for promoting "ethnic cleansing" and violating the 1995 treaty. Hungarian spokesmen feared that ethnic Magyars' status could further plummet if Slovakia experienced serious economic decline as a result of its international isolation. Minorities could be targeted by the state in order to distract public attention from the government's policy failures.

In July 1996, a new administrative law divided the country into eight large regions and seventy-nine districts.[28] This measure elicited protests among the democratic opposition and Hungarian minority leaders, who feared the centralization of government and the elimination of local self-government. The measures were opposed by the Association of Cities and Towns, which petitioned for a greater devolution of power. Political leaders in eastern Slovakia—an area with traditionally strong support for regionalism and autonomy—were especially worried. They complained that Bratislava was seeking to narrow local government responsibilities.

Under the constitution, the president was elected by a two-thirds majority in parliament. Kováč's term officially expired in March 1998. Mečiar was intent on ousting his major political adversary and further undercutting the office of the presidency. Neither the ruling coalition nor the opposition could muster the votes necessary to elect a new president. With a prolonged stalemate, the remaining presidential powers could simply pass to the prime minister and his cabinet—a situation that clearly benefited Mečiar.

After parliament was unable to elect a president after five votes, the post became vacant. According to the Slovak constitution, in the absence of a president all presidential responsibilities were handed over to the prime minister. Immediately after President Kováč left, Mečiar displayed his eagerness to concentrate power in his own hands. He recalled numerous ambassadors and granted amnesty to key figures implicated in the politically motivated 1995 kidnapping of President Kováč's son. He also cancelled the intended replay of the failed 1997 referendum, despite the fact that President Kováč had already announced it before he left the post. Slovakia was without a head-of-state for more than a year and faced a constitutional crisis after 2 March 1998 when President Kováč stepped down at the end of his regular term of office.

Mečiar's maneuvers caused serious concerns about the upcoming parliamentary elections. Soon after President Kováč left office, the ruling coalition, in order to disadvantage the opposition, enacted several controversial laws. The Slovak constitution was amended so that elections would be held in a single constituency instead of the four that had existed previously. These amendments favored parties with strong leaders, because single-candidate lists allowed each party to feature its best-known personality across the entire country.[29]

In addition, a new clause required each party within a coalition to gain at least 5% of votes to be seated in parliament. This clause was apparently aimed against opposition parties that might be able to enter parliament as members of a coalition. However, Mečiar's move had the unintended consequence of strengthening opposition unity, as the democrats were forced to cooperate with each other. On 30 March 1998, five reformist parties formed an anti-MDS bloc called the Slovak Democratic Coalition (SDC), which included the post-communist Party of the Democratic Left, the Christian Democratic Movement, the newly formed Party of Civic Understanding (PCU), the Democratic Union, and a coalition of Hungarian parties.

The election law also restricted substantially the use of independent media in the campaign process. Another means of securing an electoral victory was the privatization of state assets. The largest and most important factories and enterprises were sold, or the top managerial posts were given, to a group closely linked to Mečiar's MDS in return for future political favors. For example, Alexander Rezeš, the biggest shareholder in one of the largest East European steel industries, became a leading figure on Mečiar's election team.

Despite Mečiar's efforts to maintain power through legal measures and media controls, the parliamentary elections on September 1998 were won by the opposition, parties. They mustered a clear majority in parliament: the Slovak Democratic Coalition (SDC) obtained 42 seats, the Party of the Democratic Left 23, the Party of the Hungarian Coalition 15, and the Party of Civic Understanding 13. The nationalist Slovak National Party only garnered 14 deputies.[30] Although the MDS actually obtained the largest number of seats (43), no major party was willing to enter into a coalition with it. Mečiar failed to form a majority government and went into opposition, while the SDC successfully created a new administration on 30 October 1998. The governing coalition consisted of leftist, centrist, and rightist parties committed to placing Slovakia on track for European integration.

Bratislava inherited various economic, legal, and institutional problems, and it was challenged by the political diversity within the coalition. Some conflict arose between representatives of the SDC and their parent parties and between minority members in government. Perhaps the only uncontroversial matter for the Coalition was a law on the procedure for direct presidential elections, which passed in March 1999. As a result, Slovakia held its first direct presidential elections on 15 and 29 May 1999. The former mayor of Košice, Rudolf Schuster, won decisively against Mečiar in the second round of balloting. Schuster captured 57.18% of the vote, while Mečiar gained 42.82%.

The Slovak parliament approved measures by the end of June 1999 that enabled the EU to place Slovakia on the "fast track" in accession talks. The regulation of language use by minorities was one of Brussels's most important conditions for Slovakia's admission to the Union. The law was finally passed on 10 July 1999, after disputes within the governing coalition. Hungarian deputies opposed the bill, arguing that it did not reduce the negative impact of the existing law on the state language because it did not cover those areas where the state law restricts the usage of minority languages. However, the European Commission commended Slovak officials for adopting the law.

Another issue that challenged coalition unity was a disparity of views over the direction of the Slovak economy, between liberal-conservative and leftist-socialist wings. The Minister of Finance was a PDL official, Brigita Shmögnerová. On the other side of the spectrum stood the Deputy Prime Minister Ivan Mikloš, who was responsible for economic affairs. Some analysts accused Shmögnerová of blocking necessary reforms proposed by Mikloš because of their potential negative social impact.[31] In June 1999, the prime minister confirmed that the sharp decline in the *koruna*'s exchange rate convinced the government of the absolute priority of economic reforms.[32] There was some danger that Prime Minister Dzurinda could be left with a minority government because of disputes over economic policy. However, an important factor that kept the coalition together was that Slovakia's sole political alternative was another Mečiar government, which could again set back the country's progress.

At the end of 1999, Mečiar petitioned for a parliamentary vote of no-confidence in the government, for a public referendum on new general elections, and for a new coalition with the MDS. Nevertheless, all the major parties refused to cooperate with Mečiar. A referendum on new elections was held on 11 November 2000, after the MDS gathered the required number of votes and gained approval from the presidency. The vote failed to pass the 50% threshold necessary for validity: only 20.03% of eligible voters participated. The referendum itself stirred disputes over constitutional interpretation and created new tension between the president and government. Disputes were also evident between the governing coalition and its Hungarian partner over plans for administrative reorganization that would subdivide Hungarian-populated southern Slovakia into several new regions. Nevertheless, the Hungarian parties remained in government, where they could exert more influence over state policy.

POLITICAL PARTIES

Socialists and Social Democrats

Party of the Democratic Left (PDL)
Strana Demokratickej Ľavice (SDL)

The Party of the Democratic Left (PDL) emerged from the Slovak Communist Party in October 1990 and was led by Chairman Peter Weiss. Other prominent party members included Pavol Kanis, Milan Ftáčnik, Brigita Shmögnerová, and Peter Magvasi. After 1989, the Slovak communists became increasingly independent of the federal Communist Party of Czechoslovakia and introduced a number of internal political reforms. During its October 1990 congress, the party changed its name to the Party of the Democratic Left and agreed to form a provisional coalition with the Communist Party of Bohemia and Moravia in November 1990.

In January 1991, PDL leaders decided to remove conservative communists by mandating a re-registration of all members. Younger activists came to the fore after the retirement of the old guard. Some critics accused the PDL of being an opportunistic party that adjusted its program simply to suit current requirements, whether this was independence or privatization. In reality, the younger leadership attempted to steer the organization toward a European-type social democratic position and curtailed its support for a welfare system.

In March 1991, when Mečiar's pro-sovereignty MDS broke away from the PAV, PDL leaders increasingly sensed that the national issue, combined with a social democratic economic orientation, could help them harness significant public support. As a result, the PDL initially emphasized its support for Mečiar's program and was considered a quasi-nationalist party in its own right. By April 1991, the party reported 20,000 re-registered members. While this represented a drop of some 100,000, public opinion polls revealed that the PDL remained the second strongest party in Slovakia, benefiting from about 16% of public support. Due to the party's social democratic and pro-nationalist orientation, it moved away from traditional communism while some marginal Leninist parties emerged to fill this gap. During the June 1992 elections, the party scored particularly well in eastern Slovakia, where it obtained 21.5% of the popular vote. The PDL gained 14.7% of the national vote, winning 29 seats in the Slovak National Council.[33]

The PDL was the second strongest party in parliament until 1994. It attempted to find a new political identity, trying to distance itself from its communist legacy. The PDL defined itself as left-centrist with a social democratic orientation, which tried to realize the principles of "democratic socialism as an organic connection of the values of humanism, social justice, pluralist democracy, and self-rule." The PDL used its supporters' nostalgia for the era before November 1989 but at the same time declared its support for the values of a modern, open society. PDL leaders voiced support for a process of social transformation through the "minimization of social losses; [and] resistance to the tendency of reducing the role of the state."

In the September–October 1994 elections, the party gained 13 seats in parliament out of a total of 18 for the leftist bloc "Common Choice." In early 1996, the PDL expressed interest in entering the Mečiar government, which it was claimed would increase Slovakia's foreign stature and contribute to the resolution of its domestic problems. However, the PDL never received a firm offer to enter the administration. The party leadership later defended their intent to enter a minority government with the MDS during the June 1996 coalition crisis as necessary to prevent political destabilization and an early election that would have apparently benefited the MDS.

In April 1996, at its fourth congress in Nitra, the PDL elected a new chairman, Jozef Migaš, who was then serving as Slovak ambassador to Ukraine and who was regarded as a member of the party's pragmatic wing. Delegates to the congress spoke in favor of continuing the party's independent leftist opposition stance. Despite its strong criticism of specific policies pursued by the Mečiar government, the PDL did not regularly take part in joint events organized by the emerging democratic coalition, which it considered excessively radical and confrontational. It refused to support the opposition's petition drive for a referendum on direct presidential elections, arguing that it was more appropriate to consider the issue within a broader package of constitutional reforms.

The PDL strongly opposed what it viewed as efforts to revive fascist ideas, such as attempts by *Matica Slovenská* (Slovak Motherland), the Slovak cultural association, to rehabilitate Jozef Tiso, president of the wartime Slovak state. The party supported Slovakia's membership in NATO and the EU and blamed the Mečiar government for Bratislava's failure to gain membership in the first wave of enlargement. In September 1996, the PDL was admitted to the Socialist International. It maintained contacts with parties sharing its social democratic orientation and participated in the activities of the socialist faction of the Parliamentary Assembly of the Council of Europe.

In the September 1998 elections, the PDL gained 23 out of 150 parliamentary seats and became the third strongest party in the legislature, and thus was able to secure several governmental posts. The PDL was a member of the coalition government and held five ministerial positions, among them the Ministries of Finance and Defense. Through their Finance Minister, the PDL participated in regulating Slovakia's economic reforms. As a result, Minister Shmögnerová was blamed for Slovakia's economic hardship by some SDC coalition partners.

Common Choice (CC)
Spoločná Voľba (SV)

Following the September–October 1994 general elections, Common Choice (CC) became the second strongest grouping in parliament, having received 10.41% of the vote. It included the Party of the Democratic Left (PDL), the Social Democratic Party of Slovakia (SDPS), the Green Party of Slovakia (GPS) and the Agricultural Movement of the Slovak Republic (AMSR). As these parties stated in their joint program, they were united by an adherence to common values such as social justice, solidarity, democracy and human rights, peace, good international relations, national tolerance, and ecological awareness. The coalition was an attempt by the PDL to integrate the left-oriented political forces into a powerful social democratic movement. The big surprise of the election was that the creation of the Common Choice coalition did not bring the PDL more votes. According to some surveys, Common Choice voters were mostly from the PDL, and only a minority were from other political formations. On the other hand, only 49.3% of former PDL voters chose to vote for Common Choice, while 11.9% turned to MDS, 6% to the Association of Slovak Workers (ASW), 3.7% to the Communist Party of Slovakia (CPS), and 7.5% to other parties. The PDL failed to elaborate its own set of solutions to urgent social problems and proved unable to appeal to disillusioned leftist voters, especially white-collar and industrial workers.

Social Democratic Party of Slovakia (SDPS)
Socialno Demokratická Strana Slovenska (SDSS)

The Social Democratic Party of Slovakia (SDPS) was a small, urban-based party whose identity revolved around the figure of Aleksander Dubček. Prominent party members included Boris Zala, Ľubor Bystrický, and Chairman Jaroslav Volf. The party had two deputies in the National Council after the September–October 1994 general elections and attempted to become a significant opposition force despite internal party schisms. The party condemned the government's privatization policies and what it called glaring cases of social corruption. The SDPS also demanded democratic reforms within parliament and supported public protest actions such as the Save Our Culture initiative. Unlike the PDL, its election partner, the SDPS openly participated in mass rallies and citizen protests organized by the parties of the Blue Coalition and the Hungarian Coalition against the Mečiar government. When the PDL expressed its willingness to support a minority MDS administration, representatives of SDPS announced their intention to establish an independent social democratic parliamentary caucus. The SDPS supported the opposition initiative to amend the Slovak constitution to permit direct presidential elections, and supported the petition drive for a referendum. The party was for European integration and rejected the notion of Slovak neutrality. As a member of the Socialist International, the SDPS maintained extensive contacts with social democratic and socialist parties abroad.

For the September 1998 elections, the SDPS entered the Blue Coalition. Later, it helped create the Slovak Democratic Coalition (SDC). The SDPS and the Greens also formed a common socialist platform within the opposition coalition. When Mečiar amended the election law in May 1998, just a few months before the balloting, all potential deputies had to become members of the newly established party, the Slovak Democratic Coalition. On its own, the SDPS remained fairly marginal and only registered 1% to 2% in public opinion polls after the sudden death of Dubček on 7 November 1992.

At the SDPS congress in June 1999, its Chairman Jaroslav Volf was reelected. He announced the launching of a project called "New Social Democracy" that was designed to consolidate the party's political leadership and its expert bodies. Volf blamed the party's poor standing on legislation on political parties that provided little space for the survival of small organizations. However, he praised the SDPS's presence in the SDC, even though following the September 1998 elections the party earned few governmental posts.

Liberals

Slovak Democratic Coalition (SDC)
Slovenská Demokratická Koalicia (SDK)

Throughout 1996 and 1997, leaders of the Slovak opposition increasingly acknowledged the need for more coordinated action in their campaigns for the September 1998 parliamentary elections. An earlier expression of such cooperation was the short-lived Blue Coalition, encompassing the Christian Democratic Movement (CDM), the Democratic Party (DP), and the Democratic Union

(DU). In July 1997, after months of negotiation, the chairmen of those parties and of the Social Democratic Party of Slovakia (SDPS) and the Slovak Green Party (SGP), signed an agreement to form a joint electoral entity called the Slovak Democratic Coalition (SDC). Its members pledged to run joint candidate lists and specified how candidates would be chosen. They also agreed to campaign on a common platform, and in August announced a fifteen-point "Martin Declaration," which committed the parties to a pro-Western reform agenda.

The chairmen of the five member-parties served as co-chairmen of the SDC. Mikuláš Dzurinda, deputy chairman of the CDM, was named as the SDC's official spokesman. The SDC also signed a cooperative agreement with the three ethnic Hungarian parties, whose support proved essential in forming a new government.[34] The SDC contained something for everyone: religious-based conservatism, *laissez-faire* capitalism, and center-left socialism. The coalition was committed to economic reform and to meeting the criteria for NATO and EU membership.[35] On 4 July 1998, the SDC formally merged to form a party and elected Dzurinda as its chairman. The move was prompted by the amendment to the electoral law, passed by parliament in June 1998, that required each member of an electoral alliance to obtain at least 5% of the vote.[36]

The MDS technically won the elections but proved unable to form a government. Because the SDC gained only approximately one third of votes, it had to agree to cooperate with other parliamentary parties. A post-election pact was signed in June 1999 to establish the arrangement of inter-party relations. The pact contractually defined each party's support for the new cabinet and other guidelines regulating the SDC presence in parliament. It was based on the acceptance of double membership in the SDC and in its member-parties, thus refraining from enlarging SDC membership while settling decision-making mechanisms between the SDC and the member-parties.

Democratic Party (DP)
Demokratická Strana (DS)

Between 1993 and 1994 several small political parties merged to form a center-right liberal organization. The process started with the transformation of the Civic Democratic Union (CDU), the successor to the Public Against Violence, into the Party of Conservative Democrats. In May 1993, this party united with the Civic Democratic Party of Slovakia and changed its name to the Conservative Democratic Party. This party, in turn, merged in May 1994 with the Democratic Movement (DM) and adopted the name of Democratic Party (DP). The resulting party retained this name, which had a long tradition in Slovakia. The process of party formation was often complicated by personal tensions and the ambitions of its leaders. In July 1997, the DP joined the Slovak Democratic Coalition (SDC). Ján Langoš succeeded Peter Osuský as party chairman and was re-elected at the November 1996 party congress in Prešov. Langoš was elected on the CDU candidate list in 1994. When he later became chairman of the DP, he chose to represent it in parliament but remained a close ally of his former CDU colleagues.

Electoral support for the DP hovered slightly below the 5% level required for representation in parliament, but stabilized in 1996 at the threshold of electability. Like its larger allies, the DP strongly opposed the policies of the MDS government in the realms of privatization, territorial and administrative redistricting, internal security, education, and the media. The DP initiated or supported votes of no confidence in several government officials, including Foreign Minister Juraj Schenk, security services director Ivan Lexa, and Štefan Gavorník, president of the National Property Fund. The DP proposed that in the event of Slovakia's exclusion from the first round of NATO enlargement talks, the Mečiar government should resign for failing to fulfill a key item of its program declaration. In August 1996, the DP prepared its own list of democratic reforms required for Slovakia's entry into the EU and NATO. This list later became the basis for coalition negotiations with the SDC.

The DP presented itself as a strictly anti-communist and anti-fascist force. For example, it condemned open and covert revivals of fascism, such as the participation of representatives of the governing coalition and *Matica Slovenská* in events commemorating the wartime Slovak state. The opening of the Jozef Tiso memorial room in Bytca, during which Bishop Rudolf Baláž, chairman of the Conference of Slovak Bishops, called Tiso an outstanding and exceptional personality, was viewed as an act of covert propagation of fascism.

The party promoted close cooperation among non-leftist opposition forces. Although it actively supported Slovakia's membership in NATO and the EU, the DP initially opposed holding a referendum on Slovakia's entry into NATO. Once the 1997 referendum was announced, party leaders strongly supported citizens' participation. As an integral part of the SDC, the DP pursued liberal-conservative values in the coalition government. As a reaction to developments within the SDC, one of the DP deputies, Peter Zajac, stated that the possible emergence of a sixth party would mean the fragmentation of the coalition. The Deputy Economics Minister Ivan Mikloš, representing the DP's neoliberal view on the transformation of the Slovak economy, consistently pushed for more far-reaching economic reforms. However, he was often overruled by Finance Minister Shmögnerová.

Democratic Union of Slovakia (DUS)
Demokratická Únia Slovenska (DUS)

Prominent Democratic Union of Slovakia (DUS) members included Roman Kováč, Milan Knažko, and Ján Budaj. The Democratic Union was created as a result of the gradual split of the parliamentary caucus of the MDS. First, the MDS was abandoned by a group surrounding Milan Knažko that formed the Alliance of Democrats, and later another group called the Alternative for Political Realism split from the MDS under the leadership of Josef Moravčík, the former prime minister. The merger of both political groups led to the creation of the DUS in April 1994. The Union contained a broad group of activists, including centrists, liberals, conservatives, and independents. In the September–October 1994 elections, the Union received 8.57% of the votes, ensuring it 15 parliamentary seats.

The Mečiar government attempted to expel fifteen parliamentary deputies who were elected on the MDS ticket and subsequently formed the DUS. The DUS developed in opposition to the MDS and it strongly advocated traditional liberal values. It emphasized the significance of personal initiative and responsibility for family and country. The party favored a restrictive financial policy directed at lowering taxes, which it argued would stimulate private business. The DUS stressed the role of the country's regions and promoted their further development, as well as the redistribution of power in favor of regional self-administration. One of the factors that attracted new voters to the DUS was the fact that many prominent former government officials were among its members. Most DUS support came from students, intellectuals, business people, and white-collar workers, while its backing was lowest among industrial workers and peasants.

The DUS had fifteen parliamentary deputies after 1994, but lost one early in 1997, when Anton Hrnko resigned from the party caucus. The DUS was strongly opposed to the policies of the Mečiar government and coordinated its activities closely with the CDM and the Democratic Party. Early in 1996, Moravčík called for early parliamentary elections to reverse the harm done by the Mečiar government to Slovakia's prospects for Western integration. In February 1996, DUS deputies presented in parliament their Constitutional Law on Implementing Basic Rights, Liberties, and Self-Government, which aimed at strictly enforcing the principles of a civil society and individual rights. The parties of the Hungarian Coalition, however, announced in advance that they would not support the DUS proposals. The DUS itself, while supportive of minority rights, was strongly in favor of the civic option and opposed any moves toward territorial or ethnic autonomy.

Some delegates criticized their own parliamentary representatives for their actions during the debates on laws pertaining to the state language and ratification of the Slovak-Hungarian Treaty. A number of dissatisfied DUS members participated in the May 1996 founding congress of the Civil Liberal Party, whose creation DUS representatives suspected was an MDS plot to splinter the opposition. At the third DUS congress in Piešťny in March 1997, Eduard Kukan was elected chairman. DUS deputies backed all proposals in parliament for votes of no confidence in the Mečiar cabinet. They demanded the recall of Michal Valo, the prosecutor-general, and for conclusive investigations of the abduction of Michal Kováč's son and the death of journalist Robert Remiáš. The DUS espoused a clearly pro-Atlantic, pro-integration foreign policy and rejected as dangerous and unworkable the idea of Slovak neutrality. In June 1996, the DUS was admitted to the Liberal International.

The Democratic Union of Slovakia held a congress in May 1999 where members elected a new chairman, Ľubomír Harach. He represented a non-conflictive position that promoted close cooperation with the SDC. Dual membership was also a burning problem. All SDC member-parties tried to find a feasible way to satisfy their parties while keeping their mandates. Opinion polls showed that the population still preferred the SDC to the liberal DUS and that only approximately 1% of voters would support the DUS if there were new elections. Delegates also confirmed the inter-party accord, called for a strong DUS, and voiced strong support for Dzurinda's cabinet.

Party of Civic Understanding (PCU)
Strana Občianskeho Porozumenia (SOP)

Rudolf Schuster, the popular mayor of Košice, formed the Party of Civic Understanding (PCU) and filled its ranks with well-known political, business, and entertainment personalities. The PCU's message was that both the MDS and the SDC parties forfeited their political credibility in unsuccessfully dealing with Slovakia's transition process and that a new political dynamic was needed in the country. In the October 1998 elections, the PCU performed extremely well. Thanks to its popular leadership, the party gained 13 parliamentary seats and was included in the SDC government. For a new political body, the PCU was successful in gaining two ministerial posts and one deputy prime minister. The peak of their triumph was the election of Chairman Schuster as the first directly elected Slovak president in May 1999.

The PCU platform was strongly supportive of EU and NATO membership and drew support mostly from the undecided part of the population. On the one hand, the party backed improvements in the living standards of pensioners and students. Yet on the other hand, it did not demand unconditional reprivatization—a fact that contributed to its popularity among businessmen. Among other liberal formations, Slovakia also had the Party of the Democratic Center (PDC) *(Strana Demokratického Centra)*, and the Party of Civic Concord (PCC) *(Strana Obcianskej Svornosti, SOS)*.

Direction (D)
Smer (S)

The Direction (D) movement was established during 1999 by parliamentary deputy Robert Fico, a former leading official in the PDL. Fico founded the party, evidently as an alternative to both the leading governmental and opposition parties, and rapidly garnered substantial public support. By the close of 1999, Direction reportedly was the second most popular party in the country, with over 20% support in public opinion polls. Much of Fico's support came from former backers of the ruling democratic coalition who became dissatisfied with its policies, and from the PDL in particular. Direction also benefited from support among several interest groups that had formerly backed the MDS. Fico adopted a populist position on many pressing issues. He was critical of both the government and the opposition, and excluded the possibility of forming any future coalition with ex-premier Vladimir Mečiar. He also peddled a "soft xenophobia" directed against the Roma population. Although he supported European integration for Slovakia, stress was laid on defending the country's sovereignty during this process. Direction endorsed the November 2000 referendum on early elections, which was organized by the MDS, and welcomed the prospect of an early national ballot. The referendum failed to pass the threshold of votes to become valid, but Direction remained poised to play a significant role in the next parliamentary ballot.

New Slovakia Movement (NSM)
Hnutie Nové Slovensko (HNS)

The New Slovakia Movement (NSM), chaired by Rudolf Mosný, was established in the late 1990s and consisted of young professionals who recently entered the political scene. The Movement adopted a social liberal agenda. For example, the NSM aimed to lower unemployment to less than 10% by supporting small and mid-size entrepreneurs, initiating appropriate agricultural policy, and favoring regional development. It also sought to ensure adequate housing for families, improve the status of women through establishment of a ministry for women, raise wages, improve economic conditions for pensioners, and enhance state support of health care. The NSM also wanted to increase spending on education and ensure the allocation of adequate funding for scientific research. The NSM promoted the development of specific regions by decentralizing decisionmaking and budgeting to the local level. It wanted to provide three-year tax breaks for investors in regions with high unemployment. NSM leaders sought the prosecution of illegal privatization and wanted to open up the Slovak market to foreign capital. The Movement was a strong supporter of Slovakia's membership in the European Union.

Christian Democrats

Christian Democratic Movement (CDM)
Kresťanskodemokratické Hnutie (KDH)

The Christian Democratic Movement (CDM) was founded in February 1990 and evolved from the underground church under communist rule. Most of the initial members were Catholic, anti-communist lay people and activist priests who operated a "secret church" during the 1970s and 1980s. It kept the party's original name following a schism in the Movement in March 1992. Prominent party members included Ivan Šimko, Mikuláš Dzurinda, and František

Mikloško. Led by former Slovak Prime Minister Ján Čarnogurský, the majority of registered Christian Democratic Movement members reportedly resided in the countryside. However, the party also included several urban organizations with a professional orientation. Many members in Čarnogurský's CDM welcomed the movement's division, claiming that it would cleanse the movement of leftist and ultranationalist elements and enable it to become a traditional right-of-center Christian democratic party. Throughout the 1990s, the Catholic Church did not become influential in Slovakia and priests or lay people were generally uninvolved in politics.

In its initial statements, the CDM supported the Czechoslovak federation, although it preferred a looser inter-republican relationship. However, some leaders proclaimed their ultimate goal to be the dissolution of Czechoslovakia. The CDM developed into the strongest competitor of the Public Against Violence (PAV), emerging from the June 1990 elections as the second most popular party. It subsequently joined the Federal Assembly's ruling coalition with the Civic Forum and the PAV and vigorously supported the adoption of a constitutional amendment in December 1990 that ceded many of the federation's powers to the two republics.

During the summer of 1990, the CDM adopted a more nationalist orientation. In July 1990, the leadership issued a statement advocating a Czechoslovak confederation and a future "sovereign and equal" Slovakia. The Movement's growing image as a defender of Slovak rights was reflected in its increasing popularity. After recasting its program in a more nationalist fashion, it became the strongest political force in the republic at the local level, gaining 27.5% of the vote during the local elections in November 1990. Following the PAV split in March 1991, the CDM became the strongest political force in the Slovak National Council, with 31 seats. However, due to pressure from its pro-federation coalition partners, the CDM diluted its confederalist stance and advocated a looser federation instead. This change in orientation was widely seen as a setback for Slovak sovereignty. It also appeared to diminish the CDM's popularity, which slipped to 12% in public opinion polls, while the pro-sovereignty MDS increased its support to over 30%.

Internal factionalism became evident in the MDS by the summer of 1991. Despite its official support for preserving the federation, the Movement allied itself with Slovak nationalist parties in the Federal Assembly in vetoing proposals to hold a referendum on the country's constitutional setup. But the CDM also blocked attempts by nationalist parties in the Slovak National Council to adopt a Declaration of Slovak Sovereignty. In February 1992, leaders of the Czech and Slovak National Councils tentatively agreed on the text of a state treaty for which Čarnogurský had campaigned vigorously. However, the presidium of the Slovak National Council rejected the draft, and four members of the CDM voted against the treaty. This was a clear signal that the CDM could no longer remain unified. Čarnogurský gave the nationalist wing an ultimatum: either follow the party line, or leave; and the Klepác faction, responded by announcing its departure.

In March 1992, František Mikloško, the chairman of the Slovak National Council and a member of the PAV, announced that he would join Čarnogurský's party. He suggested that the party should become a "modern conservative party" similar to other European Christian democratic parties. The CDM continued to advocate the maintenance of the federal state on a temporary basis, with eventual independence for Slovakia. But it insisted that the adoption of the federal constitution, scheduled for the end of 1991, be preceded by a state treaty between the Czech and Slovak republics.

The party platform advocated a degree of state intervention in the economy, and gradual market transformation, in order to reduce social tensions in Slovakia. The CDM fared poorly in the June 1992 general elections, scoring only 8.89% of the popular vote, winning only 18 out of 150 seats in the Slovak National Council, and losing more than half of its previous supporters. While Čarnogurský was effectively removed from power, he remained a member of the Slovak National Council.[37]

The September–October 1994 elections, in which the CDM won 10% of the vote, demonstrated that its voter base remained stable. Most of the votes received were from intellectuals, students, pensioners, businesspeople, and white-collar workers, while support was lowest among industrial workers. CDM leaders claimed in their platform that the movement had shifted from centrist to rightist positions. In its document "Better Slovakia," the party declared itself for the principles of democracy, a legal state, and a market economy with an emphasis on private property and self-responsibility. The CDM declared "unbridled liberalism" its political enemy.

With 16 deputies in parliament, the CDM was the largest opposition party. It regarded the policies of the Mečiar government as a betrayal of democratic values. The party repeatedly complained about the exclusion of the opposition from oversight of the intelligence services and the privatization process. In March 1996, Mikuláš Dzurinda, CDM deputy chairman, claimed to have uncovered a so-called "model 34," by which 34% of a privatized company was earmarked for persons close to the governing coalition. In October 1996, the CDM presented its new economic program, which included proposals to reduce official corruption and to apply transparent rules in the administration of state finances.

The CDM opposed the idea of regional autonomy for the Hungarian minority and criticized the positions of the Coexistence movement. In June 1996, on the occasion of the unveiling of a memorial of the 1,100th anniversary of the arrival of Hungarians in the Carpathian Basin, Chairman Čarnogurský objected both to the text of the memorial and to the construction of such memorials in general. The party's ninth congress in November 1996, held in Banská Bystrica, featured a leadership contest between Čarnogurský and Dzurinda, who differed primarily in the way they depicted the party in public.

The congress re-elected Čarnogurský, who then promised to improve the CDM's popularity by promoting expertise and professionalism in politics, supporting those victimized by current government policies, and uniting the opposition against the Mečiar government. One example of the latter was the signing of a pre-election agreement among the CDM, the DU, and the DS in October 1996; this became known as the Blue Coalition.

The CDM vigorously supported Slovakia's membership in NATO and EU and warned that the government's domestic policies and style of governing were leading Slovakia toward international isolation. As a member of the European Democratic Union, the CDM maintained close contacts with other conservative and Christian democratic parties in Europe. In September 1996, it organized a meeting in Bratislava of representatives of such parties from the Czech Republic, Hungary, and Slovenia.

After the party's successful performance in the September 1998 elections, when it received the second largest amount of votes, the CDM helped form a coalition government, and Dzurinda became prime minister. In April 1999 a national congress changed the party's statute, which permitted CDM members within the SDC to possess dual membership. However, they were not able to apply for any elected functions in the CDM. Chairman Čarnogurský was re-elected for a new term in office. Čarnogurský preferred that the SDC return to a coalition of independent parties rather than a single organization, and the Movement's leadership continued to build the CDM's separate identity while supporting Dzurinda's cabinet.

A new Slovak Democratic and Christian Union (SDCU) was founded in November 2000. At its opening congress, Prime Minister Dzurinda was elected the Union's chairman. The SDCU was one of the proto-parties earmarked to succeed the Slovak Democratic Coalition (SDC), which was gradually disintegrating by the end of the year. Dzurinda remained chairman of the SDC. However, the SDCU was not slated to participate in the country's political life until the scheduled 2002 general elections, so as not to undermine the coalition government. Meanwhile, nine deputies of the CDM, a component of the SDC, decided to leave the Movement's parliamentary caucus and form a separate grouping.

Christian Social Union (CSU)
Kresťansko Socialná Unia (KSU)

The Christian Social Union (CSU) was established in 1992 as a result of the separation of the radical nationalist wing from the CDM. This organization emphasized the positive significance of the Slovak state during World War II, and it supported the concept of a social market economy with strong statist elements. The Union did not perform well in the September–October 1994 elections, gaining only 59,217 votes and 2.05% of the total, and thus failing to qualify for parliamentary seats. It subsequently disappeared from the political scene.

Agrarians

New Agrarian Party (NAP)
Nová Agrárna Strana (NAS)

A merger congress between the Agricultural Party of Slovakia (APS) *(Roľnícka Strana Slovenska, RSS)* and the Movement of Peasants (MP) *(Hnutie Poľnohospodárov, HP)* gave birth to the New Agrarian Party (NAP). Former APS Chairman Pavol Delinga became the NAP chairman, while Jozef Klein became honorary chairman. The congress delegates also elected a ten-member presidium and four deputy chairmen. According to documents approved by the delegates, the NAP's policies would be based on the APS's agrarian programs and activities aimed at protecting the interests of farmers, the food industry, forestry, water management workers, and the rural population at large. According to the NAP program, the party wanted to positively influence life in the Slovak countryside and engage in activities aimed at self-sufficiency in food and at making domestically produced food affordable to the widest possible cross-section of the population. Chairman Delinga made no secret of the fact that he favored NAP cooperation with the MDS and with Prime Minister Mečiar. The NAP was thereby accused by the democratic opposition of being a virtual MDS front organization. The party failed to gain any parliamentary seats in the two sets of general elections since Slovakia achieved independence.

Greens

Green Party of Slovakia (GPS)
Strana Zelených na Slovensku (SZS)

The declared aim of the Green Party of Slovakia (GPS) was to promote sustainable economic development while improving social and environmental conditions in the country. The GPS was critical of the government's territorial and administrative redistricting of the country, its regulation of the nongovernmental sector, universities, and cultural institutions, its amendments to the penal code, and the privatization process. Electoral support for the GPS throughout the decade remained slightly below the electoral threshold, and the party failed to gain parliamentary seats. However, in comparison with those of other political entities in the National Council, the activities of the GPS were poorly publicized in the media.

Slovakia's entry into NATO and the EU were considered foreign policy priorities for the GPS. As a member of the European Federation of Green Parties (EFGP), the GPS maintained regular contacts with other environmental parties. It was particularly close to the Green Party in Germany. In June 1996, a delegation of the GPS took part in the EFGP congress in Vienna, where its efforts resulted in the adoption of a resolution against the construction of nuclear power plants in Central-Eastern Europe. Jozef Pokorný was the GPS chairman.

During 1998, the Greens formed a leftist fraction in the Slovak Democratic Coalition with the Social Democrats. As a result of the SDC's success in the September 1998 elections, the Greens gained access to the decision-making process. However, their support according to opinion polls in 1999 still remained marginal.

Another environmentalist organization was the Slovak Green Alternative (SGA) *(Slovenská Zelená Alternatíva, SZA)*, which had little public influence.

Communists

Association of Slovak Workers (ASW)
Združenie Robotníkov Slovenska (ZRS)

The Association of Slovak Workers (ASW) was established in March 1994 and was chaired by Ján Lupták, a former communist "worker-hero." The party sought to appeal to blue-collar workers and other sectors of society negatively affected by the economic reforms. As a result of the failure of the PDL and SDPS to attract many traditional leftist voters, the ASW unexpectedly gained 7.34% of the votes and received 13 seats in the September–October 1994 elections. Party voters were mainly blue-collar workers who recalled the past with nostalgia and found it difficult to adapt to new conditions. Only 33% of ASW adherents believed that the Slovak economy prior to 1989 needed any significant changes, while 59% characterized the new property differences that emerged after 1989 as more unfair than the inequality that existed during the socialist period. ASW supporters remained susceptible to leftist demagoguery and to populist "solutions" to complex problems. Surveys indicated that the majority of ASW votes came from industrial workers and the unemployed, and the fewest came from businesspeople and students.

Despite the fact that the ASW had 13 deputies on the National Council after the 1994 elections, it was the coalition's weakest member in 1996–1997 because of its unprofessional leadership and various structural weaknesses in the party. The ASW violated its own election program by supporting government policies, and consequently lost many of its original supporters. Some critics believed that the ASW was secretly sponsored by the MDS to draw support away from other democratic leftist formations. Lupták himself was considered a demagogue and a curiosity factor for the media.

ASW leaders were sympathetic to the SNP position in the coalition crisis, but in the end chose to remain in the three-party agreement. Although critical of privatization in general, the ASW found ways to benefit from the coalition's privatization policies in practice. In October 1996, information came to light showing that the party had been demanding a so-called "privatization fee" for its support for the passage of selected privatization projects.

The ASW adopted positions identical to those of MDS and SNP with regard to President Kováč and the opposition parties. According to Ľupták, the ASW's greatest enemy was the PDL, which it described as an ostensibly left-wing party controlled by right-wing leaders who deceived Slovak workers. The ASW opposed Slovakia's membership in NATO and the EU and insisted on holding a referendum on Slovakia's entry into NATO in the spring of 1997. In the October 1998 elections, the Association performed poorly and did not pass the required parliamentary threshold; hence it went into political oblivion. One other notable quasi-communist grouping was the Real Social Democracy of Slovaks (RSDS) *(Reálna Sociálna Demokracia Slovákov, RSDS).*

Communist Party of Slovakia (CPS)
Komunistická Strana Slovenska (KSS)

Following the collapse of the communist system and the disintegration of the Czechoslovak Communist Party, several Marxist-Leninist fractions continued to operate with marginal public support and political influence. The most notable was the Communist Party of Slovakia (CPS). The second party congress, held in Bratislava on 29–30 June 1996, formulated as its strategic goal the building of a socialist society, support for small and medium-sized entrepreneurs, and the complete elimination of unemployment. The program, which also criticized the political system that had been built in the country according to West European and U.S. models, was approved unanimously by all 315 delegates.[38] The CPS had virtually no impact on political developments in the country, as much of its leftist rhetoric and program were either discredited or adopted by alternative parties.

Nationalists

Movement for a Democratic Slovakia (MDS)
Hnutie za Demokratické Slovensko (HZDS)

The Movement for a Democratic Slovakia (MDS) splintered off from the pro-federalist Public Against Violence (PAV) coalition on 5 March 1991, in response to a decision by the PAV leadership to remove Vladimír Mečiar as Slovakia's prime minister. Much of its membership was initially associated with the Trnava group within the PAV, which exhibited nationalist leanings in the fall of 1990. Led by Mečiar, the MDS depicted itself as a centrist political group with a measured approach toward market reform and the elimination of state economic control. The MDS program ranked Slovak national concerns above all other issues and adopted a much more pronounced nationalist stance than the PAV. It favored a loose confederal structure based on separate republican constitutions and a new inter-state agreement. The party asserted that a Slovak constitution had to be adopted before the conclusion of a state treaty between Slovakia and the Czech Republic.

By March 1992, Mečiar's party had become the strongest political force in Slovakia, with an estimated 40% support in public opinion polls. It increasingly spoke out against radical economic reforms, pointing to the growing unemployment rate in Slovakia. For the general elections of June 1992, the MDS program specified the following steps: the unconditional declaration of Slovak sovereignty, without consultation with Prague; the adoption of a Slovak constitution; and a referendum on the form of coexistence with the Czech Republic. It also called for a slower pace of privatization to guard against economic disruption and potential social unrest. In October 1991, party chairman Mečiar provocatively suggested a union between Slovakia and Moravia if the Slovak and Czech Republics failed to reach agreement on a state treaty.

In the June 1992 general elections, the MDS missed winning an absolute majority in the Slovak National Council by only two votes, gaining 74 out of 150 seats and capturing 37.26% of the popular vote. But opposition to Mečiar's party in the Council proved weak and splintered, especially as the PAV and the Christian Democratic Movement (CDM) fared poorly in the balloting. Support for the MDS was highest in the industrialized areas of western and central Slovakia, where Mečiar's pledge, contrary to Prague's policies, to continue Slovak arms manufacturing boosted his popularity. His evident anti-Hungarian stance and his support for restrictions on Magyar autonomy also had some appeal among the electorate.

Although public opinion polls indicated that the majority of Slovaks favored preserving the federation, they also demonstrated that Mečiar was by far the most popular Slovak politician. The substantial MDS mandate in the 1992 elections invigorated Mečiar's push toward Slovak independence. Following failed negotiations with Prague in the summer of 1992, a timetable for separation was mutually agreed upon in the fall. Slovakia formally attained its independence in January 1993 and Mečiar became the new prime minister. The MDS formed the core of the new government, capturing 11 of the 14 ministries; one minister was a member of the Slovak National Party and the other was unaffiliated. MDS member Michal Kováč was elected Slovak president by the National Council in February 1993.[39]

The political elite of the MDS included supporters of the reformist communist experiment in the years 1968–1969 belonging to the *Obroda* (Revival) club, former members of the Communist Party, and nationalists. The electoral program of MDS contained strong welfarist and statist elements to protect society from economic disruption. It also had an ambiguous approach toward NATO and EU membership and used the issue of integration and absorption to pose as the defender of Slovak independence and sovereignty. Observers believed that different factions within the MDS favored differing approaches to integration; while some supported a rapid approach, others articulated a neutralist stance.

In March 1994, premier Mečiar was ousted in a vote of no-confidence engineered by leaders displeased with the government's increasingly autocratic tendencies. An interim government was formed. Mečiar made a notable comeback in the September–October 1994 elections and went on to forge a coalition with the SNP and the ASW. With 61 deputies on the National Council, the MDS remained the strongest entity in parliament and in the governing coalition. Described by Augustín Marián Húska, its vice chairman, as a people's party of the center, the MDS was difficult to define ideologically. Rather than espousing a set of abstract political beliefs, the MDS promoted the concentration of political and economic power while rewarding its loyal supporters through the privatization process.

The September 1998 elections were technically won by the MDS, as the Movement gained the highest percentage of votes nationwide and 43 seats in parliament. However, the five-party opposition coalition obtained an overall majority. Mečiar was unable to stitch together a government, as none of the opposition parties were willing to cooperate with him. Although he declared that he had finished with politics, he was resurrected when the law on direct presidential elections was changed and he decided to run for president in spring 1999. He survived the first round of balloting, with 37% of the popular vote. But in the second round, on 29 May 1999, he lost to Rudolf Schuster, the mayor of Košice, with 42.82% as opposed to 57.18% of the vote for the latter. After the parliamentary and presidential elections, the MDS functioned as a standard opposition party critical of government policies and initiatives. It also petitioned for a referendum for new elections during 2000, seeking to exploit public disaffection with economic conditions. However, the MDS had a ceiling of support in the country, and few other parties were willing to collaborate with it.

Slovak National Party (SNP)
Slovenská Národná Strana (SNS)

Established in February 1990, the Slovak National Party (SNP) was initially headed by the controversial leader Víťazoslav Móric. Critics charged that the party was sponsored by the ex-communist apparatus and secret police agents who jumped on the bandwagon of nationalism and independence without any firm ideological commitments. They were linked neither with the civic activists nor with the more nationalistic CDM. The SNP finished third in the June 1990 Slovak National Council elections, winning 22 seats, and gaining 15 seats in the Federal Assembly. During 1990, public support for the SNP climbed significantly; by late summer, sympathy for the party had reportedly grown to 14%, and at the time of the general elections, to over 20%.

The party's popularity dropped substantially during the local elections of November 1990, when it rallied only 3% of the vote. This appeared to be the result of internal conflicts, competition with other nationalist groups, and because the Christian Democrats and some PAV deputies had taken aboard some nationalist issues. An inner crisis became evident in the SNP, propelled by a power struggle in which prominent leaders were accused of programmatic inconsistency and their inability to increase the party's share of the popular vote. The party performed poorly in many villages, where it had failed to build a viable network, and its pro-sovereignty position was skillfully espoused by several competing forces. Following a party shake-up, the former trade union leader Jozef Prokeš became the SNP's new chairman, and the party became increasingly supportive of Mečiar's MDS when the latter dropped its pro-federalist position.

The SNP displayed its willingness to capitalize on popular frustrations by organizing street rallies and other protest actions in support of outright independence and against alleged Czech domination and Hungarian subversion. For instance, it helped organize some of the first anti-Magyar demonstrations in Bratislava and Nové Zámky in February 1990. It also sought to revitalize Slovak cultural traditions and contended that all nationalities in the republic had to respect Slovakia's national and state sovereignty, in accordance with the rules of international law. The SNP underscored the primacy of "Slovak national interests" and the position of Slovaks as a "state-forming nation." It fully supported the March 1991 Declaration of Slovak Sovereignty, formulated by several nationalist groups. This declaration demanded that Slovak laws take precedence over those of the federation.

The party advocated short-term solutions to various pressing issues, rather than adhering to a consistent political philosophy, and kept its attention fixed on the goal of complete Slovak independence. In the June 1992 general elections, the SNP performance was modest, obtaining 7.93% of the total vote and 15 Slovak National Council seats. Its center of support was in Bratislava, where it gained 17% of the ballots, and in southern and western counties where anti-Hungarian sentiments remained pronounced. Despite its poor showing, the SNP gained one ministry in Slovakia's first independent government in coalition with the MDS. In the summer of 1993, talks were initiated between the SNP and MDS to form a new coalition government, potentially giving the nationalists a bigger profile in the administration.[40]

Until 1994, the SNP constituted the fourth largest political formation in the Slovak parliament. Party leaders made strenuous efforts to attract private businesspeople, and their new economic program emphasized support for private economic activity but with emphasis on social security. SNP activists sought to recruit members of the "industrial lobby" or directors of big industrial and weapons factories. In February 1994, Ján

Slota, the controversial mayor of the central Slovak city of Žilina, became the SNP chairman. Following his appointment, six parliamentarians left to form the moderate National Democratic Party, which merged into the Democratic Union (DU).

In the September–October 1994 elections, the SNP received 5.4% of the votes and nine parliamentary seats. When the party joined the coalition government with the MDS, some moderate members left, as they opposed the MDS policy of confrontation. Radical nationalist tendencies gained prominence in the SNP, reflected in the election of new party leaders as well as in the rhetoric of their election campaigns. The SNP electorate consisted primarily of industrial workers, pensioners, and the unemployed. Authoritarian inclinations were characteristic among many SNP voters, who preferred "national unity" over democracy and pluralism.

The party described itself as a "conservative party with pro-national attitudes." Its traditional themes included defending Slovak national interests, particularly with respect to the Hungarian question. It also became a strong advocate of the death penalty. The SNP used its presence in the governing coalition to secure certain policy initiatives. For example, as a condition of its assent to the long-postponed ratification of the Slovak-Hungarian Treaty, the SNP demanded that parliament amend the penal code and pass the law on the new territorial-administrative division and a law on state of emergency.

The coalition crisis of June 1996 centered on SNP objections to the management staff dismissals at the Slovak Insurance Company, imposed by the MDS. But an offer by the opposition PDL to enter into a minority government with the MDS pushed the SNP back into the coalition. The SNP opposed changing the electoral system from a proportional to a majority system. It proposed, however, to implement proportional voting in elections for local governments, to correct what it considered the underrepresentation of Slovaks in local councils in southern Slovakia.

SNP activists also held radical views on how to "solve" the Romani question—through deportation or the building of "reservations." Roma organizations initiated a petition demanding that SNP Chairman Ján Slota lose his parliamentary immunity because of his anti-Romani statements. The SNP maintained contacts with ultranationalists in Western Europe, and in September 1997, Jean-Marie Le Pen (the French anti-immigrant leader) visited Slovakia at the party's invitation. The SNP also strongly opposed NATO membership and regularly criticized NATO representatives for their alleged interference in Slovakia's domestic affairs. After the September 1998 elections, the SNP went into opposition, having gained 15 mandates. The party established an expert group that sought to remake the SNP's image among voters as a reformist and pragmatic organization, and selected a more moderate chairperson, Anna Malíková, to replace Slota. The SNP evidently wanted to become a party that "stabilizes" Slovak society and is in favor of reform and modernization.

Slovak Motherland (SM)
Matica Slovenská (MS)

This national-cultural association was originally established in 1863, during the period of Hungarian occupation, to promote and defend Slovak identity. It was disbanded by the Hungarian authorities in 1875 but resuscitated during the first Czechoslovak Republic. Throughout the most repressive Stalinist years (1948–1968) the Slovak Motherland (SM) was suppressed, but it was once more reinstated during the 1968 Prague Spring and again in the wake of the 1989 "Velvet Revolution." The SM held annual national gatherings and significantly expanded its membership, program, activities, and influence. Its first post-communist president was Jozef Markus, who was elected in August 1990 by the SM general assembly. The SM issued a major national program calling for outright Slovak statehood and independence.

By mid-1992, it claimed to have nearly 400 local branches, a membership of some 140,000, over 600,000 sympathizers, and cells in the Czech Republic, Poland, and the West. The SM was reported to have extensive influence among the nationalist-minded Slovak intelligentsia, placing enormous emphasis on strengthening Slovak culture and education; it also established extensive publishing ventures. The SM program focused on alleged "deformations" in Slovak education caused by decades of communist and Czech influences. It underscored that it would strive to rebuild the educational system and cultural life in a "national spirit" and cooperate closely with all relevant government organs.

Although the movement's program declared that it would protect the rights of all minorities, it claimed above all to work against the "denationalization" of Slovaks, and other anti-Slovak phenomena, clearly alluding to demands by Hungarians for more extensive collective rights. SM leaders strongly supported a version of the language law that would make Slovak the exclusive language in the republic in all administrative affairs and public communications.

The SM issued strong statements on the position of Slovaks in the southern part of the country, claiming that Slovak language, culture, religious services, and national identity were dying out in the region as a result of mounting Hungarian discrimination. It asserted that Hungarian political parties were creating an atmosphere of "national, cultural, and existential insecurity" for Slovaks in mixed population areas. The SM protested against all efforts at local autonomy that allegedly violated the "cultural and territorial integrity" of the Slovak republic. It proposed to parliament that the law on local self-government needed to be amended to prevent domination of Slovaks by the Hungarian minority. (Ethnic Slovaks evidently had to be ensconced in all leading positions in public administration to "eliminate opportunities for Hungarian discrimination.") Should tensions between Magyars and Slovaks increase, the Slovak Motherland seemed ready to provide the ideological underpinnings for any anti-minority measures.[41]

Other nationalist cultural organizations also became active in the 1990s, including the Štúr Society led by Vladimír Repka, which published one of the more xenophobic newspapers, *Nový Slovák* (New Slovak).

Slovak Christian Democratic Party (SCDP)
Slovenská Kresťanskodemokratická Strana (SKDS)

The Slovak Christian Democratic Party (SCDP) emerged as an overtly nationalist wing of the Christian Democratic Movement (CDM). It formally seceded in March 1992, as its leaders were dissatisfied with the CDM's stance on Slovak independence. It was led by Ján Klepáč, the deputy chairman of the Slovak National Council. Eleven of the thirty-one deputies representing the CDM in the Slovak National Council decided to join Klepáč, together with five of the 25 deputies in the Federal Assembly. Four members of the Slovak government also defected to Klepáč's party. The SCDP's economic platform opposed the methods and consequences of privatization and instead advocated a "social market economy" with pronounced state intervention. Most members of the former Economic Club of the CDM joined Klepáč's party, including the Club's most prominent member, Forestry Minister Vilém Oberhauser. But aside from a strong emphasis on Slovak sovereignty, the SCDP platform remained vague. Potentially an ally of Mečiar's MDS, the SCDP attracted only 3% of the popular vote during the June 1992 elections. Its failure to garner sufficient votes for parliamentary seats was blamed by party leaders on the large number of contenders who had adopted populist and nationalist orientations. The party subsequently faded from the political scene.

Movement for an Independent Slovakia (MIS)
Hnutie za Nezávislé Slovensko (HNS)

Established in July 1990 by Vojtech Vitkovský, the Movement for an Independent Slovakia (MIS) became a militant nationalist organization committed to full Slovak independence. It consistently voiced discontent with the proposed constitutional and political solutions to Slovak sovereignty, maintaining that conditions were ripe for the assertion of Slovak statehood. The MIS considered absolute Slovak independence the only recipe for the country's development. The leadership also contended that coexistence with minority ethnic groups was guaranteed by "Slovak good will" and that whenever this was violated it was primarily the consequence of minority activities and foreign subversion. The MIS remained in favor of close economic cooperation with the Czech Republic after Slovak-Czech relations were stabilized and equalized by the creation of two independent states. The party remained fairly small, although its ultranationalist and anti-minority sentiments gave it appeal.[42]

Slovak National Democratic Movement (SNDM)
Slovenské Národné Demokratické Hnutie (SNDH)

The Slovak National Democratic Movement (SNDM) was founded in Bratislava in July 1990, on the initiative of members of the nationalist cultural grouping the Štúr Society and of the Independent Party of Slovaks. The Movement was led by Chairman Peter Brnák, elected in January 1991 as an independent deputy to the Slovak National Council. The SNDM stressed that Slovak "national unity" was the most important step toward the creation of an independent Slovakia. It presupposed that the Slovak language would become the only official language of the future Slovak state. Its goal was to maintain the "well-being" of Slovaks during the transformation of the republic. It called for full Slovak sovereignty and the speedy adoption of a Slovak constitution. Representatives of the SNDM displayed a marked anti-Hungarian position. For example, during July 1991, they claimed that weapons were being smuggled to "Magyar extremists" in southern Slovakia, and they called on Slovaks to be vigilant and prepared for violent confrontations. Like other ultra-nationalist groupings, the Movement viewed specific political and economic programs as less important than the achievement of national independence.[43]

Several other smaller Slovak nationalist and pro-independence organizations were formed during the 1990s, including the Party of Freedom—Party of National Unity (PF-PNU) *(Strana Slobody—Strana Národnej Jednoty, SS-SNJ),* Movement for a Free Slovakia, the Party for National Prosperity, the Party of Slovak Unity, the Slovak Heritage Foundation, the National Salvation Movement, the National Liberal Party, the Freedom Party (FP) *(Strana Slobody, SS),* the Association for the Republic (AR) *(Asociácia pre Republiku, AR),* the Republican Party (RP) *(Republikánska Strana, RS),* and the Slovak People's Party, which styled itself as a successor to Anton Hlinka's pre–World War II nationalist party.[44] All focused on questions of independence and had pronounced anti-Czech and anti-Hungarian tendencies.[45]

Ethnic Minority and Religious Parties

Party of the Hungarian Coalition (PHC)
Strana Maďarskej Koalície (SMK)

The Party of the Hungarian Coalition (PHC) was formed by the country's three Hungarian parties, which cooperated in a coalition in 1994 to support the Moravčík government and subsequently continued their cooperation.[46] The PHC ranked third in the 1994 parliamentary elections. It collected 10.18% of the votes and received 17 seats in parliament. The coalition included three different political parties: the Hungarian Civic Party (HCP), based on civic principles; the Hungarian Christian Democratic Movement (HCDM), which adhered to the principles of conservatism; and the liberal-conservative Coexistence

(Együttelés). The slogan of the coalition, "Not a single Hungarian vote in vain," implied a nationalist approach. In their election campaign, the PHC emphasized the protection of the rights of the Hungarian minority and demanded the acceptance of the "Komárno" documents as well as a law on the protection of the national minorities. The "Komárno" documents recommended a territorial reorganization of Slovakia on the basis of ethnic regions—a proposal that was unanimously rejected by practically all Slovak political parties.

The PHC remained a stable coalition despite the divergence of its voters and leadership. Of the Coalition's 17 deputies, 9 were from Coexistence, 7 from HCDM, and one from the HCP. Most PHC parliamentarians abstained from voting on the ratification of the Slovak-Hungarian Basic Treaty in March 1996 because of the inclusion of a declaration with no legal significance by the MDS ruling coalition. All three parties strongly opposed amendments to the penal code proposed by the SNP as well as the law on the Territorial Administrative Division of the Slovak Republic, which they claimed did not account for the particular needs of the ethnically mixed territories and which contradicted the European Charter of Self-Government.

Representatives of the HCP rejected the irredentist label forced upon them by representatives of the ruling coalition, and signed a common declaration reaffirming their loyalty to the Slovak Republic. László Nagy, chairman of the HCP, promised not to use the confrontational term "autonomy," and Béla Bugár, HCDM chairman, stated that his movement did not support territorial autonomy. On the other hand, Miklós Duray, chairman of Coexistence, declared that until a solution to minority problems could be implemented according to the self-government principle, some form of territorial autonomy could not be ruled out.

In an effort to rectify the situation that arose in 1995 by the passage of the law on the state language, which excluded the use of minority languages in official business, representatives of the PHC proposed a law clarifying minority language rights. The Coalition also complained that government policies in education, culture, and the media were inconsistent with provisions of the Slovak-Hungarian Basic Treaty. An election law amendment pressured the three parties to merge into a single organization in June 1998. However, the three parties continued to maintain their separate platforms within the coalition which won 15 seats in the September 1998 elections. The PHC faced disputes with its government partners during 2000, over plans for a administrative reorganization of the country that would subdivide the Hungarian population along the Danube into several newly formed regions.

Coexistence (C)
Spolužitie (S)

Coexistence (C), the former Forum of Hungarians in Czechoslovakia, was founded in February 1990 by the prominent dissident and national rights activist Miklós Duray. Its immediate forerunner was the Committee for the Pro-

tection of Hungarian Minority Rights (Legal Defense Community) in Czechoslovakia, an organization established in the late 1970s to campaign for Magyar
causes under the communist regime. Coexistence was the third Hungarian
party to emerge after the "Velvet Revolution," following the Independent
Hungarian Initiative (IHI) and the Hungarian Christian Democratic Movement (HCDM). Within a few months, it claimed a membership of some 40,000
people. It declared itself free of any particular ideology and pledged to represent the interests of all national minorities in Czechoslovakia. Its membership included some Poles, Germans, Ukrainians, and Ruthenians. Coexistence
aimed to deal with all problems faced by the country's minorities and called
for firm legal safeguards that would protect their interests. For instance, it
proposed the creation of a Ministry of Nationalities in the federal government, and it opposed high percentage thresholds for gaining seats in the Federal Assembly, as this excluded minority parties from parliament.

Coexistence differed from other Hungarian parties in its approach toward
minority rights. Whereas the IHI believed that such campaigns should not
take precedence over the broader process of democratization in the initial
post-communist phase, Coexistence viewed the nationality question as re-
solvable alongside the democratization program. As a result, it was viewed as
radical and nationalist even by some pro-federalist Slovaks. With the rise of
anti-Hungarian sentiment among several Slovak nationalist parties, Coexistence became a target for frequent political and media attacks and was accused
of supporting revisionist territorial demands emanating from Budapest. Duray
consistently rejected such interpretations of its policies, viewing them as a
smokescreen for denying various rights to the Magyar community. Coexistence leaders believed that the Slovak authorities viewed Hungarian culture as
"imported" and thereby unworthy of support and protection.

Coexistence consistently supported the federal system as the best environment for protecting minority rights, as opposed to outright Slovak independence. Its leaders felt that none of the Slovak parties had clear minorities'
policies with which the Hungarians could remain comfortable. Coexistence
claimed to understand Slovakia's national aspirations but voiced concern that
an independent Slovak state would become intolerant toward its minorities.
With the attainment of Slovak statehood, Coexistence envisioned the creation of regional self-governing bodies and substantial decentralization of the
state administration. Its program underscored "collective rights" for
Czechoslovakia's minorities, including cultural autonomy for all ethnic groups
and political autonomy in regions containing compact Magyar communities,
particularly in southern Slovakia. Its economic goals stressed privatization,
private ownership, and the transformation of collectives into private farms.

Coexistence formed a coalition with the HCDM for the elections of June
1990. It won 12 seats in the Federal Assembly and 14 seats in the Slovak
National Council, capturing over 8% of the total vote and nearly 80% of the
ethnic Magyar vote. However, during the November 1990 local elections, it

only secured 6.25% of the ballot, although performing reasonably well in counties containing large Hungarian populations. For example, it managed to elect 105 mayors, while other Hungarian parties only gained 62 mayorships.

Coexistence objected to the package of language laws introduced by Bratislava in October 1990, which ensured that Slovak was the sole official language even in minority areas, with the use of Hungarian limited to districts containing 20% or more Magyar inhabitants. Instead, it proposed legislation on the public use of minority languages in all areas with significant minority populations. However, Magyar leaders pointed out that at least the new law nullified the variant proposed by the Slovak National Party, which would have made Slovak the exclusive language in all districts, regardless of minority proportions.

In mid-July 1991, Coexistence, together with the HCDM, objected to the newly introduced land law at a joint session of the Czechoslovak Federal Assembly. The law purportedly discriminated against some minorities: for example, Hungarians were only entitled to 50 hectares of private land, while members of other nationalities could receive as much as 250 hectares. Coexistence protested against the Slovak government's decision in the summer of 1991 to cut subsidies to ethnic minority cultural organizations. It also lodged complaints over the federal law on rehabilitation that set February 1948 (when the communists seized power) as the retroactive limit for material compensation to unjustly dispossessed individuals. Magyars had lost much of their property between 1945 and 1948, under pressure from local communists and the Soviet occupation forces.

Coexistence issued a series of legal and political proposals, including a draft supplement to the new federal constitution regarding minority rights, its own draft language law for Slovakia, and a comprehensive proposal on ways to improve the position of minorities. It requested the creation of a constitutional committee of representatives of all national minorities, a body that would draft a separate paragraph in the new constitution, on the rights of national minorities. The party also called for the expansion of Hungarian-language educational and media activities, including the establishment of a Hungarian university in the southern city of Komárno.

Coexistence feared that the achievement of Slovak statehood would prove unfavorable for minority groups. It also expressed strong apprehensions that economic deterioration could exacerbate social and ethnic unrest, for which Magyars would invariably be blamed. For the June 1992 elections to the Slovak National Council, the party formed a coalition with the Hungarian Christian Democratic Movement; the Hungarian People's Party joined the coalition in the campaign for seats in the Federal Assembly. In its election campaign, the coalition called for the right of all minorities to their own schools, with instruction in their mother tongue from elementary to university levels; for equitable political representation at the republican and federal levels; for the right to use their mother tongue at all tiers of public administration in districts where minorities formed a large proportion of the population; and for the right to have their own churches. The coalition won 14 out of 150 seats on the Slovak National Council, nine of which went to Coexistence, garnering 7.42% of the popular vote. It also elected twelve deputies to the Federal Assembly, eight of whom represented Coexistence.

At its fourth congress in Komárno, in February 1993, Coexistence delegates condemned repressive government policies and called for "political and economic self-administration" for the Hungarian areas of southern Slovakia. Delegates drafted a document on the "Principles of Regional Self-Government and Personal Autonomy," in which the notion of "regional self-rule" was elaborated. Three kinds of areas were defined: "majority areas," in which Magyars formed over 50% of the population; "minority areas," where they formed between 10% and 50%; and "sporadic areas," where they totaled less than 10%. In the former, Hungarians should be able to establish local governments linked together in a Hungarian "ethno-region." Such proposals were interpreted by Slovak politicians as precursors of demands for territorial autonomy based on ethnic principles, which could lead to the separation of Hungarian-majority municipalities from southern Slovakia.[47]

Coexistence entered the PHC prior to the September 1998 general elections and participated in its decisionmaking. Although many aspects of its program were shared by other Magyar parties, some Hungarian leaders tended to distance themselves from its pronouncements on territorial autonomy. They viewed these as unnecessarily provocative and potentially destructive of the coalition administration.

Social and Democratic Union of Hungarians in Slovakia (SDUHS)
Sociálny a Demokratický Zväz Maďarov na Slovensku (SDZMS)

This organization, founded in April 1993 and formerly known as *Csemadok* (Democratic Union of Hungarians in Czechoslovakia), was led by Viktór Bauer. Originally formed in November 1949 as the Cultural Association of Hungarian Working People in Czechoslovakia, *Csemadok* was the sole Hungarian organization in Slovakia approved by the communist government. The party functioned in cooperation with the regime, as the communists did not allow ethnic minorities to form independent political groups. During its four decades of existence, the organization attracted the largest membership of all Hungarian groups in Slovakia. However, when the organization attempted to move into the political arena after the 1968 Prague Spring, it was excluded from Czechoslovakia's "normalized" National Front in 1971. After December 1989, it attempted to transform itself into an umbrella political organization representing the interests of the Hungarian minority in Czechoslovakia's new political system. Reflecting this changing profile, *Csemadok*'s general assembly voted at its March 1990 extraordinary session to omit the designation "cultural" from its name and to add the appellation "democratic."

The SDUHS gave its support to the Coexistence–Hungarian Christian

Democratic Movement coalition in the June 1990 general elections and became an outspoken proponent of minority rights. It sought to prevent the political splintering of the Hungarian community, arguing that factionalism would deprive the minority of representation in public life commensurate with its numeric strength. Its platform displayed similarities to that of Coexistence, and it unequivocally supported the Czechoslovak federal system as the best solution for guaranteeing minority rights. It called for the creation of a Ministry of Nationalities at the federal level, and vehemently protested the 1990 Slovak language law that made Slovak the republic's exclusive official language. *Csemadok*'s reputation remained tarnished because of its links with the previous regime. After 1989, its membership dropped from some 100,000 to 80,000, although it still claimed to possess the largest membership of all Hungarian groups in Slovakia. Following moves toward Slovak independence, the SDUHS contended that the most important task for ethnic Hungarian parties was to work with Slovak politicians who supported the safeguarding of minority rights. Its leaders believed that an independent Slovakia was unlikely to tolerate any form of political or territorial autonomy for the Magyar minority. The SDUHS also severely criticized the Slovak state media for their belligerent anti-Hungarian tone.[48]

Hungarian Christian Democratic Movement (HCDM)
Maďarské Kresťansko Demokratické Hnutie (MKDH)

Founded in March 1990 and headed by President Kálmán Jánics, the Hungarian Christian Democratic Movement (HCDM) was the second Magyar political group to emerge in the wake of the democratic changes. The party grew out of the Hungarian Christian Democratic clubs in Slovakia but was not welcomed by the Slovak Christian Democrats. The HCDM became the second most significant Magyar movement in the republic, with regard to the number of its local chapters and local representatives. Shortly after its creation, the movement experienced internal ideological and personality disputes among its estimated 50,000 members. This resulted in the April 1991 expulsion of its four Federal Assembly deputies, who had accused the, HCDM leadership, headed by chairman Béla Bugár, of being undemocratic and of distancing itself from Coexistence. These four deputies joined the Hungarian People's Party.

The HCDM stood as a coalition partner with Coexistence during the June 1992 election campaign for seats in the Slovak National Council, and its representatives obtained five seats in Bratislava. The coalition was joined by the Hungarian People's Party in competing for seats in the Federal Assembly. Although it partially cooperated with the Slovak Christian Democratic Movement, the HCDM platform became almost identical to that of Coexistence, including its stance toward Slovak independence. Nevertheless, it was considered to have a more moderate and conciliatory stance on the ethnic question.

After the general elections of June 1992, the party demanded educational, cultural, and partial territorial autonomy for its compatriots in southern Slovakia. It declared that if the rights of ethnic minorities were not guaranteed by the independent state, the party would consider intervening in the European parliament against Slovak independence and would be compelled to ask the Hungarian government for assistance from international organizations.[49] The HCDM subsequently became one of the three parties that formed a Hungarian coalition for the September 1998 general elections, which together gained 15 parliamentary seats. The Hungarian coalition then entered the Slovak government together with the Slovak Democratic Coalition (SDC).

Hungarian Civic Party (HCP)
Madǎrská Občianska Strana (MOS)

The Hungarian Civic Party (HCP) emerged from the Independent Hungarian Initiative (IHI) in January 1992. The original IHI was established in November 1989 and was chaired by László Nagy. Its most prominent leaders were longtime dissidents Lajos Grendel, Kálmán Balla, and Károly Tóth. Similarly to Coexistence, the IHI regarded Duray's Committee for the Protection of Hungarian Minority Rights in Czechoslovakia as its forerunner. Various professionals gathered in the organization, including writers, artists, teachers, and technical intellectuals. The IHI was among the first groups to pledge support for the Civic Forum in Prague and was also represented in the national coordination plans of the Public Against Violence. It published its "declaration of principles" in November 1989, describing itself primarily as a "civic initiative." It was viewed as a liberal-rightist organization focusing on individual rather than collective rights.

While Coexistence maintained that nationality problems should be solved simultaneously with political democratization, the IHI/HCP believed that a stable democracy must first be established before the minorities could fully gain their group rights. It contended that the fast pace at which Coexistence demanded the institutionalization of minority rights would unnecessarily antagonize Slovak leaders. The HCP supported Slovak self-determination but feared that a breakup of the federation would have negative consequences for ethnic minorities. It rejected charges leveled by Coexistence activists that it had compromised too often with Slovak organizations. The HCP's stated goal was minority rights within a democratic framework, but it did not support territorial autonomy for the Magyar community.

In December 1989, the IHI proposed that the new federal government should include a minister of nationality affairs, and nominated Duray for the position. The proposal was vetoed by the newly appointed Czechoslovak Prime Minister Marián Calfa, who argued that such a position was not envisioned in the constitution and that if a Magyar minister was appointed, then every minority would demand a cabinet seat. In the June 1990 elections, the party ran on the PAV ticket and won a total of six seats in the republican assembly. In

February 1991, the IHI became a member of the three-party Slovak coalition government, in which it had a parliamentary vice chairman, László Nagy, and a deputy prime minister, Gábor Zászlós, after June 1991. By 1992, the party claimed to have 102 local groups and a 30-member leadership. László Nagy was elected party chairman and Károly Tóth, former chairperson of the Slovak National Council, became the secretary-general.

While Coexistence accused the IHI/HCP of collaborating with Slovak parties, its leaders maintained that it was more effective to work inside the government and have the opportunity to influence policy than to stand outside, in permanent opposition. The party remained open to compromise with various Hungarian political and cultural organizations and established its own "minority council." In early 1991, the HCP was denied a partnership in the Coexistence-HCDM minority coalition unless it withdrew from the Slovak government and reevaluated its participation in drafting legislation that was deemed harmful to Magyar interests. The HCP refused, and subsequently failed to find another coalition partner. The PAV also denied the HCP a coalition partnership, as it had lost an estimated 20,000 Slovak votes in June 1990 by allowing the former IHI to run candidates on its election lists. Thus, the HCP was forced to run alone in the second multiparty election, in June 1992, and failed to obtain parliamentary seats.[50] The IHI/HCP entered the three-party Hungarian coalition for the September 1998 general elections. The coalition gained 15 parliamentary seats and entered the Slovak government with the Slovak Democratic Coalition (SDC).

Hungarian People's Party (HPP)
Madărská Ľudová Strana (MLS)

The Hungarian People's Party (HPP) was established in December 1991 and became the first Hungarian political party, as distinct from a political movement, to officially register. It was led by Chairman Gyula Popély, a historian and former member of Coexistence, and Vice Chairman Ferenc Szocs, one of the four Federal Assembly deputies expelled from the HCDM. The HPP advocated Christian moral values, national reconciliation, an "environmentally secure" social market economy, and universal human rights. The HPP was the only Hungarian party asserting that Slovak independence would have a positive impact on the Magyar minority. The party also maintained that a comprehensive law guaranteeing minority rights should become part of the new Slovak constitution.

In July 1991, Popély criticized the poor organizational efforts among Magyar political movements as the main reason for their inability to effectively defend minority interests in the Slovak parliament. The HCDM subsequently accused the HPP of attempting to divide the Hungarian community. The party joined a coalition with Coexistence and the HCDM during the June 1992 elections for seats in the Federal Assembly. But it could not enter this coalition for balloting to the Slovak National Council, because it could not gather the 10,000 signatures required under the electoral law. It could, however, include its candidates on the Coexistence-HCDM candidate lists.

Other significant Hungarian organizations included the Association of Hungarian Students, the Federation of Hungarian Teachers, the Association of Hungarian Writers, and the Cultural Association of Magyars.

Union of Ukrainians and Ruthenians in Czechoslovakia (UURC)
Zväz Ukrajincov a Rusínov v Česko-Slovensku (ZURCS)

The Union of Ukrainians and Ruthenians in Czechoslovakia (UURC) changed its name from the Cultural Association of Ukrainian Workers soon after the November 1989 revolution. It supported the preservation of a federal Czechoslovak state and opposed efforts by various Slovak parties to establish an independent republic. It feared that in such an eventuality, the rights of various minorities would be denied while Prague would lack the leverage to protect their distinct interests. Three deputies representing the Ruthenian-Ukrainian nationality were elected to the Slovak National Council in the June 1992 balloting.

Ruthenian Revival (RR)
Rusínska Obroda (RO)

This social and cultural organization considers the Ukrainian-Ruthenian population in Slovakia a separate ethnolinguistic group. It set out to cultivate Ruthenian cultural and linguistic traditions and help develop a distinct self-identity among the population. Activists asserted that the process of Slovakization and Ukrainianization, visible since the close of World War II, needed to be reversed. Ruthenian Revival (RR) organized the First World Congress of Ruthenians in eastern Slovakia in March 1991, during which participants pressed for the full recognition and registration of Ruthenian cultural, social, and educational organizations.

In May 1993, another Ruthenian grouping, the Ruthenian Association of Subcarpathia (RAS), based in neighboring Ukraine, set up a "provisional government" in preparation for a referendum on Ruthenian independence and eventual unification with Slovakia. Many of the Ruthenian Association officials reportedly resided in Slovakia, but there was little appetite for any border changes or Ruthenian independence among the majority of the population.[51]

Democratic Union of Roma in Slovakia (DURS)
Demokratický Zväz Rómov na Slovensku (DZRS)

The Democratic Union of Roma in Slovakia (DURS) sought to ensure that the Roma were recognized as members of a distinct ethnic group, with all the rights to which minorities were entitled, and that this recognition is enshrined in the Czechoslovak constitution. The DURS subsequently united with the Democratic Association of Roma (DAR) to prevent unnecessary fragmentation and to contest elections to the Federal Assembly, the Slovak National Council, and local government organs. Romani organizations subsequently failed to gain legislative representation at the republican level. Leaders of various Romani bodies appealed to Slovak leaders to promote the cultural and social development of Gypsy communities, claiming that the population was ignored by the government. Some Roma also called for OSCE observers to be dispatched to Slovakia to investigate the observance of human rights.[52] Although Slovakia has a large Roma population, deep divisions and disputes over leadership have seriously undermined the Romani influence on the political process.

Party for Romani Integration (PRI)
Strana za Rómsku Integráciu (SRI)

Founded in Slovakia in February 1990, the Party for Romani Integration (PRI) was headed by Chairman Koloman Gunár. The party's platform underscored the improvement of living conditions for the Roma throughout Czechoslovakia. It differed from the DURS in that it did not seek the recognition of Roma as a distinct national minority. It regarded the Roma as an ethnic group that was part of the larger Slovak nation. It campaigned to increase the percentage of Romani children attending school and to solve the community's severe housing problems. The PRI formed the League of Romani Unity (LRU) in February 1991 in order to unite and coordinate the activities of all the divergent Romani organizations.[53]

Representatives of various Romani organizations also formed a Romani National Congress (RNC) for the June 1992 general elections. Its leaders lodged a strong protest against the Prague-based Romani Civic Initiative Party and other Gypsy groups that they depicted as extreme right-wing organizations no longer representing the true interests of Roma. Since it considered that basic human rights and minority freedoms were abused in Slovakia, the Romani Congress intended to form a united opposition and build a "nationalities institution" enabling each minority to solve its specific problems. Other significant Romani organizations in Slovakia included the Roma Civic Initiative (RCI) (Rómska Občianska Iniciatíva, ROI), established in 1989 and chaired by E. Scuka; the Party of Gypsies; the Movement of Involved Gypsies; the Democratic Association of Roma; and the Association of Romani Intelligentsia.[54]

Slovakia's smaller minorities also established their own cultural and social organizations, including the Croatian Cultural Union in Slovakia, the Independent Organizations of Romanians, and the Carpatho-German Association in Slovakia.

POLITICAL DATA

Name of State: Slovak Republic *(Slovenska Republika)*
Form of Government: Parliamentary democracy
Structure of Legislature: Unicameral National Council of the Slovak Re-public *(Národná Rada Slovenskej Republiky)*, 150 seats and four-year terms
Size of Territory: 18,917 square miles
Size of Population: 5,392,982 (1998 estimate); 5,396,193 (1999 estimate)

Composition of Population (1991):

Ethnic Group	Number	% of Population
Slovaks	4,511,679	85.63
Hungarians	566,741	10.76
Roma (Gypsies)	80,627	1.53
Czechs	53,422	1.01
Ruthenians	16,937	0.32
Ukrainians	13,847	0.26
Germans	5,629	0.11
Moravians	3,888	0.07
Poles	2,969	0.06
Others	13,196	0.25
Total minorities	757,256	14.37
Total population	5,268,935	100.00

Sources: From Peter Procházka, "Position of National Minorities in the Slovak Republic," and "The Hungarian Minority in Slovakia and the Autonomy Issue," in *International Issues: A Revue of Foreign Policy, Law, Economics, and Culture,* Vol. 1, No. 3, November 1992, Bratislava, Ministry of Foreign Affairs. See also *CIA World Factbook* and *Transitions On-line Country Reports,* Slovakia.

ELECTION RESULTS

Presidential Election, 15 and 29 May 1999

First Round, 15 May 1999

Turnout: 73.89%

Candidate	Votes	% of Vote
Rudolf Schuster	1,396,950	47.48
Vladimír Mečiar	1,097,956	37.31
Magda Vášaryová	194,635	6.61
Ivan Mjartan	105,903	3.61
Ján Slota	73,836	2.50
Boris Zala	29,697	1.00

Juraj Švec	24,077	0.82
Juraj Lazarčík	15,386	0.52
Ján Demikat	4,537	0.15
Total	2,942,977	100.00

Second Round, 29 May 1999

Turnout: 75.45%

Candidate	Votes	% of Vote
Rudolf Schuster	1,727,481	57.18
Vladimír Mečiar	1,293,624	42.82
Total	3,021,105	100.00

Source: http://volby.statistics.sk/volby99/results/tab6.asp.

Presidential Election (Indirect), 15 February 1993

Candidate	Votes	% of Vote
Michal Kováč	106	72.6
Against	20	—
Abstained	19	—
Invalid	1	—
Total	146	100.0

Source: Radio Free Europe/Radio Liberty, archived at http://www.friends-partners.org.

Parliamentary Elections, 25–26 September 1998

Turnout: 84.15%

Party/Coalition	Votes	% of Vote	Seats
Movement for a Democratic Slovakia	907,103	27.00	43
Slovak Democratic Coalition	884,497	26.33	42
Party of the Democratic Left	492,507	14.66	23
Party of the Hungarian Coalition	306,623	9.12	15
Slovak National Party	304,839	9.07	14
Party of Civic Understanding	269,343	8.01	13
Communist Party of Slovakia	94,015	2.79	—
Association of Slovak Workers	43,809	1.30	—
Other parties	56,419	1.72	—
Total	3,359,155	100.00	150

Source: http://www2.essex.ac.uk/elect/eledter/slovakia_er_nl.htm.

Parliamentary Elections, 30 September–1 October 1994

Turnout: 75.65%

Party/Coalition	Votes	% of Vote	Seats
Movement for a Democratic Slovakia	1,005,488	34.97	61
Common Choice (PDL, SDPS, AMSR, GPS)	299,496	10.42	18
Hungarian Coalition	292,936	10.19	17
Christian Democratic Movement	289,987	10.08	17
Democratic Union	246,444	8.57	15
Association of Slovak Workers	211,321	7.35	13
Slovak National Party	155,359	5.40	9
Democratic Party	98,555	3.43	—
Communist Party of Slovakia	78,419	2.72	—
Christian Social Union	59,217	2.06	—
New Slovakia Movement	38,369	1.33	—
Party Against Corruption	37,929	1.31	—
Movement for a Prosperous Czechia and Slovakia	30,292	1.05	—
Romani Civic Initiative	19,542	0.68	—
Social Democracy	7,121	0.25	—
Real Social Democracy of Slovaks	3,573	0.12	—
Association for the Republic– Republican Party	1,410	0.05	—
Total	2,875,458	100.00	150

Sources: Sonja Szomolányi and Gregorij Mesežníkov (Eds.), *Slovakia: Parliamentary Elections, 1994*, Bratislava: Slovak Political Science Foundation, 1995; and the Slovakia News Agency, 1994 Parliamentary Elections in the Slovak Republic, 27 September 1994. Also consult http://www2.essex.ac.uk/elect.

Parliamentary Elections, 5–6 June 1992

Slovak National Council

Turnout: 83%

Party/Coalition	Votes	% of Vote	Seats
Movement for a Democratic Slovakia	1,148,625	37.26	74
Party of the Democratic Left	453,203	14.70	29
Slovak National Party	244,527	7.93	15
Christian Democratic Movement	273,945	8.89	18
Coexistence/Hungarian Christian Democratic Movement	228,885	7.42	14
Civic Democratic Union	124,503	4.04	—
Social Democratic Party	123,426	4.00	—
Hungarian Civic Party	70,689	2.30	—
Democratic Party/Civic Democratic Party	102,058	3.31	—
Other parties	312,835	10.15	—
Total	3,082,696	100.00	150

Sources: Jirí Pehe, "Czechoslovakia's Political Balance Sheet, 1990–1992," RFE/RL Research Report, 19 June 1992.

Parliamentary Elections, 8–9 June 1990

Slovak National Council

Turnout: 95.39%

Party/Coalition	Votes	% of Vote	Seats
Public Against Violence	991,285	29.34	48
Christian Democratic Movement	648,782	19.20	31
Slovak National Party	470,984	13.94	22
Slovak Communist Party	450,855	13.43	22
Coexistence/Hungarian Christian Democratic Party	292,636	8.66	14
Democratic Movement	148,567	4.39	7
Green Party	117,871	3.48	6
Alliance of Farmers	85,060	2.51	—
Social Democratic Party	61,401	1.81	—
Freedom Party	60,041	1.77	—
Democratic Union of Roma	24,797	0.73	—
Movement of Czechoslovak Understanding	13,417	0.39	—
People's Democratic Party	7,023	0.21	—
Free Bloc	3,326	0.09	—
Czechoslovak Socialist Party	1,166	0.03	—
Czechoslovak Democratic Forum	515	0.02	—
Total	3,377,726	100.00	150

Sources: Sharon L. Wolchik, *Czechoslovakia: Politics, Economics, and Society*, London: Pinter Publishers, 1991, pp. 72, 75. See also http://www2.essex.ac.uk/.

Federal Czechoslovak Elections, 5–6 June 1992

Chamber of the People (Slovak Republic results)

Turnout: 83%

Party/Coalition	Votes	% of Vote	Seats
Movement for a Democratic Slovakia	1,036,459	33.53	24
Party of the Democratic Left	446,230	14.44	10
Slovak National Movement	290,249	9.39	6
Christian Democratic Party	277,061	8.96	6
Coexistence/Hungarian Christian Democratic Movement/Hungarian People's Party	227,925	7.37	5
Social Democratic Party	150,095	4.86	
Civic Democratic Union	122,359	3.96	—
Democratic Party/Civic Democratic Party	122,266	3.95	—
Hungarian Civic Party	72,877	2.36	—
Other parties	345,453	11.18	—
Total	3,090,974	100.00	51

Sources: http://www.eunet.sk/slovakia/slovakia/history-politics/politics.html. June 1996 and Grigorij Meseznikov, "The Program of Political Parties in Slovakia: In Practice and In Declarations," in Sonja Szomolanyi and Grigorij Meseznikov (Eds.), *The Slovak Path of Transition to Democracy,* Slovak Political Science Association, Bratislava, 1994, p. 84. Also consult the University of Essex, Political Transformation and the Electoral Process in Post-Communist Europe, located at www2.essex.ac.uk/elect.

Chamber of Nations (Slovak Republic results)

Party/Coalition	Votes	% of Vote	Seats
Movement for a Democratic Slovakia	1,045,395	33.85	33
Party of the Democratic Left	433,750	14.04	13
Slovak National Party	288,864	9.35	9
Christian Democratic Movement	272,100	8.81	8
Coexistence/Hungarian Christian Democratic Movement/Hungarian People's Party	228,219	7.39	7
Social Democratic Party	188,223	6.09	5
Civic Democratic Union	124,649	4.04	—
Democratic Party/Civic Democratic Party	113,176	3.66	—
Hungarian Civic Party	71,122	2.30	—
Other parties	322,928	10.47	—
Total	3,088,426	100.00	75

Source: http://www2.essex.ac.uk/elect.

Federal Czechoslovak Elections, 8–9 June 1990

Chamber of the People (Slovak Republic results)

Turnout: 95.39%

Party/Coalition	Votes	% of Vote	Seats
Public Against Violence	1,104,125	32.54	19
Christian Democratic Movement	644,008	18.98	11
Slovak Communist Party	468,411	13.81	8
Slovak National Party	372,025	10.96	6
Coexistence/Hungarian Christian Democratic Movement	291,287	8.58	5
Democratic Party	149,310	4.40	—
Green Party	108,542	3.21	—
Alliance of Farmers	87,604	2.58	—
Social Democratic Party	64,175	1.89	—
Freedom Party	49,012	1.44	—
Democratic Union of Roma	22,670	0.67	—
Movement of Czechoslovak Understanding	13,947	0.41	—
People's Democratic Party	8,557	0.25	—
Free Bloc	6,145	0.18	—
Czechoslovak Socialist Party	2,086	0.06	—
Movement for Civic Liberty	580	0.02	—
Czechoslovak Democratic Forum	562	0.02	—
Total	3,393,046	100.00	49

Chamber of Nations (Slovak Republic results)

Party/Coalition	Votes	% of Vote	Seats
Public Against Violence	1,262,278	37.28	33
Christian Democratic Movement	564,172	16.66	14

Slovak Communist Party	454,740	13.43	12
Slovak National Party	387,387	11.44	9
Coexistence/Hungarian Christian Democratic Movement	287,426	8.49	7
Democratic Party	124,561	3.68	—
Green Party	87,366	2.58	—
Alliance of Farmers	71,204	2.10	—
Social Democratic Party	51,233	1.51	—
Freedom Party	42,111	1.24	—
Democratic Union of Roma	20,445	0.60	—
Movement of Czechoslovak Understanding	16,934	0.50	—
People's Democratic Party	7,169	0.21	—
Free Bloc	5,643	0.18	—
Czechoslovak Socialist Party	2,073	0.06	—
Movement for Civic Liberty	914	0.03	—
Czechoslovak Democratic Forum	499	0.01	—
Total	3,386,155	100.00	75

Source: See Federal Czechoslovak Elections, 5–6 June 1992, p. 331.

NOTES

1. For recent histories of Slovakia consult Stanislav J. Kirschbaum, *A History of Slovakia: The Struggle for Survival*, New York: St. Martin's Griffin, 1995; Francis Dvornik, *The Making of Central and Eastern Europe*, Gulf Breeze, FL: Academic International Press, 1974; Josef Kalvoda, *The Genesis of Czechoslovakia*, Boulder, CO: East European Monographs, 1986; Joseph M. Kirschbaum (Ed.), *Slovakia in the 19th and 20th Centuries*, Toronto: Slovak World Congress, 1978;Stanislav J. Kirschbaum and Anne C. R. Roman (Eds.), *Reflections on Slovak History*, Toronto: Slovak World Congress, 1987; Carol Skalnik Leff, *National Conflict in Czechoslovakia: The Making and Remaking of a State, 1918–1987*, Princeton, NJ: Princeton University Press, 1988; Gordon H. Skilling (Ed.), *Czechoslovakia, 1918–1988*, London: Macmillan, 1991; and Zdenek Suda, *Zealots and Rebels: A History of the Ruling Communist Party of Czechoslovakia*, Stanford, CA: Hoover Institution Press, 1980.

2. Check Jiří Pehe, "The Inevitable Divorce," *Freedom Review*, Vol. 23, No. 6, November-December 1992.

3. Ján Obrman and Jiří Pehe, "Difficult Power-Sharing Talks," Radio Free Europe/Radio Liberty Research Institute (RFE/RL), *Report on Eastern Europe*, Vol. 1, No. 49, 7 December 1990.

4. See the statement by Vladimír Mečiar in *Národná Obroda*, Bratislava, 26 July 1990.

5. Consult "An Appeal to Slovak Citizens," *Verejnost*, Bratislava, 24 July 1991.

6. For the text of the declaration check *Lidové Noviny*, Prague, 9 November 1991.

7. See Jiří Pehe, "The State Treaty Between the Czech and Slovak Republics," RFE/RL, *Report on Eastern Europe*, Vol. 2, No. 23, 7 June 1991. For text of the draft Czech-Slovak Constitutional Treaty see *Hospodárske Noviny*, Prague, 11 February 1992.

8. See "Václav Havel: Separation is Better Than Confederation," *Rude Pravo*, Prague, 1 July 1991, and the Speech at the 17th Joint Session of the Federal Assembly, *Prague Radio Network*, 24 September 1991, in Federal Broadcast Information Service, *Daily Report: East Europe*, *FBIS-EEU-91-186*, 25 September 1991. See also Havel's "Address to the Nation," on *Prague Federal TV Network*, 17 November 1991, in *FBIS-EEU-91-222*, 18 November 1991.

9. Ján Obrman, "President Havel's Diminishing Political Influence," RFE/RL, *Research Report*, Vol. 1, No. 11, 13 March 1992.

10. See Oskar Krejcí, "Czech Nationalism and Separatism," *Pravda*, Bratislava, 14 June 1991.

11. See Jiří Pehe, "Czechoslovakia: Parties Register for Elections," *Radio Free Europe/ Radio Liberty Research Report*, Vol. 1, No. 18, 1 May 1992.

12. See Ján Obrman, "The Czechoslovak Elections," *Radio Free Europe/Radio Liberty Research Report*, Vol. 1, No. 26, 26 June 1992.

13. Jiří Pehe, "The New Slovak Government and Parliament," RFE/RL, *Research Report*, Vol. 1, No. 28, 10 July 1992.

14. *Hospodárske Noviny*, Prague, 10 September 1992.

15. Jiří Pehe, "Czechs and Slovaks Define Postdivorce Relations," RFE/RL *Report on Eastern Europe*, Vol. 2, No. 45, 13 November 1991.

16. See Jiří Pehe, "Czechs and Slovaks Prepare to Part," RFE/RL, *Research Report*, Vol. 1, No. 37, 18 September 1992, and Ján Obrman, "Czechoslovakia's New Governments," RFE/RL, *Research Report*, Vol. 1, No. 29, 17 July 1992.

17. Consult Ann E. Robertson, "How to Succeed at Seceding: The Value of Federalism in Political Divorce," in John S. Micgiel (Ed.), *State and Nation Building in East Central Europe: Contemporary Perspectives*, New York: Columbia University, Institute on East Central Europe, 1996, pp. 199–224.

18. See the interview with Václav Klaus, "A Chance for Czechoslovakia," *Respekt*, Prague, No. 26, 29 June–2 July 1992.

19. Constitution of the Slovak Republic, published in *Hospodárske Noviny*, Prague, 8 September 1992, in *FBIS-EEU-92-179-S*, 15 September 1992; *Hungarians in Slovakia*, Information Bulletin, September 1992, compiled on behalf of the Political Movement Coexistence, Bratislava; *Memorandum on the Slovak Republic's Future Admission to the Council of Europe*, issued by the Coexistence Political Movement, Hungarian Christian Democratic Movement,

Hungarian People's Party, and Hungarian Civic Party, Bratislava, 4 February 1993; and "Excerpts from Speeches by Ethnic Hungarian Representatives in the Slovak Parliament," '*Uj Szo*, 24 April 1993, in *Federal Broadcast Information Service/Joint Publications Research Service, Daily Report: East Europe, JPRS-EER-93–046–S*, 26 May 1993.

20. See Ján Obrman, "Language Law Stirs Controversy in Slovakia," RFE/RL *Report on Eastern Europe*, Vol. 1, No. 46, 16 November 1990; and Georg Brunner, "Minority Problems and Policies in East-Central and South-East Europe," *International Issues*, Vol. 1, No. 3, 1992.

21. From *Hungarians in Slovakia*, September 1992, compiled on behalf of the Political Movement Coexistence, Bratislava.

22. See the statement by Slovak Minister for Culture Dušan Slobodník in *Národná Obroda*, Bratislava, 25 May 1993, in *FBIS-EEU-93–103*, 1 June 1993.

23. For the full text of the law on state citizenship of the Slovak Republic see *Pravda*, Bratislava, 21 January 1993.

24. Dušan Leška and Viera Koganová, "The Elections 1994 and Crystallization of the Political Parties and Movements in Slovakia," Slovakia Parliamentary Elections 1994, Slovak Political Science Association, Friedrich Ebert Foundation, Bratislava, 1994, p. 86.

25. See Sharon Fisher, "Tottering in the Aftermath of the Elections," *Transitions*, Vol. 1, No. 4, 29 March 1995, pp. 20–24.

26. Consult Sharon L. Wolchik, "Democratization and Political Participation in Slovakia," in Karen Dawisha and Bruce Parrott (Eds.), *The Consolidation of Democracy in East-Central Europe*, Cambridge: Cambridge University Press, 1997, pp. 197–244.

27. For a useful synopsis of Mečiar's politics see Steve Kettle, "Slovakia's One-Man Band," *Transition*, Vol. 2, No. 17, 23 August 1996, pp. 12–15, 64.

28. Ľudmila Malíková, "Political Reflections on the Transformation of Power in Local Government," Localities and Polities in the Transformation Process: The Slovak and Czech Experiences, Conference proceedings, 8–9 June 1995, Bratislava, Slovak Republic, Bratislava, 1995, pp. 14–16.

29. http://www.ivo.sk/show.asp?Id=32.

30. *CTK*, Bratislava, 12 June 1999, in *FBIS-EEU-1999–0612*, "Slovak Voting Patterns Analyzed."

31. *CTK*, Bratislava, 8 June 1999, in *FBIS-EEU-1999–0608*, "Leftwing Daily Stability Pact Not Feasible."

32. Interview with Slovak Prime Minister Mikuláš Dzurinda by Vladimír Tvaroška, *Pravda*, Bratislava, 25 May 1999.

33. *CTK*, Prague, 28 May 1990, in *FBIS-EEU-90–104*, 30 May 1990; Jiří Pehe, "Divisions in the Communist Party of Czechoslovakia," RFE/RL, *Report on Eastern Europe*, Vol. 2, No. 30, 26 July 1991.

34. http://www.iri.org/C_E_Europe/Publications/Slovakia_Political_Update98.htm.

35. Robert Norris, National Democratic Institute, Bratislava, "Slovakia: Political and Election Report," Vol. 1, 17 June 1998.

36. http://www.rferl.org.newsline/3–cee.html.

37. Jiří Pehe, "The Local Government Elections," RFE/RL, *Report on Eastern Europe*, Vol. 1, No. 50, 14 December 1990; Jiří Pehe, "Growing Slovak Demands Seen as Threat to Federation," RFE/RL, *Report on Eastern Europe*, Vol. 2, No. 12, 22 March 1991; Jiří Pehe, "The Changing Configuration of Political Forces in the Federal Assembly," *RFE/RL, Report on Eastern Europe*, Vol. 2, No. 16, 19 April 1991; Jiří Pehe, "Bid for Slovak Sovereignty Causes Political Upheaval," *RFE/RL, Report on Eastern Europe*, Vol. 2, No. 41, 11 October 1991. See also Jiří Pehe, "Slovak Nationalism Splits Christian Democratic Ranks," *RFE/RL, Research Report*, Vol. 1, No. 13, 27 March 1992.

38. "Slovakia: Communist Party Holds Congress, Elects Leadership," *Bratislava Pravda*, 1 July 1996, p. 2, *FBIS-EEU-96–129*, 3 July 1996, p.18.

39. Michael J. Deis, "A Study of Nationalism in Czechoslovakia," RFE/RL, *Research Report*, Vol. 1, No. 5, 31 January 1992; Jiří Pehe, "Political Conflict in Slovakia," RFE/RL, *Report on Eastern Europe*, Vol. 2, No. 19, 10 May 1991; Ján Obrman, "The Czechoslovak Elections," RFE/RL, *Research Report*, Vol. 1, No. 26, 26 June 1992; and Jiří Pehe, "The New Slovak Government and Parliament," RFE/RL, *Research Report*, Vol. 1, No. 28, 10 July 1992.

40. "The Stand of the Slovak National Party," *Smena*, Bratislava, 30 June 1990, in *FBIS-*

EEU 90–130, 6 July 1990; "Deputy Panis Is Leaving," *Pravda*, Bratislava, 31 January 1991, in *FBIS-EEU-91–025*, 6 February 1991; Pehe, "Growing Slovak Demands Seen as Threat to Federation"; Jirí Pehe, "The State Treaty Between the Czech and The Slovak Republics," RFE/RL, *Report on Eastern Europe*, Vol. 2, No. 23, 7 June 1991; and Jirí Pehe, "Czechoslovakia's Changing Political Spectrum," RFE/RL, *Report on Eastern Europe*, Vol. 1, No. 5, 31 January 1992.

41. See the material on the *Valné Zromaždenie Matice Slovenskej, 1992*, Bratislava, 33/1992; and the *Second Memorandum of Slovaks from Southern Slovakia* adopted at the April 1993 *Matica Slovenská* meeting in Surany, Slovakia.

42. Interview with Vojtech Vitkovský by Renatá Havranová, "Breaking Up Czechoslovakia?" *Práce*, Prague, 8 August 1990, in *FBIS-EEU-90–157*, 14 August 1990.

43. *Bratislava Domestic Service*, 27 July 1990, in *FBIS-EEU-90–146*, 30 July 1990; interview with Peter Brnák by Ján Felix, "A New Boat in Slovak Politics," *Smena*, Bratislava, 28 January 1991, in *FBIS-EEU-91–022*, 1 February 1991; editorial report on news conference held by representatives of the Slovak National Democratic Movement in *Smena*, Bratislava, 26 July 1991.

44. *Bratislava Domestic Service*, 28 January 1991, in *FBIS-EEU-91–019*, 29 January 1991. See also Frank Cibulka, "The Radical Right in Slovakia," in Sabrina P. Ramet (Ed.), *The Radical Right in Central and Eastern Europe Since 1989*, University Park, Pennsylvania State University Press, 1999, pp. 110–131.

45. Jirí Pehe, "Czechoslovakia: Parties Register for Elections," RFE/RL, *Research Report*, Vol. 1, No. 18, 1 May 1992; and Ján Obrman, "The Czechoslovak Elections: A Guide to the Parties," RFE/RL, *Research Report*, Vol. 1, No. 22, 29 May 1992.

46. www.europeanforum.bot-consult.se/cup/slovakia/parties.htm.

47. Edith Oltay, "Hungarians in Slovakia Organize to Press for Ethnic Rights," RFE/RL, *Report on Eastern Europe*, Vol. 1, No. 22, 1 June 1990; Peter Miklósi, interview with Miklós Duray, president of the Coexistence Political Movement, "Time Trap: It Would Be Our Homeland That Would Give Us Strength in Facing Our Problems," *Vasárnap*, Bratislava, 17 July 1992, in *JPRS-EER-92–103*, 10 August 1992; Edith Oltay, "Hungarian Minority in Slovakia Sets Up Independent Organizations," RFE/RL, *Report on Eastern Europe*, Vol. 1, No. 11, 11 March 1991.

48. "Anxiety about the Incitements of Frictions," *Národná Obroda*, Bratislava, 27 August 1990, in *FBIS-EEU-90–174*, 7 September 1990; Alfred A. Reisch, "Hungarian Ethnic Parties Prepare for Czechoslovak Elections," RFE/RL, *Report on Eastern Europe*, Vol. 1, No. 18, 1 May 1992; "*Csemadok* With A New Name," *Republika*, Bratislava, 5 April 1993.

49. Edith Oltay, "Hungarians in Slovakia Organize to Press for Ethnic Rights"; Reisch, "Hungarian Ethnic Parties Prepare for Czechoslovak Elections"; "We Want Educational, Cultural, and Partial Territorial Autonomy," *Národná Obroda*, Bratislava, 23 July 1992, in *JPRS-EER-92–103*, 10 August 1992.

50. See Alfred Reisch, "Hungarian Ethnic Parties Prepare for the Czechoslovak Elections"; announcement by the Independent Hungarian Initiative, *CTK*, Prague, 1 August 1991, in *JPRS-EER-91–115*, 5 August 1991; "Every Knife Would Flick Open," by István Lékó, *Respekt*, Prague, 14–20 October 1991, in *FBIS-EEU-91–202*, 18 October 1991.

51. Interview with Paul Robert Magocsi, "Ruthenians Are No Longer in Parentheses," *Smena*, Bratislava, 29 March 1991; Jaromír Horec, "Subject: Ruthenia," *Lidové Noviny*, Prague, 21 September 1990; Peter Juscák, "Ruthenian Renaissance," *Hlas Demokracie*, Kosice, No. 7, 1991; RFE/RL, *Daily Report*, No. 98, 25 May 1993.

52. "Unification of Romanies in Slovakia," *CTK*, Prague, in *FBIS-EEU-90–082*, 27 April 1990.

53. Editorial Report, *Pravda*, Bratislava, 5 March 1990, in *FBIS-EEU-90–046*, 8 March 1990; "Environmentally and Socially," *Pravda*, Bratislava, 25 February 1991, in *FBIS-EEU-91–039*, 27 February 1991.

54. Text of Romani National Congress, *Lidové Noviny*, Prague, 7 August 1991, in *JPRS-EER-91–131*, 4 September 1991; *Bratislava Rozlasová Stanica*, 21 January 1993, in *FBIS-EEU-93–013*, 22 January 1993.

Hungary

HISTORICAL OVERVIEW

The Central European, or Danubian, basin formed part of the ancient Roman province of Pannonia and was occupied by various tribal groupings before the arrival of the Hungarians. These included Celts, Goths, Huns, Avars, and Slavs during the first nine centuries AD. Hungarian, or Magyar, tribes arrived in the region at the end of the ninth century AD and quickly proceeded to gain control of the area. The original home of the Hungarians, a Finno-Ugric people, was on the upper reaches of the Volga and Kama rivers in present-day Russia and subsequently on the lower Don River. They were organized in a loose federation of seven tribes, each under a hereditary chieftain. In 889 AD attacks by the Pechenegs drove the Magyars westward and in 892 AD they were invited by the Carolingian emperor Arnulf to assert his authority over the Moravian Empire.

The Hungarians made forays into the Danubian basin several times before their settlement there. In 894, they came to the help of the Moravian king, Svätopluk, fighting the Bavarians. Then, in 895, led by Árpád, the leader of the most powerful tribe, the Magyars crossed the Carpathians and easily subjugated the already decimated local inhabitants. They destroyed the Moravian empire in 906 AD and occupied the entire Pannonian region. Renouncing their customary raiding pursuits after their decisive defeat by the Holy Roman Empire under Otto I in 955 AD at the battle of Lechfield, the Hungarians developed a sedentary lifestyle. Stephen I (969–1038) was crowned as the first Hungarian king in 1000, was recognized by the Holy See, and proceeded to convert his people to Christianity. Tribal authority was transformed into a hereditary landowning class under the supervision of royal officials.[1]

After Stephen's death, Hungary was beset by dynastic rivalries for the next century that seriously weakened the state and left it open to foreign incursions and loss of territories. By the end of the eleventh century, King László I successfully extended the Hungarian domain to the Carpathian mountains and incorporated Transylvania, including the eastern regions inhabited by Szeklers, a people related to the Magyars. German Saxon settlers were invited to colonize the major towns in the Transylvanian region. King László's successor, King Kálmán, occupied Slavonia, Croatia, and Dalmatia and assumed the Croatian crown at the beginning of the twelfth century. But the state suffered a major disaster in 1242 when the country was overrun by Mongol invaders and lost about half of its population together with most of its towns and wealth. The Árpád dynasty died out in 1301.

The fourteenth century proved a "golden age" for Hungary under the Angevin kings, as its neighbors were preoccupied with their internal problems and the state was able to recover from the Mongol incursions. Lajos I (1342–1382) surrounded his kingdom with dependencies in the Balkans and the lower Danube regions, became king of Poland (1370–82), and significantly built up its wealth. However, in the fifteenth century, Hungary faced a new threat from the Ottoman Turks, who had steadily advanced through the Balkans to the Danubian territories. The famous General János Hunyadi successfully defended the country's borders from the Turks until his death in battle in 1456. Under King Matthias Corvinus, Hunyadi's son (1458–1490), the Ottomans were held at bay and Hungary acquired control over territories along its western borders, as Matthias was crowned as the Czech king (1472) and gained control over Silesia (1472).

In 1526 Hungarian forces suffered a stunning defeat at the battle of Mohács as Turkish forces under Sultan Sulejman the Magnificent overran the southern part of the country and reached the capital Buda before retreating. The Ottoman-occupied territories were devastated and depopulated and by 1568 the Hungarian lands were divided into three parts: the westernmost, Royal Hungary, fell under Austrian-Habsburg domination; Transylvania, in the east, gained a measure of autonomy as an electoral principality under Turkish suzerainty; and the central plains fell under direct Ottoman control. The Turkish areas in particular witnessed an inflow of non-Magyar nationalities including Serbs, Romanians, Croats, and Germans. In the late seventeenth century, the Habsburgs took over most of the Hungarian lands from the retreating Turks, after the latter's defeat at the battle of Vienna in 1683 and Buda in 1686. Under the Treaty of Carlowitz (1699), Turkey relinquished all of Hungary except the Banat region, which it kept until 1718, while Transylvania remained a separate principality. Throughout the eighteenth century, Hungary was ruled by a succession of autocratic Austrian kings against whom the princes of Transylvania and Upper Hungary revolted.

As the nineteenth century progressed, Hungary gained a measure of autonomy within the Habsburg Empire as Vienna authorized the government in Budapest to help administer its large multi-national state. Periodic Hungarian nationalist revolts to gain full state independence were subdued, and the Habsburgs pursued a policy of divide and rule, playing off one nationality against another by providing selective political and economic benefits. At this time,

Hungary underwent a cultural renaissance that became increasingly politicized under the oppressive Habsburg dictatorship. This spawned a broad reform movement calling for economic, social, and political changes. It was led by such notable patriots as Ferenc Deák, Baron József Eötvös, and Lajos Kossuth. Kossuth led the movement for national liberation and Hungarian independence, which culminated in the 1848 revolution. The revolt was brutally suppressed by Vienna in 1849 with the assistance of armies from Tsarist Russia.

With the Habsburg Empire racked by escalating internal conflicts and defeat by Prussia, Vienna decided to make some far-reaching concessions to the Hungarians. When the Empire was transformed into a "dual monarchy" in 1867, the Hungarians could set up their own government and parliament, with only defense, foreign affairs, and the treasury remaining in joint control with the Austrians. As a result, the Hungarian Government regained administrative control over territories that included substantial Hungarian populations in Transylvania, Slovakia (then Upper Hungary), Croatian Slavonia, and Ruthenia. This new arrangement served to intensify hostilities between Hungarians and the subordinate Romanian, Slovak, Ruthenian, Ukrainian, and Croatian populations. Croatians gained a measure of autonomy and their own parliament in 1868, but other nationalities did not obtain similar privileges. Moreover, Hungarian activists continued to press for full independence from Austria and for extensive social and economic reforms.

At the close of World War I in 1918, the Habsburg Empire disintegrated. Hungary declared its independence but was forced to relinquish large tracts of territory in central and southeast Europe under the 1920 Treaty of Trianon. In fact, Hungary lost about two-thirds of its lands as punishment for its alliance with the Central Powers of Austria and Germany and was only left with some territories where Magyars predominated. Still, more than three million ethnic Hungarians were left outside of the post-war state, in the Slovak and Ruthenian regions of the newly created Czechoslovakia, in Transylvania and Banat in Romania, in the Vojvodina region of the newly created Yugoslavia, and in the Burgenland region attached to Austria. These drastic border changes left a lingering sense of resentment in Hungary and stimulated the activities of revisionist and irredentist forces both inside and outside the country.

At the same time, the border changes also eliminated sizable ethnic minorities from the Hungarian state and diluted a potential source of internal friction. The minority population in inter-war Hungary did not exceed 10% of inhabitants. In general, they were not a major point of contention, either domestically or internationally. The Hungarian government adopted a nationality decree providing for the equality of all Hungarian citizens regardless of their language, religion, or ethnicity. Native tongues were also permitted as the language of instruction in schools with minority students, and a high degree of tolerance was shown for the cultural development of minority groups.

In 1920, Admiral Miklós Horthy was elected regent, the provisional head of state pending the full restoration of a monarchy. But the country was economically depressed following the prolonged war, a short-lived communist takeover in 1919, and a Romanian invasion. As in much of Central Europe, the Great Depression and the world financial crisis in the early 1930s hit Hungary hard and spawned the popularity of rightist radicals. During the late 1930s, Budapest increasingly allied itself with Nazi Germany and Fascist Italy, as both powers appeared to be the most promising patrons for regaining former Hungarian territories. With the onset of World War II, Hungary regained parts of southern Slovakia and Ruthenia in November 1938, as the Germans carved up the Czechoslovak Republic. Hungary also recovered portions of northern Transylvania in August 1940 and the Vojvodina region in Yugoslavia following the German invasion in 1941. But these lands were lost again at the close of World War II, as a consequence of the Axis defeat by the Allied powers.

The minority population in Hungary shrank substantially after the war. The number of Germans decreased by half to about 220,000, following mass expulsions by the post-war administration, and thousands of Germans continued to leave the country over the following decades. The number of Jews decreased dramatically during World War II from about 825,000 to 250,000; the majority perished in the Holocaust following mass deportations to Nazi death camps after the German occupation of Hungary in March 1944. By the late 1960s, thousands more had emigrated to Israel and the West. The Gypsy (Romani) population also sustained serious losses as a result of deportations and Nazi exterminations, although precise numbers proved difficult to ascertain.

After the defeat of the Axis powers at the end of World War II, Soviet troops occupied Hungary, as they did all of Central and Eastern Europe. The Paris Peace Treaty in February 1947 restored the Trianon frontiers, and Hungary was forced to pay reparations for maintaining an alliance with Nazi Germany. An elected coalition government and a quasi-democratic system were maintained for three years in the face of pressures from the communists backed by a large Soviet army. The Communist Party "merged" with the remaining, but subdued, Social Democrats in 1948, forming the Hungarian Workers' Party, and a communist dictatorship was imposed along Stalinist lines. Stalin's death in 1953 brought changes to the dictatorial style; Imre Nagy, a reform communist, became prime minister, but by 1955 he was expelled from the Hungarian Workers' Party as a result of an internecine struggle within party ranks. In October–November 1956, Hungarians rose up against communist rule and Soviet domination. Fueled by Soviet leader Khrushchev's denunciation of Stalin and by general discontent, what started as a struggle within the Communist Party between reformer Imre Nagy and hard-line Leninists turned into a nationalist, bloody, anti-Soviet revolution.

Large sectors of the population joined the 1956 revolution, including intellectuals, students, and workers. Hungarian leaders, with Imre Nagy again as prime minister, declared an independent and neutral Hungarian state. Soviet armed forces intervened in November 1956 and crushed the revolution thereby ensuring the survival of the communist system and Hungary's membership in the Warsaw Pact. Between 25,000 and 50,000 insurgents were killed in the fighting together with about 7,000 Soviet soldiers. More than 200,000 Hungarians fled the country to the West in the wake of the revolt, while thousands remaining at home were imprisoned, executed, or deported to Soviet labor camps.

Moscow installed a new, loyal government under the strict control of the renamed Hungarian Socialist Workers' Party (HSWP), led by Secretary-General János Kádár. Although the Hungarian revolution failed to achieve its aims, the new regime introduced various liberalizing economic measures in order to gain recognition from the populace, which viewed Kádár as a traitor, and to forestall any future unrest. In 1961, Kádár denounced the practice of making party membership a prerequisite for jobs that demanded specialization and technical expertise. In November 1962, the Central Committee of the HSWP replaced many Stalinists and incompetent officials holding leading party positions. Then, in late 1965, the party set up a committee to examine the country's economic system. The result was a series of reforms that modified Hungary's rigid, centrally planned economy and eventually introduced elements of a free market in 1968 known as the "New Economic Mechanism" (NEM), led by Rezső Nyers. One measure dealt with private ownership. In 1959, the recollectivization of land was imposed, and by 1962, 75% of farms had been collectivized, during the 1960s, cooperative farms became largely autonomous units and the regime became more tolerant of personal ownership over small plots of land.[2]

During the Kádár era, from 1956 until 1988, Hungary became the most "liberal" communist state, especially in the economic and cultural spheres, and some limited private enterprise was permitted. By standards prevailing elsewhere in Eastern Europe, Kádár's New Economic Mechanism (NEM), introduced in January 1968, was considered reformist, although it failed to resolve Hungary's underlying structural problems. During the early 1960s, the government made trade with the West and with COMECON (Soviet bloc) countries a priority.

The opposition movement began to organize more effectively in the mid-1980s. For example, in 1987 dissident economists produced a radical critique of the Hungarian system; these ideas became increasingly accepted by reform communist leaders such as Imre Pozsgay, Rezső Nyers, and Miklós Németh. In June 1987, the *samizdat* periodical *Beszélő* (Speaker) published a "Social Contract" calling for political pluralism, an autonomous parliament, and a free press. In September 1988, opposition leaders and reform communists met in Lakitelek and created the Hungarian Democratic Forum (HDF), the first significant political organization outside of communist control. Two months later, the Alliance of Free Democrats (AFD) was formed. All of these initiatives contributed not only to undermining communist rule but to promoting political pluralism and providing a political alternative to the one-party state. However, Hungary did not possess a broad, mass-based opposition movement either before or during the dismantling of one-party rule. Paradoxically, in many respects, this promoted the emergence of distinctive political parties early in the democratization process.

POST-COMMUNIST DEVELOPMENTS

Under growing internal pressure and with the threat of Soviet intervention lifted in the late 1980s, as a result of Mikhail Gorbachev's reformist policies in Moscow, the Hungarian communists abandoned their monopoly on power in 1989. A series of important steps away from one-party rule were undertaken during 1988–1989. Liberalizers in the communist regime realized that some political concessions were essential as the economic reforms had run out of steam and the prospect of social unrest was mounting. The ruling Hungarian Socialist Workers' Party (HSWP) tried to capture some popular legitimacy by taking credit for the reforms, transforming itself into an electable organization, and benefiting from important symbolic acts such as the June 1989 reburial of Imre Nagy, who had been executed by the Soviet-imposed regime. This culminated in Pozsgay's announcement in January 1989 that the 1956 revolution had indeed constituted a "popular uprising" rather than a "counter-revolution" as it had been portrayed by communist propaganda.

At an HSWP conference in May 1988, younger reformist leaders and the technocratic elite were successful in removing Kádár and several of his closest comrades from the leadership of the party and the state. The HSWP Central Committee subsequently relieved Kádár of his remaining official posts, and although the centrist Károly Grósz was appointed as party leader, his powers were curtailed by the appointment of key reformers in the HSWP presidium. Dozens of "reform circles" were also established within the party, demanding more far-reaching political measures.

The country also witnessed the flowering of numerous independent political movements between 1988 and 1989, including the Alliance of Free Democrats (AFD), the Hungarian Democratic Forum (HDF), and the Federation of Young Democrats (AYD). Nine of the largest independent organizations (seven political parties and two civic groups) formed an Opposition Roundtable to present a united front in negotiations with the communist authorities for a transition to a pluralistic democracy. Opposition candidates also won several by-elections to the National Assembly (parliament) during 1989, as multicandidate and multiparty elections were gradually introduced.

In December 1988 and January 1989, the parliament passed legislation allowing for the right to association and assembly. In February 1989, laws permitting a multi-party system were enacted. In April 1989, draft laws on political parties were published to liberalize the political system, and the HSWP accepted conditions for roundtable discussions with the opposition for transforming the political system. In the summer of 1989, representatives of the HSWP, the Opposition Roundtable, and various official organizations entered into detailed negotiations on a transition to democratic pluralism and a market economy. By September 1989, in this "negotiated revolution," agreements were reached on a multi-party system and on new laws for national elections. The agreement also created a relatively weak presidency but stipulated that the first president should be elected by popular vote.

In October 1989, the Hungarian parliament adopted changes to the constitution eliminating the principles of the HSWP's "leading role" in society and creating the legal framework for multi-party elections. With the reformist wing taking control within the ruling party, at its congress in October 1989, the HSWP dissolved and formed the Hungarian Socialist Party (HSP) in its place. An authoritative Constitutional Court was established on 1 January 1990 and was assigned the role of protecting the rule of law and of safeguarding the separation and balance of powers in the government.

The amended constitution augmented the already recognized human and civil rights. It also enfranchised the country's minorities, stating that they retained the right to their own culture, religion, and the use of their native language. Providing redress for any human rights violations, the constitution allowed for the creation of the office of a Commissioner for Human Rights in the National Assembly to act as an ombudsman.[3] Parliament also voted to disband the communist-controlled Workers' Militias, to ban political groups from workplaces, and to create a parliamentary body to assess the assets accumulated by the ruling party during its decades in power.

In November 1989, the Alliance of Free Democrats (AFD) and several other groups called for a referendum on the timetable for deciding on direct presidential elections. They feared that an early ballot favored the HSP, because the opposition did not have enough time or media exposure to mount an effective campaign. The ex-communists also favored the creation of a stronger presidency elected through a direct popular ballot.[4] Early elections would have enabled the reformed communists to maintain control over the state even if they were defeated in subsequent parliamentary elections. The November referendum was narrowly won by the Free Democrats' proposition, with 50.07% of the vote, thereby delaying the presidential balloting until after the parliamentary elections in March 1990.

Most of the political parties were formed or reconstituted during 1988 and 1989. Some of them had historical roots, such as the Independent Smallholders' Party (ISP) and the Social Democrats, while others, including the liberal AFD and the more conservative, nationalist HDF, evolved from the democratic opposition movement of the 1970s and 1980s, while the youngest party, the Alliance of Young Democrats (AYD) was established in 1989. In general, the transition to a multiparty system was peaceful, aside from sporadic acts of police brutality against peaceful demonstrators. However, some argued that the nature of the transformation, through behind-the-scenes debates and agreements, raised public skepticism as to the ultimate legitimacy of the process.[5]

In the months preceding the first multi-party parliamentary elections on 25 March 1990, the HSP reformists steadily lost ground to the opposition groups. Although 65 parties were officially registered, only twelve obtained a sufficient number of candidate nominations to be included on national lists for the elections. The first round of the ballot was narrowly won by the conservative, anti-communist HDF, ahead of the AFD and the ISP. The HSP obtained a mere 10.89% of the popular vote. After the decisive second round of balloting on 8 April 1990, the HDF increased its score to 42% of the seats in parliament, with the AFD garnering 24%, the ISP 11%, and the HSP under 9% of the parliamentary mandates.

HDF leader József Antall became the prime minister and in May 1990, the HDF formed a coalition administration with the ISP and the Christian Democratic People's Party (CDPP). Only three more parties gained enough of the popular vote to enter the National Assembly: the Alliance of Free Democrats, the Alliance of Young Democrats, and the Hungarian Socialist Party. In a compromise arrangement in August 1990, the new Hungarian parliament elected Alliance of Free Democrats member Árpád Göncz as speaker of the house and interim national president.[6] This followed a failed referendum in July 1990 calling for a popular election of the country's president, a move sponsored by the HSP, which felt confident of victory. In fact, a mere 13% of the electorate actually turned out to vote, thus making the ballot invalid.

Conflicts arose early on between the president and the government as a result of the unusual arrangement whereby an HDF-majority legislature elected an essentially oppositionist AFD president. Although presidential powers were largely ceremonial, Göncz played a more active role than the government initially envisaged and there were clashes over certain coalition decisions, such as the appointment of directors in the mass media. According to the constitution, the president had no veto powers over legislation and had no real executive authority. Moreover, because he was elected by parliament, his position ultimately depended on its consent. Despite his conflicts with the legislature, Göncz was re-elected for a second term in office on 19 June 1995, primarily because he had gained substantial public popularity.

Although it served its full four-year term in office, the conservative governing coalition gradually lost its popularity. It confronted various problems, including a poor public relations policy in explaining the necessity of painful economic reforms in the midst of comprehensive market restructuring. Furthermore, although the post-communists were formally out of power, they had connections at every level in the public administration and in the media, such that the governing coalition confronted both obstruction and opposition at various levels and in several institutions.

Other problems materialized within the largest governing party, the HDF, as Antall struggled against more extremist elements within the organization. He was caught in a dilemma between pushing them out of the Forum and thereby risking an early governmental collapse and new general elections in which the HDF confronted a potential defeat. Most of the Smallholders' deputies left and formed another parliamentary faction. The nationalist demagogue István Csurka left the HDF and formed the Hungarian Justice and Life Party (HJLP) on 22 June 1993.

Antall died prematurely in office on 12 December 1993, and his successor as premier, Péter Boross, only served one year in office before new elections took place. For the parliamentary elections in May 1994, three main poles existed on the Hungarian political scene: leftist, liberal, and nationalist. At that time, the popularity of the Socialists was at its height. Many people were nostalgic for the relatively inexpensive life and the full employment that prevailed under the previous regime and expected the HSP to restore much of the welfare umbrella. The liberal electoral bloc contained two main liberal parties, the Alliance of Free Democrats (AFD) and the Alliance of Young Democrats (AYD). Before the elections, the AYD leaders were clear that they would not form a coalition with the ex-communists, while the Free Democrats were more ambiguous. The third center-right bloc consisted of the Hungarian Democratic Forum (HDF), the Independent Smallholders' Party (ISP), and the Christian Democratic People's Party (CDPP). All three were more oriented toward a nationalist position but with differing economic prescriptions.

In the 1994 ballot, only seven parties qualified for seats. The HSP won an absolute majority in parliament with 209 out of 386 seats. The AFD garnered 70 seats, while the former governing party, the HDF, suffered a major defeat by only managing 38 seats. The other center-right parties also fared poorly: the ISP gained 26 deputies, and the CDPP only 22 deputies. The liberal AYD managed only 20 seats.

The HSP formed a coalition government in June 1994 with the ADF, led by the reform communist HSP Prime Minister Gyula Horn. Although the Socialists could have governed alone, they did not have the two-thirds parliamentary majority enabling them to alter the constitution or to pass "fundamental laws." Moreover, the HSP calculated that a broader coalition would provide additional legitimacy for conducting tough economic reforms such as tightening the budget and introducing of long-overdue austerity measures after March 1995.

The socialist-liberal coalition in Hungary constituted the first example of a successful coalition government between a post-communist party and a post-dissident organization in the Central European region. Although the HSP claimed that it would reduce the social costs of economic reform and better protect the more vulnerable social groups, paradoxically they implemented even more stringent austerity measures and cuts in state spending than the previous, rightist administration. The influence of the liberal and pro-market ADF proved important in maintaining the reformist momentum.

Although there were four center-right parties in the National Assembly, they were unable to forge any coalition pact and had an insufficient number of parliamentary seats to form a government. Splits even appeared within some of the rightist formations. For example, some former HDF deputies founded the Hungarian Democratic People's Party (HDPP), and fractions also appeared within the CDPP. The majority of Christian Democrats wanted closer relations with the Smallholders, but the party leadership refused such overtures.

The two-party governing coalition held a 72% majority in the legislature between 1994 and 1998. It launched a more extensive economic reform program and cut the state's welfare expenditure. But although it attained impressive macroeconomic results, corruption remained a burdensome problem, and many former communist functionaries reportedly acquired their own businesses and adroitly used their old connections. The coalition survived its term in office despite Budapest's tough social spending program that provoked broad public disquiet. Anger and cynicism were also prevalent as a consequence of several financial scandals concerning the privatization program.

In seeking to curtail spending, the authorities trimmed the extensive social security program, leading to protests by traditional socialist and trade union leaders.[7] In order to stay on track for European Union (EU) membership and to avoid a major financial crisis, Budapest was compelled to pursue such a program despite the initial social costs. The HSP re-elected Premier Horn as party chairman in April 1996 and reaffirmed support for the government's economic stabilization program. Although Horn was a more traditional leftist, and the liberal finance minister László Békesi lost his post in February 1995 as a result of pressure from the premier, Horn ultimately supported the liberal program, calculating that there was no viable alternative.

A major government scandal was uncovered in October 1996. Serious illegal financial dealings in the Privatization and Holding Company, which conducted the privatization program, led to the dismissal of the entire board of directors and the resignation of finance minister Lajos Bokros; he was replaced by Péter Medgyessy, who pledged to continue the tough economic reforms. The authorities promised to make the privatization process more transparent to the public in order to avoid future scandals. At the same time, the government pledged to continue reforms in the pension and health insurance systems and to scale down state expenditures on industry and welfare.

Budapest took several important steps to stabilize its relations with neighboring states. In May 1996, Hungary and Slovakia exchanged ratification documents on their bilateral treaty that was designed to smooth years of tension and mistrust, particularly over the status of the sizable Hungarian minority in southern Slovakia. A basic treaty with Romania was also signed in September 1996

A dispute over NATO's use of Hungarian air space and airports occurred between the HSP and the ruling coalition. The HSP wanted to modify the text of a parliamentary resolution allowing NATO to use Hungarian air space and airports for its attacks on Serbia so that no attack could be launched on Serbia from Hungarian territory. On 14 July 1999, the HSP also submitted a motion to the parliament to amend the constitution to allow for direct presidential elections.

Hungarian Social Democratic Party (HSDP)
Magyar Szociáldemokrata Párt (MSzDP)

The origins of the Hungarian Social Democratic Party (HSDP) date back to 1889. It operated as an underground body during the German occupation in 1944, and in 1948 it was forced to merge with the communist party. Although it was re-created in 1989, the HSDP failed to establish itself as a viable political party, even after merging with other social democratic formations in 1993. In the March–April 1990 general elections, the HSDP failed to meet the necessary threshold for parliamentary seats, which was set at 4%. Its aging leadership, the absence of a solid constituency, and the transformation of the Hungarian Socialist Party (HSP) into a credible social democratic formation, undermined HSDP aspirations and its public appeal.

In the May 1994 parliamentary elections, the party again performed poorly, mostly because of its internal problems and because the HSP had successfully captured most of the left-leaning constituencies. It was unable to enter the legislature, as the minimum requirement for seats was established at 5%. In the May 1998 general elections, the party received a mere 0.07% of the vote. The fact that the HSP had gained international recognition as a social democratic party was received with bitterness in the HSDP, whose leaders still remembered their persecution under the communist regime. By the late 1990s, the party had virtually disappeared as a player on the political scene. The party's leader was László Kapolyi.[14]

Liberals

Alliance of Free Democrats (AFD)
Szabad Demokraták Szövetsége (SzDSz)

The Alliance of Free Democrats (AFD) had its origins in the democratic opposition movement in the 1970s and 1980s. From the late 1970s onward, the group had stood for uncompromising anti-communism and an insistence on Western democratic values, rights, and liberties.[15] Its predecessor, the Network of Free Initiative, called for a democratic transformation of Hungarian society during the late 1980s. The AFD itself was formed on 13 November

1988 and became an important member of the National Round Table (NRT), a forum for negotiating the peaceful demise of one-party rule during the summer of 1989. The Alliance, initially led by the philosopher and former dissident János Kis, was drawn mostly from intellectual and professional circles and from groups with single-issue platforms. However, the party steadily evolved to embrace a wider social sphere including new entrepreneurs and young people.

Péter Tölgyessy was elected as Kis's successor in November 1991. Then in November 1992, the party underwent a re-organization, making Iván Pető, formerly the leader of the parliamentary group, president of the party. In February 1993, Gábor Kuncze was elected as the leader of the party's parliamentary group. In July 1993, the party formally gained admission to the Liberal International.

During the first multi-party parliamentary elections in March–April 1990, the AFD gained 92 seats. It thereby became the most significant opposition party in the legislature and forged an agreement with the leadership of the governing HDF about basic constitutional questions. For example, the two parties agreed that the National Assembly would elect the president of the republic rather than arranging for a popular vote.

In the May 1994 elections, the AFD became a member of the liberal electoral bloc and won 69 parliamentary seats. After the elections, the Alliance of Free Democrats formed a coalition with the HSP and placed three ministers in the new government. But the coalition lost significant popularity as a result of the tough austerity measures it imposed in order to cut government spending and rescue the country's currency. As a result, in the May 1998 elections, the AFD suffered a significant defeat, gathering only 24 legislative seats.[16] The AFD's poor showing was attributed both to the unpopular economic measures and to rancorous disputes within the coalition itself that became public.

As a self-proclaimed liberal party, the AFD emphasized the importance of the free market in economic development and full respect for the rule of law. It strenuously pushed for privatization and state budgetary discipline. Supporters of the Alliance were largely from the better-educated and urban middle class.[17] The AFD also developed a strong connection with minority groups and supported the expansion of their rights and their involvement in the political and economic process. Before the 1998 elections, Gábor Kuncze was president of the AFD, but he subsequently resigned. Bálint Magyar then became the party is president.

Alliance of Young Democrats–Hungarian Civic Party (AYD-HCP)
Fiatal Demokraták Szövetsége–Magyar Polgári Párt (AYD-MPP)

College students representing the young, anti-communist generation founded the Alliance of Young Democrats (AYD), or *Fidesz*, on 30 March 1988. The police initially warned and harassed the organizers, declaring the AYD an illegal organization. In 1989, the party took part in the National Round-table, which brought the democratic opposition forces together in negotiations with communist reformers. In the same year, the AYD contacted the Liberal International for membership. On 16 June 1989, AYD leader Viktor Orbán delivered a speech at the re-burial of Imre Nagy (the prime minister during the 1956 anti-communist revolution), where he called for Soviet forces to vacate Hungary.

During the first elections, in April–May 1990, the AYD gained 22 National Assembly seats. In the same year, during the local elections, the party doubled its popular support after it recast itself as a right-of-center liberal formation. But as a result, the party's popular deputy leader, Gábor Fodor, defected to the Alliance of Free Democrats (AFD). During its period in parliamentary opposition, the AYD proved a tough critic of the conservative governing parties. In 1992, the AYD became a member of the Liberal International. Viktor Orbán was later elected vice president of this organization.

During 1993, the party rescinded its age limit of 35 for membership and changed its name to the Alliance of Young Democrats–Hungarian Civic Party. During this time, the party experienced an internal crisis. Some well-known members of the party decided to leave the organization, fearing that the party was veering too far toward the nationalist right in its political orientation. Because these defections occurred only seven months before the May 1994 elections, they proved extremely harmful for the party, whose popularity had steadily declined, from heading the opinion polls in mid-1993 to barely passing the 5% threshold for parliamentary seats in May 1994. The party leader who had defected to the Alliance of Free Democrats, Gábor Fodor, later became a minister in the Socialist and Free Democrat government.

For the 1994 elections the AYD-HCP organized an electoral bloc together with the Alliance of Free Democrats, the Entrepreneurs' Party, and the Agrarian Alliance. The purpose of the electoral bloc was to provide a viable liberal alternative, but it failed to generate public enthusiasm. With the Entrepreneurs' Party and the Agrarian Alliance unable to enter the National Assembly and the Free Democrats forming a coalition with the Socialist Party, the liberal electoral bloc broke up. The AYD-HCP attracted under 10% of the vote, giving it a mere twenty parliamentary seats.

After the elections, despite the party's poor showing, Orbán was re-elected president of the party. In the new political environment, two major poles had emerged: the center-left, with the governing coalition of the Socialist Party and the Free Democrats; and the center-right, with the Hungarian Democratic Forum, the Christian Democrats, and the AYD-HCP. In the years following the elections, party leaders worked hard to bring the center-right parties together, and they created another electoral bloc by the time of the May 1998 elections, with the Hungarian Democratic Forum (HDF), the

Independent Smallholders Party (ISP), and the Christian Democratic People's Party (CDPP).

In the May 1998 parliamentary elections, the AYD-HCP won 148 seats and became the strongest party in the legislature. Centrist-liberal and rightist-conservative voters tended to support the party, viewing it as a fresh and effective political force. László Kövér was elected president of the party and Viktor Orbán was selected by parliament as the new prime minister. The center-right bloc gained the majority of parliamentary seats as the governing coalition faltered. The Independent Smallholders' Party (ISP) won 48 seats and the Hungarian Democratic Forum (HDF) did not pass the 5% threshold for representation in the party-list voting but did maintain a parliamentary presence by winning 17 seats in single-member constituency races. Out of the 16 ministerial positions, AYD-HCP ended up with ten, the ISP with four, and the HDF and CDPP with one each.

As a center-right bloc, the AYD-HCP and its partners appealed particularly to middle-class voters. Moreover, the new government came into power at an auspicious time. The economy was beginning to prosper, the country was to be formally inducted into NATO on the date of the organization's fiftieth anniversary, 4 April 1999, and the administration would have the privilege of overseeing the thousandth anniversary of the Hungarian state in 2000.

The AYD-HCP was accused of having an aggressive style of governing that caused some consternation among Hungary's neighbors. For instance, Orbán was critized for publicly expressing his support for a Hungarian-language university in Romania. In August 1999 he "promised" Hungarian-language education from nursery school to university level for ethnic Hungarians in Transylvania by the year 2000. Later, at the inauguration of the Office for Hungarians Abroad, Orbán stated that his government wanted guarantees that Hungarians living in neighboring countries would be granted full educational and cultural opportunities. This was reminiscent of former HDF Prime Minister József Antall's statement when inducted into office that he was prime minister of 15 million Hungarians, meaning the 10 million citizens living within Hungary's borders and the 5 million living in neighboring countries. According to Premier Orbán, all Hungarian citizens, as well as Hungarians outside of the country's borders, were members of a single and indivisible nation. Such statements incited fears in both the Slovak and Romanian governments, raising questions about the status of their Hungarian minority populations.

Hungarian Democratic People's Party (HDPP)
Magyar Demokrata Néppárt (MDNP)

Former members of the Hungarian Democratic Forum (HDF) formed the Hungarian Democratic People's Party (HDPP) in 1993. Many ex-ministers or well-known politicians of József Antall's government joined the party. But the HDPP proved unable to build a constituency and to gain any parliamentary seats in the May 1994 elections. The party received 61,004 valid votes, totaling 1.36% in the first round. This was not enough to gain entry to the parliament.[18] The party was led by Iván Szabó.

Other small liberal organizations also emerged during the 1990s, including the Liberal Civil Alliance–Entrepreneurs' Party (LCA-EP) (*Vállalkozók Pártja, LPSz -VP*) led by Péter Zwack, which became a member of the liberal electoral bloc but failed to win parliamentary seats in the May 1998 elections. The party received only 2,409 votes, or 0.05% of the total.

Christian Democrats

Hungarian Democratic Forum (HDF)
Magyar Demokrata Fórum (MDF)

The Hungarian Democratic Forum (HDF) was a Christian-conservative party established in the town of Lakitelek on 3 September 1988. It was closely associated with national liberalism, populist-national traditions, and with Christian democracy. József Antall, HDF president from 1989 to 1993, was elected as the first post-communist prime minister of Hungary in 1990. In 1990, the HDF created a coalition with the Christian Democratic People's Party (CDPP) and the Independent Smallholders' Party (ISP).[19] The Forum defined itself as a center-right "national party" and won the first multi-party parliamentary elections, in March–April 1990, gaining 164 out of 386 seats. The HDF was composed of three broad political-ideological trends: Christian democrats, populist-nationalists, and national liberals; all were recognized as integral components of the Forum. Its chairman and new premier, Antall, was considered to belong to the HDF centrist Christian democratic stream. He consistently tried to balance the three HDF wings and to prevent the growth of nationalist extremism.

The HDF endeavored to have a national and ethnic minorities law passed by the Hungarian National Assembly. It advocated the drafting of a regional charter providing for the rights of all European minorities. The government supplied financial assistance for all minorities, including Romas, to help support their political and cultural organizations and to fund their election campaigns.[20] The HDF was referred to as a "national party" because one of its primary activities after assuming office was the protection of Magyar minorities abroad. Through organizations such as the Secretariat for Hungarians Abroad, the government made the position of Magyar minorities one of its core foreign policy priorities.

Some critics accused the HDF of anti-Semitism and other extreme nationalistic tendencies, although such trends were visible only in one section of the Forum. In August 1992, *Magyar Fórum* published an article by István Csurka, a writer and deputy president of the HDF, which was peppered with anti-Semitic and other racist remarks. It suggested that Hungary was the victim of the ubiquitous Jewish "conspiracy" that obstructed the country's democratic transformation. Csurka attributed the apparent deterioration of Hungary to "genetic causes" and discussed the need for Hungarian *Lebensraum* (living space). The virulent nationalism that underlay the tract caused a political uproar in Hungary and spawned a pro-Csurka ideological movement called *Magyar Út* (Hungarian Way).

In October 1992, Csurka's supporters started to establish their own network of "circles" or "workshops" within the HDF, financed by the Hungarian Way Foundation. Their objective was to educate a new class of politicians concerned with "national and patriotic" questions and to gain broad support among rank-and-file Forum members. Because of Csurka's high position in the party, there was a pronounced fear that the HDF would swing toward the radical right, elevating a xenophobic ideology to the forefront of Hungarian politics. Alternatively, there were fears that the HDF could split into two or more small parties prior to the next general elections.

A number of parliamentary deputies from the HDF and the Independent Smallholders' Party (ISP) displayed some sympathy toward Csurka's views, although HDF leaders claimed Csurka's supporters were clearly in the minority in the National Assembly. HDF leaders met on two occasions in late August 1992 to discuss Csurka's tract, but no official condemnation was issued, as they calculated that the storm would subside. But Csurka's activities continued to fuel controversy by tacitly lending support to the burgeoning neo-Nazi skinhead movement, clearly hurting Hungary's reputation as a model post-communist state.

Csurka's policies were eventually condemned by Prime Minister Antall, who asserted that Csurka wanted to seize political power in the country through a takeover in the HDF. Meanwhile, the HDF Presidium ruled that the Hungarian Way circles were not permitted to operate within the Forum's basic party organization. In response, at its first national congress in February 1993, *Magyar Út* was launched as a "national movement" that would operate alongside the HDF. Csurka evidently estimated that although the time was not yet ripe to establish a distinct political party, *Magyar Út* could attract support from a broad range of citizens dissatisfied with the adverse effects of economic reform.

Csurka claimed that *Magyar Út* had some 60,000 followers, organized in about 400 local groups. It cooperated closely with the "Imre Mikó Circle" within the HDF parliamentary caucus, which sought to "strengthen Hungarian consciousness and the Society for the Protection of the Hungarian Spirit." In May 1993, a handful of Forum deputies established a "Hungarian Truth National Policy" inside the party's parliamentary faction. One of the group's leaders, Lajos Horváth, declared that it would support Csurka if he were ousted from the HDF. Some sources estimated that about 10% of the HDF's membership backed Csurka's extremist positions. In June 1993, the HDF's national steering committee voted to expel Csurka from the party. Csurka announced the creation of a new Hungarian Justice and Life Party (HJLP) that would include the *Magyar Út* network and about ten parliamentary deputies. The party intended to promote a more "national-oriented policy" and keep a close eye on "Hungarian national interests."[21]

After losing the May 1994 general elections, the HDF suffered a major internal rupture and a sharp drop in its popularity. In March 1996, the party split into two separate parties. The newly elected chairman, Sándor Lezsák, one of the Forum's founders, led the remaining HDF. Lezsák selected György Gemesi as the new executive deputy chairman. Lezsák supported cooperation between with the Christian Democrats and more openness toward the Independent Smallholders Party. Meanwhile, Iván Szabó, who resigned from his post as HDF parliamentary group leader soon after the election of Lezsák, founded a new party, the Hungarian Democratic People's Party (HDPP). The Szabó faction supported a more moderate national-liberal direction, including closer cooperation with the AYD-HCP, while the more populist-national wing, under Lezsák, backed the National Alliance and collaboration with the Smallholders. Justice Minister Ibolya Dávid was elected HDF chair, defeating Lezsák, on 30 January 1999. Dávid received nearly two-thirds of the vote.[22] She stated that the party must alter the way it presented itself to the public and that it must welcome back former members.[23]

The HDF performed poorly in the May 1998 parliamentary elections, having lost most of its support base to stronger center-right formations. It only managed to seat 17 deputies. Soon after the balloting, the HDF elected Ágoston Székelyhidi as its board chairman in an attempt to revive its sagging fortunes. Nevertheless, HDF was included in the new government coalition.

Christian Democratic People's Party (CDPP)
Keresztény Demokrata Néppárt (KDNP)

The Hungarian Christian Democrats claim a long historical pedigree. In 1947, the Democratic People's Party (DPP) won 62 seats in the Hungarian legislation, but in 1949, when the communists took power, some party leaders were arrested or fled into exile. In 1988, former members of the DPP formed a civil association (the Márton Áron Society) to bring together the Hungarian Christian Democrats, and finally they formed a party in September 1989. In the first democratic elections, in March–April 1990, they won 21 seats in parliament and joined the governing coalition. After the May 1994 elections, in which the CDPP captured 22 seats, the party went into opposition and underwent a major debate about its future policy. Most of the parliamentary deputies wanted to create an electoral bloc with the Alliance of Young Democrats (AYD-HCP) and the Hungarian Democratic Forum (HDF), but the majority of CDPP members sought to involve the extremist Hungarian Justice and Life

Party (HJLP) as well. The center-rightist deputies subsequently joined the Young Democrats and split off from the CDPP, forming the Christian Democratic Union (CDU). During the May 1998 general elections, the party failed to secure parliamentary representation. In the second round of voting, the party garnered 104,892 of the votes, or 2.31% of the total.[24] The president of the party was György Giczy.

Agrarians

Independent Smallholders' Party (ISP)
Független Kisgazda Földmunkás és Polgár Párt (FKgP)

The Independent Smallholders' Party (ISP) was originally founded in the early 1920s and was well represented in parliament before World War I. It became the largest party after the war, gaining 57% of votes in the first post-war elections, in November 1945. But the ISP was suppressed by the communists, who perceived the party as a major threat to their monopoly of power. Its leadership was jailed or fled into exile in the West. The party was revived in 1989 as a mainstream organization and became one of the HDF's coalition partners in government between 1990 and 1994. It sought to attract rural voters in particular, even though its traditional base of small farmers had been dispossessed and collectivized under communist rule. Through the early 1990s, the ISP began to benefit from growing support in rural areas.

The ISP was led by József Torgyán, who increasingly made provocative and extremist nationalist statements. In 1992, most of the ISP deputies split off from the governing coalition in order to pursue a more populist policy. They were instrumental in establishing a new nationalist bloc in January 1993, called the Christian National Union, that would allegedly "save the Hungarian people." But despite these claims, the ISP was able to win only twenty-six seats in parliament in May 1994. Torgyán and his faction forced many activists who did not accept his policy and authority to leave the party. But before the May 1998 parliamentary ballot, Torgyán abandoned his militant nationalistic line and started to attract center-rightist votes as well. The party performed well in the election, garnering 48 parliamentary seats. The Alliance of Young Democrats (AYD), which headed the new government coalition, initially did not want the ISP to join the electoral bloc and declared that it would not cooperate with the Smallholders' Party. However, after the elections it proved impossible to form a governing coalition without the ISP, which thus obtained four ministerial posts in the new administration.

In April 1999, tensions between the coalition partners, the AYD-HCP and the ISP, were provoked by disputes over the properties of the Vasas sports club. The majority of the Smallholders, including Torgyán, voted against the

Minister of Youth and Sports, Tamás Deutsch. At the same time, disputes within the ISP parliamentary faction raised calls for the dismissal of the Environment Minister, Pál Pepo, an ISP member. Torgyán refused to replace Pepo despite allegations of shady business dealings surrounding Pepo. Despite these crises, the coalition survived and resisted demands for early general elections.

Hungarian People's Party (HPP)
Magyar Néppárt (MNP)

The Hungarian People's Party (HPP) was established shortly after World War II as a radical leftist organization based in the countryside, that supported the communist remolding of society. Most of the party leadership decided to merge with the communists after 1947, and remained loyal agrarian allies of the ruling party. The HPP was recreated in 1988 by reform communists who wanted to establish a rural base for the newly formed Hungarian Socialist Party. In the March–April 1990 general elections, the HPP barely gained 0.75% of the vote and failed to capture any parliamentary seats. The party subsequently faded from the political scene.

Other, smaller agrarian and rural-based parties included the Agrarian Alliance (AA) (Agrárszövetség, ASZ), which registered under 4% of the vote in the March–April 1990 and May 1994 parliamentary elections.

Greens

Greens (G)
Zöldek (Z)

Hungary's environmentalist movement at the political level remained largely insignificant during the 1990s. Green parties existed as small, single-issue political formations. For example, the Greens (G) obtained less than 5% of the vote in the May 1998 general elections. The Green Alternative (GA) participated in the May 1994 parliamentary ballot and scored under 1% of the total. In the same elections, the Hungarian Green Party (HGP) garnered less than 1% of the national vote. Prior to that, in the March–April 1990 parliamentary ballot, the HGP also performed miserably. Ecological issues evidently were not high on the public agenda. However, the environmental disasters along the Tisza and Szamos rivers in January 2000 created by a cyanide leak originating in Romania raised public concerns over the country's susceptibility to ecological challenges, and the issue was likely to figure more prominently in future political campaigns. However, it remained uncertain whether the small green movements could benefit from heightened public concern.

Communists

Hungarian Workers' Party (HWP)
Magyar Munkáspárt (MM)

The hard-line communist party, the Hungarian Workers' Party (HWP), consisted of remnants of the former ruling Hungarian Socialist Workers' Party (HSWP). The HWP, led by Gyula Thürmer, opposed NATO membership, allegedly because of the high costs involved and the potential loss of Hungarian sovereignty. It advocated Hungarian neutrality, more trade with Russia, and a lessened focus on the European market. The party gained little influence and narrowly missed achieving the 5% threshold for entry into parliament for all three parliamentary elections during the 1990s. Moreover, the reformist wing of the former communist ruling party had successfully transformed itself into a pan-European social democratic formation. As in all other Central European states, hard-line communism and its reformist variations had only marginal public appeal and was closely associated in public perceptions with decades of Soviet domination.

Nationalists

Hungarian Justice and Life Party (HJLP)
Magyar Igazság és élet Pártja (MIéP)

This nationalist party was established and chaired by István Csurka, a former member of the Hungarian Democratic Forum, who was expelled from the HDF in June 1993.[25] Its platform included a revision of privatization, the abolition of "anti-Hungarian racial discrimination," the establishment of a national civic guard, and the creation of a civil disobedience movement. The HJLP was widely considered an anti-Semitic party. Csurka often made racist speeches and published anti-Jewish tracts calling for a "Christian-national" Hungary.[26]

Like most ultranationalist formations, the HJLP supported state protection over the national economy in order to keep it "purely Hungarian" and to prevent an alleged takeover by foreign capital and "alien" business interests. The party feared the "globalization" process, seeing it as a major threat to the independence and survival of the Hungarian nation. The HJLP garnered significant public support among disenchanted and frustrated sectors of the population susceptible to populist and nationalist demagoguery. However, in the May 1994 parliamentary elections it only scrambled together a mere 1.59% of the national total.

During the May 1998 general elections, the party narrowly crossed the 5% threshold necessary to acquire parliamentary representation, and won 14 seats in the legislature. During the environmental disaster in the Tisza and

Szamos rivers in late January 2000, which the ultranationalists described as deliberate sabotage by the Romanian authorities, Csurka called for an independent Transylvania. He also demanded the annexation of the Hungarian-inhabited parts of Vojvodina by Hungary after the end of the NATO war against Serbia in the summer of 1999. According to the party's own website, it called itself the "mouthpiece of national radicalism."[27] In September 1998, the Council of Europe referred to the HJLP in its report as a "xenophobic, anti-Semitic party."

Christian National Union (CNU)
Keresztény Nemzeti Unió (KNU)

The Christian National Union (CNU) was one of several right-wing organizations that appealed for a "renewal" of the Hungarian nation after decades of imposed communist "internationalism." Like other extremist groupings, it regarded the stipulations of the 1920 Trianon Treaty as unjust, and it called for a redefinition of Hungary's borders to include the Magyar minorities in neighboring states. On the seventieth anniversary of the treaty, the CNU staged a protest rally in Budapest. Despite its revisionist pronouncements, the CNU appeared to be less militant than other nationalist groups. It advocated a "peaceful" way of redrawing borders and did not seem to espouse an explicitly racist philosophy. Despite the CNU's vehemently Christian pronouncements, no significant political groups or religious bodies supported the organization.

Neofascists

Holy Crown Society (HCS)
Szentkorona Társulat (SzT)

The Holy Crown Society (HCS) was an openly neofascist grouping that claimed to exert substantial influence over the activities and organization of Hungary's nascent skinhead movement. Its leadership and goals were not widely known, but there was a suspected connection with László Romhányi, the editor of the neofascist political journal *Szent Korona* (Holy Crown). The skinhead groups were loosely structured, although there appeared to be some direction from extreme rightist groups such as the 1956 Anti-Fascist and Anti-Bolshevik Association. Indeed, skinhead youths acted as security guards for these organizations. Most skinhead spokesmen espoused a Nazi-like philosophy regarding the alleged superiority of the Magyar "race." There were strong parallels with other skinhead groups in Europe and North America in their appearance, the youthful age of members, their political inclinations, and their avid use of violence. Skinhead formations have not formed any distinct political parties, but they are asso-

ciated with various nationalist youth groups, some of which are legally registered. According to police reports, skinheads had several hundred active gang
members in Budapest alone.

Independent National Youth Front (INYF)
Független Nemzeti Ifjúsági Front (FNIF)

This neofascist organization established in October 1992 claims nearly 2,000
members nationwide, most of whom are active, or former, skinheads. The
INYF has branches in the towns of Eger, Veszprém, Szeged, Miskolc, and
Debrecen. According to István Szöke, the self-proclaimed "patron of the Hungarian skinheads," the INYF aimed to "organize the military and patriotic
education of young people" and to provide physical education, sports training, and camping programs for nationalist youth. Its political goals included
the removal of Jews and former communist activists from positions of power
(it alleged that this small "elite" still controlled national life).

If skinheads could be considered to have a common goal, it would be the
creation of an ethnically pure Hungary. Most skinhead activities have involved
violent acts, such as the beating and stabbing of non-Magyars, usually Roma
(Gypsies). Often these juveniles have shouted fascist slogans and displayed
Nazi relics, such as swastikas, pictures of Adolf Hitler, and symbols of the
Arrow Cross movement, Hungary's wartime fascist organization. Skinhead
groups in Hungary were also believed to have maintained contacts with
neofascist Hungarian organizations in the West. On 23 October 1992, skinheads
sporting Nazi symbols disrupted a rally commemorating the anniversary of
the 1956 uprising and the 1989 proclamation of a post-communist Hungary,
forcing President Göncz to leave without speaking. The Interior Ministry was
criticized for allegedly ignoring the growing danger of neo-Nazi violence in
Hungary.[28] The skinhead movement continued to attract a small following
throughout the 1990s but did not have any significant impact on national
politics.

Hungarian National Alliance (HNA)
Magyar Nemzeti Szövetség (MNSz)

Until his arrest in July 1992, László Romhányi was the chairman of the ultra-
nationalist Hungarian National Alliance (HNA) party. The subsequent Alliance leader was reputed to be Romhányi's deputy, Imre Bosnyák. The HNA
had its origins in the initial burgeoning of opposition to the communist regime. In April 1987, Romhányi was appointed director of the Jurta Theater,
which later became the center for opposition parties, including the Hungarian
Democratic Forum, the Alliance of Free Democrats, and the Alliance of Young
Democrats. After the parliamentary elections in March–April 1990, the Jurta
Theater became a center catering to extreme nationalist political entities. The

HNA, the CNU, the Hungarian Legitimist Party (HLP) chaired by László Pálos, and other rightist groups congregated at Jurta to formulate an ultranationalist ideology later referred to as the "Spirit of Jurta." In May 1992, Romhányi delivered a speech at the "national ceremonies" at the Jurta Theater in which he urged cooperation between all nationalist and rightist forces, called for the disbanding of parliament, and demanded the resignation of the government. In July 1992, Romhányi and four associates were arrested and accused of torturing and then murdering a homeless man whom they had employed as a courier. Romhányi's arrest appeared to thwart his political ambitions.

Hungarian National Front (HNF)
Magyar Nemzeti Front (MNF)

Formerly known as the Hungarian National Socialist Action Group, the Hungarian National Front (HNF) became an openly neo-Nazi organization, led by the radical fascist István Györkös. The HNF intended to transform itself into a mass-based political party based on the heritage of the wartime Arrow Cross movement, which engaged in atrocities against Hungary's Jewish population. Györkös claimed to have contacts with several skinhead gangs, other ultranationalist groupings in Hungary, and with neofascist émigré organizations and neo-Nazi movements in Germany, Austria, and Spain. In February 1993, Györkös was arrested and charged with inciting hatred against minorities and aliens, and with the illegal possession of firearms. He received a one-year suspended sentence.[29]

1956 Anti-Fascist and Anti-Bolshevik Association (AAA)
1956–os Antifasiszta és Antibolseviszta Szövetség (AASz)

A neofascist organization led by Sándor Hajós and István Porubsky, the 1956 Anti-Fascist and Anti-Bolshevik Association (AAA) was allied with extreme nationalist political groups such as the Hungarian National Alliance. Providing what Hajós described as history lessons and physical training, the Association became a youth group for skinhead gangs in Budapest, referred to by the AAA as "national conservative–thinking youth." It claimed to have the support of elements of the Independent Smallholders' Party as well as István Csurka and Interior Minister Péter Boross. Its objective was to counter the government's "lukewarm centrist politics," which were strongly criticized in Csurka's anti-Semitic tract.[30]

Another neofascist organization was the Hungarian Welfare Society (HWS), or the Association for the Welfare of the Hungarian People (AWHP) (*Verband der Ungarischen Volkswohlfahrt*), led by Albert Szabó, whose chief plank was a struggle against "foreign oppression." It called for U.S. troops to leave Hungary and demanded the resignation of the "Western-leaning" government.[31]

In March 1999, the organization held a public rally under police supervision where Szabó destroyed a NATO emblem and a Star of David, which he called symbols of "inhuman actions enforced under the banner of Zionism."[32]

Ethnic Minority and Religious Parties

National Minority Roundtable (NMR)
Kisebbségi Kerekasztal (KK)

Toso Doncsev became the executive chairman of this umbrella lobbying group created in January 1991. The NMR was composed of representatives from minority organizations and was directly involved in the creation of the law on ethnic and national minorities. Groups participating in the Roundtable included the Phralipe Independent Gypsy Association, the Roma Parliament, the Association of Germans in Hungary, the Democratic Union of Slovaks in Hungary, the Croatian Democratic Alliance, the Democratic Federation of Romanians in Hungary, the Federation of Slovenes in Hungary, and the Democratic Federation of Serbs. The NMR garnered support from liberal opposition parties such as the AFD and the AYD-HCP. It was created to draw on minority support in negotiations with the government and to play an active role in the formulation of a minority law.

Another primary goal of the Roundtable was to ensure cooperation and promote understanding among the country's various minorities. A first draft of the minorities bill, drawn up by the Justice Ministry at the end of 1990, was rejected by several minority organizations, which decided to establish the NMR. Two subsequent drafts were drawn up independently by the NMR and the government's Office of National and Ethnic Minorities (ONEM), from which a common version was finalized. Because of unacceptable modifications, the NMR rejected this draft, which was accepted by the Hungarian government in December 1991. According to the Roundtable, the bill, resubmitted by relevant government ministries, applied rules that allegedly discriminated against certain minorities. However, it remained unclear which stipulations were being questioned or which minorities would be affected. The revised bill also purportedly limited cultural autonomy through self-governing bodies established for minorities, and it did not solve the problem of parliamentary representation. NMR representatives approved the final version of the Minority Code, which was passed in July 1993.[33]

Nationality Council of Gypsies in Hungary (NCGH)
Magyarországi Cigányok Nemzetiségi Uniója (MCNU)

Roma (Gypsy) numbers have long been underreported in the national census. For example, the official count in 1960 was about 25,000, but the unofficial estimate exceeded 200,000. Many Roma continue to resist integration into

Hungarian society and experience persistent public prejudice. The Roma population possessed only rudimentary political, religious, and cultural organizations under communism, but various governmental economic programs have since been launched to improve their material conditions and employment opportunities.

The Nationality Council of Gypsies in Hungary (NCGH) was created in June 1990 and regards itself as the highest organ of the Romani community. It became an umbrella organization for seven Roma parties and groups, the most important of which were Phralipe, the Democratic Alliance of Hungarian Gypsies (DAHG), and the Hungarian Gypsy Party (HGP). Other organizations forming the Council included the Social Democratic Party of Gypsies in Hungary, the Budapest Gypsy Band Union, the Gypsy Workers' Federation, the Baranya County Cultural and Education Union, and the Justice Party of Hungarian Gypsies. The main goal of the NCGH was to promote cooperation among the often quarrelsome Romani organizations and to try to end the fragmentation that had plagued Gypsy politics since 1989.[34]

Notable among the Roma parties were the Hungarian Gypsy Party (HGP) *(Magyar Cigány Párt, MCP)* established in June 1989, which grew into the largest Gypsy party, and the Hungarian Gypsy Social Democratic Party (HGSDP) *(Magyar Cigány Szociáldemokrata Párt, MCSzP)* created in October 1989 as an ally of the Hungarian Social Democratic Party (HSDP), which included more than 15,000 members. Although the HGSDP and the HSDP provided each other with mutual assistance prior to the 1990 elections, by the end of March 1990 their alliance had collapsed. The HGSDP accused the HSDP of failing to abide by its promise to field Romani candidates on the Social Democrat ticket, while the HSDP proved unable to win any seats in parliament. The Gypsy community remained highly fractured in its political and group loyalties.[35]

Roma Parliament (RP)
Magyarországi Romaparlament (MRP)

The Roma Parliament (RP) became the governing body for different Romani (Gypsy) political factions, chaired by Aladár Horváth. Although not a political party, the Roma Parliament (RP) played an important role in articulating Gypsy demands to the Hungarian authorities. It wanted the government and the National Assembly to specifically ensure human, constitutional, and national minority rights for the Roma population. In the summer of 1991, the RP presented a petition to the government demanding parliamentary representation for all national and ethnic minorities. It also requested that a national minorities bill be presented to parliament by the end of September 1991, and asked the National Assembly for two billion forints (Hungarian currency) to be used for Gypsy vocational retraining and employment programs.

The RP maintained an adversarial relationship with the Antall government. For instance, there were disputes over what the RP viewed as government antipathy toward Gypsies. In November 1991, the RP asked the prime minister to remove János Báthory, the deputy director of the Office for National and Ethnic Minorities, because of his alleged anti-Gypsy remarks. The Roma Parliament also accused another Gypsy organization, DAHG, of complicity in the theft of one million forints from the office of Deputy Chairman Béla Osztojkán. The ensuing polemical dispute between the RP leadership and DAHG Chairman Gyula Náday resulted in demands to dismiss Horváth from the major opposition party, the Alliance of Free Democrats (AFD). The RP, together with other groups, undertook various initiatives to coordinate Romani interests. For instance, it helped establish a National Coordinating Center of Roma Communities in January 1993: the Center was designed to prepare individuals for local and national elections. In July 1993, the RP helped organize a Romani rally in the town of Eger, labeled as Hungary's "skinhead capital," protesting against skinhead attacks on Romani communities.[36]

Democratic Alliance of Hungarian Gypsies (DAHG)
Magyarországi Cigányok Demokratikus Szövetsége (MCDSz)

Gyula Náday became the chairman of this leftist Roma political party formed in January 1989. It tried to gain representation in the National Assembly in order to pursue its program of Romani "societal renewal." One of its prime objectives was to ensure economic progress and self-sufficiency by patterning Gypsy village settlements along the lines of the Israeli *kibbutz* system. The DAHG was one of the major players in the ongoing conflict among Roma organizations. Náday orchestrated demonstrations at the Roma Parliament (RP) headquarters to protest alleged moral misconduct of the three main RP leaders. He also sought to persuade Péter Tölgyessy, the chairman of the Association of Free Democrats (AFD), to review and revoke the membership of Aladár Horváth, the RP chairman. Charges of corruption against Alliance leaders, stemming from a substantial infusion of government money, led to a factional split in the DAHG in December 1989.[37]

Phralipe Independent Gypsy Association (PIGA)
"Phralipe" (Testvériség) Független Cigány Szervezet (PFCSz)

Established in April 1989, *Phralipe*, which means "brotherhood" in Romani, became an organization dominated primarily by Romani intellectuals and was openly critical of government policies toward the Gypsies during the 1980s. Its aim was to consolidate an awareness of Romani identity and to strengthen Gypsy community solidarity. It endeavored to ensure Romani rights in the workplace and in dealings with the authorities. It reported on racist violence against Gypsy communities by skinhead gangs and abuses perpetrated by policemen.

A similar organization, the Amalipe Union for Promotion of Gypsy Culture and Tradition (AUPGCT), was created to represent the traditional, trade-oriented Gypsy clans, such as the Tinkers and the Bear Trainers.[38]

An Anti-Fascist Organization of Hungarian Gypsies (AFOHG) (*Magyar Cigányok Antifasiszta Szervezete, MCASz*) was formed to protect Gypsies against racially motivated attacks. During German Chancellor Helmut Kohl's visit to Hungary for the signing of the German-Hungarian Treaty, the organization (along with the Roma Parliament's Presidium) sent the German leader a letter requesting compensation for the relatives of the estimated 70,000 Hungarian Gypsies deported and killed by the Nazis during World War II. According to the letter, in 1970 the West German government gave the Hungarian Communist government DM 100 million as compensation for war crimes, none of which was channeled to the Roma.[39]

Association of Germans in Hungary (AGH)
Magyarországi Németek Szövetsége (MNSz)

In the early 1990s, Géza Hambuch became the executive secretary and Karl Manhertz (Károly Manherz) the vice president of the Association of Germans in Hungary (AGH). It did not style itself as a political party, but rather as an umbrella organization articulating the demands of the German minority. Its primary goal was to promote German educational and cultural needs, such as expanding the German-language school system and providing for more German radio and television programs. The AGH opposed the restoration of land to the pre-communist, pre-1947 owners, regarding this as an injustice against the German minority. It demanded an accurate count of ethnic Germans in the country in order to establish German-language schools corresponding to the size of the population. German-language education evidently needed to be instituted from kindergarten through high school in order to help preserve the language. According to Hambuch, the German language in Hungary had become a "grandmother language, spoken only by elderly people." During a meeting of the AGH national board in January 1990, a call was issued for the direct election of three German representatives to the national parliament.

At the completion of the February 1992 German-Hungarian Treaty, Secretary Hambuch met with Chancellor Kohl to request assistance for teaching the German language in schools. The German government has spent about DM 2 million per annum since 1987 on cultural and educational aid to Hungary's German minority. The AGH published a weekly, *Neue Zeitung* (New Newspaper), which received assistance from the German Danubian Swabian Cultural Foundation. German activists also established the Association of German Writers and Artists in Hungary (AGWAH) in February 1992 to revive and promote German artistic traditions in Hungary.[40]

Democratic Union of Slovaks in Hungary (DUSH)
Magyarországi Szlovákok Szövetsége (MSzSz)

The Slovak population in Hungary has been relatively dispersed in several northern and western counties. Their numbers decreased from approximately 200,000 at the close of World War II to under 22,000 in the 1970 census. Much of the loss was the consequence of a major population exchange with Czechoslovakia after World War II, when about 73,000 Slovaks were transferred to Slovakia and a commensurate number of Magyars were dispatched to Hungary. At various times, Slovak nationalists claimed that the Slovak minority bore the brunt of human rights violations and sustained assimilationist pressures. But despite claims of persecution and enforced Magyarization under the post-Stalinist governments, the Slovaks were able to establish their own national organizations, schools, and cultural groups. Nonetheless, the departure of a large intellectual stratum after World War II had a negative impact on ethnic coherence and cultural development among the remaining Slovaks.

Although approximately forty years old, the Democratic Union of Slovaks in Hungary (DUSH) was finally allowed to create a membership base in 1989. Mária Jakab, its chairwoman, was also the parliamentary representative-at-large for national minorities. She was transferred from the post of general secretary at the November 1990 party congress. The Union became a political interest bloc representing different Slovak organizations dispersed among 104 Slovak communities in Hungary. Other Slovak organizations not affiliated with DUSH included the Association of Slovak Writers in Hungary, whose chairman was Gregor Papucsek, and the Organization of Slovak Youth in Hungary, led by Anton Pavlik. The DUSH's main goal was to halt the assimilation of Hungarian Slovaks.

The DUSH wanted to strengthen Slovak national consciousness and to preserve the community's mother tongue. It sought to create a self-governing body that would represent Slovak interests on a national level and coordinate the activities of local organizations. The DUSH supported the passage of a nationality law that could economically empower ethnic minorities. Jakab also voiced opposition to proposals issued by the Slovak Heritage Foundation and the Institute for Slovaks Living Abroad to allow international forums to settle the status of Slovaks in Hungary. The DUSH's Deputy Chairwoman Anna István complained about a discrepancy in the Hungarian government's aid to Magyars residing outside of Hungary's borders versus that given to ethnic minorities inside Hungary. According to her, there was too much official emphasis on the well-being of Magyars abroad.[41]

Jewish Cultural Federation (JCF)
Magyar Zsidók Kulturális Egyesülete (MZsKE)

Jewish political and cultural life was stifled by the communist regime, but after Stalin's death Jews were able to resume many of their cultural, religious, and educational activities. In fact, Jewish life in Hungary—particularly in Budapest, where the vast majority of Jews resided—was the most vibrant in communist-controlled Eastern Europe. The JCF was formed in 1988, shortly before the democratic changes, under the chairmanship of Endre Rózsa, a radio journalist. It was the first major Jewish organization created independently of the communist-supervised communal structures, and its leaders were critical of the subservient role played by various Jewish religious and cultural bodies. The JCF organized lectures on Jewish topics and published the magazine *Szombat* (*Sabbath*). Several of its leaders became active in the liberal opposition grouping the Alliance of Free Democrats and were elected to parliament.

In 1991, the former communist-sponsored National Representation of Hungarian Israelites (NRHI) was renamed and revamped and a democratic constitution was adopted. At the same time, the Council of Jewish Organizations (CJO) was created to reorganize various aspects of Jewish communal affairs. Gusztáv Zoltai, a former director of the Central Board of Hungarian Jews (CBHJ), was the first president of the newly created Alliance of Hungarian Jewish Religious Communities (AHJRC) *(Magyarországi Zsidó Hitközségek Szövetsége, MAZsIHISz)*. These organizations were instrumental in preserving and reviving the Jewish religious, cultural, and educational heritage. In March 1990, the Hungarian Zionist organization (HZO) was re-established, headed by Tibor Englander, as an affiliate of the World Zionist Organization based in Jerusalem, and an office of B'nai B'rith was also opened in Budapest.[42]

Croatian Democratic Alliance (CDA)
Magyarországi Horvátok Szövetsége (MHSz)

Hungary's south Slav population declined after the two World Wars as a result of territorial changes and demographic movements. From approximately one quarter of a million people in 1941, the total Slav population barely reached 100,000 after the war. The Croats along the Drava River formed the largest group, followed by Serbs and Slovenes who were settled in a few territorial pockets. These populations did not present a significant source of dispute between Hungary and Yugoslavia and were permitted to create their own cultural and social associations.

The Croatian Democratic Alliance (CDA) was created in January 1990 in Baja and Pécs, as a result of the schism within the Democratic Alliance of South Slavs (DASS); independent Serb and Slovene groups were also formed at this time. Its President, Djuro Franković (György Frankovics), was the former secretary of the DASS. The CDA pushed for the rejuvenation of Croat culture by re-establishing Croatian elementary schools and training Croatian clergy to serve churches in the seventy to eighty Croat settlements in western Hungary.[43]

A Federation of Slovenes in Hungary (FSH) *(Magyarországi Szlovének Szövetsége, MSzSz)* was established in 1990 and led by President József Hírnök. In June 1992, it signed a five-year cooperation agreement with the local administration of Murska Sobota district in Slovenia. The agreement dealt with economic, transportational, cultural, and sports-related cooperation between Murska Sobota and the FSH-represented districts in western Hungary.

Democratic Federation of Serbs (DFS)
Szerb Demokratikus Szövetség (SzDSz)

A Serbian Action Committee was created in January 1990, in the wake of the dissolution of the Democratic Alliance of South Slavs. During a gathering of the DFS assembly in November 1992, its leaders underscored that the Serb minority was entitled to parliamentary representation following the general elections scheduled in 1994. The DFS also announced that it would allocate a larger share of its budget to the cultural and educational activities of local branches, and it pressed for the return of property previously confiscated from the Serbian Orthodox Church. Complaints were raised that Budapest only had one Yugoslav school, which split into Serb and Croat factions. Serbs sought assurances that they would receive financial support from the state to open a purely Serbian school. Among other minority organizations the Federation of Bulgarians in Hungary (FBH) *(Magyarországi Bolgárok Szövetsége, MBSz)*, represented about 2,500 Bulgarian residents. Its executive chairman, Toso Doncsev, was also the executive chairman of the National Minorities Roundtable.[44]

A youth organization, the Mladost Youth Association (MYA) *(Ifjúsági Szervezet–Mladost, ISzM)*, representing young Croats, Serbs, and Slovenes, was established in January 1990. Ivica Djurok became its first leader. It sought institutional guarantees for the political representation of national minorities. It also demanded that minority members elected to parliament achieve their posts through mainstream political organizations already represented in the legislature, rather than through the direct election of minority parties. *Mladost* called for an infusion of minority professionals into ethnic organizations, to "enable national minorities to have a serious and genuine influence on the issues that concerned them in the areas of politics, economics, legislation, as well as state administration."[45]

Democratic Association of Romanians in Hungary (DARH)
Magyarországi Románok Demokratikus Szövetsége (MRDSz)

The Romanian population in the eastern counties of Hungary declined from about one million in 1940 to a little over 12,000 in the 1970 census. The Democratic Association of Romanians in Hungary (DARH) was originally founded in 1949 to promote cultural traditions and the Romanian mother tongue. It was formerly known as the Democratic Federation of Romanians in Hungary (DFRH), one of the numerous minority organizations created under the auspices of the communist regime. Because of mistrust among the Romanian minority, the DARH decided to dissolve and restructure itself in June 1990. National Assembly Deputy György (Gheorghe) Márk became the Association's executive secretary, while Gheorghe Mihaiescu was elected chairman of the board and the national council. Headquartered in Gyula, the DARH endeavored to play a part in the creation of a law governing the rights of all minorities in Hungary. The DARH promoted Romanian-language instruction in schools and took part in negotiations with the government to develop a nationalities law.

Like most other minority organizations in Hungary, the DARH was an advocate of the 1990 law awarding direct parliamentary representation to all minorities, over and above the 386 members of parliament elected under the rules of the electoral law. The Association wanted to maintain close relationships with Romania, but condemned the human rights abuses committed in Romania against resident minority groups—specifically, against Magyars in Transylvania. DARH members aided Romanian refugees fleeing to Hungary in the last months of the Ceauşescu regime by distributing Romanian-Hungarian dictionaries and by finding temporary shelters for them in the homes of Hungarian Romanians.[46]

Another Romanian organization, the Federation of Romanians in Hungary (FRH) (*Magyarországi Románok Szövetsége, MRSz*), was established in December 1990 in Gyula as an avowedly democratic and grassroots-oriented alternative to the DARH. Its president, Gheorghe Petruşan (György Petrusan), claimed it represented the interests of all ethnic Romanians living in Hungary, as a mass movement rather than as a partisan political organization. The FRH's primary concern was the preservation of Romanian culture, manifested in the use of the Romanian language. It supported the passage of the national minorities bill in order to obtain government resources for the establishment of ethnic schools. The Federation also concerned itself with the cultural reawakening of the Romanian people based around its intellectual heritage.

POLITICAL DATA

Name of State: Republic of Hungary (*Magyarország*)
Form of Government: Republic
Structure of Legislature: Unicameral legislature (Országgyűlés, National Assembly) electing the Prime Minister and the President. The 386 members of parliament are elected by popular vote under a system of direct and proportional representation.
Size of Territory: 35,919 square miles
Size of Population: 10,106,017 (July 2001 est.)

Composition of Population:

Ethnic Group	Number	% of Population
Hungarians	9,477,362	91.35
Roma (Gypsies)	404,461	3.90
Germans	175,000	1.69
Slovaks	110,000	1.06
Jews	80,000	0.77
Croats	80,000	0.77
Romanians	25,000	0.24
Greeks	6,000	0.06
Serbs	5,000	0.05
Slovenes	5,000	0.05
Armenians	3,000	0.03
Bulgarians	2,500	0.02
Poles	2,000	0.02
Total minorities	897,961	8.65
Total population	10,375,323	100.00

Sources: By East European standards, Hungary's population was ethnically homogeneous. According to official Hungarian statistical estimates in 1991, out of a population of 10,375,323, approximately 8.71% were members of national, ethnic, and religious minorities. Population figures are conservative estimates provided by minority organizations, official or semiofficial sources, and media reports. See also Andre Leibich, "Minorities in Eastern Europe: Obstacles to a Reliable Count," Radio Free Europe/Radio Liberty Research Institute (RFE/RL), *Report on Eastern Europe*, Vol. 1, No. 20, 15 May 1992; and Alfred A. Reisch, "First Law on Minorities Drafted," RFE/RL, *Report on Eastern Europe*, Vol. 2, No. 50, 13 December 1991. For other census data, see "National and Ethnic Minorities in Hungary," *Fact Sheets on Hungary*, No. 9, 1991 Budapest: Hungarian Ministry of Foreign Affairs.

ELECTION RESULTS

Known for its complexity, Hungary's general election is held in two rounds. The 386 parliamentary seats are divided and gained through voting on three lists: single-member or individual lists; regional or territorial lists; and national lists.

Candidates running on single-member lists who obtain more than 50% of the vote in the first round are elected directly to parliament. Such an occurrence is rare. Candidates who obtain more than 15% of the vote, or the top three candidates (whichever number is greater) in the first round advance to the second round of voting. Out of the 386 mandates of parliament, 176 are distributed on the single-member lists.

Regional or territorial mandates are won on the basis of proportional representation. Out of the 386 parliamentary seats, 128 were distributed on the regional lists in 1998; 125 seats in 1994; and 120 seats in the 1990 election.

National lists: National mandates are allocated on the basis of "residual" votes. Votes are apportioned between parties that obtain more than 5% of the national vote, but which fail to win a seat on the regional or single-member lists. Out of the 386 mandates of parliament, 82 were distributed on the national lists in 1998; 85 in 1994; and 90 in the 1990 election.

Sources: Martyn Rady. The 1994 Hungarian General Election, http://www.igc.apc.org and the Hungarian Central Election Commission, http://www.valasztas.hu.

Presidential Election (Indirect), 6 June 2000

Candidate	Votes	% of Vote
Ferenc Mádl	243	69
Against and invalid	108	31
Total	351	100

Presidential Election (Indirect), 19 June 1995

Candidate	Votes	% of Vote
Árpád Göncz	259	77
Against and invalid	76	23
Total	335	100

Presidential Election (Indirect), 3 August 1990

Candidate	Votes	% of Vote
Árpád Göncz	295	95
Total	310	100

Source: MTI Hungarian News Agency, 7 July 1995.

Parliamentary Elections, 10 and 24 May 1998

Turnout: 56.26% First Round, 57.01% Second Round

Parliamentary Seats divided by three voting lists:

Party/Coalition	Regional List	National List	Individual List	Total
Alliance of Young Democrats	48	10	90	148
Hungarian Socialist Party	50	30	54	134
Independent Smallholders' Party	22	14	12	48
Alliance of Free Democrats	5	17	2	24
Hungarian Democratic Forum	—	—	17	17
Hungarian Justice and Life Party	3	11	—	14
Independents	—	—	1	1
Total	128	82	176	386

Sources: (for all three parliamentary elections): The Hungarian Ministry of Interior, Central Data Processing, Registration and Election Office, http://www.valasztas.hu; Economic University of Budapest, http://www.bke.hu/politologia/adatok/vaszt.html; Political Transformation and the Electoral Process in Post-Communist Europe, University of Essex, http://www2.essex.ac.uk/elect/electer/hu_er_nl.htm; István Stumpf, "The Realignment of Political Power after the Elections," in Luca Gabor (Ed.) *Parliamentary Elections,* Budapest, 1994, pp. 574–575; and Magyar Kozlony, Budapest, No. 25, 1990; and György Szoboszlai (Ed.), Parliamentary Elections, 1990, Budapest, MTA, 1990, pp. 455–476.

Parliamentary Elections, 8 and 29 May 1994

Turnout: 68.92% First Round, 55.11% Second Round

Parliamentary Seats divided by three voting lists:

Party/Coalition	Regional List	National List	Individual List	Total
Hungarian Socialist Party	53	7	149	209
Alliance of Free Democrats	28	25	16	69
Hungarian Democratic Forum	18	15	5	38
Independent Smallholders' Party	14	11	1	26
Christian Democratic People's Party	5	14	3	22
Alliance of Young Democrats–Hungarian Civic Party	7	13	—	20
Agrarian Alliance	—	—	1	1
Joint Candidate	—	—	1	1
Total	125	85	176	386

Parliamentary Elections, 25 March and 8 April 1990

Turnout: 65.09% First Round, 45.50% Second Round

Parliamentary Seats divided by three voting lists:

Party/Coalition	Regional List	National List	Individual List	Total
Hungarian Democratic Forum	40	10	114	164
Alliance of Free Democrats	34	23	35	92
Independent Smallholders' Party	16	17	11	44
Hungarian Socialist Party	14	18	1	32
Alliance of Young Democrats	8	12	1	22
Christian Democratic People's Party	8	10	3	21
Agrarian Alliance	—	—	1	1
Independents	—	—	6	6
Joint Candidates	—	—	4	4
Total	120	90	176	386

NOTES

1. For recent histories of Hungary see Stephen Borsody (Ed.), *The Hungarians: A Divided Nation*, New Haven: Yale University Press, 1988; Jorg K. Hoensch, *A History of Modern Hungary, 1867–1986*, London: Longman, 1988; Bennett Kovrig, *Communism in Hungary: From Kun to Kádár*, Stanford: Hoover Institution Press, 1979; Hans-Georg Heinrich, *Hungary: Politics, Economics and Society*, Boulder: Lynne Rienner, 1986; and Charles Gati, *Hungary and the Soviet Bloc*, Durham: Duke University Press, 1986.

2. See R.J. Crampton, *Eastern Europe in the Twentieth Century*, London: Routledge, 1994, p. 316.

3. For background on the constitutional changes see Edith Oltay, "Constitutional Amendments Strengthen Civil Rights, Pave Way for Multiparty System," RFE/RL, *Situation Report: Hungary*, SR/17, 30 November 1989.

4. See Attila Agh, "The Strength of Hungary's Weak President," *Transition*, Vol. 2, No. 25, 13 December 1996, pp. 24–27.

5. For an excellent concise analysis of the Hungarian political transformation see Rudolf L. Tokes, "Party Politics and Political Participation in Postcommunist Hungary," in Karen Dawisha and Bruce Parrott (Eds.), *The Consolidation of Democracy in East-Central Europe*, Cambridge: Cambridge University Press, 1997, pp. 109–149. See also Rudolf L. Tokes, *Hungary's Negotiated Revolution: Economic Reforms, Social Change, and Political Succession, 1957–1990*, Cambridge: Cambridge University Press, 1996.

6. Sources include: "Hungary and Its People," Fact Sheets on Hungary, 1992, Ministry of Foreign Affairs, Budapest, MTI Printing Shop, March 1992; and "A Short History of Coalition Governments in Hungary," Fact Sheets on Hungary, 1994, Ministry of Foreign Affairs, Budapest, MTI Printing Shop, September 1994.

7. For a helpful analysis see Linda J. Cook and Mitchell A. Orenstein, "The Return of the Left and Its Impact on the Welfare State in Poland, Hungary, and Russia," in Linda J. Cook, Mitchell A. Orenstein, and Marilyn Rueschemeyer, *Left Parties and Social Policy in Postcommunist Europe*, Boulder: Westview Press, 1999, pp. 47–108.

8. *MTI*, Budapest, "Local Elections Start in Hungary," in *FBIS-EEU-98–291*, 19 October 1998.

9. Kossuth Radio, Budapest, in *FBIS-EEU-98–292*, 19 October 1998.

10. See Hungary 1999: Country Commercial Guide, U.S. State Department, http://www.state.gov.

11. For details on the HSP see Ivan Szelenyi, Eva Fodor, and Eric Hanley, "Left Turn in Post-Communist Politics: Bringing Class Back In?" *East European Politics and Societies*, Vol. 11, No. 1, Winter 1997.

12. www.europeanforum.bot-consult.se/cup/hungary/socdem.htm.

13. Radio Free Europe, *Newsline*, 24 June 1999.

14. See http://www.europeanforum.bot-consult.se/cup/hungary/socdem.htm.

15. http://www.centraleurope.com/special/huelect/freedemo.php3.

16. James Toole, Country Files: Hungary: Annual Report 1998; and http://www.transitions-online.org/countries/hunar98.html.

17. László Keri, Parties in the Run-Up to the 1998 Elections, http://www.hungary.com/hungqno149/82.html.

18. 1998, évi Parlamenti Választás 1.Forduló országosan összesített szavazási adatok, http://www.mdf.hu/val98.html.

19. See the chapter on the Antall government in Joseph Kun, *Hungarian Foreign Policy: The Experience of a New Democracy*, New York: Praeger, CSIS, 1993.

20. For election results see Zoltán D. Bárány, "The Hungarian Democratic Forum Wins National Elections Decisively," RFE/RL, *Report on Eastern Europe*, Vol. 1, No. 17, 27 April 1990. Background information on the Hungarian Democratic Forum is taken from Alfred A. Reisch, "The Democratic Forum at the Finish Line," RFE/RL, *Report on Eastern Europe*, Vol. 1, No. 14, 6 April 1990; *Magyar Hírlap*, Budapest, 17 December 1991, in *JPRS-EER-92–011*, 28 January 1992; Zoltán D. Bárány, "Democratic Changes Bring Mixed Blessings for Gypsies," RFE/RL, *Research Report*, Vol. 1, No. 20, 15 May 1992.

21. For a summary of the Csurka article see *Népszabadság*, Budapest, 27 August 1992; and Judith Pataki, "István Csurka's Tract: Summary and Reactions," RFE/RL, *Research Report*, Vol. 1, No. 40, 9 October 1992. The complete text of the tract plus official responses can be found in *JPRS-EER-92–132–S*, 17 September 1992. Further analysis of the consequences of the article is found in J.F. Brown, "A Challenge to Political Values," RFE/RL, *Research Report*, Vol. 1, No. 40, 9 October 1992. See also Edith Oltay, "A Profile of István Csurka," RFE/RL, *Research Report*, Vol. 1, No. 40, 9 October 1992; Edith Oltay, "Hungarian Democratic Forum Rent by Dispute Over Extremism," RFE/RL, *Research Report*, Vol. 1, No. 47, 27 November 1992; Edith Oltay, "Hungary: Csurka Launches "National Movement," RFE/RL, *Report on Eastern Europe*, Vol. 2, No. 13, 26 March 1993; and Csurka's speech on the "Hungarian Way," in *Magyar Fórum*, Budapest, 29 April 1993, in *JPRS-EER-93–052–S*, 9 June 1993.

22. HVG on-line, 6 February1999, No. 99/05, www.hvg.hu/new/english/9905.htm.

23. Radio Free Europe/ Radio Liberty, *Newsline*, 1 February 1999.

24. http://www.valasztas.hu/v98din2a/l120.htm.

25. For a valuable synopsis of Hungarian post-communist nationalism see László Karsai, "The Radical Right in Hungary," in Sabrina P. Ramet (Ed.), *The Radical Right in Central and Eastern Europe Since 1989*, University Park: Pennsylvania State University Press, 1999, pp. 133–146.

26. See the 16 March 1996 *Népszabadság*, Budapest, editorial about FkgP leader Torgyán's speech and the 23 March 1996 *Héti Világgazdaság* article, "Message Behind Rallies of FkgP, MIEP," in *FBIS-EEU*, 25 March 1996.

27. http://www.miep.hu/part/enbmiep.htm.

28. Interview with István Szöke by László Bartus, "The Police Provided Protection to the Skinheads," *Magyar Hírlap*, Budapest, 2 November 1992, in *FBIS-EEU-92–216*, 6 November 1992.

29. *MTI*, Budapest, 7 December 1992, in *FBIS-EEU-92–237*, 9 December 1992; and *Country Reports on Human Rights Practices for 1992*, Department of State, Washington, D.C., February 1993.

30. Information on Hungarian right-wing organizations is taken from a series of articles reprinted in *Tallózó*, Budapest, 30 July 1992, in *JPRS-EER-92–126*, 9 September 1992; Elemer Magyar, "Neofascists in Eger," *Beszélö*, Budapest, 9 November 1991, in *JPRS-EER-91–175*, 3 December 1991; Judith Pataki, "Increasing Intolerance of Foreigners," RFE/RL, *Research Report*, Vol. 1, No. 19, 8 May 1992; interview with Mihály Hansély, "Not Skinheads But

National Youth—Are Fascism and Anti-Fascism Only Political Terms for Right Wing?" *Magyar Hírlap*, 5 October 1992, in *FBIS-EEU-92–198*, 13 October 1992.

31. *FBIS-EEU-96–053*, Hungary, 18 March 1996, "Szabó Wants U.S. Troops To Leave," *MTI*, Budapest Television Network in Hungarian 1830 GMT, 15 March 1996.

32. For more information on anti-Semitic incidents in Hungary during 1999, see "Hungary: A Growing Tolerance for Anti-Semitism," http://www.adl.org/international/Hungary4_Anti_Semitism.html.

33. Alfred Reisch, "First Law on Minorities Drafted"; Rimas, "Bill on National Minorities: Dissatisfaction"; "Hungary's National Minorities Reject the Bill," *Népszabadság*, 21 February 1992, in *FBIS-EEU-92–037*, 25 February 1992.

34. Zoltán D. Bárány, "Hungary's Gypsies," RFE/RL, *Report on Eastern Europe*, Vol. 1, No. 29, 20 July 1990.

35. For more information on the Hungarian Gypsy Party and the Hungarian Gypsy Social-Democratic Party see Bárány, "Hungary's Gypsies."

36. Z.O., "Roma Parliament: Báthory Should Resign," *Magyar Hírlap*, Budapest, 26 November 1991, in *JPRS-EER-92–001*, 2 January 1992; P. Sz., "Gypsies Demonstrated Against Gypsies"; RFE/RL, *Daily Report*, No. 21, 2 February 1993.

37. Bárány, "Hungary's Gypsies"; "Gypsies Demonstrated Against Gypsies," *Magyar Hírlap*, Budapest, 19 December 1991, in *JPRS-EER-92–011*, 28 January 1992; and RFE/RL, *Daily Report*, No. 138, 22 July 1993.

38. "Representation in Parliament!" *Magyar Hírlap*, Budapest, 29 July 1991, in *JPRS-EER-91–113*, 1 August 1991. See also *Helsinki Watch Report*, Vol. VII, No. 39, 1 August 1990.

39. Alfred A. Reisch, "Hungarian-German Treaty Cements Close Relations," RFE/RL, *Research Report*, Vol. 1, No. 10, 6 March 1992.

40. For more information on the German minority see "Germans in Hungary Expect More Assistance from the State and from Society," *Népszava*, 8 January 1990, in *JPRS-EER-90–016*, 7 February 1990; Alfred Reisch, "Hungarian-German Treaty Cements Close Relations," RFE/RL, *Daily Report*, No. 46, 6 March 1992.

41. "Short of Priests," *Zemedelské Noviny*, Prague, 20 February 1991, in *FBIS-EEU-91–038*, 26 February 1991. See also Ján Babak, "Slovaks in Present-Day Hungary," *Literarny Tyzednnik*, Bratislava, 7 July 1989, in *JPRS-EER-89–129*, 22 November 1989; interview with Mária Jakab by Péter Matyuc, "The Cry for Help of a Diminishing National Group," *Népszabadság*, Budapest, 12 November 1990, in *FBIS-EEU-90–223*, 19 November 1990; interview with Mária Jakab and György Popovic by Katalin Decsi, "If Circumstances Do Not Change, National Minorities in Hungary Will Be Threatened by Assimilation—Rights on Paper, Sad Reality," *Népszabadság*, Budapest, 23 May 1990, in *FBIS-EEU-90–109*, 6 June 1990; series of articles by Frigyes Varju, "To Be a Slovak in Hungary," *Népszava*, Budapest, 4–6 April 1991, in *FBIS-EEU-91–069*, 10 April 1991.

42. See Charles Hoffman, *Gray Dawn: The Jews of Eastern Europe in the Post-Communist Era* (New York: Harper Collins, 1992), pp. 55–112; and *MTI*, Budapest, 27 February 1990, in *FBIS-EEU-90–040*, 28 February 1990.

43. Jovo Paripovic, "Three Alliances Instead of One," *Vjesnik*, Zagreb, 28 January 1990, in *JPRS-EER-90–029*, 8 March 1990.

44. Interview with Toso Doncsev and Pero Lasztity by Andrea M. Rimas, "Bill on National Minorities: Dissatisfaction," *Népszabadság*, Budapest, 1 August 1992, in *FBIS-EEU-92–154*, 10 August 1992.

45. János Gyurok, "Why Are There No National Minority Representatives in Parliament?" *Népszabadság*, Budapest, 15 October 1990, in *FBIS-EEU-90–202*, 18 October 1990.

46. Interview with György Márk by Imre Szenes, "The Way the Leader of Romanians in Hungary Sees It," *Népszava*, Budapest, 14 November 1989, in *JPRS-EER-90–003*, 4 January 1990. Information on Romanian organizations is taken from *Budapest Domestic Service*, 15 June 1990, in *FBIS-EEU-90–118*, 19 June 1990; interview with Gheorghe Petrusan by Livmos Ágoston, "We Need a Law on National Minorities," *Magyar Nemzet*, 18 December 1991, in *FBIS-EEU-91–245*, 20 December 1991.

Serbia

HISTORICAL OVERVIEW

The central Balkan areas became part of the Roman Empire after the first century AD. During the fourth century AD, the Empire was divided between Rome and Constantinople and the Balkan region was subject to raids and invasions by a number of Germanic and Turkic tribes. Slavic tribes settled in the region that is now Serbia in the fifth and sixth centuries AD, after migrating from an area north of the Black Sea.[1] Like other Slavic groups, their social and political structure was based on a system of clans under the military and political leadership of a *župan*. As the Serbian tribes settled they absorbed many of the indigenous inhabitants, including the local Vlachs.

The main center of the initial Serb settlement was in the Raška region, in present-day Sandžak, in Serbia. At the end of the ninth century, *župan* Vlastimir recognized the suzerainty of the Byzantine Empire and opened up the Serb-inhabited lands to conversion to Eastern Orthodox Christianity. *Župan* Mutimir was converted in 879 AD. The first kingdom claimed by Serbian historians was established in the early part of the eleventh century, in present-day Montenegro, in an area known as Zeta. The local leader, Constantine Bodin, declared his allegiance to Rome. The kingdom disintegrated after his death, and the locus of Serbian power shifted to Raška.

Under the Nemanja dynasty, during the 1160s, Serbian unity and power expanded significantly. In 1169, Stefan Nemanja became *župan* of Raška and initiated a dynasty that was to rule for two hundred years. The Nemanjas expanded their control over modern-day Montenegro, Bosnia, Herzegovina, and central Serbia (Šumadija) and pledged allegiance to the Orthodox faith. In 1219, Stefan's son, who was later canonized as Saint Sava, became the first archbishop of a newly autocephalous Serbian Orthodox Church. This link between monarchy and Church was to remain a central feature of Serbian identity.

Under King Milutin, at the beginning of the fourteenth century, Serbia seized a sizeable chunk of Macedonian territory from the Byzantine Empire. Under Milutin's son, Tsar Stefan Dušan, in the middle of the fourteenth century, the Nemanjić dynasty reached the peak of its power, ruling a territory stretching from the Danube river to the Aegean Sea and toward central Greece. Dušan had himself crowned Emperor of the Serbs and Greeks and presided over the most powerful state in the Balkans. But after Tsar Dušan's death in 1355, Serbian power substantially declined and the state disintegrated into a number of principalities, including Zeta, Raška, Macedonia, and Kosovo.

Serb forces suffered a series of defeats by invading Ottoman Turkish forces. A critical defeat at Kosovo Polje in 1389 sealed Serbia's fate and by 1459 the country was overrun by the Ottomans. For the next three centuries, Serbia remained under Turkish domination. During this period, mass migrations out of Kosovo and southern Serbia shifted the Serbian population northward into what are now Vojvodina and Slavonia. Tens of thousands of Serbs also settled in Croatia and Bosnia, along the "military frontier" that was created by the Habsburgs to guard against Turkish penetration.

In 1699, Ottoman armies were pushed south of the Danube by Austrian Habsburg forces, while the rest of present-day Serbia remained under Turkish control. Several failed uprisings took place in central Serbia against onerous Turkish rule, including a revolt in 1804 led by Karadjordje Petrović, who briefly succeeded in liberating most of the Belgrade *pashalik* (Ottoman administrative region). After the Russo-Turkish war of 1828–1829, Serbia became an internationally recognized autonomous principality, although still under Ottoman rule and with overall Russian protection. The reborn state gradually expanded southward as Ottoman rule diminished. A number of prominent Serb intellectuals, including Vuk Karadžić and Ilija Garašanin, helped stir a national consciousness and formulated a national ideology with the objective of establishing a Greater Serbia.

Following an insurrection in Bosnia-Herzegovina in 1875, Serbia and Montenegro went to war against Turkey in 1876–78 in support of the Bosnian rebels and suffered significant military losses. With assistance from Russia, and following the Treaty of San Stefano in March 1878 and the Congress of Berlin in June 1878, Serbia gained more territory as well as formal independence. However, the Habsburgs obtained Bosnia-Herzegovina and Sandžak and thus created enormous resentments in Serbia. When Austria-Hungary formally annexed Bosnia-Herzegovina in 1908, the Sandžak region was restored to Ottoman rule in order to prevent any expansion of Serbian or Russian influence.

In the First Balkan War (1912), Serbia formed an alliance with Montenegro, Bulgaria, and Greece, to seize the remaining Ottoman territories in the Balkans. Serbia retook the Sandžak and Kosovo. In the Second Balkan War (1913), in which Bulgaria lost to its former allies, Serbia gained the region of Vardar Macedonia. However, Vienna compelled Belgrade to surrender Albanian lands that it had seized and that would have given Serbia direct access to the Adriatic Sea. Nevertheless, Serbia almost doubled in size and population.

On 28 June 1914, a Serbian activist, Gavrilo Princip, belonging to the Young Bosnia organization, assassinated the Austrian Archduke Francis Ferdinand in the Bosnian capital, Sarajevo. The attack precipitated World War I, as Vienna feared that Serbian subversion would incite other south Slavs within the Habsburg lands to revolt. Serbia was defeated and overrun by Austrian and Bulgarian forces and the country lost about a quarter of its population. Some Serb leaders helped form the Yugoslav Committee with Croatian and Slovenian activists, with a program of creating a united, south Slavic state.

With the collapse of Austria-Hungary at the end of the war, Serbia and other southern Slavic lands were liberated, and a new Kingdom of Serbia, Croatia, and Slovenia was established on 1 December 1918. Serbia became the domi-nant power despite the demands of Croatian and other leaders for a more decen-tralized federal state. A centralist constitution was approved by a Serb-dominated parliament on 28 June 1921. As protests against Belgrade's rule mounted and political turmoil accelerated, Serbian King Alexander I Karadjordjević declared a royal dictatorship in January 1929, abolished the parliament, and changed the country's name to Yugoslavia ("land of south Slavs").

The Yugoslav state was split into nine new administrative units *(banovinas)* that terminated the historic regional boundaries; this accentuated Croatian resistance. The Serbian king was assassinated by Croatian and Macedonian gunmen in 1934, and a regency council ruling on behalf of the young King Peter II attempted to pacify Croatian grievances by restoring the traditional national regions. This agreement came too late, however, on the brink of World War II.

After a coup in Belgrade reversed Yugoslavia's acquiescence to a pact with the Axis powers, German forces attacked Serbia on 6 April 1941 and dis-membered Yugoslavia. A Croatian puppet state was established that included Bosnia-Herzegovina, and the remaining Serbian territories were divided and occupied by Germany, Hungary, Bulgaria, and Italy. A rump Serbian state was left, largely within its 1912 boundaries, and an essentially puppet regime was installed by Berlin under Serbian General Milan Nedić.

A Serb nationalist resistance movement *(Četniks)* loyal to the monarchy was active in Serbia, Bosnia-Herzegovina, Montenegro, and other parts of the former Yugoslavia. *Četnik* units led by General Dragoljub Draža Mihailović were accused of collaborating with the occupying powers and of failing to mount an effective armed campaign. *Četnik* leaders contended that they were trying to save Serbian civilians from reprisal massacres by the Nazis. They were also accused of murdering Muslim and Albanian civilians in areas under their control and seeking to carve out an ethnically pure Greater Serbia. Com-munist partisan forces, with Allied and Soviet assistance, gained victory by the close of the war. They brutally eliminated rival military and political groups, including the *Četniks*, both during and after seizing power. The total number of wartime deaths was estimated at about one million, and about half of this number were Serbs in the three central republics (Serbia, Croatia, and Bosnia-Herzegovina).

Post-war Communist Yugoslavia restored its pre-war borders and gained some additional territory from Italy in the northwest. Yugoslav leader Josip Broz Tito established a federal communist state and limited the powers and ambitions of any single national unit. Serbian influence was substantially reduced with the creation of the separate republics of Macedonia, Montenegro, and Bosnia-Herzegovina. The granting of autonomous provincial status to Kosovo and Vojvodina within the Serbian republic during the 1950s further undercut Serbian influence and bred resentment among Serb nationalists. However, the creation of two autonomous provinces as distinct federal units contributed to the partial satisfaction of the demands of Hungarian and Albanian leaders for decentralization.

Vojvodina underwent a significant shift in ethnic composition after the expulsion of the large German population at the close of the war. The traditional Croatian area of eastern Srem was incorporated into the province. Large numbers of Serbs were resettled in Vojvodina and Magyar numbers fell to about 20% of the population. Nonetheless, the community benefited from a large measure of administrative and economic decentralization and extensive linguistic and educational rights. Stability in the province was also assured by the area's relative prosperity and the absence of any overt Hungarian territorial pretensions. The province held a complex ethnic mix. In addition to Serbs and Hungarians, sizable pockets of Croats, Slovaks, Ruthenians, and Romanians were present. But there was no evident ethnic conflict, and the region was renowned for its tolerance and diversity.

By contrast, in Kosovo-Metohija (the full Serbian name) there were pronounced ethnic and cultural divisions between Serbs and Albanians. The Albanian population in the province had grown substantially since the seventeenth century, especially as Serbian families moved northward and westward to escape Turkish rule. This pattern continued into the twentieth century: between 1953 and 1981, Serbian numbers dropped from 27.9% to 14.9% of the population. Although the majority evidently left for primarily economic reasons, some vacated the province due to pressure from the Albanian majority. Meanwhile, Kosovo's Albanian population underwent a dramatic growth, from 733,000 in 1948 to about 1.3 million by 1981. Serbian depopulation of this historically sensitive region raised popular resentment against Albanians. This was heightened during the 1960s and 1970s when Kosovo attained constitutional status within Yugoslavia virtually equal to that of the other republics.

During the 1960s and 1970s, Albanians attained a predominant position in the communist apparatus, local administration, and the police forces, while able to expand their educational, cultural, and linguistic rights. Serb leaders remained perturbed by the high Albanian birthrate, estimated at about four times the national average. Tito's policy was one of measured appeasement and inter-ethnic balance, designed to give Albanians a stake in the Yugoslav federation without provoking a Serbian backlash. But Belgrade's policies generated resentment on both sides: among Serbs, over alleged Albanian dominance; and among Albanian leaders, over the lack of full self-government and republican status.

During the late 1960s and 1970s, Yugoslavia was further decentralized and the republican party structures obtained significant autonomy under the 1974 constitution. After Tito's death in 1980, Serbia's communist leaders began to reassert the republic's position in the Yugoslav federation and sought to recentralize the state. With his ascent to the leadership of the League of Communists of Serbia (LCS) in 1986, Slobodan Milošević took up the Serbian nationalist cause. His initial successes focused on centralizing the Serbian republic and limiting the autonomy of both Kosovo and Vojvodina. Milošević's policies were reinforced by a memorandum produced by the Serbian Academy of Arts and Sciences in September 1986, which established the justification and agenda for a renewed "Greater Serbia" project.

Milošević was selected as Serbian President on 8 May 1989, and his regime proceeded to strengthen direct controls over Kosovo on the pretext that the regional government dominated by Albanians was persecuting Serbs and seeking to detach the region from Yugoslavia. Various measures were taken to restrict Albanian political and social life: the powers of the regional government were undermined, states of emergency were imposed to limit protests, the public security organs were taken over by Belgrade, and the Serbian regime claimed the right to appoint or dismiss members of all legislative and judicial bodies.

In July 1990, Belgrade suspended the Kosovo Provincial Assembly, days after the legislature had declared the independence of Kosovo as a sovereign Yugoslav republic. Albanian legislators from the dissolved parliament met secretly in September 1990 to pass a law on Kosovo's republican status; this became known as the Kačanik Constitution. The Serbian authorities suspended the operations of much of the Albanian-language media, and under the new Serbian constitution Kosovo's autonomous statehood was eliminated. In March 1991, the Kosovo provincial presidency was officially abolished, thus sealing the province's full integration into Serbia. The curtailment of Albanian educational and cultural activities, together with discrimination in public employment, sparked protest actions and the growth of independent political activism as Albanian leaders demanded full independence and separation from Serbia. In May 1992, Albanians held their own general elections and appealed unsuccessfully for international recognition.

Milošević also reasserted Belgrade's control over Vojvodina. In October 1988, the Vojvodina provincial authorities were replaced in a purge designed to eliminate "pro-autonomist forces" allegedly conspiring against Serbia. These moves intensified tensions in the region, increased protests against the centralist state apparatus, and stimulated the resurgence of ethnically based organizations. Although the crackdown against minority educational and cultural pursuits was not as comprehensive as in Kosovo, state policy clearly favored Serbs and Milošević loyalists in the administration and security forces. Moreover, the powers of the provincial government were curtailed, and Vojvodina was governed directly from Belgrade.

The collapse of the Yugoslav federation began in early 1991, with the secessions of Slovenia and Croatia, and later Bosnia-Herzegovina and Macedonia, which directly affected Serbia's national minorities. Albanians in Kosovo pushed toward separation from the rump Yugoslavia, fearful not only of Serbian domination but of the forcible expulsion of non-Serbs to alter Kosovo's demographic structure. Hungarian and Croatian minorities grew concerned about similar operations in Vojvodina as Belgrade began to exert pressure on minority inhabitants and resettled Serbs in the province from other parts of Yugoslavia. The large Muslim Slav population in the Sandžak area of southern Serbia was also subjected to intimidation by security forces and radical Serbian paramilitaries. The Milošević regime maintained a tight grip over the Serbian government, economy, army, and security forces. The promulgation of the "Greater Serbia" doctrine and the support given to militant Serb formations alarmed minority leaders.

POST-COMMUNIST DEVELOPMENTS

After his rise to the leadership of the League of Communists of Serbia in May 1986, Slobodan Milošević set the political and national agenda in the republic. Recognizing that the communist and Yugoslav causes had lost their potential for mass mobilization, Milošević fixed his attention on reviving Serb nationalism and manipulating national grievances to consolidate and expand his hold on power. Reiterating the position expressed in the 1986 memorandum issued by the Serbian Academy, Milošević contended that Serbia had been deliberately weakened by the Tito regime.[2] The 1974 Yugoslav constitution allegedly undermined Serbia's sovereignty over its two autonomous provinces, Vojvodina and Kosovo, which obtained equal representation in the federal administration and were able to veto decisions in Serbia's National Assembly.

Moreover, large numbers of Serbs (about 42% of 8.1 million Serbs in Yugoslavia) resided in Croatia and Bosnia-Herzegovina, allegedly without sufficient constitutional protection. Milošević focused his efforts on reversing this situation and restoring a centralized Serbian administration. To achieve his aims, he removed the most threatening political rivals and placed much of the Belgrade media under his strict supervision. He organized mass demonstrations to rally popular support behind Serbian unification in Belgrade, Montenegro, Vojvodina, and Kosovo.[3] In exploiting various political, ethnic, and economic grievances, Milošević orchestrated the ouster of the entire Montenegrin state and party leadership in January 1989, replacing them with pro-Belgrade loyalists.

A new Serbian constitution was promulgated on 28 September 1990, making Serbia the first republic to actually undermine the federal structure.[4] A unicameral parliament, the National Assembly (*Narodna Skupština*), was inaugurated, with 250 seats. The Assembly had constitutional and legislative powers with representatives elected by citizens in direct and multiparty elections for a four-year term. Officials in Belgrade claimed that the constitution fully protected the rights of national minorities because Serbia was not defined as a "national state", but a "democratic state of all citizens." Citizens were "guaranteed the freedom to express their nationality and culture and the freedom to use their language and script."[5] Albanians charged that such provisions failed to address the key issue of the status of their population and continued to relegate them to the position of a "nationality" or "minority." The constitution also underscored that Serbia was "unified and unalienable," thus formally restricting the autonomy of Kosovo and majority demands for self-determination. The constitution buttressed the powers of the Serbian presidency, reaffirmed Serbia's sovereignty, and removed constitutional mechanisms for self-government among the largest national minorities. It was rushed through parliament before Serbia's first multiparty elections in December 1990.

Milošević consolidated his position in July 1990 when the LCS and the Socialist Alliance, its front organization, united to create the Socialist Party of Serbia (SPS) under Milošević's leadership. The new party adopted an openly nationalist platform, and its dominant position in the mass media contributed to limiting the appeal of newly formed Serbian opposition parties. With pressures mounting throughout Yugoslavia, opposition parties were legalized in Serbia in August 1990, but the SPS maintained its unfair advantage in the first multiparty elections, in December 1990. It benefited from state resources, maintained a republic-wide political apparatus, and monopolized the media. Milošević was elected president of Serbia with 65.34% of the vote; his nearest challenger, Vuk Drašković, from the newly formed opposition group the Serbian Renewal Movement (SRM), barely reached 16.4%.

In the parliamentary ballot, the Socialists gained a clear majority by capturing 194 of 250 seats, amid charges of various voting irregularities.[6] The closest opposition party, the SRM, managed to win only 19 seats and 15.78% of the vote. As in other authoritarian, post-communist systems, the ruling party also sponsored the creation of numerous small parties across the political spectrum. This served to confuse the public, to undercut the opposition vote, and to limit television airtime for any single organization.

In the new Serbian constitution, the autonomy of Vojvodina was practically abolished and most executive, administrative, and judicial functions were transferred to Belgrade. These measures led to protests not only by spokesmen of the large Hungarian population but also among several smaller, independent groupings that sprang up in defense of an autonomous Vojvodina. They argued that Belgrade's policies eliminated the unique status that the province had enjoyed since the collapse of the Austro-Hungarian Empire. Moreover, the rise of Serbian nationalism and its advocacy by the ruling party threatened to undermine the region's peaceful inter-ethnic relations. The ethnification of Yugoslav politics and growing Serbian nationalism also sparked ethnically based movements among Vojvodina's smaller minorities.

In late 1989, several Hungarian organizations were formed to defend minority interests and campaign against increasing pressures from Belgrade. The Democratic Community of Vojvodina Hungarians (DCVH) became the largest and most active body, and it published a program on redressing minority grievances and codifying minority rights. Unlike the Kosovor Albanians, the DCVH stood in the multiparty elections in December 1990, calculating that with parliamentary representation the Magyars would be in a better position to defend their interests. The authorities allowed for the participation of ethnically based parties, and the DCVH together with the Alliance of Vojvodina Hungarian (AVH) won eight seats in the republican assembly. Magyar leaders contended that the Serbian authorities were whittling away minority rights and were gerrymandering electoral districts to disperse Hungarian votes and limit Hungarians' participation in the Serbian parliament. In January 1992, Vojvodina was divided into seven administrative districts, replacing the fifty previous ones and making Magyars a minority in all districts.

The DCVH appeared unconcerned about the suspension of the Vojvodinian Assembly, arguing that the institution had not adequately served minority interests in the first place.[7] The DCVH spoke out for the "cultural autonomy" of Hungarians not based on territorial principles. The idea was to establish a "self-government council" for all Magyar residents, with an advisory status in the Serbian parliament, that could represent their collective interests in relations with state institutions. It also envisaged a measure of political self-government at the local commune level in areas where Hungarians constituted clear majorities, as in the northern portions of Bačka. During 1991, these concepts were overwhelmingly rejected by the Serbian Assembly, as were proposals to establish a republican ministry for national minorities.

Pressures on the Hungarian and other minorities in Vojvodina continued throughout the early 1990s. For instance, the number of Magyar schools and language classes was further decreased, on the pretext that the state was reorganizing the school system. Belgrade intensified its supervision over the Hungarian-language media by appointing directors of all newspapers, journals, and radio and television stations. Moreover, anti-Hungarian sentiments were fanned by the state-controlled media, which accused the DCVH of seeking separation from Serbia, despite the fact that the community had explicitly recognized the inviolability of existing borders. A further nail in the coffin of minority rights was delivered in July 1991, with the passage of a new language law by the Serbian Assembly that made Serbian the sole official language, thus ruling out the use of Hungarian in public life.

In April 1992, the DCVH issued a formal Memorandum on Hungarian Autonomy in Vojvodina as an initiative to enshrine minority rights in the Serbian constitution.[8] It proposed the concept of tripartite autonomy: individual or cultural autonomy; a special status for communes in which Magyars formed clear majorities; and local self-government for dispersed minority towns and villages. The proposal exceeded the principles of cultural autonomy outlined the previous year, although it did not specify the content of self-government in the various branches of state administration. It amounted to a declaration of principle that a "measure of self-government should be granted to a defined territory" inhabited primarily by Hungarians, referring to eight municipalities in northern Bačka and Banat.

The memorandum also called for the settlement of Vojvodina's constitutional status through a public referendum, with a clear choice between autonomy and incorporation into an integral Serbia. In addition, DCVH leader András Ágoston underscored that the community was not declaring territorial autonomy in northern Vojvodina. The DCVH proposals were rejected outright by the Serbian authorities and some media outlets and parliamentary delegates charged the DCVH with seeking secession. Several non-Hungarian oppositionist parties also criticized the DCVH program for its exclusive focus on Hungarian interests, to the neglect of Vojvodinian autonomy as a whole or the democratization of the Serbian state. Vojvodinian groups also feared that the Hungarian program would serve Belgrade's interests by fostering division among the region's diverse ethnic groups.

Throughout the 1990s, Vojvodina's regional assembly with curtailed powers was dominated by the Socialists, Radicals, and other Milošević allies. However, in the September 2000 elections, regionalist and democratic forces gained ascendancy in the assembly. The League of Social Democrats won 24 seats in the 120-strong body, while the Democratic Party captured 27 seats. Among other regionalist formations, the Hungarian organizations gained 17 seats, the Reformists of Vojvodina eight, and the Coalition for Vojvodina seven. The Socialists barely managed to garner two deputies. The regional authority looked set to push toward greater autonomy for the territory and prepared for negotiations over regional powers and responsibilities with the next Serbian government, following the December 2000 republican elections.

The large Slavic Muslim minority in the Sandžak region, which spanned southwestern Serbia and northeastern Montenegro, also grew restless during the late 1980s. Although the Sandžak did not exist as a distinct political entity in either republic, Muslims formed absolute majorities in three districts *(opštine)* in the eastern part of the region, and they organized to protect their distinct interests as Yugoslavia began to disintegrate. The largest Muslim political organization, the Party for Democratic Action (PDA), was formed in August 1990 as an all-Yugoslav party for Muslims in Bosnia-Herzegovina, Sandžak, and Kosovo. The PDA initially sought cultural and educational autonomy for the Sandžak region, but its leaders declared that if Yugoslavia disintegrated and Serbia and Montenegro were to form a new state, then Muslims would demand territorial autonomy and a political link with a sovereign Bosnia.

In the Serbian elections of December 1990, the PDA won in all the electoral units where Muslims constituted clear majorities. As inter-republican tensions increased throughout Yugoslavia, the PDA formed the Muslim National Council of the Sandžak (MNCS) in May 1991 as a parliamentary and quasi-governmental body. The council consisted of representatives from all Sandžak municipalities under the chairmanship of PDA leader Sulejman Ugljanin. Its role was purportedly one of "self-defense" in case a state of emergency was declared by Belgrade. MNCS leaders underscored that they saw no credible future for Muslims in a revamped Greater Serbia. Serbian authorities did not recognize this body, asserting that it had no legal status in the republic.

After Croatia and Slovenia declared their independence in the summer of 1991, Muslim leaders organized a referendum on the status of the Sandžak. Several options were considered by council leaders: autonomous status, a new federal unit, merger with Bosnia-Herzegovina, or the creation of a new state to include all regions in Yugoslavia in which Muslims formed a majority of the population. Despite warnings from Belgrade that the vote was illegal, a referendum was held in the region in October 1991. Muslim residents in ten Sandžak municipalities balloted overwhelmingly in favor of political and territorial autonomy. According to the PDA, 70.19% of the population participated in the plebiscite, of which 98.92% voted for Sandžak autonomy.

The referendum was reportedly less successful in the Montenegrin Sandžak, where the position of local Muslims was less threatening. In January 1992, the MNCS voted to establish a "special status" for the Sandžak as an "optimal solution for the autochthonous Muslim nation in the remnants of Yugoslavia." Although the Sandžak was not declared an independent republic, the region's government would remain exclusively responsible for education, culture, media, privatization, agriculture, mining, social services, police, justice, banking, and taxation.[9]

Serbia's National Assembly maintained that the Sandžak did not constitute a "legal territorial entity" and could not be granted autonomy.[10] Belgrade also claimed that the Muslim referendum had been organized under the auspices of the PDA leadership in Bosnia, whose objective was to annex Serbian and Montenegrin territory. Tensions sharply increased in the region after the outbreak of hostilities in neighboring Bosnia during the spring of 1992. As in Kosovo, Serbian government propaganda claimed that Serbian residents were being pushed out of the Sandžak by Islamic fundamentalists and Muslim nationalists intent on "ethnically cleansing" the area. Conversely, PDA leaders alleged that Muslim residents were increasingly subject to intimidation by Serbian security forces and paramilitary units.

Due to fears of violence and military conscription, about 70,000 Muslims reportedly fled the region by early 1993. In particular, the western border area with Bosnia was reportedly being cleared of Muslim residents in order to break the connection between Muslims in both states. Serbian leaders also claimed that Muslims had established armed units in the Sandžak in preparation for an uprising and attacks on the Serbian population. The PDA dismissed such assertions as ludicrous, given the heavy army and police presence, and as a pretext to arm local Serbs, increase the number of Yugoslav troops, and allow ultranationalist irregulars to terrorize the local population.

During 1991, Milošević strengthened direct Serbian controls over the remaining Yugoslav federal institutions and conducted a sweeping purge of the armed forces. In Serbia itself, Milošević maintained a tight grip over the mass media, the legal system, major sectors of the economy, and the extensive security apparatus. An opposition movement was permitted to function, to preserve an image of democratization and tolerance. Nonetheless, the development of a pluralist democracy was stymied as the Socialists manipulated the key media outlets, cracked down on public demonstrations, and exploited nationalist sentiments to question the patriotism of democratic opposition parties. The opposition was largely bereft of funding, media time, organization, and staff, and had restricted public identification.

Furthermore, Milošević cultivated the activities of the ultranationalist Serbian Radical Party (SRP) both to undermine the potential appeal of alternative national parties and to present the Socialists as a comparatively moderate political formation defending Serbian national interests. The opposition itself remained deeply divided on programmatic questions and on their approach toward republican and federal elections. Personal rivalries also contributed to undermining any unified front. They were also largely focused on the national question, where Milošević had successfully set the agenda, and were unable to put forward a coherent anti-authoritarian and anti-nationalist program.[11]

When it was no longer feasible to hold the federation together, the Milošević regime calculated that a Serb-dominated and smaller Yugoslavia could be crafted from the remaining territories. The optimal goal was to keep Bosnia-Herzegovina and Macedonia in the federation in addition to the captured areas of Croatia. When Muslim and Croat leaders declared the independence of Bosnia-Herzegovina in February 1992 and the Macedonian government followed suit, Milošević adopted a twin-track approach to preserve Serb-inhabited territories outside the new state entities. A war of partition was launched in Bosnia, similar to the one in Croatia the previous year, with the direct assistance of Belgrade and the Yugoslav army.

Although Serbia's population was officially estimated at approximately 10,500,000 by the late 1990s, there had been a huge refugee inflow from Croatia, Bosnia-Herzegovina, and Kosovo. In the period between 1991 and 1993, Serbia took in about 550,000 refugees, of whom over 80% were ethnic Serbs. There were also significant changes with respect to Vojvodina and Kosovo. In Vojvodina, according to the 1991 census, the percentage of Serbs grew from 54.4% in 1981 to 57.3% in 1991. Many refugees from Croatia and Bosnia were resettled in Vojvodina. The number of Hungarians declined by several tens of thousands, either in avoidance of military conscription or because of intimidation by Serbian nationalists. Around 170,000, primarily Serbs and Roma from Kosovo, were internally displaced in Serbia and Montenegro.

The remaining members of the federal presidency declared the founding of a new Federal Republic of Yugoslavia on 27 April 1992.[12] It consisted of two republics, Serbia and Montenegro. A federal constitution was rushed through, explicitly leaving open the possibility that other entities could join the new state. According to the constitution, "the Federal Republic of Yugoslavia may be joined by other member republics, in accordance with the present constitution."[13] The objective may have been to allow for the future accession of Serbian Krajina (captured from Croatia) and the Serbian Republic (partitioned from Bosnia- Herzegovina).

Federal elections were staged on 31 May 1992 to provide a veneer of legitimacy for the new state. They were won by the Socialists and their allies in Montenegro. Opposition parties boycotted the ballot, claiming that the elections were illegal and unconstitutional, that the election law was a sham document, and that the campaign period was too short for proper multiparty competition. Among the few parties that participated in the elections were the Radicals, sponsored and encouraged by the regime, and the DCVH, whose leaders calculated that a boycott would leave them without any voice in federal decisions pertaining to the position of the Magyar minority. Following the ballot, Dobrica Ćosić was selected as federal president in June 1992, and the emigré businessman Milan Panić, as prime minister, by the federal assembly in July 1992.

During the fall of 1992, tensions visibly increased within Serbia, not only between opposition parties and the ruling Socialists but also among various governing institutions.[14] Milošević had sponsored Panić's premiership as a way of buying time and deflecting international criticism of Belgrade's policies. However, the premier became more outspoken and active, criticizing Milošević for his support of the war in Bosnia and his thwarting of democracy in Serbia. Panić also made some overtures toward Albanian leaders in Kosovo and offered the prospect that Yugoslavia could recognize the independence of Slovenia and Croatia. This approach led to vehement attacks by Socialist spokesmen and to bitter denunciations by the Radicals, who organized two votes of no-confidence in the federal government on the grounds that Panić was betraying Serbian interests.

Panić survived the vote and elicited the tacit support of Yugoslav President Dobrica Ćosić and the backing of the Montenegrin leadership and the oppositionist DEPOS *(Demokratski Pokret Srbije)* coalition, which was founded on 23 May 1992 by the Serbian Renewal Movement, the Democratic Party, the Serbian Liberal Party, the People's Peasant Party, and New Democracy. However, despite Panić's growing popularity in Serbia, he neglected to form a credible and structured opposition alliance, and delayed his entry for the Serbian presidential elections. Moreover, Ćosić hesitated in lending his support to Panić's candidacy, thus undermining the premier's popularity. Suspicions persisted that either Ćosić was trying to maintain a balance between Milošević and Panić to avoid allying with the losing side, or that he was working in tandem with Milošević while appearing as the moderate voice of Serbian nationalism. Indeed, observers pointed out that Milošević had faithfully applied the program laid out in the famous 1986 memorandum to unite all Serb-inherited territories—of which Ćosić was one of the leading architects.

The opposition parties found themselves at an enormous disadvantage in the December 1992 federal, republican, and local elections, held to relegitimize the Milošević regime and to deflate oppositionist claims to widespread popularity.[15] In addition to its privileged access to the chief media organs the ruling party skewed the election laws and procedures in its favor. Serious questions were raised over voter registries, the security of voting materials, the rights of refugees to vote, and party funding; the opposition also alleged large-scale fraud. The Albanian population boycotted the balloting and charged that Panić had failed to deliver on his promise to restore the Albanian educational system, while intimidation and repression were intensifying in the province. Muslim parties in the Sandžak also boycotted the elections, but some Muslim voters cast their ballots for the Serbian opposition. Milošević won the Serbian presidential election with 55.9% of the vote, while Panić scored 34.3% and was swept out of the political arena in the December 1992 election. The SPS gained 47 out of 138 seats in the federal Chamber of Citizens and 12 seats in the 40-member Chamber of Republics. The SRP captured 34 seats in the Chamber of Citizens and eight in the Chamber of Republics. These results gave the pro-Milošević forces a working majority at the federal level in coalition with the Montenegrin Socialists, even though Ćosić was maintained as Yugoslav president. In February 1993, a new Serbian government was installed, headed by Premier Nikola Sainović, an SPS loyalist.

The Socialists captured 101 seats in the 250-member unicameral Serbian parliament, and the Radicals, 73, giving the regime an absolute majority at the republican level. The opposition Civic Alliance scored only one seat in the federal assembly and five in the republican assembly; three of the latter were gained by the Farmers Party of Vojvodina, a non-ethnic regionalist grouping. The Vojvodinian bloc also obtained two seats in the federal assembly, while the DCVH gained nine seats, in addition to nine seats in the Serbian assembly. The Serbian Renewal Movement obtained 20 seats at the federal level and 50 at the republican level, making it the largest democratic opposition party represented in both legislatures. The Group of Citizens from Kosovo and Metohija, led by the alleged war criminal Arkan, obtained five seats in the Serbian legislature. The majoritarian voting system in each district clearly favored the ruling party.

The Socialists and the Radicals also performed well at the local level, as did the DCVH in the eight Hungarian-majority districts. Hungarian and other Vojvodinian activists were concerned that the Radicals' capture of the mayorship of Novi Sad, the Vojvodinian capital, was a prelude to further political restrictions. Elections to the Vojvodina regional assembly were also held.

Out of 120 deputies, 58 were from a loose coalition of democratic Serbian, non-ethnic, and minority parties, while 62 were Socialists and Radicals. The democratic bloc walked out of the first Vojvodina Assembly session in protest at its limited powers and its subordination to the Serbian republican assembly. Despite an evidently conciliatory gesture in May 1993, when the Novi Sad Assembly passed amendments giving the Hungarian language equal status with Serbian in official affairs, minority leaders expressed fears of discrimination and persecution.

Pressures against Serbian moderates increased during the spring of 1993, and the opposition claimed that Serbia was gradually being transformed into a fascist state. Ćosić was ousted from the Yugoslav presidency in May 1993, after a vote of no-confidence sponsored by the Radicals, and he was replaced by Milošević loyalist Zoran Lilić. DEPOS leader Vuk Drašković was arrested and beaten up by the police before being placed on trial on charges of provoking riots in Belgrade. Milošević successfully used the Radicals to overthrow the Panić federal government in the summer of 1993. There were also indications of a struggle for power brewing between Milošević and Šešelj. The latter had created his own political power base and captured the support of sectors of the armed forces as well as militant Serbs in Bosnia and Croatia. Milošević was prepared to abandon Šešelj in order to consolidate his power and pose as the reasonable voice of Serbian nationalism vis-à-vis the international community.

New Serbian parliamentary elections were held in December 1993 after the SPS engineered a governmental collapse following a vote of no-confidence. The Socialists easily won the ballot with nearly 37% of the vote and gained 123 parliamentary seats. DEPOS increased its support to almost 17% and 45 seats, while the SRP only obtained 13% of the vote and 39 seats, after Milošević had largely excluded the Radicals from the state-controlled media. The Democratic Party achieved 11.6% and 29 seats; the remaining seats were shared among Hungarian and Muslim parties.

In early 1993, the Yugoslav federal government prepared a draft law on the "liberties and rights of minority communities and of their members."[16] The authorities were evidently seeking to counter growing international condemnation of their treatment of minority groups. Belgrade proposed to provide proportional representation for all minorities in federal, republican, and local assemblies; to establish the office of ombudsman and a commission in the federal government to monitor the rights of minority communities; and to grant various forms of autonomy for minorities that did not undermine the integrity of the state. Despite these positive declarations, the document also contained stipulations that further undermined the position of the Albanian community. For instance, the representative of any minority could only be someone who had been elected in a "democratic and free ballot" determined by the Yugoslav or Serbian authorities and who participated in the country's parliamentary life. If such rules were applied, not a single party in Kosovo would be authorized to represent the Albanian community.

During 1995, Milošević increased pressures against Serbia's domestic opposition. Several independent media outlets were either closed down or taken over by the state. Official propaganda depicted Milošević as a peacemaker who had weathered the storm of international sanctions. The economic sanctions imposed by the United Nations were removed in the spring of 1996. But the lifting of an "outer wall" of penalties, including access to international credits and financial institutions, remained contingent on progress in domestic political and economic reforms.

On 3 November 1996, elections were held to the Yugoslav federal assembly, consisting of deputies from Serbia and Montenegro, as well as to the Montenegrin republican assembly. Milošević's Socialist Party, in coalition with the Yugoslav United Left (YUL), captured a narrow majority of seats in the Yugoslav federal legislature but fell short of a two-thirds majority. In Montenegro, the ruling Democratic Party of Socialists (DPS) won 45 out of 71 seats to the republican assembly. The remainder of seats in both parliaments were divided among Serb nationalists and an assortment of moderate parties, including the oppositionist *Zajedno* coalition, which was formed by the Serbian Renewal Movement, the Democratic Party, and the Civic Alliance on 2 September 1996.

To the surprise of observers, in the local runoffs in Serbia, held in mid-November 1996, *Zajedno* scored several major victories in Belgrade and a number of Socialist bastions, including the cities of Niš and Kragujevac. While *Zajedno* claimed success in twelve cities, the local election commissions overturned the results, claiming various irregularities in the voting. By the end of November, massive demonstrations shook Belgrade and several other towns as protestors claimed the government was defrauding the electorate. The federal election results had evidently lulled the Socialists into a false sense of security about their inevitable success. Although municipal governments were not critical institutions in Serbia's highly centralized system, they nevertheless provided a basis for future political challenges to Milošević's rule. In addition, local authorities controlled thousands of local jobs and owned dozens of television and radio stations, thus potentially undermining the Socialist media monopoly.

In response to the regime's brazen dismissal of the vote and the staging of repeat elections, demonstrators took to the streets in a dozen cities. In Belgrade, tens of thousands of protestors marched through the center of the city; participants included students, teachers, and many ordinary, impoverished Serbs. Milošević refrained from intervening with violence, evidently calculating that the protests would fizzle out, and instead imposed a media blockade. His strategy was to prevent the protests from spreading to the working class. The opposition refrained from calling for mass strikes and other industrial actions, fearing that this could provoke severe government retaliation. Nevertheless, discontent with economic conditions was growing among urban residents and blue-collar workers.

The opposition attempted to benefit from the growing disquiet, but was divided in its political programs and strategies. Serious personality conflicts between Drašković and the Serbian Democratic Party leader Zoran Djindjić undermined any coherent resistance to Milošević's rule. In fact, the local election results were less a vote for *Zajedno* than a vote against Milošević and his corrupt officials. The protests gained momentum despite the failures of *Zajedno,* whose leaders initially demanded only the reinstatement of the local election results. But as the protests spread, some opposition spokesmen called for Milošević's resignation.

With rallies continuing late into December 1996, Milošević seemed willing to make some concessions by removing several Socialist officials and reassigning some local governments to the *Zajedno* opposition. The Serbian administration clearly feared that thousands of ordinary workers might join the protests and seriously undermine Socialist rule. The working class in Serbia was increasingly frustrated by falling living standards, unpaid wages, and rising unemployment, but they had not been mobilized by the opposition.

Milošević was concerned that opposition victories in the local elections could erode support for the Socialists during the national ballot, but he eventually conceded, and *Zajedno* gained control over 34 city governments. The Serbian leader calculated that the opposition would be held responsible for the failures of city government services because of their lack of financial resources. Djindjić became mayor of Belgrade, but *Zajedno* itself split on the eve of presidential and parliamentary elections, on 21 September 1997. While Djindjić called for an election boycott, Drašković participated and lost in the presidential ballot. Milošević faced no credible democratic alternative that could rally citizens behind any realistic program. Instead, the former opposition leaders spent more time attacking each other than they did the ruling Socialists. Infuriated with the outcome of republican elections, Drašković lashed out at Djindjić and made it his mission to remove his rival from the Belgrade mayoralty. Meanwhile, the election boycott called by Djindjić and Civic Alliance leader Vesna Pešić proved a statistical failure.

In the first round of the elections for the Serbian presidency, on 21 September 1997, no candidate received the required 51% of the vote to be elected. As a result, the two contenders who received the most votes, Vojislav Šešelj and Zoran Lilić, participated in a second round of balloting. On 5 October 1997, Šešelj received a majority, but voter participation was below the 50% needed to elect a president. A new election was scheduled for 7 December 1997, as required by Serbia's election law. Because no candidate received the majority of votes in the December balloting, a second round was required. On 21 December 1997, the new SPS candidate Milan Milutinović received nearly 60% of votes, while Šešelj obtained less than 38%. Milutinović became president of Serbia on 29 December 1997.

In the parliamentary elections on 21 September 1997, the SPS won 110 out of 250 parliamentary seats, the Serbian Radical Party gained 82, and the Serbian

Renewal Movement, 45. The ruling Socialists were unable to form a single-party government, and entered into a coalition with the Radicals. Milošević himself was elected Yugoslav president by the Federal Assembly after he was constitutionally barred from standing for a third term in Serbia. The SPS retained the right to appoint the prime minister (Mirko Marjanović), and the Radical Party obtained two deputy prime minister positions (Šešelj and Tomislav Nikolić) plus the Ministry of Information (Aleksandar Vučić). Although the Yugoslav United Left (YUL) party won an insignificant number of votes, they were given three ministerial positions—a measure designed to satisfy Mirjana Marković, Milošević's wife and YUL leader.

The Serbian and Yugoslav economy remained in dire straits. Industrial production was estimated at about half of its level before the disintegration of Yugoslavia, and the government had failed to introduce essential structural reforms. Economists predicted rampant inflation, as the authorities had printed vast amounts of money to pay for wages and pensions in order to preempt large-scale public unrest. Moreover, Yugoslavia continued to be subject to an "outer wall" of U.S.-led sanctions that denied the country credits, investments, and access to international financial institutions.

Following the balloting, the socialist-nationalist coalition proceeded to impose tighter restrictions on oppositionist activities. On 21 October 1998, the Serbian parliament passed a new media law curbing the dissemination of news, especially from the foreign media. The bill imposed high taxation, restrictions on domestic and foreign donations, and placed bans on re-broadcasting foreign programs on state-run radio and television networks. Journalists were closely monitored by the authorities, and there was a comprehensive imposition of censorship. Serbian information minister Aleksandar Vučić, a member of the SRP, announced that the new law on information pertained to the Internet as well as other mass media. Under this decree, several daily newspapers were banned, including *Danas* (Today), *Dnevni Telegraf* (Daily Telegraph), and *Naša Borba* (Our Struggle). Serbian authorities also targeted independent radio stations.

Milošević conducted purges in the military to ensure the loyalty of top commanders. On 24 November 1998, the Chief of Staff of the Yugoslav National Army, Momčilo Perišić, was replaced by Dragoljub Ojdanić, a general considered close to the SPS. The head of Serbian state security and a close Milošević ally, Jovica Stanišić, resigned in protest against Belgrade's preparations for a major crackdown in Kosovo. As compared to the army, the state security service was completely subordinated to Milošević. Its newly appointed head, Rade Marković, who succeed the ousted Jovica Stanišić, was promoted to the rank of police general. Appointments in the security services were closely controlled by Mirjana Marković.

With the failures of the opposition parties to mobilize the public against Milošević, a new student-based movement called *Otpor* (Resistance) was formed during 1998. It had no structure or leadership, but staged spontaneous demonstrations and actions against the regime. For example, on 6 December 1998, *Otpor* activists arranged a protest march though central Belgrade, demanding the reinstatement of deans who were dismissed from various universities in the spring of 1998. Meanwhile, the president of the League of Vojvodina Social Democrats, Nenad Čanak, asserted that his party would advocate the creation of a Republic of Vojvodina. He added that this concept implied the federalization of Serbia and not the declaration of an independent Vojvodina.

On 30 December 1998, the most influential opposition parties, except for the SRM, formed the Alliance for Change (AFC). Its members included the Democratic Party, the Serbian Civil Alliance, the Serbian Demo-Christian Party, the Social Democratic Party, the Democratic Alternative, the Democratic Center, and the Alliance of Hungarians in Vojvodina. Nebojša Čović, the spokesman for the Alliance, stated that it was a nucleus for "all progressive people in Serbia."

At the beginning of 1999, the SRM made an alliance with the SPS. Drašković, once the harshest critic of Milošević and his government, became the vice president of Yugoslavia. This move was seen as treason by Alliance for Change leaders. Drašković claimed that he joined the regime to be able to change it "from inside," a laughable idea, given the degree of Milošević's control over the key levers of power. Drašković's maneuver further split the opposition movement and undermined its credibility.

Milošević launched a major military campaign against the Albanian population in Kosovo in the spring of 1999 and intensified the mass murder and expulsion of civilians following NATO's attack on Serbia on 24 March 1999. In turn, the Belgrade regime manipulated the alleged threat of Albanian terrorism and the NATO offensive to whip up nationalist sentiments and to discredit oppositionists as national traitors. Following Belgrade's capitulation to NATO in June 1999, Milošević immediately claimed victory and asserted that his government was rebuilding the devastated country.

During the Kosovo war, Milošević was formally indicted as a war criminal, by the international tribunal in The Hague—an event that further isolated the regime internationally. After the war, several protests were organized by the opposition in a number of Serbian cities, but their impact was limited. Most citizens were either preoccupied with questions of economic survival or fearful of police repression if they participated in demonstrations. Moreover, most of the opposition leaders had lost trust and credibility among wide sectors of the public. Apathy and despair were widespread, having been promoted and exploited by the Milošević administration. Furthermore, the government staged crackdowns on the alternative media and the young people's movement, and threatened to pass a new "anti-terrorism" law that would virtually turn Serbia into a police state.

In July 2000, the federal parliament amended the Yugoslav constitution, primarily to prolong Milošević's term in office. According to the 1992 constitution, the president of the Federal Republic was elected by secret ballot by the federal assembly. The same individual could not be reelected for a second term, and the president and the federal prime minister could not be from the same republic. However, according to amendments to the 1992 constitution adopted on 9 July 2000, the president was henceforth to be elected through direct elections, by a secret ballot, for a four-year term.[17]

Despite these maneuvers, Milošević seriously miscalculated growing public frustration with his rule and the popularity of the opposition candidate Vojislav Koštunica. Koštunica, the leader of the small Democratic Party of Serbia (DPS), had not been discredited, corrupted, or co-opted by the Milošević regime over the previous decade. He won the Yugoslav presidency outright in the first round of voting on 24 September 2000, despite massive fraud by the Socialist administration. Following large-scale demonstrations and the storming of the federal parliament on 6 October 2000, Milošević lost the loyalty of the military and police forces and was unable to stage a crackdown. He finally capitulated on 7 October 2000 and resigned from office. A behind-the-scenes deal was evidently struck by DOS leaders and Serbia's military and police commanders to sideline Milošević while launching a process of measured reform that would preclude any major purges in the security apparatus.

In the Yugoslav parliamentary elections on 24 September 2000, the broad coalition the Democratic Opposition of Serbia (DOS) gained 58 out of 138 federal seats in the Chamber of Citizens, while the Socialists, who had dominated the body throughout the 1990s, managed to gain only 44 seats. In Montenegro, an extensive boycott of the Yugoslav elections was called by the governing coalition in protest against unilateral constitutional changes in Belgrade. Only 28% of citizens took part in the balloting—primarily supporters of the oppositionist Socialist People's Party (SPP), which was tied to the Serbian Socialists.

In mid-October 2000, Serbia's DOS coalition formed a new federal government with the support of the Montenegrin SPP, which had switched its loyalties to Koštunica after the elections. Their candidate Zoran Žižić was appointed the new federal Prime Minister. The appointment was not recognized by the Montenegrin administration, which claimed that the elections and the new federal structures were illegitimate. Following the formation of the federal government, Serbia entered a new era of institutional reconstruction; but it still faced a legion of political, economic, ethnic, and social problems inherited from the Milošević years.

Politically, the new administration confronted the task of keeping together a disparate coalition of 18 parties while removing Socialist stalwarts from public office without provoking new instabilities. Economically, Belgrade needed to implement a tough reform program involving wholesale restructuring, budgetary discipline, and competitive privatization, while undermining and curtailing the interest groups that controlled the Serbian economy. Socially, the authorities needed to maintain sufficient public support while implementing wrenching reforms, in order to forest all populist and nationalist reactions as a result of deflated expectations over economic prosperity.

Constitutionally, Serbia and Montenegro had to reformulate their inter-republican relations on a more equitable basis. Otherwise, the government in Podgorica looked determined to seek independence, a move that would effectively terminate the Yugoslav federation. Moreover, the conflict between Serbia and Kosovo looked destined to continue because of the irreconcilable positions of Belgrade and Priština on the question of Kosovo's independence.

The Serbian republican elections on 23 December 2000 strengthened the position of the anti-Milošević forces. The ballot was comfortably won by the Democratic Opposition of Serbia (DOS) with over 64% of the vote and 176 out of 250 parliamentary seats. The Socialist Party of Serbia (SPS) finished with a mere 13.67% of the vote and 37 seats, and their Serbian Radical Party (SRP) colleagues obtained 8.55% and 23 seats. Zoran Djindjić, leader of the Democratic Party (DP) within the DOS coalition, was appointed Serbia's new prime minister.

Throughout the early part of 2001, growing divisions were evident among factions of the broad ruling coalitions at both the federal and republican levels over appropriate political and economic reforms. Due to intensive international pressure to bring the former Serbian leader to justice, in April 2001, Milošević was finally arrested and a trial was gradually prepared. However, the federal authorities in Belgrade resisted demands to dispatch Milošević to the Hague on war crimes charges, arguing that he first had to be tried in Serbia for an assortment of domestic indictments. In July 2001, the Serbian republican authorities unilaterally extradited Milošević to the Hague despite opposition within the federal government and from the Yugoslav constitutional court. Prime Minister Djindjić asserted that without this move, Serbia would have faced international isolation and a loss of critically needed financial assistance. The evacuation of Milošević led to the collapse of the federal government as the Montenegrin party in the federation, the Socialist People's Party (SPP), was adamantly opposed to the Hague war crimes process. Although a new federal administration was put together in mid-July under Prime Minister Dragiša Pesić (of the SPP), the Yugoslav structure remained highly volatile and unstable, with conflict increasing between FRY President Koštunica and the Serbian authorities.

POLITICAL PARTIES

Socialists and Social Democrats

Socialist Party of Serbia (SPS)
Socialistička Partija Srbije (SPS)

On 16 July 1990, the League of Communists of Serbia (LCS) *(Savez Komunista Srbije, SKS)* and its mass organization, the Socialist Alliance, united to form the Socialist Party of Serbia. Most of the 111 members of the party's main committee were former members of the LCS. The SPS was perceived primarily as a new structure for former communists who now formally accepted the idea of a multi-party democracy. However, some reformists also joined the SPS, including the socialist critic of Titoism, Mihailo Marković, who became the party's vice president.

This new party was forged and led by Slobodan Milošević, who in May 1986 was selected president of the LCS and proceeded to purge any potential rivals. In May 1989, the Serbian National Assembly *(Skupština)* elected him president of Serbia in an indirect ballot and in a December 1989 referendum 86% of voters expressed confidence in his presidency. Milošević became the undisputed leader of the SPS after its inception. He was first elected during the founding congress on 16–18 July 1990 and subsequently re-elected at the second congress on 23–24 October 1992, at the third congress on 2 March 1996, and at the fourth congress on 17 February 2000. The vice-president of the party at the end of the 1990s was Mirko Marjanović, who also served as Serbia's prime minister. The SPS secretary general was Gorica Gajević. The party leadership was elected at the SPS's fourth congress on 17 February 2000.

According to its statute the SPS was organized on a territorial principle with 5,000 communal organizations, 189 municipal and city committees, 29 district committees, and two provincial committees.[18] The party claimed to have approximately 600,000 members, including 70,000 belonging to Serbia's national minorities. The youth organization of the party claimed to have over 100,000 members under the age of 30. However, in general, the SPS relied on the following groups for support: the elderly, the less educated, pensioners, unqualified and semi-qualified workers, farmers, civil servants, and unemployed housewives.[19]

With its new socialist guise, its increasingly nationalist agenda, and its firm control over the state bureaucracy, the security forces, and the mass media, the SPS gained 194 of 250 seats in Serbia's first multi-party elections in December 1990. Milošević was elected president of Serbia, gaining 65.3% of the vote. The party maintained enormous support among bureaucrats, military veterans, and factory managers, as well as large sections of the peasantry and working class that were dependent on the state. The Serbian Orthodox Church and the Serbian Academy of Sciences also lent their support to the SPS, largely because of its nationalist-oriented program at a time when Yugoslavia appeared to be on the verge of dissolution. As war erupted in Slovenia and Croatia in the summer of 1991, the Serbian regime, led by SPS, depicted itself as the defender of Serbian interests. The party easily won federal elections to the newly declared two-member Yugoslav government in May 1992, in a ballot that was boycotted by the majority of opposition parties in Serbia, which condemned the elections as illegal and unconstitutional. The Serbian authorities claimed that despite the boycotts 60% of eligible voters had participated.

The SPS leadership deliberately undercut the popularity of the opposition by capitalizing on nationalist sentiments, sponsoring the ultranationalist Serbian Radical Party, and depicting democrats and moderate nationalist forces as traitors because they criticized the war in Croatia and Bosnia. Despite the imposition of international economic sanctions on Serbia and Montenegro as punishment for Belgrade's sponsorship of the conflict in Bosnia, the SPS preserved its hold on power. Economic decline, falling living standards, and increasing unemployment precipitated by a failed economic policy and the UN embargo were presented by the SPS as an international conspiracy against the Serbian nation. SPS leaders and bureaucrats also benefited from the thriving sanctions-busting black-market economy and assured much of the ex-communist *nomenklatura* that they could preserve their privileges.

The SPS maintained enormous advantages in the federal, republican, and local elections in December 1992, particularly in terms of funds and media access. The opposition remained weak, confused, disunited, and kept off balance. In addition, various balloting and legal irregularities assured the Socialists and their Radical allies a victory at each administrative level. The SPS obtained 101 seats in the 250-member Serbian Assembly, 47 out of 138 deputies in the federal Chamber of Citizens, and 12 out of the 20 Serbian seats in the 40-member federal Chamber of Republics in the December 1992 federal ballot. In May 1993, Socialist deputies in the federal assembly voted with the Radicals in passing a vote of no-confidence against Yugoslav President Dobrica Ćosić, who was condemned for his moderating policies and public criticisms of the Bosnian Serb leadership. The democratic opposition attacked the removal of Ćosić as an unconstitutional coup that heralded the consolidation of totalitarian or quasi-fascist rule.[20]

In the parliamentary elections on 21 September 1997, the SPS ran in a coalition with the Yugoslav United Left (YUL) and New Democracy (ND).[21] The Socialists won 110 seats out of 250 parliamentary seats and entered into a coalition with the Radicals. Milošević himself was elected Yugoslav president by the Federal Assembly after he was constitutionally barred from standing for a third term in Serbia. The SPS retained the right to appoint the Prime Minister, Mirko Marjanović.

In spite of its authoritarian grip on power and its nationalistic policies, in its party programs the SPS depicted itself as a party of the left, dedicated to the values of freedom, peace, social justice, solidaritity, and humanism. In a party program adopted at its fourth congress, the party reaffirmed as its basic goals "to create a modern, democratic society in which: all problems will be resolved peacefully and by democratic means; all human rights are guaranteed; and economic processes will be regulated by free market within established legal frameworks."[22] Observers believed that the party contained factions that were dissatisfied with Milošević's policies, especially in the economic and business sphere, and that could form the nucleus of more concerted opposition given the right impetus from the military or security apparatus. However, they remained too weak and disorganized to challenge Milošević directly.

With respect to the numerous national minorities in Serbia, the SPS declared the principle of "national equality" according to which members of minorities, as individuals, had the same rights as members of the majority nation. However, the SPS explicitly declared itself against the political autonomy of national minorities, which would involve the possibility of secession. The party reaffirmed its support for a "United Serbia," from which the autonomous provinces (Kosovo and Vojvodina) could not secede.

SPS leaders rejected any responsibility for what occurred in Kosovo during the past decade, including the atrocities against the Albanian population. Instead, they placed all the blame on "militant Albanian separatists." The party refused to recognize the reality of the changed balance of power in Kosovo after the entry of NATO forces and Kosovo's new status as a virtual international protectorate. SPS leaders denounced the role of the international community in Kosovo and demanded full compliance with the provisions of the Security Council Resolution 1244, in which Serbian authority was supposedly to be restored. The SPS suffered a political disaster in September 2000, when Milošević lost the federal presidential elections and the party was pushed out of power in the Yugoslav federal government. The Socialist-controlled Serbian republican administration was also pressured to step down by the victorious Democratic Opposition of Serbia (DOS) after new general elections in December 2000.

Democratic Alternative (DA)
Demokratska Alternativa (DA)

The DA was founded on 16 July 1997 by Nebojša Čović, the former mayor of Belgrade and a high functionary of the Socialist Party of Serbia. Its vice presidents were Djordje Petrović and Nada Kolundžija, and it claimed to have over 30,000 members. In the December 1997 parliamentary elections, the party won only one seat in the Serbian parliament. The party was a member of the Alliance for Change coalition, but subsequently formed the DAN (The Day) coalition, together with the Democratic Center and New Democracy. The party's political platform was centrist with a social democratic orientation. As an opposition party, it was highly critical of the Milošević regime and pushed for economic, political, and social reforms based on the principles of social democracy. According to the DA, the Federal Republic of Yugoslavia needed a high degree of decentralization. The DA asserted that Serbia and Yugoslavia were multinational and multiconfessional states and that national minorities should be provided the full array of minority rights according to international law.

Social Democracy (SD)
Socijaldemokratija (SD)

Social Democracy was formed in 1997 and led by its president Vuk Obradović and vice presidents Slobodan Orlić and Slobodan Lalović. The SD declared itself a party of the center but with a social democratic orientation. The SD participated in the September 1997 presidential and parliamentary elections in Serbia. Obradović was the party's candidate for Serbian President, and he won just over 3% of the votes. The SD did not win any seats in the Serbian parliament and failed to meet the electoral threshold by winning only 102,000 votes. The party was part of the opposition bloc Alliance for Change (AFC) until 22 October 1999, when it left the opposition. Nevertheless, it remained dedicated to the efforts of the opposition to dislodge the Milošević regime. The SD supported all the key demands of the broad opposition movement, including free and fair elections, political democratization, economic reforms, and the integration of Serbia and Yugoslavia into all international institutions. All of these demands were repeated in the party's program document "The Foundations of European Serbia," adopted on 12 February 2000.[23] With respect to the Kosovo question, the SD, like other parties, called for the implementation of UN Security Council Resolution 1244, which stated that Kosovo should remain a province of Yugoslavia.

Social Democratic Union (SDU)
Socijaldemokratska Unija (SDU)

The SDU was founded on 13 May 1996 by its president Zarko Korać, a deputy in the Serbian parliament from 1993 to 1997. He was known for his opposition to the Milošević regime and for his anti-war activities. The party's vice presidents were Miroslav Hristodulo, Vera Marković, and Branko Pavlović. The SDU was a small political party with no governmental representation at local, republican, or federal levels, but it was very active in opposition circles. It defined itself as a party of the democratic center, with a social democratic, anti-nationalistic, and anti-war orientation. Since 1997, SDU has been a member of the coalition the Alliance of Democratic Parties (ADP), which includes the League of Social Democrats of Vojvodina, the Alliance of Vojvodina Hungarians, the Sandžak Coalition, the Banat Coalition, and the Šumadija Coalition. However, social democratic groups have not been significant players in Serbian politics, and they have gained few adherents from ex-SPS supporters.[24]

Liberals

New Democracy (ND)
Nova Demokratija (ND)

New Democracy was formed on 10 July 1990 through the unification of the Social Democratic League of Serbian Youth and the Movement of Cities for Serbia. It was led by President Dušan Mihajlović, Secretary-General Tahir Hasanović, and Vice Presidents Nebojša Leković, Radivoje Lazarević, Slobodan Radulović, and Rebeka Srbinović. The party operated as an umbrella political movement in that it respected the relative independence of local organizational units and fostered the creation of academic, cultural, business, and other clubs. It claimed to have around 55,000 members and considered itself a centrist party with liberal principles.[25] In its statute, the ND stressed that it did not propagate any ideology but supported three core goals: reintegration in Europe, development of private property, and a regional approach to local problems.

The ND was a founding member of the DEPOS coalition. It withdrew from the opposition alliance in February 1994, when it decided to support the SPS administration. From the beginning of 1994 until March 1998, ND was in coalition with the Socialist Party of Serbia and the Yugoslav United Left in the Serbian and federal parliaments. During the November 1996 federal elections, New Democracy ran on a joint ticket with the SPS and YUL. In its newsletter, published in February 1996, ND explained why it decided to join the National Unity Government in which the SPS held a majority. Apparently, as part of the government, it could promote peace and cooperation instead of confrontation with Europe and the world; it could work on the suspension of UN sanctions against Yugoslavia; and it could provide support for the economic reforms formulated by the economist Dragoslav Avramović.[26] However, on 16 July 1999, the coalition between ND, SPS, and YUL collapsed and the Serbian Assembly expelled the ND ministers from government. After that, ND joined the democratic opposition and became a member of the DAN coalition, together with the Democratic Center and the Democratic Alternative.

Civic Alliance of Serbia (CAS)
Gradjanski Savez Srbije (GSS)

The CAS was founded by members of the Alliance of Reform Forces of Yugoslavia (ARFY) *(Savez Reformskih Snaga Jugoslavije, SRSJ)*, led by the last Yugoslav Prime Minister Ante Marković and chaired by Vesna Pešić; the Republican Club, chaired by Nebojša Popov; and the People's Peasant Party, chaired by Dragan Veselinov. The founding assembly took place on 12 February 1994. According to its program, the Civic Alliance aimed toward "harmony between a civic state and people's national feelings towards the community to which they belong."[27] The party strongly discouraged "malignant, primitive and aggressive nationalism that arouses fear, hatred and violence." It also strongly advocated the principles of parliamentary democracy, the rule of law, social justice, a market economy, and respect for human rights.

Goran Svilanović became the Civic Alliance president in 1998. Between 1992 and 1998, the CAS president was Vesna Pešić, one of the most prominent Serbian opposition politicians, who was one of the leaders of the coalition *Zajedno* (Together) in the 1996 federal and local elections. The CAS vice presidents included Dragor Hiber, Aleksandar Pošarac, Miroslav Filipović,

and Konstantin Obradović. The Alliance claimed to have 59 local committees. Its members were primarily educated people with an anti-war, anti-nationalist, and civic political orientation. Many of its prominent members were
founders or members of numerous NGOs, such as the Belgrade Circle, the
Center for Anti-war Action, the Center for Advancement of Law Studies, and
the Belgrade Center for Human Rights.

The CAS was one of the main opponents of the Milošević regime, but was
against the isolation of Serbia and Yugoslavia by the international community. Immediately after the end of the NATO war against Serbia on 5 July
1999, the party expressed its views in a document titled *The Need for a New
Policy towards Yugoslavia.*[28] The party believed that isolation would only
lead to right-wing radicalization; to a civil war between the ultra-nationalists
and the opponents of the regime; to a conflict between Serbia and Montenegro;
and to conflicts in ethnically mixed areas of Yugoslavia. The Alliance believed that Yugoslavia had to be included in the South East European Stability Pact. Domestically, CAS wanted to broaden the opposition coalition
Alliance for Change. With respect to the Kosovo issue, CAS believed that the
long-term solution could only be found within Yugoslavia. It called for cooperation between Albanian and Serbian democratic forces, to enhance democratic changes as a precondition for establishing a democratic government,
the rule of law, and respect for human rights.

Alliance for Change (AFC)
Savez za Promene (SAP)

The Alliance for Change (AFC) was an umbrella opposition bloc formed on
30 December 1998 by the Democratic Party, the Civic Alliance of Serbia, the
Demo-Christian Party, New Serbia, the popular professor of economics
Dragoslav Avramović, and Milan Panić, the former prime minister of Yugoslavia. According to the *Coalition Agreement on the Alliance for Change*, the
AFC was an "association of political parties, nongovernmental organizations,
unions, and other organizations, associations, and distinct individuals, for
achieving the goal of democratic transformation and economic reforms in
Serbia."[29]

The AFC assembled most of the major opposition parties, excluding the
Serbian Renewal Movement but including the Democratic Party, the Civil
Alliance of Serbia, the Serbian Demo-Christian Party, the Social Democratic
Party, New Serbia, the Democratic Movement for Pančevo, the Yugoslav
Democratic Party, the Liberal Democratic Party, the Progressive Party, the
Progressive Radical Party, the People's Radical Party, the Roma Congress
Party, the Alliance of Citizens of Subotica, Serbian National Renewal, the
Party of Independent Entrepreneurs, the Alliance of Hungarians in Vojvodina,
and the Democratic Community of Vojvodina Hungarians.

Other AFC member organizations included the Association of Free and

Independent Unions, the Serbian Democratic Club *Odbrana*, the Movement for Protection of Human Rights, the Movement for Unification of Serbia and Montenegro, the Association of Tenants of Yugoslavia, the Independent Union of Agricultural Producers, My Vojvodina, and the University Board for the Protection of Democracy.

The Alliance had a political-promotional team composed of several distinguished opposition politicians, including Dragoslav Avramović, Vladan Batić (Demo-Christian Party), Milan Protić (Serbian Democratic Club *Odbrana*), Dragan Milovanović (Association of Free and Independent Unions), Goran Svilanović (Civic Alliance of Serbia), Zoran Djindjić (Democratic Party) and Velimir Ilić (New Serbia). With respect to the program and goals of the Alliance, Nebojša Čović, the AFC spokesman, stated that the most important goal was to overthrow Milošević and to initiate democratic changes.

An elaboration of Alliance goals was stated in the *Declaration of the Alliance for Change,* adopted on 15 July 1999, in the aftermath of the Kosovo war.[30] Its political goals included a democratic transformation of the political system; the rule of law and constitutional guarantees for individual and collective human rights; territorial decentralization based on the principles of local, regional, and provincial self-government; opening Serbia to international organizations; complete protection of private property; the building of democratic institutions with a high degree of self-government for Kosovo; respect for the sovereignty and territorial integrity of Serbia and Yugoslavia; and a rearrangement of relations between Serbia and Montenegro on the basis of "mutual agreement."

According to its declaration, the immediate goals of the AFC were the removal of Milošević and his regime from power, the formation of a transitional government, and democratic elections with new electoral laws, under international monitoring. Members of the Alliance agreed to participate in all elections as a coalition, according to the stipulations of the coalition agreement. The AFC announced that it would participate in the federal and local elections on 24 September 2000, and would submit common lists for the balloting as part of the wider Democratic Opposition of Serbia (DOS), a coalition consisting of eighteen oppositionist parties. Although DOS hoped to nominate a joint candidate with the SRM to oppose Milošević in the Yugoslav presidential elections, both organizations fielded their own nominees. With the victory of DOS and the election of Vojislav Koštunica as the federal President, several former AFC members were included in the new Yugoslav administration.

Another small centrist liberal grouping, the Democratic Center (DC) *(Demokratski Centar, DC)*, was founded in 1996 by a fraction of the Democratic Party, led by one of its founders, Dragoljub Mićunović. It sought to "maintain the original spirit of the Democratic Party" and took part in the *Zajedno* coalition, but remained largely on the sidelines. It defined itself as an anti-nationalist party, but it only played a minor role on the Serbian political scene.

Christian Democrats

Christian Democratic Party (CDP)
Demohrišćanska Stranka (DS)

The Christian Democratic Party (CDP) was established on 6 May 1997 in Kragujevac, in central Serbia, as an opposition party to the Milošević regime. It strongly believed in a united opposition as the only way to overthrow communism in Serbia. The main goal of the party was to establish a democratic parliamentary system. It was absolutely respectful of the Serbian Orthodox Church and possessed a monarchist stream, recognizing the legitimacy of the Karadjordjević dynasty and believing that the Church and the crown should be the two pillars of a modern Serbian state. The CDP president was Vladan Batić, an international lawyer from Belgrade University. The party's honorary president was the Serbian American businessman Milan Panić. [31]

Agrarians

People's Peasant Party (PPP)
Narodna Seljačka Stranka (NSS)

The People's Peasant Party (PPP) was one of the founding members of the DEPOS coalition in May 1992—a group that sought to dislodge the Milošević regime from power. It remained a small formation, capturing only 1.35% of the vote in the Serbian parliamentary elections on 9 December 1990 and four legislative seats. DEPOS itself gained only 16.89% of the vote in the Serbian parliamentary elections on 20 December 1992, and 50 seats. The PPP leader Milan Paroški also stood in the Serbian presidential elections in December 1992 but finished with only 3.31% of the vote and remained a relatively minor figure on the political stage. In the Serbian parliamentary elections in December 1992, the PPP gained 2.71% of the vote and three seats. Thereafter, the party was submerged by more effective oppositionist forces.

Greens

Serbian Green Party (SGP)
Zelena Stranka Srbije (ZSS)

The Serbian Green Party (SGP) was established on 2 October 1990, but it was largely inactive for most of the 1990s because of political conditions in the country and the limited appeal of ecological issues at a time of profound social, political, economic, and national crisis. In 1997, the party held a "reestablishment conference." Jelena Vuković became president of the party but failed to resuscitate it. On 27 February 2000, the party held another conference, and elected Budimir Babić as its president. During 2000, it formed a coalition called the Union of Greens (UOG) with two other environmentalist formations—the Ecological Party of Serbia (EPS) and the Ecological Party *Hrast.* The UOG became a member of the Democratic Opposition of Serbia (DOS).[32]

Communists

Yugoslav United Left (YUL)
Jugoslovenska Ujedinjena Levica (JUL)

The Yugoslav United Left (YUL) was founded on 23 July 1994 through the unification of twenty-three parties, all with leftist and pro-Yugoslav orientations. It was therefore regarded more as a political movement than a political party. The YUL considered itself as the mother party of all "left-wing and progressive forces that believed that the general interest always comes above private interest." The YUL was a successor to the League of Communists–Movement for Yugoslavia (LC-MY) *(Savez Komunista–Pokret za Jugoslaviju, SK-PJ)*, a now-defunct party that was led by Dragomir Drašković and was regarded as the organization of generals and the hard-line faction of the former ruling communists. Mirjana Marković, the wife of Yugoslav President Slobodan Milošević, was a prominent member of this party before she launched the YUL political movement.

The YUL inherited a large portion of the LC-MY membership and much of its property, including a building in New Belgrade that was later destroyed in the NATO bombardment in the spring of 1999. According to its political platform, the party welcomed communists, socialists, social democrats, and greens into its ranks. In 1995, Ljubiša Ristić became the YUL president; he was a representative in the Civic Chamber of the federal parliament. Its secretary-general was Zoran Todorović. The chair of the YUL directorate was Mirjana Marković, the high-profile wife of Slobodan Milošević. She was a professor of sociology at the faculty of natural sciences and mathematics at Belgrade University. Marković was considered the most influential YUL politician and the movement's ideological force.

The party was organized on the principle of territoriality, both in Serbia and Montenegro, with 4,600 local boards, 209 municipal boards, 36 district boards, and five city boards. The party claimed a membership of around 200,000 by the end of the decade but this was difficult to verify. Membership in the YUL was considered invaluable for personal enrichment or career promotion. The YUL's membership included well-known Serbian intellectuals, government ministers, managers of companies, ambassadors, and press editors, many of whom had switched from the SPS.

Up until the November 1996 federal elections, the YUL had no seats in parliament. Nevertheless, it quickly grew into one of the most influential parties in Serbia. The YUL never took part in the parliamentary elections independently but always in coalition with the SPS and New Democracy. Together with the SPS and New Democracy, the YUL participated in the 1996 federal parliamentary elections and in the 1997 parliamentary elections in Serbia. The YUL took part independently in local elections in November 1996 and won 785 seats in the local assemblies and 17.5% of the popular vote.[33] The party's program and rhetoric are almost identical to those of the Socialists, primarily because of the personal and political symbiosis of the two parties' leaders.

Nationalists

Serbian Renewal Movement (SRM)
Srpski Pokret Obnove (SPO)

Initially an offshoot of the Serbian National Renewal, the Serbian Renewal Movement (SRM) was founded in August 1990 and was directed by the charismatic orator and writer Vuk Drašković. At the outset, the party was fervently nationalistic, anti-communist, and monarchist. It promoted the idea that in the case of Yugoslavia's breakup, the western borders of Serbia needed to be extended to incorporate the territories of Croatia and Bosnia-Herzegovina where the Serbian population formed a majority. The party maintained overall pan-Serbian goals but increasingly focused its attention on democratizing the Serbian political system. The SRM modified its extreme nationalist position in the wake of its poor showing in the December 1990 elections, particularly after Milošević and the Socialists successfully swayed many ultra-nationalist supporters over to their favored "opposition" party, the SRP. Drašković finished second to Milošević in the Serbian presidential race, capturing 16.4% of the vote, while the movement only gained 19 parliamentary seats in the December 1990 republican elections. The SRM was obliged to broaden its political appeal by moving toward the center and promoting the establishment of a constitutional monarchy under the exiled king Aleksandar Karadjordjević, avowedly in order to democratize the state.

The SRM, like other nationalist groupings, initially sponsored its own paramilitary formation, the Serbian Guard, to participate in the Croatian war during the summer and fall of 1991. However, its numbers shrank due to competition with the SRP and as Milošević's campaign against Drašković gathered momentum. With the adoption of a more moderate policy, the Serbian Guard lost its importance and Drašković was condemned by the state media for abandoning the goal of a Greater Serbia. In order to bolster its opposition to the Socialist regime, the SRM initiated a new anti-Milošević coalition, the Democratic Movement of Serbia (DEPOS), in late May 1992. It included the pro-monarchist Democratic Party of Serbia (DPS), the Serbian Liberal Party (SLP), the New Democracy–Movement for Serbia (NDMS), and the People's Peasant Party (PPP). DEPOS leaders contended that Milošević's Socialist government had to be replaced in order to reintegrate Serbia with the rest of the world. The SRM criticized the regime for conducting a brutal war in Bosnia, but SRM leaders were loath to abandon the goal of an enlarged Serbian state.

In the elections of December 1992, the DEPOS bloc gained 20 seats to the federal Chamber of Citizens and 50 seats to the Serbian Assembly, thereby becoming the largest oppositionist party in both legislatures. In June 1993, protesting the ouster of Yugoslav President Dobrica Ćosić, the SRM staged a rally outside the federal parliament that was violently dispersed by the police. Drašković and his wife, Danica, were arrested and severely beaten by police, and the authorities began proceedings in the constitutional court to ban the SRM altogether. Once Drašković was released from prison in July 1993, he pledged to unite the opposition movement and dislodge Milošević from power.[34] However, his popularity diminished together with his capability to mobilize the Serbian public, especially given the weak performance of *Zajedno* at the federal elections in November 1996. It won only 23.8% of the vote in the election for the Civic Chamber of the federal parliament, in contrast to the 45.4% gained by the ruling coalition of the SPS, Yugoslav Left, and New Democracy. It was estimated that many SRM voters did not like the newer, more moderate tone of the party and voted for the Serbian Radical Party.[35]

Unlike the federal elections, the November 1996 local elections proved to be a much greater success for SRM. The *Zajedno* coalition won the majority of votes in 40 out of 189 municipalities, including the two biggest cities in Serbia, Belgrade and Niš. When the Milošević regime tried to nullify the outcome of the elections by doctoring the results and manipulating the electoral and judicial organs, the SRM, together with other *Zajedno* partners (Democratic Party and the Civic Alliance), organized mass protests attended by over 200,000 people that lasted 88 days. These protests forced Milošević to validate the election results. However, during and after the protests there were visible cracks in the coalition due to personal animosities between the SRM and SD leaders and their differing political platforms. This was most clearly expressed by Drašković's presidential campaign in 1997, when he promoted the idea of restoring the monarchy together with "national reconciliation" between *Četnik*s and partisans.

The SRM allied itself with the SPS against DP leader Zoran Djindjić, and it managed to strip him of the mayoralty of Belgrade by replacing him with the SRM candidate, Vojislav Mihajlović. In January 1999, the SRM joined the federal government coalition, composed of the SPS, YUL, and the Socialist People's Party of Montenegro. Four ministerial posts went to SRM candidates, including Vuk Drašković, who became deputy prime minister from January 1999 until April 1999, in a government led by Momir Bulatović. During the NATO war against Yugoslavia, Drašković was the leading government official who presented its views to the foreign media. However, in the midst of the NATO campaign, Drašković became increasingly critical of Belgrade's conduct of the war, and especially of Milošević, whom he accused of hiding the real human and military cost of the war. As a result, he and the SRM were excluded from the government at the end of April 1999.

Following the war, Drašković criticized the Milošević regime, especially for the deterioration of relations between Belgrade and Montenegro. The SRM believed that the Serbian opposition had to side with the government in Podgorica and help it for "political and historical reasons."[36] The SRM also attacked the NATO and UN missions in Kosovo, especially with regard to the alleged "ethnic cleansing" of Serbs by returning Albanians, and the destruction of historic monuments.

Relations between the SRM and the governing coalition were publicly strained, but critics speculated that behind the scenes Drašković was collaborating with Milošević to weaken the opposition movement. Some believed that Milošević had accumulated information on Drašković's corruption and was, in effect, blackmailing him. It remained unclear whether the assassination attempt on Drašković on 15 June 2000 in the Montenegrin tourist resort of Budva was genuine or a performance staged to raise Drašković's prestige. Nevertheless, the regime in Belgrade continued to apply pressure against the opposition, including arrests of SRM activists and the closure or repression of sympathetic media, such as the radio stations Studio B and Radio B92. The SRM responded by initiating protest rallies and demonstrations. The federal elections in September 2000 proved disastrous for the SRM as the party had failed to enter the DOS (Democratic Opposition of Serbia) coalition and its electoral base virtually disappeared. Some local SRM leaders voiced strong dissatisfaction with Drašković's leadership of the movement.

New Serbia (NS)
Nova Srbija (NS)

In the spring of 1998, a part of the Serbian Renewal Movement (SRM) led by former functionaries Jovan Marjanović and Velimir Ilić, formed the party Serbia Together. However, as the result of a power struggle, Ilić subsequently founded his own party, New Serbia (NS). Ilić was the mayor of Čačak, and his party also held power in the municipalities of Lučani and Šumadija. As a new party, NS did not have a broad organizational network throughout Serbia, but it claimed to have approximately 10,000 members and sympathizers and was part of the coalition Alliance for Change (AFC).

Serbia Together (ST)
Srbija Zajedno (SZ)

Serbia Together (ST) was founded on 10 February 1998 by a fraction of the Serbian Renewal Movement. It gathered some disappointed members of the SRM and other opposition parties, who wanted to overcome the weaknesses of the Serbian opposition. Jovan Marjanović, president of ST, was a former high functionary in the SRM and a close adviser to Drašković, the SRM president. Within a short period after its formation, the party had managed to develop an extensive organizational network throughout Serbia, with branches in over 100 towns and municipalities. ST declared as its immediate goals: crushing the communist regime, fighting nepotism and corruption in government, struggling against crime, depoliticizing the state apparatus, pursuing privatization and foreign investment, and repatriating Serb refugees to their homes.[37] The party voiced strong anti-communist and anti-regime rhetoric. The ST claimed to be an "anti-leader-centered" party. The ST gained some seats in local assemblies in Obrenovac, Leskovac, Vladimirci, and Belgrade, because of the defection of representatives from other parties.

Serbian National Renewal (SNR)
Srpska Narodna Obnova (SNO)

Founded by the "cultural-historical" Sava Society, the Serbian National Renewal (SNR) was launched in Nova Pazova (in Vojvodina) in January 1990. The Sava Society originally represented the nationalist demands of Serb activists in Vojvodina. It subsequently developed to represent nationalist goals throughout Serbia and the other former Yugoslav republics. The SNR was founded in order to preserve the Serbian language, the Cyrillic alphabet, and the historical truth as well as to defend Kosovo. Mirko Jović was selected president of the Sava Society and the chairman of the Executive Committee of the SNR.

After the SNR declared itself an independent political party in January 1990, Vuk Drašković, the party's chief ideologist at the time, proclaimed the goal of an enlarged Serbian state based on historical and ethnic borders that would include parts of Bosnia-Herzegovina and Croatia, the autonomous regions of Kosovo and Vojvodina, and all of Macedonia and Montenegro. Drašković abandoned the party during the summer of 1990 to lead the Serbian Renewal Movement, after falling out with Jović and opposing his strong pro-Milošević stance. During 1991, Jović established an irregular paramilitary formation, the White Eagles, which became active in anti-Muslim massacres in Bosnia and in terrorizing the Slav Muslim population in the Sandžak region of southern Serbia and northern Montenegro. The SNR itself did not become a significant political force in either of the two remaining Yugoslav republics.[38]

Democratic Party (DP)
Demokratska Stranka (DS)

The Democratic Party (DP) was founded on 11 December 1989. It has an avowedly liberal and democratic orientation, and it was recognized as the first opposition party in Serbia. Led by Belgrade intellectuals, the DP defined itself as " a modern party of the political center."[39] The party claimed its roots in the Democratic Party founded at the beginning of the twentieth century when some members of the ruling Radical Party set up the Independent Radical Party (IRP) with a European leaning. After the establishment of the Kingdom of Serbs, Croats, and Slovenes in 1919, the IRP merged with democratic groups in Slovenia and Croatia and founded the Democratic Party. After World War II, the DP was banned by the communists.

The future president of the restored DP, Zoran Djindjić, was active in the student opposition movement and was arrested and sentenced to a year in prison for attempting to set up an autonomous student organization. He later cofounded the DP and was elected chairman of the DP executive board in 1990. The same year he was elected a member of the Serbian parliament, becoming the party's parliamentary group whip. In 1993, he became deputy in the Chamber of Republics in the federal parliament. In 1994, after the resignation of the first party president, Dragoljub Mićunović, he became president of the DP. In 1996, Djindjić was given a suspended four-month prison sentence after being found guilty of libel because of his accusations of corruption against the Serbian prime minister.

On 21 February 1997, after eighty-eight days of civic and student protests over the regime's defrauding of the local elections, Djindjić was elected as the first non-communist mayor of Belgrade. However, due to personal animosities and a power struggle between Djindjić and Drašković, the SRM leader, the *Zajedno* coalition fell apart. Djindjić was subsequently ousted as major in September 1997. The SRM, by forming a coalition with the Socialist Party of Serbia, gained the mayor's position for Vojislav Mihajlović.[40]

DP's vice presidents included Predrag Filipov, Zoran Živković, Boris Tadić, and Slobodan Gavrilović. Party founders included Zoran Djindjić, Miodrag Perišić, Gojko Djogo, Dragoljub Mićunović, Borislav Pekić, Vojislav Koštunica, Slobodan Inić, Vladimir Gligorov, Milovan Danojlić, Kosta Čavoski, Marko Janković, Radoslav Stojanović, and Dušan Vukajlović.[41] The first party president was Dragoljub Micunović, who resigned on 29 January 1994 at an extraordinary party conference called by more than 80 municipal party branches and the party main board.

DP membership was primarily composed of intellectuals and successful businessmen. Party leaders declared their commitment to a democratic multiparty system, democratic political institutions, the rule of law, protection of human and minority rights, a market economy, privatization, denationalization, the fight against organized crime and state corruption, the decentralization of government, and promotion of a new foreign policy that would reintegrate Serbia and Yugoslavia in the international community. The party regularly submitted legislative projects based on its program, such as laws on privatization and denationalization. The DP also possessed a youth organization called the Democratic Youth.

The DP was one of the most active opposition parties in Serbia in the 1990s and one of the most serious opponents of the SPS. In 1992, the party collected over 840,000 signatures calling for the resignation of Serbian President Milošević. In May 1992, the DP did not participate in the federal elections, as a protest against unfair electoral conditions. The party supported Dobrica Ćosić for the federal presidency and the government of Milan Panić. It was one of the main organizers of demonstrations against the Milošević regime, most notably the protests in 1996 together with the SRM and the Civic Alliance. This later grew into the serious opposition coalition, *Zajedno*. This coalition managed to win the 1997 local elections in the major cities in Serbia, where approximately 67% of the Serbian population lived. The nullification of the election results provoked massive protests organized by the DP and its coalition partners.

For a while, the DP resisted the creation of a single opposition movement. When DEPOS was formed in June 1992, one wing of the DP chose to join the movement. This wing was led by Vojislav Koštunica. It subsequently broke off from the DP and formed the Democratic Party of Serbia (DPS). However, the departure of Dragoljub Mićunović from the party, and a swing toward nationalism, caused the party's exit from the DEPOS opposition coalition. Later, the DP was the main initiator of the unification of opposition parties. As a result of its efforts, on 26 November 1995 the coalition Democratic Alliance was formed; it was joined by the Democratic Party of Serbia, the Serbian Liberal Party, and the People's Party of Milan Paroški.

The DP was vocal in the field of foreign policy. It was a harsh critic of Milošević's isolationist politics, which had alienated Serbia from the international community. With respect to the war in Bosnia-Herzegovina, the DP supported "Serbian self-determination" and eventually the Dayton peace agreement in November 1995. The DP was a harsh critic of the government's mishandling of the Serbian refugees pouring into Serbia from Croatia and Bosnia and it organized humanitarian and political support for the refugees.

The DP was initially very critical of the 1998 Milošević-Holbrooke Agreement on Kosovo because it allegedly failed to take the interests of the Serbian people into consideration.[42] The DP believed that the Kosovo problem could only be solved by "political means," taking into consideration the interests of both the Serbian and Albanian communities, but within the framework of Yugoslavia. During the 1999 Kosovo war, the DP was critical both of Milošević's policies of ethnic cleansing and of the NATO air strikes.[43] In the aftermath of the war, the DP insisted on radical political changes and the reintegration of Yugoslavia into the international community. After the September 2000 federal elections, DP leader Zoran Djindjić became close adviser to Yugoslav President Vojislav Koštunica and his major political rival. Djindjić was selected as prime minister of Serbia on 25 January 2001, following general elections in December 2000.

Democratic Party of Serbia (DPS)
Demokratska Stranka Srbije (DSS)

The Democratic Party of Serbia (DPS) was established on 26 July 1992, shortly before the 1992 general elections, by a small faction of the Democratic Party that wanted to join DEPOS. The DPS left DEPOS as a result of disagreement within the coalition on the question of relations with the government and the Serbian national question. The DPS president, Vojislav Koštunica, was one of the founders of the Democratic Party, but formed the DPS in 1992 out of one of its fractions. He remained president of DPS from its inception. He was a member of the Serbian parliament between 1990 and 1997 and was a dissident during the communist period, having been expelled from Belgrade University in 1974 and denounced as a "liberal."

The vice presidents of the DPS included Vladeta Janković, Aleksandar Pravdić, Dušan Budišin, Marko Jakšić, and Zoran Šami. The party had 16 regional boards and party branches. Most of its membership was composed of defecting members of the DP, especially from Serbia's smaller towns. In 1996, the DPS formed a "technical" coalition with the *Zajedno* coalition, but it still ran separately in some municipalities. It boycotted the September 1997 Serbian parliamentary elections.

The DPS declared itself a party of the center, but it had very strong anti-communist and nationalistic elements. It held radical stands on the national questions, often more radical than those of the government. When there was a breakdown in relations between Milošević and the Bosnian Serb leader Karadžić on the acceptance of the Contact Group plan for Bosnia-Herzegovina, the DPS took the side of Karadžić, and supported the Bosnian Serbs in their ambitions to join Serbia. The party believed that the experience of the two previous Yugoslav states demonstrated that all federal arrangements placed Serbs in a weak position, and therefore, any future state should have "Serb" in its name. The DPS believed that Serbian refugees expelled from other parts of Yugoslavia should be given Yugoslav citizenship. The DPS was very critical of all the agreements on Kosovo, denouncing them as violations of Serbian and Yugoslav sovereignty, and it strongly denounced "Albanian separatism."[44]

The DPS was one of the few opposition parties that never cooperated with the Milošević regime. Its leader, Koštunica, was selected as the opposition candidate for the September 2000 federal presidential elections, which he won in the first round of the ballot. After mass public protests, the federal election commission recognized Koštunica as the new Yugoslav president.[45]

Movement for a Democratic Serbia (MDS)
Pokret za Demokratsku Srbiju (PDS)

The Movement for a Democratic Serbia (MDS) was founded on 8 August 1997, during a period of significant unrest against the Milošević regime. Its president was Momčilo Perišić, a general in the Yugoslav People's Army and its supreme commander until 1998 when he was sacked by Milošević for questioning Milošević's Kosovo policy. Other leading members of the MDS included Boris Karaičić, Ljubivoje Tadić, and Vojkan Tomić. The idea of the MDS was to create a broad-based citizens' movement to enhance Serbia's democratic forces. The party was critical of the Milošević regime, considering it to be destructive of national interests. On 24 September 1997, the MDS issued a "Call to the Representatives in the Federal Assembly," which included a demand for the dismissal of President Milošević by the Federal Assembly.[46] The MDS accused Milošević of violating many constitutional norms regarding the powers of the president.

The MDS did not join the Alliance for Change, but starting on 10 January 2000, it participated in deciding opposition strategies. The MDS took part in the presidential, parliamentary, and local elections in September 2000, because it believed that change could only come about through massive participation in the elections.[47]

Other, smaller nationalist formations included the People's Assembly Party (PAP) *(Narodno Saborna Stranka, NSS),* led by Slobodan Rakitić. Formed in January 1995, the PAP claimed to be based on "democratic and Christian values."

Neofascists

Serbian Radical Party (SRP)
Srpska Radikalna Stranka (SRS)

The Serbian Radical Party (SRP) was founded in the fall of 1990 by Vojislav Šešelj and became the main ultranationalist party advocating the creation of a "Greater Serbia." Šešelj had been a nationalist dissident in the 1980s and had spent time in prison for his anti-communist views. Šešelj started his political career in 1988, in the Sava Society. In early 1990, Šešelj founded the Serbian *Četnik* Movement, but the authorities refused to register the party. Shortly afterwards, he formed the Serbian Freedom Movement, and then on 10 March 1990 he cofounded the Serbian Renewal Movement (SRM), together with Vuk Drašković. However, Šešelj and Drašković displayed their animosity soon after the formation of the SRM. Šešelj believed that Drašković had abandoned the nationalistic purpose of the party and that he was more interested in promoting democracy than in elevating Serbian national interests. As result, on 31 May 1990, Šešelj announced that he was leaving the SRM.

Šešelj became a member of the Serbian parliament in 1991, as an independent candidate, after the death of Miodrag Bulatović of the SPS. He was reelected to parliament in the September 1992 elections as a representative of his newly formed Serbian Radical Party (SRP). In May 1992, campaigning for the elections, Šešelj summarized the party's militant position when he claimed that Albanians should be driven from Kosovo to Albania, Muslims should be expelled from Sandžak, and Croats driven out of Serbia. In the December 1992 elections, the party gained 73 out of 250 seats in the Serbian Assembly. In the December 1992 federal elections, the SRP captured thirty-four seats in the federal Civic Chamber and eight seats in the Chamber of Republics.

The vice presidents of the SRP included Maja Gojković and Tomislav Nikolić, and its secretary-general was Aleksandar Vučić. The SRP was one of the few Serbian parties with an organizational net throughout the Federal Republic of Yugoslavia.[48] The party claimed to have more than a million members, but this was clearly an exaggeration. The clash between Šešelj and Drašković was maximally used by Milošević, who saw Šešelj as a useful wedge inside the opposition. Milošević helped engineer Šešelj's election to the Serbian parliament in 1992 and allowed him to promulgate his ultra-nationalist views on state television, thereby drawing support away from the SRM. This also helped Milošević to manipulate Serbian nationalism, deflect attention from deepening economic problems, and present the Socialist regime as a patriotic but moderate force.

The Radicals were provided with resources and opportunities by Belgrade to establish paramilitary "volunteer" forces. Known as the White Eagles, these forces engaged in atrocities during the Serbian offensives in Croatia and Bosnia. For his role in the Bosnian war, Šešelj was denounced in the West as a neofascist and war criminal. Radical leaders were also given a slice of the lucrative black market in Serbia.

In the aftermath of the 1992 elections, SRP representatives in the Serbian and federal parliaments continued to be the most outspoken in supporting the Bosnian Serb leadership and the creation of a Greater Serbian state. Their persistent and aggressive criticisms of Yugoslav President Ćosić for his moderating influence culminated in a successful vote of no-confidence in May 1993. The ouster of Ćosić and the crackdown on the democratic opposition appeared to further expand the SRP's influence. In addition to his xenophobic stance toward Serbia's minorities and his condemnation of all democratic opponents, Šešelj took a combative stance against the UN intervention in Bosnia.[49]

In the fall of 1993, Milošević's support of the Vance-Owen plan for Bosnia strained the relationship between Milošević and Šešelj. Mira Marković, Milošević's wife, labeled Šešelj a "primitive chauvinist," to which Šešelj responded by accusing Milošević of being "the greatest criminal in Serbia." In this period, the SRP started to cooperate with the opposition parties in the Serbian parliament, building a "technical coalition" with the Democratic Party and the Democratic Party of Serbia. However, in the November 1996 local and federal ballots, the SRP entered the elections alone. It won the municipality of Zemun and gained sixteen seats in the Civic Chamber and six seats in the Chamber of the Republics of the federal parliament.

Šešelj stood in the Serbian presidential elections on 21 September 1997.

Because of the boycott by the Democratic Party and the Democratic Party of Serbia, he managed to enter the second round and to win 49.1% of the votes, more votes than Zoran Lilić, the presidential candidate of Milošević's SPS, with 47.9%. But Milošević had the final word as the results were nullified. When the election was repeated on 7 December 1997, Šešelj lost to the SPS candidate, Milan Milutinović, primarily as a result of the regime's manipulation of votes in the electoral units of Kosovo.

In April 1998, after three months of negotiations, the SRP and Drašković's SRM entered the so-called "war" government. Šešelj became a deputy prime minister and used his position to pass draconic information laws and to help launch propaganda offensives against the Albanians in Kosovo. In November 1998, he promoted the notion of a Russian–Belarusia Yugoslav federation. He launched his proposal on his official governmental visit to Russia in November 1998. Except for Russian nationalists and communists, few expressed open support for the idea. After NATO forces occupied Kosovo, Šešelj and his party initially resigned from the government on 10 June 1999; but his resignation was not accepted by the Socialists, who enticed the Radicals to re-enter the administration. The SRP was soundly defeated during the September 2000 federal elections and was excluded from the Democratic Opposition of Serbia (DOS)–dominated government. It gained 8.5% of the vote and 23 seats in Serbia's parliamentary elections in December 2000.

Radical Party of Nikola Pašić (RPNP)
Radikalna Stranka Nikola Pašić (RSNP)

The Radical Party of Nikola Pašić (RPNP) was created on 28 January 1995 by the separation of a part of the SRP and was led by its President, Siniša Vučinić, a former leader of the Serbian Hawks paramilitary formation, which assisted Serb forces during the war in Bosnia-Herzegovina. The party's vice presidents were Zoran Pešović, Vlada Nešović, Vladica Kežović, and Milenko Petrić. The RPNP organizational network consisted of 16 county and 57 communal boards, and the party claimed to have approximately 11,400 members. These "new radicals" wanted a "better application of Serbian national interests" as developed by Serbian socialist Svetozar Marković and by the founder of the New Radical Party, Nikola Pašić. In a 1997 interview, RPNP leader Vučinić explained the political differences between his party and the SRP. He claimed the RPNP was a democratic and patriotic party that did not want to eliminate Serbia's national minorities, as contrasted with Šešelj's SRP. Nevertheless, the RPNP opposed any form of autonomy or special status for Vojvodina, Kosovo, or Sandžak. The party opposed street demonstrations and placed state and national interests above "narrow ideological interests."[50]

There were many indicators that the RPNP was primarily a satellite of the regime. For example, the party supported the signing of the Dayton peace agreement and backed Milošević's role in the process. Vučinić accused the opposition coalition *Zajedno* of being a "fifth column" that served American and German interests. The party also denounced the opposition protests of 1996–1997 and the frequent election boycotts. The RPNP considered the state media objective and protective of Serb national interests, unlike the opposition media.

Party of Serbian Unity (PSU)
Stranka Srpskog Jedinstva (SSJ)

The Party of Serbian Unity (PSU) was an ultranationalist party founded by Željko Ražnjatović (Arkan) prior to the 1993 December elections. Its founder, a commander of the Tigers paramilitary group, had been linked to a variety of atrocities committed during the wars in Croatia, Bosnia, and Kosovo. In September 1997, Arkan was indicted for war crimes by the Hague Tribunal, but the indictment was kept under wraps until 31 March 1999, when the Head Prosecutor of the Hague Tribunal, Louise Arbour, announced the indictment. Arkan was elected as a representative of the Serbian parliament from a Kosovo electoral unit as an independent candidate. Despite substantial financial backing from Arkan, the PSU failed to gain influence among Serbian voters and did not win seats in parliament. After their 1993 election failure, the party leadership virtually abandoned politics and reverted to their illicit business activities.

After the conclusion of the Dayton peace agreement in November 1995, Arkan kept a low profile until the Kosovo war of 1999, where his paramilitaries were involved in the massacres of Albanian civilians. On 15 January 2000, Arkan was shot dead in the lobby of a Belgrade hotel. The circumstances surrounding his murder were unclear. Some Serbian independent media reported rumors that there was government involvement because Arkan was preparing to negotiate with the Hague Tribunal to offer evidence against Milošević in exchange for an acquittal. Serbia's Information Minister accused the Hague Tribunal and NATO of arranging Arkan's murder. Arkan's demise made it all the more uncertain whether the PSU would survive the death of its founder. Nevertheless, the PSU gained over 5% of the vote and 14 parliamentary seats in the December 2000 elections.

Homeland Non-Party Serbian Association (HNPSA)
Domovinsko Nepartijsko Srpsko Udruženje (DNSU)

The Homeland Non-Party Serbian Association (HNPSA) was formed in early 1991 as a Serbian ultranationalist organization based in Priština, Kosovo. It regularly called on citizens to defend the Serbian people and Serbian territories "with weapons in hand." In particular, it claimed to be concerned about the "genocidal threat" posed by the Croatian Ustašas and by Albanian separatists in Kosovo. Reports indicated that the HNPSA had close ties with paramilitary units of the SRP and with the Tigers, a unit led by the alleged war criminal Arkan (Željko Ražnjatović) and reportedly coordinated by Yugoslav army commanders. In December 1992, Arkan and four of his followers were elected to the Serbian Assembly in a body styled as the Group of Citizens from Kosovo and Metohija. The HNPSA also supported the arming of Serbian residents in Kosovo by the Yugoslav and Serbian security forces.[51]

Ethnic Minority and Religious Parties

Democratic Union of Bulgarians in Yugoslavia (DUBY)
Demokratski Savez Bugara Jugoslavije (DSBJ)

Created in October 1990 in Niš, southeastern Serbia, the Democratic Union of Bulgarians in Yugoslavia (DUBY) was led by Kiril Georgiev, a journalist who worked for the Bulgarian-language *Bratstvo* (Fraternity) paper, issued in Niš. The founders established the union as a voluntary, independent, and democratic organization of Yugoslav citizens of Bulgarian origin as well as representatives of other nationalities. It formed branches in the Bulgarian-populated towns of Dimitrovgrad and Bosilegrad. The union apparently excluded ethnic Bulgarians who displayed "nationalist, chauvinist, and separatist leanings." The DUBY aimed to enhance the national awareness of the Bulgarian minority, to safeguard the civil and national rights of Bulgarians, and to reach a rapprochement between Serbs and Bulgarians. Marin Mladenov, vice president of DUBY, underscored that Bulgarians were in a very different position than either the Hungarian or Albanian populations. The latter had consistently defended their ethnicity and culture, while Bulgarians apparently allowed themselves to become much more assimilated.

Union leaders asserted that their chief problem was not with the Serbian people but with the policies of the Serbian government, which endeavored to assimilate the shrinking Bulgarian population and constrict its cultural, educational, and political activities. DUBY was the only ethnic party to join the opposition coalition DEPOS for election-related activities.

In May 1993, a Bulgarian organization with claims to eastern Serbia also declared its existence in Sofia, Bulgaria. The Congress of the Western Bulgarian Outlands (CWBO), led by Stefan Rangelov, demanded the recognition of former Bulgarian territories and their placement under the jurisdiction of Slovenia and Croatia, which it viewed as the lawful successors to the first Yugoslavia (the Kingdom of Serbs, Croats, and Slovenes). It condemned Belgrade for pursuing assimilationist measures toward the Bulgarian population.[52]

Democratic Alliance of Vojvodina Romanians (DAVR)
Demokratski Savez Rumuna Vojvodine (DSRV)

The Democratic Alliance of Vojvodina Romanians (DAVR) was established during 1990 because of growing fear over the status of minority ethnic groups if the Yugoslav federation were to collapse. The organization was led by Ion

Marković and was organized according to territorial principles. The DAVR did not claim to be a political party but a broad movement intent upon "preserving the collective identity of the Romanian nationality." In May 1993, the new president of the alliance, Pavel Gaetan, met with the Yugoslav president, apparently "for the first time in decades," and reported on the problems of schooling and publishing among the Romanian minority. Gaetan underscored that the Romanian community had no representative in the Vojvodina parliament.[53]

Alliance of Ruthenians and Ukrainians (ARU)
Savez Rutenca i Ukrajinca (SRU)

The Alliance of Ruthenians and Ukrainians (ARU) was founded in Novi Sad in May 1990 to defend the national identity of the Ruthenians and Ukrainians, of which there were an estimated 30,000 throughout the former Yugoslavia. The organization did not claim any party affiliation and was open to everyone, regardless of national identity or religious conviction. The organization sought to promote "positive ethnic relations" while stressing the importance of protecting the cultural and educational rights of Ukrainians and Ruthenians, as specified in the Serbian constitution.[54]

Slovak National Heritage Foundation (SNHF)
Osnivanje Slovačka Narodna Nasledstva (OSNN)

The Slovak National Heritage Foundation (SNHF) officially renewed its activities in August 1990 in order to protect and represent the approximately 67,000 Slovaks living in Vojvodina. Chairman Mihal Spevak described the emphasis of the organization as on the preservation of Slovak identity, particularly through the creation of a minority educational system. SNHF leaders protested the new Serbian education law because it allegedly "did not provide for the specific needs of ethnic minorities and did not guarantee schools for minorities." In response to questions regarding the armed conflict among the Yugoslav nations, Spevak expressed his support for everyone struggling for truth, sovereignty, the right to self-determination, and the preservation of his own identity. But the group studiously avoided issuing statements of support for any single Yugoslav nation.[55]

Democratic Political Party of Roma (DPPR)
Demokratska Politička Partija Roma (DPPR)

The Democratic Political Party of Roma (DPPR) was based in Kragujevac, in central Serbia. The party advocated the cultural, economic, and social emancipation of the Roma population so that they could emerge from their "state of backwardness." It wanted to see more Roma in schools and work organizations, to have representatives in all official bodies, and to obtain a "national status" for the Gypsy population in a democratic Yugoslavia.[56]

Vojvodina Regionalists

Democratic Community of Vojvodina Hungarians (DCVH)
Demokratska Zajednica Madjara Vojvodine (DZMV)

Founded in April 1990, the DCVH became the largest and most active of the Hungarian organizations in the former Yugoslavia. The party promoted the presence of Hungarians in public office and the right to publicly use their own language. The DCVH defined itself as an "independent political organization that sought to represent the collective rights of Hungarians and to participate in establishing a multi-party parliamentary democracy and a free democratic state based on the rule of law." Under the direction of its President, András Ágoston, the DCVH demanded that the Hungarian national minority be provided with an array of cultural and political rights, including the opportunity to establish a local minority self-government. At the outset, Ágoston claimed that his organization viewed a united Yugoslavia as the most suitable state structure, whether this would be a federation or a confederation. But the DCVH increasingly blamed the Socialist Party for deteriorating relations between the Serbian government and the Hungarian minority. The DCVH dismissed all attempts to reform the communist system and condemned the rise of ultranationalism sponsored by the Milošević regime.

The Community described itself as right-of-center politically, supporting social and economic reform, constitutional changes, and a full-fledged market economy. Although the DCVH acknowledged Serbia's "historical right" to protect the territorial integrity of the state, it maintained that Hungarians in Vojvodina should be governed according to the principles of "cultural autonomy in the framework of minority self-government," not territorial autonomy. In the DCVH's concept of self-government, all ethnic Hungarian citizens of Serbia, regardless of where they lived, would have the option of enrolling in a minority self-government, a provision that was evidently consistent with the 1974 constitution.

For the most part, the DCVH stressed its loyalty to the state, despite Serb nationalist attempts to portray the organization as secessionist and a threat to Serbian national interests. The DCVH supported efforts to resolve the crisis between Serbia and Croatia through negotiations. In August 1991, Ágoston demanded that Hungarian soldiers be demobilized and withdrawn from the military conflict in Croatia because they did not wish to take part in inter-Slav conflicts. One of the twelve members of the DCVH's governing body, Béla Csorba, was arrested when he refused to comply with the draft papers he was issued.

In the elections of December 1990, the DCVH won 8 of the 250 seats in the Serbian parliament; but cooperation with Serbian opposition parties proved

difficult, because most of them did not support the DCVH's position of codifying minority rights and promoting minority autonomy. Only the Democratic Community of Croats in Vojvodina backed the DCVH on minority
questions. With the breakup of Yugoslavia, from mid-1991 onward, the DCVH
grew increasingly anxious over remaining in a truncated, Serb-dominated state,
particularly as anti-minority policies were accelerating and the media were
accusing DCVH leaders of being separatists. In addition, Serb refugees from
Croatia and Bosnia were resettled in Vojvodina; and in some areas of the
province, minority communities were encouraged or pressured to leave the
country (thousands of Hungarians left Vojvodina during 1991 and 1992).

The DCVH won four federal and eight republican assembly seats in the
December 1992 elections, three of the latter being lost in the December 1993
balloting. The party later disclosed that pro-autonomy Hungarian organizations in Vojvodina had been financially supported by Hungary. Thereafter,
the DCVH became divided between those favoring autonomy for Vojvodina
and others supporting some measure of cooperation with Belgrade. Policy
and personality rifts eventually led to a group breaking off from the DCVH
and forming the Alliance of Vojvodina Hungarians (AVH) in June 1994.

In April 1992, the DCVH issued a memorandum on autonomy, proposing a
tripartite system consisting of "personal autonomy," whereby the minority
would ensure the protection of its ethnic, cultural, linguistic and religious
identity; "territorial autonomy," with self rule in those municipalities where
Hungarians formed a majority; and "local self-rule" in isolated villages in
which Hungarians made up more than 50% of the population. The memorandum was rejected by the Serb authorities, and the DCVH was accused of
separatism and irredentism.

The DCVH participated in the federal and republican elections in December 1992, and performed well in the eight Hungarian-majority districts, winning the mayoralty of Subotica. DCVH deputies were elected to the
reconstituted Vojvodinian Provincial Assembly, forming a bloc of 58 out of
120 seats, composed of various democratic and minority parties. Together
with other oppositionist parties, DCVH deputies stormed out in protest after
the first parliamentary session, describing the Assembly as a mere appendage
of the Serbian parliament, with no authentic legislative powers.[57] In the republican elections in December 1993, the DCVH won five seats with only
112,456 votes. In the September 1997 Serbian parliamentary elections, the
DCVH won four seats and subsequently selected Sándor Páll as its new leader.

Non-Hungarian intellectuals and seventeen political parties and associations with a civic orientation from Vojvodina co-signed the Manifesto for an
Autonomous Vojvodina on 6 December 1995. They criticized the tripartite
autonomy concept of the DCVH because of its allegedly ethnocentric orientation, while pointing out that autonomy for the whole of Vojvodina was the
ideal solution for all inhabitants. Within the Hungarian community, divergent
interpretations for protecting Magyar interests led in 1994 to the appearance

of a new political force, the Alliance of Vojvodina Hungarians (AVH), following a split in the DCVH. The differences in the programs of these two organizations, according to Ferenc Czubela, the first leader of the new party, were not fundamental but tactical, with the AVH favoring a more pragmatic approach.

Alliance of Vojvodina Hungarians (AVH)
Savez Vojvodjanskih Madjara (SVM)

The Alliance of Vojvodina Hungarians (AVH) was founded on 18 June 1994 as an association of citizens, by a breakaway faction of the DCVH. On 17 June 1995 it was transformed into a political party with the aim of promoting the interests of the Vojvodina Hungarians by participating in Serbia's and Yugoslavia's political process. Its leaders argued that an election boycott would simply assist the ruling party, while participation would allow at least some influence over political decision-making. Its president was József Kasza, who in 1988 was elected mayor of Subotica. In 1990 he was elected to the Serbian parliament, where he served three terms. He was elected president of the AVH in 1995, and re-elected in 1997. The Alliance's vice presidents were László Józsa, Attila Juhász, Károly Pál, and Mihály Szecsei.

The AVH obtained three seats in the lower house of the federal parliament in 1996 and gained four deputies to the Serbian parliament in the September 1997 parliamentary elections. It also won 13 out of 120 seats in the Vojvodinian provincial parliament and 139 seats to the municipal assemblies in the 1996 local elections. The DCVH gained only one seat in the Vojvodinian assembly. The goals of the AVH were to preserve Hungarian language, culture and identity; to support the autonomous aggregation of Hungarians by establishing associations, organizations, and professional circles in the fields of education, information, and language; to develop local governments and economic activities; to implement minority autonomy; and to deepen unity between Vojvodina Hungarians and Hungarians abroad. The AVH supported the "special territorial autonomy" of Vojvodina within Serbia, which would resemble the status of Vojvodina in the 1974 Yugoslav constitution.[58]

In 1997, the AVH became a member of the oppositionist Alliance of Democratic Parties. Several other Hungarian parties were formed by the close of the decade, including the Civic Movement of Vojvodina Hungarians (CMVH), established in March 1995 and headed by József Borocz, and the Hungarian Christian Democratic Movement (HCDM), led by Tibor Várga.

Association of Hungarians for Our Fatherland, Serbia
and Yugoslavia (AHOFSY)
Udruženje Madjara za Našu Domovinu, Srbiju i
Jugoslaviju (UMDSJ)

The Association of Hungarians for Our Fatherland, Serbia and Yugoslavia (AHOFSY) was established in 1991 as a front organization for the Socialist regime, to undermine the independent Hungarian movements and to draw distinctions between "loyal" and "disloyal" Hungarians. József Molnár became chairman of this Belgrade-sponsored organization, and he vehemently denounced the DCVH and its leader, Ágoston, for requesting that Hungarians be released from the Yugoslav army. Molnár claimed that such military separation would be tragic for Hungarians because it would pit them against Serbs and make Hungarians "enemies in our own republic." Parroting the official Serbian government position, Molnár claimed that Hungarians in Serbia enjoyed civic and national rights greater than the rights enjoyed by any national minority in any country. The AHOFSY made direct appeals to the Magyar minority to "resist the secessionists and the foes of Serbia and Yugoslavia," referring implicitly to the DCVH.

The organization regularly disagreed with other Hungarian parties over even the least controversial issues. For example, the association did not agree that the names of villages in Magyar areas should be written in both Serbian and Hungarian. Despite the funds and resources it received from Belgrade, the AHOFSY failed to gain any significant support from the Hungarian population and was perceived as a Socialist proxy.[59]

Democratic Alliance of Croats in Vojvodina (DACV)
Demokratski Savez Hrvata u Vojvodini (DSHV)

The Croatian minority in Vojvodina formed the Democratic Alliance of Croats (DACV) to defend its interests against growing centralization and potential repression. The DACV also sought cultural autonomy and the control of its local affairs. It issued protests over increasing assimilationist pressures, Croat mobilization in the Yugoslav army, and the abandonment of the province by over 35,000 Croats in the early 1990s as a consequence of intimidation by Serb nationalists and security forces. Croat and Magyar leaders claimed that a low-visibility policy of "ethnic cleansing" was being pursued by the Serbian authorities in Croatian villages to diminish minority numbers so that Vojvodina could be resettled by loyalist Serbs transplanted from war zones in Croatia and Bosnia-Herzegovina.

The DACV was established in 1990 and Bela Tonković was elected president. The organization complained that Croats in Vojvodina had been prevented from nurturing their own national identity. Unlike most of the other ethnic opposition parties, the DACV took part in the May 1992 federal elections. Alliance leaders explained their participation as giving voters a "democratic option" and not as legitimizing the newly proclaimed Federal Republic of Yugoslavia. The DACV proposed a referendum for Vojvodina's citizens, concerning the type of autonomy the province should be granted and what relations it should maintain with other components of the Serbian state. The alliance contended that Vojvodina should benefit, at the very least, from the autonomy specified under the 1974 Yugoslav constitution.

The DACV won local seats in the December 1992 elections in Subotica after forming a coalition with the Democratic Community of Vojvodina Hungarians. Croat leaders regularly voiced concerns about Belgrade's policies that were evidently intended to push the majority of Croats out of Vojvodina and replace them with Serbs from Croatia and Bosnia. Between 1991 and 1993, Radical Party activists, in cooperation with Serbian security forces, reportedly forced over 35,000 Croats out of the province, particularly from the western Srem and Bačka areas. Croatian activists were sacked from work, beaten by police, and unjustifiably imprisoned. The DACV found it difficult to cooperate with the Serbian opposition, as the latter evidently feared that including Croats in their coalitions would diminish their popularity.[60]

Farmers' Party of Vojvodina (FPV)
Seljačka Stranka Vojvodine (SSV)

The Farmers' Party of Vojvodina (FPV) was founded in late 1991 by Dragan Veselinov, a democratic activist who supported a civic-oriented program and a multi-ethnic Vojvodina with a large measure of autonomy. By the close of 1992, the party claimed a membership of some 5,000. Despite its name, most of its activists were intellectuals and students. The FPV voiced concern about the expulsion of minorities from Vojvodina and lodged protests against the "ethnic cleansing" of Croatian communities. In June 1992, the FPV, together with the League of Social Democrats of Vojvodina, the Reformist Party, and the Republican Club, founded the Civic Alliance of Serbia as an alternative democratic coalition to the Socialist-Radical alliance and the quasi-monarchist DEPOS coalition. DEPOS in turn maintained links with the Democratic Reformists of Vojvodina, who were not strong autonomists but favored a decentralized state structure.

The FPV considered Milošević's rule autocratic and the formation of the Federal Republic of Yugoslavia illegal because it took place without public consent. Party leaders proposed the dissolution of the Serbian Assembly, the resignation of Milošević, and the formation of a new, transitional Serbian government. The coalition was supported by political independents, intellectuals, civic-oriented groups, and peace organizations. The Civic Alliance coalition scored poorly in the December 1992 elections, gaining only one seat in the federal assembly and five in the Serbian Assembly; three of these were gained by the FPV. The alliance only registered 1.5% of the popular vote.

In the aftermath of the ballot, the FPV and the League of Social Democrats founded an unofficial Vojvodina Coalition and the rest of the Civic Alliance transformed itself into a party under the leadership of Vesna Pešić and Radomir Tanić.[61] The Vojvodina Coalition (VC) incorporated the League of Social Democrats, the National Peasants' Party, the Reformist Party of Vojvodina, and the Banat Forum. The Coalition adopted a political declaration that openly demanded autonomy for the province as a federal unit in a federalized Serbia.

League of Social Democrats of Vojvodina (LSDV)
Liga Socialdemokrata Vojvodine (LSV)

The League of Social Democrats of Vojvodina (LSDV) was established on 14 July 1990 by activist Nenad Čanak, who became its chairman. Prior to the formation of the LSDV, Čanak was not a member of any political party. The League's vice presidents included Emil Fejzulahi, Bojan Kostreš, and Zoran Bošković, and its secretary-general was Antun Katić. The LSDV claimed to have the support of 15% to 20% of the Vojvodina population, basing its claim on public opinion surveys. It also claimed that its membership reflected the national structure of Vojvodina's population and that its support was mostly drawn from the younger generation.

The LSDV cast itself as a multi-ethnic organization, seeking autonomy for Vojvodina in a democratic, tripartite Serbian federation, consisting of Vojvodina, Kosovo, and Šumadija. It claimed to have significant support across the ethnic spectrum among the old settlers in Vojvodina, but recognized that most of the Serbian newcomers were Milošević supporters. The League co-operated with all parties that shared its views either on Vojvodinian autonomy or on the civic option in Serbian politics. It entered into an oppositionist coalition with the Civic Alliance for the December 1992 elections, but the coalition performed poorly, gaining only one seat in the Federal Assembly and five in the Serbian Assembly.

The LSDV claimed that many of its members also belonged to the Farmers Party of Vojvodina, with which it cooperated in an unofficial "Vojvodina bloc." In the November 1996 federal parliamentary elections, the LSDV ran in coalition with the People's Peasant Party and won two seats in the federal parliament. The party had more success with the 1996 elections for the province's parliament, where it won seven seats. In the September 1997 Serbian parliamentary elections, the LSDV won four seats in the Serbian parliament, including one for its leader, Nenad Čanak. In 1997, the LSDV became a member of the Alliance of Democratic Parties.

The League was critical of the Hungarian parties for allegedly placing their ethnic ambitions above that of pan-Vojvodinian interests. It also suspected that Belgrade could be planning to split the province. If Belgrade ceded the northern portion to Hungary, the position of the autonomist movement in the rest of Vojvodina would be seriously undermined. Hungarian and Socialist leaders dismissed such speculations as groundless.

In the September 2000 elections, regionalist and democratic forces gained ascendancy in the Vojvodina assembly. The LSDV won 24 seats in the 120-member body, while the Democratic Party captured 27 seats, Hungarian organizations 17, the Reformists of Vojvodina eight, and the Coalition for Vojvodina seven. The Socialists barely managed to garner two deputies. Vojvodina's regional authority looked set to push toward greater autonomy for the territory in negotiations with the post-Socialist Serbian government.

Vojvodina Coalition (VC)
Koalicija Vojvodina (KV)

The Vojvodina Coalition (VC) was founded in 1996 and its president was Dragan Veselinov, the FPV chairman. Its political activities focused on the territory of Vojvodina, where it had branches in 44 municipalities. It maintained that Vojvodina had a separate historical development, with unique economic, cultural, and social traditions. As a result, Vojvodina should have "permanent legislative, executive and judiciary independence within the state of Serbia."[62] According to the VC, the status of Vojvodina within Serbia should be decided through a referendum by all Vojvodina citizens. In the November 1996 federal parliamentary elections, the VC won two seats in the Civic Chamber, while in the September 1997 elections it gained four seats in the Serbian parliament.

Reformist Democratic Party of Vojvodina (RDPV)
Reformsko-Demokratska Stranka Vojvodine (RDSV)

The Reformist Democratic Party of Vojvodina (RDPV) was founded on 13 October 1990 and its president was Miodrag Isakov. After 1996, he was a member of the federal parliament. Its vice presidents included Ratimir Svircevic, Miroslav Šproh, Blaško Kopilović, Aleksandar Popov, and Ivica Predojev. The party mainly operated on the territory of Vojvodina and developed an organizational structure in several municipalities. The RDPV claimed to have more than 20,000 members. Its origins were from the Vojvodina branch of the Alliance of Reform Forces, founded by the last Prime Minister of Socialist Yugoslavia, Ante Marković, in an attempt to preserve the federation. However, after the dissolution of Yugoslavia, in 1992 the party renamed itself the RDPV. In its statute, it defined itself as a "social democratic political organization operating in Serbia and Vojvodina."[63] It became a strong advocate of national minorities' rights and called for the decentralization of Serbia, with autonomous provinces and regions, including Vojvodina. After 1997 the party became a member of the Alliance of Democratic Parties.

Vojvodina Movement (VM)
Vojvodjanski Pokret (VP)

The Vojvodina Movement (VM) was founded on 25 April 1998 in the Vojvodinian capital of Novi Sad as an "alliance of political parties, nongovernmental organizations, citizen's associations, unions, and other interest-based organizations." It advocated advancing the rights of Vojvodina's ethnic minority movements and other organizations active in Vojvodina whose goals were "peace, political plurality, parliamentarism, rule of law, a decentralized state with autonomous provinces, local and regional self-

government, religious tolerance, a market economy, and international cooperation."[64] Its president was Slobodan Budakov, and its vice presidents were
Branislav Zarić and Stevan Plestović. The president of the VM's political
council was Stanimir Lazić.

The membership in the VM was individual or collective. It claimed twelve
collective members, including the Democratic Alliance of Croatians in
Vojvodina, the Civic Movement of Vojvodina Hungarians, the Alliance of
Citizens of Subotica, the All-National Democratic Front of Vojvodina, the Society for Truth about the World War II National Liberation Struggle, the Hungarian Language Society, the Society for Tolerance, the Group for Peace Action
"M," the Movement for Peace in Vojvodina, the Vojvodina Club, the Sombor
Party for Prosperity, and the Autonomous Movement of Vojvodina. All of the
collective members preserved their legal identity and organizational and programmatic independence.

The VM was organized in eighteen Vojvodina cities and covered 74 out of
120 electoral units in Vojvodina. In practice, the main goal of the VM was
wider autonomy for Vojvodina within Serbia and Yugoslavia, and the removal
from power of the Milošević regime. The VM did not participate in national
elections throughout the 1990s but contested the ballot on 24 September 2000
in support of the DOS coalition.

Sandžak Regionalists

Party of Democratic Action (PDA)
Stranka Demokratske Akcije (SDA)

The Party of Democratic Action (PDA) was founded on 29 July 1990 with the
aim of representing Muslim interests in the Sandžak and throughout Serbia.
Its leadership included Numan Balić, chairman of the Kosovo-Metohija PDA,
Harun Hadžić, chairman of the Montenegrin PDA, Sulejman Ugljanin, chairman of the Sandžak PDA, and Riza Halili, chairman of the Preševo PDA. In
December 1993, the PDA contested the Serbian Assembly election in an alliance with the Democratic Party of Albanians, which won two seats. The more
militant Sandžak PDA had come under pressure from the federal authorities,
with party members being detained on firearms offenses in late 1993. In mid-
1994 about two dozen Sandžak PDA leaders were tried on charges of plotting
armed attacks on public targets.

The party maintained close links with the PDA in Sarajevo even after the
secession of Bosnia-Herzegovina from Yugoslavia in early 1992. The party
had to close its section in Belgrade but maintained branches in the Serbian
and Montenegrin Sandžak and in Kosovo. The PDA declared early on that if
Yugoslavia disintegrated and the unification of Serbia and Montenegro intensified, the party would demand cultural and political autonomy for Muslims
in the Sandžak region. Sandžak Muslims claimed to speak the Bosnian lan-

guage and to write in the Latin script, and their leaders declared that they would not accept the Serbian language and the Cyrillic alphabet.

In April 1991, Milošević dispatched police reinforcements to the Sandžak on the pretext that there was a possibility of widespread rioting sparked by Muslim unrest. After that, repression against the Muslim population increased, and the PDA initiated several steps toward forming an independent political structure. In October 1991, the Muslim National Council of Sandžak (MNCS), a quasi-governmental body established in May 1991 whose authority purportedly extended to the Montenegrin Sandžak, organized a referendum on autonomy. Of Muslim voters in ten Sandžak municipalities, 98.92% out of the 70.19% who participated voted for political and territorial autonomy. The exercise was condemned by Belgrade as unconstitutional.

After the plebiscite, the Muslim National Council selected a new Sandžak government. PDA Secretary-General Rasim Ljajić was chosen as prime minister and Ugljanin remained president of the MNCS. The PDA maintained a majority of seats in the new government; it also included members of the Liberal Bosniak Organization and the Party of National Equality. However, conflicts between moderate and radical elements of the PDA intensified during the 1990s and were exploited by the Milošević administration.

In January 1992, the MNCS declared the creation of a "special status" for the Sandžak that would give the region far-reaching autonomy. The initiative was not recognized by the Yugoslav or Serbian governments. As Serb ultranationalist paramilitaries became active in the region during 1992, the western regions of the Sandžak in the districts of Priboj (Serbia) and Pljevlja (Montenegro) were deliberately cleared of Muslim residents through bombings, assaults, intimidation, and economic discrimination. The PDA consistently protested against government policies and boycotted the federal, republican, and local elections in December 1992. However, divisions also appeared in the party over the question of participation and potential Muslim support for Yugoslav prime minister Milan Panić.

Throughout the 1990s, the party was unable to forge any meaningful cooperation with the Serbian opposition; the latter evidently perceived Muslim organizations as more of a liability than an advantage in election campaigns.[65] For example, in the federal election campaign for the September 2000 ballot, the PDA put forward its own presidential candidate in objection to the choices offered by the Serbian opposition. Moreover, rival factions emerged within the PDA, with the parent body led by Ugljanin forming a coalition with smaller groups such as the Democratic Alliance of Sandžak, the Party for Modern Sandžak, and the Reform Party of Sandžak. Meanwhile, Rasim Ljajić created the Sandžak Coalition (SC) and forged agreements with such organizations as the Liberal Bosniak Organization, the People's Congress of Bosniaks, and the Reform Democratic Party of Sandžak.

Liberal Bosniak Organization (LBO)
Liberalna Bošnjačka Organizacija (LBO)

The Liberal Bosniak Organization (LBO) was established during 1990 as the Sandžak branch of the Bosnia-based Muslim Bosnian Organization, but declared its independence once Yugoslavia began to disintegrate. The party emphasized a multi-ethnic "Bosniak" identity rather than a narrower Muslim religious-ethnic identification as defined by former communists and nationalists. The LBO focused on the democratization and decentralization of the Sandžak, and like to the PDA, claimed "special status" or autonomy for the region but opposed secession or any changes in existing republican borders. Led by Mehmed Slezović, the LBO claimed about 3,000 members and many more sympathizers. It also established an "initiative council" in the Montenegrin Sandžak. The LBO claimed it was open to all nationality groups, cooperated with the much larger PDA, and had members in the Muslim National Council and the National Assembly in Novi Pazar, the chief city in the Serbian Sandžak.

POLITICAL DATA

Serbia's republican structure consisted of a directly elected presidency and a directly elected parliament comprising 250 seats, which nominated the Serbian Prime Minister and cabinet. While the federal structure was supposedly the foremost authority in the Yugoslav state, especially in matters of defense, foreign policy, and economic policy, in practice under the Milošević administration, power was largely personalistic and tended toward gravitate to whatever office Milošević held, whether as Serbia's President or as Yugoslavia's President.

Name of State: Republic of Serbia *(Republika Srbija)*
Size of territory: 48,033 square miles
Size of population: 10,500,000
Form of government: Republic
Structure of Legislature: Unicameral Assembly of the Republic of Serbia (Skupština Republike Srbije)

Composition of Population:

Ethnic Group	Number	% of Population
Serbs	6,485,596	62.69
Albanians	1,727,541	16.70
Montenegrins	520,508	5.03
Hungarians	345,376	3.34
Muslims	327,290	3.16
Roma	137,265	1.11
Croats	115,463	1.12
Slovaks	67,234	0.65
Macedonians	48,437	0.47
Romanians	42,386	0.41
Bulgarians	25,214	0.24
Vlachs	17,557	0.17
Turks	11,501	0.11
Slovenes	8,747	0.08
Others	465,349	4.50
Total minorities	3,859,868	37.31
Total	10,345,464	100.00

Source: UNHCR/OSCE Update on the situation of ethnic minorities in Kosovo: period covering February through May 2000, www.unhcr.ch. (1991 census incomplete, boycotted by Albanians in Kosovo)

Vojvodina (Province)

Ethnic Group	Number	% of Population
Serbs	1,143,723	54.4
Hungarians	339,491	18.9
Yugoslavs	174,225	8.1
Croats	74,808	5.4
Slovaks	63,545	3.5
Montenegrins	44,838	2.1
Romanians	38,809	2.3
Others	—	5.3
Total	1,879,439	100.0

Kosovo (Province). See page 479, below.

ELECTION RESULTS

Serbian Presidential Election, 7 and 21 December 1997

First Round, 7 December 1997

Turnout: 52.75%

Candidate	Votes	% of Vote
Milan Milutinović	1,665,822	43.43
Vojislav Šešelj	1,227,076	33.18
Vuk Drašković	587,776	15.41
Vuk Obradović	115,580	3.03
Dragolub Mićunović	86,583	2.27
Miodrag Vidojković	29,180	0.56
Miodrag Vuletić	21,353	0.56
Total	3,182,448	100.00

Sources: International Foundation For Electoral Systems (IFES), http://www.ifes.com/eguide. Also see Center for Political Analysis, www.cpa.org.yu.

Second Round, 21 December 1997

Turnout: 53%

Candidate	Votes	% of Vote
Milan Milutinović	2,181,808	61.2
Vojislav Šešelj	1,383,868	38.8
Total	3,565,676	100.0

Sources: British Helsinki Human Rights Group and the Republic of Serbia, Republic Bureau of Statistics, December 23, 1997.

Serbian Presidential Election, 21 September and 5 October 1997 (Invalidated)

First Round, 21 September 1997

Turnout: 57.4%

Candidate	Votes	% of Vote
Zoran Lilić	1,474,924	37.70
Vojislav Šešelj	1,126,940	27.28
Vuk Drašković	852,800	20.64
Mile Isakov	111,166	2.43
Vuk Obradović	100,523	2.43
Nebojsa Čović	93,133	2.23
Sulejman Ugljanin	68,446	1.66

Milan Paroški	27,100	0.66
Miodrag Vidojković	14,105	0.34
Predrag Vuletić	11,463	0.27
Dragan Djordjević	10,864	0.26
Milan Mladenović	10,112	0.24
Djordje Drljacić	9,430	0.22
Branko Cicić	7,097	0.17
Gvozden Sakić	3,293	0.06
Total	3,921,396	100.00

Second Round, 5 October 1997

Turnout: 48.97%

Candidate	Votes	% of Vote
Vojislav Šešelj	1,733,859	49.1
Zoran Lilić	1,691,354	47.9
Invalid ballots	104,223	3.0
Total	3,529,436	100.0

Source: Serbia 1997: Parliamentary and Presidential Elections, British Helsinki Human Rights Group at http://www.bhhrg.org.

Serbian Presidential Election, 20 December 1992

Turnout: 68.23%

Candidate	Votes	% of Vote
Slobodan Milošević	2,515,047	55.90
Milan Panić	1,516,693	34.30
Milan Paroški	147,693	3.31
Dragan Vasiljković	87,847	1.97
Jezdimir Vasiljević	61,729	1.38
Miroslav Jovanović	28,010	0.63
Blažo Perović	20,326	0.46
Others	—	2.05
Total	4,377,345	100.00

Sources: Commentary on the December 1992 Elections in Serbia and Montenegro, International Republican Institute, Washington, DC, 1993. See also Center for Political Analysis, www.cpa.org.yu.

Serbian Presidential Election, 9 December 1990

Turnout: 71.50%

Candidate	Votes	% of Vote
Slobodan Milošević	3,285,799	65.34
Vuk Drašković	824,674	16.40
Ivan Durić	277,398	5.52

Sulejman Ugljanin	109,459	2.18
Vojislav Šešelj	96,277	1.91
Blažo Perović	57,420	1.14
Slobodan Matić	28,978	0.58
Dragan Jovanović	22,458	0.45
Ljuben Alen Aleksov	19,123	0.38
Ljubomir Grujić	17,675	0.35
Total	4,739,252	95.00

Sources: The 1990 Elections in the Republic of Yugoslavia, National Republican Institute for International Affairs, Washington, DC, 1991. Also see http://www.sps.org.yu/izbori/dec90.html.

Serbian Parliamentary Elections, 23 December 2000

Turnout: N/A

Party/Coalition	Votes	% of Votes	Seats
Democratic Opposition of Serbia	—	64.21	176
Socialist Party of Serbia	—	13.67	37
Serbian Radical Party	—	8.55	23
Party of Serbian Unity	—	5.33	14
Serbian Renewal Movement	—	3.50	—
Yugoslav United Left	—	0.33	—
Others	—	4.41	—
Total	—	100.00	250

Source: Zagreb Hina (in English), December 26, 2001. Serbian election results analyzed.

Serbian Parliamentary Elections, 21 September 1997

Turnout: 57.4%

Party/Coalition	Votes	% of Vote	Seats
Socialist Party of Serbia/Yugoslav United Left/New Democracy	1,415,456	38.71	110
Serbian Radical Party	1,159,868	31.72	82
Serbian Renewal Movement	793,224	21.70	45
Democratic Community of Vojvodina Hungarians	112,215	3.07	4
Alliance of Vojvodina Hungarians	50,960	1.39	4
Sandžak Coalition	49,486	1.35	3
Coalition Democratic Alternative	60,855	0.66	1
Democratic Coalition Preševo-Bujanovac	14,179	0.39	1
Total	3,656,243	100.00	250

Sources: Center for Political Analysis, http:// www.cpa.org.yu. Also see http://www.mfa.gov.yu/facts/institutions/ass_sr_e.htm; and *Election Today News* from the International Foundation for Election Systems, Vol. 7, No. 3, p. 60.

Serbian Parliamentary Elections, 19 December 1993

Turnout: 62%

Party/Coalition	Votes	% of Vote	Seats
Socialist Party of Serbia	1,576,287	36.65	123
DEPOS/Serbian Renewal Movement	715,564	16.63	45
Serbian Radical Party	595,467	13.84	39
Democratic Party	497,582	11.57	29
Democratic Party of Serbia	218,056	5.05	7
Democratic Community of Vojvodina Hungarians	112,456	2.61	5
Party of Democratic Action– Democratic Party of Albanians	29,34	0.68	2
Total	3,921,396	88.00	250

Serbian Parliamentary Elections, 20 December 1992

Turnout: 69.7%

Party/Coalition	Votes	% of Vot	Seats
Socialist Party of Serbia	1,359,086	28.77	101
Serbian Radical Party	1,066,765	22.58	73
DEPOS/Serbian Renewal Movement	797,831	16.89	50
Democratic Community of Vojvodina Hungarians	140,825	2.98	8
Democratic Party	196,347	4.16	6
Group of Citizens from Kosovo and Metohija	17,352	0.37	5
People's Peasant Party	128,240	2.71	3
Farmers' Party of Vojvodina	71,865	1.52	3
Democratic Reform Party of Moslems	6,336	0.13	1
Total	3,784,647	100.00	250

Source: Commentary on the December 1992 Elections in Serbia and Montenegro, International Republican Institute, Washington, DC, 1993.

Serbian Parliamentary Elections, 9 and 23 December 1990

Turnout: 71.48%

Party/Coalition	Votes	% of Vote	Seats
Socialist Party of Serbia	2,320,507	46.08	194
Serbian Renewal Movement	794,786	15.78	19

Democratic Community of Vojvodina Hungarians	132,726	2.63	9
Group of Citizens (Independents)	456,318	9.06	8
Democratic Party	374,887	7.44	7
Party for Democratic Action	84,156	1.67	3
Alliance of Reform Forces for Yugoslavia	74,748	1.48	6
People's Peasant Party	68,045	1.35	4
New Democracy–Movement for Serbia	67,356	1.33	—
People's Radical Party	63,041	1.29	—
Party of the League of Peasants of Serbia	52,663	1.04	—
Serbian National Renewal	40,359	0.80	—
Total	4,529,592	100.00	250

Source: Center for Political Analysis, http://www.cpa.org.yu.

Electoral data for the Federal Republic of Yugoslavia appear on pages 441–445.

NOTES

1. For recent histories of Serbia consult Ivo Banac, *The National Question in Yugoslavia: Origins, History, Politics*, Ithaca and London: Cornell University Press, 1992; Stephen Clissold (Ed.), *A Short History of Yugoslavia: From Early Times to 1966*, Cambridge: Cambridge University Press; Alex N. Dragnich, *The First Yugoslavia: Search for a Viable Political System*, Stanford: Stanford University Press, 1983; and Barbara Jelavich, *History of the Balkans*, 2 Volumes, Cambridge: Cambridge University Press, 1989.

2. For an analysis of the nationalist memorandum, see Slobodan Stenković, "The Serbian Academy's Memorandum," Radio Free Europe/Radio Liberty Research Institute (RFE/RL), *Yugoslav Situation Report*, No. 11, 20 November 1986.

3. Valuable background on the early Milošević years can be found in Milan Andrejevich, "Yugoslavia's Lingering Crisis," RFE/RL, *Report on Eastern Europe*, Vol. 1, No. 1, 5 January 1990. For an invaluable analysis of the Milošević strategy to maintain power see Eric D. Gordy, *The Culture of Power in Serbia*, University Park, Pennsylvania: Pennsylvania State University Press, 1999.

4. See *Službeni Glasnik Republike Srbije*, January 1990.

5. For the official Serbian position on constitutional and legal questions, see Prvoslav Ralić, *Minority Rights in Serbia: Facts, Figures, Orientation.*

6. For a report on the elections with full documentation, see *The 1990 Elections in the Republics of Yugoslavia*, National Republican Institute for International Affairs, Washington, D.C., 1991.

7. See Edith Ottay, "Hungarians in Yugoslavia Seek Guarantees for Minority Rights," RFE/RL, *Report on Eastern Europe*, Vol. 2, No. 38, 20 September 1991.

8. *Memorandum on the Self-Government of Hungarians in the Republic of Serbia*, Working Document of the General Assembly of the Democratic Community of Hungarians in Vojvodina, 25 April 1992.

9. For some details, see M. Antic and F. Hamidović, "Muslim National Council of Sandžak Formed: Sandžak out of Serbia?" *Borba*, Belgrade, 20 May 1991; and the *Memorandum on the Establishment of a Special Status for Sandžak*, Muslim National Council of Sandžak, Novi Pazar, June 1993.

10. For details, see Milan Andrejevich, "The Sandžak: The Next Balkan Theater of War?" RFE/RL, *Research Report*, Vol. 1, No. 47, 27 November 1992.

11. Check Nicholas J. Miller, "A Failed Transition: The Case of Serbia," in Karen Dawisha and Bruce Parrott (Eds.), *Politics, Power and the Struggle for Democracy in South-East Europe*, Cambridge: Cambridge University Press, 1997, pp. 146–188.

12. Article 2 of the 1992 Constitution of Federal Republic of Yugoslavia stipulates, "The Federal Republic of Yugoslavia shall be composed of the Republic of Serbia and the Republic of Montenegro." See http://www.gov.yu/regulations/constitution/constitution.html.

13. See the *Constitution of the Federal Republic of Yugoslavia*, Belgrade, 1992.

14. Useful analysis is contained in Milan Andrejevich, "What Future for Serbia?" RFE/RL, *Research Report*, Vol. 1, No. 50, 18 December 1992.

15. See the *Commentary on the December 1992 Elections in Serbia and Montenegro*, International Republican Institute, Washington, DC, 1993.

16. See Branislav Radivojsa, "Law for Minority Communities Prepared: Anyone Can Be in a Minority," *Politika*, Belgrade, 9 March 1993.

17. See the Amendments to the Constitution of the Federal Republic of Yugoslavia, http://www.mfa.gov.yu. Also see, www.gov.yu/regulations/constitution/constitution.html.

18. See www.sps.org.yu/eng/documents/statute/index.html.

19. Srbobran Branković, *Serbia At Work With Itself: Political Choices in Serbia, 1990–1994.* Belgrade: Institute of Political Studies, 1995, p. 280.

20. *Tanjug*, Belgrade, 13 June 1990, in *FBIS-EEU-90–116*, 15 June 1990; Ljuba Stojić, "Pluralistic Ballot," *Nin*, Belgrade, 28 September 1990; Milan Andrejevich, "Milošević and the Serbian Opposition," RFE/RL, *Report on Eastern Europe*, 19 October 1990; *Belgrade Domestic Service*, 4 November 1990, in *FBIS-EEU-90–214*, 5 November 1990; RFE/RL, *Daily Report*, No. 103, 1 June 1992.

21. SPS Issues Statement on SPS-JUL-ND Coalition Platform, 3 June 1997.

22. See the Socialist Party of Serbia, *Program of the Socialist Party of Serbia*, IV Congress, 17 February 2000.

23. See *Socijademokratija, Temelji Evropske Srbije*, http://www.socijaldemokratija.org.yu.

24. Check the International Crisis Group, "Serbia's Embattled Opposition," 30 May 2000, *ICG Balkans Report No. 94*, Washington/Brussels, pp. 15–17.

25. See http://www.novademokratija.org.yu.

26. *New Democracy Newsletter*, Belgrade, February 1996.

27. See http://gradjanskisavez.org.yu.

28. See Civic Alliance of Serbia, *The Need for a New Policy Towards Yugoslavia*, 5 July 1999, Belgrade.

29. See *Savez za Promene, Koalicioni Sporazum Koalicije Savez za promene*, http://www.szp.org.yu.

30. See *Savez za promene, Deklaracija Saveza za Promene*, http://www.szp.org.yu.

31. Demohrišćanska Stranka Srbije at http://www.dhss.org.yu/licna.html.

32. Zelena Stranka Srbije at www.zelenastranka.da.ru.

33. Embassy of Federal Republic of Yugoslavia, Results of the Election Commission for the November 1996 Local Elections.

34. *Belgrade Domestic Service*, 4 November 1990, in *FBIS-EEU-90–214*, 5 November 1990; *Tanjug*, Belgrade, 10 June 1992, in *FBIS-EEU-92–113*, 11 June 1992; Nešo Djurić, "Prosecutor Calls for Ban of Serb Opposition Party," UPI, Belgrade, 6 June 1993.

35. See Vladimir Goati, *Izbori u SRJ od 1990 do 1998: Volja gradjana ili izborna manipulacija*, Centar za slobodne izbore i demokratiju, Belgrade, 1999.

36. Serbian Renewal Movement Archive from 30 July 2000 on http://www.spo.org.yu.

37. See *Srbija Zajedno, Prioritetni zadaci*, http://www.srbijazajedno.org.yu.

38. *Belgrade Domestic Service*, 6 January 1990, in *FBIS-EEU-90–009*, 12 January 1990; Milan Andrejevich, "The Yugoslav Army in Kosovo: Unrest Spreads to Macedonia," RFE/RL, *Report on Eastern Europe*, Vol. 1, No. 8, 23 February 1990.

39. See http://demokratska.org.yu.

40. See Vladimir Goati, *Izbori u SRJ od 1990 do 1998: Volja gradjana ili izborna manipulacija*, Centar za slobodne izbore i demokratiju, Belgrade, 1999.

41. http://www.demokratska.org.yu/English/history/index.html. p. 6 of 6.

42. Press Release of the Democratic Party from 23 October 1998, http://www.demokratska.org.yu.

43. Press Release of the Democratic Party from 22 April 1999, http://www.demokratska org.yu.

44. Demokratska Stranka Srbije, *Deklaracija o Kosovu i Metohiji*, http://www.dss.org.yu.

45. *New York Times*, 7 August 2000. Also see Demokratska Stranka Srbije, Konferencija za Novinare, Belgrade, 7 August 2000.

46. Pokret za Demokratsku Srbiju, *Poziv poslanicima Savezne skupstine*, www.pokret.org.yu.

47. Press conference of the President of the Movement for Democratic Serbia, held on 2 August 2000, http:// www.pokret.org.yu.

48. See OTN Guide to Kosovo: Serb Plans: The Radical Party, http://www.negastories.com/kosovo/plan/radical.htm.

49. Interview with Vojislav Šešelj, *Heti Vilaggazdasag*, Budapest, 18 May 1991, in *FBIS-EEU-91–099*, 22 May 1991.

50. See Interview with Siniša Vučinić, *Intervju Magazine*, from 8 May 1997, Belgrade.

51. *Tanjug*, Belgrade, 4 November 1991, *in FBIS-EEU-91–214*, 5 November 1991.

52. BTA, Sofia, 21 October 1990, in *FBIS-EEU-90–206*, 24 October 1990; *Tanjug*, Belgrade, 20 October 1990, in *FBIS-EEU-90–205*, 23 October 1990; Elena Urumova, "The Bulgarian Voice in Serbia Needs to Be Heard," *Demokratsiya*, Sofia, 30 May 1992, *in JPRS-EER-92–101*, 4 August 1992; BTA, Sofia, 22 December 1992, in *FBIS-EEU92–247*, 23 December 1992; BTA, Sofia, 28 May 1993, in *FBIS-EEU-93–103*, 1 June 1993.

53. *Borba*, Belgrade, 19 May 1990, in *FBIS-EEU-90–106*, 1 June 1990; *Tanjug*, Belgrade, 13 May 1993, in *FBIS-EEU-93–092*, 14 May 1993.

54. *Tanjug*, Belgrade, 12 May 1990, in *FBIS-EEU-90–093*, 14 May 1990.

55. *Tanjug*, Belgrade, 30 July 1991, in *FBIS-EEU-91–147*, 31 July 1991.

56. *Belgrade Domestic Service*, 13 October 1990, in *FBIS-EEU-90–224*, 20 November 1990.

57. *Borba*, Belgrade, 19 May 1990, in *FBIS-EEU-90–106*, 1 June 1990; *Magyar Nemzet*, Budapest, 2 June 1990, in *JPRS-EER-90–116*, 14 August 1990; Milan Andrejevich, "Vojvodina Hungarian Group to Seek Cultural Autonomy," RFE/RL, *Report on Eastern Europe*, Vol. 1, No. 41, 12 October 1990; *Tanjug*, Belgrade, 4 February 1991, in *FBIS-EEU-91–026*, 7 February 1991; Miloš Antić, "Division of Serbs and Montenegrins Into 'Natives' and 'Newcomers' Increasingly Pronounced in Kosovo: Divide, Alienate, and Rule," *Borba*, Belgrade, 19 April 1991, in *JPRS-EER-91–065*, 14 May 1991; interview with Ándras Ágoston by Nandor Pilcz in Novi Sad, *Nepszabadsag*, Budapest, 21 January 1992, in *FBIS-EEU-92–016*, 24 January 1992; "Serbian Authorities Arrest Ethnic Hungarian Leader," Hungarian Human Rights Foundation, *HHRF Alert*, New York, 9 February 1992.

58. See Alliance of Vojvodina Hungarians, "Agreement on the Political and Legal Frameworks of the Self-Government of Vojvodina and the National Communities of Vojvodina," http://www.vmsz.org.yu.

59. *Tanjug*, Belgrade, 15 August 1991, in *FBIS-EEU-91–159*, 16 August 1991; *Kossuth Radio Network*, Budapest, 25 July 1991, in *FBIS-EEU-91–144*, 26 July 1991.

60. *Danas*, Zagreb, 30 April 1991, in *JPRS-EER-91–071*, 28 May 1991; Bela Tonković, President, Democratic League of Croats in Vojvodina, "Evaluation of the Political Situation and the Attitudes of the Democratic League of Croats in Vojvodina," Subotica, June 1992.

61. *Tanjug*, Belgrade, 10 June 1992, in *FBIS-EEU-92–113*, 11 June 1992.

62. See Koalicija Vojvodina, *Program: Politicki sistem Vojvodine*, http://www.koalicijavojvodina.org.yu.

63. See *Statut Reformsko-Demokratske Stranke Vojvodine*, http://www.rdsv.org.yu.

64. See Vojvodanski pokret, *Sporazum o osnivanju Vojvodanskog pokreta*, http://www.vp.org.yu.

65. *Vjesnik*, Belgrade, 30 July 1990, in *FBIS-EEU-90–150*, 3 August 1990; *Radio Sarajevo Network*, 27 July 1991, in *FBIS-EEU-91–145*, 29 July 1991; *Tanjug*, Belgrade, 7 April 1991, in *FBIS-EEU-91–067*, 8 April 1991.

Appendix

Federal Republic of Yugoslavia

The Federal Republic of Yugoslavia (FRY) was established in 1992 following the collapse of the Socialist Federal Republic of Yugoslavia (SFRY), which had contained six republics (Serbia, Montenegro, Slovenia, Croatia, Bosnia-Herzegovina, and Macedonia) and two autonomous regions (Kosovo and Vojvodina). The FRY consisted of two republics, Serbia and Montenegro, and no autonomous regions—the latter's status had been eliminated by the Serbian government of Slobodan Milošević in the late 1980s.

According to the FRY constitution, the top federal offices rotated between the two republics so that if the Yugoslav President was from Serbia, the federal Prime Minister had to be a Montenegrin, and vice versa. While the federal structure was supposedly the foremost authority in the Yugoslav state, especially in matters of defense, foreign policy, and economic policy, under Milošević's administration, power was largely personalistic and tended to gravitate to whatever office Milošević held, whether as Serbia's President or as Yugoslavia's President.

Elections to the federal parliament took place in the two republics and culminated in the formation of a federal government. According to the FRY constitution, the federal structure was divided into two houses: the Civic Chamber, or lower house, and the Chamber of Republics, or upper house. The Civic Chamber or Chamber of Citizens consisted of 138 seats, of which 108 were allocated to Serbia, as the larger Yugoslav republic, and 30 seats to Montenegro. The 40-seat Chamber of Republics was divided equally between Serbia and Montenegro. The two chambers elected a federal government consisting of a Prime Minister and a cabinet, while elections to the federal presidency became direct through a popular vote according to constitutional amendments initiated in the summer of 2000.

Yugoslav Federal (Indirect) Presidential Election

Presidents of the Federal Republic of Yugoslavia	Period in Office
Dobrica Ćosić	May 1992–May 1993
Zoran Lilić	May 1993–July 1997
Slobodan Milošević	July 1997–September 2000
Vojislav Koštunica (direct election)	October 2000–

Yugoslav Federal Presidential Election, 24 September 2000

Turnout:

Candidate	Votes	% of Vote
Vojislav Koštunica	2,470,304	50.24
Slobodan Milošević	1,826,799	37.15
Tomislav Nikolić	289,013	5.88
Vojislav Mihajlović	145,019	2.95
Miodrag Vidojković	45,964	0.93
Total	4,777,099	97.15

Yugoslav Federal Parliamentary Elections, Chamber of Citizens, 24 September 2000 (both Serbia and Montenegro)

Turnout: 71.29%

Party/Coalition	Votes	% of Vote	Seats
Democratic Opposition of Serbia	2,040,646	43.86	58
Socialist Party of Serbia/Yugoslav Left	1,532,841	32.95	44
Serbian Radical Party	406,196	8.73	5
Serbian Renewal Movement	238,343	5.12	0
Socialist People's Party of Montenegro	104,198	2.23	28
Others	330,159	7.10	3
Total	4,652,383	99.99	138

Parliamentary Elections, Chamber of Republics, 24 September 2000

Serbia

Party/Coalition	Votes	% of Vote	Seats
Democratic Opposition of Serbia	2,092,799	46.23	10
Socialist Party of Serbia/Yugoslav Left	1,479,583	32.68	7
Serbian Radical Party	472,820	10.44	2

	Votes	% of Vote	Seats
Serbian Renewal Movement	281,153	6.21	1
Party of Natural Law	102,062	2.25	0
Radical Party of the Left/			
Nikola Pasić	98,822	2.18	0
Total	4,527239	100.00	20

Montenegro

Party/Coalition	Votes	% of Vote	Seats
Socialist People's Party	103,425	83.28	19
Serbian People's Party	9,494	7.64	1
Serbian Radical Party	5,586	4.50	—
Yugoslav Left for Montenegro	1,928	1.55	—
Total	120,433	96.97	20

Sources: All three sets of data for the 2000 elections are from International Foundation for Election Systems at http://www.ifes.org/eguide.

Yugoslav Federal Parliamentary Elections, 3 November 1996

Civic Chamber (138 seats)

Montenegro (30 seats)

Turnout 67.1%

Party/Coalition	Votes	% of Vote	Seats
Democratic Party of Socialists	146,221	50.88	20
People's Party of Montenegro	66,165	23.02	8
Party of Democratic Action	12,327	4.29	1
Social Democratic Party	26,128	9.90	1
Total	250,842	88.09	30

Serbia (108 seats)

Turnout: 60.33%

Party/Coalition	Votes	% of Vote	Seats
Socialist Party of Serbia/Yugoslav Left/			
New Democracy	1,848,669	45.41	64
Zajedno: Serbian Renewal Movement/			
Democratic Party of Serbia	969,296	23.81	22
Serbian Radical Party	764,430	18.78	16
Alliance of Vojvodina Hungarians	81,311	2.00	3
"Vojvodina" Coalition	57,645	1.42	2
Sandžak Coalition	62,111	1.53	1
Total	3,783,462	92.95	108

Chamber of Republics (40 seats)

(Party representation in the Chamber of Republics based on the number and % of votes in the Civic Chamber)

Montenegro (20 seats)

Party/Coalition	% of Vote	Seats
Socialist People's Party	35.0	14
Serbian People's Party	15.0	6
Total	50.0	20

Serbia (20 seats)

Party/Coalition	% of Vote	Seats
Socialist Party of Serbia	17.5	7
Serbian Radical Party	15.0	6
Serbian Renewal Movement	10.0	4
Yugoslav United Left	5.0	2
Alliance of Vojvodina Hungarians	2.5	1
Total	50.0	20

Source: Overall results for the elections of the FRY Federal Assembly, November 1996, Federal Republic of Yugoslavia at http://www.szs.sv.gov.yu/izbori/izbeng.htm accessed 18 August 1998. The total votes listed take into account invalid votes or votes for smaller parties and are therefore not reflective of the total number of votes cast in the election. This is due to the separate reporting of the Montenegrin and Serbian chambers in this chapter.

Yugoslav Extraordinary Federal Parliamentary Elections, 20 December 1992 and 3 January 1993

Civic Chamber (138 seats)

Montenegro (30 seats)

Turnout: 67.6%

Party/Coalition	Votes	% of Vote	Seats
Democratic Party of Socialists	130,431	47.5	17
Socialist Party of Montenegro	36,390	13.5	5
People's Party of Montenegro	34,436	11.9	4
Serbian Radical Party	31,556	11.5	4
Total	232,813	84.4	30

Serbia (108 seats)

Turnout: 67.4%

Party/Coalition	Votes	% of Vote	Seats
Socialist Party of Serbia	1,478,918	31.4	47
Serbian Radical Party	1,056,539	22.4	34
DEPOS/Serbian Renewal Movement	809,731	17.2	20
Democratic Party	280,183	6.0	5

Democratic Community of Vojvodina Hungarians	106,036	2.3	3
Democratic Party/Reform Democratic Party of Vojvodina	101,234	2.2	2
Democratic Party/Civic Alliance of Serbia/ DRPV	58,505	1.3	1
Invalid ballots	273,614	5.8	
Other	545,232	11.4	
Total	4,709,992	100.0	112

Chamber of Republics (40 seats)

Montenegro (20 seats)

Party/Coalition	% of Vote	Seats
Democratic Party of Socialists	36.0	15
People's Party of Montenegro	6.2	3
Serbian Radical Party	3.0	2
Total	45.2	20

Serbia (20 seats)

Party/Coalition	% of Vote	Seats
Socialist Party of Serbia	32.0	12
Serbian Radical Party	18.0	8
Total	50.0	20

Source: International Republican Institute, Commentary on the December 1992 Elections in Serbia and Montenegro, Appendix G, Washington, DC 1993; and Chronicle of Parliamentary Elections and Developments: 1 July 1992–30 June 1993, General Interparliamentary Union, 1994.

Yugoslav Federal Parliamentary Elections, 31 May 1992

Civic Chamber (138 seats)

Montenegro (30 seats)

Turnout: 56.7%

Party/Coalition	Votes	% of Vote	Seats
Democratic Party of Socialists	160,040	68.4	23
Serbian Radical Party	22,256	7.7	3
Communist Alliance–Yugoslav Movement	14,205	6.1	2
Independents	—	3.0	2
Total	196,501	85.0	30

Serbia (108 seats)

Turnout: 56%

Party/Coalition	Votes	% of Vote	Seats
Socialist Party of Serbia	1,665,485	43.0	73
Serbian Radical Party	1,166,933	30.0	30
Democratic Community of Vojvodina Hungarians	106,831	3.0	4
Independents		2.0	1
Others	445,858	12.0	—
Total	3,385,107	90.0	108

Kosova

HISTORICAL OVERVIEW

The region of Kosova formed part of the Illyrian kingdom until the Roman occupation in the first century AD. The Albanian-speaking population is believed to be descended from the ancient Dardanians, a subgroup of the Illyrians, with subsequent admixtures of Vlachs, Slavs, and other settlers. Slavic groups settled in the area after the middle of the sixth century AD, although the chief region of Slavic Serbian settlement was in the Raška area to the northwest of Kosova and in the Montenegrin (Zeta) region. Here, Slavic chiefdoms were first developed, and by the seventh century AD Slavic settlers had penetrated the traditionally Albanian-inhabited territories.[1]

The Albanians did not possess a state structure or kingdom but were loosely organized into tribal groups. The first Slavic state that incorporated much of Kosova was that of the Bulgarians in the middle of the ninth century AD. Indeed, Kosova formed a part of the Bulgarian empire between 850 and 1018, until Bulgaria's Tsar Samuel died and his empire crumbled. For the next two centuries the region remained under Byzantine rule, until the last decade of the twelfth century.

In 1160 the Nemanjia dynasty took over Raška and gradually expanded Serbian control as the Byzantine Empire contracted. By the beginning of the thirteenth century, Serbian rule extended over Zeta-Dioclea, northern Albania, present-day southern Serbia, northern Macedonia, and Kosova. This expansion was accompanied by an acceleration in Serbian settlement throughout the territory. Under Nemanjid rule, the autocephalous Serbian Orthodox Church established its patriarchate in the town of Peja (Peć), Kosova, and a number of important monasteries were built in the territory.

With the death of Tsar Stefan Dušan in 1355, the Serbian empire's strength declined and local potentates took over various territories between northern Greece and Montenegro. Serbian and other Slavic forces suffered a devastating defeat at the hands of the Ottoman Turks in the 1371 battle of Marica in Bulgaria. This allowed for further Turkish penetration into the Balkans and the defeat of a combined Christian force of Serbs, Hungarians, Montenegrins, and Albanians at Kosova Polje in 1389. The battle was later glorified and mythicized by Serbian leaders, clergy, and intellectuals and turned into a core element of Serb nationalist ideology. Kosova was portrayed as the "heart of Serbia," and the avenging of the 1389 defeat became a historical priority.

Ottoman forces had overrun the medieval Serbian state by 1459 and dominated the Kosova region until the beginning of the twentieth century. Most of the Albanian population converted to Islam, although a sizeable Catholic Albanian element continued to exist in parts of western Kosova. Albanians remained the majority ethnic group throughout the period of Ottoman occupation, particularly in the western part of the province and in many towns. There were various migrations into Kosova by Albanians and Serbs alike, particularly from the mountainous areas of northern Albania and Montenegro.

Kosova was briefly occupied by Austrian forces in 1689, before their crushing defeat by the Turks. Both Serbs and Albanians fought on the side of Vienna, against Ottoman forces. But during the Austrian retreat, tens of thousands of Serbs fled Kosova for fear of Turkish reprisals. Ottoman and Tatar troops launched a reign of terror on the territory, with large-scale killing and plundering of the local population. Sporadic revolts against various onerous features of Turkish rule occurred during the eighteenth and nineteenth centuries, but they were interspersed with long periods of calm, as the Ottomans allowed for a measure of self-government through the *millet* system and were tolerant of the Orthodox Church.

Following the Congress of Berlin in July 1878, the Serbian state, originally established in 1817 around the Belgrade area, became a fully independent entity. However, it was denied any territory in Kosova, and the province remained under firm Ottoman control. From the late nineteenth to the early twentieth centuries, the Albanian population in Kosova experienced a national renaissance amidst increasing calls for Albanian autonomy and even independence and statehood. Abdyl Frasheri became the intellectual leader of an autonomist movement intended to unite the entire Albanian nation in a single political entity. In 1877 he established an Albanian Committee to press for the unification of all Albanian majority territories into a single *vilayet* (Ottoman province). Under his guidance, the League of Prizren was created in the town of Prizren, Kosova, in June 1878, as an essentially military organization that would defend any Albanian territory from foreign occupation. Frasheri was also a social and economic reformer who opposed the influence of Muslim traditionalists in Albanian society.

In 1880, the League of Prizren was effectively in control of Kosova as a *de facto* government while Ottoman power continued to crumble. However, in March 1881, Turkish forces staged a crushing attack on the League, and thousands of Albanian activists were arrested and deported to Asia Minor. This repression sparked a number of Albanian uprisings in the next three decades. During this time there was also an increased exodus of Serbs from the province and a mass expulsion of Albanians and other Muslims from Serbia and Montenegro, many of whom settled in Kosova. By the beginning of the twentieth century, the Serbian population in Kosova stood at about 25%.

The First Balkan War was sparked in western Kosova by an Albanian revolt against Turkish rule in the spring of 1912. The rebellion quickly spread to Albania itself, and the Ottomans agreed to the creation of an Albanian quasi-state. But within a few months, Turkish forces were driven out of the Balkans by a coordinated Bulgarian, Serbian, and Montenegrin offensive. Serbian forces advanced into Kosova in October 1912 and captured the province within a few weeks and then pushed on toward the Adriatic. In order to prevent a Serbian conquest and the division of Albania among Serbia, Greece, and Montenegro, a group of Albanian politicians led by Ismail Qemal proclaimed a new Albanian state on 28 November 1912.

In Kosova itself, Serbian troops pursued a repressive policy to alter the area's demographic structure, primarily through murders, forced conversions, and mass expulsions. Between 1918 and 1941, over 100,000 Albanians emigrated from Kosova. In response to Serb policies, Albanian *kacak*s (rebels) mounted attacks against the Serbian authorities. Although the Great Powers recognized Serbian annexation of Kosova, they also prevented Serbia from gaining access to the Adriatic Sea by accepting the existence of a separate, independent Albanian state.

In the aftermath of World War I, a Serb-dominated Yugoslav state was created in which Kosova was considered an integral part of Serbia. During the first royalist Yugoslavia, Belgrade imposed a repressive regime in which the Albanian language was suppressed and Albanian publications and schools were prohibited. Under a large-scale colonization program, tens of thousands of Serbs and other Slavs were settled in the region and land was confiscated from Albanian villagers. Belgrade planned to expel around 200,000 Albanians to Turkey, but its schemes were cut short by the outbreak of World War II.

Yugoslavia was rapidly overrun by German, Italian, Bulgarian, and Hungarian forces in April 1941. Kosova was divided into three parts: a sliver of eastern Kosova was taken by Bulgaria, the Germans held the industrial region in the north, and Italy claimed the bulk of the territory, annexing it to Italian-controlled Albania. Kosovar Albanian forces launched attacks against Serbian colonists in order to reclaim their ancestral land, and thousands of Serbs fled the province. When Italy capitulated, German forces seized both Albania and Kosova and declared the combined territory an independent state under German protection.

When Yugoslav communist forces seized power at the end of World War II, following the German withdrawal from Yugoslavia, Kosova was declared an autonomous region within Serbia. Although use of the Albanian language was allowed in public life and in the educational system, the first two decades of communist rule ensured the dominance of Serbs in the state and police apparatus. After Tito's break with Stalin in 1948, the Yugoslav regime broke off relations with Albania and cracked down on any signs of Albanian political opposition and separatism.

A communist-directed thaw was implemented in the late 1960s after the removal of the notorious Serbian Interior Minister Aleksander Ranković. In 1968, the status of Kosova was elevated to that of an autonomous province and various concessions were made to the Albanian population in their local affairs and in the creation of a university in the capital, Prishtina. By the late 1970s, the proportion of Albanians in the ruling League of Communists had risen to about two-thirds; a similar pattern prevailed in the police services.

The 1974 Yugoslav constitution gave Kosova and the autonomous province of Vojvodina a status that was virtually identical to that of the country's six republics. Serbs in Kosova now claimed that they were subject to harassment and discrimination by the Albanian majority, and they appealed to Belgrade to protect their interests and restore their previous privileged position. Meanwhile, the Serbian population steadily declined by about 100,000 between 1961 and 1981. While the majority who left were economic migrants, others evacuated the province fearing repression and revenge attacks by the Albanian community.

The Yugoslav authorities feared that the rise of Albanian activism could trigger calls for democratic reform and separation from Yugoslavia. A massive crackdown was staged by police units in March and April 1981 against thousands of young protestors demanding improved living and working conditions and a distinct Kosovar republic within the Yugoslav federation. Dozens were reportedly killed and hundreds imprisoned. Throughout the 1980s, the situation remained tense as both Albanians and Serbs held grievances against each other and against a government in Belgrade that was perceived to be neglecting their distinct national interests.

POST-COMMUNIST DEVELOPMENTS

Slobodan Milošević focused public attention on Kosova during his rise to power in the late 1980s. According to the government in Belgrade, Serbs had suffered harassment and discrimination in the province since the mid-1970s at the hands of the Albanian-dominated provincial government. Serbian government propagandists claimed that Albanian leaders were planning to expel the remaining Serb and Montenegrin population, declare a separate republic, and eventually unify with Albania. Starting in the summer of 1988, Milošević staged a number of Serbian rallies in Kosova at which inflammatory speeches were delivered condemning the Albanianization of the province and pledging to protect the purportedly endangered Serbian and Montenegrin populations.

A series of political steps were also taken by Belgrade to restrict and eliminate Kosovar autonomy, beginning with constitutional changes passed by the Serbian National Assembly in March 1989 that gave Serbia more direct control over security, justice, territorial defense, foreign policy, finance, and social planning in both Kosova and Vojvodina. Two leading Albanian politicians, Azem Vlassi and Kaqusha Jashari, were removed from the provincial communist apparatus and Rahman Morina was appointed by Belgrade as the Communist Party chief in Kosova. Large-scale Albanian demonstrations that included workers from the large Trepča mine protested these measures and were violently suppressed by federal units and Serbian police. At least twenty-four people were killed in March 1989 and six more in October 1989.

In June 1990, the Serbian National Assembly passed a package of "special measures" further eroding the autonomy of Kosova. The legislation bolstered the size and prerogatives of the security forces; enabled the republic's executive, legislative, and judicial branches to suspend the activities of any government authority in the provinces; and empowered the Serbian government to appoint new provincial officials. Albanian deputies stormed out of the Serbian parliament in protest, declaring the new measures unconstitutional. Belgrade also made preparations to adopt a new constitution in order to eradicate the sovereignty of its two provinces.

Fearing the imminent dissolution of the Kosova Provincial Assembly, in July 1990, 114 ethnic Albanian deputies in the 183-seat Assembly issued a "constitutional declaration" proclaiming Kosova an "independent and equal entity in the framework of the Yugoslav federation."[2] The Serbian authorities condemned this move as illegitimate and a few days later formally dissolved the Kosova Assembly and its Executive Council on the pretext that Albanian leaders were seeking to secede from Yugoslavia. The rights and duties of the provincial government were taken over by the Serbian Assembly for the first time since 1946, when Kosova was constituted as a distinct region. According to Belgrade, the Provincial Assembly would be unable to reconvene until a new Serbian constitution was adopted and multiparty elections were held.

Albanian deputies sought several measures to reverse Serbian centralization. For instance, they demanded a new republican constitution that would enshrine Kosova's status as an equal Yugoslav republic. They declared Albanians a "nation" and not a "national minority" (Albanians outnumbered four of the six recognized Yugoslav "nations"). They also demanded that all Serbian constitutional amendments enacted since March 1989 be declared null and void. Serbian pressures against all semblance of Albanian independence continued unabated. For example, in August 1990, Belgrade closed down the Albanian-language daily *Rilindja* after suspending the Albanian-language broadcasts of Prishtina Radio and Television.

Freedom of movement and assembly were curtailed in the province. Albanian politicians were subjected to threats and intimidation. Leading intellectuals and community leaders were fired from their posts and a virtual state of siege was imposed in Kosova by a large police and military presence. As repressive measures mounted, Albanian deputies from the disbanded Kosova Assembly adopted a new "Kaçanik Constitution" in September 1990 and proclaimed a new "Republic of Kosova." This move was condemned by Belgrade as a direct attack on Yugoslav and Serbian territorial integrity. At the end of September 1990, the Serbian Assembly proclaimed a new Serbian constitution that formally terminated Kosova's autonomy. Albanian leaders in turn condemned its passage as unconstitutional and nonbinding.[3]

The overwhelming majority of Albanians in Kosova boycotted the republican elections in December 1990. Albanian leaders grouped in the newly formed Democratic League of Kosova (DLK) asserted that because Kosovars had already voiced their support for Kosova's new constitution, proclaiming the province an equal and independent republic, the Serb elections were irrelevant. Analysts also contended that the Serbian election law discriminated against potential Albanian voters by limiting the number of seats assigned to Kosova in the Serbian parliament. The first round of balloting fell well under 50%, the minimum required to elect deputies. But despite a continuing boycott by Albanians, in the second round, Serb representatives were formally elected in all Kosovar constituencies.

Following the 1990 elections in all six Yugoslav republics and the demise of both integral communism and Yugoslavism, nationalist disputes accelerated both within and among the federal entities. A spiral of conflict was set into motion as Slovenian and Croatian demands for a looser confederal system clashed with the Serbian resurgence and Milošević's opposition to permanently detaching from Yugoslavia the large Serbian minority populations resident in neighboring republics. Fears were also raised in Belgrade that the restless Albanian Kosovars would exploit the opportunity to pursue their separation from Serbia. The specter of Albanian secessionism was in turn adroitly exploited by Milošević to invigorate Serbian nationalist passions, and Milošević himself was cast in the role of the principal defender of Serbian national and religious interests.

Throughout 1991 and 1992, state repression dramatically increased in Kosova and assumed a multitude of forms.[4] Its most egregious examples included the shooting of protestors, kidnappings, beatings, torture, arbitrary arrests, the jailing of political dissidents and human rights activists, summary legal procedures, widespread purges and dismissals from a variety of professions, strict censorship or elimination of the Albanian media, politically imposed mergers between Kosovar and Serbian enterprises, mass firings of Albanian workers, the closure of Albanian schools and cultural institutions, violent police raids on Albanian villages, the ransacking and closure of churches and mosques, and the eviction of Albanian residents from their homes.

Paramilitary ultranationalist groups, under the direct sponsorship of Milošević, were dispatched to Kosova to intimidate and terrorize the Albanian population. The Albanian leadership adopted a nonviolent approach to official provocations and proceeded to construct a parallel political structure, separate economic operations, and a virtually underground educational and cultural life. Following the declaration of independence by Slovenia and Croatia in June 1991, Ibrahim Rugova, the DLK leader, declared that Albanians would not remain in a truncated, Serb-dominated Yugoslavia. However, he insisted that only peaceful means would be used to defend Kosovar interests.

During the summer of 1991, a Coordinating Council of Albanian Political Parties was established in Prishtina to prepare contingencies for creating a provisional "government of national salvation." When armed conflicts erupted in Slovenia and Croatia, the Assembly of the Republic of Kosova in exile (some of whose members were resident outside of Kosova) endorsed a resolution that Kosova would be transformed into a sovereign republic. It also announced the holding of a referendum on Kosova's sovereignty and plans to form a newly elected government.

Despite a heavy police presence, a reported 87% of the Albanian population voted in the referendum in September 1991, of which over 95% supported Kosova's sovereignty and independence. Albanian majorities in three southern Serbian municipalities outside of Kosova, making up over 60% of the population, also voted for autonomy, with the possibility of merging with Kosova. In October 1991, the parallel Kosovar Republican Assembly elected a new provisional coalition government, headed by Bujar Bukoshi, and the single-party Executive Council was replaced by a multiparty governing body.[5] Albanian leaders demanded a new agreement among the Yugoslav republics that would provide Kosova with equal status in a confederal arrangement. They also raised the option of separating from Yugoslavia altogether if Slovenia, Croatia, and the other republics proved successful in their bids for statehood.

At the end of May 1992, the Albanian community in Kosova staged its own unrecognized parliamentary and presidential elections despite substantial police harassment. Competing in the parliamentary ballot were 22 parties and 490 candidates; 89.32% of registered voters participated, including representatives of several minority groups, including Muslims, Turks, Romas, and Croats. The Democratic League of Kosova (DLK) gained 96 out of 125 direct election seats; the Parliamentary Party of Kosova obtained 13 seats; the Peasant Party of Kosova and the Albanian Christian Democratic Party (ACDP), 7 seats each; and the remaining two seats were acquired by independent candidates.

Election organizers also devised a system of proportional representation for Kosova's nationalities. According to their percentage of the population, Muslims were allocated 4 seats. In addition, a Muslim candidate won in direct voting, and two Turks were elected on the DLK ticket. Fourteen seats were left vacant for potential Serbian and Montenegrin candidates. Ibrahim Rugova was elected Kosova's president by an overwhelming majority. Although the imminent partition of Bosnia-Herzegovina by Serbia and Croatia was condemned by Albanian leaders, Rugova pointed out that it could set a precedent for the partition of Serbia and the separation of Kosova. He dismissed speculation that Belgrade was seeking to solve the Kosova problem by dividing the province between Albania and Serbia, saying that neither the Serbian regime nor the DLK would be willing to accept a truncated Kosova.

Throughout the 1990s, the mood of the Albanian majority in Kosova appeared to be reaching the boiling point. Their calls for independence from Serbia had been ignored by the international community. In the summer of 1996, a clandestine Kosova Liberation Army (KLA) *(Ushtria Çlirimtare e Kosovës, UCK)* guerrilla movement was established and its units staged several successful assassination attempts against Serb policemen and Albanian collaborators. Meanwhile, students undertook street protests in the capital Prishtina and other towns to challenge Belgrade's ban on Albanian schooling. The moderate Albanian leadership of President Rugova came under severe criticism from political opponents and younger activists who were frustrated with his insistence on passive resistance to Serbian rule.

The diametrically opposed positions of the two parties, with Belgrade adamant about the territorial integrity of Serbia and Prishtina unwilling to backtrack on demands for outright independence, presented a major challenge for U.S. policymakers and international mediators. The Kosova crisis entered an unpredictable phase during 1997 as a consequence of three destabilizing factors. First, growing sectors of the Kosovar Albanian population became disenchanted with the peaceful approach of their leaders and increasingly supported radical measures as social and economic conditions deteriorated. Second, the moderate Albanian leadership became fearful of losing control over the masses, particularly as the Serb authorities threatened to provoke wide scale violence in order to forcefully pacify the territory. And third, the international community was widely perceived in Kosova as being unable or unwilling to promote Albanian interests. Indeed, the omission of Kosova from the Dayton agenda in the fall of 1995 and the persistent opposition to Kosova's independence among Western governments disillusioned many Albanians who had counted on international intervention. Some Kosovar leaders feared that the Albanians had been sacrificed and abandoned by the West in the forlorn hope of democratizing Serbia and unseating Milošević.

The position of Rugova and other Albanian leaders had been clear-cut since the formal declaration of Kosova's independence in September 1991. Neither the strategies nor the objectives of the DLK underwent significant change. With state sovereignty as the ultimate goal, the key activity involved the creation of a separate political and social structure, including a system of media channels, economic activities, educational institutions, justice organs, health care networks, and cultural activities. Some activists described Kosova as a giant NGO (nongovernmental organization) in which the Serbian state only controlled the instruments of repression. Kosova remained a territory of apartheid, divided from Serbia and divided internally, as Serbs and Albanians rarely intermingled or cooperated.

Albanian strategies were based upon the principles of nonviolence and passive resistance despite frequent provocations by Serb police and paramilitary forces sanctioned by Belgrade. Even public demonstrations were deliberately avoided by Albanian leaders in order not to provide the pretext for a crackdown that could thwart all independent activities. Rugova and his colleagues also calculated that the "internationalization" of the conflict was essential to give Kosova high priority on the American and European foreign policy agendas. The Prishtina leadership courted numerous international institutions and foreign government, hoping they would establish a presence in the province that would not only deter Serb repression but also raise Kosova's status as a distinct international subject.[6]

Rugova's strategies appeared to be paying some dividends in the early days of the standoff. Bloodshed was minimized and the Albanians won praise and support from various governments for their steadfast and peaceful approach. Locals even believed that the authorities in Prishtina were poised to gain international recognition. But as the stalemate continued, the benefits of pacifism and "organic work" in creating a parallel sociopolitical structure seemed to dwindle. An increasing number of Albanians began to question both the wisdom and the direction of the DLK's policies. Independence was at a standstill and high initial expectations were turning to frustration and resentment.

More radical options began to emerge in Kosova, represented primarily by the writer Redžep Qosja and the former political prisoner Adem Demaçi, as well as by a clandestine organization, the KLA, advocating armed resistance to Belgrade's policies. Qosja was opposed to Rugova's Gandhian methods, which he believed to have stifled the drive for independence. Although he did not represent any organized political force in Kosova, he advocated more active opposition through mass rallies and demonstrations. His stance reflected the belief that the Albanians may have missed the opportunity for independence when Yugoslavia disintegrated in 1991. Instead of opting for passive declarations, Albanian leaders should have mobilized their people for active resistance, even though casualties may have been sustained.

Leaders of the opposition Parliamentary Party of Kosova were equally critical of the DLK and proposed more active measures against "Serbian occupation." These proposals involved a broad range of resistance tactics, including demonstrations, strikes, and other protest actions that would have made Kosova ungovernable while intensifying international attention. Paradoxically, these objectives appeared more "moderate" than that of the DLK, in that Parliamentary Party leader Adem Demaçi proposed some form of confederation with Serbia once Kosova attained independence.[7] However, his proposition contained both a contradiction and a danger. Analysts wondered why Kosova would want to confederate with Serbia once statehood had been accomplished. Furthermore, Milošević could capitalize on Albanian unrest to declare a state of emergency and conduct a sweeping crackdown.

The extent of Albanian frustration with the *status quo* was evident in the late 1990s even within the DLK leadership. Prime Minister Bujar Bukoshi asserted that the government's moderate tactics had "come to a dead end" and called for stronger forms of civil disobedience.[8] Student leaders also grew more outspoken and openly petitioned the DLK for public demonstrations against the Milošević regime.

The slippage in DLK control over the Albanian population became evident in two ways: in the growing criticism of its leadership and policies and in the emergence of militant armed groupings. Opposition spokesmen complained about the DLK's political monopoly in Kosova's parallel institutions, as exemplified in the postponement of parliamentary and presidential elections scheduled for the end of 1996.[9] DLK spokesmen countered that given the prevailing repression, conditions were simply not conducive for parliament to meet or for elections to take place. They feared a police crackdown and the wholesale arrest of the Albanian leadership.

The first organized violent anti-Serb incidents were launched in the summer of 1995 and became more and more common in the following two years. Such incidents included attacks and assassinations targeted at Serbian policemen and officials and at those Albanians suspected of collaborating with Belgrade. The clandestine KLA was reportedly the military arm of the National Movement for the Liberation of Kosova (NMLK), which claimed responsibility for the deaths of some thirty people by the summer of 1997. In May 1997, the KLA issued a proclamation to the citizens of Kosova to "reject the peacemaking policy of Rugova and accept the liberation struggle against the invader."[10] Although Serb police arrested, tried, and convicted several dozen young people on charges of belonging to the KLA/NMLK, Albanian leaders claimed that this was merely a pattern of state-sponsored intimidation. Indeed, some believed that the KLA was actually a creation of the Serbian security services.

More troubling for both Serbian and Albanian leaders was evidence of rising sympathy for the KLA among young people. Many jobless youths were frustrated with the cul-de-sac of pacifism and incessant police intimidation and sought alternative outlets to their anger. Even premier Bukoshi admitted that many Kosovars sympathized with the KLA.

Serbian officials also accused "Albanian terrorists" of receiving training and weapons in neighboring Albania, although there was no verifiable evidence that the government in Tirana was involved in such operations. Nonetheless, a substantial volume of weapons undoubtedly crossed the border after the arms bonanza blossomed in Albania in the wake of the public rebellion against the Sali Berisha government during the spring and summer of 1996. No major party inside Albania publicly affirmed its support for the KLA, although the more nationalist groupings, such as *Balli Kombëtar*, criticized Rugova and his peace policy and were outspoken about the necessity for a liberation struggle and the creation of a "Greater Albania." In any case, such parties exerted no influence on the Socialist administration in Tirana.

Albanian government policy toward Kosova was characterized by caution. Tirana's prudence was encouraged by Washington and the European powers concerned by the specter of a Serbian-Albanian war. In the fall of 1991, the first democratically elected Albanian parliament recognized the independence of Kosova. However, Berisha's Democratic Party administration did not formalize this recognition as it feared provoking a crisis with Yugoslavia at a time when it was preoccupied with its own internal problems. Although Berisha verbally supported the DLK program, he was not in a position to offer any tangible assistance. Indeed, Rugova privately complained about Tirana's lack of concrete support and was dismayed over Berisha's recommendation that negotiations should begin on restoring Kosova's "autonomy" within Yugoslavia, a position vehemently opposed by the DLK.

The crisis in Albania during 1996 left the Kosovars feeling even more isolated. They had viewed Albania as a potentially stable ally whose rising international position would reverberate positively on U.S. and EU policy toward Kosova. But the newly installed Socialist government looked unlikely to engage in any bold initiatives toward the region. It remained preoccupied with its domestic crisis and could not afford to pay significant attention to Prishtina. In addition, the new Albanian President, Rexhep Meidani, had a less influential international role, as presidential powers were curtailed.

Throughout the 1990s, Belgrade's repressive policies in Kosova were generally low-key enough not to provoke any strong international reaction but sweeping enough to instill a sense of fear in Kosovars. During 1996 about 14 Albanians were killed by the police, and about a dozen died in 1997. Moreover, hundreds of people were reportedly imprisoned or beaten by the security forces. Milošević used the Kosova issue throughout the 1990s in the Serbian and Yugoslav elections. It suited him to promote a sense of threat to Serbia's territorial integrity—a threat that he then claimed to be combating through forceful rhetoric, resolute policies, and international exclusion from the region.

In June 1997, Milošević revisited Prishtina (the place where he launched his Serbian nationalist career ten years before) for a public rally in which he claimed Serbia would not "yield an inch of Kosovo and Metohija."[11] In August 1997, the Serb government held its first session in Prishtina since the elimination of the region's autonomy in 1990. Officials made promises about investment and economic development in order to secure the votes of Kosovar Serbs in the September 1997 Serbian republican elections. Because of the mass Albanian boycott, a small number of Serbs decided who would occupy the 42 (out of 250) parliamentary seats allocated for the republican assembly.

The Serbian opposition also expressed fears that Milošević could engineer a crisis in Kosova as a pretext for imposing martial law and eliminating dissent and independent activism throughout the country. Indeed, during the Belgrade demonstrations in the winter of 1996–1997, the state media tried to link the opposition movement *Zajedno* with "Albanian separatism." Wary of any association with opposition parties whose position on Kosova seemed no more accommodating than that of the Socialist regime, DLK leaders avoided public protests or any show of support for *Zajedno*. The Serbian opposition was probably grateful for being ignored in Prishtina, as it undermined the government's propaganda campaign against alleged *Zajedno* support for Albanian separatism.

Serbian opposition parties gave no evident support to Albanian aspirations and publicly avoided the Kosova question for fear of being branded as national traitors. On occasion, the most prominent leaders declared their opposition to Kosova's sovereignty in order to gain nationalist support. Democratic Party leader Zoran Djindjić warned against independence, claiming that this would lead to civil war.[12] Djindjić displayed his position on Kosova in January 1997 when he accused Albanians of terrorism, following the assassination attempt on the rector of Prishtina University, without offering any hard evidence as to who was responsible. Vuk Drašković, leader of the Serbian Renewal Movement, proved even more hostile to Albanian demands. During the 1997 Serb presidential election campaign, he declared that Kosova should be renamed "Old Serbia," indicating his archaic and essentially nationalistic approach to the crisis.

For their part, Kosovar leaders did not express overt support for any of the Serb opposition parties. Premier Bukoshi asserted that the DLK only backed "those forces in Serbia that have the political courage to support self-determination for the people of Kosova."[13] Nevertheless, he did not completely discount a dialogue with the opposition. Parliamentary Party leader Demaçi did express backing for *Zajedno* and even visited Belgrade during the mass demonstrations and granted interviews to the Serbian press. His presence was misinterpreted as a climb down from Kosovar independence, heralding the supposed initiation of a historic compromise with the Serbian opposition. The collapse of *Zajedno* and the subsequent statements on Kosova by Djindjić and Drašković injected a dose of reality into Serbian-Albanian relations.

Western governments avidly looked for signs of agreement between Belgrade and Prishtina. In order to deflect Western criticism and improve prospects for the lifting of economic sanctions, Milošević occasionally made some gestures toward easing repression in Kosova. For instance, in September 1996 he signed an agreement with Rugova to reintegrate Albanian youths into the state school system, which they had boycotted for six years. But the agreement, by which Albanian students and teachers would be given access to all levels of education from which they were banned by Belgrade, was never implemented. During 1996 and 1997, a vibrant student movement was formed in Prishtina, led by Bujar Dugolli and Albin Kurti, that endeavored to stage more active demonstrations against state repression.

Milošević periodically offered the carrot of confidence-building measures to Albanian leaders. The impact was negligible: Socialist officials were absent from talks organized by American institutions, and participants from the Serbian opposition were branded by the media as traitors to the national cause. One additional ingredient of Milošević's strategy was to weaken and divide the Albanian movement by driving a wedge between the Kosovars and their leadership. Hence, he offered talks and illusory concessions in order to discredit any willing participants. Nevertheless, no major Albanian figure took the bait or undermined the united pro-sovereignty front.

Contrary to Belgrade's propaganda, the NATO states did not support independence for Kosova but instead focused attention on two questions: containment and the "restoration of human and political rights." U.S. Presidents Bush and Clinton both publicly affirmed that in case of armed conflict in Kosova, the United States would unilaterally intervene to protect the Albanians. However, the precise threshold for intervention was not specified. This deliberate ambiguity was designed to keep both sides in check. The policy may have deterred massive Serb repression while not initially encouraging an Albanian revolt. Washington's overriding concern was an armed spillover into Albania and Macedonia; hence the policy of containment involved measured pressures on Milošević together with consistent restraint on the Kosovars.

Milošević for his part exploited other crises to mute the Kosova question. During the Dayton process in Bosnia-Herzegovina after the fall of 1995, he cast himself as an indispensable peace broker, calculating that this would provide him with greater leeway in Kosova. The Kosovar Albanian leaders were dismayed when Kosova was omitted from the Dayton agreement despite Prishtina's incessant appeals. Their anger was aggravated during the visit to Kosova by then U.S. Assistant Secretary of State John Kornblum, who reportedly told Rugova to abandon the idea of independence and take part in the Serbian republican elections. Albanian leaders complained that the question of Kosova's self-determination should not be tied to Serbian democratization, and that a dual track policy needed to be pursued.

Despite Albanian fears, Washington did not fully abandon Kosova to Belgrade. Following the Dayton accords, an "outer wall" of sanctions was maintained against the Federal Republic of Yugoslavia (FRY), which denied Belgrade access to international financial institutions. One of the conditions for lifting the sanctions was "substantial progress in Kosova." Indeed, the U.S. proved consistently more engaged than the European countries that granted significant trading privileges to Belgrade in April 1997 despite appeals from Prishtina. In a letter to Milošević in February 1997, Secretary of State Madeleine Albright urged Belgrade to "take positive steps to resolve the situation in Kosova" and cautioned against the use of force.[14]

Washington underscored its engagement in Kosova by opening up a U.S. Information Office in Prishtina in June 1996 and inviting Rugova to Washington in August 1997 to meet with Albright. Indeed, Albright injected a new sense of urgency in seeking to defuse the Kosova time bomb and maintaining pressure on Milošević. The administration realized that an official and continuous American presence in Kosova was essential to demonstrate support for Rugova's peaceful strategy and undercut the militant option, even if Washington disagreed with the DLK's ultimate objectives.

But questions remained whether the balance between Belgrade and Prishtina could be maintained by Washington. The State Department relied on Serbian democratization to help resolve its policy challenges in Kosova. As prospects for an opposition takeover receded and talks between Albanian and Serbian leaders remained stalemated, the U.S. evidently understood that some fresh initiatives needed to be undertaken. In the wake of Milošević's takeover of the Yugoslav presidency and the failures of the opposition to democratize Serbia, the administration was clearly concerned that the confluence of economic collapse, public unrest, and Albanian militancy could destabilize the *status quo* and precipitate a violent showdown.

Given the prospect of further turmoil in Kosova, the Serbian government was ultimately faced with four options: homogenization, partition, disassociation, or federalization. In option one, Belgrade could attempt to forcefully Serbianize the region in a Bosnian-type scenario of "ethnic cleansing." In option two, Belgrade could territorially divide Kosova and allow the region next to the Albanian border to separate, a proposal once mooted by former Yugoslav President Dobrica Ćosić. In option three, Belgrade could simply disassociate itself from Kosova and allow the region to gain *de facto* independence.

Option four would involve federalization, in which Kosova would obtain the status of a republic in a three-way federation, alongside Serbia and Montenegro. Even DLK leaders privately conceded that this could be the only way of defusing tensions in the absence of international support for outright independence. The institutional underpinnings of such an arrangement already existed. The constitution of the FRY contained provisions for absorbing additional federal units, while the independence resolution of the Republic of Kosova affirmed that the state had the "right of constitutive participation in the Alliance of states-sovereign republics (in Yugoslavia) based on full freedom and equality."[15]

Some Albanian leaders viewed granting Kosova the status of a third republic within Yugoslavia as a transitional stage in achieving Kosova's independence. This option was attractive to the international community, as it did not result in the changing of or creation of new international borders. But Serbia rejected this concept, taking the position that Kosova remained Serbia's internal matter. By mid-1998 the Kosovar views of federalization were equally negative: an international protectorate and demilitarization were seen as the most credible interim steps towards independence.

The federal option was mooted by the escalation of armed conflicts within Kosova. At the same time the KLA, formed in June 1996 as a more unified guerrilla organization, started to execute attacks on police patrols and Albanians who allegedly collaborated with Serbian authorities. Unlike Rugova's DLK, which believed that a peaceful solution could be found,

KLA leader Hashim Thaçi asserted that there should be no dialogue with the Serbian government and that Kosova should fight for independence. Belgrade immediately declared the KLA a terrorist organization.

KLA units conducted hit-and-run attacks against the Serbian police operating in the province. Indeed, the Yugoslav army became increasingly visible as the police failed to combat armed KLA units. The professed long-term goal of some KLA leaders was to unite the Albanian populations of Kosova, Macedonia, and Albania into a "Greater Albania," although such ambitions were not shared by Albanian politicians. In late February 1998, following an unprecedented series of clashes in Kosova between Serbian police forces and members of the KLA, Serb police raided villages in Kosova's Drenica region, a KLA stronghold. Security forces reportedly burned homes and killed dozens of ethnic Albanians during these raids.

Thousands of Albanians in Prishtina peacefully protested against Belgrade's actions and were attacked by the police with tear gas, water cannons, and clubs. As a result of the fighting and government reprisals in the countryside, thousands of Kosovar Albanians were displaced from their homes, many taking refuge with host families, while a smaller proportion took to the hills and forests to escape capture.

On 9 March 1998, the International Contact Group for the former Yugoslavia announced eleven demands to be met by Belgrade by 19 March 1998. These demands included the cessation of actions by the security forces; the withdrawal of special police units; support for the Organization for Security and Cooperation in Europe (OSCE) mission to Kosova; cooperation with the International War Crimes Tribunal; and permission for an independent team of forensic experts to investigate possible war crimes and atrocities against civilians.

In response to the Contact Group's demands, Milošević launched a media campaign against foreign interference and called for a referendum regarding foreign mediation in Kosova. On 27 April 1998, 97% of Serbian participants voted against foreign involvement. This was intended to create a new mandate for Milošević in his campaign against the Kosovars. Faced with time constraints and new atrocities in Kosova, the Contact Group eased the requirements for the Belgrade government. Backing away from its original eleven demands, the Contact Group simply asked for the cessation of repression and the reopening of the OCSE mission in the FRY, including Kosova. Washington suggested on 28 April 1998 that there would be a gradual lifting of remaining sanctions if Milošević agreed to negotiate a settlement to the crisis. But the Serb leader remained defiant to all propositions and incentives from the international community.

Instead of negotiating peace with the Kosovar Albanian leadership, Belgrade initiated large-scale violence against Albanian villagers during the summer of 1998. This resulted in a displacement of some 300,000 people, with over 60,000 refugees finding shelter in neighboring states. After July 1998,

Milošević steadily increased the level of violence against the Albanian majority and sought to depopulate entire districts where KLA guerrillas were believed to operate. Due to pressure from Western states, a cease-fire was agreed to in October 1998, which enabled refugees to find shelter and averted an impending humanitarian crisis over the winter. As a result of Serbian attacks, over 210,000 Albanians were reportedly displaced from their homes by February 1999.

An international verification mission was deployed in Kosova under the auspices of the OSCE and was led by U.S. Ambassador William Walker. The OSCE and the Yugoslav government reached an agreement whereby a 2,000-member international inspection force would be deployed in the province to monitor conditions. The force was unarmed and was primarily required to verify compliance with the demands of a UN Security Council resolution, including the withdrawal of Yugoslav special forces from Kosova. Under the agreement, partial self-government was to be established in Kosova and a general amnesty issued for people accused of criminal acts related to the conflict, but war crimes would still be prosecuted. By 9 November 1998, an agreement of procedures for elections needed to be completed and the ballot held within nine months.

Aware of the disastrous effect that war in Kosova could have on the wider Balkan region, Western leaders pressed the Serbian government for a peace agreement on Kosova. On 6 February 1999, a peace process was initiated in Rambouillet, France. The Belgrade delegation was led by Serbian President Milan Milutinović and the Albanian delegation by Ibrahim Rugova and Hashim Thaçi. The agreement provided for a three-year interim period for democratic self-government, security, and peace. An international meeting was to be convened following the three-year period to determine the mechanism for a final settlement of Kosova's status. In the meantime, Kosova would obtain a constitution; free elections would be held nine months after the agreement entered into force; and the territory would remain part of Yugoslavia.

Under the Rambouillet proposals, Kosova would have had the authority to make certain laws not subject to revision by Serbia or the Yugoslav authorities, including levying taxes and instituting programs of economic, scientific, technological, regional, and social development. In the sphere of security, NATO would deploy a military force (KFOR), and the Yugoslav army would have to withdraw completely from Kosova, except for a limited border guard force contained within five kilometers of the border zone. Simultaneously, the KLA was to be demilitarized.

Albanian leaders were willing to make a temporary compromise by postponing the question of national independence for a transitional period of three years in return for a substantial NATO presence in the territory. The Albanian delegation to the peace talks in France formed a provisional government on 23 February 1999, headed by the political commander of the KLA, Hashim Thaçi, and including representatives of several smaller parties.

Established in direct opposition to the existing parallel Kosova government led by DLK leader Rugova, this new "provisional government" officially began operating on 2 April 1999, under the premiership of Thaçi. Although it included a range of political parties, in practice the KLA political leaders dominated its proceedings and held all the important posts, such as those in security and finance. Rugova and the DLK refused to assume the ministerial posts they were assigned in this body and continued to operate their own shadow government. Neither body could claim any real decision-making powers in the administration of the territory.

The Rambouillet process was perceived by the Yugoslav government as interference in the internal affairs of a sovereign country. Officials began an aggressive media campaign against any potential agreement under U.S. or EU auspices. The Serbian oppositionist Alliance for Change, not wanting to be outdistanced by Milošević, declared that the agreement should be modified in order to protect the Serbian minority in Kosova. They also stated that Kosova had to remain part of Serbia. On the other side, KLA leaders were dissatisfied with the agreement because they sought outright independence and not a three-year waiting period within Serbia. As a result, neither side proved willing to sign the agreement. After tough negotiations between KLA representatives and U.S. officials, the Albanian delegation finally signed the accord on 18 March 1999.

The following day, the peace talks collapsed after Serbia refused to initial the agreement. Belgrade argued that the accords favored the Albanian side. It strongly opposed the prospect of a NATO presence in Kosova, claiming that this would violate Yugoslav sovereignty. Kosovar Albanian leaders maintained that without a sizeable NATO deployment, Milošević could not be trusted to implement the autonomy agreement. The Contact Group threatened military action if either side rejected the Rambouillet agreement, and this move was fully endorsed by NATO leaders.

In January 1999, Belgrade had expelled William Walker, the head of the OSCE mission, from Kosova after accusing him of meddling in Serbian politics. On 20 March 1999, the OSCE's Kosova Verification Mission (KVM) withdrew its monitors from Kosova, citing a lack of security and cooperation from the Serbian authorities. OSCE Chairman Knut Vollebaek asserted that the Serbian government had failed to provide OSCE staff with information and support, and with access to suspected mass murder sites in the province.

Richard Holbrooke, U.S. special envoy for the Balkans, visited Milošević in a final attempt to resume the peace talks. His mission failed, and NATO initiated a bombing campaign against Serbian military targets on 24 March 1999.[16] The NATO effort lasted for 11 weeks. The operation was code-named "Joint Guardian" and was intended to dislodge Yugoslav and Serbian forces from Kosova and to provide protection for the besieged Albanian population.

In February and March 1999, the Serbian government had launched a major military campaign against the Albanian population on the pretext of eradicating the rebel KLA ,whom they dismissed as "terrorists." The objective was to expel the bulk of the two-million-strong community and eliminate any resistance to Serbian rule. German Foreign Minister Joschka Fischer claimed that "Operation Horseshoe" was masterminded by Milošević in order to expel or eradicate the Albanian population from Kosova and to permanently alter the ethnic balance in favor of Serbs.

Within a few weeks, Serbian police, paramilitary, and army troops expelled around one million Albanians from Kosova or forcefully displaced them within the territory. The Serbian opposition was generally silent during the war, criticizing NATO's policy rather than that of Belgrade. Only Montenegro's President, Milo Djukanović, raised his voice against Serbian policy toward the Kosovar Albanians, asserting that it had led to destruction, war, and ethnic cleansing. The media in Serbia were strictly controlled, and any politician who made a political statement against Milošević was branded a traitor.

Meanwhile, NATO announced that bombing would continue until Belgrade met five key demands: an end to the killing and expulsion of civilians; the withdrawal of armed forces from Kosova; the acceptance of international peace-keepers in the province; the return of expelled refugees; and the official acceptance of the Rambouillet accords. Belgrade refused to comply with these demands, calculating that as the war continued NATO's cohesion would dissipate and Serbia could gain more favorable conditions from the international community.

During the NATO bombing, disputes became evident within the Atlantic Alliance. Proponents of more widespread and intensive military strikes disagreed with voices calling for moderation and compromise. The question of preparing for a ground invasion also created rifts within the NATO leadership. Above all, some military leaders, including America's NATO commander General Wesley Clarke, complained that there was too much civilian interference by Western leaders, hindering the success of the military operation. The NATO campaign initially consisted of air strikes against Yugoslav and Serbian military targets. When Belgrade refused to capitulate, the bombing was intensified and expanded to include various governmental, infrastructural, and transportation targets throughout Yugoslavia. Dozens of Serbian cities were shelled, and several hundred soldiers and civilians reportedly perished in the NATO bombing. Belgrade used the pretext of Serbia's war footing to further stifle any domestic opposition to Milošević's repressive rule.

On 20 May 1999, the International Criminal Tribunal for the Former Yugoslavia in the Hague indicted Slobodan Milošević; Milan Milutinović, the President of Serbia; Nikola Šainović, the deputy prime minister of Yugoslavia; Dragoljub Ojdanić, the chief of the general staff of the Yugoslav Army; and Vlajko Štojljković, the Serbian Minister of Internal Affairs, for crimes against humanity and violations of the laws or customs of war. International agencies estimated that approximately 11,000 Albanian civilians were slaughtered by Serbian forces and tens of thousands of homes were looted and destroyed, together with farm buildings, crops, and livestock.

Several other measures were undertaken by the Western countries against the Milošević government. They included a travel ban imposed on top government officials, a ban on the shipment of oil and oil products to Serbia, a ban on export credits guaranteed by private banks, a tightening of restrictions on investments, and the prevention of companies from providing technical assistance to targets destroyed by NATO. All commercial air links with Belgrade were also suspended by the NATO countries.

After eleven weeks of bombing, with the growing possibility of a NATO ground war against Serbia, the Serbian parliament signed the text of the Kosova Peace Plan on 3 June 1999. It included an imminent and verifiable end to the violence against civilians in Kosova; the withdrawal of Serbian army, police, and paramilitary troops from Kosova; the deployment of international forces in Kosova under UN auspices and with a NATO core; the establishment of an interim administration in the territory; and the safe return of all refugees. On 9 June 1999, the Serbian government and NATO signed a military agreement providing for the deployment of NATO troops and establishing a precise timetable for the Serbian police and military withdrawal.

NATO dispatched almost 50,000 troops to the territory under a United Nations (UNMIK) mandate and effectively terminated Belgrade's military and political control. Kosova was divided into five military operational sectors, controlled by the United States, Britain, France, Germany, and Italy. Several international organizations were entrusted with controlling and developing the province over the next few years. NATO was given the task of ensuring security; the United Nations was responsible for establishing a political authority and providing humanitarian assistance; the OSCE was charged with developing public institutions (including local police forces), monitoring human rights, and organizing general elections; and the European Union (EU) was empowered to coordinate economic reconstruction.

However, the future status of the territory was not determined. This contributed to rising fears among the Kosovar Albanian population that Kosova would revert to Belgrade's control once NATO vacated the area. As Serbian forces fled the territory, Kosovar Albanians flooded back into the country. By the end of July 1999, more than 500,000 refugees had returned home. On the other side, about half of the approximately 200,000 Serbian population fled the region, fearing Albanian revenge attacks. Over the following months, there were hundreds of incidents of attacks against Serbian civilians, houses, and churches.

The Russian government was adamantly opposed to the NATO campaign against Serbia-Yugoslavia and suspended various contacts with the NATO states during the war. Its warnings to the Alliance early in the conflict may have been wrongly interpreted by Belgrade as evidence of impending Russian military assistance to Serb forces, and this may have stiffened Belgrade's resolve. During NATO's ground entry into Kosova, a Russian contingent from Bosnia, with Belgrade's cooperation, rushed to take the airport in Prishtina in a show of defiance against NATO. However, despite Moscow's demands, Russian forces were not allocated a separate sector within Kosova, as Western leaders feared that this would lead to a partition of the territory.

Although Kosova was liberated by NATO from the repressive policies of the Milošević regime, numerous problems materialized in building the foundations of a functioning multiethnic democracy. The lack of a legitimate Kosovar Albanian authority and persistent conflicts between two rival Albanian jurisdictions (the "shadow state" of Ibrahim Rugova, and the political descendants of the Kosova Liberation Army) paralyzed the development of political institutions and the emergence of a civic society. Although the KLA-dominated "provisional government" and the DLK parallel government were disbanded following an agreement made on 15 December 1999, and a new Interim Administrative Council (IAC) was formed, conflicts persisted between the two political factions.

Continuing criminality also threatened the security of residents; perpetuated a climate of revenge against the minority Serbian community as well as against Roma residents, who were widely viewed as collaborators with the Belgrade regime; and undermined the emergence of a democratic system. An OSCE report published at the end of 1999 described the province as completely polarized ethnically with both Serbs and Albanians being subject to violence by gunmen and vigilantes. Attacks on Serb civilians were particularly worrying. At least 200 were reportedly murdered in revenge killings in the first three months of the UN administration. In addition, Serb properties were burned or confiscated and harassment of civilians was widespread.

By the fall, the Serbian population in Kosova was estimated at 70,000. Serb leaders accused NATO of turning a blind eye to the anti-Serb violence. Military commanders responded that they simply did not possess the manpower to patrol every neighborhood in Kosova. Meanwhile, there were persistent delays in the training and deployment of an indigenous police force and the establishment of a credible and professional judiciary that could promote law and order in the territory.

In a careful investigation of Serbian atrocities during the war, international war crimes experts estimated that mass graves in Kosova contained the bodies of approximately 11,000 Albanians. The exact figure was unknown because Serb forces reportedly burned thousands of bodies and carefully disguised the evidence of mass murder. In addition, over 2,000 Albanians were taken hostage by retreating Serb units and were incarcerated in various Serbian prisons. Some of these were believed to have been tortured and killed.

Various measures were taken by the international community to create a workable administration and a functioning economy in Kosova. For example, the German mark was made the legal currency in the province, new license

plates were introduced, and various public institutions were established outside of Belgrade's supervision. The UN-sponsored Transitional Council was
established with a multi-ethnic membership, with the aim of fostering dialogue between Albanian and Serbian leaders and finding solutions to local
problems. But the council obtained only advisory powers, and Kosovar leaders were disappointed by its lack of decision-making authority.

International agencies operating in Kosova paradoxically undercut the
emergence of embryonic local authorities. The establishment of a Kosova
advisory council under the supervision of UN Special Representative Bernard Kouchner failed to fill the political vacuum, as it did not possess any real
decision-making powers. Some observers argued that the large-scale international presence actually contributed to suffocating the development of indigenous political institutions and a local civil society.[17] Political parties and a
range of civil groups and NGOs faced an uphill struggle in making the transition from clandestine organizations to more formal legal entities.

Despite substantial resistance, the KLA was officially disbanded in September 1999. A section of the KLA was transformed into the Kosova Protection Corps (KPC) *(Trupat Mbrojtes të Kosovës, TMK)*, which was to contain
3,000 full-time members and 2,000 reservists and to be empowered to respond
to civilian emergencies throughout the territory. Several Serbian members of
the Kosova Transitional Council resigned in protest against the creation of the
KPC, including the Orthodox Bishop Artemije. They argued that the largely
Albanian force could be employed against Serb civilians and would promote
Kosova's ultimate separation from Serbia. KLA leaders had expected to play a
pre-eminent role in post-war Kosova, but instead their military structure was
disbanded and the political commanders split into several political factions that
intended to contest the planned local and territory-wide elections.[18]

Disputes between the major Albanian parties continued to hinder the establishment of a single indigenous authority in Kosova. The DLK leadership
refused to recognize the legitimacy of the KLA commanders and the legality
of the "provisional government" established by KLA leader Hashim Thaçi.
Conversely, KLA commanders dismissed the DLK and President Rugova as
anachronisms in the post-war setting. The creation of the multi-party Interim
Administrative Council did not fully alleviate the problem. Moreover, observers feared that criminal organizations had become active in the province
and undermined the emergence of a democratic and law-abiding society. Some
of the gangs were operating from Albania and engaged in various forms of
smuggling, intimidation, and even assassinations.

While the overwhelming majority of Albanians continued to demand
Kosova's independence, some Serbian leaders pushed for the province's
cantonization. They wanted Serb majority districts in northern Kosova,
around the town of Mitrovica, to gain their own local administration and to
retain special ties with Serbia. This proposal was rejected by UN Special
Representative Kouchner on the grounds that it would herald a formal parti-

tion of Kosova along ethnic lines. Albanian leaders adamantly opposed such a solution and demanded full territorial integrity under a single government.

After the NATO entry, four major shortcomings of the Kosova operation were visible. First, the territory was torn by political polarization among the majority Albanian population and persistent conflicts with the Serbian minority. This was accompanied by the lack of a viable Kosovar Albanian authority. Disputes between the two major Albanian factions continued to hinder the establishment of a single indigenous government. Albanian divisions also paralyzed the development of political institutions and the emergence of a civic society. In some respects, such a situation suited those UN officials who argued that the Kosovars simply could not govern themselves and needed to be shepherded by the international community toward some future Yugoslav framework. The creation of a joint Kosova advisory council under the supervision of the UN Special Representative did not resolve the underlying political tensions.

Second, the problem of criminalization and the lack of the rule of law became widespread in Kosova. Observers feared that criminal organizations were undermining the emergence of a democratic and law-abiding society. Corruption and crime resulted not only in a lack of security for residents but also in the corrosion of economic and political institutions, many of which were controlled by special interest groups. In addition, Serbian special forces, paramilitaries, and intelligence agencies continued to operate in parts of Kosova, deliberately provoking violence to discredit international institutions, to undermine the longevity of the NATO mission, and to discount any realistic possibility of Kosovar self-government.

The third negative factor in Kosova was the institutional shortcomings of international agencies. These were visible in a lack of serious reconstruction resources, an insufficient number of international police officers, turf battles between international organizations, the undercutting of embryonic Albanian local authorities, and the creation of deliberative councils without any credible decision-making powers. There were also persistent delays in the training and deployment of an indigenous police force and the establishment of a professional judiciary system that could enforce law and order on the territory.

In such inauspicious conditions, a dependency relationship was emerging between Kosovars and international institutions that could become difficult to overcome, the longer the "stalemate" continued. Moreover, such a relationship could seriously threaten the development of indigenous institutions and democratic procedures. To counter this phenomenon, an election process was launched in Kosova through a campaign of voter registration, political party development, and civic education. This could help establish structure, legitimacy, and authority for elected Kosovar leaders. Observers noted that local and central Kosovar authorities needed to obtain the authority and resources to govern and not simply to consult with international agencies. The OSCE prepared to hold local elections for Kosova's 28 municipal councils and to make preparations for general elections to a central Kosovar authority, to be held sometime in fall 2001. But there was a persistent lack of clarity as to the power of the proposed central government and its relationship with the UN authorities and the Serbian and Yugoslav governments.

Municipal elections took place in Kosova on 28 October 2000 and resulted in a sweeping victory for the DLK. Figures released by the OSCE showed that Ibrahim Rugova's Democratic League of Kosova won 58% of all votes and 504 seats in 27 municipalities, gaining control of 21 local governments. Hashim Thaçi's Democratic Party of Kosova (DPK) won 27.3% of the vote, 267 municipal seats, and control in six local councils. The Alliance for the Future of Kosova won 7.7% of the vote. Voter turnout was estimated at 79% of registered voters, indicating a high commitment to a self-governing Kosova state.

The OSCE mission claimed that the results in the Serb-dominated areas of Leposavić, Zubin Potok, and Zvečan could not be validated but that Kouchner should appoint Serbian leaders to those municipalities. Although international mediators were hopeful that the revitalized authority of Rugova could lead to some breakthrough agreement with the new President of Yugoslavia, Vojislav Koštunica, the Kosovar leader immediately underscored that his goal remained the full independence of Kosova and that no political link with Serbia or Yugoslavia would be acceptable to the population.

The fourth and most important failing that can be directly attributed to international institutions has been the lack of a final legal status for Kosova as an independent state. Western leaders believed that postponing the decision on Kosova's status would allow for democratic changes to take place inside Serbia and enable a new relationship to emerge between Serbia and Kosova following the ouster from power of Yugoslav President Milošević. However, critics charged that NATO would simply be faced with escalating anger among the Albanian community if the UN insisted on preserving Kosova within Serbia, regardless of leadership changes in Belgrade. Meanwhile, for the indefinite future, Kosova looked set to remain an international ward without any inspiring vision for its future status.

A strong argument has been advanced that in order to avoid long-term dependence on outside agencies, self-determination and independence for Kosova should be the primary and openly stated objectives of the international community. Such a step could have several positive symbolic, political, and security ramifications. It would restore Kosovar confidence in the international community and prevent a potential radicalization of Albanian politics, whereas long-term ambiguity on the status question could undermine the region's democrats and favor its demagogues. Acceptance of future independence could also undercut the threat of a new Serbian takeover by delegitimizing Belgrade's provocations on the territory. Additionally, criteria and timetables for a democratic independent state would give both the internationals and the locals a concrete goal toward which political, institutional, and economic reconstruction could be directed. Local and national elections would help empower local actors, who have felt largely excluded from the governing process, or in limbo, pending the resolution of the status question. Legitimate central elections would also contribute to undercutting political polarization by removing the two Kosovar Albanian shadow "governments," which had not faced an internationally supervised election.

Kosova also needed a new indigenous democratic constitution to help concentrate political energy, give credence to legality, and provide a more solid basis for democratic development. All Albanian leaders in Kosova evidently supported such an approach in order to create the foundations of statehood. The organs of government would then win the confidence of the public and the commitment of all major political players. In this context, extremist parties advocating ultranationalist and authoritarian solutions could be exposed and marginalized to prevent them from undermining the legitimacy of the new state.

The question of minority rights also needed to be comprehensively tackled, whether through granting cultural and educational autonomy, some measure of territorial self-administration, regional decentralization, or a guaranteed proportion of seats in the future territorial parliament. The protection of minority rights is not in the exclusive purview of national governments but has become a legitimate component of international human rights conventions. Hence, a future Kosova administration will be required to pass legislation and pursue policies that comply with its international obligations.

POLITICAL PARTIES

Kosovar Albanian Parties

Democratic League of Kosova (DLK)
Lidhja Demokratike e Kosovës (LDK)

As the largest Albanian party in Kosova, the Democratic League of Kosova (DLK) was founded on 23 December 1989 in Prishtina. Its president was Ibrahim Rugova, a well-known Kosovar intellectual and president of the Association of Writers of Kosova, which emerged as the vanguard of political activism and protest during the 1980s. Fehmi Agani was the League's vice president and chief strategist. Other prominent members included Edita Tahiri, the DLK's "foreign minister" and a respected political activist. At its founding, the League promoted the concept of "a democratic, federal, socialist Yugoslavia and reform of the political system." The DLK was legally registered under federal law but did not apply for registration within Serbia.

The DLK initially held valid the constitutional declaration adopted by ethnic Albanian deputies to the Kosova Provincial Assembly in July 1990 that proclaimed the autonomous republic of Kosova a fully equal unit in the Yugoslav federation. Due to the DLK's opposition, the Albanian population overwhelmingly boycotted the December 1990 Serbian elections. With the collapse of the Yugoslav communist federation in 1991 and the imminent independence of Slovenia and Croatia, the DLK advocated the creation of an independent, demilitarized republic in Kosova and a change of its status to an autonomous province of Serbia.

The DLK won the majority of seats in a "constituent republican assembly" organized by Kosovar activists but unrecognized by the Serbian or Yugoslav governments. The DLK leader was then proclaimed the president of a self-declared Republic of Kosova. In September 1991, the DLK helped organize a referendum on the independence and sovereignty of Kosova; the vote was reportedly supported by over 95% of Albanian voters.

The plebiscite was followed in October 1991 by Kosova's declaration of independence from the crumbling Yugoslavia. In November 1991, Rugova asked the West to exempt ethnic Albanians from any sanctions imposed against Serbia for fomenting war in Croatia. In February 1992, he requested that the European Community (EC) and the United States recognize the independence of the state of Kosova. Rugova contended that such recognition would prevent mass bloodshed in the region. The Albanian population boycotted elections in the newly created Federal Republic of Yugoslavia (FRY) in May 1992 and held separate legislative and presidential elections in the Republic of Kosova the same month.

The ballot was intended to legitimize the Albanian political structures and win international recognition for Kosova's drive for independence. Rugova was the only candidate for the presidency, and the DLK won the majority of seats to the Kosova Assembly, gaining 96 out of 125 deputies in direct elections. Serbia's government immediately declared the elections, and the call for international recognition, illegal and provocative, and accused Albanian leaders of seeking to merge Kosova with Albania. Rugova discounted the charge and declared that the Albanian population sought sovereignty, independence, and neutrality rather than outright unification with Albania.

Kosova's new Prime Minister, Bujar Bukoshi, announced an eight-point peace plan in early 1993 that called for Kosova to be placed under international UN protection, but this scheme was discounted by Western leaders as unrealistic. The creation of a UN protectorate was viewed by Albanians as an important step toward international recognition and as a means of defending the Albanian majority from further repression and possible mass expulsions. Linked with the DLK was the Kosova Women's Association (KWA), led by its President, Luljeta Beqiri, as well as a youth wing. The party, together with all Kosovar Albanian political organizations, boycotted the December 1993 and November 1996 federal elections in Yugoslavia.

The DLK also sponsored and financed the independent Albanian educational system, publishing activities, cultural life, and economic ventures, and was largely reliant on funding from Albanian exiles and workers in the West. As state repression persisted throughout the 1990s and the position of Albanians continued to deteriorate, Rugova came under criticism from some local activists for being too passive and patient in his approach. Kosova's president contended that any combative moves by a largely unarmed community would result in a bloodbath. Nonetheless, he recognized that Albanians' frustration was growing and that young Albanians in particular were becoming increasingly radicalized.[19]

Rifts were evident within the DLK even before the eruption of armed hostilities in Kosova. In particular, Rugova and Bukoshi were in conflict over the dispersal of funding from the Kosovar diaspora and over tactical and strategic questions inside the territory. Bukoshi was responsible for fund raising for Kosova, but after his break with Rugova in 1997, he terminated funding to the DLK parallel state institutions. Instead, he attempted to establish a rival to the KLA guerrilla movement known as the Armed Forces of the Republic of Kosova, units of which subsequently cooperated with the KLA during operations against Serb forces. After the 1999 war, Bukoshi remained in dispute over funds, both with the DLK and the post-KLA leaders who wanted to use the money, estimated at close to 400 million DM, to support various programs in Kosova.

During the March 1998 parallel presidential elections, most parties boycotted the process, aside from the DLK and its sister organizations, and Rugova won without any competition. When fighting erupted in central Kosova in February 1998, many local DLK activists left the organization to join the KLA, being critical of the DLK's passive and pacifist stance. Even several prominent members of the League abandoned it, including the former political prisoners Mehmet Hajrizi and Hydajet Hyseni. The DLK suffered a stunning blow during Milošević's "ethnic cleansing" campaign in May 1999, when Fehmi Agani, the movement's chief strategist and a close advisor to Rugova, was murdered by Serb forces.

Rugova and the DLK were largely sidelined during the NATO-Serbian war in the spring of 1999, although Rugova did participate in the Rambouillet peace process. Milošević attempted to manipulate Rugova during the conflict, to depict him as a collaborator and thereby to dent Albanian resolve and unity. But his efforts failed and Rugova maintained significant prestige among the Kosova population. Following NATO's entry into Kosova, the DLK joined the UN-appointed Transitional Council as one of the three major political forces in the territory, alongside the ex-KLA groups and the UDM coalition.

Despite the setbacks, the DLK rebuilt much of its pre-war organizational structure and retained significant support, especially in urban areas. However, bitter political rivalries led to several assassinations and violent attacks on DLK activists. The League captured most of the local council seats in municipal elections held in Kosova under international supervision on 28

October 2000. The high turnout indicated the mass nature of popular support for Rugova's leadership.

Parliamentary Party of Kosova (PPK)
Partia Parlamentare e Kosovës (PPK)

The Parliamentary Party of Kosova (PPK) was formed during 1990 to "help achieve a real parliamentary democracy and civil society in Kosova." It declared its commitment to political pluralism and civil rights and initially insisted on the distinct political, legal, and cultural status of Kosova within the framework of the Yugoslav federation. With the breakup of Yugoslavia, the PPK supported the DLK's position on Kosova's sovereignty. The party primarily relied on the work accomplished by the Kosova Youth Parliament and was led by its chairman Veton Surroi.

In May 1991, Surroi created a coalition of opposition groups that included: the Albanian Christian Democratic Party (ACDP), the Social Democratic Party (SDP), the Committee for Protection of Human Rights and Freedoms (CPHRF), the Party of Democratic Action (PDA), the Kosova Women's Forum (KWF), and the Forum of Albanian Intellectuals (FAI). In the parallel Kosova elections of May 1992, the PPK gained 13 deputies to the "Republic's" parliament. The party recommended that Albanians in Kosova make preparations for possible "ethnic cleansing" by Serb paramilitaries, and criticized the DLK for adopting an overly pacifist position. Despite this, the PPK did not engage in arming Kosovar Albanians, contrary to charges by the Serbian media. Belgrade tried to present Surroi and the PPK as violent, armed secessionists in order to foster divisions among the Albanian opposition.[20]

Surroi distanced himself from politics and concentrated on developing an independent newspaper—the prestigious *Koha Ditore*. He was replaced as PPK chairman in 1993 by Bajram Kosumi. The former political prisoner Adem Demaçi subsequently took over the leadership of the party in 1996 and pursued a more active campaign against Serbian repression. Kosumi resumed the party leadership after Demaçi briefly became a spokesman for the KLA at the close of 1998. Demaçi resigned from the KLA on 2 March 1999, in opposition to the Rambouillet agreement. He had insisted on provisions for a binding referendum on Kosova's future. His influence in the independence movement greatly declined. The PPK joined the United Democratic Movement (UDM) coalition in opposition to the DLK bloc at the end of the NATO-Serbian war.

United Democratic Movement (UDM)
Lëvizja e Bashkuar Demokratike (LBD)

The United Democratic Movement (UDM) was established during 1998 as the crisis in Kosova began to escalate and there was increasing opposition to the pacifist policies of Rugova's DLK. The Movement was a coalition of seven small parties and was headed by writer Rexhep Qosja. The UDM established good relations with the KLA and supported the premise of an armed struggle against the Milošević regime. It attracted several former members of the DLK, who were frustrated with Rugova's pacifist policies, including Mehmet Hajrizi, Hydajet Hyseni, and Bajram Kosumi. The UDM was Western-oriented, regarded itself as a centrist force in economic and social issues, and viewed the DLK as a classic post-communist leftist party, most of whose members were former communist *apparatchiks*.[21]

The seven UDM coalition partners included: the Albanian Democratic Movement (ADM) *(Lëvizja Demokratike Shqiptare, LDS)*, led by Qosja himself; the Parliamentary Party of Kosova (PPK); the Albanian Unification Party (AUP), headed by Ukshin Hoti; the Albanian Liberal Party (ALP), led by Gjergj Rrapi; the Albanian National Party (ANP), headed by Milaim Kadriu; the Greens, led by Daut Maloku; and the Albanian Republican Party (ARP), chaired by Skëndër Hoti. As a broad-based alliance, the UDM faced problems of coherence, identity, and consistency in its program and platform.

Democratic Party of Kosova (DPK)
Partia Demokratike e Kosovës (PDK)

The Democratic Party of Kosova (DPK) was formed in September 1999 as the political successor party for the Kosova Liberation Army (KLA) leadership. It was chaired by Hashim Thaçi, the key guerrilla commander and KLA representative at the Rambouillet peace talks in March 1999. The DPK gained significant popularity among Albanian Kosovars disillusioned with the DLK's (Democratic League of Kosova) passive resistance vis-a-vis Belgrade. The DPK gained 27% of the vote in Kosova's municipal elections in October 2000 and captured 26 seats to the newly formed Kosova assembly after the November 2001 general election.

Alliance for the Future of Kosova (AFK)
Aleanca per Ardhmërinë e Kosovës (AAK)

The Alliance for the Future of Kosova (AFK) was established in May 2000 as a coalition of several smaller political groups, some of whom emerged from the defunct Kosova Liberation Army (KLA). It was led by Ramush Haradinaj, a prominent commander in the KLA who challenged the traditional DLK leadership in Kosova's politics. The Alliance gained 8% of the voted in the October 2000 municipal elections and garnered 8 seats in the November 2001 general election.

Albanian Christian Democratic Party of Kosova (CDPK)
Partia Shqiptare Demokristiane e Kosovës (PSHDK)

Founded during 1990, the Albanian Christian Democratic Party of Kosova (CDPK) was led by Mark Krasniqi and Zef Morina, deputy speaker of the disbanded Kosova parliament. Despite its name, this Prishtina-based party counted among its members both Christian and Muslim Albanians; indeed, about 90% were reported to be Muslim. The CDPK emphasized Albanian unity, both culturally and geographically. According to the secretary of the party, Ramush Tahiri, the CDPK did not believe in the existence of two Albanian nations, and it advocated the creation of branches and organizations "in all parts of the world where Albanians live." He reiterated this position in May 1991, when he stated that if Yugoslavia disintegrated, the party would promulgate full unification with Albania, respecting the "ethnic principle" in defining new state borders.

The Serbian Federal Secretariat for Justice refused to register the party because it was avowedly demanding the right to secede from the Yugoslav federation. The CDPK won seven seats to the Kosova Assembly in the "illegal" elections of May 1992. The same number of seats were gained by the Peasant Party of Kosova, led by Hifzi Islami. Among other centrist Albanian parties during the 1990s, the Social Democratic Party of Kosova (SDPK), led by Bajram Krasniqi, claimed to have significant support among intellectuals, and one deputy in the underground Kosova parliament. The Christian Democrats had close links with the DLK and with its president Rugova, but it did on occasion criticize the League for its overly passive approach. However, the CDPK avoided any overt conflicts that could play into Milošević's hands.[22] It remained a small organization with limited public influence on the eve of the NATO-Serbian war in the spring of 1999 and was largely submerged by newly emerging political formations after the war.

Several other parties also were closely connected with the DLK and served in the parallel parliament during the period of Serbian control during the 1990s. They included the Social Democratic Party (SDP) led by Kaqusha Jashari and Iliaz Kurteshi, and the Liberal Party (LP) led by Gjergj Dedaj.

People's Movement of Kosova (PMK)
Lëvizja Popullore e Kosovës (LPK)

The People's Movement of Kosova (PMK) was formed in 1982 and operated during the 1980s and 1990s as a clandestine movement, with many of its activists exiled in Switzerland. Some of its members and supporters were reportedly linked to the communist regime in Albania and were supported by Tirana's secret services. The PMK's goal was the liberation of Kosova from Yugoslav control and the construction of a "Greater Albania." After the fall of communism in Albania in 1991, the PMK discarded any communist ideological precepts but maintained its uncompromising nationalist stance. During the early 1990s, the PMK leadership decided that armed struggle was the only way to liberate Kosova, and it vehemently opposed the pacifist policies of Rugova and the DLK. One of its recruits was Hashim Thaçi, a former student at Prishtina University. The PMK became closely involved in organizing the guerrilla group the Kosova Liberation Army (KLA). The party effectively ceased to exist during the NATO-Serbian war, but many of its activists formed new parties. The Democratic Union Party (DUP) became its most prominent successor.

Party of Democratic Progress of Kosova (PDPK)
Partia e Progresit Demokratik të Kosovës (PPDK)

The Party of Democratic Progress of Kosova (PDPK) was established in September 1999 following a merger between the Democratic Union Party (DUP) *(Partia e Bashkimit Demokratik, PBD)* and Hashim Thaçi's supporters. The DUP itself was created on 4 July 1999 as a post-war outgrowth of the KLA. Bardhyl Mahmuti became the DUP president, with Jakub Krasniqi and Martin Berishaj as vice presidents. Other prominent members included Shaban Shala and Jashar Salihu. In the first weeks after the NATO-Serbian war, KLA activists gained control over the local administration in 27 municipalities where Albanians formed a majority of the population, but were not recognized as legitimate by international representatives. During its first year, the party was active in setting up local branches and developing its organization in preparation for the local elections scheduled for the fall of 2000. However, not all former KLA notables joined the DUP, including Thaçi himself. Following the merger, the PDPK represented a broad cross-section of the ex-KLA leadership, including former activists of the People's Movement of Kosova (PMK) based in Switzerland.

National Movement for the Liberation of Kosova (NMLK)
Lëvizja Kombëtare për Çlirimin e Kosovës (LKCK)

The National Movement for the Liberation of Kosova (NMLK) began as an underground movement led by Valon Murati in 1993. It began with a mass distribution of pamphlets calling for full mobilization and an uprising to liberate Kosova. It aimed to organize and lead the armed struggle of the Albanian people for national liberation. Some military analysts calculated that Albanian militants in the early 1990s had indeed mobilized diversionary and reconnaissance units in Kosova in preparation for armed conflict. Other explicitly separatist organizations that did not discount the possibility of armed insurrection against the "Serbian occupation forces" included the Party of National Unity (PNU), which broke away from the DLK in May 1991 under the leadership of Ali Alidemaj; the Albanian Revolutionary Organization (ARO), formed by former Albanian communists; and the Movement for the Republic of Kosova (MRK), which strongly criticized Rugova for his cautious pacifism.

The NMLK staunchly supported the KLA during the armed struggle against Serbian forces and obtained two posts in the "provisional government" established by Hashim Thaçi on the eve of the Rambouillet peace process. The Movement was not only highly critical of the DLK but also voiced dissatisfaction with the KLA leadership for agreeing to postpone the imperative of independence in an unnecessary compromise with the international community. Some KLA units and the NMLK itself was suspected of providing assistance to guerrilla forces active in the neighboring Serbian municipalities of Bujanovac, Presevo, and Medvedja, where Albanians formed a majority of the population. They considered the region "eastern Kosova" and sought to provoke a NATO reaction to "liberate" these territories. Milošević's police forces escalated pressure on Albanian villages suspected of harboring guerrillas after NATO forces had deployed in Kosova during the summer of 1999.

For a while, there were also suspicions that the NMLK and other small ultramilitant groups were sponsored, funded, or penetrated by the Serbian security services to divide the Albanian political movement, to give credence to Belgrade's charges of Albanian extremism, and possibly to prepare for an armed provocation in Kosova. Belgrade also helped form a pro-Yugoslav movement in Kosova, styled as the Association of Albanians, Serbs, and Montenegrins (AASM), but it obtained virtually no support among the Albanian community.[23]

Coordinating Council of Albanian Political Parties (CCAPP)
Këshilli Koordinues i Partive Politike Shqiptare (KKPPSH)

The Coordinating Council of Albanian Political Parties (CCAPP) was established in the summer of 1991 by leaders of several Albanian organizations in the former Yugoslavia. The Council was based in Prishtina and was intended to enhance cooperation among parties aiming to maintain "the sovereignty of the Albanian people" and to oppose any threats from the Yugoslav regime. DLK leader Ibrahim Rugova was elected chairman of the council, signaling his high prestige among Albanian activists in all former Yugoslav republics. In December 1991, the committee formally asked the EC to recognize the Republic of Kosova as an independent political entity.[24]

Council for the Protection of Human Rights and Freedoms (CPHRF)
Këshilli për Mbrojtjen e të Drejtave dhe Lirive të Njeriut (KMDLNJ)

The Council for the Protection of Human Rights and Freedoms (CPHRF), under the leadership of Secretary Zenon Çelaj, promoted pan-Albanian goals and sought ultimately to unite Kosova with Albania. The Council believed that the core of the Kosova problem was that the Serbian authorities treated the Albanian majority as an ethnic minority. According to the Serbian media, the Chairman of the Council, Adem Demaçi, was also the leader of the military wing of the "Skipetar national-separatists," which advocated "secret mobilization." (The term "Skipetar" was a pejorative name for Albanians used by Serb nationalists.) The Serbian claims were denied as preposterous by the Council's leaders, who contended that the Albanian population was virtually unarmed and that any violent provocations would be suicidal because they could precipitate a brutal Serbian crackdown.[25] Demaçi himself had been imprisoned for more than twenty years for advocating Kosovar independence and Albanian unification through peaceful means since the early 1960s. Most of the Council's activities consisted of gathering, compiling, publishing, and distributing information on the repressive policies and human rights abuses of the Serbian regime in Kosova.

Minority Political Parties

Serbian Resistance Movement (SRM)
Srpski Pokret Otpora (SPO)

Following the end of the NATO-Serbian war, few local Serbian parties survived in Kosova, as more than half of the Serbian population had fled the province. However, the Serbian Resistance Movement (SRM), led by Momčilo Trajković, continued to operate and participated in the Transitional Council established under United Nations supervision. Trajković's participation was condemned by Serbian nationalists and the Milošević government, which considered the SRM and moderate Serbian Bishop Artemije national traitors. In the early 1990s, Trajković had been an ally of Milošević and the Socialist regime, and had served as governor of Kosova. He subsequently became a strong critic of the Yugoslav President, charging him with manipulating the Kosovar Serbs for his own political objectives. During 1997–1998, the SRM advocated dialogue with the Albanian leadership, but it had limited public influence. Trajković became an ally of the Serbian Orthodox Church, and after the NATO-Serbian war, worked closely with Bishop Artemije. He initially advocated the partition of Kosova and subsequently supported the cantonization of the province into ethnic majority areas—a proposal that was rejected by the Albanian leadership and by international representatives.

Party of Democratic Action for Kosova (PDAK)
Stranka Demokratske Akcije Kosova (SDAK)

Founded in 1989, and linked with the PDA in Bosnia and Sandžak, the Party of Democratic Action for Kosova (PDAK) was composed of Albanians, Muslims, and Turks from Kosova and neighboring areas of southern Serbia with a sizable non-Serb population. Under its chairman, Numan Baliq, the PDAK sought cultural and educational autonomy and local rule for the non-Albanian, Muslim nationality in Kosova. It demanded the right to use the Latin alphabet of the "Bosnian language" and for Muslim history and culture to be introduced into local textbooks. According to the PDAK, the best option for the status of Kosova was that of an independent and sovereign republic. It underscored that an independent Kosova could only be achieved through democratic and peaceful means. A PDAK member, Nasuf Behuli, was the only Albanian deputy in the Serbian Assembly, having been elected in December 1990.[26]

Other ethnic minority groups in Kosova also established their own political representations. They included the Turkish People's Party (*Stranka Turska*), led by Sezair Shaipi, which participated in the proceedings of the Transitional Council established by the United Nations representatives in Kosova at the close of the NATO-Serbian war, in the summer of 1999.

POLITICAL DATA

Although Kosova remained technically a part of the Federal Republic of Yugoslavia, developments in the territory effectively severed its political system from Belgrade's control. Local political leaders and the majority of Kosovar citizens aspired to separate statehood and boycotted all Yugoslav federal and Serbian republican elections throughout the 1990s. Kosova became a protectorate of the United Nations and the NATO alliance in the summer of 1999 and was administered without any involvement by the Yugoslav federal government. Under international supervision, Kosova held local elections in October 2000, and preparations were made by the UNMIK (United Nations Mission in Kosova) for general parliamentary elections by the end of 2001: the first legislative ballot in the quasi-independent entity.

Name of Entity: Kosova (*Kosova*)
Size of Territory: 4,189 square miles
Size of Population: 1,956,000 (1991 Yugoslav census)

Composition of Population:

Ethnic Group	Number	% of Population
Albanians	1,596,072	82.20
Serbs	194,190	9.90
Muslims	66,189	0.38
Romas	45,745	2.34
Montenegrins	20,356	1.04
Turks	10,446	0.54
Croats	8,062	0.41
Others	3,716	0.19
Total	1,956,176	100.00

Source: The 1991 Yugoslav census. See Serbia Info/Fact and Figures, http://www.serbia-info.com/facts/kosovo.html. More recent figures indicate that through the 1990s the Albanian population grew to some 1.9 million and constituted over 90% of Kosova's population. According to some Kosovar Albanian sources, the territory had a total population of 2.1 million, of which 90% were ethnic Albanians, 8% Serbs, and 2% other ethnic groups. According to figures accepted by both NATO and the Kosovar leadership, there were an estimated 1.89 million ethnic Albanians and 168,000 Serbs in Kosova at the start of the 1999 war. Since the NATO intervention in June 1999, the Serbian proportion has further declined.

ELECTION RESULTS

On 17 November 2001, the first national elections were held in Kosova under United Nations supervision. Although the ballot did not formally empower the proclamation of independence or legitimize statehood for Kosova, the elections created a legitimate parliament, government, and presidency that will be able to deal with the UN and other international agencies on a more equitable basis.

Ibrahim Rugova's Democratic League of Kosova (DLK) won 47 out of 120 legislative seats, with 46.29% of the vote. But the DLK needed to enter into a coalition with other parties in order to form a workable government. Hashim Thaçi's Democratic Party of Kosova (DPK) gained 26 seats with 25.54% of the vote, while Ramush Haradinaj's Alliance for the Future of Kosova (AFK) captured 8 seats and 7.8% of the vote. The Serbian coalition "Return" *(Povratak)* finished third in the elections and garnered 22 seats, by obtaining 10.96% of the vote. A total of 14 parties were represented in the new parliament. The process of forming a coalition government began in earnest, as well as attempts by parliament to elect Kosova's first president.

In order to ensure stability and democratic development, UN functions needed to be diminished and the Kosovar government empowered to govern rather than simply consult with international agencies. Confusion and uncertainty over the powers of the government in Prishtina could otherwise breed paralysis or radicalism among Kosovars, encourage nationalist revanchism in Belgrade, and actually prolong the necessity for a foreign presence.

NOTES

1. For recent histories of Kosova consult Noel Malcolm, *Kosovo: A Short History*, New York: New York University Press, 1998; Miranda Vickers, *Between Serb and Albanian: A History of Kosovo*, New York: Columbia University Press, 1998; Julie A. Martus, *Kosovo: How Myths and Truths Started a War*, Berkeley: University of California Press, 1999; Ivo Banac, *The National Question in Yugoslavia: Origins, History, Politics*, Ithaca and London: Cornell University Press, 1992; Stephen Clissold (Ed.), *A Short History of Yugoslavia: From Early Times to 1966*, Cambridge: Cambridge University Press; Alex N. Dragnich, *The First Yugoslavia: Search for a Viable Political System*, Stanford: Stanford University Press, 1983; and Barbara Jelavich, *History of the Balkans*, 2 Volumes, Cambridge: Cambridge University Press, 1989.

2. See *Priština Domestic Service*, 2 July 1990, in Federal Broadcast Information Service, *Daily Report, East Europe*, FBIS-EEU-90–128, 3 July 1990.

3. For mutual criticisms of the two constitutions, check *Tanjug*, Belgrade, 20 September 1990, in *FBIS-EEU-90–184*, 21 September 1990; and Blerim Reka and Emin Azemi, "Life Under Two Constitutions," *Flaka e Vëllazërimit*, Skopje, 30 September 1990, in *FBIS-EEU-90–196*, 10 October 1990.

4. For valuable chronicles of human rights violations in Kosovo, see *The Crisis in Kosovo: Heading Towards an Open Conflict*, Priština Branch of the Yugoslav Helsinki Committee, Priština, February 1991; Dismissals and Ethnic Cleansing in Kosovo, International Confederation of Free Trade Unions, Brussels, October 1992.

5. See Milan Andrejevich, "Kosovo: A Precarious Balance Between Stability and Civil War," *RFE/RL, Report on Eastern Europe*, Vol. 2, No. 38, 20 September 1991.

6. For a valuable discussion refer to Fabian Schmidt, "A Strategic Reconciliation in Kosovo," *Transition*, Vol. 1, No. 15, 25 August 1995.

7. From the author's conversations during a visit to Kosova in July 1997. See also Janusz Bugajski, "Close to the Edge in Kosovo," *Washington Quarterly*, Vol. 21, No. 3, Summer 1998; and "The Kosovo Volcano," *Transition: Changes in Post-Communist Societies*, Vol. 4, No. 5, October 1997.

8. See *Radio Free Europe/Radio Liberty Newsline*, No. 96, Part II, 15 August 1997.

9. Consult the interview with the former chairman of the Parliamentary Party, "The Parliament Will Avoid Splits," *Flake e Vëllazërimit*, Skopje, 4 January 1997.

10. *Reuter*, Belgrade, 19 May 1997.

11. *Reuter*, Belgrade, 25 June 1997.

12. See *Agence France Presse*, Belgrade, 28 January 1997.

13. Quoted in *Kosova Infofax*, No. 213, Washington D.C., 13 December 1996.

14. *Kosova InfoFax*, No. 215, Washington D.C., 13 February 1997.

15. See http://www.gov.yu/regulations/constitution.htlm.

16. For an excellent account of the NATO-Serbian war see Ivo H. Daalder and Michael E. O'Hanlon, *Winning Ugly: NATO's War To Save Kosovo*, Washington, DC: Brookings Institution Press, 2000.

17. Refer to Janusz Bugajski, "Balkan In Dependence," *Washington Quarterly*, Vol. 23, No. 4, Autumn 2000.

18. A useful analysis can be found in The International Crisis Group, *Balkans Report*, No. 88, "What Happened to the KLA," Prishtina/Washington/Brussels, 3 March 2000.

19. *Priština Domestic Service*, 8 March 1990, in *FBIS-EEU-90–047*, 9 March 1990; *Ljubljana Domestic Service*, 13 July 1990, in *FBIS-EEU-90–185*, 24 September 1990; *Tanjug*, Belgrade, 8 November 1991, in *FBIS-EEU-91–219*, 13 November 1991; *Radio Belgrade Network*, 7 February 1992, in *FBIS-EEU-92–027*, 10 February 1992; RFE/RL, *Daily Report*, No. 99, 25 May 1992; RFE/RL, *Daily Report*, No. 99, 23 May 1993.

20. Emin and Blerim Reka, "When Will the Emigrants Return to Kosovo?" *Flaka e Vëllazërimit*, Skopje, 18 November 1990, in *FBIS-EEU-90–229*, 28 November 1990; Milovan Drecun, "Preparations of the Skipetars for an Armed Rebellion," *Politika*, Belgrade, 14 July 1991, in *JPRS-EER-91–111*, 30 July 1991.

21. For invaluable summaries on the post-war parties in Kosova check the International Crisis Group, *Balkans Report*, No. 76, "Who's Who in Kosovo," Prishtina, 31 August 1999.

22. *Vjesnik*, Zagreb, 18 May 1991; Emin Azemi and Blerim Reka, "Hunger Will Not Bring the Albanians to Their Knees," *Flaka e Vëllazërimit*, Skopje, 16 November 1990, *in FBIS-EEU-90–225*, 21 November 1990; and interview with Shkelzen Maliqi by Nadira Avdic-Vllasi, *Vjesnik*, Zagreb, 1 September 1991, *JPRS-EER-91–143*, 25 September 1991.

23. *Kosova Daily Report*, Prishtina, 1 April 1993, in *FBIS-EEU-93–063*, 5 April 1993; *Borba*, Belgrade, 13 May 1991, in *FBIS-EEU-91–099*, 22 May 1991; *Radio Croatia*, Zagreb, 19 November 1991, in *FBIS-EEU-91–225*, 21 November 1991; "Letters from the Illegal Movement for the Republic of Kosovo to Ibrahim Rugova," *Vecer*, Skopje, 7 June 1993, in *JPRS-EER-93–057–S*, 22 June 1993.

24. Bexhet Halili, "The Albanians Must Also Be Included in Talks with Europe," *Bujku*, Priština, 31 August 1991, in *FBIS-EEU-91–176*, 11 September 1991; ATA, Tirana, 20 December 1991, in *FBIS-EEU-91–246*, 23 December 1991.

25. Milovan Drecun, "Preparations of the Skipetars for an Armed Rebellion," *Politika*, Belgrade, 14 July 1991, in *JPRS-EER-91–111*, 30 July 1991; *Tanjug*, Belgrade, 5 February 1992, in *FBIS-EEU-92–025*, 6 February 1992.

26. See *Flaka e Vëllazërimit*, Skopje, 17 October 1990, in *FBIS-EEU-90–205*, 23 October 1990; *Tanjug*, Belgrade, 21 January 1992, in *FBIS-EEU-92–015*, 23 January 1992; and interview with Riza Halimi, *Vjesnik*, Zagreb, 16 March 1992, in *FBIS-EEU-92–068*, 8 April 1992.

Montenegro

HISTORICAL OVERVIEW

Under the Roman Empire, the Montenegrin territories formed part of the province of Illyricum. Montenegro acquired its name from the Venetian-Italian word for "black mountain." The region was settled by Slavic tribes in the seventh century AD, and an independent province of Zeta or Duklja existed during the tenth and eleventh centuries.[1] The area was incorporated into the Serbian empire at the end of the twelfth century, but after the death of the Serb ruler Stefan Nemanja, Serbian power declined and the area was ruled by a succession of local Montenegrin princes.

Montenegro retained its independence throughout the Ottoman Turkish occupation of the Balkans between the fifteenth and early twentieth centuries. Despite repeated incursions, Turkish forces were unable to fully subdue the country, partly because of the inhospitable terrain and partly due to stubborn local resistance, particularly in the central-southern core of "Old Montenegro." Although Constantinople claimed that Montenegro was an integral part of the Ottoman Empire, it was incapable of collecting taxes or tribute from the Montenegrins and was unable to have any influence over their internal administration.

After 1516, Montenegro became a type of theocracy ruled by bishop-princes *(vladike)* elected by popular assemblies. However, the authority of the central ruler was severely restricted by the powers held by tribal leaders. After 1697, succession to the *vladike* was restricted to the Petrović branch of the Njegoš tribe. Montenegrin tribes frequently conducted raids against the Ottomans and Albanians. At the beginning of the eighteenth century, Montenegro's rulers formed an alliance with Russia whereby St. Petersburg provided financial assistance to the desperately poor state. In 1798, an assembly of tribal chiefs met in the capital Cetinje to coordinate the defense of the territory and to establish a central court with administrative and judicial functions. But the *vladike* were unable to establish an authoritative central government, even though in theory the bishop-prince was the undisputed secular and religious leader.

Montenegro's rulers sought to balance Austrian and Russian influence in the region. The Congress of Berlin in 1878, after the Russo-Turkish war, doubled Montenegro's size and formally recognized the country's independence. Nevertheless, Montenegro was prohibited from acquiring a fleet and the Austrians were entrusted with policing its coastline, as Vienna feared growing Russian influence in the Adriatic Sea. As a result of Albanian resistance, the country's southern border remained unsettled until 1880, when Montenegro gained a short coastline on the Adriatic Sea, as well as the plain of Podgorica.

Nicholas I reigned from 1860 until 1918. Under pressure from reformist elements, he established a state council that acted as a legislative body in 1879 and approved a parliamentary constitution in 1905. He proclaimed himself King of Montenegro in 1910. His essentially autocratic rule spurred resentment among many young Montenegrins, who began to favor unification with Serbia in order to help modernize the country and inaugurate a constitutional government. During the Balkan wars of 1912–1913, Montenegro collaborated with Serbia against Turkish forces and helped expel them from most of the Balkan region. As a result of these successes, Montenegro obtained new territory in the north and east, in the Sandžak region, and thus came to share a border with Serbia.

Montenegro supported Serbia during World War I and was unilaterally incorporated into the newly formed Kingdom of Serbs, Croats, and Slovenes at the close of hostilities. King Nikola fled into exile in January 1916. A pan-Serbian Montenegrin Committee for National Unification was formed in February 1917 by pro-Belgrade activists. A national assembly met in the capital Podgorica,under Serbian control, on 26 November 1918, and officially dethroned Nicholas and absorbed the country into Serbia under the rule of the Karadjordjević dynasty.

Throughout the inter-war years, in the first Yugoslavia, Montenegrin society was divided between the traditionalists, who maintained the distinct heritage of Zeta as a fountain of their distinct nationhood, and the Serb-centered faction, which viewed Montenegro as the vanguard in the restoration of the medieval Serbian empire. As Montenegro expanded in the late nineteenth and early twentieth centuries, the newly acquired territories incorporated a larger Serbian ethnic population that did not identify with Montenegrin statehood. During the first post–World War I elections in the common state, the traditionalists became known as Greens *(zelenaši)* and the Serbists as Whites *(bjelaši),* because of the color of paper on which their candidate lists were printed. During the first decade of royalist Yugoslavia, there were periodic revolts by Green guerrillas that were brutally crushed by the Serbian army and by White militias. Although the Green forces that supported an equal Serb-Montenegrin confederation or a fully independent state benefited from larger public support, they were poorly organized and disunited throughout the inter-war period.

Following the Nazi German invasion and division of Yugoslavia in 1941, Italian troops occupied parts of Montenegro, and after forming a puppet national assembly, they declared Montenegro an independent state under the ultimate authority of the Italian king. Rebellions broke out in various parts of the country, and by 1944 communist partisans had gained control over most of the territory and Marshal Josip Broz Tito established a second Yugoslavia under a communist regime.

The federal constitution of 1946 transformed Montenegro into one of six Yugoslav republics, and the country received further territories around the Gulf of Kotor and the Adriatic. Under the Tito regime, the Montenegrins were declared a distinct south Slav nation. The regime sought to preserve an inter-republican balance in the communist federation and to undercut the preponderance and dominance of the Serbs by removing Montenegro from under direct Serbian jurisdiction. These measures heightened resentment among Serbian leaders and nationalist politicians who emerged during the 1980s, and who exploited them as another pretext for reasserting Serbian authority throughout post-Titoist Yugoslavia.

In January 1989, the entire leadership of the League of Communists of Montenegro (LCM) and the republican government leadership in the capital Titograd were replaced following large-scale public demonstrations sponsored by the regime in Belgrade. This "anti-bureaucratic" coup ousted the older Yugoslav leaders and republican-oriented Titoist politicians and installed pro-Belgrade activists loyal to Serbian President Slobodan Milošević. The new leadership pledged to introduce political pluralism, and prepared for republican elections as the Yugoslav federation came under increasing strain.

Montenegro's first multiparty general elections in December 1990 were won convincingly by the League of Communists of Montenegro (LCM), which continued to control the media and benefited from a preponderance of funds, assets, and an extensive political apparatus in comparison to the newly formed opposition parties. Following the elections, the LCM changed its name to the Democratic Party of Socialists (DPS) and proceeded to control closely the pace of political and economic reform.

Titograd openly sided with the Serbian authorities as the federation began to disintegrate during the course of 1991, and indeed the dominant position enjoyed by Montenegrin Socialists was largely the consequence of Belgrade's political, military, and economic support. The core of the DPS included a broad stratum of bureaucrats, security personnel, factory directors, and military veterans with a direct personal stake in preserving the Yugoslav federation and curtailing Montenegro's autonomy. President Momir Bulatović rushed through a republican referendum in March 1992 that approved Montenegro's continuing association with Serbia in the newly created Federal Republic of Yugoslavia (FRY).

The opposition Liberal Alliance of Montenegro (LAM), the strongest Green force in the republic, staged demonstrations in several cities, claiming that the wording of the referendum did not inform voters on the alternatives to a close federation with Serbia. The DPS comfortably won the federal Yugoslav elections in May 1992—a ballot boycotted by virtually all opposition parties, which charged that the elections were unconstitutional. The election victory assured the DPS of continuing control over the key instruments of government, the mass media, and the economy.

Montenegro's Albanian and Muslim minorities grew concerned about Serbian control over the republic and the spread of the Croatian and Bosnian conflicts into Montenegro. Albanian and Muslim leaders were generally supportive of Montenegrin sovereignty and independence and campaigned for greater collective rights in education, culture, language, and local administration. But they asserted that they harbored no separatist ambitions, and they tacitly supported the democratic Montenegrin oppositionist parties. Belgrade and the Montenegrin regime charged that the minority leaders were extremists intent on dismembering the republic and creating a large Islamic or Albanian state. As the war in Croatia and Bosnia-Herzegovina escalated, radical Serbian guerrillas also become active in parts of Montenegro. Muslim communities in the Montenegrin Sandžak region, along the border with Serbia and Bosnia-Herzegovina, became subject to harassment and intimidation.

The government in Podgorica (the restored, pre-communist name for Titograd) did not condone the activities of militant Serb guerrilla formations sponsored or tolerated by Belgrade. In fact, following the appointment of Milan Panić as Yugoslav prime minister in the summer of 1992, the Bulatović regime appeared to distance itself from Milošević, initially calculating that his days in power could be numbered. Some elements of the Montenegrin Socialist leadership seemed to be repositioning themselves for a major crisis in Serbia and not excluding the possibility of detaching the republic from Yugoslavia. Meanwhile, Serbian radicals continued to claim that Albanian and Muslim separatists were preparing to mount an uprising; such charges were intended to rally Montenegrin citizens behind Belgrade.

According to the 1991 Montenegrin census, 380,484 (61.84%) persons out of a total population of 615,267 were registered as ethnic Montenegrins.[2] Muslims formed the largest minority, numbering 89,932, or 14.62% of the population, and were mostly resident in the Sandžak area. Self-declared Serbs totaled 57,176, or 9.29% of the population. The figures continued to fuel disputes between those who considered Montenegrins a distinct ethnic group and those who viewed them simply as a subdivision of the Serbian nation. Indeed, Serb nationalists contended that the majority of those who declared themselves Montenegrins actually identified themselves as "Montenegrin Serbs." Montenegrin nationalists disputed such assertions. Albanians constituted the third largest minority in the republic, totaling 40,880 people, or 6.64% of the population.

POST-COMMUNIST DEVELOPMENTS

The December 1990 elections marked the first multiparty ballot in Montenegro since 1938. The bulk of the 125 contested seats in the National Assembly went to the League of Communists of Montenegro (LCM), which was subsequently renamed the Democratic Party of Socialists (DPS).[3] The LCM had utilized its monopoly over state funds and the media to achieve an electoral victory, winning 85 seats in parliament. The Alliance of Reform Forces of Montenegro (ARFM), a pro-Yugoslav coalition of the Socialist Party, the Social Democratic Party, the Liberal Alliance, the Independent Communists of Bar, the Party of National Equality, and several smaller groupings, won a total of 17 seats. The Serb nationalist People's Party of Montenegro (PPM) benefited from its affinity with Belgrade and was able to garner 12 seats. The Democratic Coalition (DC), a minority-centered alliance of smaller Muslim and Albanian parties, won 12 seats in the republican assembly.

By October 1992, the political composition of the Montenegrin legislature had changed somewhat. The DPS had been reduced to 82 seats when three of its deputies resigned from the party in September 1992. The ARFM, now renamed the Reform Coalition (RC), lost four seats as a result of the departure of the Party of National Equality (PNE); the PNE subsequently joined the Democratic Coalition minority bloc. The PPM was reduced to just two seats in the National Assembly in late 1992, when eight deputies joined the ranks of the newly formed People's Democratic Party (PDP), a Serbian nationalist formation with close ties to the Serbian Radical Party in Belgrade.[4]

The loyalty of the Montenegrin government to Milošević was assured during the protracted and ultimately futile negotiations to confederate Yugoslavia during the early part of 1991, but when war erupted in the summer of 1991 Podgorica began to show signs of distancing itself from Belgrade. There were several reasons for this change of track, although the Montenegrin opposition initially dismissed it as mere opportunism. First, President Momir Bulatović calculated that Milošević was purposely drawing Montenegro into a destructive and unpopular war with Croatia from which the republic was unlikely to benefit. Second, a long, drawn-out conflict and a deteriorating economy would broaden support for Montenegrin sovereignty and even independence from Yugoslavia. In such a scenario, the DPS could have lost its respectable public backing and faced the prospect of having to surrender power. Third, the government wanted to avoid direct responsibility for the war, particularly for the atrocities committed by Serb-Yugoslav forces in Croatia and Bosnia in the name of Serb unity. As a result, in September 1991, Prime Minister Milo Djukanović announced preparations for a declaration of Montenegrin sovereignty within a Yugoslav framework; and the following month, President Bulatović called for the withdrawal of Montenegrin reservists from battle fronts in Croatia.

Podgorica's delicate balancing act between Yugoslav integralism and Montenegrin sovereignty was further displayed during 1992 after war erupted in neighboring Bosnia-Herzegovina. With reports of systematic war crimes against Muslim residents by Serbian guerrillas and paramilitary formations operating from both Serbia and Montenegro, the Bulatović leadership increasingly adopted a pacifist stance. After the appointment of Milan Panić as Yugoslav prime minister in July 1992, the Montenegrin deputies consistently supported his overtures for a peaceful resolution to the Yugoslav wars and opposed Socialist and Radical criticisms. Indeed, Panić survived two votes of no-confidence largely because of Montenegrin support in the Federal Assembly. In addition, Bulatović publicly voiced his backing for the Vance-Owen plan for decentralizing Bosnia-Herzegovina despite persistent Bosnian-Serb and Belgrade government opposition.

Nevertheless, to prevent outright condemnation by Milošević and forceful attempts to unseat the government, in March 1992 Podgorica moved ahead with a referendum on Montenegrin membership in the newly initiated two-republic federation, the Federal Republic of Yugoslavia (FRY), despite the resistance of opposition parties. Sixty-three percent of the electorate reportedly voted in favor of the new federation, although little time was allowed for a public debate on the issue. The DPS participated in drafting the new federal constitution that was pushed through in April 1992 and heralded the proclamation of the FRY. Montenegro's opposition parties boycotted the proceedings in protest. Montenegrin leaders stated that through their involvement in federal assembly sessions the republic would maintain some degree of influence over Belgrade's policies, express its opposition to the war in Bosnia, and suggest proposals for resolving the regional crisis.

The Podgorica authorities were also apprehensive that Milošević and his Radical allies in Montenegro were planning to destabilize the republic by provoking conflicts with the Muslim and Albanian minorities, then using this scenario as a pretext for replacing the regime and raising support for Belgrade's policies. With a large army and Serb paramilitary presence in Montenegro, Bulatović was clearly wary of a direct confrontation with his erstwhile political sponsor.

After a hurried entrance into a rump Yugoslav federation with Serbia in March 1992, and the subsequent passage of a new federal constitution in April 1992, Montenegro adopted its own constitution in October 1992. The constitution asserted Montenegrin sovereignty in all realms not already explicitly claimed as the responsibility of federal institutions. The document changed the official state language from Serbo-Croatian to the Serbian *jekavian* dialect and addressed the rights of minorities in several articles. It asserted specifically the rights of national and ethnic groups to protect their national, ethnic, cultural, and linguistic identities in accordance with prevailing international standards. These included access to education and information in an individual's native language, the right to display national symbols, and the right to establish educational and cultural associations with material assistance from the state. The constitution also asserted that it was illegal for citizens to "provoke others" and "stir up trouble" on the basis of ethnic identity or racial animosity.

The Muslim population in the Sandžak was singled out for provocative assaults by Serb paramilitaries during the summer and fall of 1992. Serbian radicals were reportedly intent on clearing Muslim residents from the Montenegrin-Bosnian border areas through intimidation, harassment, and outright acts of violence. The Montenegrin authorities intervened belatedly to try and defuse rising tensions in the region, but they displayed great caution for fear of provoking ultranationalist Serb attacks elsewhere in the republic and outright condemnation by Belgrade. On the other hand, Podgorica also earned some credit by providing assistance to several thousand Muslim refugees from eastern Bosnia who had fled across the border from advancing Serbian forces or were expelled during brutal "ethnic cleansing" operations.

Although occasional incidents of violence were reported against the Albanian minority, criticisms of the Montenegrin government by Albanian leaders primarily focused on occupational discrimination and educational disadvantages. According to minority spokesmen, the powers of the local authorities were curtailed in the early 1990s, including in districts containing large Albanian populations. In addition, the key institutions, including police, finance, education, and culture, were directed by Montenegrins, and the official language even in minority regions remained Serbian. All official documents, including private contracts and birth and teaching certificates, were drafted in Serbian, and it was obligatory to add a Serbian suffix to all family names of the Albanian minority.

A salient point of the language dispute revolved around the media issue. Montenegrin state radio reserved only 30 minutes a day for Albanian-language programming, and there were no Albanian programs on Podgorica Television. No ready outlet existed in the print media, since there was no Albanian press agency and no state-funded minority news publication. Since 1982, the Montenegrin authorities had also prohibited the use of the Albanian flag, in violation of the federal law. Furthermore, Albanians were not authorized to celebrate their national holidays publicly.[5]

Albanian leaders also grew concerned over Montenegro's inclusion in the Federal Republic of Yugoslavia in March 1992, the rapid passage of the new Montenegrin constitution, and the rushed federal elections in May 1992. Some minority activists planned to hold a referendum on Albanian autonomy in districts where Albanians formed a relative majority of the population. In September 1992, the largest Albanian party, the Democratic Alliance of Montenegro (DAM), issued a Memorandum on the Special Status of Albanians. The document was criticized by both the government and the opposition parties for encouraging separatism and playing into the hands of Serbian militants. Although some Albanian leaders voiced fears of potential

Montenegrin nationalism, they remained more perturbed over the activities of Serb paramilitaries, and participated in the republican and local elections of December 1992 to undercut the nationalist vote.

In the second multiparty elections, on 20 December 1992, the Democratic Party of Socialists (DPS) gained 46 seats in the Montenegrin National Assembly; the total number of deputies had been constitutionally reduced from 125 to 85 seats. Despite complaints over the election law and the unfair advantage maintained by the DPS in terms of funding, resources, and access to the media, all major opposition parties participated in the republican and local elections. The People's Party finished second, with 14 seats; the Liberals third, with 13 seats; the Radicals fourth, with 8 seats; and the Social Democrats fifth, with 4 seats. The Democratic Alliance of Montenegro (DAM) failed to exceed the threshold for parliamentary representation, and the Muslim Party of Democratic Action (PDA) did not participate.

In December 1992, the 20-seat Montenegrin section of the federal Chamber of Republics, the DPS, elected 15 deputies, the People's Party 3, and the Radicals 2. To the 138-seat federal Chamber of Citizens (or Civic Chamber), the DPS elected 17 deputies, the Socialists 5, the People's Party 4, and the Radicals from Montenegro also gained 4 deputies. Momir Bulatović was re-elected Montenegrin President. In a runoff with Radical Party candidate Branko Kostić, Bulatović obtained 63.3% of the popular vote after the opposition decided to support his ticket against the Radicals. Former Montenegrin prime minister and DPS member Radoje Kontić was nominated for Yugoslav prime minister, to replace Milan Panić.

Following the ballot, the DPS seemed to display its wariness of Belgrade by moving to form a coalition government with several opposition parties. With the defeat of Panić in the Serbian presidential election, increasing pressure on Dobrica Ćosić to step down from the Yugoslav presidency, and the success of the Radicals in the Serbian ballot, Podgorica appeared to be more exposed to a potential crackdown by Belgrade. It therefore proceeded to build a broader umbrella movement with the Montenegrin opposition. A new government was formed in April 1993. While the DPS retained the premiership and a number of key ministries, the Liberals and Social Democrats obtained two portfolios each, while the People's Party took one deputy premiership and two ministries without portfolio. The coalition government appeared to stabilize the republic by lessening political tensions while isolating the Serbian Radicals as the primary instigators of conflict.

Some analysts believed that out of political opportunism and sheer self-preservation, the Bulatović regime would adopt a more openly pro-sovereignty position, while closely watching for any hostile intervention by Milošević. After the ouster of Yugoslav President Ćosić, the evaporation of the threat of Western military intervention against the Serb militias and Yugoslav-Serb forces in Bosnia, and the collapse of the Vance-Owen plan in Bosnia, for which Bulatović had declared his support, Podgorica appeared to soften its stance toward Milošević and a rapprochement with Belgrade became evident.

In June 1993, Serbian Socialist Party secretary general Milomir Minić announced that talks were under way to merge the Socialists with the Montenegrin DPS.[6] According to Serbian Socialists the objective was to ensure that the federal administration was streamlined and made more efficient. In reality, the move appeared designed to undermine the independent stance of the DPS, to sow dissension within the Montenegrin political elite, and to prepare for the formation of a new pan-Serbian federation that would undermine Montenegro's republican status. The merger, however, did not take place.

The Montenegrin authorities supported the Dayton peace plan for Bosnia, viewing it as a positive factor in stabilizing the republic's western borders. But the government in Podgorica became increasingly dissatisfied with Milošević's policies and Serbian domination within the FRY, particularly after the failures of the Serbian opposition to dislodge him from power during the mass protests in Belgrade in the winter of 1996.

In October 1997, former Prime Minister Milo Djukanović was elected President of the republic after beating the Belgrade loyalist Bulatović in a second-round ballot. Djukanović favored broad autonomy for Montenegro and had grown frustrated with Belgrade's reluctance to conduct any meaningful economic reforms. Bulatović accused his rival of fraud, and he organized demonstrations on 14–15 January 1998, prior to Djukanović's inauguration. The protests failed to ignite any mass opposition to the Djukanović presidency. The Djukanović faction of the DPS claimed it was the legal successor of the original DPS, and the Montenegrin High Court upheld this position. The Bulatović faction subsequently formed a new pro-Milošević party, the Socialist People's Party (SPP).

Djukanović's DPS formed a coalition, For a Better Life (Da Živimo Bolje), with the Social Democratic Party (SDP) and the People's Party of Montenegro (PPM), and won the Montenegrin republican elections on 31 May 1998 with 49.5% of the vote. The extraordinary elections had been scheduled because of the split in the former ruling party. Following the ballot, the DPS-led coalition government, with representatives from the minority groups, proceeded to enact various measures to distance itself from the Serbian authorities and from Milošević's policies. It pursued closer relations with Western countries, initiated economic reforms, and adopted an increasingly pro-independence position for Montenegro. Its public support remained stable in spite of its neutrality in the NATO-Serbian war over Kosova in 1999 and despite difficult economic conditions in the republic.

Podgorica pledged to conduct a separate foreign policy if Serbia remained isolated in the international community. This would constitute the first step toward the formal declaration of independence. The Montenegrin independence movement, associated with the major opposition parties, also expanded its influence and enlisted support from the country's Albanian and Muslim minorities. At the same time, Milošević grew concerned that Montenegrin representatives in the federal assembly might attempt to remove him from the Yugoslav presidency, the office he had assumed in July 1997, as he was constitutionally barred from another term as President of Serbia.

Having made numerous overtures to gain Western investment, including trips to Washington, the government of President Djukanović attempted to extricate itself from Serbia's political and economic control. Evidently in retaliation for these initiatives, the Montenegrin foreign minister, Janko Jeknić, who was instrumental in pursuing a pro-Western course, was killed in a mysterious car crash in mid-January 1998. Montenegro opened a separate trade mission in Washington, whose spokesmen distanced themselves from the nearby Yugoslav embassy. Podgorica also threatened to introduce its own currency if Serbia did not stop printing money to shore up Milošević's authority. The government subsequently introduced the German mark as the republic's official currency. Montenegrin officials desperately wanted to avoid hyperinflationary pressures that could destroy the crippled economy and provoke major social unrest. Serbia continued to print millions of dollars worth of dinars to subdue popular protests by paying off frustrated workers.

Montenegrin leaders prepared an "alternative economic program," launching a sweeping privatization of state firms in order to attract foreign investment. They were frustrated by Belgrade's reluctance to conduct any meaningful economic reforms and by the dominance of die-hard communists in the country's leadership. The official daily *Pobjeda* (Victory) accused Milošević of brazenly "lecturing the West" instead of conducting radical political and economic reforms. Although Montenegrin leaders expressed sympathy for the Serbian opposition, the reinstatement of Serbia's defrauded local election results in 1997 made little difference to Podgorica and there was general disappointment with the failure of anti-Milošević forces in Serbia to topple the government.

During the course of 1998, Montenegro's deputy premier, Slavko Drljević, declared that the republic was prepared to "defend itself by all means necessary" against Belgrade's pressures. The temperature visibly heated up between Belgrade and Podgorica when President Djukanović launched a scathing attack on Milošević, warning the Yugoslav President that he would not have Montenegrin support in votes that he needed in the federal Yugoslav assembly to strengthen the powers of the federal office. In an outspoken interview for *Vreme* (Time), Djukanović asserted that Milošević's political views were "outdated" and he was surrounded by people who kept him misinformed about the real scale of Yugoslavia's problems.

In response to Djukanović's criticisms of Milošević, Serbia's state-run media launched a scathing attack on the Montenegrin leadership, linking Djukanović to organized crime and murky business pursuits. Montenegrin television, in a display of independence, cut off the Serbian broadcasts, and the offices of the pro-Milošević *Dnevnik* daily in Podgorica were attacked. In a major show of defiance, the influential Montenegrin writers' association appealed to the government to put an end to Milošević's dictatorship and to finally secede from Yugoslavia.

Various measures were taken to counter Milošević's influence in Montenegro. For example, President Djukanović and Serbian Democratic Party leader Zoran Djindjić declared on 1 December 1998 that they agreed to launch a new independent Yugoslav satellite TV station. Montenegro also announced the opening of its own "liaison" offices in five foreign capitals. Podgorica was also critical of Milošević's policy toward Kosova and remained largely neutral during Yugoslavia's war with NATO in the spring of 1999.

For the Djukanović government, Montenegrin sovereignty became a question of political and economic survival. The proposals lodged by Podgorica in its negotiations with Belgrade during 1999, calling for a restructured "confederation," seemed a last-ditch attempt at decentralizing power in the FRY. A cross section of Montenegrin politicians and intellectuals concurred that it was not possible to build a democratic Montenegro within an autocratic Yugoslavia run by indicted war criminals.

The confederation proposal lodged by the Djukanović government in the summer of 1999 appeared to be a political cover for an eventual referendum on national independence. A team of leading Montenegrin academics led by economist Veselin Vukotić drafted a blueprint for economic sovereignty. Not surprisingly, its basic premises were unacceptable to Belgrade. The program called for fiscal independence through the introduction of a separate Montenegrin currency; the creation of an internationally monitored currency board to control state spending; full control by Montenegro over its own budget; accelerated privatization; and far-reaching legal reforms to encourage foreign investment.

This virtual declaration of economic independence also included some crucial political and security demands that outraged Belgrade. These involved constitutional reforms to balance power in all "confederal" institutions, Montenegrin control over any Yugoslav army units stationed on its territory, and full Montenegrin supervision of the country's borders. Support for independence mounted in the wake of the Kosova war and the NATO victory over Serbia in June 1999. Djukanović and his previously hesitant government were clearly testing the waters for public support. In some opinion polls, almost 70% of the population declared that they would back the administration if it opted for independence or managed to negotiate a confederation arrangement, and only 12% of Montenegrins were strongly in favor of preserving the status quo and the common state.

For the political leadership in Podgorica, economic and political independence became imperative. If Montenegro proved unable to detach its economy from that of Serbia, its chances of obtaining any substantial assistance or investment through the South East European Stability Pact remained slim and its goal of joining the process of European Union integration would be indefinitely postponed. As far as Belgrade was concerned, the alternative to independence was not "confederation" but comprehensive absorption by the Serbian state. Ominously for President Milošević, without Montenegro, Yugoslavia as a "federal" state would cease to exist, together with all of its offices and institutions.

To prevent such an outcome, Milošević kept several potential scenarios up his sleeve. First, analysts calculated that he could try to engineer a military coup in Podgorica after replacing many commanding officers with handpicked loyalists. However, this could have provoked substantial armed resistance from Montenegro's specially trained, 15,000-strong police force, loyal to President Djukanović. Second, Belgrade could have engineered ethnic tensions with Albanian and Muslim minorities through actions staged by Serb paramilitaries relocated from Kosova and Serbia. But this could have also precipitated an armed confrontation with the Montenegrin police and spiraled into an all-out civil war. Djukanović remained dependent on Albanian and Muslim support to maintain his coalition government and feared any deterioration in ethnic relations in the republic.

Third, some observers speculated that Milošević could have offered Djukanović a new political deal in which the DPS would nominate the next Yugoslav federal Prime Minister after the removal of Bulatović. However, if Djukanović had accepted such an arrangement, Montenegro's coalition government would have likely collapsed. In the midst of the ensuing political paralysis, Milošević could have engineered some new "state of emergency" and implanted his own loyalists in Podgorica.

An armed conflict in Montenegro, provoked by Belgrade, might have rapidly spiraled into a civil war between "Greens" (traditional, pro-independence lobbies) and "Whites" (pro-Serbian forces) as well as between diverse political factions. Such a conflict might not have been containable inside Montenegro and may have spread to Serbia itself. Some analysts calculated that Podgorica might have missed its chance for gaining statehood by failing to declare Montenegrin independence during the war over Kosova, when Belgrade was preoccupied on other fronts. This could have enabled the country to automatically gain NATO protection against Yugoslav military and Serbian paramilitary formations—protection that proved more difficult to secure in post-war conditions.

Montenegro's position in the FRY was further undercut by the Socialist-dominated federal assembly on 9 July 2000. According to the 1992 federal constitution, the election and the termination of the mandates of the Chamber of Republics (upper house) of the federal assembly were to be regulated by the laws of each republic. However, according to the July 2000 amendments, the FRY constitution henceforth mandated direct elections for the Chamber of Republics. Under the original constitution, 20 deputies each represented the Montenegrin and Serbian republican parliaments in the upper chamber. In effect, the introduction of direct elections further limited the influence of the Montenegrin legislature at the federal level.[7]

These constitutional measures were unacceptable to Podgorica, and the Djukanović government declared that Milošević had in effect staged a "constitutional coup" in the federation. It also announced that it would not participate in the federal assembly and presidential elections scheduled for 24 September 2000, elections that would simply serve to legitimize Milošević and further extinguish Montenegro's sovereignty.

Following the unexpected victory of Vojislav Koštunica in the FRY presidential elections, the Montenegrin authorities refused to recognize him as the President of Yugoslavia, as they considered the June constitutional changes had effectively terminated the federation. Nevertheless, in order to avoid a full-scale confrontation, the Djukanović administration offered to engage in negotiations with Belgrade in an effort to establish an alliance or confederation of two independent states. Podgorica was pressed by Western governments into some accommodation with the new administration in Belgrade. At the same time, it prepared to hold a national referendum on independence, which it felt confident of winning, as the majority of Montenegrin citizens favored either outright statehood or only a loose association with Serbia.

The Djukanović government clearly did not want to be drawn into Serbia's deep internal problems or to be submerged as a mere province of Serbia without any beneficial international recognition. Preservation of the FRY was perceived as a regressive step that could hinder Montenegro's domestic reforms and undercut its international standing. Podgorica declared that it would wait for the outcome of the Serbian republican elections in December 2000 in order to negotiate a new bilateral arrangement with Serbia that would recognize the existence of two independent states prepared to share certain prerogatives, such as defense and foreign policy, without an intermediate federal level of decisionmaking. If Belgrade proved unwilling to compromise, then Podgorica looked determined to hold a national referendum on statehood and Montenegro's complete detachment from Serbia.

The republican elections took place on 22 April 2001 and were narrowly won by the pro-independence bloc Victory for Montenegro, which gained 42.36% of the vote and 36 seats. The anti-statehood Montenegrin coalition, Together for Yugoslavia, captured 40.9% and 33 seats. However, the independence parties captured a majority in the legislature as the Liberal Alliance of Montenegro (LAM) obtained six seats, and the two Albanian parties, two seats. After several weeks of negotiations, a new government was formed at the beginning of July 2001. It consisted of a coalition between the Democratic Party of Socialists (DPS) and the Social Democratic Party (SDP), with the DPS's Filip Vujanović as prime minister. The government pledged to hold a referendum on independence by early 2002 as tensions persisted within the federal structure, between the two republican administrations and the Yugoslav authorities.

POLITICAL PARTIES

Socialists and Social Democrats

Democratic Party of Socialists (DPS)
Demokratska Partija Socijalista (DPS)

The Democratic Party of Socialists (DPS) was the direct successor of the League of Communists of Montenegro (LCM), which changed its name at the party congress in June 1991. It acquired the property and cadres of the LCM and easily won the December 1990 republican elections, obtaining 83 out of 125 seats in Montenegro's parliament. Its young leadership had been brought to the fore by Milošević during the "anti-bureaucratic" purge of potentially disloyal Montenegrin activists in January 1989. These new leaders were denounced by both the reformist and the pro-independence opposition as stooges, careerists, and opportunists. The DPS remained committed to preserving Yugoslavia, and its leader, Montenegrin President Momir Bulatović, consistently voted with Milošević in the federal presidency against a looser confederal arrangement in Yugoslavia proposed by Slovenia and Croatia during the early part of 1991.

The DPS's top leadership included Momir Bulatović, president of the party; Milo Djukanović, Montenegrin prime minister; Radoje Kontić, the federal prime minister; and Svetozar Marković, the party's general secretary. When Yugoslavia began to disintegrate, the DPS staged a much-criticized referendum in March 1992 on Montenegro's continuing federation with Serbia. Sixty-three percent of the electorate reportedly voted in favor of this option, although little time was allowed for a public debate on the issue. The DPS participated in drafting the new federal constitution, which was rushed through in April 1992 and resulted in the proclamation of the Federal Republic of Yugoslavia (FRY). Montenegrin opposition parties boycotted the proceedings in protest. In May 1992, the DPS and the Serbian Radical Party between them elected all the deputies to the 20-member Montenegrin section of the federal assembly's Chamber of Republics and the federal Chamber of Citizens.

During the fall of 1992, a rift appeared between Bulatović and Milošević. The Montenegrin leader sided strongly with Yugoslav Prime Minister Milan Panić in his dispute with Milošević over ending the war in Bosnia-Herzegovina. DPS deputies cast their ballots against the votes of no confidence in Panić sponsored by the Serbian Radicals and Socialists in the federal assembly.

The DPS dominated Montenegrin politics throughout the 1990s and monopolized all public institutions. In the December 1992 election, it gained 46 out of 85 seats to the Montenegrin Assembly, with almost 44% of the vote. It also garnered 17 out of 138 seats to the federal Chamber of Citizens in the December 1992 federal ballot, and 15 out of 20 seats to the Montenegrin section in the federal Chamber of Republics. Bulatović was reelected as Montenegro's President in a second-round run-off with the Serbian Radical candidate Branko Kostić. The pro-independence opposition forces, including the Liberals, supported Bulatović in the second round, considering his candidacy preferable to the militant pro-Milošević position of Kostić.

With the failure of Panić to be elected as Serbian President and the weakening position of Dobrica Ćosić in the federal presidency, Bulatović appeared to fall into disfavor with Milošević. After the elections, the DPS initiated the formation of a broad-based coalition government in Montenegro and appeared to move closer to a pro-sovereignty option for the republic. Opposition leaders remained undecided whether Bulatović had genuinely converted into a Montenegrist or was trying to protect himself domestically against political pressure from Belgrade. Some even speculated that Bulatović continued to coordinate his policies closely with his mentor Milošević and was simply trying to defuse or absorb the appeal and impact of Montenegro's pro-sovereignty opposition.[8]

After the December 1992 elections, the DPS itself appeared to be increasingly divided between federalist and pro-sovereignty factions. Its parliamentary delegates and middle echelons seemed to be moving closer to the Social Democrats and Liberals. The DPS leadership expressed concern over the growing influence of the Radicals in Serbian politics and feared that the relationship between Serbia and Montenegro could be further unbalanced to the disadvantage of the latter. This became evident when only Serbian Socialists and Radicals were nominated to the Serbian section of the Chamber of Republics, and their vote, together with that of the two Radical deputies from Montenegro, unseated Ćosić from the Yugoslav presidency in June 1993.

DPS leaders also voiced fears about the radicalization of Montenegrin politics and remained apprehensive about the activities of the Radical Party and Serbian paramilitary units sponsored by ultranationalists in Serbia. Svetozar Marović, secretary of the DPS Main Board, gave indications that the party would use the Montenegrin constitution to protect its republican status vis-à-vis potential Serbian domination. However, if it proved impossible to defend Montenegro's equal status through constitutional means, then the DPS appeared willing to conduct a new referendum on the republic's future.

In the FRY elections in November 1996, the party obtained 20 of the 30 Montenegrin seats in the federal Chamber of Citizens and maintained an absolute majority at the republican level, with 45 seats. Throughout this period, the party stressed the importance of maintaining close ties with Belgrade. However, as the Yugoslav economy continued to contract and the country became isolated and was sanctioned by most of the international community, the DPS looked increasingly disunited and fractious by the spring of 1997. Two major fractions crystallized: one centered around Prime Minister Milo

Djukanović, which endeavored to end Montenegro's international isolation, and a second grouping led by President Momir Bulatović, which displayed its continuing loyalty to Belgrade. In July 1997, the party split into two factions when Milica Pejanović Djuršić replaced Bulatović as the party's president and called for more autonomous Montenegrin foreign and domestic policies.[9] Bulatović declared his ouster to be illegitimate and claimed that he was still the party leader. However, he proved unable to call a party congress, as he had lost control over key positions and personnel in the DPS. Prime Minister Djukanović had captured the loyalty of the security services and the party finances while controlling all important state institutions.

On 6 August 1997, Bulatović summoned together a rump congress, and those who attended the proceedings formed a new party, the DPS-Momir Bulatović. In the Montenegrin presidential elections in October 1997, Djukanović stood against his former leader Bulatović and narrowly won the ballot in the second round of voting. Bulatović accused his rival of fraud and organized demonstrations on 14–15 January 1998 prior to Djukanović's inauguration. Although some violence broke out, the protests failed to ignite any mass opposition to the Djukanović presidency. The Djukanović faction of the DPS claimed it was the legal successor of the original DPS, and the Montenegrin High Court upheld this position. The Bulatović faction subsequently was renamed the Socialist People's Party (SPP), on 21 March 1998.

The DPS formed the For a Better Life *(Da Živimo Bolje)* coalition, together with the Social Democratic Party (SDP) and the People's Party of Montenegro (PPM), and won the Montenegrin extraordinary republican elections on 31 May 1998, with 49.5% of the vote. The coalition then proceeded to enact various measures to distance itself from the Serbian authorities and from Milošević's policies. In particular, it pursued close relations with Western countries, initiated certain economic reforms, and adopted an increasingly pro-independence position for Montenegro. Its public support remained stable in spite of its neutrality in the NATO-Serbian war over Kosova in 1999 and the difficult economic conditions in the republic.

Following the NATO intervention in March 1999, the Djukanović government was increasingly perceived in Western capitals as the staunchest opponent of the Milošević regime, and the government obtained political support and financial assistance from the West. Indeed, Podgorica provided shelter to several opposition leaders and independent journalists from Serbia who were fearful of assassination by Milošević's henchmen. Djukanović maintained the support of the overwhelming majority of party members and he adopted an increasingly pro-independence position as the crisis in Yugoslavia deepened. The DPS refused to participate in the September 2000 federal presidential and parliamentary elections and did not recognize the eventual victor, Vojislav Koštunica, as the legitimate president of Yugoslavia. Following the ouster of Milošević, President Djukanović inaugurated negotiations with Koštunica on a new equal political arrangement between the two republics while simultaneously preparing for a referendum on Montenegro's statehood and independence.

Socialist People's Party (SPP)
Socjalistička Narodna Partija (SNP)

As a pro-Milošević and pro-Yugoslav splinter of the ruling Democratic Party of Socialists (DPS), the Socialist People's Party (SPP) was established on 21 March 1998, following a split between the two erstwhile colleagues Bulatović and Djukanović.[10] With full support from Belgrade, Bulatović claimed that the SPP was the most popular party in Montenegro; and he was appointed as the Yugoslav federal prime minister on 20 May 1998. The DPS protested that this move was illegitimate because the federal assembly no longer reflected the legitimate political authorities in the Montenegrin republic. As a result, the Montenegrin administration refused to cooperate with all federal bodies, while Bulatović refused to resign from the premiership and continued to benefit from the support of the non-DPS federal deputies together with the Serbian Socialists and Radicals.

The SPP was essentially a Yugoslavist party loyal to Prime Minister Bulatović, strongly opposed to Montenegro's independence, and closely tied to the ruling circles in Serbia. It was financed directly by Belgrade and managed to capture most of the republic's pro-Serb votes. Its estimated support at the close of 1999 stood at around 30% of the electorate and included many pensioners and rural inhabitants. The party was particularly visible in the northern parts of the province that maintained a strong Serbian identity. It tried to forge an anti-Djukanović Montenegrin tribal alliance, the Council of People's Assemblies, but this initiative fizzled due to lack of public support.

Bulatović and his supporters claimed that the Djukanović government was corrupt and a stooge of the NATO countries aiming to break up the FRY. Observers believed that the SPP leadership itself was involved in various smuggling and sanctions-busting operations. Although there were persistent rumors of a split in the SPP, with a smaller faction favoring compromise with the DPS, Bulatović remained in control of the party structure. A more reformist wing based in Podgorica and led by Predrag Bulatović, the vice president of the SPP, became increasingly active during 2000 but it did not question the party's vehement anti-independence stance.

The SPP gained the majority of Montenegrin seats in the federal assembly following the September 2000 elections, especially given the nonparticipation of some 75% of Montenegrin voters. In late October, the party entered the federal government with Koštunica's Democratic Opposition of Serbia (DOS). SPP member Zoran Žižic was selected as the new Yugoslav prime minister. At the same time, the DPS refused to enter into what it considered an illegitimate federal institution.

Social Democratic Party (SDP)
Socijaldemokratska Partija (SDP)

The Social Democratic Party (SDP) was formed at a unification congress in June 1993 through a merger between the Social Democratic Party of Reformers (SDPR) *(Socijaldemokratska Partija Reformatora, SDPR)* and the Socialist Party of Montenegro (SPM) *(Socijalistička Partija Crne Gore, SPCG)*. The SDPR itself consisted of a coalition between the Coastal Reformers (CR) and the Independent Communists of Bar (ICB). The latter had changed its name to the Social Democratic Party of Montenegro (SDPM) in November 1992. These organizations held 12 seats in the Montenegrin Assembly following the December 1990 elections and were particularly active at the local level in opposition to the ruling Democratic Party of Socialists (DPS) and the radical pro-Serbian forces. The SDP became a strong advocate of a sovereign and independent Montenegrin state.

The Independent Communists of Bar (the major Montenegrin port on the Adriatic Sea) openly opposed the Milošević coup in 1988 and established their own separate organization in May 1990, which won the December 1990 local elections in Bar municipality *(opština)*. Its president Mico Orlandić was also elected deputy to the republican assembly. The SDPR and the ICB boycotted the national referendum in March 1992 and the federal elections of May 1992 because they opposed the centralism and radicalization of Serbian policy. However, the SPM did participate in the ballot and garnered five seats in the federal parliament.

As Yugoslavia disintegrated, the various reformist forces moved closer to the "Montenegrin option," although they initially criticized the Liberals for placing too much stress on national questions above social and economic programs. Because all the SDPR components welcomed members from other nationalities, they were condemned by Serbian nationalists as anti-Serb traitors. In the December 1992 republican elections, the SDPR alliance gained four seats in the Montenegrin Assembly but did not compete for the federal ballot. The party's relatively poor performance was probably due to its unclear stance on the national question and its focus on social and economic reforms. Under prevailing conditions, in which nationalism had become a burning issue, such positions did not elicit wide popular resonance.

After the ballot, SDPR president Žarko Rakčević declared that the ruling DPS was undertaking some positive steps away from Milošević's "Greater Serbia" program. However, he remained skeptical whether Bulatović's moves to form a coalition government were merely a tactical ploy. The SDPR itself appeared to adopt a more forthright pro-sovereignty position, claiming that about 75% of the population under "normal circumstances"—in other words, without fear of Serbian military intervention—would favor some model of Montenegrin independence. SDPR leaders also underscored that the Montenegrin political opposition, including the Liberals and Social Democrats, would fully cooperate with the international community in bringing to trial known war criminals operating in the republic who had engaged in atrocities against civilians in Bosnia-Herzegovina.

The first SDP president was Ilija Vujošević, who was replaced by Rakčević in late 1993. Rakčević remained the party's president for the rest of the decade. The SDP performed poorly in the November 1996 Montenegrin elections, when it failed to gain any seats, and it captured only one seat to the Civic Chamber in the November 1996 federal ballot. The SDP was the most pro-Western and pro-reform member of the ruling coalition after the May 1998 Montenegrin elections. Although it won only five seats following the ballot, the party suddenly found itself indispensable in forging a governing coalition after the split in the DPS.

Party leaders helped steer the Djukanović government toward an increasingly pro-independence position through such notable figures as deputy Prime Minister Dragiša Burzan. On several occasions, the SDP president Rakčević threatened that the party would pull out of the government if the DPS did not initiate a referendum on Montenegro's independence. It also criticized the authorities for moving too slowly on privatization and structural economic reform. Its support base was mostly among young people and the republic's middle-class voters. The party gained observer status at the Socialist International in 1996.

Socialist Party of Montenegro (SPM)
Socijalistička Partija Crne Gore (SPCG)

The Socialist Party of Montenegro (SPM) was founded in July 1990; its members were formerly active in the Alliance of Socialist Youth but grew increasingly restless after the "anti-bureaucratic revolution" in early 1989. SPM president Srdjan Darmanović criticized President Bulatović and the Democratic Party of Socialists (DPS) leadership for their opportunism and neglect of Montenegrin interests. The party sought a sovereign and independent Montenegro and differed with the Liberals on methods rather than objectives, contending that the Liberal Alliance of Montenegro (LAM) engaged in too much demagogic rhetoric and neglected to address vital socio-economic questions.

The Socialists gained three seats after the December 1990 republican elections but boycotted the March 1992 referendum on federation with Serbia, demanding a new plebiscite and a prolonged period of open debate. SPM leaders understood Podgorica's difficult strategic position, in that any declaration of independence could provoke violent Serbian retribution. As a result, they urged a more pragmatic approach than the Liberals through the building of a broad pro-Montenegrin front in preparation for a more opportune occasion when Milošević was not in a position to intervene violently. The Socialists failed to gain seats in the December 1992 elections to the Montenegrin Assembly for the same reasons that explain the Social Democratic Party of Reformers (SDPR). However, the SPM did manage to elect five deputies to the federal assembly's Chamber of Citizens.

Unlike the other members of the "Montenegrin bloc," the SPM urged close cooperation with the "national democratic bloc" in Serbia, including the Democratic Movement of Serbia (DEPOS),[11] as well as the Civic Alliance. It calculated that support for Montenegrin statehood and independence was still not fully developed, as sentiments for the old Yugoslavia continued to predominate among broad sectors of the population. The SPM merged with the SDPR to form the Social Democratic Party (SDP) in a unification congress in June 1993. As the rifts between Serbia and Montenegro widened during the mid to late 1990s, the former Socialist activists became increasingly outspoken on behalf of Montenegrin independence.

Liberals

Democratic Party (DP)
Demokratska Stranka (DS)

Established in December 1989 as an opposition party to the declining League of Communists of Montenegro (LCM), the Democratic Party (DP) elected Slobodan Vujošević as president. The DP was granted observer status in the Montenegrin National Assembly, an ostensible first step toward the recognition of the party as a legal entity. In September 1990, due to irreconcilable conflicts among members concerning the issue of Montenegrin statehood, the DP split into two parties. The larger wing remained close to the Democratic Party in Serbia, with a strong pro-federalist and pro-Serbian stance. Meanwhile, the smaller offshoot took a more Montenegrist position on the issue of republican sovereignty. Neither wing performed well in the first republican elections, and the party disappeared from the political mainstream.[12]

Communists

Yugoslav United Left (YUL)
Jugoslovenska Ujedinjena Levica (JUL)

Yugoslav United Left (YUL) was founded on 23 July 1994 through the unification of 23 parties with leftist and pro-Yugoslav orientations. It was therefore regarded more as a political movement than a political party. YUL considered itself the mother party of all "left-wing and progressive forces that believe that the general interest always comes above private interest."[13] YUL could also be considered a successor of the former League of Communists–Movement for Yugoslavia (LC-MY) because it included a large portion of the LC-MY membership and inherited much of the party's property, including a building in New Belgrade, which was later destroyed during the NATO bombardment in 1999.

According to its political platform, the party welcomed communists, socialists, social democrats, and greens. In 1995, Ljubiša Ristić became the YUL president; he was a representative in the Civic Chamber of the federal parliament. Its secretary general was Zoran Todorović. The chair of the YUL directorate was Mirjana Marković, the high-profile wife of Slobodan Milošević. She was a professor of sociology at the faculty of natural sciences and mathematics at Belgrade University. Marković was considered to be the most influential YUL politician and the movement's ideological force.

The party was organized on the principle of territoriality, both in Serbia and Montenegro, with 4,600 local boards, 209 municipal boards, 36 district boards, and 5 city boards. The party claimed a membership of around 20,000 people. Membership in YUL was considered the best opportunity for personal enrichment or career promotion, and YUL's membership included some well-known Serbian intellectuals, governmental ministers, managers of companies, ambassadors, and media editors.

Up until the November 1996 elections, YUL had no seats in parliament. Nevertheless, it quickly grew into one of the most influential parties in Serbia, but with less influence in Montenegro. YUL never took part in parliamentary elections independently, but always in coalition with the Socialist Party of Serbia (SPS) and New Democracy (ND).[14] YUL participated in the 1996 federal parliamentary elections and in the 1997 parliamentary elections in Serbia—in both cases, in coalition with the SPS and New Democracy. But it was unable to gain any seats in the Montenegrin parliament in the May 1998 republican elections and possessed limited public support. YUL's program and rhetoric, as well as its political practice, were almost identical with those of the Socialists, primarily because of the personal and political symbiosis of the two party leaders.

League of Communists–Movement for Yugoslavia (LC-MY)
Savez Komunista–Pokret za Jugoslaviju (SK-PJ)

Led by Dragomir Drašković, the League of Communists–Movement for Yugoslavia (LC-MY) was regarded as the party of Yugoslav army generals and the hard-line faction of the former ruling communist party. Mirjana Marković, the wife of Yugoslav President Slobodan Milošević, was a prominent member of this party before she launched her own political creation, Yugoslav United Left (YUL), in July 1994.

In addition to YUL and the LC-MY, a New Communist Party of Yugoslavia (NCPY) also operated in the country, led by its president Branko Kitanović. None of these formations could garner any significant popular backing, and they virtually vanished as organized forces by the late 1990s.

Nationalists

Liberal Alliance of Montenegro (LAM)
Liberalni Savez Crne Gore (LSCG)

The strongest pro-independence organization in Montenegro, the LAM was established in the historical capital of Cetinje in January 1991. It sought to engage all political forces that believed in a sovereign Montenegro and the curtailment of central controls from Belgrade. Slavko Perović was elected executive president and Velimir Kudević president of the LAM. Perović was previously active in the League of Communists of Montenegro and in the Alliance of Reform Forces led by Yugoslavia's former Prime Minister Ante Marković, which scored poorly in the December 1990 republican elections.

During the early 1990s, the Liberals were vilified by the state-controlled media as agents in the pay of Croatia, the Vatican, and U.S. security services, intent on destroying the unity of the Serbian nation. Despite threats and police intimidation, the LAM managed to gather 13,000 members by mid-1992. These were mostly intellectuals, students, younger workers, and members of the "Old Montenegrin" families in the coastal and central regions of the country, the pro-independence heartland. The Liberals organized several rallies in March 1992 against the rushed referendum on Montenegro's membership in the Federal Republic of Yugoslavia, and backed a substantial boycott of the ballot. They demanded a new plebiscite, preceded by a proper debate in the media concerning the content and consequences of federalism. Its leaders maintained that they did not exclude belonging to a federation of equal republics but were opposed to Belgrade's centralism and the "ethnic assimilation" of Montenegro by Serbs.

The LAM protested against the activities of paramilitary, ultranationalist Serbian formations on Montenegrin territory and the tolerance exhibited toward them by the Podgorica government of President Bulatović. It claimed that Montenegro was a multiethnic and multireligious state in which Montenegrin and Serb Orthodox, Croat Catholics, and Slav and Albanian Muslims could coexist. LAM spokesmen pointed out that Serbian Radicals were intent on stirring conflicts with the minorities in order to depict Albanians and Muslims as separatists. Liberals contended that the minorities would only demand autonomy or secession from an integral Serb-dominated state and not from an independent Montenegro. The Liberals adopted an anti-war position as Serb forces sought to detach territories in the newly independent states of Croatia and Bosnia-Herzegovina between 1991 and 1995.

In order to strengthen Montenegrin identity, Perović suggested the reinstatement of the Montenegrin Autocephalous Orthodox Church and even a referendum on the establishment of a constitutional monarchy under the exiled Prince Nikola Petrović Njegoš. Although the Alliance tried to avoid being provoked by radical Serb forces that occasionally disrupted its election campaigns, Liberal leaders also contended that they could not remain passive if Montenegrin integrity was further undermined.

The LAM became the staunchest supporter of independence for Montenegro. It boycotted the federal elections of May 1992 and December 1992, asserting that participation would simply give credence to the illegitimate federal structure. Instead, they demanded a public referendum on the question of sovereignty, calculating that in a free ballot more than 70% of the population would vote for independence. The LAM stood in the republican elections of December 1992 and was allowed some access to the media, enabling it to mount a proper election campaign. It gained 13 seats in the 85-member Montenegrin Assembly, and a Liberal deputy, Djemal Perović, was nominated as one of the Assembly's three vice presidents. Party leaders claimed that their support would have been much greater if the Yugoslav media had not painted them as armed radicals and if they had benefited from more funding and media exposure.

The LAM entered the coalition government in April 1993 led by the Democratic Party of Socialists (DPS), calculating that President Bulatović was adopting a more pronounced Montenegrinist position after supporting the failed candidacy of Milan Panić against Milošević. It obtained the ministries of environment and urban development but simultaneously reserved the right to withdraw from the government. Liberal leaders claimed that public respect for the LAM increased, as it was seen as a responsible political force concerned with avoiding violent confrontations. In particular, the Liberals reported making inroads in gaining popular support in the northern regions of Montenegro, which were traditionally more Serbia-oriented. Following the crackdown on the Serbian opposition in Belgrade, the LAM, together with the Social Democratic Party of Reformers (SDPR), the Socialist Party of Montenegro (SPM), and the civil resistance movement Public Against Fascism, organized a rally in Cetinje in June 1993 under the slogan "Democratic Montenegro for a Democratic Serbia."[15]

During the November republican 1996 balloting, the party established an alliance with the People's Party of Montenegro and secured 19 seats. Besides supporting an independent Montenegrin state, the LAM promoted the international recognition of Montenegro and its integration into the international community. The Liberals accused the ruling party in Podgorica of working closely with Milošević to establish a new federation of Serbian states from the ruins of Yugoslavia. Following internal conflicts in the LAM, Perović was replaced by Miodrag Živković as president. Perović was accused of authoritarian tendencies and of purging dozens of leading LAM activists because of various policy and personal disagreements.

Increasing support for independence within the DPS coalition pushed the Liberals into the background, and the LAM gained only 5 seats in the May 1998 republican elections and 6.29% of the popular vote. The LAM claimed its election performance was disappointing because the For a Better Life coalition had appropriated many of its policies. It subsequently refused to be part of the governing coalition, considering Djukanović a crypto-communist imposter rather than a genuine supporter of Montenegrin statehood.

The LAM consistently pressed for a referendum on Montenegro's statehood, feeling confident that the majority of voters would support independence. It sought to revive the Montenegrin Orthodox Church and based its support primarily in the heart of "Old Montenegro" with its capital in Cetinje.

The Liberal leadership distanced itself from the Djukanović coalition government, claiming that the government was usurping the independence question while maintaining a criminalized and essentially communist regime. It subsequently remained in opposition, hoping to pull the Social Democrats out of the coalition government. It continued to claim a growing support base throughout the republic.

People's Party of Montenegro (PPM)
Narodna Stranka Crne Gore (NSCG)

The People's Party of Montenegro (PPM) started out in 1990 as a vehemently pan-Serbian nationalist party that strongly advocated the maintenance of Montenegro's ties with Serbia. It won 13 out of 125 seats to the Montenegrin National Assembly in the December 1990 elections, and its leaders benefited from easy access to the media, in which they advanced Belgrade's political line. In April 1991, the PPM called upon the republican authorities to arm the citizens of Montenegro in the event of a Yugoslav civil war. The statement warned of Croatian, Sandžak Muslim, and Albanian claims to Montenegrin territory and demanded armed preparations to defend the Montenegrin-Serb people. The party was reported to have organized its own paramilitary units with several hundred men under arms. In November 1991, People's Party leaders criticized President Bulatović for accepting Lord Carrington's confederal proposal for Yugoslavia, which defined Montenegro as a nominally sovereign state. PPM deputies were among the 42 legislators who boycotted the National Assembly vote to uphold the government's decision.

Headed by Novak Kilibarda, a university professor, the People's Party began its life as a movement strongly favoring unification between Montenegro and Serbia and supportive of Serbian nationalism. The PPM declared that if the Yugoslav federal structure fell apart, Montenegro should join Serbia to form a separate, integral state. It viewed the territories of Montenegro and Serbia as being populated by one essentially Serbian people, as evidenced by religious, ethnic, and linguistic affinities, and it thereby advocated the "spiritual unification and moral renaissance of Serbianism."

The PPM initially supported Milošević's ambitions in Croatia and Bosnia-Herzegovina and backed the March 1992 Montenegrin referendum on federation with Serbia in the Federal Republic of Yugoslavia. However, the party did not fully condone the new federal constitution, and it boycotted the May 1992 federal elections. During the course of 1992, the People's Party evidently moderated its position in a fashion parallel to that of the Serbian Renewal Movement and the DEPOS coalition in Serbia, with which it maintained close ties. It distanced itself from the ultranationalist Serbian parties and paramilitary formations engaged in war crimes in Bosnia, criticized Milošević and the DPS for being undemocratic, and tried to appeal to more moderate Serb voters, to Orthodox believers, and to monarchists in Montenegro. The

Montenegrin opposition suspected that Kilibarda realized that Milošević's days could be numbered and that Montenegro could attain statehood; hence, to avoid marginalization or charges of supporting war criminals, he purposely distanced himself from his prior militant stance.

In the run-up to the December 1992 elections, the PPM claimed that it was defending Montenegrin interests in an equal federation with Serbia. It also criticized Montenegro's Albanian and Muslim minorities for allegedly seeking to separate from the republic. Kilibarda asserted that the party had successfully cleansed itself of "communist and fascist elements" that wanted to provoke conflicts in Montenegro. He even claimed that if the majority of Montenegrin citizens voted in a referendum for an independent state, the party would accept their decision. In the December 1992 elections, the People's Party, with 13% of the vote, gained 14 seats in the Montenegrin Assembly, 4 seats in the federal Chamber of Citizens, and 3 seats in the federal Chamber of Republics.

During the mid to late 1990s, the PPM began to adopt a more reformist position and stopped opposing the possibility of Montenegrin independence. Kilibarda purged the more Serbia-oriented nationalists from the party and accepted new cadres into the organization. The PPM even forged a political deal with the Liberal Alliance in an effort to create an unprecedented White-Green coalition, agreeing to postpone the question of Montenegrin independence until a proper national referendum could be organized. It also criticized the monopolistic position of the Democratic Party of Socialists (DPS) and was staunchly anti-communist in its rhetoric. In the November 1996 elections, the party won 8 seats in the federal lower house, while the National Unity alliance of the PPM and the Liberal Alliance gained 19 seats in the Montenegrin Assembly.

The party joined the For a Better Life coalition in the May 1998 general elections and gained seven parliamentary seats and representation in the new government. Party leaders sought a new identity for the organization, as it had lost most of its Serbian support base. The power struggle between moderates and Serbian nationalists again intensified, and although Kilibarda initially won the dispute, the PPM fractured, with the radical Serbian faction forming the Serbian People's Party (SPP) and the PPM's support base correspondingly diminished. Kilibarda adopted a strong anti-Milošević position and even favored Montenegrin independence in some of his pronouncements.

After prolonged internal conflicts, Kilibarda was forced to resign from the PPM leadership in February 2000 and was replaced by Dragan Šoć, the Minister of Justice in Montenegro's coalition government. The PPM aimed to attract a broader following among moderate Serb voters dissatisfied with the support of the opposition SPP for the Milošević regime. However, the new leaders did not favor Montenegro's statehood, and it was unclear whether they would ultimately support a referendum on independence.

Serbian Nationalists

Serbian Radical Party (SRP)
Srpska Radikalna Stranka (SRS)

This extremist nationalist party was established during 1991 with close links to the Serbian Radical Party (SRP) in Serbia headed by Vojislav Šešelj. The Radicals also created a paramilitary wing, based in Montenegro, that supplied weapons and manpower to Serb forces involved in the war in Bosnia-Herzegovina. When the People's Party moderated its stance, the SRP assumed the mantle of the most vehement pro-Serbian formation. Under the direction of self-proclaimed Četnik Major Deko Dačević, SRP paramilitaries were allegedly behind the armed provocations and attacks on Muslims in Pljevlja and other cities in the Montenegrin Sandžak during the summer and fall of 1992.

The Radicals obtained 8 seats in the Montenegrin Assembly during the December 1992 elections, as well as three seats in the federal Chamber of Republics. Together with the Serbia-based SRP, they gained a total of 34 seats in the 138-seat federal Chamber of Citizens. In the Montenegrin presidential election, Radical candidate Branko Kostić lost in a runoff ballot to Momir Bulatović but managed to gain 36% of the popular vote. In the May 1998 republican elections, the Radicals gained only 1.18% of the vote and failed to win any parliamentary seats. However, they did manage to gain seats in several local governments, particularly in the northern parts of the country.

Both the Democratic Party of Socialists (DPS) and the pro-independence opposition believed that the SRP was financed and employed by Milošević to destabilize Montenegro and undermine the new government. For example, the SRP organized rallies against the government's evident neglect of environmental problems: in 1992, Montenegro had been declared an "ecological state" by the National Assembly. The SRP established a "Serbian Council of Zeta" in an area of Montenegro where Serb nationalists believed that an essentially Serbian state had been forged by tribal leaders in the eleventh century. It also proposed the creation of autonomous Serbian regions in Boka, Pljevlja, and Zeta; engaged in anti-Muslim attacks in the Sandžak area, and attempted to stimulate conflicts with the Muslim and Albanian minorities by depicting these groups as anti-Montenegrin and anti-Serbian separatists.

The Radicals were also intent on capitalizing on social disquiet over deteriorating economic conditions. There were indications that SRP leaders were in favor of a second "anti-bureaucratic" revolution to unseat the Bulatović and later the Djukanović administration. Similarly to the SRP in Serbia, the Radicals' long-term objective was the creation of a new pan-Serbian federation incorporating Serb-held territories in Croatia and Bosnia together with Serbia proper and Montenegro.[16] By the late 1990s, the Radicals largely disappeared from Montenegro's political scene, having failed to attract a sizeable number of votes or to win parliamentary seats. Under the Djukanović administration, the SRP's paramilitary gangs were barred from Montenegro and its leadership was closely monitored by Montenegrin security services.

People's Democratic Party (PDP)
Narodna Demokratska Stranka (NDS)

This party was created in late 1992 by militant pro-Serb elements in the People's Party of Montenegro (PPM). Eight PPM parliamentary deputies in the Montenegrin legislature, two-thirds of their total number of seats, defected to the People's Democratic Party (PDP) because of Kilibarda's support for federal president Dobrica Ćosić. PDP leaders established close contacts with the Serbian Radical Party (SRP), and to increase their numbers they endeavored to appeal to jobless people and other disaffected elements of society. A similarly militant party, the Serbian People's Party (SPP) *(Srpska Narodna Stranka, SNS)*, led by Želidrag Nikčević, stood in the May 1998 elections but gained only 1.92% of the vote and no parliamentary seats. However, it did manage to place some of its representatives in several municipal assemblies. In sum, none of the ultranationalist Serbian parties benefited from any significant popular support in Montenegro, especially because, unlike in Serbia, they were not officially or clandestinely sponsored by the government and its security services.

Serbian Democratic Party of Montenegro (SDPM)
Srpska Demokratska Stranka Crne Gore (SDSCG)

This pro-Serb party was created in January 1992 as a branch of the Serbian Democratic Party in Bosnia-Herzegovina, the separatist party led by Radovan Karadžić, whose family origins were in Montenegro. Its initiative committee stressed that the formation of a Montenegrin branch would "influence the creation and strengthening of the new Yugoslavia that has been created by the two Serbian states, Montenegro and Serbia." The Serbian Democratic Party of Montenegro (SDPM) did not delineate between Serbs residing in Serbia proper and Serbs living in neighboring republics, and explicitly supported the coalescing of all Serbs in one state. Moreover, the party did not recognize either Muslims or Montenegrins as separate nations or distinct ethnic groups.[17]

Movement for Montenegro's Autonomous Accession to Serbia (MMAAS)
Pokret za Autonomni Pristup Crne Gore u Srbiju (PAPCGS)

Established in May 1990, this Belgrade-based organization declared in its founding act that its chief purpose was to make Montenegro an autonomous province of Serbia. The Movement for Montenegro's Autonomous Accession to Serbia (MMAAS) did not consider itself engaged in a struggle for political power; rather, it depicted itself as a broad political movement open to all Montenegrin and Serbian citizens. It also proposed that a public referendum be held in Montenegro concerning the republic's autonomous status. A number of similar organizations were established during the 1990s to uphold a close Serb-Montenegrin relationship in the event of a Yugoslav breakup, including the Serbian-Montenegrin Unification Movement (SMUM).[18]

Ethnic Minority and Religious Parties

Democratic Alliance of Montenegro (DAM)
Demokratski Savez Crne Gore (DSCG)

Mehmet Bardhi became the president and Ljeka Ljuljudjuray the vice-president of this Albanian-based political organization founded during 1990. It was based in the southern town of Ulcinj, where 80% of the population was ethnic Albanian. By mid-1992, the Democratic Alliance of Montenegro (DAM) claimed about 3,000 members, with branches in all major Albanian communities, including Bar, Tuzi, and Ostrog. Following the December 1990 elections, the minority alliance, the Democratic Coalition (DC), which included the DAM and the Muslim Party of Democratic Action (PDA), gained 13 seats in the Montenegrin National Assembly. The DAM performed well in local elections in Albanian-inhabited districts; for example, in Ulcinj it elected 35 out of 40 local councilors.

The Alliance initially favored a Yugoslavia consisting of equal federal units and opposed a truncated and recentralized Yugoslavia comprising only Serbia and Montenegro. Moreover, the DAM platform stated that Montenegrin Albanians had the right to decide on the future of Montenegro and its relationship with Serbia. With the disintegration of the six-republic federation, Albanian and Muslim leaders grew concerned over both the status of Montenegro and the position of non-Serb minorities. The DAM boycotted the March 1992 referendum on Montenegro's membership in the newly formed Federal Republic of Yugoslavia (FRY) and, together with other opposition parties, abstained from the federal elections in May 1992.

In response to the overwhelming approval in the plebiscite for Montenegro's continued association with Yugoslavia, there were rumors about a possible Albanian referendum to decide on autonomy for Albanian majority districts. President Bardhi reiterated that his party regarded unification with Serbia as unfeasible, and he condemned Milošević's anti-minority policies. In September 1992, the DAM leadership demanded the establishment of a special status for the Albanian minority, guaranteeing it a large measure of local autonomy.

In their Memorandum on the Special Status of Albanians in Montenegro, the DAM claimed that the Albanian minority in Montenegro was being excluded from decisionmaking by the Bulatović administration. Meanwhile, the power of municipal authorities was undercut, in that they did not control the police, education, and cultural life. Albanian leaders asserted that police units, often brought in from outside the district, engaged in provocative acts against the minority through harassment and tight surveillance. Such policies visibly increased tensions in the minority areas and seemed designed both to foster Albanian resentment against the Montenegrin authorities and to raise Montenegrin suspicions about the growth of Albanian separatism.

DAM leaders contended that their relations with "real Montenegrins" remained cordial, and they maintained a certain level of cooperation with the Liberals, Social Democrats, and Socialists. By contrast, relations with the Democratic Party of Socialists (DPS) and the People's Party were strained, while the Serbian Radicals were rabidly anti-Albanian and intent on altering the demographic structure by pushing ethnic minorities out of their traditional areas of settlement. The DAM said it did not support the creation of a "Greater Albania" but favored an independent Montenegro as such an entity could evidently better protect Albanian minority rights. Nonetheless, the DAM joined the Coordinating Council of Albanian Political Parties (CCAPP) under the leadership of Kosova's Albanian leader Ibrahim Rugova to canvass for Albanian "national rights" throughout the former Yugoslavia.

The DAM objected to the election law for the December 1992 ballot because the system of proportional representation diminished the number of elected deputies. In addition, thousands of Albanians had reportedly left the republic during the previous year to escape military conscription, growing unemployment, and a potential Serbian crackdown. The DAM boycotted the federal elections and failed to win seats to the Montenegrin Assembly. Its coalition with the Muslim PDA broke down a few days before the ballot as the PDA withdrew from all the elections, while the 4% threshold for gaining seats proved debilitating. DAM leaders calculated that with only a few hundred more votes they would have obtained three parliamentary seats.

The Alliance performed better in the local elections, particularly in Ulcinj, where it held 19 of the 32 town council seats, and in the coastal city of Bar. Bardhi was elected mayor of Ulcinj. After the elections and the formation of a coalition government from which minorities were excluded, DAM leaders voiced concern about rising Montenegrin nationalism in addition to pressures from radical Serbs. Fears were expressed that a sovereign Montenegro might prove more restrictive of minority rights and cut the Albanian community off from Kosova. Nonetheless, given a choice between Montenegrin independence and Serbian domination, Albanian leaders clearly favored the former.

Some militant activists continued to harbor the goal of eventually separating Albanian-majority districts and unifying them with Albania, but they were in a minority in the republic.[19] Although the DAM claimed to represent all Albanians, it never reached this target, especially as many Albanians voted for the major political formations such as the DPS and the SDP. Albanian ethnics obtained five seats in the Montenegrin parliament after the May 1998 elections: one was captured by DAM and one by the Democratic Union of Albanians (DUA). Most Albanians evidently voted for the larger, multiethnic Montenegrin parties.

Democratic Union of Albanians (DUA)
Demokratska Unija Albanaca (DUA)

The Democratic Union of Albanians (DUA) was led by Fuad Nimani and Ferhat Dinosha, who obtained a seat in the republican assembly following the May 1998 general elections. The party itself gained a ministerial post in the Djukanović coalition government, when Luigj Juncaj became Minister for the Protection of Minorities, even though the DUA was not formally part of the ruling coalition. The Union maintained cordial relations with the Democratic Alliance of Montenegro and held similar positions in campaigning for the rights of Albanians. It complained that the Albanian population, which constituted 7% of the total in Montenegro, lacked proper representation in government, public institutions, and educational facilities. However, DUA leaders confirmed that they had obtained effective protection from the Montenegrin police against threatened attacks by Serbian paramilitaries. Both the major Albanian organizations strongly supported Montenegrin independence, as this would evidently undercut Serb nationalism, enable easier cross-border contacts with Albania and Kosova, and provide Albanians with more opportunities in the independent state.

Party of Democratic Action–Montenegro (PDA-M)
Stranka Demokratske Akcije–Crna Gora (SDA-CG)

Harun Hadžić became the leader of this largest Montenegrin Muslim party. It was principally a branch of the Party of Democratic Action (PDA) in the Serbian Sandžak and formerly of the PDA in Bosnia-Herzegovina. The Party of Democratic Action–Montenegro (PDA-M) sought to articulate the demands of the Muslim population, situated primarily in the northern regions of Montenegro. It became a member of the Democratic Coalition, with the Albanian Democratic Alliance of Montenegro (DAM), a coalition that gained 12 seats in the December 1990 republican elections. Following the outbreak of war in Bosnia-Herzegovina, the PDA came under increasing pressure on both sides of the Serb-Montenegrin border, from Serb paramilitaries and local police forces evidently instructed by Belgrade to curtail Muslim political life. Its leaders were also subjected to constant vilification in the state-controlled media and were accused of preparing for armed confrontation and a rebellion against the Yugoslav federation. The PDA denied these charges and continued to participate in the political system. However, the party boycotted the federal elections and the December 1992 Montenegrin referendum on joining the new Yugoslav Federation with Serbia, arguing that these were illegitimate acts orchestrated by Belgrade.

The PDA-M withdrew from the minority election coalition shortly before the ballot, on the grounds that repression against the Muslim population was increasing and participation may have legitimized the Yugoslav authorities. Indeed, during the previous year, attacks on Muslim shopkeepers and families were reported from the northern parts of the Montenegrin Sandžak, close to the Bosnian border. Serbian paramilitaries also kidnapped and presumably murdered Muslim passengers from a train en route from Belgrade to Bar at the end of 1992. The Montenegrin authorities made some attempts to pacify any potential escalation by sending in police units and restraining Serb militants. However, they were in no position to completely outlaw the irregular forces armed and sponsored by the Serbian government and the Yugoslav army.

Although the PDA officially boycotted the 1992 ballot, it did not discourage Muslims from casting their votes; indeed, some activists encouraged them to vote for the "Montenegrin bloc," either Liberals, Socialists, or Social Democrats.[20] After 1996, the party largely vanished from the political scene, having won only three legislative seats. It was increasingly compromised by internal scandals and accusations of sabotage and spying for the Milošević regime. In the May 1998 general elections, the Muslim population largely supported the Djukanović coalition and Muslim representatives gained seats in local elections in several Montenegrin Sandžak towns, including Plav, Rožaje, and Bijelo Polje.

Party of National Equality (PNE)
Stranka Narodne Jednakosti (SNJ)

A predominantly Muslim party based in the Sandžak, the Party of National Equality (PNE) came into conflict with the Party of Democratic Action (PDA) over the political representation of Montenegrin Muslims. It viewed the PDA, and its parent organization in Bosnia-Herzegovina, as too extremist and militant in seeking special rights for Yugoslav Muslims. A statement issued by the PNE in September 1990 denied that the PDA in Bosnia-Herzegovina had the right to speak on behalf of Montenegrin Muslims. On the other hand, PNE leaders underscored that the Muslims in Montenegro were dissatisfied with their status and resented being referred to as "an invented nation" by Serbian nationalists. The PNE was a member of the Democratic Coalition (DC), together with the Albanian DAM and the Montenegrin Muslim based PDA, during the December 1990 republican election. The coalition won 13 out of 125 seats in the Montenegrin National Assembly.

In February 1992, the party declared its opposition to a republican referendum concerning the future status of Montenegro, on the grounds that the wording did not adequately delineate between the establishment of a new federal Yugoslav state and a "Greater Serbia" or "Serboslavia." In a Serb-dominated state, the PNE believed, the position of the Muslims would inevitably deteriorate. The PNE participated in the minority coalition during the election campaign for the December 1992 ballot but did not formally take part in the elections, although its members and sympathizers were not discouraged from voting against the "Serbian bloc."[21] Through the late 1990s, the PNE did not garner any substantial public backing and it did not obtain representation in the republican legislature.

Boka Mariners' Association (BMA)
Bokaljska Mornarica (BM)

Tracing its origins to an organization founded in 1463, this Croatian association was based in the Boka Kotorska region of southwestern Montenegro. It endeavored to preserve the historical and cultural heritage of the republic's estimated 12,000 Catholics. Because of political pressure from the Montenegrin authorities at that time, and fear of persecution by the Yugoslav authorities after the outbreak of Serb-Croat hostilities, the Boka Mariners' Association (BMA) separated from its Zagreb branch during 1991.[22] The BMA remained a small grouping, especially as many Croats left Montenegro during the early 1990s, while others were fearful of open political activity under the Bulatović government. The condition of the remaining Croatian population improved after the installment of the Djukanović government, as Podgorica established good relations with the new democratic coalition in Zagreb following the death of Croatian President Franjo Tudjman. In the spring of 2000, President Djukanović formally apologized to the Croatian people for the destruction perpetrated by Montenegrin troops during the Yugoslav army attacks along the Dalmatian coast in the summer of 1991.

POLITICAL DATA

Name of State: Republic of Montenegro *(Republika Crna Gora)*
Form of Government: Democratic republic
Structure of Legislature: Unicameral assembly of Montenegro *(Skupština)*
Size of Territory: 5,333 square miles
Size of Population: 635,442 (July 1996 est.)

The Montenegrin republican structure consisted of a directly elected President and a directly elected single-chamber parliament, in which the number of seats decreased from 102 in the May 1998 elections to 77 in the April 2001 ballot.

Composition of Population (1991):

Ethnic Group	Number	% of Population
Montenegrins	380,484	61.84
Muslims	89,932	14.62
Serbs	57,176	9.29
Albanians	40,880	6.64
Yugoslavs	25,854	4.20
Croats	6,249	1.02
Macedonians	860	0.14
Slovenes	407	0.07
Others	13,425	2.18
Total minorities	234,783	38.16
Total population	615,267	100.00

Sources: CIA World Factbook 2000, http://www.odci.gov/cia/publications/factbook; Arthur Banks, Alan J. Day, and Thomas C. Muller, *Political Handbook of the World: 1997*, Binghamton: CSA Publications, 1997, pp. 953–954.

ELECTION RESULTS

Presidential Election, 5 and 19 October 1997

First Round, 5 October 1997

Turnout: 74.88%

Candidate	Votes	% of Vote
Momir Bulatović	147,615	48.20
Milo Djukanović	145,348	47.42
Novica Stanić	5,109	1.66
Acim Višnjić	4,635	1.51
Dragan Hajduković	1,988	.64
Novica Vojnović	785	.25
Milan Radulović	620	.20
Slobodan Vujačić	383	.12
Total	306,483	100.00

Second Round, 19 October 1997

Turnout: 73.07%

Candidate	Votes	% of Vote
Milo Djukanović	174,745	50.80
Momir Bulatović	169,257	49.20
Total	344,002	100.00

Source: Center for Free Elections and Democracy, Centar za slobodne izbore i demokratiju. http://www.cesid.org.yu.

Presidential Election, 20 December and 10 January 1992

First Round, 20 December 1992

Turnout: 68.94%

Candidate	Votes	% of Vote
Momir Bulatović	123,183	41.80
Branko Kostić	68,296	23.16
Slavko Perović	52,736	17.90
Novak Kilibarda	25,979	8.80
Dragan Hajduković	10,270	3.50
Slobodan Vujošević	1,770	.60
Veselin Kaludjerović	1,606	.54
Predrag Popović	1,419	.50
Veselin Kiro Radović	1,399	.50
Invalid	8,150	2.70
Total	294,808	100.00

Second Round, 10 January 1992

Turnout: 59.11%

Candidate	Votes	% of Vote
Momir Bulatović	158,722	62.58
Branko Kostić	92,045	36.29
Invalid	2,863	1.13
Total	253,630	100.00

Source: Center for Free Elections and Democracy, Centar za slobodne izbore i demokratiju. http://www.cesid.org.yu.

Montenegrin Parliamentary Elections, 22 April 2001

Turnout: n/a

Party/Coalition	Votes	% of Vote	Seats
Victory for Montenegro–Democratic Coalition Milo Djukanović	153,946	42.36	36
Together for Yugoslavia	148,513	40.90	33
Liberal Alliance of Montenegro	28,746	7.91	6
People's Socialist Party of Montenegro/Momir Bulatović	10,702	2.80	—
Serbian Radical Party/Vojislav Šešelj	4,275	1.18	—
Democratic Union of Albanians	4,232	1.17	1
Bosniak Muslim Coalition in Montenegro	4,046	1.11	—
Democratic Alliance of Montenegro/Mehmet Bardhi	3,570	1.00	1

Communist and Labor Party for Yugoslavia–Power to the Working Class	1,640	0.45	—
Osman Redza/Party of Democratic Prosperity	1,572	0.43	—
Foreign Currency Savers Party	639	0.20	—
Natural Law Party of Montenegro	512	0.14	—
LDP Voice for Montenegro	354	0.10	—
People's Unity Party/ Novak Kilibarda	268	0.10	—
Protection of Savings Accounts and Social Security Party	199	0.10	—
Yugoslav Left in Montenegro	190	0.05	—
Total	363,404	100.00	77

Sources: Center for Monitoring, Podgorica, Montenegro, Election 2001, http://www.cemi.cg.yu/NovostiUk.htm; Parlamentarni Izbori Republika Crna Gora 2001 (Parliamentary elections in the Republic of Montenegro 2001), http://www.izbori.cg.yu/liste/rezultati.htm.

Montenegrin Extraordinary Parliamentary Elections, 31 May 1998

Turnout: 76.04%

Party/Coalition	Votes	% of Vote	Seats
For a Better Life	170,080	49.5	42
Socialist People's Party	123,957	36.1	29
Liberal Alliance of Montenegro	21,612	6.3	29
Democratic Alliance of Montenegro	5,425	1.5	1
Democratic Union of Albanians	3,529	1.0	1
Others	18,747	5.6	—
Total	343,350	100.0	78

Sources: CNN Election Watch and the International Foundation for Electoral Systems (IFES); British Helsinki Human Rights Group-Montenegro, 1997–2001.

Montenegrin Parliamentary Elections, 3 November 1996

Turnout: 60.3%

Party/Coalition	Votes	% of Vote	Seats
Democratic Party of Socialists	150,237	51.2	45
Liberal Alliance/People's Party	74,963	25.6	19
Party of Democratic Action	10,167	3.5	3
Democratic Alliance of Montenegro	5,289	1.8	2
Democratic Union of Albanians	3,849	1.3	2
Others	8,698	16.6	—
Total	253,203	100.0	71

Source: Embassy of the Federal Republic of Yugoslavia. "Results of the Election Commission for the November 1996 Local Elections," p. 8.

Montenegrin Parliamentary Elections, 20 December 1992

Turnout: 56.7%

Party/Coalition	Votes	% of Vote	Seats
Democratic Party of Socialists	125,578	43.78	46
People's Party of Montenegro	37,532	13.08	14
Liberal Alliance of Montenegro	35,564	12.40	13
Serbian Radical Party	22,265	7.76	8
Social Democratic Party of Reformers	12,994	4.53	4
Total	233,933	82.00	85

Montenegrin Parliamentary Elections, 9 December 1990

Turnout: 75.5%

Party/Coalition	Votes	% of Vote	Seats
League of Communists of Montenegro	171,316	56.16	83
Reform Forces of Montenegro	41,346	13.56	17
People's Party of Montenegro	39,107	12.82	13
Democratic Coalition	30,760	10.08	12
Others	11,354	3.80	—
Total	293,883	96.42	125

Electoral data for the Federal Republic of Yugoslavia appear on pages 441–445.

NOTES

1. For recent background histories of Montenegro consult Ivo Banac, *The National Question in Yugoslavia: Origins, History, Politics*, Ithaca and London: Cornell University Press, 1992; Stephen Clissold (Ed.), *A Short History of Yugoslavia: From Early Times to 1966*, Cambridge: Cambridge University Press; Alex N. Dragnich, *The First Yugoslavia: Search for a Viable Political System*, Stanford: Stanford University Press, 1983; and Barbara Jelavich, *History of the Balkans*, 2 Volumes, Cambridge: Cambridge University Press, 1989.

2. Census figures can be found in *Stanovništvo SR Crne Gore Po Popisima Prema Nacionalnoj Pripadnosti*, Titograd (Podgorica), Republièki Zavod Za Statistiku, Broj 42, 25 June 1991.

3. For an election report, see the National Republican Institute, *1990 Elections in the Republic of Yugoslavia*, Washington, DC, 1991, pp. 26–34.

4. Milan Andrejevich, "The Elections in Montenegro," Radio Free Europe/Radio Liberty, Research Institute (RFE/RL), *Report on Eastern Europe*, Vol. 1, No. 51, 21 December 1990.

5. Dom Nike Ukguni, *Demand for the Defense of the Rights of Albanians in Montenegro*, paper presented by the Democratic Alliance of Montenegro to the Conference on Peace in Yugoslavia, Brussels, 17 May 1992.

6. See *Radio Belgrade Network*, 30 June 1993, in Federal Broadcast Information Service, *Daily Report: East Europe*, FBIS-EEU-93–125, 1 July 1993.

7. See Amendments to the Constitution of the Federal Republic of Yugoslavia; Constitutional Law of the Implementation of Amendments II to VIII to the Constitution of the Federal Republic of Yugoslavia, http://www.mfa.gov.yu.

8. For example check Željko Ivanović, "The Šešelj Enigma," *Monitor*, Podgorica, 11 June 1993, in *FBIS-EEU-93–115*, 17 June 1993.

9. For details see *Pobjeda*, Podgorica, 12 July 1997.

10. For a valuable summary of the DPS split, see the International Crisis Group, "Montenegro's Socialist People's Party: A Loyal Opposition?" *Balkans Report*, No. 92, 28 April 2000.

11. For more information on DEPOS and its constituent parties see the chapter on Serbia.

12. "To Power Legally," *Borba*, Belgrade, 18 December 1989, in *FBIS-EEU-90–008*, 11 January 1990; Milan Andrejevich, "Montenegro to Introduce Multiparty Elections," RFE/RL, *Report on Eastern Europe*, 23 February 1990; *Tanjug*, Belgrade, 12 September 1990, in *FBIS-EEU-90–178*, 13 September 1990.

13. "Yugoslav Left Expects to Enter Parliament," *FBIS-EEU*, 29 December 1995.

14. "Serbia: Political Aims of Milošević's Wife Detailed," *FBIS-EEU*, 29 January 1996.

15. Janusz Bugajski, "Is Montenegro Next?" *Post-Soviet Prospects*, No. 15, Center for Strategic and International Studies, Washington, DC, September 1992; M. Pavicević and S. Djukanović, "Fascism Must Be Stopped," *Pobjeda*, Podgorica, 9 June 1993, in *FBIS-EEU-93–114*, 16 June 1993.

16. *Vreme*, Belgrade, 24 August 1992, in Federal Broadcast Information Service/Joint Publications Research Service, *Daily Report, East Europe, JPRS-EER-92–127*, 10 September 1992; "Weekly Review," RFE/RL, *Research Report*, Vol. 1, No. 33, 21 August 1992.

17. *Tanjug*, Belgrade, 3 January 1992, in *FBIS-EEU-92–003*, 6 January 1992.

18. "A Third Serbian Province," *Borba*, Belgrade, 14 May 1990, in *FBIS-EEU-90–097*, 18 May 1990; *Tanjug*, Belgrade, 30 June 1990, in *FBIS-EEU-90–127*, 2 July 1990.

19. B. Milošević, "Announcement of Another Referendum of Albanians," *Politika*, Belgrade, 25 March 1992, in *FBIS-EEU-92–063*, 1 April 1992; Milan Andrejevich, "Montenegro Follows Its Own Course," RFE/RL, *Report on Eastern Europe*, Vol. 2, No. 47, 22 November 1991.

20. Z. Ivanović, "Conversation With the President and the Gentleman," *Borba*, Belgrade, 30 July 1992, in *JPRS-EER-92–109*, 18 August 1992; Velizor Brajović, "Montenegro: Pljevlja on a Powder Keg," *Vreme*, Belgrade, 24 August 1992, in *JPRS-EER-92–127*, 10 September 1992.

21. *Tanjug*, Belgrade, 11 September 1990, in *FBIS-EEU-90–178*, 13 September 1990; Milan Andrejevich, "Montenegro Follows Its Own Course," RFE/RL, *Report on Eastern Europe*, Vol. 2, No. 47, 22 November 1991; *Tanjug*, Belgrade, 21 February 1992, in *FBIS-EEU-92–036*, 24 February 1992.

22. "Croatian Minorities in Vojvodina, Italy, Montenegro, and Bosnia and Herzegovina," *Newsletter 9: Current Affairs*, Croatian Ministry of Foreign Affairs, Zagreb, 16 March 1993.

Bosnia-Herzegovina

HISTORICAL OVERVIEW

The territory of Bosnia-Herzegovina was once part of the Illyrian kingdom that stretched across the northwest Balkans. The Illyrians are believed to have settled in the area in about 1800 BC. Most of the region became part of the Roman province of Illyricum in the first century BC. A stretch along the Sava River in the North was assigned to the Roman province of Pannonia. Following the collapse of the Roman Empire during the fourth and fifth centuries AD, Gothic tribes conquered the northwestern and central Balkan territories. They were followed by Turkic Avars and by Slavic tribes, who gained control of the Pannonian area and gradually settled throughout the region.[1] The Avars were defeated by the Frankish king Charlemagne in 796 AD and the Slavic populations accepted overall Frankish suzerainty.

For the next four centuries, various Slavic princes ruled the mountainous Bosnian area. The Croatian kingdom from the late ninth century until the eleventh century controlled much of the Bosnian and Herzegovinian territories. At the end of the twelfth century, a powerful Serbian kingdom was founded under the rule of Stefan Nemanja; his descendant King Stefan Dušan controlled a region stretching from the Adriatic to the Aegean Sea by the middle of the fourteenth century, an area that included parts of eastern Bosnia and eastern Herzegovina. While much of the Croatian population accepted Roman Catholicism, the Serbs and local Vlachs converted to Orthodox Christianity. Thus the dividing line culminating in and deriving from the Christian schism passed through Bosnia-Herzegovina. Bosnian historians claim that most of the local population felt no particular allegiance to either Croatia or Serbia, as control over the territory was changeable and often nominal. Many inhabitants either belonged to an autonomous and schismatic Bosnian Church or to a heretical dualist sect known as the Bogomils.

During the twelfth century, Hungary conquered large parts of Bosnia and turned the region into one of its dominions as a *banat* (province), under the control of a *ban* (governor) of Bosnian, Croat, or Hungarian origin. However, Bosnia's rulers gained increasing independence from their Hungarian over-lords following the rule of Ban Kulin at the beginning of the thirteenth century. During the fourteenth century, Ban Stjepan Kotromanić extended Bosnia's territory to include the Orthodox province of Hum (or Zahumlje), later known as Herzegovina, and much of the Adriatic coast. Krotomanić's nephew and successor, Stjepan Tvrtko, further extended the boundaries of these territories, and in 1376 proclaimed himself King of Serbia and Bosnia.

The Bosnian kingdom began to disintegrate after the death of Tvrtko. A rebellious Bosnian chieftain seized the Hum region early in the fifteenth century and established it as Herzegovina ("independent duchy"). The Ottoman Turks invaded Bosnia in 1386, and by 1463 most of the region became a Turkish province following a series of battles. Herzegovina subsequently fell to the Turks in 1483. The two territories remained provinces of the Ottoman Empire for the next 400 years, although unsuccessful uprisings against the Turks occurred periodically during the nineteenth century. Bosnia remained an important outpost in Turkey's wars with Venice and Austria.

The population of the area included Roman Catholic Croats, Orthodox Serbs, and Bosnian Slavs who converted to Islam during Ottoman rule. The conversion process was gradual through the centuries, and the result of several factors: a lack of allegiance to either Catholicism or Orthodoxy, an absence of well-organized Christian churches, and the promise of improved political, social, and economic positions under Turkish rule. As a result, a local Muslim hereditary nobility developed together with a class of landowners. These new Muslims began to develop a strong sense of ethnic and regional identity, which produced tensions with their Catholic and Orthodox neighbors. Unrest among the various ethnic groups, coupled with the deterioration of the Ottoman Empire, led to a general economic decline and increasingly repressive rule. Both Christians and Muslims grew resentful of Constantinople's interference. At the same time, the relative independence of the Orthodox Church under Ottoman rule stimulated Serbian nationalism in the traditional Orthodox areas of eastern Herzegovina and in areas in northwest Bosnia that were more recently settled by Serbs.

In 1875, a large Christian uprising against the Muslim elite was put down by the Turks, but it provoked Great Power intervention, and the Ottomans were forced to surrender control over Bosnia. During the Congress of Berlin in 1878, following the Russo-Turkish war, the dual monarchy of Austria-Hungary negotiated with other European rulers for administrative rights over the area. In 1908, it annexed the two Bosnian provinces. Austro-Hungarian rule did little to quell tensions in the region, and Bosnia became a center of nationalist agitation for political independence and cultural autonomy. Europe began to take sides in the disputes: Austria-Hungary and Germany opposed growing Serbian nationalism, while Russia and Britain generally supported it. The evident weakness of Ottoman rule encouraged some Slavic activists within the Austro-

Hungarian Empire to press for union with kindred peoples elsewhere in the Balkans. Their "Yugoslav" movement for south Slav unification was countered by nationalist pan-Serbian and pan-Croatian groupings.

The Bosnian Muslim political emergence became more pronounced during the short period of Austrian rule between 1878 and 1918. Vienna encouraged a Bosnian national identity as a counterpoint to Serbian and Croatian irredentism and Yugoslavism, and it tolerated Islamic cultural activism to promote a separate ethno-religious identity. Such policies inadvertently stimulated religious differentiation that coincided with the development of ethnic identity at a time of rising nationalism throughout the Balkans. Croatian nationalists, such as Ante Starčević's Party of Rights, rejected a south Slav union and sought a Greater Croatia including all of Bosnia-Herzegovina. They considered all Bosnian Muslims to be Croats who had converted to Islam during Ottoman rule. Similarly, Serb nationalists demanded a Greater Serbia including Bosnia-Herzegovina and claimed the Muslims were converted Serbs. Both sides tried to absorb Bosnia's Muslims and to elicit their political and ethnic loyalty in order to gain a majority in the country.

In June 1914, the heir to the throne of Austria-Hungary, Archduke Francis Ferdinand, and his wife were assassinated in the Bosnian capital Sarajevo, an act that precipitated World War I. Gavrilo Princip, the assassin, was a Serbian student from Bosnia whose Young Bosnia movement believed that Vienna's policies would deny Serbia's territorial ambitions. Most of the Bosnian Muslim and Croatian population rejected Serb nationalist claims and sought to develop Bosnia-Herzegovina into an autonomous entity within the Habsburg monarchy.

During World War I, some Croats and Serbs fought together, hoping to create a kingdom that would unite all the south Slavic peoples, while others pursued an exclusively nationalist agenda. The Muslim population remained divided in its political allegiances. On 1 December 1918, following the defeat of Austria-Hungary at the close of the war, Bosnia-Herzegovina became part of the independent Kingdom of Serbs, Croats, and Slovenes, ruled by Serbian monarch Aleksandar I from 1921 to 1934. When political conflicts between Croats and Serbs exacerbated national tensions, Aleksandar tightened control over the country, and in 1929 he renamed the kingdom Yugoslavia ("land of the south Slavs"). Croat and Serb leaders clashed over the structure of the state, with the Croats favoring a looser federal state, and the Serbs, a more centralized system.

Once again, Bosnia's Muslims were caught in the middle of this struggle and were pressured to support either Croatian or Serbian separatism or the centralized monarchy. While Muslim leaders generally supported the centralist constitution, a growing number of activists claimed that Bosnian Muslims should be recognized as a distinct national group. However, Serbia's royal dictatorship denied the existence of separate nations in Yugoslavia and established new administrative districts *(banovinas)* that cut across ethnic and historical boundaries. Bosnia-Herzegovina was partitioned between four such *banovinas,* each with a Muslim minority, thus alienating the Muslim population from the monarchist state.

On 6 April 1941, the Axis powers invaded and dismembered Yugoslavia. Germany and Italy supported the formation of a fascist puppet state encompassing much of Croatia and Bosnia-Herzegovina, which was headed by ultra-nationalists in Croatia. The *Ustaše* leadership of the Independent State of Croatia sought to annex Bosnia and engaged in a policy of genocide against the Serbian population, while Serbian monarchists (*Četniks*) slaughtered Muslims because of their alleged collaboration with Zagreb and their supposed "Turkish" identity. Although some Muslims engaged in anti-Serbian massacres, a significant number of Bosnians in all three ethnic groups favored the multi-ethnic communist partisan forces led by Marshal Josip Broz Tito.

Tito's units fought against the Croatian fascist puppet state and the Serbian monarchists. At the end of the war, Tito restitched the various parts of Yugoslavia into a Yugoslav federation, with Bosnia-Herzegovina as one of its constituent republics. This was accomplished despite insistence by Serb activists that the region be transformed into a province of Serbia and despite Croatian demands for closer links with Bosnia. The republic was a multi-ethnic unit, precluding domination by any of the three constituent groups. Federation was supported by Muslim leaders as a means of preserving their national and religious identity and gaining benefits from the Yugoslav system. During the 1960s, Tito's regime granted Bosnia's Muslims a distinct ethnic status, in a policy designed to place them on an equal footing with Serbs and Croats. They received their own power base in an increasingly decentralized or "republicanized" communist structure.

One of Tito's objectives was to prevent either Serbia or Croatia from dominating the federation and reviving claims to Bosnian territory; hence, the political and economic infrastructure of the republic was substantially expanded. Tito sought to balance Yugoslavia's national units and promote the growth of an overarching "Yugoslav" identity as well as a multi-ethnic Bosniak consciousness within Bosnia-Herzegovina. He also endeavored to strengthen Muslim identity to counteract Serb and Croat ambitions, and helped forge a distinct Muslim political base in the republic.

In the 1961 census, the communist authorities allowed citizens to register for the first time as "Muslims in the ethnic sense" rather than "Muslims ethnically undeclared." In the 1971 census, Slavic Muslims were finally elevated to the status of a distinct nation (and not only in Bosnia), equal to that of Serbs, Croats, Slovenes, Montenegrins, and Macedonians. Further constitutional reforms strengthened the *de facto* autonomy of each republic. During the 1970s, the government adopted a more tolerant approach toward organized religion, including Islam, and Bosnia's Muslims experienced a cultural, educational, and religious revival. Many Muslim leaders concluded that like the other Yugoslav republics, Bosnia-Herzegovina should be defined as their national territory. This sparked opposition among Serbian and Croatian leaders, who feared that they would become minorities in the republic.

Yugoslavia's federal arrangement thwarted the potential chauvinism of the two largest nations, the Serbs and Croats, and provided a modicum of protection for the smaller nations: Muslims, Macedonians, Montenegrins, and Slovenes. While it did not offer them statehood or internal democracy, the system guaranteed their territorial integrity, defense against Serbian centralism and Croatian annexation, and a sustained period of economic development through industrialization, urbanization, and the provision of a large slice of the state budget.

In this federal arrangement, Bosnia-Herzegovina became the only republic without a predominant nation, as all three groups (Muslims, Serbs, and Croats) were considered equal political and constitutional entities, even though Croats and Serbs had their own "home" republics. The 1974 constitution underscored the equality of Bosnia's "constituent nations," an arrangement designed not only to prevent the dominance of one ethnic group but to avoid any compacts between two nations that would "minoritize" the third. Muslims were formally defined as a nation; thousands of people who had previously declared themselves Serbs, Croats, or Yugoslavs assumed this definition in the new censuses.

Under the 1974 federal constitution, and particularly following Tito's death in 1980, political power continued to devolve to the six republics in order to ensure that none of the federal units would become dominant. Nonetheless, widespread mistrust, accompanied by a resurgence of nationalist and separatist sentiments, crept to the political foreground. This trend was further heightened by Yugoslavia's poor economic performance during the 1980s and what was increasingly perceived as the unequal distribution of economic resources among the republics. Croatian and Slovenian authorities complained that their republics were subsidizing the poorer southern regions, without receiving any commensurate material benefits.

Communist controls were decentralized to the republics, and various economic reforms were instituted without eliminating one-party rule. In the late 1970s, Belgrade expressed fears about a potential Islamic resurgence in Bosnia. Hence, periodic crackdowns were undertaken against political dissenters who favored either Islamic or democratic rule. Muslim leaders dismissed charges of a fundamentalist resurgence and calculated that Belgrade was concerned over closer Muslim-Croatian cooperation following the rise of Croatian nationalism earlier in the decade.

Bosnia-Herzegovina was in a unique position among the former Yugoslav republics, in that no single nation or nationality formed an absolute majority of the population.[2] By the late 1980s, Bosnia's ethnic balance was compounded by a complex territorial mix among the three major communities. In the 99 municipalities outside the capital Sarajevo, Muslims formed absolute majorities in only 32, and few of these were territorially contiguous: the biggest concentrations were in northwestern, eastern, and central Bosnia. Serbs constituted absolute majorities in 30 municipalities, most of these in western, northeastern, and southeastern Bosnia. Croats formed absolute majorities in only 14 municipalities, the majority in the western Herzegovina region. In 23 municipalities, no ethnic group possessed a clear majority; and even in districts where one ethnic group predominated, there were large minorities of one of the other two nationalities.

Yugoslavia's complex system of presidential and governmental succession did not allow for effective central rule while the republican administrations sought an accelerating devolution of powers. During the 1980s, following Tito's death, the disintegration of the ruling League of Communists of Yugoslavia and growing national and ethnic polarization aggravated the position of Bosnia-Herzegovina as the central contested region between Serbia and Croatia. Economic difficulties also fueled inter-republican competition for scarce funds and resources and increased social and ethnic tensions throughout the federation.

POST-COMMUNIST DEVELOPMENTS

Political and economic liberalization in Yugoslavia was evident in the late 1980s under the government of federal Prime Minister Ante Marković. But the unraveling of communist rule also sparked demands for republican autonomy among all recognized nations and for ethnic self-determination among the smaller nationalities. The situation in Bosnia-Herzegovina remained especially complex, as none of the three national groups, Muslim, Serb, or Croat, had an absolute demographic majority. As political liberalization gathered pace in all six republics, in February 1990 the Bosnian Assembly passed a law allowing for political parties to be formed freely in preparation for the first post-war multi-party elections.[3] More than forty new groupings were created, although only thirteen fielded candidates in the November 1990 general elections.

In July 1990, the Assembly declared the republic a "democratic and sovereign state with full and equal rights for all its citizens," signaling the first step toward a looser federal arrangement, but avoiding any explicit moves toward separation from Yugoslavia. Constitutional amendments were simultaneously passed to legalize the holding of multi-party elections. The result of the November 1990 elections read like a census of the republic's population, with nationalist parties of the three major groups taking 80% of the vote in proportions reflecting their percentages of the population. Residents elected deputies to the 240-seat bicameral legislature, divided between a Chamber of Citizens (130 seats) and a Chamber of Municipalities (110 seats), as well as members of the collective presidency. Ethnic parity was to be maintained in all three institutions.

The republican elections in November 1990 were designed to balance the representation of the three constituent nations in the Bosnian presidency, government, and parliament. Each ethnic group formed its own party to stand in the ballot: the Muslim-based Party of Democratic Action (PDA), the Serbian Democratic Party (SDP), and the Croatian Democratic Union (CDU). Although non-nationalist parties won a quarter of the seats in the Chamber of Citizens, they had no lasting impact on political developments and could find no coalition partners.[4] Although 41 parties and associations were registered, only a handful won seats. Aside from the three largest, ethnicity-based parties, the most credible contenders included the Social Democratic Party (SDP), formerly the League of Communists, and the Alliance of Reform Forces (ARF), led by Yugoslav Prime Minister Ante Marković. A Party of Yugoslavs also contested for seats, as did several smaller, ethnicity-based organizations, including the Muslim Bosnian Organization (MBO), the Serbian Renewal Movement (SRM), and the Herzegovinian Democratic Union (HDU).

The election law stipulated that in order to maintain an ethnic balance in the Assembly, each ethnic group had to receive a proportion of seats that matched, within 15%, their proportion of the Bosnian population according to the 1981 census. Although the purpose of this ruling was to maintain ethnic balance, leaders of non-ethnic parties expressed reservations about the quota system, as it encouraged voting according to ethnic identification rather than political or economic program. The law specified that if the correct proportions were not achieved, the elections could be annulled and new ones staged until the required balance was attained. Leaders of the main parties recognized the elections as legitimate, even though they had voiced fears that the ex-communists would manipulate the balloting. In the final tally, the PDA gained 86 seats in the Assembly, the SDP 71, and the CDU 45; the 38 remaining mandates were shared among eight political groups.

The victory of the three large ethnic parties both reflected and encouraged national identification among citizens. The key government positions were awarded to the three ethnic groups. Alija Izetbegović, head of the PDA, was chosen as president of the nine-member presidency, a post that was envisioned as rotating among the three ethnic components. Jure Pelivan of the CDU was chosen as Prime Minister, head of the republic's government, and Momčilo Krajišnik of the SDP became speaker of the National Assembly. Bosnia's ethno-political divisions were clearly displayed in the final election tally to the Chamber of Citizens. The PDA received 33% of the popular vote; the SDP gained 26%; the CDU scored 16%. Only 21% of the electorate voted for the smaller ethnic parties, for the Yugoslav organizations, or for the non-ethnic political associations. Although the results preserved a tri-ethnic balance in the legislature and the presidency, they also further polarized the electorate and its political representatives.

Since no party won a clear majority, leaders of the three national parties formed a coalition government. Muslims obtained ten ministries, Serbs seven, and Croats five. While the three ethno-parties agreed to share power at the national level, in various municipalities *(opštinas)* the victorious parties proceeded to assume absolute control in local governments. The Serb *opštinas* increasingly refused to recognize Sarajevo's authority. Beneath the facade of cooperation at the republican level, an intense power struggle was brewing. This became evident when parliament attempted to enact new legislation in response to the accelerating disintegration of the federation. It proved impossible to pass a new constitution, as the agreement of all three major parties was required. The Serbian side refused to countenance any constitutional changes propelling Bosnia toward statehood, while Muslim and Croat leaders feared that the secession of Slovenia and Croatia would leave the republic in a precarious position by strengthening Serbia's position in the shrunken federation.

As Slovenia and Croatia pressed for independence after the collapse of talks on a looser confederation, Bosnia-Herzegovina found itself caught in the middle of a tightening vise. Leaders of the republic's chief ethnic groups were increasingly pressured to side with either Serbia or Croatia. Serb leaders voiced concern about an emerging Muslim-Croat alliance that would exclude Serbs from key government posts. Serb activists also calculated that Croats and Muslims would seek closer political and military ties with Croatia. Meanwhile, Muslim and Croat leaders grew anxious that local Serbian activists in league with the Socialist regime in Belgrade were planning to engineer a crisis in the republic in order to detach large areas of Bosnia from Sarajevo's control.

Hostilities among leaders of the three national communities escalated throughout 1991, following the outbreak of armed warfare in neighboring Croatia and the seizure of large stretches of Croat territory by the Yugoslav army and Serbian guerrillas. Sarajevo's position was made even more difficult by differences within the republican presidency and government on the future of Yugoslavia. While the Muslim side favored a loose alliance rather than outright secession, having little experience of independent statehood, the Serbian side sought to preserve a unified Yugoslav state with some measure of republican autonomy. Croatian leaders veered toward Bosnian sovereignty and independence. Caught between demands for Bosnian separatism and Yugoslav federalism, Bosnia's Muslim leaders simply could not afford to take a neutral position: either option would have led to confrontation with Serbs or Croats.

As war raged in neighboring Croatia and the prospect of international recognition appeared as a distinct possibility, the Muslim leadership leaned toward secession from Yugoslavia and the preservation of a unitary Bosnian state. While this move largely satisfied Croatian aspirations, the Serb leadership was dismayed and warned that they would not accept Bosnian independence, as this would allegedly leave 1.5 million Serbs stranded in the new state. The slide into all-out conflict and a savage anti-civilian war had begun in earnest.

Throughout late 1991 and early 1992, Serb leaders carved out their own jurisdictions in Bosnian municipalities where Serbs formed absolute or relative majorities, and threatened civil war if Sarajevo moved toward statehood. Croat leaders in Herzegovina also began to make preparations for territorial autonomy in the event that Bosnia remained in a truncated Yugoslavia. Meanwhile, the Belgrade government accused the Bosnian Muslim leadership of planning to transform the republic into an Islamic state and of harboring pretensions to other Muslim-inhabited areas of Serbia. The charge was vehemently denied by President Izetbegović, who considered it a propaganda ploy designed to mobilize both Serbs and Croats against Bosnian independence.

The Bosnian Assembly remained deadlocked over the issue of sovereignty, even though the three ethnic parties appeared to agree on maintaining the republic's territorial integrity. In February 1991, the SDP rejected a joint PDA-CDU proposal on declaring sovereignty and giving Bosnian laws precedence over federal legislation. Serb leaders contended that such moves would institutionalize the "minority status" of Serbs. In April 1991, the PDA and CDU rejected SDP proposals for the "economic regionalization" of Bosnia, whereby each ethnic group would have control over its own economic interests. They calculated that this would constitute the first step toward partition and the creation of a "Greater Serbia." Through the summer of 1991, conflicts continued to rage over a draft proposal for Bosnian sovereignty. SDP leaders appeared to be stalling, evidently seeking to prolong the political deadlock until the military situation in Croatia became clarified.[5]

As tensions mounted, Muslim and Croat deputies in Bosnia's National Assembly in October 1991 declared the republic's full sovereignty and neutrality, stopping just short of declaring independence. Serb leaders boycotted the session, declared the vote illegal and unconstitutional, and announced that they would not recognize Bosnian laws. Fearing an assault by the Yugoslav army similar to the one in Croatia, Muslim and Croat leaders decided to hold a referendum on independence. The ballot in February 1992 was boycotted by the majority of Serb residents, but over 64% of the electorate turned out and voted overwhelmingly for Bosnian independence. Sarajevo promptly declared an independent state and gained comprehensive international recognition. The move proved unacceptable to local Serb leaders, who launched an armed offensive within the republic, with the active support of the Yugoslav army, charging that Sarajevo's policies threatened their national rights and even their physical existence.

In many respects, Bosnia-Herzegovina found itself in a position similar to that of the Yugoslav federation after Slovenia and Croatia withdrew from the federal government. It was marked by virtually unbridgeable polarization between the leaders of the component nations.[6] In November 1991, in a clear challenge to the declaration on sovereignty, the SDP organized its own referendum among Bosnian Serbs. According to Serb sources, the overwhelming majority participated in the ballot and voted for maintaining the federation with Yugoslavia, regardless of agreements between Muslims and Croats. Serb leaders asserted that they would not accept minority status in an independent Bosnia, as this would allegedly leave them vulnerable to official persecution. Conversely, Croat leaders charged that Serb activists in league with the Milošević regime were preparing a crisis similar to the one engineered in Croatia.

A series of pre-planned steps were undertaken during 1991 to solidify exclusive Serb control over the bulk of Bosnian territory, evidently as a prelude to secession. As far back as October 1990, the SDP had set up a Serbian national council in the town of Banja Luka and demanded the creation of three national chambers in the republican parliament. The establishment of parallel organs of power was condemned by the government for violating Bosnia's sovereignty.[7] In April 1991, a Serb Community of Municipalities of Bosnian Krajina was declared, consisting of 14 Serb majority municipalities in western Bosnia that bordered the Serb-held territories in Croatian Krajina. Municipal governments in heavily Serb-populated areas of eastern, northern, and southeastern Bosnia also prepared to form autonomous communities avowedly to protect Serb interests against Muslim-Croatian separatism.

Sarajevo charged that the self-proclaimed communities negated the rights of local minorities and undermined the Bosnian administration. They were viewed as the first steps toward establishing autonomous regions that would presage the fracturing of the republic into contested ethnic zones. At a joint session in June 1991, deputies of the assemblies of Bosnian Krajina municipalities and the Serbian Autonomous Region of Krajina (in Croatia) adopted a "treaty on cooperation" and promulgated a "declaration of unification" of the two regions. These measures served to confirm that Serb leaders in both republics were intent on linking up their territories and creating an enlarged Serbian state that would remain in Yugoslavia.

In September 1991, Serb leaders announced the formation of a Serbian Autonomous Region of Eastern and Old Herzegovina; it covered eight municipalities in southeastern Bosnia inhabited primarily by Serbs. Meanwhile, the Bosnian Krajina region was declared the Serbian Autonomous Region of Krajina. Even more ominously, local Serb police forces and party radicals proceeded to establish armed "volunteer units" and steadily eliminated Sarajevo's jurisdiction in these areas. The Bosnian presidency and legislature and all Muslim and Croatian organizations condemned these initiatives as illegal and provocative. Serb leaders claimed that they were simply protective measures designed to ensure "self-determination" for Yugoslavia's largest nation.

During the fall of 1991, three more autonomous Serbian regions were proclaimed in northeastern Bosnia, northern Bosnia, and the Mount Romanija region east of Sarajevo. Recognizing the authority of the self-proclaimed Assembly of the Serbian People in Bosnia-Herzegovina, leaders of the new territorial units threatened to establish a unified Serbian republic, secede from

Bosnia, and remain in a federal Yugoslavia. They asserted that a declaration of Bosnian independence and the non-recognition of Serbian territorial autonomy would provoke even more radical steps toward separation and could precipitate bloodshed. Muslim and Croat leaders declared that no autonomous regions could be formed on the republic's territory and dismissed as null and void any planned referendums on autonomy. Serbian representatives responded that Bosnia would need to be divided into three distinct ethnic territories if civil war was to be avoided. In February 1992, they adopted a constitution of the Serbian Republic of Bosnia-Herzegovina.

Although CDU leaders criticized Serbian steps toward secession, activists in Croatian-majority municipalities, in close liaison with the authorities in Zagreb, proceeded to form their own quasi-autonomous regions.[8] They claimed that they did not want to live outside of Croatia if a large wedge of Serbian-controlled territory separated them from other republics. In November 1991, a Croatian Community of Herceg-Bosna was established. It included 30 municipalities containing a large Croatian population in western Herzegovina and central Bosnia. The community was declared a distinct political entity that would recognize the government in Sarajevo only as long as the republic upheld its sovereignty. During the same month, a Croatian Community of the Bosnian Sava Valley was established to incorporate eight municipalities in northern Bosnia. In January 1992, a Croatian Community of Central Bosnia was formed, comprising four municipalities. Croat leaders declared themselves in favor of union with Croatia.

Serb moves toward secession were accompanied by a propaganda barrage emanating from Belgrade, alleging that Muslim extremists led by President Izetbegović were intent on transforming Bosnia-Herzegovina into a militant Islamic state in which Serbs would be subject to persecution and genocide.[9] They cited passages from Izetbegović's previously banned *Islamic Declaration* as proof of his allegedly "fundamentalist" aims; the passages were taken out of context and presented as a manifesto for restructuring Bosnia into a Muslim state. These charges were strenuously denied by the PDA, which asserted that it supported a tolerant, secular, multi-ethnic, and democratic state.

Indeed, on the eve of the hostilities there was no perceptible threat from either Muslims or Croats to the safety of Bosnian Serbs. However, Belgrade's propaganda elicited resonance among segments of the rural Serb population and provided ammunition to radicals intent on carving out a "pure" Serbian state. Muslim leaders and their followers were denounced as "Turks" and "fundamentalists" and the conflict was depicted as a primarily religious war in which Serbs were merely seeking defense against an internationally sponsored Islamic *jihad* (holy war). In January 1992, the self-styled Serb Assembly claimed it was entitled to control 60% of the republic's territory, and disclosed plans to establish its own security forces and governmental institutions.

In December 1991, EC foreign ministers decided to recognize the independence of all Yugoslav republics fulfilling four fundamental conditions, including commitments to various human rights accords and guarantees of rights to national groups and minorities; respect for the inviolability of frontiers; and agreement to settle state succession and regional disputes. Bosnia-Herzegovina, Croatia, Macedonia, and Slovenia submitted applications for international recognition, whereas Serbia and Montenegro claimed that they already represented Yugoslavia. The EC Arbitration Commission, chaired by Robert Badinter, concluded that only Macedonia and Slovenia had fully met the EC conditions. But in January 1992, under German pressure, Slovenia and Croatia were recognized while Macedonian recognition was blocked by Greece. Bosnia-Herzegovina met most of the EC requirements, but it was not granted recognition because no referendum had taken place to ascertain "the will of the inhabitants" for constituting an independent state.

In response to the EC decision, the Bosnian presidency, with the approval of the National Assembly, authorized a referendum. With the exception of the SDP deputies, who left the session in protest, the Assembly slated the referendum on independence for late February and early March 1992.[10] The SDP, led by its chairman Radovan Karadžić, declared the referendum illegal because it was not approved by the full Assembly and did not have the support of all three constituent nations. Although Serbian leaders did not comprehensively disrupt the plebiscite, local officials in Serb-dominated areas refused to cooperate.

Observers contended that SDP leaders feared that without an active boycott, a substantial percentage of Serbs may have opted for independence and derailed the efforts of militants such as Karadžić, who endeavored to prove that Serbs remained united against Bosnian statehood. Sixty-four percent of eligible voters participated in the referendum, and 99.7% cast their ballots for independence. The constitutionally required two-thirds majority was thereby attained. The figures indicated that the overwhelming majority of Muslims, Croats, Yugoslavs, and other minorities favored Bosnian statehood, while the Serb boycott was comprehensive. Immediately after the balloting, a shooting incident in Sarajevo suddenly raised tensions and Serb militias established barricades around various cities, evidently in preparation for armed confrontation.

Bosnia-Herzegovina was recognized as an independent state in early April 1992. The day after recognition, the Serbian Republic of Bosnia-Herzegovina was formally proclaimed and SDP representatives withdrew from all governmental institutions and openly recognized the authority of their own separate administrative organs. Krajišnik, the former president of the Bosnian Assembly, assumed the presidency of the Serbian Assembly, and Karadžić, the presidency of the Serbian Republic. Meanwhile, three moderate Serbs entered Bosnia's collective presidency, which under wartime conditions assumed the powers of the republican Assembly.

The EC-sponsored talks on a new constitutional order remained deadlocked over territorial delineations: it proved impossible to devise any scheme that would be acceptable to all three sides. Muslim leaders remained wary of any regional divisions based on ethnic criteria, arguing that the populations were so intermingled that any form of cantonization needed to take account of existing administrative and economic criteria. A division based primarily on ethnic grounds would lead to discriminatory measures against minority groups in each canton and an eventual division of the embryonic state. Stilted debates over cantonization also brought into focus persistent rumors of a secret deal between Zagreb and Belgrade to partition the republic. They were fueled by meetings between Serbian and Croatian leaders that heightened anxieties among Muslim officials. During the summer of 1991, presidents Milošević and Tudjman allegedly held two secret meetings to divide the republic even though no firm agreements were reached.[11]

In April 1992, the political impasse in Bosnia was transformed into an outright armed conflict launched by Bosnia's Serb leaders.[12] The Sarajevo government had already lost administrative control in most of the Serbian autonomous regions. Militarily, Sarajevo was incapable of either neutralizing the Serb forces or protecting Muslim residents. As the war in Croatia died down in early 1992, the Yugoslav army transferred much of its heavy equipment and troops into Bosnia; under instructions from Belgrade, military stocks were made readily available to local Serb forces. Militia detachments had been formed in the five Serbian "autonomous regions" and a military command was already functioning parallel to the Serb Assembly. In June 1991, the Serb-dominated Yugoslav Army General Staff had ordered that all weapons belonging to Bosnia's Territorial Defense Forces be placed under the federal army's control. Much of this weaponry was apportioned to Bosnian Serb commanders, and additional war materiel began to flow in from Serbia and Montenegro. Between March and May 1992, the bulk of the Yugoslav army stationed in Bosnia was transformed into a new Serb army commanded by a former Yugoslav army general, Ratko Mladić.

With overwhelming firepower and material support from Belgrade, Serbian forces overran nearly two-thirds of Bosnian territory by the close of 1992, including municipalities where Serbs constituted a relative minority of the population. Bosnia's Muslim forces were caught unprepared and defenseless and suffered severe casualties across the republic. Serbian "ethnic cleansing" operations were comprehensively applied to terrorize Muslim communities and create pure, contiguous Serbian territories across western, northern, and eastern Bosnia. Over a million people were displaced from their homes.

As the conflict escalated, Croatian leaders in western Herzegovina formed their own army and government structures while nominally pledging allegiance to the government in Sarajevo. Suspicions persisted that if Bosnia-Herzegovina were allowed to fracture, then Croatia would claim its share of about one-fifth of the republic, particularly those municipalities in Herzegovina where Croats formed absolute majorities. As Serb forces consolidated their hold over captured territories, a separate Serbian Republic was declared with the avowed aim of linking up with Serb-captured territories in Croatia and eventually joining the rump Yugoslavia. But although Serb forces controlled the major towns in about 70% of Bosnia's territory, Sarajevo remained under siege and the countryside became a battleground between competing guerrilla forces.

About 150,000 people were presumed dead or missing by the spring of 1993 and nearly two million were refugees. What began as a rebellion against Bosnian statehood by radical elements of one of the major nationalities had turned into an ethnic war among the three communities seeking outright territorial control. Bosnia's Muslim and Serb leaders continued to uphold diametrically opposed positions on the republic's future. While Serb spokesmen sought a far-ranging "cantonization" tantamount to partition, the Muslim leadership wanted to maintain a unitary state with extensive territorial and political decentralization but not based on ethnic criteria. The Croats increasingly veered toward partition as the Bosnian government proved unable to control the republic or to regain territories from Serb forces. With the collapse of UN-sponsored peace plans, by the summer of 1993 Bosnia stood on the verge of partition. The refusal of the Bosnian government to accept the *fait accompli* simply encouraged Serb and Croat forces to carve out more extensive territories and to push the outgunned Muslims into shrinking territorial pockets.

The Bosnian government was caught unprepared for armed conflict. It calculated that under the umbrella of international recognition, the Serbs would desist from open warfare and a political compromise would be reached under an EC mandate. Although Sarajevo had established special security units to suppress civil disorder, it had not bargained for the kind of sustained offensives organized by Serbian militants. Bosnia's military structure remained poorly organized, undermanned, and underarmed.[13] Sarajevo seriously underestimated the escalating threat and was slow in organizing an appropriate defense. Some local Muslim leaders acting on their own initiative began to form paramilitary groups. The presidency formally established an Army of Bosnia and Herzegovina in May 1992 and only declared a state of war in June 1992, by which time Serb forces had already overrun much of the republic.

According to reliable estimates, by the close of 1992 the Bosnian army consisted of about 80,000 combatants, although only half that number were adequately armed. By contrast, the Serbian side was able to field about 60,000 well-armed troops and about 10,000 paramilitaries. Moreover, the Serbs had an enormous advantage in all armament categories: from tanks and helicopters to artillery pieces of all calibers. The Croatian side mustered nearly 40,000 soldiers, with direct assistance from Zagreb, and deployed a respectable number of tanks and artillery. Bosnian army inferiority was compounded by the absence of a strong central command and the operation of various local forces pledging only nominal allegiance to Sarajevo.

Serbian military objectives were twofold: to link up and expand the territories they controlled in northern and eastern Bosnia, thus creating a contiguous Serb republic between Croatian Krajina and Serbia proper; and to eliminate the non-Serb populations in this new political entity, whether through threat, eviction, or outright murder. A campaign of terror was unleashed against non-Serb civilians; atrocities committed by irregular forces were loudly publicized to intimidate remaining residents and escalate the war psychosis.

The anti-civilian offensive, euphemistically described as "ethnic cleansing," had already been set in motion in Croatia the previous year.[14] In Bosnia, the practice became more widespread and brutal, and it was largely defenseless Muslim civilians who fell victim to this centrally planned "civil war." With overwhelming firepower, Serb militias and irregular paramilitaries targeted Muslim villages and neighborhoods, rounding up residents and executing or imprisoning males of military age. Older people, women, and children were largely expelled. In many cases, however, virtually all residents were slaughtered, and reports of rape, torture, and mutilation became widespread. As word of Serb atrocities spread through Muslim towns, local resistance was organized. In such cases, Serb artillery would first be deployed to destroy or weaken the defenders before the location was captured and its residents murdered or expelled. As the conflict expanded, thousands of civilians were imprisoned in concentration camps; while many died of starvation, execution, or torture, others were used in prisoner exchanges with Muslim and Croat forces.

The systematic nature of the "ethnic cleansing" campaign indicated that the policy had been planned and approved at the highest political levels. It served several purposes: to eliminate the non-Serb population as a potential source of future resistance; to create demographic problems for Muslim-majority areas outside the regions designated for the "Serb Republic" by flooding them with refugees; to provide war booty for local guerrillas and gunmen recruited in Serbia; to gain the loyalty of Serbs evacuated from other locations by allowing them to occupy captured houses and land; and to entrap non-combatant Serbs in a permanent conflict with Muslims in which the militias could pose as defenders protecting ordinary Serbs from Muslim revenge attacks. An "ethnic conflict" was thereby engineered across Bosnia, buttressed by an incessant propaganda barrage claiming that Serbs simply could not live with Muslims and that Serbs primarily wanted "self-determination" to protect them from the tide of "fundamentalism".

The rapid success of Serb forces in gaining absolute control over more than 60% of Bosnian territory galvanized Bosnia's Croat leadership and strengthened the position of those favoring partition. The moderate CDU leader, Stjepan Kljujić, who had strongly favored an integral Bosnia, was replaced, and the more radical Herzegovinian Mate Boban, under the patronage of Zagreb, took charge of political and military operations in Croatian-majority regions. Initially, Croat forces did not engage in "ethnic cleansing" operations, particularly as they largely confined their operations to Croatian-majority municipalities and entered into a loose alliance with the Bosnian armed forces as protection against the Serbian onslaught.

Boban criticized the Bosnian leadership for its lack of preparedness and its military incompetence, and established a separate military structure in western Herzegovina, central Bosnia, and the Posavina region, along the Sava River border with Croatia, styled as the Croatian Defense Council (CDC). The CDC also recruited thousands of local Muslims to fight in its ranks, while claiming that only Croats were able to offer a proper defense of their "national space." Although the CDC pledged nominal allegiance to the government in Sarajevo, under the chairmanship of Jadranko Prlić it also made preparations to establish a separate Croatian republic with the option of joining Croatia at some future date.

Bosnia's Croat forces received military supplies and logistical assistance from Zagreb, as the border with Croatia virtually ceased to exist and thousands of soldiers from Croatia were reportedly active in Herzegovina. Boban dismissed accusations that he was intent on partitioning Bosnia, claiming that Croat forces were simply organizing effective resistance against Serbian aggression and actually protecting the integrity of Bosnia-Herzegovina. Conversely, to justify their control of approximately 20% of Bosnian territory, Croatian leaders occasionally imitated Belgrade's propaganda line that the PDA was intent on establishing an Islamic state in which non-Muslims would figure as second-class citizens. Such charges laid the groundwork for future attempts to divide the republic.

Suspicions continued to surface that Boban and Karadžić had fashioned a secret deal to partition Bosnia. These were reinforced in July 1992 when Boban declared the autonomy of "Herceg-Bosna," with its capital in Mostar, and proceeded to consolidate a separate administrative structure. Croat spokesmen contended that this was merely a temporary arrangement designed to ensure political stability and the security of Croat municipalities in wartime conditions. President Tudjman regularly signaled his support for Bosnian independence and territorial integrity and offered a closer Croat-Bosnian military alliance. Sarajevo's response remained lukewarm, as the Bosnian presidency was wary of committing itself to an unstable accord with Zagreb. Observers believed that Tudjman's statements were designed to placate international opinion and to single out the Serbs as the prime aggressors, leaving Croats with the option of remaining in Bosnia or forging their own political entity depending on both internal and international developments.

The Croat side retained its membership in the Bosnian presidency and continued to provide military assistance to the beleaguered Muslim forces. However, on several occasions Croat forces appeared to avoid all-out confrontations with the Serb army. In some instances, they reportedly abandoned Muslim positions as Bosnian forces proceeded to lose their foothold in several key locations. Nonetheless, in Sarajevo, Tuzla, and other large towns, a marked degree of political and military cooperation remained visible. Many urban Serbs and Croats in Bosnian-controlled territory refused to recognize either the Karadžić or the Boban leadership and upheld their allegiance to the principle of a single multi-ethnic state.

Nevertheless, the process of ethnic polarization and segregation was proceeding apace. At the highest political levels, the Croat Bosnian Prime Minister Mile Akmadžić criticized Izetbegović for failing to abide by the principles of presidential rotation and claimed that he did not fully represent all three national communities. Izetbegović countered that under emergency conditions the presidency could not function normally. The situation on the ground was even more discouraging. By the close of 1992, a separate Serbian state was already functioning. In August 1992, a Serb Assembly meeting in Banja Luka renamed the new entity the Serb Republic *(Republika Srpska)*.

In June 1992, the United Nations mounted a humanitarian operation in Bosnia, and approximately 7,000 troops were dispatched to the republic. Their mission was largely confined to providing relief supplies to Sarajevo and other besieged cities. Food and medical aid also became a weapon in the siege of Bosnian cities. Serb and Croat militias periodically blocked U.N. convoys and severed essential water, electricity, and gas supplies in order to demoralize and starve out Muslim defenders. In August 1992, under the direction of Cyrus Vance, the personal representative of the U.N. secretary general, and David Owen, an EC-appointed mediator, the London Conference on Yugoslavia made efforts to find a political solution and enforce an agreement.

Following several rounds of negotiations, in October 1992, a document was formulated that became known as the Vance-Owen plan.[15] It advocated the creation of a decentralized state consisting of nine largely autonomous provinces, three for each nationality, and a central region around the capital Sarajevo. In each province one of the three ethno-national groups would predominate, thus opening up the possibility of population transfers under international supervision. The central government would have only minimal responsibilities, including foreign affairs, international commerce, taxation, and national defense. The nine provinces would control all other governmental functions such as education, media, energy, finance, and local police. The demilitarization of the republic was envisioned under international supervision.

Although the constitutional and political arrangements appeared to be largely acceptable to all three sides since Serb and Croat leaders viewed them as a step toward cantonization and partition and the Muslims calculated that under international protection an integral Bosnia would be maintained, the delineation of provincial borders proved highly contentious. The Vance-Owen map was acceptable only to the Croats, who stood to gain pockets of territory outside the regions they already controlled, particularly in northern and central Bosnia. The Muslims would lose land in the north and the center but would regain some territories in eastern Bosnia that had been captured by Serb forces. The Serbs were outraged by the proposed maps: acceptance would have meant the surrender of nearly a quarter of the occupied territories, with extensive territorial fragmentation in eastern Bosnia and the loss of their northern corridor. The Croatian side promptly accepted the plan. The Muslims held out until March 1993, realizing that further opposition would simply prolong the war and ensure further Serbian conquests. In accepting the plan, Sarajevo estimated that significant international pressure would be exerted on the Serbs, particularly as calls for U.N. intervention escalated.

Fearful of international military involvement, Serb leaders adopted a dual-track approach. They continued to procrastinate in giving a final decision on the plan while launching new offensives in eastern Bosnia during March and April 1993 to eradicate the remaining Muslim pockets. Karadžić initialed the Vance-Owen plan under pressure from Milošević, who feared that the combined effect of tightening U.N. sanctions against Yugoslavia and the possibility of bombing assaults on Bosnian-Serb supply lines, communications, and armaments factories would precipitate a major crisis inside Serbia itself. But the validation of Karadžić's signature was made contingent upon the acceptance of the plan by the self-styled parliament, which in April 1993 further delayed a decision by calling for a referendum among the Serb population. The ballot took place in May 1993, and the Vance-Owen plan was overwhelmingly rejected by voters.

The relationship between Karadžić and the Bosnian Serb military and their patron Milošević gave rise to intensive speculation. Milošević's acceptance of the Vance-Owen plan and his public criticisms of the Bosnian Serb Assembly could have been taken at face value as a split over strategy and programs. Conversely, it may have been a tactical ploy intended for foreign consumption, whereby Belgrade could avoid further economic sanctions and any military retaliation for the rejection of the plan by Bosnian Serbs. Even though Serbia continued to supply military provisions to Serb separatists, there were indications that Milošević did not fully control his former proxies. Strong ideological differences also materialized between an essentially neocommunist leadership in Belgrade and a monarchist and Orthodox-oriented Serb leadership in Bosnia. Milošević may have gauged that a swift unification of Serbian territories could strengthen the position of nationalist rivals in Serbia, Bosnia, and Krajina.

Western indecision was quickly exploited by Bosnia's Serb leaders, who pressed on with their military offensives. By the end of May 1993, the republic had descended into an all-out land-grabbing operation. Croatian forces launched offensives against their erstwhile Muslim allies in central Bosnia and proceeded to expel the remaining Muslim population from western Herzegovina. Serbs intensified their assaults on the surviving Muslim enclaves in eastern Bosnia, reducing them to barely defendable pockets that the U.N. declared "safe havens" but failed to protect. In sheer desperation, Bosnian government forces launched offensives in central Bosnia to regain territory lost to the Croats, but they simply did not possess the firepower to dislodge Serbian forces from the occupied territories.

In June 1993, Serb and Croat leaders finalized a new plan for the division of Bosnia-Herzegovina into three ethnic provinces or mini-states with only a nominal central government. According to the proposals, Serbs would give back a small portion of their territory, while the Muslim quasi state would be contained in central Bosnia, with Sarajevo as the capital, and with a small enclave in the northwestern Bihać pocket. Croatia would avowedly guarantee Muslim access to the sea at the Adriatic port of Ploče.[16] The plan was deemed unacceptable by the Bosnian government, which continued to favor a multi-ethnic federal arrangement. However, rifts began to appear in the collective presidency between the majority of Muslim leaders, who vehemently opposed the proposal, and some Croat members together with Fikret Abdić, the Muslim leader representing the Bihać-Cazinska area, who felt that without a speedy accord the state would be dismembered and the Bosniaks would be left with a fragmented area overflowing with refugees.

On 1 March 1994, fighting between Bosnian Muslims and Croats ended when the two groups signed a comprehensive cease-fire agreement in Washington. They also created a joint federation, and a new constitution was promulgated on 30 March 1994. Further documents envisaged a confederal arrangement with Croatia.[17] The federation was based on territory amounting to 58% of Bosnia-Herzegovina, contingent upon the recovery of territory from the Serbs. The federation was based on eight cantons, four of which would be Muslim-dominated; two controlled by Croats; and the remaining two of mixed ethnicity. The new federation would coexist with the established government of the republic of Bosnia-Herzegovina, which remained under the control of President Izetbegović.

In late May 1995, NATO aircraft bombed Serb-held positions in Bosnia to prevent further attacks on U.N. "safe havens." In retaliation, and to prevent further attacks, the Serbs took more than 300 U.N. troops as hostages, but they were all eventually released. Events moved quickly during the summer of 1995. Serbian forces overran the "safe havens" of Srebrenica and Žepa and massacred thousands of Muslim civilians. NATO forces mounted a major air-strike campaign against Serbian positions to prevent further attacks. In cooperation with Bosnian Croat units, Bosnian government forces captured large areas of western Bosnia, and the Serbs suffered their first major defeat of the war. The Bosnian government also eliminated a Muslim rebellion in the Bihać area of western Bosnia led by Abdić, who had collaborated with Serbian forces.

By late summer 1995, the Muslim-Croat federation controlled more than 50% of the country's territory. Following lengthy negotiations mediated by U.S. assistant secretary of state Richard Holbrooke, Izetbegović, Tudjman, and Milošević initialed a comprehensive agreement in November 1995 near Dayton, Ohio. Signed in Paris the following month, the Dayton accord was intended to guarantee a lasting peace in Bosnia and to reconstruct the country as a single state consisting of two entities: the Federation of Bosnia-Herzegovina (also known as the Muslim-Croat federation), which would receive 51% of the territory, and the Serb Republic, which would receive 49%.

The accord established Sarajevo as a unified city under the control of the central government. It also called for free elections to posts in both the central government and entity administrations, to be held in September 1996 under the supervision of the Organization on Security and Cooperation in Europe (OSCE). Milošević struck two deals: one with Zagreb and Sarajevo, promising that the Serbs would withdraw to 49% of Bosnian territory; and one with the international community, that he would sign the Dayton agreements and remove the leading indicted war criminals. This maneuver served several objectives. Primarily, it won Milošević favors with the U.S., pushed Karadžić to the sidelines, and made Milošević appear indispensable for regional stability.

To ensure the peace, a NATO implementation force (I-FOR) was placed in Bosnia in January 1996 on a one-year mandate. The force consisted of 60,000 troops from more than 20 nations, including approximately 20,000 U.S. soldiers and large numbers of French and British troops. The troops were stationed primarily along the demarcation line between the Muslim-Croat federation and the Serb Republic. The three parties complied with the main military provisions of the Dayton accord by withdrawing their weapons and troops from the zones of separation and releasing most of their prisoners of war. However, other provisions of the agreement proved more difficult, as Serbian and Croatian nationalists resisted the integration of ethnically divided communities and delayed the return of refugees to their homes.

It took several months of negotiations before the Bosnian government at the central level was finally formed. The first session of the two-chamber Bosnian parliament took place in early January 1997 after months of obstruction by Serb representatives. Under the Dayton accords, the House of Peoples consisted of 15 delegates (five each of Muslims, Serbs, and Croats), and the House of Representatives, of 42 members (28 from the Muslim-Croat Federation and 14 from the Serbian entity). The parliament confirmed nominations to the central government Council of Ministers with seats being allocated among Muslims, Croats, and Serbs. Prime Ministers were to rotate on a weekly basis. In addition, the state presidency consisted of three members, one from each ethnic group. The power-sharing arrangements demonstrated that ethnic proportionality combined with the separatist objectives of Serb and Croat representatives could paralyze the central government institutions. The Bosnian Federation parliament maintained limited powers in the Croat majority areas, as the "Herceg-Bosnia" parallel regime continued to function despite repeated promises that it would be disbanded.

In early 1996 the International Criminal Tribunal for the Former Yugoslavia (ICTY), established in late 1993 in the Hague, the Netherlands, stepped up its activities. More than 50 Bosnians, the majority of whom were Serbs, were indicted by the ICTY for massacring civilians during the war. Those indicted included Radovan Karadžić and General Ratko Mladić. Several lower-ranking war crimes suspects also were apprehended, but other, more important leaders evaded capture. In July 1996 the ICTY issued international arrest warrants for Karadžić and Mladić on charges of genocide and crimes against humanity. Later that month, U.S. officials secured Karadžić's resignation. Mladić was dismissed from power in November 1996 by Biljana Plavšić, who had replaced Karadžić as President of the Serb Republic.

In keeping with the provisions of the Dayton accord, national elections were held in Bosnia in September 1996. Six other ballots also took place for cantonal assemblies (in the Federation), the House of Representatives of the Bosnian Federation, the National Assembly of the Serb Republic, the Presidency of the Serb Republic, the House of Representatives of Bosnia-Herzegovina, and the Presidency of Bosnia-Herzegovina. The election campaign was riddled with violations that would disqualify the ballot under normal conditions. No free movement existed between Muslim-Croat and Serb territories, many war criminals were on the ballot, freedom of assembly remained tenuous, and the major media outlets were dominated by nationalists who wanted to seal Bosnia's division, not achieve its reunification.

The ruling Muslim, Serb, and Croat nationalist parties scored major victories, each capturing about 80% of the vote of their ethnic constituencies. The Party of Democratic Action (PDA) won the largest number of seats in Bosnia's central legislature. Seats on the three-member collective presidency went to Bosnia's Muslim president Alija Izetbegović, Serb leader Momčilo Krajišnik, and Croat leader Krešimir Zubak. Izetbegović received the most votes and thus was to chair the presidency. Disputes surfaced between Muslim and Serb leaders over the role and power of the collective presidency. For example, Serb leaders insisted that the post of chairman should rotate between the three members every eight months. The Dayton accords were not precise on the arrangement, as with numerous other procedural issues, and their interpretation remained a major source of dispute. The Serb side often raised such questions to sow confusion and paralyze the newly constituted governing bodies.

The Serbian Democratic Party (SDP) won the majority of seats in the assembly of the Bosnian Serb Republic, and Biljana Plavšić, a member of the SDP, continued as president of the Serb Republic. The PDA won the largest number of seats in the Muslim-Croat federation's House of Representatives, followed by the Croatian Democratic Union (CDU). The presidency of the Muslim-Croat federation was chosen by the federation's parliament and thus was not contested. The overwhelming victory of the country's ruling parties reflected the suppression of opposition parties in the weeks leading up to the elections. Many observers feared that the success of nationalists would serve to ratify Bosnia's partition along ethnic lines. Instead of cementing together the two halves of Bosnia, the general elections consolidated the power of the three ethno-nationalist political forces. For example, the PDA and the CDU obtained 24 out of 28 seats in the Bosnian Federation parliament. The moderate democratic parties that favored a multi-ethnic society gained few seats to either the cantonal, regional, or central authorities.

The Karadžić faction withdrew its representatives from the joint Council of Ministers and blocked meetings of the Bosnian collective presidency. This "Pale clique" was essentially controlled by five hard-liners: Karadžić,

Krajišnik, Dragan Kalimić (speaker of the Serbian Republic parliament), Gojko Kličković (the Prime Minister), and Dragan Klijać (the interior minister). Their battles with Plavšić revolved around control over the army, police forces, political and economic networks, and the mass media. Police units divided into two: about half of the 20,000 officers backed Plavšić's attempt to take over Serbian institutions. The remainder, together with an estimated 3,000 "special police" troops, remained loyal to the old SDP leadership.

Two rival power centers emerged in the Serb Republic. Plavšić created her own party in Banja Luka and attracted some former Karadžić loyalists. For example, vice president Dragoljub Mirjanić defected to Plavšić, and two deputy prime ministers and the finance minister resigned from the SDP and endorsed Plavšić. At least 40 former SDP notables switched camps and became members of the new party's initiative board. The Serbian media also split and became the propaganda mouthpiece of two factions: Karadžić hard-liners in Pale and Trebinje and Plavšić rebels controlling Banja Luka television.

In December 1996, NATO launched a new, 31,000-strong stabilization force (S-FOR) in Bosnia to replace the 60,000-member I-FOR, whose one-year mandate had expired. The S-FOR mission was to deter new hostilities and provide a secure environment for civilian peace efforts. Washington contributed 8,500 troops to the new force. In February 1998, NATO leaders decided to extend the S-FOR's mission past June 1998, while the ICTY delivered a historic verdict when it convicted Dušan Tadić, a Bosnian Serb, of crimes against humanity for participating in an ethnic cleansing campaign against Muslims. This trial marked the first time an international court had tried and convicted someone for war crimes since the close of World War II.

During 1997, Serb Republic President Plavšić clashed with a Serb Assembly dominated by hard-line nationalist supporters of her predecessor Karadžić. With Western backing, Plavšić formed a new party, the Serb People's Alliance (SPA), in August 1997. On 3 July 1997, the Serb Assembly called for Plavšić's dismissal, accusing her of betraying the Serbian cause. She responded by dissolving the Assembly, and legislative elections were called for 22–23 November 1997. In total 1,158,000 people were eligible to cast ballots for 83 seats. Three coalitions, 28 political parties, and 18 independent candidates registered for the elections.[18] Following the vote, a new National Assembly included the Serbian Democratic Party, with 24 seats; the Coalition for a Single and Democratic Bosnia and Herzegovina, 16 seats; the Serbian Radical Party, 15 seats; the Serbian People's Alliance, 15 seats; the Socialist Party of the Serb Republic, 9 seats; and the Independent Social Democratic Party, 2 seats.[19]

Eighteen members of the Bosnian Serb Assembly were Muslims, elected by Muslim refugees voting in their home areas under complex election provisions. These new legislators combined with Plavšić supporters in January 1998 to elect as Prime Minister businessman Milorad Dodik, who had only limited ties with the Bosnian Serb wartime leadership. For the first time since the war began, the Bosnian Serb government was not controlled by the

SDP. Dodik led a minority government dependent on the support of the PDA and the CDU; but the latter two were formally excluded from the government for fear of losing Serb support for Dodik. Dodik sought to minimize SDP influence in the Serb entity, especially by breaking that party's hold over the media. He also moved the government of the Serb Republic from Pale, a Serb nationalist stronghold, to Banja Luka, where Plavšić had more influence. Dodik's government made further efforts to comply with the Dayton accords, including encouraging suspected war criminals to surrender to the ICTY.

Bosnia's first post-war municipal elections took place on 13–14 September 1997; 136 municipal councils were at stake, and 2.5 million Bosnian citizens were registered to vote. The elections were designed to reverse the results of "cleansing" campaigns that had driven hundreds of thousands people from their homes. By the time of the balloting, only 235,000 people had actually returned, mainly to areas where they were of the majority. In administering the elections, strong efforts were undertaken to deter fraud. Indeed, the international controls exerted over the electoral process were more thorough than during the September 1996 elections to national, entity, and cantonal offices. Of the 136 municipal councils, 75 were in the Bosnian Federation and 61 in the Serb Republic, each having between 15 and 70 seats. Except for 159 independent candidates, however, the seats were allotted by a proportional vote among political parties, of which 91 participated. In many cases, political parties ran partly or wholly as members of coalitions, of which nine existed—four in the Federation and five in the Serb entity.

The ruling parties, the PDA, the SDP, and the CDU, won the most seats on local councils, and achieved majorities in areas where they traditionally predominated. Only in a few municipalities did alternative political parties or coalitions win absolute or even relative majorities. The main exception to this was the SDP, whose votes were highly concentrated in the eastern half of the Serb Republic. Nationalist parties continued to rely on fears of domination by other ethnic groups. Even though civic parties scored some success in cities such as Sarajevo and Tuzla, nationalists retained power in the majority of local councils. Their control over local police and economic resources also consolidated ethnic exclusivity. Because refugees voted in large numbers, some towns elected nationalist parties from rival ethnic groups.

Opposition parties, especially the Socialist and Radical parties, scored well in the Serb entity. Opposition parties in the Federation made smaller gains, but the Joint List coalition maintained its majority in Tuzla, and Fikret Abdić's party won in Velika Kladuša. The Social Democrats scored well in the Sarajevo area. forty-five political parties or coalitions won at least one seat on a municipal council somewhere in the country. Karadžić's allies in the SDP were determined to resist efforts to reunite Bosnia, and called for the expulsion of the OSCE mission. They also obstructed the functioning of mixed-ethnic local councils. Ten local councils failed to form new governments because nationalist authorities resisted the sharing of power in territories conquered during the war.[20]

Despite the assurance of security and the termination of armed hostilities, NATO failed to guarantee the return of refugees and freedom of movement for all Bosnian residents. By 1998, out of about two million refugees, only 250,000 had returned to their original homes, and few families had ventured across the inter-entity line dividing the republic. Nationalists on all three sides hampered the free movement of people, and the process of ethnic homogenization continued. Moreover, Serb leaders hampered the functioning of the central government in Sarajevo. Although the three-person Bosnian presidency, consisting of one Muslim (Izetbegović), one Serb (Krajišnik), and one Croat (Zubak), was formed together with an executive cabinet in which all three ethnic groups were represented, the powers of the central government remained limited while the entity authorities retained substantial control.

Fears remained that the unresolved territorial issue around the northern Bosnian town of Brčko could result in new hostilities. The city linked Serb-controlled territories in western and eastern Bosnia. The international arbitration commission regularly postponed its decision on the region. Observers believed that if the commission awarded the city to the Muslim-Croat Federation or placed it under an international protectorate, Serb resistance could result in new fighting. Western leaders also remained concerned about the commitment of Milošević and Tudjman to Bosnia's territorial integrity. Suspicions persisted that they continued to support the partition and eventual annexation of the country. Furthermore, neither Milošević nor Tudjman proved cooperative in surrendering indicted war criminals resident on the territories under their control.

Within the Bosnian Federation, the Muslim side consistently complained that Croat leaders were sabotaging the agreements and constructing their own state structure. Croat representatives claimed that their counterparts in Sarajevo were refusing to approve true power-sharing institutions for the Federation. Moreover, they voiced fears that a "unitary federation" would give the Muslims a dominant role in the midst of growing Islamic nationalism. In effect, federal institutions remained largely paralyzed, and cantonal and local authorities exercised more effective control. Croatian nationalists retained strong vested interests in a permanent division of the country. Millions of black-market dollars were earned from the war and from the peace. Politically connected criminal gangs in the Croatian territories were manipulating nationalist sentiments, instilling fear in the local population, preventing the normalization of life throughout western Herzegovina, and syphoning off vital funds from the government in Sarajevo. Furthermore, ethnically separate political and military structures continued to operate within the Federation.

In the Serb Republic, President Plavšić realized that without Western economic assistance the entity faced catastrophe. In order to gain popularity and power she challenged Karadžić, Krajišnik, and other war profiteers. Her campaign against corruption struck a chord among many ordinary Serbs. Some observers believed that the Serbian power struggle was also exploited by

Milošević in order to maintain his influence in the para-state. Milošević may have encouraged Plavšić to undermine Karadžić's influence by dismissing the Assembly and publicly attacking Karadžić and his supporters as fascists and terrorists. Plavšić had created her own political party and challenged the monopoly of the SDP. Some observers feared that the Serb entity could dissolve into an all-out civil war and a split into two antagonistic parts: the western section based around the Plavšić and Dodik leadership in Banja Luka, and the eastern, Karadžić group in Pale.

Meanwhile, both the CDU and the SDA sought to benefit from the Serb conflict. Local officials continued to block the implementation of Dayton by disallowing any significant return of refugees and thwarting the operation of multiethnic institutions. The CDU in particular remained a monopolistic organization that eliminated all space for free mass media and political pluralism. In such circumstances, the municipal elections provided another endorsement for separatist nationalism. Even though the civic parties scored some success in the major Federation cities, their actual powers were limited by the ruling nationalists. The latter's control over the security forces and economic purse strings guaranteed the consolidation of ethnic exclusivity and political favoritism.

Croatia's proposal to create a monetary and customs union with the Bosnian Federation raised concerns in Sarajevo about President Tudjman's long-term ambitions. Critics contended that instead of strengthening Bosnian integrity and independence, Zagreb's confederation initiative could precipitate Bosnia's partition and absorption by its more powerful neighbors. The Croatian government contended that it was seeking to strengthen the development of Bosnia's economy. Zagreb's offer was rejected by Izetbegović, who argued that the proposals undermined Bosnian integrity and sovereignty. An economic union would place the Federation in a subservient position by increasing Sarajevo's economic dependence on Zagreb. Suspicions remained that Zagreb wanted to tie the Federation economy to the *kuna*, similarly to the Herceg-Bosnia areas, while blocking attempts to create a Bosnian currency. Observers believed that instead of promoting mergers with Croatia, the Federation itself first needed to be merged, as it did not constitute a single economic unit.

The Bonn Conference in December 1997 empowered Carlos Westendorp, the international mediator for Bosnian civil reconstruction, to impose solutions on the three Bosnian protagonists. The High Representative was authorized to make binding decisions on how to run the central government, impose interim solutions during disputes, and fire Bosnian officials who blocked progress toward integration. Some observers considered Westendorp's new mandate to be the first step toward transforming Bosnia into an international protectorate. Westendorp complained that the country lacked human and minority rights protection, laws on foreign investment, customs rules, national political parties, and public corporations. The Bonn Document called for a sustained campaign against official corruption and efforts to break the links between nationalist politicians and criminal rackets.

Fresh elections to the Bosnian Serb presidency and for the Serb member of the collective Bosnian presidency took place on 12–13 September 1998. The latter ballot was won byŽivko Radišić from the Socialist Party of the Serb Republic (SPSR), who gained 51.2% of the vote. His nearest challenger was the SDP leader Momčilo Krajišnik, who captured 44.9%. Nikola Poplašen, a leader of the Serbian Radical Party, won the vote to the Serbian presidency but was barred from taking office by Westendorp because of his staunch opposition to Bosnian integration. A new series of municipal elections took place in April 2000, but showed mixed success in integrating Bosnia and curtailing the powers of nationalist forces. Serb nationalists won in 49 municipalities, while Croatian nationalists captured 25. The Muslim Party of Democratic Action won in 23 by itself, and in 11 more in coalition with the more moderate Party for Bosnia-Herzegovina. There were some encouraging signs in that the multi-ethnic Social Democrats won in 15 municipalities and made important electoral advances.

Although Milošević's relationship with the Bosnian Serb leadership deteriorated during the war, the quasi-state was initially dependent on Belgrade for military and economic support. Moreover, all major political forces in the Serb Republic, including the opposition parties, supported a separate, Serb-dominated entity that would eventually merge with Yugoslavia. The main differences between them appeared to be over timetables and tactics rather than objectives. Similarly, leaders of the major opposition parties in Serbia indicated their support for an enlarged Serbia even as they paid lip service to Bosnian integration.

Tudjman's ties with the separatist Bosnian Croats also remained close. Indeed, several members of his inner circle were from the region and backed the "Greater Croatia" project. While Tudjman expressed his support for the Bosnian Federation, he reserved the long-term option of Herceg-Bosna's unification with Croatia. Nonetheless, unlike the situation in Serbia, the strongest opposition parties in Croatia opposed Tudjman's hidden agenda and remained openly committed to an integral Bosnia-Herzegovina.

The international community provided several billion dollars in aid to Bosnia after the signing of the Dayton accords. But there were persistent complaints that funds had been misused and primarily benefited the ruling nationalists. No major boost in production was registered, and the Serb entity in particular remained pauperized and devoid of any significant reconstruction assistance because of the obstruction of nationalist politicians. The reconstruction of Bosnia-Herzegovina as a single state and the promotion of a central political authority frustrated the international community. Nationalist politicians, especially from the major Serbian and Croatian parties, persistently blocked the process of state integration. The country remained polarized along ethnic lines as nationalist parties controlled decision-making in the two entities. In the municipal elections in April 2000, exclusivist nationalist parties again predominated in the Serb

and Croat majority areas as they effectively posed as the defenders of allegedly endangered "national interests."

International agencies favored the marginalization of nationalist hard-
liners of all three ethnic groups. For example, during his term in office,
Westendorp dismissed the President of the Serb Republic, Nikola Poplašen,
for interfering in the country's democratic process and for supporting partition. Westendorp also tried to intensify the state-building process by various
unilateral measures such as deciding on the country's new flag, national anthem, a joint currency, a common passport, and common national license
plates. In a number of cases, nationalist politicians in several cantons and
municipalities who openly violated the Dayton provisions were either removed
from office or barred from standing in future elections. Westendorp also began to restructure the Bosnian media by wresting control of several television
stations from the ruling nationalist parties. Although the High Representative
did not technically command any military force to put pressure on recalci-
trant politicians, his control of major aid and reconstruction resources enabled him to enforce most of his decisions.

But the degree of Westendorp's intervention led to complaints about externally imposed solutions among various Bosnian activists. Others believed
that the High Representative had not sufficiently exercised his authority and
had unnecessarily delayed the full implementation of the Dayton accords.
Simultaneously, international organizations were severely criticized for failing to arrest the two most senior indicted war criminals—Radovan Karadžić
and General Ratko Mladić.

Westendorp's successor, Wolfgang Petrisch, concentrated his efforts on
reforming Bosnia's corrupt judicial system, buttressing its precarious independent mass media, and improving its educational system. International representatives also condemned the activities of the Croatian Herzegovinian
ultranationalist networks as having thwarted the development of a functioning democracy and prevented the emergence of a competitive market economy.
They criticized the Tudjman government in Croatia for supporting illicit structures inside Bosnia and for harboring designs on Bosnian territory. But with
the election of a democratic coalition government in Croatia in January 2000,
Zagreb displayed its commitment to an integral Bosnia and thus improved
prospects for eliminating separatist trends in Croatian Herzegovina.

Human rights violations among rival ethnic groups persisted in Bosnia,
including discrimination in obtaining housing, education, and employment,
as well as sporadic acts of violence against returning refugees. Serbian leaders in particular continued to block the return of Muslim residents expelled
from their homes during the 1992–1995 war. A similar situation prevailed in
the Croatian-dominated parts of western Herzegovina. Nevertheless, without
international pressures and financial incentives the position of Bosnia's refugees and local minorities would be even more precarious.

International dependence was also evident in the Bosnian economy. Real growth continued to stagnate as a consequence of numerous factors, including widespread corruption and mismanagement, over-dependence on international agencies, and limited indigenous economic development. Since 1995, Bosnia had benefited from substantial foreign economic aid, particularly from the World Bank and the International Monetary Fund (IMF). But reports also surfaced that government leaders had misappropriated up to $1 billion from public funds or from international aid projects. The embezzled funds were believed to amount to about 20% of all state finances. The allegations were vehemently denied by both entities but they soured the climate for further foreign assistance and investment. International agencies also bemoaned the lack of a proper banking system and an effective tax and tariff collection agency in the country. Both factors encouraged illegitimate business activities and undermined the authority of the central government in Sarajevo.

The survival of Bosnia-Herzegovina as a single state remained dependent primarily on the presence of NATO and other international institutions to provide physical security, state resources, economic reconstruction, institutional continuity, and territorial integrity. Hard-line nationalists calculated that international resolve would weaken over time and that their resistance to ethnic reintegration and civic democracy would eventually pay off as international organizations disengaged from Bosnia and *de facto* recognized the existence of two sovereign states. Meanwhile, Bosnia's democrats were frustrated by the initial weak pressures exerted by international organizations on nationalist "warlords" and the slow development of civic institutions. But the civic activists and integralists were also cognizant that over-dependence on international actors could undermine the authenticity and indigenous development of Bosnia's multi-ethnic, civic-democratic institutions.

Centrist and civic forces gained a greater share of parliamentary representation in the general elections of 11 November 2000. Nevertheless, the all-Bosnia legislature remained extremely fractured, with 13 parties claiming the 42 seats. The multi-ethnic and moderate Social Democratic Party of Bosnia-Herzegovina captured nine seats, but the three major mono-ethnic formations gained a combined tally of 19 seats. Parliament eventually blocked the nomination of Croatian nationalist Martin Raguz as Prime Minister and elected the moderate Croat Božidar Matić as premier on 12 March 2001. Matić was backed by a broader anti-nationalist coalition, the Alliance for Change, which was strongly supported by the international community.

The nationalist Croatian Democratic Union (CDU) charged that the formation of the Bosnian Council of Ministers was unconstitutional and claimed discrimination against the Croatian community. In protest against the formation of a pro-integralist administration, in early March 2001 the CDU threatened to withdraw from all governmental institutions at the central, federal level and to create a parallel authority in the Croatian majority areas of western Herzegovina. CDU leader Ante Jelavić claimed that Croatian authorities would establish "temporary self-rule" through a separate "national assembly" and "inter-cantonal council" in the Herzegovinian capital Mostar. The separatist initiative was condemned by international agencies, and as tensions escalated in April 2001, NATO forces moved to freeze CDU bank accounts and to prevent the formation of a separate Croatian entity.

In the Serbian entity, Mirko Sarović of the Serbian Democratic Party (SDP) won the presidency in the first round of voting on 11 November 2000, while the more moderate Mladan Ivanić and Milorad Dodik finished a long way behind. Sarović's victory ensured a nationalist stranglehold over all state institutions in the Serb Republic and continuing resistance to Bosnia's political integration.

POLITICAL PARTIES

Socialists and Social Democrats

Social Democratic Party (SDP)
Socijaldemokratska Stranka (SDS)

The Social Democratic Party (SDP) emerged from the League of Communists and was first known as the Democratic Party of Socialists (DPS). It was led by its president Zlatko Lagumdžija. The party was created in 1989 but traced its heritage to democratic socialist movements in pre–World War II Yugoslavia. It voiced pride in the wartime communist partisans who resisted Nazi occupation and created the second Yugoslavia. It supported the communist decision after the war to establish a Bosnian republic within the Yugoslav federation.

According to its official history, by the end of the 1980s the SDP accomplished a historic step toward a multi-party democracy by condemning the principles and practices of the ruling communists. The SDP gained 15 seats in the November 1990 republican elections, with just over 11% of the total vote. After the ballot and the success of the nationalist formations, the SDP warned about the menace of ethnicity-based parties that were intent on instigating nationality conflicts and that favored the territorial aspirations of Serbia and Croatia. SDP leaders warned against attempts at provoking war and partition in Bosnia. During the 1992 referendum, the SDP called upon its members and supporters to vote for an independent and united state.

The first SDP congress took place on 27 December 1992, at which the old name of the party was adopted. The congress also expressed its orientation towards the "European" concept of social democracy. The party expressed its commitment to a multi-party parliamentary democracy, inter-ethnic cooperation, and a "legal and social state." The SDP wanted primarily to be a party that advocated the interests of labor and all sectors of society oriented towards a civil state. The SDP participated in the September 1996 elections as a part of the coalition Joint List for Bosnia-Herzegovina, which captured only two seats in the national parliament.[21] The SDP ran on its own in the 12–13 September 1998 elections and gained two out of the 28 federation seats in the national parliament.

Despite this relatively poor showing at the national level, the position of the SDP after the Dayton accords proved more favorable than that of most other multi-ethnic, civic-based parties. The SDP gained 19 out of 140 seats in the Federation parliament in the September 1998 elections. Lagumdžija was able to mobilize voters across entity boundaries, and some observers believed that the SDP had an opportunity of becoming one of the strongest parties in the country if the influence of nationalists declined.

Alliance of Reform Forces of Yugoslavia (ARFY)
Savez Reformskih Snaga Jugoslavije (SRSJ)

The Alliance was formed in August 1990 throughout Yugoslavia in an effort to support the federal Prime Minister Ante Marković, who was seeking to maintain a democratized Yugoslav federation. Marković launched a program of economic reform and marketization but was increasingly sidelined because of growing nationalist mobilization throughout the country. In Bosnia-Herzegovina, the ARFY branch was headed by Nenad Kečmanović, rector at Sarajevo University and a prominent liberal. In fact, the Alliance functioned as an umbrella organization for numerous small local groupings with reformist policies that appealed across ethnic boundaries. The ARFY captured 12 seats in the November 1990 elections in the Chamber of Citizens and one in the Chamber of Municipalities. As the country slid toward armed conflict, the Alliance became increasingly irrelevant and disappeared from the political radar screen.

Independent Social Democratic Party (ISDP)
Stranka Nezavisna Socijalistička Demokratska (SNSD)

The Independent Social Democratic Party (ISDP) was initially established in February 1992 in Banja Luka. During the 1992–1995 war, its founder Milorad Dodik worked in difficult conditions on behalf of inter-ethnic cooperation but was also believed to be involved in some of the sanctions-busting and smuggling networks commonplace across Bosnian-Serb territories. Following the Dayton accords, the party emerged in a more public setting. In September 1996, the ISDP participated in the Alliance for Peace and Progress, in Bosnia's first post-war parliamentary elections. Dodik and his party were the initiators of the *Sloga* coalition, which consisted of the ISDP, the Serbian People's Union (SPU), and the Socialist Party of the Serb Republic (SPSR). Together with their *Sloga* partners, the ISDP became the main opposition to the nationalist SDP/SRP bloc in the Serb entity.

The ISDP was generally Western-oriented and focused on cooperation with parties from other ethnic groups. Party leader Dodik was the only candidate for prime minister who was acceptable to the High Commissioner Westendorp. However, his political course remained unstable, as he could not ignore substantial nationalist sentiments in the Serb Republic. For example, whenever tensions rose in Bosnia, the position of the ISDP altered, as Dodik did not want to be perceived as a puppet of international policy and calculated that the High Representative would support him because of a lack of credible non-nationalist alternatives. The international ruling over the city of Brčko provoked severe anger in Bosnian Serbian politics, and the ISDP publicly expressed resentment against the ruling, together with other Serbian parties.

Dodik recognized that collaboration with the international community was more likely to bring tangible rewards than tying the Serb entity to Milošević's Yugoslavia. However, during his tenure the gap between east and west in the Serb Republic increased, and most international aid flowed into the western sector in order to encourage the "liberals" in Banja Luka and to discourage the "hard-liners" in Pale. But Dodik was also vulnerable to criticism that he had not delivered results commensurate with the political and financial support he received. For example, refugee returns were negligible despite his declaration early in 1998 that up to 70,000 would return that year. Dodik argued that he could not go too far against public opinion or he would lose votes and power. International agencies largely accepted this argument, because Dodik appeared to be independent of Belgrade. The ISDP gained 6 out of 83 seats in the Serb Republic assembly in the September 1998 elections, and 11 seats in the November 2000 ballot, with a possibility of entering a new coalition government.

Liberals and Integrationists

Party for Bosnia-Herzegovina (PB-H)
Stranka za Bosnu i Hercegovinu (SB-H)

The Party for Bosnia-Herzegovina (PB-H) was established in April 1996 by former Bosnian Prime Minister Haris Silajdžić as a multi-ethnic organization, although it came to represent a moderate Muslim constituency. Silajdžić, who was a PDA leader and the country's premier until January 1996, resigned because he thought that the PDA's policies had become too Muslim oriented. Moreover, Silajdžić advocated the unity of Bosnia-Herzegovina, an ideal he believed had been squandered by the PDA leadership. The PB-H became a component of the Whole and Democratic Bosnia (CWDB) *(Koalicija za Cijelu i Demokratsku Bosnu)* election coalition in 1996, together with the PDA and other largely Muslim Bosniak groupings. Although membership was open to all ethnic groups, the party was Muslim-based and obtained strong Muslim backing in urban areas such as Tuzla and Sarajevo. The PB-H ran as an independent party in the September 1996 Federation elections and won 10 out of

140 seats.[22] In the November 2000 general elections, the PB-H gained 5 seats in the all-state (Bosnian Federation and Serb Republic) House of Representatives and 21 of 140 seats in the Federation parliament.

Muslim Bosnian Organization (MBO)
Muslimanska Bošnjačka Organizacija (MBO)

The Muslim Bosnian Organization (MBO) was formed after a split in the leadership of the PDA. It was founded in October 1990 by the former PDA vice president Adil Zulfikarpašić, as well as by Muhamed Filipović and Hamža Mujagić, PDA members who had been expelled from the party. The MBO called for a democratic Yugoslavia, contending that Yugoslavia as a union of republics was the best solution for its component nations. The party claimed that it did not use Islam for political ends, although one of its main objectives was to ensure the rights of Bosnian Muslims to practice their faith freely. The leadership announced that the new party would have a liberal-democratic orientation and would not be ideological or nationalistic. The party also stood for the religious rights of all Bosnian citizens and explicitly distanced itself from the more Muslim-oriented PDA. But its appeal did not extend deeply into the Muslim community and was largely confined to intellectual circles.

Zulfikarpašić, a former partisan major general, was once an ideologist of the Bosnian Brotherhood, an organization that had urged all Muslims to remain in the Yugoslav federation. He also founded the Institute of Bosnian Studies in Zurich, which propagated the theory of *Bošnjastvo*—that Bosnians were a separate ethnic group regardless of religious affiliation. In early 1990, Zulfikarpašić returned to Bosnia, where he founded the PDA together with Izetbegović. But differences soon emerged, and Izetbegović accused Zulfikarpašić of being a Yugoslav counterintelligence agent. When Zulfikarpašić proposed to Radovan Karadžić that a Serb-Muslim agreement be signed without the participation of the PDA, the largest Muslim party in the republic, Bosnian Muslim and Croat leaders declared him a traitor.

Meanwhile, in 1991, leaders of the MBO accused Alija Izetbegović of sponsoring militant PDA groups that were said to be terrorizing members of the MBO. A letter was sent to Izetbegović by MBO leaders stating that there was evidence of assaults on MBO members. These incidents had allegedly occurred after the MBO and SDP agreed on a joint platform to form a federative order in Yugoslavia in August 1991. The draft agreement called for Muslims and Serbs to join together to preserve Yugoslavia as a single state and to maintain a "whole and indivisible" Bosnia-Herzegovina within the federation. Zulfikarpašić continued to criticize the Sarajevo leadership throughout the Bosnian war for its failure to reach an accord with the Serbs and for bearing responsibility for the collapse of the state and its descent into civil war.[23] However, the MBO failed to gain any significant support after the 1992–1995 war and remained a small political formation.

Democratic Party (DP)
Demokratska Stranka (DS)

The Democratic Party (DP) was formerly known as the People's Democratic Union (PDU) (*Demokratska Narodna Zajednica, DNZ*) and was founded by Fikret Abdić, a popular businessman and political leader in the Bihać-Cazin region of western Bosnia. In the presidential elections on 18 November 1990, Abdić gained the majority of Muslim votes for the collective office, scoring over 44% as compared with 37% for his main rival Alija Izetbegović. Abdić sided with Croatian forces and against Izetbegović after the initial Croat-Muslim alliance fell apart in 1993–1994. He took control of the Bihać region with a small local force, operating between Serbian-held areas in Croatian Krajina and Bosnia's Serb Republic. His forces opposed the incorporation of Bihać into the emerging Muslim entity when Bosnia appeared to be on the verge of collapse and partition. He established a self-proclaimed Autonomous Province of Western Bosnia.

Observers believed that Abdić skillfully steered between Croatian and Serbian nationalists and conducted illicit trade with both sides to maintain the autonomy of the Bihać pocket. At the end of the war, in 1995, Abdić fled to Croatia, where he remained in hiding through the end of the decade. The Hague Tribunal indicted Abdić for committing war crimes during the Bosnian war, and the Sarajevo government issued a warrant for his arrest on charges of state treason. Nevertheless, Abdić's party, the DS, was allowed to stand in the post-Dayton elections in September 1996 and obtained one seat in the national House of Representatives and three seats in the Federation parliament.

Serbian People's Union (SPU)
Srpski Narodni Savez (SNS)

The Serbian People's Union (SPU) was founded in July 1997 by Biljana Plavšić, the former successor of Radovan Karadžić as President of the Serb Republic. During the 1992–1995 war, Plavšić was a hard-line nationalist, claiming large parts of Bosnia for the Serb para-state. After the war, the international community was able to drive a wedge between Plavšić and Karadžić. She was transformed into a "dove," inclined to cooperate with the West and with the Muslim and Croat leadership. The "doves" formed a minority within the ruling Serbian Democratic Party (SDP). Plavšić left the SDP and founded the SPU while moving toward the political center. The SPU became a member of the *Sloga* coalition, which included the Socialist Party of the Serb Republic (SPSR), and the Independent Social Democrats (ISD). The SPU gained 12 seats out of 83 in the National Assembly of the Serb Republic in the September 1998 elections.

Differences became apparent within the SDP after the signing of the Dayton accords that reflected broader political disagreements between nationalist interest groups in Pale and Banja Luka. By 1997, these differences led to an open split, provoked by Plavšić's criticism of those within the SDP who engaged in massive corruption and who were mostly loyal to the Pale-based representative of the collective Bosnian presidency, Momčilo Krajišnik. A catalyst for the split was the apprehension in June 1997 by British S-FOR units of two persons in Prijedor wanted for war crimes, and the death of a third, who resisted arrest. This act prompted Serbian officials to take more seriously the international community's determination to implement the Dayton provisions. As the international actors expressed similar resolve by backing Plavšić, the population in Banja Luka and the western part of the Serb entity genuinely seemed to support her efforts, and the second half of 1997 saw the steady reduction of Pale's influence, particularly within the police forces and local administration.

The SPU was founded too late to participate in the municipal elections in September 1997. However, Plavšić succeeded in pushing through new parliamentary elections within the Serb Republic, the results of which finally broke the SDP stranglehold on power. Plavšić formed an alliance with the moderate Milorad Dodik, who had established his own Independent Social Democrats Party (ISDP). Meanwhile, the SDP gained the support of the Serbian Radical Party (SRP), a branch of the Belgrade-based political party of the same name and led by the extreme nationalist Vojislav Šešelj.

Republican Party (RP)
Republikanska Stranka (RS)

The Republican Party (RP) was founded in 1994 in Sarajevo and claimed about 12,000 members. It was led by Stjepan Kljujić, the former leader of the Croatian Democratic Union (CDU), who fell out of favor with Croatian nationalists and the irredentist policies of Croatian President Franjo Tudjman. Kljuić dissented on the issue of ethnic coexistence, which he deemed necessary for the preservation of Bosnia. The RP failed to gain any parliamentary representation while maintaining its position as a centrist party that advocated "civic patriotic" policies. According to the party statute, the RP had two main objectives: the struggle for the liberation and integrity of Bosnia-Herzegovina, and the struggle for democracy. Bosnian Republicans upheld close contacts with several like-minded parties, including the Croatian Independent Democrats (CID). The RP was active inside the Patriotic Front in the Bosnian Federation but staunchly opposed the narrow nationalism of the ruling PDA and CDU. The Republicans established a multinational membership structure, which they claimed was almost identical with the structure of the Bosnian population of Bosnia. However, in the September 1998 and in the November 2000 elections, the party did not pass the threshold for parliamentary representation.

New Croatian Initiative (NCI)
Nova Hrvatska Inicijativa (NHI)

The Bosnian based Croatian Democratic Union (CDU) split after the party's fifth convention in May 1998, and the moderate faction around Krešimir Zubak, the then Bosnian Croat representative on the country's joint presidency, established a new party, the New Croatian Initiative (NCI). The party promoted an integrationist political agenda but was unable to determine a decisive shift away from the agenda of exclusive ethnic nationalism among Croats in western Herzegovina in particular. Ante Jelavić, the new Bosnian CDU hard-line president, had declared his commitment to carrying out the Dayton agreement. But this did not signify that his cooperation would be genuine nor that the CDU had given up its ultimate goal of joining the parts of Bosnia where ethnic Croats formed a majority with Croatia itself. The NCI performed poorly in the national elections in November 2000, gaining only 2% of the vote and one seat in the all-state House of Representatives and 1.6% of the vote and two seats in the Federation parliament.

Party of Democratic Progress (PDP)
Partija Demokratskog Progresa (PDP)

Led by Serbian activist Mladen Ivanić, the Party of Democratic Progress (PDP) was established in September 1999 and declared itself a party of "new people and European standards." The first congress of the party took place in Banja Luka on 26 February 2000, at which the party named its leadership and declared its program. Ivanić was a professor of political economy at the university of Banja Luka who became known in public life as the *Sloga* presidential candidate for the Bosnian presidency during the first general elections after the 1992-1995 war. After the dismissal of the Serb assembly, Plavšić appointed Ivanić as Prime Minister; but after failing to obtain SDP support, he turned his mandate down. He subsequently established his own party, whose goal, at least publicly, was to fulfill the Dayton agreements. Most members of the PDP were university professors and intellectuals. The PDP gained 5% of the vote and two seats in the Bosnian House of Representatives in the elections on 11 November 2000, and 12.2% of the vote and 10 seats in the Serbian National Assembly. It looked set to join the coalition government in the Serbian entity.

Christian Democrats

Croatian Christian Democratic Union (CCDU)
Hrvatska Krščanska Demokratska Unija (HKDU)

The Croatian Christian Democratic Union (CCDU) was established in 1997 during Bosnia's local elections. The first president was Zeljko Nuić, who was replaced by Ante Pašalić Djinda in 1998. The same year, the CCDU joined the coalition with the New Croatian Initiative (NCI), hoping for better election results. However, it gained only one seat in the Bosnian parliament in the September 1998 elections. The party's parliamentary representative was Petar Milić, who did not work in accordance with the party statute and was removed from his position. Following his removal, Milić created his own political party under the name of the Croatian Christian Democrats (CCD) *(Hrvatski Demokrščani, HD)*. Both parties remained minor political actors on the Bosnian stage and claimed little support either within or outside the Croatian community.

Agrarians

Croatian Peasants Party (CPP)
Hrvatska Seljačka Stranka (HSS)

The Croatian Peasants Party (CPP) was established and led by Ivo Komčić as a non-nationalist party, in opposition to the nationalist and separatist CDU sponsored by the regime in Zagreb. The party strongly supported the Bosnian state. Its backers primarily consisted of moderate Croats from central and northern Bosnia who vehemently opposed Tudjman's policies. The CPP advocated a decentralized administration, according to which the regional cantons would acquire most power. The party was linked to the CPP in Croatia, which was founded in 1904 and played a major role in inter-war Yugoslavia. The Bosnian CPP was close to social democratic political thinking, but some of its top members tended toward a more centrist political standpoint. The party was hindered from attracting broad public support by the nationalist atmosphere that prevailed in western Herzegovina, where only the CDU had unlimited freedom of action. Indeed, CPP representatives were harassed and assaulted in the Croatian nationalist strongholds and were unable to campaign freely in local or national elections. The CPP obtained only one seat in the Federation's House of Representatives in the elections on 12–13 September 1998 and failed to win any seats in the November 2000 elections.

Greens

Ecological Party (EP)
Zelena Stranka (ZS)

The green movement in Bosnia-Herzegovina has not played any significant role in political or social life, although several small political organizations did exist in the republic, including the Ecological Party (EP), the Ecological Movement (*Ekološki Pokret*), and the Bosnian Greens (*Bosanski Zeleni*). None of these formations were successful in gaining seats to the federal or entity parliaments, as public attention was focused on more immediate problems of physical survival and gaining a livelihood.

Communists

League of Communists–Social Democratic Party (LC-SDP)
Savez Komunista–Socijalistička Demokratska Partija (SK-SDP)

During the political upheavals in 1990, the League of Communists of Bosnia-Herzegovina (LCBH) transformed itself into an organization supporting pluralism and democracy. Party membership was generally multiethnic, but the LCBH began to disintegrate as ethnicity-based parties were established among Bosnia's three national groups. The League of Communists–Social Democratic Party (LC-SDP) was led by Nijaz Djuraković, a Muslim, and it worked closely with the former communist front organization, which adopted the name Democratic Socialist Alliance (DSA) *(Demokratski Socijalistički Savez, DSS)*. The LC-SDP gained 15 seats in the November 1990 elections to the Chamber of Citizens and 4 seats in the Chamber of Municipalities. The DSA captured one seat on its own, and one seat in coalition with an environmentalist party. Another communist splinter, the Socialist Youth Organization (SYO), also won one parliamentary seat. All these groupings essentially became bystanders during the bloody war that erupted in 1992, and had almost no political impact on developments in the republic during the 1990s.

Nationalists

Party of Democratic Action (PDA)
Stranka Demokratske Akcije (SDA)

The Party of Democratic Action (PDA) was founded in May 1990 under the leadership of Alija Izetbegović and in the presence of 1,500 supporters. The PDA not only claimed to rally Bosnia's Muslims but also sought a political alliance of all Yugoslav citizens with an affinity for Muslim cultural, historical, and religious traditions. Hence, the party established branches or affiliates in other republics, including Serbia, Montenegro, and Macedonia. However, the latter's links with the Bosnian party became increasingly tenuous as Yugoslavia dissolved and Bosnia approached open conflict. The PDA's founding assembly was attended by representatives from 73 locations, including the larger towns of Mostar, Banja Luka, Zenica, Velika Kladuša, and Kladanj, and even from Croatian capital of Zagreb, where the PDA claimed more than 10,000 supporters.

In the November 1990 elections, 37.8% of the electorate voted for the PDA, and the party won 86 of the 240 seats in the Bosnian Assembly as well as 3 out of 7 open seats in the Bosnian national presidency. As envisaged in election stipulations, soon after the ballot, Izetbegović, who was elected to the nine-person Bosnian presidency, formed a coalition government with the major Serb and Croat parties. Consequently, he was nominated as the first president in the rotating Bosnian presidency. In its program, the PDA called for economic reform with an emphasis on the denationalization of government-owned enterprises and the privatization of property. It called for the return of land confiscated by the communists after 1945. The party also advocated that restrictions on landholding by private citizens should be removed.

As part of its economic liberalization program, the party stressed modern market production in agriculture as well as a reduction in budgets and personnel with respect to government offices, the police force, and the military. At its inaugural meeting, the PDA declared its principles to include freedom and equality of all citizens, without any distinction in regard to religion, nationality, race, sex, language, social status, or political beliefs. The party proposed legislation guaranteeing the national, cultural, and religious rights of Bosnian Muslims and the free activity of all religious communities. In addition, the PDA called for preserving the integrity and inviolability of the borders of Bosnia-Herzegovina. The PDA, which by early 1991 claimed to have over 400,000 members, considered itself the representative of various strata in society. In fact, the party's initial calculations showed that during the pre-election period, Bosnians were registering in the party at a rate of 100,000 a month.

Throughout 1991, the PDA condemned Serbian steps toward territorial autonomy. According to Muslim leaders, the newly formed Serb authorities in self-declared autonomous municipalities were created without prior consultation with the Bosnian government and contrary to the legislature's recommendations. PDA leaders asserted that the formation of such bodies negated and denied the rights of Muslims and other nations living in that territory. Moreover, the proposed unification of Croatian Krajina and Bosnian Krajina constituted a "violation of the territorial integrity, sovereignty, and constitutional order of Bosnia-Herzegovina." Sarajevo declared this move null and void. In mid-September 1991, in response to the creation of Serbian autonomous regions, the PDA warned that it would form an autonomous Muslim region in the Mostar area of Herzegovina.

The head of the Islamic Religious Community (IRC), Hadji Jakob Efendi Selimoski, claimed that the Muslims were undergoing a religious revival in Bosnia. Apparently, an increasing number were observing the holy month of Ramadan, participating in Islamic rituals, and learning about their faith. As a result of this revival movement, during the summer of 1991, Belgrade claimed that Muslim extremists were calling for the transformation of Bosnia into a separate Islamic state. The new entity, according to Serb leaders, was slated to incorporate other areas of Yugoslavia with large Muslim populations. The PDA denied any such intentions. But despite this disclaimer, the Serbian media vilified Izetbegović for his alleged pan-Islamic sympathies.

In August 1991, the leader of the Muslim Bosnian Organization (MBO), Adil Zulfikarpašić, argued that Izetbegović should accept a proposal endorsed by Karadžić for remaining within Yugoslavia. Zulfikarpašić believed that without Yugoslavia there would be no Bosnia-Herzegovina and that the problem could not be solved without the participation of Serb leaders. Such statements were vehemently opposed by Izetbegović, who at that time did not want to enter into any agreement that would exclude a third party, in this case the Croats. He affirmed that the PDA would not take sides in the Serb-Croat dispute, as this would endanger Bosnia's political integrity and provoke an all-out war. While the MBO supported preserving an indivisible Bosnia within a Yugoslav federation, regardless of whether Slovenia and Croatia seceded, the PDA favored a confederal Yugoslavia without the loss of Bosnian territory.

As tensions mounted within the republic, in October 1991 Muslim and Croat leaders in the Bosnian Assembly voted to declare the republic's sovereignty and neutrality. However, Serbian leaders boycotted the session and declared the vote illegal because it breached an agreement that called for consensus among all three major parties in passing legislation and undertaking constitutional changes. The PDA envisioned Yugoslavia as either a federation with various confederal elements or a confederation with federal elements.

In March 1992, the party spoke out against the idea of dividing the state according to ethnic principles alone and claimed that it would support a unitary and civil Bosnia-Herzegovina, taking into account the multi-ethnic characteristics of the republic. This position was maintained by the party leadership throughout the war launched by Serb guerrillas in April 1992, despite some division between more pragmatic and militant factions. The war itself contributed to radicalizing a segment of the Muslim population and the PDA leadership, although Izetbegović, his deputy Ejup Ganić, and Foreign Minister Haris Silajdžić were able to preserve the party's unity.[24]

Throughout the 1990s, the PDA remained one of the strongest parties under the leadership of Izetbegović. In the second multi-party election, in September 1996, the PDA won 19 out of 42 seats in the House of Representatives of the parliamentary assembly of Bosnia-Herzegovina. The candidate of the party was elected a member of the presidency, and later on the chair of the presidency, of the Bosnian state. In the House of Representatives of the parliament of the Federation of Bosnia-Herzegovina, the PDA won 78 out of 140 seats, and in the National Assembly of the Serbian Republic, 14 out of 83 seats. In the same year, the PDA won the majority vote in 6 out of 10 cantons on the territory of the Federation. At the local elections in 1997, the Coalition for an Integrated and Democratic Bosnia-Herzegovina, consisting of the PDA, the Party for Bosnia and Herzegovina, the Civic Democratic Party, and the Liberal Party, won the greatest number of votes in 56 out of 135 municipalities in which elections took place.

At the general elections in September 1998, the PDA again participated within the Coalition for an Integrated and Democratic Bosnia-Herzegovina. The Coalition candidate, Izetbegović, was elected again as the Bosniak member of the presidency of Bosnia-Herzegovina. In the House of Representatives of the parliamentary assembly of Bosnia-Herzegovina, the Coalition won 17 out of 42 seats. In the House of Representatives of the Federation of Bosnia-Herzegovina, the Coalition captured 68 out of 140 seats, and in the National Assembly of the Serb Rèpublic, the Coalition gained 15 out of 83 seats. Representatives of the Coalition also garnered a majority in 6 out of 10 cantonal assemblies in the Bosnian Federation.[25] In the November 2000 ballot, the PDA gained eight of the 42 seats in the Bosnia-Herzegovinian House of Representatives and 38 out of 140 seats to the Bosnian Federation parliament.

Bosniak Organization (BO)
Bošnjačka Organizacija (BO)

The Bosniak Organization (BO) was founded in 1990 as the Muslim Bosniak Organization (MBO) after a split within the PDA. It was led by chairman Adil Zulfikarpašić. At that time the party advocated Bosnian emancipation, which to its opponents signified Muslim nationalism. After the war the party transformed itself into a moderate party and described itself as a multi-ethnic, multi-confessional, and liberal party that abandoned any ethnocentric preoccupations. The party name was changed, and the word *Muslim* was deleted. The BO advocated the return of refugees to their original homes; in order to achieve this goal, trans-ethnic and inter-entity cooperation was an absolute necessity. The BO maintained good relations with the Social Democratic Party and other centrist formations. The BO also became a member of the Joint List for the elections in September 1996.

Muslim Democratic Party (MDP)
Muslimanska Demokratska Stranka (MDS)

The Muslim Democratic Party (MDP) was established during 1992 to challenge the policies of President Izetbegović and the PDA leadership. It was led by President Armin Pohara, who attacked the Sarajevo government for failing to prepare for the Serbian onslaught and keeping the Croatian side at arm's length. Indeed, the MDP advocated "complete unity" between Bosnian Muslims and Croats and a confederation between Bosnia-Herzegovina and Croatia, possibly culminating in an integrated state, to oppose Serbian aggression. It defended the CDU leadership and the self-styled president of "Herceg-Bosna," Mate Boban, and proposed a joint Croatian-Muslim command of Bosnia's armed forces. Pohara claimed that a Muslim member of the Bosnian presidency, Fikret Abdić, who controlled the Bihać–Cazinska Krajina pocket and was a long-time critic of Izetbegović, was planning to join the party. However, it remained unclear how much support the MDP actually had on the ground, especially as Muslim-Croat relations deteriorated throughout Bosnia in the wake of mutual "ethnic cleansing" campaigns during the spring and summer of 1993.[26] The party practically disappeared from the political scene in the mid-1990s.

Serbian Democratic Party (SDP)
Srpska Demokratska Stranka (SDS)

The Serbian Democratic Party (SDP) was founded in July 1990 by Radovan Karadžić, a psychiatrist by profession, in the presence of 8,000 members. The party was initially a branch of the Croatia-based SDP, which led Serbian opposition to the independent Croatian state and was instrumental in establishing a parallel authority in the Krajina region. In Bosnia-Herzegovina, the SDP drew its support and ideological orientation from Serb intellectuals, professionals, military leaders, and the Milošević leadership in Belgrade. With regard to social programs, the SDP was considered a centrist party with some leftist leanings. The party's stated aim was to ensure the full and unconditional civil, national, cultural, religious, and economic equality of Serbs in Bosnia. It called for the "national, cultural, and spiritual unification" of Serbs in Bosnia-Herzegovina and other Yugoslav territories. The SDP also advocated freedom of religion, the complete restructuring of the educational and social service administrations, the depoliticization of government agencies, and the establishment of a modern army. The SDP initially encountered some competition from rival Serbian parties, including the Serbian Renewal Movement (SRM), but their political impact was curtailed by the support offered to Karadžić by the regime in Belgrade and by the extensive political apparatus inherited from the former communist *nomenklatura*.

The prime objective of the SDP was to defend "Serbian interests" in the republic. In pursuit of this objective, during 1990 the SDP established a self-governing Serbian National Council that was sharply criticized by both Muslim and Croat leaders for encouraging ethnic polarization and Bosnian disintegration. In the November 1990 elections, ethnic parity was maintained in the Chamber of Citizens, the Chamber of Municipalities, and the collective presidency. The SDP won a total of 71 seats in the 240-seat bicameral legislature. Following the elections, the SDP joined the PDA and the CDU to form a coalition government representing the republic's three major ethnic groups.

After the balloting the SDP claimed that Serbs living in predominantly Serbian areas of Bosnia-Herzegovina opposed Bosnian independence and were in favor of a union or close association with Serbia. Serb spokesmen affiliated with the SDP claimed that their rights would be endangered in an independent Bosnia. Karadžić and his followers asserted that an independent Bosnian state would be a unitary entity in which a combined Muslim and Croatian majority would disenfranchise and persecute the Serbian minority. The SDP claimed that all Serbs had the inalienable right to live in one state and asserted that only nations and not republics had the right to separate from Yugoslavia.

The political and military strategies of Serbian forces in Bosnia led by the SDP focused on gaining control over territories inhabited predominantly by Serbs. Karadžić denied that he and his supporters sought to separate Bosnian territory and annex it to a planned Greater Serbia. Instead, he proposed the division of Bosnia-Herzegovina into communal cantons that would function as autonomous entities under the control of the majority national group in each canton. Under such an arrangement, Karadžić and his followers believed that Serbian-controlled cantons would include about 70% of Bosnian territory, despite the fact that Serbs constituted only 31% of the republic's population. The SDP leaders justified their claim by the fact that Serbs, who were mostly farmers and rural residents, purportedly owned 70% of the land.

In a referendum in March 1992, the Bosnian Assembly asked citizens whether they supported a sovereign and independent Bosnia-Herzegovina. The SDP declared the act illegal and encouraged all Bosnian Serbs to boycott the plebiscite. The boycott was comprehensive among the Serbian electorate, as 63.4% of Bosnian voters participated in the ballot. Of those who did participate, mostly Muslims and Croats, the vast majority voted in favor of independence. Having met the requisite EC criteria, the republic was internationally recognized as an independent state in April 1992.

Immediately after Bosnia's recognition, the SDP withdrew its representatives from the Bosnian presidency, the Bosnian Assembly, and all other governmental institutions and proclaimed the formation of the Serbian Republic of Bosnia-Herzegovina. As the war escalated during the spring and summer of 1992, it became evident that the governments of Yugoslavia and Serbia were providing economic, military, and political support to the Bosnian Serbs. It was widely believed that Karadžić was directly sponsored by President Milošević. Indeed, Belgrade both openly and clandestinely supported the SDP's military and political objectives. Despite the militant stance of the SDP, many Serbs in Bosnia-Herzegovina reportedly did not share its program of ethnic division, particularly those living in multi-ethnic cities such as Sarajevo. Similarly, Serb democrats in Serbia and some members of the academic community opposed the position of the SDP and its promulgation of conflict in Bosnia.[27]

The SDP retained the majority of seats on the quasi-governmental Serb Assembly, based in the Bosnian town of Pale near Sarajevo. Its activists adopted the most militant positions, pushing for the creation of a fully separate state, rejecting the EC-sponsored peace proposals, organizing a referendum on independence in May 1993, and calling for the political and military unification of the Serb Republic (in Bosnia-Herzegovina) and the Serb Republic of Krajina (in Croatia). Some rifts were visible both in the Assembly and in the party over strategic approaches toward Serbian unification and merger with Yugoslavia. Karadžić himself remained close to his patron Milošević, while balancing the uncompromising position of local activists and military commanders with those of more moderate politicians who preferred a longer-term approach and seemed willing to make short-term concessions.

The militant line prevailed, especially when it became evident that the United Nations was not prepared to engage in military intervention. SDP ideologist Jovan Spremo and SDP activists from the radical stronghold of Banja Luka proposed early unification between the Serb and Krajina republics. At a joint session between the two republican assemblies, SDP delegate Vojo Kuprešanin also proposed that the new state be declared a monarchy or a duchy under the constitutional rule of Prince Tomislav Karadjordjević. In this scenario, Tomislav's nephew Aleksandar would be slated to inherit the throne as king of Yugoslavia. The two monarchies would then move toward royal and administrative unification in one Greater Serbian state. Although Prince Tomislav reportedly viewed the proposal favorably, Milošević was not well disposed to an initiative that challenged his influence in Serb-held territories in Bosnia and Croatia.[28]

In the September 1998 Bosnian elections, the SDP gained four seats in the House of Representatives, all of which were allotted to candidates from the Serb Republic. Until the 1998 ballot, the SDP was the leading Serbian party in the Serb entity, with its headquarters in Pale. The party's ideological orientation remained ultra-nationalist to the neglect of economic and social issues. During and after the Bosnian war, SDP maneuvers and positions revolved around its political leader, the indicted war criminal Karadžić. Karadžić was forced to resign from his positions in the party he helped to found, because according to the Dayton accords indicted individuals were not allowed to hold public posts or run in any elections. Initially, neither the SDP nor Karadžić were inclined to obey this ruling, but with strong international pressure, the more moderate wing within the SDP removed him from office. Aleksa Buha became the new party leader. After Karadžić's downfall, SDP popularity diminished somewhat. It won 45 seats in the 83-member parliament of Serb Republic elections in 1996, but only scored 19 seats after the 1998 elections. The SDP and the SRP formed a joint list for the 1998 elections.

Despite various setbacks and challenges from moderates, the SDP maintained its popularity among Serb voters. Many of them, especially in the eastern Serb Republic, viewed it as the most effective protector of their "national interests" and remained fearful of Bosnian integration and their potential minority status. The party scored 36% of the vote in elections to the Serb Assembly in November 2000 and garnered a total of 31 seats: it formed the basis of a new coalition government in the Serb entity.

Socialist Party of the Serb Republic (SPSR)
Socijalistička Partija Republike Srpske (SPRS)

The Socialist Party of the Serb Republic (SPSR) was a branch of the Socialist Party of Serbia, the party of Slobodan Milošević, even though its leaders claimed otherwise. The original party leadership was made up of officers of the Bosnian Serb army. It was the main Serbian opposition party against the SDP, although it shared the SDP's position on the future of the Serb Republic—i.e., that it should become part of Yugoslavia. For the September 1996 elections, the party was part of the Alliance for Peace and Progress coalition. The SPSR was the only Bosnian Serb organization to run in the whole of Bosnia-Herzegovina and not only in the Serb entity. The party's views changed over the years from radical Serbian nationalism towards a more moderate position of cooperation with the international community. For the September 1998 elections, the SPSR joined the *Sloga* coalition and was led byŽivko Radišić. It gained two seats in the Federation parliament and 10 seats in the National Assembly of the Serb Republic, but only four seats in the Serb Assembly after the November 2000 elections. Several smaller nationalist organizations were also formed in the Serb Republic, including the sister party of the Belgrade-based Serbian Renewal Movement (SRM) (*Srpski Pokret Obnove, SPO*).

Croatian Democratic Union (CDU)
Hrvatska Demokratska Zajednica (HDZ)

The Croatian Democratic Union (CDU) was founded in October 1990 and was led by Stjepan Kljujić, a journalist, until March 1992, when Miljenko Brkić was elected acting president. The party initially propounded a liberal orientation, promoting all forms of private ownership, a market economy, and the entry of Bosnia into the EC. The CDU described itself as the "only party that would guarantee the rights of Croats in Bosnia." The party sought a constitutional guarantee that Croats in the republic would have the right to "self-determination." As one of the three largest ethnicity based parties, and with the additional support of its sister organizations in Zagreb, the CDU managed to gain 45 legislative seats, out of a total of 240, in the November 1990 republican elections. A number of other Croatian parties were also formed during 1990, including the ultra-nationalist Zagreb-based Croatian Party of Rights (CPR), but their influence in Bosnia-Herzegovina was dwarfed by the CDU.

The programs of Croat activists in Bosnia and Croatia varied significantly, in particular with respect to the status of western Herzegovina and their cooperation with the Bosnian government. Even though CDU members technically remained members of the Bosnian presidency, they barely participated in its deliberations. Liberal and moderate Croats supported an independent Bosnia. This position was best exemplified by Kljujić, a member of the Bosnian presidency and supporter of an integral Bosnia, who was removed from the CDU leadership shortly after the outbreak of armed conflicts in March 1992. A nationalist wing of the CDU sought autonomy for the predominantly Croatian areas of western Herzegovina as a prelude to secession and union with neighboring Croatia. This position was represented by CDU leader Mate Boban, president of the Croatian Community of Herceg-Bosnia, who was regarded as a close collaborator of Croatian President Franjo Tudjman. Soon after the outbreak of hostilities, Boban established a separate military structure in the Herzegovina area, known as the Croatian Defense Council (CDC).

Some Croatian ultra-nationalists, including the CPR, remained staunchly opposed to any partition of Bosnia-Herzegovina, contending that the entire republic should form a confederation with Croatia to counter Serbian pressures. The CPR established its own paramilitary units, styled as the Croatian Defense Forces (CDF), which were active in parts of Bosnia after the outbreak of war. As Boban moved to solidify his control, tensions between the CDC and CDF mounted, resulting in occasional firefights and culminating in the ouster or absorption of CDF units by the much more powerful CDC structure with the full backing of Zagreb.

The position of the Zagreb government with regard to the status and integrity of Bosnia was contradictory. On one hand, Croatia recognized the republic's independence and territorial integrity in April 1992 and offered Sarajevo a formal military alliance. On the other hand, various incidents indicated that Tudjman and Boban had secretly planned to divide the republic. In March 1991, Tudjman and Milošević met clandestinely in Karadjordje, in Serbia, to discuss the division of Bosnia-Herzegovina between the two republics. In May 1992, Boban met with Karadžić in Graz, Austria, to deliberate on Bosnia's future. Since both leaders were collaborating with Tudjman and Milošević, respectively, the meeting was believed to have been engineered by the Croatian and Serbian presidents.

In July 1992, Boban proclaimed a quasi-independent Croatian state within Bosnia-Herzegovina—"Herceg-Bosna"—with its capital in Mostar. The territory claimed by Boban comprised a region of 30 municipalities in which Croats formed clear majorities, with planned extensions toward central Bosnia and the Posavina region in northern Bosnia. According to both Boban and Tudjman, the crisis in Bosnia could be resolved only by organizing the republic as a community of three constituent nations on a cantonal basis. The CDU leadership and the quasi government in Mostar promptly accepted the Vance-Owen plan in early 1993, which envisaged decentralizing Bosnia into ten self-administered provinces including Sarajevo.

Under the proposals, each ethnic group would have been allocated three provinces. Croat leaders supported the planned territorial delineations primarily because they allocated more territory to the Croatian side than it already controlled militarily. But the partition of Bosnia remained a divisive issue among Croats in Bosnia and in Croatia. Moderate parliamentary deputies, Croat members of the Bosnian presidency, and opposition parties in Croatia opposed partition principally on the grounds that it could set a dangerous precedent for the future partition of Croatia. Nonetheless, as the military situation deteriorated during the summer of 1993 and Sarajevo's authority evaporated, CDU leaders increasingly favored a three-way division of Bosnia.[29]

The CDU maintained its dominance among the Croatian community throughout the 1990s. In the first post-war elections in September 1996, it captured 36 of 140 seats in the Federation parliament, and 8 of 28 federation seats in the national parliament. In the September 1998 general elections, it gained six seats in the national House of Representatives and 28 seats in the Federation House of Representatives. The majority of Croats in Herzegovina continued to vote for the CDU, viewing it as a protector of their national interests. Moreover, rival Croatian parties were unable to campaign freely in the nationalist enclaves of western Herzegovina. The political agenda of the party included full national autonomy for Croats within the Bosnian Federation and a confederal structure with Croatia. After the violent death of party official Jozo Leutar on 28 March 1999, all CDU officials were pulled out of the central and federation institutions.

The Bosnian CDU split after the party's fifth convention in May 1998, and the moderate faction around Krešimir Zubak, the Bosnian Croat representative in Bosnia's joint presidency, established a new party, the New Croatian Initiative (NCI), which promoted an integrationist political agenda. But the CDU failed to shift away from its agenda of exclusive ethnic nationalism promoted by the new hard-line president Ante Jelavić. Although he declared his commitment to carrying out the Dayton agreement, this did not imply that such cooperation would be genuine or that the CDU had given up its ultimate goal of joining parts of Bosnia with Croatia. In the November 2000 general elections, the CDU captured 5 of the 42 seats in the House of Representatives and 25 of 140 seats in the Federation parliament and remained the most significant Croatian formation.

Neo-Fascists

Serbian Radical Party (SRP)
Srpska Radikalna Stranka (SRS)

The Bosnian branch of the Belgrade-based Serbian Radical Party (SRP) was founded at the outset of the war in Bosnia. Its main branch in Serbia was led by Vojislav Šešelj, the Deputy Prime Minister of Serbia. Banja Luka was the initial stronghold of the party, where it propounded its ultra-nationalist idea of a Greater Serbia. The party deployed paramilitary units during the Bosnian war that were responsible for the mass murder and expulsion of Muslim civilians, earning itself a xenophobic and neo-fascist reputation. The party's main post-war goal was the international recognition of the Serb Republic as an independent state, which would allow it to strengthen ties with Serbia and the Federal Republic of Yugoslavia. The SRP was a mainstay of the Milošević government. But a rift between Šešelj and Milošević became apparent after Milošević's election victory in 1993. Moreover, Belgrade's policies toward Bosnia changed during 1994–1995, and Šešelj became a burden to the regime. Šešelj was later rehabilitated by Milošević and was allowed to join the Serbian government.

Nikola Poplašen became the SRP leader in Bosnia, and under his leadership, the SRP's ultra-nationalist policies were somewhat toned down. After the September 1998 elections and the difficult position of Poplašen, who was not allowed by international community representatives in Bosnia to assume the Serb Republic presidency, the SRP's isolation increased.[30] The SRP only gained two seats in the Bosnian House of Representatives and 11 seats in the National Assembly of the Serb Republic, and it failed to win any mandates in the November 2000 elections.

Other Ethnic Minority and Religious Parties

Democratic Alliance of Albanians (DAA)
Demokratski Savez Albanaca (DSA)

The Democratic Alliance of Albanians (DAA) was formed during the post-1990 election period and was based in Mostar, in Herzegovina. It issued warnings on several occasions that any agreement on a new Yugoslav or Bosnian structure of equal nations would not be acceptable without the participation of legitimate Albanian representatives. The party maintained that if Albanians were not allowed to express their political will on an equal basis with the other Yugoslav nations, this would have unforeseeable implications for the whole of Yugoslavia. Several other smaller parties and associations were formed in Bosnia-Herzegovina to represent minority populations, including Albanians, Slovenes, and Montenegrins. However, their role during the armed conflicts and the post-war reconstruction remained negligible.[31]

POLITICAL DATA

Name of State: Republic of Bosnia and Herzegovina *(Bosna i Hercegovina)*
Form of Government: Central government with two political entities, the Muslim (Bosniak)/Croat Federation of Bosnia-Herzegovina and the Bosnian Serb Republic.
Structure of Legislature: Bicameral parliamentary assembly *(skupština)* composed of the House of Representatives *(predstavnički dom)* and the House of Peoples *(dom naroda)*. House of Representatives with 42 members directly elected by a system of proportional representation for two-year terms. Two-thirds (28) of seats in House of Representatives allocated to representatives of the Federation of Bosnia-Herzegovina and one-third (14) allocated to representatives of the Serb Republic.
Size of Territory: 19,741 square miles
Size of Population: 3,922,205

Composition of Population:

Ethnic Group	Number	% of Population
Bosniaks*	1,725,770	44.00
Serbs	1,215,884	31.00
Croats	666,775	17.00
Yugoslavs	215,721	5.50
Others	98,055	2.50
Total population	3,922,205	100.00

*Bosniak is the term for Bosnian Muslims whose sense of Bosnian identity was strengthened during the breakup of Yugoslavia.

ELECTION RESULTS

Bosnian Presidential Election (Collective Presidency), 12–13 September 1998

Turnout: 70%

Bosniaks

Candidate	Votes	% of Vote
Alija Izetbegović	511,541 (elected)	86.8
Fikret Abdić	36,438	6.2
Sefer Halilović	33,687	5.7
Hajrija Rahmanović	7,694	1.3
Total	589,360	100.0

Croats

Candidate	Votes	% of Vote
Ante Jelavić	189,438 (elected)	52.9
Gradimir Gojer	113,961	31.9
Krešimir Zubak	40,880	11.4
Senka Nožica	11,089	3.0
Saša Nisandžić	2,638	0.8
Total	358,006	100.0

Serbs

Candidate	Votes	% of Vote
Živko Radišić	359,937 (elected)	51.2
Momčilo Krajišnik	314,236	44.9
Zoran Tadić	27,388	3.9
Total	701,561	100.0

Bosnian Presidential Elections (Collective Presidency), 14 September 1996

Bosniaks

Candidate	Votes	% of Vote
Alija Izetbegović	730,592	80.00
Haris Silajdžić	124,396	13.62
Six other candidates	58,289	6.38
Total	913,277	100.00

Serbs

Candidate	Votes	% of Vote
Momčilo Krajišnik	690,646	67.30
Mladen Ivanić	207,461	29.96
Two other candidates	28,050	2.28
Total	1,026157	100.00

Croats

Candidate	Votes	% of Vote
Krešimir Zubak	330,337	88.70
Ivo Komšić	37,684	10.11
Two other candidates	4,405	1.19
Total	372,426	100.00

Bosnian Presidential Elections (Collective Presidency), 18 November 1990

Turnout: 74%

Bosniaks

Candidate	Votes	% of Vote
Fikret Abdić	867,702	43.00
Alija Izetbegović	726,567	36.00
Nijaz Djuraković	466,887	21.00
Total	2,061,156	100.00

Serbs

Candidate	Votes	% of Vote
Biljana Plavšić	482,914	35.00
Nikola Koljević	470,595	34.00
Nenad Kečmanović	421,012	31.00
Total	1,374,527	100.00

Croats

Candidate	Votes	% of Vote
Stjepan Kljujić	413,432	21.10
Franjo Boraš	365,532	18.65
Ivo Komšić	298,176	15.22
Total	1,077,140	100.00

Others

Candidate	Votes	% of Vote
Ejup Ganić	584,090	29.81
Ivan Čerešnjec	307,649	15.70
Josip Pejaković	266,225	13.58
Total	1,157,964	100.00

Bosnian Parliamentary Elections, House of Representatives, 11 November 2000

Turnout: 63.7%

Party/Coalition	Votes	% of Vote	Seats
Social Democratic Party of Bosnia and Herzegovina	268,270	18.8	9
Party for Democratic Action	279,548	18.0	8
Serbian Democratic Party	248,576	17.8	6
Croatian Democratic Union	169,821	11.7	5
Party for Bosnia and Herzegovina	168,995	11.4	5
Party of Democratic Progress	87,497	6.4	2
Independent Social Democratic Party	79,137	5.1	1
Socialist Party of the Serb Republic	20,712	2.6	1
Serbian People's Union	n/a	1.9	1
Bosnian Patriotic Party	n/a	1.1	1
Party of Pensioners	n/a	1.8	1
New Croatian Initiative	n/a	1.6	1
BiH Patriot Party	n/a	1.8	1
Total	1,043,008	100.0	42

Bosnian Parliamentary Elections, House of Representatives, 12–13 September 1998

Turnout: 70%

Elected from Federation

Party/Coalition	Votes	% of Vote	Seats
Coalition for a Whole and Democratic Bosnia	455,668	47.90	14
Croatian Democratic Union	187,707	19.73	6

Serbian Democratic Party	138,004	14.57	4
Social Democratic Party	28,740	3.02	2
New Croatian Initiative	28,572	3.00	1
Democratic National Union	21,452	2.26	1
Others	91,114	9.58	—
Total	951,257	100.00	28

Elected from Serb Republic

Party/Coalition	Votes	% of Vote	Seats
Together Coalition	214,716	33	4
Serbian Democratic Party	162,721	25	4
Coalition for a Whole and			
Democratic Bosnia	128,277	19	3
Serbian Radical Party	118,522	18	2
Radical Party of the Serb Republic	27,686	4	1
Total	651,922	100	14

Bosnian Parliamentary Elections, House of Representatives, 14 September 1996

Elected from Federation

Turnout: 73%

Party/Coalition	Votes	% of Vote	Seats
Party of Democratic Action	725,417	54.22	16
Croatian Democratic Union	338,44	25.30	8
Joint List for Bosnia	105,918	7.92	2
Party for Bosnia	93,816	7.01	2
Ten other parties and coalitions	74,304	5.55	—
Total	1,337,895	100.00	28

Elected from Serb Republic

Party/Coalition	Votes	% of Vote	Seats
Serbian Democratic Party	578,723	54.49	9
Party of Democratic Action	184,553	17.38	3
Alliance for Peace and			
Democracy	136,077	12.81	2
Seven other parties or coalitions	162,626	15.32	—
Total	1,061,979	100.00	14

Bosnian Parliamentary Elections, 18 November 1990

Turnout: 74%

Chamber of Citizens

Party/Coalition	Votes	% of Vote	Seats
Party of Democratic Action	760,840	33.08	43
Serbian Democratic Party	601,450	26.15	34
Croatian Democratic Union	371,450	16.15	21
League of Communists–			
Social Democratic Party	265,420	11.54	15
Alliance of Reform Forces	212,290	9.23	12
Muslim Bosnian Organization	35,420	1.54	2
Democratic Socialist Alliance	17,710	0.77	1
Ecological Movement	17,710	0.77	1
Socialist Youth Organization	17,710	0.77	1
Democratic Party/ Ecological Movement			
Total	2,300,000	100.00	130

Chamber of Municipalities

Party/Coalition	Votes	% of Vote	Seats
Party of Democratic Action	897,000	39.09	43
Serbian Democratic Party	773,720	33.64	37
Croatian Democratic Union	501,860	21.82	24
League of Communists–			
Social Democratic Party	83,720	3.64	4
Alliance of Reform Forces	20,930	0.91	1
Serbian Renewal Movement	20,930	0.91	1
Muslim Bosnian Organization	—	—	—
Democratic Socialist Alliance	—	—	—
Ecological Movement/ Socialist Youth			
Organization/ Democratic Party	—	—	—
Total	2,298,160	100.00	110

Bosnian Federation Parliamentary Elections, House of Representatives, 11 November 2000

Party/Coalition	Votes	% of Vote	Seats
Party of Democratic Action	232,674	26.8	38
Social Democratic Party of BiH	226,440	26.1	37
Croatian Democratic Union	151,812	17.5	25
Party for Bosnia and Herzegovina	128,883	14.8	21

Democratic People's Union	17,999	2.1	3
BiH Patriot Party	14,681	1.7	2
New Croatian Initiative	9,439	1.6	2
Croatian Party of Rights	9,026	1.0	1
Total	790,954	100.0	140

Bosnian Federation, Parliamentary Elections, 12–13 September 1998

House of Representatives

Party/Coalition	Votes	% of Vote	Seats
Coalition for a Whole and Democratic Bosnia	456,657	49	68
Croatian Democratic Union	184,603	20	28
Social Democratic Party	126,649	14	19
Social Democrats	29,427	4	6
New Croatian Initiative and Christian Democrats	27,435	3	4
Democratic National Union	19,491	2	3
Bosnian-Herzegovinian Patriotic Party	12,585	1	2
Socialist Party of Serb Republic	10,742	1	2
Democratic Pensioners Party	10,126	1	2
Croatian Party of Rights	10,120	1	2
Bosnian Party	9,427	1	1
Center Coalition	4,953	1	1
Bosniak Party of Rights	3,789	1	1
Croatian Peasants Party	2,226	1	1
Others	19,587	—	—
Total	927,817	100	140

Bosnian Federation, Parliamentary Elections, 14 September 1996

House of Representatives

Party/Coalition	Votes	% of Vote	Seats
Party of Democratic Action	725,810	54.34	78
Croatian Democratic Union	337,794	25.29	36
Joint List for Bosnia	105,897	7.93	11
Party for Bosnia-Herzegovina	98,207	7.35	10
Croatian Party of Rights	16,344	1.22	2
Seven other parties and coalitions	27,995	2.10	—
Total	1,335,707	100.00	140

[Bosnian] Serb Republic, Presidential Election, 11 November 2000

Candidate	Votes	% of Vote
Mirko Sarović	313,607	50.0
Mladen Ivanić	54,433	8.7
Milorad Dodik	162,154	25.9
Zijad Mujkić	42,834	6.8
Slobodan Popović	52,411	8.4
Total	625,439	100.0

[Bosnian] Serb Republic, Presidential Election, 12–13 September 1998

Candidate	Votes	% of Vote
Nikola Poplašen	322,684	38.00
Biljana Plavšić	286,606	34.00
Zulfo Nišić	107,036	12.00
Mihajlo Črnadak	16,079	2.00
Predrag Sekulović	3,295	0.38
Total	735,700	86.38

[Bosnian] Serb Republic, National Assembly Elections, 11 November 2000

Party/Coalition	Votes	% of Vote	Seats
Serbian Democratic Party	226,226	36.0	31
Independent Social Democratic Party	81,467	13.0	11
Party of Democratic Progress	76,810	12.2	10
Socialist Party of the Serb Republic	30,636	4.9	4
Democratic Socialist Party	25,763	4.1	4
Democratic People's Union	22,083	3.5	3
Serbian People's Union	14,239	2.3	2
Social Democratic Party of BiH	31,176	5.1	4
Party of Democratic Action	47,379	7.6	7
Party for BiH	32,450	5.2	4
Others	36,258	6.1	3
Total	624,487	100.0	83

[Bosnian] Serb Republic, National Assembly Elections, 12–13 September 1998

Party/Coalition	Votes	% of Vote	Seats
Serbian Democratic Party	160,594	24	19
Coalition for a Whole and Democratic Bosnia	125,546	19	15
Serbian People's Union	95,817	14	12
Serbian Radical Party	97,244	13	11
Socialist Party of the Serb Republic	79,179	12	10
Independent Social Democratic Party	54,058	7	6
Radical Party of the Serb Republic	27,119	4	3
Serbian Coalition for the Serb Republic	19,198	2	2
Social Democratic Party	10,742	2	2
Croatian Democratic Union	11,471	1	1
New Croatian Initiative and Christian Democrats	10,546	1	1
Bosnian Party	9,427	1	1
Coalition for the King and Country	3,044	—	1
Others	38,756	—	—
Total	741,761	100	83

[Bosnian] Serb Republic, National Assembly Elections, 22–23 November 1997

Turnout: 70.07%

Party/Coalition	Votes	% of Vote	Seats
Serbian Democratic Party	n/a	n/a	24
Coalition for a Whole and Democratic Bosnia	n/a	n/a	16
Serbian Radical Party	n/a	n/a	15
Serbian National Party– Bilijana Plavsic	n/a	n/a	15
Socialist Party of the Serb Republic	n/a	n/a	9
Independent Social Democratic Party	n/a	n/a	2
Party for BiH	n/a	n/a	2
Total	n/a	n/a	83

Source: OSCE, Office for Democratic Institutions and Human Rights (ODIHR), National Assembly Election in Republica Srpska, 22–23 November 1997, Final Report. http://www.osce.org/odihr/documents/reports/election_reports/ba/.

[Bosnian] Serb Republic, National Assembly Elections, 14 September 1996

Party/Coalition	Votes	% of Vote	Seats
Serbian Democratic Party	568,980	52.31	45
Party of Democratic Action	177,388	16.31	14
Alliance for Peace and Changes	125,372	11.53	10
Serbian Radical Party	72,517	6.67	6
Democratic Patriotic Bloc	32,895	3.02	2
Party for Bosnia-Herzegovina	25,593	2.35	2
Joint List for Bosnia	22,329	2.05	2
Serbian Party of Krajina	17,384	1.60	1
Serbian Patriotic Party	14,508	4.32	1
Seven other parties and coalitions	30,800	2.83	—
Total	1,087,763	100.00	83

Source: Bosnia Report, http://www.bosnia.org.uk/bosrep/no96ja97/election. htm#top.

NOTES

1. For recent histories of Bosnia-Herzegovina see Robert J. Donia, *Islam Under the Double Eagle: The Muslims of Bosnia and Herzegovina, 1878–1914*, Boulder: East European Monographs, 1981; Robert J. Donia and John V. A. Fine, *Bosnia and Herzegovina: A Tradition Betrayed*, New York: Columbia University Press, 1994; Francine Friedman, *The Bosnian Muslims: Denial of a Nation*, Boulder: Westview Press, 1996; Mark Pinson (Ed.), *The Muslims of Bosnia-Herzegovina: Their Historic Development from the Middle Ages to the Dissolution of Yugoslavia*, Cambridge: Harvard University Press, 1994; Peter F. Sugar, *Southeastern Europe Under Ottoman Rule, 1345–1804*, Seattle: University of Washington Press, 1977; Charles Jelavich and Barbara Jelavich, *The Establishment of the Balkan National States, 1804–1920*, Seattle: University of Washington Press, 1977; Ivo Banac, *The National Question in Yugoslavia: Origins, History, Politics*, Ithaca: Cornell University Press, 1984; Joseph Rothschild, *East Central Europe Between the Two World Wars*, Seattle: University of Washington Press, 1974; Sabrina P. Ramet, *Nationalism and Federalism in Yugoslavia, 1963–1983*, Bloomington: Indiana University Press, 1992; and Noel Malcolm, *Bosnia: A Short History*, New York: New York University Press, 1994.

2. Information on the Yugoslav census in Bosnia-Herzegovina in 1991 can be found in various official documents in Sarajevo, Belgrade, and Zagreb. See also G. Golubic, S.E. Campbell, and T.S. Golubic, "The Crisis in Bosnia-Herzegovina: Is an Ethnic Division of Bosnia-Herzegovina Desirable or Possible?" Center for the Study of Small States, Boston University, June 1992.

3. Details on the 1990 elections and the election campaign can be found in the National Republican Institute for International Affairs, *The 1990 Elections in the Republics of Yugoslavia*, Washington, DC, 1991; D. Stanišić, "At Least One, At Most Seven," *Oslobodjenje*, Sarajevo, 11 November 1990, in *Federal Broadcast Information Service, Daily Report: East Europe, FBIS-EEU-90–223*, 20 November 1990; "Elections in Bosnia and Herzegovina," *Borba*, Belgrade, 10 November 1990; Milan Andrejevich, "Bosnia-Herzegovina: Yugoslavia's Linchpin," Radio Free Europe/Radio Liberty Research Institute (RFE/RL), *Report on Eastern Europe*, Vol. 1, No. 49, 7 December 1990; and Milan Andrejevich, "Moslem Leader Elected President of Bosnia and Herzegovina," RFE/RL, *Report on Eastern Europe*, Vol. 2, No. 3, 18 January 1991.

4. For a useful analysis see Steven L. Burg, "Bosnia-Herzegovina: A Case of Failed Democratization," in Karen Dawisha and Bruce Parrott (Eds.), *Politics, Power, and the Struggle for Democracy in South-East Europe*, Cambridge: Cambridge University Press, 1997, pp. 122–145.

5. See Milan Andrejevich, "The Future of Bosnia and Herzegovina: A Sovereign Republic or Cantonization?" RFE/RL, *Report on Eastern Europe*, Vol. 2, No. 27, 5 July 1991; and Milan Andrejevich, "Bosnia and Herzegovina Moves Toward Independence," RFE/RL, *Report on Eastern Europe*, Vol. 2, No. 43, 25 October 1991.

6. Valuable discussions on ethnic questions and growing unrest in Bosnia can be found in Milan Jajcinović, "What Will Happen to Bosnia?" *Danas*, Zagreb, 10 July 1990, in *Federal Broadcast Information Service/Joint Publications Research Service, Daily Report: East Europe*, JPRS-EER-90–119, 20 August 1990; A. Kaurin, "Bosnia Too Has Gotten Its Kosovo," *Večernji List*, Zagreb, 30 August 1990, in *FBIS-EEU*-90–172, 5 September 1990; Nenad Kečmanović, "My Grave Is My Freedom," *Nin*, Belgrade, 13 September 1991; and Urog Komnenović and Bogdan lvanišević, "Nothing Cheerful from the Drina," *Nin*, Belgrade, in *JPRS-EER-91–146*, 30 September 1991.

7. For Serbian moves toward autonomy, consult *Belgrade Domestic Service*, 15 October 1990, and 16 October 1990, in *FBIS-EEU-90–201*, 17 October 1990; *Tanjug*, Belgrade, 29 April 1991, *in FBIS-EEU-91–084*, 1 May 1991; *Tanjug*, Belgrade, 27 June 1991; Zoran Odić, "Constitutional Occupation of Bosnia-Herzegovina," *Oslobodjenje*, Sarajevo, 2 October 1991; *Tanjug*, Belgrade, 13 September 1991; *Tanjug*, Belgrade, 22 October 1991, in *FBIS-EEU-91–205*, 23 October 1991.

8. Discussions on the Croat position can be found in Goran Moravczek, "The Opening of the Croatian Question," *Delo*, Ljubljana, 9 March 1991; *Radio Croatia Network*, Zagreb, 18 November 1991, in *FBIS-EEU-91–223*, 19 November 1991; K. Kožar, "Self-Organization of the Sava Valley and Herceg-Bosnia," *Oslobodjenje*, Sarajevo, 20 November 1991; Radovan Pavić, "Fantasy Becomes Reality," *Danas*, Zagreb, 11 June 1991, in *JPRS-EER-91–094*, 28 June 1991; published material by Vlado Pogarčić, Foreign Affairs Advisor to the President of the Croatian Community of Herceg-Bosnia; Mate Boban; "Why the Croatian Community of Herceg-Bosnia Was Founded," July 1993.

9. See *Borba*, Belgrade, 27 May 1991; and Patrick Moore, "The Islamic Community's New Sense of Identity," RFE/RL, *Report on Eastern Europe*, Vol. 2, No. 44, 1 November 1991.

10. Consult the Commission on Security and Cooperation in Europe, *The Referendum on Independence in Bosnia-Herzegovina, 29 February–1 March 1992*, Washington, DC, 12 March 1992.

11. See V. Janković and A. Borden, "National Parties and the Plans for Division," *Balkan War Report*, London, No. 16, November–December 1992.

12. For early reports on the war in Bosnia-Herzegovina see Milan Andrejevich, "Bosnia and Herzegovina: In Search of Peace," RFE/RL, *Research Report*, Vol. 1, No. 23, 5 June 1992; and material from the Institute for Strategic Research, Sarajevo, 1992 and 1993.

13. Military estimates of the contending forces are taken from Milan Vego, "The Army of Bosnia and Herzegovina," *Jane's Intelligence Review*, February 1993, and from private sources in Zagreb, Belgrade, and Ljubljana. See also D. Pusonjić, "New Detachments on Zelengora," *Borba*, Belgrade, 13 September 1991, in *JPRS-EER-91–145*, 27 September 1991.

14. See Janusz Bugajski, "Blood and Soil in Bosnia," *Orbis: A Journal of World Affairs*, Vol. 40, No. 4, Fall 1996; Janusz Bugajski, "Bosnian Blunders," *The World & I*, Vol. 7, No. 11, November 1992. For reports on atrocities perpetuated primarily, but not exclusively, by Serb militias, check Helsinki Watch, *War Crimes in Bosnia-Herzegovina*, New York, August 1992; *Country Reports on Human Rights Practices for 1992*, Department of State, Washington, DC, February 1993; and "The Ethnic Cleansing of Bosnia-Herzegovina," Committee on Foreign Relations, U.S. Senate, Washington, DC, August 1992. See also Filip Svarm, "War Crime: Fighting to the Last Booty," *Vreme*, Belgrade, 8 March 1993, in *FBIS-EEU-93–065*, 7 April 1993; Krešimir Meler and Mirjana Glušac, "Rape as a Means of Battle," *Delo*, Ljubljana, 23 February 1993, in *FBIS-EEU-93–054*, 23 March 1993; Patrick Moore, "Ethnic Cleansing in Bosnia: Outrage But Little Action," RFE/RL, *Research Report*, Vol. 1, No. 34, 28 August 1992.

15. "Paper Solutions Move Across the Ocean," *Ljiljan*, Zagreb, 15 March 1993, in *FBIS-EEU-93–077*, 23 April 1993. For a valuable overview of political fragmentation and Western

involvement see Robert M. Hayden, "The Partition of Bosnia and Herzegovina, 1990–1993," RFE/RL, *Report on Eastern Europe*, Vol. 2, No. 22, 28 May 1993.

16. Discussions on the partition plan can be found in Duško Topalović, "Creation of a Corridor-State," *Danas*, Zagreb, 28 June 1993, in *FBIS-EEU-93–123*, 29 June 1993.

17. For details on the Bosnian Federation see Thomas Ambrosio, "The Federation of Bosnia and Herzegovina: A Failure of Implementation," in John S. Micgiel (Ed.), *State and Nation Building in East Central Europe: Contemporary Perspectives*, New York: Columbia University, Institute on East Central Europe, 1996, pp. 225–241.

18. OSCE (Organization for Security and Cooperation in Europe) report on Bosnia, http://www.osce.org/odihr/elecrep-bih.htm.

19. OSCE final report , http://www.osce.org/odihr/election/bih3–3.htm.

20. For more details on the Bosnian elections see http://www.house.gov/csce/bosnianelec.htm).

21. For more details on the SDP see http://www.sdpbih-centar.com/statut.htm.

22. See "Political Parties in BiH": http://www.europeanforum.bot-consult.se/cup/bosnia.

23. See M. Lučić, "Without Islam for Political Purposes," *Borba*, Belgrade, 27 September 1990, in *FBIS-EEU-90–199*, 15 October 1990; and the interview with Adil Zulfikarpašić by Semra Saracević, "Izetbegović Is Worse Than the Muslims' Worst Enemy!" *Globus*, Zagreb, 23 February 1993, in *FBIS-EEU-93–059*, 30 March 1993.

24. See the interview with Alija Izetbegović by Azra Kaurin, *Vecernji List*, Zagreb, 3 June 1990, in *FBIS-EEU-90–113*, 12 June 1990; *Oslobodjenje*, Sarajevo, 23 October 1990, in *FBIS-EEU-90–210*, 30 October 1990; *The 1990 Elections in the Republics of Yugoslavia*, National Republican Institute, Washington DC, 1991; Fahrudin Radončić, "Goodbye, Bosnia," *Danas*, Zagreb, 2 July 1991, in *JPRS-EER-91–107*, 19 July 1991; "Can Bosnia Be an Islamic State, Asks the Sarajevo Weekly Ekspres 071: New Story on an Old Dilemma," *Borba*, Belgrade, 27 May 1991, in *JPRS-EER-91–089*, 21 June 1991; and interview with Bosnian presidency member Mirko Pejanović by Zdravko Latal, "On Conflicts in the Presidency," *Delo*, Ljubljana, 17 June 1993, in *FBIS-EEU-93–130*, 9 July 1993.

25. Consult www.bih.net.ba/~sda.

26. See the interview with Armin Pohara by Andrej Rora, "We Offer Survival to the Muslim People," *Vjesnik*, Zagreb, 25 May 1993, in *FBIS-EEU-93–04*, 2 June 1993.

27. "Can Bosnia Be an Islamic State, Asks the Sarajevo Weekly Ekspres 071: New Story on an Old Dilemma," *Borba*, Belgrade, 27 May 1991, in *JPRS-EER-91–089*, 21 June 1991. Also see the interview with Radovan Karadžić by Jovan Janjic, *Nin*, Belgrade, 10 January 1992, *FBIS-EEU-92–020*, 30 January 1992.

28. Milena Dražić, "Could Prince Tomislav Become Duke of Western Serbia: I Would Accept If It Would Not Divide the Seth Nation," *Borba*, Belgrade, 19 May 1993, in *JPRS-EER-93–055–S*, 16 June 1993.

29. Milan Andrejevich, "Bosnia-Herzegovina: Yugoslavia's Linchpin," RFE/RL, *Report on Eastern Europe*, 7 December 1990; *Radio Belgrade Network*, Belgrade, 31 March 1992, in *FBIS-EEU-92–063*, 1 April 1992; *Tanjug*, 12 February 1992, in *FBIS-EEU-92–031*, 14 February 1992; "War Crimes in Bosnia-Herzegovina," *Helsinki Watch Report*, prepared by Human Rights Watch, August 1992.

30. Check www.odci.gov/cia/publications/factbook/fields/political_parties_and_leaders.html.

31. *Tanjug*, Belgrade, 8 January 1991, in *FBIS-EEU-91–006*, 9 January 1991.

Croatia

HISTORICAL OVERVIEW

Croatia formed part of the province of Illyricum during the time of the Roman Empire. Illyricum was subsequently divided into the provinces of Pannonia and Dalmatia, both of which were besieged by Goths in the fourth century AD and conquered by the Avars, a Mongolian people, in the sixth century AD as the Roman Empire decayed. During the seventh century, Croatian clans settled in the region, having migrated with other Slavic tribes from an area north of the Carpathian mountains.[1] Some Croatian historians have posited a theory that the Croatians were a community of Iranians who lived at the mouth of the Don River around 200 BC. Other theorists believe that the Croats emerged from a blend of Slavic and Ostrogoth tribes along the Adriatic coast.

The Croatian territories were subdivided into counties (*župe*) ruled by local *župan*s and by princes (*knez*) at a higher level, or principality. One of these principalities, Dioclea, became Montenegro, while another, Zahumlya, was later called Herzegovina. One of the Croatian clans that occupied the heartland of Dalmatia was known as Hrvat (Croat) and from this clan the name of the country evolved. In 800 AD, the Frankish armies of Charlemagne conquered Dalmatia and conducted a policy of evangelization among the local rulers. The Croatian Duke Višeslav accepted Christianity shortly afterwards, and under his successors, Vladislav, Mislav, Trpimir, and Zdeslav, the Croatian dukedom expanded inland into present-day Bosnia, even though the entire region remained under overall Frankish control.

In 925 AD Croatia became an independent kingdom. Under its most prominent king, Tomislav (910–929), the state reached its zenith and united Dalmatia with Pannonia. Croatian sovereignty lasted until the end of the eleventh century, when a period of political fragmentation and dynastic rivalry led to intervention by Venice in the west and Hungary in the northeast. While Venice acquired a number of Dalmatian cities, in 1102 a pact was signed by the major Croatian clans recognizing Hungarian King Kálmán as the ruler of Croatia. In return for its loyalty, Kálmán granted Croatia virtual self-rule under a *ban*, or local ruler. Pannonian Croatia was called the Kingdom of Slavonija and placed under the jurisdiction of a separate *ban*. Croatian rulers had entered the union with Hungary principally as a defense against Venice, but the Venetians nevertheless managed to acquire several important Dalmatian cities.

Except for a brief period of Mongol occupation and devastation in the 1240s, periodic Ottoman Turkish incursions and conquests between the fifteenth and eighteenth centuries, and a brief period of French occupation at the beginning of the nineteenth century, most of Croatia was an autonomous principality under Hungarian and Habsburg rule from 1102 until the Hungarian revolution of 1848. In the late fourteenth century, Croatia lost large tracts of Bosnia and southern Dalmatia to the Bosnian King Trvtko, and the country became narrower and less defensible. By 1420, Venice gained control over virtually the entire Dalmatian coast, which it maintained until the Napoleonic wars at the end of the eighteenth century. Only the city of Dubrovnik (Ragusa) managed to retain a large measure of independence, and it grew into a major trading center at the crossroads of western and eastern Europe.

In 1493, Croat forces lost a major battle at Krbavsko Polje to the Ottoman armies, and the country's leaders were slaughtered. The loss opened up the Croatian lands to Turkish penetration, and large tracts of Slavonija and Dalmatia fell under Ottoman control. As Hungary increasingly came under Turkish domination, in the 1520s Croatian nobles decided to switch their loyalty to the Austrian Habsburgs as a defensive measure against the Turks. In 1527, they elected Austria's Archduke Ferdinand as king of Croatia, thus terminating the joint kingdom with Hungary. A line of fortresses was established by the Habsburgs along the Croatian-Ottoman boundary, and this area became known as the Military Frontier (*Vojna Krajina*). In 1533, the Krajina was placed under a military commander who was virtually independent of the Croatian *bans,* provoking significant protests in Zagreb that the Austrians had in effect created a state within the Croatian state. These fears were compounded when the area was settled at Vienna's invitation by Serbs and Vlachs who belonged to the Serbian Orthodox Church. Over time, historians believe, the Vlachs began to identify themselves as ethnic Serbs, largely due to the activities of the Orthodox clergy. Croatia suffered further blows in the 1670s when the power of the major feudal families was broken and their lands were confiscated and distributed to German and Hungarian settlers. With direct Habsburg rule over the Krajina region, Croatia was effectively subjugated by Austria.

In the 1780s, the Croatian province was virtually eliminated as new units of local government were created and the post of *ban* was made irrelevant. In 1790, the Croatian assembly (*sabor*) surrendered most of its prerogatives to the Hungarian parliament, and Budapest launched a policy of Magyarization while incorporating Slavonija into Hungary proper. At the same time, Dalmatia was placed under direct Austrian control even though each major city continued to be controlled by the Italian elites. After Austria's crushing military defeat by France in 1805, Vienna was forced to cede Dalmatia to Paris. But under the short-lived Napoleonic administration, Croatian language, publishing, education, and culture were restored, thus stimulating a national revival after the Habsburgs regained control over the territory following the Congress of Vienna in 1815.

Several notable Croatians were active in the nineteenth century, laying the foundations for future Croatian nationalism. They included historian Ljudevit Gaj, who favored closer links between subjugated south Slavic peoples in the Austrian and Ottoman empires and was one of the founders of the Slavic Illyrian movement, and *ban* Josip Jelačić, a popular officer in Krajina who sought Croatia's liberation from Hungary and a more equal relationship with Austria. But following the crushing of the Hungarian independence movement in 1848 by Vienna, Croatia fell under stricter Austrian control and the Germanization process was intensified. Croatian frustrations were reflected in the latter nineteenth century in the activities and policies of Bishop Strossmayer, who asserted the need for a joint Slavic state to counter both Austrian and Hungarian pressures.

In 1867, Vienna and Budapest created the dual monarchy of Austria-Hungary. Most of Croatia was assigned to Hungarian control, but Dalmatia remained under Austrian jurisdiction. Under an agreement known as the *Nagodba*, Croatia gained a measure of autonomy, retaining the *ban* as the president of the Croatian government, as well as the *Sabor*, a supreme court, a home guard, and the right to use the Croatian language in administration and education. In the 1880s, the Krajina region was administratively reincorporated into Croatia. The Austrians now occupied neighboring Bosnia-Herzegovina.

During World War I (1914–1918), Croatian and Serbian leaders formed a Yugoslav Committee and tried to build a common front against Austrian domination. Their objective was to establish a kingdom that would unite all the south Slavic peoples. On 29 October 1918, the Croatian *Sabor* formally declared the country's independence. On 1 December 1918, following the defeat of the Austrian monarchy, Croatia joined the independent Kingdom of the Serbs, Croats, and Slovenes under the constitutional Serbian monarchy. But instead of the decentralized or federalized state demanded by Croatian leaders, Belgrade sought to create a centralized system. This was evident in the 1921 constitution, which abolished Croatia's traditional institutions, including the *ban* and the *sabor*, and broke the country up into departments governed by Belgrade-appointed prefects. Croatian leaders, led by the head of the People's Peasants Party, Stjepan Radić, protested, and boycotted the parliament in Belgrade.

As conflicts between Croatian and Serbian leaders intensified following the assassination of Radić in August 1928 by Serb nationalists, the Serbian

King Aleksandar tightened control over the country. On 6 January 1929, he proclaimed a royal dictatorship and renamed the state the Kingdom of Yugoslavia ("land of the south Slavs"). The king abolished all political parties, and the country was reorganized into nine provinces, or *banovinas*, in a move designed to undermine national unity among the Croats. Tensions between the two nations continued; the entire post-war history of the first Yugoslav state was marked by the Croatian struggle for greater political autonomy. Croatian and Macedonian extremists assassinated King Aleksandar in 1934, and more radical nationalist movements began to garner support among both Croats and Serbs. However, in order to forestall a potential disintegration of the state, in August 1939 Serbian and Croatian leaders signed an agreement (*sporazum*) that reorganized the country's administrative divisions and created a new Croatian *banovina*. The new understanding did not last long, as Yugoslavia was dismembered during World War II.

On 6 April 1941, Nazi Germany invaded and occupied Yugoslavia. The country was partitioned among its neighbors (Italy, Hungary, Bulgaria, Albania). A large Independent State of Croatia was formed, which included most of Slavonija and Bosnia-Herzegovina; the Dalmatian coast reverted to Italy. The new Croatian state was a puppet of the Axis powers, and was governed by the fascist *Ustaše* regime under the leadership of Ante Pavelić. Yugoslavs fought against each other during the remainder of the war; in particular, the forces of Josip Broz Tito, a Croatian-Slovenian communist, fought against the Italian-backed *Ustaše* regime and the Serb royalist-nationalist *Četniks*.

The *Ustaše* persecuted Jews, Gypsies, and Serbs; most of the Jewish population was murdered, along with approximately 200,000 Serbs. The *Četniks* exterminated Croats and Muslims in the areas under their control. Meanwhile, Tito's partisans murdered any suspected German collaborators, nationalists, and democrats among all ethnic groups. In sum, about one million Yugoslavs perished during the war, of which approximately 487,000 were Serbs, 207,000 Croats, 86,000 Muslims, and 60,000 Jews. As the war came to a close, Tito's communists seized power and established a new Yugoslav state made up of six republics and two autonomous regions, in an effort to balance the country's diverse nationalities. Croatia became one of the constituent republics. By the terms of the peace treaty with Italy in 1947, most of Istria, formerly part of Italy, was ceded to Croatia.

Tito eliminated all rival political groups and imposed a harsh Stalinist regime in the late 1940s. But after the break with the Soviet Union in 1948, Belgrade sought to balance Western and Eastern influence in the country and some decentralizing elements were introduced at the republican level, particularly with the passage of the 1974 Yugoslav constitution. During the 1960s and 1970s, some Croatian leaders began to agitate for greater autonomy and liberalization. This "Croatian Spring" began as a reform movement within the Communist Party but increasingly attracted non-party activists, including students and intellectuals, much as Czechoslovakia's "Prague Spring" of 1968 did. However, Croatian demands were suppressed by Tito in late 1971, and any hope of reforming the communist system was crushed.

Croatian self-assertiveness mounted again following Tito's death in 1980 amidst growing resentment against alleged Serbian political domination and economic exploitation. As communist controls began to unravel during the mid to late 1980s, each of the Yugoslav republics pushed toward sovereignty. In 1989, preparations were made for multi-party republican elections, while many former communist politicians adopted nationalist positions in order to garner public support. Croatian nationalism was also spurred by the rise of Slobodan Milošević in Serbia, with indications that Belgrade was seeking to recentralize the Yugoslav federation. Most notably, a former Titoist general and political prisoner after the "Croatian Spring," Franjo Tudjman, was elected president of the newly established Croatian Democratic Union (CDU) on 17 June 1989.

The republic's communist leadership, led by the reformer Ivica Račan, initiated a program of political liberalization and permitted the creation of various political parties. More than 1,700 candidates vied for 356 seats in Croatia's tricameral legislature in a set of elections in May 1990 that would shape the future of Croatia's status within Yugoslavia. The elections were essentially a contest among three entities: the Croatian Democratic Union (CDU), the Party for Democratic Change (formerly the League of Communists of Croatia, LCC), and the centrist National Coalition for Understanding, composed of the five major liberal parties: the Croatian Social Liberal Party, the Social Democratic Party, the Democratic Party, the Christian Democratic Party, and the Croatian Peasant Party. The Coalition also included several smaller groupings, including the Croatian Peace Party, the Democratic Alliance of Albanians in Croatia, and the Muslim Democratic Party.

Several organizations ran independently of these coalitions, including the Serbian Democratic Party and the Green Party. The voting was considered to be relatively fair by outside observers, and the final tabulations showed that the CDU won comfortably, with 206 seats, gaining a clear majority in the 351-seat legislature. The CDU had grown into a broad-based political movement whose main plank was the achievement of national sovereignty. Tudjman was elected Croatian President and he appointed Stipe Mesić as the first non-communist Prime Minister.[2]

When talks stalled within the federal presidency on restructuring and further decentralizing the Yugoslav state, Croatia held a referendum on independence on 18 May 1990. An overwhelming majority of voters cast their ballots in favor of separation from Yugoslavia: 83.56% cast their ballots; of these, 93.24% voted in favor of Croatian sovereignty and independence with the right to enter into alliances with other republics. The secession of Slovenia seemed acceptable to the Serbian government, as it would strengthen Serbia's ethnic demographics and political position vis-à-vis the remaining nationalities. But the separation of Croatia proved much more problematic for Belgrade.

The Milošević regime asserted that Croatia could theoretically leave Yu-goslavia, but it could not take with it the large Serbian minority. It thereby implied that Zagreb's secession would provoke claims to Serb-inhabited ter-ritories in Croatia and other Yugoslav republics. This in turn would lead to the establishment of either a smaller, Serbian-dominated Yugoslavia or a larger Serbian state. An independent although much reduced Croatia would also remain subject to pronounced political and economic pressure from Belgrade, as Serbia would become the strongest regional power.

POST-COMMUNIST DEVELOPMENTS

With Croatia moving toward separation, leaders of the large Serb minority grew restless and claimed growing discrimination and persecution in the emerging state. The restoration of Croatian national insignia and the reor-ganization of the republican bureaucracy and security forces alarmed many local Serbs. Hundreds of Serbs reportedly lost their jobs. Croat leaders claimed that this was because they held a preponderant number of positions under the communist system, but Serbs charged Zagreb with deliberate eth-nic discrimination.

Leaders of Serb political groups began to demand their own territorial au-tonomy, especially in areas such as the Krajina, where Serbs formed com-pact majority communities. Belgrade and local Serb spokesmen asserted that if Croatia gained its independence, then it would stand to lose about a quarter of its territory, where Serbs outnumbered Croats. Zagreb was not opposed in principle to granting cultural autonomy to the Serbs but remained convinced that steps toward territorial self-determination were orchestrated by the Milošević regime in collusion with local radicals, in order to undermine and fracture the Croatian republic.

Although the Croatian Democratic Union (CDU) was formed as a national movement with a broad political spectrum and portrayed itself as the cham-pion of democratic reform and political moderation, it made little effort dur-ing the election campaign to acquire the support of the country's Serb population. President Tudjman and his associates sought to transform nation-alist sentiments into electoral support and ended up making a number of in-flammatory statements. For example, he implied that the republican borders would need to be revised in order to draw together elements of the Croatian nation resident outside Croatia. He claimed that the Muslims of Bosnia-Herzegovina did not constitute a separate ethnic group but were an integral part of the Croatian nation. He also called for the overhaul of the administra-tive structure, which had extended too many important positions of power to Serbs, in numbers that were disproportionate to their share of the population.[3]

Tudjman's nationalist pronouncements rang alarm bells among Serbian leaders, and the situation was made more tense by the context in which they were issued. As communist controls in Yugoslavia began to unravel in the late 1980s, an ideological struggle erupted over the structure of the state, and the ammunition for this conflict became the historical record. In particular, during 1988 the Serbian press and the Belgrade government's propaganda machine began to refocus attention on the atrocities of the *Ustaše* regime. When the CDU reintroduced Croatia's traditional national insignia, their display was depicted as the revival of the wartime Independent State of Croatia.

The Zagreb authorities declared the Latin alphabet to be the country's official script and proceeded to remove signs bearing the Cyrillic script, an action widely viewed as gratuitous and unnecessarily provocative. Serbian leaders also charged that non-Croats were being pressured to abandon their home villages. The government's decision to reorganize the republican bureaucracy and security forces cost hundreds of Serbs their jobs and suggested deliberate ethnic discrimination by Zagreb. Many local Serbs, keenly sensitized to the bloody episode of *Ustaše* rule during World War II, perceived these acts to be the first steps toward the reintroduction of a new fascist regime. As a result, when Croatian authorities began to build a "Croatian guard" to take over the functions of the republican police and territorial defense forces, Serb policemen, particularly in Serb-majority municipalities, refused to be disarmed and replaced.

Growing tensions in the Krajina culminated in Serb calls for territorial autonomy. In June 1990, the self-appointed Assembly of Knin (the unofficial capital of Krajina) announced the establishment of a Community of Serb-Administered Areas in the regions of northern Dalmatia and Lika, a move that was promptly overturned as illegitimate by the Croatian Constitutional Court. In July 1990, the Serbian National Council was created; this body, led by Milan Babić, formally declared Serb autonomy at the end of September 1990. Subsequent steps toward secession included the introduction of the Cyrillic alphabet to administrative institutions in Knin and the discontinuation of tax payments to the republican government. On the military side, local police chief Milan Martić began to distribute weapons to Knin residents and other volunteers and quickly built up an irregular force of several thousand combatants.[4]

The political and military insurrection of Serbs in Krajina appeared to be fully supported by the Serbian authorities in Belgrade. In October 1990, the Yugoslav People's Army, in which 70% of the officers were either Serbs or Montenegrins and which was increasingly becoming a tool of the Milošević regime, actively began to support rebel Serbs in the Knin district and dispatched arms to Serb fighters. The intricate planning behind this operation, in which trains carrying weapons were unexpectedly rerouted to Knin, where local Serbs unloaded the cargo, strongly suggested that Belgrade had been planning the Knin rebellion before the outbreak of hostilities and was simply waiting for the appropriate opportunity.[5] Serbia's intervention on behalf of the Knin insurgents caused the authorities in Zagreb to view the Krajina Serbs as puppets of Milošević rather than as citizens with legitimate concerns about their status. As a result, the Tudjman government was at first reluctant to negotiate seriously with the Serbs and unwilling to discuss the question of territorial autonomy—a discussion that Zagreb calculated would fuel "Greater Serbian" irredentist pressures.[6]

While Tudjman proceeded cautiously over the question of Serb autonomy, Serb demands accelerated. In July 1990, the president of the Serbian Democratic Party (SDP), Jovan Rašković, met with Tudjman to discuss the ongoing problems in Krajina. At that time, Rašković stated that the Serbs were interested neither in independence nor in annexation by Serbia but in autonomy.[7] However, he reserved the right to hold a referendum that would decide the status of Krajina in the event of the breakup of Yugoslavia. Indeed, in August 1990 the Serbs staged a referendum on cultural and territorial autonomy that the Croatian authorities attempted to ban. The Serbs voted in favor of a rather vaguely defined autonomous status, and shortly afterward established road-blocks and took up arms, ostensibly to defend themselves against expected reprisals by Croatian security forces.

The draft of the new Croatian constitution was opposed by leaders of the SDP, who were dissatisfied with its lack of provisions for minority rights and the assertion that Croatia was the homeland of the Croatian nation alone. In December 1990, the SDP-dominated Serbian National Council in Krajina announced that it was adopting a statute to establish a fully autonomous Serbian region before Zagreb passed a new constitution. The region was to include all territories in which Serbs constituted a majority, as well as neighboring municipalities where no single group predominated. The new authorities in the autonomous region were to assume responsibilities for judicial and policing functions independently of the Croatian state. At the end of December 1990, the Serbian Autonomous Region of Krajina was proclaimed. It incorporated ten municipalities in the Knin region adjacent to northern Dalmatia. Zagreb immediately annulled the decision, contending that it was contrary to the republican constitution, which provided no legal basis for forming autonomous districts within Croatia.

Serbia promptly accused the Croatian government of imposing a state of siege in minority areas through the creation of its own national guard. It also charged Zagreb with anti-Serbian discrimination and with creating an "ethnocracy" based along wartime *Ustaše* lines. Purges in the old communist apparatus, which displaced many prominent Serbs, were depicted by the Yugoslav media as a racist policy designed to turn Serbs into second-class Croatian citizens. The Croatian President himself came under severe criticism for allegedly concentrating too much power in his hands, for enacting various press restrictions, and for maintaining exclusive control over defense policies. Zagreb justified such measures as temporary but essential to preserve national unity during a national emergency, especially in the face of mounting pressures from Belgrade.

In February 1991, as the Serb-Croat conflict escalated at the republican level, the Serbian National Council in Knin declared the independence of Krajina from Croatia. The city of Knin was named as the region's capital, but the legality of the move was not recognized by Zagreb. In April 1991, the Krajina Executive Council adopted a declaration on separation from Croatia and on federation with Serbia. A few weeks later the decision was endorsed in a public referendum among Serbs in the region. Serb leaders in western and eastern Slavonija, Baranja, and western Syrmia (Srem) also sought to link up with Krajina, and in August 1991 proclaimed an autonomous region as an integral part of Serbian Krajina.

The federal government, presumably to avoid international censure and not to be seen as breaking up the federation, did not formally acknowledge these decisions. It declared the creation of any new autonomous regions to be unconstitutional, particularly the secession of territory from one republic and its incorporation into another republic. The Serbian regime itself did not automatically approve the Krajina decision or accept the region as a constituent part of Serbia.[8]

The crisis in Croatia intensified in January 1991 after the Yugoslav defense minister asserted that no republic would be allowed to create paramilitary units outside the federal military structure. The Croatian legislature had approved constitutional amendments giving republican governments jurisdiction over territorial defense and foreign relations. An armed confrontation was narrowly averted when Zagreb agreed to demobilize its reserve militia forces although not its main national guard contingents. Despite this partial compromise, tensions remained high. Croatia stood accused by the Serbian authorities of creating illegal armed formations, of importing weapons from abroad, and of planning to sabotage Yugoslav army operations.

At the end of June 1991, Croatia declared its independence and "disassociation" from Yugoslavia. Initially, the Yugoslav People's Army (the only intact federal institution) focused its attention on crushing the Slovenian rebellion, but it also moved its troops and equipment to saturate Croatian territory. The bulk of YPA forces that subsequently withdrew from Slovenia were repositioned in Croatia. Having failed to subdue Slovenia, the army leadership put its weight behind the Serbian government program. This focused on one of two objectives: either to ensure that Zagreb remained in a centralized Yugoslavia controlled from Belgrade, or to carve away about a third of Croatia's territory and establish a "Greater Serbia" or a "Community of Serbian States" stretching to the Adriatic coast. Serb guerrillas in Krajina, with logistical and military assistance from the YPA, launched offensives across the republic to capture a contiguous tract of territory and to push out Croat residents from the contested zones. Reports also surfaced that Serbs were being resettled in some captured territories from other parts of the country in order to alter the demographic structure.

During the summer and fall of 1991, Serb insurgents gained control over about a quarter of Croatian territory against the poorly armed Croatian national guard. By December 1991, over 5,000 deaths were reported in the fighting, countless thousands were injured, and over a quarter of a million refugees had fled or been expelled from the conflict zones. With the expiration of the EC-brokered Brioni moratorium on independence in October 1991, the Croatian parliament restated the republic's statehood and negated all federal laws and Yugoslav jurisdiction in Croatia. These moves neither forestalled the armed conflict nor ensured international recognition for the republic. Although the Serbian government expressed agreement for a United Nations peace-keeping force to enter Croatia, there was little indication that any of the captured territories would be surrendered by Serb guerrillas or by the Krajina government.

In order to obtain diplomatic recognition from the EC member states, the Croatian authorities moved to provide stronger guarantees of minority rights. Certain assurances were contained in Croatia's December 1990 constitution, which declared all of Croatia's constituent nationalities equal, and guaranteed their members freedom to express their nationality, language, and cultural autonomy. It underscored that all citizens would enjoy rights and freedoms regardless of race, color, language, sex, religion, political opinion, national or social origin, and it provided for the cultural autonomy of members of all nations and minorities. Nonetheless, serious concerns remained that the document was not explicit enough in institutionalizing minority rights and insuring against the domination of political life by ethnic Croats.[9] Serbian leaders charged that it was not forthright enough in recognizing and assuring the "collective rights" of the Serb minority. While the human rights of all citizens were verbally guaranteed in the constitution, together with the cultural and educational rights of minorities, the issue of political or territorial self-determination was not clearly enunciated. Such omissions were condemned by Serbian leaders as a deliberate negation of specifically Serbian interests and an indication of growing Croatian repression.

As conflicts escalated, Croatian government officials came under mounting international pressure to make some clear concessions to the Serb population and to underscore their commitment to minority rights. In July 1991, Zagreb offered an olive branch by agreeing to negotiate on the question of granting Serbs some form of limited political autonomy. Croatian officials proposed forming districts with a special status, in which the municipal Serbian authorities would have legislative powers and some control over local police, education, and culture. These were to include the areas of Knin, Krajina, Banja, Kordun, and parts of eastern Slavonija. But such proposals came too late to have any impact on the armed struggle, and the rebel government in Krajina rejected the status of an autonomous region within Croatia as a way of settling the crisis.

In May 1992, the Croatian parliament ratified a Constitutional Law of Human Rights and Freedoms and the Rights of National and Ethnic Communities or Minorities. This legislation institutionalized within Croatian law the special position of minorities, with emphasis on the Croatian Serbs. The goal of the Constitutional Law was to amplify constitutional provisions that dealt with the rights of minorities to cultural autonomy. It guaranteed a special self-governing status for the Knin and Glina districts, proportional representation for all minority groups that comprised more than 8% of the population, the right to special education in one's own language upon request, and stipulations for international supervision in the implementation of the law.[10]

The legislation would assign to Serbs almost complete internal governance of the two Krajina districts, including the authority to police and to raise taxes in the area, to run local courts, schools, and the media. The system of proportional representation required that Serbs be represented in parliament in numbers commensurate with their share of the population, thus ensuring that Serb deputies would have at least 12% of *Sabor* seats. However, the law was largely irrelevant as long as Serbian guerrillas refused to surrender their territories. Such legal initiatives and government pronouncements failed to reassure Serbian leaders.

In December 1991, a Republic of Serbian Krajina was officially proclaimed to include the autonomous regions of Krajina, Slavonija, Baranja, and Srem. The Krajina authorities were evidently prepared to weigh only three political options: unification with Bosnian Krajina as a separate federal unit within Yugoslavia, the creation of a Krajina republic within a federal Yugoslavia, or the transformation of Krajina into a component region of an expanded Serbia. All three options were unacceptable to Zagreb. The government refused to countenance any loss of territory, particularly as a result of armed aggression. Despite the war raging on its territory, Croatia reaffirmed its declaration of independence in October 1991.

In January 1992, Croatia was officially recognized by the international community after largely meeting a set of conditions laid down by the EC. In the same month, a UN-sponsored cease-fire came into effect. An agreement was reached among Zagreb, Belgrade, Yugoslav military commanders, and local Serb authorities in Krajina to implant a UN peace-keeping force in the disputed territories. This was known as the Vance Plan, after the former U.S. secretary of state who helped to forge the agreement. But the United Nations proved unable to complete its mandate, including the restoration of the pre-war demographic structure, the disarming of Serb paramilitaries, and the reestablishment of a multi-ethnic police force in preparation for a return of Croatian authority.

The only persistent opposition to the UN proposals came from Milan Babić, the Serbian president of the Krajina region. He feared that Serbian militia forces would be disbanded and the local population subjected to Croatian control once the UN troops were withdrawn. Babić was accused by some of his SDP colleagues of creating an autocratic system in Krajina and abusing the rights of the Serbian community. In the internal power struggle that followed, Babić was replaced by Goran Hadžić, an avowed moderate who benefited from Belgrade's support. Although the Milošević government, facing mounting opposition to the war in Serbia, appeared to back away from a "Greater Serbia" policy, suspicions persisted that this was merely a tactical ploy to subdue domestic criticism and elicit international support for the beleaguered Yugoslav regime.

In January 1992, the UN Security Council adopted a resolution establishing the United Nations Protection Force (UNPROFOR), numbering 14,000 troops. in four UN protected areas. UN troops were to act as a buffer between Croat and Serb forces in the Krajina area and the surrounding "pink zones." Under the UN plan, the Yugoslav army was to be withdrawn from Croatia and irregular Serbian and Croatian detachments were to be disarmed. Existing local authorities and police forces were to function on an interim basis under UN supervision, pending an overall political solution. Croatian authorities expressed reservations about the UN mission, fearing that it could legitimize the separation of the Krajina region.

Croatia's second multi-party elections to the presidency and to the Croatian Chamber of Deputies took place on 2 August 1992. They were marred by instances of intimidation, an excessive degree of CDU influence over the mass media, irregularities in election procedures, incomplete voter registries, and the fact that elections could not be conducted in the Serb-held territories. Tudjman was reelected president for a five-year term, with 56.73% of the vote; his nearest challenger, Dražen Budiša, leader of the Social Liberal Party, captured 21.87%. Opposition parties were larger and better organized than in the first elections, but only six parties and one regional alliance received the minimum 3% of the vote necessary to capture a parliamentary seat. The CDU maintained its dominant position by gaining 85 out of 138 seats in the *Sabor*, aided by the state bureaucracy, the media, and an electoral law that evidently favored the party in power.

Other pertinent results included a relatively reasonable showing by the regionalist party coalition in Istria, which gained 6 seats; the Social Liberal Party, which obtained 14 seats; and the Social Democratic Party (the successor to the communists) which won 11 seats. There were serious setbacks for the ultra-nationalist Croatian Party of Rights, which managed to gain only five seats, as well as for smaller oppositionist parties including the Croatian People's Party and the Croatian Peasant Party. The Serbian National Party, which had been strongly supportive of Croatian independence, gained only 3 seats. The elections included voter and candidate lists for the occupied territories, although in several cases only a few hundred displaced people were able to elect deputies to constituencies in which Croatian authority did not function. The election law allocated 13 seats for Serbs in the lower house under a system of proportional representation for minorities. The individuals were designated by the election commission to officially represent the Serb population.[11]

The Tudjman government was charged with maintaining authoritarian controls over most aspects of public life. It responded by claiming that in conditions of war it was unrealistic to launch an extensive economic reform program and allow unfettered criticism of the government in the mass media. It also pointed out that political pluralism had been reestablished in the country, as dozens of parties and associations were allowed to operate. Some analysts believed that Croatia had only a brief spell of liberalism and democracy during the election campaign, before a new authoritarian system was installed.[12] The authorities linked nationalism with democracy, whereby democratic rule meant national liberation and independent statehood. Individual liberties evidently had to be subsumed to the process of preserving independence.

Political tensions increased in June 1993 when Serb leaders in Croatia abandoned peace talks and held a referendum on the unification of the Serb Krajina Republic with the Serb Republic in Bosnia. A government of "technocrats" was subsequently installed in Zagreb with the appointment of Nikica Valentić as Prime Minister in April 1993. Nonetheless, harder-line elements in the CDU and the army appeared to gain ascendancy during the summer of 1993, intent primarily on recapturing territory lost to the Serbs. President Tudjman repeatedly made it clear that Croatia would not countenance any diminution of its territory. Ultimately, for the government and opposition alike, there could be no peace without the reintegration of the Krajina region. Throughout 1992 and 1993, UNPROFOR stood as a buffer between Croatian and Serb forces, thus preventing Croatia from taking military action to regain these areas. Observers calculated that Zagreb's military position remained too weak to launch any major offensives, even though it continued to stockpile weapons and established a more professional fighting force.

The task assigned to UNPROFOR was to provide basic peace-keeping functions, to ensure the restoration of law and order, and to allow for the return of populations driven away by the fighting.[13] The UNPROFOR force, however, proved unable to complete its mandate of restoring the pre-war demographic structure, compelling the Serbs to lay down their arms, and permitting Croatian populations to return to their pre-war homes. Tudjman stated that although Croatia's goal was to regain the Krajina region through peaceful means, Zagreb could not tolerate the permanent occupation of its territory.[14]

In order to regain its territories, the Zagreb government either had to convince Serb leaders that their interests would be protected within the Croatian state, or it had to achieve victory on the battlefield. The former option called for a strategy of reconciliation that would limit the extent of post-war reprisals. In keeping with this concept, the Croatian parliament passed an amnesty act in October 1992 that guaranteed the safety of all citizens who were actively involved in the 1991 war, provided that they had not engaged in war crimes. This promise failed to encourage any Serb leaders to break ranks. A relatively moderate Serb faction in western Slavonija that appeared willing to negotiate with Zagreb was disciplined by hard-line leaders. Furthermore, the Serbian authorities in Krajina employed a relatively effective self-policing mechanism based on fear and intimidation that tended to keep desertion rates low.

As Tudjman seemed unable to woo the Serbs from their barricades, he intended to reverse at least some of their military gains. This was evident in actions such as the liberation of the Maslenica bridge in January 1993, in which Croatian forces recaptured some territory and provisionally reopened traffic routes to the Dalmatian coast. While lacking the resources to launch a general offensive against Serbian Krajina, Zagreb may have calculated that it could successfully prosecute a more limited military campaign to regain strategic positions.

Continuing Serb policies of "ethnic cleansing" in the occupied areas, coupled with frustration over the UN mission, were clearly building a momentum for intervention. The Zagreb government came under increasing domestic pressure to resolve the Krajina issue, while the failure of UN operations in both Croatia and Bosnia-Herzegovina to dislodge the Serb guerrillas from captured territories served to reinforce the war option in Croatia.[15] Negotiations between Zagreb and the Krajina authorities were stalled and tensions again mounted when the Serbian leadership organized a referendum in June 1993 in which over 98% of the electorate, of the 95.6% who voted, reportedly favored joining the area with Serbian Bosnia.

A power struggle ensued in the Krajina between a more pragmatic faction supported by Milošević, which gave indications that it would countenance trading full independence for far-reaching autonomy within Croatia, and more militant elements supported by radicals in Belgrade who remained determined to move swiftly toward Serbian unification. Rumors persisted that Tudjman and Milošević had discussed plans to exchange territory in Krajina and Bosnia. Following the Krajina referendum, a commission was appointed to draw up a joint constitution of the Serbian territories west of the Drina River, but no announcement was made about imminent reunification. The perceptible moderation of the Serbian position led to another extension of the UN mandate in Croatia, which expired at the end of June 1993.

The UN Security Council prolonged the mission for another three months, while Zagreb pledged that it would not agree to further extensions unless the Serbian side signed a binding agreement to implement fully the peace plan by disarming its militias, allowing for the return of refugees, and setting a timetable for the restoration of Croatian authority. The outcome in Krajina was also closely linked to the war in Bosnia, where Croatian-Serbian agreements on partition placed the Krajina issue temporarily on hold. The danger remained that with the consolidation of Croat and Serb control over Bosnia, significant numbers of troops would be freed for combat duty in Croatia.

It remained unclear as to what the CDU leadership believed the ultimate borders of Croatia should be. Although Tudjman opposed attempts by the Serbs to detach areas from Croatia and was putatively in favor of maintaining intact all internal frontiers of the former Yugoslavia, including the border with neighboring Bosnia, he also asserted that the people of Bosnia must be given the right to decide by referendum in which state they preferred to live.

In a February 1991 speech, Tudjman did not deny that a plan had been concocted to divide up Bosnia-Herzegovina between Croatia and Serbia. He noted that Croatia maintained a special interest in the approximately 800,000 Croats living in Bosnia.[16] Such comments indicated that the CDU viewed portions of Bosnia as belonging to Croatia.

Furthermore, Croatian nationalists claimed that the Bosnian Muslims did not constitute a separate nation with sovereign rights but were in reality an Islamicized branch of the Croatian nation. The Hercegovinian lobby in Zagreb proved particularly tenacious in pressuring Zagreb to adopt a more combative stance in campaigning for the incorporation of western Herzegovina into Croatia. In addition, hard-line elements of the CDU were evidently intent on establishing a state in which Croat ethnicity would become a prerequisite for full citizenship and equal treatment in the country's political system. Such positions undermined the regime's commitment to a multi-ethnic society and laid the basis for ongoing tensions with Bosnian Muslims.

The Croatian-Bosnian relationship was also complicated by the tremendous refugee burden that Zagreb confronted. During 1992–1993, more than half a million refugees fled Bosnia to find shelter in Croatia. This situation strained the already decimated Croatian economy, which had lost billions of dollars as a result of the collapse of the Adriatic tourist trade. Without the resources to provide for these refugees adequately, Croatia attempted to manipulate citizenship and naturalization criteria in order to prevent Bosnians from permanently settling in Croatia. A relatively strict immigration policy came into effect in which individuals needed to renounce their current citizenship, have at least five years of continuous residence in Croatia, know the Croatian language and Latin alphabet, and demonstrate "that they respected the legal order and customs in the Republic of Croatia and accepted Croatian culture."[17] The ambiguous criteria left open the possibility that officials could interpret the policy arbitrarily in such away that whereby Serbs or other minorities could be denied citizenship in order to further ethnic homogenization. Furthermore, without citizenship, individuals were not permitted to own property, obtain employment, or receive retirement pensions.

The process of effecting shifts in the demographic balance was a recurrent theme in CDU ideology. Tudjman's 1990 inaugural address claimed that the policies of the previous several decades had brought the Croatian national corpus into a state of demographic endangerment. These problems had to be combated by taking "urgent and purposeful steps with a view to both stemming the flow of our citizens leaving the country and increasing our birthrate."[18] Such assertions tapped into traditional nationalist ideas about reestablishing more extensive ties with the Croatian diaspora and reining in the number of Croatian guest workers.[19]

Some schisms appeared in Croatia during the 1990s on the basis of regional affiliation. In particular, there was a growing tide of opposition to Zagreb's policies in several Istrian municipalities, including Rijeka and Pula.

Istria, an ethnically mixed region that generated a large portion of Croatia's tourist trade, had been contested by Italy and Yugoslavia since World War I. Its mix of Italian, Croatian, and Slovenian cultures and its strong regionalist identity contributed to stirring opposition to the CDU government. Democratic forces, including the Social Liberals and various regionalist movements, polled successfully in the area, campaigning against Zagreb's centralism and Tudjman's penchant for power. There was a growing popular movement aiming at regional autonomy, perhaps in a joint relationship between Slovenia, Croatia, and Italy.[20]

The war in Croatia produced a legion of human rights abuses, including the summary execution of civilians and unarmed combatants; the torture and mistreatment of detainees; arbitrary arrests and disappearances; destruction of civilian property; and the killing of journalists covering the war. The most serious human rights abuses were associated with the policy of "ethnic cleansing" undertaken primarily by Serb militants against non-Serb residents in the Krajina region. In pursuit of ethnically homogeneous areas, Serb paramilitaries, with the complicity of local authorities, conducted a campaign of intimidation, arrest, torture, and murder in order to force Croats to vacate their homes.[21]

Prior to the outbreak of armed hostilities, the majority of Serbs lived in Zagreb and other larger towns. They constituted an absolute or relative majority in only 11 out of 115 Croatian municipalities along the Krajina's border with Bosnia-Herzegovina, including Knin, Donji Lapac, Gračac, Obrovac, Benkovac, Titova Korenica, Vrginmost, Vojnić, Glina, Koštajnica, and Dvor, where they totaled a little under 150,000 inhabitants. According to official estimates, by early 1992, when the conflict subsided, over 10,000 people had perished or disappeared in the war and over a quarter of a million had been expelled or fled their homes. The demographic structure in the affected municipalities was significantly altered, and they became purely Serbian enclaves. Serb numbers outside the Krajina continued to shrink as hundreds of families left Croatia for fear of intimidation. By the close of 1992, only about 150,000 Serbs were believed left in areas under Zagreb's control.

About 20,000 Serb settlers were reportedly transferred to the Baranja region in eastern Croatia, thus dramatically altering the demographic structure. By mid-1992, Serbs constituted over 90% of the inhabitants of Baranja, as compared to about 25% before the war. The serbianization of these enclaves was not reversed or halted by the UN deployment, while Croatian patience with international forces visibly diminished. As displaced Croats from Krajina registered to vote in the Croatian elections, they generated an increasing amount of support for recapturing occupied territories.

Croatian paramilitaries also engaged in atrocities against Serb civilians. It remained unclear whether the government in Zagreb was unable or unwilling to control these violations. The forces most implicated in war crimes were irregular formations such as the armed wing of the neo-fascist Croatian Party of Rights, styled as the Croatian Defense Force. Although the Croatian government prohibited the formation of paramilitary organizations and claimed by late 1991 that all former irregulars were under the command of the Ministry of Defense, the degree to which Zagreb actually exercised control over these units remained highly ambiguous. Another disturbing development was the harassment of government critics, whether Croats or Serbs, by extremists, policemen, and government officials. Members of the Serbian Democratic Party and veterans of the Yugoslav army were targeted and accused of being spies.

By mid-1993 it became clear that the Vance-Owen peace plan, proposed by Lord Owen of the EC and Cyrus Vance of the UN in October 1992, had failed. But negotiations continued and a bilateral accord between Croatia and Serbia was signed in January 1994, pledging the restoration of communication and transportation links between the two republics. Nevertheless, Serb guerrillas still occupied 25% to 30% of Croatian territory. President Milošević refused to include a mutual recognition clause in the agreement that would have solidified Croatia's claim to the Krajina region. In March 1994, the Bosnian government and Bosnian Croats signed a charter for a new federation, linking the remaining territory of Bosnia controlled by the two groups. At the same time, the new federation signed an agreement with Croatia to facilitate economic cooperation. But the tense standoff between Croats and Croatian Serbs continued. The cease-fire was held in place chiefly by the UN peacekeeping force. The Z-4 peace plan presented by U.S. and Russian ambassadors in November 1994 proposed restoring the original boundaries of Croatia while giving Serbs local autonomy in Serb-dominated regions. Both sides rejected this plan.

The uneasy peace in Croatia was threatened by Tudjman's efforts in early 1995 to end the UN mandate and force out foreign troops, whose presence Zagreb feared was solidifying the Serbian hold on the Krajina. Tudjman finally agreed to let a UN force remain in Croatia through November 1995, but he insisted that the name of the force be changed to reflect Croatia's independent status and that the number of troops occupying Croatia be reduced by about one third. On 29 April 1995, Croatian forces crossed UN lines and attacked the Serb-held enclave in western Slavonija; the Serbs immediately responded by shelling Zagreb. The Serb population was forced to evacuate the region, giving the Croatian army a victory and reducing the Croatian territory controlled by Serb militants.

Despite these initial fears, the Yugoslav army did not intervene and neither did the Bosnian Serb forces. On 22 July 1995, a joint Croatian-Bosnian declaration was signed on a common defense against Serbian aggression. On 4 August 1995 Croatian forces mounted "Operation Storm"—a large-scale offensive across the entire Krajina region—and quickly reconquered all occupied territories aside from a narrow strip of land in Eastern Slavonija. Serbian forces put up little resistance, and most armed units fled before the civilian population. Hundreds of thousands of Serbs evacuated Croatia, most of them taking refuge in Bosnia and Serbia. Once again the Yugoslav army did not intervene, thereby avoiding a war between Croatia and Serbia. Some observers speculated that Tudjman and Milošević had arranged a secret deal over, the return of the Krajina region.

On 29 October 1995, Croatia held elections for its House of Representatives, as Tudjman hoped to benefit from the recapture of the Krajina. Although the CDU won 75 of the 119 seats in the chamber, this actually represented a decline from its previous holdings. A five-party coalition, which included the Croatian Peasant Party, the Croatian People's Party, and the Croatian Christian Democratic Union, won 20 seats. The largest opposition party, the Croatian Social Liberal Party, gained 11 seats.

In the months following the elections, there was increasing public disaffection with Tudjman's autocratic rule and the corruption that was rampant in the CDU. Tudjman's popularity was slipping, particularly in the larger cities. On four occasions, Tudjman blocked the Zagreb mayoral candidacy of the seven-party opposition coalition, and eventually he dissolved the Zagreb City Council. The opposition had won control of the City Council in October 1995. Despite public protests and charges of manipulation, the President appointed his own political loyalist as mayor of Zagreb. The opposition subsequently boycotted assembly sessions, leading to gridlock in the functioning of the city administration. They also staged walkouts from the national parliament, where the CDU maintained a governing majority.

In December 1995, President Tudjman joined Serbian President Milošević and Bosnian President Alija Izetbegović in the signing of the Dayton peace accord, which ended the war in Bosnia. The previous month, an international plan had been arranged to address continued Serb occupation of the regions of eastern Slavonija and Baranja. According to the plan, these regions were to revert to Croatian control during a twelve-month transition period that could be extended for another year at the request of either party. In the meantime, a UN-mandated force consisting of 5,000 troops remained in the area to maintain peace and security.

In August 1996, the foreign ministers of Croatia and the Federal Republic of Yugoslavia (FRY) signed a mutual recognition agreement in which they pledged to establish diplomatic relations and restore trade and transportation links between the two countries. The agreement sent a message to Serbs in eastern Slavonija that the FRY would not support their campaign to establish the region as a special international zone and would not hinder its return to Croatian rule. In January 1997, the UN Security Council decided to extend its mandate in eastern Slavonija and Baranja following a request by Serb authorities in the regions to allow for a gradual and peaceful reintegration into Croatia. The US and its European allies pressed Zagreb to live up to its agreement by allowing exiled ethnic Serbs to return to their homes. Western leaders also criticized the Croatian government for failing to make full provisions to accommodate the 120,000 Serbs living in eastern Slavonija, many of whom had been forced out of other parts of Croatia in 1995.

On 13 April 1997, Croatia held elections to the parliamentary House of Districts. Candidates of the ruling CDU scored a decisive victory, increasing their number of seats in the 68-member chamber from 37 to 40. The largest opposition party, the Croatian Social Liberal Party, only obtained 11 seats. On 15 June 1997, presidential elections were held and Tudjman won another five-year term as President, with more than 61.4% of the vote. His nearest challenger, Zdravko Tomac of the Social Democratic Party, only gained 21%, and Vlado Gotovac, leader of the Social Liberals, obtained 17.5%. However, only 55% of the voters went to the polls. Monitors from the Organization on Security and Cooperation in Europe (OSCE) criticized the elections and the campaign, citing strong favoritism towards Tudjman within the state media, vastly unequal campaign resources among candidates, and the denial of voting rights to minority Serbs.

In January 1998, after a two-year transition period, eastern Slavonija and Baranja were finally turned over to Zagreb. UN troops departed, although international observers were sent to the region to monitor Croatia's treatment of Serb residents. In the months that followed, large numbers of Serbs left eastern Slavonija and Baranja for the FRY and other countries, complaining of job discrimination, harassment, intimidation, evictions, and unemployment. A program approved by parliament in June to safeguard returning refugees had not been fully implemented by the end of 1998.

The West remained adamant that Zagreb needed to cooperate with the international war crimes tribunal; ensure that Bosnian Croats fully abided with all of Dayton's provisions, including the return of refugees and the operation of joint federation institutions; and reintegrate Serb refugees in eastern Slavonija and other formerly occupied territories. Serious questions remained whether the surrender of the Croatian military leader Dario Kordić and his cohorts from western Herzegovina to the Hague War Crimes Tribunal indicated a genuine long-term policy shift by Zagreb or merely a concession to cushion against further American pressures on the beleaguered Tudjman regime. The U.S. and EU also insisted on domestic political and economic reforms, a concerted government campaign against officially sanctioned corruption, and greater respect for human rights and freedom of speech.

During 1998, President Tudjman proposed changing Croatia's constitution to define the country as a Central European state and to prohibit membership of any future Balkan alliances. Unfortunately, Zagreb could not determine a country's geopolitical position or internal evolution by simply issuing a decree. The ruling party stifled the development of a competitive democracy and an open market economy through a series of regressive measures. The notion propounded by official propaganda that Croatia needed a strongman was fundamentally anti-democratic. The state media remained susceptible to historical revisionism. For example, the idea implanted in citizens that Tudjman gained independence for Croatia through his far-sighted policies was highly questionable. Croatia won independence despite having leaders who made little preparation for war, gullibly believed that Milošević could be trusted, diverted weapons from the siege of Vukovar to their nationalist allies in western Herzegovina, and launched a war of partition against Bosnia.

Throughout the 1990s, Zagreb employed nationalist xenophobia. Official statements promulgated an "us versus them" syndrome. The purpose of this threat-mongering was to maintain public support for the CDU. The political opposition was depicted as basically anti-Croat and pro-Yugoslav. Even the US was vilified by the government as an alien force seeking to subvert Croatian statehood through its support for various democratization programs. Various non-governmental organizations were harassed by officials. Indeed, Tudjman claimed that "internal enemies" such as human rights groups were part of an international plot to undermine Croatia's independence.

The CDU implanted itself in all administrative institutions. This did not simply involve the temporary appointment of key personnel, but the creation of a politically loyal *nomenklatura* not subject to independent checks and balances. For example, judges at all levels were CDU loyalists, officers in the military were promoted according to party loyalty, and CDU membership remained essential in a range of professions. The major media outlets were tightly controlled by the ruling party. Several formerly independent papers were squeezed out or bought by the CDU. The rest were subject to harassment, including fines and court cases, amidst a constant sense of threat that they could be closed down. A notorious media law protected the President and other officials from press criticism; critics could be fined or imprisoned, even if they were simply presenting facts about government policy.

Croatia faced an uphill struggle in implementing democratic reforms and curtailing the influence of the CDU patronage network. Numerous reports surfaced on how the clandestine privatization process benefited a narrow circle of political loyalists and family members. This form of corruption and misappropriation of public property became a major campaign issue in the 2000 parliamentary and presidential elections, especially as the gap between rich and poor continued to widen and sparked protests by angry workers. Moreover, two major criteria for both NATO and EU membership were transparency in privatization and a proper legal and regulatory system: Croatia under Tudjman failed on both counts.

In November 1996, President Tudjman was suddenly rushed to a hospital in the US, reportedly suffering from stomach cancer. While American reports signaled that Tudjman had less than two years to live, the official Croatian media refused to report on his state of health. In order to thwart independent news, officials threatened to close down the major non-governmental broadcast outlet, Radio 101, by revoking its license. This move outraged the citizens of Zagreb and on 21 November 1996 about 100,000 demonstrators gathered in the capital to protest. The authorities quickly restored Radio 101's license in order to defuse public anger. The radio incident indicated how much the authorities feared freedom of information. During the late 1990s, pressures were applied on various independent newspapers despite the protests of the international community. Croatia gained admittance to the Council of Europe under extreme reservations that democratization was threatened by Tudjman's autocratic policies.

The resignations of Defense Minister Andrija Hebrang and President Franjo Tudjman's Chief of Staff Hrvoje Šarinić in October 1998 brought into the open the deep-seated disputes within the ruling elite. Both men criticized blatant abuses of office by hard-line factions in the CDU. They revealed that Zagreb's intelligence services regularly spied on the political opposition and the independent media and intimidated rivals within the government. The resignation of CDU moderates strengthened the hard-line Herzegovinian lobby. Croatia's democratic opposition parties formed a coalition bloc and won a number of local elections during 1998 in several major cities, including Dubrovnik and Split. By the close of the year, opposition leaders were pressing for early parliamentary elections while seeking to benefit from growing social discontent over deteriorating economic conditions among workers and pensioners. Living standards fell among sectors of the population after the government introduced a 22% VAT (value-added tax) on most consumer items in January 1998. Railway workers, teachers, farmers, and other groups staged strikes to demand wage increases and to protest growing reports of corruption among state officials.

By the close of 1999, Croatia's progress toward democratic rule and membership in international institutions remained stalled by its quasi-authoritarian government. A broad range of domestic reforms continued to be obstructed, including reform of the election law, an end to persecution of the independent media, the rooting-out of corruption and political patronage, and the unhindered return of Serbian refugees to their pre-war homes. Zagreb was also criticized by the international community for concentrating too much power within the central government, and particularly in the President's office. Tudjman held substantial constitutional powers enabling him to block democratic reforms.

With the death after a long illness of President Tudjman in December 1999, the popularity of the CDU plummeted. Parliamentary elections to the House of Representatives were held on 3 January 2000, with a voter turnout of 71%. The two-party opposition coalition, consisting of the Social Democratic Party and the Croatian Social Liberal Party, gained 47.02% of the vote and 71 seats. The CDU scored 30.46% and captured 46 seats. A smaller opposition coalition of five parties (the Croatian Peasant Party, the Istrian Democratic Assembly, the Croatian People's Party, the Liberal Party, and the Action of Social Democrats of Croatia) garnered 15.89% of the vote and 24 seats. A coalition of the ultra-nationalist Croatian Party of Rights and the Croatian Christian Democratic Union gained only 3.31% of the vote and 5 parliamentary seats.

The Serbian National Party and several smaller formulations captured the remaining seats, together with unaffiliated candidates.

The splits within the CDU became even more apparent during the presidential elections on 24 January 2000. With a voter turnout of 60.88 % in the second round, on 7 February 2000, two opposition candidates battled for the office. Mate Granić, the moderate CDU candidate, only managed 22.47% of the vote in the first round and was eliminated. Stjepan Mesić, the former Prime Minister, won the presidency in the second round with 56.01%. Dražen Budiša, the leader of the Social Liberal Party, captured 43.99% of the popular vote. The two elections signaled the end of the CDU era and the beginning of a democratic administration that faced numerous problems during its first year in office, not least of which was to keep the diverse government coalition together during the implementation of long-overdue political and economic reforms. Topping the political agenda was the constitutional reduction of presidential powers, restructuring of the state administration, and elimination of widespread corruption in privatization.

POLITICAL PARTIES

Socialists and Social Democrats

Social Democratic Party of Croatia (SDPC)
Socijaldemokratska Partija Hrvatske (SDPH)

The Social Democratic Party of Croatia (SDPC) was originally founded on 1 August 1937 and was revived as a legal party on 3 November 1990. It claimed a membership of between 35,000 and 40,000 and was led by Ivica Račan. The SDPC was the direct successor to the former League of Communists in Croatia and became the major leftist party in the country. In the first free elections, the SDPC attempted to signal its break with the communist past and its commitment to political and economic reform, and it added the Party of Democratic Change to its original title. By continuing to call for a "socialist" Republic of Croatia and by campaigning on a platform of maintaining Yugoslavia, the party was hindered in efforts to convince voters it was serious about far-reaching change. As a result, party membership dropped to under 15,000 by the time of the parliamentary elections in April–May 1990. Many of the groups that supported the party feared the consequences of opposition calls for an independent Croatia. After the first elections, the SDP became the strongest opposition party, with 73 parliamentary delegates.

The SDPC went through a crisis of identity and in the elections of 2 August 1992 it won only eleven seats to parliament. In April 1993, the organization declared itself the Social Democratic Party of Croatia. Another social democratic party with the same name already existed, with Antun Vujić as its president. On 30 April 1994, the two parties united in a new SDPC. The party regained strength in the parliamentary elections on 29 October 1995. It won 9% of the state list and by its number of seats in the parliament the SDPC became the third strongest party in Croatia and the only leftist party that succeeded in crossing the 5% threshold for entry into parliament. The party was extremely successful in the local government elections for the city of Zagreb, in which it received nearly 19% of the vote.

The SDPC was dedicated to "protecting the interests of the labor force of medium and low purchase power, as well as the interests of all social groups that due to their minority character need special care and protection." The party, which had a significant number of members of Serbian and other nationalities, was a member of the Socialist International. With the ruling CDU losing support in the late 1990s, the SDPC emerged as the most credible and popular opposition party, and in the general elections of 3 January 2000, it won 47% of the national vote in a coalition together with the Croatian Social Liberal Party (CSLP). The SDPC itself became the largest party in the *Sabor*, with 43 seats, and its leader Račan became Croatia's new Prime Minister.

Croatian People's Party (CPP)
Hrvatska Narodna Stranka (HNS)

The Croatian People's Party (CPP) is a center-left opposition party that was organized after the 1990 elections by Savka Dabčević-Kučar, who had been Croatia's premier in the late 1960s but was removed from the political scene for involvement in the 1971 Croatian autonomy movement known as the "Croatian Spring." The party was outspoken in its demands for a free press and for the role of the state to be reduced. It advocated equal rights for all citizens, the rule of law, the division of powers, and the protection of ethnic and cultural minorities and social groups with special needs. In an interview given to *Danas* in May 1994, Dabčević-Kučar advocated strengthening the constitutional role of the parliament with new operating procedures, because the existing ones were allegedly defined to suit the incumbent party. She criticized the merger of the party and the state, as well as Croatian government policy toward Bosnia-Herzegovina.

The CPP experienced a number of defections after the 1992 elections, as well as in 1995, when three distinguished parliamentary representatives left to join the CDU. The defectors stated that the party leaders' deviation from a populist policy was the reason for their departure. After Dabčević-Kučar ceded her position as CPP president to Radimir Čačir, many members expressed their dissatisfaction with his style, arguing that he was cooperating too closely with leftist parties. Some observers believed the defections experienced by the CPP and other opposition parties were the result of the ruling party's tactic to destabilize the opposition before parliamentary elections. The party claimed a membership of some 24,700 and was part of a small opposition coalition of five parties that garnered nearly 16% of the vote and a total of 24 seats following the parliamentary elections of 3 January 2000.

Action of Social Democrats of Croatia (ASDC)
Akcija Socijaldemokrata Hrvatske (ASH)

The Action of Social Democrats of Croatia (ASDC) was established on 22 October 1994 and claimed a membership of 3,800 by October 1996. Its first president was Miko Tripalo, then a representative in the *Sabor*. Three other members of the *Sabor* followed him into the ASDC, as did several members of the Croatian People's Party and the Social Democratic Union, as well as numerous intellectuals. After Tripalo's death on 11 December 1995, Silvije Degen was elected party president. The proclaimed goal of the Action was to overcome the alleged crisis in the Croatian left wing by implementing a new program through which Croatia would offer a social democratic alternative founded on the experience of European social democrats.

The party also promoted the protection of human rights and supported democratic institutions, a market economy, and free enterprise, as well as the establishment of the institutions of a modern welfare state. At the party's founding assembly the following principles were stated as the party's program: a democratic, free, and European Croatia; respect for the anti-fascist struggle; peaceful reintegration of the UN Protected Areas; and an integrated Bosnia-Herzegovina. ASDC urged respect for Serbian rights in Croatia and Serb autonomy in line with European standards. They also supported local and regional self-administration, provided that this did not threaten Croatia's integrity.[22]

The party was formed in response to the marginalization of the political left. President Tripalo criticized CDU practices in the transformation of the economic system, particularly the massive looting of property, claiming that in Croatia "an unscrupulous capitalism of the Latin American type" had been created. He also pointed out the totalitarian tendencies on the Croatian political scene. The ASDC remained dedicated to unification of all social democratic parties. It entered the small five-party opposition coalition for the general elections on 3 January 2000. The coalition gained nearly 16% of the vote, and 24 seats in the *Sabor*.

Liberals

Croatian Independent Democrats (CID)
Hrvatski Nezavisni Demokrati (HND)

The Croatian Independent Democrats (CID) was created on 30 April 1994 as a CDU splinter group by several former senior members of the ruling party—

in particular, by Stjepan Mesić, who served as Croatia's representative on the former Yugoslav collective presidency, and Josip Manolić, once a close friend of Tudjman and Croatia's Prime Minister. Mesić and Manolić were both ousted from the CDU by a vote in the Croatian Assembly, in a process some commentators labeled as "terrorism of the majority." By June 1995, the CID claimed a membership of 10,568, and 12,680 by April 1996. Stjepan Mesić was the party's president, while other prominent leaders included Josip Manolić, Slavko Degorica, and Perica Jurić.

The Independent Democrats stressed as their goals the protection of the sovereignty and territorial integrity of the Croatian state within its internationally recognized borders; securing the rights of ethnic minorities; development of local self-government; and ensuring the rule of law through efficient supervision of the executive branch by the representative bodies. Party founders, in particular Manolić, were displeased with Tudjman's perceived anti-Muslim views and his collusion with Gojko Šušak, the Minister of Defense, who was widely considered responsible for Croatia's involvement in the war against Bosniaks in the early 1990s.

Manolić claimed that his call for Šušak to retire was the main reason for his removal from the party. Manolić supported the 1994 Washington accord, which called for a federation between Croats and Bosnians, and he perceived Šušak as the man fully responsible for the war between Croats and Muslims. He accused Tudjman of supporting the accord only on paper, without any intention to implement it. In an interview with *Novi List*, an independent Croatian daily, Manolić listed three main issues in his disagreement with his once close friend Tudjman: Croatian policy in Bosnia-Herzegovina, the functioning of the civic state, and the way Tudjman led the party.

The Manolić-Tudjman power struggle, which led to the formation of the Independent Democrats, dealt with several issues. Concrete points of disagreement were the legal limits in the relationship between the ruling party and the Croatian state, the pace of privatization and denationalization, and Zagreb's policy toward Bosnia. Tudjman's attitude toward anti-fascism, though not a concrete party issue, constituted another point of disagreement between Tudjman and Manolić. The latter claimed that Tudjman did not pay enough respect to Croatia's role in fighting fascism during World War II and in fact supported some neo-fascist overtures, as evinced in restoring Ante Pavelić's state insignia and national currency, the *kuna*. Manolić felt that anti-fascism was one of Croatia's strong cards, which it should point to when seeking international recognition. Nonetheless, the Independent Democrats' platform echoed many of the CDU's principles, and there were indications that Manolić hoped to replace the CDU with his Independents.[23]

The main goals and policies of the CID as declared by its president Stipe Mesić were: the separation of power into three branches of government; freedom of the media; protection of minorities and respect for human rights; decentralization of power through the strengthening of local administration and promotion of regional particularism; and decreased state influence over the economy and free enterprise.

In September 1994 Mesić claimed that part of the CDU conducted isolationist politics. He also pointed out the danger of Croatia becoming hostage to the politics of Herceg-Bosna. He asserted that the war between the Croats and Bosniaks was a mistake, that Herceg-Bosna should not have been a response to the formation of the Serbian Republic, and that the alliance with the Muslims should have been preserved. In total, 17 deputies joined the party at its formation, which made it the largest opposition party in the *Sabor.* In later national and local elections, the CID failed to attract a large number of voters.

In 1997, Mesić and the entire CID membership joined the Croatian People's Party. Mesić was elected Croatia's new President in 2000, following the second round of elections, on 7 February. With a voter turnout of 61%, Mesić obtained 56% of the vote and a total of 1,433,921 ballots. His rival from the Social Liberal Party, Dražen Budiša, gained 44% and 1,125,969 ballots. Mesić's popularity soared during the election campaign partly because of the poor showing of his nearest rivals and partly because of his credentials as an uncorrupted reformer. In the wake of the elections, both the new parliament and the presidency began to draft plans to change the constitution in order to curtail the presidential powers that had accumulated during Tudjman's tenure.

Croatian Social Liberal Party (CSLP)
Hrvatska Socijalno Liberalna Stranka (HSLS)

The Croatian Social Liberal Party (CSLP) was the first opposition party in communist Croatia, founded in May 1989. Its membership stood at 9,000 in June 1995, and 12,500 in October 1996. It was initially led by Slavko Goldstein, the first president of the party. Dražen Budiša was elected CSLP president in 1990, and Vlado Gotovac became president in February 1996. Gotovac eventually left the CSLP in January 1998 to found the Liberal Party. At the first democratic elections, the party was a member of the Coalition of National Agreement, which sought to provide an alternative to both communism and nationalism. The coalition drew little support, however, due to the lack of a clearly defined program and personal leadership. In the April–May 1990 republican elections, the CSLP won only three seats in the National Assembly. In later elections, the CSLP affirmed itself as the strongest opposition force. Its greatest success was registered in regions that felt that their interests were neglected by Zagreb.

The party's program exemplified classic social liberalism and had greatest appeal in urban areas and among intellectuals. It supported free enterprise and parliamentary democracy and presented itself as the most viable political alternative to the CDU. In the parliamentary elections to the House of Districts on 7 February 1993, the party won 28% of the vote, obtaining 16 seats. The party performed impressively in several cities, including Osijek, Split, Varaždin, Trogir, Omiš, Rijeka, Crikvenica, Našice, Kutina, Koprivnica,

Zabok, and Ivanić Grad, although in some instances it lost the control of the mayor's post because of the defection of some members to the CDU. The party suffered disagreements within the leadership and displayed division between the "populists" and "elitists." In the parliamentary elections to the House of Representatives on 29 October 1995, the party won only 11 seats, but it did better in the elections to the Zagreb assembly, where it obtained ten seats.

At the fourth CSLP convention, president Budiša spoke out against: the "instrumentalization of patriotism, that as a form of authoritarian populism discloses itself in politics, culture, education; the disintegration of Bosnia-Herzegovina; the semipresidential system; existing process of the transformation of state property which leads to a type of society that exists in Latin America; and the incumbent party's monopoly over state-owned television." At the convention, the party adopted resolutions on economic development, media freedom, local self-government, human rights, the position of youth in society, and social problems in Croatia.

The CSLP is essentially a party of the political center, and it places emphasis on individual freedom. The party emphasizes the European tradition and orientation of Croatia. In an interview with *Nedjeljna Dalmacja*, its first president Slavko Goldstein claimed that the party was founded with three goals: "Croatia, liberal democracy, and social justice." The last two have not yet been achieved and they remain the party's major objectives for the coming years. In the parliamentary elections of 3 January 2000, the CSLP ran in a major two-party opposition coalition that captured 47% of the popular vote and gained a total of 71 parliamentary seats. The CSLP itself seated 25 deputies in the *Sabor*.

Liberal Party (LP)
Liberalna Stranka (LS)

The Liberal Party (LP) was founded in Zagreb on 24 January 1998 by Vlado Gotovac, until then one of the leaders of the CSLP. A faction of the CSLP, including Gotovac and other prominent members such as Milan Vilfan, Bozo Kovačević, and Zlatko Kramarić, defected from the party because of their distaste for the CSLP's increasing orientation toward the CDU. Gotovac and other like-minded former CSLP members found Budiša's willingness to cooperate with the CDU to be in violation of the spirit of an opposition party, and therefore left to found the Liberal Party.

At the time of its foundation, aside from marginal leftist and regional parties, the Liberal Party was the only political party in addition to the SDP not to include the word "Croatian" in its name. Initially, defectors from CSLP accounted for approximately 80% of the LP's membership; individuals previously not belonging to other parties composed the remaining 20%. The LP's program, as revealed at its founding ceremony in January 1998, focused on ending CDU rule. Gotovac proclaimed: "It is difficult to imagine a country in which intellectuals and public servants have so forgotten their morals. The only way to change Croatia is to eliminate the CDU."[24] He also asserted: "If it is true that the CDU can be removed only by revolutionary methods, Croatia is not a democratic country."[25] Vilfan put forth additional indictments of the CDU regime, based on its control over the military and the media.[26]

The Liberal Party placed itself in the political center, committing itself to the values and traditions of Croatian and European liberal democracy. Its fundamental tenets, as stated in its statute, were equality, freedom, responsibility, solidarity of all citizens, a balanced society, and freedom of enterprise and individual initiative. The LP supported a multi-party, liberal-democratic parliamentary political system and the development of local government. The party aimed to integrate Croatia into international political and economic institutions.[27] It had two parliamentary seats and participated in the small democratic coalition that garnered a total of 24 seats in the January 2000 elections. The Ministry of Environmental Protection and Zoning was awarded to the Liberal Kovačević.

Christian Democrats

Croatian Democratic Center (CDC)
Hrvatski Demokratski Centar (HDC)

The Croatian Democratic Center (CDC) was formed on 2 April 2000 in Zagreb by two former moderates in the ex-ruling CDU: Mate Granić, the previous foreign minister, and Vesna Škare-Ozbolt. Both had withdrawn from the CDU when the latter began to disintegrate following its monumental losses in the parliamentary and presidential elections in January–February 2000, in which Granić had been the CDU candidate for president. The party was soon renamed as simply the Democratic Center (DC). Granić and Škare-Ozbolt placed their inchoate DC at the center of the political spectrum, introducing it as a Christian, populist party with a pro-European orientation and a commitment to human rights and the rule of law. It demanded transparency and professional, civilian control over the intelligence services after years of misuse and political exploitation by the Tudjman regime. The DC attracted to its ranks Žarko Domljan, one of the founders of the CDU, and Hrvoje Šarinić, the chief of Tudjman's cabinet, as well as a large share of the CDU Youth. Prominent moderates such as Nikica Valentić, Pavle Miljevac, Zlatko Mateša, and Franjo Gregurić also expressed support for the DC.[28]

Croatian Christian Democratic Union (CCDU)
Hrvatska Kršćanska Demokratska Unija (HKDU)

The party was formed in December 1992 by the merger of two rightist groups: the Croatian Christian Democratic Party (CCDP), led by Ivan Cesar, and the

Croatian Democratic Party (CDP), led by Marko Veselica, who became the president of the CCDU. It claimed about 40,000 members by the mid-1990s. The party asserted that it was based upon the Christian principles of faith, hope, and love. A good part of its program was devoted to the exposition of very general ideals of an ethical nature. A high priority was given to reversing the perceived decline of the Croatian population, and the traditional Catholic focus on "pro-life" issues figured prominently in its manifesto. The party did not benefit from any significant public support.

Agrarians

Croatian Peasant Party (CPP)
Hrvatska Seljačka Stranka (HSS)

The Croatian Peasant Party (CPP) was the oldest political party in Croatia, originally founded by the brothers Radić in 1904. The party was an influential force in Croatian and Yugoslav politics during the 1930s. Its leaders were interned by the *Ustaše* fascists during World War II, and after the war, fled to Canada, where the party maintained its existence. The party was resurrected in Croatia during 1989. Shortly before the republican elections in April 1990, the CPP split into two factions, one remaining in the Coalition of National Understanding, and the other becoming part of the Croatian Democratic Bloc with five other small nationalist parties, including the CDU.

The party's vision for Croatian society combined radical liberalism, pacifism, commitment to localism, and mutual cooperation. The affairs of agriculture and small business figured high on its agenda. It advocated complete privatization of the economy, with comprehensive social welfare for the disadvantaged. In the February 1993 local elections the party won 12% of the vote, hence becoming the third strongest party in Croatia at the local level. It claimed a membership of 40,000 people. During 1994 about 50 members defected, criticizing the party leadership. This faction was headed by Drago Stipić, who founded a new formation under the name State-Building Initiative. By the late 1990s, the CPP claimed to have 40,000 members, and its president was Zlatko Tomčić. In the January 2000 general elections, the CPP ran in a five-party coalition of small democratic parties and it subsequently claimed 16 parliamentary seats, with 10.6% of the popular vote.

Greens

Croatian Green Party (CGP)
Hrvatska Stranka Zelenih (HSZ)

The Croatian Green Party (CGP) was founded in Zagreb on 14 May 1996. It participated in the parliamentary elections for the House of Representatives held on 3 January 2000, gaining a total of 12,972 votes, or slightly less than 0.50% of the total.[29] It did not gain any parliamentary seats. The party's president was Zlatko Sviben. The CGP's platform stressed the importance of preserving nature and the environment and striving for balanced and sustainable economic, regional, and social development. Additionally, the party advocated the development of a welfarist democratic state that would provide its citizens with social security, health care, and education, as well as promote culture and scientific research. Public health was a significant concern of the Greens, as they stressed the need for healthy and safe food, as well as fighting the spread of HIV-AIDS by providing citizens with information on prevention.[30]

Green Party (GP)
Zelena Stranka (ZS)

The Green Party (GP), established in 1996, operated under the name Green Community until the party assembly in April 1999. At the assembly, the party adopted the guiding principles of the European Federation of Green Parties (EFGP) and expressed its hope to be included in the federation. The GP cited its ten fundamental values to be environmental consciousness, immediate and decentralized democracy, social justice, nonviolence, a decentralized economy, cooperation, tolerance, personal and global responsibility, and a focus on the future.[31] Though it was not fully organized until 1996, the Green Party claimed limited success in the first free parliamentary elections, in April 1990. The ballot for these included 23 Green candidates, one of whom ran in a coalition with the communists and consequently won a seat in the parliament. He lost his mandate two years later.[32]

Green Party leaders believed that economic development and environmentally responsible policies were not at odds with one another. Hence, an ecologically conscious economic program should be a priority for Croatia's economic development and would result in as much productivity as a fast-paced program of economic growth based on pumping resources into output growth. Furthermore, the Green Party stressed that it was not exclusively an environmental party. It cited economic instability, war and violence, inequality in living standards, violations of human rights, and the inequality of the sexes as problems that needed to be addressed and solved. Ideally, improvement would result from civic action within the parameters of decentralized democracy, though the party recognized that purely civil initiatives do not always yield results in representative democracies such as is Croatia.

The GP advocated a gradual move toward a decentralized democratic process, in which local and civil organizations decided on certain issues. This would free the central government to concern itself with programs affecting the state as a whole and which could best be administered from the center, such as foreign policy and defense. The Green Party conceded that Croatian democracy was still highly centralized, and until its stated ideals could be enacted, it urged citizens to keep local democracy viable through active membership in civic associations.[33]

Movement for Human Rights–Party of Environmentally Conscious Citizens (MHR-PECC)
Pokret za Ljudska Prava–Stranka Ekološki Svjesnih Gradana (PLP-SESG)

The Movement for Human Rights (MHR) was founded in Zagreb on 13 March 1999 by Rikard Moritz, who became the party's president. It focused on such issues as religious discrimination, combating cancer, supplying pensions to senior citizens, work-related injuries, war injuries, unemployment, and eroded savings accounts. According to the party, various violations had accrued since the early 1990s, and the cost of social, economic, and political realignment was compounded by the CDU's mismanagement of the economy and government.

The MHR was a non-parliamentary, activist party, concerned with protecting the environment, human rights, and democracy. It advocated government provision of social security, but at the same time extolled private property and private initiative as key to economic success in Croatia. The MHR viewed itself as a progressive, grassroots party with a detailed program addressing political, family, environmental, economic, scientific, educational, cultural, and medical issues.[34] It participated in the parliamentary elections on 3 January 2000, but won only 0.1% of the vote in Zagreb and a negligible amount elsewhere.[35] Moritz attempted to gather the 10,000 signatures needed to support his candidacy for the presidential elections, but some of his signatures were deemed inadmissible. His subsequent hunger strike, staged in a Zagreb shopping center, attracted more attention than his actual bid for presidential candidacy. The MHR was a minor political actor; it proved more significant in putting forward various ideas than in achieving results.

Nationalists

Croatian Democratic Union (CDU)
Hrvatska Demokratska Zajednica (HDZ)

The Croatian Democratic Union (CDU) was formally established in Zagreb on 17 June 1989. Franjo Tudjman remained its president from the party's inception until his death on 10 December 1999. By the end of 1996, the CDU claimed a membership of 400,000. Its greatest strength was in the Zagorje region in northern Croatia, and in parts of Slavonija, and it was weakest in Istria and Dalmatia. The CDU was successful in mobilizing the support of Croatians in the *diaspora,* who viewed it as the party most committed to national independence. It was considered a center-right formation and was highly centralized. It had its own youth organization, the HDZ Youth.

The CDU dominated the political life of independent Croatia during the first decade. Billing itself as the "most Croatian of all parties," the CDU was created while Yugoslavia was still extant. It originally tried to present itself as the singular alternative to the old Yugoslav structure, and its program called for national sovereignty, free elections, and market reform. Led by the former Titoist army general and ideologist of the 1971 Croatian nationalist movement, Tudjman, the CDU drew support from across the political spectrum and was able to translate this endorsement into a sweeping victory during the April–May 1990 republican elections.

Out of 351 seats in the Croatian Assembly, the CDU won 206, the communists and Socialist Alliance finished in second place with 90 seats, the Coalition of National Understanding gained 11, the Croatian Democratic Party 10, the Serbian Democratic Party five, and the remaining seats went to independents. Tudjman was subsequently elected as Croatia's President by the new legislature. At that time, the CDU claimed nearly half a million members and had branches around the country; much of its political apparatus was simply appropriated from the former League of Communists of Croatia.

In late 1990 and early 1991, Tudjman engaged in protracted negotiations within the federal presidency on restructuring relations among the six Yugoslav republics. Zagreb maintained that Croatia and Slovenia were paying the lion's share of the state budget, and remained concerned over centralizing trends in Belgrade. However, even before the breakdown of negotiations over a new confederal arrangement, Croatia made important strides toward secession. The Tudjman administration began to purge Serb and Yugoslav loyalists from the bureaucracy and security forces, restored Croatia's historical state symbols, and held a plebiscite on independence in May 1991, in which the overwhelming majority of voters opted for full sovereignty. The outbreak of armed conflict with Serb guerrillas and the Yugoslav army in the summer of 1991 appeared to strengthen Tudjman's position and that of the CDU, which was depicted in the state-controlled media as the prime defender of Croatian interests.

Zagreb was not militarily prepared for the Serb-Yugoslav assault and lost over a quarter of its territory during the war. A cease-fire was put in place in January 1992 through the creation of a UN-protected zone, while the Tudjman government capitalized on the grievances of expelled Croats and the state of emergency to impose restrictions on media activities that were deemed unpatriotic. A personality cult developed around Tudjman, fostered by depictions of his critical role in regaining Croatian statehood. The CDU itself penetrated all the former communist bureaucracies as a monolithic organization, controlling or supervising all major economic, cultural, educational, and media organs. The ruling party portrayed itself as the defender of Croatian statehood against the perennial Serbian threat, and prior to the August 1992 general elections it endeavored to show that it had restored a marked degree of normality in the country.

The *Sabor* elections of 2 August 1992 were marred by various irregularities, such as problems with voting lists, and by the impossibility of implementing voting procedures on Serb-held territory. Tudjman was returned to the presidency with 56.73% of the popular vote. The CDU maintained its dominant position in Croatia's lower house of parliament, the House of Deputies, gaining 85 out of 138 seats with 43% of the popular vote. In elections held for the upper house in February 1993, the CDU also retained a nearly two-thirds majority, though defeats in certain opposition strongholds, such as Split, Rijeka, Pula, and Osijek, stripped the party of its aura of invincibility. Nonetheless, the CDU performed well in municipal elections, including areas directly affected by the war.

The CDU leadership viewed Croatia as a state of ethnic Croats. Furthermore, it maintained that the Croatian people extended beyond current state borders, implying that Croatia's frontier with Bosnia-Herzegovina was not necessarily inviolable. During 1992, Zagreb entered a loose alliance with the Bosnian government against Serbian attacks, partly as a form of self-protection, partly to curry favor with the international community, and perhaps with a view to a future Croatian-Bosnian confederation. But in 1993 it was instrumental, with its sister organization in Bosnia, in conducting a brutal policy of "ethnic cleansing" in parts of central Bosnia and western Herzegovina, against its former Muslim allies.

The CDU also actively promoted an expansion of the ethnic Croatian population, and it deliberately sought to alter the demographic balance by attracting Croatian emigrants to return, placing tight stipulations on granting Croatian citizenship, and increasing the birthrate. While Croatia provided shelter to a large number of Bosnian refugees, it was slow in extending citizenship to Yugoslavs who were not of Croatian origin. These policies pointed to a long-term CDU interest in creating an ethnically homogeneous state.

During the mid-1990s, there were increasing signs of a rift in the CDU between a conservative nationalist faction led by Deputy Prime Minister Vladimir Šeks and Defense Minister Gojko Šušak, and a more centrist-liberal wing. The latter, informally led by former Yugoslav president Stjepan Mesić, called for greater press freedom and the curtailment of political party interference in the country's media. Even though differences persisted in approaches to the Serbian issue, with some activists criticizing any land swaps with Serbia, Tudjman prevailed in keeping the CDU together.[36]

The CDU maintained one important advantage over other opposition parties—its connections with the Croatian *diaspora* and through it a reliable channel for campaign funds. The *diaspora* had a guaranteed 12 posts in the Croatian Assembly, which constituted almost 10% of the total number of seats. To have seats reserved for emigres was not controversial in itself, but when considering the size of the potential voting population abroad, estimated at about 400,000, the number of seats reserved appeared inflated.[37]

In April 1994, the Union suffered the defection of a number of its leading figures, who founded the Croatian Independent Democrats. This was accompanied by the rise of such people as Gojko Šušak and Ivica Pašalić on the CDU's nationalist right; their mainstays were support for a strong Croatian state and military and an interventionist policy in Herzegovina. During the mid to late 1990s, the position of technocrats in the party weakened even further, and according to some observers this marked the sliding of the CDU toward "right-wing radicalism." In such conditions, any demands for more pluralism and a decentralized governing structure were portrayed by CDU leaders as attempts to destabilize the country.

Meanwhile, opposition discontent grew over the ruling party's stance on the war in Bosnia, while the public became increasingly disenchanted with domestic economic issues, most importantly with the fall in living standards and the growth of cronyism and corruption among the CDU elite. This discontent was especially notable among the urban population. The first big blow to the party came during the local elections in Zagreb in 1995, when the CDU won only 16 of the 50 city council seats.[38] However, President Tudjman refused to approve the opposition nominees for mayor, marking the beginning of what became known as the "Zagreb crisis." This was the beginning of the party's decline due to the loss in the credibility of its proclaimed commitment to democracy both among domestic and international observers. However, some commentators believed that the party had accumulated so much power that only an internal conflict over the distribution of authority and wealth among the party factions could further its self-destruction.

Though the severity of Tudjman's illness was not publicly reported, the CDU was well aware of Tudjman's ill health, and candidates for the post of president began to appear even before his demise. The party intimated that Mate Granić, then foreign minister, would win the CDU nomination.[39] At the same time, Vlatko Pavletić, who was practically unknown to the public until Tudjman was incapacitated by illness, expressed his intention to seek the candidacy for Croatian President. Vladimir Šeks also voiced his interest in the post. Tudjman's death brought the latent dissension within the CDU to the fore. The battle for the party's endorsement for the presidential candidacy was the immediate symptom of deeper ideological divisions within the party as well as of clashing personal political ambitions.

Granić was reasonably popular with the Croatian people and with the Catholic Church and was viewed favorably by the international community for his conciliatory attitude, which contrasted with Tudjman's often quarrelsome personality. Thus, his candidacy for President seemed almost certain, until Vladimir Šeks expressed severe reservations about endorsing him. He held Granić, as foreign minister, responsible for the lackluster turnout of foreign heads of state at Tudjman's funeral. Granić openly stated his intention to run for President, implying that he would seek the post as an independent candidate if the CDU refused to endorse him. Granić ultimately did win the CDU's support, but the process not only exposed the disunity within the organization but actually made its fall from power imminent.

With the death of President Tudjman on 10 December 1999, the CDU began to implode.[40] Several party factions vied for power and leadership, as Tudjman had failed to prepare a credible successor. At least two major factions were visible by the end of 1999: a hard-line ultra-nationalist group linked with the "Herceg lobby" and led by the former deputy speaker of parliament Ivica Pašalić, and a more centrist Christian Democratic stream grouped around Granić. Granić abandoned the Union after its failure in the national elections on 3 January 2000 and formed his own political organization. In the parliamentary elections for the House of Representatives, the CDU captured only 30% of the popular vote and 46 seats in the *Sabor.*

The CDU's chief rivals, grouped in a two-party coalition, won the national ballot and formed the first non-CDU government. The Union's weak performance in the parliamentary elections paved the way for its defeat in the presidential ballot. Immediately prior to the elections, Granić attempted to improve his chances at the polls by withdrawing from CDU party posts, but to little avail.[41] In the first round of the presidential elections on 24 January 2000, Granić gained only 22.47% of the popular vote and consequently was eliminated from the contest. This ensured that the CDU would no longer have control over any branch of government. Following the elections, there were major disclosures regarding corruption scandals and economic mismanagement by the outgoing administration, and pressures increased to bring some former officials to trial. By the summer of 2000, there were signs that a more pragmatic faction of the CDU, grouped around former Prime Minister Nikica Valentić, would either take over the Union or would leave to found a new party, thus further isolating the nationalist core.

Neo-Fascists

Croatian Party of Right (CPR)
Hrvatska Stranka Prava (HSP)

The Croatian Party of Right (CPR) was originally formed in 1861 by Ante Starčević and Eugen Kvaternik. It was outlawed on 6 January 1929 when Belgrade imposed a royal dictatorship over Yugoslavia, like all other parties, it was banned throughout the communist period. The CPR was reestablished on 25 February 1990, under the leadership of Dobroslav Paraga, a former nationalist dissident. Paraga openly advocated secession from Yugoslavia and called for a Croatia with expanded borders that would include large parts of Bosnia-Herzegovina.

According to its general statutes, the CPR championed "absolute sovereignty and national independence on the entire ethnic and natural territory of the Croatian people." According to its understanding, this included the whole of Bosnia-Herzegovina and even parts of Serbian Vojvodina. The CPR brooked no thought of compromise with Serbian insurgents in Krajina and Bosnia.

Instead, it openly advocated the creation of a Greater Croatia, which would extend the country's borders to its "historic frontiers" of the tenth century. Unlike the ruling CDU, the CPR rejected the idea of dividing Bosnia between Zagreb and Belgrade. Such proposals, it claimed, actually fueled "Serbian revanchism." Instead of allowing Serbia to expand, Paraga's group advocated reducing Serbia to its pre-1912 borders. It also claimed that the Bosnian Muslims were an integral part of the Croatian nation, a part that converted to Islam during Turkish occupation.

The CPR remained strongly opposed to what it called the "cantonization" of Croatia through the extension of autonomy to Serb-dominated regions, as specified in the Constitutional Law on the Rights of Minorities. Instead of unilaterally extending advantages to the Serbs, Paraga advocated defeating the insurgents in an outright war and bargaining from a position of strength. However, a war with the Serbs could not be conducted while the UN Protection Force stood as a buffer between the two sides. Since UNPROFOR had not succeeded in returning Serb-held territory to Croatian administration, the CDU demanded that UN contingents leave the country and permit Croatian forces to recapture the occupied lands. This policy was one of the chief CPR campaign planks during the August 1992 elections, when Paraga accused the Tudjman leadership of betraying Croatian interests by not engaging in an all-out war with Serbian guerrillas. The party performed poorly in the ballot, capturing a mere five seats in the National Assembly, and Paraga received only 5.4% of the vote in the presidential election.

The CPR did not limit itself merely to advocating victory in war and criticizing the CDU government for its lack of military preparation. Paraga's group established an armed wing, a paramilitary organization called the Croatian Defense Forces (CDF) *(Hrvatske Oružane Snage, HOS)*, which engaged in armed attacks against Serbian positions in Croatia and Bosnia. Officially, the Croatian government outlawed the formation of paramilitary organizations and claimed that CDF forces (estimated to number between 300 and 2,000 troops) and other volunteer units came under the full control of the Croatian Ministry of Defense during late 1991. Paraga attacked the Tudjman regime for betraying both Croatia and Bosnia by arranging secret deals with Serbia to carve up Bosnia-Herzegovina. He claimed that the CPR supported Bosnian unitarism and independence; but his critics charged that Paraga envisaged this merely as a prelude to absorption by Croatia.

In June 1993, Paraga and three of his associates were placed on trial in Zagreb, accused of forming a paramilitary organization to overthrow the elected government. The following month, the CPR was forcibly expelled from its Zagreb headquarters. Paraga had been previously acquitted in 1991 of armed rebellion against the state. It appeared that the Tudjman regime was intent on both reining in the opposition and displaying its determination to eliminate renegade armed units with contingents in Bosnia-Herzegovina.[42]

In 1992, there was a split between Paraga and his deputy, Ante Djapić, who was considered a vassal of the ruling party. Paraga subsequently formed a new party—the 1861 Croatian Party of Right. Although Paraga was the loudest exponent of the *Ustaše* and the war-time Independent State of Croatia, he began to advocate as the chief goals of his new party free elections, the removal of the CDU from power, denationalization, and a coalition with other opposition parties. Meanwhile, the Djapić CPR became a virtual subordinate of the CDU and did not challenge its policies or its monopoly of power. In the 3 January 2000 elections, the CPR gained 2.65% of the popular vote and four parliamentary seats.

Several smaller Croatian nationalist parties were also formed before the republic's first multi-party elections and adopted a strong pro-independence stance. Moreover, after the collapse of talks on loosening the Yugoslav federation, most Croatian parties came out in favor of secession from Yugoslavia. With the onset of independence and war in the summer of 1991, a number of parties adopted a critical stance toward the CDU government for its lack of preparedness in resisting the Yugoslav army and Serb guerrilla assault, and some adopted a more forthright nationalist position. They included the Croatian Democratic Party (CDP), which held 10 seats after the first election but whose support base subsequently eroded when it failed to gain representation after the August 1992 balloting, and the Croatian National Party (CNP), which captured three seats in the House of Representatives in the August 1992 elections but subsequently disappeared from the political scene.

Ethnic Minority and Religious Parties

Serbian National Party (SNP)
Srpska Narodna Stranka (SNS)

The Serbian National Party (SNP) was established in May 1991 and claimed a membership of about 18,000 people. Its president was Milan Djukić. The party represented the accommodationists among Croatia's Serb population who did not support Jovan Rašković and his separatist Serbian Democratic Party. The latter managed to rally Serbs only in the Krajina region where it was instrumental in creating the Serbian Autonomous Region of Krajina. The SNP operated exclusively in the regions controlled by the Croatian government. Following the elections of 2 August 1992, the SNP gained three representatives in the lower house of parliament, all elected on the national level rather than for specific constituencies. The party acted as the voice of those Serbs who regarded Croatia as their homeland. Its main concerns revolved around constitutional issues. It sought to secure an adequate representation for Serbs and other minorities and was very critical of the gerrymandering of constituency boundaries, especially in relation to the new *županije* (districts). It also concerned itself with issues relating to the cultural heritage of Serbs within Croatia.

Critics charged that the SNP was an entity created by the CDU during 1992 to provide Croatian Serbs outside the Krajina with organized representation and to counter the radical demands of Serbian nationalists. The SNP was therefore denounced by Serb militants as well as by some Croatian opposition politicians as a stooge of the ruling party. Its program stipulated that the SNP would work to reconstruct Croat-Serb relations and generally improve the position of Croatia's Serbian community. Its leaders officially distanced themselves from ex-communists as well as from the Serbian Democratic Party and sought in particular to appeal to urban Serbs living outside the Krajina region, who totaled nearly 200,000 at the time Croatia gained independence. SNP leaders contended that the preconditions for a lasting peace and healthy ethnic relations were already in place in the country. SNP spokesmen condemned the Krajina referendum in June 1993, asserting that Serbs had no right to secede from Croatia and that the Krajina was dominated by a military junta.

Several other Serbian organizations were formed in Croatia during the 1990s to try and pacify Serb-Croat relations and lend support to Croatia's independent status, including the Croatian Serb Alliance (CSA) and the Alliance of Serbs of Istria, Rijeka, and Gorski Kotor (ASIRGK). In many cases, suspicions persisted that these were merely front organizations for the ruling CDU and not properly representative of the Serbian population. Many of their leaders proved hesitant in asserting minority rights, for fear of retribution. However, the SNP on occasion also criticized the Zagreb authorities for failing to enforce minority rights legislation and for encouraging discrimination against Croatian Serbs.

Serbian Democratic Party (SDP)
Srpska Demokratska Stranka (SDS)

The Serbian Democratic Party (SDP) was formed in the town of Knin, in Krajina, in late 1989. It was originally established to protect the interests of Serbs in Croatia during the breakup of Yugoslavia. Under the leadership of Jovan Rašković, the SDP sought to achieve an extensive guarantee of Serbian rights in Croatia. When the new Croatian government headed by Tudjman and the CDU came to power in April 1990 and began to display nationalist inclinations, Rašković and the SDP concluded that the Serbs in Croatia must secure some kind of institutionalized autonomy in order to guarantee their rights. Although it was ostensibly committed to working within the parliamentary system to accomplish these goals, the SDP pulled its five elected representatives out of the Croatian Assembly shortly after the April–May 1990 elections and proceeded to rally support within the Serbian community for more combative actions to assert Serb autonomy.

The SDP organized a mass rally in July 1990 in order to galvanize support for its calls for autonomy. Rašković pronounced the demonstration "a rebellion, an unarmed uprising," but underscored that the SDP would make every effort to avoid violent actions. The SDP leadership, however, with the evident support of Belgrade, was not interested in backing away from confrontation. Within several days, Rašković organized a referendum on political autonomy for Serbs in the Krajina region. When Zagreb attempted to ban the referendum, it touched off an armed confrontation between Serb gunmen and the Croatian authorities. The new SDP leader, Milan Babić, who replaced Rašković because of the latter's evident willingness to compromise with Zagreb, drew upon the party's close ties to Slobodan Milošević and the Yugoslav People's Army in order to arm and equip Serbian militias in Krajina. In June 1990, a self-proclaimed Serbian National Council was established, based in Knin and presided over by Babić. It functioned as an informal parliamentary body largely controlled by SDP activists.

According to the organizers of the August 1990 Serb referendum, nearly 100% of voters cast their ballots in favor of an extremely vague concept of Serbian autonomy. Bolstered by these results, the SDP announced that if Croatia separated from Yugoslavia, then the Serbs in Croatia would secede to form their own independent state. The SDP was at the forefront of establishing the Serbian Autonomous Region of Krajina and later pushed for the region's annexation to Serbia proper. Babić and his associates centered their efforts on securing the independence of Serb-dominated regions, and unilaterally declared the establishment of the Republic of Serb Krajina in December 1991. During this time, evidence also surfaced of a bitter power struggle among the Serb leadership in the Krajina. Babić and his supporters in the SDP were seeking to consolidate their territorial gains and move rapidly toward unification with Serbia.

By contrast, Milošević and his proxies in the Krajina calculated that such a move was premature and could both prolong the war in Croatia and precipitate international sanctions against the rump Yugoslavia. Milošević exerted intense pressure against the Krajina leadership and replaced Babić with loyalist Goran Hadžić as president of the Republic of Serb Krajina. Hadžić displayed his willingness to reach an accord with Zagreb through UN mediation, and in January 1992 a UN-protected area was established in the occupied areas of Croatia. Babić asserted that a virtual *coup d'etat* had taken place in which dissenters were excluded from decisionmaking and only people benefiting from the full support of Belgrade remained in the Krajina administration.

The Assembly of the Republic of Serbian Krajina was composed of several parts: representatives of Knin Krajina, western Slavonija, and eastern Slavonija; Baranja; and western Srem. Although several parties were included in the government, including the SDP and the Serbian Socialist Party (a branch of Milošević's Socialist Party in Serbia), a normal parliamentary system did not function in the region but rather a civilian-military dictatorship. Although a relative peace was maintained in the area throughout 1992 and early 1995, tensions remained high as Zagreb was giving signals that it was intent on restoring its lost territories.

In January 1993, Croatian forces launched an assault in the northern Dalmatian region and regained control over an airport and a key bridge linking central Croatia with the coast. Serb authorities used the occasion to remobilize their forces and initiate the shelling of Croatian positions outside the occupied territories. In June 1993, the Krajina government held a referendum on linking the region with the newly carved Serb quasi state in neighboring Bosnia. Plans were drawn up to establish a joint assembly and a single government structure. The initiative was placed on hold pending the outcome of negotiations between Zagreb and Belgrade on partitioning Bosnia-Herzegovina.[43] The entire plan collapsed in August 1995 when Croatian forces launched a rapid assault on the occupied territories and regained all sections except Eastern Slavonija. The Serb Krajina's political and military leadership did not receive armed backing from Belgrade and they fled the territories ahead of the Croatian onslaught. With the Serbian depopulation of the Krajina region, the SDP disappeared from the political scene.

Serbian Democratic Forum (SDF)
Srpski Demokratski Forum (SDF)

The Serbian Democratic Forum (SDF) was established in early 1993 as a non-partisan umbrella body to represent the interests of Serbs in Croatia. It claimed a small membership, mostly consisting of Serbian intellectuals and professionals resident in Zagreb and other major cities. Vice president Petar Ladjevid underscored that the SDF would try to build contacts with Serbian intellectuals in the Krajina region, ties that had been severed since the start of the war. In addition, the SDF tried to establish communication with Serbian organizations in the rump Yugoslavia and advocated the mutual recognition of both states: this would avowedly help to reconcile Croats and Serbs in Croatia itself. Forum leaders issued criticisms of the SNP, which they perceived as a puppet of the ruling CDU with little real influence among the Serb community. They criticized the government for generating perceptions of collective responsibility by the Serbian people for launching the war in the summer of 1991, as well as for failing to stem violations of human rights against the Serbian community.[44]

National Community of Croatian Montenegrins (NCCM)
Nacionalna Zajednica Crnogoraca Hrvatske (NZCH)

Under its chairman Drago Kastratović, the National Community of Croatian Montenegrins (NCCM) distanced itself from the policies of the Montenegrin government and its alliance with Milošević during the early 1990s. It attempted to clear the names of all "honorable members" of the Montenegrin people following the Serb-Croat war in which Montenegrin volunteers had taken part in attacks on Dubrovnik and across southern Croatia and evidently besmirched the reputation of the Montenegrin nation.[45]

Hungarian People's Party (HPP)
Madjarska Narodna Stranka (MNS)

When the Hungarian People's Party (HPP) was set up in June 1989, József Csorgics became the party chairman. The party claimed to represent the political interests of the Hungarian minority, demanding equal rights for Hungarians, the opportunity to use the Hungarian language, and the provision of general schools with Hungarian-language instruction regardless of the number of students. Other aims of the HPP included the protection of human rights, religious freedom, and the natural environment.[46]

Croatian Muslim Democratic Party (CMDP)
Hrvatska Muslimanska Demokratska Stranka (HMDS)

The Croatian Muslim Democratic Party (CMDP) was established in Zagreb during 1991 under the presidency of Mirsad Bakšić. It cast itself as a secular organization representing the interests of "Croats of Islamic faith" as well as Muslims who since 1968 had declared their nationality in Yugoslavia as Muslim. The CMDP also tried to organize cells in Bosnia-Herzegovina, representing the Croatian nationalist position that Bosnian Muslims were in origin Croatian Catholics. The CMDP vehemently attacked the Sarajevo-based Muslim Party of Democratic Action (PDA) for claiming to represent all of Bosnia's Muslims. Bakšić himself became a colonel in the Croatian Army. He claimed that over 25,000 "Croat Muslims" participated in the defense of Croatia against "Serbian aggression."[47]

Romani Party of Croatia (RPC)
Stranka Roma Hrvatske (SRH)

The Romani Party of Croatia (RPC) was formed in July 1990 with the stated goal was to seek recognition of the Romani (Gypsy) nationality and guarantee full minority rights. In this endeavor, it appealed to Croatia's National Assembly for primary- and secondary-level classes and textbooks in the Romani language.[48]

A number of other ethnicity based minority organizations were established in Croatia during the 1990s, some even before Croatia achieved independence. They included the Democratic Alliance of Albanians in Croatia (DAAC), the Democratic Union of Croatian Muslims (DUCM), the Albanian Christian Democratic Party (ACDP), the Alliance of Czechs and Slovaks (ACS), the Alliance of Germans and Austrians (AGA), the Slovak Association (SA), the Alliance of Ruthenians and Ukrainians (ARU), the Alliance of Germans in Croatia (AGC), the Alliance of Slovenians in Croatia (ASC), the Italian Union of Istria and Rijeka (IUIR), and the National Community of Macedonians (NCM).

Regionalists

Istrian Democratic Assembly (IDA)
Istarski Demokratski Sabor (IDS)

Established in February 1990 in the city of Pula, with branches throughout the Istrian peninsula and with a membership of 3,800 by 1996, the Istrian Democratic Assembly (IDA) was initially led by its president Ivan Jakovčić. The IDA represented the regional interests of the population of the Istrian peninsula, in the northwest of the country, where it became the dominant political force. It co-operated closely with the other regional parties, including Dalmatian Action (DA) and the Rijeka Democratic League (RDL), especially during national elections. The party platform stated that the central government should deal with issues such as the army, police, finances, and foreign policy, while all other issues should be left to regional governments. The specific motivation for this platform was the party's belief that Croatia's central government under the CDU did not recognize true regional interests, and in the case of Istria, the rights of its significant Italian minority. The IDA's leadership disputed the existing territorial organization of the country, which in their view under the CDU had become a centralized and totalitarian system.

Jakovčić complained that only 7% of the region's funds were left in Istria while the rest went to the central treasury; before the CDU came to power, this figure stood at 40–45%. According to him, the state was "being organized in such a way that everyone has to come to the central cashier begging for money, and only the politically suitable will get it." Not surprisingly, relations between the CDU and the IDS and Istria in general remained strained throughout the decade. The IDS tapped into the dissatisfaction of its constituents with the economic and political decisions of the incumbent party, and it regularly won all local elections in Istria.

Similarly to the regionalist Dalmatian Action, the IDA believed that its region, one of the most developed in the former Yugoslavia, possessed a distinctive history, culture, and identity differentiating it from the rest of Croatia. IDA leaders claimed that Istrian identity was a symbiosis of Slavic, Latin, and.Germanic cultures, and historically it had benefited from a large measure of autonomy. They contended that the region was unfairly deprived of its special status in post-war Yugoslavia, when Tito artificially divided the region between Slovenia and Croatia in order to assure the domination of Slavs over other ethnic groups.

The IDA sought to restore Istria as an "inter-state region" and multi-ethnic unit without undermining the sovereignty of any neighboring state. In particular, it backed economic self-determination and the opportunity to deal directly with other "Euro-regions" in developing tourism and privatization. The authorities in Zagreb endeavored to discredit the IDA, claiming that its members were separatists in the service of Italian irredentists and Serbian agents. The IDA asserted that it had no radical or secessionist stream even though it encompassed a broad spectrum of political trends. Instead, it supported a form of "intergovernmental autonomy" or home rule with close contacts among Croatia, Slovenia, and Italy.

The IDA remained troubled by what it considered the excessive nationalism and ethnocentrism of the Croatian regime. It felt that the government's emphasis on nationality would undermine the delicate multi-ethnic character of the Istrian region. Furthermore, the IDA pointed out that the path that the CDU chose to create a nation-state was a nineteenth-century model and obsolete at the end of the twentieth century. Instead, the IDA advocated a state that respected the rights of all its citizens, regardless of their nationality, religion, race, or language. It therefore tried to distance itself from decisionmaking in Zagreb and avoided being drawn into the acrimonious debates over Croat-Serb relations.

The CDU, in turn, viewed the IDA very unfavorably in the first half of the 1990s. In its almost paranoid search for "enemies of the state," the CDU periodically leveled accusations against the IDA. In early 1994, Tudjman single-handedly created the Istria Committee, an advisory committee to the president of the republic; the members chosen to staff this committee learned about their new assignment only after reading about it in the newspaper. The IDA charged that Tudjman's action constituted an affront to Istria and to democracy, especially since none of the seventeen members of the Istria Committee were Istrian, and other distinct cultural regions of Croatia, such as Slavonija, Baranija, or Dalmatia, did not have advisory committees named after them. Zagreb's action invited censure from factions of the Italian right that saw attempts at subverting Istrian local rights as an affront to the Italian minority in that region.[49] Throughout the mid-1990s, the government in Zagreb continued to label IDA activities as irredentist agitation threatening the unity of the Croatian state.

In the summer of 1996, the IDA was rocked by an internal crisis stemming from an argument over how to apportion the city of Pula's treasury funds. To resolve the crisis, the IDA appealed to the CDU to mediate. The aftermath left the IDA weakened. In January 1998, Ivan Pauletta, one of the founders of the IDA, revealed a project called the "Land of Istria." The program called for a constitution for Istria, a separate fiscal, judicial, and police system, and the demilitarization of the peninsula. This initiative was important because it came after a two-year period of strained relations within the IDA, which resulted in numerous defections of original party members either to the CDU or to the opposition parties. The Land of Istria project was interpreted by some as a call upon the IDA to reexamine its current status and return to its founding values. To preserve its unity, the IDA subsequently abandoned some of its sharp regionalism, and with it some of its popularity.[50]

In the August 1992 general elections to the House of Representatives, the IDA formed a loose coalition with Dalmatian Action, the Rijeka Democratic Alliance (RDA), and the List for Osijek (LFO), a small regionalist movement in eastern Slavonija that had only marginal influence in the region and was linked with the main opposition group, the Social Liberal Party. The IDA obtained 55% of the vote in three Istrian districts and elected four deputies to the Croatian parliament. In the second round of elections in February 1993, to the upper house, or Chamber of Municipalities, the IDA scored 72% of the vote and elected three more deputies. As a result, it established a parliamentary club consisting of eight members, including a representative from the Italian Union for Istria and Rijeka (IUIR).

In addition, the IDA won all the local elections in Istria, scoring majorities in thirty-seven town councils as well as in five towns outside the Istrian *županja* (district). In the 1993 local elections, it captured 72% of the votes. IDA leaders expressed anxiety about the depopulation of the peninsula and the resettlement there of citizens from other parts of Croatia who had little knowledge of Istrian culture. IDA spokesmen noted that Zagreb could become more receptive to their demands and thus boost the region's economy and directly assist the struggling Croatian economy. The CDU even gave indications that it would seek a coalition with the IDA. Indeed, the IDA representative for the city of Poreč, Ivan Herak, was offered a post as deputy prime minister and minister of tourism. IDA leaders remained hesitant in accepting such overtures. The IDA also organized a branch in Slovenian Istria but did not establish a branch or affiliate in Italy, being cognizant of Zagreb's political sensitivities.[51]

In the general elections of 3 January 2000, the IDA ran in a coalition with four other small parties which together gained 15.89% of the national vote and captured 24 parliamentary seats. The IDA itself obtained four seats in the *Sabor* and asserted that it would continue to push for regional devolution and the economic development of Istria. Its leaders felt that the IDA could work more constructively with the new democratic government in Zagreb.

Dalmatian Action (DA)
Dalmatinska Akcija (DA)

This regionalist organization was formed in Split in December 1990 and therefore did not participate in the first Croatian general elections. It remained a relatively small organization, claiming a membership of some 2,000 people by mid-1992, under president Mira Ljubić-Lorger and secretary Radovan Kečkemet. Dalmatian Action (DA) leaders asserted that Croatia consisted of several distinct regions, including Dalmatia, Istria, Slavonija, and Lika, that should be allowed to develop their specific economies, cultures, and regional self-governments. It claimed that the CDU and most of the opposition parties were Zagreb-centered and intent on maintaining a monolithic and centralized state. Ljubić-Lorger criticized Croatia's new administrative division into *županije*, describing them as offices of the central power that simply hierarchized the system of local administration. The *županije* evidently had little opportunity to take any significant economic decisions.

Croatian nationalists depicted the DA as anti-Croat separatists in league with militant Serbs intent on breaking up Croatia. DA leaders strenuously denied such charges and asserted that they simply wanted to restore greater regional decision making through, for example, budgetary control over culture and education. A regional assembly would also ensure closer Dalmatian links with the Alpe-Adria economic association, leaving Zagreb in control of defense, foreign policy, foreign trade, and the economic infrastructure.

According to DA spokesmen, a more autonomous Dalmatian region could purportedly also include much of the Knin Krajina region. The DA stressed that it was a multi-ethnic organization, considering regional issues more significant than questions of nationality. In the August 1992 general elections, the DA entered into an election coalition with Istrian, Rijekan, and Slavonijan regionalists but was unable to gain any seats for Dalmatia in the National Assembly. DA spokesmen claimed that they were ignored by Croatian television during the election campaign and some of their candidates were harassed or threatened by the police. Moreover, they suffered from a debilitating shortage of funds, premises, and resources.

DA leaders believed that there was widespread latent sympathy for the DA's position which would continue to grow if the Tudjman government became more authoritarian and if regionalists could offer an attractive and profitable alternative to central control. Tudjman's highly publicized opening of the Maslenica bridge in July 1993 was evidently designed not only to signal defiance of the Krajina Serbs but to indicate to Dalmatians that Zagreb was determined to reestablish normal communications with the region and to provide it with economic assistance.[52] In subsequent national elections, the DA failed to capture any seats in the country's parliament, but the victory of a democratic coalition in January 2000 was likely to spur DA demands for decentralization and regional development.

Dalmatian National Party (DNP)
Dalmatinska Narodna Stranka (DNS)

Launched in mid-December 1990, this radical regionalist party rallied citizens who regarded Dalmatia as their homeland. Similarly to the DA, the party urged that Dalmatia regain the status of a special region and complained about the centralizing policies of the Tudjman administration. Its program laid stress on Dalmatia's legendary enterprising spirit, free market traditions, and ecological concerns that had evidently been sorely neglected by Zagreb.[53]

Rijeka Democratic Alliance (RDA)
Riječki Demokratski Savez (RDS)

The Rijeka Democratic Alliance (RDA) was formed in early 1990 to press for a special status for the port city of Rijeka. Its leaders were concerned that protectionist policies and other forms of state interference were harming the economic well-being of the city. They wanted Rijeka to acquire the status of a free port that would be able to operate like a "Hong Kong of the Mediterranean" and profit economically from more intensive European integration. The RDA stood in an election coalition with three other regionalist organizations for the August 1993 ballot and performed reasonably well in the local city elections. As with other regionalist groupings, its leaders welcomed the election of a new democratic coalition government in Zagreb in January 2000 as an opportunity for expanding administrative decentralization and regional development.

Istrian Radical Organization (IRO)
Istarska Radikalna Organizacija (IRO)

The Istrian Radical Organization (IRO) was created in October 1991 as a reestablishment of the illegal TIGR (Trieste–Istria–Gorica–Rijeka) organization under a new name. In its previous incarnation during World War II it was a joint Slovenian-Croatian organization that, in opposition to the wartime fascist regime, trained young people for an uprising and was involved in sabotage operations. The organization avowedly supported the democratic opposition in Croatia, particularly those formations that wanted to restore a large measure of local autonomy to the Istrian peninsula.[54]

POLITICAL DATA

Name of State: Republic of Croatia *(Republika Hrvatska)*
Form of Government: Parliamentary democracy
Structure of Legislature: Bicameral Assembly *(Sabor)*: House of Districts *(Županijski Dom)*, 68 members; and House of Representatives *(Zastupnički Dom)*, 127 members, directly elected for a four-year term
Size of Territory: 21,829 square miles
Size of Population: 4,784,265 (1991 census); 5,004,112 (July 1996, est.)

Composition of Population:

Ethnic Group	Number	% of Population
Croats	3,736,356	78.10
Serbs	581,663	12.16

Yugoslavs	106,041	2.22
Muslims	43,469	0.91
Slovenes	22,376	0.47
Hungarians	22,355	0.47
Italians	21,303	0.46
Czechs	13,086	0.27
Albanians	12,032	0.25
Montenegrins	9,724	0.20
Roma	6,695	0.14
Macedonians	6,628	0.14
Slovaks	5,606	0.12
Ruthenians	3,253	0.07
Germans	2,635	0.06
Ukrainians	2,494	0.05
Smaller minorities	4,080	0.08
Regional affiliation	45,593	0.95
No affiliation	73,376	1.53
Unknown	62,926	1.32
Total minorities	1,047,909	21.90
Total	4,784,265	100.00

Sources: The 1996 CIA World Factbook, via Internet, http://www.odci.gov/cia/publications/nsolo/factbook/hr.htm.

For demographic statistics on Croatia, see the Yugoslav population census of 1991, "Refugees and Displaced Persons in the Republic of Croatia," Republic of Croatia, Ministry of Information, Zagreb, July 1992.

ELECTION RESULTS

Presidential Election, 24 January and 7 February 2000

First Round, 24 January 2000

Turnout: 65.88%

Candidate	*Votes*	*% of Vote*
Stjepan Mesić	1,100,671	41.11
Dražen Budiša	741,837	27.71
Mate Granić	601,588	22.47
Slaven Letica	110,782	4.14
Ante Djapić	49,282	1.84
Ante Ledić	22,845	0.85
Tomislav Merčep	22,845	0.85
Ante Prkačin	7,401	0.28
Zvonimir Šeparović	7,235	0.27
Total	2,664,486	99.52

Source: http://www.hidra.hr/STR/501rp2000.htm.

Second Round, 8 February 2000

Turnout: 60.88%

Candidate	Votes	% of Vote
Stjepan Mesić	1,433,921	56.01
Dražen Budiša	1,125,969	43.99
Total	2,559,890	100.00

Source: http://www.vjesnik.com/Izbori_2000/Predsjednik/.

Presidential Election, 15 June 1997

Turnout: 54.62%

Candidate	Votes	% of Vote
Franjo Tudjman	1,337,990	61.41
Zdravko Tomac	458,172	21.03
Vlado Gotovac	382,630	17.56
Total	2,178,792	100.00

Source: Presidential Election Results Report, Election Commission of Republic of Croatia, Zagreb, 24 June 1997.

Presidential Election, 2 August 1992

Turnout: 74.90%

Candidate	Votes	% of Vote
Franjo Tudjman	n/a	56.73
Dražen Budiša	n/a	21.87
Savka Dabčević–Kučar	n/a	6.02
Dobroslav Paraga	n/a	5.40
Silvije Degen	n/a	4.07
Marko Veselica	n/a	1.70
Ivan Cesar	n/a	1.61
Antun Vujiæ	n/a	0.70
Invalid Ballots	n/a	1.90
Total	n/a	100.00

Sources: Parliamentary and Presidential Elections in an Independent Croatia, Commission on Security and Cooperation in Europe, Washington, DC, August 1992, pp. 24–25.

Parliamentary Elections, House of Representatives, 3 January 2000

Turnout: 71%

Party/Coalition	Votes	% of Vote	Seats
Coalition SDP/CSLP:	1,302,816	47.02	71
Social Democratic Party	789,115	28.48	(43)*
Croatian Social Liberal Party/	458,839	16.56	(25)
Croatian Party of Slavonija-Baranija	36,574	1.32	(1)
Primorsko-Goranski Assembly	36,574	1.32	(2)
Croatian Democratic Union	843,976	30.46	46
Coalition CPP/IDA/CPP/LP:	440,275	15.89	24
Croatian Peasant Party (CPP)	295,364	10.60	16
Istrian Democratic Assembly (IDA)	73,425	2.65	4
Croatian People's Party (CPP)	36,574	1.32	2
Liberal Party (LP)	36,574	1.32	2
Coalition CPR/CCDU:	91,712	3.30	5
Croatian Party of Rights (CPR)	73,425	2.65	4
Croatian Christian Democratic			
Union (CCDU)	18,289	0.66	1
Ethnic Minorities Election Unit:	91,712	3.31	5
Total	2,770,491	99.99	151

*Numbers within brackets denote the number of seats allocated to an individual party within a coalition.

Sources: http://kuna.hidra.hr/STR/501rz2000.htm; and http://www.croatiaemb.org/politics/vote2000/012000.htm.

Parliamentary Elections, House of Districts, 13 April 1997*

Turnout: 71.37%

Party/Coalition	Seats
Croatian Democratic Union/Croatian Party of Rights/	
Croatian Christian Democratic Union	40
Croatian Social Liberal Party/Croatian Peasant Party	15
Social Democratic Party	4
Istrian Democratic Assembly	2
Croatian Party of Rights	2
Appointed by Croatian President	5
Total	68

*Full data not available.

Sources: The April 1997 Parliamentary, County and Municipal Elections in Croatia, Commission on Security and Cooperation in Europe, Washington, DC, June 1997, p. 13; and Information Packet on Elections, 13 April 1997, Embassy of Republic of Croatia, Washington, DC.

Parliamentary Elections, House of Representatives, 29 October 1995

Turnout: 68.80%

Party/Coalition	Votes	% of Vote	Seats
Croatian Democratic Union	1,093,403	45.23	75
Coalition:	441,390	18.26	20
Croatian Peasant Party			
Istrian Democratic Assembly			
Croatian People's Party			
Croatian Christian Democratic Union			
Croatian Party of Slavonija-Baranja			
Croatian Social Liberal Party	279,245	11.55	11
Social Democratic Party	215,839	8.93	9
Croatian Party of Rights	121,095	5.01	4
Social Democratic Union	78,282	3.24	—
Croatian Independent Democrats	72,612	3.00	—
Action of Social Democrats of Croatia	40,348	1.67	—
1861 Croatian Party of Rights	31,530	1.30	—
Croatian Christian Democratic Party	16,989	0.70	—
Croatian Party of Rights	7,835	0.32	—
Croatian Conservative Party	6,858	0.28	—
Independent Party of Rights	6,608	0.27	—
Homeland Civic Party	5,343	0.22	—
Total	2,417,377	99.98	119

Source: Chronicle of Parliamentary Elections, Volume XXX (1995–96), Inter-Parliamentary Union, Geneva 1997, p. 61.

Parliamentary Elections, House of Districts, 7 February 1993

Turnout: 62.6%

Party/Coalition	% of Vote	Seats
Croatian Democratic Union	45.49	37
Croatian Social Liberal Party	27.94	16
Croatian Peasant Party	11.62	5
Istrian Democratic Assembly	4.45	3
Social Democratic Party	2.80	1
Croatian People's Party	1.03	1
Total	93.33	63

Source: Nenad Zakosek, "Pregled rezultata izbora za domove Sabora Republike Hrvatske i za županijske skupštine," Politićka Misao, Vol. XXXIV, 1997, pp. 129–143.

Parliamentary Elections, House of Representatives, 2 August 1992

Turnout: 75.6%

Party/Coalition	Votes	% of Vote	Seats
Croatian Democratic Union	1,176,437	43.72	85
Croatian Social Liberal Party	466,356	17.33	14
Party of Democratic Change	145,419	5.40	11
Croatian People's Party	176,214	6.55	6
Croatian Party of Rights	186,000	6.91	5
Croatian National Party	111,896	4.16	3
Serbian National Party	28,620	1.06	3
Independents	—	11.76	5
Regional groups	83,623	3.11	6
Total	2,374,565	100.00	138

Source: *Chronicle of Parliamentary Elections and Developments* (1992–993), Vol. XXVII, Inter-Parliamentary Union, Geneva 1994, p. 73.

Parliamentary Elections, April–May 1990

(First Round) 22–23 April 1990, (Second Round) 6–7 May 1990

Turnout: 84.5%

Party/Coalition	Votes	% of Vote	Seats
Croatian Democratic Union	2,373,066	58.7	206
League of Communist	840,882	20.8	73
Communist Party/Socialist Alliance	194,049	4.8	17
Coalition of National Understanding	125,325	3.1	11
Croatian Democratic Party	117,238	2.9	10
Serbian Democratic Party	56,597	1.4	5
Socialist Alliance	36,384	0.9	3
Independent	149,580	3.7	13
Others	149,580	3.7	13
Total	4,4042,071	100.0	351

Source: *Elections in Central and Eastern Europe, A Compendium of Reports on the Elections Held from March through June 1990*, Commission on Security and Cooperation in Europe, Washington, DC, July 1999, p. 90.

NOTES

1. For recent histories of Croatia consult Marcus Tanner, *Croatia: A Nation Forged in War*, New Haven: Yale University Press, 1997; Charles Jelavich and Barbara Jelavich, *The Establishment of the Balkan National States,1804–1929*, Seattle: University of Washington Press, 1977; Paul Shoup, *Communism and the Yugoslav National Question*, New York: Columbia University Press, 1968; and Ante Kadic, *From Croatian Renaissance to Yugoslav Socialism: Essays*, The Hague: Mouton, 1969.

2. See *The 1990 Elections in the Republics of Yugoslavia*, National Republican Institute for International Affairs, Washington DC, 1991.

3. *Glas Koncila*, Zagreb, 30 July 1989, 24 September 1989, and 8 October 1989.

4. Olga Ramljak, "Dossier: Beginnings of Aggression: Anatomy of Seth Rebellion: Those Issuing Orders From Serbia Had Good Servants in War Criminals," *Danas*, Zagreb, 26 February 1993, in Federal Broadcast Information Service, *Daily Report, East Europe, FBIS-EEU-93–057*, 26 March 1993. For a valuable appraisal of the military situation, see James Gow, "Military-Political Affiliations in the Yugoslav Conflict," Radio Free Europe/Radio Liberty Research Institute (RFE/RL), *Research Report*, Vol. 1, No. 20, 15 May 1992.

5. *Zagreb Domestic Service*, 17 October 1990, in *FBIS-EEU-90–202*, 18 October 1990.

6. Milan Andrejevich, "Croatia Between Stability and Civil War (Part II)," RFE/RL, *Report on Eastern Europe*, Vol. 1, No. 39, 28 September 1990.

7. "Serbian People's Uprising," *Vjesnik*, Zagreb, 25 July 1990, in *FBIS-EEU-90*145, 27 July 1990.

8. *Tanjug Domestic Service*, Belgrade, 16 March 1991, in *FBIS-EEU-91–052*, 18 March 1991; *Tanjug Domestic Service*, Belgrade, 1 April 1991, in *FBIS-EEU-91062*, 1 April 1991; *Tanjug*, Belgrade, 1 April 1991; *Tanjug*, Belgrade, 4 April 1991; *Tanjug Domestic Service*, Belgrade, 23 December 1991, *in FBIS-EEU-91–247*, 24 December 1991. For the Charter of the Serbian Autonomous Region of Krajina, check *Borba*, Belgrade, 4 January 1991.

9. See *The Constitution of the Republic of Croatia*, Zagreb, 1991.

10. Republic of Croatia, Constitutional Law of Human Rights and Freedoms and the Rights of National and Ethnic Communities or Minorities in the Republic of Croatia (Articles 21, 18, 14, 58), Zagreb, December 1991.

11. Milan Andrejevich, "Croatia Between Stability and Civil War (Part I)," RFE/RL, *Report on Eastern Europe*, Vol. 1, No. 37, 18 September 1990; Ivo Bicanic and Iva Dominis, "Tudjman Remains Dominant After Coalition Elections," RFE/RL, *Research Report*, Vol. 1, No. 37, 18 September 1992.

12. See Vesna Pusic, "Dictatorships with Democratic Legitimacy: Democracy Versus Nation," *East European Politics and Society*, Vol. 8, No. 3, Fall 1994, pp. 383–401.

13. Paul Shoup, "The UN Force: A New Actor in the Croatian-Serbian Crisis," RFE/RL, *Research Report*, Vol. 1, No. 13, 27 March 1992.

14. Information Report, Ministry of Foreign Affairs, Republic of Croatia, Zagreb, February 8, 1993.

15. Kresimir Meler and Mirjana Glugac, "Both Sides Already Have Plans," *Delo*, Ljubljana, 1 March 1993, in *FBIS-EEU-93–060*, 31 March 1993.

16. Samo Kobenter report on news conference by Croatian president Franjo Tudjman, "Open Border Question on the Balkans," *Der Standard*, Vienna, 22 February 1991, in *FBIS-EEU-91–038*, 26 February 1991.

17. Svetlana Vasovic-Mekina, "Slovenia and Croatia: How to Become a Citizen: State as Prison," *Vreme*, Belgrade, 8 March 1993, in *FBIS-EEU-93–065*, 7 April 1993.

18. Excerpts of inaugural address by Franjo Tudjman, "We Do Not Need Political 'Solidarity,'" *Vjesnik*, Zagreb, 31 May 1990, in *FBIS-EEU-90–118*, 19 June 1990.

19. Milan Andrejevich, "Croatia Between Stability and Civil War (Part II)" RFE/RL, *Report on Eastern Europe*, Vol. 1, No. 39, 28 September 1990.

20. Interview with Ivan Pauleto, president and founder of the Istrian Democratic Assembly, by Rajko Djurdevic, "Istria: Why We Are Demanding Autonomy," *Nin*, Belgrade, 11 January 1991, in Federal Broadcast Information Service/Joint Publications Research Service, *Daily Report, East Europe, JPRS-EER-91–018*, 11 February 1991.

21. See the Country Reports on Human Rights Practices for 1992, Department of State, Washington, DC, February 1993; and Helsinki Watch, *Yugoslavia: Human Rights Abuses in the Croatian Conflict*, Vol. 3, No. 14, September 1991.

22. http://www.hinet.hr/ash/onama.html.

23. http://www.aimpress.org, "Manolić Returns the Blow," Zagreb; 3 April 1994.

24. http://aimpress.org, "Osnivanje Liberalne Stranke," Zagreb, 24 January 1998.

25. http://www.aimpress.org, "New Croatian Political Geography," Zagreb, 28 January 1998.

26. http://aimpress.org, "Osnivanje Liberalne Stranke," Zagreb, 24 January 1998.

27. "The Goals and Values of the Liberal Party," from http://ww.liberali.hr/99glava2.html.

28. http://www.aimpress.org, "HDZ Disappearing from the Croatian Political Scene," Zagreb, 29 March 2000. See also RFE/RL, *Balkan Report*, Vol. 4, No. 53, 18 July 2000.

29. http://kuna.hidra.hr/STR/501int7–zast2000.htm#Hrvatska stranka zelenih.

30. http://kuna.hidra.hr/STR?s001746h.htm.

31. http://mesopust.com/zeleni/vrednote.htm. These ten fundamental values have been adapted from the 1984 proclamation of the United States' Green Party.

32. http://mesopust.com/zeleni/english1.htm.

33. http://mesopust.com/zeleni/deklar1.htm.

34. http://www.haa.hr/pol/program.htm.

35. http://www.hidra.hr/STR/501int7–zast2000.htm#Pokret za ljudska prava, stranka ekološki svjesnih građana.

36. Dejan Jović, "Who Is Preserving Yugoslavia?" *Danas*, Zagreb, 6 March 1990, in *JPRS-EEU-92–212*, 21 May 1990; Milan Andrejevich, "Nationalist Movements in Yugoslavia," RFE/RL, *Report on Eastern Europe*, 23 February 1990; RFE/RL Research Institute, *Daily Report*, No. 114, 18 June 1993.

37. 1995 Parliamentary Elections in Croatia, Commission on Security and Cooperation in Europe, Washington, DC, February 1996, p. 11.

38. 1995 Parliamentary Elections in Croatia, Commission on Security and Cooperation in Europe, Washington, DC, February 1996, p. 27.

39. http://www.aimpress.org, "Tudjman Is Dead: Let Us Do It All Over Again," Zagreb, 11 December 1999.

40. http://www.rferl.org/newsline/1999/12/131299.html.

41. http://www.aimpress.org, "Presidential Elections in Croatia," Zagreb, 25 January 2000.

42. Croatian Party of Rights, Constitution of the Croatian Party of Rights, Zagreb, 24 February 1991; Croatian Party of Rights, Electoral Declaration of the Croatian Party of Rights, Zagreb, 1992; *Die Presse*, Vienna, 27 January 1992, in *FBIS-EEU-92–018*, 28 January 1992. See also the Open Letter to Franjo Tudjman, Helsinki Watch, 13 February 1992; ORF Television Network, 5 November 1991, in *FBIS-EEU-91–215*, 6 November 1991; and Die Presse, Vienna, 27 January 1992, in *FBIS-EEU-92–018*, 28 January 1992.

43. Zoran Daskalovic and Milan Curuvija, "They Have Proclaimed Autonomy," *Vjesnik*, Zagreb, 26 July 1990, in *FBIS-EEU-90–149*, 2 August 1990; Milan Andrejevich, "Croatia Between Stability and Civil War (Part II)," RFE/RL, *Report on Eastern Europe*, Vol. 1, No. 39, 28 September 1990; 'The Right Is Gaining in Strength," *Borba*, Belgrade, 29 October 1990, in *FBIS-EEU-90–219*, 13 November 1990; Olga Ramljak, *Danas*, Zagreb, 26 February 1993, in *FBIS-EEU-93–057*, 26 March 1993; and interview with Milan Babić by Srdjan Radulović, "Milan Babić: The Krajina Administration Is a Puppet," *Borba*, Belgrade 2 April 1993, in *FBIS-EEU-93–067*, 9 April 1993.

44. See the interview with Petar Ladjević "Anything But War," *Monitor*, Podgorica 21 May 1993, in *FBIS-EEU-93–116*, 18 June 1993.

45. HTV, Zagreb, 21 December 1991, in *FBIS-EEU-91–246*, 23 December 1991.

46. Budapest Domestic Service, 7 March 1990, in *FBIS-EEU-90–047*, 9 March 1990; Patrick Moore, "The Question of All Questions: Internal Borders," RFE/RL, *Report on Eastern Europe*, Vol. 2, No. 38, 20 September 1991.

47. See the interview with Mirsad Baksic, "Izetbegović Does Not Represent Us All," *Vjesnik*, Zagreb, 5 April 1993, in *FBIS-EEU-93–085*, 5 May 1993.

48. "Romany Party of Croatia Founded," 22 July 1990, in "Weekly Record of Events," RFE/RL, *Report on Eastern Europe*, Vol. 1, No. 31, 3 August 1990.

49. http://www.aimpress.org, "Istria does not trust Tudjman," Zagreb, 22 April 1994.

50. http://www.aimpress.org, "Project of the Land of Istria," 27 January 1998.

51. Interview with Ivan Pauleto by Rajko Djurdjevič, *Nin*, Belgrade, 11 January 1991, in *JPRS-EER-91–018*, 11 February 1991.

52. Program Declaration of Dalmatian Action, Split, 30 May 1992; and interview with Mira Ljubič-Lorger by Petar Grubišić, "Hostages to Zagreb and Knin," *Danas*, Zagreb, 4 June 1993, in *JPRS-EER-93–060–S,* 30 June 1993.

53. Tanjug Domestic Service, Belgrade, 17 October 1990, in *FBIS-EEU-90–204*, 22 October 1990.

54. Tanjug Domestic Service, Belgrade, 5 October 1991, in *FBIS-EEU-91–195*, 8 October 1991.

Slovenia

HISTORICAL OVERVIEW

Slavic tribes settled in the Alpine-Adriatic region in the middle of the sixth century AD after a long period of migration from their original homes north of the Black Sea. Early distinctions between Slavic tribes are difficult to ascertain, but those settling in the territories that later became Yugoslavia were split into three main branches: the Slovenes in the northwest, the Croats in the center, and the Serbs in the southeast.[1] Most of the indigenous inhabitants of these regions were gradually Slavicized. Between 627 and 658 AD, a Slavic prince, Samo, ruled an empire that stretched from present-day Austria and Bohemia to the Sava River in Croatia. This political entity was known as Karantania, and its center was near the present-day Austrian town of Klagenfurt. This was the only state that the Slovenes could claim as their own historical heritage, and its rulers became vassals of the Moravian emperor.

Between the eighth and twelfth centuries, the Slovenes successively came under the domination of Bavaria, the Frankish kingdom, and Hungary, before their absorption by the Holy Roman Empire under the rule of King Charlemagne. Slovenian-inhabited territories at this time were almost double the present extent of the country and included much of central Austria; war, conquest, and migration reduced their size. German bishops and missionaries from Austria converted the population to Christianity. Austro-German princes and barons acquired land and enserfed the Slovenian peasantry and the latter were unable to develop an indigenous ruling stratum. German colonists, including merchants and craftsmen, were encouraged to settle in the Slavic areas. Many Slovenes were absorbed into the dominant German culture and some entered the Austro-German nobility, but the mass of peasants retained their Slavic culture and language.

During the tenth and eleventh centuries, the Slovenian lands were divided into a number of smaller duchies, including Carniola, Karantania (later Carinthia), Gorizia, Gradiška, Istria, and Styria. For the following two centuries, the Slovenes were ruled by a succession of princes, until the entire region fell under Austrian Habsburg control between 1335 and 1382. Thereafter, Slovenia's history and the development of its social, economic, and religious life remained closely linked with that of western Europe. Apart from brief periods of outside occupation, the territories remained under Austrian control until the close of World War I in 1918 and the creation of the first Yugoslavia. (Although, between the fifteenth and seventeenth centuries the Slovenes were subject to repeated raids by Ottoman forces, the Turks failed to gain control over any part of these territories.)

In the early sixteenth century, the Protestant Reformation initially had a major impact among the Slovenian population and stimulated the birth of the Slovenian literary language and educational system. The first Slovenian literary works became a major inspiration for the movement for national emancipation in the nineteenth century. The Habsburg-led Counter-Reformation and the determination of the Austrian nobility to retain their power reinforced the influence of the Catholic Church and the traditional feudal system, but it also afforded recognition to a Slovenian national identity.

Increasing Habsburg centralization during the course of the seventeenth century, particularly during the reign of Maria Theresa and Joseph II, escalated the process of Germanization. German was declared the official language for all governmental affairs and in the local educational system. Nevertheless, during the pan-European Enlightenment movement in the late seventeenth century, Slovenian national consciousness was preserved and stimulated while the mass of peasants continued to use their native language. The Catholic clergy played an important role in promoting Slovenian identity, language, and culture. The Carniola (Kranj) region became the center of the Slovene national awakening.

France briefly gained control over the Slovenian lands through the 1809 Treaty of Vienna following Napoleon's campaign against Austria. Slovenia, Croatia, and Dalmatia were formed into the province of Illyria under a French proconsul. The brief period of French rule resulted in some cultural liberalization as the Slovenian language was given more pronounced recognition. After the defeat of Napoleon's forces during the Russian campaign, the 1815 Congress of Vienna restored Slovenia, Dalmatia, and Croatia to the Habsburg Empire. The Slovenian lands were again divided among the three Austrian provinces of Carinthia, Carniola, and Styria.

During the nineteenth century, a growing sense of national unity and assertiveness was evident among Slovenian intellectuals, some of whom demanded autonomy, a federation with Austria and Hungary, outright independence, or unification within a new south Slav state. Many of these national spokesmen stemmed from the substantial educated Slovenian middle class that had emerged under Austrian occupation. A number of individuals had studied in various European universities and were imbued with the ideals of national and social liberation. The idea of a south Slavic union was spawned at this time and the Napoleonic Illyrian province provided a point of inspiration for some Slovenian activists. However, the majority sought a "United Slovenia" through the merger of all Slovene-inhabited lands of the Habsburg Empire into one administrative unit.[2] They envisaged autonomy and federation within the Austrian state rather than outright national independence.

Following the reorganization of the Habsburg domains into a dual Austrian-Hungarian monarchy in 1867, the Slovenes found themselves further divided territorially. About 27,000 were included in Italy and 45,000 in Hungary, out of a total population of some 1.1 million. To counter the pressures of division and assimilation, some pan-Slavist Slovenian liberals formulated a program stressing the equality of Slavic nations and religions and calling for a united south Slavic entity as one of three units in a proposed "triple monarchy." Meanwhile, Slovenian socialists more explicitly demanded a single and separate Yugoslav state in which Slovene identity would be submerged. A few activists, such as the writer Ivan Cankar, advocated a fully independent Slovenian state, especially in the context of increasing Germanization in the latter part of the nineteenth century.

During World War I (1914–1918), Slovenian politics was radicalized, and with the collapse of the Austro-Hungarian Empire, an independent south Slavic state was created on 1 December 1918. It was initially named the Kingdom of Serbs, Croats, and Slovenes. But the country was not able to regain territories from Italy, including the city of Trieste, nor lands from Austria, inhabited by substantial Slovene populations estimated to number about 400,000 people. The new Slavic state was declared a constitutional and democratic monarchy, but it soon fell under centralized Serbian domination. Serbs formed almost 40% of the population, and Slovenes represented only 8% of the Yugoslav total, or approximately one million people.

Two conflictive views emerged on the structure of the new state. Slovenian and Croatian leaders advocated a federal structure with substantial national autonomy, whereas Serbian leaders envisaged a more centralized state and a unitary form of government. This sowed the seeds of persistent discord and a growing disenchantment with the pan-Yugoslav ideology.[3] One of the strongest and most influential Slovenian parties that emerged during the inter-war period was the autonomist and federalist Slovenian Catholic Party.

On 6 January 1929, the Serbian King Aleksander attempted to counter the forces of Yugoslav disintegration by nullifying the 1921 constitution and imposing dictatorial rule. He centralized the administration and limited the autonomy of other nationalities while maintaining Serbian hegemony. The country was renamed the Kingdom of Yugoslavia and the traditional territorial units were reorganized into nine entities (*banovinas*) and renamed to undercut ethnic separatism. The Slovenian territory was known as the *Dravska Banovina*. The 1931 Yugoslav constitution banned political organizations based on ethnic or religious criteria. Slovenian politicians soon became disillusioned by these developments and campaigned for a looser federation, but without any success. They were also concerned that their economically developed republic would be exploited by Belgrade and its progress would be correspondingly slowed down. Aleksander's autocracy failed to forge a transethnic Yugoslav identity or to foster loyalty to the new state.

Following the Nazi invasion and dismemberment of Yugoslavia in 1941, the country descended into a brutal civil and inter-ethnic war. Slovenia was partitioned into several parts: the western coastal area was annexed by Italy, a northern segment was occupied by Germany, a northeastern section was occupied by a pro-Nazi Hungarian state, and a southern sliver was assigned to the pro-Nazi Independent State of Croatia. The occupying powers pursued a policy of de-Slovenization, and the country's political and intellectual elites were decimated. Slovenia did not spawn a fascist movement that could be entrusted with administering a pro-Nazi state. Instead, an anti-fascist resistance movement emerged, although it was split between nationalist and communist forces. The latter organized a Liberation Front of the Slovene Nation; the former were split between the conservative, Catholic Church-oriented White Guard and the broader-based Home Guard (*domobranci*).

At the close of the war in 1945 and following the takeover by communist Yugoslav forces, Slovenia was incorporated into a re-created Yugoslav federation dominated by Marshal Josip Broz Tito. The Titoist regime eliminated all political opponents on grounds of treason and collaboration with the fascist powers, in order to guarantee its unchallenged rule. Several thousand nationalists, democrats, and liberals were executed by communist units. But Slovenia emerged relatively unscathed from World War II, in comparison to the other Yugoslav republics. Slovenia regained some territories from Italy at the Paris Peace Conference in 1946, although the city of Trieste was left outside of the new Yugoslavia. Slovenian claims to southern Carinthia were also settled in favor of Austria.

During the late 1940s and 1950s, Yugoslavia resembled a Soviet-type federal system, in which power was concentrated at the apex of the unified party-state apparatus. With administrative reforms enacted during the 1960s, Slovenia, together with the five other Yugoslav republics, gained a relative degree of autonomy, and a more reformist leadership emerged in the capital Ljubljana. By the close of that decade, the Yugoslav republics emerged as growing centers of political power, although a crackdown by Belgrade in the early 1970s suspended many reformist policies. The ethnic and linguistic distinctiveness of Slovenia prevented a mass inflow of Serbian communist bureaucrats like that witnessed in neighboring Croatia. Slovenia also became the most industrially developed and productive republic, and its pronounced ethnic homogeneity precluded any significant nationality conflicts. Slovenes remained strongly Catholic despite the prevailing communist ideology.

The 1974 Yugoslav constitution, framed by Tito and the leading Slovenian communist Edvard Kardelj, introduced the "delegate system" in the federation, whereby greater powers devolved to the Communist Party apparatus at the republican and provincial levels. This both enhanced republican autonomy and weakened central decisionmaking where unanimity was required by the leaders of six republics and two autonomous provinces in order to formulate policy. A major point of contention in Slovenia throughout the post–World War II era was the issue of the federal government's financing of the development of the less-developed Yugoslav regions. Essentially this meant that tax revenues and investment capital were diverted away from the richer, northern republics of Slovenia and Croatia, where funds would earn the best return on investment, and toward the southeastern republics of Montenegro, Macedonia, Bosnia-Herzegovina, and Serbia.

The inefficient use of resources under the republican bureaucracies seemed to many in Slovenia to be evidence of Belgrade's efforts to exploit Slovenia and to promote its patronage networks in the underdeveloped republics. Although payments to Yugoslavia's Federal Fund for the Accelerated Development of the Underdeveloped Regions and Kosovo (FADURK) never amounted to huge contributions, they nevertheless provided additional fuel for the rise of nationalist resentments. This became especially apparent when the Yugoslav economy as a whole began to decline during the 1980s, with rising inflation, high unemployment, a huge foreign debt, and severe food shortages. Slovenian leaders felt that remaining part of Yugoslavia increasingly hampered their republic's aspirations toward integration in the major European institutions. During 1986, a more reformist wing of the League of Communists of Slovenia (LCS) gained dominance over the conservative factions, and a younger leadership headed by Milan Kučan took control of the party.[4]

The impulse toward reform was ignited in May 1988, when rumors began to circulate that the Yugoslav army was planning to stage a coup in Slovenia to purge the republic of its liberal elements. When a sergeant major in the Yugoslav army, Ivan Borštner, brought word of this plot to the weekly magazine of the Socialist Youth Alliance, *Mladina*, Borštner and three of the journalists he contacted were promptly arrested. The public outcry against the arrests was widespread and continued to accelerate throughout the summer of 1988 as crowds of over 10,000 people regularly gathered in Ljubljana to protest the army's actions and called for the prisoners' release.[5] Yugoslav military authorities sentenced the four men after a sham trial that only further antagonized the Slovenian public. The "Trial of the Four" was clearly a political move directed against the Slovenian democratic movement and Slovenian "separatism." It dominated the attention of citizens, created a sense of threat, and further legitimized the embryonic opposition forces.

By early 1989, several dozen grass-roots organizations and ten independent political groups were active in the country. A Committee for the Protection of Human Rights was established to monitor and oppose what was widely perceived as Yugoslavia's drift toward a police state, and the Slovenian League of Communists actually granted the organization its support.[6] By midsummer over 70,000 individuals joined the Committee as well as numerous ecological, peace, and feminist groupings. A group of intellectuals centered around the publication *Nova Revija* formulated a national program calling for Slovenian self-determination, democracy, a market economy, and statehood.

During 1988 and 1989, the Slovenian Communist Party threw its support behind systemic reform and tried without much success to push the federal party in the same direction. Slovenian communist willingness to recognize an alternative voice on policy matters paved the way for the founding of several new democratic parties during 1989. They included the Social Democratic Alliance of Slovenia (SDAS), the Slovenian Democratic Union (SDU), the Slovenian Christian Socialist Movement (SCSM), and the Slovenian Green Party (SGP).[7] The SDU was founded on 16 January 1989 as the first political alternative to the League of Communists, with about 1,100 members and led by Dimitrij Rupel.

An important step in these democratizing developments was the decision on 27 September 1989 to delete from the Slovenian constitution the official vanguard role that had been accorded to the League of Communists since Tito's takeover. This allowed for freer political discourse and encouraged the non-communist opposition to broach new ideas on the future of the republic. One of the most important instances of this was the so-called May Declaration of 1989, which envisioned a future in which the Slovene nation would enjoy full sovereignty. It proved to be a vision more compelling to the public than anything that the reinvented communist parties could offer. Constitutional amendments also included the explicit right to self-determination—that is, secession from Yugoslavia.

The position of opposition forces was also enhanced by the electoral law of December 1989, which enabled the non-communist organizations to coalesce into a single movement, the Democratic Opposition of Slovenia (*Demokratična Opozicija Slovenije*, DEMOS). By the time of the April 1990 elections, the DEMOS alliance incorporated six parties: the Slovenian Democratic Alliance (SDA), the Social Democratic Alliance of Slovenia (SDAS), the Slovenian Green Party (SGP), the Liberal Party (LP), the Slovenian Christian Democrats (SCD), and the Slovenian Farmers' Party (SFP).

Throughout 1989, Ljubljana felt increasingly threatened, as events in Yugoslavia seemed to forebode the breakdown of the old federal structure. Of particular concern were Serbian actions toward the provinces of Kosovo and Vojvodina and amendments to the Serbian constitution that essentially eliminated the autonomous status of both regions and paved the way for a unitary Serbian state. In Slovenia, such measures were perceived as a direct challenge to other republics that could presage Belgrade's efforts to eliminate Slovenian autonomy.

During the course of 1989, Slovenian political organizations and citizens' groups organized rallies to protest Serbian policies vis-à-vis Kosovo, which provoked the wrath of Serbian President Slobodan Milošević. He dubbed the

Slovene regime "fascist" and instituted an economic blockade of the republic. The embargo caused some hardships for the public and adversely affected the republic's productive capacity. However, it also proved beneficial
in the long run, as Slovenia was forced to find new markets for its imports
and exports, to liquidate some unproductive state-owned enterprises, and to
seek a greater degree of foreign investment.[8] As a result, Slovenia became
relatively better prepared for life after Yugoslavia disintegrated than most
of the other republics.

By early 1990, Slovenian leaders felt increasingly alienated from the
Yugoslav state: they were struggling under an economic blockade and remained focused on their long-term autonomy. During the fourteenth emergency session of the League of Communists of Yugoslavia, between 20–22
January 1990, all Slovenian proposals for decentralization were blocked, and
the Slovenian delegation stormed out of the session in frustration and protest.
Shortly afterwards, Slovenia's republican Assembly announced that new multi-
party general elections were to be held. In March 1990, the Slovenian Assembly adopted proposals that dropped the word "socialist" from the constitution,
defined Slovenia as a state founded on the sovereignty of its citizens, and
began preparations for the republic's economic independence. The political
climate for the first pluralistic elections on 8 April 1990 was therefore extremely restless, and there were great misgivings about the future of the communist system and the Yugoslav federation.

Slovenian citizens participated in several simultaneous elections: for the
republic's president, for members of the Slovenian state presidency, and for
the three chambers of the National Assembly: the Sociopolitical Chamber
(101 seats), the Chamber of Municipalities (80 seats), and the Chamber of
Associated Labor (59 seats). Fifteen parties and three "civil lists" were registered for the ballot, and a total of 2,103 candidates took part. However, the
parties spanned a fairly narrow ideological and programmatic range, and there
was little ethnicization of the political scene, primarily because of the small
size of Slovenia's minorities. Moreover, none of the parties defined itself as
"Yugoslav," and all expressed their goal of achieving sovereignty for the republic. The one significant difference was in the pace and method of achieving Slovenian sovereignty. Two major forces competed in the polling: the
DEMOS coalition, comprised of seven major registered parties, and the former
League of Communists, which had changed its name to the Party of Democratic Renewal (PDR).

The DEMOS coalition, led primarily by the People's Party, the Christian
Democrats, and the Democratic Alliance, displayed its soaring popularity by
gaining 124 seats to the three-chamber, 240-member National Assembly. The
Liberal Democratic Party gained 40; the PDR scored 35; the Alliance of Socialists 12; two candidates canvassed as independents; and the Italian and
Hungarian communities obtained one parliamentary seat each. The two minority representatives gained seats in the two additional districts for election

to the Sociopolitical Chamber. DEMOS representative France Bau čar was selected president of the National Assembly, and another DEMOS leader, the Christian Democrat Lojze Peterle, became prime minister with the installa-tion of the new government in May 1990.[9]

In its election campaign, DEMOS promised its voters that Slovenian state-hood would be achieved when the republic gained a distinct political, eco-nomic, military, and international legal status. Once in power, the new government pursued a policy consistent with these promises. President Milan Kučan, who was elected the same month, conferred closely with the newly elected president of Croatia, Franjo Tudjman, in crafting a design for a confederal Yugoslav arrangement that would replace the old federal struc-ture. Belgrade charged that such a loose political structure would be tanta-mount to the dissolution of Yugoslavia. Ljubljana was still sending mixed messages at this time concerning its commitment to independence. On 2 July 1990, the Slovenian parliament passed a fundamental declaration on sover-eignty. But in September 1990, Ljubljana offered proposals that would have converted Yugoslavia into an "alliance of sovereign states," purportedly on the model of the Benelux countries or the European Community.

The Slovenian notion was to establish a "confederation" in order to main-tain an economic community, a customs union, a common defense force, a very limited ministerial council, a confederal court (for interpreting the agree-ment of confederation), and various other organs for dealing with matters of common concern. According to this proposal, each state would retain the right to pursue an independent foreign policy and would receive a share of the property of the former Yugoslavia, in proportion to the republic's contribu-tion to the national budget. This last element became especially problematic when it came to dividing and apportioning the value of federal property.[10]

Nonetheless, there were stark differences between the European Commu-nity (EC) and any imagined future confederal Yugoslavia. The former was composed of states with similar political and economic systems, which had voluntarily surrendered some elements of their national sovereignty, while the latter included both authoritarian socialist republics and nascent free-market democracies. This systemic disparity ensured that any project for creating an alliance on the EC model would prove extremely daunting.[11] In light of the wide differences among the Yugoslav republics, certain Slovenian leaders thought it wiser to create a smaller sphere of cooperation comprising Slovenia, Croatia, and Bosnia-Herzegovina. A smaller alliance would have benefited from more pronounced political and economic convergence and would have possessed a historical border: the old frontier of the former Habsburg Empire. Other leaders, including Prime Minister Lojze Peterle, also suggested the idea of a bilateral union or federation with Croatia; such calculations failed to materialize in the wake of Yugoslavia's violent dissolution

In 1990, Slovenia's leaders still calculated that there would be some ben-efits from retaining an association with the other Yugoslav republics: for example, the establishment of an economic community, a tariff union, and perhaps even a joint monetary policy. The Slovenian leadership, however, was not determined to maintain this association at all costs. The Serbian economic blockade begun in 1989 demonstrated to Slovenia that its relations with Croatia and Bosnia were of far more importance economically than its relations with the southern Yugoslav republics.

Even more important to Ljubljana was the country's eventual integration into the EC: such a step was considered to be a panacea for most of the country's problems. It would supposedly offer an unparalleled market for Slovenia's exports, long-term protection for its cultural distinctiveness, confirmation of its identity as a European rather than a Balkan society, and a workable system of regional security cooperation that would defuse any dangerous bilateral conflicts with its neighbors. Because this idea was so potent, Slovenia had little interest in being fettered to any confederation of states that might opt for a slower pace of entry into the EC. The government sought to confirm its national sovereignty so that it would not be consigned to the role of a subnational interest when European integration finally embraced Yugoslavia.[12]

POST-COMMUNIST DEVELOPMENTS

With the loosening of federal controls and the disintegration of the League of Communists throughout the 1980s, Slovenia moved swiftly to assert its sovereignty and eventual "disassociation" from Yugoslavia. On 2 July 1990, the Slovenian National Assembly adopted a proclamation on the republic's sovereignty and began to draft a new, independent constitution that would negate the validity of all Yugoslav federal laws in the republic. A national plebiscite was held on the question of independence on 23 December 1990, and 88% of the 95% of the electorate who cast their ballots opted in favor of sovereignty and independence.

The results further aggravated Ljubljana's relations with the federal authorities. The new government sought a much looser confederal arrangement with the other Yugoslav republics. But agreements on a new political system could not be reached with the Serbian and Montenegrin leadership. As a result, Ljubljana took a major step toward secession in February 1991, when the National Assembly annulled all federal laws and Slovenia's obligations to Belgrade. Slovenia's communist leader Milan Kučan steered among conflicting factions within the party and slowly prepared to sever all ties with Belgrade.

After several months of fruitless negotiation for some novel confederative structure within Yugoslavia, Slovenia finally declared its independence from Yugoslavia on 25 June 1991. The declaration was the culmination of the republic's attempts to safeguard its status as a unique nation from the encroachments of the Yugoslav federal structure. Slovenian leaders had long expressed reservations about their position in the Yugoslav federation, fearing that their national and linguistic identity would melt away into the Serbian-Croatian mainstream, and resenting the fact that their tax revenues were being diverted to support Yugoslavia's less-developed southern regions. As Slovenians became increasingly wary of Milošević's attempts to subvert the country's relatively decentralized federal structure, Slovenia's newly formed opposition forces found common cause with the reform-oriented League of Communists in seeking a more democratic polity and a greater measure of sovereignty.

Slovenia's act of "disassociation" from Yugoslavia was rejected by the federal government and provoked a Yugoslav army intervention in an effort to coerce Ljubljana into rescinding its decision on independence. Instead of intimidating Slovenia, however, the attempted army crackdown had the reverse effect, stiffening Slovenian resistance and uniting virtually the entire political spectrum behind the administration. The objective of the Yugoslav People's Army intervention in June 1991 was evidently to disarm the Slovenian territorial defense forces, destabilize the government, and reverse the decision on independence. The maneuver failed, and Slovenian forces were able to resist the assault and inflict some damage on the Yugoslav military. In fact, the invasion force was too small and inflexible to operate in mountainous terrain unsuitable for conventional warfare.

The Yugoslav incursion and the "ten-day war" proved a disaster in that the cumbersome military units were outmaneuvered by highly mobile and motivated Slovenian defense forces that had managed to make significant operational and logistical preparations for such an encounter. Indeed, the Slovenian Defense Minister Janez Janša had skillfully and clandestinely organized special units within and outside the old territorial defense force structure. These units were at the forefront of resistance to the Yugoslav army. Some observers speculated that the incursion itself was either half-hearted or prematurely aborted. It remained unclear, however, whether this was the result of political conflicts between the political and military leadership in Belgrade, or whether the whole episode had been designed to fail by Belgrade as it busily prepared for the forthcoming war in Croatia.

Analysts believed that Milošević was prepared to allow Slovenia to secede in order to increase the demographic strength of Serbs in the remaining federation. He also used the opportunity to discredit some high-ranking Yugoslav military commanders in preparation for a thorough overhaul of the military structure and its full subordination to the Serbian leadership. After ten days of hostilities and only a dozen or so casualties, both sides agreed to an EC-sponsored cease-fire. The agreement stipulated that Slovenia and Croatia both consented to suspend their declarations of independence for three months. During this time Yugoslav forces, numbering about 20,000 troops, were withdrawn from Slovenia and repositioned inside Croatia and Bosnia-Herzegovina.

Ljubljana had agreed to place its independence on hold for three months pending a new series of inter-republican negotiations to restructure the federation. When the moratorium expired on 8 October 1991 without any notable progress, Slovenia again declared its independence and separation from Yugoslavia. During the early part of 1992, the new state finally obtained comprehensive international recognition as an independent republic.

After achieving statehood Slovenia made steady progress toward a pluralistic democracy. It was not beset by any significant territorial or minority problems, either domestically or with its neighbors. Tensions with Croatia were visible throughout the 1990s, particularly over such issues as direct access to the Adriatic and the delineation of sea borders. But there was little danger of any major confrontation between Ljubljana and Zagreb. Leaders of the Italian minority in Slovenian and Croatian Istria and the Hungarian minority in the eastern corner of the republic campaigned for greater protection and collective rights. Ljubljana appeared to achieve some success in satisfying their demands and improving its relations with both Italy and Hungary.

On 23 December 1991, Slovenia adopted a new constitution that proclaimed the country to be a democratic republic governed by the rule of law. The document enacted a multi-party parliamentary system and provided a charter of human rights and fundamental freedoms that would establish the normative basis for the state. The president was the head of state, directly elected for a maximum of two consecutive five-year terms. Slovenia adopted a unicameral legislature, the National Assembly *(Državni Zbor),* with 90 deputies, 88 elected by proportional representation and two by ethnic minorities, for four-year terms. In addition, the National Council *(Državni Svet)* was created as an advisory body with 40 members elected to represent social, economic, professional, and local interests for five-year terms. The prime minister was the head of government, and the judiciary consisted of a Constitutional Court, regular courts, and an attorney general.

Of all the former Yugoslav republics, Slovenia was clearly the most successful in rapidly disentangling itself from federal institutions, pressures, and conflicts. Significant success was also achieved in establishing a stable democracy and a market economy. Slovenia's second multi-party parliamentary elections (and the first in an independent state), on 6 December 1992, resembled Western ballots and it was generally free of irregularities. The DEMOS coalition had fractured by late 1991, resulting in intense competition for political office. The Liberal Democratic Party (LDP), which was created by ex-communist reformers from the Communist Youth Union, emerged as the strongest force, gaining 22 seats in the 90-seat National Assembly. It evidently captured the public's support by championing privatization and more rapid movement toward a market economy. The Christian Democrats finished second and improved on their 1990 result with 15 seats. The third-best showing, with 14 seats, was achieved by the United List (UL), a coalition of four left-of-center parties that included the former communists, renamed the Social Democratic Party of Reformers (SDPR).

The radical nationalist Slovenian National Party (SNP) achieved a respectable showing; it appealed in particular to impressionable young people and residents of the Italian and Austrian border regions. This ultra-nationalist party captured 12 seats in the legislature, while playing on popular fears over allowing Bosnian refugees into the country. The Slovenian People's Party (SPP), a successor to the Slovenian Democratic Alliance, managed to elect 10 deputies, while the Democratic Party, the Green Party, and the Social Democratic Party shared the remaining 15 seats. One seat each was allocated to the Hungarian and Italian minorities.

On 25 January 1993, Prime Minister Janez Drnovšek, the Liberal Democrat leader, assembled a five-party governing coalition and proceeded to implement various economic and social reforms. The government was controlled by the United List and the Liberal Democrats: both parties were direct descendants of the former Communist League and retained much of its apparatus, resources, and *nomenklatura* networks. They surfed to power on the wave of independence and managed to preserve many of their privileges and positions at both the central and local levels. In particular, their control over much of the mass media, especially the major television channels, assured them of constant access to voters and the interpretation of events favoring the ruling coalition, especially as the opposition was increasingly divided into rival parties. The other members of the coalition included the Social Democrats, the Christian Democrats (whose leader Lojze Peterle became foreign minister), and the Greens. Despite post-communist domination in the cabinet, Slovenia consolidated its political progress throughout the 1990s with the formation of fairly stable multi-party coalition governments.

In the first post-independence presidential elections, on 6 December 1992, Milan Kučan, the former president of the League of Communists, was elected head of state. Out of nearly one and a half million people eligible to vote, a total of 85.9% did so. Kučan gained 63.9% of the total valid votes. He benefited from a good measure of popularity as a result of his efforts to limit potential domination by Belgrade, although some anti-communists charged that his late conversion to the cause of Slovenian independence was due more to personal motives than any strong patriotic sentiments. Kučan evidently gained the support of some nationalists by backing Slovenia's drive for independence and maintained the support of the leftist United List, despite his formal break with the communist party.[13]

Slovenian non-post-communist democratic opposition remained broad and divided, and it faced an uphill struggle in the elections. The Social Democrats were initially the most popular party, led by Janez Janša, the former defense minister, who was instrumental in creating an independent Slovenian army on the eve of independence. He had been ousted from the ministry at the behest of ex-communists who resented his popularity and non-dependence on their patronage network. His standing in opinion polls placed him above Prime Minister Drnovšek, but the media consistently portrayed Janša as a loose cannon who could endanger the reform process.

The People's Party, led by Marjan Podobnik, steadily climbed in public opinion polls through the 1990s, and the party gained substantial support among young rural voters. The Christian Democrats, led by Lojze Peterle, initially shared government in the post-communist coalition but subsequently went into opposition in September 1994 after resigning largely in protest against the coalition's choice for parliamentary speaker. The Christian Democrats' support base evidently declined partly because of their past associations with the United List and the Liberal Democrats.

The local elections on 4 and 18 December 1994 were conducted in the 147 newly established municipalities and they proved a major test for the country's post-communist and reformist leadership. Voters elected mayors and members of local councils and clearly favored the oppositionist Slovenian Spring parties, eroding the local power base of the post-communist parties.[14] The Drnovšek government was increasingly seen by the public as responsible for various economic scandals and unsuccessful reform policies. The Christian Democrats gained 18.4% of the vote, the Liberal Democrats 17.2%, the Social Democratic Party 13.8%, the United List 13.2%, the People's Party 12.0%, the Greens 3.0%, the Democratic Party of Retired People 4.0%, and independents 9.47%.

The ex-communist United List left the government on 21 January 1996, disagreeing with the coalition parties about the course to be taken in economic and social policy. The minority government was only able to survive for a few more months. In the parliamentary elections on 10 November 1996, the Liberal Democratic Party (LDP) gained 25 seats, the Slovenian People's Party (SPP) 19, the Social Democratic Party (SDP) 16, the Christian Democratic Party (CDP) 10, the Democratic Party of Pensioners of Slovenia (DPPS) 5, and the Slovenian National Party (SNP) 4. The results indicated that the political pendulum was swinging back toward the former anti-communist opposition.

An attempt to line up the Liberal Democratic Party, the United List of Social Democrats, and the Slovenian National Party was rejected on 7 February 1997. Talks between the LDP and the Slovenian Spring parties fell apart even earlier. But after lengthy negotiations, the Liberal Democrats, led by premier Drnovšek, formed a coalition with the former oppositionist Slovenian People's Party and the Democratic Party of Pensioners of Slovenia (DPPS). The new government gained the support of 52 out of 90 deputies and was approved by parliament on 27 February 1997.

The cabinet consisted of 19 ministers, including the Prime Minister: 10 were from the LDP, 8 from the SPP, and one from the DPPS. The SPP, led by

Marjan Podobnik, was one of the three major opposition groups belonging to the Slovenian Spring, which sought to replace former communist officials with a more progressive administration. The coalition agreement included plans to prepare the nation for European Union (EU) and the North Atlantic Treaty Organization (NATO) membership, to reform the pension system, to restructure agriculture, to curb inflation, and to reduce unemployment. The three disparate formations worked reasonably well together, particularly on foreign policy issues. Nevertheless, they still needed to handle several pressing domestic questions, including the privatization of state industry, the rooting out of corruption, and the decommunization and transformation of state institutions into accountable and transparent organs of government.

The new parliament passed a number of important laws to bring the country into line with European standards. For example, in July 1997 it amended the constitution in order to allow foreigners to own property in the country. Prime Minister Drnovšek and Archbishop Franc Rode also reached an agreement to return the Roman Catholic Church property seized and nationalized by the communists after World War II.

Slovenia's second post-independence presidential elections took place on 23 November 1997. Milan Kučan received 55.57% of the vote and was reelected for another five-year term. His nearest rival was Janez Podobnik, the speaker of parliament and a leader of the People's Party. Kučan had attained significant popular prestige and authority for his handling of the Yugoslav crisis in 1991 and his evident success in avoiding mass bloodshed. Nevertheless, he was criticized for upholding a system of informal patronage and privilege among the former *nomenklatura* and awarding them prestigious positions and benefits from the privatization process. Some observers speculated that elections would signal whether Slovenia was making a clean break with the past or was maintaining some post-communist elements during its transition. However, regardless of the election's outcome, the country's political leaders appeared uniformly committed to a process of democratization and European integration.

On 24 February 2000, the People's Party and the opposition Christian Democrats announce their merger. Nine ministers of the People's Party resigned to form a new election coalition with the Christian Democrats. Premier Drnovšek nominated eight experts who did not belong to any political party to join his cabinet. The legislature rejected his nominees and Drnovšek lost a vote of confidence on 8 April 2000. After several months of dispute within the governing coalition and amidst various public scandals, the Liberal-People's coalition government collapsed.[15] On 28 April 2000, a new coalition government was formed. The oppositionist Social Democratic Party joined forces with the already governing Slovenian People's Party and the Christian Democratic Party. The three parties signed a three-party agreement to form the "Coalition Slovenia" (*Koalicija Slovenija*). By joining forces, the three formations gained a majority in parliament and obtained the right to nominate a prime minister.

Coalition Slovenia chose Andrej Bajuk as prime minister, and he was elected with 46 parliamentary votes on 3 May 2000. Lojze Peterle, the Christian Democrat leader, was appointed minister of foreign affairs while Janez Janša, the Social Democratic Party leader, was appointed defense minister. The interim government, which remained in power until the elections in October 2000, had one major goal: to make progress on harmonizing Slovenian laws with those of the EU. Slovenia was falling behind in its schedule of harmonization, and by June 2000 it needed to adopt at least ten new laws or forfeit its chance to join the EU in the first round.

As result of differences over the new election law between Prime Minister Bajuk and the SPP, the premier established his own political party to contest the ballot. His New Slovenian People's Christian Party (NSPCP) held its founding meeting on 11 August 2000. The new center-right coalition was unable to hold together because of personality and policy conflicts. The more coherent and better organized Liberal Democrats regained a large measure of public support during the summer under the leadership of Janez Drnovšek who had served as the country's prime minister for most of the 1990s.

Slovenia's parliamentary elections were held on 15 October 2000 according to a majoritarian rather than a proportional system. Since the Coalition Slovenia pressed for a new government, several other parties thought it would be wise to simply hold early elections and avoid the prospect of two parliamentary elections within six months. Members of Coalition Slovenia asserted that with early elections, Slovenia would not have time to work on harmonizing its laws with the EU. In the ballot, the Liberal Democrats gained over 36% of the vote and captured 34 seats. Their nearest challenger, the Social Democrats, managed to muster only 16% of the vote and 14 seats. The ex-communist United List gathered 12% of the vote and 11 seats. The Slovenian People's Party bloc gained just over 9% of the vote and 9 parliamentary seats. Bajuk's party, the NSPCP, captured only 8 seats in the legislature.

On 17 November 2000, parliament approved Janez Drnovšek, the Liberal Democratic leader, as the new Prime Minister, although the Social Democrats and the New Slovenia Party abstained from the ballot. The LDP signed a government coalition pact with the United List of Social Democrats, the Slovenian People's Party, and the Pensioners' Party. The coalition controlled 58 out of 90 parliamentary seats and looked set to continue the policies of the pre-April 2000 administration.

With regard to ethnic questions, Article 3 of the country's new constitution defined Slovenia as "a state of all its citizens" that was "based on the permanent and inalienable right of the Slovene nation to self-determination." The constitution addressed the question of minority protection by affording special rights to autochthonous Hungarian and Italian minorities. It prohibited all incitements to discrimination and formally guaranteed the free expression of national allegiance, language, and script. For example, although the country's official language was Slovenian, the Italian and Hungarian languages were also stipulated as official in those areas where the respective national communities resided. The constitution also affirmed that the state remained responsible for ethnic Slovenian minorities in neighboring states, including emigrants and migrant workers, and would promote their ties with the homeland.[16]

Some uncertainties remained about how extensive minority rights in Slovenia actually were. Ljubljana institutionalized the rights of indigenous Hungarian and Italian minorities, who in 1991 together constituted less than 0.6% of the country's population. However, Yugoslav groups referred to as "immigrant communities," Croats, Serbs, Bosniaks, and others, who made up 11.7% of the population, did not benefit from constitutionally recognized cultural or group rights. The 1991 constitution seemed to indicate that Slovenia was establishing a three-tiered set of nationality definitions and privileges.[17] At the pinnacle were ethnic Slovenes. The language of the constitution remained unclear on whether the state fully guaranteed the "right of self-determination" to all citizens or specifically to ethnic "Slovene people."

In second position were the "autochthonous minorities," or the Hungarian and Italian communities that possessed historical homelands on Slovenian territory. The two groups enjoyed some special rights, particularly within the designated "nationally mixed areas." These rights were guaranteed by the constitution and further elaborated in various laws. The most important of these included the right to use their native language where Slovenian and the minority language had equal status in nationally mixed territories, the free use of national symbols, the establishment of autonomous organizations and institutions, the development of their own culture, education in their own language, and the pursuit of cooperation with their homelands. The constitution placed a financial obligation on the republic to support the implementation of these rights. Both minorities were entitled to "self-governing national communities" that represented their interests through municipal assembly councils. Furthermore, both minorities had the right to direct representation in the National Assembly; each community obtained a permanent seat in parliament without having to contend with the system of proportional representation.[18]

When Slovenia gained independence in 1991, everyone who was a permanent resident and was living in the country at the time was entitled to citizenship. The immigrant population that obtained citizenship represented about 10% of the total population. There were some calls from nationalistic parties to change the law and reconsider citizenship granted to non-ethnic Slovenes, and opinion polls showed reasonably high public support for a more restrictive policy. New restrictions on naturalization and citizenship came into force in April 1993, when the government instituted a supplemental requirement within Article 40 of the citizenship law.

Henceforth, people applying for citizenship needed to furnish proof of the termination of any other citizenship.[19] This stipulation was evidently aimed at people seeking to avoid difficult economic, military, or political conditions in their home republic by assuming Slovenian citizenship as a temporary or permanent measure. Such moves barely masked the fact that Slovenes were fearful of the effects of continued mass immigration. There was criticism that the discretionary powers of the administrative bodies in conferring citizenship were too wide and that little possibility existed for appeal against negative decisions.[20]

Polls on ethnic relations in Slovenia revealed that a majority of respondents felt threatened by the influx of immigrant workers and many criticized the government's liberal legislation. There was resentment that foreigners were taking jobs away from Slovenes, especially at a time when Slovenia was experiencing high rates of unemployment. A lingering anxiety also existed that these workers could be exploited politically by Belgrade or Zagreb, possibly providing an excuse for intervention in Slovenia's internal affairs. As a result of these concerns, 23.9% of those polled argued that immigrants should not be allowed to establish their own organizations, and 45.8% felt that immigrants should only be permitted to form cultural associations and not political parties.[21]

Slovenia's treatment of its ethnic minorities also had a bearing on its foreign relations. One case in point was Ljubljana's relationship with Croatia. Slovenia disallowed many Croatian and Bosnian refugees from remaining in the country, instead forcing many to choose between returning to Croatia or moving on to Germany. The nationalist government in Croatia contended that it was betrayed by Slovenia, which refused to carry more of the refugee burden at a time when Croatia was flooded with refugees from the Bosnian war in addition to its simmering conflict with rebel Serbs. Zagreb was also perturbed by the fact that Croat residents in Slovenia were denied the constitutional status that was accorded to Italians and Hungarians. As Croatian President Tudjman increasingly adopted a siege mentality, neighboring Slovenia was portrayed in collaborationist terms, as a treacherous former ally. Various disputes over fishing rights off the Istrian peninsula, land-border delineations, and foreign-policy objectives became symptomatic of the gulf between two erstwhile anti-federalist allies who proved unable to conclude a friendship treaty throughout the 1990s.[22]

Slovenia was one of the wealthiest of the former Yugoslav republics, with a manageable foreign debt. By the late 1990s, over 60% of its trade was with EU member-states. One of the most industrialized and economically advanced of the former Yugoslav republics, Slovenia had only 8% of the former Yugoslavia's population but produced 20% of its GDP.[23] It became a haven of political and economic stability among the former Yugoslav republics. Slovenia signed the Central European Free Trade Agreement (CEFTA) on 25 November 1995. The key domestic economic issues included curbing wage increases and reforming the pension structure. As with all other ex-communist states, funds to cover pensions had to be raised and the institutional system needed to be changed.[24]

For most of the 1990s, Slovenia placed some restrictions on foreign direct investment, due to fears that foreigners would purchase the country's valuable assets.[25] The Slovenian parliament amended the constitution to permit foreigners to own property. This removed the last major obstacle to Slovenia's ratifying its agreement of association with the EU. The property issue was politically sensitive because many Slovenes feared that lifting the ban would lead to massive purchases of property by Italians whose families fled Slovenia at the close of World War II. After 1 January 1997, the day the EU associate agreement went into effect, Slovenia allowed Italian citizens who lived in Slovenia for at least three years to reacquire real estate that was nationalized by the Yugoslav government. Fears of Italian irredentism and substantial property claims had significantly receded by this time. Slovenia was hoping to be in the next group of nations admitted into the EU as full members—possibly, by 2003—having met most of the necessary criteria.

NATO membership was another priority for Ljubljana. Slovenia depicted itself as a crossroads between eastern and western Europe and between the Mediterranean and the Baltic.[26] An estimated 66% of Slovenian citizens supported the government's endeavors to join NATO, and Alliance membership became one of the top government priorities.[27] While some members of the opposition remained hesitant about the costs and benefits of EU membership, all the major parties supported NATO entry. Only the nationalist SNP was skeptical and opposed the opening of foreign military bases or placement of nuclear weapons on Slovenian territory.

Throughout the 1990s, Slovenia made strides toward constitutional democracy, market reform, and European assimilation. Indeed, compared to its former Yugoslav neighbors, Slovenia appeared to be an island of stability, prosperity, and democracy. The country developed a competitive multi-party system, and its economic potential steadily increased. However, although Slovenia was a relative success story, analysts contended that it would take several elections to strengthen the foundations of a pluralistic democracy. Like its neighbors, Slovenia was not immune from the dangers of elitist patronage and quasi-authoritarianism, and it needed to pay close attention to fully meeting the criteria for NATO and EU membership.

Alliance policy makers closely monitored such factors as the degree of media freedom, the development of civil democracy and minority rights, as well as the influence of nationalists, populists, and former communist *apparatchiks* in the political process. The extent and transparency of the economic reform program was also under close scrutiny, including the connections between the political elite and the process of denationalization and privatization, the extent of corruption and the role of special interests in the economy, and whether there was genuine market competition or a pervasive system of patronage. The state of civil-military relations also featured prominently in NATO decision making. For instance, the role of the military establishment in security planning, personnel policy, and the political process were closely monitored, as were Slovenia's defense budgets, the size, structure, and potential contribution of the armed forces to Alliance missions, and the development of military and intelligence cooperation.

At NATO's summit in Madrid in May 1997, Alliance leaders excluded Slovenia from the first wave of expansion despite the political and economic progress the country had achieved since gaining independence. Ljubljana met most of the broad criteria for NATO membership, even though it fell short in some details. For example, it had constructed a pluralistic and democratic parliamentary system, restructured its civil-military relations, settled its outstanding disputes with neighbors (aside from some remaining difficulties with Zagreb over access to the Adriatic), and faced no important internal ethnic or territorial disputes.

The Alliance decision raised important questions about Slovenia's foreign policy priorities, including the country's relations with Central Europe and South East Europe. Government critics charged that despite its ambitious policy priorities, Ljubljana was not sufficiently prepared for admission to NATO. Nevertheless, the country was singled out as a prime candidate for the "second wave" of NATO expansion if it continued to pursue political and military reforms. Ljubljana took steps to restructure its military and to cooperate with its neighbors on various international projects including peacekeeping and humanitarian crisis management. On 25 June 1996, Slovenia became the tenth country to gain associate partner status in the Western European Union (WEU), the defense structure of the European Union.

Between 1997 and 1999, Slovenia largely settled its tense relations with both Italy and Croatia. For example, visa-free travel was arranged with Italy and Hungary, while Zagreb and Ljubljana finally agreed to seek international assistance in their border dispute in the Gulf of Piran, on the Adriatic Sea. The two countries also started a joint administration of the Krško nuclear power plant in Slovenia, ownership of which had been a subject of dispute between the two post-Yugoslav governments since they gained independence. The demise of President Tudjman and the election of a new democratic coalition government in Zagreb in January 2000 signaled that most remaining disputes could be quickly resolved.

As in much of Central and Eastern Europe, it would take Slovenia several elections to institutionalize and strengthen the foundations of a pluralistic democracy. However, all the former mono-party communist states needed to ensure that their political and economic development was not sidetracked toward some new form of authoritarianism or elitist patronage. Slovenia's political reforms were not always as deep as they were broad. In particular, the debate over administrative reorganization and the professionalization of the Interior, Justice, Defense, and other ministries preoccupied politicians through the 1990s.

With the questions of national sovereignty and statehood resolved, attention was focused on the shortcomings of internal reform. The ex-communists in both the United List and the Liberal Democrats were charged by their opponents of profiting unfairly from the economic reform process by transferring funds and businesses into the hands of party loyalists. Yugoslav "self-management" was evidently transformed into self-enrichment for a stratum of well-connected bureaucrats through the privatization program. Accusations of corruption and the misuse of state funds figured prominently in election campaigns. A proposed law to ban former communists from office was sharply attacked by President Kučan and other ex-communist officials claiming that the names of individuals who violated human rights under the old regime were well known and there was no need to punish all former officials. Opposition leaders Janez Janša and Lojze Peterle countered that Slovenia needed to firmly break with its communist past.

Slovenia registered one of the healthiest economies and highest living standards in Eastern Europe. Nevertheless, the government had to grapple with a number of negative trends, including a rising budget deficit fueled by a growth in state expenses and increasing unemployment among workers laid off from the unprofitable heavy industrial sector. Slovenia was included with four other Central and East European countries in early negotiations for EU membership. The accord on associate membership of the EU was ratified on 15 July 1997 by the Slovenian parliament, more than one year after it was signed. Slovenia was the only former Yugoslav republic to have such an agreement at that time. The process of negotiation for EU entry formally commenced in March 1998.

POLITICAL PARTIES

Socialists and Social Democrats

United List of Social Democrats (ULSD)
Združena Lista Socialnih Demokratov (ZLSD)

The United List of Social Democrats (ULSD) was formed prior to the December 1992 general election as a coalition of several groups deriving from the former ruling League of Communists and its various fronts. Subsequently, the Democratic Party of Retired People of Slovenia (DPRPS), the Social Democrat Union (SDU), the Social Democratic Renewal Party (SDRP), and the Labor Party of Slovenia (LPS) formally merged into the ULSD in May 1993. Janez Kocijančič became the leader of this new, leftist social democratic coalition.

The United List was part of the first post-independence government elected in December 1992 but abandoned the governing coalition in January 1996 because it would not consent to changes in the pension system that resulted in a drop in pensions. United List leaders distrusted its coalition partner's intention to change the Retirement Act, aimed to save the retirement fund, which was about to collapse. Some observers concluded that this was merely a form of pre-election maneuvering by the ULSD in order to appeal to some 600,000 Slovenian pensioners. It was also a convenient excuse to leave the government after their economics minister Maks Tajnikar was allegedly entangled in suspicious business transactions.

Pressed by the other coalition partners because of these scandals, Prime Minister Janez Drnovšek did not waste the opportunity to make the United List a scapegoat. The moment Minister Tajnikar was asked to resign, the other three United List ministers left. At the end of January 1996, Tajnikar was replaced by Metod Dragonja. Only two of the four coalition partners remained in the government. Andrej Umek and Janez Dular took the offices of minister of science and minister of culture to replace the ULSD ministers.

In the November 1996 elections, almost half a million of the United List's votes came from retired people. The ULSD gained nine parliamentary seats. United List leaders included Janez Kocijančič (president), Cvetka Tinauer (vice president), Borut Pahor (vice president), Vlado Rancigaj (vice president), Dušan Kumer (general secretary), and Miran Potrč (leader of the parliamentary group). Several unions and interest groups were associated with the party, including the Labor Union, the Women's Union, the Youth Organization, and the Seniors' Organization. On 15 March 1997, the party selected a new leadership including Borut Pahor as president, Aurelio Juri and Miloš Pavlica as vice presidents, and Dušan Kumer continuing as the general secretary.

Since 1996, the party has been affiliated with the Socialist International, the largest international organization of socialist, social democratic, and labor parties. The ULSD was also active in the Party of European Socialists (PES), which united similar parties from the countries of the EU.[28]

A few marginal ultra-leftist and communist organizations also continued to operate in Slovenia but without any appreciable public support. They included the National Party of Work (NPW) *(Nacionalna Stranka Dela, NSD)* and the Communist Party of Slovenia (CPS) *(Komunistična Partija Slovenije, GCP)*.

Social Democratic Party of Slovenia (SDPS)
Socialdemokratska Stranka Slovenije (SDS)

The Social Democratic Party of Slovenia (SDPS) was founded by France Tomašič and led by its president Janez Janša, with Barbara Medved as vice president. Other party notables included Jože Pučnik, Ivo Hvalica, and Branko Grims. The SDPS was created in 1987, when workers in the Litostroj plant organized a strike led by France Tomašič who proposed the establishment of the first non-communist party.[29] It subsequently became one of the five Slovenian Spring parties that first pressed for democratic reform and subsequently for full national independence from Yugoslavia.

The SDPS was affiliated with the Socialist International and described itself as a social democratic party in the tradition of European democracy and the "social state." Despite its social democratic label, the SDPS was widely perceived as a right-leaning party primarily because it favored fast-paced market reform and was outspoken about investigating ex-communists over their control of the privatization process. The party was closely linked with its leader Janša, who had made numerous enemies in the ex-communist parties; they subsequently lambasted him as an authoritarian demagogue and extremist. Critics charged that the charismatic Janša had a populist and autocratic disposition.

In the December 1992 elections, the SDPS barely managed to enter parliament because it failed to attract many voters from the left. The party won only 3% of the popular vote and four legislative seats, but subsequently participated in the coalition government led by the Liberal Democratic Party. Following the dismissal of party leader Janez Janša as Slovenian defense minister in March 1994, the SDPS left the government coalition and joined the parliamentary opposition. The party had significant success at the local elections in December 1994 despite Janša's dismissal from his ministerial post and frequent attacks on him in the state media.

After the November 1996 parliamentary elections, the Social Democrats obtained sixteen seats. They remained part of the oppositionist Slovenian Spring Coalition with the People's Party and the Christian Democratic Party until February 1997, when the People's Party decided to leave the opposition grouping and join the new government in a coalition with the Liberal Democrats. Although they were invited to join the government, SDPS leaders asserted that they would leave the opposition only if the Slovenian Spring parties gained a majority in the government; this did not happen.[30]

At the end of November 1996, the presidents of the Slovenian People's Party (SPP), the Slovenian Christian Democrats (SCD), and the SDPS signed an agreement on cooperation among the Slovenian Spring parties and coordinating the work of their deputies' clubs in parliament. The agreement specified that the signatories would support harmonized nominations for the parliamentary speaker and deputy speaker, the Prime Minister–designate, the government, and the presidents and members of parliamentary working committees.[31]

The parties discussed the formation of a stable coalition. The People's Party agreed to enter the coalition on the condition that Marjan Podobnik obtain the position of temporary Prime Minister until the next elections.[32] In September 1997, Janša developed the idea that the Social Democrats and the Christian Democrats needed to establish an effective political representation of the Slovenian Spring that could attain a relative majority even without the People's Party. This would mean that the alliance would be able to stand in elections with one candidate list where the majority system was used, whereas in a proportional system the allied parties would oblige themselves to be together either in government or in opposition.[33]

Coalition Slovenia was eventually formed in the spring of 2000 and included the People's Party. The three parties gained a majority in parliament and the right to nominate a new Prime Minister and cabinet. Under the premiership of Andrej Bajuk, Janša once again became Slovenia's defense minister with the installation of the new government in May 2000. In the October 2000 general elections, the SDPS came in second but managed to muster only 16% of the vote and 14 seats in parliament. The party returned to opposition politics.

Party of Democratic Reform (PDR)
Stranka Demokratskih Reform (SDR)

The leadership of the Party of Democratic Reform (PDR) included president Peter Bekeš and Ciril Ribičič. The PDR emerged in February 1990 from the ashes of the League of Communists of Slovenia (LCS). The parent party had long exhibited a Euro-communist posture with a commitment to internal democracy. Milan Kučan, the LCS's most prominent figure since 1986, became increasingly opposed to the federal authorities in Belgrade over the question of Yugoslav decentralization. Elected president of the republic as the party's candidate in April 1990, Kučan stood as a nominal independent in December 1992, winning reelection with 64% of the vote. Tied for second place in the National Assembly elected in April 1990, the PDR did not gain seats in parliament following the November 1996 general elections, and in effect the party expired soon afterwards.

Other small and uninfluential social democratic parties included the Labor Party of Slovenia (LPS) (*Delavska Stranka Slovenije*, DSS) and the Socialist Party of Slovenia (SPS) (*Socialistièna Stranka Slovenije*, SSS).

Liberals

Liberal Democracy of Slovenia (LDS)
Liberalna Demokracija Slovenije (LDS)

The Liberal Democracy of Slovenia (LDS) was led by Janez Drnovšek, the country's prime minister for most of the 1990s and party president, and by Igor Bavčar, the vice president. The LDS was formed on 12 March 1994 in Bled, through the merger of the Liberal Democratic Party led by Drnovšek and several smaller groupings, including a faction of the Democratic Party (with three deputies), the Green Ecological Social Party (five deputies), and the Socialist Party of Slovenia led by Viktor Žakelj. Their merger increased the number of LDS representatives in the National Assembly. Two deputies subsequently withdrew from the party. The recreated LDS was backed by 30 out of 90 deputies in parliament. Of the three newcomers into the LDS only the Socialist Party, descended from the front organization of the communist era, was not represented in the parliament elected in December 1992.

The original Liberal Democratic Party (LDP) descended from the former Federation of Socialist Youth of Slovenia (FSYS) and was formally launched in November 1990. According to some analysts, unlike most communist youth organizations the Federation had been a substantially independent formation supportive of liberal values such as individual rights and freedoms since the early 1980s. Having been among the runners-up in the 1990 election, the LDS became the strongest parliamentary party in the 1992 balloting, gaining 22 seats, with its leader Drnovšek becoming Prime Minister. The LDS was considered a center-left party with liberal leanings. After the November 1996 parliamentary elections, having captured 25 seats, Drnovšek was designated to form a new government that would include the LDS, the United List, the National Party, and two representatives of the Italian and Hungarian minority. But talks on a broader coalition government failed, as Drnovšek did not want to accept a cabinet in which Slovenian Spring ministers would occupy half of the cabinet seats. As a result, he initially proposed a leftist government composed of the LDS, the United List, and the Democratic Union of Pensioners.

In February 1997, the LDS finally formed a government coalition with the People's Party. The coalition agreement between the two parties primarily served to calm the People's Party's voter base, which felt that too many compromises were being arranged with ex-communists. The agreement included detailed program goals as well as specifics on relations among the coalition partners.[34] The Minister of Labor, Family, and Social Welfare, Tone Rop, and Igor Bavčar shared the vice president position in the party while Drnovšek remained party leader.[35]

After a number of ministerial resignations, including that of Foreign Minister Zoran Thaler in July 1997, the coalition looked increasingly fragile and vulnerable.[36] It finally collapsed in April 2000 when the People's Party withdrew and formed a new provisional coalition government with the Social Democrats and the Christian Democrats.[37] The Liberal Democrats were left outside of government for the first time since Slovenia gained its independence. However, in the October 2000 general elections, the LDS acquired 36% of the popular vote and captured 34 parliamentary seats. Party leader Drnovšek established a new coalition government.

Democratic Party of Slovenia (DPS)
Demokratična Stranka Slovenije (DSS)

The Democratic Party of Slovenia (DPS) was led by its president, Tone Peršak. It was descended from the Slovene Democratic League (SDL), which registered as a party in March 1990. One of the strongest supporters of Slovenian secession from Yugoslavia, the DPS participated in the April 1990 republican elections as a member of the opposition DEMOS coalition. It won six seats in the parliament in November 1992, after which it absorbed a small social democratic grouping to become the DPS. In March 1994, three DPS deputies joined the restructured Liberal Democracy of Slovenia. Of the other three, two deputies opposed the dissolution of the DPS and one became an independent. The DPS did not gain any parliamentary seats following the November 1996 elections and subsequently vanished from the political scene.

Several other essentially liberal or centrist parties were active in the country during the 1990s. They included the Slovenian Entrepreneurial Party (SEP) *(Slovenska Obrtno Podjetniška Stranka, SOPS)*, the Liberal Party (LP) *(Liberalna Stranka/ Slovenski Liberalci, LS)*, the Civil Initiative for Slovenia (CIS) *(Civilna Iniciativa za Slovenijo, CIS)*, and the Republicans of Slovenia (RS) *(Republikanci Slovenije, RS)*.

Christian Democrats

Slovenian Christian Democrats (SCD)
Slovenski Krščanski Demokrati (SKD)

The Slovenian Christian Democrats' (SCD) leaders included president Lojze Peterle; Ivan Bizjak; Ignac Polajnar, the parliamentary leader; and Vida Čadonič-Špelič, the party's secretary-general. In the late 1980s, the SCD formed one of the first independent democratic parties in the country. It grew into the second largest party, with its leaders coming predominantly from Catholic circles. The party proceeded to strengthen its international ties with other European Christian democratic parties. The SCD's major policy planks included the privatization of property, the creation of a market economy, a commitment to the European Union, and security within NATO and the WEU. The party supported increasing competitiveness, a decrease in bureaucratic red tape in business, an expansion of foreign markets, a reasonable policy toward foreign investment, support of family farms, greater individual responsibility, and private initiative. It also had links with the Catholic Church and supported the clergy's calls for religious instruction in public schools and a ban on abortion.

The SCD leader Peterle resigned as foreign minister in November 1994, when the party became embroiled in a political dispute with its coalition partner, the Liberal Democrats. Prime Minister Drnovšek and the LDS accused Peterle of betraying Slovenia and selling its land during negotiations with Italy over the EU Agreement. In addition, coalition deputies were voting differently in parliament than they had agreed to in their initial meetings. According to Peterle, the absence of a reasonable "political culture" in the country also contributed to his decision. Peterle stayed on in his post an extra month in order to prepare the *Aquilea* document between Italy and Slovenia, so that Italy would open the way for Slovenia to sign the EU Agreement. Other SCD ministers resigned from the cabinet, including interior minister Andrej Šter, culture minister Janez Dular, and agriculture minister Jože Osterc.[38]

The party obtained ten seats in the November 1996 parliamentary elections. The elections led to an altered picture in parliament. The number of parties was reduced from ten to seven, and both coalition parties faced some decline in public support at the ballot box. The Christian Democrats found themselves in a difficult situation as the party was basically appealing to the same electorate as the other major opposition parties while at the same time having served as the junior partner in a government dominated by leftist parties. The vote in the 1996 general elections became a vote against the outgoing government. The SCD was subject to attacks from both left and right, from former and current political partners. However, the three Slovenian Spring formations—the People's Party, the Social Democrats, and the SCD—increased their total score from 31 to 45 seats in the 90-seat house. This was the highest score that the democratic forces had achieved since Slovenia attained independence. Even the first democratic elections in April 1990 assembled a democratic majority in only two out of the three chambers that constituted parliament at that time.[39]

Simultaneously with the search for a joint presidential candidate, the Slovenian Spring bloc was also considering the possibility of forming a Christian Social Union.[40] This would involve creating a "party of the relative majority" on the right of the political spectrum, something akin to the 1994 merger of the Liberal Democrats, the Democrats, and the Socialists in Bled. The heads of the Social Democrats and the Christian Democrats, Janez Janša and Lojze Peterle, respectively, discussed the idea but did not reach an agreement. It remained unclear whether such a party, if it materialized, would emerge from a two-party coalition or from some other alliance. Some analysts believed that no one could bring the Christian Democrats and the Social Democrats together because of practical differences between them—for example, when appointing joint councillors or joint candidates in local elections.

Before the November 1996 parliamentary elections, the SCD signed a coalition agreement with the People's Party and the Social Democrats. However, during talks on the new government, SCD deputy Ciril Pucko defected from the SCD parliamentary group and announced that he would give his vote to Prime Minister Drnovšek. After lengthy negotiations, the People's Party decided to follow Pucko and suddenly broke the three-party agreement, forming a coalition with the Liberal Democrats. Meanwhile, the SCD, after being in government for almost six years, opted to remain in opposition.

There was some similarity with several other anticommunist parties in Eastern Europe that led the reform process in the first democratically elected governments and subsequently lost their base of public support. Despite their defeat at the general elections, the SCD congress in June 1997 reelected Peterle as party leader and entrusted him with the renewal of the party. Party documents confirmed that the SCD would remain a mainstream and moderate organization as represented by Peterle.

In April 1999, the SCD joined forces with the governing People's Party, and together they formed a coalition with the Social Democratic Party under the name Coalition Slovenia (*Koalicija Slovenija*). By joining forces, the *troika* gained the majority in parliament and successfully nominated the new independent Prime Minister, Andrej Bajuk.[41] In February 2000, the SCD and the People's Party announced their merger. On 17 April 2000, the new grouping formed a center-right coalition called SPP+SCD–People's Party. The coalition, chaired by France Zagožen, and the Social Democrats, nominated Andrej Bajuk as their joint candidate for Prime Minister. He was formally selected by parliament on 3 May 2000 and served in office with SCD members in the interim government until the parliamentary elections of October 2000. The SPP/SCD coalition only managed to attract 9.5% of the popular vote in the ballot and obtained only nine parliamentary seats.

One other notable Christian Democratic party, the Christian Social Union (CSU) (*Krščansko Socijalna Unija, KSU*), can be mentioned. It was led by chairman Franc Miklavič and founded in early 1995 by Christian activists who claimed that they had a "social conscience." It failed to gain any seats in the November 1996 or the October 2000 parliamentary elections.

Agrarians

Slovenian People's Party (SPP)
Slovenska Ljudska Stranka (SLS)

Claiming descent from the pre-war party of the same name, the Slovenian People's Party (SPP) was founded in May 1988 as the non-political Slovene Peasant League (SPL), which registered as a party in January 1990. Party leaders included President Marjan Podobnik, his brother Janez Podobnik, Ivan Oman, and Marjan Šinkovec. It won eleven general assembly seats in the April 1990 parliamentary elections as a member of the DEMOS opposition and adopted its present name in 1991. In the December 1992 elections, it won ten legislative seats and gained 8.7% of the popular vote.

Originating as a farmers' union, it attracted a broader electorate. Its leaders came from the same Catholic circles as the Christian Democrats. The Slovenian Christian Democrats (SCD) introduced the idea of merging into one party but the SPP refused. The People's Party called itself the authentic center party, claiming that other opposition parties had either moved towards the left or to the right.[42] The SPP was originally a member of the Slovenian Spring coalition with the Social Democrats and Christian Democrats, but left the coalition after the November 1996 elections, when the party gained 19 parliamentary seats and entered the government in a coalition with the Liberal Democrats and the Democratic Party of Pensioners of Slovenia (DPPS). The SPP was intent on joining the government with or without the other Slovenian Spring parties and sought to raise its prestige and influence. This led to some disputes within the party, as some factions were more inclined to cooperate with the Social Democrats and Christian Democrats than with the post-communist formations. However, the party's main committee decided to join the coalition government.

The SPP's principal goals were to move Slovenia towards the "establishment of democratic institutions, building the rule of law, keeping a resolute grip on economic crime, particularly when linked to privatization, building up ties between Slovenes at home and those abroad, and calming down the radical political tensions that have recently increased in Slovenia." At the end of 1999, the SPP decided to unite with the Christian Democrats, and provisionally entitled their coalition SPP+SCD–People's Party. A few months later, in April 2000, the SPP decided to expand the coalition to include the Social Democrats. By recombining the three Slovenian Spring partners, this new formation, entitled Coalition Slovenia *(Koalicija Slovenija)*, obtained a majority in parliament.

According to the Slovenian constitution, the majority party in parliament could choose the Prime Minister. In May 2000, Andrej Bajuk was selected as Prime Minister by the Coalition Slovenia, and the SPP was back in government pending legislative elections in October 2000. The party performed poorly in the fall ballot; in coalition with the Christian Democrats it only managed to attract 9.5% of the popular vote and obtained nine parliamentary seats.

Greens

Greens of Slovenia–Ecological Social Party (GOS-ESP)
Zeleni Slovenije–Ekološko Socialna Stranka (ZS-ESS)

The Greens of Slovenia–Ecological Social Party (GOS-ESP) led by Dušan Puh was formally launched in June 1989. It had been active as a non-political environmentalist group for a number of years. The GOS-ESP was a participant in the democratic, pro-independence coalition DEMOS. In the April 1990 elections the party achieved an unexpected success, gaining 9% of the popular vote and capturing a total of 17 parliamentary seats. All the Green deputies joined the restructured Liberal Democrats in 1994, leaving the parent group without any parliamentary representation. In the November 1992 parliamentary elections, the Greens received only 3.7% of votes, due to various programmatic inconsistencies in the party and the waning influence of ecological issues among the Slovenian public. It captured only 5 legislative seats. The party was administratively erased from the register of Slovenian parties, which caused confusion among voters about whether the party still existed. This contributed to the party's poor showing in subsequent general and local elections.

Other environment-focused Slovenian organizations included the Greens–Ecological Social Party (G-ESP), led by Peter Tancig, and the Green Alternative of Slovenia (GAS) *(Zelena Alternativa Slovenije, ZAS)*, led by Metka

Filipič. The G-ESP and the GAS were due to run together in the parliamentary elections in October 2000 without forming a coalition, although they did reportedly plan to merge soon after the balloting.

Nationalists

Democratic Opposition of Slovenia (DOS)
Demokratska Opozicija Slovenije (DEMOS)

Founded in December 1989, Democratic Opposition of Slovenia (DOS), popularly known as DEMOS, was conceived of as a credible alternative to the ruling Communist League. Its original members included the Slovenian Democratic Alliance (SDA), the Social Democratic Alliance of Slovenia (SDAS), and the Slovenian Christian Democrats (SCD). In January 1990, two more parties, the Slovenian Farmers' Alliance (SFA) and the Greens of Slovenia (GS), joined the coalition, followed by the Liberal Party (LP). In the general elections of April 1990, the DEMOS coalition captured 47 of 80 seats in the Sociopolitical Chamber of the National Assembly. The six-party coalition, made up of leftist, centrist, and rightist parties, formed the government that gained independence for Slovenia.

The DEMOS parties had canvassed in favor of market reform, the abolition of social ownership, and Slovenia's rapid and deeper involvement in the political, economic, and cultural life of Western Europe. The main issue in the 1990 elections, however, was the achievement of national sovereignty. DEMOS captured strong public support by promising that it would quickly achieve Slovenia's independence. In this sense, DEMOS can be defined as a pro-independence, moderate nationalist formation. Statehood for Slovenia was envisaged as an important starting point for full political freedom, economic prosperity, and European integration.

The DEMOS platform was partially shaped by the more vehemently pro-independence members of the coalition. The Slovenian Democratic Alliance (SDA) in particular argued for the primacy of Slovenia's national interests and strongly advocated the republic's withdrawal from all federal Yugoslav structures that were perceived as draining Slovenia's resources and subverting its national identity. The SDA found common cause with the Slovenian Farmers' Alliance, which campaigned for the imposition of tougher conditions for gaining Slovenian citizenship and a reduction in the privileges of immigrants from other republics. However, Slovenia's first elections were generally devoid of radical nationalist competition or rhetoric. Following the April 1990 elections, the DEMOS coalition unraveled and several distinct parties emerged spanning a traditional political spectrum; the majority espoused a reasonably moderate agenda. They included Social Democrats, Socialists, Agrarians, Greens, Liberals, Liberal Democrats, and Christian Democrats.[43]

On 30 December 1991, DEMOS virtually expired. In October 1991, the influential Democratic Alliance had split off and seriously weakened the coalition. Moreover, each of the constituent parties developed their own political identities, leadership structures, and public constituencies and had little need for an umbrella movement. Public criticism of the Christian Democrat Prime Minister Lojze Peterle also intensified over economic issues, thus further weakening the coalition. DEMOS, as a distinct political entity, only gained 9,143 votes in the elections on 6 December 1992, or 0.77% of the popular vote, and failed to gain any parliamentary seats. The formation subsequently vanished from the political scene.

Slovenian National Party (SNP)
Slovenska Nacionalna Stranka (SNS)

Led by its president Zmago Jelinčič and secretary-general Jure Jesenko, the Slovenian National Party (SNP) was founded in Ljubljana in April 1991 as an offshoot of the former Slovenian Farmers' Alliance. (Jelinčič was previously the head of the Farmers' Alliance.) The SNP criticized the DEMOS government and most of its component parties for vacillating on the question of national independence, and sought to portray itself as the first genuinely Slovene party. It excluded non-Slovenes and former members of the communist party, because it allegedly did not want its national mission diluted by individuals whose loyalties to Slovenia were questionable. The party publicly stated that the League of Communists of Slovenia (LCS) was an implacable enemy of the Slovenian nation. It thereby advocated that individuals in positions of authority who were formerly members of the LCS should be ferreted out and dismissed from public life. Indeed, in order to undermine their democratic opponents, SNP leaders argued that the DEMOS coalition was a hiding place for many communists endeavoring to salvage their political careers.

Jelinčič's vision for his country was of a pure "Slovenia for the Slovenes," an essentially ultra-nationalist platform. According to him, the benefits of the state should first and foremost be made available to ethnic Slovenes. Jelinčič contended, for instance, that guest workers should not be allowed to take jobs away from Slovenian citizens; indeed, according to him, for as long as there was unemployment in Slovenia, guest workers should be sent home. The SNP was adamant about not accepting any more refugees into the country, especially as it claimed that there were many citizens who were underfed and homeless. The SNP asserted that it would abolish Article 40 of the law on citizenship and make the naturalization process more restrictive. In Jelinčič's calculations, immigrants who wanted to acquire citizenship should reside in Slovenia for at least twenty years, and have absolute mastery of the language and complete financial independence. In effect, the SNP advocated the mass deportation of Bosnian and Albanian refugees.

The SNP painted an apocalyptic vision of the country's future if migration were not halted. Claiming there were already 100,000 refugees in the country by the early 1990s, Jelinčič asserted that the figure could quickly multiply unless Ljubljana took stringent measures to halt the influx. Refugees would evidently mushroom into a political problem, claiming minority rights and state funds for their cultural and religious pursuits. If unchecked these demands would rapidly escalate and provoke serious inter-communal hostilities and a growing crime wave. Both the SNP and the post-communist parties also attacked the West for failing to provide appropriate refugee assistance, using the issue in their sometimes less-than-subtle anti-Western attacks.

In the foreign policy arena, Jelinčič sharply criticized the Ljubljana administration for accepting the current borders with Croatia and Italy, which the SNP considered to be unjust. He asserted that the border with Croatia should be on the Mirna River, not on the Dragonja, while claiming that Italy had stolen the border belt with Slovenia. The party also voiced pretensions to the Carinthian region of Austria, inhabited by a sizable Slovenian minority. In addition, Jelinčič complained about the status of Istria: in SNP estimations, the peninsula should be reunited and attain autonomy within the Slovenian state. The SNP claimed that if a referendum were to be held in the area, the majority of Istrians would choose Slovenia over Croatia. Jelinčič's accusations against Zagreb and an alleged Vatican-Croatian conspiracy to absorb Slovenia led some observers to believe that the SNP may have been acting in the interests of Belgrade in the early 1990s to deepen the Croatian-Slovenian rupture. In sum, the SNP promulgated a "Great Slovenia" program and a policy of territorial expansion vis-à-vis Italy, Austria, and Croatia.

The SNP emerged as a more important player on the Slovenian political scene during the December 1992 elections, when it entered parliament as the fourth strongest party. Its main source of popularity was opposition to the influx of Bosnian refugees, who were estimated to make up nearly 4% of Slovenia's population by the close of 1992. According to post-election assessments, the SNP gained considerable support among citizens aged under 25, as well as among people living along the Italian-Austrian border, a highly developed area with a strong tourism base. In February 1993, the SNP split into two factions, each retaining six seats in parliament. After a prolonged legal dispute for possession of the SNP name, the breakaway, more xenophobic wing led by Marjan Stanid and Sašo Lap named itself the National Party of Slovenia (NPS).[44]

The SNP remained an essentially radical nationalist grouping that stood for a militarily strong and sovereign Slovenia and focused on the preservation and restoration of the country's cultural heritage. It won 10% of the vote and 12 lower house seats in December 1992 but entered a fissiparous phase in 1993 after party leader Jelinčič was accused of being a federal Yugoslav agent. Also contributing to the party's disunity were disclosures that prominent members were listed in police files as informers in the communist era. The party was viewed by its critics as a United List affiliate that played on nationalistic and xenophobic tendencies in Slovenian politics.

As a result of internal party scandals, five of its assemblymen, led by Sašo Lap, formed an "independent SNS Deputy Group," three others launched a breakaway Slovenian National Right (SNR), and one withdrew to become an independent. The SNP became the smallest party in parliament following the November 1996 elections, with four Assembly seats out of its original twelve. Jelinčič attempted to steer the party in a more leftist direction by supporting anti-clericalism and a prohibition on foreigners' purchasing of land in Slovenia, but he failed to garner any substantial support.[45] In the October 2000 elections, the SNP captured only 4% of the vote and four parliamentary seats.

Slovenian Alliance (SA)
Slovenska Zveza (SZ)

In early 1993, a new initiative, Slovenian Alliance (SA), was launched among Slovenia's marginal radical rightist groupings to forge a more effective union. Its initiator Aleš Žužek sought to capitalize on public trepidation over the refugee problem and over fears of growing unemployment. The SA's essentially xenophobic program was avowedly based on similar populist solutions espoused by radical right forces in Germany and France. Žužek underscored that the major goal of the Alliance was an "ethnically pure" Slovenia in which all immigrants and refugees would be returned to their original homelands. The Alliance issued a tentative "Plan for Returning Immigrants and Refugees as a final solution to the foreigner question." The planned return would encompass all residents who were not of Slovenian descent and who moved to Slovenia after 1945. To gain public support for its initiatives, the party planned to hold a referendum, offering the country a clear choice between becoming an economically successful European state or a "Balkan charitable institution." The SA also propounded the idea of a militarily strong Slovenia that would defend the "ethnic rights" of Slovenian minorities in Italy, Austria, Hungary, and Croatia. The SA leadership also proposed the possibility of border adjustments with neighbors, in Slovenia's favor.[46]

National Democratic Party (NDP)
Narodna Demokratska Stranka (NDS)

Led by its president, Marjan Vidmar, the National Democratic Party (NDP) was formed in 1994 by a militant splinter group of the SCD (Slovenian Christian Democrats). It did not obtain any parliamentary seats after the November 1996 general elections and was considered a marginal phenomenon in Slovenian politics. Other marginal ultra-nationalist formations formed during the 1990s included the Slovenian National Right (SNR), the neo-fascist National Social League of Slovenia (NSLS), headed by Matjaž Gerlanc, and the Slovenian Falcons (SF) *(Slovenski Sokoli, SS).*

Ethnic Minority and Religious Parties

Italian Union for Istria and Rijeka (IUIR)
Italijanska Zveza za Istro in Reko (IZIR)

The Italian Union for Istria and Rijeka (IUIR) was established during 1989, before the breakup of Yugoslavia, to defend the interests of the Italian population in Slovenia and Croatia. Following the attainment of independence by these two states, the IUIR tried to maintain one organization despite the new frontier. After the December 1992 elections, Roberto Battelli became the parliamentary representative of the Italian community. In addition, the IUIR elected councillors in each local commune inhabited by the Italian minority. Although generally satisfied with the status of the minority in Slovenia, Battelli located several problem areas, including emigration by young people, lack of Italian teachers in local schools, and insufficient legislation on minority rights. For instance, the IUIR sought more specific laws to regulate the status of minorities at local levels.

Nonetheless, Italian activists expressed more concern about the minority's status in Croatia, where Italians purportedly did not benefit from official bilingualism and other minority rights. Battelli believed that interstate agreements between Rome and Ljubljana regulating the position of minorities in both countries would greatly help the Italian minority. Reportedly, some of the estimated 200,000 Italians who emigrated from Istria and Rijeka after World War II were interested in buying back their property. Their organizations were believed to have some influence on Italian politics, but few activists other than a small minority of neo-fascists were demanding outright border changes with Slovenia or Croatia.

Interest Community of the Hungarian Minority (ICHM)
Interesna Skupnost Madžarske Manjšine (ISMM)

Following the December 1992 elections, the Interest Community of the Hungarian Minority (ICHM) activist Marija Pozsonec became the Hungarian deputy to the Slovenian parliament according to stipulations for automatic Magyar and Italian representation. The Community was not a specifically political organization but simply a representative body inherited from the former communist self-management structures that once included committees for local minorities. It published the weekly *Népújság* (People's Paper). Hungarian spokesmen contended that they encountered few problems in Slovenia and maintained good contacts with Hungary. In addition, they organized the delivery of aid to the Magyar minority in Serbian Vojvodina; ironically, economic and political assistance formerly flowed in the opposite direction. A Bosniak party was also established in the early 1990s, linked with the major Muslim party in Bosnia-Herzegovina and known as the Party of Democratic Action of Slovenia (PDAS) *(Stranka Demokratske Akcije Slovenije, SDAS)*.

Regionalists

A number of regionalist organizations were established in Slovenia during the 1990s, focusing on the specific problems of their respective regions and campaigning for governmental support. They included the Union for the Primorska Region (UPR) *(Zveza za Primorsko, ZZP)*; the Union for Progress of Radeče and the Radeče Region (UPRRR) *(Zveza za Napredek Radeč in Radeškega Območja, ZNRRO)*; the Country Party of Stajerska (CPS) *(Deželna Stranka Štajerske, DSS)*; the Union for Ljubljana (UL) *(Zveza za Ljubljano, ZZL)*; the Union for Gorenjska (UG) *(Zveza za Gorenjsko, ZZG)*; the Independent List for Maribor (ILM) *(Neodvisna Lista za Maribor, NLM)*; and the Istrian Democratic Convention (IDC) *(Istrski Demokratski Zbor–Dieta Democratica Istriana, IDZ-DDI)*.

Independents and Others

Democratic Party of Pensioners of Slovenia (DPPS)
Demokratska Stranka Upokojencev Slovenije (DeSUS)

The Democratic Party of Pensioners of Slovenia (DPPS) was established specifically to support the growing community of elderly in Slovenia. The party defended the interests of pensioners by favoring a much-needed pension reform since the post-independence pensions were not privatized.[47] Anton Delak was head of the party's parliamentary caucus, which was affiliated with the United List. The DPPS entered the government coalition with the Liberal Democrats and the People's Party, having gained five seats in parliament following the general elections of November 1996. The party's leadership decided unanimously at its presidency session on 13 November 1996 that it would support the candidacy of Janez Drnovšek for prime minister. This refuted a rumor that some DPPS deputies supported a prime minister designate from the Slovenian Spring parties. The DPPS then entered in February 1997 the coalition government, with the Liberal Democrats and the People's Party. In the October 2000 general elections, the DPPS gained 5% of the vote and captured four parliamentary seats. It joined the new coalition government led by the Liberal Democrats and Premier Drnovšek.

A rival pensioners' organization, reportedly with more nationalist leanings, was also established in the early 1990s. It styled itself as the Patriotic Party of

Retired People–League for Slovenia (PPRP-LS) *(Domoljubna Enotna Upokojenska Stranka–Liga za Slovenijo, DEUS-LZS)*, but had no visible public impact.

POLITICAL DATA

Name of State: Republic of Slovenia *(Republika Slovenija)*
Form of Government: Parliamentary democracy
Structure of Legislature: Unicameral National Assembly *(Državni Zbor)*
Size of Territory: 7,820 square miles
Size of Population: 1,970,570 (1999)

Composition of Population

Ethnic Group	Number	% of Population
Slovenes	1,727,018	87.84
Croats	54,212	2.76
Serbs	47,911	2.44
Muslims	26,842	1.37
Yugoslavs	12,307	0.63
Hungarians	8,503	0.43
Macedonians	4,443	0.23
Montenegrins	4,396	0.22
Albanians	3,629	0.18
Italians	3,064	0.16
Romas	2,293	0.12
Regional affiliation	5,254	0.27
Others	3,514	0.18
Unspecified	9,011	0.46
Unknown	53,589	2.73
Total minorities	238,968	12.16
Total population	1,965,986	100.00

Source: Slovenski Almanah 93, Delo Novice, Ljubljana, December 1992.

ELECTION RESULTS

Presidential Election, 23 November 1997

Turnout: 68.29%

Candidate	Votes	% of Vote
Milan Kučan	575,169	55.57
Janez Podobnik	190,647	18.42
Jožef Bernik	97,221	9.39

Marian Cerar	73,127	7.07
Marjan Poljšak	33,322	3.22
Total	969,486	94.00

Source: Radio Slovenia Network, Ljubljana, 2 December 1997, in *FBIS-EEU-97–336*, 7 December 1997; *Delo*, Ljubljana, 30 November 1997, in *FBIS-EEU-97–334*, 2 December 1997; http://www.sigov.si/cgi-bin/spl/elections/preds97/candidates.htm; and http://www.sigov.si/cgi-bin/spl/elections/preds97/erez_sl.htm?language=csz.

Presidential Election, 6 December 1992

Turnout: 85.84%

Candidate	Votes	% of Vote
Milan Kučan	793,851	63.90
Ivan Nizjak	262,847	21.60
Jelko Kacin	90,711	7.30
Stanislav Buser	24,042	1.94
Darja Lavtičar Bebler	22,681	1.83
Alenka Slana	21,603	1.74
Ljubo Sirc	18,774	1.51
France Tomašič	7,849	0.30
Total	1,242,358	100.00

Presidential Election, 22 April 1990

Turnout: 73.5%

Candidate	Votes	% of Vote
Milan Kučan	611,073	44.30
Joze Pučnik	362,781	26.30
Ivan Kramberger	260,706	18.90
Marko Demšar	144,836	10.50
Total	1,379,396	100.00

Parliamentary Elections, 15 October 2000

Turnout: 70.14%

Party/Coalition	Votes	% of Vote	Seats
Liberal Democratic Party	390,306	36.26	34
Social Democratic Party	170,228	15.81	14
United List of Social Democrats	130,079	12.08	11
Slovenian People's Party/Slovenian Christian Democrats	102,691	9.54	9
New Slovenia/People's Christian Party	93,247	8.66	8
Democratic Party of Pensioners	55,694	5.17	4
Slovenian National Party	47,214	4.39	4

Party of Young People (SMS)	46,674	4.34	4
Total	1,036,133	96.25	88

Parliamentary Elections, 10 November 1996

Turnout: 73.7%

Party/Coalition	Vote	% of Vote	Seats
Liberal Democratic Party	288,783	27.01	25
Slovenian People's Party	207,186	19.38	19
Social Democratic Party	172,470	16.13	16
Slovenian Christian Democrats	102,852	9.62	10
United List of Social Democrats	96,597	9.03	9
Democratic Party of Pensioners	46,152	4.32	5
Slovenian National Party	34,422	3.22	4
Hungarian and Italian Minorities	—	—	2
Democratic Party of Slovenia	28,624	2.68	—
Green Party of Slovenia	18,853	1.76	—
Slovenian Craftsmen/ Entrepreneurial Party	12,335	1.15	—
Slovenian Forum	11,383	1.06	—
Liberal Party	7,972	0.75	—
National Labor Party	5,827	0.54	—
Green Alternative of Slovenia	5,602	0.52	—
Republican Association of Slovenia	5,071	0.47	—
Communist Party of Slovenia	5,027	0.47	—
Christian Social Union	4,767	0.45	—
Slovenian National Right Party	3,327	0.31	—
Patriotic Unionist Party of Retirees/ League for Slovenia	2,025	0.19	—
The New Party	1,104	0.10	—
Forward Slovenia	886	0.08	—
Party for the Equality of Regions	541	0.05	—
Total	1,061,806	99.29	90

Source: Radio Slovenia Network, Ljubljana, 18 November 1996, in FBIS-EEU-96–224, 20 November 1996.

Parliamentary Elections, 6 December 1992

Turnout: 85.6%

Party/Coalition	Votes	% of Vote	Seats
Liberal Democratic Party	278,851	23.46	22
Christian Democratic Party	172,424	14.51	15
United List of Social Democrats	161,349	13.58	14

Slovenian National Party	119,091	10.02	12
Slovenian People's Party	103,300	8.69	10
Democratic Party of Slovenia	59,487	5.01	6
Greens of Slovenia	44,019	3.70	5
Social Democratic Party	39,675	3.34	4
Socialist Party	32,696	2.75	—
National Democrats and Slovenian Party	25,852	2.18	—
Liberal Party	19,069	2.01	—
Slovenian Handicraft and Business Party	18,965	1.60	—
Liberal Democratic Party of Slovenia	16,892	1.42	—
Party of Independence	16,178	1.36	—
Independent candidates	11,850	1.00	2
Total	1,119,698	94.63	90

Parliamentary Elections, 8 April 1990

Turnout: 77%

Party/Coalition	Votes	% of Vote	Seats
DEMOS coalition	834,536	55	124
Slovenian People's Party			(34)
Slovenian Christian Democrats			(26)
Slovenian Democratic Union			(25)
Social Democratic Party of Slovenia			(18)
Greens of Slovenia			(17)
Liberal Party			(4)
Unaffiliated			3
Liberal Democratic Party	242,774	16	40
Party of Democratic Renewal	257,947	17	35
Alliance of Socialists	182,080	12	12
Total	1,517,338	100	214

Parliamentary Elections, Sociopolitical Chamber, 8 April 1990

Party/Coalition	Votes	% of Vote	Seats
Party of Democratic Reform	186,928	17.3	14
Liberal Democrats	156,843	14.5	12
Slovenian Christian Democrats	140,403	13.0	11
Slovenian People's Party	135,808	12.6	11
Democratic Party of Slovenia	102,931	9.5	8
Greens of Slovenia	95,640	8.9	8
Social Democratic Party	79,951	7.4	6
Socialist Party of Slovenia	58,082	5.4	5
Liberal Party	38,269	3.5	3
Total	994,855	92.0	78

NOTES

1. For background histories on Slovenia see Francis Dvornik, *The Slavs in European History and Civilization*, New Brunswick: Rutgers University Press, 1962; R.W. Seton-Watson, *The Southern Slav Question and the Habsburg Monarchy*, London: Constable, 1977; Fred Singleton, *A Short History of the Yugoslav Peoples*, Cambridge: Cambridge University Press, 1985; Ivo Banac, *The National Question in Yugoslavia: Origins, History, Politics*, Ithaca: Cornell University Press, 1984; Carole Rogel, *The Slovenes and Yugoslavism, 1890–1914*, New York: East European Monographs, 1977; Peter Vodopivec, "Slovenes and Yugoslavia, 1918–1991," *East European Politics and Society*, No. 6 (3), 1992, pp. 230–241; and Peter Vodopivec, "Slovenes in the Habsburg Empire or Monarchy," *Nationalities Papers*, No. 21, 1993, pp. 159–170.

2. Consult Carole Rogel, "In the Beginning: The Slovenes from the Seventh Century to 1945," in Jill Benderly and Evan Kraft (Eds.), *Independent Slovenia: Origins, Movements, Prospects*, New York: St. Martin's Press, 1994, pp. 3–21.

3. See Lenard J. Cohen, *Broken Bonds: The Disintegration of Yugoslavia*, Boulder: Westview Press, 1993, p. 13–17.

4. See Sabrina Petra Ramet, "Democratization in Slovenia-the Second Stage," in Karen Dawisha and Bruce Parrott, (Eds.), *Politics, Power, and the Struggle for Democracy in South-East Europe*, Cambridge, UK: Cambridge University Press, 1997, pp. 189–217.

5. Dušan Nečak, "A Chronology of the Decay of Tito's Yugoslavia 1980–1991," *Nationalities Papers*, Vol. 21, No. 1, Spring 1993.

6. *Danas*, Zagreb, 29 November 1988; *Delo*, Ljubljana, 26 July 1988.

7. Sabrina P. Ramet, *Nationalism and Federalism in Yugoslavia 1962–1991*, 2nd Edition, Bloomington: Indiana University Press, 1992, p. 211.

8. Speech by Dušan Šinigoj, president of the Slovenian Executive Council, to the Republican Assembly, 7 February 1990.

9. For information on the Slovenian elections, consult the National Republican Institute for International Affairs, *The 1990 Elections in the Republic of Yugoslavia*, Washington, DC, 1991.

10. V. Zagorac, "Everything—Only Not a Federation," *Večernji List*, Zagreb, 18 September 1990, in Federal Broadcast Information Service/Joint Publications Research Service, *Daily Report: East Europe*, FBIS-EEU-90–185, 24 September 1990.

11. Jana Taskar, "Only an Independent Slovenia or a Confederate Union," *Delo*, Ljubljana, 4 October 1990, in *FBIS-EEU-90–197*, 11 October 1990; interview with Slovenian Democratic Alliance president Jože Pučnik by Hans-Henning Scharsach, "Slovenia Remains Sovereign Even If It Cooperates with Belgrade," *Kurier*, Vienna, 7 October 1990, in *FBIS-EEU-90–197*, 11 October 1990; and the interview with Slovenian prime minister Lojze Peterle by Rudolf Gruber, "Looking for Franz Ferdinand," *Profil*, Vienna, 30 July 1990, in *FBIS-EEU-90–148*, 1 August 1990.

12. Interview with Slovenian foreign affairs minister Dimitrij Rupel by B. Cukov and M. Gregorič, "We Will Not Enter Europe Through Belgrade," *Borba*, Belgrade, 11 June 1990, in *FBIS-EEU-90–121*, 22 June 1990; Valentin Hribar, "Slovenes and European Transnationality," in *The Case of Slovenia*, Ljubljana: Nova Revija, 1991.

13. See *The Slovene Elections: A Report on the December 6, 1992, Presidential and Parliamentary Elections in Slovenia*, The Libra Institute, Ljubljana, January 1993.

14. See http://www.skd.si/english/polit96/c23.html; and Stan Markotich, "Stable Support for Extremism?" in *Transition*, Vol. 1, No. 4, 29 March 1995, pp. 31–32.

15. Some details can be found in "Slovenia and Elections: Drnovšek's Government in a Crisis," *AIM Press*, Ljubljana, 26 March 2000.

16. *Constitution of the Republic of Slovenia*, Ljubljana, Uradni List Republike Slovenije, 1992.

17. Vojin Dimitrijevič, "Ethnonationalism and the Constitutions: The Apotheosis of the Nation-State," paper presented at the conference "Issues of Identity in Contemporary Yugoslavia," University of Kent at Canterbury, England, 20–23 August 1992.

18. "Italian and Hungarian National Communities (Minorities) in the Republic of Slovenia," *Report on Nationalities from the Government of the Republic of Slovenia*, 16 November 1992.

19. Meta Roglič, "Fewer Slovene Citizens," *Dnevnik*, Ljubljana, 3 May 1993, in Federal Broadcast Information Service/Joint Publications Research Service, *Daily Report: East Europe JPRS-EER-93–047–S*, 23 May 1993.

20. www.ecri.coe.int/en/02/02/05/e02020551.htm.

21. Zoran Medved, "That Is Slovenia," *Danas*, Zagreb, 20 February 1990, in *JPRS-EER-90–070*, 18 May 1990.

22. "Analysis of Current Events," *Association for the Study of Nationalities*, New York, Year 4, No. 7, May 1993. See also James Gow, "Slovenia: Stabilization or Stagnation?" *RFE/RL Research Report*, Vol. 3, No. 1, 1 August 1994, p. 136.

23. *Political Handbook of the World*, 846.

24. Http://wnc.fedworld.gov/cgi-bin/ret.1z7cad&CID=C43026733398437557750789; *FBIS-EEU-97–041*, "Drnovšek Views New Government, EU, NATO Membership."

25. "Slovenia: Drnovšek Interview Focuses on Economy," *FBIS-EEU-96–228*, 14 September 1996.

26. "Slovenia: Article Views Pros, Cons of Joining NATO," *FBIS-EEU-96–229*, 16 November 1996.

27. "Slovenia: Integration Issues Seen to Dominate Elections," *FBIS-EEU-96–219*, 9 November 1996.

28. www.zlsd.si/preds.html.

29. www.sds.si/ostranki.htm.

30. *Mag*, Ljubljana, 2 March 1998, in *FBIS-EEU-98–061*, 5 March 1998.

31. *Radio Slovenia Network*, Ljubljana, 17 February 1997 in *FBIS-EEU-97–032*, 19 February 1997.

32. www.si-int-news.com/ln/politika/volitve96/volitve96–clanki.html.

33. *Mag*, Ljubljana, 2 March 1998, in *FBIS-EEU-98–061*, 5 March 1998.

34. *Delo*, Ljubljana, 20 February 1997, in *FBIS-EEU-97–038*, 27 February 1997.

35. www.lds.si.

36. *Dnevnik*, Ljubljana, 5 August 1997, in *FBIS-EEU-97–217*, 6 August 1997; and *Radio Slovenia Network*, Ljubljana, 31 July 1997, in *FBIS-EEU-97–212*, 1 August 1997.

37. www.eon.si/novice/StaCustoms81.asp.

38. *Mag*, Ljubljana, 29 May 1996, in *FBIS-EEU-96–111*, 10 June 1996.

39. http://www.skd.si/english/polit97/c02.html.

40. *Delo*, Ljubljana, 20 October 1997, in *FBIS-EEU-97–293*, 22 October 1997.

41. www.sds.si/novice.htm.

42. http://wnc.fedworld.gov/cgi-bin/retrieve.

43. Bojan Balkovec, "Political Parties in Slovenia," *Nationalities Papers*, Vol. 21, No. 1, Spring 1993, pp. 189–192.

44. For information on the Slovenian National Party, see Miha Štamcar, "Pure Slovenia," *Mladina*, Ljubljana, 2 April 1991, in *JPRS-EER-91–071*, 28 May 1991; and *Tanjug*, Belgrade, 22 March 1993, in *FBIS-EEU-93–054*, 23 March 1993.

45. For a useful synopsis of Slovenian nationalism, although with an evident personal bias against the pro-independence activist and former defense minister Janez Janša, see Rudolf M. Rizman, "Radical Right Politics in Slovenia," in Sabrina P. Ramet (Ed.), *The Radical Right in Central and Eastern Europe Since 1989*, University Park: Pennsylvania State University Press, 1999, pp. 147–170.

46. See Sveto Krašnik, "Union of the Slovene Radical Right," *Dnevnik*, Ljubljana, 9 February 1993, in *FBIS-EEU-93–Mi*, 4 March 1993.

47. www.europeanforum.bot-consult.se/cup/slovenia/parties.htm.

Albania

HISTORICAL OVERVIEW

According to most scholars, the Albanians are descended from Illyrian people who settled in the Balkan region during the latter part of the Bronze Age, in about 1000 BC.[1] During the seventh and sixth centuries BC, the Greeks established several colonies along the Albanian coast, including Epidamnus (present-day Durrës) and Apollonia (near present-day Vlorë). By the third century BC, the colonies began to decline, and eventually they disappeared. As the Greeks left, the small Illyrian groups that pre-dated them evolved into more complex political units, including federations and kingdoms. The most important of these kingdoms, the Adrians kingdom, flourished between the fifth and second centuries BC. It reached its peak under the rule of King Agron (250–231 BC).

The Romans viewed Illyria as a bridgehead for their eastern conquests, and in 229 BC, Roman forces crossed the Adriatic. By 168 BC, the Roman force had established effective control over the region and had named the province Illyricum. Rome ruled the region for the next six centuries, but the Illyrians resisted assimilation, and their distinctive culture and language survived. Illyrians gained significant influence in the Roman armed forces, and several became Roman emperors, including Aurelian (AD 270–275), Diocletian (284–305), and Constantine the Great (306–337). Christianity had a growing impact in Illyricum by the middle of the first century AD, and in 58 AD, Saint Paul placed an apostle in charge of Epidamnus. Seats for bishops were later created in Apollonia and Scodra (present-day Shkodër).

In 395 AD the Roman domains were split into western and eastern empires; the lands of modern Albania became part of the eastern, Byzantine Empire. Several Illyrians became Byzantine emperors, including Justinian I (527–565). By the fifth century, Christianity had become the established religion and Albanian Christians were under the religious jurisdiction of the Roman Pope, despite being subjects of the Byzantine Empire. In the fourth and fifth centuries, invading Visigoths, Huns, and Ostrogoths devastated the region, and between the sixth and eighth centuries, Bulgars and Slavs settled in Illyrian territories.

The Slavs assimilated many of the Illyrians in what is today Slovenia, Croatia, Bosnia-Herzegovina, and Serbia. However, the southern Illyrian peoples, including those in modern Albania, resisted assimilation. In 732 AD, Byzantine emperor Leo III detached the Albanian Church from Rome and placed it under the patriarch of Constantinople. When the Christian Church formally split in 1054 into Eastern and Western branches, southern Albania retained its ties to the Orthodox Church in Constantinople while northern Albania reverted to the jurisdiction of the Roman Catholic Church in Rome.

From the eighth to the eleventh centuries, Illyria gradually became known as Albania, from the Albanos group that inhabited central Albania. In the ninth and tenth centuries Byzantine power began to weaken as Norman Crusaders, Italian Angevins, Serbs, and Venetians invaded the region. After the tenth century, a feudal system developed in Albania in which peasant soldiers who had served military lords became serfs on landed estates. At this time some of the region's provinces became virtually independent of Constantinople. In 1190, the Albanian prince Progon established an independent state, which lasted until the middle of the thirteenth century, after which the country was faced with new outside pressures and internal fragmentation.

The Serbian occupation after 1347, under Stefan Dušan, prompted a mass migration of Albanians to Greece. Byzantine and Serbian rule declined by the middle of the fourteenth century, and in 1388 the Ottoman Turks invaded Albania and conquered most of the country by 1430. During the 1440s, Gjergj Kastrioti (1405–1468) organized the country's feudal lords to fight the Ottomans. Kastrioti, popularly known as Skënderbeg, successfully resisted Ottoman control for twenty-five years with military help from Rome, Naples, and Venice. Albanian resistance collapsed after Skënderbeg's death and the Ottomans reoccupied the country by 1506. About one quarter of the country's population fled to Italy, Sicily, and the Dalmatian coast along the Adriatic. Skënderbeg's name was subsequently invoked throughout Albanian history to inspire national unity and the struggle for independence.

During four centuries of Ottoman rule, the Turks failed to control all of Albania. In the highland regions, Ottoman power was weak and the Albanians refused to pay taxes or perform military service. Albanians staged several rebellions, partly in defense of their Christian faith. At the end of the sixteenth century, the Ottomans began a policy of Islamicization as a way of preventing future unrest. By the end of the seventeenth century, about two-thirds of the population had converted to Islam, many to avoid the heavy taxes levied on Christians. The Ottomans also extended their control through a feudal-military system under which military leaders who were loyal to the Empire received landed estates.

As Ottoman power declined in the eighteenth century, the power of some military lords and native princes increased. The Bushati family dominated most of northern Albania between 1750 and 1831, while Ali Pashë Tepelena ruled southern Albania and northern Greece from 1788 to 1822. These local rulers created separate states until they were overthrown by Ottoman Sultan Mahmud II. A number of Albanians also rose to high positions in the Ottoman government in the eighteenth and nineteenth centuries, with more than two dozen becoming grand viziers or prime ministers. However, Albania failed to develop an effective political leadership during the mid-1800s, at a time when national liberation movements were proliferating throughout the Ottoman Empire.

In 1878, Albanian leaders met in the town of Prizren, in Kosova, where they founded the League of Prizren, also called the Albanian League, to promote a free and unified Albania in all Albanian-populated territories. They also sought to prevent the cession of Albanian-inhabited regions to Serbia and Montenegro. The League endeavored to develop Albanian language, education, and culture, and in 1908 Albanian leaders adopted a national alphabet based on the Latin script. Between 1910 and 1912, Albanian nationalists waged an armed struggle against the Ottomans, who had refused to grant Albania autonomy. In October 1912, Ottoman occupation forces were attacked and defeated by Serb, Montenegrin, Greek, and Bulgarian armies in the First Balkan War.

The Ottoman defeat precipitated Albanian moves toward statehood. Under the leadership of Ismail Qemal, Albania proclaimed its independence from the Ottoman Empire on 28 November 1912 in the coastal city of Vlorë. At the London Conference, which began on 16 December 1912 and ended on 30 May 1913, Britain, Germany, Russia, Austria, France, and Italy signed the Treaty of London, in which they agreed to accept Albanian independence. But because of strong pressures from Albania's neighbors, the Great Powers gave the Albanian-inhabited region of Kosova to Serbia and much of the southern Çamëria region to Greece. Roughly half of the predominantly Albanian territories and 40% of the population were left outside the new country's borders.

The Great Powers also appointed a German prince, Wilhelm zu Wied, as Albania's ruler, but he was in power only six months before the outbreak of World War I. During the war, Austrian, French, Italian, Greek, Montenegrin, and Serb armies occupied Albania, and the country lacked any political leadership. At the Paris Peace Conference after the war, U.S. President Woodrow Wilson vetoed a plan by Britain, France, and Italy to partition Albania among its neighbors. In January 1920, the Albanians established a provisional government and the country was admitted to the newly formed League of Nations, thereby gaining international recognition as an independent state.

During the 1920s, Albania was deeply divided between two major political forces. A conservative class of landowners and tribal leaders, led by Ahmed Zogu, wished to maintain the *status quo,* while liberal intellectuals, politicians, and merchants wanted to modernize Albania. The liberals were led by Fan S. Noli, a U.S.-educated bishop of the Orthodox Church. In 1924, a popular revolt against the conservatives forced Zogu to flee to Yugoslavia. Noli became prime minister of the new government and set out to build a Western-style democracy. But six months later, beset by internal opposition and lacking international support, Noli was overthrown by Zogu. Zogu reigned for fourteen years, first as president (1925–1928) and then as King Zog I (1928–1939) when a constituent assembly proclaimed Albania a "parliamentary hereditary kingdom." Zog's dictatorial rule was marked by economic stagnation, although he helped create a modern school system and made the country somewhat more stable. During his reign, the Albanian Orthodox Church obtained autocephalous status from the Patriarch of Constantinople. However, Zog failed to resolve the problem of land reform, and the peasantry remained impoverished.

Under Zog, Italy exercised considerable influence over Albania's affairs and the state evolved into a virtual Italian protectorate. In April 1939, shortly before the start of World War II, Italy invaded and occupied Albania, sending Zog fleeing to Greece. After Nazi Germany defeated Yugoslavia and Greece in 1941, Kosova and Çamëria were taken from those countries and joined to Albania, which remained under Italian supervision until 1943, when German forces assumed control after the Italian surrender. The wartime state disintegrated in November 1944 when the Germans withdrew their forces. Kosova was then returned to Serbia (by then part of Yugoslavia) and Çamëria reverted to Greece.

During World War II, nationalists, monarchists, and communists in Albania actively resisted Italian, German, and Albanian fascism. The Albanian Communist Party, which had been established in November 1941, eventually prevailed in a civil war over the *Balli Kombëtar* (National Front) and the pro-Zog *Legaliteti* (Legality) movement. They seized power in Tirana in November 1944 with help from Yugoslav communists. The secretary-general of the Albanian Communist Party, Enver Hoxha, was installed as the country's new leader. On 11 January 1946, a constituent assembly proclaimed Albania a People's Republic; a new constitution was promulgated in March 1946, and a government was formed. All political opposition as well as the pre-war political elite were ruthlessly eliminated.

Supported by impoverished peasants and some intellectuals, the party launched a radical reform program that destroyed the power of landlords; nationalized industry, banks, and commercial properties; and created a state-controlled socialist society. Agriculture was collectivized, and by 1967, almost all peasants worked on collective farms. The Hoxha regime also gained firm control over the northern highlands and largely eliminated the traditional authority of patriarchal clans and tribal leaders. Tirana pursued a particularly harsh policy against the largely Roman Catholic Geg population in northern Albania, who forcefully resisted communist rule into the late 1940s. However, some positive results were also evident, including the virtual elimination of illiteracy and the elevation of women to legal equality with men.

Initially, Albania depended on Yugoslavia for economic and military aid, but it feared Yugoslav political domination. In 1948, when Stalin expelled

Yugoslavia from the Communist bloc for ideological reasons, Albania backed the Soviet leader, broke ties with Belgrade, and expelled Yugoslav advisers from the country. Hoxha also purged Albania's pro-Yugoslav faction, headed by Koçi Xoxe, his chief rival. The Communist Party was renamed at its first congress in November 1948 as the Albanian Party of Labor (APL). Tirana copied the Soviet model of fast-paced industrialization and strict central economic planning and became a loyal ally of Moscow between 1948 and 1955. With the death of Stalin in 1953, Albanian-Soviet relations began to sour, especially as the new Soviet leadership sought an accommodation with Yugoslavia. Hoxha refused to relax his grip on Albanian society or to conduct a de-Stalinization campaign, unlike Moscow's other East European satellites.

When the Soviet Union and China argued over control of the world communist movement in the early 1960s, Albania supported China, which Hoxha viewed as having a "purer" form of Marxism-Leninism. Hoxha was also disillusioned with other communist allies, whom he accused of "revisionism," of abandoning the socialist revolution, and of seeking accommodation with the capitalist West. In December 1961, diplomatic ties were broken between Albania and the Soviet Union. Soviet aid, credits, and technical assistance, which had enabled Albania to create a modern industrial and agricultural base, were severed. China took the Soviet Union's place as Albania's main trading partner and supplier of economic aid.

Until the late 1960s, Albania remained virtually isolated from the rest of the world. Following the Soviet invasion of Czechoslovakia in 1968, Albania sought to protect itself by renewing ties with neighboring European states and formally withdrawing from the USSR-led Warsaw Pact. During the 1970s, Albania's relations with China became strained by China's detente with the United States. In 1978, China canceled its trade agreements with and its aid to Albania. Tirana subsequently pursued closer economic contacts with several European states, but in terms of political and social ties, Albania remained one of the most isolated countries in the world until the early 1990s.

Under Hoxha's rule, political oppression was severe. In order to eliminate dissent, all political parties except the APL were banned and the regime periodically purged potential opponents from the ruling party. Thousands were dismissed from their jobs, imprisoned in labor camps, or killed. The state tightly controlled and censored all public institutions and organizations, including trade unions, the press, cultural associations, women's and youth organizations, and all economic enterprises. In addition, Tirana sought to eliminate the regional differences between northern Gegs and southern Tosks, which were manifest in dialectical and cultural divergences, in order to create a single Albanian identity under strict party control.

In a tightly controlled "Cultural Revolution" in the mid-1960s, Hoxha purged the party and the government of potential opponents and rivals who favored some liberalization in the political and economic systems. Another extensive purge of the nation's political, military, and economic elites was conducted in the early 1970s. Albania's three major religious communities—Muslim, Orthodox Christian, and Roman Catholic—were also subject to attack. Most of the property belonging to religious organizations was confiscated, and prominent religious leaders were executed, imprisoned, or exiled. In 1967, religion was officially outlawed and Albania was declared the world's first atheist state.

The state security network, or *Sigurimi*, kept a close eye on the entire population and eliminated any signs of dissent. Unlike elsewhere in Eastern Europe, Albania failed to develop a *samizdat* underground dissident press. The state-controlled media were tightly censored, no independent information was allowed to circulate, and foreign contacts were kept to a minimum. The only indications of organized opposition appeared within the ruling party itself. For example in 1981, Mehmet Shehu, the chairman of the Council of Ministers (Prime Minister) died in mysterious circumstances; he was believed to be the leader of a plot designed to unseat Hoxha. In 1983, a number of former party officials were executed by the *Sigurimi*.

Hoxha died on 11 April 1985 and was promptly replaced as APL First Secretary by Ramiz Alia, who tried to preserve the essence of the system while introducing tentative reforms to revive the economy, which had been declining for several years.[2] However, he was cautious not to unleash a liberalization program that could threaten the party's rigid hold on power and control over the economy.[3]

POST-COMMUNIST DEVELOPMENTS

As communist rule in Eastern Europe collapsed in 1989, increasing numbers of Albanians demanded more far-reaching political reforms. The protestors included intellectuals, members of the working class, and frustrated young people. However, the dissidents were unable to establish any significant oppositionist organization. In response to growing unrest and public protests, President Alia initiated some cautious reformist steps by restoring religious freedom, cutting back the power of the *Sigurimi*, and adopting some modest market reforms.

In December 1990, the government endorsed the creation of independent political parties, thereby ending the communist monopoly on power. Five opposition parties were formed within the following month. The judicial system was reformed, with the reestablishment of a ministry of justice and the reduction of capital offenses. Albanians were also granted the right to foreign travel. Throughout 1990, thousands of citizens had tried to flee the country through Western embassies. A multinational relief operation arranged for the safe evacuation of more than 5,000 Albanians, and 20,000 more sailed illegally to Italy in vessels seized at civilian ports.

An interim constitution was passed in April 1991 and the country was re-named the Republic of Albania. The state had a unicameral legislature known as the People's Assembly (*Kuvendi Popullor*) with 140 members elected for a four-year term, 115 members in single-seat constituencies spread among the 26 electoral districts, and 25 members elected through proportional represen-tation. According to the 1991 constitution, the president was the head of state and the commander-in-chief of the armed forces. He was elected by the People's Assembly for a five-year term. Presidential powers were enhanced: the incumbent could declare a state of emergency, dissolve parliament, and call for new general elections. With the approval of the People's Assembly, the President also appointed the prime minister, who chaired the Council of Minis-ters. The prime minister and the Council of Ministers formed the executive branch of the government, while the president and prime minister were jointly responsible for the country's foreign relations and security affairs.

Albania was divided into 37 districts (*rrethe*) in which government at the district and city levels operated through people's councils. The councils were elected for three-year terms and they administered most of the social, cul-tural, and economic affairs of their geographic areas. In 1992, a new, decen-tralized system of local administration was introduced. Thirty-seven districts replaced the previous 27 and were subdivided into 310 communes and 43 municipalities. In 1993, the government announced plans to establish 12 pre-fectures as a new intermediate regional tier of local government.[4]

Anti-government protests continued in Albania in the early part of 1991, leading to the removal of several hard-line communists from the government and the party politburo. At public demonstrations in early 1991, several pro-testors were killed by the police, who had remained under communist con-trol. In March 1991, a general amnesty for all political prisoners was declared. Multi-party elections to the People's Assembly took place the same month. The snap elections were designed by the ruling party to gain electoral legiti-macy and to disable the opposition from effectively organizing.

The opposition had few resources at its disposal, limited access to the mass media, and insufficient time to coordinate an effective election campaign. With a much more extensive organizational base, the communists and their allies won 169 of the 250 seats, while the newly formed Democratic Party won 75 seats. *Omonia* (Harmony)*,* an ethnic Greek party, gained five seats, and the National Veterans' Committee obtained one seat. The communist sup-port base in the countryside remained especially strong, while the Democrats were successful in the larger cities. In fact, the communist victory served to polarize society and provoked new public protests in which police killed four people in the city of Shkodër on 2 April 1991.

In indirect presidential elections in March 1991, a communist majority in parliament elected Ramiz Alia to the new post of Albanian President, and the communist leader Fatos Nano became prime minister. But with unrest mount-ing, and following a general strike in May 1991 by thousands of workers, the government resigned, and a coalition government was formed on 4 June 1991. Led by new Prime Minister Ylli Bufi, it included the Albanian Party of Labor (communists), the Democrats, Republicans, and Social Democrats. Demonstrations continued through the summer as protestors demanded the arrest of former communist leaders and full freedom for the media. In December 1991, the coalition government collapsed and an interim administration was appointed.

New elections were held on 22 March 1992, giving the Democrats 92 of the 140 seats in the reorganized People's Assembly. The Socialist Party (the renamed Party of Labor) won 38 seats, the Social Democrats 7, and the Greek minority Unity Party for Human Rights 2. The assembly overwhelmingly elected the leader of the Democratic Party, Sali Berisha, as Albania's new president on 9 April 1992, following Alia's early resignation. Berisha appointed Aleksandër Meksi as the new premier. Under Berisha, several former communist officials, including Alia and Nano, were arrested, tried for corruption and abuse of power, and sentenced to long prison terms.

Observers believed that the trials were politically inspired and that President Berisha had used them to conveniently eliminate potential rivals. However, both Alia and Nano were released within a few years of their convictions. Under harsh economic conditions—an inevitable concomitant of structural reform—the Democrats' support base began to erode and in the local elections in July 1992 the party lost almost 20% of its electorate, winning 43% of the popular vote; the Socialists won 41%. Public euphoria over the collapse of communism had not been accompanied by a realistic appraisal of the government's capabilities in delivering rapid economic prosperity. Hence, large sectors of society quickly became disillusioned with the Democrats' performance.

A draft constitution supported by the Democrats was rejected by voters in a national referendum on 6 November 1994. Out of a turnout of 84.43% of the population, 53.9% voted against the new constitution and 41.7% in favor. Opponents charged that the proposed draft vested too much power in the presidency and diminished the role of parliament. They also complained that there was insufficient consultation in drafting the document. The president stood accused of implementing authoritarian measures by restricting press freedoms, persecuting former communist officials, controlling the judiciary, increasing presidential powers, and limiting the prerogatives of the prime minister and his cabinet.[5] The parliament was charged with being a pliant body, with few Democrat deputies challenging Berisha's decisions. By contrast, supporters of the government accused the Socialists of attempting to discredit the country's democratization program and undermining the government. They argued that Albania needed a strong executive that could make speedy decisions during a potentially destabilizing transition process.

Albania emerged from its isolation, established relations with all Western states, and joined various international bodies, including the Organization for Security and Cooperation in Europe (OSCE) and the Organization of the Islamic Conference (OIC). Albania also applied for membership in the North

Atlantic Treaty Organization (NATO) and the European Union (EU). However, its relations with neighboring Greece and Yugoslavia remained tense. The status of the Greek minority in Albania proved problematic and Athens claimed that the Greek population suffered from discrimination. Tirana asserted that extremist groups in Greece were supporting separatism in southern Albania and protested the mistreatment of Albanian workers in Greece. Five members of a Greek minority organization were tried in July 1994 on charges of espionage. They were initially sentenced to imprisonment but were later released with suspended sentences.

Relations with Greece began to improve during 1995 and Athens withdrew its veto on EU aid to Albania. But contacts with Yugoslavia remained tense, particularly over Serb repression of the Albanian majority in the province of Kosova, whose autonomy had been terminated by Belgrade in 1989. The Albanian leadership in Kosova subsequently declared the region's independence from Yugoslavia. Albania continued to campaign on Kosova's behalf and wanted UN monitors dispatched to the province; but this proposal was persistently rejected. Albania feared that major unrest and a military crackdown in Kosova could lead to a massive outflow of refugees and destabilize the entire Balkan region. Albania's relations with the republic of Macedonia were also subject to dispute over the position of the large Albanian minority in that new state. Albanian leaders sought equal status for their language with Macedonian and greater representation in the government. The governments in Tirana and Skopje established diplomatic relations and worked to solve their mutual problems.

The Albanian-Greek dispute remained evident, even over the question of population statistics. According to the 1981 Albanian census, the Greek community numbered some 55,000 out of a total population of over three million. By contrast, Greek sources on both sides of the border estimated the figure to be somewhere in the region of 200,000—a number that remained constant in Greek statements despite the large outflow of Greek refugees. Tirana claimed that Athens deliberately exaggerated the total by including various categories of people with little or no Hellenic background, including all Orthodox Christians in southern Albania regardless of their ethnic origins and cultural identity.

With the onset of political liberalization during 1990–1991, Greek activists formed their own political party and won seats in the National Assembly in the first multi-party general elections. Increased Greek activism inside Albania and growing suspicions about the influence of extremist revisionist circles in Greece spurred the new parliament to ban ethnic or regional parties from standing in future elections. The issue soured relations between Tirana and Athens, which had steadily improved under the Alia administration. Although a newly formed and predominantly Greek organization was allowed to function and participate in the elections of 1992, Albanian-Greek relations remained tense as the country began to undergo profound political and economic changes. Further controversies arose over the question of Greek maltreatment of Albanian refugees, over the activities and sponsorship of irredentist organizations in Greece with overt claims to Albanian territory, and over the influence of Greek organizations during and after the Albanian election campaigns.

Minority rights were officially acknowledged only for those villages deemed "minoritarian" by the government. Such was the case with 99 villages in the southern districts of Sarandë and Gjirokastër, where the Greek population was concentrated. Greek spokesmen claimed that 34% of the population of Gjirokastër and 42% of the population of Sarandë was Greek. If a few Albanian families settled in one of these villages, its minority inhabitants lost their distinct rights: they were no longer provided with an education in their own language or the opportunity to publish their own newspaper. The same principles applied to other areas inhabited by ethnic minorities but which were not granted a special minority status.

As a result of these policies, Greek educational and linguistic rights were largely absent in several cities heavily populated by Greeks, such as Korçë, Himarë, Tepelenë, Fier, Vlorë, Shkodër, Berat, Përmet, and Elbasan. In regions where Greek education was allowed, courses were designed to terminate at the fourth grade of elementary schooling, and Greek activists sought to extend optional classes through the secondary level. Even the cities of Sarandë and Gjirokastër were excluded from the minority rights guarantees, although both were capitals of the two districts eligible for designation as minority areas. Despite the fact that a compact Greek population inhabited the area, in official legislation prior to the democratic changes the minority was technically considered of non-Greek origin.[6]

In 1991, a draft constitution proposed by the ruling Albanian Party of Labor (APL) (after June 1991, known as the Albanian Socialist Party) was presented to parliament. Its first chapter outlined the basic rights of all Albanian people, including national minorities. The constitution recognized minority rights as guaranteed by international law. However, Article 8 evinced strong criticism from Greek minority representatives, as well as from various international organizations and human rights groups. It declared that political parties and organizations could not be created on the basis of nationality or ethnicity. Also barred were political organizations of a "fascist or racial character, or those that by their program and activities threaten to overthrow by force the constitutional order, against the independence and territorial integrity of the country."[7] Greek leaders raised serious objections to stipulations prohibiting the formation of minority political organizations. They claimed that such provisions violated the right of minorities to express their political will and limited their participation in the country's political life.

The draft constitution defined Albanian as the official language, but "in special localities, where the majority is made up of national minorities, the language of the minority may be used side by side with the Albanian language according to conditions foreseen by law."[8] According to leaders of the Greek minority, while in theory the right of ethnic minorities to use their mother tongue was recognized, the required conditions for applying this ruling were not specified in the legislation and in practice could prove extremely restrictive. In addition, the article did not mention any regulations concerning the right of education in languages other than Albanian.

The second section of the draft constitution dealt with the basic rights and freedoms of all citizens. It declared that freedom of thought, conscience, and religious and political beliefs were inviolable. With regard to the rights of ethnic minorities, the state guaranteed "free preservation and development of their ethnic, cultural, religious, and linguistic identity."[9] Moreover, individuals belonging to ethnic minorities were free to establish contacts with people of the same ethnic origin inside the country and with foreign nationals of the same ethnic origin, cultural heritage, and religious belief outside the country. During 1990, the government also legalized the private and public practice of all religions, and the law on major constitutional provisions declared Albania a "secular state" respecting freedom of religious faiths, and obliged the government to create conditions enabling all denominations to exercise these liberties.

However, certain "collective rights" in the religious realm continued to be denied to the Greek minority, including the freedom to practice their religion in the Greek language. Albanian laws provided that in Albanian Orthodox churches, masses were to be held only in the Albanian language, which in effect contradicted provisions included in the draft constitution. Controversies also surfaced during 1992 in the appointment of bishops to the Albanian Autocephalous Orthodox Church. When the Ecumenical Patriarch in Istanbul named three bishops of Greek origin to the Dioceses of Korçë, Berat, and Gjirokastër, the government refused to agree to their installation. When an ethnic Greek was named the Orthodox Archbishop of Albania, a storm of protests erupted. Although Anastas Janullatos was formally installed, Tirana only accepted him on a provisional basis, until a suitable ethnic Albanian replacement could be found.[10] President Berisha's draft constitution that was rejected in a public referendum on 11 November 1994 outraged the Greek minority, as it specified that the heads of large religious denominations must be native-born Albanians. This provision would have disqualified Greek-born Archbishop Janullatos.

The law on major constitutional provisions, which served as a substitute for a full constitution, provided for the "human rights and fundamental freedoms of national minorities, as accepted by international documents." In practice, however, limitations were placed on the extent to which minorities could exercise their rights—especially those groups that were not officially recognized by Tirana. Schooling in the mother tongue of different ethnic groups was not allowed in regions other than southern Albania, where the Greek minority was concentrated. However, Tirana Radio periodically broadcast Greek-language programs, and a Greek-language newspaper, *Liko Vima*, was published in the southern town of Gjirokastër.[11]

Although the Greek organization *Omonia* gained five seats in the March 1991 general elections, controversies over the electoral participation of ethnic parties culminated in the formulation of a new law that prohibited political activities by parties based on ethnic or regional criteria. The draft of the election law submitted in January 1992 initially contained an article allowing for the participation of ethnicity-based parties. But after a serious dispute in the National Assembly over the role of ethnic parties, a last-minute change effectively disqualified *Omonia* from participating in the elections. This enraged Greek activists and led to vehement protests by Athens.

The election controversy was partially eased when the Albanian government agreed to register the Greek-based Unity Party for Human Rights (UPHR) and permitted it to stand in the March 1992 parliamentary elections. The new party succeeded in gaining two seats for the southern districts of Sarandë and Gjirokastër in the newly constituted National Assembly. But the election campaign itself was marred by conflicts, as some Albanian officials charged that irredentist Greek organizations were campaigning for the Unity Party and distributing campaign literature printed in Greece.

The National Assembly elections of March 1992 were held according to the electoral law passed by the Albanian parliament in February 1992. Certain provisions of that law affected the political rights of minorities. In order to qualify for the ballot, every candidate had to present a list of 400 signatures of voters who supported his or her candidacy. Considering the fact that the country was divided into 100 voting districts, the number of signatures required proved relatively high, compared to the number of eligible voters. Consequently, the collection of 400 signatures proved difficult for the smaller parties, especially those attempting to represent minority populations.

Small parties that were formed to represent the interests of minority groups remained at a clear disadvantage during the balloting. According to the election law, only parties presenting candidates in at least thirty-three electoral counties and nine electoral districts could participate in the subsequent, proportional distribution of additional parliamentary seats. These provisions guaranteed that minority parties had little chance of gaining seats after the second round of voting. Furthermore, voter registration lists had to be completed at least 25 days prior to election day. This requirement created a practical problem for Albanian citizens of Greek origin who were working in Greece and were unable to register on time.[12]

The local elections of July 1992 were held according to provisions barring the participation of ethnicity-based parties. The Unity Party for Human Rights (UPHR) was permitted to field candidates for mayoral positions and local council representatives posts. However, tensions were evident in the south of the country on election day, particularly in Gjirokastër and Sarandë. For example, some emigrants who worked in Greece or resided there as refugees and returned to Albania in order to vote discovered that they were not registered on the electoral lists. Albanian authorities accused political groups in Greece of pressuring people to return to Albania and vote for the UPHR, a party that clearly represented the interests of the Greek minority. This created a political crisis in the Sarandë district, where Albanian political parties protested against brazen interference by the Greek government.

But despite this localized storm and the grievances of some political leaders, the election results in Greek minority regions were accepted as legitimate. The UPHR received 5.69% of the district council seats and 4.96% of the municipal council seats, electing 53 district councillors (out of 932) and 32 municipality councillors (out of 645). It also managed to elect one of the 42 municipal mayors and 13 commune chairmen in the country's 314 communes.[13]

In the first three years of the Democratic Party government, Albania registered economic progress while facing continuing political turbulence over the policies and ruling style of President Berisha. The political atmosphere simmered as Berisha was accused by his opponents of developing an authoritarian style and an autocratic state. The Socialist opposition charged Berisha with persecuting his rivals and suppressing dissent. The most publicized case of alleged persecution was the trial and conviction of Fatos Nano, the former chairman of the Albanian Socialist Party, who was sentenced to twelve years for stealing state property, nepotism, and falsifying documents. Nano became the rallying point for Socialists demanding curbs on presidential powers. Berisha failed to pass his "presidential" constitution in the fall of 1994 and in 1995 several opposition parties, including the Social Democrats, the Democratic Alliance, and the Unity Party for Human Rights, published their own draft "opposition constitution" as an alternative to Berisha's proposal.

After they assumed power, the Democrats purged most of the existing administration and appointed many party loyalists in their place. Albania presented a stark example of the operation of patronage, or the "spoils system." Loyalty and obedience were prized above merit and competence, and any incoming administration expected to replace all appointees of the previous government. In addition, much of the Democratic Party (DP), faithful to Berisha, originated in the north of the country, thereby exacerbating resentment in the capital and in the southern regions.

As in communist times, the local governments remained closely tied to the central administration in terms of political loyalty and financial dependence. In order to deflect attention from his own authoritarian tendencies, Berisha accused the opposition of seeking to undermine his position and to destabilize the political system for their own political gains. Conflicts were also visible within the ruling Democratic Party between Berisha and party chairman Eduard Selami. At its annual congress in April 1995, the party voted overwhelmingly to dismiss Selami, thereby strengthening the president's position in the organization.

In late 1994, five members of the Greek minority organization *Omonia* were arrested, convicted, and imprisoned on charges of espionage and the unlawful possession of arms. Initially, Berisha pardoned one of the accused but the remaining four were expected to serve long jail sentences. However, in February 1995, the Supreme Court reviewed the case of the remaining four and freed them from prison. The release appeared to be a politically motivated move by the judge—a challenge to the presidency. Both the judge and the president were members of the ruling DP, and the decision indicated a split in the party between Berisha's supporters and detractors. Critics charged that the president had been too harsh in his treatment of political adversaries and was unnecessarily creating divisions in society. In September 1995, when the head of the Supreme Court was dismissed by parliament, he expressed fears of political persecution.

Although the Greek government obtained assurances that the approximately 60,000-strong Greek minority was well treated, complaints continued to be lodged by local Greek leaders and by the Helsinki Commission in Albania that the position of minorities had been aggravated by the strong-arm tactics of local police forces. But although several incidents were reported by human rights observers, these were neither systematic nor part of state policy. The Helsinki Commission also claimed that some extremist nationalist parties were publishing and distributing offensive propaganda against minorities. According to human rights monitors, the judicial system was in need of reform to eliminate various abuses and to bring it into line with European standards.

During 1996, Albania's ruling DP consolidated its position through overwhelming victories in the country's parliamentary and local elections. While the Democrats strengthened their political position in all governing institutions, they came under increasing international attack for alleged anti-democratic tendencies and human rights abuses. Human rights organizations concluded that five years after Albania's first free elections, the country was still plagued by serious violations, including restrictions on freedom of expression and association, manipulation of the legal system, and police violence. The justification for these measures was allegedly the ongoing campaign to root out communist influence. The government arrested several members of the former communist regime, including ex-President Ramiz Alia, on charges of political persecution and the repression of civilians. Tirana also banned several dozen candidates from the general elections, on the basis of the screening law that prohibited former high-ranking communists from running for public office for ten years.

In April 1996, Tritan Shehu was elected as the new chairman of the Democratic Party; he was considered to be closely tied to Berisha. In the parliamentary elections on 26 May 1996, the Democrats won overwhelming majorities in most of the electoral districts. Because of the new electoral law, which introduced a strong majoritarian system, the Democrats obtained 122 seats in the 140-member national assembly, or over 87% of the legislature, although they won only 55.5% of the vote. This gave the party a two-thirds parliamentary majority, enabling it to make constitutional changes.

The Socialist Party obtained 20.4% of the vote but only ten seats, the Republicans three, the Unity for Human Rights Party two, and the nationalist National Front (NF) (*Balli Kombëtar*) three. International election monitors observed several irregularities in the voting process and recommended the rescheduling of elections in a number of constituencies.[14] The Democrats stood accused of using violence against opposition parties, although this was reportedly exaggerated by the Socialist opposition. Indeed, the Socialists deliberately contributed to some of the irregularities on election day by suddenly withdrawing all of their representatives from election commissions before the vote counting could begin.

In light of these problems, the OSCE stated in its report that Albania should consider holding new elections under more favorable conditions. The Council of Europe also called for new elections, indicating that the voting had not been fully free and fair. The Democrats refused to schedule another election, and the Socialists announced that they would boycott the new parliament until new national elections were held. Alexandër Meksi was reappointed prime minister on 2 July 1996, and the government established a new privatization ministry in an attempt to push through economic reforms. Opposition parties eventually boycotted the parliament, which in early 1997 elected Berisha to another five-year term as president.

The Democratic Party further consolidated its position during the local elections on 20 October 1996 and subsequently controlled all levers of power. It gained 88% of the vote and won control of 37 districts and the vast majority of communes and town councils. The rest of the local seats were distributed among Socialists, Social Democrats, nationalists, and the Greek minority party. The rightist National Front and Legality parties won the mayoralty in the largest northern city of Shkodër but were unable to repeat their success in any other part of the country. Once again, the government was criticized for voting irregularities and for its monopoly of the mass media and the electoral commissions. Nevertheless, foreign observers believed the balloting was generally free and fair.

Although it remained the poorest country in Europe, Albania also continued to have one of the fastest growing economies but its starting point was very low. Much of Albania's traditional industrial infrastructure was obsolete and uncompetitive, and it failed to attract foreign investors. Some industrial unrest was evident as a result of price hikes in bread, gas, and other products.

In the international arena, Albania continued to improve its relations with a number of states and institutions. In March 1996, Berisha signed a friendship and cooperation treaty with Greece. After years of dispute and conflict with Athens, Tirana pledged to respect the human rights of the Greek minority, and Athens agreed to regulate the status of the large number of illegal Albanian immigrants in Greece. The bilateral treaty aimed to boost military and economic ties and increase the number of border crossings. Tirana also signed various military cooperation agreements with NATO members. Although Albania was not considered a prime contender for NATO membership, the government vigorously pursued closer contacts in order to present itself as a viable future candidate.

During the spring and summer of 1997, Albania was shaken by an armed rebellion against the Berisha government. This followed the collapse of several fraudulent investment (or "pyramid") schemes in which over half of the population lost their life savings.[15] By March 1997, a sporadic rebellion had broken out and several parts of the country were virtually ungoverned. The authorities in Tirana rapidly lost control of large areas of the country after the military and police forces rapidly disintegrated. The southern part of Albania, including the cities of Vlorë and Sarandë, was controlled by local militias or armed citizens defending themselves against rioters.

The rebels accused Berisha's government of directly benefiting from the failed "pyramids" and demanded his resignation. Tirana asserted that opposition Socialists orchestrated the unrest in order to overthrow the government. Indeed, the Socialists exploited the opportunity to undermine the Democratic government and in some instances incited public revolt, thus contributing to the chaos and breakdown of Albanian institutions. Rebels and ordinary citizens captured arms from military stocks and by March 1997 the entire southern part of the country was controlled by local militias, former *Sigurimi* members, criminal gangs, or armed citizens defending themselves against looting and banditry. Albania's armed forces and police units were powerless and an estimated 1,500 people died in the clashes. But despite fears among some observers, the anti-government rebellion did not have a regionalist, autonomist, nationalist, or separatist component.

The Democrats failed to stem the growing unrest even while adopting increasingly authoritarian measures. Indeed, they added fuel to the flames by re-electing Sali Berisha president, through a parliamentary vote on 3 March 1997, in the midst of the escalating crisis. In order to prevent the outbreak of all-out civil war and the complete disintegration of the state, Berisha declared a state of emergency on 2 March 1997. After an agreement with opposition parties, an interim government of "national reconciliation" was appointed, headed by the Socialist Bashkim Fino. In a major depatrure from his previous uncompromising stance, the president also agreed to hold early general elections in June 1997 and promised to compensate the victims of the failed pyramid schemes.

The interim administration proved ineffective in providing order and security, and appealed for an international military force to restore law and order in the country. However, the 7,000-strong multinational contingent led by Italian forces, which arrived in the country in April 1997, stayed for only four months. It was primarily mandated to protect the delivery of humanitarian assistance to the most destitute areas of the country, and it avoided confrontations with armed civilians.

The situation was calmed somewhat after the holding of new general elections on 29 June 1997, in which the Socialists returned to power in a landslide victory. The amended electoral law expanded the number of seats allocated under a proportional system. The Albanian Socialist Party (ASP) formed an election pact with the Social Democratic Party of Albania (SDPA) and the Albanian Democratic Alliance Party (ADAP). Despite poor security conditions, the Organization for Security and Cooperation in Europe (OSCE) declared the elections acceptable by international standards. The Socialists overwhelmingly won the ballot, gaining 101 of the 155 seats in the Albanian National Assembly and garnering 65% of the vote against the 25% drawn by the Democrats. The smaller parties allied with the Socialists took 17 seats, giving the coalition more than a two-thirds majority in the parliament and enabling it to change the constitution in order to weaken the powers of the presidency.

The ruling Albanian Democratic Party (ADP) was decimated in the ballot and won a mere 27 seats, three of which were allocated to their coalition partners. Shortly afterwards, President Berisha resigned from office. The ADP had formed a rightist electoral coalition with the monarchist Movement of Legality Party (MLP), the Christian Democratic Party, the Social Democratic Union, and the Democratic Union Party, but their contribution proved insignificant. Another election bloc, the United Albanian Right, composed of the Republican Party, the National Front, the Christian Democratic Union Party, the Movement for Democracy, the Conservative Party, and the Right Democratic Party, also failed to gain any substantial public support. The coalition leaders had tried but failed to establish a viable third alternative to Albania's increasingly polarized and fractured political system.

Parliament elected Socialist Rexhep Meidani president, and Socialist leader Fatos Nano became the new prime minister. The Socialists formed a coalition government with representatives from the Social Democratic Party, the Democratic Alliance, the Agrarian Party, and the Union for Human Rights. In a public referendum that was held during the general elections, more than 60% of the voters opted for keeping Albania a republic and rejected the creation of a monarchy. In protest against what they perceived as Socialist manipulation of the electoral process, the Democrats boycotted parliament for the rest of the year. In August 1997, the government announced that the army and police had restored order to Vlorë and other riot-torn towns and the multinational force left that same month. The pretender to the Albanian throne, King Leku, returned to the country during the crisis but was unable to muster any significant support.

The new government faced a daunting task in rebuilding the impoverished country. It underscored three priorities: reestablishing law and order in all regions affected by unrest, rebuilding the paralyzed government institutions, and reconstructing the shattered economy. In order to re-establish the rule of law, the government set about reforming and rebuilding the discredited police and security forces and restoring public confidence in national institutions. The state of emergency was lifted and an amnesty was offered to citizens who surrendered captured weapons. Several of the most threatening gangs were disarmed by the security forces.

The Democratic Party, now in opposition, re-elected Berisha as party leader and asserted its intention to push for early general elections. The Democrats also claimed that the Socialists were conducting mass purges in all governmental, educational, and judicial institutions, as well as in the mass media, severely restricting the purviews of local authorities, and failing to compensate the victims of the pyramid schemes despite their election pledges. Socialist leaders asserted that they were simply depoliticizing all official bodies and restoring public trust in the administration.

The Nano government signaled its commitment to strict fiscal discipline in order to reduce the budget deficit and to introduce free market reforms based on the privatization of state-owned enterprises. The authorities were unable to repay investors their losses because they did not possess available funds. Analysts warned that the large-scale printing of cash to compensate citizens who lost their savings would spark hyperinflation. The Italian-led humanitarian mission approved by the United Nations Security Council helped the Nano government to restore a sufficient measure of security. A number of other measures were undertaken by the international community to assist Tirana. Italian, Greek, and Turkish military advisers remained in the country to help train and organize the police and the military. Meanwhile, NATO Secretary General Javier Solana signed an agreement with premier Nano whereby the Atlantic Alliance would help rebuild the Albanian armed forces.

The Western European Union (the EU's military arm) launched a six-month police training mission. Concerns remained that instability in Albania could have spillover effects throughout the Balkans. In particular, NATO feared that public unrest or civil war in Albania could destabilize the Albanian populated province of Kosova in neighboring Serbia, as well the Albanian-inhabited regions of neighboring Macedonia. Indeed, reports surfaced that weapons looted in Albania were increasingly finding their way to armed groups in both Kosova and Macedonia.

During 1998, Albania remained torn by severe political conflicts that threatened the country's precarious reform process. These disputes led to the replacement of the country's prime minister and a failed coup attempt against the Socialist government. The rift between the Socialist Party government and the Democratic Party opposition widened. The Democrats, led by Berisha, boycotted the parliament throughout most of the year and tried to stir public unrest against the Nano administration. Berisha charged that the government was illegitimate and unrepresentative and called for early general elections.

In August 1998, Albanian police arrested six officials appointed by the previous DP government. They were charged with "crimes against humanity" in conjunction with their alleged roles in suppressing the public rebellion the previous year. Berisha accused the authorities of political persecution and violations of the constitution. After the assassination of Azem Hajdari, one of the founders of the Democratic Party, on 12 December 1998, opposition pro-testors occupied several government buildings in Tirana. At least three people died in the unrest before the police recaptured the buildings. Tirana charged Berisha with plotting to stage a *coup d'état*.

In the midst of the escalating crisis, Nano stepped down as prime minister in September 1998 and was replaced by Socialist Party secretary-general Pandeli Majko. Majko became Europe's youngest head of government. He sought a dialogue with the Democrats and the passage of a new constitution to limit the dangerous spiral of political polarization. He also declared the launching of an anti-crisis package to resuscitate the Albanian economy. Berisha refused to allow his deputies to return to parliament and called for a boycott of the November referendum on the new constitution.

The country continued to veer between authoritarianism and state disintegration. Some northern parts of the country around the Tropojë region were largely outside of governmental control. In addition to destabilizing political battles, Albania was riddled with organized criminal gangs tied to various political interest groups and engaged in smuggling operations across the country's borders. Large parts of Albania remained unsafe for travel because of the presence of armed gangs. The World Bank declared Albania the most corrupt country in Europe. Corruption was reportedly endemic in all administrative organs as well as in state enterprises, the judicial and prison systems, and among customs officials.

Albania remained a weak state, having shifted from hard-line communism to ungovernability and political fragility. Cronyism and nepotism were rampant in an unstable economic climate. The country's economic development was undermined by political polarization, organized crime and corruption, and the negative impact of the Kosova war. Albania remained polarized between the governing Socialists and the opposition Democrats, with no real middle ground of dialogue and compromise.

Most of the smaller parties were tied in with one of the major organizations. The Socialist bloc Alliance for the State included the Social Democrats, the Democratic Alliance, the Union for Human Rights, the Agrarians, and the National Unity Party. The Democratic bloc Union for Democracy included the Movement of Legality Party, the Christian Democratic Party, the Liberals, the National Front, and the Democratic Union Party. A third, smaller bloc, the United Right Coalition, consisted of the Republicans, the Conservatives, the Democratic Movement Party, and the Democratic Christian Union. Only thirteen parties actually held parliamentary seats, and only the two largest formations really mattered, as the electoral system had cultivated an essentially bipolar party system.

After a prolonged boycott, the return to parliament of the Democratic Party during the summer of 1999 proved insufficient to engender political stability and institutional reform. The differences between Socialists and Democrats had little to do with ideology or policy and more to do with access to power and resources. Both government and parliament remained largely paralyzed amidst bitter power and personality struggles. The public exhibited little trust in the government. No credible centrist party emerged and young people invariably shunned politics altogether. Indeed, many young professionals continued to leave Albania because of limited opportunities and general disillusionment.

Socialist Ilir Meta was appointed prime minister in October 1999, after a loss of confidence in the Majko administration. During 1999 and 2000, the Meta government managed to restore public order in the major cities and began to implement measures to more effectively combat organized crime with international assistance. Nevertheless, official corruption and vigilantism remained serious challenges to economic reform and national stability.[16] Analysts noted a persistent symbiosis between politics and crime where many politicians and policemen were believed to be corrupt and where special interest groups controlled substantial sectors of the economy. Albania was a transit point for cross-Balkan smuggling, money laundering, and trafficking routes while developing a vibrant domestic industry focusing on prostitution, cigarette smuggling, refugee smuggling, drug and arms trafficking, and sanctions busting vis-à-vis Yugoslavia. The state lost enormous amounts of money each year on customs and tax evasion, while some members of the administration as well as local police chiefs were widely believed to profit from corruption.

With international assistance, the Meta administration introduced various measures to curtail corruption and organized crime and to build legitimate government institutions. Although public dissatisfaction with economic conditions was widespread, the Socialists maintained a significant degree of popularity because of their reformist endeavors and because the opposition parties failed to put forward a viable and attractive program for citizens. After two rounds of voting in parliamentary elections, held on 24 June and 8 July 2001, the Socialist Party returned a majority, with 73 of the 140 seats contested. The Democratic Party, which headed the coalition, obtained 25 direct seats and a total of 46. Of the smaller parties, the newly formed New Democratic Party (NDP) gained 5 parliamentary deputies. The Socialists formed the next Albanian government, and their majority in the legislature would enable them to elect the next Albanian President in an indirect presidential ballot scheduled for 2002.

The role of Albania remained important in Kosova's development. The country clearly passed some major tests during the two-month war between NATO and Serbia in the spring of 1999, both as a NATO ally and as a factor of regional stability. Tirana opened up the country to the Allies with no hesitation and assisted NATO in its mission against the Milošević regime. Meanwhile, the Albanian people spontaneously opened up their homes to Kosovar refugees and thereby helped to ease a potentially heavy burden on the European Union and the United Nations.

Both of the major Albanian political parties maintained connections with nascent Kosovar parties. Their influence could have proven negative if they had primarily replicated the cleavages evident in Tirana. Exclusive links between Socialists and the parties that were formed by political leaders from the former Kosova Liberation Army, and between Democrats and the Democratic League of Kosova, encouraged polarization and countered attempts to forge a broad-based reformist agenda in Kosova. There were also indications during 1999 and 2000 that criminal elements had moved into Kosova from Albania to replace the Serbian mobsters who ruled the territory during the previous decade. Criminal gangs acted as parasites on the developing economy and subverted the process of democratization and reform.

Both Albania and Kosova remained highly dependent on the international community for their stability and security, and for any prospects of economic development. But long-term external dependence tended to breed internal stagnation and stifled indigenous initiative. Because of political uncertainty and rampant criminality for much of the 1990s, most foreign investors had shied away from Albania. The international community maintained a presence in Albania both during and after the war over Kosova. NATO troops were stationed in the country to provide logistical support for the large Allied presence in neighboring Kosova after Serbian forces fled the province in early June 1999.

POLITICAL PARTIES

Socialists and Social Democrats

Albanian Socialist Party (ASP)
Partia Socialiste Shqipërisë (PSS)

The Albanian Communist Party (ACP) was founded on 8 November 1941 and was renamed the Albanian Party of Labor (APL) in September 1948. Following the collapse of communist rule, the party adopted its present name, the Albanian Socialist Party (ASP), at its tenth congress, in June 1991. Its chairman for most of the 1990s was Fatos Nano, its general secretary was Gramoz Ruçi, and its vice-chairmen were Servet Pëllumbi, Ilir Meta, and Namik Dokle. The party claimed to have about 115,000 members by the mid-1990s, and with an estimated core national support of some 19% of the population. The APL changed its name to separate itself from the repressive policies of Enver Hoxha.

Under the communist system, only the APL was allowed to operate; all other parties were banned, and political opposition and ruthlessly suppressed.

The ASP emerged from the defunct APL when reformist elements realized that the days of single-party rule were numbered. A more orthodox stream within the APL, which sponsored anti-reformist organizations such as the Enver Hoxha Voluntary Activists Union, tried to restore hard-line communism; but they were rapidly outpaced by events and had negligible public support. In the general elections on 31 March 1991, the APL won 169 seats in the 250-seat parliament, while the main opposition formation, the Democratic Party (DP), won only 75. The Socialists received most of their support from the rural areas and from the older population. Widespread civil unrest, a series of four unstable governments, and the inability to transform Albania into a functioning democratic state forced new elections a year later.

In the elections of 22 March 1992, the ASP garnered only 25% of the vote, while the DP obtained 62%. Following this political defeat, the ASP struggled to redefine itself as the only significant opposition to the DP. However, the party made some impressive gains in Albania's first democratic local elections in July 1992. This produced a difficult political situation in which a large proportion of the local government ended up in the hands of the ASP while the central government was controlled by Democrats. The ASP received 41% of the local vote, only slightly less than the DP. Out of a total of 43 municipalities, the ASP won 22 mayoralties.

Shaken by its crushing defeat in the parliamentary elections, the ASP tried hard not to lose further votes while increasing its share in certain areas, particularly in the south of the country. It primarily targeted groups of people who fell into the category of underprivileged, or those who felt the full impact of the tough economic reforms. The loss of jobs and steep rises in the cost of living that followed the lifting of price controls pushed hundreds of thousands of people below the poverty level despite promises of government compensation.

ASP propaganda was aimed at exploiting any internal dissent within the DP. Dismissed by the DP as "communists," ASP leaders claimed that they had created a modern European left-wing party with a pro-Western, pro-market, pluralist, and democratic orientation. The party was shaken in 1992–1993 by a series of arrests and trials of members of the previous government. In July 1993, chairman Fatos Nano was arrested and charged with corruption during his term as prime minister in 1991. The ASP alleged that the conviction was politically motivated and engineered by the DP. In protest, the ASP boycotted parliament throughout July and August 1993.[17]

The ASP claimed that it was committed to the defense of democracy, freedom, and human rights, and supported a new democratic constitution. It pledged support for economic reform and transformation into a market system with certain social and welfare provisions. It evidently favored an economy open to the world and integrated with European and global markets. Party leaders claimed that economic progress was impossible without European integration and closer ties with all European structures, including the Council of Europe and the European Union (EU). The ASP also stated its commitment to developing close relations with the United States.[18] Despite these pronouncements, some party leaders continued to play on populist and statist themes, particularly among the broad sector of the population that remained impoverished throughout the reform program.

Despite their initial financial and organizational advantages, the ASP suffered numerous setbacks in the early 1990s. First and foremost, party leaders were unable to convince the majority of voters that the ASP was no longer the same party that had been responsible for decades of repression. To many Albanian citizens, the Socialists still represented the old communist regime, which was blamed for the country's dire economic problems. As a result of their diminishing support in the early 1990s, the ASP heavily lost both the general and the local elections in 1996. In the parliamentary ballot on 26 May 1996, it gained just ten seats in the People's Assembly. Party leaders later claimed that the voting system discriminated against the opposition. In the local elections on 20 October 1996, the ASP won control over only four cities and 12 out of 310 communes.

During the nationwide unrest in the spring and summer of 1997, following the collapse of several "pyramid" investment schemes, the Socialists were accused of provoking armed revolt against the central and local governments controlled by Democrats. Indeed, Socialist leaders were charged with disruptive policies throughout their years in opposition. On 29 June 1997, the ASP regained power in a landslide general election victory, capturing 52.7% of the vote and 101 out of 155 parliamentary seats. The ASP clearly benefited from widespread public anger with the discredited and enfeebled Berisha administration. The Socialists formed a new government in coalition with several smaller, allied parties, including the Social Democratic Party, the Democratic Alliance, the Agrarian Party, and the Union for Human Rights. Parliament elected Socialist Rexhep Meidani as president and Socialist leader Fatos Nano became the new prime minister.

Nano stepped down as premier in September 1998 and was replaced by Socialist Party secretary-general Pandeli Majko. Majko became Europe's youngest head of government and launched a new anti-crisis program to restore security in the country. Majko was replaced by Ilir Meta as prime minister in October 1999, after a loss of confidence in the Majko administration. Meta's government began to register some success during 2000 in combating organized crime and pursuing economic stabilization. The ASP scored significant successes in the October 2000 local elections, gaining control over 252 out of 398 municipalities with over 50% of the popular vote. The ballot decimated Democratic Party control over the local administration throughout most of Albania, including the capital Tirana.

Despite the significant changeover in the party's personnel during the 1990s, the ASP retained its communist predecessor's extensive organizational network throughout the countryside. It maintained 36 district offices and had representation in nearly every town and village, with 3,777 branches. All of the district branches had a paid staff, including a chairman, secretary, and administrator. Most of the offices possessed the equipment and vehicles necessary to conduct a proper election campaign. The ASP's newspaper, *Zëri i Popullit*, was the largest circulation daily in Albania.The Socialists retained poser following the general elections in June 2001.

Social Democratic Party of Albania (SDPA)
Partia Socialdemokratike e Shqipërisë (PSDS)

The Social Democratic Party of Albania (SDPA) was established during 1991, just as the March general elections were taking place. It was led by chairman Skënder Gjinushi, a former minister of education in the last communist government. Its general secretary was Gaqo Apostoli, and other prominent personalities included Haxhi Aliko and Paskal Milo. The SDPA was largely composed of intellectuals. It gained support relatively quickly and was able to field 97 candidates in Albania's first pluralistic elections, making it the fourth party to qualify for supplemental seats according to the proportional system used in the ballot. It claimed a membership of some 23,000 by the mid-1990s and estimated its overall popular support at some 4% of the electorate. One of the SDPA's main achievements was to gain entry into the Socialist International, which opened the party to foreign contacts and precluded the possibility of membership by the Socialist Party. The ASP was seeking to become the Albanian representative as a way of gaining legitimacy in its claim to be a fully reformed party.

Although the SDPA finished third in the parliamentary elections in March 1992, gaining 4.38% of the votes and seven seats, it subsequently failed to elicit support from the population. As a party consisting predominantly of intellectuals, it lacked a well-developed grassroots organization. The SDPA spent most of the late 1990s devising a broad national strategy rather than building up its grassroots base. The SDPA's campaign slogan, "Work, Security, and Justice," reflected its priorities. The party's election campaigns concentrated on political issues such as the leadership style of President Berisha, the absence of a national constitution, and the lack of an independent judiciary. But it experienced difficulties in directly addressing issues that concerned voters, particularly their growing sense of economic insecurity. The SDPA formed the other half of the "Center Pole," along with the Democratic Alliance Party. Through this informal coalition, their joint candidates had a greater political base to work from than the meager nationwide support that the SDPA had managed to develop.

Gjinushi was consistently re-elected chairman of the SDPA despite the fact that he was unable to run as a candidate under the new electoral law in the early 1990s because he had been a minister in the last communist government. The SDPA maintained government-funded national headquarters in Tirana, with a small paid staff; it also possessed staff in all 36 districts of the country. Following the 1992 local elections, it had 308 officials at district and city levels. The party produced a party newspaper, *Alternative SD*, which was published two or three times per week, with a small circulation. In the June 1997 elections, the SDPA garnered nine legislative seats and entered the coalition government led by the Socialist Party.

Social Democratic Union (SDU)
Bashkimi Socialdemokrat e Shqipërisë (BSSH)

The Social Democratic Union (SDU) was formed as a splinter party by members of the Social Democratic Party (SDPA), including member of parliament Teodor Laço, writer Bardhyl Londo, and former Deputy Foreign Minister Arian Starova. Laço was a minister in the 1992–1996 Democratic Party–controlled government and left the SDPA in late 1994 in opposition to the party's decision to leave the coalition with the Democrats. Laço was the SDU's chairman, and its general secretary was Ferdinand Dafa. The SDU failed to develop an independent identity that translated into support for its candidates. Critics charged that the party was actually sponsored by the Democratic Party to foster division among potential political rivals. The party held its first national congress in April 1996 and subsequently staged campaign events throughout the country. However, the SDU was unable to expand its support base and gain any additional parliamentary seats, and was perceived by its rivals as a mere appendage of the Democratic Party. In the June 1997 general elections, it received only one parliamentary seat.

Liberals

Albanian Democratic Party (ADP)
Partia Demokratike e Shqipërisë (PDS)

The Albanian Democratic Party (ADP) was originally founded on 12 December 1990 by dissident intellectuals who were largely disillusioned ex-communists. Its unofficial, symbolic leader was Ismail Kadare, a renowned writer and a secretary of the Albanian Academy of Sciences. Its seventeen-member steering committee was initially led by student activist Azem Hajdari, charismatic cardiologist Sali Berisha, and general secretary Besnik Gjongecaj. The ADP was a diverse assortment of individuals and ideologies bound together by their opposition to communist rule. In March 1990, the party openly called for an end to the Leninist regime; this marked the beginning of the intellectual revolt against communism. On 19 December 1990, the ADP became the first independent party to receive formal recognition from the Ministry of Justice and began the process of forming a viable political opposition.

The party experienced resistance from the government at all stages of its development. The first priority of the ADP leadership was to postpone the planned March general elections until May 1991 in order to allow the pro-democratic forces time to organize and develop their campaign. At first the government denied the request; however, after large popular rallies and a threat of a boycott, the government postponed the elections until 31 March 1991. The ADP demanded the establishment of an opposition press and the release of all political prisoners. Eventually, the government conceded to these demands. With few financial and material resources, the ADP struggled to build up its membership and infrastructure throughout the early 1990s.

By the time of the first parliamentary elections in March 1991, the ADP managed to establish branches throughout the country, thus becoming a genuinely national party. Its estimated membership stood at some 120,000, and its popular support in opinion polls reached 41%. The charismatic leadership of Sali Berisha and the professionalism of his colleagues helped to put the ADP at the forefront of the electoral race in all major cities. The party emphasized the importance of human rights, improved relations with neighboring states, the introduction of a market economy, and the foundations of a state based on the rule of law. The economic program presented by the ADP frightened some people, especially those in rural areas, where pro-Socialist propaganda claimed that the ADP program sought to sell their land to foreigners.

The ADP's program of creating a Western-type political system and fully opening up the country to foreign influence, assistance, and investment created substantial support in urban areas and among young people. Party leaders pledged to fight for the creation of a democracy based on human rights and fundamental freedoms, prosperity through economic freedom and social justice, and the unification of the nation with historic developments taking place throughout Europe. The ADP's program denounced the Enverist version of Stalinism as wholly anti-democratic, anti-national, and "anti-human," and persistently accused the Socialists of being secret Enverists.

On 31 March 1991, in the first multiparty elections, the ADP won 75 seats in the People's Assembly, despite losing to the APL. The very fact that the Democrats were able to organize in just three months and win parliamentary seats in the face of enormous obstacles was a considerable achievement. Despite being in opposition, the ADP nevertheless had political momentum on its side. It obtained the economic and finance portfolios in the Socialist-led government, and became vulnerable to criticism due to the continuous deterioration of the economy. As a result, Berisha declared any further cooperation with the Socialists as unworkable and withdrew ADP members from the government in December 1991.

As the leading and most effective opposition force in Albania, the ADP attracted many individuals with widely divergent views and backgrounds. With the development of political pluralism, these differences led to the formation of factions within the ADP. At the end of 1991, policy differences over continued participation in the Socialist government marked the beginning of the first split in ADP ranks. This resulted in the expulsion of many of its prominent members, including Gramoz Pashko, who formed the Albanian Democratic Alliance Party, in opposition to what they claimed was the "autocratic rule" of Berisha. In order to solve some of the problems that kept the ADP from winning in the 1991 elections, the party received considerable foreign assistance, as it desperately needed office equipment and vehicles, which were critical for access to the countryside.

In the general elections on 31 March 1992, the ADP won 92 out of 140 People's Assembly seats, and on 9 April Berisha was elected President of Albania, following the resignation of former President Ramiz Alia. Berisha asked ADP member Aleksandër Meksi to form a new government. The elections were held in a significantly more open environment than a year before. The opposition, and the ADP in particular, had increased its ability to communicate with voters throughout Albania, and greater media freedom led to more accurate and balanced reporting on developments in the country.

After the 1992 elections, the ADP demonstrated an increasing intolerance toward the political opposition and press criticism. Both the Republican and Social Democratic parties left the coalition with the Democrats. The Social Democratic Party was soon labeled by the government as a "communist sympathizer" party, while the Republican Party, which remained supportive of the ADP and President Berisha, experienced milder attacks. The Democratic Alliance Party formed by several of the original founders of the ADP was discriminated against by the government in terms of access to the media and financial resources. Another split within the ADP occurred in August 1993, when two prominent members of the nationalist faction *Balli Kombëtar* (National Front) were dismissed from the party. They later created a new party: the Democratic Party of the Right.

The ADP suffered a major setback during the July 1992 local elections, as a result of which a large portion of local government ended up in the hands of the Socialists. This was primarily a consequence of continued economic hardship and policy mistakes during the ADP's four months in power. The local elections showed that there was a growing gap between local and central power, threatening the stability of the country at the same time as it was battling severe economic difficulties and struggling to establish a market economy. Only 70.5% of the Albanian electorate took part in the local elections—down from over 90% in the March 1992 general elections. The ADP won 43% of the vote—only 2% more than the Socialists. Following the elections, the ADP pledged to continue the economic reforms regardless of the outcome of the local elections.

The immediate reaction by the ADP leadership in general, and by Berisha in particular, was to fault others for the poor election results. He blamed ADP activists for their failure to wage an effective public relations campaign, despite the fact that a lot of campaigning was done by Berisha himself. Meanwhile, ADP Chairman Eduard Selami and Prime Minister Aleksandër Meksi began to gradually and quietly seek some distance from Berisha. Selami, the second most important politician in Albania, eventually was removed from his position as chairman because of his disagreement with Berisha regarding the role of the party in its relations with the government. Selami was replaced by Tritan Shehu in April 1995 at the ADP's national congress.

In the general elections on 26 May 1996, the ADP obtained an absolute majority of Assembly seats because of the proportional representation system that was employed. Despite winning only 55.5% of the vote, it gained 122 seats, or 87% of the parliament. This result reinforced opposition claims that the ADP and Berisha were establishing authoritarian rule. They were blamed for election fraud and for extending their power over the legislative, executive, and judicial branches of government, as well as over the media. In protest against what he viewed as Berisha's "personality cult," Azem Hajdari, one of the founders of the party and a former student leader, broke with the ADP and was elected leader of the Union of Independent Trade Unions in November 1996. Hajdari charged the government with corruption, authoritarianism, and monopolization of the mass media.

On 20 October 1996, the Democrats emerged as the absolute winners of the local elections, gaining representation in 58 out of 64 town halls and in 268 out of 309 communities. Despite the difficulties and disputes, the 1996 elections gave the ADP a clear mandate to govern and took international pressure off the administration, enabling its leaders to further increase their hold on power. The party had developed an effective organizational network throughout the country. It maintained a large national headquarters in Tirana as well as offices in all 36 districts of Albania, in addition to most of the smaller communes and villages. Every district branch had a paid staff consisting of a chairman, secretary, and financial specialist. The ADP published a daily national newspaper, *Rilindja Demokratike*, which propagated the ADP's party line; and when in government, it maintained editorial control over state television and radio.

During the armed revolt in the spring and summer of 1997, following the bankruptcy of the "pyramid" investment schemes, the Democrats' support base rapidly shrank and the popularity of President Berisha plummeted, despite his reelection as President of Albania by the legislature on 3 March 1997. The party itself experienced internal turmoil, and a new faction, led by former deputy prime minister Dashamir Shehi, left the ADP to form the new Movement for Democracy Party (MDP). However, the group proved unable to garner any significant public support. In the early general elections of 29 June 1997, the Democrats were decimated, President Berisha resigned from office, and the Socialists returned to power. The Socialists gained 101 of the 155 seats in the National Assembly, garnering 52% of the vote, against 25% for the Democrats. After the ballot, the ADP faced an uphill battle in trying to regain its credibility and authority in the country, although it did maintain a hard-core group of supporters. The party suffered further setbacks when a rival faction led by Genc Pollo emerged within it. The ADP suffered major losses in the October 2000 local elections and the June 2001 parlimentary ballot.

Albanian Republican Party (ARP)
Partia Republikane e Shqipërisë (PRS)

The Albanian Republican Party (ARP) was the second party to register when the political opposition was legalized during 1990. Its leadership included Chairman Sabri Godo, Vice Chairman Fatmir Mediu, and General-Secretary Çerçiz Mingomataj. The ARP sought to become a Western-style political party with a conservative and rightist direction. The ARP's platform included the protection of human rights and the democratization of Albania, but it chose a less radical, confrontational platform than the ADP. It emphasized social and economic rights rather than the privatization of industry and property. In the first general elections on 31 March 1991, the ARP did not win any seats in the parliament, but it built a modicum of political influence in the country. It claimed a membership of some 20,000 people by the early 1990s. The Republican platform was geared towards moderate Albanians desiring a more measured and protective emergence from isolation and central planning.

Just before the first general elections, the ARP made a strategic mistake that alienated a large number of potential supporters. Party Chairman Godo endorsed certain Albanian Party of Labor (APL) candidates on national television and radio, suggesting that Albanians should support reform-minded communists, which would allow the country to begin emerging from isolation. This convinced many Albanians that the ARP was actually controlled by the Socialists. Only by subsequently directing its supporters to vote for the Democrats was the ARP able to restore some of its legitimacy.

After the parliamentary elections on 22 March 1992, in which the ARP won only one seat, the party joined the ADP-dominated government, with one minister and two deputy ministers. The ARP held its first congress in June 1992, during which major divisions within the party emerged. This eventually led to splits and the creation of two parties: the Albanian Republican Party and the Party of Republican Alliance. The ARP sought to develop a broader constituency in several ways. First, it aligned itself with the position of former land-and property owners and made the return of property confiscated by the communist regime the centerpiece of its platform. Second, it initiated the formation of the "Right Front" of political parties to compete in the parliamentary elections of 26 May 1996. However, this attempted coalition actually disintegrated before the balloting took place.

The ARP's slogan "Land will belong to those who work it" proposed a rebuilding of the countryside by the peasants, as well as privatization with less interference from the state. In addition, the ARP developed an effective series of posters for the national campaign, and some of its candidates prepared individual brochures. The ARP aggressively pursued a strategy of broadening its base in the districts, communes, and villages in preparation for the May 1996 elections, in which the party received almost 6% of the votes and obtained three seats in the People's Assembly.

The Albanian Republican Party also experienced some success in the local elections on 20 October 1996, finishing third, behind the ADP and ASP, but continued to suffer from a lack of resources and grassroots support. In the general elections of June 1997, the Republicans could only muster 2.4% of the vote, and gained only one parliamentary seat. The ARP possessed a government-provided national office in Tirana with a small, paid staff, and maintained 38 district branches with offices. The party's main power base was in the Tosk areas, in the south of the country. It also produced a party newspaper, *Republika* (Republic), published two to three times a week. During the course of the mid to late 1990s, the party moved gradually toward a more nationalist position, and strongly adopted the controversial policy of restitution for property owners dispossessed by the communist regime. Such a policy alienated many residents and peasants, who feared that they would be evicted from their homes and farms if the ARP program was implemented. By the late 1990s, the party was led by a younger and more ambitious team than its original leadership and was grouped around the well-known Fatmir Mediu.

Albanian Democratic Alliance Party (ADAP)
Aleance Demokratike e Shqipërisë (ADS)

The Albanian Democratic Alliance Party (ADAP) was formed in late 1992 as a splinter group of the Albanian Democratic Party (ADP), including two of the original founders, Gramoz Pashko and Secretary-General Arben Imami, as well as the ADAP President Neritan Ceka. It claimed to have 15,000 members and an estimated national support of some 5%. Following Berisha's announcement on 6 December 1991 that the ADP was withdrawing from the Ylli Bufi government, in contradiction to the view of the party's Deputy Chairman Pashko, the ADP parliamentary leader, Ceka, left the party. He was supported by six other members of parliament: Pashko; Perikli Teta, former minister of defense; Arben Imami, former ADP secretary-general; Ridvan Peshkëpia; Teodor Keko; and Afrim Jupi. All of these activists were formally expelled from the ADP in July 1992. ADAP leaders complained that under Berisha's authoritarian rule the ADP was evolving into a "right-wing party" controlled by a narrow interest group tied to the president.

The ADAP members of parliament were not recognized as a separate parliamentary caucus but as a group of independents. Although the ADAP had six deputies in the first democratic parliament, the number needed to form a parliamentary group, they were denied such recognition. In addition, they received no government funding, and asserted that they were regularly harassed and threatened by the authorities. Lacking in material resources, ADAP leaders focused their campaign on individual races rather than trying to run a unified national campaign. The party did not have a single campaign slogan; rather, individual candidates devised their own slogans and formulated agendas based on local conditions. The most common theme of the ADAP was an emphasis on creating a "normal" Albania. It concentrated its resources on producing individual brochures for candidates.

The most important strategic decision by the ADAP was to join with the Social Democratic Party in forming the "Center Pole." Under an agreement within this informal coalition, the two parties chose to evenly divide the majority of the electoral zones in Albania between them and run only one candidate in each zone. Their hope was that the "Center Pole" would draw former ADP supporters who were disenchanted with Berisha's leadership style, as well as those voters who leaned to the left but who were not comfortable voting for the former communist party. Because they occupied the center of the political spectrum, they expected that any of their candidates who made it to the second round of voting would be able to defeat the ADP or ASP candidates.

Although the state did not provide office space, the ADAP did operate a small headquarters with a few paid staff. They had branches in most districts but maintained offices in less than a dozen and possessed few material resources or vehicles. The ADAP pursued a grassroots strategy and possessed a youth-oriented core, but it still faced a great number of obstacles in becoming a truly nationwide party. Its support was largely confined to intellectuals and the small, emerging class of entrepreneurs. The ADAP program was not dissimilar to that of the ADP. But the party was critical of what it called authoritarian tendencies within the Democratic Party leadership. It advocated a faster pace to and an expansion of economic reforms, as well as the diminution of the state sector.

In October 1993, the party leadership paid a controversial visit to Belgrade aimed at opening a dialogue, during which they held talks with Serbian government officials. The visit was sharply criticized by the ADP on the grounds that the mission gave the internationally isolated Milošević the basis to claim that he was talking with Albanians. The ADAP remained a small and mostly intellectual-based formation for the remainder of the decade, gaining only two parliamentary seats in the June 1997 elections and a mere 2.7% of the popular vote.

Christian Democrats

Christian Democratic Party (CDP)
Partia Demokristiane (PD)

The Christian Democratic Party (CDP) sought to embrace the Christian democratic tradition of parties in Western Europe. Its Chairman, Zef Bushati, was one of the founders of the Albanian Republican Party and then became actively involved in building a national Christian democratic party. The CDP claimed about 8,000 members by the mid-1990s and maintained its support base primarily in the northern and more Catholic regions of the country, in and around the city of Shkodër, but it proved unable to compete on a nation-wide scale. Its platform was generally on the center-right of the political spectrum with regard to economic issues. In the May 1996 general elections it failed to win parliamentary seats, taking only 1.3% of the popular vote. However, in the June 1997 elections, it took one legislative seat even though it scored less than 1% of the popular vote. The CDP maintained close ties with the Albanian Democratic Party and became part of the larger opposition bloc after the 1997 ballot.

Agrarians

Albanian Agrarian Party (AAP)
Partie Agrare e Shqipërisë (PAS)

The AAP was founded in 1991 before the March national elections. Its president was Lufter Xhuveli and it claimed a membership of 20,000 people. Despite the fact that an overwhelming majority of the Albanian population lived in the countryside, the party only managed to attract limited support among rural dwellers due to the strong conservatism of the peasantry as well as the minuscule resources of the party. The AAP proposed a program of rescuing Albania's agricultural sector and the peasant population devastated by four decades of collectivization. It demanded new laws to regulate the privatization of former collectivized property and land; the setting up of credit arrangements for farmers; the establishment of the right to form new and voluntary arrangements, including cooperatives; and a concerted effort to create new jobs for the large percentage of unemployed, particularly youths, in the countryside. In the elections of June 1997, the AAP managed to gain one parliamentary seat after forming an election alliance with the Socialist Party. Agrarian issues did not attract a sizable public following, largely because of their narrow focus and the preponderant influence of the two largest political parties.

Greens

Albanian Ecological Party (AEP)
Partia Ekologjike e Shqipërisë (PES)

The Albanian Ecological Party (AEP) was founded on 1 January 1991 and was led by Namik Hoti. It claimed a membership of between 1,500 and 2,000 people. A second environmentalist party, the Albanian Green Party (AGP) (Partia e Blertë Shqiptare, PBS), was led by Chairman Nasi Bozhegu and claimed a membership of some 3,000 citizens. However, environmentalist parties in Albania were unable to attract any substantial popular support because of their narrow focus and the general lack of public awareness of ecological issues. Moreover, the AEP was widely believed to have been sponsored by the ex-communists to undercut the appeal of larger opposition parties.

Communists

Albanian Communist Party (ACP)
Partia Komuniste Shqiptare (PKS)

The Albanian Communist Party (ACP) was founded in December 1991 and promptly outlawed in June 1992, although it claimed to have a membership of several thousand people. The party was formed by hard-line Enverists opposed to the policies of the reformed Albanian Socialist Party and the democratic opposition. It produced a political platform for the March 1992 parliamentary elections, but the Albanian parliament imposed a ban on the activities of the party and on the formation of similar communist or fascist organizations in the future.

The party's program issued for the 1992 parliamentary elections warned of the perils of "counter-revolution" in Albania. It appealed to the electorate to follow the teachings and instructions of the "genius" Enver Hoxha, who evidently contributed to the freedom and independence of Albania. In trying to mobilize nationalist appeal, the Communist Party expressed support for the Republic of Kosova and the territorial autonomy of Albanians in Macedonia, Montenegro, and Serbia, with the prospect of uniting all these territories in a single nation-state. It also supported the "legitimate human and national rights" of the Albanians violently expelled from or living under a system of discrimination in the territory of Çamëria, in northern Greece.

Nationalists

Democratic Party of the Right (DPR)
Partia Demokratike e Djathtë (PDD)

The Democratic Party of the Right (DPR) emerged during 1994 as a result of a split within the Democratic Party when two prominent members of the right-wing faction *Balli Kombëtar* (National Front), Abdi Baleta and Petrit Kalakula, left the party. Kalakula became the DPR chairman. Following internal personality conflicts, Baleta was expelled from the DPR in May 1995. He went on to form the Party of National Restoration, which advocated the union of Kosova with Albania. The platform of the DPR was aggressively nationalist and anti-communist. It also vehemently advocated the restoration of pre-communist property rights. The party was involved in an attempt to form a "Right Front" in Albanian politics but decided to enter the May 1996 elections alone and gained no parliamentary seats. The party supported the complete return of property nationalized in 1945, including land, to its former owners. DPR leaders voiced strong backing for the creation of a "Greater Albania," without which there would allegedly be no stability in the Balkans. Despite its efforts, the DPR failed to build a national party structure; it possessed a national office but no district offices. It also ran a party newspaper, *E Djathta*, which was published once a week.

National Front (NF)
Balli Kombëtar (BK)

The National Front (NF) was originally formed before World War II to fight against Italian fascists and then the Albanian communists. It was the major anti-communist resistance group during World War II. The party was outlawed and severely repressed by Hoxha's communist regime but was resuscitated soon after Albania's democratic breakthrough in 1991. Its chairman was Abaz Ermenji, who led the party when it was a guerrilla partisan movement during World War II. The party's vice chairman was Hysen Selfo. The NF claimed a membership of 12,300 by the mid-1990s. It had elected officials in several districts following the 1996 local elections, and received substantial financial resources from Albanian émigré organizations, enabling it to maintain a national office and a few district offices and to publish a party newspaper twice a week. Most of the NF's support came from older Albanians and expatriates. Following the parliamentary elections of 26 May 1996, Ermenji left Albania and returned to exile in Paris, in protest against the NF's recognition of the election results in which *Balli Kombëtar* gained only three seats. The National Front gained only three seats and 2.3% of the popular vote in the June 1997 elections, and remained a marginal political player.

Movement of Legality Party (MLP)
Partia Lëvizja e Legalitetit (PLL)

The Movement of Legality Party (MLP) was dedicated to restoring the monarchy of King Leka Zogu, the son of Zog I, who was two days old when his parents fled Albania in the wake of the Italian invasion in 1939. The MLP claimed to be one of the oldest political parties in Albania and had been banned under the communist system. It maintained a small core of monarchist supporters, and sponsored visits from King Zogu during the 1990s. Its chairman was Guri Durollari, and its membership was estimated at some 6,200 people. But it failed to revive significant public interest in the monarchy, even though Zogu returned to Albania during the public revolts in April 1997 in order to mobilize public support for the restoration of a constitutional monarchy. During the March 1992 elections, several MLP candidates were elected to district and communal councils. In 1993, major divisions emerged within the party, which led to a split that further weakened its impact. The party's support came primarily from older Albanians who remained nostalgic for the monarchy and favorably viewed the rule of Zog I in the 1920s. During the mid-1990s, the MLP split into several factions, thus further eroding its chances of gaining any mass appeal.

Another essentially monarchist party, the National Democratic Party (NDP), was formed in 1991 and competed for the same constituency as the MLP. It was equally unable to build a nationwide organization and did not possess a credible economic program. Various attempts were made to unite the nationalist and monarchist rightist parties in local and national election campaigns, but the efforts failed to create any coherent mass movement. For example, six parties formed an Albanian Right League in February 1995, with a coordinating committee and rotating leadership. But the coalition collapsed before the 1996 elections, because of intense inter-party rivalries.

Albanian National Unity Party (ANUP)
Partia e Unitetit Kombëtar (PUK)

The Albanian National Unity Party (ANUP) was registered in March 1991 under the chairmanship of Idajet Beqiri. The program of the ANUP included calls for the creation of a pan-Albanian confederation encompassing all the territories inhabited by Albanian majorities in Kosova, Serbia, Montenegro, Macedonia, and Greece. ANUP leaders demanded that Tirana take a more forthright role in support of Albanian rights in Kosova. They recognized the independent Kosovar constitution passed in September 1990 by the Kosovar Assembly and the subsequent declaration of independence in late September 1991. It voiced its readiness to work together with all political and non-political organizations whose goals were to "protect Albanian national interests" inside and outside of the country. Observers believed that the ANUP included many former hard-line communists who were seeking to capitalize on latent nationalist sentiments among the population. Although they openly sought to annex territories inhabited by Albanian majorities to neighboring countries before World War I, ANUP leaders claimed they did not propose forceful reintegration. In ANUP estimations, the peaceful creation of a second Albanian republic, to include Kosova and parts of Macedonia and Montenegro, would purportedly be followed by a formal union with Albania after a public referendum.

ANUP membership remained small, although the party claimed latent support within other political parties and evidently received financial and material assistance from exiled Kosovar Albanians, enabling it to publish a weekly newspaper. It failed to win seats in the general elections of March 1992, gathering under 1% of the total national vote. Although the major Albanian parties, including the Democrats and Socialists, also contained deputies, members, and sympathizers who periodically voiced militant nationalist sentiments, they did not manage to form significant political factions within the two major parties. In July 1993, Beqiri was sentenced to six months in prison for allegedly insulting and slandering President Berisha. Beqiri had publicly claimed that Berisha was installing a "fascist dictatorship" in Albania. Critics claimed that the government's measures were reminiscent of the former communist system and signaled an unsettling trend toward autocracy. The ANUP only managed to gain less than 1% of the popular vote in the June 1997 elections but was allotted one parliamentary seat as a result of its coalition with the ADP.

Motherland Political Association (MPA)
Shoqata Politike Mëmëdheu (SPM)

The Motherland Political Association (MPA) was founded in July 1991. Its leadership worked in close alliance with the ANUP, declaring their main goal to be the creation of a pan-Albanian confederation in the Balkans. The MPA, together with the ANUP and the Kosova Patriotic and Political Association, demanded that Tirana take a more visible role in support of Albanian interests in Kosova and unreservedly recognize the independent Kosovar constitution and the sovereignty and independence of the Kosovar republic. Like the ANUP, the MPA was critical of both the Albanian authorities and the Albanian leadership in Kosova for remaining too passive and conciliatory in the face of Serbian intransigence and constant provocations. In the event of armed confrontations in Kosova, both the ANUP and MPA appeared intent on mobilizing Albanians to actively defend their threatened kinsmen.[19]

Several other explicitly nationalist, revanchist, and expansionist organizations have also surfaced in Albania. Although ultra-nationalist influence in Albania remained restricted, dire economic conditions coupled with regional instability could provide them with wider public resonance. Such a scenario could also elevate nationalist sentiments within the more mainstream Albanian parties.

Kosova Patriotic and Political Association (KPPA)
Shoqata Patriotike Atdhetare Kosova (SPAK)

The Kosova Patriotic and Political Association (KPPA) was established in March 1991. A militant pro-Kosovar group, it held its founding congress in Tirana in June 1991 and claimed a membership of about 12,700 people. A number of similar pro-Kosovar groups and cultural associations were created in both Tirana and the northern city of Shkodër. The Association was headed by Murat Gjonbala, and the initiating commission also included Husamadin Ferraj, Ibrahim Shatri, Agim Haxhia, and Shkëlzen Berisha.

The KPPA claimed to be an "all-national association." Although it did not participate in the parliamentary and local elections in the early 1990s, it declared its backing for political forces that supported the independence of the territories in the former Yugoslavia inhabited predominantly by Albanians. Its main goal was to achieve the "social, cultural, and political freedom of the Albanian majority in Serbian-ruled Kosova," and eventually to facilitate the national unification of all Albanians and the peaceful creation of a single Albanian state. The KPPA's platform encouraged pan-national unification in a "European context," claiming this to be in accordance with the basic documents of international justice, such as the UN Charter, the Helsinki Final Act, and OSCE documents. It considered the development of educational, cultural, and economic links with Kosova not as final goals but rather as the fastest road toward Albanian unification.[20]

Çamëria Political and Patriotic Association (CPPA)
Shoqata Patriotike Atdhetare "Çamëria" (SPAC)

The Çamëria Political and Patriotic Association (CPPA) was formed in January 1991 and was registered by the Ministry of Justice one month later. It was headed by Abaz Dojaka and claimed a membership of some 40,000 people by the end of the year. In March 1991, the first national conference of the CPPA was held in Tirana, with many of its activists drawn from the Albanian community expelled from Çamëria, an area of northwestern Greece occupied and then lost by Albania during World War II. Delegates demanded the protection of the legitimate rights of the Albanian minority in Greece and called for the Greek authorities to recognize the persistence of the "Çam question." They urged the Albanian government to take up the issue with Athens at the highest bilateral levels and to be more assertive in defending the rights of Çam Albanians remaining in Greece. The CPPA intended to bring to international attention the neglected and suppressed linguistic, cultural, and educational rights of both Orthodox and Muslim Albanian Çams, who had been subjected to a policy of "Greek assimilation."

The group also launched campaigns on behalf of dispossessed Çam exiles in Albania. Although the CPPA did not participate in parliamentary elections, it claimed to represent the majority of an estimated 200,000-strong Çamërian population in Albania, which resided primarily in the southern part of the country. Çamërian exiles in Albania claimed that about 250,000 of their co-ethnics were still resident in Greece (although not all in Çamëria) and were deprived of all elementary collective rights. Dojaka specified that his organization had three main demands for Athens: respect for international conventions on the treatment of minorities, including all relevant OSCE documents; the opening of Albanian schools; the return of property confiscated from expelled Çams or the payment of appropriate compensation by Athens; and permission for Albanian Çams to return to their ancestral lands and maintain contacts with family members and kinsmen. The CPPA asserted that the Greek government continued to prevent Çams from obtaining visas to visit Greece.

The CPPA claimed a structure of some 23 local branches, primarily in southern Albania, and the support of a broad cross-section of Albania's political forces, as well as the Çam population in Greece. Çamërian leaders contended that they were expanding their influence across Albania's political spectrum and that several political parties had taken their cause aboard in their programs. It favored granting human and group rights to the Greek minority in Albania but opposed any steps toward political or territorial autonomy and demanded similar rights for the Çam population in Greece.

The CPPA staunchly opposed any Greek territorial pretensions and believed that some elements of *Omonia* and the Unity Party for Human Rights (UPHR) were radicals supported by chauvinistic and annexationist forces in Greece. Dojaka alleged that these elements sought to provoke ethnic conflicts in Albania in order to hasten Greek government intervention. The CPPA denied that it was involved in attacks on Greek stores in Sarandë in February 1992, evidently in retaliation for the mistreatment of Albanian refugees in Greece, or that it sought to heighten ethnic tensions in Albania. It claimed to have some contact with Çams in Albania where Greek policy made it difficult to organize pressure groups. Çamërian leaders confirmed that the Association supported the Democratic Party in the March 1992 elections, although some suspicions were initially voiced about the CPPA's links with the former communists. The CPPA managed to raise public and governmental interest in the Çam issue and both Democratic and Socialist administrations raised the question with Athens throughout the 1990s as a counterweight to Greek campaigns on behalf of the Greek minority in Albania.[21]

Ethnic Minority and Religious Parties

Democratic Union of the Greek Minority "Omonia" (DUGM)
Bashkimi Demokratik i Minoritetit Grek "Omonia" (BDMG)

The Democratic Union of the Greek Minority "Omonia" (DUGM), otherwise known as the *Omonia* Sociopolitical Organization (OSO), was created in February 1991, in accordance with a decree dated December 1990, on the creation of political organizations and associations. It was not originally a political party but a cultural association that subsequently engaged in political activities. *Omonia* (Harmony) placed strong emphasis on monitoring the alleged repression of the Greek population, and received substantial support from the ethnic Greek minority concentrated in the southern districts of Sarandë and Gjirokastër.

Omonia became Albania's largest minority organization representing the Orthodox Christian, ethnic Greek community. Its leaders, including President Thoma Sharra and Secretary-General Vangjel Papakristo, called for an end to

Albania's isolationism and the persecution of its minorities. They expressed concern over the mass exodus of refugees to Greece during 1990–1991, and they appealed for a maximum commitment on the part of both the government and the local authorities to stabilize the situation in the minority areas affected by the exodus. Omonia's subsequent president was Sotir Qirjazati and its chairman was Theodori Bezhani.

The Greek minority in Albania, estimated at 60,000 by Tirana and around 300,000 by Athens in the early 1990s, inhabited the villages of southern Albania, with a large share residing in the larger cities. In the March 1991 elections, *Omonia* presented its candidates in southern Albania and won each of the five constituencies it contested, thus becoming the third largest party in parliament. At that time, there were widespread suspicions that *Omonia* was principally an ALP front designed to subdue or dilute demands for minority rights and to divide the burgeoning opposition movement. In fact, *Omonia* proved itself to be an authentic and legitimate political body that occasionally cooperated with the Democratic Party against the Socialists in the Albanian legislature.

The ban on all parties of ethnic, regional, or religious character, which was ratified by the Albanian parliament before the March 1992 ballot, changed *Omonia*'s political status, and the party was unable to participate in the second general elections. As a result, Greek minority political leaders complained that the restrictions violated OSCE principles. They threatened to boycott the elections, but subsequently backed the candidates of the newly-formed Unity Party for Human Rights (UPHR) for the 1992 balloting; many of these were also *Omonia* members. The position of *Omonia* was closely related to the state of official Albanian-Greek relations. As a purely ethnic Greek party, *Omonia* was a regional organization, exclusively concerned with local Greek minority issues. *Omonia* openly opposed Tirana's official policies toward the Greek minority, particularly the purported attempts to assimilate the minority by force and deprive it of its ethnic and cultural identity. To express these concerns, *Omonia* sent a memorandum to the OSCE during the International Human Dimension Conference held in Moscow in September and October 1992.

Following an internal party shake-up in early 1992, some of the relatively moderate *Omonia* leaders were replaced by more militant elements who demanded a referendum to determine the future status of Greek-inhabited areas in southern Albania. In June 1993, *Omonia* presented a petition to the Albanian parliament, calling for Greek children to be taught in their mother tongue at all school levels and for Greek to be used in Orthodox church services. In addition, Greek minority spokesmen wanted the freedom to play the Greek national anthem during major festivities and to hoist the Greek flag alongside the Albanian one. They also requested the restoration of property belonging to Greek families forced to leave Albania after the communist takeover in 1944.[22]

Unity Party for Human Rights (UPHR)
Bashkimi i të Drejtave të Njeriut (BDN)

The Unity Party for Human Rights (UPHR) was formed on 24 February 1992 in response to the ban on ethnicity-based political parties. For the second national elections on 31 March 1992, the UPHR presented 36 candidates, enough to be eligible for supplemental seats; but the Central Election Commission disqualified eleven of them for having invalid signatures on their petitions for candidacy. In the national elections, the UPHR won two People's Assembly seats as compared with Omonia's five seats in March 1991. It gained 2.9% of the popular vote, and Sotir Qirjazati and Thoma Miço were elected deputies. Its new co-chairmen were Vasil Melo and Thoma Miço.

Although it only had a few weeks to conduct an effective campaign, had little access to Albanian television or radio, and possessed insufficient funds to establish its own newspaper, the UPHR submitted 36 candidacies in as many electoral districts in order to assure its participation in the second round of seat distribution. Thoma Xhai was elected chairman of the UPHR, which consisted of minority Greeks, *Omonia* activists, and a handful of Albanians. According to the initiating documents, the main objective of the party was to register electable candidates and represent the interests of all minorities in parliament. It did not openly seek political or territorial self-determination for the Greek minority, and claimed to "oppose the policies of some chauvinistic circles in Greece." The influence of the UPHR increased in the following months, and in the elections for local representatives in July 1992, it received 4.3% of the popular vote and elected several dozen ethnic Greek mayors and other local officials.[23]

The UPHR was reportedly created to protect human rights for all citizens. But it was generally accepted as a Greek minority party, despite the fact that its chairman sought to demonstrate that it was a national party with a broad agenda. The promotion and protection of ethnic Greeks was its main concern. The party advocated far-reaching economic reforms leading toward a market economy to ensure a fast rate of development and a higher standard of living. The UPHR's program supported close economic relations with foreign countries, bilateral relations with all states, and the encouragement of foreign investment.

The UPHR possessed the third highest total of local elected officials, although these officials were located primarily in the country's southern regions, bordering Greece. The party did not have a government-provided national office, but it maintained a small office in Tirana and district offices primarily in southern districts. The UPHR did not possess a true nationwide presence. In the June 1997 general elections, the UPHR maintained its level of support among ethnic Greeks, gaining 2.7% of the vote and taking four parliamentary seats.

Association of Montenegrins (AM)
Shoqata e Malazezëve (SM)

The Association of Montenegrins (AM) was formed in Vraka, near the town of Shkodër, in northern Albania, as a social-cultural organization and not as an avowedly political group. Although the Montenegrins were not recognized by the Albanian authorities as a distinct national minority, the Association claimed to have over 1,000 members representing the interests of a 2,500-strong minority residing mainly in the area around Shkodër. The AM challenged the official statistics issued by Tirana in the early 1990s, in which the number of Montenegrins and Serbs was placed at only 100. Some Albanian officials contended that several hundred Slavs had left the country since the onset of the democratic changes, including both Serbs and Montenegrins, and that the numbers were accurate. Members of the Association advocated promoting the culture and customs of Montenegrins and urged the recognition of Montenegrin and Serbian minorities in Albania and the return of original Slavic names to members of these minorities. The AM planned to reopen elementary schools in the mother language and to form a Montenegrin-Serbian cultural club.[24]

Another Slavic minority grouping, the "Bratska" Political Association of Macedonians in Albania (BPAMA) *(Shoqata "Bratska" e Maqedonasve të Shqipërisë, SBMS)*, was established in September 1991 as an openly political group. It claimed to represent the interests of the small Macedonian minority located primarily in Albania's Macedonian border region. In August 1992, Tirana and Skopje agreed that the Macedonian government would help to fund Macedonian-language education in several villages near the border.[25]

Association of Arumanians in Albania (AAA)
Shoqata e Arumunëve të Shqipërisë (SAS)

The Association of Arumanians in Albania (AAA) was established in October 1991 by activists in the town of Selenicë, near Vlorë, which has a substantial Arumanian population. Delegates at the first conference in April 1992 confirmed the existence, authenticity, and legitimate rights of the Arumanian (or Vlach) population in Albania to its ethnic identity, language, customs, and culture. A council composed of 42 members was elected. Janko Ballamaci became its chairman; Anastas Buneci, Arqile Dhamaj, and Anastas Kaporeni, vice chairmen; and Nikolla Seferi, secretary-general. The conference specified the basic goals of the organization and issued a resolution demanding that the Arumanian community in Albania enjoy full ethno-cultural rights, like all other ethnic communities.

The Association intended to conduct a census of the Arumanian population through its fifteen local branches, although it recognized that many Vlachs were fully assimilated into Albanian culture and barely preserved their traditional language or identity. The AAA assumed a cultural character; but although it did not involve itself directly in the political process, some of its demands could be classified as essentially political. Its members believed that the state had to create all necessary conditions to enable the Arumanians to maintain their language and to develop their religious and cultural heritage in their mother tongue.

The AAA demanded that the government guarantee Arumanians the right to have their own language classes in local schools, as well as radio and television programs, newspapers, magazines and other publications, and to restore several delapidated churches and monasteries. Because of their minority's chronic impoverishment, Vlach leaders sought financial aid from the state to support these endeavors. The AAA also tried to promote contacts and develop relations between Albanian Arumanians and Romania (a country with which they claim historical links), as well as with Arumanian communities elsewhere in Eastern Europe and in the West. The AAA invited Vlachs from Vojvodina, Macedonia, Romania, Greece, Bulgaria, and Ukraine to take part in their April 1992 conference. The Association proposed that the Romanian government allow the Arumanians to travel in and out of the country without visas in order to enhance the exchange of ethno-cultural values and personal contacts.

The Roman (Gypsy) community also has become more active since the democratic changes in Albania. Reportedly, Jerg Romani activists formed an association during 1992 to press for various cultural liberties; but little solid information has been available about this and other Romani initiatives in Albania.[26]

POLITICAL DATA

Name of State: Republic of Albania *(Republika e Shqipërisë)*
Form of Government: Semi-presidential system
Structure of Legislature: Unicameral legislature, People's Assembly *(Kuvendi Popullor)*
Size of Territory: 11,100 square miles
Size of Population: 3,249,000 (1996)

Composition of Population

Ethnic Group	Number	% of Population
Albanians	3,117,600	97.96
Greeks	58,758	1.85
Macedonians	4,697	0.15
Serbs and Montenegrins	100	—
Others	1,261	0.04

Total minorities	64,816	2.04
Total population	3,182,416	100.00

Sources: Transitions On-line Country Reports, Albania, Statistics, http://www.tol.cz/ countries/albania.htm. The most recent official population statistics are taken from the *Statistical Yearbook of Albania 1991*, Tirana, 1991. According to *Koha Jone* of 18 October 1995, Albania's population only reached 3,256,000 in mid-1995. Despite the high birth rate and a yearly increase of approximately 60,000, the actual population increase was modest because of the large outflow of refugees since the early 1990s: this exodus was estimated at over half a million people.

ELECTION RESULTS

Presidential Election (Indirect), 24 July 1997

Candidate	Votes	% of Vote
Rexhep Meidani	110	70.96
Non-participants, against, abstentions, invalid	45	29.04
Total	155	100.00

Presidential Election (Indirect), 3 March 1997

Candidate	Votes	% of Vote
Sali Berisha	122	87.14
Non-participants, against, abstentions, invalid	18	12.86
Total	140	100.00

Presidential Election (Indirect), 9 April 1992

Candidate	Votes	% of Vote
Sali Berisha	96	68.57
Non-participants, against, abstentions, invalid	44	31.43
Total	140	100.00

Presidential Election (Indirect), 30 April 1991

Candidate	Votes	% of Vote
Ramiz Alia	172	68.80
Namik Dokle	2	0.80
Non-participants, against, abstentions, invalid	76	30.40
Total	250	100.00

Parliamentary Elections, 24 June 2001

Turnout: 54.95%

Party/Coalition	Votes	% of Vote	Seats
Socialist Party	549,589	41.513%	73
Union for Victory	487,314	36.809%	46
Democratic Party of Albania			
Party of the Albanian National Front			
Republican Party of Albania			
Movement of Legality Party			
Liberal Democratic Union			
New Democratic Party	67,349	5.087%	6
Social Democratic Party	48,253	3.645%	4
Unity Party for Human Rights	34,607	2.614%	3
Agrarian Party	33,993	2.568%	3
Democratic Alliance Party	33,718	2.547%	3
Independents	—	—	2
Total	1,254,823	94.783%	140

Sources: Albanian Central Election Commission; Agence France Presse 2001; Deutsche Presse-Agentur 2001; British Broadcasting Corporation, BBC Monitoring Europe 2001.

Note: Final election results were declared by the Albanian Central Election Commission on 21 August 2001. A total number of five rounds of voting took place between 24 June and 19 August. Out of the 140 seats in parliament, 100 deputies are elected by a majority vote and 40 deputies are elected by proportional representation.

Parliamentary Elections, 29 June 1997

Turnout: 72.96%

Party/Coalition	Votes	% of Vote	Seats
Socialist Party	690,003	52.71	101
Democratic Party	336,167	25.82	24
Social Democratic Party	32,537	2.49	9
Unity Party for Human Rights	37,191	2.71	4
National Front	30,693	2.34	3
Movement of Legality Party	42,567	3.28	2
Democratic Alliance Party	35,598	2.73	2
Republican Party	31,573	2.41	1
Christian Democratic Party	12,728	0.98	1
Social Democratic Union	10,457	0.80	1
Democratic Union Party	10,977	0.84	1
National Unity Party	3,784	0.29	1
Agrarian Party	10,421	0.80	1

Right Democratic Party	9,837	0.76	—
Movement for Democracy	3,802	0.29	—
Christian Democratic Union	3,734	0.29	—
Conservative Party	3,400	0.26	—
National Covenant Party	1,865	0.14	—
Democratic Progress Party	669	0.05	—
United Right Coalition	—	—	—
Independents	—	—	—
Total	1,308,023	100.00	151

Source: Central Election Commission, *Buletin: Rezultatet e Zgjedhjeve Parlamentare, Qershor 1997* (Bulletin: Results of the June 1997 Parliamentary Elections), Tirana, 1997.

Parliamentary Elections, 26 May 1996 and 2 June 1996[*]

Turnout: 89.08%

Party/Coalition	Votes	% of Vote	Seats
Democratic Party	914,218	55.50	122
Socialist Party	335,402	20.40	10
Unity for Human Rights Party	94,567	5.70	3
Albanian Republican Party	81,822	5.00	3
National Front	66,529	4.00	2
Movement of Legality Party	34,019	2.10	—
Social Democratic Union	32,430	2.00	—
Democratic Alliance Party	25,679	1.50	—
Social Democratic Party	25,019	1.50	—
Christian Democratic Party	21,068	1.30	—
Democratic Union Party	11,789	0.70	—
National Unity Party	3,939	0.20	—
Total	1,646,481	99.99	140

[*]Fourth polling was held on 16 June in 17 constituencies after previous balloting was invalidated due to fraud.

Sources: The International Republican Institute, IRI Observation Report on the Albanian Parliamentary Elections of May 26, 1996, Washington, D.C., 1996, p. 32 and *Urgent: Council of Europe Wants New Elections in Albania*, 1996 France Press.

Parliamentary Elections, 22 March 1992

Turnout: 90.35%

Party/Coalition	Votes	% of Vote	Seats
Democratic Party	1,046,193	62.09	92
Socialist Party	433,602	25.73	38
Social Democratic Party	73,820	4.38	7
Unity Party for Human Rights	48,923	2.90	2
Republican Party	52,477	3.11	1
Others	30,022	1.79	—
Total	1,685,037	100.00	140

Sources: *Fletorja Zyrtare e Republikës së Shqipërisë* (The Official Gazette of the Republic of Albania), No. 2, May 1992, p. 99; and *Rilindja Demokratike*, Tirana, 11 April 1992.

Parliamentary Elections, 31 March 1991

Turnout: 98.9%

Party/Coalition	Votes	% of Vote	Seats
Party of Labor	1,046,120	56.17	169
Democratic Party	720,948	38.71	75
Republican Party	27,393	1.47	—
Omonia Democratic Union	13,538	0.73	5
Committee of Veterans	5,241	0.28	1
Agrarian Party	1,379	0.07	—
Ecological Party	65	0.00	—
Others	47,836	2.57	—
Total	1,862,520	100.00	250

Source: Zëri i Rinise, Tirana, 20 April 1991.

NOTES

1. For recent histories of Albania see Edwin E. Jacques, *The Albanians: An Ethnic History from Prehistoric Times to the Present*, London: MacFarland & Company, 1995; H.T. Norris, *Islam in the Balkans*, Columbia: University of South Carolina Press, 1993; Nicholas C. Pano, *The People's Republic of Albania*, Baltimore: Johns Hopkins University Press, 1998; Anton Logoreci, *The Albanians: Europe's Forgotten Survivors*, Boulder, Colorado: Westview Press, 1977; Arshi Pipa, *Albanian Stalinism: Ideo-Political Aspects*, Boulder: East European Monographs, Columbia University Press, 1989; Peter R. Prifti, *Socialist Albania Since 1944: Domestic and Foreign Developments*, Cambridge, MA: MIT Press, 1978; Elez Biberaj, *Albania: A Socialist Maverick*, Boulder, Colorado; Westview Press, 1990; Miranda Vickers, *The Albanians: A Modern History*, London: I. B. Tauris, 1995; Stavro Skendi, *The Albanian National Awakening, 1878–1912*, Princeton, NJ: Princeton University Press, 1967; and S. Swire, *Albania: The Rise of a Kingdom*, New York: Arno Press and the New York Times, 1971.

2. See *The Europa World Year Book*, 1995, Vol. 1, Europa Publications, 1996; *Encyclopedia Brittannica*, 1995; and the Economist Intelligence Unit, "Country Profiles: Bulgaria and Albania: 1995–96," London: Economist Intelligence Unit, 1996.

3. For an excellent analysis of the fall of communism and Albanian political developments during the 1990s see Elez Biberaj, *Albania in Transition: The Rocky Road to Democracy*, Boulder, Colorado: Westview Press, 1998.

4. *The Europa World Factbook* 1996.

5. For more details see Nicholas Pano, "The Process of Democratization in Albania," in Karen Dawisha and Bruce Parrott (Eds.), *Politics, Power, and the Struggle for Democracy in South-East Europe*, Cambridge, UK: Cambridge University Press, 1997, pp. 285–352.

6. See *Human Rights Worldwide*, No. 5, November 1991; and Greek Helsinki Committee for Human Rights, *Report on the Parliamentary Elections of March 23, 1992 and the Political Rights of the Greek Minority*, Thessaloniki, May 1992.

7. The proposed constitutional provisions are cited from an unauthorized translation of the Draft Constitution of the Republic of Albania. Also see the statement by the Labëria Association, "Provocative and Insulting Acts by Greek Chauvinists," *Republika*, Tirana, July 16,1992, in Foreign Broadcast Information Service/Joint Publications Research Service, *Daily Report: East Europe*, *JPRS-EER-92–106*, August 13, 1992. See also *Country Reports on Human Rights Practices for 1992*, U.S. Department of State, February 1993.

8. Ibid.

9. Ibid.

10. The proposed constitutional provisions are cited from an unauthorized translation of the Draft Constitution of the Republic of Albania. Also see the statement by the Labëria Association, "Provocative and Insulting Acts by Greek Chauvinists," *Republika*, Tirana, 16 July 1992, in Foreign Broadcast Information Service/Joint Publications Research Service, *Daily Report: East Europe*, *JPRS-EER-92–106*, 13 August 1992. See also *Country Reports on Human Rights Practices for 1992*, U.S. Department of State, February 1993.

11. Refer to Section 5, "Discrimination Based on Race, Sex, Religion, Language, or Social Status," in *Country Reports on Human Rights Practices for 1991*, U.S. Department of State, February 1992.

12. Details about electoral procedures in 1991 and 1992 and provisions relating to the participation of ethnic minorities can be found in Greek Helsinki Committee for Human Rights, *Report on the Parliamentary Elections of 22 March 1991 and the Political Rights of the Greek Minority*, Thessaloniki, May 1992; National Democratic Institute for International Affairs, *Albania: 1991 Elections to the People's Assembly*, Washington, D.C., April 30, 1991; Helsinki Watch, *Albania*, New York, 19 April 1991; and International Republican Institute, *Albania Election Information, Parliamentary Elections of 22 March 1992*, Washington, D.C., April 1992.

13. For local election results see *Tirana Radio Network*, 13 August 1992, in Foreign Broadcast Information Service, *Daily Report: East Europe*, in *FBIS-EEU-92–157*, 13 August 1992. Also check *Tirana Radio Network*, 26 July 1992, in *FBIS-EEU-92–144*, 27 July 1992; *Tirana Radio Network*, 31 July 1992, in *FBIS-EEU-92–149*, 3 August 1992; and *Tirana Radio Network*, 3 August 1992, in *FBIS-EEU-92–150*, 4 August 1992.

14. See Fabian Schmidt, "Election Fraud Sparks Protests," *Transition*, Vol. 2, No. 13, 28 June 1996, pp. 38–39, 63; Fabian Schmidt, "An Old System Blends Into the Present," *Transition*, Vol. 2, No. 18, 6 September 1996, pp. 50–53; and Fabian Schmidt, "Albania's Democrats Consolidate Power," *Transition*, Vol. 3, No. 2, 7 February 1997, pp. 47–48.

15. See Fabian Schmidt, "Pyramid Schemes Leave Albania on Shaky Ground," *Transition*, Vol. 3, No. 4, 7 March 1997, pp. 8–10, 56; and Fabian Schmidt, "Albania's Fledgling Democracy Runs Aground," *Transition*, Vol. 4, No. 2, July 1997, pp. 62–65.

16. Consult the *1999 Country Reports on Human Rights Practices*, Bureau of Democracy, Human Rights, and Labor, U.S. Department of State, 25 February 2000, chapter on Albania.

17. International Republican Institute, *Political Party Survey*, Washington, D.C., 1996.

18. Marianne Sullivan, "Socialists on the Campaign Trail," *Transition*, Vol. 2, No. 11, 31 May 1996.

19. Some information on the Albanian National Unity Party and the Motherland Political Association is contained in *Tirana Radio Network*, 24 September 1991, in *FBIS-EEU-91–188*, 27 September 1991.

20. Details on Kosovar movements in Albania can be found in *ATA*, Tirana, 8 March 1991, in *FBIS-EEU-91–046*, 8 March 1991; *ATA*, Tirana, 3 February 1992; and the "Program and Statute of the Kosova Patriotic and Political Association," *Kosova*, Tirana, 21 July 1991, in *JPRS-EER-91–118*, 7 August 1991.

21. For more about the Çamëria question check *Zëri i Popullit*, Tirana, 19 March 1991, in *FBIS-EEU-91–058*, 26 March 1991; and *ATA*, Tirana, 17 September 1991.

22. For details about *Omonia* see *Tirana Domestic Service* and *Tirana Radio Network*, 18 May 1991, in *FBIS-EEU-91–098*, 21 May 1991; *Tirana Domestic Service*, 26 February 1991, in *FBIS-EEU-91–039*, 27 February 1991; Louis Zanga, "Albanian-Greek Relations Reach a Low Point"; Greek Helsinki Committee for Human Rights, *Report on the Parliamentary Elections*.

23. See *Elliniki Radiofonia Radio Network*, Athens, 25 February 1992, in *FBIS-EEU-92–038*, 26 February 1992; Greek Helsinki Committee for Human Rights, *Report on the Parliamentary Elections*.

24. Check *Tanjug*, Belgrade, 27 February 1991, in *FBIS-EEU-91–040*, 28 February 1991.

25. See *Tirana Radio Network*, Tirana, 8 September 1991, in *FBIS-EEU-91–174*, 9 September 1991.

26. Information about the Arumanian Association is taken from "Aremenil Din," The Albania "Cultural Association," Tirana, February 1993; and *ATA*, Tirana, 12 February 1993, in *FBIS-EEU-93–030*, 17 February 1993.

Macedonia

HISTORICAL OVERVIEW

The Macedonian region in the central Balkans witnessed successive waves of settlers and invaders. During the Bronze Age, until about 2000 BC, the area was inhabited by people who spoke a non–Indo-European language. Greek settlers began to arrive in the region during the first millennium BC and most of them moved south into the present-day Greek peninsula.[1] In the seventh century BC, one of the local tribes, which had evidently intermingled with Greeks, created a kingdom of Macedonia in the region's coastal plains. Their descendants were the Macedonians of the Classic period. According to historians, the Macedonians in general did not consider themselves to be Greek, their language was not comprehensible to contemporary Greeks, and their political systems differed significantly from the Greek city-states.

Under Philip of Macedon and his son Alexander the Great, in the fourth century BC, the Macedonian empire greatly expanded. It dominated Greece and Anatolia and stretched as far as India and North Africa. Following Alexander's death, the empire split into three parts—Macedon (including Greece), Syria, and Egypt. Roman legions conquered Macedonia in 167 BC and incorporated the territory as a Roman province. However, the region continued to be subject to repeated invasions from the north by Goths and Huns.

In the seventh century AD, proto-Bulgarians (a Turkic people) and various Slavic tribes settled in the region and founded the first Bulgarian state in AD 681. Bulgaria's conversion to Christianity in AD 864, under the rule of King Boris, enabled them to merge with the Slavs, who had already undergone Christianization, and to extend the Bulgarian state to encompass all of Macedonia. The local Slavic language was codified by two brothers, Cyril and Methodius, whose ethnic origin remains in dispute but who founded the Church Slavonic or "Old Bulgarian" alphabet. There has also been considerable debate, with political implications, as to the identity of the Macedonian

Slavs themselves—whether they were Bulgarian or formed a distinct ethnic group. Historians conclude that there were significant linguistic, cultural, and regional differences among Slavic tribes inhabiting the central Balkan region.

Under Bulgaria's King Simeon the Great, at the end of the ninth century, the country's boundaries were expanded to the Adriatic and Aegean Seas. The empire declined during the tenth century but revived again at the turn of the eleventh century, under King Samuil. He was based in the Ohrid region of Macedonia, and the location of his court provoked later disputes about his ethnic identity; at the time such categories were not considered important. Samuil's army suffered a major defeat in 1014 at the hands of Basil II, the emperor of Byzantium, and Macedonia fell under Byzantine control until 1230. The region was subsequently divided among Greeks and Serbs. In 1282, the Serbian King Milutin captured the Macedonian town of Skopje and established control over much of the Balkans. The Serbian empire reached its high point under Stefan Dušan, who was crowned in Skopje in 1346. After his death in 1355, the empire disintegrated and the entire Balkan region confronted Ottoman Turkish incursions.

Having defeated the Byzantines, the Ottomans invaded the rest of the Balkan peninsula through Macedonia, which they dominated for about five centuries, from the end of the fourteenth century. Under the Ottoman *millet* system, Ottoman territories were divided and administered according to religious affiliation. The Christian Orthodox Balkan population was controlled by the Greek patriarchate in Constantinople (Istanbul). The patriarchate was instrumental in hellenizing the Slavic Macedonians, Albanians, Vlachs, and other Balkan peoples.

As the Ottoman Empire began to implode at the end of the nineteenth century, Bulgarian leaders who had re-established an independent state claimed most of the Macedonian territories. At the close of the Russo-Turkish war of 1875–1878, the Treaty of San Stefano initially awarded Macedonia to Bulgaria, but the Great Powers (Austria-Hungary and Britain) were opposed to a large Bulgaria dominating the Balkans as a potential client of Russia. In response, they signed the Treaty of Berlin in 1878, which removed the Macedonian regions from Bulgarian control and placed them under Turkish rule. A series of uprisings followed in which Macedonian revolutionaries sought to free themselves from the Ottomans. (Bulgarian historians interpret these as Bulgarian protests against the Berlin Treaty.)

Macedonian national identity had been slow to develop under Turkish overlordship, as the intelligentsia was small and the local language had not been codified. Indeed, many Macedonians identified themselves as part of a religious and local community rather than a distinct ethnicity or nation. However, on 23 October 1893, the Internal Macedonian Revolutionary Organization (IMRO) was formed in opposition to the partition of Macedonia among its neighbors. One of its key figures was Goce Delčev, who was instrumental in organizing uprisings against the Turks. The largest, the Ilinden uprising, was staged on 2–3 August 1903 but was suppressed by October. During the uprising, IMRO leaders briefly declared a Macedonian republic in the town of Kruševo.

Another organization, the Supreme Macedonian Committee (Supremacists), was established in Bulgaria in 1895 in order to direct the liberation movement. Although both organizations demanded an autonomous Macedonia, the Supremacists pressed for Bulgaria's outright annexation of the region while the IMRO was divided between pro-Bulgarian and pro-independence factions, which fought a bitter struggle for leadership in the movement.

Two Balkan wars were fought in 1912–1913. In the first, a coalition of Balkan states, including Bulgaria, Serbia, Montenegro, and Greece, succeeded in driving the Turks out of most of the region. The second war was fought over the future of Macedonia, and it pitted Bulgaria against its former allies. With Bulgaria losing the war, Serbia and Greece carved up most of Macedonia between them. Athens gained the larger, southern part of the region, including the city of Salonika; Serbia annexed the northern Vardar region (more or less equivalent to the contemporary Republic of Macedonia); Bulgaria was left with a small slice of the territory in the eastern Pirin area; and Albania received a tiny portion in the west. Serbian and Greek repression in Macedonia was particularly harsh. Belgrade and Athens executed independence activists, terrorized the population, closed down Bulgarian schools and churches, and pursued a program of Serbianization and Hellenization. Serbia's leaders designated Macedonia "southern Serbia."

During World War I (1914–1918), Bulgaria regained control over most of Macedonia. Serbs and Greeks were persecuted by the new administration while most of the local Macedonians reportedly welcomed Sofia's rule. With Bulgaria finding itself on the losing side in 1918, Sofia again lost control over the bulk of Macedonia. A new state of Yugoslavia was created, and Vardar Macedonia was included as its southernmost province. Serbian control was reestablished in the area, and Macedonian or Bulgarian identity was systematically suppressed. The local Orthodox community was incorporated under the jurisdiction of the Serbian Orthodox Church.

With the collapse of Yugoslavia during World War II, the "Macedonian question" was reopened. The region was once again carved up—this time, between Bulgaria, Albania, Germany, and Italy. Bulgarian occupation was initially welcomed, but Sofia's heavy-handed rule alienated much of the population and increased calls for Macedonian autonomy. A Macedonian communist movement supported Tito's plan for a new Yugoslav federation, and on 29 November 1943, Tito's Anti-Fascist Council for the National Liberation of Yugoslavia (AVNOJ) formally recognized the existence of a Macedonian nation.

On 2 August 1944, Tito's communist regime accorded Macedonia the status of a constituent Yugoslav republic, equal with the other five. But the federal arrangement was initially more nominal than substantive. Central communist controls were maintained until 1974, when the new Yugoslav constitution conceded more wide-ranging administrative powers to each of the six federal units. The creation of a distinct Macedonian republic was partially designed to undercut the dominant position of the Serbs and to maintain an inter-republican balance among the major Yugoslav nations.

Tito originally planned to create a larger Balkan communist federation, to include an enlarged and united Macedonia, together with Bulgaria and Albania. While Tito wanted Bulgaria to join as another federal unit, the Bulgarian leadership under Georgi Dimitrov was receptive only to the idea of an equal Bulgarian-Yugoslav federation, and opposed a formal union. The whole project was eventually capsized because of Stalin's opposition and the defeat of communist insurgents in Greece in the late 1940s. Tito's policy goals heightened tensions with Greece; and after Yugoslavia's expulsion from the Soviet bloc, hostilities with Bulgaria also increased. As Moscow's relations with Belgrade deteriorated, Sofia stepped to the forefront of the anti-Yugoslav campaign and revived its claims to Yugoslav Macedonia at the same time as it eliminated the separate status of its own Macedonian population.

After the break with Bulgaria, Tito continued to promote a distinct Macedonian identity and to combat pro-Bulgarian sentiments. For example, the Macedonian language, based on four central Macedonian dialects, was officially recognized and scripted and deliberately distinguished from Bulgarian. Macedonian cultural societies were established and Macedonian identity was promoted in the educational system. On 18 July 1967, an autocephalous Macedonian Orthodox Church was inaugurated in an officially engineered schism with the Serbian Orthodox Church. These moves were condemned by Serbian and Bulgarian Orthodox clergymen, but they corresponded with Macedonian aspirations for autonomy and self-determination and helped anchor Macedonian identity.

The Macedonian issue was played down somewhat by Belgrade in the foreign policy arena while Moscow attempted to re-establish closer ties with Belgrade and held Sofia in check. But the issue was revived again during the Yugoslav-Bulgarian disputes in the 1970s and 1980s. The Yugoslav authorities periodically charged Sofia with violating the United Nations Charter and the Helsinki Agreements by refusing to recognize Macedonians as a distinct national minority, and with undermining the integrity of Yugoslavia by denying legitimacy to one of its constituent republics. Communist Bulgaria, in turn, claimed that it harbored no pretensions to Yugoslav territory, and charged Belgrade with promoting annexationist ambitions toward Bulgarian territory.

While Macedonia had a certain degree of protection as a distinct entity under the Titoist regime, following Tito's death in 1980 Yugoslavia's political crisis fueled nationalist demands in all six republics and energized calls for full Macedonian sovereignty. Macedonian activists became fearful of either being swallowed up by the new centralist regime in Serbia or becoming pawns in a wider Balkan conflict in the event that Yugoslavia disintegrated.

POST-COMMUNIST DEVELOPMENTS

Macedonia prepared for its first multiparty elections as central Yugoslav controls weakened and the communist stranglehold increasingly gave way to nationalist and autonomist forces. The balloting on 11 and 23 November 1990 produced a fractured parliament in which no party or coalition benefited from a clear majority. The elections were held against a backdrop of ethnic tension, resurgent nationalism, growing ruptures among the Yugoslav republics, and accelerating economic deterioration. All six of Yugoslavia's republics were in the throes of the most serious constitutional crisis in the country's post-war history, particularly after the victory of pro-independence movements in the Slovenian and Croatian elections earlier in 1990.

One hundred twenty seats were contested for the unicameral Macedonian National Assembly *(sobranie)*, and the ballot was widely considered to be a referendum on both communism and Yugoslav federalism. To gain electoral support, the League of Communists of Macedonia (LCM) emphasized its commitment to a multi-party system and a modern market economy, whereas most of the other parties blamed the communists for Macedonia's economic and political problems. A process of political ethnicization was also visible as the two major nationalities, Macedonian Slavs and Albanians, founded their own ethnicity-based parties. They were less concerned with specific economic prescriptions than with protecting their "national interests" and gaining a measure of self-determination.

Of the twenty registered parties, sixteen put forward candidates for the parliamentary elections. They included: the League of Communists of Macedonia–Party of Democratic Transformation (LCM-PDT); the Alliance of Reform Forces in Macedonia (ARFM), linked with Yugoslavia's reformist Prime Minister Ante Marković; the Party for Democratic Prosperity (PDP), the largest Albanian party; the Socialist Party–Socialist Alliance of Working People (SP-SAWP); the Movement for Pan-Macedonian Action (MPMA); and the Internal Macedonian Revolutionary Organization–Democratic Party of Macedonian National Unity (IMRO-DPMNU), two nationalist organizations seeking outright Macedonian independence; the Party of Yugoslavs (PY); the Democratic Alliance of Turks (DAT); and the Party for the Complete Emancipation of Roma (PCER).

After three rounds of balloting, no single party obtained a clear governing majority. A precarious balance was achieved in parliament among three major political forces: reform communists, Macedonian nationalists, and Albanian nationalists.[2] The LCM-PDT, which later renamed itself the Social Democratic Alliance (SDA), won 31 seats in the 120-seat National Assembly. The Party for Democratic Prosperity (PDP) gained 17 seats, and its coalition partner, the National Democratic Party (NDP), 5 seats. IMRO-DPMNU captured 38 seats. The Alliance of Reform Forces obtained only 11 deputies, the Socialist Party four, the Party for Yugoslavia 2, the PCER 1, while 3 seats went to independent representatives. Although IMRO-DPMNU performed poorly in the first round, the initial success of the PDP and IMRO's adroit use of nationalist issues helped the party to take the largest bloc of seats after the runoffs.

The Albanian parties lodged complaints about the election process, claiming that the republican electoral commission had gerrymandered districts with large Albanian populations to restrict Albanian representation in parliament. Despite this, the majority of Albanian voters evidently cast ballots along ethnic lines, electing a total number of deputies commensurate with the estimated size of the Albanian community. Given the impressive performance of the PDP in gaining 20% of parliamentary seats, charges of district gerrymandering were subsequently dropped.

In November and December 1990, the Macedonian electorate also cast ballots for local government officials in the 34 county or commune administrations, including the capital, Skopje. In the 34 Macedonian communes, a total of 1,510 councilors were elected, including 1,911 Macedonians, 221 Albanians, 22 Turks, 16 Serbs, 15 Roma, 12 Vlachs, and 33 individuals of various smaller nationalities. Albanians obtained clear majorities in the three western municipalities of Gostivar, Debar, and Tetovo. The LCM-PDT gained the largest number of local seats, 512, followed by the ARFM with 313, the PDP with 226, IMRO-DPMNU with 199, the Socialists with 175, the MPMA with 34, the Social Democrats with 10, the Albanian NDP with seven, the PCER with seven, and the rest allocated among smaller parties. Albanian leaders asserted that in Tetovo, Gostivar, and Debar, local councils were not properly constituted and remained under a "compulsory government." Officials initially refused to transfer power to the victorious Albanian councilors. Indeed, a parallel authority operated, as two municipal assemblies continued to function—one dominated by Macedonians, and the other by Albanians.

A Macedonian government was finally installed on 20 February 1991, following intense maneuvering by the major political parties, as no organization had gained an overall majority. Neither IMRO-DPMNU nor the PDP were in a position to form an administration or to choose a President acceptable to all sides. The only serious candidate proved to be Kiro Gligorov, former president of the Federal Assembly, former Yugoslav deputy prime minister, and LCM-PDT leader, who was elected President by the republican legislature on 27 January 1991. The new coalition "government of experts" was headed by Prime Minister Nikola Kljusev. The three deputy premiers were Blaze Ristovski, Beqir Zuta, and Jovan Andonov. The ministries were distributed among the coalition partners. One deputy premier and two government ministers were ethnic Albanians, but only two of the fifteen ministers had any party affiliation. The new administration seemed determined to avoid any escalation of tensions with the Albanian minority. In addition to gaining ministerial portfolios, the PDP obtained two presidencies and one vice-presidency in key parliamentary committees, as well as representation in the supreme, district, and communal judicial bodies and in Macedonia's constitutional court.

The question of the constitution remained a sore point in relations between Macedonian and Albanian leaders. Various proposals were tabled for a new republican constitution that would underscore Macedonian statehood. In April 1989, the republican parliament discussed 32 constitutional amendments that had been drafted during several months of intense and sometimes acrimonious debate. The most controversial amendment redefined Macedonia as "the national state of the Macedonian nation," thereby significantly altering the 1974 constitution, in which Macedonia was defined as a state of the "Macedonian people and the Albanian and Turkish minorities." Albanian leaders expressed strong opposition to the amendments and viewed them as a negation of Albanians' national rights that could lead to severe discrimination. Despite Albanian protests, several constitutional revisions were adopted in October 1989 after a series of private and public fora.[3]

In August 1990, the Macedonian government rejected a petition drafted by several Albanian organizations and civil leaders. Albanians demanded the right to use their native language in teaching and in the school administration, wide-ranging reform of the curriculum, and the reinstatement of Albanian teachers previously suspended on political pretexts. The government claimed that the demands contained in the petition deviated from existing legal regulations and constitutional provisions. The National Assembly became more outspoken on the question of Macedonian identity and less constrained by the position of the Yugoslav government. In June 1990, parliament adopted a declaration concerning Macedonia's relations with neighboring countries and expressed growing concern for the neglected status of ethnic Macedonian minorities. The document claimed that Greece, Albania, and Bulgaria continued to apply discriminatory policies toward Macedonian Slavs and refused to recognize their national distinctiveness. It denounced such measures as repressive and assimilationist.[4]

President Gligorov at first moved cautiously on the question of independence. He calculated that a renovated confederal Yugoslavia could be established with a much looser relationship between Belgrade and the republics. But following the "disassociation" of Slovenia and Croatia and the armed conflict in both republics during the summer of 1991, Macedonia affirmed that it would not remain in a Serbian-dominated "rump Yugoslavia." Macedonia and Bosnia-Herzegovina had originally supported a looser or "asymmetric" federal arrangement with the other republics, but after Slovenia and Croatia seceded, Skopje moved to protect its integrity and sovereignty and organized a nationwide referendum on independence. On 8 September 1991, 68.32% of registered voters cast their ballots in support of Macedonian sovereignty and independence.[5] The ballot also stipulated that a sovereign Macedonia would reserve the right to join a union of independent Yugoslav states at some future date.

Much of the Albanian population boycotted the independence referendum on the grounds that it would become a vulnerable minority in a sovereign Macedonia. The PDP did not discount the possibility of endorsing Macedonian statehood if the government guaranteed Albanian rights in education, culture, language use, and local administration. To allay the fears of its neighbors, premier Kljusev declared that Skopje harbored no territorial claims on Bulgaria, Greece, or Albania. The Milošević regime responded by asserting that Macedonia would not be permitted to secede from Yugoslavia and that the Belgrade authorities were prepared to use force to prevent separation.[6]

The government in Skopje declared Macedonia an independent state in September 1991 and appealed for international recognition. Although Macedonia evidently fulfilled all the European Community criteria for independent statehood, recognition was effectively blocked by Greece. Athens insisted that Macedonia change its name and desist from adopting any symbols linked with ancient Macedon, which Athens claimed was a purely Hellenic entity. The Greek authorities charged that the new republic harbored designs on Greek Macedonia; it was evidently anxious about international campaigns in defense of the minority rights of Greece's Slavic population. Skopje refused to comply with these demands, but it explicitly renounced all territorial pretensions in its new constitution and declared all of its borders permanent.

Cognizant of Macedonia's potentially precarious position in any direct conflict with Serbia in a smaller Yugoslavia, the republican Assembly adopted a declaration on sovereignty and statehood on 17 September 1991. This was done despite the concerns of Albanians and other minorities over possible ethnic discrimination in a sovereign Macedonia. Albanian deputies, in particular, charged that the authorities had failed to dispel persistent fears of minority persecution and manifestations of Macedonian chauvinism. Macedonian deputies responded by pointing to Albanian participation in the legislature and in the executive, while expressing fears of Serbian domination in a truncated Yugoslavia. Some Albanian leaders demanded a binational federation with the equality of the Albanian language in public life; proportional representation for Albanians in local and republican governments, the military, and the police; and a separate, Albanian-language university.

As Macedonia moved toward separation from Yugoslavia, tensions perceptibly increased between the Slav majority and the large Albanian minority, which formed its own political organizations. Amendments to the Macedonian constitution had redefined the republic as a "nation-state of the Macedonian people," thus alienating Albanian and Turkish activists fearful of anti-minority discrimination. Skopje also feared that the large Albanian minority might seek closer links with both Kosova and Albania if Macedonia experienced increasing internal turmoil. In the worst-case scenario, a conflict over Macedonia could spread through the Balkans, embroiling Bulgaria, whose government recognized Macedonian independence but not the existence of a separate Macedonian nation; Greece, whose tilt toward Serbia strengthened suppositions that it could be drawn into a partition of Macedonia; Albania, which could seek to defend its co-ethnics; and Turkey, which would find it difficult to remain on the sidelines in the event of Greek involvement and Serbian expansionism.

Skopje managed successfully to negotiate the withdrawal of about 60,000 Yugoslav troops in early 1992. However, suspicions remained pronounced that Serbia's Milošević regime harbored territorial ambitions toward Macedonia and might deliberately aggravate Macedonian-Albanian tensions to destabilize the republic or provoke a major conflict in neighboring Kosova that would spill over into Macedonia. Such scenarios would provide an appropriate pretext for intervention in which Belgrade could pose as a defender of Macedonian sovereignty against alleged Albanian expansionism.

The government in Skopje had initially adopted a more cautious approach than Slovenia and Croatia toward independence, fearing both a possible Yugoslav army assault and claims to its territories by hostile neighbors. The stridently pro-independence IMRO-DPMNU remained in a minority position in the republican parliament and could not push unilaterally for independence. Once the European Commission (EC) announced its conditions for recognizing the statehood of former Yugoslav republics, the Macedonian authorities reconfirmed the republic's independence in December 1991 and canvassed for comprehensive international recognition. Indeed, Macedonia met all the EC conditions for statehood as laid out by the arbitration body, the Badinter Commission, in accordance with CSCE (Conference on Security and Cooperation in Europe) commitments.

At the outset, only a handful of states, including Bulgaria, Turkey, and Russia, recognized the new state. The Greek government successfully blocked comprehensive EC recognition on the grounds that Greece held exclusive rights to the name "Macedonia." It also charged Skopje with annexationist pretensions to northern Greek territory where a sizable Slavic population was resident. In order to reassure the international community that Macedonia harbored no expansionist ambitions, a constitutional amendment was promulgated in January 1992 explicitly prohibiting any territorial aspirations. President Gligorov noted that he was willing to enter into a bilateral agreement with Athens guaranteeing the permanence of borders.[7] Greece rejected these overtures and Macedonia was left in a precarious state of limbo. In April 1993, the republic was finally accorded United Nations (UN) membership under the provisional name the Former Yugoslav Republic of Macedonia (FYROM), pending a final agreement between Skopje and Athens under international mediation.

The Macedonian Assembly adopted a new sovereign constitution on 17 November 1991, despite the abstention of most Albanian deputies.[8] It defined Macedonia as the "national state of the Macedonian people in which the integral civil equality and enduring coexistence of the Macedonian people with Albanians, Turks, Vlachs, Gypsies, and other nationalities are protected." All nationals and residents of Macedonia were defined as citizens and could not have their citizenship revoked. The Macedonian language, written in the Cyrillic alphabet, was the official state language. However, in local self-governing entities in which the majority of inhabitants were members of non-Macedonian ethnic groups, their languages and alphabets would also have official status and could be used in administrative transactions. Although the Macedonian Orthodox Church was singled out in the constitution, it was not provided with any special legal status or preeminence vis-à-vis other denominations.

The constitution underscored the free expression of national affiliation and declared that Macedonia respected the universally accepted standards of international law. It proclaimed freedom of religious belief and ensured freedom of assembly so that citizens could exercise and protect their political, economic, social, and cultural rights and beliefs. Citizens were able freely to establish associations and political parties and were at liberty to join or to withdraw from these bodies. However, the programs and the activities of citizen associations and political parties could not be aimed at violating the constitutional order by encouraging "military aggression, or promoting national, racial, or religious hatred or intolerance."

The constitution proclaimed that members of ethnic groups possessed the right to express their ethnicity freely and to "promote and develop their identity and special ethnic character." Members of ethnic groups had the right to establish their own cultural and artistic institutions as well as scientific and other associations in order to express, promote, and develop their identities. In addition, members of all ethnic groups had the right to be taught in their own language at primary and secondary school levels. Despite protests by Albanian leaders that their educational, cultural, and publishing needs remained underfulfilled, the Macedonian government claimed that the republic had an exemplary record in providing appropriate schooling and cultural and media outlets for the minorities. Albanians contended that there was no Albanian-language university and only minimal language instruction at the national university, and that the number of Albanian-language schools at the secondary level remained insufficient.

A Council on Inter-Ethnic Relations was established in October 1992 and was comprised of Macedonians and two representatives from each of the five minority groups: Serbs, Roma, Vlachs, Turks, and Albanians. The primary function of the council was to debate issues related to inter-ethnic relations and to submit suggestions for the resolution of impending problems. The President of Macedonia was empowered to nominate the members of the council.[9] Albanian leaders complained that the council was only a consulting body whose decisions were not obligatory for state organs, and that its composition did not proportionally represent the national minorities.

Albanian leaders lodged complaints that, according to constitutional provisions and despite numerous nominal guarantees, Albanians did not enjoy equal rights with Slav Macedonians. Their principal claim was that Albanians should not figure in the constitution as a "national minority" but as a constituent "nation" with equal rights vis-à-vis other nations. Alternatively, the document should not differentiate on the basis of ethnicity but simply focus on citizenship. Albanians warned that if constitutional stipulations proved unsatisfactory, then they would organize a separate referendum, declare the Macedonian constitution non-binding, and take measures toward "cultural and territorial independence."[10] This could culminate in the proclamation of an Autonomous Region of Western Macedonia that would have the right to enter into alliances with other states.

Indeed, in early January 1992, a referendum on "political and territorial autonomy" was held among the Albanian minority despite government charges of illegality. The turnout reportedly exceeded 90%, and over 95% of the ballots were cast in favor of political and cultural autonomy for Albanian areas in western Macedonia. The outcome was dismissed as invalid by the government. In April 1992, activists in several predominantly Albanian municipalities declared the region the "Republic of Ilirida," centered on the town of Tetovo. The PDP leadership distanced itself from this decision, which was officially condemned by the government in Skopje. The PDP was opposed to a partition of Macedonia but favored wide-ranging autonomy. Despite the pressures exerted by some Macedonian nationalist groupings to clamp down on Albanian activism, the authorities tried to pacify inter-ethnic relations by offering Albanian leaders several posts in the coalition government.

During its first congress in February 1992, the PDP passed a resolution asking the Macedonian authorities to recognize the independence of Kosova and the autonomy of Albanian regions of western Macedonia.[11] Neither declaration was forthcoming from Skopje, as it tried to avoid antagonizing Serbia or setting any precedents for the partition of Macedonian territory. Despite the referendum, PDP leaders did not push forward on the question of autonomy, calculating that this would further destabilize the state and give ammunition to Macedonian nationalists. Indeed, the autonomy question was manipulated as a tool to wrest various concessions from the government. Albanian spokesmen complained about a host of discriminatory measures against the minority in job opportunities, in media access, and in representation in the military and police forces. The government claimed that it was introducing limited measures to ameliorate the ethnic imbalance and to counter the pattern of discrimination.

Tensions with the Albanian minority mounted visibly on several occasions. In November 1992, thousands of Albanians demonstrated in central Skopje after the Macedonian police allegedly beat an Albanian cigarette vendor. The rallies turned into riots and three Albanians and one Macedonian bystander were shot dead. Although the incident did not trigger an escalation of communal conflicts, it served as a warning that ethnic grievances could be exploited to destabilize the country. A government enquiry subsequently implied that foreign agents might have been responsible for the November events.

Albanian leaders claimed that the police had used excessive force against protesters. Although Macedonia and Albania established reasonably cordial relations, several border incidents during 1992 and 1993, in which Macedonian guards shot and killed Albanian citizens illegally crossing into the republic, aggravated tensions within and between both states.

IMRO-DPMNU and other nationalist groupings adopted a militant stance toward both the Albanian leadership and the incumbent government. IMPRO-DPMNU accused Albanians of planning to overrun the republic numerically, pointing to the high Albanian birthrate; and with calling for autonomy as a preliminary step toward outright secession and annexation by Albania. In addition, the PDP was charged with deliberately fanning ethnic tensions and with being an appendage of the pro-independence Albanian movement in Kosova. Conversely, IMRO-DPMNU accused the Skopje administration of being overindulgent with Albanian politicians, a policy that simply stimulated more extremist demands. Nationalists asserted that Albanians had no right to any special status. They opposed any extension of Albanian educational rights or moves toward decentralization, federalism, or autonomy in western Macedonia.

The Gligorov leadership resisted calls for early elections by the nationalists, claiming that they could lead to intolerable ethnic polarization at a precarious juncture in Macedonia's quest for international status. Throughout 1992, IMRO-DPMNU continued to attack the administration for failing to win outright international recognition, accusing Gligorov and his associates of being Serb-Yugoslav agents. (The party took a pro-Bulgarian position.) Conflicts over international recognition, Skopje's foreign policy, and the position of the Albanian minority virtually paralyzed the legislative process. Meanwhile, the destructive impact of UN sanctions on Yugoslavia adversely affected the Macedonian economy, which was dependent on Belgrade for over 60% of its trade, and thus raised social tensions in the republic.

After months of bitter dispute, the Kljusev government lost a vote of confidence in July 1992 and was replaced by a broad-based coalition in September 1992. IMRO-DPMNU was given the opportunity to form a government, but proved unable to elicit sufficient parliamentary support. Branko Crvenkovski, a member of the Social Democratic Alliance of Macedonia (SDAM), eventually assembled a coalition of SDAM, ARF, and PDP representatives, together with several smaller parties. IMRO-DPMNU was once again left out of the equation. Albanian representatives received five out of the 21 ministries, including one deputy premiership, but they complained that this figure did not properly reflect their numbers and thereby diminished their influence in decisionmaking. The SDAM retained 11 ministries, including the key portfolios of defense, internal affairs, and justice. One minister was an ethnic Turk. This fairly moderate and broad coalition survived a no-confidence vote lodged by IMRO deputies in April 1993 over the unresolved issue of Macedonia's international recognition.

In the second multiparty elections, on 16 October 1994, the majority of parliamentary seats were won by the Alliance for Macedonia, a three-party coalition composed of the SDAM, the Liberal Party, and the Socialist Party.[12] The SDAM won 56 seats, the Liberal Party 28 seats, and the Socialist Party six. The largest Albanian party, the PDP, gained 11 seats, the People's Democratic Party five seats. The Social Democratic Party, the Party for Full Emancipation of the Romanies, and the Democratic Party of Turks together with the Party for Democratic Action each obtained one seat. After the first round of voting, IMRO-DPMNU and the Democratic Party proclaimed the elections a fraud; they also boycotted the second round. The second multiparty elections were conducted under a majority voting system, and 120 members of parliament were elected in two rounds, for a four-year term. Each electoral unit mandated one representative.

The second multiparty, unicameral National Assembly was constituted on 19 November 1994, and the government was formed by Prime Minister Branko Crvenkovski. The Alliance for Macedonia formed a coalition government with the PDP, and the Liberal leader Stojan Andov was selected as speaker of parliament. After the breakup of the Alliance in February 1996, when the Liberals left the government coalition, Andov was succeeded as parliamentary speaker by Tito Petkovski, from the SDAM. Following a government reshuffle, Crvenkovski remained Prime Minister in a coalition consisting of the SDAM, the SP, and the PDP.

Relations were troubled among Macedonia's minorities. Tensions surfaced between Albanians and Turks, as some Turkish activists claimed that Albanian leaders were exaggerating their population estimates by including other Islamic communities—e.g. Turks, Roma, and Slavic Muslims. In January 1992, the Association of Macedonian Muslims issued a public statement opposing the Albanian referendum on autonomy. The party declared that the referendum was an anti-Macedonian act directed against the international recognition of the state and leading the Albanian population to further ghettoization.[13] Tensions also were manifested between Slav Muslim and Turkish leaders, with the former evidently fearful of potential Turkicization campaigns.

Serbian radicals were active in Macedonia, capitalizing on the country's precarious international position. In the early 1990s, local followers of Serbian Radical Party leader Vojislav Šešelj reportedly made plans to create a Serbian Autonomous Region of the Kumanovo Valley and Skopska Crna Gora in northern Macedonia. Leaders of Serbian parties explicitly objected to the omission of the "Serbian nation" from the republic's constitution and claimed that Serbs were denied elementary rights in education, employment, and in access to the mass media. Tensions occasionally erupted in protest actions, and on New Year's Day 1993, Macedonian police clashed with Serbian youths in the village of Kucevište. The authorities suspected that the incidents were provoked by nationalists in Belgrade.

Conflicts also persisted in relations between the Serbian and Macedonian Orthodox churches, particularly as the latter was not officially recognized by the former, which sought to have the Church returned to its jurisdiction. In December 1992, the Serbian Orthodox Church created a Patriarchate in Niš (Serbia) to administer all former "Serbian" dioceses until a new Metropolitan of Skopje was appointed. In May 1993, the Serbian Church appointed Archimandrite Jovan its administrator of the diocese of the Macedonian Orthodox Church. The authorities in Skopje described this as a provocation confirming that Serbia was interfering in Macedonia's internal affairs. The government also remained concerned over potential Serb-Greek collaboration in carving up the Macedonian state. To counter such threats, it demanded full diplomatic recognition by Western states and credible security guarantees, in addition to economic assistance to help stabilize the country. The small UN peacekeeping force dispatched to the country and augmented by a unit of U.S. troops during the summer of 1993 was viewed as a positive step in this direction.[14]

In October 1992, the Macedonian government promulgated a new citizenship law with a fifteen-year residency requirement that placed many citizens of the former Yugoslavia in an ambiguous position. In particular, Albanians charged that the measure would have a deleterious impact on the status of ethnic Albanians, Serbs, and Muslims. Under the law, non-Macedonians resident in the republic for less than fifteen years would be eligible for citizenship only if they could prove a permanent source of income and if they were above 18 years of age; those who did not meet these stipulations would be deported.[15] Albanian leaders sought a maximum five-year residency requirement, asserting that the measure would disenfranchise a large segment of the Albanian population that had been evacuated from Kosova. The passage of the citizenship law demonstrated that even a measure designed to limit the potential for ethnic strife by placating nationalist opposition and preserving the country's ethnic balance, could in itself foster conflict and polarization.

Although it was surrounded by turmoil throughout the Balkans, Macedonia remained comparatively stable throughout the 1990s. The major source of conflict revolved around the aspirations of the large Albanian minority. The government of President Gligorov did not face any major challenges to its authority, despite the political upheavals that rocked neighboring Albania, Bulgaria, and Serbia. Prime Minister Crvenkovski conducted a cabinet reshuffle and launched an anti-corruption drive among state officials following the collapse of a major "'pyramid" investment scheme in early 1994, in which thousands of citizens lost their deposits. The scheme's owner and the governor of the National Bank were arrested in connection with the scandal. The government's actions helped stave off public unrest, particularly as the Bank pledged to reimburse investors. The country's stability was also buttressed by a reasonable macroeconomic performance. Gligorov was reelected President in October 1994 with 52.6% of the vote, in a clear indication that the electorate rejected nationalist solutions.

Albanians continued to campaign for their own university and the use of their own flags in public places. In July 1997, two Albanians were killed and several dozen wounded in the town of Gostivar during clashes with Macedonian police. The riots erupted when Macedonian policeman pulled down Albanian flags that had been hoisted over the city hall. Rufi Osmani, the ethnic Albanian mayor of Gostivar, was arrested on charges of inciting unrest and promoting ethnic hatred.

The Gligorov administration sought to avoid further ethnic polarization and proposed a draft law in which minorities could choose their own national symbols in any private, cultural, or sporting events. However, they would not be able to fly their flags over public buildings. Albanian politicians were split on the issue. Some Albanian parliamentarians urged compromise with the government; a more radicalized faction sought greater confrontation with the state. Gligorov feared that too many concessions on the question of autonomy would provoke separatism. His difficult balancing act was acknowledged by the special envoy of the U.N. Human Rights Commission to the former Yugoslavia, Elizabeth Rehn. She stated that Macedonia had improved human rights but that concerns remained over police abuses and the plight of the Albanian minority.

During the spring 1997 uprising in Albania, Macedonia placed its military on a high state of alert fearing a massive inflow of refugees. The threat subsided by the end of the summer, after the elections in Albania. Nevertheless, the defense ministry remained concerned over armed incidents in the border areas between Albanian groups and Macedonian security forces. To underscore the importance of preserving Macedonian stability, the United Nations extended the mandate of its Preventive Deployment Force (UNPREDEP), which included a 350-strong American contingent.

During 1998, Macedonia was faced with a number of internal and external challenges to its stability. General elections in the fall looked set to install a more nationalist coalition government that could increase conflicts with the country's large Albanian minority. Meanwhile, fears were heightened that the war in neighboring Kosova could spill over into Macedonia. After two rounds of parliamentary elections in October and November 1998, a new government centered around IMRO-DPMNU took office. IMRO leaders asserted that they had discarded their nationalist orientation; but Albanian spokesmen remained concerned that difficult economic conditions, coupled with escalating regional tensions, could help to revive anti-minority policies.

IMRO's popularity had soared largely because of its attacks on the incumbent government's economic policies. It charged the administration of premier Crvenkovski with widespread corruption and economic mismanagement. The country was experiencing a deepening recession and an unemployment rate of some 40%. President Gligorov's position looked increasingly vulnerable as his Social Democratic Alliance, which had governed Macedonia since the country gained independence in 1992, lost the elections. IMRO-DPMNU won 43 seats, the SDAM 27, the PDP 14, the DA 13, the DPA-NDP

11, and the LDP four. The new National Assembly consisted of 120 representatives, 85 of whom were elected by the majority principle in the 85 electoral districts in Macedonia, and 35, by the proportional principle.

Relations between the Macedonian authorities and leaders of the Albanian minority remained tense as the latter demanded greater autonomy and more significant representation in state institutions. In May 1999, several thousand Albanians staged a protest march in Skopje to demand the release of the mayor of Gostivar, Rufi Osmani, imprisoned for seven years for illegally flying an Albanian flag from his town hall and for "inciting national and religious hatred." In September 1997, police arrested an ethnic Albanian suspected of carrying out several bombing attacks. Macedonian police believed that cells of the Kosova Liberation Army (KLA) were active in the country, recruiting volunteers for the independence struggle in Kosova, channeling weapons to the insurgents through Macedonian territory, and encouraging Albanian separatism in Macedonia. The government also feared the prospect of a massive wave of refugees from the fighting in Kosova—an influx that could heighten ethnic tensions and strain the state's limited resources.

As the conflict in Kosova accelerated, the international community expressed fears that Macedonia itself could be destabilized and drawn into a wider Balkan war. In July 1998, the U.N. Security Council extended the UNPREDEP mandate as the force continued to monitor the borders with Serbia and Albania. With the signing of an agreement between Yugoslav President Slobodan Milošević and U.S. envoy Richard Holbrooke in October 1998, Macedonia was also poised to host North Atlantic Treaty Organization (NATO) contingents for possible deployment in Kosova.

During the spring of 1999, Macedonia survived a major crisis stemming from the inflow of Albanian refugees fleeing the war in neighboring Kosova. The government managed to handle the destabilizing effects of the crisis as a quarter of a million Albanian refugees poured into the country. The authorities coped with the challenge despite provocations by Serbian extremists and growing resentment among Macedonia's Slavic majority. The bulk of the expellees returned to Kosova in June 1999 after NATO's victorious campaign against Belgrade. The government welcomed a larger NATO presence in the country and took a number of initiatives to enhance regional security in the Balkans.

Boris Trajkovski won the Macedonian presidential election on 14 November 1999, defeating his nearest challenger from the oppositionist Social Democratic Party. He was the candidate of the ruling party, IMRO-DPMNU, and was inaugurated on 15 December 1999. The presidential elections sharpened the country's political disputes and threatened to unsettle ethnic coexistence. In the first round of the ballot, on 31 October 1999, the SDAM candidate Tito Petkovski gained 33% of the vote, while Trajkovski registered only 21%. Petkovski deliberately whipped up the specter of Albanian separatism to frighten and mobilize Macedonian voters. In stark contrast, Trajkovski and

IMRO Prime Minister Ljubčo Georgievski focused on pressing economic issues in their election campaign and rejected nationalism and ethnic division. The elections also brought to a close the term of President Gligorov, who had steered the country toward independence and successfully avoided bloodshed in Macedonia during the breakup of Yugoslavia.

The government coalition that was forged at the end of 1998, following parliamentary elections on 18 October and 1 November 1998, weathered a series of domestic and regional storms. It combined the former nationalist IMRO-DPMNU and the largest Albanian party, the PDA (Party of Democratic Action). IMRO had captured 43 parliamentary seats, while the DPA-NDP gained 11; the third coalition partner, the Democratic Alternative (DA), garnered 13 seats. The SDAP won only 27 seats, and its former Albanian coalition partner, the PDP, 14 seats. IMRO's policies turned out to be pragmatic and steered clear of nationalist provocations. In a series of moves to defuse tensions, the Albanians were offered positions in various government organs; several high-ranking Albanian political prisoners were released; and concessions were made regarding Albanian-language higher education.

But the new government faced serious economic problems. The Macedonian economy was severely unsettled by the war in neighboring Serbia. Macedonia estimated that its losses from the war, including trade, investment, and refugee assistance, totaled some $1.5 billion by the end of 1999. Foreign investments dropped off dramatically, and many contracts with European and American companies were cancelled.

Macedonia was shaken in February 2001 with the emergence of an armed Albanian insurgency movement styling itself as the National Liberation Army (NLA). Militant leaders of the rebel force initiated attacks on Macedonian security forces, capturing several villages in the northern and western parts of the country. The NLA consisted of Albanian radicals and warlords from both Macedonia and Kosova who were intent on exploiting the accumulated grievances of sizeable sectors of the Albanian minority in Macedonia. Their leaders asserted that they were not seeking to partition Macedonia but simply demanding the recognition of various minority rights and constitutional changes to equalize the position of the Albanian population.

Albanian leaders harbored some justifiable grievances against the Macedonian government. They criticized the Macedonian constitution for defining the republic as a state of Macedonians, and demanded that the document be redrafted to provide for equality between the two major ethnic groups, or that the state not be defined by nationality but by citizenship. They also contended that Albanian should become a second official language and that a greater share of Albanians should be incorporated in government organs and security structures.

Slavic Macedonians pointed out that the generally unfavorable economic conditions affected all citizens regardless of ethnicity and that Albanians were not being singled out for discrimination. Macedonians feared that any major concessions to the Albanian community would provoke more expansive demands for territorial or political autonomy, the federalization of the state, and eventual separation. Hence, the Macedonian government was trapped in a dilemma between Albanian and Macedonian nationalism. A weak response to the guerrillas could alienate it from the Slavic population, while an overly strong response could alienate it from the Albanian community.

Attempts at forging an inter-ethnic agreement led to the creation of a broad, multiparty coalition government in May 2001, and as the insurgency restarted, political leaders sought to hammer out an acceptable formula for politically disarming the NLA. Government attempts to destroy the guerrillas by force proved largely ineffective, and the indiscriminate shelling of Albanian villages threatened to further divide and polarize the ethnic communities. President Trajkovski issued an extensive settlement plan including a partial amnesty for the guerrillas, extensive linguistic rights, the inclusion of greater numbers of Albanians in state institutions, comprehensive educational reform, and potential changes in the Macedonian constitution. Negotiations on a comprehensive inter-ethnic agreement were held in July 2001, with high-level international mediation led by American and European Union (EU) representatives. A comprehensive accord was eventually signed on 13 August 2001.

One of Macedonia's most significant foreign policy achievements during 1999 was the breakthrough in relations with Bulgaria. This was symbolized by the signing in February of a declaration settling the language dispute and stating that the two countries harbored no territorial claims on each other. The declaration was signed in the official languages of the two countries, ending a conflict that arose when Bulgaria refused to recognize Macedonian as a language separate from Bulgarian. Several other agreements in the area of trade and investment were initialed. In March 1999, Macedonian Defense Minister Nikola Kljusev and his Bulgarian counterpart, Georgi Ananiev, signed a framework accord on military cooperation between armies of the two countries. The IMRO administration proved more determined and capable of improving relations with Bulgaria than its Social Democratic predecessor, and did so without undermining Macedonian sovereignty and integrity.

Macedonia's relations with Serbia remained strained for several reasons. Belgrade refused to recognize the border between the two states, despite years of negotiations. Skopje believed that Serbian delays were deliberately designed to keep Macedonia off balance and to maintain some leverage over the government. Belgrade also tried to blackmail Macedonia by threatening to provoke inter-ethnic incidents inside the country through the use of militant members of the Serbian minority. During the NATO-Serb war, Yugoslav President Milošević tried to destabilize Macedonia by pushing Kosovar refugees into the country and by promoting anti-Albanian and anti-NATO unrest among the Serb minority. Skopje weathered the storm, and the early return of Albanians to Kosovo relieved pressure that otherwise could have been exploited by Belgrade. A border agreement with Belgrade was finally reached in early 2001.

Throughout the 1990s, the name dispute between Macedonia and Greece remained unresolved. Talks were periodically held at the UN between government representatives without any results. The name issue aside, relations at most levels between Athens and Skopje developed well. This was evident in the mushrooming of Greek economic investment in the latter part of the decade, while the Macedonian authorities viewed Greece as a potential gateway to the European Union (EU). Paradoxically, by the end of the 1990s, Greece had become one of the strongest proponents of Macedonian independence and territorial integrity, viewing these as a guarantee against possible Albanian irredentism and radicalism in the south Balkans.

POLITICAL PARTIES

Socialists and Social Democrats

Social Democratic Alliance of Macedonia (SDAM)
Socijaldemokratski Sojuz Makedonije (SDSM)

At its congress on 21 April 1991, the League of Communists–Party for Democratic Renewal, which had altered its name to the Party for Democratic Transformation (PDT) shortly before the first multiparty republican elections in Macedonia in November 1990, changed its name to the Social Democratic Alliance of Macedonia (SDAM). It elected Branko Crvenkovski as its president and Nikola Popovski as vicepresident. It adopted statutes that abandoned Leninist socialism and espoused the values of West European social democracy. Crvenkovski denied the existence of factions within the SDAM and affirmed that the party remained broad but united.

The SDAM managed to retain many of the assets and organizational networks of the former communist apparatus and a large degree of its popular support. Its overall head was Kiro Gligorov, the country's President through most of the 1990s, who steered Macedonia to independent statehood. In the November–December 1990 general elections, the SDAM gained 31 parliamentary seats and 25% of the popular vote, after which proceeded to form a coalition government.

According to its programmatic declaration, the SDAM focused on civic values and social democratic principles, and it discarded ethno-nationalism. With Yugoslavia still existing, the party favored a confederated state, and it was consequently accused by its nationalist rivals of being a communist apparatus and a Yugoslavist front. Its rivals also accused party leaders of benefiting from the selective privatization of state enterprises during the 1990s. SDAM spokesmen countered that they sought a peaceful transition to independence and the maintenance of ethnic and social stability in Macedonia. SDAM leader Crvenkovski was selected as Prime Minister at the end of June 1992.

In the general elections on 16 October 1994, the SDAM captured 58 parliamentary seats and became the leading party in the new governing coalition with the Liberals and Socialists. However, the party came into conflict with its coalition partner, the Liberal Party. The Liberals accused the SDAM of usurping power and slowing down the democratization processes with the help of the police and through its control over the media. At the same time, the SDAM administration was charged by nationalists with pandering to the demands of the Albanian minority. The party's popularity slipped throughout the decade under difficult economic conditions, and it lost the parliamentary elections on 18 October 1998 and 1 November 1998 and only managed to garner 27 seats. For the first time since independence, the SDAM went into opposition.[16]

The party's presidential candidate, Tito Petkovski, lost the second round of the national ballot on 14 November 1999, with 46.2% of the popular vote, after being the prime candidate in the first round. Petkovski had employed ethno-nationalist rhetoric during the campaign and alienated the country's large Albanian minority, which voted overwhelmingly for his rival from the Internal Macedonian Revolutionary Organization-Democratic Party for Macedonian National Unity (IMRO-DPMNU), Boris Trajkovski.

Socialist Party of Macedonia (SPM)
Socijalisticka Partija na Makedonija (SPM)

The Socialist Party of Macedonia (SPM) was created in Skopje on 28 September 1990.[17] In the first multiparty elections in November–December 1990, the Socialists gained four parliamentary deputies—one seat won jointly with the Alliance of Reform Forces in Macedonia, and another, with the Party for the Complete Emancipation of Roma. The SPM struggled to transform itself from its previous identity as the communist front organization, the Socialist Alliance of Working People, and it was often viewed as an opportunistic post-communist formation. It had positions on international affairs identical to those of other centrist or center-left parties, while its attitude toward the economy was more or less in line with the economic programs elaborated by the Yugoslav reformist and Prime Minister Ante Marković.

The SPM held its first congress in June 1991 and it supported the transformation of Yugoslavia into an association of equal republics and sovereign states. The congress also criticized nationalist tendencies and "abuse of patriotic feelings" by certain political forces. The Socialists made drastic changes in their concept of the future Macedonian state. As Yugoslavia fractured during 1991, the party's position switched in support of Macedonian independence and sovereignty. It chose to struggle for a "sovereign, independent and democratic Macedonian state, as an economically, politically and socially equal subject in the Balkans and Europe," and for the country to only rely on "its own defense forces, serving to protect the territorial integrity and independence of Macedonia."

Despite its transformation into a democratic party, the SPM underwent no major internal struggles and schisms, and its membership remained relatively stable. It participated in the Social Democratic Alliance of Macedonia (SDAM) government coalition until the general elections of October 1998, when it won only one seat in the legislature. Commentators described the party as the smallest and most obedient of the SDAM partners. Notwithstanding these charges, there were bitter debates between the Socialists and the biggest coalition member, especially during the last two years of the SDAM government.

Disputes with the SDAM also revolved around the sale of state-owned business. SPM leaders accused the SDAM of not offering them a sufficient number of cabinet seats: the party had only one minister and one parliamentary vice president. Socialist leaders believed the party was the true democratic leftist formation in Macedonia. It did not regard the nationalist parties as either leftist or rightist, as the labels were easily changeable. Most parties struggled to secure a position in the center of the political spectrum, including the SDAM and the Liberals, while the SPM prided itself on being genuinely leftist. Kiro Popovski was the leader of the SPM until his death in 1995. Ljubisav Ivanov Dzingo subsequently assumed this position, and remained the party's undisputed leader into 2000.[18]

Democratic Party of Macedonia (DPM)
Demokratska Partija na Makedonija (DPM)

The Democratic Party of Macedonia (DPM) was founded in March 1992 and was officially registered on 1 April 1992. The party was reportedly established to draw attention to the poor inter-ethnic situation in the western part of Macedonia and to meet the requests of citizens for adequate participation in public life. The members of the party founding committee were Sveto Tomoski, Sveto Boskoski, Zoran Efremov, Tomislav Stojanovski-Bombaj, and other personalities from the Tetovo region. Tomoski was elected the party's first president, and branches of the DPM were established in Gostivar, Kicevo, Skopje, Stip, and other major cities. Stojanovski-Bombaj became president of the party in the summer of 1993 with the objective of improving its organization.

The first party congress was held in June 1994, in Tetovo, and was attended by 400 delegates. The congress adopted a decision to participate in the October 1994 general elections with candidates from almost all cities in Macedonia. The party succeeded in winning one seat in the 1994 ballot. Stojanovski-Bombaj, the leader of the party, became a deputy after the party won 29,000 votes. He was outspoken in parliament and in the media about the difficult position Macedonians faced in Albanian majority areas in the western parts of the country. The DPM also took part in the local elections in 1996 and gained nine councilors' posts. The party participated in the October–November 1998 elections, in a coalition with the Liberal Democratic Party, For a Better Life. It only managed to gain a combined total of four seats. Other parties of a social democratic orientation included the Social Democratic Party of Macedonia (SDPM), led by Branko Janevski, and the Macedonian People's Party (MPP), led by Vladimir Stefanovski.

Liberals

Liberal Democratic Party (LDP)
Liberalno-Demokratska Partija (LDP)

The Liberal Democratic Party (LDP) was founded on 19 April 1997 through a unification of the former Liberal Party of Macedonia (LPM) *(Liberalnata Partija na Makedonija, LPM)* and the Democratic Party (DP). The LPM had emerged during 1991 from the Macedonian remnants of the former Yugoslav Prime Minister Ante Marković's Alliance of Reformist Forces and the Young Democratic Progressive Party. The DP was formed on 17 May 1993 by Petar Goshev and Georgi Marianovich. Within a few months of its inception, the Liberal Democratic Party claimed to have 45,000 members organized in 90 municipal organizations. The leadership of the LDP consisted of Petar Gosev, president; Stojan Andov, president of the LDP Council; and Risto Penov, vice president. The LDP positioned itself in the political center with a clear free-market orientation and a determination to push through economic reforms. However, it was accused by critics of monopolizing the privatization process, as many of the party's activists were former enterprise managers who reportedly benefited from the economic reforms.

On the national question, the LDP was a moderate party oriented towards the building of inter-ethnic tolerance and the integration of minorities into all spheres of social life. The Liberal Democrats were part of the coalition government formed with the Social Democratic Alliance after the October 1994 elections. When President Gligorov was incapacitated after a failed assassination attempt in October 1995, LDP leader Stojan Andov temporarily assumed the position of acting President of Macedonia. On 23 February 1996, Andov resigned as speaker of parliament and withdrew the party from government, calling for early elections. Among other disputes, Andov objected to a disproportionate representation of Albanians in the Crvenkovski cabinet, to the neglect of other coalition partners.

The Liberal Democratic Party took part in the parliamentary elections in October–November 1998 together with the Democratic Party of Macedonia, in the coalition For a Better Life. The coalition nominated candidates in all 85 electoral units, and 35 candidates for the proportional list. Five of those from the majority list and three from the proportional list were candidates of the

Democratic Party of Macedonia (DPM). The first person listed on the LDP-DPM ticket was Petar Gosev, and the chief of the coalition's central electoral headquarters was Risto Ivanov. The coalition gained a mere four seats. After the poor showing, Petar Gosev resigned as president of the party. The LDP's new leader was Risto Penov, the mayor of Skopje, elected in 1996.

Democratic Party (DP)
Demokratska Partija (DP)

The Democratic Party (DP) was established in 1993 as a centrist organization seeking to become a viable alternative to both the Social Democratic Alliance of Macedonia (SDAM) and the Liberal Democratic Party (LDP). It was initially led by Petar Gosev, the former president of the Central Committee of the League of Communists in Macedonia, who resigned from the ruling SDAM claiming that it was corrupt and incompetent. The DP emphasized its national-democratic and reformist character in standing for the "legitimate historical and national interests of the Macedonian people and the citizens of Macedonia." As a political party of the self-defined "radical national center," the Democratic Party was committed to the defense of the civil concept of the Macedonian people as stipulated by the constitution, securing and guaranteeing all human rights regardless of ethnic origin, religious belief, gender, and other status, and in accordance with international norms concerning individual and collective rights. It claimed to have a membership of some 12,000 people, but its actual influence was more limited. In the October 1994 parliamentary elections the DP obtained one seat, and in the October 1998 elections it failed to win any seats. Its new leadership after 1999 included Denko Skalovski as chairman.

Democratic Alternative (DA)
Demokratska Alternativa (DA)

The Democratic Alternative (DA) was formed during 1998 and led by its president Vasil Tupurkovski, the last Macedonian representative to serve on Yugoslavia's collective presidency. He returned to domestic politics after several years abroad. Tupurkovski consistently scored high in public opinion polls and the party effectively served as a vehicle for his political ambitions. Other DA leaders included Radmila Kiprijanova-Radovanović, the former president of the University of Skopje, and Savo Klemovski, former president of the Skopje university senate. The party claimed to be a centrist and civic organization that wanted to unite Macedonia's disparate ethnic and religious groups in a modern civic state. Its program included the following tasks: deepening and widening human rights and freedoms; protecting the political, economic, social, and cultural rights of citizens; scientific, educational and technological readiness of Macedonia for the twenty-first century; economic welfare for all Macedonian citizens; and the development of inter-ethnic and inter-confessional relations based on mutual respect and common interests and values. In the October 1998 parliamentary elections, the DA formed a coalition with the Internal Macedonian Revolutionary Organization–Democratic Party for Macedonian National Unity (IMRO-DPMNU), which won a combined total of 56 seats.

Civil Liberal Party of Macedonia (CLPM)
Gradjansko Liberalna Partija na Makedonija (GLPM)

The Civil Liberal Party of Macedonia (CLPM) was founded on 7 June 1991. The president of the party since its foundation has been Boris Gegaj. The party participated in the parliamentary elections in 1994 and 1998 and in the local elections in 1996 but failed to capture any seats and had only limited public appeal. Other essentially centrist or liberal organizations have included the League for Democracy (LD), led by its president Aleksandar Tortevski.

Christian Democrats

Macedonian Alliance (MA)
Makedonski Sojuz (MS)

The founding assembly of the Macedonian Alliance (MA) party was held on 14 January 1996, electing Gjorgija Atanasoski as president. The basic aim of the Macedonian Alliance was to strengthen the state and the legal status of Macedonia as a "free, sovereign, autonomous, independent, unitary, democratic and social state," with recognized international legal status. It supported, in the field of foreign policy, an active role in the United Nations (UN) and the European Union (EU) and membership in all multinational European and transatlantic organizations. The MA also wanted to build equitable relations with its neighbors in a peaceful manner through negotiations concerning all issues in the interest of peace and stability of the Balkans.

The Alliance has expressed concern about the position and rights of Macedonians in other states and their ability to express their cultural and ethnic identity. The party has supported the principles of the republican constitution, the multi-party system, private initiative, the return of previously confiscated private possessions, the reconstruction of infrastructure, reform of the tax system, and low tax rates. The Macedonian Alliance pledged to take particular care of the protection of human rights of all citizens, regardless of their national and ethnic origin and religious affiliation, and thereby to ensure their confidence in the country's institutions, the rule of law, and in its independent professional judicial system. The MA participated in the October–November 1998 elections in the Macedonian National Coalition together with the MAAK–Conservative Party and the Democratic Party.

A number of smaller Christian democratic organizations have been formed in Macedonia in recent years, including the Macedonian Christian Party (MCP), led by Miroslav Todorovski, and the Socialist Christian Party of Macedonia (SCPM), led by Vasil Risteski. Neither grouping has garnered any visible public support.

Agrarians

Democratic Alliance–Party of Farmers (DA-PF)
Demokratski Sojuz–Partija na Zemjodelcite (DS-PZ)

The Democratic Alliance–Party of Farmers (DA-PF) existed briefly during 1990 but fell apart soon afterward. Macedonia failed to develop any notable agrarian or farmers' parties despite the fact that agriculture constituted a major economic sector and much of the population lived and worked on the land. The party briefly entered the National Front coalition after the November–December 1990 elections, together with three others —the Internal Macedonian Revolutionary Organization–Democratic Party for Macedonian National Unity (IMRO-DPMNU), Movement for Pan-Macedonian Action–Conservative Party (MPMA-CP), and the People's Party (PP). The PP was founded in the village of Gorni Polog, near Kočani, and in Novo Selo, near Strumica. It was registered at the beginning of June 1990, with Dimitar Galev as president. The membership and leadership of both the DA-PF and the PP fluctuated between different political formations.[19] By the late 1990s, no visible agrarian formation existed on the political scene.

Communists

League of Communists of Macedonia (LCM)
Sojuz na Komunistite na Makedonija (SKM)

With the introduction of pluralism in Macedonia, the main body of the Communist League of Yugoslavia (CLY) transformed itself into the Party for Democratic Renewal and ultimately into the Social Democratic Alliance of Macedonia (SDAM). One faction of the original party, however, did not embrace the democratic changes, and proceeded to register the communist party as the League of Communists of Macedonia (LCM). The party established its headquarters in Skopje and was headed by Milan Pancevski, a high-level party official of the former regime known for his hard-line communist stance. A rival Communist Party of Macedonia (CPM) *(Komunisticka Partija na Makedonija, KPM)* was also established, led by Todor Pelivanov, but both parties played very minor roles in the country's politics.

Nationalists

Internal Macedonian Revolutionary Organization–Democratic Party for Macedonian National Unity (IMRO-DPMNU)
Vnatresna Makedonska Revolucionerna Organizacija–Demokratska Partija za Makedonsko Nacionalno Edinstvo (VMRO-DPMNE)

Several nationalist parties were established in June 1990 demanding complete Macedonian sovereignty and statehood in the face of mounting Yugoslav turmoil. The Internal Macedonian Revolutionary Organization–Democratic Party for Macedonian National Unity (IMRO-DPMNU) held its founding congress in June 1990, in Skopje. The party's platform called for a "spiritual, economic, and ethnic union of the divided Macedonian people and the creation of a Macedonian state in a future united Balkans and united Europe." IMRO-DPMNU was led by Ljubčo Georgievski, who had previously been a member of the Movement for Pan-Macedonian Action (MPMA). He was elected chairman in April 1991, replacing Vladimir Golubovski, who left the party after bitter divisions over its leadership and program. IMRO-DPMNU advocated the creation of a parliamentary democracy respecting the equality of citizens. Georgievski specified, however, that "because of the aggression of Albanian nationalists and their parties, Macedonia can be the national state only of the Macedonian people."

In the first multiparty elections, in November–December 1990, IMRO-DPMNU gained 38 seats in the 120-seat National Assembly, a number surpassing all other parties but insufficient to form a government. Georgievski became vice president of Macedonia after the ballot, but he resigned during 1991, to indicate his dissatisfaction with both President Gligorov and the incumbent government. When the new administration was formed, IMRO-DPMNU went into parliamentary opposition. Although renouncing IMRO's pre-war terrorist heritage, it pledged to continue its political traditions and opposed any amendments to the republican constitution that would limit Macedonian sovereignty.

IMRO-DPMNU also called for the recognition of Macedonian minorities by neighboring states and appeared to depart from its traditional pro-Bulgarian orientation by calling for a sovereign Macedonia in a future Balkan confederation. Nevertheless, its critics asserted that the organization was "supremacist" and in the service of "Greater Bulgarianism." IMRO-DPMNU initially advocated a looser political arrangement in Yugoslavia but expressed apprehension about Serbian domination in a smaller federation. Some IMRO factions also expressed more ambitious irredentist objectives, seeking the union of all former Macedonian territories in Yugoslavia, Bulgaria, and Greece. IMRO-DPMNU activists also claimed that the Albanians were a subversive element in Macedonian society. They accused Albanian leaders of turning the republic into a center for smuggling and black-marketeering while hatching plans to tear away Macedonia's western regions.

In April 1991, IMRO-DPMNU held a congress in Prilep and passed a resolution emphasizing that the party would struggle for an independent
Macedonian state that would embody the ideals of the Kruševo uprising and
the revolutionary hero Goce Delcev. Party leaders insisted that the defense
and security of the Macedonian state must be ensured through the immediate
creation of a Macedonian army. Spokesmen also advocated the demilitarization of the "Macedonian national space," thereby implying claims to parts of
Bulgaria and Greece. By the close of 1992, IMRO-DPMNU boasted a membership of some 150,000, with branches in every region of the country as well
as ten sections abroad among Macedonian exiles. It also established a youth
organization and published the newspaper *Glas* (Voice) at irregular intervals.
However, because of factional disputes, the number of IMRO-DPMNU seats
in parliament was reduced to 35 during the course of 1991–92.

IMRO-DPMNU deputies criticized the government on both national and
socio-economic grounds. They claimed that the governing coalition had failed
to ensure Macedonia's prompt international recognition and internal security
and that it had pursued an essentially neo-communist economic agenda. IMRO-
DPMNU periodically staged nationalist rallies in Skopje and other large cities to mobilize popular support for its cause. In February 1993, IMRO-DPMNU
and the Movement for Pan-Macedonian Action (MPMA) organized a two-
day anti-Muslim demonstration, protesting a government decision to construct a camp in Skopje's suburbs to house refugees from Bosnia-Herzegovina.
Nationalist leaders argued that the mass inflow of refugees would tilt the ethnic balance in Macedonia in favor of Albanians and other Muslims, thus undermining Macedonia's independence.[20] The party boycotted the October 1994
parliamentary elections but was diligent in reorganizing its national networks
during the following years.

IMRO-DPMNU deputy leader Dosta Dimovska claimed on several occasions that the Macedonian parliament was illegitimate because more than
half of the voters did not have representatives in it. She charged that the government had skewed the elections by failing to register more than 10% of the
voters. Dimovska also accused the government of leading the country into a
deep economic crisis and of dominating the country's mass media. IMRO-
DPMNU leader Georgievski strongly denied his party's involvement in the
assassination attempt on President Gligorov in October 1995.[21] Some critics
of the organization issued reminders about IMRO's past terrorist record during the leadership of Vancho Mihailov in the 1920s. However, Georgievski
claimed that the Bulgarian IMRO, rather than his party, was the ideological
successor to Mihailov's organization.

IMRO-DPMNU claimed over 60,000 members by the mid-1990s, and a
well-developed organizational network throughout the country. In the 1996
local elections, IMRO-DPMNU in coalition with the Democratic Party and
MPMA-CP won control in 29 towns. In order to distance themselves from
their nationalist and anti-minority past, during the late 1990s IMRO-DPMNU

leaders asserted that the organization was founded as a modern political party with a European Christian democratic orientation. IMRO-DPMNU participated in the October 1998 general elections, for the majority list, in coalition with the Democratic Alternative and the League for Democracy. The Organization's message to voters was the need for political change and a stable and dignified life. It played down its previous nationalist rhetoric and instead lay stress on pragmatic economic issues.

IMRO-DPMNU won the parliamentary ballot, gaining 43 out of 120 seats. Together with its election coalition partner the DA, and the Democratic Party of Albanians (DPA), it formed a coalition government by the close of 1998.[22] In the October–November 1999 presidential elections, IMRO-DPMNU candidate Boris Trajkovski won in a second-round runoff against the Social Democratic Alliance of Macedonia (SDAM) candidate Tito Petkovski. The party thereafter controlled all branches of government and pursued an essentially centrist program in cooperation with its coalition partners.

Internal Macedonian Revolutionary Organization–Democratic Party (IMRO-DP)
Vnatresna Makedonska Revolucionerna Organizacija–Demokratska Partija (VMRO-DP)

The Internal Macedonian Revolutionary Organization–Democratic Party (IMRO-DP) was first constituted in Ohrid, in 26 January 1991, as an offshoot of Internal Macedonian Revolutionary Organization–Democratic Party for Macedonian National Unity (IMRO-DPMNU), and registered as an independent political party on 4 February 1992. It was founded and directed by Vladimir Golubovski, who had previously led IMRO-DPMNU in the town of Veles but left the organization as a result of serious political and personality disputes. He claimed that IMRO-DPMNU had been captured by outside forces and was pro-Bulgarian. Golubovski refused to recognize the new leadership and threatened to file charges against his replacements in IMRO-DPMNU, especially against the new president Ljubčo Georgievski.

Golubovski initially advocated a confederal status for Macedonia within the Yugoslav community, as well as a confederal army and new legislative elections to "overcome the incompetence of the delegates in the Macedonian Assembly." With the collapse of Yugoslavia in the middle of 1991, IMRO-DP adopted a staunchly pro-independence program while continuing to attack the ambitions of Albanian minority leaders. Golubovski repeatedly criticized the republican government for pursuing "an indulgent policy toward the Albanians." He denied that the party upheld an anti-minority position, and proclaimed its willingness to recognize the rights of all minorities according to standards set by international conventions.

IMRO-DP was consistently critical of Albanian activists for their incessant demands for self-determination and autonomy, which allegedly would truncate Macedonian territory and leave the country exposed to renewed foreign domination. Golubovski stated that the national question would remain at the center of the party's program. Although IMRO-DP benefited from only limited public support, it claimed it would rapidly acquire a broader membership in an independent Macedonia. IMRO-DP was also accused by critics of adopting a militant pro-Bulgarian position and of favoring the eventual unification of Macedonia with Bulgaria. Party leaders stated that they simply wanted to reorient Macedonia away from its economic dependence on Serbia, toward other regional powers.[23]

At its congress in September 1995, Golubovski claimed that IMRO-DP was committed to the Western economic model, in that the state should guide only certain economic sectors while creating conditions for free enterprise. The party's economic platform emphasized low taxation, liberal laws to encourage free enterprise, and the development of free trade. IMRO-DP wanted to distance itself from IMRO-DPMNU, especially regarding economic issues, and posed as a more pro-market force. Like other nationalist parties, it did not take part in the second round of the October 1994 general elections. It won nine councilors' mandates in the local elections of 1996. According to the State Electoral Commission, it was the fifth most influential Macedonian political party, according to the election results, and the seventh strongest party in the country. IMRO-DP participated in the parliamentary elections of October–November 1998 but failed to win any seats in competition with its larger and more established IMRO-DPMNU rival. Nevertheless, it managed to put forward 53 candidates and claimed a membership of 20,000 people.

IMRO–Movement for Restoration of Macedonia (IMRO-MRM)
VMRO–Dvizenje za Obnova na Makedonija (VMRO-DOM)

In accordance with the IMRO–Movement for Restoration of Macedonia (IMRO-MRM) statute from January 1998, the party was organized in regional, city, municipal, and "cross-border" committees. It participated in the October 1998 general elections but failed to gain any parliamentary seats. The president of IMRO-MRM was Tomislav Stefkovski, a former parliamentary deputy. Its vice presidents were Stoile Stojkov and Pece Jovevski, and its secretary was Blagoja Petrusev.

The IMRO-MRM claimed to be a "people's party of national-social orientation based on Christian values." One of the stated objectives of the party was to "respect and cherish" the Macedonian people's historical strivings through IMRO and ASNOM (Anti-Fascist Assembly of the People's Liberation of Macedonia)—the wartime communist front. Its leaders pledged themselves to work for the full spiritual, political, economic, and ethnic unification of Macedonians people within a united Europe. In accordance with the

Macedonian constitution, IMRO-MRM wanted to build a national state of the Macedonian people with a unitary character under majority rule. According to the party program, no one would be allowed to rename the state as a multi-ethnic community.

Several other IMRO offshoots sprouted in Macedonia during the 1990s. They included IMRO–Fatherland Party (IMRO-FP) *(VMRO–Tatkovinska Partija, VMRO-TP),* headed by Dimitar Crnomarov and registered as an independent political party after a split within IMRO-DPMNU; and IMRO-IMRO *(VMRO-VMRO)* or the "real" IMRO, as its leader Boris Zmejkovski called it. IMRO-IMRO was founded after a power struggle between two streams in VMRO-DPMNU led by two of the closest collaborators of its leader Georgievski, Dosta Dimovska and Boris Zmejkovski, that evolved into the so-called pro-Bulgarian and pro-Macedonian wings. IMRO-DPMNU leaders, stood on the side of Dimovska. Zmejkovski and his followers left, and created IMRO-IMRO.

Movement for Pan-Macedonian Action–Conservative Party (MPMA-CP) Dvizenje za Semakedonska Akcija–Konservativna Partija (MAAK-KP)

The Movement for Pan-Macedonian Action–Conservative Party (MPMA-CP) was founded by nationalist intellectuals on 4 February 1990 as the first political party in Macedonia to openly compete with the ruling communists. Its name at that time was simply the Movement for Pan-Macedonian Action. Gane Todorovski was its first president, followed by Ante Popovski, a renowned Macedonian poet. The party announced that it represented all Macedonian people, no matter where they lived. Its leaders, Todorovski and Popovski, outlined the Movement's objectives at its founding assembly, stressing that the MPMA program advocated the "accelerated development" of the republic, the productive use of its human resources and natural wealth, and the free exchange of ideas, know-how, and experience. The Movement avowedly supported a law-governed, democratic state with a multiparty system, and claimed to oppose any form of discrimination.

In August 1990, the organization reaffirmed its position when it issued a manifesto on a free, sovereign, and independent state of Macedonia in front of the tomb of Macedonian revolutionary hero Goce Delcev, in the Holy Salvation church in Skopje. The declaration affirmed that Macedonia needed independent statehood in order to gain the attributes of a modern European nation, and criticized the government for failing to attain this objective. Following national elections in November 1990, MPMA leaders demanded that a ban be placed on Albanian parties because their activities were allegedly a threat to the constitutional order and incited national and religious intolerance. They claimed that Macedonian Slavs in the western part of the country were subjected to fear and uncertainty under an accelerated process of Albanianization.

Prior to the general elections in November 1990, MPMA, Internal Macedonian Revolutionary Organization–Democratic Party for Macedonian

National Unity (IMRO-DPMNU), the People's Party (PP), and a number of smaller nationalist organizations formed a National Front for Macedonian Unity in order to gain a sizable block of seats in parliament and to counter the electoral success of the reform communists and Albanian parties. In its program, the Front called for a sovereign Macedonia in a confederal Yugoslavia and proposed forging a united platform against the Albanian political movement. Despite its nationalist agenda, the MPMA failed to gain seats in the November 1990 elections. The party claimed it had been denied sufficient time to organize a proper election campaign; in any case, it barely reached 3.2% of the popular vote. Much of its nationalist appeal was captured by the better organized IMRO-DPMNU, and a significant number of MPMA members reportedly joined the larger national bloc.

Following the ballot, the MPMA expanded its organization, and by early 1993 it claimed branches in 31 districts with a membership of 20,000 people. It also established a youth wing. Critics of MPMA claimed that the organization was sponsored by Belgrade in an effort to disrupt the republic. Pro-Bulgarian nationalists also charged that MPMA leaders were providing clandestine assistance to the *Ilinden* organization in Bulgaria, an "illegal" grouping allegedly backed by Belgrade to wrest Pirin Macedonia from the Bulgarian state and to create conflictive rifts between Skopje and Sofia. In November 1991, the MPMA pushed for the immediate adoption of a Macedonian constitution, declaring statehood an urgent necessity for protection against encroaching extremist forces. It also displayed some moderation in the security arena, calling for the demilitarization of the republic under United Nations and CSCE (Conference on Security and Cooperation in Europe) guarantees of Macedonia's security.[24]

The party assumed its full name at the second congress in 1995, when the "conservative political option" was adopted. Straso Angelovski was elected president; this was confirmed at the third extraordinary congress, held on 8 February 1998, in Prilep. The party claimed to have 65 municipal organizations and about 11,000 members. It won 27 councilor posts in local elections and participated in the October–November 1998 general elections as a member of the Macedonian National Coalition founded on 23 April 1998. Its other members included the Macedonian Alliance and the Democratic Party.

MPMA's priorities included the "development of national consciousness," promotion of Macedonian identity and the Macedonian literary language, opposition to the creation of "ethnically pure" communities, spiritual unification of Macedonians from all four parts of their traditional territory, protection of the ethnic and cultural identity of immigrants from Macedonia, and deepening of relations with neighboring countries. The Movement's economic prescriptions were essentially liberal and included full privatization of the economy, a free market, reform of tax policy and the banking system, and the creation of favorable legal regulations to stimulate foreign investments.

One faction of MPMA split from the main body of the party and became an independent entity. Its president was the prominent Macedonian lawyer Jagnula Kunovska. Other nationalist Macedonian parties formed in the 1990s included the Macedonian Unity Party (MUP) led by president Branislav Sinadinovski, and the Macedonian National Front (MNF) led by president Ivan Spirkoski.[25]

Macedonian Alliance (MA)
Makedonski Savez (DS)

The Macedonian Alliance (MA) was established on 14 January 1996. At its founding assembly, Georgi Atanasovski was elected its president. The MA focused its attention on strengthening the unitary Macedonian state and building relations with Macedonians around the world. Its economic agenda was reformist and market-oriented, concentrating on the return of private property appropriated by the communist regime. The MA participated in the October–November 1998 parliamentary elections as part of the Macedonian National Coalition, together with the Movement for Pan-Macedonian Action–Conservative Party (MPMA-CP) and the Democratic Party (DP).

More radical nationalist splinter groups also formed in Macedonia during the last decade, unequivocally calling for a "united Macedonia" to embrace the Aegean (Greek), Pirin (Bulgarian), and Vardar (post-Yugoslav) regions, together with some border adjustments with Serbia in favor of Macedonia. They were banking on increasing their appeal among young people and workers experiencing economic deprivation in one of the poorest regions in the former Yugoslavia. They also seemed intent on garnering support among approximately 400,000 Macedonian Slavs living in Macedonia who traced their family origins to northern Greece. Several nationalist Macedonian groupings, including the Internal Macedonian Revolutionary Organization (IMRO) and MPMA, have supported the recognition and ethnic revival of the contested Macedonian Slav minority in northern Greece. In 1990 the Assembly of Aegean Macedonians (AAM) reportedly established its headquarters in Skopje, as did the Dignity (Dostoinstvo) human rights organization focusing on violations of minority rights in Greece.

While these groups claimed that the Slav population in Greece totaled over 300,000 and was denied basic minority rights, Athens charged they were intent on provoking separatist tendencies in Greece. A group styling itself as the Central Committee for Macedonian Human Rights (CCMHR) was formed in Thessaloniki during 1989. Such organizations regularly condemned Greek policy, called for closer border ties between Macedonians in both states, and sponsored protest actions on frontier crossings. In early 1992, Macedonian activists in the Greek town of Sopotsko established a Macedonian Movement for Balkan Prosperity (MMBP); among its leadership was the former Orthodox cleric Archimandrite Nikodimos Carknjas, who was thrown out of the Greek Church on charges of being an "autonomist" and a "Skopje agent." The Movement was refused registration by the Greek authorities, who sought to thwart any manifestations of a Slavic cultural or political revival in northern Greece.

MMBP leaders called for the respect of human rights, schooling for Macedonian children in their native language, and permission for holding church services in the Macedonian language under the jurisdiction of the Macedonian Orthodox Church. The Movement also demanded that the Greek state grant rights of free communication and of repatriation to all refugees and ensure free information on clubs and societies fostering Macedonian culture. The MMBP periodically held "Pan-Macedonian" congresses, calling for closer cooperation between Macedonians in Greece and their compatriots in the diaspora, while affirming respect for the inviolability of borders.[26]

Ethnic Minority and Religious Parties

Party for Democratic Prosperity (PDP)
Partija za Demokratski Prosperitet (PDP)

The Party for Democratic Prosperity (PDP) was founded by Albanian minority leaders on 15 April 1990, in the village of Dzepciste near Tetovo. Its first president was Nevzat Halili who was replaced in 1994 after a prolonged power struggle in the party. Halili, went on to establish his own organization, the Party for the People's Union (PPU). The PDP's strongest base was in the western municipalities of Macedonia where the majority of the Albanian population was concentrated, although it also claimed some Turkish, Roman, and Vlach members. The PDP's president Halili and vicepresident Sami Ibrahimi indicated early on that the PDP primarily represented Albanian interests although it was also prepared to defend the rights of other minorities.

The party called for constitutional changes to provide Albanians with a more equitable position in Macedonia; greater educational rights; the comprehensive use of the Albanian language; the release of all political prisoners; and an end to all forms of discrimination. The PDP quickly grew into the largest Albanian organization, claiming to have 18 local branches and several sections abroad. In coalition with the National Democratic Party, the PDP won 22 seats to the republican legislature in November–December 1990, as well as sizable majorities on local councils in three municipalities during the subsequent local elections.

PDP leaders claimed that the party would have obtained a much larger parliamentary representation if a proportional election law had been in effect and if the election authorities had not gerrymandered several electoral districts. Party leaders asserted that approximately 40% of the country's population were Albanian, contrary to the official statistic of around 22%. In a display of protest against allegedly rising Macedonian nationalism, the party urged a boycott of the 1991 republican census, asserting that the number of Albanians represented among census takers was not proportional to the size of the Albanian population, thereby opening up the possibility of statistical fraud.

The PDP abstained from voting on the new Macedonian constitution, arguing that the document did not provide sufficient provision for the group rights of Albanians. Halili asserted that he would continue to press for amendments in the constitution to redefine the Albanians as a constituent nation and more solidly guarantee their "collective rights." If this proved impossible to achieve, then the PDP would consider the constitution invalid and would undertake steps toward full minority autonomy.

PDP leaders supported some measure of territorial autonomy for regions containing Albanian majorities within an independent Macedonia. According to Halili, such regions could form an Assembly of Citizens that would be eligible to pass laws on education, the local economy, police, and local courts. A referendum on autonomy among the Albanian community in January 1992 was won overwhelmingly by a pro-autonomy vote, but the plebiscite was immediately dismissed as invalid by the Macedonian government.

After the ballot several local leaders in predominantly Albanian communes in western Macedonia declared the region the "Republic of Ilirida," stating their objective as the unification of all Albanians in the former Yugoslavia. In the interim, they favored the federalization of Macedonia, in which Ilirida would cover approximately half of the republic's territory. In response, the Macedonian government vowed to combat any anti-constitutional attempts to create parallel authorities in the country. PDP leaders also criticized the Ilirida proclamation and denied that they intended to partition Macedonia and join the region with an independent Kosova or with Albania.

Despite their participation in the government and legislature, PDP leaders remained concerned about official discrimination, the provocation of ethnic conflicts in the republic, and a potentially damaging spillover from the conflict in Kosova. They attacked the various Internal Macedonian Revolutionary Organization (IMRO) groups for their alleged anti-Albanian chauvinism and suggested that Serbian security forces were seeking to infiltrate these groups in order to engineer ethnic unrest. The PDP held its first congress in February 1992 and passed a resolution recognizing the independence of Kosova from Serbia and the principle of Albanian autonomy in western Macedonia. Some radical activists wanted eventually to unite the area with the Kosova republic, a position that was publicly opposed by the party leadership.

At a mass rally in April 1992, in central Skopje, Halili declared that Albanians considered Macedonia their home and that Skopje itself held many of their graves. He underscored that Albanians remained dissatisfied with their status as "second-class citizens" and condemned the EC for not providing sufficient support to the Albanian population in all the former Yugoslav republics. Among other demands, the PDP called for a petition drive to conduct a referendum on changing the constitution; proportional representation for nationalities in local government organs; a greater measure of local autonomy; and equal status for the Albanian and Macedonian languages.

In September 1992, the PDP received five ministries in the Crvenkovski coalition government, including a deputy premiership, but complained that it had been excluded from the most important portfolios. Despite their criticisms of various government policies, PDP representatives realized that their withdrawal from the executive would further limit their influence and simply place them in long-term opposition.[27]

At its annual congress in August 1993, more radical PDP members called for the resignation of the party leaders on charges that their participation in the Macedonian government had brought no positive results. A final split came on 4 December 1993 when the 15-member party leadership together with the PDP's government ministers resigned and formed a separate organization called the PDP–Party of Continuity.[28] They protested against the takeover of the party's Tetovo branch by the more militant activist Menduh Thaçi. Xeladin Murati, the deputy speaker of the Macedonian parliament, became the chairman of this group, which claimed to be the authentic PDP and was recognized as such for the October 1994 general elections. Murati himself resigned at the party's third congress in July 1994 and was succeeded by Abdurrahman Aliti.

The PDP participated in the parliamentary elections in October–November 1998, with 19 candidates on the majority system list and 17 candidates on the proportional list, in coalition with the People's Democratic Party (PDP) and the Party for Democratic Prosperity of Albanians (PDPA). After its poor performance during the ballot, the party underwent a change in leadership and elected Ymer Ymeri its new president. Most of the party's old guard was replaced; its new vice presidents were Qemal Musliu and Shpëtim Pollozhani, Mahi Nesimi became secretary-general. Ymeri was previously arrested by Macedonian authorities on charges of being a member of a paramilitary group seeking to overthrow the government.

In the post–1998 election period the PDP went into opposition, and its rival, the Democratic Party of Albanians (DPA), became a coalition partner in the Macedonian government. As a party in opposition, the PDP assumed more radical standpoints on Albanian issues. One such question was higher education in the Albanian language. The PDP opposed proposals for a private university that would provide higher education in Albanian and instead demanded full recognition of the Mala Rečica University in Tetovo and state funding for its operations. Conversely, the DPA's previous more hard-line stand was modified as it supported the idea of a private university.

Democratic Party of Albanians (DPA)
Demokratska Partija na Albancite (DPA)

The Democratic Party of Albanians (DPA) originated as a splinter from the official Party for Democratic Prosperity (PDP). As activists became dissatisfied with the performance of the party leadership, they initially formed the breakaway *(Partija za Demokratski Prosperitet na Albancite (PDPA)*, led by Arben Xhaferi and Menduh Thaçi, and then merged with the People's Democratic Party (PDP) to form the DPA in June 1997. Other prominent leaders included Iljaz Halimi, Adem Ademi, Fejzullah Shabani, and Bedredin Ibraimi. The party's original program was considered radical, as it called for the cantonization of Macedonia along ethnic lines. The party refused to work with the government, and opposed any compromises on issues central to the Albanian community, such as the acceptance of Albanian as a state language. The statutes of the DPA prevented the party from officially registering under that name, because of its objections to Macedonia's constitutional provisions. As a result, the DPA name was not recognized by the official law on political parties and the organization was still referred to under its original name—the Party for Democratic Prosperity of Albanians (PDPA).

Despite its conflicts with the PDP, the DPA entered an electoral alliance with its rival for the October 1998 parliamentary elections. Together the two parties gained over 19% of the national vote and elected 25 deputies, of which 11 belonged to the DPA. Following the elections, the party entered a coalition government with Internal Macedonian Revolutionary Organization–Democratic Party for Macedonian National Unity (IMRO-DPMNU) and the Democratic Alternative (DA). It obtained three ministries in the cabinet: Justice, Labor and Social Policy, and Local Self-Government. It also pushed for various changes in government policy in order to incorporate Albanians more fully into Macedonia's public life. However, the party leaders came under growing criticism from the PDP and from more radical factions within the DPA, which thought the leaders had made too many compromises with their Macedonian coalition partners without gaining any significant advantages for the Albanian community.

People's Democratic Party (PDP)
Narodna Demokratska Partija (NDP)

The People's Democratic Party (PDP) was created in early 1990 and was chaired by Iljaz Halili, of Tetovo. It entered into an electoral coalition for the first parliamentary elections in November 1990 and gained one deputy to the National Assembly. In parliament, the PDP maintained its coalition with the much larger Party for Democratic Prosperity, while often adopting more radical positions in its criticisms of the government and in its approach toward Albanian political and territorial autonomy. The PDP was active in organizing a boycott of the Macedonian census as well as the referendum on Macedonian independence, and its leaders were outspoken critics of the new constitution. During 1992, the party promoted a "Draft Platform for National Equality in Macedonia," calling for the country's federalization and the creation of an autonomous Albanian region. It also proposed the formal redefinition of Macedonia as a binational state.[29] The party was not a major political player through most of the 1990s, in comparison with the two larger Albanian formations.

Republican Party (RP)
Republikanska Partija (RP)

Founders of the Albanian-based Republican Party (RP) announced their program in July 1992. The RP was organized by an initiative committee that included its chairman Myftar Zyberi, one of the founders of the original Party for Democratic Prosperity, and parliamentary deputy Muhamed Halili. The party aimed to establish a broad base among Albanian intellectuals but claimed that it would remain open to all ethnic groups and seek to promulgate an essentially civic program. RP leaders believed that there were many uncommitted intellectuals in the country who would be willing to join the party and who sincerely supported the existence of an independent Macedonia. The RP appeared to distance itself from the more assertive agendas of the larger Party for Democratic Prosperity and the People's Democratic Party.[30]

Albanian Democratic Union–Liberal Party (ADU-LP)
Albansko Demokratski Sojuz–Liberalna Partija (ADS-LP)

The Albanian Democratic Union–Liberal Party (ADU-LP) was founded in 1996. Its chairman, Xhemail Idrizi, stated that the party's fundamental goals for the Albanian nation in Macedonia included full civil liberties, equality, open borders, and the free flow of goods. Idrizi declared that Macedonia did not consist solely of one nation but was multi-national and multi-confessional and that the constitution should acknowledge this state of affairs. The party condemned the forceful denationalization allegedly imposed on Albanian ethnics in the past and advocated the independent decision of all citizens, including Slavic Muslims, to choose their own national identity. The ADU-LP placed emphasis on a civic orientation rather than an ethnicity-based platform. On occasion it was critical of the PDP-DPA alliance for its more radical stance. The ADU-LP strongly supported Macedonian sovereignty and independence.[31]

Other Albanian parties included the Republican Party for National Unity (RPNU), founded in 1995 and led by Nevzat Halilii; the Democratic Union of Albanians (DUA), founded in February 2000 and led by Besnik Telai; and the Democratic Alliance of Albanians (DAA), established in March 2000 and led by Mevaip Ramadani.

Association of Macedonian Muslims (AMM)
Zdruzenie na Makedonci Muslimani (ZMM)

The Association of Macedonian Muslims (AMM), led by Dzevat Djulioski, who replaced Ljatif Pajkovski, aspired to work for the cultural and national renaissance of Slavic Muslims in Macedonia. According to the AMM, Muslim Macedonians encountered serious problems of awareness regarding their national identity. In addition, Muslim leaders claimed that both Albanian and Turkish activists were attempting to Turkicize them. They resolutely opposed any attempts to denationalize segments of the Macedonian population on the basis of ethnicity, religion, or politics. Leaders of the AMM asserted that the Party for Democratic Prosperity (PDP) and other Albanian nationalist groups had used the Muslim religion for separatist goals, and they strenuously decried the manipulation of Islam for political purposes. The AMM urged all Macedonian Muslims to fight with "all available means" the alleged nationalism of some minority parties that were trying to recruit Slavic Muslims for the separatist idea of a "Greater Albania," asserting that this would fan religious intolerance and cause a rift among Macedonian citizens.

The AMM transformed itself into a political party during 1992 so that it could function more effectively among its Muslim constituents. Party leaders claimed that Muslims were subject to serious restrictions and threats by elements of some Albanian parties, including the PDP and the NDP, and subjected to Turkicization by leaders of the Turkish community. They protested the Albanian referendum of January 1992, considering it a provocation directed against the recognition of Macedonia as an independent state, and urged all Slavic Muslims to boycott the ballot.[32]

Islam has not been strong enough anywhere in the Balkans to transcend ethnic boundaries. Islamic religious leaders have had only a limited role in the political process, and rarely have been in the vanguard of nationalist or separatist movements.[33]

Democratic Party of Turks (DPT)
Demokratska Partija na Turcite (DPT)

The Democratic Party of Turks (DPT), initially called the Democratic Alliance of Turks (DAT) *(Demokratski Sojuz na Turcite vo Makedonija, DSTM)*, was converted from a union into a political party at its second extraordinary congress, in June 1992, after the Macedonian parliament changed the legislation so that only parties could participate in national elections. Its chairman Avni Engülü emphasized the necessity of a more organized national orientation among Turks so that they would be viewed as an equal national community in an independent Macedonia. DPT leaders contended that Turks had not fully understood that in an embryonic pluralistic democracy it was necessary to form their own political party. The union pledged to support a free, sovereign, united, and independent Macedonia, and called for the defense of its territorial integrity and the equality of all citizens before the constitution. It urged the full participation of Turks in Macedonia's political life and sought equitable representation for Turks in all government structures, as this would help to stabilize the republic. The DPT did not promote political or territorial autonomy, being cognizant of the dispersal of the Turkish population and concerned about ethnic polarization in Macedonia. However, it demanded an expansion of educational programs for Turkish speakers and the inclusion of Turks in the country's security and police forces.

DPT leaders claimed discrimination at the hands of local authorities in parts of the republic. Some charges were investigated and dismissed by the administration as exaggerations. DPT president Erdoğan Saraç once claimed that Turks in Macedonia were "threatened with extinction," and in April 1993 he declared a "state of emergency" for DPT members and threatened to urge all ethnic Turks to emigrate to Turkey unless Macedonian authorities "take seriously this final warning to stop the harassment of Turks." Saraç issued several demands, including the withdrawal of police forces from the Debar area in western Macedonia, the return of expelled Turkish teachers to their schools, and the appointment of ethnic Turks to ministry-level positions. Radical elements of the DPT have also openly demanded the conversion of Muslim Slavs into ethnic Turks, leading to charges of "pan-Turkism" by Macedonian nationalists and Muslim leaders alike.[34]

During the October 1994 parliamentary elections, the DPT was the only political party of the Turkish people in Macedonia and was led by its new president Saraç. Fifty-four candidates participated in the elections but only one candidate entered the legislature: Kenan Hasipi, from the village of Vrapciste. The DPT won about 22,000 votes in the 1994 elections. The party also participated in the local elections in 1996, winning two mayoral posts and 42 councilor posts in 17 municipalities. Upon the DPT's initiative, the Movement for Cultural Tolerance and Civil Cooperation (MCTCC) was created before the October 1998 general elections. Members of the Movement included the Party for the Complete Emancipation of Roma (PCER), the Democratic Progressive Party of Roma (DPPR), and the Party for Democratic Action (PDA). Ferid Muhic, one of the most eminent intellectuals in Macedonia, was appointed coordinator of this inter-ethnic initiative. The DPT was listed on the national ballot in coalition with the Socialist Party of Macedonia, which won four parliamentary seats.

Party for Democratic Action (PDA)
Partija za Demokratska Akcija (SDA)

The Party for Democratic Action (PDA) was established in October 1990 and its registration was confirmed in March the following year. It did not participate in the first and the second parliamentary elections. The first president of the party was Sadrija Hasanović, followed by Rizvan Halilović, who was subsequently replaced by Avdija Pepić. The party claimed to have over 5,000 members throughout the country. The programmatic objectives of the PDA included the promotion of basic human rights and freedoms, support for democracy in social and political life, preservation of the sovereignty and territorial integrity of Macedonia, support for a neutral and peaceful international policy, and Macedonia's integration into all international economic, political, and cultural associations. PDA leaders also spoke out for equitable inter-ethnic relations and the protection of the environment.

The PDA participated in the October 1998 elections in coalition with the Socialist Party and the Movement for Cultural Tolerance and Civil Cooperation of Macedonia. The Movement's coordinator was Ferid Muhic. A rival Slavic Muslim organization was also established, called the Party for Democratic Action–The True Way (PDA-TW) *(Partija za Demokratska Akcija–Vistinski Pat, PDA-VP)*, led by its president Kenan Mazlimi.

Party for the Complete Emancipation of Roma (PCER)
Partija za Celosna Emancipacjia na Romite (PCER)

The primary objectives of the Party for the Complete Emancipation of Roma (PCER), as stated by Abdi Faik, the party's president, were to secure more substantive rights for the Roma population in Macedonia. Faik became a member of the Macedonian parliament for the Šuto Orizari township and displayed pride in citing the progress that the Roma had made in achieving recognition as a national minority. In September 1990, Roma leaders called on the population to stop identifying themselves as Albanians or Turks simply on the basis of their religious affiliation. In 1992, the PCER claimed to have 36,000 members in local branches throughout the country.

The party held its third plenary meeting in Skopje in November 1992 and addressed several issues regarding the provision of education and information in the Gypsy language. It called for the standardization of the Romani language and its use in elementary and secondary schools and in daily newscasts on television and radio. Some progress was subsequently achieved, and a Romani educational program prepared by the Ministry of Education was introduced in elementary schools in September 1993.

The PCER was also successful in securing the opening of a department of Romani studies at Skopje University, as well as the transmission of television and radio programs in Romani. Some Macedonian nationalists claimed that the PCER was being pressured to adopt more militant positions; its leaders reportedly suggested that a Gypsy state called "Romanistan" be established in the Balkans, claiming that nearly 220,000 Roma lived in Macedonia. However, the PCER condemned the more radical position of its rival, the Democratic Progressive Party of Roma in Macedonia (DPPRM), and repeatedly expressed its support for the Skopje leadership. The "Romanistan" concept was not an outright separatist demand but appeared designed to underscore the existence of a Roma nation in the Balkans and to canvass for international protection.[35] The PCER president at the end of the 1990s was Bajram Berat.

Democratic Progressive Party of Roma in Macedonia (DPPRM)
Demokratska Progresivna Partija na Romite vo Makedonija (DPPRM)

The Democratic Progressive Party of Roma in Macedonia (DPPRM) was formed on 27 December 1991, at the first constitutional assembly in opposition to what many in attendance considered the moderate stance of the Party for the Complete Emancipation of Roma (PCER). Arif Bekir was elected DPPRM president, Iskender Jakupov and Sali Bekirov became vice presidents, and Gunesh Mustafa was elected general secretary. Mustafa complained that the Romani population was subject to social and political experimentation and assimilation. As proof he cited an alleged agreement between Skopje and Bonn to return and reintegrate Gypsy refugees living in Germany. The DPPRM asked the government to take into consideration the possible consequences for Romani workers of the conversion of industry from public to private ownership, claiming Roma were often considered mere surplus labor. Mustafa also made statements in support of establishing a separate state of "Romanistan" in the Balkan region that would encompass parts of Macedonia.

The party took part in the second parliamentary elections, in October 1994, with no success. The party membership stood at about 2,800 in 1995. Four new municipal branches were established later, and the membership grew to about 5,400. The DPPRM representative won the mayor's seat in the Šuto Orizari municipality during the local elections in 1996. In the October–November 1998 parliamentary elections, the DPPRM took part in a coalition with the Movement for Cultural Tolerance and Civil Cooperation of Macedonia, but failed to win any legislative seats. The DPPRM's most recent president was Vekir Arif. Another Roma organization was formed in the mid-1990s, the Alliance of Roma in Macedonia (SRM) *(Sojuz na Romite vo Makedonija, SRM)*, led by its president Amdi Bajram.

Egyptian Association of Citizens (EAC)
Zdruzenie na Egipjanite (ZE)

The Egyptian Association of Citizens (EAC) was established in Ohrid in 1990, shortly before the first multi-party elections. Led by Nazim Arifi, it claimed a membership of 4,000 in the Ohrid and Struga areas of southwestern Macedonia. These people had renounced their Romani identity and asserted their purportedly Egyptian heritage. The EAC claimed that there were close to 30,000 people of Egyptian descent in Macedonia and petitioned for the inclusion of this category in the 1991 census. The government complied with their demands, although the number of people declaring themselves Egyptian fell below EAC expectations. The EAC also calculated that a further 100,000 Egyptians lived in Kosova, a claim that was ridiculed by Serbian and Albanian leaders. The basis of the claim revolved around the notion that thousands of Gypsies had migrated from Asia to Egypt during the Middle Ages and some of these people later crossed to the Balkans. Despite these assertions, the EAC experienced only limited success in canvassing for a separate nation and in gaining public support among the Romany populace.[36] The Association grew into the Party for the Democratic Movement of Egyptians of Macedonia (PDMEM) *(Partija za Demokratsko Dvizenje na Egipjanite vo Makedonija, PDDEM)*. Its headquarters were situated in Struga, and its president was Kamberi Napoleon.

Democratic Party of Serbs (DPS)
Demokratska Partija na Srbite (DPS)

The Democratic Party of Serbs in Macedonia (DPS) was founded on 16 March 1992. Although it was legally registered, the DPS asserted that Serbs were the most discriminated-against population in Macedonia. The party protested the exclusion of Serbs and Montenegrins from mention in the Macedonian constitution, which explicitly guaranteed minority rights to Albanians, Turks, Roma, and Vlachs. It claimed that there were numerous problems regarding the status of Serbs in Macedonia: for example, in pursuing education in the Serbian language, maintaining cultural traditions, and observing religious practices in Serbian churches. The party was founded and based in the northern Macedonian town of Kumanovo, near the Serbian border. Kumanovo was seen as one of Macedonia's most volatile areas, as Albanians composed 36% of the population and Serbs 15%.

DPS president Borivoje Ristić outlined the party's intentions in an interview in January 1993. He discussed several goals, such as codifyingthe legal status of Serbs and Montenegrins as distinct nations; the right to education in the mother tongue; full religious freedom; and Serb and Montenegrin broadcasts on state television. Ristić asserted that there was no reason for Serbs to be condemned for maintaining ties with their country of origin. However, Macedonian nationalists countered that although Serbs made up only 2% of the Macedonian population, they could be used as a pretext for Serbia to intervene in the republic and claim territory for a "Greater Serbian" state.

As Macedonia moved toward independence, some DPS leaders asserted that the aim of the Macedonian government was "the deliberate elimination of Serbs as a group." They underscored the necessity for Serbs to organize themselves, democratically struggle for their rights, and deter their "quiet assimilation." On the basis of the Albanian example, a motion was submitted by Serbian leaders to stage a referendum among Serbs and Montenegrins and to develop a Serbian autonomous region in northern Macedonia. During 1992, Serbs in the Kumanovo area began to organize themselves in associations and political parties and held demonstrations in support of the Serbian cause in Croatia and Bosnia-Herzegovina. Ristić intensified the party's demands for collective rights, improved economic conditions, and the possibility of dual citizenship, both Yugoslav and Macedonian.

DPS vicepresident Dobrivoje Tomić stated that if the demands of Serbs were ignored, "the natural thing would be to demand and count on protection by the mother country, Serbia." Some Serb activists expressed support for Serbian Radical Party leader Vojislav Šešelj, who consistently called for the absorption or partition of Macedonia, claiming that Macedonians were in reality Serbs with no claims to independent statehood. Šešelj sympathizers made efforts to establish a Serbian Autonomous Region of the Kumanovo Valley and Skopska Crna Gora. Macedonian nationalist organizations alleged that the DPS intended to destabilize Macedonia and claimed that accusations about anti-Serb discrimination were inaccurate and deliberately misleading. Macedonian nationalists argued that Western failures to recognize the sovereignty of the republic fueled Serb resistance. Despite official confirmations of the inviolability of existing frontiers, the Serbian regime seemingly viewed the borders as alterable administrative lines and refused to recognize them throughout the 1990s.

In January 1993, 500 Serb nationalists gathered in the town of Kucevište, north of Skopje, to protest police repression of a Serb rally on New Year's Eve. They claimed that the police attacked Serbian youths and injured thirteen people for hoisting a Yugoslav flag and displaying pictures of Šešelj. DPS leaders countered that the entire incident was incited by Macedonian nationalists in order to draw the United Nations Protection Force into the region. They also asserted that if Serbs continued to be mistreated by Macedonian authorities, they would undertake measures for "self-protection." Conflicts between Serbs and Macedonians have persisted over the status of the Prohor Pčinski Monastery, which technically is on the Serbian side of the border but is claimed as a major Macedonian shrine. Macedonian leaders issued several protests over the treatment of Macedonian citizens who visited the monastery to celebrate their national holiday. Nationalists have called for border adjustments to place the monastery within Macedonia.[37]

From the outset, the DPS focused its attention on promoting the cultural and national identity of the Serbian people and their unimpeded material, cultural, and scientific development. The party made efforts to ensure the active participation of Serbs in the Macedonian parliament, government, and other state institutions. It also strove to promote Serbian cultural and art societies, theatres, and publication. The DPS claimed to have 20,000 members and supporters. Its president after 1993 was Dragisa Miletić. Ristić formed his own party, the Democratic Alliance of Serbs in Macedonia (DASM), with essentially the same program but with more limited public influence.

Another essentially Serbian organization, the Association of Serbs and Montenegrins in Macedonia (ASMM) *(Zdruzenie na Srbite i Crnogorcite vo Makedonija, ZSCM),* cooperated closely with the DPS but on occasion adopted even more militant positions toward the Macedonian authorities. In June 1993 the association rejected a draft agreement between Skopje and local Serb leaders concerning the regulation of the status of the Serb population proposed by the chairman of the Geneva Conference on the Former Yugoslavia. It insisted that Serbs and Montenegrins be explicitly mentioned in a new Macedonian constitution as constituent nations and be afforded the full range of collective rights.

League of Vlachs (LOV)
Liga na Vlasite (LV)

The League of Vlachs (LOV) president, Mitko Kostov, stated that the goals of the organization were to resolve all problems revolving around Vlach

(Arumunian) culture, education, and religion without any covert political aspirations. As in other Balkan states, the process of Vlach assimilation in Macedonia over the decades had seriously undermined the cultural and linguistic cohesiveness of this small and essentially rural population. In a League meeting in March 1993, steps were undertaken toward the completion of a Vlach-language grammar book as well as the reintroduction of the Vlach-publication *Feniks*, which had been interrupted for almost a year. The group united with other Vlach organizations to form an International Vlach League (IVL) in the town of Kruševo in August 1992. The IVL was created as the official representative body of the Vlach people in dealings with all external entities, including the European Union nations, the Organization for Security and Cooperation in Europe (OSCE), and the United Nations.[38] Other ethnic minority organizations have also been active in Macedonia during the past decade. They include the small but vocal Society of Bulgarians (SOB), which denied the whole concept of a separate Macedonian nation and campaigned for outright unification with Bulgaria.

POLITICAL DATA

Name of State: Republic of Macedonia *(Republika Makedonija)*
Size of Territory: 9,928 square miles
Form of Government: Parliamentary Democracy
Structure of Legislature: Unicameral Assembly *(Sobranje)*, 120 seats
85 members are directly elected by popular vote, 35 members are elected proportionally through party lists.
Size of Population: 2,046,209 (July 2001 estimate)

Composition of Population (1991)

Ethnic Group	Number	% of Population
Macedonians	1,314,283	64.62
Albanians	427,313	21.01
Turks	97,416	4.79
Roma	55,575	2.73
Serbs	44,159	2.17
Vlachs	8,129	0.40
Others	87,089	4.28
Total minorities	719,681	35.38
Total population	2,033,964	100.00

Sources: Basic Statistical Data, Republic of Macedonia, Statistical Office, Skopje, December 1991; Yugoslavia 1918–1988 Statistical Yearbook, Federal Institution for Statistics, Belgrade 1989; and Statistical Yearbook of the Socialist Republic of Macedonia 1990, Republic Bureau of Statistics, Skopje, 1991.

ELECTION RESULTS

Presidential Election, 31 October and 14 November 1999

First Round, 31 October 1999

Turnout: 72.9%

Candidate	Votes	% of Vote
Tito Petkovski	304,168	33.33
Boris Trajkovski	188,826	20.69
Vasil Tupurkovski	146,835	16.10
Muharem Hexhipi	131,291	14.40
Stojan Andov	102,550	11.24
Muhamed Halili	38,705	4.24
Total	912,375	100.00

Second Round, 14 November 1999

Turnout: 69.87%

Candidate	Votes	% of Vote
Boris Trajkovski	592,118	53.80
Tito Petkovski	514,735	46.20
Total	1,106,853	100.00

Presidential Election, 16 and 30 October 1994

Candidate	Votes	% of Vote
Kiro Gligorov	715,774	52.60
Ljubčo Georgievski	197,210	14.49
Other	n/a	32.91
Total	n/a	100.00

Presidential Election (Indirect), 27 January 1990

Candidate	Votes	% of Vote
Kiro Gligorov	114	95.00
Total	120	100.00

Source: British Broadcasting Corporation, 4 November 1994.
Note: Voting was repeated on October 30 in eleven polling stations due to irregularities in the first round.

Parliamentary Elections, 18 October and 1 November 1998

Turnout: 72.9%

Party/Coalition	Votes	% of Vote	Seats
Internal Macedonian Revolutionary Organization–DPMNU	n/a	n/a	43
Social Democratic Alliance of Macedonia	n/a	n/a	27
Party for Democratic Prosperity	n/a	n/a	14
Democratic Alternative	n/a	n/a	13
Democratic Party of Albanians	n/a	n/a	11
Liberal Democratic Party/ Democratic Party of Macedonia	n/a	n/a	4
Socialist Party of Macedonia	n/a	n/a	1
Party for Complete Emancipation of Romas	n/a	n/a	1
Total	n/a	n/a	120

Source: CIA World Factbook 2001.

Note: Results provided by the Macadonian State Electoral Commission listed preliminary seats won by party. No official percentages nor vote tally were available.

Parliamentary Elections, 16 and 30 October 1994

Turnout: 77.76% (First Round), 53.15% (Second Round)

Party/Coalition	Votes	% of Vote	Seats
Alliance for Macedonia	n/a	n/a	90
Social Democratic Alliance of Macedonia			
Liberal Party of Macedonia			
Socialist Party			
All others	n/a	n/a	
Party for Democratic Prosperity			11
People's Democratic Party			5
Party for Complete Emancipation of Roma			1
Social Democratic Party of Macedonia			1
Democratic Party of Turks/ Party of Democratic Action			1
Democratic Party of Macedonia (Tetovo)			1
Independents			9
Total	n/a	n/a	120

Sources: Fabian Schmidt, from National Consensus to Pluralism. *Transitions* Vol. No. 4, 29 March 1995; Skipje Radio Macedonia Network thorugh FBIS reporting, *FBIS-EEU-94-211*; and BBC Summary of World Broadcasts, 5 November 1994.

Parliamentary Elections, 11 November 1990

Turnout: 85%

Party/Coalition	Votes	% of Vote	Seats
Internal Macedonian Revolutionary Organization/ Party for Macedonian National Unity	238,367	24.80	38
League of Communists of Macedonia/ Party for Democratic Transformation	243,259	25.39	31
Party for Democratic Prosperity	162,642	16.90	17
Alliance of Reform Forces	135,635	14.13	11
Democratic and Progressive Party	63,446	6.60	7
National Democratic Party	36,297	3.98	5
Socialist Party	44,977	4.68	4
Independent candidates	12,769	1.32	3
Party for Yugoslavia	13,331	1.38	2
Social Party of Macedonia and People's Democratic Party	4,105	0.42	1
Party for Complete Emancipation of Roma	3,961	0.40	1
Total	958,789	100.00	120

Source: Unless otherwise stated, election data are from www.sinf.gov.mk/ IZBORI%2098/Izbori_DefaultMK.htm.

NOTES

1. For recent histories of Macedonia see Hugh Poulton, *Who Are the Macedonians?* Bloomington: Indiana University Press, 1995; N. G. L. Hammond, *Migrations and Invasions in Greece and Adjacent Areas,* Park Ridge, NJ: Noyes Press, 1976; and Done Ilievski, *The Macedonian Orthodox Church,* Skopje, 1973.

2. See National Republican Institute for International Affairs, *The 1990 Elections in the Republics of Yugoslavia,* Washington, DC, 1991; and Milan Andrejevich, "Macedonia's New Political Leadership," Radio Free Europe/Radio Liberty Research Institute (RFE/RL), *Report on Eastern Europe,* Vol. 2, No. 20, 17 May 1991.

3. See "Macedonia Cracks Down on Legal Status on Minorities," RFE/RL, Situation Report: Yugoslavia, SR/7, 26 May 1989; and *Vecernje Novosti,* Belgrade, 13 May 1989.

4. "Declaration on Respecting Rights of Minorities," *Borba,* Belgrade, 8 June 1990, in *Foreign Broadcast Information Service, Daily Report: East Europe,* FBIS-EEU-90–118, 19 June 1990.

5. *Tanjug,* Belgrade, 8 September 1991.

6. Check *The Financial Times,* London, 20 September 1991.

7. See Duncan M. Perry, "The Republic of Macedonia and the Odds for Survival," RFE/RL, *Research Report,* Vol. 1, No. 46, 20 November 1992.

8. For full text of the constitution see *Nova Makedonija,* Skopje, 25 November 1991.

9. See "Constitution of the Republic of Macedonia," in *Foreign Broadcast Information Service/Joint Publications Research Service, Daily Report: East Europe,* JPRS-EER-92–016–S, 10 February 1992; letter from the Party of Democratic Prosperity, Tetovo, 19 January 1992; and *Country Reports on Human Rights for 1992,* U.S. Department of State, Washington, DC, February 1993.

10. See the interview with Halili in *Kossuth Radio Network,* Budapest, 9 September 1991, in *FBIS-EEU-91–178,* 13 September 1991.

11. RFE/RL, *Daily Report,* No. 28, 11 February 1992.

12. For a valuable analysis of Macedonian politics in the early 1990s see Duncan M. Perry, "On the Road to Stability—Or Destruction?" *Transition,* Vol. 1, No. 15, 25 August 1995, pp. 40–48.

13. *Radio Macedonia Network,* Skopje, 29 December 1991, *FBIS-EEU-91–251,* 31 December 1991.

14. See Hugh Poulton, "The Republic of Macedonia After UN Recognition," RFE/RL, *Research Report,* Vol. 2, No. 23, 4 June 1993; "War Games: Hell Bridge," *Puls,* Skopje, 26 November 1992, in *JPRS-EER-92–168,* 14 December 1992; Pance Zafirovski, "Political Irrationality," *Puls,* Skopje, 19 November 1992, in *JPRS-EER-92–172,* 22 December 1992.

15. *Tanjug,* Belgrade, 20 August 1992, *FBIS-EEU-92–163,* 21 August 1992.

16. Check www.sdsm.org.mk.

17. http://www.b-info.com/places/Macedonia/republic/partiesSocialist.shtml.

18. See http://www.vmacedonia.com/politics/soc.html.

19. Check at binfo.com.places/Macedonia.

20. See Duncan Perry, "The Macedonian Question Revitalized," RFE/RL, *Report on Eastern Europe,* 24 August 1990; Nenad Batkoski, "The Victim of New and Alien Domination," *Borba,* Belgrade, 17 August 1990; Velizar Encev, "The International Macedonian Revolutionary Organization Prilep Congress: Between Realities and Illusions," *Zora,* Sofia, 16 April 1991, in *JPRS-EEU-91–091,* 25 June 1991; Julijana Kocovska, "Greeks Among Us," *Nova Makedonija,* Skopje, 7 March 1992, in *JPRS-EER-92–043,* 8 April 1992; and interview with Ljubčo Georgievski, "Macedonia Will Not Sink to Its Knees," in *Zora,* Sofia, 25 February 1992, in *JPRS-EER-92–043,* 8 April 1992.

21. *FBIS-EEU-95–196,* 11 October 1995.

22. Check www.vmro-dpmne.org.mk.

23. *Borba,* Belgrade, 31 May 1991, in *JPRS-EER-91–084,* 15 June 1991; and *Borba,* Belgrade, 29 January 1991, in *FBIS-EEU-91–028,* 11 February 1991.

24. *Tanjug,* Belgrade, 4 February 1990; *Belgrade Radio Network,* 12 November 1991, in *FBIS-EEU-91–219,* 13 November 1991; RFE/RL, *Daily Report,* No. 136, 19 July 1990; inter-

view with Emil Anastasov, *Borba*, Belgrade, 10 April 1990, in *FBIS-EEU-90–074*, 17 April 1990.

25. Consult www.maak.org.mk.

26. Check Milan Andrejevich, "Yugoslav Macedonians Demand Recognition of Aegean Macedonians," RFE/RL, *Report on Eastern Europe*, Vol. 1, No. 22, 1 June 1990; Draško Antov, "Secret Document for a Pogrom Against Macedonians," *Nova Makedonija*, Skopje, 15 May 1992, in *FBIS-EEU-92–107*, 3 June 1992; "First Congress of the Macedonian Movement for Prosperity in the Balkans," *Nova Makedonija*, Skopje, 5 February 1993, in *JPRS-EER-93–026–S*, 2 April 1993; see the interview with Archimandrite Nikodimos Carknjas in *Nova Makedonija*, Skopje, 28 March 1993, in *JPRS-EEU-93–036–S*, 29 April 1993; and Vanjo Hadziev, "The Aegeans and Macedonian-Greek Relations," *Puls*, Skopje, 28 May 1993, in *JPRS-EER-93–062–S*,1 July 1993.

27. "Nevzat Halili Elected Chairman," *Flaka e Vëllazërimit*, Skopje, 12 February 1992, in *FBIS-EEU-92–035*, 21 February 1992; Daut Dauti, "Macedonia: Europe's Common Homeland," *Flaka e Vëllazërimit*, Skopje, 1 April 1992, in *FBIS-EEU-92–069*, 9 April 1992.

28. For background on the split in the PDP see Fabian Schmidt, "From National Consensus to Pluralism," *Transition*, Vol. 1, No. 4, 29 March 1995, pp. 26–30.

29. See Iljaz Halimi, "The Constitution of the Republic of Macedonia and the Status of the Albanians," *Nova Makedonija*, Skopje, 4 January 1992, in *FBIS-EEU-92–019*, 29 January 1992; and Branko Geroski, "Losing Stance and Political Boss," *Vecer*, Skopje, 15–16 May 1993, in *JPRS-EER-93–057–S*, 22 June 1993.

30. Interview with Muhamed Halili in *Nova Makedonija*, Skopje, 14 July 1992, in *JPRS-EER-92–113*, 21 August 1992.

31. See the interview with Dzemail ldrizi, "Macedonia Is Pursuing a Peace-Loving Communicative Policy," *Nova Makedonija*, Skopje, 16 May 1993, in *JPRS-EER-93–057–S*, 22 June 1993.

32. Check the report by Panta Dzambazovski, "Muslim Macedonians Will Form Party," *Nova Makedonija*, Skopje, 13 February 1992, in *JPRS-EER-92–028*, 9 March 1992; interview with Dzevat Djulioski by Panta Dzambazovski, "We Must Be Taken Into Account," *Nova Makedonija*, Skopje, 5 December 1992, in *JPRS-EER-93–006*, 22 January 1993; Panta Dzambazovski, "Muslim Macedonians Will Form Party," *Nova Makedonija*, Skopje, 13 February 1992, in *JPRS-EER-92–028*, 9 March 1992; and *Vecer*, Skopje, 4 March 1993, in *JPRS-EER-93–029–S*, 9 April 1993.

33. Consult Duncan M. Perry, "The Republic of Macedonia: Finding Its Way," in Karen Dawisha and Bruce Parrott (Eds.), *Politics, Power, and the Struggle for Democracy in South-East Europe*, Cambridge, UK: Cambridge University Press, 1997, pp. 226–281.

34. J. Mirovski, "From an Association, a Political Party: Second Extraordinary Congress of the Association of the Democratic Union of Turks," *Nova Makedonija*, Skopje, 28 June 1992, in *JPRS-EER-92–104*, 11 August 1992.

35. Hugh Poulton, "The Roma in Macedonia: A Balkan Success Story?" RFE/RL, *Research Report*, Vol. 2, No. 19, 7 May, 1993; A. L., "The Gypsy Language in Education," *Nova Makedonija*, Skopje, 16 November 1992, in *JPRS-EER-93–001*, 5 January 1993; *Nova Makedonija*, Skopje, 21 October 1992, in *JPRS-EER-92–170*, 17 December 1992.

36. See Hugh Poulton, "The Roma in Macedonia: A Balkan Success Story?" RFE/RL, *Research Report*, Vol. 2, No. 19, 7 May 1993.

37. *Nova Makedonija*, Skopje, 10 September 1992, in *JPRS-EER-92–139*, 29 September 1992; interview with Vojislav Šešelj, "The Serbs Will Not Surrender," *Otechestven Vestnik*, Sofia, 27 April 1993, in *FBIS-EEU-93–083*, 3 May 1993; Mirka Velinorska, "JNA Soldiers in Border Provocations," *War Report*, London, No. 15, October 1992; *Nova Makedonija*, Skopje, 23 January 1993, in *JPRS-EER-008–S*, 17 February 1993; *Puls*, Skopje, 21 January, 1993, in *JPRS-EER-93–016–S*, March 3, 1993; *Belgrade Radio Network*, Belgrade, 15 January 1993, in *FBIS-EEU-93–011*, 19 January 1993.

38. A.D., "International Vlach League Formed at Kruševo Congress," *Nova Makedonija*, Skopje, 16 August 1992, *JPRS-EER-92–133*, 18 September 1992; *Vecer*, 17 March 1993, in *JPRS-EER-93–038–S*, 6 May 1993.

Bulgaria

HISTORICAL OVERVIEW

During the Bronze Age, from the twelfth century BC onward, the Bulgarian lands were inhabited by Thracians who, by the fifth century BC, had established a thriving civilization and a centralized state structure.[1] The Thracians were weakened by waves of Greek colonization, especially in the Aegean coastal areas. The Romans established full control over these territories in the first century AD and formed the provinces of Thrace and Moesia (between the Balkan mountains and the Danube). As Rome was Christianized, so were these territories. With the division of Christendom in the fourth century AD, the Bulgarian lands became part of the Byzantine Empire, ruled from Constantinople.

The current Bulgarian territories were subject to successive invasions by Goths, Huns, and Avars. By the end of the fifth century AD, there were increasing incursions by Slavic tribes from the north, many of which settled in the area. Proto-Bulgarian groups of Turkic origin, from a region between the Ural Mountains and the Volga River, entered the Balkan area in the seventh century AD. They possessed a developed political system based around their ruler, the Khan, and a powerful military structure. During the 630s, a loose federation of proto-Bulgarian tribes was formed, and in AD 680 Khan Asparuh gained control of the region. In 681, Emperor Constantine V Pogonatus signed a treaty with Asparuh recognizing the existence of a Bulgarian state with its capital in Pliska.

The Bulgarian state grew rapidly at the start of the eighth century AD. With the collapse of the Avar Empire, it expanded westward as far as the river Tisza in present-day Hungary. In 864, king Boris launched a mass conversion of the Bulgarians, a process that helped facilitate the merger of Slavs and proto-Bulgarians and the development of a common Slavic language. In 870 an autocephalous Bulgarian Orthodox Church was established, free of the Byzantine patriarchate. The first Slavic alphabet was developed in the latter half of the ninth century by the monks Cyril and Methodius.

Under Simeon the Great at the start of the tenth century, Bulgaria's frontiers were extended to the Adriatic Sea in the west and the Aegean Sea in the south. Simeon was given the title of *tsar* by the Byzantine Emperor. By the end of the tenth century, the center of the state was Ohrid, in present-day Macedonia. But Bulgarian forces suffered a major defeat in 1014 at the hands of the Byzantine Emperor Basil II, and by 1018 Bulgaria had been incorporated into the empire.

A second Bulgarian empire was established between 1185 and 1393, based in the religious capital of Turnovo. It freed itself from Byzantine domination and came to control an area between the Balkans and the Danube River. Its more notable rulers included Tsar Kaloyan (1197–1207) and Tsar Ivan Assen II (1218–1241). But the empire was increasingly torn by conflicts between opposing magnates and was weakened by Tatar incursions from the north and east at the end of the thirteenth century. By the beginning of the fourteenth century, Tatar domination was broken, and Bulgaria reestablished control over Thrace under its ruler Mihail Shishman (1323–1330).

Two new threats appeared during the fourteenth century, from Serbia in the west and from the Ottoman Turks in the east. In 1362, Turkish forces took Edirne (Adrianople). They captured Sofia in 1385 and Turnovo in 1393. Soon all of Bulgaria was under Ottoman control, and it remained as for almost 500 years. The traditional Bulgarian state structure was destroyed and the Bulgarian Orthodox Church was placed under the authority of the Greek patriarch. Periodic resistance to Turkish rule was offered by bands of *hajduks* (anti-Turkish guerillas), but they were not a serious threat to Ottoman domination.

During the early part of the nineteenth century, Bulgaria underwent a cultural renaissance that gradually was transformed into a national revival, with attempts to reestablish an independent, Bulgarian Orthodox Church. Several armed uprisings were staged, but they were brutally put down by Istanbul. Secret independence cells were established by such patriots as Georgi Rakovski and Vasil Levski. Bulgaria achieved independence from Ottoman rule in 1878, following the Russo-Turkish war. The initial Treaty of San Stefano created a large state stretching from the Danube to the Aegean and including most of present-day Macedonia. These territories were diminished by the Treaty of Berlin in July 1878, at the insistence of the Great Powers, because of fears of Russian influence throughout the Balkans. Bulgaria proper now included the region between the Danube and the Balkan Mountains; the area between the Balkan and Rhodope Mountains in the south formed the autonomous Ottoman province of Eastern Rumelia. These border readjustments and Bulgaria's reversion to a semi-autonomous Ottoman principality under a German ruler created resentments in the state. However, during the last few decades of the nineteenth century, Sofia adopted the progressive Turnovo constitution, which guaranteed individual rights. A number of political parties were established, including the National Liberal Party and the Bulgarian Agrarian Union.

The country finally proclaimed its full independence from Turkey in 1908, after several popular revolts, including the Ilinden uprising in August 1903, centered in the Macedonian and Thracian regions. Bulgaria's territorial claims helped fuel two Balkan wars in 1912 and 1913. In the first war, the new Balkan states combined their forces to drive the Turkish armies out of the region. In the second war, Bulgaria was unsuccessful in its military campaign against Serbia and Greece and once again lost territories in Macedonia and Thrace to its two neighbors. The result left a lasting sense of injustice in Sofia with regard to Bulgaria's rightful frontiers. Sofia retained only a small slice of Pirin Macedonia and a sector of the Thracian coastline. During World War I, Bulgaria allied itself with Germany and Austria, but with the defeat of the Central Powers it was again forced to accept a harsh peace treaty at Neuilly in November 1919, and lost all access to the Aegean Sea.

The Macedonian region and its Slavic population presented an intractable problem for neighboring states that claimed the inhabitants as co-ethnics. Macedonia achieved a very brief period of independence before it was partitioned among Serbia, Greece, and Bulgaria. After World War I, the Macedonian population itself was divided as to its ethnic identity. The most vocal political forces tended to consider themselves as a subdivision of the Bulgarian nation and campaigned for the liberation of territories under Serb-Yugoslav and Greek control. However, some activists favored a separate Macedonian state that would incorporate the three traditional regions: Vardar (in Yugoslavia), Pirin (in Bulgaria), and Aegean Macedonia (in Greece). Macedonians were not registered as a distinct nationality in the inter-war Bulgarian censuses, even though many Macedonians were active in Bulgaria's political life. Their total numbers were therefore difficult to estimate.

For most of the inter-war period, Bulgaria witnessed political turmoil and economic crisis, particularly after the overthrow of the Agrarian government led by Aleksandur Stamboliyski in 1923. In a military *coup d' état* supported by their political rivals and by Macedonian activists, Stamboliyski and other Agrarian leaders were murdered. After a decade of political instability and conflict, another coup led by military officers in May 1934 resulted in the formation of a personalistic regime under King Boris III. During World War II, Sofia imposed a royal dictatorship, and capitalized on the German occupation of Yugoslavia and Greece to forge an alliance with Berlin and regain parts of Macedonia and Thrace. Sofia also repossessed the region of southern Dobrudja from Romania. King Boris died in August 1943, and for the rest of the war the country was ruled by a regency, as Boris's successor Simeon was only six years old.

Bulgaria's territorial advances were again reversed at the close of World War II, following the defeat of the Axis powers. Communist forces with Soviet assistance seized power on 9 September 1944 and proceeded to eliminate all organized opposition by the end of 1947. The former Comintern agent

Georgi Dimitrov returned to Bulgaria and assumed leadership over the Communist Party and the state. A new, Stalinist, "Dimitrov" constitution was passed on 4 December 1947. The communist regime, under Soviet supervision, placed tight restrictions on cultural and political life, conducted a full-scale drive toward state control over the economy, and pursued agricultural collectivization. Dimitrov died on 2 July 1949 and was replaced by Vulko Chervenkov. He in turn was replaced by Todor Zhivkov on 17 April 1956, during the process of de-Stalinization. Zhivkov maintained tight control over the country for the next 34 years, until the collapse of the communist system. His absolute loyalty to Moscow and his ability to thwart any organized domestic opposition to Leninist rule earned him the complete support of the Soviet leadership.

Although the majority of Bulgarians considered the Macedonians their ethnic compatriots, during the late 1940s the communist regime accepted the existence of a distinct Macedonian republic in Yugoslavia and accorded its own Macedonians national minority status. At that time, both Sofia and Belgrade appeared well disposed toward the creation of some kind of Balkan communist federation, in which Macedonia would figure as one component political entity. In the 1956 census, nearly 188,000 Macedonians were registered, constituting 2.5% of the Bulgarian population. However, as tensions increased between Belgrade and Sofia after Tito's break with Stalin in 1948, the Bulgarian government stepped to the forefront of the anti-Yugoslav campaign and revived its claims to Yugoslav Macedonia, eliminating at the same time the minority status of its own Macedonian population.

Henceforth, Bulgarian patriotism was strenuously propagated and Macedonia was described merely as a geographic region. Residents in the Pirin region of geographic Macedonia were required to declare their nationality as Bulgarian. While some citizens complained that they had been forced to identify themselves as Macedonian during the 1940s and 1950s, others claimed they were coerced after 1964 into accepting new internal passports with a Bulgarian designation. From the early 1960s, the identity of Macedonians plagued relations between the two communist capitals, with each charging the other with unacceptable territorial pretensions.

Under the communist regime, Sofia renounced its claims to Greek Macedonia and Turkish and Greek Thrace. But the large Turkish minority in Bulgaria, estimated at around 10% of the population, remained a serious bone of contention between Sofia and Ankara. Soon after the communist takeover, collective rights in education and cultural life were abolished and about 150,000 Turks were pressured to emigrate: these were primarily the least assimilable and most devout Muslims. Although Bulgarian Turks did not campaign for political or territorial autonomy, periodic drives were launched by the authorities to eradicate their distinct ethnic and religious identity. Similar assaults were made against the Pomak Muslims and the Muslim Roma (Gypsies), with communist propagandists claiming that these were ethnic Bulgarians who had converted to Islam due to pressure and persecution by the Ottoman administration.

Ethnic Turks were periodically subject to the most intensive assimilationist pressures. Under Zhivkov's rule, official anti-Turkish sentiments gave rise to a number of government-sponsored campaigns culminating in major persecution during the mid-1980s. The campaign was officially justified as a means of enlarging the Bulgarian population, which was allegedly threatened by excessive Turkish demographic growth. The authorities forced Turks to Bulgarize their names and abandon their Islamic rituals and cultural traditions. The campaign provoked riots and clashes with police, and several dozen people were shot dead. About 350,000 Turks left the country; after the democratic changes in Bulgaria in 1989, between 120,000 and 180,000 returned from Turkey. Sofia's human rights violations were terminated and most Turkish minority rights were restored. With the fall of communism, Turks were allowed again to use their original names, to restore their religious practices, and to legally establish their own political, social, and cultural organizations.

The position of the Turkish community remained a barometer of relations between Sofia and Ankara during the 1990s. Turkish activists were closely watchful for the impact of Bulgarian ultra-nationalist groups that campaigned to limit the educational and linguistic rights gained by ethnic Turks. Some Bulgarian spokesmen also remained concerned about the potential growth of Turkish nationalism and of autonomist and separatist trends among minority organizations.

In the early stages of democratization, some ex-communists capitalized on widespread anti-Turkish feelings in order to gain public support. Party officials in provincial cities were fearful of losing their jobs and property, seized during the Turkish exodus, and of being held responsible for the anti-Turkish campaign. They helped organize anti-Turkish demonstrations around the country and fanned ethnic tensions. Former communists, in league with newly formed ultra-nationalist organizations, accused Turkish activists of seeking autonomy, secession, and annexation by Ankara, followed by the dispossession and expulsion of Bulgarian Christians. Such charges played on fears of demographic decline and economic turmoil among ordinary Bulgarians, but seemed to bear little resemblance to reality.

POST-COMMUNIST DEVELOPMENTS

Before Bulgaria's democratic breakthrough at the end of 1989, a number of reformist groups were established in the late 1980s. One of the first anti-communist groupings, the Turkish Democratic League (TDL), was founded in the town of Krumovgrad, in southeast Bulgaria, in 1986. The TDL protested against the forced assimilation of Bulgaria's Turkish population. The sociologist Zheliu Zhelev, expelled from the Bulgarian Communist Party, formed the Club for the Support of Glasnost and Perestroika. A free trade union, *Podkrepa* (Support), was established by Konstantin Trenchev. In the heavily polluted city of Ruse (on the Danube river) an ecological group was formed which came to be known as *Ecoglasnost* and which challenged Sofia's neglect and destruction of the environment. Several major pre-war political parties were also revived, including the Bulgarian Agrarian National Union-Nikola Petkov (BANU-NP) and the Social Democrats.

Other groupings were established to push for human rights and religious liberties. A growing number of intellectuals refused to be cowed by the Zhivkov regime. By 1989, various cultural groups were active and increasingly criticized the regime. In the spring of 1989, protest movements spread among Turks through hunger strikes and other protest actions. By the fall of 1989, there were sporadic demonstrations in Sofia calling for reforms, although their scale and political impact remained limited.

Following a wave of public protests and increasing political pressures against the communist regime, on 10 November 1989 the Bulgarian Communist Party (BCP) Central Committee announced the resignation of Todor Zhivkov as secretary-general and his replacement by Foreign Minister Petar Mladenov. The new leader promised sweeping political and economic measures to transform Bulgaria into a "modern democratic state." The BCP organized pro-Mladenov rallies, depicting itself as the initiator of progressive reforms, scapegoating the Zhivkov leadership for all the country's maladies, and seeking to deny the reformist initiative to the emerging but still embryonic democratic opposition.

Although organized dissent was modest in Bulgaria, the *Ecoglasnost* group gathered several thousand signatures on petitions to the regime and staged several small public rallies. The Independent Association for the Defense of Human Rights held its first demonstration in October 1989 and demanded political reform. In November 1989, the Independent Discussion Club for the Support of Glasnost and Perestroika held its first public meeting in Sofia and demanded freedom of speech and democratic reform. An umbrella organization, the Union of Democratic Forces (UDF), was established in December 1989 to help coordinate the growing opposition movement; it was initially made up of representatives of ten unofficial organizations.

Mladenov held meetings with dissident activists in mid-November 1989 and pledged to implement substantive democratic reforms and legalize all manner of independent groups and activities. The BCP's subordinate bodies, including the *Komsomol* youth association, were allowed a more critical role, in a move designed to deflate some of the opposition demands. Reshuffles were conducted in the BCP Politburo and Central Committee, and Mladenov declared himself in favor of free elections. The regime dropped the BCP's "guiding force" role from the constitution and promised to curtail the repressive role of the security services. This paved the way to the creation of a multi-party system. While the BCP endeavored to maintain the political initiative, dozens of new political groups were formed.

Some reform communists demanded the resignation of the entire BCP Central Committee, amid growing signs of factionalism with the emergence of the inner-party Alternative Socialist Association. In early December 1989, a preparatory meeting was held between BCP officials and representatives of some independent groups. Mladenov promised that the authorities would hold a constructive dialogue with all groups supporting socialism. In order to incorporate leading opposition elements in some workable coalition and to prevent destructive splits within the party, in January 1990 the BCP initiated roundtable discussions with officially sponsored organizations and some newly formed opposition groups.[2]

The regime continued to be treated with mistrust by opposition groups that refused to enter the "Government of National Consensus" proposed by the communists. At its Extraordinary Congress in early February 1990, the BCP selected Alexander Lilov as its new secretary-general and replaced the Central Committee with a smaller Supreme Party Council and the Politburo with a new presidency. BCP leaders also initiated steps to separate the party from the state. The party itself was renamed the Bulgarian Socialist Party (BSP).

The National Assembly (parliament), controlled by the BSP, elected Andrei Lukanov as the new prime minister. Lukanov attempted to form a broader-based coalition government, but the initiative was rejected by the UDF, which had grown into the chief opposition alliance. The new cabinet became an all-communist body as the BSP's former coalition partner, the Agrarian National Union, refused to join the Lukanov government and purged itself of compromised older leaders. In addition, reformist BSP intellectuals established an Alternative Socialist Party (ASP) and cast serious doubts on the party's ability to democratize. Meanwhile, the UDF organized public demonstrations to protest the slow progress in the roundtable negotiations.

By mid-March 1990, an agreement was reached between the BSP and the UDF on the transition to a democratic system and the scheduling of pluralistic elections. Parliamentary elections on 10 and 17 June 1990 were won by the BSP with 47% of the vote; the party gained 211 parliamentary seats. The UDF obtained a disappointing 36% and 144 seats, while the Agrarian Union took 8% and 16 seats, and the Turkish organization, the Movement for Rights and Freedoms (MRF), 6% and 23 seats. The UDF accused the regime of ballot rigging and of maintaining a monopoly over the media, while the opposition had insufficient time to organize an effective election campaign and scored particularly poorly in rural areas, where the communist apparatus remained largely intact.

In April 1990, parliament had formally created the office of president, limiting its authority to security matters and ceremonial functions, with no veto powers over parliamentary legislation. On 6 July 1990, acting President

Mladenov resigned and the BSP threw its support behind Zheliu Zhelev as the country's new head of state. With the UDF refusing to form a coalition to ensure a two-thirds parliamentary majority, the Lukanov government was stalemated. The BSP Lukanov government resigned at the end of November 1990 and was replaced a month later by a coalition headed by Prime Minister Dimitur Popov and including the BSP, the UDF, Agrarians, and independents.

The National Assembly served as a constitutional assembly, drafting Bulgaria's new constitution. The document stressed that Bulgaria was a unitary state, and prohibited any forms of territorial autonomy or the creation of political parties founded on an ethnic, racial, or religious basis. Parliament was given legislative supremacy, and the presidency was given a veto on legislation passed by the National Assembly. The constitution was adopted on 12 July 1991, despite opposition from some UDF factions.

Prior to the October 1991 elections, the UDF split because the Union's largest coalition partners, the Social Democratic Party and the Agrarian Union, were refused a more prominent voice in the UDF Council or a greater number of candidates on the UDF electoral list. In addition, the Union was divided between advocates of a moderate line toward the BSP ("light blues") and a majority who demanded far-reaching decommunization ("dark blues"). The former wing withdrew from the Union and formed the UDF-Liberals; the latter faction became known as the UDF-Movement, and inherited the coalition's organizational network and media outlets.

In the October 1991 elections, the UDF-Movement narrowly won a plurality of votes amidst declining support for the BSP. The UDF received 34% of the vote, with 110 of the 240 parliamentary mandates, while the BSP achieved 33%, with 106 seats. The only other party to clear the 4% threshold and gain parliamentary seats was the MRF. Not surprisingly, the legislature became highly polarized and the UDF had to form a coalition government with the MRF, headed by Prime Minister Filip Dimitrov, who was installed in November 1991. The new government gave qualified support for Zheliu Zhelev in the indirect presidential ballot in January 1992. The president was pressured to accept running mate Blaga Dimitrova, from the UDF-Movement, in return for the party's endorsement. Zhelev received only 45% of the votes in the first round of balloting and 53% in the second round against the BSP candidate Velko Vulkanov. However, there was incessant hostility between the UDF administration and President Zhelev, who represented a more moderate policy line. Both the government and parliament criticized Zhelev for appointing ex-communists to the presidential office, and they tried to further undercut presidential powers.

One of the top priorities of the UDF-MRF administration was decommunization in all public institutions and the elimination of subversive activities by secret service officers who were trying to obstruct market reform. This task proved difficult because of the entrenched interest groups that pervaded most state bodies and enterprises. The National Assembly passed a law to confiscate communist property, and the prosecution of former officials was intensified: about fifty prominent figures were indicted, including Zhivkov. However, the decommunization campaign was depicted by members of the old *nomenklatura* as a "witch-hunt" that undermined economic progress and failed to assist ordinary citizens. The UDF leadership asserted that without the ouster of communist officialdom and the elimination of special interests that were parasitical on the Bulgarian economy, the market reform program could not be successful.

By the summer of 1992, the Dimitrov government faced internal splits over such issues as the return of the monarchy, the leadership of the Bulgarian Orthodox Church, and the pace of economic reform. The MRF was particularly disturbed that declining economic conditions seriously affected the Turkish rural population, as the land reforms favored former Bulgarian owners, and the state was slow to redistribute property from the state land fund to minorities. MRF leader Ahmed Dogan called for a change of policy, and absent such change, in October 1992, the MRF parliamentary delegation joined with the BSP in a vote of no confidence in the government. This motion was supported by Zhelev, who accused Dimitrov of undermining the presidency and alienating the population.

Between 1989 and 1997, Bulgaria had eight governments. Prime Minister Dimitrov resigned on 28 October 1992, after the no-confidence vote. His administration was replaced by an "expert" government headed by the Socialist Lyuben Berov, which survived until 2 September 1994. It came under mounting criticism for rampant corruption and ties to often clandestine business interests. It was replaced by a caretaker administration under Reneta Indzhova on 17 October 1994, pending early general elections. The Socialist administration was accused of maintaining secret connections with business conglomerates that were siphoning off state funds for the benefit of the old communist apparatus. Failure to follow through on reform measures led to a rapid downturn in the economy and seriously affected living standards. The Berov cabinet was transient, as no majority coalition government could be formed. Policy differences between reformists and conservatives became insurmountable, and UDF deputies frequently called for votes of no confidence.

The BSP was returned to power in the elections of 18 December 1994, winning 43.5% of the popular vote and 125 parliamentary seats. Only five parties were able to cross the 4% threshold to gain parliamentary seats. BSP leader Zhan Videnov was selected as prime minister.[3] Two allied parties, the Bulgarian Agrarian People's Union "Aleksandar Stamboliyski" and the Political Club *Ecoglasnost*, which were on the same list as the BSP in the elections, joined the government coalition. The popular swing toward the BSP was confirmed during local elections in October 1994, when Socialist candidates received 41% of the votes and the UDF only 25%.

The UDF further losses in the December 1994 elections, gaining only 24% of the vote and 69 seats. It was largely blamed for the economic downturn and for internal squabbling that disabled a coherent and determined policy line. Following their defeat, the UDF leadership resigned en masse. Ivan Kostov was elected to replace Filip Dimitrov as the Union leader. He moved to better coordinate the UDF, to undercut the independence of its constituent parties and factions, and to improve relations with the MRF and the Popular Union. The slow progress of the BSP during 1995 and 1996 in implementing reforms, and its mishandling of the economy, led to a host of financial, social, and economic problems that reached crisis proportions by the mid-1990s. Meanwhile, the UDF gradually began to regain its popular support by promoting a pro-reform and pro-Western agenda.

The year 1996 proved to be a watershed in Bulgaria. The country experienced serious economic difficulties caused by the absence of systematic market reforms, and by widespread corruption and outright theft by government officials. With social dissatisfaction growing, the Socialist Party lost the presidential elections in October–November 1996, and pressures increased for an early parliamentary ballot that could dislodge the former communists from power. The BSP and its coalition partners maintained a secure parliamentary majority despite growing pressures from the major opposition bloc, the UDF. The political scene was polarized between these two formations, and their ideological differences were evident in all major issues affecting Bulgarian society. The Socialists were determined to maintain the economic status quo, and stalled the mass privatization program, leading to serious economic decline. Moreover, the government was opposed to membership of the North Atlantic Treaty Organization (NATO), and pursued closer relations with Russia despite criticisms from the opposition.

Rifts also were evident within the Socialist Party, between the harder-line members linked to Prime Minister Zhan Videnov and reformist elements critical of government policy. These divisions widened after the assassination of former premier Andrei Lukanov at the beginning of October 1996. Lukanov had become an outspoken critic of official resistance to reform. Allegedly, he also possessed information on corruption at the highest levels of government that he reportedly planned to make public.[4] Observers contended that Lukanov himself was deeply involved in corruption and that his killing resembled a gangland assassination. The presidential elections further undermined the Socialist administration. The UDF candidate Petar Stoyanov gained an overwhelming percentage of votes (44%) over the Socialist Ivan Marazov (27%) in the first round of voting, on 27 October 1996. Stoyanov was elected president in the second round, on 3 November 1996, gaining nearly 60% of the vote to Marazov's 40%.[6] Although the post of president was primarily ceremonial, this result emboldened the opposition to push for a no-confidence vote in the Socialist government.

During 1996 Bulgaria faced a major financial crisis. Its hard currency reserves plummeted, and there were growing doubts that Sofia could meet its critical foreign debt payments. The government continued to prop up obsolete and uncompetitive state-owned industries. Moreover, the former communist *nomenklatura* controlled and exploited much of the economy through shady "economic groups," where corruption was rampant. An ambitious mass privatization program remained stalled in parliament because of powerful vested interests. As the financial crisis deepened and the currency collapsed, prices soared dramatically. Bread shortages were reported in various parts of the country, and observers expected food and fuel shortages during the winter months.

Following several months of popular demonstrations, the increasingly isolated Socialist government of Prime Minister Videnov resigned in December 1996, and the newly inaugurated President Stoyanov called for early parliamentary elections. Large sectors of the public were angry at rapidly declining living standards amidst reports of widespread corruption among government officials. The 17 April 1997 ballot was won overwhelmingly by the UDF coalition. It gained 52% of the vote and 137 out of 240 parliamentary seats; the BSP only obtained 22% of the vote and 58 seats. Ivan Kostov, the UDF leader, was appointed prime minister. The composition of his cabinet reflected Bulgaria's commitment to intensive economic and political reforms. The new administration benefited from broad public support, even though the impact of the economic reforms would be painfully felt by workers in state industries.

The key priorities of the UDF-led coalition government were economic stabilization, crime control, and Euro-Atlantic integration. The UDF-dominated legislature passed a number of important measures to root out the corruption that had become endemic among state officials and industrial managers. A new law passed in September 1997 prohibited members of the former communist apparatus from obtaining high positions in the civil service for a period of five years. Parliament also approved the opening up of secret police files to determine which top officials had collaborated with the communist-era security services. This move indicated that the authorities favored openness and transparency in government operations. Investigations against large-scale corruption were launched, as some former Socialist officials were believed to have embezzled millions of dollars from state funds.

The authorities were determined to pursue a radical economic reform program in order to avert a major financial crisis. In consultation with the World Bank, Sofia launched a far-reaching "stabilization program" that lifted most price controls, pegged the national currency to the German mark, and established a currency board to control government spending. As a result, the inflation rate dramatically decreased. Parliament also approved a new budget that cut state spending and subsidization of unprofitable industries. An extensive privatization program was launched, affecting the majority of state-owned enterprises. The possibility of social unrest remained present, should living standards sharply decline as a result of the government's austerity measures and budgetary discipline.

The new government was also determined to pursue Bulgaria's integration into various Euro-Atlantic institutions. In particular, President Stoyanov declared that Bulgaria was seeking membership in NATO and was willing to undertake the necessary reforms of its military structure. The outgoing Socialist administration had been ambiguous about Alliance membership. The new pro-NATO policy dismayed Bulgaria's traditional ally Russia, and relations between Sofia and Moscow grew tense. Bulgaria's interior minister accused Moscow of racketeering through its manipulation of gas prices and control over Bulgarian energy supplies.

At the end of the 1990s, Bulgaria made steady progress in stabilizing its economy. The parliamentary majority held by the UDF ensured that the reform program was not seriously challenged by the Socialist opposition. Stoyanov retained his high popularity despite the application of a painful austerity program. However, the local elections in October 1999 proved a setback to the UDF, which only narrowly defeated the Socialists in a majority of municipalities. Growing public frustration with layoffs and state spending cuts was evident in a low voter turnout of some 50%. However, the UDF retained control of the two major cities, Sofia and Plovdiv.

Despite the progress achieved by the UDF in securing macro-economic stability and fulfilling the criteria for international loans, the living standards of the majority of citizens stagnated or fell. The Bulgarian political scene changed dramatically in April 2001, with the return to the country of the exiled king, Simeon II. The king formed his own political party, styled as the National Movement Simeon II (NMS) *(Nacionalno Dvizhenie Simeon II, NDS)*, a center-right grouping which proceeded to draw support away from both the UDF and the opposition Socialists. In the parliamentary elections on 17 June 2001, the NMS scored a landslide victory, gaining 42.73% of the vote and 120 seats in the 240-seat legislature. The UDF finished a distant second, with 18.18% and 51 seats. Two other parties passed the electoral threshold: the Socialist Party captured 17.15% of the vote and 48 seats, and the Turkish Movement for Rights and Freedoms (MRF) garnered 7.45% and 21 seats.

Simeon II became the first monarch to return to power in post-communist Eastern Europe. His party won the protest vote of impoverished elements of the Bulgarian population, and his selection of young Western-educated professionals as potential parliamentarians and ministers also increased public support. The king himself did not run in the elections and seemed unlikely to thrust himself forward as prime minister. He also denied that there were any plans to restore the monarchy, and pointed out that the country had far more pressing issues to contend with, such as unemployment, poverty, and corruption. Critics charged that the NMS message was too populist and insufficiently specific on economic policies. NMS leaders countered that they would continue with the reform program launched by the UDF but would pay more attention to combating corruption, attracting foreign investment, and creating new employment opportunities. Moreover, Simeon underscored that his government would remain committed to Euro-Atlantic integration.

Bulgaria's essentially two-party model was mooted by the NMS triumph. However, the victors indicated that they were intent on creating a coalition government to achieve broader political consensus and ensure effective government during a difficult reform process. The Bulgarian public seemingly rejected the continued polarization of public life by voting for a movement that pledged to unify the nation. The MRF was the first party to offer its cooperation, indicating a valuable opportunity for involving the sizeable Turkish population in the governing process.

The government remained focused on privatizing the major state-owned enterprises, and proved successful in stabilizing the banking sector. Bulgaria made substantial progress in developing its relations with its Balkan neighbors. The most significant development was the breakthrough in relations with Macedonia, symbolized by the signing in February 1999 of a declaration settling the language dispute and stating that the two countries harbored no territorial claims. Several other deals were signed, including agreements on trade and investment. The two countries also negotiated the creation of a free trade area.

Bulgaria's relations with Serbia deteriorated. NATO's war with Serbia was a landmark event for Bulgaria. Sofia became outspoken about the culpability of Milošević for Balkan instability and supported NATO in its efforts in Kosova despite some opposition inside the country. Bulgaria suffered from a loss of trade as a result of the war, primarily through the blockage of traffic on the Danube River inside Serbia. Sofia continued to develop good relations with both Greece and Turkey, seeking to balance its ties with the two Balkan rivals. The government was also active in developing regional initiatives to enhance security and cooperation across Balkan borders. In July 1999, finance ministers from Bulgaria, Macedonia, and Albania negotiated a common approach to infrastructural projects in southeastern Europe. At a trilateral meeting of the Bulgarian, Albanian, and Macedonian foreign ministers, Bulgaria proposed that it become the host for an information Center for Democracy, which would work towards the establishment of civil society.

With regard to minority issues, after Zhivkov's ouster Bulgarian officials made strenuous efforts to improve the country's minority policies and to repair the damage suffered by ethnic Turks. In December 1989, the BSP renounced forcible assimilation, allowing Muslims the freedom to choose their own names, practice Islam, observe traditional customs, and speak their native language. In January 1990, the National Assembly recommended the adoption of a special statute for minority rights. With Sofia's policy reversal, thousands of ethnic Turks returned to Bulgaria—and faced new problems of adjustment. Most had lost their jobs and sold their houses for less than their true value and now demanded appropriate reparations. Ahmed Doğan, the political leader of Bulgaria's Turks, demanded a legal resolution that would restore property to victims of the exodus. Turkish deputies in parliament eventually introduced a law that was adopted by parliament in July 1992. It stipulated that all Turks be permitted to buy back their properties by April 1993 for the same prices at which they were originally sold. Those who proved unable to buy back their former homes would be given a loan at a low interest rate toward the purchase of alternative housing.[6]

The issue of minority rights, particularly language use, education, and access to the mass media, continued to generate controversy. According to the 1991 constitution, Bulgarian was to be the sole official language. Under the Zhivkov regime, ethnic Turks were forbidden to officially use their mother tongue. The legacy of language discrimination persisted and was evident in a variety of forms; for example, parliament hesitated in implementing Turkish language programs in secondary schools, for fear of ultra-nationalist reactions.[7] In January 1991, a consultative council, which included the Bulgarian prime minister, decided that the teaching of Turkish as part of the secondary school curriculum was constitutional. The Bulgarian parliament promised to implement a state-controlled Turkish program in all public schools where there was significant minority enrollment. Bulgaria's nationalist opposition claimed that these programs were unconstitutional, but parliament issued assurances that the programs would not jeopardize the "unity of the Bulgarian nation."[8]

During Zhivkov's assimilation campaign, Turkish names had been subjected to a process of "Bulgarization." Typically, a Slavic suffix was added to a Muslim name, or an entirely new name was chosen from a list of acceptable Bulgarian names. In March 1990, the country's major political forces agreed to pass a Bulgarian citizens' names law that made the restoration of names possible for all victims of forcible assimilation. New birth certificates were issued, and the process of changing names was simplified from a judiciary process to a straightforward administrative measure. Nevertheless, Muslims who did not act before 31 December 1990 had to endure a more complicated procedure accompanied by the payment of an appropriate fee.[9]

The new Bulgarian constitution prohibited the creation of political parties based on "ethnic, racial, or religious lines" and organizations "which seek the violent usurpation of power." While these stipulations were intended to protect the Bulgarian state, they were frequently cited by nationalists in efforts to undermine the rights of minorities. Nationalist organizations capitalized on Bulgarian fears of Turkish subversion and applied pressure on government organs to outlaw ethnicity-based associations on the grounds that they were politically motivated and therefore "anti-state."

The main Turkish organization, the Movement for Rights and Freedoms (MRF), was singled out for attention. In August 1991, the Sofia city court decided that a political party formed by the MRF was unconstitutional due to its ethnic basis, and could not participate in elections. The MRF claimed that it was not founded on an entirely ethnic basis and that it harbored no separatist ambitions. In September 1991, the Supreme Court banned the Rights and Freedoms Party (the political wing of the MRF) from participation in general elections on the grounds that it propounded an exclusivist ethnic and religious platform.[10] Nonetheless, the MRF itself and various Turkish cultural and social organizations were not prohibited from functioning and the MRF legally competed in the second general elections in October 1991. It gained 24 parliamentary seats, with 7.55% of the popular vote, making it the third strongest party in Bulgaria and a coalition partner for the UDF.

During the summer of 1989, at the height of the Turkish exodus from Bulgaria to Turkey, the bulk of the Pomak (Slavic Muslim) population opposed efforts at forcible integration and some sought to emigrate. The authorities proved reluctant to allow them to leave the country and denied passports to persons residing in predominantly Pomak regions. These policies resulted in several substantial Pomak protests. Pomak regions continued to suffer from steep economic decline with the closure of local industries; observers feared that material hardships would intensify political tensions. Bulgarian officials warned that unemployment and economic deprivation in regions with ethnically and religiously mixed groups was alarmingly high and that minorities were increasingly complaining about discrimination in employment. After 1989, many Pomaks adopted a Turkish identity or demanded Turkish-language education, viewing it as advantageous to associate with a stronger and more influential minority.

In some respects, Macedonian groups have borne even more onerous treatment than both Turks and Pomaks. The Bulgarian government, together with a broad spectrum of Bulgarian political parties, refused to accept Macedonians as a legitimate minority, defining them as Slavic Bulgarians with the same language and a common history. According to Bulgarian leaders, a Macedonian minority did not exist in the Pirin region despite the activities of local radicals. An openly Macedonian organization styled as *Ilinden*, was established in the Pirin area and it applied for official registration. In July 1990, the Blagoevgrad district court denied it the right to legal recognition.

Protests by *Ilinden* supporters were suppressed, and Bulgaria's Supreme Court ruled that *Ilinden* violated the unity of the Bulgarian nation. *Ilinden*'s statutes, which promoted the recognition of a sovereign Macedonian minority, evidently served as evidence that the organization intended to achieve "a united Macedonian state." *Ilinden* was ordered to disband, but it persisted in a covert fashion, claiming that the decisions of the Bulgarian courts were in violation of international law.[11] In November 1998, the local court in Blagoevgrad finally allowed the registration of a Macedonian organization, OMO *Ilinden*-Pirin, with headquarters in Blagoevgrad.[12]

The Macedonian question also left an imprint on Bulgarian foreign policy, especially after the collapse of the Yugoslav federation. Bulgaria was one of the few countries to immediately recognize Macedonia when the republic declared its independence in early 1992. However, the Bulgarian authorities did not recognize the existence of a separate Macedonian nation and refused to countenance the recognition of a Macedonian ethnic minority within Bulgaria. Nationalist pro-Macedonian groupings became more active in Bulgaria, calling for closer social, economic, and political links with the republic—links that they hoped would culminate in re-absorption by Bulgaria. At the same time, some autonomist Macedonian organizations became active in western Bulgaria, amid suspicions that they were funded by Belgrade and by militant groups in the Macedonian Republic to sow discord within Bulgaria and press for the separation of the Pirin region from the Bulgarian state.

Bulgaria and Macedonia ended a period of political deadlock with the signing of a joint declaration and a number of accords on 22 February 1999. Bulgarian Prime Minister Ivan Kostov and his Macedonian counterpart Ljubčo Georgievski sealed an agreement to settle the language dispute and to open the way to normalize relations. The joint declaration, signed in both Bulgarian and Macedonian, stipulated that the two countries would not undertake, incite, or support unfriendly activities against each other, including territorial claims or pressures for ensuring minority rights. Seven other bilateral agreements were signed to promote cooperation, trade, and investment.

Unlike the Turks, whose leaders perceived the gravest threat coming from forcible assimilation, Romany spokesmen have been particularly concerned about the segregation and marginalization of the Gypsy population. Many have opposed separate schooling for Roma children, asserting that it results in inferior education and insufficient exposure to the Bulgarian language, and stymied career advancement. Other Roma leaders have supported a revival of Gypsy culture, education, and ethnic identity, fearing gradual assimilation by either the Bulgarian or the Turkish community. In addition, the law on political parties, adopted by parliament in April 1990, that prohibited the registration of organizations established on ethnic or religious criteria, worked to the detriment of Gypsy self-organization. Even though the Roma clearly did not represent a threat to Bulgaria's "territorial integrity" and the "unity of the nation," or "incite national, ethnic, and religious hostilities," they were barred from forming electoral associations.[13]

Although Bulgaria seemed to address its most pervasive ethnic problems at an official level during the 1990s, there remained much room for improvement. Bulgarian officials claimed that the country's policies were guided by the Human Rights Charter and the Bulgarian constitution. International human rights organizations, however, urged the Bulgarian government to develop more coherent legislation that balanced concerns over national security and state integrity with full respect for minority rights and ethnic aspirations.

POLITICAL PARTIES

Socialists and Social Democrats

Bulgarian Socialist Party (BSP)
Bulgarska Sotsialisticheska Partiya (BSP)

The Bulgarian Socialist Party (BSP) was the successor party of the Bulgarian Communist Party (BCP), which ruled the country between 1944 and 1989.

The BCP was founded in 1891 as the Bulgarian Social Democratic Party. The party split several times before a pro-Soviet, revolutionary wing took power on 9 September 1944 in a Red Army–backed coup. On 10 November 1989, the leader of the BCP and Chairman of the State Council, Todor Zhivkov, resigned from his posts. With the acceleration of the democratization process, the BCP's only chance to save itself politically was a transformation of its image and policies. In early February 1990, the party held its 14th extraordinary congress, at which a Manifesto on Democratic Socialism was adopted. In April 1990, the BCP renamed itself the Bulgarian Socialist Party (BSP). In September 1990, the party held its 39th congress, which "confirmed the course toward reforms and transforming the BSP into a modern leftist party of democratic socialism."

Alexander Lilov, a Politburo member who had been ousted by Zhivkov, assumed the post of chairman of the BSP's new governing body, the Supreme Party Council, on 1 April 1990. After losing the general elections in October 1991, the BSP leadership resigned under pressure from the party's congress. A new generation of BSP activists, eager to renovate the party, obtained a majority at the party's 41st congress and elected a new leadership from their ranks. On 17 December 1991, Zhan Videnov was elected Chairman of the Supreme Party Council–the party's policy-making body.[14] It contained 50 members elected by congress delegates. Videnov was reelected with an overwhelming majority of party delegates on 6 June 1994.

Although its socialist doctrine theoretically discouraged nationalism, the BSP tended to condone it. Like the more outspoken nationalist groups, the BSP evidently felt threatened by Turkish participation in the Bulgarian National Assembly. BSP leaders asserted that ethnic political parties stood in violation of the Bulgarian constitution and formed a barrier in the transition to democracy. Elements of the BSP, particularly at the local level, were accused of helping to establish ultra-nationalist parties in order to tap potential anti-minority sentiments, to undercut the position of democratic forces, and to maintain *nomenklatura* privileges. The BSP was also accused of creating a special task force that deliberately staged acts of violence against Slavic Bulgarians and then blamed them on ethnic Turks. BSP officials allegedly calculated that such simulated attacks would undermine the popularity of the Movement for Rights and Freedoms (MRF) prior to the elections. The Bulgarian newspaper *Demokratsiya* called this scheme a "mass psychosis" campaign and alleged that the BSP's prime motive was to procure an extra 5% to 10% of the popular vote in the fall 1991 parliamentary elections.

The Socialists stood in an electoral alliance with five nationalist groups for the October 1991 national ballot and obtained 106 seats in the 240-seat National Assembly, capturing 33.14% of the popular vote. The BSP had lost nearly 14% of its electoral support since the June 1990 ballot. After the elections, the BSP focused most of its attention on socio-economic issues and criticized the fast pace of market reform. It was not averse to capitalizing on nationalist and anti-Turkish sentiments when it sensed that it stood to benefit politically.[15]

The BSP formed a pre-election alliance with seven small parties, each of which had very limited support. The apparent intention of the BSP leadership was to convince its constituents that the party had decisively broken with its intolerant and authoritarian past. The participating parties in the pre-election alliance were the Bulgarian Liberal Party (BLP), the People's Liberal Party (PLP), the Fatherland Party of Labor (FPL), the Socialist Youth Union (SYU), the Federation of Bulgarian Socialist Youth (FBSY), the Christian Republican Party (CRP), and the Christian Women's Movement (CWM).

Former BSP leader Lilov remained prominent in the party as director of the Center for Strategic Analysis. This institution played an important role in devising the party platform for the 1994 elections. The Center supported the idea of a European security system based on NATO, but rejected the necessity of Bulgarian accession to NATO, due to the conviction that Bulgarian security was not seriously threatened. In the economic realm, Lilov called for a slow transition to a free market economy and was not adverse to the idea of implementing the Chinese model of socialism in Bulgaria.[16]

According to the BSP statute, "ideological movements" could exist within the party. The main factions that developed included the Alliance for Social Democracy (ASD) chaired by Chavdar Kyuranov, the Alternative Socialist Alliance (ASA), Marxist Alternative, and the Road to Europe. In addition to the formal divisions, informal groups struggled for control over the party. Although these groups harbored ideological differences they were based primarily on a personal competition for leadership. The ASD conflict with Videnov dated back to the summer of 1994, when Georgi Pirinski and other prominent ASD members withdrew from the Supreme Party Council.

In the December 1994 parliamentary elections and the fall 1995 local elections, the BSP participated in a coalition with the Bulgarian Agrarian National Union (BANU) "Aleksandar Stamboliyski" and the Political Club *Ecoglasnost*.[17] The party also signed a pre-election agreement with the nationalist Patriotic Alliance that included the BSP's former coalition partner, the FPL. In the parliamentary elections on 18 December 1994, the BSP participated in the Democratic Left (DL) coalition as the Political Coalition BSP, together with BANU "Aleksandar Stamboliyski" and the Political Club *Ecoglasnost*. The DL was founded in November 1994 with the signing of a political agreement by the chairmen of the three formations. The coalition won the 1994 general elections and the October–November 1995 local elections. In the presidential elections of October–November 1996, the DL was the backbone of the coalition Together for Bulgaria, whose candidate was Ivan Marazov. For the April 1997 parliamentary elections, the chairman of BANU, Svetoslav Shivarov, rejected a renewal of the coalition, and only two parties remained in the DL.

When the BSP assumed power after the 1994 parliamentary elections, tensions within the party intensified. Videnov was accused of having an authoritarian leadership style. After his reelection as party leader in 1994, he told a

Duma reporter that he could be considered extreme in seeking a "unity of ideas, words, and deeds."[18] Videnov came under pressure from two groupings in the party—the neo-communists and the social democrats.[19] He managed to consolidate his position within the party and regained some influence. There were persistent tensions within the ruling BSP coalition, due to the independent posture of some minor parties. Even though BANU and *Ecoglasnost* only had eight deputies, both of them received a seat in the Council of Ministers. Their leverage stemmed from the fact that without their votes the BSP would lose its absolute majority in parliament.[20]

The BSP declared its core values to be peace among nations; internal ethnic and social stability; protection of the environment; freedom of the individual; justice and democracy; housing for all; and the advancement of national traditions. Respect for private property was not mentioned.[21] In its economic prescriptions the BSP sought to boost industrial production; implement an economically effective and socially just structural reform of the economy; stop the decline of the population's real income; create new jobs; provide free health care; protect the real incomes of agricultural producers through governmental control over prices; and discourage "disloyal," external competition.

In terms of internal security, the BSP pledged to fight organized crime; to combat corruption though a reduction in the state bureaucracy; to promote strong local government, and to provide financial support for underdeveloped regions. In its foreign policy program, the BSP sought to speed up the process of Bulgaria's integration into European structures. Other important goals included keeping Bulgaria out of the Yugoslav conflict; strengthening bilateral relations with other Balkan states; achieving "spiritual unity" between all Bulgarians around the world; pursuing an independent foreign policy; placing Bulgaria on an equal posture in relations with powers like Russia and the U.S.; and maintaining "active neutrality"—that is, refraining from joining any existing security structures.[22]

With regard to minority issues, the BSP vehemently opposed the creation of ethnic parties, and perceived their existence as threatening national security. It wanted to develop economic programs to support the underdeveloped regions, where a big percentage of the population were Roma, but it rejected the idea of disbursing aid on an ethnic foundation.[23] BSP decisively opposed the "national minority" concept and instead proposed the use of the concept of "ethnic group" or "ethnic community." The party believed that although a certain portion of the population was Muslim by religious choice and tradition, the entire nation was Bulgarian by origin. The BSP rejected claims that a Macedonian minority existed within the Pirin region. But because Macedonia was Bulgaria's closest ally in the Balkans, the BSP felt that Sofia should support its consolidation as an independent state.

In 1994, the BSP claimed to have over 400,000 members organized in 10,000 local organizations. Even though statistics from 1995 showed that party membership had decreased to approximately 350,000, it still remained the largest party in the country. Indications that the BSP might split after decades of unity came when four members of the Alliance for Social Democracy (ASD), Dimitur Yonchev, Andrey Raychev, Andrey Bundzhulov, and Rose Karadimov, publicly threw their party membership cards away. On 18 January 1997, the ASD, the Civic Alliance for the Republic (SAR), the Alternative Socialist Association (ASA), and a group that split from the Bulgarian Social Democratic Party, formed the BSP-2, a new leftist party without Georgi Purvanov, who was elected BSP leader. Preparations for forming a BSP-2 were first mentioned in mid-1996, when it became clear that Videnov not only controlled the BSP apparatus but that his policies had become the trademark of a party incapable of rising above the political stature of its leader.

The focus of interest in the BSP was on two formations—the Movement for Unity and Development of the BSP (MUD) and the Open Forum. These groups gathered together activists with connections to business and to centers of power within the party. MUD leaders represented themselves as people who possessed the skills and experience to govern. Members of the Open Forum also took pride in the past, but not the communist period, and declared that they knew how to lead the BSP toward a resurgence. The two groupings were united not so much by ideas as by common interests. On 21 January 1997, BSP leader Purvanov was elected chairman of the Democratic Left parliamentary group, replacing Krasimir Premyanov, who resigned from the post.

About 126 leftist representatives met near Veliko Tŭrnovo on 18 July 1998. Among the organizations represented were the Euro-Left, the BSP, *Ecoglasnost*, the United Labor Bloc, the Bulgarian Social Democratic Party, the Bulgarian Socialist Youth, the European Left Youth Alternative, and the Confederation of Independent Trade Unions. The participants discussed the tasks of Bulgaria's leftist forces under the motto: "New Left—Social Democracy 2001." The main points of discussion included strengthening democracy and civil society, an independent judiciary, the supremacy of the law, elimination of corruption among leaders, and establishing democratic local governments. In the economic arena the leftists favored redistributing property "justly and transparently in the interest of all Bulgarians," as well as reducing taxes, encouraging small and medium-sized businesses, conducting an active policy on employment, ensuring certain minimum social guarantees, and guaranteeing health protection for all citizens.

Bulgarian Euro-Left (BEL)
Bulgarska Evrolevitsa (BEL)

The Bulgarian Euro-Left (BEL) was founded on 22 February 1997 in Sofia. It described itself as "a modern social democratic movement." Among its founding organizations were the Civil Union for the Republic, the Alternative Socialist Union, the Movement for Social Humanity, and four deputies who left the BSP in February 1997. For the April 1997 parliamentary elections, the Bulgarian Euro-Left was registered under the name Civil Union for the Republic–Bulgarian Euro-Left. After capturing 5.5% of the popular vote, BEL obtained a parliamentary group of 14 deputies, with two deputies from the Bulgarian Business Bloc (BBB) joining the organization in February 1998. At the end of February 1998, the Bulgarian Euro-Left held its first congress and transformed itself into a social democratic party. Aleksandar Tomov became its chairman.

The Alliance for National Salvation (ANS) and the Euro-Left agreed to hold regular consultations on principal policy issues, with a view to protecting democracy against alleged attempts to establish a one-party or personalistic regime. The main criticisms made by Euro-Left leaders were that the economy was being portioned out by means of licenses, control was being exercised over the media, freedom of speech was restricted, and the citizens' right to choose was being violated. According to some spokesmen, the government had no desire to conduct a dialogue with the opposition, and prime ministerial control was overwhelming.

Bulgarian Social Democratic Party (BSDP)
Bulgarska Sotsialdemokraticheska Partiya (BSDP)

Founded in 1891 as the Bulgarian Workers' Social Democratic Party, it participated in the government coalition before 1944 and in the Fatherland Front in 1944–45. The party was disbanded in 1944, and in 1947 some of its members joined the Bulgarian Communist Party. The Bulgarian Social Democratic Party (BSDP) was restored after 1989 and became one of the founders of the Union of Democratic Forces (UDF). As a member of UDF, the party was represented in the first post-communist National Assembly. During 1991, as a result of internal splits in the UDF, some party members founded the Social Democratic Party (SDP), which preserved its membership in UDF.

In the parliamentary elections of October 1991, BSDP participated in a coalition with the Political Club *Ecoglasnost*, under the name UDF-Center. In the elections of December 1994, the BSDP joined the Democratic Alternative for the Republic coalition. In the local elections of October–November 1995, the BSDP took part both independently and in different coalitions, most often with the UDF. In May 1995, the Movement for Social Humanism was created within the party, aimed at bringing it closer to the BSP. In the presidential elections in January 1992, the BSDP supported the nomination of Zheliu Zhelev, and in the presidential elections in October 1996 it favored Petar Stoyanov. BSDP also became a member of the Socialist International and was chaired by Petar Dertliev. In February 1997, the Movement participated in the founding congress of the Bulgarian Euro-Left, and in December

1995 the BSDP and the SDP founded the Social Democratic Alliance. In March 1997, the BSDP participated in the parliamentary elections in the UDF coalition, which won the national ballot.

Democratic Alternative for the Republic (DAR)
Demokratichna Alternativa za Republika (DAR)

The "political union" Democratic Alternative for the Republic (DAR) was founded in September 1994. It united four left-of-center parties: the Alternative Social Liberal Party (ASLP), the Bulgarian Social Democratic Party (BSDP), the Civic Alliance for the Republic (CAR), and the Green Party (GP). ASLP and CAR had been BSP factions, and BSDP and GP had been among the founding members of the Union of Democratic Forces (UDF). ASLP had also been a member of UDF until it was expelled from the Union for its support of the Berov cabinet in 1993. Before the fall 1995 local elections, the BSDP left the coalition. In February 1996, the GP was expelled from the coalition and a two-party alliance was formed between ASLP and CAR.

The leader of the coalition was originally appointed on a rotational basis among the leadership of the participating parties, but after August 1995 the chairman was elected. CAR leader Aleksander Tomov was the initial chairman of the coalition. According to Asen Michkovski, an ASLP deputy, the coalition's supporters were mainly state employees, intellectuals, new businessmen, and people disappointed by both the BSP and the UDF. He estimated that the coalition had between 300,000 and 350,000 sympathizers.[24] However, in the December 1994 parliamentary elections the coalition garnered only 3.79% of the votes and did not return any deputies to parliament.[25]

In the 1994 ballot, the coalition acquired the image of a populist formation without a firm and clear stand on any issue. Moreover, critics charged that it represented precisely what it claimed to fight against—political demagogy and populist rhetoric.[26] In the parliamentary elections of 18 December 1994, DAR could not pass the 4% limit for gaining seats. In the local elections of October–November 1995, DAR participated independently or in coalition with other political forces, although the BSDP temporarily left the coalition before the local elections. At the beginning of February 1996, the Green Party was also expelled from the coalition. The Civil Union for the Republic was the last to leave the coalition, after participating in the founding congress of Bulgarian Euro-Left.

In March 1997, DAR attracted four new members: the Alternative Social Liberal Party-Constitutional Forum, chaired by Nikolay Genchev; the Republican Party, chaired by Aleksander Popov; Will for Bulgaria, chaired by Yordan Velichkov; and the New Bulgaria Party, chaired by Boyan Chukov. The revived coalition under the DAR name participated in the April 1997 parliamentary elections. Its policy goals included acquittals for the victims of communist show trials after 1944; respect for the memory of the victims of fascism and Stalinism; fostering inter-ethnic tolerance by creating more jobs in multi-ethnic regions; adopting a National Unity Charter; declaring war on organized crime; strengthening the military; maintaining free health care, social security, and education; and protection of the environment.

DAR economic policy goals included replacing "shock therapy" with a policy that would purportedly guarantee economic growth, create new jobs, and foster financial stability. The leadership wanted to create a modern, ecologically conscious, social market economy; to implement "civilized economic nationalism"; to establish better incentives for foreign investors; to speed up the privatization process while providing support for employees of enterprises earmarked for privatization; ro reduce inflation; and to make agriculture a priority sector. Its foreign policy goals included strengthening relations with the U.S., restoring close ties with Russia, and fostering cooperation with all Balkan neighbors. DAR wanted to affirm Bulgaria's neutrality and to seek security guarantees from NATO and the Western European Union (WEU).

Liberals

Union of Democratic Forces (UDF)
Sayuz na Demokratichnite Sili (SDS)

The Union of Democratic Forces (UDF) was founded on 12 December 1989 by various dissident groups and recently restored, traditional parties.[27] The dissident groups that formed the backbone of the coalition included *Ecoglasnost*, the Club for Glasnost and Restructuring, the Independent Society for the Defense of Human Rights, and the Committee for the Defense of Religious Rights, Freedom of Conscience, and Moral Values. A major scandal beset the Union during 1990 when its first chairman Petar Beron was pressured to resign over allegations that he had been a police informant. He was replaced by Filip Dimitrov, the vice chairman of the Green Party.

Before the October 1991 elections, the UDF split when the largest coalition partners, the Social Democratic Party and the Agrarian Union, were denied a more prominent voice in the Union council or an increase in their number of candidates on the UDF electoral list. In addition, the Union was divided between advocates of a moderate line toward the Bulgarian Socialist Party (BSP) ("light blues") and a majority who demanded far-reaching decommunization ("dark blues"). The former wing withdrew from the Union and formed the UDF-Liberals; the latter faction became known as the UDF-Movement, which inherited much of the coalition's organizational network and media outlets.

In the October 1991 general elections, UDF-Movement narrowly won a plurality of votes and formed a coalition government with the Movement for Rights and Freedoms (MRF), headed by Prime Minister Filip Dimitrov, who was installed in November 1991. The new government gave qualified support to Zheliu Zhelev in the presidential ballot in January 1992. The President was pressured to accept running mate Blaga Dimitrova from the UDF-Movement in return for the party's endorsement. There was incessant hostility between the UDF administration and President Zhelev, who represented a more moderate policy line.

The top priority of the UDF-MRF administration was decommunization and the removal of communist officials who thwarted the reform process. The constant battles over this question contributed to the frustration of Bulgarians who did not understand the connection between economic stagnation and communist control and who remained preoccupied with declining material conditions. The UDF-dominated parliament passed a law to confiscate communist property, and it intensified the prosecution of former officials. By the summer of 1992, the Dimitrov government faced internal splits over such issues as the return of the monarchy, the leadership of the Bulgarian Orthodox Church, and the pace of economic reform. The administration also lost the support of its coalition partner, the MRF. The MRF parliamentary delegation joined with the BSP in a vote of no confidence in the government. This motion was supported by Zhelev, who accused Dimitrov of undermining the presidency and alienating the population. Dimitrov resigned on 28 October 1992, after the no-confidence vote.

After the signing of a new political agreement on 6 September 1994, the UDF consisted of the following political parties and movements: the Bulgarian Democratic Forum, led by Dianko Markov; the Agrarian Democratic Union, led by Vladislav Kostov, the Civic Initiative Movement, led by Zakhari Krustev, Loreta Nikolova, and Stanislav Ikonomov, the Conservative and Ecological Party, led by Svetlana Diankova, the National Club for Democracy, led by Svetoslav Luchnikov, the National Movement *Ecoglasnost,* led by Edvin Sugarev; the New Social Democratic Party, led by Vassil Mikhailov; the United Christian Democratic Center, led by Ekaterina Mikhailova; the Radical Democratic Party, led by Aleksander Iordanov, the Republican Party, led by Lenko Rusanov, the Social Democratic Party, led by Ivan Kurtev, the Union of the Persecuted after 1944, led by Ivan Stanchev, the Federation of Independent Student Associations, led by Plamen Panaiotov; the Christian Democratic Union, led by Assen Agov, and the Democratic Party 1896, led by Stoian Rajchevski.

The UDF suffered substantial losses in the general elections of 18 December 1994, gaining only 24% of the vote and 69 seats. Following their defeat, the UDF leadership resigned en masse. Ivan Kostov was elected to replace Dimitrov. He moved to better coordinate the Union, to undercut the independence of its constituent parties and factions, and to improve relations with the MRF and the Popular Union. The UDF gradually began to regain its popular support by promoting a reformist and pro-Western agenda and criticizing the BSP for its abject failure in government.

The coalition United Democratic Forces (UDF) *(Obedineni Demokratichni Sili, ODS)* was founded in June 1996 to nominate a candidate for Bulgaria's presidential elections. In the period between August 1996 and February 1997, members of the coalition included the Union of Democratic Forces (UDF), the People's Union, and MRF. The governing body was the Political Council, in which each party was represented by its chair. In February 1997, a new agreement between the UDF and the People's Union was signed. MRF refused to initial this and formed a new coalition—the National Salvation Union. Subsequently, other small parties and organizations joined the UDF, as did MRF activists led by Gyuner Tahir. The UDF, led by Kostov, won the April 1997 general elections with 52% of the vote and garnered 137 parliamentary seats. Kostov was selected as the new Prime Minister, and he kept the Union together throughout its term in government.

Bulgarian Liberal Party (BLP)
Bulgarska Liberalna Partiya (BLP)

By the end of the 1990s, there were 11 registered liberal parties in Bulgaria. However, only three of them were significant: the Bulgarian Liberal Party (BLP), the Alternative Social Liberal Party (ASLP), and the Liberal Congress Party (LCP). None of these groups were represented in the National Assembly. The LCP was visible largely due to the notoriety of its leader Yanko Yankov, who won a lawsuit in the Sofia district court that found the original registration of the Bulgarian Socialist Party to be unlawful; it had proclaimed itself a successor to the Bulgarian Communist Party, which was never legally registered.

The BLP claimed to be the successor to the first dissident group, the Club for Support of Glasnost and Democracy, formed in November 1988. The Club was among the founders of the Union of Democratic Forces (UDF) in December 1989. As many similar clubs had sprung up throughout the country by 1990, delegates at the national conference in January 1990 decided to create a Federation of Democracy Clubs. At another national conference in November 1991, the delegates decided to rename the federation as the Liberal Party. The party was officially registered with the court on 20 December 1992. Through all these transformations, the leader of the formation was Petko Simeonov.

After the schism in the UDF over the signing of the constitution during the summer of 1991, the Federation of Democracy Clubs left the coalition. In the 1991 elections, the Federation participated in the UDF-Liberal coalition with the Green Party. The coalition failed to pass the 4% barrier and did not return deputies to parliament. From the mid to late 1990s, the Liberal Party diminished. On 7 October 1994, the leadership made a desperate attempt to recover the party's position by taking part in another coalition, this time with the Fatherland Party of Labor, the *Volya* Movement, and the Fatherland Union. The newly formed nationalist alliance, the Patriotic Union, turned out to be even more unsuccessful than the UDF-Liberals coalition. In the 18 December 1994 elections it barely received 1% of the national vote.

The BLP platform in 1992 contained mostly vague generalizations about pragmatism, respect for democracy, and tolerance. What the party stood for could be inferred from its choice of coalition partners in the Patriotic Union coalition. The Fatherland Party of Labor was a nationalist party, and the Union for the Fatherland was the successor of the communist-controlled Fatherland Front. The BLP election platform published before the 1994 elections also pointed to its nationalist and populist character. Among the main principles enumerated in the document were private property, preferences for Bulgarian businesses, and a united Eastern Orthodox Church.[28] In the June 1990 elections, the party had obtained 17 seats as part of the UDF coalition; but in the December 1994 elections, the Patriotic Union received less than 2% of the vote.

Liberal Democratic Alternative (LDA)
Liberalno Demokratichna Alternativa (LDA)

The Liberal Democratic Alternative (LDA) was founded by 200 people, mainly intellectuals, on 30 November 1996. Its founding members included former President Zheliu Zhelev. Among the party's basic ideas was the creation of a presidential republic. The Liberal Democratic Alternative (LDA) was the driving force behind the founding of the coalition Liberal Forum (LF), which contained two more members—the Radical Democratic Party (RDP), (which was not in the UDF at the time), and its youth organization, the Federation of Radical Democratic Youth (FRDY). The LF was registered for the April 1997 parliamentary elections. The chair of the National Executive Council was Boris Galabov, and his deputies included Georgi Spasov and Momchil Doychev.[29] In the 1997 parliamentary elections, the Liberal Forum failed to win any seats, gaining less than 1% of the popular vote.

"New Choice" Union (NCU)
Sayuz Nov Izbor (SNI)

The "New Choice" Union (NCU) was founded in July 1994 as a coalition between the New Policy Center and the Alliance for Democracy. Both formations were splinter groups of the Union of Democratic Forces (UDF), formed by deputies who were expelled or voluntarily left the Union between 1992 and 1994, mainly as a result of their support for Berov's cabinet. The Center for New Policy was founded on 12 December 1993 by Dimiter Ludzhev, the first defense minister in Dimitrov's cabinet, who was forced to resign in June 1992. After premier Berov's resignation in September 1994, the attempt to form a new government was given to Ludzhev's New Policy Center. The Bulgarian Socialist Party refused to hold talks about a coalition cabinet, and Ludzhev did not seek rapprochement with his former UDF colleagues. In the end, he failed in his attempt to form a new administration. A caretaker government was appointed by the President, and elections were set for 18 December 1994. At the beginning of 1994, Ludzhev claimed that 10% of the electorate would vote for his New Policy Center, but no precise data on membership of the New Policy Center or the Alliance for Democracy were available.[30]

"New Choice" aimed at accomplishing several goals: effective and responsible management of state enterprises; establishment of a protectionist regime to encourage the development of Bulgarian industry; speedy privatization; increased foreign investment; preferential tax treatment of private business; lifting of price controls; and the creation of export incentives for the agricultural sector. In October 1996, the NCU was a co-founder of the Liberal Union. In March 1997, it joined the coalition National Salvation Union (NSU). The party was represented in the National Assembly by Ludzhev, who co-chaired the NCU with Ivan Anev.

Bulgarian Business Bloc (BBB)
Bulgarski Biznes Blok (BBB)

The Bulgarian Business Bloc (BBB) was founded on 10 January 1990 as a rightist formation, on the initiative of the Union of Entrepreneurs. At its second congress, the party split into two formations. One, led by George Ganchev, kept the name the Bulgarian Business Bloc. The other wing, chaired by Aleksander Cherpokov, adopted the name Bulgarian Business Party (BBP), later renamed the New Bulgaria Party (NBP). The latter subsequently disappeared from political life.

The leader of the BBB from its founding was Ganchev, an emigre who returned to Bulgaria in 1990. The relative success of the party in the December 1994 elections could be attributed almost solely to Ganchev's charisma. Few other BBB figures were known to Bulgarian voters. In the 1992 presidential elections, Ganchev formed a team with ex-UDF leader Petur Beron. They managed to capture 17% of the vote, and some observers dubbed Ganchev "Bulgaria's Ross Perot." Analysts claimed that Ganchev's success was due to voters who abhorred communism but were suspicious of anyone in power. Velko Vulkanov, the candidate endorsed by the Bulgarian Socialist Party (BSP) for President, insisted that had Ganchev not been in the race, Zhelev would have lost to Vulkanov because Ganchev drew votes from the leftist electorate.

Ganchev viewed his seat in parliament as a springboard to the presidency. However, his career as a parliamentarian was short-lived. In April 1995 he was forced to leave the National Assembly after his election was declared invalid by the Constitutional Court on the grounds that he had U.S. citizenship at the time of the ballot. After his expulsion, the BBB parliamentary group split. Six of the twelve deputies left the party on 28 June 1995 after a dispute with Ganchev over the appointment of the deputy chairman of the National Assembly. They became independent parliamentarians. In November 1995, three BBB deputies abandoned the BBB to found the New Democracy Party (NDP), claiming that the Bloc did not fulfill its pre-election program once it achieved representation in the legislature.[31] As a result, the initial group of 13 BBB deputies following the December 1994 elections split into three factions.

According to its statute, the BBB espoused liberal values: "economic democracy" and "technological progress." But the party platform for the 1994 election also included nationalist issues with a populist approach. The main goals of the BBB were identified in its pre-election program entitled "A Policy of National Dignity." In the economic sphere, the state should become a "shield" for Bulgarian business by creating conditions to protect national business from outside competition. The market, not the state, should be responsible for the distribution of resources; privatization should be swift, but "selling national capital to foreign countries, beyond certain limits to preserve sovereignty, should be precluded." It also supported the development of infrastructure in sparsely populated regions along the country's borders.

In September 1997, the BBB split again after two simultaneous congresses. After losing his parliamentary group and his control over the Bloc's business strategy, by November 1997 Ganchev had no party and was left an independent parliamentary deputy. In parliament, Petrushev and his lieutenant Yasho Minkov sought points of contact for forming a "liberal democratic alternative" with the Alliance for National Salvation (ANS) and the Movement for Rights and Freedoms (MRF). Having shed Ganchev, the BBB advertised its claim to be a centrist formation. According to the new BBB chairman, Khristo Ivanov, the party had to regain the lost confidence of voters, some of whom were learning toward the Euro-Left. In effect, the BBB lacked a coherent ideology and a clear program. Meanwhile, Ganchev's claims that he was the real opposition had little credibility.

National Salvation Union (NSU)
Obedinenie za Natsionalno Spasenie (ONS)

The National Salvation Union (NSU) coalition was founded in March 1997 by the Movement for Rights and Freedoms, the "New Choice" Union, the Bulgarian Agrarian National Union–"Nikola Petkov," the Green Party, the Federation "Bulgarian Kingdom," and the Democratic Center Party. The coalition described itself as a right-of-center liberal formation. In the 19 April 1997 parliamentary elections it won 19 seats and was chaired by Ahmed Dogan. Other small liberal formations included the Party of New Democracy (PND) (Partiya "Nova Demokratsiya," PND), founded in October 1995 by three MPs who left the parliamentary group of the BBB—Ivo Traykov, Nikolay Kisyov, and Orlin Draganov. The first PND congress was held in November 1996; in March 1997, the party became an observer member in the National Salvation Union coalition. The PND was chaired from the outset by Ivo Traykov; its deputies included Nikolay Kisyov and Orlin Draganov.

Christian Democrats

Popular Union (PU)
Naroden Sayuz (NS)

The Popular Union (PU) was founded on 12 October 1994 by Stefan Savov, leader of the Democratic Party (DP), and Anastasiya Mozer, leader of the Bulgarian Agrarian National Union (BANU).[32] In March 1995, the coalition was joined by the Democratic Center Party.[33] The DP was established in 1896 by three of the most prominent Bulgarian politicians of the twentieth century, Petko Karavelov, Petko Slavejkov, and Dragan Tzankov. This rightist formation ruled the country several times during the first half of the century. On 22 September 1908, its Prime Minister Aleksander Malinov proclaimed Bulgaria's independence from the Ottomans. The party was disbanded in 1947 by the communist government, but was revived in the early 1990s. The PU coalition obtained 18 seats in parliament following the elections of 18 December 1994, and captured 6.51% of the popular vote, but failed to amass any further public support. On 16 June 1995, PU leaders signed a cooperation memorandum with the Union of Democratic Forces (UDF).[34] The Union failed to gain any seats in the parliamentary elections of 19 April 1997. The PU cooperated with both the UDF and the MRF on key legislation.

Democratic Party (DP)
Demokraticheska Partiya (DP)

The Democratic Party (DP) was originally founded in 1896 and disbanded between 1934 and 1945 and from 1947 until 1989. From the beginning of 1990 until October 1994, the revived DP was a member of the Union of Democratic Forces (UDF) coalition. The Party was restored on 19 December 1989, and became one of the first members of the UDF. Stefan Savov was elected chairman of the DP's central bureau at the thirteenth party congress in December 1990. He was chairman of UDF's parliamentary group in the first post-communist legislature. By the early 1990s, the DP claimed about 25,000 members. It had little initial influence in the UDF coalition. Only 17 out of a total of 391 UDF candidates for the June 1990 general elections were nominated by the DP. Gradually, with Savov's popularity increasing due to his activeness and political skills, the party attracted new members.

By 1994, the DP had developed into the largest party in the UDF.[35] Its leadership grew frustrated with the UDF rules for distribution of decision-making power, according to which all parties in the coalition, regardless of their size, had equal representation in the National Coordinating Council (NCC). In addition, the DP blamed Filip Dimitrov and his associates for gambling away UDF's victory in the 1991 elections, and believed that he had to take full political responsibility for the fall of the government. The DP became a member of the European Democratic Union and of the European Christian Democratic Union.

By July 1994, cool relations between Savov and Dimitrov culminated in a head-on confrontation that Savov lost. On 26 July 1994, the NCC adopted a decision to freeze the DP's membership in the coalition. Humiliated and furious, the DP leadership decided to leave the coalition, and when time came on 6 September 1994 for a new political agreement to be signed by all member formations in the UDF, the DP refused. In order to assure that the party passed the 4% hurdle in the December 1994 elections, the DP leadership looked for possible coalition partners. An agreement for the creation of a DP-BANU coalition was signed on 12 October 1994. The party drew support mostly from intellectuals and middle-class voters. DP was a very active advocate of the restitution of property seized by the communist regime and therefore counted on the votes of those who benefited from the restitution process.

DP leaders claimed that the Christian democratic values that the DP and BANU shared were the glue of their coalition. Both parties were observers at the Christian Democratic International. The DP claimed it wanted to curtail the BSP's drive for "total domination," while building a socially oriented market economy, returning land to its pre-1944 owners, respecting private property, creating incentives for the rich to help the poor instead of expanding the welfare system, and building a democratic society in which the rights and interests of individuals stood above state interests.[36]

Democratic Center Party (DCP)
Demokratichna Partiya Tsenter (DPT)

The Democratic Center Party (DCP) succeeded the United Christian Democratic Center (UCDC), which was founded in 1990. It was established within the already existing Popular Union on 20 March 1995. The leader of the DCP at its founding was Ventseslav Dimitrov, a prominent economist and one of the initial key UDF figures.

By the end of the 1990s, eleven registered parties were contending for center-right votes. In addition to the DCP, they included the Bulgarian Christian Democratic Party–Center (BCDP-C), the Bulgarian Christian Democratic Union–Unity (BCDU-U), New People's Christian Democratic Party (NPCDP), the United Christian Democratic Center (UCDC), the Christian Agrarian Party (CAP), the Christian Democratic Union (CDU), the Christian Democratic Party (CDP), the Christian Radical Party (CRP), the Christian Radical Democratic Party (CRDP), and the Christian Republican Party (CRP).[37]

Agrarians

Bulgarian Agrarian National Union "Nikola Petkov" (BANU-NP)
Bulgarski Zemedelski Naroden Sayuz "Nikola Petkov" (BZNS-NP)

Through the first half of the twentieth century Bulgarian Agrarian National Union (BANU) was the political voice of agrarian workers, and since Bulgaria had a predominantly agricultural economy, the BANU possessed a broad electoral base. Nevertheless, it managed to rule the country only between 1919 and 1923 due to its notorious infighting, which over the years produced more than a dozen splinter groups. After the communist ascension to power in 1944, the BANU leadership split over the issue of whether the party should support the Bulgarian Communist Party (BCP). By 1947 all the leaders who had advocated opposition to the BCP had been executed, jailed, or forced to immigrate to the West. In December 1947, the union's leadership accepted the leading role of the BCP in political life and endorsed the Communists' program for building a Soviet-type socialist society.

Due to this political sellout, during the next forty years the BANU remained the only party besides the BCP to legally exist, participate in elections, and obtain seats in parliament. However, because of its perfunctory role in political life, it lost its connection to the electorate, and after 1989 it was in a situation similar to the BCP: it had to change or disappear from the political scene. The main BANU faction, which was disbanded and persecuted by the communist regime after the execution of BANU leader Nikola Petkov, was restored in December 1989. Soon afterward the agrarian movement recuperated its traditional dynamics as numerous BANU factions mushroomed. By 1994, there were five agrarian formations claiming the vote of rural constituents: two within the UDF, one in coalition with the BSP, and two independent ones.

After 1990, the official BANU had to change its image of passivity and compete for rural votes with a revived BANU "Nikola Petkov," whose leaders had political credibility because most of them had been imprisoned under the communist system. In the June 1990 elections, agrarian votes were split between the independent BANU and BANU "Nikola Petkov." In June 1991, BANU "Nikola Petkov" fractured the signing of the new constitution. Also in 1991, some BANU "Nikola Petkov" deputies signed an agreement with BANU and created BANU-United. The latter, however, proved to be an unstable alliance, and in November 1992 a new congress was held at which Anastasia Mozer won the leadership. She was the daughter of a famous agrarian leader of the 1940s, G.M. Dimitrov. Due to the multiple transformations of BANU, many splinter groups emerged that claimed to be the "true successors" of Alexander Stamboliyski, the preeminent pre-war agrarian leader. There were 11 Bulgarian Agrarian National Unions registered as political parties, but Mozer's BANU was by far the most influential agrarian party. According to Mozer, in 1994, BANU had 150,000 members.[38]

A Union congress in September 1996 led to a new split in the party. Part of the organization refused to take part in the congress and in December 1996 held an alternative meeting. This wing, chaired by Petko Iliev, preserved the name BANU. Mozer's wing had to register the party with a new name: the Bulgarian Agrarian National Union–People's Union. Both agrarian wings were in the UDF coalition, with Mozer's BANU joining in February 1997. BANU became a member of the European Christian Democratic Union. It was considered a strongly decentralized organization, in which significant authority was delegated to the governing council.

Bulgarian Agrarian National Union "Aleksandar Stamboliyski" (BANU-AS)
Bulgarski Zemedelski Naroden Sayuz "Aleksandar Stamboliyski" (BZNS-AS)

This Bulgarian Agrarian National Union (BANU-AS) was founded in November 1993 by agrarian leaders, who rejected the decisions of the restoration congress of the BANU in November 1992. The platform of the party encompassed the 25 ideas and principles defined by pre-war agrarian leader Aleksandar Stamboliyski. BANU-AS considered itself a party of the political center. It supported an open and socially oriented market economy, priority for the development of agriculture and the food industry, and socially just privatization. In November 1994, BANU-AS signed a political agreement with BSP and the Political Club *Ecoglasnost* for participation in general elections and for a common parliamentary group. Svetoslav Shivarov, chair of BANU-AS, refused to renew the Democratic Left coalition agreement for the 19 April 1997 parliamentary elections.

Greens

Political Club "Ecoglasnost" (PCE)
Politicheski Klub "Ekoglasnost" (PKE)

The Political Club *Ecoglasnost* (PCE) was founded in March 1990 as a political wing of the Independent Society *Ecoglasnost* created in April 1989. *Ecoglasnost* was one the founders of the Union of Democratic Forces (UDF) coalition on 7 December 1989. In the first post-communist legislature, *Ecoglasnost* had 17 deputies organized in a parliamentary group within the parliamentary UDF. In the summer of 1991, most of the *Ecoglasnost* deputies endorsed the new national constitution promulgated by the BSP and were expelled from UDF. As a result, two organizations emerged from *Ecoglasnost*: the National Movement *Ecoglasnost*, a member of UDF, and the Political Club *Ecoglasnost*. The Political Club *Ecoglasnost* advocated the protection of nature and the fundamental values of humanism. It participated consecutively in the coalitions UDF-Center (1991–1992) and Bulgarian Democratic Center (1992–1994). After November 1994, the PCE had a political agreement with BSP and BANU-AS for participation in the December 1994 elections; the agreement was renewed for the local and presidential elections. At the third national PCE conference in April 1995, Petar Slabakov was reelected chairman. Later he resigned, and the deputy chair Stefan Gaytandiiev replaced him. After March 1997, *Ecoglasnost* formed the Democratic Left coalition together with the BSP-PC. By April 1995, the PCE claimed to have 36 organizations and 750 members; but its support dwindled through the 1990s as new parties emerged and the ecological question lost much of its gravity for the public.[39]

Bulgarian Green Party (BGP)
Bulgarska Zelena Partiya (BZP)

The Bulgarian Green Party (BGP) was founded in December 1989. It was a member of the Union of Democratic Forces (UDF) coalition in 1990–1991. In the first post-communist National Assembly, the BGP had its own parliamentary group within the parliamentary UDF. In the 1991 parliamentary elections, the Green Party participated together with the Clubs for Democracy in the coalition UDF-Liberals. In the December 1994 parliamentary elections and in the local elections in October–November 1995, the Green Party participated in the coalition Democratic Alternative for the Republic (DAR), but, was it expelled the following year. In March 1997, the BGP joined the coalition National Salvation Union (NSU) and was represented in parliament by two deputies within the NSU. The chair of the BGP since its foundation has been Aleksandar Karakachanov.

Communists

Bulgarian Communist Party (BCP)
Bulgarska Komunisticheska Partiya (BKP)

Several parties claimed to represent the communist ideal, but among them the Bulgarian Communist Party (BCP), led by Vladimir Spasov, was the most significant. The BCP was founded in April 1990 with the initial name Party of Labor People. After an internal party referendum in the spring of 1990 the name of the ruling BCP was changed to the Bulgarian Socialist Party, and the Party of Labor People adopted the name of the Bulgarian Communist Party. The majority of its members were Marxist-oriented former BCP members. The party participated independently in the parliamentary elections in 1991 and 1994, in the local elections in 1995, and in the presidential elections in 1996.

On 1 May 1996 all communist formations met in Sofia in order to unite, but the BCP walked out, accusing the other participants of paying membership dues to the BSP.[40] The main goals of the communists were identified at a meeting in May 1996. They included preventing the restoration of the monarchy; preventing Bulgaria from joining NATO; hindering the process of privatization; and preparing for renationalization once communists returned to power. In the December 1994 parliamentary elections, the BCP came in a surprising sixth place with 1.5% of the vote, and in the April 1997 elections it garnered 1.2% of the vote. On neither occasion did it obtain any legislative seats. The BCP published the newspaper *Komunistichesko Delo*. Vladimir Spasov was reelected secretary-general at the party congress in 1996.

Nationalists

Bulgarian National Radical Party (BNRP)
Bulgarska Natsional Radikalna Partia (BNRP)

The Bulgarian National Radical Party (BNRP) traced its origins to the Bulgarian Nationalist Party, an underground formation founded in 1955 and forcefully disbanded in 1957. In 1962 the party re-registered as the Bulgarian National Revolutionary Party, but it was again disbanded in 1983. Finally, it was registered again, as the BNRP, on 18 April 1990. It scored a mere 0.06% of the vote in the June 1990 general elections. The leader of the party in all its permutations was Ivan Georgiev.[41] BNRP leaders claimed they were fighting for the freedom and independence of the Bulgarian nation. This evidently involved the unification of Bulgaria in its historical and ethnic boundaries; outlawing of ethnicity and religion-based parties; preventing the participation of individuals with different "ethnic self-awareness" in solving Bulgaria's national problems; the building of a modern army; the restoration of capital punishment for grave crimes; the creation of a society characterized by order and the rule of law; the establishment of a strong and incorruptible police; encouraging ethnic Bulgarian families to have more children; giving preference to ethnic Bulgarians in the social security system and job market; pursuing stable economic development, defense of national capital, and annulment of the foreign debt; and unconditional land restitution.

The BNRP also focused its attacks on the Turkish Movement for Rights and Freedoms (MRF). So disturbed was the BNRP at the National Assembly's acceptance of 23 victorious MRF representatives in June 1990, that it threatened to surround the parliament building on the day the new democratically elected legislature was scheduled to convene and force away any "individuals with a foreign national self-awareness." In a provocatively worded statement in June 1990, Georgiev protested the participation of ethnic Turks in the National Assembly.

The National Radicals protested against the teaching of Turkish as part of a standard curriculum in secondary schools with large numbers of Turkish students. They claimed joint responsibility with other nationalist groups for protests against the Turkish language issue in the city of Kardzhali. The BNRP appealed to Slav Bulgarian parents to keep their children at home until the language issue was resolved to their liking. Party leaders claimed a membership of approximately 38,000 and asserted that the BNRP became a member of the European Nationalist Union (ENU) in August 1991. It received moral and material support from the ENU, which struggled to "protect Christian values against the offensive of Islam in Europe." Georgiev also spoke out for Bulgarian unification with Macedonia on the basis of a public referendum.[42]

Fatherland Party of Labor (FPL)
Otechestvena Partiya na Truda (OPT)

The Fatherland Party of Labor (FPL) was established on 3 April 1990 as the political wing of the Committee for Defense of National Interests. The FPL's leader and representative in the National Assembly was Mincho Minchev. In the 1990 parliamentary elections, the FPL ran on an individual ballot only in single-member constituencies. It returned one deputy, Minchev, to the National Assembly from the Kardzhali district. Nationally, the party only obtained 0.6% of the vote. In March 1991, Minchev withdrew from parliament in protest of the Assembly's handling of the nationality issue. In the October 1991 parliamentary elections, the FPL participated in the Bulgarian Socialist Party (BSP)–led coalition and gained three deputies. In the December 1994 parliamentary elections, the FPL participated in the Patriotic Alliance, together with the Fatherland Union and the Liberal Party. This coalition received 1.43% of votes and did not obtain representation.

FPL leaders viewed the main national priorities as the unity and integrity of the nation, and the sovereignty, security, and indivisibility of Bulgaria. The party defined itself as left-of-center and nationalist, evidently distancing itself from chauvinism and linguistic, religious, or racial hatred. Nevertheless, it opposed the establishment of parties along ethnic lines. The claim that it was leftist stemmed from its economic policy, as it supported a socially oriented market economy. The party's membership was estimated between 4,900 and 5,600 people.[43]

Rumen Popov became the FPL's chairman, and Dimitar Arnaudov, a parliamentary representative, its deputy chairman. The party's membership was composed mostly of middle-income shop owners, artisans, farmers, and sectors of the local communist *nomenklatura*. FPL ideologists claimed that Bulgaria contained only one ethnic group and that the Turks were in reality forcibly converted Bulgarians who were now being misled by radicals promoting pan-Turkic objectives. In this scenario, Bulgaria stood on the front line against Muslim penetration into Europe.

In its own historiography, the FPL purportedly emerged due to pressure from ordinary Bulgarian citizens who were outraged when the Turkish Movement for Rights and Freedoms (MRF) was permitted to participate in the June 1990 parliamentary elections. Arnaudov argued that the party's complaints regarding MRF participation stemmed from a legal rather than an ethnic dispute, because the Bulgarian constitution explicitly prohibited political parties from organizing along ethnic, racial, or religious lines. The FPL leadership rejected a host of Turkish-oriented initiatives, and accused ethnic Turks of intentionally flooding the southeastern Bulgarian cities of Kardzhali, Haskovo, and Varna in order to register as residents and vote in strategic blocs to boost MRF support in local elections. According to FPL statistics, the massive influx of Turks into Kardzhali had forced fifteen Slav Bulgarian families per month to relocate away from Turkish-populated areas.

At the party's first congress in Sofia in April 1991, chairman Popov announced that the party was not ashamed to be anti-Turkish and anti-Islamic. Although the FPL and other ultra-nationalist groupings obtained less than 1.5% of the vote in the October 1991 elections, they claimed to possess an extensive infrastructure and to benefit from substantial local sympathy in mixed-population areas. During 1993, the FPL claimed to be building a left-of-center alliance in preparation for future elections; the coalition would evidently be open to all left wing and patriotic Bulgarian parties. FPL leaders persistently warned that Turkey was intent on annexing parts of Bulgaria and was using the MRF as a vehicle in this long-range endeavor. The party claimed that while the MRF leadership appeared to be moderate, it contained ultra-nationalist elements with a secret agenda to dismember Bulgarian territory.[44] The FPL was a member of the Patriotic Union coalition between 1994 and 1996.

Several other leftist-nationalist organizations emerged during the 1990s; many of them grouped in the People's Patriotic Leftist Front, which held its constituent meeting on 22 January 1997. The Front founders included the FPL; the Movement for Protection of Pensioners, Unemployed, and Socially Handicapped Citizens, chaired by Ivan Mitev; the Communist Party of Bulgaria, which united five communist parties and elected Aleksandur Paunov as its leader; the Bulgarian Unified Communist Party; the *Fakel* (Torch) Political Club; the "Baba Paraskeva" Club; the Bulgarian Communist Party–Bolsheviks; the International League of Women for Peace and Freedom; the Movement for National Democracy; the Central Club of the BSP (Bulgarian Socialist Party) Veterans; and the *Nasoka* (Direction) Movement.

Committee for Defense of National Interests (CDNI)
Komitet za Zashtita na Natsionalnite Interesi (KZNI)

The Committee for Defense of National Interests (CDNI) was the most influential Bulgarian nationalist group after the onset of democratization. It served as an umbrella organization for several nationalist political parties. In November 1990, it claimed some 40,000 members nationwide. Under the chairmanship of Dimitar Arnaudov, a member of parliament, the main goals of the Committee were to protect the "territorial integrity" and "ethnic space" of Bulgaria by including all patriotic Bulgarians, regardless of their political or religious orientation. To achieve this objective, the CDNI attacked the agendas of any organization that it felt threatened the integrity of the Bulgarian state.

Its principal target was the Movement for Rights and Freedoms (MRF), the largest organization representing ethnic Turkish interests. The Committee challenged the legitimacy and participation of the MRF in the political system, claiming that the group harbored separatist intentions. When the MRF was allowed to participate legally for the first time in National Assembly elections in June 1990, outraged CDNI supporters attempted to embarrass lawmakers who backed the MRF's right by publicly circulating a list of their names. The Committee also pressured the Ministry of Internal Affairs to publish statistics on crimes committed by members of various pro-Turkish groupings in order to promote public hostility toward minority activists.

The CDNI did not limit itself to rhetoric and publishing. In April 1990, members of the Committee rallied in the town of Haskovo, protesting against the sympathy allegedly shown by the Council of Ministers toward ethnic Turks returning home from Turkey to reclaim their names and property. In July 1990, the organization planned several strikes in the city of Kardzhali, in a region of southern Bulgaria where Turks formed over 70% of the population and where the CDNI claimed to have a strong base. It protested against the seats gained by the MRF to parliament as well as against the introduction of schooling in Turkish. In early October 1991, a series of violent outbreaks occurred between nationalists and Turkish activists in Razgrad in northeastern Bulgaria, incited by the controversial issue of Turkish language lessons in Bulgarian schools.

Bulgarian nationalist forces tried to benefit from difficult economic conditions and continuing political uncertainty in the country. In November 1990, as the Socialist government faced massive social unrest and mounting political opposition, nationalist groups in the Razgrad area, inhabited by large numbers of Turks, declared an "independent Bulgarian republic." They refused to recognize Sofia's authority in the region because the government had purportedly displayed too much leniency toward Turks. Protests were staged against the restoration of Turkish family names, and nationalist leaders called for acts of civil disobedience to counter alleged Turkish radicalism.

The CDNI and other groups opposed giving Turks the status of a national minority because this would supposedly threaten Bulgaria's state integrity. In late November, the Razgrad Republic was renamed the Association of Free Bulgarian Cities, linking several towns containing large Turkish minorities. A civil parliament was to be formed to counterbalance the National Assembly, which the CDNI accused of betraying Bulgaria's national interests. In recognition of mounting tensions fueled by the nationalist initiative, President Zheliu Zhelev appeared on national television to appeal for calm. Following his intervention, the Free City campaign subsided.

The absence of a clear-cut official language policy left the question of teaching Turkish as an optional course in elementary schools open to various interpretations by nationalists as well as by ethnic Turks. Committee members held the view that Bulgarian, as the country's official language, should be the only language course offered to citizens. Many ethnic Turks felt that Turkish should become part of the Bulgarian school curriculum so that their children would continue to use their mother tongue. When parliament prepared to vote on the issue in February 1991, tensions soared, and the CDNI, in conjunction with other nationalist groups, formed a Bulgarian National Union (BNU) and organized protests in a dozen cities. They declared that Slav Bulgarian parents should keep their children away from school until Turkish was taken off the curriculum. The BNU specifically opposed the introduction of optional classes in Turkish to schools attended by large numbers of Muslims: this was depicted as the Turkicization of Bulgarian education. The wave of protests subsided when the National Assembly voted to postpone the introduction of Turkish as an optional subject during the 1991 school year.

The move was condemned by Turkish leaders as unconstitutional. The beginning of the school year in September 1991 was marred by boycotts in some Turkish areas, in protest against government failures to meet demands for Turkish language instruction. In October 1991, parliament passed laws prohibiting the teaching of minority languages in state schools. This essentially anti-Turkish legislation was proposed by nationalist deputies and drew overwhelming support from the Socialist parliamentary majority. However, in November 1991, the new Bulgarian government decreed that ethnic minority pupils in municipal schools could receive instruction in their native languages as an optional subject for a few hours a week.

The CDNI leadership announced a list of demands to prevent "Turkification." Their first issue of concern was the implementation of an official minorities policy. The Committee suggested that any new program should be subject to public scrutiny and approval. The second issue revolved around Bulgarian names: they advocated a law that would enforce a Unified National System of Names in order to "preserve tradition" and Bulgaria's state identity. Suspicions persisted that the CDNI and other radical national associations were created, supported, and financed by local BSP activists whose leaders were implicated in assaults on Turkish spokesmen during the Zhivkov era. An indication of these close ties was the forging of a pre-election alliance in October 1991 between the BSP and five nationalist groupings. Meanwhile, the UDF was accused of entering an "unholy alliance" with the MRF, which was allegedly financed by irredentist circles in Turkey.

CDNI delegates met in February 1992 and voted to dissolve the group as a "public supra-party political organization." They criticized the "unconstructive political approaches" of the Committee's leadership, which avowedly failed to "consolidate the interests" of Bulgarian citizens. Ultimately, these delegates transferred their allegiance to a new party they created, the National Democracy Party (NDP). A more moderate agenda was adopted, focusing mostly on national and social issues. Dimitar Arnaudov, who also served as deputy chairman of the FPL, was appointed to chair the NDP.[45] Some prominent personalities cooperated with the CDNI, including historian Petur Beron and the former rector of Sofia university, Nikolay Genchev. CDNI also published the weekly newspaper *Zora*, which advocated the notion of a Slavic front against Islamic fundamentalism.

All-Bulgarian Union (ABU)
Obshto-Bulgarski Sayuz (OBS)

This nationalist organization was established in early 1990 to campaign for Bulgarian "cultural integrity." Its leaders pledged to wage a legal struggle against "pan-Serbian chauvinism" and "Macedonianism" and against Serbian attempts to assimilate "Bulgarians" in Vardar Macedonia. The All-Bulgarian Union (ABU) contested the right of *Ilinden* to register as a legal political organization, concluding that it was too small to represent "Macedonian" interests and was aiming to detach the Pirin region from Bulgaria and place it under Serbian domination. The ABU emphasized the national unity and single identity of the Bulgarian and Macedonian peoples and their historic struggle for fraternity. It promoted the expansion of Bulgarian social, cultural, and economic links with the sovereign Macedonian republic, with a view to drawing this state closer to Bulgaria and eventually absorbing it. ABU leaders also asserted that they would defend the interests of "Macedonian Bulgarians" in Thrace (Greece) and northern Dobrudja (Romania). A small Society of Bulgarian Macedonians (SOBM) expelled from Aegean Greece, which was also operating in Bulgaria, cooperated with the ABU. The Association was believed also to have developed close links with the nationalist Internal Macedonian Revolutionary Organization (IMRO) groups in Macedonia as well as with the Society of Bulgarians (SOB) in Skopje, which campaigned for the rebirth of Macedonia's "Bulgarian heritage."[46]

Fifth of October Society (FOS)
Obshtestvo Peti Oktomvri (OPO)

Chaired by Ivan Obetsanov and composed of representatives from various political organizations, the Fifth of October Society (FOS) promoted a "non-distorted view" of Bulgarian and Macedonian history, emphasizing the community of the two groups in their liberation from Ottoman rule. The Society was formed in Bansko in May 1990, by the same group that founded the All-Bulgarian Union (ABU). (The fifth of October was the date when Bansko had been freed from Ottoman occupation.) Together with the ABU, the FOS appealed to the Bulgarian public to condemn the *Ilinden* organization and denounce its claims about the existence of a "Macedonian minority" in Bulgaria. It contended that *Ilinden* was responsible for the dangerous "rift in national consciousness" within the Bulgarian state.[47] Other ultra-nationalist organizations have included the Bulgarian Democratic Forum (BDF), led by Vasil Zlatarov, and the Bulgarian Liberal Democratic Party (BLDP), led by Veselin Koshev (which has ties to the Liberal Democratic Party in Russia).[48]

Ethnic Minority and Religious Parties

Movement for Rights and Freedoms (MRF)
Dvizhenie za Prava i Svobodi (DPS)

The Movement for Rights and Freedoms (MRF) was founded on 4 January 1990 in Varna as a successor formation to the Turkish National Liberation Movement (TNLM). The TNLM was established during the early 1980s with the goal of fighting the communist regime for the rights of the Turkish ethnic minority. It sprang up in direct response to the anti-Turkish "revival" movement undertaken by the communist regime in 1983. Its supporters were evidently even prepared to adopt violent means of resistance. Some members of the TNLM were believed responsible for planting a bomb that killed several people at a train station near Plovdiv in 1985.

Ahmed Doğan, a Turkish activist during the communist era, chaired the MRF after its inception. Doğan had spent time in prison for organizing resistance to Zhivkov's anti-Turkish "rebirth" campaign of 1984–1989. He was arrested in June 1986 and sentenced to ten years in prison for violating Bulgarian laws forbidding "anti-state" activities. The Zhivkov government considered Doğan politically dangerous, and he served nine months in solitary confinement. He subsequently stood trial, was found guilty, and was imprisoned. Doğan continued his protest against government assimilationist measures by organizing strikes and sit-ins from his prison cell. His followers included ethnic Turks and members of other minority groups. Doğan was released under an amnesty following Zhivkov's ouster in November 1989.

While in prison, Doğan formulated an agenda to serve the interests of Bulgarian Turks. His demands included freedom to use one's original name, freedom of language and religion, an amnesty for political prisoners, and the right to emigrate to Turkey. He later transferred this agenda to the MRF platform and broadened it, incorporating new goals such as the promotion of tolerance in all nationality issues; the opening of membership to all ethnic groups; the overcoming of economic problems among minorities; the creation of a moderating role for the MRF between the Bulgarian Socialist Party (BSP) and the Union of Democratic Forces (UDF); and the struggle to overcome anti-Turkish sentiments prevailing in Bulgaria, a deep-rooted legacy of 500 years of Ottoman rule.

The MRF was established in January 1990 and promptly legalized. The MRF organized campaigns for educational, religious, and linguistic rights, and pressed for the political representation of all minority groups. By early 1991, the MRF claimed a membership of some 120,000, together with more than one million sympathizers. This made the MRF the fourth largest political organization in the country. The movement won 23 seats in the Bulgarian parliament at the June 1990 general elections and finished third in the ballot. However, it could not contest the elections as a distinct political organization representing only the Turkish community. The Socialist regime had arrived at an agreement with the UDF that parties organized along ethnic or religious lines would not be registered. To avoid accusations of being an exclusively Turkish party, the MRF opened itself to all ethnic and religious groups while renouncing any autonomist or separatist ambitions. Even so, over 90% of the MRF's members were Turkish.

The MRF tried to appeal to the Bulgarian Muslim (Pomak) population. Opinion polls conducted in August 1990 showed that the majority of Pomaks (51%) were not politically active. About one-third were members of a national political organization, and of that number, approximately 20% were affiliated with the MRF. Three-quarters of the Pomaks polled approved the program and actions of the MRF, and only a tiny percentage disapproved. In general, Pomak approval ratings of the MRF were lower than similar ratings among ethnic Turks, even though Doğan remained a highly popular figure.[49] Nationalist Bulgarians accused the MRF of launching a Turkicization drive among Pomaks by pressing them to declare themselves Turks and by campaigning for Islamic unity under the MRF umbrella. Movement leaders denied any ulterior motives in forging a multi-ethnic political movement, particularly as Pomaks were unable to form an effective political organization to represent their interests. A parliamentary report issued in May 1993 accused local Turkish leaders of pressuring Pomaks to renounce their "Bulgarianness." It called on parliament to prosecute local authorities guilty of such practices, to declare invalid all ethnic statistics compiled in Pomak regions, and to cancel the opening of Turkish-language schools in these areas.

In August 1991, the MRF announced that it was establishing a separate political party, the Rights and Freedoms Party (RFP), to stand in upcoming national elections. The Sofia city court refused to register the organization, on the grounds that according to the constitution, parties could not be formed on the basis of ethnicity or religious conviction as this would threaten the "unity of the nation." However, the MRF was allowed to register by the Central Election Commission as a multi-ethnic movement, despite the protests of Bulgarian nationalists. In the October 1991 general and local elections, the MRF gained 24 parliamentary seats, over 1,000 local councilors, 650 village mayors, and 20 district mayors. Its position in the Bulgarian parliament generated serious consternation among nationalist groups and even among more moderate forces fearful of growing Turkish influence and the possibility that the MRF could hold the balance of power in a parliament divided between Socialists and Democrats.

The MRF was one of the most highly structured ethnic organizations in Bulgaria. Spanning the country and targeting areas of Turkish density, the MRF possessed nearly 900 branches and 22 regional offices run by urban and rural local committees. A central administrative bureau, consisting of an executive committee and several regional coordinators, managed the organization's affairs. At the top of the hierarchy stood a central council that gathered every two months; a national congress of MRF representatives held the principal authority. Every group of 500 MRF members was served by one representative who participated in a congress that convened at least once every three years.

MRF leaders denied that they were seeking either territorial autonomy or political self-determination for the Turkish community. Instead, they were pressing for an end to job discrimination against Turks, for greater cultural autonomy in education and language use, and for full political representation in the administrative structures. Doğan attributed the poor relations between Muslim Turks and Christian Bulgarians not to a fundamental inability to co-exist, but to interference by the central authorities and to manipulation and provocation by ultra-nationalist forces. The position and treatment of the Turkish minority was also one of the main barometers of relations between Sofia and Ankara: any curtailment of Turkish rights could seriously jeopardize relations between the Turkish and Bulgarian governments—ties that had significantly improved since the fall of communism.[50]

Despite the threats of disqualification from the October 1991 election on the grounds of its being an unconstitutional political force, the MRF managed to replicate its 1990 vote. It became the only party represented in parliament besides the BSP and the UDF.[51] It received 7.55% of the votes, which translated into 24 seats. The percentage achieved by the MRF was almost equal to the percentage of the population that had identified themselves as members of the Turkish minority. Filip Dimitrov's government came into power with MRF support in November 1991 and left power prematurely in September 1992—again with the MRF's blessing. Although there were no initial major problems between the two coalition partners, the MRF was disappointed in falling living standards and rising unemployment in Turkish areas, which the government had done little to rectify. MRF deputies sided with the BSP in toppling the UDF government and supported the nomination of BSP Prime Minister Berov on 30 December 1992.

The sudden switch of alliances from the UDF to BSP, and the subsequent backing of the Berov government, cost the MRF its unity in parliament and part of its support base. On 30 December 1992, a BSP cabinet with MRF support was formed. The MRF held only the post of deputy Prime Minister and minister of labor and social care. In the December 1994 elections, the MRF was no longer the only ethnically based party to solicit the Turkish vote. Aden Kenan's Turkish Democratic Party (TDP) and Mehmed Hodzha's Party for Democratic Change (PDC) took away almost a third of the MRF's 1991 vote. However, the Movement succeeded in remaining the only political force representing the Turkish minority in parliament by winning 5.4% of the vote and gaining 15 seats.

According to its platform, the MRF pledged to contribute to the unity of the Bulgarian people; to work against any form of discrimination; to promote respect for the rights and freedoms of all ethnic, religious, and cultural communities; to facilitate the peaceful transition to democracy; to participate in the defense of Bulgaria's sovereignty and territorial integrity; and to advocate tolerance and national consensus.[52] The Movement's principal parliamentary tasks were creating legal guarantees for the observance of human rights and freedoms; devising mechanisms for the implementation of legal norms; setting up nationwide conditions for the application of human rights legislation; and participating in drafting laws that defended the right of self-determination for each ethnic community. The platform emphasized the MRF's rejection of regional autonomy and of any form of separatism.

The MRF called for the preservation of cultural and educational traditions through the restoration of newspapers, magazines, and radio stations using the Turkish language. It supported the obligatory study of one's mother tongue and called for extracurricular religious education. In the social sphere, the MRF insisted on the immediate restitution of property to all Bulgarian Turks returning from Turkey. It demanded the eradication of the policy of discrimination against citizens of non-Bulgarian descent in government institutions. In the economic sphere, the MRF supported the building of a socially oriented market economy and economic development programs in predominantly Turkish regions. The MRF published the weekly *Prava i Svobodi* (Rights and Freedoms), issued in Bulgarian and Turkish.

Turkish Democratic Party (TDP)
Turska Demokraticheska Partiya (TDP)

The Turkish Democratic Party (TDP) was founded in 1993 by Aden Kenan, a Movement for Rights and Freedoms (MRF) activist and parliamentarian who became disillusioned with Doğan's policies. Due to the constitutional provision that prohibited the formation of parties on an ethnic basis, the TDP was not officially registered.[53] The party claimed approximately 10,000 members, all of them ethnic Turks. The majority were blue-collar workers, and some, representatives of the intelligentsia. The latter were accepted only after voluntarily disclosing their past, because, in Kenan's words, "most of the well-educated Turks were strongly influenced by the state security services." The TDP demanded that Bulgaria be turned into a federation of Bulgarian and Turkish republics. Its leaders believed that the TDP was needed to fill the vacuum that was created after Doğan's MRF "betrayed" the Turkish electorate by creating a national civil rights party. The main goals of the organization were the recognition of Turkish as an official language and the abrogation of the constitution, which was perceived as an example of Bulgarian "national chauvinism." Since the TDP was unconstitutional, it did not participate in any elections.

TDP leaders accused Doğan of appeasing former communists with an overly compromising political platform. They even labeled Doğan and the MRF an "assimilationist grouping." The main goals of the TDP were the achievement of "national self-determination" and "self-preservation" among the Turkish minority. It sought the creation of two autonomous regions where Turks formed local majorities, and in effect, the federalization of Bulgaria. Doğan viewed the TDP as an essentially extremist clique, unrepresentative of the Turkish community and probably working in the service of ultra-nationalist forces intent on provoking ruptures between Turks and Bulgarians.

Apart from the MRF and the TDP, two other parties claimed the support of ethnic Turks: the Party of Democratic Change (PDC), led by Mukaddes Nalbant, and the Democratic Party of Justice (DPJ), led by Ali Ibrahimov. The former was founded in May 1994, by former MRF deputy Mehmed Hodzha; the latter, in October 1993. Neither of them gained parliamentary representation, because they failed to reach the 4% barrier. The PDC received 0.27%, and the DPJ received 0.46% of the popular vote.[54]

United Roma Organization (URO)
Obedinena Organizatsia Roma (OOR)

Under the leadership of Chairman Manush Romanov, the Roma Democratic Union (RDU) was founded in Sofia in November 1989. It changed its name to the United Roma Organization (URO) in October 1992. It claimed to serve as a non-party union of all Bulgarian Gypsies, and by early 1991 it declared a membership of some 50,000. Delegates at the founding conference in March 1990 discussed the political, economic, social, and cultural disadvantages that Roma had historically endured. Their grievances included the forcible changing of Muslim Gypsy names under the Zhivkov regime and other forms of pressurized assimilation—the absence of Romani newspapers, the closure of Roma clubs, and laws forbidding the use of the Romani language—and the disappearance of Gypsy customs. URO goals have included solving the severe housing and educational problems of Romani communities and pursuing political and social advancement for Gypsies to counter large-scale unemployment and a rising crime rate. The Union was denied registration as a political party for general elections because of its ethnic basis, but it could function as a social and cultural organization and was permitted to publish its own newspaper.

Romanov was elected to parliament in the first multi-party elections in June 1990 as a Union of Democratic Forces (UDF) representative. He became an energetic campaigner for social and economic improvements among the Roma population. Romanov complained that the UDF had avoided supporting Romani causes for fear that such action could estrange a sizable number of Bulgarian voters. Christian Roma have also been wary of backing the Turkish-based Movement for Rights and Freedoms (MRF), fearful of hastening the Islamization of Roma communities. The URO has suffered from a persistent lack of political cohesion among Romani leaders, and it has not explicitly challenged the official prohibition on declaring itself a political party.[55]

Police forces periodically conducted large-scale raids of Roma neighborhoods, claiming they were searching for stolen goods, but local human rights groups suspected the raids were intended to intimidate Roma and collectively to punish the community for its perceived criminality. Residents of the neighborhoods were occasionally beaten, and homes and goods were destroyed. Witnesses and victims have informed the Bulgarian Helsinki Committee that they were too afraid to file official complaints, and were convinced that the complaints would have no effect.

By the late 1990s, there were nearly 400 Roma organizations in the country. They included the Confederation of Roma in Bulgaria (CRB) *(Konfederatsia na Romite v Bulgaria, KRB)*, a pressure group formed in Sofia in May 1993 and chaired by Petar Georgiev; the Movement for Cultural, Educational, and Social Development of Gypsies (MCESDG*) (Dvizhenie za Kulturno, Obrazovatelno i Sotsialno Razvitie na Tsiganite, DKOSRT)*, which promoted community awareness; the Independent Democratic Socialist Association of Gypsies in Bulgaria (IDSAGB*) (Nezavisima Demokraticheska Sotsialisticheska Asotsiatsia na Tsiganite v Bulgaria, NDSATB)*, believed to include members of the former *nomenklatura* seeking to maintain their privileges; and the United Roma Union (URU) *(Obedinen Romski Sayuz, ORS)*, an independent and non–political organization chaired by Milcho Tonchev and then by Vasil Chaprasov.

Romani Christian Democratic Party (RCDP)
Romska Hristiyan Demokraticheska Partiya (RHDP)

Founded in Popovo in December 1992, this controversial Roma organization claimed to be an alternative to the Turkish-oriented Movement for Rights and Freedoms (MRF). The MRF had in fact invited other ethnic minorities to participate under its umbrella, and a Romani faction, mostly consisting of Muslims, subsequently developed under its auspices. Romanov, the leader of the Roma Democratic Union, dismissed the Romani Christian Democratic Party (RCDP) as "unserious," and other Gypsy clan leaders equally disapproved of the organization, claiming that it was created to provoke conflict among already established Romani organizations. Several clan leaders stated that they would boycott and ostracize this organization.

"Peace"
"Shalom"

Bulgaria's Jewish population survived largely intact during World War II. Although the government deported Jews into German hands from the Bulgarian-occupied areas of Macedonia and Thrace and placed onerous restrictions on its own Jewish population, it resisted Nazi pressures to ship this vulnerable minority to German death camps. The majority of the 48,000 Jews who survived in Bulgaria at the close of the War emigrated to Palestine, and by 1956 only about 5,000 remained in the country. In the 1990s, the Jewish population numbered between 3,000 and 5,000. Jews are among the few minorities, that have benefited from official recognition. Founded in Sofia in March 1990 as a renewed version of the former communist-sponsored Social, Cultural, and Educational Association of Bulgarian Jews (SCEABJ), *Shalom* was a non-partisan organization that fostered the social, economic, and cultural development of the Jewish community. A branch of *B'nai B'rith*, the international Jewish society, was also reestablished in Bulgaria in March 1992, more than 50 years after it was banned in 1941. The rebuilding of the society was linked to Prime Minister Dimitrov's visit to Israel. Members of *B'nai B'rith* asserted that they were devoted Bulgarian patriots, dedicated to solving their country's economic and ethnic problems. Their group's chairman was Emil Kalo.

Party for Democratic Prosperity (PDP)
Partiya za Demokraticheski Vazkhod (PDV)

This ethnic Albanian political party became operative in the Pirin Macedonian region and supported Albanian political and cultural rights. The Party for Democratic Prosperity (PDP) was reportedly linked to its namesake in neighboring Macedonia. The Macedonian *Ilinden* organization vociferously expressed its disapproval of the Albanian party, claiming it was unlawfully formed on an ethnic basis. Albanians numbered approximately 5,000 and were left stranded in Bulgaria after the Albanian government parted with the Soviet bloc in the 1960s. Evidence indicates that the Albanians were also subjected to a name-changing campaign under the communist regime, but few details are available. Bulgaria's other minorities, including Armenians, Gagauz, and Vlachs, also established independent social, cultural, and quasi-political organizations after 1989.

Regionalists

United Macedonian Organization "Ilinden" (UMOI)
Obedinena Makedonska Organizatsia Ilinden (OMOI)

Several Macedonian organizations were formed during the collapse of the Zhivkov regime. The Independent Macedonian Organization *Ilinden* (IMOI), created by Georgi Angelov Solunski in November 1989, had limited public impact. The United Macedonian Organization, "Ilinden" (UMOI), founded in April 1990 by its national president Stoyan Georgiev and Pirin region president Yordan Kostadinov, it largely superseded the IMOI grouping. It sought the official recognition of a Macedonian minority in Bulgaria, and the right to use the Macedonian language and to promote Macedonian culture.

Kostadinov was considered more radical than Georgiev in his demands for Macedonian recognition.

The name *Ilinden* held historical significance for both Macedonians and Bulgarians. On 2 August 1903, St. Elijah's Day or *Ilinden*, an uprising against the Ottomans was mounted by Macedonian rebels styled as the Internal Macedonian Revolutionary Organization (IMRO). They fought courageously against the larger and better equipped Turkish forces but were forced to retreat after several months and to postpone their vision of an independent Macedonia. IMRO persisted after World War I, frequently using violent tactics to campaign for a united Macedonia. It was divided between a pro-Bulgarian orientation seeking to recreate a Greater Bulgaria, and an autonomist wing that supported the creation of a large Macedonian state incorporating the three traditional regions of Vardar, Pirin, and Aegean Macedonia.

UMOI was joined at its inception by the Independent Democratic Macedonian Front of Blagoevgrad (IDMFB) and the Committee for the Defense and Rights of Macedonians (CDRM). Several cultural and educational societies also became affiliated with UMOI—among them, groups named after Macedonian heroes Yane Sandanski, Nikola Vapkarov, and Goce Delchev. *Ilinden* claimed at least 42 different regional cells or branches and estimated its membership at some 16,000 people.

The UMOI defined its purpose as "uniting every Macedonian and citizen of the republic of Bulgaria on a fraternal cultural basis." It demanded "the recognition of the Macedonian minority" and claimed that *Ilinden* members would "fight to secure the right to present alternative opinions on problems in sociopolitical developments in Macedonia." *Ilinden* was unsuccessful in implementing its statutes amidst Bulgarian reluctance to recognize the Macedonian minority. By contrast, dozens of other organizations were legally approved after November 1989, because they represented the "official" minorities (Turks, Jews, Armenians, Roma). The government defined Macedonians as Slavic Bulgarians.

In July 1990, the Bulgarian press announced the date of a UMOI congress scheduled to convene the following month. The press announcement triggered a warning from the prosecutor's office in Blagoevgrad. The UMOI was threatened with criminal prosecution on the grounds that its meeting would be deemed "anti-Bulgarian, separatist, and unconstitutional." UMOI chairman Atanas Kiryakov did not officially acknowledge the warning, but UMOI appeared to comply with the law, and cancelled the congress. UMOI's objective was primarily to unite all Macedonians in the cultural field and to organize symposiums, meetings, and discussion forums "at which documents and archival materials would be presented on the identity of the Macedonian nation."

To further its impact, UMOI held semi-clandestine meetings, disseminated leaflets, and gathered signatures for the formal recognition of a Macedonian minority. UMOI Secretary Krasimir Iliev blamed the structure of the Bulgarian economy for the generally low living standard shared by most Macedonians. He believed that Sofia intentionally avoided building industrial plants in the Pirin region so that Macedonians would be economically forced to relocate and assimilate. Other sources claimed that the Bulgarian authorities purposely built health spas and vacation resorts in the Pirin area so as to make any potential alliance between the Macedonian population and the Yugoslav Macedonian republic less attractive. According to its critics, UMOI benefited from more substantial support in the southern parts of the Pirin region and especially among younger people.

UMOI members rallied in Sofia in March 1990 demanding "cultural and national autonomy" for Macedonians. They petitioned the National Assembly to recognize the existence and rights of a Macedonian minority. Hundreds of nationalist counter-demonstrators expressed strong opposition to such recognition. In April 1990, UMOI organized a rally in Sandanski commemorating the 75th anniversary of the death of the revolutionary hero Yane Sandanski. Participants called for the promotion of freedom, peace, democracy, and unity among Balkan peoples. Several speeches openly endorsed "Macedonism" and criticized government policies toward the Macedonian issue.

In April 1991, UMOI issued sixteen demands to the Bulgarian government, including the restoration of the Macedonian language and culture in all educational institutions in the Pirin region, full access to the mass media, and the replacement of a Macedonian bishop in the Pirin area independent of the Bulgarian Orthodox Church but united with the Macedonian Autocephalous Church in the republic of Macedonia. It also demanded the withdrawal of "Bulgarian occupation troops" from Pirin and full cultural, economic, and political self-determination for the region.

Throughout the 1990s, UMOI was prohibited from holding public meetings, although a Macedonian cultural group was legally recognized in June 1992. UMOI leaders claimed a membership of some 1,000 activists in the Pirin region, who established a Society for the Defense of Human Rights to promote their Macedonian agenda. UMOI was accused by government spokesmen and by nationalist Bulgarian organizations of being a front organization sponsored and funded by Serb Yugoslav authorities seeking to separate Pirin Macedonia in order to undermine the state and to counter Bulgarian claims to the former Yugoslav Macedonia. Other critics have claimed that UMOI was an essentially pan-Macedonianist irredentist organization supported by the nationalist IMRO-DPMNU in Skopje and unwittingly playing into Serbian hands by seeking to enlarge the Macedonian republic at Bulgaria's expense.[56]

Internal Macedonian Revolutionary Organization–Independent (IMRO-I)
Vatreshna Makedonska Revolyutsionna Organizatsia–Nezavisim (VMRO-N)

This Macedonian organization was founded in Sofia in November 1989 and claimed a membership of some 600 people. According to its President, Georgi

Solunski, the organization's objectives were similar to those of the United Macedonian Organization "Ilinden" (UMOI). The two groups jointly organized campaigns for the official recognition of the Macedonian minority in Bulgaria. The Internal Macedonian Revolutionary Organization-Independent (IMRO-I) was denied registration by Bulgarian courts, as the authorities claimed they formed a separatist movement. The IMRO-I platform called for the "unification of all Macedonians living in Bulgaria on a cultural basis" and demanded the rights of citizens to "self-definition" as a distinct ethnic group. Organizers denied that the organization was terrorist or separatist, received support from outside the country, or violated Bulgaria's territorial integrity. IMRO-I and the UMOI held joint meetings to coordinate their strategy but complained that they were harassed by the authorities and prevented from gathering signatures throughout the Pirin region for a petition in support of their aims. The group's leaders have sought closer ties with Macedonian compatriots in neighboring states. In the long term, they envisaged full "Macedonian autonomy" in both the cultural and political spheres.[57]

Internal Macedonian Revolutionary Organization–Union of Macedonian Societies (IMRO-UMS) Vatreshna Makedonska Revolyutsionna Organizatsia–Obedinenie na Makedonskite Druzhestva (VMRO-OMD)

Initially called the Union of Macedonian Cultural and Educational Societies (UMES), this group changed its name to Internal Macedonian Revolutionary Organization–Union of Macedonian Societies (IMRO-UMS) at its first national congress, in December 1990. Pan-Bulgarian in nature, IMRO-UMS opposed *Ilinden*, the Internal Macedonian Revolutionary Organization-Independent (IMRO-I), and similar Macedonian "separatist" organizations, claiming that they were unconstitutional. The Union's first chairman was historian Dimitar Gotsev, a native of Vardar Macedonia. Gotsev believed that the Yugoslav authorities endeavored to invent a "Macedonian self-identity" for Bulgarian residents in the former Yugoslavia through a system of "brain-washing, terror, and repression" that could undermine Bulgaria's territorial integrity. Instead, IMRO-UMS advocated the unification of all Macedonian lands within a larger Bulgarian state.

Critics charged that IMRO-UMS and other pan-Bulgarian groupings were impregnated with former communist functionaries who deliberately manipulated the Macedonian issue in order to appear more patriotic than the UDF and other democratic forces. In March 1993, Stoyan Boyadzhiev was elected the new chairman. He insisted that the majority of members were not affiliated with other parties, although IMRO-UMS encompassed sympathizers of both the BSP and the UDF. Boyadzhiev also underscored that his organization strongly supported the recognition of Macedonia under whatever name the population chose, with a view toward eventual unification with Bulgaria.

The Union has not denied its links with IMRO organizations in Macedonia, particularly with leaders advocating closer links with Bulgaria.[58] A more radical Macedonianist organization, the All-Bulgaria Macedonian Union (ABMU), was established during 1990 by Hristov Tzavela. It sought to create a military structure in pursuit of a Greater Bulgaria in the south Balkans.

Macedonian Youth Society (MYS)
Makedonsko Mladezhko Druzhestvo (MMD)

A former affiliate of the Union of Macedonian Cultural and Educational Societies, the Youth Society was founded in April 1986 in the town of Gotse Delchev. The Society promoted the "spiritual unification" of all Bulgarian people. In order to fulfill its goals, the group was forced to address the Macedonian question, stating it was "convinced that two nations, a Bulgarian and a Macedonian, could not possibly exist considering their common language, culture, and history." The Society therefore denounced any versions of Macedonian history that ran contrary to its unitarist conceptions. In particular, it protested the interpretations propounded by *Ilinden* and by Macedonian politicians in the Republic of Macedonia.[59]

Independents and Others

Federation "Bulgarian Kingdom" (FBK)
Federatsiya "Tsarstvo Bulgaria" (FCB)

A monarchist movement also emerged in Bulgaria, seeking the restoration of a constitutional monarchy and the enthronement of King Simeon. However, the movement lacked unity, and three separate monarchist formations contested the December 1994 parliamentary elections—the Union of Monarchist Forces "Bulgarian Kingdom," the National Movement for Crowned Democracy "Bulgarian Kingdom," and the Federation "Bulgarian Kingdom"(FBK). Had the three political groups run on a single ballot, they would have garnered approximately 145,000 votes or about 2.8% of the ballot.

The FBK was founded in 1993 and included royalist organizations from different regions of the country as well as three small parties. The main task of the Federation was the rejection of the referendum of 1946 that had led to the abolition of the monarchy. However, Bulgaria's king Simeon, living in Spain, never expressed support for this party. The national secretary of the FBK was Hristo Kurtev. The Federation published the *Tsarski Vesti* (King's News) weekly. The Federation participated independently in the parliamentary elections in 1991 and 1994 but called for a boycott of the presidential elections in October 1996. For the April 1997 parliamentary elections, the FBK joined the National Salvation Union (NSU) coalition led by Ahmed Doğan, which captured 7.6% of the popular vote and 19 parliamentary seats. A smaller monarchist grouping, the Alliance for the King (AFK), gained a mere 1.1% of the popular vote.

POLITICAL DATA

Name of State: Republic of Bulgaria *(Republika Bulgaria)*
Form of Government: Parliamentary democracy
Structure of Government: Unicameral National Assembly *(Naradno Sabranie)* of 240 members, elected every four years. President elected directly for a period of five years. Council of Ministers elected by the National Assembly.
Size of Territory: 42,855 square miles
Size of Population: 8,155,828 (2000 estimate)

Composition of Population:

Ethnic Group	Number	% of Population
Bulgarians (and Macedonians)	7,206,062	85.05
Turks	822,253	9.70
Roma (Gypsies)	287,732	3.40
Pomaks (Bulgarian Muslims)	65,546	0.77
Others	91,131	1.08
Total minorities	1,266,662	14.95
Total population	8,472,724	100.00

ELECTION RESULTS

Presidential Election, 27 October and 3 November 1996

First Round, 27 October 1996

Turnout: 63.14%

Candidate	Votes	% of Vote
Petar Stoyanov	1,889,825	44.07
Ivan Marazov	1,158,204	27.01
George Ganchev	937,686	21.87
Aleksandar Tomov	135,571	3.16
Hristo Boychev	5,247	1.34
8 other candidates (Total)	109,546	2.58
Total	4,236,079	100.00

Second Round, 3 November 1996

Turnout: 61.67%

Candidate	Votes	% of Vote
Petar Stoyanov	2,502,517	59.70
Ivan Marazov	1,687,242	40.30
Total	4,189,759	100.00

Source: Rose, Munro and Mackie, *Elections in Central and Eastern Europe Since 1990,* Glasgow: University of Strathclyde Studies in Public Policy, No. 300. Accessed online at http://www.strath.ac.uk/departments/CSPP/bulgelec.html.

Presidential Election, 12 and 19 January 1992

First Round, 12 January 1992

Turnout: 75.39%

Candidate	Votes	% of Vote
Zheliu Zhelev	2,273,468	44.66
Velko Vulkanov	1,549,754	30.44
George Ganchev	854,020	16.77
Blagovest Sendov	113,864	2.24
Slavomir Tsankov	50,307	0.99
Others	249,696	4.90
Total:	5,091,109	100.00

Second Round, 19 January 1992

Turnout: 75.92%

Candidate	Votes	% of Vote
Zheliu Zhelev	2,738,420	52.85
Velko Vulkanov	2,443,434	47.15
Total	5,181,854	100.00

Source: University of Essex, *Political Transformation and the Electoral Process in Post-Communist Europe* at http://wwwz.essex.ac.uk/elections.

Parliamentary Elections, 17 June 2001

Turnout: 67.03%

Party/Coalition:	Votes	% of Vote	Seats
National Movement Simeon II	1,952,513	42.74	120
United Democratic Forces	830,338	18.18	51
Coalition for Bulgaria	783,372	17.15	48
Movement for Rights and Freedoms/ Liberal Union/Euroroma	340,395	7.45	21
Internal Macedonian Revolutionary Organization/"George's Day"	165,927	3.63	—
Coalition "Simeon II"	157,141	3.44	—

Others	338,505	7.41	0
Total	4,568,191	100.00	240

Source: Bulgarian Parliamentary results, Central Electoral Commission. http://212.50.5.11/Final2001/res/2001/kke.htm.

Parliamentary Elections, 19 April 1997

Voter Turnout: 60%

Party/Coalition	Votes	% of Vote	Seats
United Democratic Forces	2,223,714	52.26	137
Democratic Left			
(BSP and *Ecoglasnost*)	939,308	22.07	58
Alliance for National Salvation	323,429	7.60	19
Bulgarian Euro-Left	234,058	5.50	14
Bulgarian Business Bloc	209,796	4.93	12
Bulgarian Communist Party	50,864	1.20	—
Alliance for the King	46,765	1.10	—
Bulgarian Christian Coalition	26,614	0.63	—
Democratic Justice Party	20,433	0.48	—
Bulgarian Women's Party	16,061	0.38	—
Liberal Forum	13,638	0.32	—
28 other parties, total	150,639	3.53	—
10 independent candidates, total	19,335	0.45	—
Total	4,255,301	100.00	240

Source: Rose, Munro and Mackie, *Elections in Central and Eastern Europe Since 1990*, Glasgow: University of Strathclyde Studies in Public Policy, No. 300. Accessed online at http://www.strath.ac.uk/departments/CSPP/bulgelec.html; and Embassy of the Republic of Bulgaria.

Parliamentary Elections, 18 December 1994

Turnout: 75%

Party/Coalition	Votes	% of Vote	Seats
Bulgarian Socialist Party/			
Bulgarian Agrarian National Union/			
Political Club *Ecoglasnost*	2,262,943	43.50	125
Union of Democratic Forces	1,260,374	24.23	69
Bulgarian Agrarian National Union/			
Democratic Party	338,478	6.51	18
Movement for Rights and Freedoms	283,094	5.44	15
Bulgarian Business Bloc	245,849	4.73	13
Democratic Alternative for the Republic	197,057	3.79	—
Bulgarian Communist Party	78,606	1.51	—
New Choice Union	77,641	1.49	—
Patriotic Alliance	74,350	1.43	—
Federation "Bulgarian Kingdom"	73,205	1.41	—

Kingdom of Bulgaria National Movement for Monarchical Democracy	40,642	0.78	—
Kingdom of Bulgaria Union of Royalist Forces	31,884	0.61	—
Bulgarian National Radical Party	27,853	0.54	—
35 other parties and coalitions, and 8 independents	210,089	4.04	—
Total	5,202,065	100.00	240

Source: State Gazette, Sofia, No. 107, p. 9, 30 December 1994; and FBIS-EEU-95-211-A, 1 November 1995.

Parliamentary Elections, 13 October 1991

Turnout: 83.87%

Party/Coalition	Votes	% of Vote	Seats
Union of Democratic Forces	1,903,567	34.36	110
Bulgarian Socialist Party	1,836,050	33.14	106
Movement for Rights and Freedoms	418,168	7.55	24
BANU (United)	214,052	3.86	—
BANU (Nikola Petkov)	190,454	3.54	—
UDF (Center)	177,295	3.20	—
UDF (Liberals)	155,902	2.81	—
"Kingdom of Bulgaria"	100,883	1.82	—
Business Bloc	73,379	1.32	—
National Radical Party	62,462	1.13	—
Others	408,625	7.27	—
Total	5,540,837	100.00	240

Source: Final Election Results, Seat Distribution, FBIS-EEU-91-201, 17 October 1991 from Sofia BTA in English.

Parliamentary Elections, 10 and 17 June 1990

Turnout: 90.60%

Party/Coalition	Votes	% of Vote	Seats
Bulgarian Socialist Party	2,886,363	47.15	211
Union of Democratic Forces	2,216,127	36.20	144
Agrarian Union	491,500	8.03	16
Movement for Rights and Freedoms	368,929	6.03	23
Others (Fatherland Party of Labor, Fatherland Union, Social Democratic Party, Independents)	158,279	2.59	6
Total	6,121,198	100.00	400

Source: The June 1990 Elections in Bulgaria, International Delegation report, by the National Democratic Institute for International Affairs and the National Republican Institute fro International Affairs, 1990; FBIS-EEU-90-119, 20 June 1990; and FBIS-EEU-90-116, 15 June 1990.

NOTES

1. For recent histories of Bulgaria see R.J. Crampton, *A Short History of Modern Bulgaria,* Cambridge: Cambridge University Press, 1987; J.F. Brown, *Bulgaria Under Communist Rule,* New York: Praeger, 1970; Robert McIntyre, *Bulgaria: Politics, Economics and Society,* London: Pinter, 1988; John Bell, *The Bulgarian Communist Party from Blagoev to Zhivkov,* Stanford: Hoover Institution Press, 1986; and Bilâl N. Simsir, *The Turks of Bulgaria, (1878–1985)* London: Rustem & Brothers, 1988.

2. For a valuable account of post-communist Bulgaria see John D. Bell, "Democratization and Political Participation in 'Postcommunist' Bulgaria," in Karen Dawisha and Bruce Parrott (Eds.), *Politics, Power, and the Struggle for Democracy in South-East Europe*, Cambridge: Cambridge University Press, 1997, pp. 353–402.

3. Consult Stefan Krause, "Socialists at the Helm," *Transition*, Vol. 1, No. 4, 29 March 1995, pp. 33–36.

4. See Ivo Georgiev, "Indecisive Socialist Party Stumbles Into Crisis," *Transition*, Vol. 2, No. 26, 27 December 1996, pp. 26–28.

5. Stefan Krause, "United Opposition Triumphs in Presidential Elections," *Transition*, Vol. 2, No. 26, 27 December 1996, pp. 20–23.

6. Stephen Ashley, "Migration from Bulgaria," Radio Free Europe/Radio Liberty Research Institute (RFE/RL), *Report on Eastern Europe*, 1 December 1989; Stephen Ashley, "Ethnic Unrest During January," RFE/RL, *Report on Eastern Europe*, Vol. 1, No. 6, 9 February 1990; Kjell Engelbrekt, "The Movement for Rights and Freedoms," RFE/RL, *Report on Eastern Europe*, Vol. 2, No. 22, 31 May 1991.

7. Goran Ahren, "Helsinki Committee on Turkish Bulgarians: Continued Political Oppression," *Dagens Nyheter*, Stockholm, 24 December 1989, in *JPRS-EER-90–009*, 24 January 1990.

8. Mitko Krumov, "New Deputies Yuriy Borisov and Vasil Kostov Replace Dobri Dzhurov and Georgi Velichkov Who Resigned," *Duma*, Sofia, 10 January 1991, in *FBIS-EEU-91–013*, 18 January 1991. For a discussion of the major strikes in Kardzhali see *BTA*, Sofia, 26 February 1991, in *FBIS-EEU-91–038*, 26 February 1991.

9. For a discussion of cultural assimilation and the Name Change Law, see "Minority Problems Persist: Elections Set for June," in *News from Helsinki Watch*, News From Bulgaria, March 1990. On the new law on names see "Deep Tensions Continue in Turkish Provinces, Despite Some Human Rights Improvements," in *News from Helsinki Watch*, News from Bulgaria, August 1990.

10. "Second Yilmaz Letter Is Unprecedented and Greatly Alarms Nationwide Committee of Defense of National Interests," *Duma*, Sofia, 30 August 1991, in *FBIS-EEU-91–172*, 5 September 1991; Kjell Engelbrekt, "The Movement for Rights and Freedoms to Compete in Elections," RFE/RL, *Report on Eastern Europe*, Vol. 2, No. 91, 4 October 1991.

11. See Duncan M. Perry, "The Macedonian Question Revitalized," RFE/RL, *Report on Eastern Europe*, Vol. 1, No. 24, 24 August 1990; Evgeni Gavrilov, *Duma*, Sofia, 14 November 1990, in *FBIS-EEU-90–223*, 19 November 1990; *BTA*, Sofia, 23 September 1991, in *FBIS-EEU-91–185*, 24 September 1991.

12. *State Gazette*, Sofia, 23 February 1999 and 14 March 1999; and *BTA* 3 November 1998.

13. See Helsinki Watch Report, "Destroying Ethnic Identity: The Gypsies of Bulgaria," New York, June 1991.

14. Kjell Engelbrekt, "Bulgaria: The Weakening of Post-Communist Illusions," *RFE/RL Research Report*, Vol. 2, No. 1, January 1993.

15. Check Stefana Gergova and Evlogi Stoilov, "Bulgarian Socialist Party Prepare New Provocation Relating to the Ethnic Problems," *Demokratsiya*, Sofia, 19 September 1991; Kjell Engelbrekt, "Nationalism Reviving," and "The Movement for Rights and Freedoms to Compete in Elections"; RFE/RL, *Daily Report*, No. 193, 10 October 1991; and Kjell Engelbrekt, "Opposition Narrowly Defeats Socialists in National Elections," RFE/RL, *Report on Eastern Europe*, Vol. 2, No. 43, 25 October 1991.

16. *Standart News*, Sofia, 14 March 1994, p. 2, *FBIS-EEU-94–055*, 22 March 1994.

17. *Khorizont*, Sofia, 1 November 1994, *FBIS-EEU-94–215–A*, 2 November 1994.

18. *Duma*, Sofia, 7 June 1994, p. 5, *FBIS-EEU-94–113*, 13 June 1994.

19. Groups identified as such by a journalist in an article published in *Kontinent*, Sofia, 10 August 1995, p. 6, *FBIS-EEU-95–157*, 15 August 1995.

20. *24 Chasa*, Sofia, 24 March 1995, p. 10, *FBIS-EEU-95–061*, 30 March 1995.

21. From the pre-election program, *Summary of the Pre-election Platform of the BSP: Let's Stop the Destruction, Let's Reform Bulgaria.*

22. *Otechestven Vestnik*, Sofia, 1 November 1993, p. 3.

23. Based on an interview with deputy chairman of the BSP leadership Purvanov in *Trud*, Sofia, 7 December 1994, p. 9, in *FBIS-EEU-94–239*, 13 December 1994.

24. *Trud*, Sofia, 5 December 1994, pp. 1, 9, *FBIS-EEU-94–243*, 19 December 1994.

25. *State Gazette*, Sofia, No. 109, 30 December 1994, p. 9.

26. *DAR Pre-election Programme for Bulgaria*, DAR Press, Sofia, 23 September 1994.

27. See Ira Antonova, *The Union of Democratic Forces, Past and Present.*

28. *BTA*, Sofia, 2 April 1994, *FBIS-EEU-94–064–A*, 4 April 1994.

29. Bulgaria On Line, Independent News and Information Provider on Internet (www.online.bg).

30. *BTA*, 5 February 1994, *FBIS-EEU-94–026–A*, 8 February 1994 and "Not Just Choice. New Choice!" *Courier Press*, No. 238, pp. 3–4 and No. 239, pp. 8–9, *BTA*, Sofia, 5 December 1994.

31. *24 Chasa*, Sofia, 30 November 1995, p. 13, *FBIS-EEU-95–233*, 5 December 1995.

32. *Khorizont Radio Network*, Sofia, 12 October 1994, *FBIS-EEU-94–198*, p. 2.

33. *Standart News*, Sofia, 22 March 1995, *FBIS-EEU-95–058*, p. 7.

34. *Khorizont Radio Network*, Sofia, 16 June 1995, *FBIS-EEU-95–116*, 16 June 1995, p. 2.

35. *24 Chasa*, Sofia, 27 July 1994, *FBIS-EEU-94–148*, 2 August 1994, p. 5.

36. "BZNS-Democratic Party Coalition Agreement," *Zemedelsko Zname*, 13 October 1994, p. 1; *Standart News*, 22 March 1995, *FBIS-EEU-95–058*, p.7; *Kontinent*, 20 December 1994, *FBIS-EEU-94–247*, 23 December 1994, p. 4.

37. Handbook "Bulgaria," *BTA*, 1 January 1996, section 6.1.

38. *Trud*, Sofia, 21 September 1994, p. 9 in *FBIS-EEU-94–189*, 29 September 1994, p. 2.

39. Bulgaria On Line, Independent News and Information Provider on Internet (www.online.bg).

40. *Standart News*, Sofia, 2 May 1996, p. 7.

41. For the party platform see *BTA*, Sofia, Courier Press Service, No. 2, pp. 4–5, 3 January 1995.

42. "Bulgarian Nationalists Plan Human Chain," *Frankfurter Allgemeine*, Frankfurt, 9 July 1990, in *FBIS-EEU-90–132*, 10 July 1990; Kalina Bozeva and Purvan Stoyanov, *Demokratsiya*, Sofia, 3–5 July 1990, in *JPRS-EER-90–124*, 30 August 1990; Dulev, "The Banner Is Waving Again"; Kjell Engelbrekt, "Nationalism Reviving"; interview with Ivan Georgiev, BNRP chairman, by Nikolay Bozhev, "We Are Struggling for Christian Values Against the Offensives of Islam," *Otechestven Vestnik*, Sofia, 4 February 1993, *FBIS-EEU-93–026*, 10 February 1993.

43. Figures given by *BTA* in *FBIS-EEU-91–011*, 16 January 1991, and by Radio Free Europe, Vol. 2, No. 36, 6 September 1991.

44. See Kalina Bozeva and Purvan Stoyanov, *Demokratsiya*, Sofia, 3–5 July 1990, in *JPRS-EER-90–124*, 30 August 1990; Boris Kostadinov, "Bulgarian Social Democratic Party Invites SDS but not BSP to Its Congress," *Duma*, Sofia, 1 March 1991, in *FBIS-EEU-91–043*, 5 March 1991; interview with Dimitur Arnaudov by Yana Mavrodieva, "I Am a Citizen of the World," *Mladezh*, Sofia, 4 February 1991, in *JPRS-EER-91–044*, 5 April 1991; Elizabet Dafinova, "A Party of Pragmatic Nationalism," *Bulgariya*, Sofia, 13 April 1991, in *JPRS-EER-91–089*, 21 June 1991; Kjell Engelbrekt, "The Movement for Rights and Freedoms to Compete in Elections," and "Nationalism Reviving"; and interview with Rumen Popov, FPL Chairman in *Duma*, Sofia, 20 May 1993, in *JPRS-EER-93–063–S*, 2 July 1993.

45. Check Kalina Bozeva and Purvan Stoyanov, *Demokratsiya*, 3–5 July 1990 in *JPRS-EER-90–124*, 30 August 1990; and Kjell Engelbrekt, "The Movement for Rights and Freedoms to Compete in Elections"; Kjell Engelbrekt, "Nationalism Reviving," RFE/RL, *Report on Eastern Europe*, Vol. 2, No. 48, 29 November 1991; and "Official Announcement on the Dissolution of the Nationwide Committee for Defense of National Interests and the Founding of a National Defense Party," *Pressluzhba Kurier*, Sofia, 19 February 1992, in *FBIS-EEU-92–038*, 26 February 1992.

46. "Macedonian Youth Society Established," *Vecherni Novini*, Sofia, 3 May 1990, in *FBIS-EEU-90–091*, 10 May 1990.

47. *Vecherni Novini*, Sofia, 3 May 1990, in *FBIS-EEU-90–091*, 10 May 1990.

48. For a useful synopsis of Bulgarian ultra-nationalism see John D. Bell, "The Radical Right in Bulgaria," in Sabrina P. Ramet (Ed.), *The Radical Right in Central and Eastern Europe Since 1989*, University Park: Pennsylvania State University Press, 1999, pp. 233–254.

49. Hugh Poulton, "Minorities in the Balkans," *Minority Rights Group*, No. 82, Expedite Graphic Limited, London, October 1989; Article by the Center for the Study of Democracy, "Where Are We Going After the Dark Little Room?" *Kultura*, Sofia, 17 August 1990, in *JPRS-EER-90–145*, 23 October 1990.

50. Interview with Medi Doganov by Angelina Petrova, "The Neighborhood Door Is Ajar," *Pogled*, Sofia, 26 March 1990, in *FBIS-EEU-90–066*, 5 April 1990; interview with Ahmed Doğan by Ivan Staevski, "Path of Unification and Prosperity," *Zemedelsko Zname*, Sofia, 8 May 1990, in *FBIS-EEU-90–093*, 14 May 1990; Volen Siderov, "The Parliament Must Be Bulgarian!" *Demokratsiya*, Sofia, 17 July 1990, *FBIS-EEU-90–155*, 10 August 1990. For a detailed discussion of the MRF platform see Kjell Engelbrekt, "The Movement for Rights and Freedoms"; RFE/RL, *Daily Report*, No. 164, 29 August 1991; "Second Yilmaz Letter Is Unprecedented and Greatly Alarms Nationwide Committee for Defense of National Interests," *Duma*, Sofia, 30 August 1991, in *FBIS-EEU-91–172*, 5 September 1991; Kjell Engelbrekt, "The Movement for Rights and Freedoms to Compete in Elections," and "Nationalism Reviving"; and RFE/RL, *Daily Report*, No. 98, 25 May 1993.

51. Evgenii Danailov, "Bulgaria: Politics after the October 1991 Elections," *RFE/RL, Research Report*, Vol. 1, No. 2, 10 January 1992.

52. See the *Platform of the MRF for the Grand National Assembly Elections*, distributed by MRF Central Election Commission, 18 May 1990.

53. *State Gazette*, Sofia, No. 107, 30 December 1994, p. 9.

54. Handbook "Bulgaria," *BTA*, Sofia, 1 January 1996.

55. Simon Simonov, "The Gypsies: A Re-emerging Minority," RFE/RL, *Report on Eastern Europe*, Vol. 1, No. 21, 25 May 1990; Ivan Ilchev and Duncan Perry, "Bulgarian Ethnic Groups: Politics and Perceptions," RFE/RL, *Report on Eastern Europe*, Vol. 2, No. 12, 19 March 1993.

56. See Nikolay Zagorichanov, "What Is Macedonism, and Does It Have a Basis in Bulgaria?" *Duma*, Sofia, 12 May 1990, in *FBIS-EEU-90–095*, 16 May 1990; Pero Rakocevic, "According to a Well-Known Recipe," *Borba*, Belgrade, 8 June 1990, in *FBIS-EEU-90–121*, 22 June 1990. For a discussion of Macedonian history see *Demokratsiya*, Sofia, 28 January 1990, in *FBIS-EEU-90–120*, 21 August 1990; Duncan Perry, "The Macedonian Question Revitalized"; Evgeni Gavrilov, *Duma*, Sofia, 14 November 1990, in *FBIS-EEU-90–223*, 19 November 1990; interview with *Ilinden* Secretary Krasimir Iliev by Davor Ivankovic and Zelimir Zanko, "Sofia Continues To Negate Macedonians," *Vecernji List*, Zagreb, 24 November 1990, in *FBIS-EEU-90–239*, 12 December 1990; interview with Jordan Kostadinov by Mirche Tomovski, "It Is Not Easy To Be Human," *Puls*, Skopje, 3 September 1992, in *JPRS-EER-92–145*, 14 October 1992.

57. See Helsinki Watch, "Destroying Ethnic Identity: Selective Persecution of Macedonians in Bulgaria," New York, 12 February 1991.

58. Miglena Veselinova, "Will We Read the *Makedoniya* Newspaper?" *Rabotnichesko Delo*, Sofia, 1 March 1990, in *FBIS-EEU-90–053*, 19 March 1990; and *Kontinent*, Sofia, 26 March 1993.

59. "Macedonian Youth Society Established," *Narodna Mladezh*, Sofia, 8 March 1990, in *FBIS-EEU-90–049*, 13 March 1990.

Romania

HISTORICAL OVERVIEW

The first recorded tribal groups to inhabit the Romanian territories were the Thracians, Ionians, and Dorians, during the first millennium BC. Collectively they were known to Greek historians as Getians, and to the Romans as Dacians, living in the mountains north of the Danubian Plain. As Rome expanded into the Balkans, the Geto-Dacians forged a tribal union and fought a series of wars against the invaders, initially under the leadership of Burebista in the first century BC. By the second century AD, the Dacians had established a powerful state under the control of Decebalus, which threatened Rome's Danubian frontiers. Roman legions, under Emperor Trajan, overran the territory in AD 101. For the next 150 years the Transylvanian basin and the plain between the Carpathians and the Danube was the Roman province of Dacia, and much of the local population was Latinized.

Roman forces abandoned the Dacian territories by AD 275, following raids by tribal groups and new large-scale migrations from the north. The fate of the Dacian population, after the Roman withdrawal has stirred historical controversies. While Romanian scholars claim that the local people continued to inhabit all the lands of present-day Romania, Hungarian historians assert that the Transylvanian region was essentially depopulated before the arrival of Magyar tribes in the ninth century. A series of migratory waves overran the Romanian territories, including Visigoths in the third century AD, Huns in the fourth century, Gepids in the fifth century, and Avars in the sixth century. At the end of the sixth century, large numbers of Slavs settled throughout the Balkan peninsula and cut off Dacia from the Roman and Byzantine worlds.[1]

During the ninth century AD, the area fell under the control of the Bulgarian Empire, and Dacia gradually was Christianized. The local Slavic peoples, were absorbed by the more numerous Dacians, or Romanians. In the tenth century, Hungarian settlers overran the Transylvanian territories, which became part of the Hungarian kingdom by the eleventh century. In 1330, a number of small regions south of the Carpathians merged into the independent Romanian principality of Wallachia; and in 1359, a second Romanian principality, Moldova, also became independent. Both regions evolved as part of the Eastern Orthodox religious, cultural, and political sphere.

Between the fifteenth and nineteenth centuries, most of the Romanian lands remained under Ottoman Turkish domination. Initially by paying tribute to the Sultan and recognizing his suzerainty, the Romanians avoided direct incorporation into the Empire. At the end of the sixteenth century, Michael the Brave of Wallachia regained full independence for his principality and briefly united Moldova and Transylvania under his rule. But without support from the West European powers, the country was overrun by the Ottomans, who imposed a severe economic burden on the Romanians. Ottoman control reached its zenith in the eighteenth century when Romania became a bulwark for the Turks against Russian and Austro-Hungarian penetration. With Romanian autonomy drastically curtailed, the Ottomans replaced the local rulers with loyal Greek Phanariot administrators. However, some of them proved to be enlightened, abolishing serfdom and conducting legal and administrative reforms in Wallachia and Moldova.

As long as Transylvania remained under Hungarian control, the large Romanian population, which was primarily rural and Orthodox, was excluded from public affairs. Transylvania came under Habsburg rule at the end of the seventeenth century, and a substantial Uniate (or Eastern-rite) population emerged as Jesuit missionaries convinced portions of the Orthodox clergy to accept a union with Rome in return for a status equal to that of Roman Catholic priests. Romanian Uniate clerics became instrumental in forging a Romanian identity in the region and pushing for the acceptance of the Romanians as a constituent nation of Transylvania.

Russian influence in the Balkans increased during the last quarter of the eighteenth century, but the Romanian nobility (*boyars*) opposed the replacement of Turkish rule with Russian overlordship. Suspicions of Russian intentions increased after the Tsarist empire seized Moldova in 1812. A Russian protectorate over Wallachia was established following the Treaty of Adrianople in 1829, when the Ottomans withdrew from the region. This led to increasing Romanian resentment of Russian ambitions. Many Romanian *boyars* became active in the nationalist revolutionary ferment in 1848, but they lacked organization and support among the masses and were ultimately defeated by Russian forces.

The victory of the European allies over Russia in the Crimean war in 1856 terminated Russia's domination over the Romanian principalities. In 1859, Romanian *boyars* elected Alexandru Ioan Cuza as prince of both Wallachia and Moldova, and cemented a formal administrative union between the two principalities in 1861.

The role of the Orthodox clergy was diminished and a new constitution was promulgated in 1866. Formal independence was achieved after the Russo-

Turkish war of 1877–1878, and Romania was recognized as an independent kingdom in 1881 under the rule of King Carol I Hohenzollern. His chief dispute was with the Hungarian administration in Transylvania, where a process of assimilation denied Romanian identity and restricted the use of the Romanian language.

During World War I, Romania entered the conflict on the side of the French and British allies. When the Central Powers collapsed in 1918, a Greater Romania was created in which the country almost doubled in size and population. Bucharest gained the territories of Transylvania and Banat from Hungary, Bukovina from Austria, and Moldova from Russia. The large Hungarian and German Saxon populations in Transylvania resisted integration and maintained their distinctive identities.

In the inter-war period, Romania benefited from a parliamentary democracy in the 1920s, with the two largest parties, the Liberal Party and the National Peasant Party, playing a preeminent role. Increasing turmoil was evident in the country after the accession of King Carol II Hohenzollern to the throne in 1930 amid calls for a stronger authoritarian regime. At that time, an extremist, anti-Semitic, and fascistic organization, the Iron Guard, gained significant public support. In 1938, Carol II imposed a royalist dictatorship to stem leftist and rightist radicalism.

At the outset of World War II, Romania lost significant portions of its territory as Hungary seized northern Transylvania, the Soviet Union took Moldova and northern Bukovina, and Bulgaria captured southern Dobrudja along the Black Sea coast. King Carol II was forced to abdicate in September 1940 and was replaced by General Ion Antonescu, who forged an alliance with Nazi Germany. In a bitter struggle with the Iron Guard, Antonescu, supported by the army, emerged victorious and destroyed the Guard as a significant political force. The Antonescu dictatorship was, in turn, overthrown in August 1944 by King Michael, the son of Carol II, as the Axis powers were on the verge of losing the war. The new government declared its commitment to the Allies.

Soviet Red Army forces overran Romania in the summer of 1944 and they proceeded to impose a communist system on the country while re-annexing Moldova, northern Bukovina, and some of Romania's Danubian counties. However, Romania did regain northern Transylvania from Hungary. Under intensive pressure from Moscow, in March 1945, King Michael appointed a pro-communist government under the control of Petru Groza. The political opposition was suppressed, and a rigged election in November 1946 installed a fully communist regime in Bucharest. Between 1948 and 1960, the communist leadership under Gheorghe Gheorghiu-Dej imposed a totalitarian system in the country in which the Romanian Communist Party (RCP) assumed control over all aspects of public life.

A period of political relaxation was evident in the late 1960s, after the death of Gheorghiu-Dej in 1965 and his replacement by RCP First Secretary Nicolae Ceauşescu the same year. Between 1965 and 1971, Ceauşescu initiated a partial de-Stalinization, relaxing the party's ideological controls and limiting the operations of the secret police. He also sought to curtail Soviet control over the country by limiting its economic dependence on Moscow and exploiting widespread anti-Russian feelings to mobilize support for the RCP. But from the mid-1970s onward, a personalistic dictatorship was imposed on the country in which all forms of dissent were ruthlessly stifled and in which Ceauşescu's family acted as an infallible dynasty. An ideological orthodoxy was imposed together with a "cult of personality" glorifying the nation's leader.

Throughout the 1980s, as the economic situation became increasingly desperate for the population, Ceauşescu's personal dictatorship tightened and the country was turned into a virtual police state. His erratic rule and increasing paranoia even alienated much of the party bureaucracy, and he increasingly relied on the *Securitate* police units to guarantee his control. Ceauşescu's fall on 22 December 1989 was sudden and bloody. Demonstrations began in the streets of Timişoara in western Romania in mid-December as the police tried to evict the Hungarian Protestant pastor László Tökés from his parish house. Thousands of people took to the streets in Timişoara, and a massacre of unarmed civilians followed. As new protests erupted on the streets of Bucharest and other large cities, the army mutinied and supported the swelling public uprising. The Romanian dictator and his wife Elena were captured and executed on 25 December 1989 after a summary trial, while the violent resistance of his loyalist *Securitate* forces continued sporadically. It was estimated that several hundred civilians perished in the fighting.

POST-COMMUNIST DEVELOPMENTS

A provisional National Salvation Front (NSF) consisting of former communists, dissidents, and army commanders was formed on 22 December 1989 to govern the country pending the first general elections. Although the NSF claimed it was committed to a multi-party democracy, critics charged that it was led by former communist bureaucrats and ideologues, such as Silviu Brucan, who sought to preserve their powers and privileges. Evidently, Ceauşescu had been quickly eliminated without a proper trial in order to avoid any embarrassing revelations about other communist officials.[2] The Romanian Communist Party lacked a coherent reformist movement within its ranks, and the country had no organized opposition movement on eve of the revolution that could challenge the authority or legitimacy of the NSF.

Several political parties were established or recreated shortly after the December 1989 uprising, including the historic National Liberal and National Peasant parties, as well as social democratic, Christian democratic, monarchist, nationalist, and environmentalist groupings. The minority populations also began to organize, including the large Hungarian population. Immediately after the Romanian revolt, the position of the Hungarian minority visibly improved. Both Hungarians and Romanians participated in the rallies and protest actions that contributed to toppling the Ceauşescu regime. The initial revolutionary phase was marked by cooperative efforts between Romanian and Hungarian activists. Various restrictive and repressive policies were abandoned by the new NSF government. The Hungarian population was legally permitted to establish its own political organizations, and far-reaching concessions were granted in cultural and educational affairs.

Within weeks of the overthrow of Ceauşescu, democratic activists claimed that the public uprising had been hijacked by reform communists who thwarted the emergence of a genuine democratic system, maintained the privileges of the former *nomenklatura*, and used the secret police to harass the opposition. Some prominent democratic leaders issued the "Timişoara Proclamation" in March 1990, underscoring the anti-communist and pro-democratic values that had evidently been betrayed by the NSF leadership. The Proclamation called for the exclusion of former communist officials and security police commanders from public life. It was endorsed by hundreds of independent groups in the country, including the Group for Social Dialogue (GSD), which helped organize protest actions on University Square in Bucharest before the first general elections in May 1990. The GSD was established in December 1989 as an independent association dedicated to monitoring the government's observance of democratization. However, as a result of splits and internal conflicts, the Group lost its initial social impact and became largely confined to intellectual circles.

The NSF was widely accused of maintaining many elements of Ceauşescuism, including a strong leadership with limited democratic procedures, the exaltation of national homogeneity, the propaganda use of populist themes, and hostility to market relations.[3] Leaders of the National Salvation Front were also willing to employ nationalism and exploit anti-minority sentiments to garner domestic support. The regime of President Ion Iliescu, who was elected on 20 May 1990 with a landslide victory, stood accused of tolerating and even sanctioning the exploits of extremist anti-Hungarian nationalist forces in Transylvania. The activities of newly formed extremist Romanian organizations aggravated ethnic tensions in parts of Transylvania. Some were directly assisted by the old communist networks and the security forces, while factions in the NSF courted and supported the radicals.

Ultra-nationalist groups opposed granting any "national privileges" to the Magyar minority, including language classes (which were restored to some Transylvanian schools in 1990), and demanded a ban on all minority-based political organizations. They preyed on popular fears among some sectors of the Romanian population that Hungarian aspirations would undermine their economic conditions and place them in a subordinate political position. Such accusations were widely believed by thousands of Romanians who were resettled in Transylvania by the Ceauşescu regime. Ethnic tensions were on occasion exploited by ultra-nationalist Romanian groups to foster violence in Transylvania, as was evident in the city of Tîrgu Mureş in March 1990. Hungarian spokesmen contended that the Bucharest government failed to properly investigate the incidents and bring the culprits to trial. Romanian authorities, in turn, accused Magyar activists of bearing much of the responsibility for inciting ethnic conflicts in Transylvania.

The 1990 electoral law created a bicameral legislature consisting of a Chamber of Deputies and a Senate, but a semi-presidential system was maintained in which parliament remained weak and divided. In the elections to the Chamber of Deputies on 20 May 1990, the National Salvation Front captured 66.31% of the vote and 263 seats, while the opposition fared poorly: the National Liberal Party only managed 6.41% of the vote and 29 seats; the Ecological Movement of Romania, 2.62% and 12 seats; and the Christian and Democratic National Peasants' Party, 2.60% and 12 seats. Opposition leaders complained that the NSF obtained a grossly unfair advantage because it controlled all substantial assets in the country, maintained a powerful organization, and controlled the major media outlets. In addition, the NSF was accused of rigging some of the balloting in its favor. The opposition Democratic Convention (DC) was disorganized internally and plagued by factionalism and personality conflicts.

Petre Roman, a leading luminary in the National Salvation Front, became prime minister of the new government. He was unable to maintain his position when economic reform policies failed and was undermined in his struggle with the Iliescu faction in the NSF. The NSF subsequently split into two distinct parties: the Iliescu-led Democratic National Salvation Front (DNSF), later renamed the Party of Social Democracy in Romania (PSDR), and Roman's National Salvation Front, subsequently called the Democratic Party (DP). Prime Minister Roman was replaced in September 1991 by Theodor Stolojan, who retained the position until new elections were held in September 1992. In the first year, the government was backed by Iliescu's PSDR, the Christian Democratic National Peasants' Party (CDNPP), and the Democratic Farmers' Party of Romania (DFPR).

In the 1990 general elections, the Democratic Alliance of Hungarians in Romania (DAHR) had garnered 7.23% of the votes and 29 seats in the Chamber of Deputies. Of the smaller ethnic minorities, the German Democratic Union (GDU) captured 0.28% of the vote and one seat, and the Democratic Union of Roma in Romania (DURR) gained 0.21% and also one seat. Political groups representing various minorities that failed to gather the necessary number of votes acquired one seat each in the lower chamber of parliament according to the provisions of the electoral law. Several parties obtained one seat: the Armenian Union of Romania; the Bulgarian Union of Banat and the Bulgarian Cultural Association of Bucharest (one seat for the two); the Hellenic Union of Romania; the Lipovan Community of Romania; the Polish Union of Romania (*Dom Polski*); the Democratic Union of Serbians; the Democratic Union of Slovaks and Czechs;

the Muslim Turkish Democratic Union of Romania; and the Ukrainian Union of Romania.

In the Senate elections of May 1990, the National Salvation Front gained an overwhelming victory, with 67.02% of the vote and 91 of the 119 seats. The National Liberal Party only captured 7.06% and 10 seats, while the Christian and Democratic National Peasants' Party took 2.45% and one seat. The DAHR won 7.20% of the total vote and obtained 12 seats. The total number of Magyar representatives in parliament therefore reached 41. One of the four secretaries in the Chamber of Deputies was from the DAHR, in addition to the chairman of one of the 14 parliamentary commissions, and the vice-chairmen of two commissions. In the Senate, Hungarian senators included one of the four vice-chairmen, one of the four secretaries, and the chairmen in two commissions. The DAHR established parliamentary groups in the Chamber of Deputies and in the Senate. A parliamentary group consisting of members of political parties belonging to other minorities represented in parliament was also formed.

According to the law on public administration, ratified in November 1991, local government was to be based on the "principles of local autonomy and the decentralization of public services."[4] However, the institution of the prefect, which was empowered by the central government and represented the administration in the counties (*judete*), placed substantial limitations on decentralization. The law also stated that mayors were responsible for insuring "public law and order and the inhabitants' peace with police support." Mayors could take measures to "prohibit or suspend performances, or other public manifestations that contravene the order of the law or infringe upon good morals, public order, and peace." This article was subsequently used by the ultra-nationalist mayor of Cluj to forbid the holding of various Hungarian events in the spring of 1992, leading to numerous protest actions.

In December 1991, a new constitution was promulgated, strengthening parliamentary control over the executive and the president. But the president retained substantial powers in appointing the prime minister, presiding over cabinet meetings on defense issues, and remaining as head of the Supreme Council of National Defense and commander-in-chief of the armed forces. Moreover, the president could dissolve parliament if it twice failed to produce a vote of confidence in the government.

Hungarian deputies voted against the proposed constitution, as did several Romanian deputies. Representatives of other minorities approved the constitution, indicating that they acquiesced to the policies of the ruling party. According to opponents, the constitution did not mention the rights of national minorities, but provided an exhaustive list of prohibitions. For example, at any administrative level, members of a national minority could not use their mother tongue, even if they formed an overwhelming majority in that area. The new constitution did not prohibit education in the mother tongue, but neither did it determine the degree to which such education was allowed. It left such decisions to the law, and Hungarian leaders complained about the fickleness of laws. A referendum on the constitution was held in December 1991. The Hungarian population overwhelmingly rejected the document, but the draft was passed by a majority of citizens.[5]

The parliamentary elections of September 1992 were narrowly won by President Iliescu's DNSF, with 27.72% of the vote in elections to the Chamber of Deputies (117 out of 341 seats) and 28.29% to the Senate (49 out of 100 seats). The oppositionist Democratic Convention gained 82 seats in the lower house and 34 in the Senate. The three ultra-nationalist and populist parties gained a total of 59 seats in the Chamber of Deputies and 25 seats in the Senate. As a result of their slender plurality, the DNSF (subsequently renamed the Party of Social Democracy in Romania, PSDR) entered into a coalition with several smaller parties and non-party technocrats under Prime Minister Nicolae Văcăroiu, who was installed on 5 November 1992.

Iliescu was reelected president on 20 May 1992 in a runoff with Democratic Convention candidate Emil Constantinescu, gaining 61.43% of the vote after the ultra-nationalist parties had endorsed his candidature. Iliescu promoted himself as a safe and experienced leader who would avoid the perils of rapid economic reform and guarantee social stability. At the same time, DNSF propaganda depicted the opposition as anarchic and dangerous, with their minds set on restoring pre-war property and unequal social relations. The ruling party played on pervasive public fears of rapid change and nostalgia for state protection and even authoritarian rule, especially in rural areas, where the opposition voice was barely audible.

Because of Văcăroiu's narrow margin, the new government largely relied on the support of nationalists and populists to push through any significant legislation.[6] Between 1992 and 1996, the administration did not undertake a decisive break with the tradition of bureaucratic centralism and statism.[7] Democracy remained fragile, with a strong presidential office, a fractured democratic opposition movement, and a rudimentary civil society. The opposition failed to promote an attractive message or program to the electorate, and remained torn by internal rivalries. State control was maintained over much of the economy, and the privatization that was pursued largely benefited former communist functionaries.

Corruption, nepotism, and patronage were rampant, and there were no purges of the old administrative apparatus. Although a centralized command economy no longer existed, the progress of privatization was thwarted by special interest groups. Former state property was sold off cheaply to newly formed companies controlled by well-connected members of the former communist party. This restricted market competition and the development of an entrepreneurial stratum that could strengthen the democratization process and accelerate economic progress.

Bucharest maintained a sizeable and threatening secret police service that intimidated its political opponents. It also periodically mobilized miners from the Jiu valley to attack pro-democracy demonstrators in the streets of Bucharest, as in June 1990 and in September 1991. In the 1990 assaults, miners were employed to demolish the pro-democracy demonstrations; in 1991, they were used by Iliescu to force the resignation of Prime Minister Petre Roman. Iliescu was evidently concerned that his erstwhile colleague was intent on pursuing economic reforms that would undermine the conservative bureaucracy.

With regard to the minority issue, the DAHR performance in the 1992 elections was consistent with its results in the previous national ballot. The Alliance gained 7.45% of the national vote, obtaining 27 seats out of a total of 341 in the Chamber of Deputies, and 12 seats in the Senate. The remaining national minorities garnered 0.94% of the vote and according to electoral legislation were allocated a total of 13 seats in the Chamber of Deputies, having obtained at least 5% of the average number of valid votes required nationwide to elect a deputy outright.

Following the Iliescu victory, Hungarian leaders charged that the authorities had begun a systematic campaign to place DNSF loyalists in leading positions in various national institutions, including local government, education, and the legal system, and to eliminate ethnic Hungarians from influential offices.[8] Moreover, the authorities appeared willing to exploit ethnic tensions in parts of Transylvania, using the vehicle of newly created ultranationalist parties, to distract attention from economic hardships evident in growing unemployment, rising prices, and the curtailment of welfare assistance subsidies. In what was viewed as a further provocation, in March 1993, Bucharest announced the appointment of two new ethnic Romanian prefects in the Magyar-majority counties of Harghita and Covasna, in Transylvania. Vlad Adrian Căşuneanu, the Covasna prefect, admitted to being a member of the nationalist *Vatra Românească* organization, leading to vehement protests by local Hungarians. Observers believed that the government had acceded to the demands of nationalists in the appointment of Romanian prefects, in return for their continuing parliamentary support.

A new law on political parties was passed by the parliament in April 1996. According to the previous law, only 250 members were needed to make up an official party. Under the new law, a political party required at least 10,000 members from at least fifteen of Romania's forty counties. The 1989 law was basic in its provisions, and the requirements to establish and register a party were modest, leading to the formation of over 250 parties by the mid-1990s. The new law included language on organization, registration, association of parties, funding, and cessation of party activities. The new legislation drastically reduced the number of parties to less than one hundred. According to the *România Liberă* (Independent Romania) daily, at the end of October 1997 only forty-seven political parties were registered.[9]

Romania's domestic political situation underwent dramatic changes during 1996. The governing coalition between socialists and nationalists unraveled during late 1995, and new parliamentary and presidential elections were held in November 1996. The ruling Party for Social Democracy in Romania (PSDR) began to shift towards the political center following rising public discontent. The PSDR suffered a major setback in the local elections in June 1996, when the oppositionist Democratic Convention of Romania (DCR) and the Social Democratic Union (SDU) won a majority of mayoral and local council seats in the larger cities. The PSDR proved to be stronger in the rural areas. The public was becoming increasingly disenchanted with government policy.

Prior to the 1996 general elections, the governing party broke with several nationalist groupings with which it had formed a four-party coalition in January 1995. The PSDR ended its alliance with the Socialist Labor Party (SLP) in March 1995 and with the ultra-nationalist Greater Romania Party (GRP) a few weeks later. The extremist, anti-Hungarian, Romanian National Unity Party (RNUP) was dismissed from the coalition in September 1995.[10] Major cabinet reshuffles also took place in preparation for the November 1996 elections.

During 1995 and 1996, the democratic opposition parties managed to improve their organization and outreach, and they steadily increased their popularity and influence. They were assisted by the country's poor economic record and a growing anti-incumbent mood in the country. In the local elections on 16 June 1996, opposition democratic parties and coalitions scored well in the major cities, and the ruling party, the PSDR, fared worse than independent candidates. However, the ruling party performed better in the smaller towns and in rural areas. In Bucharest, the candidate of the ruling party, former tennis star Ilie Nastase, lost to Victor Ciorbea of the opposition DCR. Candidates from the DCR won the race for the mayoral offices in all six Bucharest districts. Cluj's controversial mayor, Gheorghe Funar, of the chauvinistic of Romanian National Unity Party, qualified for another four-year term.

Meanwhile, the country's economic performance barely improved and the reform process continued to be controlled by specific political groups. Narrow political interests and widespread corruption prevented the emergence of genuine competition and a free market. Inflation rose to 45% and exports dropped by about 10% as a result of mismanagement and inefficiency. The government faced a severe challenge in closing obsolete industries, curtailing spending, limiting the wasteful bureaucracy, privatizing banks, developing capital markets, and modernizing agriculture. Romania also experienced an energy crisis. Price controls on energy and other commodities were put into effect mainly for political expediency—to garner support from a public suffering rising costs of living and wage decreases. Strikes and industrial actions became commonplace, with workers demanding wage increases and full employment.

In the November 1996 general elections, the DCR won 122 seats in the Chamber of Deputies and 53 in the Senate. This enabled the Convention to form a governing coalition that finally unseated the PSDR after its seven years in office under different party labels. In the runoff for the presidency on

17 November 1996, the DCR leader Emil Constantinescu won office by gaining 54.41% of the vote and defeating the incumbent Ion Iliescu, who received 45.6%. The PSDR gained a disappointing 91 seats in the Chamber of Deputies and 41 in the Senate. The performance of the ultra-nationalist parties remained steady, with the GRP gaining seats at the expense of the PRNU. Meanwhile, the DAHR captured the majority of the Hungarian vote, with just under 7% and 25 seats in the lower house of parliament and 11 seats in the Senate. Smaller parties outside the main coalitions fared poorly in the elections. For example, with the National Liberal Alliance failed to pass the 3% barrier.

Following the ballot, a new center-right government emerged from a coalition between the DCR (primarily the Christian Democratic Peasant Party and the National Liberal Party), the Hungarian DAHR, the Social Democratic Union (subsequently the Democratic Party) led by former Premier Petre Roman, and some smaller political formations. This coalition benefited from a 60% majority in the lower house of parliament. The new government under the premiership of Victor Ciorbea, the former mayor of Bucharest, took office in December 1996. It committed itself to an accelerated economic reform program but was faced with a number of problems. Bucharest found it difficult to explain to the Romanian public the cost of reform in terms of living standards, welfare benefits, and job security. A substantial part of the population expected rapid material benefits, which proved unrealistic given the state of the economy. Social dissatisfaction with the government's performance became noticeable.

The government coalition contained parties with competing agendas and interests that undermined the implementation of an ambitious privatization and restructuring program launched in early 1997. And political infighting increased during 1998 when the Democrats temporarily abandoned the government coalition.

Bucharest did take steps to complete the decommunization of Romanian society. In October 1997, the authorities approved a draft law allowing for public access to the files of the communist-era secret police, the *Securitate*. Parliament also restored the citizenship of former King Michael, who became an informal roving ambassador for Bucharest, petitioning for the country's membership in the North Atlantic Treaty Organization (NATO).

Prime Minister Victor Ciorbea was replaced in April 1998 by Radu Vasile, also a Christian Democrat. The governing coalition was preserved, as none of the major political parties were seeking early parliamentary elections, which could have imperiled essential reforms and undermined international confidence in Romania's progress. Premature general elections could have resulted in a freeze of the reform program while returning to power a much more economically cautious or even a protectionist political constellation. The new government pledged itself to reinvigorating the economic reform program and pushing through the stalled privatization process while conducting ministerial reshuffles.

The Democratic Convention administration was the first in the post-communist era that benefited from Hungarian participation. In fact, the DAHR became one of the strongest supporters of the governing coalition, fearing that its collapse would seriously set back the progress of the Hungarian community. DAHR policy revolved around two issues: education and administrative autonomy. Hungarian leaders sought the passage of legislation ensuring the availability of Magyar-language education at all levels, particularly in parts of Transylvania with large Hungarian populations. They also pushed for administrative devolution and territorial or local autonomy, although not based on ethnic grounds. This entailed the option of using a minority's mother tongue in any dealings with the local administration. An ordinance to this effect was also passed by the government, but the draft laws on both measures (education and autonomy) were not ratified in parliament. Any legislation needed to be passed in both houses of parliament before it became law.

Hungarian proposals on education and autonomy generated vehement opposition from Romanian ultra-nationalist parties. Hungarian leaders believed that if the DAHR were pushed out of the coalition, then nationalist rhetoric could gain ground among the opposition. Although few politicians outside the nationalist circles attacked the government on ethnic grounds, some feared that if political and social instability intensified, the ethnic card could be increasingly played by elements of the opposition. Nonetheless, Romania made progress in promoting inter-ethnic cooperation. In May 1997, parliament approved amendments to the education law eliminating certain provisions that discriminated against minority groups. Negotiations also began between Bucharest and the Hungarian government to restore a Hungarian-language university in the Transylvanian city of Cluj. In recognition of Romania's progress, the Council of Europe's Parliamentary Assembly decided to end special monitoring of Bucharest's commitment to respect human rights.

The political opposition to the centrist government found itself in disarray following the elections. The PSDR, which had controlled the previous government, split after the resignation of former Foreign Minister Teodor Meleşcanu and due to growing dissatisfaction with former Romanian president and PSDR leader Ion Iliescu. The ultra-nationalist parties initially failed to gain any significant public support or to stir up ethnic disputes.

The centrist government launched a program of economic reform in order to push through long overdue marketization. It was based on three main pillars: fiscal austerity, privatization, and openness to foreign investment. The government cut its subsidies for a range of goods and services, including fuel, public transport, and telecommunications. Bucharest also decided to close several loss-making state enterprises, including most of the large mining sector. Miners initially went on strike in protest against large-scale layoffs. But the protests were defused when the government agreed to provide substantial compensatory payments to workers. The authorities approved an ordinance for the privatization of the majority of state-owned companies and banks.

Legislation was also passed to attract foreign investment, and foreigners were permitted to purchase land and real estate.

Romania made impressive progress in the international arena. Relations with Hungary continued to improve, and in March 1997, Bucharest signed a basic treaty of friendship and cooperation with Ukraine, renouncing all claims to former Romanian territory that was incorporated in Soviet Ukraine at the close of World War II. Romania also became a member of the Central European Free Trade Agreement and strengthened its ties with the European Union. Because of the progress of its domestic reforms and the restructuring of its armed forces, Romania became a contender for NATO membership. Although the country was excluded from the first round of enlargement, Washington signaled that Romania remained a front-runner for the planned second round of expansion.

Throughout the 1990s, Romania's relations with most of its neighbors continued to improve. Bucharest participated in several trilateral and multilateral regional initiatives in such areas as organized crime fighting, trade promotion, and infrastructure development. In May 1999, Pope John Paul II visited Romania in the first papal visit to a predominantly Orthodox Christian country. The main purpose of the trip was to improve relations between the Greek Catholic (Uniate) and Orthodox churches, whose disputes over church property heightened social tensions in parts of the country.

Allegations of security service ties and collaboration with the Ceauşescu dictatorship also figured in the country's political struggles. In September 1997, Foreign Minister Adrian Severin claimed that he was in possession of documents proving that editors of important daily newspapers were working for foreign secret services and that two political party leaders were spies financed by intelligence services abroad. He also claimed that some of Romania's most prominent human rights activists were ex-informers of the *Securitate* and that a number of those prominent in the fight against corruption had themselves been involved in illegal affairs and were now being blackmailed.[11] An inquiry carried out by the two Romanian information services and the National Defense Council found no evidence supporting of Severin's allegations.

Several cabinet members called on Severin to resign, including the Christian and Democratic National Peasants' Party (CDNPP) General Secretary, Radu Vasile. Severin finally resigned on 23 December 1997. The resignation of Transport Minister Traian Băsescu also added to the crisis, as Băsescu had sharply criticized the prime minister, reflecting profound divergences in the ruling coalition. Although the coalition leaders hoped that Băsescu's resignation would bring about the long-awaited thaw, the conflict carried on until late January 1998, when the Democratic Party withdrew all its remaining ministers from the cabinet.[12] The coalition government suffered from political disputes between the constituent parties, which undermined its reform program. In March 1998, Prime Minister Victor Ciorbea resigned after one of the coalition partners, the DP, left the government. Ciorbea's critics within the major coalition party, the CDNPP, charged that he was too weak and ineffectual to push through the necessary economic reforms. In April 1998, Radu Vasile, also from the CDNPP, was appointed the new prime minister, and the Democratic Party rejoined the government.

Bucharest was criticized by the international community for not doing enough to combat crime and corruption or to demilitarize its police force. Some human rights organizations also claimed that the government had failed to prevent discrimination and public hostility against the large Roma population. Disputes were also evident between Romanian officials and the large Hungarian community. The country's ambitious economic reform program stagnated, and the government was criticized for delaying the privatization program. Because of the absence of political consensus, Romania's economic transformation slowed down in the late 1990s. Officials remained nervous about the social implications of their reform measures. They feared public protests against financial austerity and the planned closure of several state enterprises. The privatization and restructuring of several major state industries was obstructed despite the government's commitment to a market economy.

Romania's economy continued to stagnate largely because of bureaucratic interference in the structural reform program. Insufficient foreign investment and the pervasiveness of corruption and inefficiency exacerbated the government's economic problems. The war in neighboring Serbia also negatively affected the Romanian economy, especially as blockages along the Danube River led to a major loss of income from trade with Western Europe. The closure of loss-making state-subsidized enterprises led to some serious protests by Romanian workers. Plans to close about 140 coal mines in the Jiu valley region in order to meet the requirements for further International Monetary Fund (IMF) loans led to miners' demonstrations and violent clashes with security forces. Miners' leader Miron Cosma was arrested in February 1999 for inciting unrest.

The popularity of the opposition parties increased in opinion polls because of widespread anger with economic austerity and rising unemployment. By the beginning of 2000, former president Ion Iliescu, leader of the PSDR, was well ahead of President Emil Constantinescu in all opinion surveys. Presidential and parliamentary elections took place on 26 November 2000 and resulted in a collapse of the Democratic Convention coalition. The CDNPP was eliminated from parliament; the PSDR received 36.6% of the vote for the Chamber of Deputies and 37.1% in the Senate, and formed a new government. The ultra-nationalist Greater Romania Party became the second largest parliamentary group, gaining 19.5% of the vote to the lower house and 21% to the Senate. Both the National Liberal Party and the Democratic Party captured less than 10% of the vote.

Iliescu was elected President in the second round of balloting, on 10 December 2000, with 66.83% of the vote, defeating the GRP's nationalist leader Vadim Tudor, who took 33.17%. The unexpected popularity of the GRP caused dismay among democrats and minority leaders who feared a turn toward ethnic confrontation. Tudor had stimulated significant appeal among young people frustrated with government policies, and he performed well in parts of Transylvania. The new government inherited a difficult economic situation and the prospect of losing its international standing if it implemented any authoritarian, populist, or nationalist measures. The administration of Prime Minister Adrian Nastase consequently committed itself to respecting human and minority rights and the pursuit of market reform and international integration.

POLITICAL PARTIES

Socialists and Social Democrats

Social Democratic Union (SDU)
Uniunea Social Democrat (USD)

On 27 September 1995, the Democratic Party (DP) and the Social Democratic Party of Romania (SDPR), which left the Democratic Convention of Romania a year before, signed an accord on setting up an alliance known as the Social Democratic Union (SDU). Conceived as an alliance for an unlimited period of time, the SDU was intended to act as an association between the two parties at parliamentary level and for running on common slates in the 1996 local, general, and presidential elections. The decision-making and executive forum of the SDU was the Political Coordination Council, which consisted of representatives designated by the two parties. The chairmanship was to alternate between the presidents of the DP and the SDPR.[13] According to their joint statement, the two parties supplemented each other: whereas the DP was born during the 1989 revolution, the SDPR was Romania's oldest party following the social democratic tradition.

The SDU became a member of the Socialist International in the spring of 1996. It entered the general elections in November 1996, with candidates from both parties running on common lists. It supported Petre Roman's candidature for the Romanian presidency. In the first round, Roman finished third, polling a little over 20% of the vote. After the first ballot, Roman and Emil Constantinescu signed a protocol in which Roman pledged to support the latter in the second ballot, in exchange for the presidency of the Romanian Senate, the second highest position in the state. According to the constitution, if the president of the country becomes incapacitated, the president of the Senate takes over the presidential duties for a limited period of time. The protocol also specified the SDU ministries in the next government, including those of Defense, Foreign Affairs, Work and Social Protection, and Transportation.[14] Constantinescu subsequently won the Romanian presidency with 54% of the vote.

Democratic Party–National Salvation Front (DP-NSF)
Partidul Democrat–Frontul Salvării Naționale (PD-FSN)

The National Salvation Front assumed power after the overthrow of the Ceaușescu regime in December 1989. It was established by former Romanian Communist Party (RCP) officials and included some democratic activists. Ion Iliescu, the NSF president at the time, won 85% of the vote in the Romanian presidential election in May 1990. The Front also created a number of small satellite parties to endorse its platform and to capture votes from the opposition parties that were formed soon after the popular revolt. The NSF established its base principally among former RCP *apparatchiks* fearful of losing their positions, and among wide sectors of the population dependent on the state, to whom it promised a "third way" economic policy that would evidently avoid the disruptions of fast-paced capitalism.

The Front's chief ideologist was the Marxist and neo-communist reformer Silviu Brucan, who was opposed to a multi-party political system. However, after the general elections, the NSF moved away from its "supra-party" concept toward a clearer social democratic orientation.[15] It claimed to advocate Western-style social democracy, and in 1991 the Front's leadership approved a free market reform program entitled "A Future for Romania," which was presented by Prime Minister Roman. At its third national convention in March 1992, the National Salvation Front split into two parties: the Democratic National Salvation Front (DNSF) led by Ion Iliescu, and a renewed National Salvation Front (NSF) led by Petre Roman. Other prominent NSF leaders included Caius Dragomir, a 1992 presidential candidate, and Radu Berceanu, vice president of the Chamber of Deputies.

Iliescu's party, the DNSF, won the September 1992 parliamentary elections. The NSF ran a distant fourth in the national presidential poll in September 1992, when Roman refused to campaign as a candidate. It won only 10% of the legislative votes, placing it behind the DNSF and the DCR. The NSF received most of its support from the agricultural and industrial bureaucracies and the civil administration, especially outside the major cities. Between 1992 and 1996, some parties changed names in an effort to redefine their identity. The Democratic National Salvation Front became the Party of Social Democracy in Romania (PSDR), and the National Salvation Front became the Democratic Party (DP). On 28 May 1993, the National Salvation Front convention decided on a merger with the Democratic Party. The official name of this fusion became the Democratic Party (DP), with "NSF" placed in parentheses after the name. The symbol of the party was a rose, intended to indicate its allegiance to European social democracy; and its publications included the daily newspaper *Azi* (Today).

In February 1996, Roman accepted nomination as the DP-NSF candidate in the November presidential elections, proclaiming his intention to stand on a social democratic platform. He gained only 20.53% of the vote and was eliminated in the first round, on 3 November 1996. For the accompanying legislative balloting, the DP-NSF entered into the Social Democratic Union, which gained a total of 53 lower house and 23 Senate seats. Meanwhile, the party was formally admitted as a consultative member of the Socialist International, and it entered the new coalition government in Romania.

The Ciorbea government was pitched into turmoil after the DP issued what amounted to an ultimatum for the prime minister to resign. The Social Democrats blamed Ciorbea for errors they said had dashed the hopes of twenty-two million Romanians to improve their living standards—the lowest in Eastern Europe. DP-NSF leader Roman pledged to remain within the coalition, provided a new government was formed by the end of March 1998. Other parties in the coalition, led by the Christian Democrats, backed the premier and dismissed Roman's maneuvers as hypocritical.

On 2 February 1998, the remaining ministers belonging to the DP sent a common letter of resignation to the prime minister. The CDNPP and the DP drafted an agreement on political collaboration and on the way the ruling coalition would function. Its leadership claimed that the party would back the reform legislation in parliament only if it was in accordance with its program. A protocol setting out the terms on which the minority coalition partner, the DP, would continue providing parliamentary support to the government was prepared. The DP subsequently suspended its demand for the premier's resignation. In the November 2000 parliamentary elections, the DP evidently suffered in public opinion as a result of its coalition with the DCR government, and managed to gain only 7% of the popular vote.

Party of Social Democracy in Romania (PSDR)
Partidul Democrației Sociale din România (PDSR)

The Party of Social Democracy in Romania (PSDR) was formed as the "presidential" party on 10 July 1993, through the merger of the Democratic National Salvation Front (DNSF), the Romanian Social Democratic Party (RSDP), and the Republican Party (RP). As a more centrist party favoring free enterprise, the RP had been formed in 1991, through the amalgamation of the existing Republican Party and the Social Liberal Party. Less reform-oriented than their colleagues, a number of pro-Iliescu parliamentary deputies, styling themselves as NSF–22 December (the date Ceaușescu was overthrown in 1989), withdrew from the parent group in March 1992 and registered under the DNSF label in April. The new formation won a plurality of seats in both houses of parliament in the September 1992 balloting, with approximately 28% of the vote for each parliamentary chamber. It also helped to secure the re-election of Iliescu as the country's president on 11 September 1992.

The PSDR was essentially a leftist formation that had once been closely allied with the original National Salvation Front. Its first chairman, Marian Cîrciumaru, was expelled in August 1990 for a variety of misdeeds. The PSDR's membership and support base was primarily among the traditional working class and among pensioners and state employees. Its welfarist platform called for social security, social equality, and economic parity. Having previously headed a minority government, the PSDR in August 1994 drew the nationalist Romanian National Unity Party (RNUP) into a coalition, attracting support also from the nationalist Greater Romanian Party (GRP) and the Socialist Labor Party (SLP).

In January 1995, the four governing parties—the PSDR, the Romanian National Unity Party (RNUP), the Greater Romania Party (GRP), and the Socialist Labor Party (SLP)—signed a quadripartite agreement to formalize their coalition. During the next year, tensions within the coalition increased, and the PSDR was accused of ignoring the interests of other parties. In October 1995, the PSDR renounced its cooperation with the nationalists.[16] The GRP and the RNUP left the governing coalition in March and September 1996 respectively, while the PSDR continued to govern as a minority government until the general elections in November 1996, after which the Văcăroiu government was replaced in December 1996.[17]

The PSDR adopted a new political program at its national conference in June 1997. The party defined itself as a modern, social democratic, center-left party.[18] After being the governing party between 1992 and 1996, the PSDR became the main opposition party after the November 1996 elections. It gained only 41 seats in the Senate and 91 in the Chamber of Deputies. This forced the party to resort to a process of restructuring and reorganization, of changing its strategy and style in order to "regain the trust of the people."

On 21 June 1997, the former Foreign Minister Teodor Meleşcanu and former Deputy Prime Minister Mircea Coşea resigned from the PSDR, as they had failed to convince party chairman Iliescu to agree to a compromise solution whereby neither the party's reformist group (headed by Meleşcanu) nor its conservative group (headed by Adrian Năstase) would be represented in the leadership team elected at the party's national conference. Two other members of the reformist group, Iosif Boda and Viorel Sălăgean, were expelled from the PSDR by their respective Bucharest branches on 20 June 1997, and a fifth member, deputy Marian Enache, resigned from the party.[19]

On 17 January 1997, a report on the activities of the party's national council, delivered by executive president Adrian Năstase, asserted that the PSDR needed a radical change of strategy, organization, action, and leadership. The report analyzed the causes of the party's defeat in the national elections and claimed there was a "big discrepancy" between the political priorities of the government and people's expectations.[20] The party elected a new leadership at its June 1997 national conference.[21] It included Ion Iliescu (president), Adrian Năstase (vice president), and Miron Tudor Mitrea (secretary-general). The party's major party publication was the daily *Dimineaţa* (Morning).

In opinion polls preceding the November 2000 parliamentary elections, the party clearly led all other political contenders, having benefited from widespread dissatisfaction with the incumbent administration. The PSDR easily won the parliamentary ballot with over 37% of the popular vote and formed the core of the next coalition government.

Socialist Party (SP)
Partidul Socialist (PS)

The Socialist Party (SP) was launched on 28 August 1997 and was led by Tudor Mohora. Its objective was to establish a broader center-left bloc that was not linked to the ex-communist structures. Mohora believed that the left had been severely divided after the 1989 revolution because of personality conflicts and an inability to find an appropriate social niche.[22] The party program focused on assisting the underprivileged sectors of society. This included the implementation of a monthly indexation system of wages and pensions and a rise in the minimum wage tied to 60% of the average wage. Where state corporations were privatized, the SP wanted 30% of their capital to be distributed to the population in the form of shares. The establishment of a free land market should take into account the maximum limits of land property of between 10 and 50 hectares. Institutionally, the Socialist Party sought a referendum to restructure the Romanian parliament into a single chamber and to reduce the number of ministries from twenty-four to ten. It also sought a stronger role for the country's labor unions. The party program was directed at halting the "pauperization of the population" and "ensuring a decent living standard."[23]

Alliance for Romania (AFR)
Alianţa pentru România (APR)

The Alliance for Romania (AFR) was established in January 1997 as a center-left party positioning itself to the right of the PSDR, with a social democratic political philosophy. The AFR was created shortly after the PSDR's national conference, when a part of the dissatisfied membership left, including several parliamentarians such as Iosif Boda and the party's spokesperson Teodor Meleşcanu, the ex-foreign minister.[24] AFR established initiative committees in 36 counties and held its first national meeting on 26 July 1997 in Bucharest. The party reportedly gathered 16,000 signatures necessary for its registration. Many of the initiative committee members present at the meeting were former PSDR members, but others were people who had not belonged to any political organization. In its economic program, the AFR's priorities were privatization, restructuring, and modernization. In the social domain, its principal goal was to halt pauperization. AFR leaders claimed to be reaching out to other political alliances and to civil society.[25]

Romanian Social Democratic Party (RSDP)
Partidul Social Democrat Român (PSDR)

The left-of-center Romanian Social Democratic Party (RSDP), descended from the historic party founded in 1893, but was forced to merge with the communists in 1948. It was recreated in late 1989 and stood on the ticket of the Democratic Convention in the September 1992 general elections. The party won ten Chamber seats and one Senate seat. Its leaders included Sergiu Cunescu, president, and Adrian Dumitriu, honorary president.

Among other, smaller social democratic formations were the Traditional Social Democratic Party of Romania (TSDPR) *(Partidul Social Democrat Tradiţional din România, PSDTR)*, formed in 1991 by the merger of the Traditional Social Democratic Party (TSDP) and the National Democratic Party (NDP). The NDP achieved some prominence following the June 1990 official crackdown on anti-communist demonstrations in Bucharest. Its leadership included Nica Leon, President Eugen Brânzan, and Secretary-General Bogdan Pascu.

Liberals

Democratic Convention of Romania (DCR)
Convenţie Democrat din România (CDR)

Based on the eight-party Democratic Union (DU) founded in 1990, the Democratic Convention of Romania (DCR) was launched as an anti-NSF alliance of parties prior to the local elections in February 1992. By embracing 18 parties and organizations, it ran second in the 1992 parliamentary balloting, while its nominee, Emil Constantinescu, was runner-up to Ion Iliescu in the presidential poll. The ethnic Hungarian movement was also affiliated with the DCR, although it presented a separate list in the September 1992 elections. In June 1995, the DCR rejected Hungarian overtures for political cooperation on the grounds that the major Hungarian alliance had become too nationalistic.

In the November 1996 elections, the following parties entered the ballot under the DCR logo: the Christian and Democratic National Peasants' Party (CDNPP), the National Liberal Party (NLP), the National Liberal Party–Democratic Convention (NLP-DC), the Romanian Ecologist Party (REP), the Romanian Alternative Party (RAP), and the Ecologist Federation of Romania (EFR). Besides political parties, the DCR also included grassroots organizations such as the Civic Alliance and the Former Political Detainees Association. The DCR entered the 1996 general elections on a platform called the "Contract with Romania." As the Convention leader, Constantinescu, was elected as Romania's president, Ion Diaconescu, the president of the CDNPP, was elected DCR leader. In the November 1996 general elections, the DCR gained over 30% of the popular vote, with a total of 122 seats in the lower house of parliament and 53 seats in the Senate.[26]

Apart from the issues of restructuring its activity and defining its role, DCR leaders had to cope with the different positions of its constituent parties on numerous policy questions. For example, the Romanian Alternative Party (RAP), one of the DCR members, wanted to issue a right-wing manifesto that CDNPP President Ion Diaconescu and National Liberal Party (NLP) leader Mircea Ionescu Quintus opposed, thus creating disputes within the alliance.[27]

Throughout the period between 1997 and the elections of November 2000, the DCR was subject to intensive personal and political clashes within the governing coalition that affected the DCR's unity and coherence. The DCR collapsed during the parliamentary elections in November 2000, and only some of its constituent organizations were able to gain parliamentary seats. Large sectors of the public were dissatisfied with its term in office, and accused the DCR-led coalition of failing to resolve the country's economic problems and of turning a blind eye to official corruption.

Civic Alliance Party (CAP)
Partidul Alianţei Civice (PAC)

The Civic Alliance (CA) was initially founded as a non-governmental organization (NGO) in December 1990 by a group of intellectuals and trade unionists to provide an extra-parliamentary umbrella for post-communist opposition parties, in partial emulation of East Germany's New Forum and Czechoslovakia's Civic Forum. The CA defined itself as neo-liberal, based on moral, civic, and democratic values. At its second congress, in July 1991, it voted to reformulate itself as a political party under the leadership of literary critic and prominent civic activist Nicolae Manolescu. It became the Civic Alliance Party (CAP) in August 1991. The party was first chaired by Marian Munteanu, a student leader who had spent time in prison for his political activities. Munteanu left the CAP after adopting increasingly strident nationalist positions. Other prominent leaders of the party included Stelian Tănase, Ana Blandiana, and Nicolae Ţăran. The CAP managed to win seats in several major cities during the local elections in February 1992 (including Bucharest, Timişoara, Braşov, Arad, Sibiu, and Constanţa), but then joined the Democratic Convention coalition for the September 1992 general elections.

In 1995, the party was weakened by the departure of a splinter group that eventually joined the National Liberal Party (NLP). Until March 1995, the CAP was part of the DCR and formed a joint parliamentary group with both the Liberal Party-'93 and the PSDR in the Senate. The CAP left the Democratic Convention in 1995 as a result of its discontent with the political decisions taken by DCR leaders.[28] For electoral purposes, the CAP, together with the Liberal Party-'93, established the National Liberal Alliance (NLA), which backed Manolescu for the presidency.[29] However, both the Alliance and its presidential candidate scored poorly in the elections, garnering less than 2% of the vote, and did not enter the parliament.

On 28 February 1998, the national councils of the NLP and the CAP approved an agreement reached by their respective leaders, Mircea Ionescu-Quintus and Nicolae Manolescu, according to which the CAP was to merge into the NLP and Manolescu was to chair of the NLP national council. Other CAP leaders were to be co-opted into the NLP's leading bodies. A joint unification congress was held at the end of March 1998. The NLP national council rejected a proposal by its vice chairman, Viorel Catarama, for setting up a Liberal Federation that would have also included the Liberal Party (LP) and the NLP–Câmpeanu wing, asserting that a liberal unification could be achieved only through mergers with and within the NLP.

Liberal Party (LP)
Partidul Liberal (PL)

The Liberal Party was formed through a merger between two center-right formations—the National Liberal Party–Democratic Convention (NLP-DC) and the Liberal Party-'93—concluded at a congress in Bucharest on 14 June 1997. NLP-DC leader Nicolae Cerveni was elected chairman, and LP-'93 leader Dinu Patriciu, executive chairman, of the new grouping. A rival NLP-DC group headed by Senator Aleksandru Popovici did not recognize the merger. Cerveni stated that the new party would continue to be a member of the Democratic Convention of Romania (DCR). But Mircea Ionescu-Quintus, whose National Liberal Party was the largest liberal formation within the DCR, underscored that its membership had first to be approved by the DCR's joint leadership.[30]

Earlier, in May 1997, the NLP-DC, the LP-'93, and the NLP-Câmpeanu announced that they would merge. NLP-Câmpeanu decided not to join, and the NLP-DC practically split over the planned unification. NLP-DC Senator Popovici was backed by the DCR in its opposition to Cerveni, who was in favor of a merger of all liberal parties. The NLP-DC, the LP-'93, and the NLP-Câmpeanu had already formed the National Liberal Union (NLU) (*Uniunea Naţionala Liberala, UNL*) in December 1996 and had taken part as an independent force in the November 1996 general elections. Although opinion polls were promising, the liberals proved unable to overcome the electoral threshold.

The NLU's rank and file were mainly intellectuals. It also included a parliamentary club and a youth organization. The NLU's leadership included Traian Tomescu, Horia Rusu, Dinu Patriciu, Dinu Zamfirescu, Adrian Moroianu, Niculae Cerveni, and Liviu Negoita. Ioan Ghise, the mayor of Braşov, was elected president of the NLU's Forum of Locally Elected Representatives, and Catalin Marculescu was elected president of the LP Youth Organization.[31]

Cerveni voiced his "openness to any concession for the idea of liberal unification."[32] But the liberal movement in Romania remained seriously divided. Apart from the two parties that merged, there was also in existence a National Liberal Party (NLP) led by Mircea Ionescu Quintus and represented in parliament, and which participated in the November 1996 elections within the DCR; another National Liberal Party (NLP), led by Radu Câmpeanu; and the Christian Democratic National Liberal Party (CDNLP), a dissenting wing, led by Popovici.

Liberal Party 1993 (LP-'93)
Partidul Liberal 1993 (PL-'93)

The Liberal Party (LP-'93) derived from the youth wing and several splinter groups of the National Liberal Party (NLP), which remained in the DCR when the main NLP withdrew in May 1992. A faction of the NLP youth wing, calling itself the New Liberal Party, returned to the NLP in February 1993. Most of the ex-NLP elements in the DCR formally united and adopted the LP-'93 label in May 1994. Having absorbed a liberal faction of the Civic Alliance Party in June 1993, the LP-'93 claimed to have twenty-five deputies in parliament. Its leaders included Horia Rusu, the president, and Daniela Crăsnaru, chair of the national council. Subsequently, the LP-'93 merged with a faction of the NLP-DC and formed the Liberal Party (LP) (*Partidul Liberal, PL*). After Constantinescu was nominated the second time for Romanian president, the LP-'93 left the DCR, having failed to get its preferred candidate nominated.[33] The party was a member of the National Liberal Alliance during the November 1996 general elections but did not achieve the 3% electoral threshold for admittance to parliament.

National Liberal Party–Democratic Convention (NLP-DC)
Partidul National Liberal–Convenţia Democratica (PNL-CD)

Rifts within the liberal parties have been frequent in Romania. For example, a dissenting wing of the National Liberal Party, the National Liberal Party–Democratic Convention (NLP-DC), emerged in February 1997 after unilaterally suspending party chairman Nicolae Cerveni. The dissidents opposed a protocol of unification Cerveni had signed with several liberal parties that were not members of the DCR. Having the support of the DCR leadership, the dissenting group called a special party conference, which elected Aleksandru Popovici (a senator) as its interim president. A dispute between NLP-DC Chairman Cerveni and Vice-Chairs Popovici and Sorin Stănescu over the latter's decision to take part in the DCR, led to the expulsion of these two party board members.

National Liberal Party (NLP)
Partidul Naţional Liberal (PNL)

Founded in 1848, the National Liberal Party (NLP) was a right-of-center party that endorsed a free market economy. The NLP had been disbanded in 1948 by the communist regime but was reorganized and registered in 1990.[34] It called for a resumption of the throne by exiled King Michael, although it advised against his return prior to 1990. In 1992, the ex-king declined nomination as the NLP's presidential candidate. The party had been weakened in 1990 by the departure of a splinter group–the Liberal Union (LU) *(Uniunea Liberala, UL)*. A founding member of the DCR, the NLP withdrew its support in 1992, shortly before the general elections, although two splinter groups, including the youth wing, refused to endorse the action. Those who chose to stay in the DCR in April 1992 formed the NLP-DC.

An NLP congress in February 1993 approved a merger with the New Liberal Party, consisting of former NLP elements that had broken from what became the LP-'93. They elected Mircea Ionescu-Quintus as chairman. The decision was contested by the outgoing Chairman, Radu Câmpeanu, who decided to set up another party, the NLP-Câmpeanu. In 1995, the NLP finalized its merger with the New Liberal Party and absorbed a faction of the Civic Alliance Party. It thus regained parliamentary representation of around twelve seats. Failing to pass the electoral threshold on its own, the NLP rejoined the DCR in December 1994. Having failed to win representation in the November 1996 parliamentary elections, the NLP groupings outside the DCR reached agreement in principle with the DCR's liberal components to form a unified Liberal Party in 1997. Its leaders included Mircea Ionescu-Quintus, president; Vice-Presidents Viorel Catarama, Dan Lăzărescu, Călin Popescu-Tăriceanu, and Radu Boroianu; and Secretary General Gabriel Bărbătescu.[35] Câmpeanu became the leader of a dissident faction. In the November 2000 parliamentary elections, the NLP gained just over 7% of the popular vote and lost significant public support, primarily because of its association with the DCR government.

Christian Democrats

Christian Democratic National Peasants' Party (CDNPP)
Partidul Naţional Ţărănesc-Creştin şi Democrat (PNŢCD)

Founded in the pre-war period and banned by the communists, the National Peasants' Party (NPP) refused to cooperate with the National Salvation Front because of the large number of former communist officials within NSF ranks. Prior to the 1990 general election, members of the "historic" NPP agreed to merge with a newly formed group of Christian democrats under the CDNPP rubric. Ion Raţiu, a former exile, ran for the Romanian presidency in 1990 but won only 4% of the vote. The party's platform called for a parliamentary democracy, a market economy, and the return of the Republic of Moldova to full Romanian control. Its domestic focus was on the privatization of state farms and far-reaching land reforms including the return of property confiscated by the communist regime. The party obtained significant support from the agricultural sector. It also became a member of the Christian Democratic International in 1990 and the largest member of the Democratic Convention of Romania (DCR).

The party's top leadership included Corneliu Coposu, a survivor of Romania's Stalinist jails, who was elected party president. Ion Puiu became vice president; Ion Raţiu, the 1990 presidential candidate; and Valentin Gabrielescu, the party's secretary-general. The party's major publications included the *Dreptatea* (Justice) weekly. The CDNPP leadership elected at the party's second congress in January 1996 included Ion Diaconescu, president; Gabriel Ţepelea, first vice president; Radu Vasile, secretary-general; and eight other vice presidents: Nicolae Ionescu Galbeni, Ion Raţiu, Remus Opris, Mircea Ciumara, Mircea Popa Zlatna, Ulm Spineanu, Vasile Lupu, and Sorin Lepşa.

A "culture clash" between the CDNPP and the Democratic Party (DP) was evident from the inception of the DCR, and it hindered the functioning of the post-1996 government. A significant element within the DP was comprised of reform-minded, former middle-ranking communist officials, and the party's leaders were in government during 1990–1991. In contrast, the larger CDNPP was dominated by older, communist-era dissidents who were disdainful of the DP's origins and record in the early years of democratic transition. The CDNPP was split between a faction that concentrated on economic reform issues and were mainly concerned with providing effective government, and a wing that promoted specific religious, economic, and regional interests. The latter were eager to reverse communist-era measures that penalized CDNPP supporters, without regard for the effect of this on economic reform or relations with the Democratic Party.

In the November 1996 elections, the CDNPP ran within the DCR bloc. In the lower house of parliament, the coalition received 30.17% of the vote and 122 seats, and in the Senate it received 30.7%, and 53 seats. All of the opposition parties running independently would not have been able to win over Iliescu's PSDR. The CDNPP and the Democratic Party (DP) established a political coalition known as the Democratic Convention of Romania (DCR), joined by the Democratic Alliance of Hungarians in Romania (DAHR) and other opposition parties in order to win the elections. They subsequently formed a coalition government between 1996 and 2000. In the November 2000 elections, the CDNPP was eliminated from parliament, having failed to achieve the threshold for seats, and the entire party leadership subsequently resigned.

Agrarians

Agrarian Democratic Party of Romania (ADPR)
Partidul Democrat Agrar din România (PDAR)

The Agrarian Democratic Party of Romania (ADPR) was an agricultural workers' party launched in 1990. It failed to secure lower house parliamentary representation in the September 1992 elections, with only 2.90% of the vote for the Chamber of Deputies. However, it obtained five Senate seats with 3.31% of the vote. The agrarian party was an ally of the Social Democrat–led coalition government between September 1992 and June 1994. However, there was no formal coalition agreement with the governing bloc, which consisted of the Party of Social Democracy, the Romanian National Unity Party, the Greater Romania Party, and the Socialist Party of Labor.

Formerly a governing partner of the Social Democratic Party, the ADPR withdrew from the alliance in April 1994 in protest of a bill introducing an IMF-mandated land tax. On 10 August 1994, the party merged with the People's Republican Party (PRP), with the latter pledging to adhere to the statute, platform, program, and electoral logo of the ADPR. Following the merger, the PRP leader Radu Teodoru became vice president of the ADPR for propaganda issues. ADPR claims of 172,000 members followers were difficult to verify.[36]

The ADPR, the Ecological Movement, and the Humanist Party on 30 July 1996 signed a protocol founding a National Centrist Union (NCU). The document stressed that the parties' complementary platforms facilitated the inauguration of the new alliance. The Union planned to nominate a joint candidate for the presidential election and welcomed the inclusion of groups with similar political positions. The ADPR's leaders included Victor Surdu, president; Dumitru Teaci; and Valeriu Pescaru.

National Romanian Party (NRP)
Partidul Naţional Român (PNR)

The National Romanian Party (NRP) was officially set up on 14 March 1998, through a merger between the Agrarian Democratic Party of Romania and the New Romania Party. During its founding congress, delegates decided that the new centrist party with a liberal doctrine would promote a "citizen-oriented policy" that served individuals rather than group interests. Following an analysis of the current social and political situation, the leaders of the two founding parties, Mihai Berca and Ovidiu Trăsnea, claimed that it was indispensable that the NRP appear on the political stage so that Romania be offered a viable alternative to overcome the ongoing crisis. The NRP's steering body elected Mihai Berca, former ADPR president, as the NRP's president, while Ovidiu Trăsnea was elected honorary president. Ioan Alecu became first vice president, while Virgil Măgureanu, the former director of the Romanian Intelligence Service, was elected as the party's secretary-general.[37]

Greens

Romanian Ecologist Movement (REM)
Mişcarea Ecologista din România (MER)

The Romanian Ecologist Movement (REM) became Eastern Europe's largest environmentalist group, with a reported membership of some 60,000 people. It finished fourth in the May 1990 Chamber of Deputies elections, with 2.6 % of the vote and 12 parliamentary seats, while in the September 1992 elections a joint Ecologist List on the Democratic Convention ticket gained four lower house seats. The Movement was led by its President Toma George Maiorescu. The REM was weakened in April 1996 when a splinter faction merged with the Green Alternative Party–Ecologists. In November 1996, REM announced its endorsement of Emil Constantinescu for the presidential election runoff.[38] In the November 1996 parliamentary balloting, the REM was affiliated with the Democratic Convention of Romania, and won one seat in the lower house and one in the Senate.

Romanian Ecologist Party (REP)
Partidul Ecologist Român (PER)

The Romanian Ecologist Party (REP) was an ecological group with a substantially smaller membership than the REM, with which it initially cooperated in 1992. Formed in early 1990, the REP was mainly based in Bucharest. It strongly backed a pro-environmental program and was the smallest member of the DCR coalition. Its leaders included Chairman Otto Weber, President Iustin Drăghici, and Vice President Raluca Marinescu. Other, smaller environmentalist organizations were also active during the 1990s, including the Green Alternative Party–Ecologists (GAP-E), which supported Constantinescu in Romania's presidential elections.[39] Three ecological parties on 19 September 2000 established the Ecologist Pole, prior to the November 2000 parliamentary elections: the Romanian Ecologist Party (REP), the Green Ecological Alternative (GEA), and the Party of Ecologist Convention (PEC). They were scheduled to run on joint lists and nominate a joint presidential candidate. REP Chairman Otto Weber chaired the Ecologist Pole.

Communists

Socialist Labor Party (SLP)
Partidul Socialist al Muncii (PSM)

The Socialist Labor Party (SLP) was launched in November 1990 by former Prime Minister Ilie Verdeţ and Adrian Păunescu, the owner of several newspapers. The appearance of this neo-communist group, which promised to revive socialism as a means of restoring stability after "almost a year of anarchy," triggered a fresh wave of street demonstrations in Bucharest. The SLP won eighteen parliamentary house seats in the September 1992 elections and thereafter provided qualified support for the new government. The SLP was led by Chairman Verdeţ and Deputy Tudor Mohora, and it drew most of its supporters from among former Ceauşescu loyalists with a strong nationalist orientation. Indeed, the party was viewed as the main successor to the defunct Romanian Communist Party. The SLP garnered 3% of the vote in the September 1992 general elections and elected thirteen deputies to the Chamber of Deputies, along with five senators to the upper house of parliament.

The party supported the government of Prime Minister Nicolae Văcăroiu on various occasions; for example, during "motions of censure" sponsored by the oppositionist Democratic Convention. Together with the RNUP and the GRP, the SLP assured the minority government of the Party of Social Democracy in Romania (PSDR) of a parliamentary majority after the September 1992 elections. In the November 1996 general elections, the SLP failed to achieve the 3% threshold and did not obtain seats in the legislature. Its leadership at the time included Verdeţ, executive president, and Adrian Păunescu, the party's 1996 presidential candidate and former court poet for Ceauşescu.

In 1995, the party split, with the dissenting wing setting up the Socialist Party (SP), led by Tudor Mohora. Unlike the SLP, the SP had little chance of getting into parliament on its own. As a result, Mohora appealed for leftist unity in the country. In April 1997, the SLP and the Greater Romania Party (GRP) signed a cooperation agreement. The GRP leadership claimed that this signaled "a decisive step on the road to the unification of the true national forces in order to create a new political pole."[40]

The SP became another communist-nationalist formation, and in 1995 it established a Union of Patriotic Forces (UPF).[41] This Union included Cluj officials of the Romanian Ecologist Movement (REM), the Social Democratic Party of Romania (SDPR), the Greater Romania Party (GRP), the Socialist Party (SP), the Socialist Workers' Party (SWP), and the Romanian National Unity Party (RNUP).[42]

Nationalists

Romanian National Unity Party (RNUP)
Partidul Unităţii Naţionale Române (PUNR)

Since early 1990, a legion of ultra-radical nationalist organizations have mushroomed in the country. Some were viewed as a continuation in a new guise of the "national communist" pro-Ceauşescu orientation; others constituted new incarnations of pre-war and wartime Romanian fascist movements seeking to draw support from sectors of the population disillusioned with the consequences of economic reform and seeking a strong, authoritarian government.

Links between these two trends could not be discounted if the centrist, liberal, and civic options failed to establish strong roots among Romanian voters.

Among the more significant nationalist groupings, the RNUP was established shortly before the May 1990 elections, with links to the old communist *nomenklatura*. It originated as the political arm of the nationalist cultural organization Romanian Hearth (*Vatra Românească, VR*). Its leadership included Chairman Radu Ceontea and First Deputy Chairman Petre Burca. Both were elected at the RNUP's extraordinary national conference in May 1991. The RNUP platform bore similarity to that of the Romanian Hearth. Most members of the RNUP were also reportedly members of *Vatra*. In particular, the RNUP claimed to represent the interests of the Romanian population in Transylvania. It opposed any claims for the establishment of administrative-territorial enclaves in the region and was decidedly anti-Hungarian in its orientation.

RNUP leaders persistently spoke out for strengthening Romanian unity, for re-unification of the country in its historical boundaries, and for the "spiritual unity" of Romanians all over the world. The RNUP staged protests against the establishment of a Hungarian consulate in Cluj, claiming that this was a dangerous step toward separatism. At its extraordinary national conference in May 1991, the organization issued a report on the DAHR, the major Hungarian organization in Romania, claiming that its activities seriously endangered the unity and integrity of the Romanian state. The RNUP appealed without success to parliament to prohibit the holding of DAHR congresses.

The RNUP gained sixteen mayoralties in the February 1992 local elections and captured 4.9% of the total votes cast, as compared to 2.12% in the general elections of May 1990. President Iliescu's Democratic National Salvation Front formed electoral coalitions with the RNUP in several Transylvanian counties. Most notably, the RNUP won the mayoral office in the Transylvanian city of Cluj-Napoca, where Hungarians constituted about 25% of the population. The controversial new mayor, Gheorghe Funar, who obtained nearly 11% of the vote in the presidential race, proceeded to enact various anti-minority policies, including a ban on bilingual shop signs, street names, foreign banners, and anthems, and restrictions on freedom of assembly and Hungarian cultural and educational activities. These prohibitions sparked outrage among Magyar leaders and escalated ethnic tensions in the region.

Although the central government declared several of Funar's actions illegal, he continued to use local statutes to harass Hungarian activists. In a gesture of defiance in October 1992, the RNUP appointed Funar the party's interim president after the suspension of former president Radu Ceontea. In the general elections of September 1992, the RNUP finished fifth and captured 7.72% of the national vote, thereby electing 30 parliamentary deputies and 14 senators, indicating a worrying turn toward ultra-nationalism by a significant number of Romanian voters.[43] The party was eventually co-opted into the government coalition in August 1994 and was allotted two ministerial portfolios. Serious coalition tensions developed in mid-1995 when the RNUP demanded the foreign affairs portfolio and criticized the government for making too many concessions in seeking better relations with Hungary. After government spokesmen threatened either to continue as a minority government or to call an early election, the RNUP moderated its position and remained in the coalition.

Romania's ultra-nationalist movements sought to capture support from sectors of the population disillusioned with the deleterious effects of economic reform and seeking an authoritarian hand.[44] In the November 1996 elections, the RNUP captured seven Senate seats and 18 seats in the Chamber of Deputies. In early 1997, Valeriu Tabără was elected RNUP chairman. In October 1997, Gheorghe Funar, the former chairman of the party, was expelled, in an attempt to steer the party away from its militant nationalistic stance. The new leadership stated that the party would embrace a more centrist and neo-liberal ideology. The RNUP's national convention on 22 March 1998 confirmed the ouster of Funar as president. It also elected interim president Valeriu Tabără and removed Ioan Gavra as secretary-general.

In February 1998, Funar, the Cluj city mayor, summoned the RNUP's Extraordinary National Council prior to his official ouster from the party. The majority of speakers emphasized the need to establish a new political party bearing the name *RNUP-Funar*. Deputy Matei defined the party as one that would include the entire political spectrum, after which he claimed that the RNUP-F did not need any doctrine in its "struggle against the internationalists and Hungarists."[45] After Tabără, the acting RNUP president, removed Funar from the party, the Cluj mayor retaliated by expelling Tabără, along with ten other leaders, from the same party. The party's two splinter groups interpreted the party statute in their own way, and each claimed that the other was illegitimate.[46] Many RNUP activists, disillusioned with the party's drift toward the political center, gravitated to the more nationalist Greater Romania Party (GRP). Indeed, the GRP captured much of the former RNUP constituency on the eve of the November 2000 general elections.

Romanian Hearth (RH)
Vatra Românească (VR)

The Romanian Hearth (RH) was established in February 1990; its leader Radu Ceontea was elected executive chairman at the RH's first national conference, in May 1990. *Vatra*'s second national conference was held in Tîrgu Mureş in June 1991. Iosif Constantin Drăgan, a former Iron Guardist who financed numerous extremist activities, became honorary president of the RH. Zeno Opriş was elected president, and Ceontea, the founding president. Drăgan also headed the Marshal Antonescu League and the Marshal Antonescu Foundation, in which the GRP leader Vadim Tudor was also prominent.

The RH claimed to be a sociocultural and civic organization whose program and activities served no political party. According to its leaders, *Vatra* had no ambitions to become a party; however, it did coordinate its efforts with the RNUP, and it boasted a membership of some four million people by early 1992. *Vatra* became an ultra-nationalist organization avowedly mobilized in response to the formation of the Democratic Alliance of Hungarians in Romania (DAHR). It considered the DAHR "a kind of communist successor party" and a danger to Romanian unity. *Vatra* leaders asserted that Hungarians should have no special rights in Transylvania, but that Hungarians nonetheless enjoyed a privileged position. *Vatra* viewed Romanian nationalism as the necessary response of a small country "under pressure from a united Europe, an internationalized world," which was allegedly diluting "national culture."

Vatra considered proposals for separate Hungarian schools in Transylvania a threat to Romania's position in the region, and demanded overt Hungarian loyalty to Romania's territorial integrity. *Vatra* helped organize anti-Magyar demonstrations in March 1990 to protest against celebrations of the Hungarian national holiday. *Vatra* was allegedly behind the Tîrgu Mureş disturbances in March 1990, which involved violent clashes between Romanian and Hungarian residents. RH leaders were suspected of maintaining relations with the government and the ruling National Salvation Front. But the RH was also a harsh critic of the Romanian government's performance, alleging that the NSF had adopted an overly conciliatory approach toward minority groups. On the other hand, according to Ceontea, NSF members constituted a majority of RH members, while *Vatra* leaders encouraged their electorate to vote for the Front in the general elections of May 1990.

The RH supported Moldova's declaration of independence and pledged to bring all Romanians inside the same frontier. *Vatra* established two publishing houses, one named *Vatra Românească* and the other *Ţara Noastra* (Our Country), in order to spread its propaganda. During 1991, its leaders demanded the passage of a new Romanian constitution without special rights for minorities, and became increasingly aggressive in their anti-minority stance. In February 1992, the RH escalated its anti-Hungarian campaign, calling for the termination of Hungarian-language radio and television programs and the annulment of the cultural treaty signed between Bucharest and Budapest, because it was allegedly "anti-Romanian."

The influence of *Vatra*'s nationalist ideas evidently grew in the judicial system in parts of Transylvania as well as in the Romanian army. The RNUP and the Romanian Hearth reportedly benefited from high-level military support, especially in the Romanian Third Army, based in Transylvania. The links between the army and nationalist forces were displayed during the local elections in Cluj in February 1992, when the commander of the Third Army, General Paul Cheler, appeared to infringe on article 40 of the Romanian constitution, that prevented the army from involvement in politics. He accused the Democratic Convention of proposing to dismember the country, in line with similar nationalistic statements he had made in *Scutul Patriei* (The Shield of the Homeland), the weekly newspaper of the Transylvanian Army.

RNUP candidate Gheorghe Funar declared that the Romanian army should be ready to act as the "right arm of the RNUP." During the election campaign, RH representatives regularly visited military bases to talk to soldiers, and *Vatra*-produced films were shown to recruits. As a result, Romanian Hearth and RNUP candidates reportedly obtained the major share of votes on military bases throughout Transylvania.[47] The RH stood in the November 1996 general elections but received less than 4% of the vote.

Several openly monarchist groupings also emerged in Romania. Some had nationalist tendencies; others were essentially liberal or Christian democratic and called for the restoration of a constitutional monarchy. The latter included the Liberal Monarchist Party of Romania (LMPR) (*Partidul Liberal Monarhist din România, PLMR*), led by Dan Cernovodeanu, and the *România Viitoare* (Future of Romania) movement. Although King Michael was allowed to visit the country on a number of occasions, only a small minority of citizens reportedly favored the establishment of a constitutional monarchy.

Greater Romania Party (GRP)
Partidul România Mare (PRM)

The Greater Romania Party (GRP) was established in May 1991 by a group of journalists writing for *România Mare* (Great Romania), a nationalist magazine created in June 1990. The founders were the chief editor of the magazine, Corneliu Vadim Tudor, and Eugen Barbu, who died in 1993. Both were writers renowned for their conspicuous contribution to hagiography under Ceauşescu as well as their links with the *Securitate* security police. The GRP became a strictly hierarchical organization, in many ways resembling the defunct Romanian Communist Party. By October 1990, the editors of *România Mare* claimed a circulation of some 600,000, making it one of the most widely read weeklies in the country. The GRP was widely viewed as the most extremist, nationalistic, chauvinistic, and anti-Semitic political group in Romania. GRP leaders believed that Romania's national unity and sovereignty were threatened from both within and outside the country, and they denounced the Romanian government for its inability to combat the danger.

The GRP disseminated propaganda against the Hungarian minority, which it believed was taking steps to truncate Romania; it viewed the DAHR (Democratic Alliance of Hungarians in Romania) as an essentially "terrorist organization." According to its spokesmen, Hungarian young people in Romania were "guided" by the Union of Hungarian Democratic Youth and led by the DAHR, which allegedly received orders from Hungary—a country that in turn, purportedly carried out the orders of the United States. *România Mare* demanded the elimination of the DAHR and the deportation of its members.

In October 1991, the party issued a statement that "the Romanian Army will once and for all cool down the hot-headed Horthyites of Hungary, if it is forced to enter Budapest for a third time." *România Mare*'s articles against Jews and Hungarians were condemned belatedly by President Iliescu in August 1991, following intense Western criticism. In the September 1992 elections, the GRP gained 16 deputies to the lower house of parliament, capturing 3.8% of the vote, and six senatorial posts. At the party's first congress in March 1993, Vadim Tudor demanded a crackdown on the DAHR, accusing it of plotting to dismember Romania. He also praised Ceauşescu for being a Romanian patriot and described the 1989 revolution as an "armed attack" against the country by Hungary and the former Soviet Union. The GRP unanimously re-elected Tudor as party chairman while adopting new statutes and a revised program.[48]

From mid-1994 onward, the GRP gave support to the incumbent government coalition led by the Social Democrats. Party membership climbed to about 32,000 people by the mid-1990s, with a further 5,000 in its youth organization. On 13 March 1997, the Romanian Senate stripped Vadim Tudor of his parliamentary immunity because of his continuously provocative statements and actions. This move caused senators representing the ruling coalition to walk out of Senate debates. There were also persistent reports that the GRP was seeking an alliance with the Socialist Labor Party (SLP) in what some commentators described as the "Red Quadrangle."[49]

Support for the GRP continued to grow in the late 1990s as a result of several factors: the virtual disappearance of significant rival nationalist groupings, public anger with the performance of the incumbent government, and Vadim Tudor's charismatic populism and messianism disseminated through the mass media. The GRP gained 21% of the vote in the November Senate elections and 19.5% in the lower house elections, thus becoming the second largest party in parliament. The victorious PSDR claimed that it would not enter into any coalition with the GRP, as such a prospect could destabilize and isolate the country. Vadim Tudor finished second to Iliescu in the first round of the presidential ballot but was defeated in the second round on 10 December 2000.

Party of National Right (PNR)
Partidul Dreapta Naţională (PDN)

The Party of National Right (PNR) was originally launched in April 1992 by the journalist Radu Sorescu, and its founding manifesto was published in the first issue of *Noua Dreaptă* (New Right) in early 1993. The party called for the creation of an "ethnocratic state" which would exclude all national minorities that refused to be assimilated by the Romanian nation. Sorescu embraced the "ethnocratic" doctrines of inter-war writer and philosopher Nichifor Crainic. Sorescu resigned as PNR leader in 1994 and was replaced by Aurelian Pavelescu. The PNR briefly obtained a seat in parliament in 1995 when the former Deputy Chairman of the RNUP, Cornel Brahas, defected to the PNR. Brahas was a former informer of the Ceauşescu secret police. The party claimed a membership of some 5,800 and branches in ten Romanian counties. It was avidly anti-Semitic and xenophobic and launched vicious press attacks on an assortment of "internal enemies" of the Romanian nation.[50]

Brahas was expelled from the PNR in 1996 after being accused of embezzling election campaign funds. Soon thereafter he set up his own Romanian Right Party (RRP), which was joined by Ion Coja in December 1997. Coja was a Holocaust denier and apologist for the fascist Iron Guard; he had switched from the National Salvation Front to the RNUP and to the Democratic Agrarian Party, all the while being a deputy chairman of *Vatra Românească*. He was also known to have close ties with the neo-Iron Guard "nests" headed by Şerban Suru.

Former premier Radu Vasile and ten parliamentary deputies resigned from the Christian Democratic National Peasants' Party (CDNPP) and joined the extra-parliamentary PNR in February 2000. Their intention was to change the party's name to the "Popular Party" and to compete in the national elections in November 2000. Vasile was elected chairman of the party, which subsequently changed its name to the Romanian People's Party (RPP). The party's manifesto espoused nationalism, close links with the Orthodox Church, authoritarianism, and the "rejection of multi-culturalism."

Romanian National Party (RNP)
Partidul Naţionala din România (PNR)

In February 2000, an extraordinary congress of the Romanian National Party (RNP) elected former Romanian Intelligence Service chief Virgil Magureanu as the party's chairman. Magureanu, who was a driving force behind this nationalist movement, took over the post of acting chairman after former chairman Viorel Catarama was forced to withdraw in 1999. The RNP claimed that it represented a "third way" in Romanian politics between left and right but was ready to forge alliances with other formations for parliamentary elections. In July 2000, the RNP agreed to merge with the RNUP.[51] Both parties fared poorly in the June local elections. The new formation was called the National Alliance (NA). Its chairman was the new party's candidate in the November 2000 presidential elections.

National Reunification Party (NRP)
Partidul Pentru Reunire Naţionala (PRN)

The National Reunification Party (NRP) was organized by former Chairman of the Moldovan Council of Ministers Mircea Druc, who was replaced as chairman of the Moldovan Popular Front in 1993 after having left the Republic of Moldova to become a Romanian citizen. The NRP declared its support for Emil Constantinescu's candidacy for the Romanian presidency in November 1996.[52]

A similar formation, the Romanian Popular Front (RPF) *(Frontul Popular Român, FPR),* was created as a Romanian branch of the Popular Front of Moldova, which supported the reunification of Moldova and Romania. The RPF was based in Iaşi, the capital of Romanian Moldova, where it published newspapers, including the first periodical in Romania dealing with Moldovan issues, *Flacăra Basarabiei*; the publication initially appeared in December 1990.[53]

A related organization, the League of Solidarity with the Popular Front of Moldova (LSPFM) *(Liga de Solidaritate cu Frontul Popular al Moldovei, LSFPM)*, was established in March 1991 by a group of writers and engineers. It coordinated its initiatives in the cultural, social, economic, and political domains with those of the Popular Front of Moldova headed by Iurie Roşca, an organization that supported reunification with Romania. The LSPFM was an ardent critic of the Soviet Union's referendum in March 1991 on preserving the federation, and believed that the Republic of Moldova had the full right to independence and self-determination.[54]

Pro-Bessarabia and Bukovina Association (PBBA)
Asociaţia Pro-Basarabia şi Bucovina (APBB)

The Pro-Bessarabia and Bukovina Association (PBBA) was formed in the spring of 1990 as an avowedly cultural association. Its leadership included president Nicolae Lupan and vice president Vasile Tipordei, replaced in 1990 by Gheorghe Muntean. The PBBA cast itself as a broad movement seeking to develop cultural relations between Romania and Moldova, but it also engaged in more overt political activities. It established branches in several parts of the country; a Transylvanian branch was founded in Braşov in October 1990. The first large meeting of the Association was held in March 1990 in order to commemorate the historical union of Bessarabia with Romania. In May 1990, the Association organized the "Bank of the Prut," a gathering on the Romanian-Moldovan border. In April 1991, it protested against the treaty of cooperation and friendship signed with the Soviet Union and called on the Bucharest government to denounce the Ribbentrop-Molotov pact and to recognize the sovereignty of the Moldovan republic. The PBBA maintained direct contacts with Moldova and collected funds to help the natives of both Moldova and Bukovina deported to Siberia under Stalin's rule. The Association called for dual citizenship status by permitting Romanian citizenship to all people of Moldovan origin, lineage, kinship, or spiritual affinity. The PBBA's political activities increased after the spring of 1992, as Moldova struggled to preserve its territorial integrity in the face of separatist pressures.[55]

Neo-Fascists

Movement for Romania (MFR)
Mişcarea Pentru România (MPR)

This radical rightist grouping was established in December 1991 by Marian Munteanu, a former leader of the Bucharest University Students' League who gained renown for his oppositionist activities against the Iliescu government.

The MFR was criticized by pro-and anti-government forces alike for its ideological links to the pre-war fascist organization, the Romanian Legionary Movement (or Iron Guard). In its program, the MFR criticized liberalism and social democracy for contradicting the "cultural and spiritual nature" of the Romanian people, and stressed Christian mysticism and collectivism above individualism. Its ideology was defined as "national democratic" and "Romanianist," underscoring the linguistic, cultural, and religious unity of the Romanian nation, and its alleged superiority among European peoples.

Munteanu also cast himself as the champion of young people, the "new generation" that had been frustrated and betrayed by developments since the 1989 revolution. The MFR developed its own publications, including the newspaper *Mişcarea* (The Movement). It established a "Veterans Corps," and reportedly received funds from Romanian neo-fascists in the West. It advocated close cooperation with other Orthodox Christian countries and with Romanian emigres who were willing to defend the country's "national interests."

The MFR's internal structure replicated the Legionnaire cell organizations, with no elected leadership but an enforced consensus based on discipline and obedience. Munteanu criticized other nationalist formations, including the GRP and the RNUP, for their links with former communist structures and Ceauşescu appointees, even though their programs were in many respects similar. Although MFR statements did not seem blatantly racist or xenophobic, critics charged that the Movement sought to severely restrict the rights of Hungarians and other minority groups and establish a neo-fascist dictatorship. Government officials condemned the revival of the "Legionary phenomenon" and singled out the MFR as the prime culprit.[56]

New Christian Romania Party (NCRP)
Partidul Noua Românie Creştină (PNRC)

The New Christian Romania Party (NCRP) was founded in May 1992 as an openly neo-fascist organization that visualized itself as the continuation of the Iron Guard movement. It was led by Şerban Suru, claimed several hundred members, and revered Corneliu Codreanu, the former Iron Guard leader, as a national hero deserving of sainthood. The NCRP staged several public meetings in Bucharest, seeking to bridge the gap between fascist veterans and a younger generation of activists disillusioned with post-Ceauşescu developments. The Bucharest Municipal Court was sharply criticized by democratic parties for allowing the NCRP to organize, as it allegedly contradicted constitutional stipulations banning the formation of extremist parties.

Several similar ultra-rightist groupings also operated in Romania during the past decade, including the National Legionary Party (NLP), established in September 1992 and led by Ionică Cătănescu, and the Christian Democratic Union–Sibiu Convention (CDU-SC). Several radical-right formations were believed to possess close ties with agents of the former *Securitate* and with

Ceauşescu loyalists seeking to benefit from populist, nationalist, and xeno-phobic sentiments among segments of the Romanian population.[57]

Ethnic Minority and Religious Parties

Democratic Alliance of Hungarians in Romania (DAHR)
Uniunea Democrată Maghiară din România (UDMR)

The Democratic Alliance of Hungarians in Romania (DAHR) was formed on 25 December 1989 in Bucharest. László Tőkés, one of the leading figures of the 1989 revolution, became its honorary chairman. The first elected President was Géza Domokos, a former member of the Romanian Communist Party Central Committee and a member of the post-revolutionary provisional government of the National Salvation Front. The DAHR became more of an alliance than a political party, and although open to all Romanian citizens, it was principally a Hungarian movement.

The DAHR included sixteen different parties and associations, including the Hungarian Christian Democratic Party of Romania, the Party of Hungarian Farmers in Romania, the Independent Hungarian Party of Romania, and the Union of Hungarian Democratic Youth. Each party was able to preserve its independent status inside the Alliance. DAHR membership was organized in a loose structure of local chapters that were in turn grouped into autonomous county branches. The Alliance's statutes granted territorial organizations wide latitude in local decision-making. The Council of Delegates became the main policy-making body, whose members were elected at the federation's congress. The DAHR's executive body consisted of a presidium with eleven members elected by congress. Twelve groups of experts were also set up at the 1992 congress to deal with political, cultural, economic, and other issues.

The DAHR's objectives were twofold: ethnic and national. The main ethnic goals were to reverse persistent discrimination and longstanding anti-Hungarian sentiments in Romania. The Alliance stressed increased cultural and social freedom: it promoted the right of Hungarians to run their own schools, operate independent radio and television stations, publish an independent press, and reopen the Hungarian Babeş-Bolyai University in Cluj. Each year on 15 March, the DAHR celebrated Hungary's national day in commemoration of the 1848 revolution. It supported demands for "cultural and functional" autonomy, including separate ethnic educational institutions and self-governing churches. It demanded local autonomy for Transylvania, with Hungarian prefects and deputy prefects appointed in the counties of Covasna and Harghita. It envisaged such moves in the context of local government reform, rather than specifically minority issues. On the other hand, the Alliance did not pursue "territorial autonomy," despite the accusations of Romanian nationalists. Its hesitancy stemmed from the recognition that such autonomy would leave many ethnic Hungarians outside the autonomous regions without benefit of collective rights. It also calculated that any demands for "territorial autonomy" would trigger unpleasant associations with the former Hungarian Autonomous Region, set up during the Stalinist era.

The DAHR wanted Romania declared a multinational state, and called for the creation of a Ministry of Minority Affairs. It also proposed that national minorities should use their own language in local government institutions. In June 1991, the Alliance recommended that the Romanian government, the governing party, and the opposition parties discuss the national minority issue at a national round-table conference. It also supported the creation of a Central European National Minority Forum or a joint association for Hungarians and other national minorities living in the Danube-Carpathian basin, based on a commonality of interests. It called for "an internationally accepted, comprehensive system of national minority rights, and the formulation of a system of international norms that will both guarantee and supervise the implementation of these rights."

From the outset, the Alliance participated in domestic politics in opposition to the National Salvation Front. It joined the National Alliance for the Proclamation of Timişoara, created in April 1990. In the presidential elections of May 1990, the DAHR called on people not to vote for Iliescu. The Alliance was close to the National Liberal Party but did not give the Liberals its official support because none of the Liberal candidates held a distinct position on minority issues. It opposed direct presidential elections, asserting that the president should be appointed by parliament. The DAHR finished second in the general election of May 1990, winning twenty-nine seats in the Chamber of Deputies and twelve in the Senate, and received approximately one million votes.

The Alliance participated in consultations on the settlement of the government crisis in September 1991 and supported the presidency of Theodor Stolojan. It declared its readiness to offer candidates for ministerial positions and called for the creation of a legal framework for national minority rights. It decided to participate in the new government and was offered three ministerial posts: economics and finance, industrial affairs, and trade. As a condition, the DAHR stated that the government should also have a Ministry for Nationalities. The government objected, and the Alliance refused to participate in the new administration.

During the local elections of February 1992, the DAHR ran on joint lists with the Democratic Convention opposition coalition in most districts, but on separate ones in Transylvania. The Alliance finished third in the elections, winning 8.7% of the vote, gaining seats in ten towns in Transylvania, and in 37 townships on common lists with the DC. The DAHR obtained 178 mayoral, 52 deputy mayoral, and 148 county council posts. It lost in many of the areas where it had run on separate lists, due to the strong showing of Romanian nationalists, who won twenty mayoralties, including Cluj-Napoca. But the Alliance won the mayoralty in Tîrgu Mureş after rescheduled elections in

May 1992. The DAHR ran on separate lists for the parliamentary elections of September 1992 while supporting the DC's presidential candidate. The Union maintained its support base and captured 7.45% of the popular vote for the Chamber of Deputies, obtaining 27 seats, and 7.59% for the Senate, where it gained 12 seats.

By the time of its second congress in May 1991, the DAHR claimed to have 533,000 members. It adopted a new program and a resolution demanding that the Hungarians be recognized as a "co-nation" or a "state-building" nation. Different trends were visible in the Alliance throughout the decade: a moderate tendency led by President Géza Domokos and Károly Király, and a more radical faction led by Géza Szöcs and Gábor Kolumbán, both vice presidents. Bishop László Tökés was increasingly sympathetic to the more radical wing. In April 1992, Domokos recognized the presence of different platforms within the DAHR: liberal, Christian democratic, and a movement favoring the involvement of young people in political life. In essence, all of these trends respected Romania's independence and unity; but while one wing used the help of democratically minded Romanians to gradually obtain minority rights, the others considered it important to more forcefully press for Magyar demands.

Domokos denied that any of these tendencies were extremist. It appeared that the younger wing, which included some former dissidents, wanted to emphasize participatory democracy with spontaneous political activities at the grassroots level, an outlook it shared with the Romanian extra-parliamentary opposition. By contrast, Domokos and like-minded leaders of his generation were accustomed to working within the institutions of the state to achieve what was possible with regard to minority interests. Some fissures emerged, based mainly on generational and tactical differences between the participants. A more extreme fraction, the Magyar Initiative in Transylvania, led by Adám Katona, wanted the DAHR to call for outright "territorial autonomy" in its program.

The DAHR held its third congress in January 1993 and avoided radicalizing the movement and thus playing into the hands of Romanian extremists. Its radical faction, which demanded a declaration of "self-determination" by the Hungarian population, failed to take over the executive leadership and to impose its demands. The radicals had pressured the Alliance to adopt the Declaration of Cluj in October 1992, in response to the anti-Magyar measures adopted by Mayor Gheorghe Funar. The Declaration defined Hungarians as a "state-building nation" rather than a national minority; sought the redefinition of Romania as a multinational, not a unitary state; and demanded "communitarian autonomy" for Magyars in Transylvania. However, it failed to specify whether this would signify territorial autonomy or simply "ethnic and religious autonomy."

The Cluj Declaration was condemned by virtually all Romanian parties, including the DAHR's partners in the Democratic Convention. The DAHR congress distanced itself from these propositions and criticized the radicals for leading the Alliance into isolation from the Romanian opposition. As a result, the new DAHR program did not propose "territorial autonomy" but the more ambiguous "local and regional self-administration," avoiding mention of the Hungarians as either a "state-building nation" or a "national minority," and opting instead for "national community." In 1993, Domokos stepped down from the DAHR presidency and was replaced by Béla Markó who adopted a moderate approach, similar to that of his predecessor, Tökés was reelected honorary president. Although divisions within the Alliance were not resolved, workable compromises were reached between different factions.[58]

The DAHR became the longest represented party in parliament. In mid-1995, the DAHR was uninterested in establishing ties or cooperating with other opposition parties, many of which viewed the Alliance as a party of extreme nationalism. After 1995, the DAHR adopted a more moderate image, and in 1996 it entered the new governing coalition with the DCR. In national elections in November 1996, the DAHR received 6.64% of the vote and won 25 seats in the lower house of parliament, and 6.82% of the vote and 11 seats in the Senate. It continued to focus on human rights for the Hungarian community through internal self-determination, within the constitutional framework.[59] The Alliance did not seek autonomy or advocate separatism. The DAHR's moderate politicians, including Béla Markó, György Frunda, György Tokay, and Csaba Takács, maintained the upper hand, but there was a danger in the late 1990s of a formal split in the organization.[60]

According to the law on political parties, organizations of national minorities had the right to participate in local, general, and presidential elections, and it was unnecessary to register as a political party.[61] The double status of the DAHR, as a cultural association of a national minority and as a political organization participating in government, enabled the Alliance to absorb various political orientations.[62] Two small parties were present within the DAHR—the Christian Democratic Party and the Smallholders' Association—four larger platforms: the Liberal Circle; the national liberal Reform Alliance; the Social Democratic New Left, composed mostly of former communists; and the Transylvanian Hungarian Initiative, based in eastern Transylvania. Irrespective of these organized factions, the greatest conflict within the DAHR was between moderates and radicals. The former were more inclined to negotiate with Bucharest; the latter were more demanding of group rights.[63]

Union of Hungarian Democratic Youth (UHDY)
Uniunea Tineretului Democratic Maghiar (UTDM)

The Union of Hungarian Democratic Youth (UHDY) was established in December 1989. Its principal leader was Chairman Tibor Toró from Timişoara. The Union defined itself as an independent organization without a political character, even as the youth affiliate of the DAHR. The Youth Union was dedicated to the realization of rights for young Magyars and equality for all nationalities, and it established an information center for young Hungarians. Eight of its members were elected to the DAHR presidium.[64]

Other Hungarian organizations included: the Hungarian Smallholders' Party, chaired by Zoltán Éltes; the Hungarian Christian Democratic Party, based in Tîrgu Mure° and led by István Tökés, the father of Bishop László Tökés; the Independent Magyar Party, located in Tîrgu Mureş; the Association of Magyar Youth Organizations; and the Cultural Society of Hungarians in Transylvania.

The Trianon Organizing Forum of the National Christian Union appeared in May 1990, calling for the condemnation of the Trianon Treaty. It was reportedly irredentist and considered by the DAHR as a provocation designed to instigate ethnic conflicts. The Pro-Transylvania Foundation was created in Budapest in August 1990, presided over by András Süto. The Transylvanian Emigré Government was reported to be active in Budapest during the fall of 1991, but was viewed as a provocation by the DAHR. It transpired that its president was an ethnic Romanian who claimed to have worked for the *Securitate*. A few days after its creation, it announced that it was disbanding itself. The *Együtt* (Together) Association was established in mid-1991 by Győző Hajdú, a member of the Romanian Communist Party Central Committee under Ceauşescu. Együtt was critical of the DAHR's alleged extremism and irredentism and aimed to "fight chauvinism" and to achieve Romanian-Hungarian fraternity. It advocated both the rights of the Hungarian minority and Romania's territorial integrity. Its creation was reportedly welcomed by *Vatra Românească*.[65]

League of Organizations of National and Ethnic Minorities in Romania (LONEMR)
Liga Organizaţiilor Minorităţilor Naţionale şi Etnice din România (LOMNER)

The League was established in July 1990, with leadership exercised by President Károly Király, a former member of the Romanian Communist Party Central Committee. LONEMR was designed as a consultative organization, created to defend human rights and the individual and collective rights of national and ethnic minorities. It became an umbrella organization for several independent ethnic parties and alliances. In April 1991, Király announced optimistically that there was a decrease in the nationalistic and chauvinistic pressures exerted on the Hungarian minority. He declared that "extremist political forces were losing their support among the masses as a result of the maturity of the Romanian society and the sober-minded policy of the Hungarian Union."[66]

Democratic Union of Roma in Romania (DURR)
Uniunea Democratică a Romilor din România (UDRR)

The Democratic Union of Roma in Romania (DURR) was created in Bucharest in February 1990. It was led by Ion Onoriu, the provisional president. Nicolae Bobu was elected president at the Roma Special Congress in Deva in July 1990. At the third congress of Roma in September 1991, held under the auspices of the DURR, Ion Cioabă was elected "King of the Roma" and Nicolae Gheorghe was elected secretary-general of the DURR. A rival Gypsy chieftain, Iulian Rădulescu, proclaimed himself the "Emperor of all Gypsies" in September 1992. The DURR became an umbrella organization for several Romani associations and parties and was dedicated to ensuring social, cultural, and political freedom for the Roma people. Six Gypsy parties were officially registered in Romania in the early 1990s.

The DURR decided to support Iliescu's presidential candidacy, while protesting against continuing anti-Gypsy incidents in the Romanian countryside. The DURR endeavored to establish an Ethnic Confederation of Roma that would promote Romani causes and publicize acts of discrimination, harassment, and violence. In addition, it proved effective in strengthening ties to the Romani community worldwide. Several other Romani organizations were formed, including the Fiddlers and Wood Carvers of Romani, the Free Romani Democratic Party, the Gypsy Party of Romania, the Tinsmith Roma Progressive Party, the Free Democratic Union of Roma, and the Christian Democratic Party of Roma. Most of these were regionally based, and some were in competition with each other. Such divisions obstructed progress toward forging a united Romani platform.[67]

Democratic Forum of Germans in Romania (DFGR)
Forumul Democratic al Germanilor din România (FDGR)

The Democratic Forum of Germans in Romania (DFGR) was created in January 1990, in Sibiu, and was led by President Naegler and Vice President Nikolaus Kleininger. It was formed as a socio-cultural organization and not a political party. The DFGR lobbied for enshrining the rights of minorities in the Romanian constitution. It advocated a German schooling system, cultural freedom, and the protection of Saxon and Swabian historical monuments. It assisted people who were deported to Russia after World War II, and aimed to stabilize the position of the approximately 120,000 Germans remaining in Romania in 1991; about 100,000 Germans reportedly emigrated during the early 1990s. The first meeting between DFGR and government representatives took place in September 1990. An Advisory Commission for Supporting Initiatives and Actions Aiming at Stabilizing the German Minority was established. DFGR leaders displayed great concern over the German exodus, and sought measures to entice Germans to stay in the country.[68]

Democratic Union of Serbs (DUS)
Uniunea Democratică a Sîrbilor (UDS)

The Democratic Union of Serbs (DUS) was formed in March 1990 in Timişoara to represent and defend the interests of Romanian citizens of Serbian and, initially, Croatian nationality in Timiş, Arad, Caraş-Severin, and Mehedinţi counties. It sought to reinvigorate their spiritual life, preserve their cultural traditions, and develop their educational system. Following the outbreak of war in the former Yugoslavia in 1991, some Serb leaders adopted a vehemently nationalist position avowedly in defense of Christian Orthodoxy against Roman Catholicism and militant Islam.[69]

Union of Ukrainians in Romania (UUR)
Uniunea Ucrainienilor din România (UUR)

The Union of Ukrainians in Romania (UUR) was established at the close of 1992 as an apolitical organization seeking to mediate fruitful contacts between the government and the Ukrainian minority. Its president was Stefan Tcaciuk, who was also a parliamentary deputy. According to Union leaders, the Ukrainian population was dispersed throughout the country, with some compact concentrations in northern regions such as Maramureş, next to the Ukrainian border. The minority benefited from a network of schools and language courses and the UUR, established a Ukrainian-language newspaper and a radio station in Maramureş county.[70] Romania signed a bilateral friendship treaty with Ukraine in July 1997, a move opposed by Romania's nationalist parties. The delineation of borders along the continental shelf in the Black Sea continued to mar relations between the two countries into the late 1990s.

Arumanian Cultural Society (ACS)
Societatea Culturală Aromână (SCA)

The Arumanian Cultural Society (ACS) was established in Bucharest in March 1990 to represent the under-reported Arumun or Vlach population in Romania. It traced its origins to the Macedonian-Romanian Cultural Society that was set up in 1880 but stopped functioning in 1949. It claimed to have no overt political character or aspirations.[71] The Arumun people were dispersed throughout the Balkans, and many of their activists viewed Romania as their natural home country and the Romanians as their ethnic kin.

Democratic Union of Slovaks and Czechs (DUSC)
Uniunea Democratică a Slovacilor şi Cehilor (UDSC)

The Democratic Union of Slovaks and Czechs (DUSC) was established in May 1990 as an avowedly political party representing and defending the interests of the small Slovak and Czech minorities in Romania.[72]

Several other ethnic minorities also established their own representative organizations, including the Armenian Union of Romania (AUR) *(Uniunea Armenilor din România, UAR)*, led by Varujan Vosganian and formed in Bucharest in August 1990 in order to cultivate contacts between Romania and Armenia, but not engaging in openly political activities.

Romania's smaller minorities also established independent social, cultural, and quasi-political organizations to protect their interests and campaign for an expansion of group rights. They included the Muslim Turkish Democratic Union of Romania (MTDUR) *(Uniunea Democratică Musulmanilor Turci din România, UDMTR)*, which campaigned for the organization of Turkish language classes in Romanian schools, for the recreation of an Islamic confessional school, and for the training of imams for the sixty-two remaining mosques in Romania. In addition, there was a Turkish Democratic Union, a Federation of Jewish Communities, a *Bratstvo* Community of Bulgarians, a Hellenic Union of Romania, a *Dom Polski* Union of Poles, an Italian Community of Romania, a Democratic Union of Tatars and Moslem-Turks, a Cultural Union of Albanians, and a Community of Lipovan Russians.[73]

POLITICAL DATA

Name of State: Romania *(România)*
Form of Government: Republic
Structure of Legislature: Bicameral parliament *(Parlamentul)* consisting of the Senate *(Senat)* and the Chamber of Deputies *(Camera Deputaţilor)*
Size of Territory: 91,699 square miles
Size of Population: 22,334,312 (1999)

Sources: The World Fact Book 2000, Central Intelligence Agency, http://www.odci.gov/cia/publications/factbook/geos/ro.html#Govt; Arthur S. Bank, Alan J. Day, and Thomas C. Muller, *Political Handbook of the World 1995–1996*, New York: CSA Publication Binghamton University, 1997; Transitions Online Country Reports, Romania, 1999, http://www.tol.cz/countries/romania.htm.

Composition of Population

Ethnic Group	Number	% of Population
Romanians	20,352,980	89.42
Hungarians	1,620,199	7.12
Roma (Gypsies)	409,723	1.80
Germans	119,436	0.52
Ukrainians	66,833	0.29
Russians and Lipovans	38,688	0.17

Turks	29,533	0.13
Serbs	29,080	0.13
Tatars	24,649	0.11
Slovaks	20,672	0.09
Bulgarians	9,935	0.04
Jews	9,107	0.04
Czechs	5,880	0.03
Poles	4,247	0.02
Croats	4,180	0.02
Greeks	3,897	0.02
Armenians	2,023	0.01
Others	8,420	0.04
Undeclared	1,017	—
Total minorities	2,407,519	10.58
Total population	22,760,499	100.00

Sources: The Romanian census figures published in January 1992 and the White Paper on The Rights of the Persons Belonging to Ethnic, Linguistic or Religious Minorities in Romania, published by the Ministry of Foreign Affairs of Romania, June 1991. See also Michael Shafir, "Preliminary Results of the 1992 Romanian Census," Radio Free Europe/Radio Liberty (RFE/RL) Research Institute, *Report on Eastern Europe,* Vol. 1, No. 30, 24 July 1992; and *Adevărul,* Bucharest, No. 19, 29 June–5 July 1992.

ELECTION RESULTS

Presidential Election, 26 November and 10 December 2000

First Round, 26 November 2000
Turnout: 65.31%

Candidate	Votes	% of Vote
Ion Iliescu	4,076,273	36.35
Corneliu Vadim Tudor	3,178,293	28.34
Theodor Stolojan	1,321,420	11.78
Mugur Isarescu	1,069,463	9.54
György Frunda	696,989	6.22
Petre Roman	334,852	2.99
Teodor Meleşcanu	214,642	1.92
Other candidates	321,042	2.86
Total	11,212,974	100.00

Source: International Foundation for Election Systems, http://www.ifes.org/eguide/resultsum/romaniares2.htm.

Second Round, 10 December 2000
Turnout: 57.50%

Candidate	Votes	% of Vote
Ion Iliescu	6,696,623	66.83
Corneliu Vadim Tudor	3,324,247	33.17
Total	10,020,870	100.00

Presidential Election, 3 and 17 November 1996

First Round, 3 November 1996
Turnout: 76.01%

Candidate	Votes	% of Vote
Ion Iliescu	4,081,093	32.25
Emil Constantinescu	3,569,941	28.21
Petre Roman	2,598,545	20.53
György Frunda	761,411	6.02
Corneliu Vadim Tudor	597,508	4.72
Gheorghe Funar	407,828	3.22
Tudor Mohora	160,387	1.27
Nicolae Manolescu	90,122	0.71
Adrian Păunescu	87,163	0.69
Ioan Pop de Popa	59,752	0.47
Gheorghe Muntean	54,218	0.43
Radu Câmpeanu	43,780	0.35
Nupu Anghelina	43,319	0.34
Constantin Mudava	39,477	0.31
Constantin Niculescu	30,045	0.24
Nicolae Militaru	28,311	0.22
Total	12,652,900	99.98
Invalid ballots	426,545	3.26

Source: Central Electoral Bureau of Romania, http://www.kappa.ro/guv/bec/r-prs-e.html.

Second Round, 17 November 1996
Turnout: 75.90%

Candidate	Votes	% of Vote
Emil Constantinescu	7,057,906	54.41
Ion Iliescu	5,914,579	45.59
Total	12,972,485	100.00

Presidential Election, 27 September and 11 October 1992

First Round, 27 September 1992

Turnout: 76.3%

Candidate	Votes	% of Vote
Ion Iliescu	5,633,456	47.34
Emil Constantinescu	3,717,006	31.24
Gheorghe Funar	1,294,388	10.87
Caius Traian Dragomir	564,655	4.75
Ioan Mânzatu	362,485	3.05
Mircea Druc	326,866	2.75
Total	11,898,856	100.00

Second Round, 11 October 1992
Turnout: 73.2%

Candidate	Votes	% of Vote
Ion Iliescu	7,393,429	61.43
Emil Constantinescu	4,641,207	38.57
Total	12,034,636	100.00

Presidential Election, 20 May 1990

Turnout: 86.2%

Candidate	Votes	% of Vote
Ion Iliescu	12,323,489	85.07
Radu Câmpeanu	1,529,188	10.64
Ion Raţiu	617,007	4.29
Total	14,469,684	100.00

Parliamentary Elections, Senate, 26 November 2000

Turnout: 65.31%

Party/Coalition	Votes	% of Vote	Seats
Party of Social Democracy in Romania	4,040,212	37.09	65
Greater Romania Party	2,288,483	21.01	37
Democratic Party	825,437	7.58	13

National Liberal Party	814,381	7.48	13
Democratic Alliance of Hungarians in Romania	751,310	6.90	12
Other parties	2,172,087	19.94	—
Total	10,891,910	100.00	140

Source: International Foundation for Election Systems, http://www.ifes.org/eguide/resultsum/romaniares.htm.

Parliamentary Elections, Chamber of Deputies, 26 November 2000

Turnout: 65.31%

Party/Coalition	Votes	% of Vote	Seats
Party of Social Democracy in Romania	3,968,464	36.61	155
Greater Romania Party	2,112,027	19.48	84
Democratic Party	762,365	7.03	31
National Liberal Party	747,263	6.89	30
Democratic Alliance of Hungarians in Romania	736,863	6.80	27
Other parties	2,512,442	23.19	18
Total	10,839,424	100.00	345

Parliamentary Elections, Senate, 3 November 1996

Turnout: 76.01%

Party/Coalition	Votes	% of Vote	Seats
Democratic Convention of Romania	3,772,084	30.70	53
Party of Social Democracy in Romania	2,836,011	23.08	41
Social Democratic Union	1,617,384	13.16	23
Democratic Alliance of Hungarians in Romania	837,760	6.82	11
Greater Romania Party	558,026	4.54	8
Romanian National Unity Party	518,962	4.22	7
Others	2,147,444	17.48	—
Total	12,287,671	100.00	143

Sources: http://www2.essex.ac.uk/elect/electer/ro_er)nl.htm; and the Central Electoral Bureau of Romania, at http://www.kappa.ro/guv/bec/r-dep-e.html).

Parliamentary Elections, Chamber of Deputies, 3 November 1996

Turnout: 76.01%

Party/Coalition	Votes	% of Vote	Seats
Democratic Convention of Romania	3,692,321	30.17	122
Party of Social Democracy in Romania	2,633,860	21.52	91
Social Democratic Union	1,582,231	12.93	53

Democratic Alliance of Hungarians			
in Romania	812,628	6.64	25
Greater Romania Party	546,430	4.46	19
Romanian National Unity Party	533,348	4.36	18
Others	2,437,928	19.92	15
Total	12,238,746	100.00	343

Sources: http://www.omri.cz/elections/Romania/General/Results-Parliament .html and http://www.universal.nl/users/derksen/election/romania.htm.

Parliamentary Elections, Senate, 27 September 1992

Turnout: 76.3%

Party/Coalition	Votes	% of Vote	Seats
Democratic National Salvation Front	3,102,201	28.29	49
Democratic Convention of Romania	2,210,722	20.16	34
National Salvation Front	1,139,033	10.39	18
Romanian National Unity Party	890,410	8.12	14
Democratic Alliance of Hungarians			
in Romania	831,469	7.59	12
Greater Romania Party	422,545	3.85	6
Agrarian Democratic Party	362,427	3.31	5
Socialist Party of Labor	349,470	3.19	5
National Liberal Party	—	2.10	—
Romanian Ecologist Movement	—	2.10	—
Republican Party	—	1.90	—
Independent candidates	52,462	0.47	—
Others	—	8.53	—
Total	9,360,739	100.00	143

Sources: Romania, Parliamentary Election Results, at http://www2.essex.ac.uk/ elect/electer/ro_er)nl.htm; Central Electoral Bureau of Romania, at http:// www.kappa.ro/guv/bec/r-dep-e.html. The Central Electoral Bureau reported 10,964,818 valid votes cast in the Senate election in September 1992 and 10,880,252 valid votes cast in the Chamber of Deputies election. However, the complete breakdown of votes was not available. Due to the missing figures, the percentage and the total votes do not always correspond. For more details see University of Essex, http:www2.essex.ac.uk/ elect/electer/ro_er_nl.htm.

Parliamentary Elections, Chamber of Deputies, 27 September 1992

Turnout: 76.3%

Party/Coalition	Votes	% of Vote	Seats
Democratic National Salvation Front	3,015,708	27.72	117
Democratic Convention of Romania	2,177,144	20.01	82

National Salvation Front	1,108,500	10.19	43
Romanian National Unity Party	839,586	7.72	30
Democratic Alliance of Hungarians in Romania	811,290	7.45	27
Greater Romania Party	424,061	3.90	16
Socialist Party of Labor	330,378	3.03	13
Agrarian Democratic Party of Romania	n/a	2.90	—
National Liberal Party	n/a	2.60	—
Romanian Ecologist Movement	n/a	2.30	—
Republican Party	n/a	1.60	—
Minorities	n/a	0.90	—
Others	n/a	9.68	—
Total	10,880,252	100.00	341

Parliamentary Elections, Senate, 20 May 1990

Turnout: 86.19%

Party/Coalition	Votes	% of Vote	Seats
National Salvation Front	9,353,006	67.02	91
Democratic Alliance of Hungarians in Romania	1,004,353	7.20	12
National Liberal Party	985,094	7.06	10
Christian and Democratic National Peasants' Party	341,478	2.45	1
Romanian Ecologist Movement	348,637	2.49	1
Romanian National Unity Party	300,473	2.15	2
Romanian Ecologist Party	192,574	1.37	1
Romanian Socialist Democratic Party	152,989	1.10	—
Independent cand. Antonie Iorgorah	—	.26	1
Other independents	—	2.81	—
Other Parties	850,041	6.09	—
Total	13,956,180	100.00	119

Parliamentary Elections, Chamber of Deputies, 20 May 1990

Turnout: 86.2%

Party/Coalition	Votes	% of Vote	Seats
National Salvation Front	9,089,659	66.31	263
Democratic Alliance of Hungarians in Romania	991,601	7.23	29
National Liberal Party	879,290	6.41	29

Romanian Ecologist Movement	358,864	2.62	12
Christian Democratic National Peasants' Party	351,357	2.60	12
Romanian National Unity Party	290,875	2.12	9
Agrarian Democratic Party of Romania	250,403	1.82	9
Romanian Ecologist Party	232,212	1.69	8
Romanian Socialist Democratic Party	143,393	1.04	5
Romanian Social Democrat Party	73,014	0.53	2
Democratic Group of the Center	65,914	0.48	2
Other parties	980,577	7.15	16
Total	13,707,159	100.00	396

Source: Association of Central and Eastern European Election Officials, the University of Essex, and the International Foundation for Election Systems: http://www.aceeco.com.

NOTES

1. For recent histories of Romania consult Charles and Barbara Jelavich, *The Establishment of the Balkan National States, 1804–1920*, Seattle: University of Washington Press, 1977; Stefan Pascu, *A History of Transylvania*, New York: Dorset Press, 1982.

2. For a valuable analysis of the overthrow of Ceauşescu see Nestor Ratesh, *Romania: The Entangled Revolution*, New York: Praeger and CSIS, 1991. See also Daniel N. Nelson (Ed.), *Romania After Tyranny*, Boulder: Westview Press, 1992; and Ion Mihai Pacepa, *Red Horizons: Chronicle of a Communist Spy Chief*, Washington, D.C.: Regnery Gateway, 1987.

3. Consult Vladimir Tismaneanu, "The Quasi-Revolution and Its Discontents: Emerging Political Pluralism in Post-Ceauşescu Romania," *East European Politics and Society*, Vol. 7, No. 2, Spring 1993, pp. 309–348.

4. See the "Law and Local Public Administration," Parliament of Romania, Bucharest, 1992.

5. Michael Shafir, "Romania's New Institutions: The Draft Constitution," RFE/RL, *Report on Eastern Europe*, Vol. 2, No. 38, 20 September 1991; Michael Shafir, "Romania: Constitution Approved in Referendum," RFE/RL, *Research Report*, Vol. 1, No. 2, 10 January 1992; Michael Shafir, "Romania: The Rule of Law," RFE/RL, *Research Report*, Vol. 1, No. 27, 3 July 1992.

6. Michael Shafir, "Romania's Elections: Why the Democratic Convention Lost," RFE/RL, *Research Report*, Vol. 1, No. 43, 30 October 1992.

7. For a valuable analysis see Vladimir Tismaneanu, "Romanian Exceptionalism? Democracy, Ethnocracy, and Uncertain Pluralism in Post-Ceauşescu Romania," in Karen Dawisha and Bruce Parrott (Eds.), *Politics, Power, and the Struggle for Democracy in South-East Europe*, Cambridge: Cambridge University Press, 1997, pp. 403–451.

8. See the interview with Béla Markó, President of DAHR, "Changes in the Administration or a Nationalist Diversionary Game," *22*, Bucharest, 8–14 April 1993, in Federal Broadcast Information Service/Joint Publications Research Service, *Daily Report: East Europe*, JPRS-EER-93–047–S, 28 May 1993.

9. See *România Libera*, Bucharest, 7 November 1997.

10. For some details see Michael Shafir, "Anatomy of a Pre-Election Political Divorce," *Transition*, Vol. 2, No. 2, 26 January 1996, pp. 45–49; and Michael Shafir and Dan Ionescu, "Radical Political Change in Romania," *Transition*, Vol. 3, No. 2, 7 February 1997, pp. 52–54.

11. *Rompres*, Bucharest, 6 October 1997, in *FBIS-EEU-97–279*, 7 October 1997; *Radio Romania Network*, Bucharest, 6 October 1997, in *FBIS-EEU-97–357*, 27 December 1997; *Radio Romania Network*, Bucharest, 23 December 1997, in *FBIS-EEU-97–357*, 29 December 1997.

12. *Rompres*, Bucharest, 31 December 1997, in *FBIS-EEU-97–365*, 2 January 1998; and *Rompres*, Bucharest, 13 January 1998, in *FBIS-EEU-98–013*, 14 January 1998.

13. See "The PD, PSDR Set Up Social-Democratic Union," in *Evenimentul Zilei*, 28 September 1995, *FBIS-EEU-95–197*, 12 October 1995.

14. *Monitorul*, Bucharest, 8 November 1996; and www.nordest.ro/romanian.monitor/elections/8_nov_96_elect_e.htm.

15. International Republican Institute, "The Major Political Parties Participating in the 9 February 1992 Romanian Local Elections," Washington, D.C., p. 2.

16. *Evenimentul Zilei*, Bucharest, 23 October 1995, in *FBIS-EEU-95–215*, 19 November 1995; and *Cotidianul*, Bucharest, 11 December 1995, in *FBIS-EEU*, 15 December 1995.

17. http://www.europeanforum.bot-consult.se/cup/romania/index.htm.

18. http://www.kappa.ro/pdsr/pdsr-e.html.

19. Michael Shafir, "Final Split in Romanian Opposition Party," RFE/RL, *Daily Report*, 23 June 1997.

20. *Rompres*, Bucharest, 17 January 1997, in *FBIS-EEU-97–013–A*, 22 January 1997.

21. http://www.kappa.ro/pdsr/pdsrpt.html, PDSR on-line.

22. *Rompres*, Bucharest, 30 August 1997, in *FBIS-EEU-97–242*, 3 September 1997.

23. *Radio Romania Network*, Bucharest, 15 November 1997, in *FBIS-EEU-97–319*, 19 November 1997.

24. *Rompres*, Bucharest, 16 July 1997, in *FBIS-EEU-97–197*, 17 July 1997.

25. *Adevărul*, Bucharest, 29 July 1997, in *FBIS-EEU-97–210*, 30 July 1997.

26. Domnita Stefanescu, "Two Years of Romanian History: A Chronology of Events from January 1995 to January 1997," Bucharest: Editura Masina de Scris, 1998.

27. *Curentul*, Bucharest, 10 July 1998, in *FBIS-EEU-98–191*, 13 July 1998.

28. *Rompres*, Bucharest, 8 July 1998, in *FBIS-EEU-98–189*, 9 July 1998.

29. *Monitorul*, Bucharest, 12 August 1996; and www.nordest.ro/romanian.monitor/elections/12.aug.96.elect_e.htm.

30. "Liberal Parties Merge in Romania," RFE/RL 16 June 1997.

31. *Ziua*, Bucharest, 16 June 1997, in *FBIS-EEU-97–118*, 20 June 1997.

32. *Rompres*, Bucharest, 17 June 1997, in *FBIS-EEU-97–168*, 19 June 1997.

33. *Monitorul*, Bucharest, 19 November 1996.

34. See the International Republican Institute, "The Major Political Parties Participating in the 9 February 1992 Romanian Local Elections," Washington, D.C., p. 3.

35. http://www.kappa.ro/election/cdr/pnl/html.

36. *Rompres*, Bucharest, 11 August 1994, in *FBIS-EEU-94–158–A*, 14 November 1995.

37. *Radio Romania Network*, Bucharest, 14 March 1998, in *FBIS-EEU-98–073*, 17 March 1998.

38. www.nordest.ro/romanian_monitor/elections/12_nov_96_elect_e.htm.

39. *Radio Romania Network*, Bucharest, 11 November 1996, in *FBIS-EEU-96–219*, 9 November 1996.

40. *Rompres*, Bucharest, 9 April 1997, in *FBIS-EEU-97–099*, 10 April 1997.

41. See *Adevărul*, Bucharest, 31 January 1995, in *FBIS-EEU-95–025*, 19 November 1995.

42. *Rompres*, Bucharest, 16 October 1997, in *FBIS-EEU-97–289*, 20 October 1997.

43. For details on the Party of Romanian National Unity check Dennis Deletant, "The Role of Vatra Românească in Transylvania," RFE/RL, *Report on Eastern Europe*, Vol. 2, No. 5, 1 February 1991; and Country Reports on Human Rights Practices for 1992, U.S. Department of State, Washington, D.C., February 1993.

44. For example see *Rompres*, Bucharest, 22 October 1996, in *FBIS-EEU-96–211–A*, 31 October 1996.

45. *Ziua*, Bucharest, 2 March 1998, in *FBIS-EEU-98–06*, 7 March 1998.

46. *Ziua*, Bucharest, 25 November 1997, in *FBIS-EEU-97–329*, 27 November 1997.

47. Details on *Vatra Românească* can be found in *Rompres*, Bucharest, 19 March 1990, in *FBIS-EEU-90–054*, 20 March 1990; Dennis Deletant, "The Role of Vatra Românească in Transylvania," RFE/RL, *Report on Eastern Europe*, Vol. 2, No. 5, 1 February 1991; and *22*, Bucharest, 15 February 1991, in *JPRS-EER-91–029*, 8 March 1991.

48. For some information on the GRP see *Adevărul*, Bucharest, 17 May 1991, in *FBIS-EEU-91–103*, 29 May 1991; Kossuth Radio Network, Budapest, 15 October 1991, in *FBIS-EEU-91–200*, 16 May 1991; and *Magyar Hírlap*, Budapest, 10 November 1991.

49. Michael Shafir, "Making Sense Out Of Left And Right," RFE/EEU, 1 April 1997.

50. See Michael Shafir, "The Mind of Romania's Radical Right," in Sabrina P. Ramet (Ed.), *The Radical Right in Central and Eastern Europe Since 1989*, University Park, Pennsylvania: Pennsylvania State University Press, 1999, pp. 214–232.

51. See Radio Free Europe/ Radio Liberty *Newsline*, 27 July 2000.

52. *Rompres*, Bucharest, 17 June 1997, in *FBIS-EEU-97–168*, 19 June 1997.

53. *Rompres*, Bucharest, 12 November 1990, in *FBIS-EEU-90–239*, 12 November 1990.

54. *Rompres*, Bucharest, 14 March 1991, in *FBIS-EEU-91–051*, 15 March 1991; *România Libera*, Bucharest, 12 March 1991, in *FBIS-EEU-91–052*, 18 March 1991; RFE/RL, *Daily Report*, No. 73, 16 April 1991; and *România Libera*, Bucharest, 26 April 1991, in *FBIS-EEU-91–089*, 8 May 1991.

55. *Rompres*, Bucharest, 28 March 1990, in *FBIS-EEU-90–064*, 3 April 1990; *Rompres*, Bucharest, 24 June 1990, in *FBIS-EEU-90–122*, 25 June 1990; *Rompres*, Bucharest, 26 October 1990, in *FBIS-EEU-90–209*, 29 October 1990; *Rompres*, 5 January 1991, in *FBIS-EEU-91–004*; and *Rompres*, 22 April 1991, in *FBIS-EEU-91–078*, 23 April 1991.

56. See Michael Shafir, "The Movement for Romania: A Party of 'Radical Return,'" RFE/RL, *Research Report*, Vol. 1, No. 29, 17 July 1992.

57. See Cornelius Antim, "After the Rampage of the Orthodox Communist Forces, an Iron Guard–Oriented Party Emerges," *România Libera*, Bucharest, 1 December 1992; and *Tineretul Liber*, Bucharest, 17 March 1993, in *FBIS-EEU-93–055*, 24 March 1993; and Michael Shafir,

"Growing Political Extremism in Romania," RFE/RL, *Research Report*, Vol. 2, No. 14, 2 April 1993.

58. For some details on the Democratic Alliance of Hungarians see News from Helsinki Watch, May 1990; *Adevărul*, Bucharest, 24 April 1990, in *FBIS-EEU-90–088*, 7 May 1990; Judith Pataki, "Ethnic Hungarians Contest Romanian Elections," RFE/RL, *Report on Eastern Europe*, Vol. 1, No. 22, 1 June 1990; Dan Ionescu, "Romania's First Post-communist Census," RFE/RL, *Research Report*, Vol. 1, No. 11, 13 March 1992; *Curierul Național*, Bucharest, 8 April 1992, in *FBIS-EEU-92–072*, 14 April 1992; Michael Shafir, "Transylvania Shadows, Transylvania Lights," in RFE/RL, *Research Report*, Vol. 1, No. 26, 26 June 1992; and Michael Shafir, "The HDFR Congress: Confrontations Postponed," RFE/RL, *Research Report*, Vol. 2, No. 9, 26 February 1993.

59. http://www.re.ro/clienti/udmr/index.html.

60. For more details see *Magyar Narancs*, 16 January 1997, in *FBIS-EEU-97–035*, 24 February 1997.

61. *Curierul National*, Bucharest, 27 August 1996, in *FBIS-EEU-96–171*, 4 September 1996.

62. *România Libera*, Bucharest, 5 May 1997, in *FBIS-EEU-97–101*, 28 May 1998.

63. See "International Relations of the Democratic Alliance of Hungarians in Romania," *International Studies*, No. 2, 1996, pp. 20–42.

64. Background on the Union of Hungarian Democratic Youth can be found in *Rompres*, Bucharest, 26 January 1990, in *FBIS-EEU-89–022*, 1 February 1990; and Edith Oltay, "The Hungarian Democratic Federation of Romania: Structure, Agenda, Alliances," RFE/RL, *Report on Eastern Europe*, Vol. 2, No. 29, 19 July 1991.

65. Information on other Hungarian organizations is taken from Budapest Domestic Service, Budapest, 22 February 1990, in *FBIS-EEU-90–038*, 27 February 1990; Edith Oltay, "The Hungarian Democratic Federation of Romania: Structure, Agenda, Alliances"; 1991, *op. cit*; *Népszabadság*, Budapest, 25 September 1991, in *FBIS-EEU-91–187*, 26 September 1991; and *România Libera*, Bucharest, 28 September 1991, in *FBIS-EEU-91–193*, 4 October 1991.

66. *Adevărul*, Bucharest, 29 July 1990, in *FBIS-EEU-90–151*, 6 August 1990; *MTI*, Budapest, 23 April 1991, in *FBIS-EEU-91–081*, 26 April 1991.

67. Dan Ionescu, "The Gypsies Organize," RFE/RL, *Report on Eastern Europe*, Vol. 1, No. 26, 29 June 1990; Budapest Domestic Service, 2 July 1990, in *FBIS-EEU-90–128*, 3 July 1990; *Rompres*, Bucharest, 15 July 1990; and Mihai Sturdza, "The National Salvation Front and the Workers," RFE/RL, *Report on Eastern Europe*, Vol. 2, No. 25, 21 June 1991.

68. See *Rompres*, Bucharest, 12 March 1990, in *FBIS-EEU-90–049*, 13 March 1990; *Neuer Weg*, Bucharest, 16 May 1990, in *FBIS-EEU-90–102*, 25 May 1990; and *Rompres*, Bucharest, 30 July 1990, in *FBIS-EEU-90–146*, 30 July 1990.

69. *Rompres*, Bucharest, 22 February 1990, in *FBIS-EEU-90–142*, 2 March 1990; and *Europa*, Bucharest, 27 April–3 May 1993, in *FBIS-EEU-93–086*, 6 May 1993.

70. *Rompres*, Bucharest, 25 March 1993, in *FBIS-EEU-93–057*, 26 March 1993.

71. *Rompres*, Bucharest, 14 March 1990, in *FBIS-EEU-90–053*, 19 March 1990.

72. *Rompres*, Bucharest, 17 May 1990, in *FBIS-EEU-90–100*, 23 May 1990.

73. *Rompres*, Bucharest, 11 November 1996, in *FBIS-EEU-96–222-A*, 18 November 1996.

Moldova

HISTORICAL OVERVIEW

The territories of present-day Moldova were inhabited by various tribal groups in the first few centuries AD, including Dacians, Antes, Ostrogoths, Gepids, Visigoths, and various Slavic tribes. The Dacians are believed to have intermingled with Roman colonists during the second and third centuries, when Rome occupied or exerted influence over these regions. During the ninth century, much of Moldova between the Siret, Prut, and Dniestr rivers fell under the control of the First Bulgarian Empire, which reached its fullest extent at the beginning of the eleventh century. With the disintegration of the Bulgarian state, the Moldovan areas were dominated by Pecheneg tribes, which did not establish any durable state structure. During the subsequent two centuries, the region fell under the nominal control of the Slavic principality of Galicia, before it was captured by Mongol armies and was used as a base for military operations against central and southern Europe. In the middle of the thirteenth century, the Mongols established a state known as the Golden Horde, which controlled the lucrative trade routes along the Black Sea coast and across the steppes. The Golden Horde encompassed all of Moldova.[1]

By the fourteenth century the Moldovan territory possessed a mixture of ethno-linguistic groups including Romanians (Wallachians), Slavs, Magyars (Hungarians), Cumans, Tatars, and Bulgarians. Since the disintegration of the Roman Empire in the third century AD, and particularly with the weakening of Bulgarian control, Wallachian tribes had established a number of small principalities in the region between the Carpathians and the Danube. In the early part of the fourteenth century a Wallachian prince named Dragos, from northern Transylvania, reportedly founded a Moldovan state between the Siret and Prut rivers. In the 1350s this entity began to expand territorially under the rule of the Wallachian prince *(voievod)* Bogdan. The terms *Moldovan* and *Wallachian* were often used interchangeably for the inhabitants of this state.

In the region south of the Carpathian Mountains, Besarab I created a unified principality from several small Wallachian fiefdoms. By the end of the 1350s, two essentially Romanian entities existed: the principality of Moldova in the north, and Wallachia (Romanian land) in the south. Moldova grew in power during the fifteenth century and successfully defended its borders against Hungarian, Tatar, and Ottoman Turkish incursions. However, after the death of Stefan the Great in 1505, Ottoman armies under Sulejman the Magnificent defeated Moldovan forces in 1538 and occupied the principality's capital, Suceava. Moldova, like Wallachia, became a vassal state of the Ottomans, although it was never fully absorbed into the Turkish Empire. Local princes continued to rule the province in exchange for annual tributes paid to the sultan in Constantinople.

Moldova's status as a tributary state ended in 1711 when the Ottomans appointed Greek nobles from Constantinople (Phanariots) to administer the territory. Moldova lost its autonomy and was exploited as a source of personal enrichment by the new rulers. The local Orthodox Church also fell under Greek control. Moldovan princes forged alliances with Russia against the Turks, and under Catherine the Great, in the latter part of the eighteenth century, Russia secured control over an area stretching to the east bank of the Dniestr River. At the same time, the Austrian Habsburgs annexed the northern portion of Moldova—Bukovina, which included the city of Suceava.

During the Russo-Turkish war of 1806–12, the Moldovan principality fell under direct Russian control. The Russians first occupied the eastern part of Moldova, known as Bessarabia, between the Prut and the Dniestr rivers, in 1806. They formally annexed the territory in 1812, under the Treaty of Bucharest. The Bessarabian nobility was initially allowed a measure of autonomy in local government, but the process of Russification gathered pace in the 1820s as the tsars sought greater control over their western borderlands.

Bessarabia's status was changed from that of an "imperial region" to a Russian province *(gubernia)* in 1871. Meanwhile, the Bessarabian Orthodox Church was subordinated to the Moscow patriarchate. Western Moldova between the Siret and Prut remained within the Ottoman Empire, and several local uprisings were suppressed by the Turks. Nonetheless, a strong Romanian identity developed in the region, and in 1859, noble assemblies in the Moldovan capital, Iaşi, and the Wallachian capital, Bucharest, elected Alexandru Ioan Cuza as their common prince, thus effectively creating a joint Romanian state. Romanian politicians began to call for the incorporation of all areas inhabited by Romanians, including Russian-controlled Bessarabia, into a unified state. Romania formally gained independence from the Turks in 1878 and became a dynastic kingdom in 1881.

Nationalist movements sprouted in Bessarabian Moldova in the early 1900s, particularly among intellectuals and cultural figures seeking a Romanian revival. Pro-Russian parties also became active in the province, especially among settlers and administrators who had migrated from Russia. Moldovan nationalists demanded the restoration of the Romanian language, an autocephalous

Bessarabian church, and the political emancipation of the province. With the collapse of tsarist rule during World War I, Moldovan activists pushed for outright independence from Russia. In October 1917, a locally convened congress declared the autonomy of the Bessarabian province, and in December 1917, an autonomous republic was proclaimed.

Romanian forces intervened in the territory in January 1918 and drove Russia's Bolshevik forces east of the Dniestr River. On 24 January 1918, an independent Moldovan Democratic Republic of Bessarabia was declared, and on 27 March 1918, a union with Romania was formally announced. The Moldovan republic was dissolved on 27 November 1918, when the national assembly ratified the union with Romania and then disbanded. Although the Treaty of Trianon in June 1920 legitimized the enlarged Romanian state, the acquisition of Bessarabia was not fully secured through international accords. Direct rule from Bucharest also created some resentment in the territory, especially due to the drive for cultural uniformity, and the lack of aid for economic development.

Communist leaders in Moscow could not resign themselves to the loss of Bessarabia, and throughout the 1920s and 1930s, Bolshevik agents were active in the region. In October 1924, Moscow established a Moldovan Autonomous Soviet Socialist Republic (MASSR) along the western borders of Soviet Ukraine, on the Dniestr River. The region, known as Transnistria in Romanian, fell within the borders of Soviet Ukraine and was not an area with traditional Romanian settlements. Although the MASSR was populated mainly by Ukrainians, it was used as a staging point and a propaganda ploy for the creation of a Soviet Moldovan republic from the territories once held by Russia's tsars. Chişinău was declared the MASSR's capital, and all of Bessarabia was included in this entity's official borders, pending the full "liberation" of Bessarabia.

Soviet leaders attempted to consolidate a distinct Moldovan ethnicity and language in order to permanently separate the region from Romania and to undercut any claims for a larger Romanian state. A Moldovan nation was thereby engineered by communist activists who claimed that the Moldovans constituted a unique ethno-linguistic group. However, attempts to forge a separate Moldovan national consciousness proved difficult to implement, as the cultural, linguistic, and educational tools employed to establish a major divide with the Romanians were widely considered artificial. For example, the Moldovan language differed little from standard literary Romanian.

According to the secret protocols of the Ribbentrop-Molotov Pact, signed by Nazi Germany and the Soviet Union in August 1939, the Bessarabian region was to revert to the USSR. On 26 June 1940, Moscow issued an ultimatum to Bucharest demanding the immediate cession of Bessarabia and northern Bukovina on the grounds that the population was closely linked to the Russian-Soviet sphere and was largely Ukrainian. Lacking support from the Western allies, the Romanian authorities, under King Carol II, acceded to

Soviet demands, and on 28 June 1940, Soviet troops occupied Bessarabia and northern Bukovina. Stalin conducted a major purge in the territory against political figures, professionals, intellectuals, entrepreneurs, and "kulaks" (landowners or rich peasants), and about 90,000 Moldovans were either executed or deported to Siberia.

Romania allied itself with Nazi Germany, and after the German invasion of the USSR in July 1941, Romanian forces retook Bessarabia and northern Bukovina and officially reintegrated them in the enlarged state. Romanian troops also occupied the area east of the Dniestr River as a buffer zone between Greater Romania and the Soviet front line. It was in this region that some of the worst anti-Jewish massacres took place as Nazi units and Romanian fascists, under the leadership of General Ion Antonescu, murdered over 123,000 Jews from Bessarabia and Bukovina.

In April 1944, Transnistria again fell under Soviet control as the Red Army advanced against retreating German and Romanian forces. Both Bessarabia and northern Bukovina were occupied by Soviet troops, a communist regime loyal to Moscow was installed in Bucharest, and the peace treaty of February 1947 set the Romanian-Soviet border along the Prut River. A Moldovan Soviet Socialist Republic (MSSR) was created, comprised of the Bessarabian region between the Prut and the Dniestr, together with a thin strip of territory east of the Dniestr River. Northern Bukovina and some southern Bessarabian counties along the Black Sea were simply added to the Ukrainian Soviet Socialist Republic by the Moscow regime.

A Stalinist regime was imposed in Moldova whereby all political opposition was ruthlessly eliminated, all public institutions and economic enterprises placed under strict Communist Party control, and the Moldovan peasantry was forcibly collectivized. Over 115,000 peasants reportedly died from hunger and disease by the end of 1947. Russian and Ukrainian workers were encouraged to settle in the republic, particularly in the industrialized urban conglomerations along the Dniestr River. The Moldovan share of the population dropped from almost 70% in 1941 to 63% by 1979. Meanwhile, the proportion of Russian residents doubled from 6% to 13% between 1941 and 1989. At the same time, the Russification process was intensified in culture, education, and language use. During the rule of Soviet leader Leonid Brezhnev, Moldovan communists were loyal supporters of Moscow, and Brezhnev himself briefly served as the Moldovan party leader. Ivan Bodyul, the Moldovan party chief from 1961 until the early 1980s, was a trusted Brezhnev supporter.

Following the accession of Mikhail Gorbachev to power in the Kremlin in 1985, a campaign for restructuring *(perestroika)* and openness *(glasnost)* was launched throughout the USSR that had reverberations in Moldova. The Moldovan Communist Party, under the leadership of party First Secretary Semion Grossu, proved intransigent and resistant to change, thus sparking a broad popular movement for reform that was initially tacitly backed by Moscow. Several "informal organizations" were established during the summer of 1988, including the Moldovan Movement in Support of Restructuring and the Aleksei Mateevici Literary-Musical Club. They gathered together writers, journalists, and other intellectuals who canvassed for an increase in the official use of the Moldovan language and for more honest histories of the Bessarabian region. These groups appealed to Moscow for support against the hard-line republican leadership. Concurrently, a struggle developed between dogmatists and reformers in Moldova's cultural institutions, which challenged the stranglehold of the Leninist conservatives.

A Popular Front of Moldova (PFM) *(Frontul Popular din Moldova, FPM)* was established in May 1989 by 200 delegates, and it proceeded to campaign vigorously through demonstrations, rallies, and petitions for the reinstatement of the Moldovan-Romanian language in public life. Many reform communists sympathized with or joined the movement, calculating that the Communist Party was losing its control and influence in the republic. The party was further weakened following elections to the Soviet Union's Congress of People's Deputies in March 1989, in which reformers sponsored by the "informals" defeated several members of the Communist Party Politburo. Ten seats were won by pro-independence activists such as Nicolae Dabija, Ion Druta, and Grigore Vieru, and the ability of communist conservatives to control the electoral process was seriously undermined.[2]

On 27 August 1989, the PFM assembled a "Grand National Assembly" in the center of the Moldovan capital Chişinău, which consisted of a mass rally attended by almost half a million people. Demonstrators denounced the Ribbentrop-Molotov Pact and the Soviet assaults on Moldovan culture. Speakers demanded the withdrawal of Soviet troops from Moldova and condemned the illegal annexation of the country by Moscow. The Assembly adopted a manifesto calling for full national sovereignty and the right of separation from the Soviet Union. Under intense public pressure, on 31 August 1989, the Moldovan Supreme Soviet adopted new language laws that declared Moldovan the "state language" of the MSSR, mandated the transition to a Latin alphabet, recognized the unity of the Moldovan and Romanian languages, and established guidelines for expanding the use of Moldovan in all national institutions.

Moves toward Moldovan self-assertion negatively impacted inter-ethnic relations in the republic, as Slavic Russians and Ukrainians, together with Turkic Gagauz, were disturbed by the replacement of Russian as the official language. They were also concerned about growing pan-Romanian sentiments, fearful of forcible assimilation, and perturbed about possible moves toward Moldova's unification with Romania. These minorities created their own organizations to protect their interests. The Gagauz Turks, who inhabited a compact region in southern Moldova, set up the Gagauz People *(Gagauz Halki)* organization in May 1989. This movement grew out of a cultural club in the city of Comrat. Meanwhile, pro-Muscovite Slavic activists in the Transnistrian region formed the *Edinstvo* (Unity) organization as a branch of the all-Union *Interfront* movement, which supported the preservation of the USSR. Many of its leaders were high-ranking Communist Party officials in the heavily industrialized cities on the east bank of the Dniestr River who feared for their jobs and privileged positions.

Grossu, who had blocked all moves toward meaningful political or economic reform, was removed from office in November 1989 and replaced as Communist Party First Secretary by Petru Lucinschi, an active reformer favored by Moscow. Moldovan Communist Party luminaries included a number of reformers. Among them was Mircea Snegur, who through his astute support for national independence and his links with the PFM would become the country's first president. Snegur used the pressures toward reform and sovereignty to challenge the dogmatic and anti-reformist Transnitrian leadership that had dominated the republic's communist apparatus.

POST-COMMUNIST DEVELOPMENTS

The elections to the Moldovan Supreme Soviet on 25 February 1990 ended the monopoly of the Communist Party and inaugurated the collapse of one-party rule. Popular Front of Moldova (PFM) candidates, where they were permitted to stand in elections, easily defeated communist candidates. As a result, 27% of all Supreme Soviet seats went to Front supporters, and most of the rest to reform communists, while the hard-liners and the Transnistrian lobby were effectively marginalized. Prominent PFM organizer Mircea Druc became the country's new prime minister. The mood for independence began to grow among the Moldovan majority, although only a small percentage favored outright unification with Romania.

Events moved swiftly during 1990, after the Supreme Soviet (parliament) ended the leading role of the Communist Party in May 1990, legitimized a multi-party democracy, and declared state sovereignty on 23 June 1990. Several dozen pro-Soviet or Russophile deputies withdrew from the republican legislature in protest and focused on establishing alternative institutions, especially in the Transnistria area. In September 1990, Snegur was elected by the legislature to the newly created position of president, and parliament adopted a version of the Romanian flag as the Moldovan state emblem. Various other independence-oriented laws were enacted over the coming months, and in May 1991 parliament proclaimed the Republic of Moldova and terminated the MSSR designation.[3]

The Moldovan authorities opposed signing Gorbachev's new Union Treaty in early August 1991, and on 27 August 1991, the parliament formally declared full state independence, during the failed hard-line coup in Moscow. Under Prime Minister Mircea Druc, the PFM-dominated government conducted a purge of non-Moldovans from the country's cultural institutions and pursued a policy of Moldovization in the educational system. However, upon gaining independence, the PFM, which was formed from a diverse assortment of groups, began to break up into competing factions, thus creating political space for the reform communists and pro-Moldovan factions. The Agrarians in particular benefited from the Front's disintegration and became the most important grouping in parliament throughout most of the 1990s.

The Front's increasingly militancy on the issue of unification with Romania alienated large sectors of the population, including Moldovans and minorities alike. A small but committed majority of Moldovan activists, mostly the intellectual elites in Chişinău, sought an outright merger with Romania, and they proved influential in the early days of independence. Journalist Iurie Rosca, one of the PFM leaders, was the most vehement supporter of a merger with Romania, which he saw as the culmination of the de-Sovietization and democratization process. The pan-Romanian activists increasingly came into conflict with the Moldovanists represented by President Snegur, who benefited from substantial public support. In a move designed to undercut the Romanianist lobby, Druc was replaced as premier in May 1991 by the more moderate Valeriu Muravschi.

President Snegur increasingly distanced himself from the PFM program and depicted himself as a pragmatist and reformer. In December 1991, he was re-confirmed as the country's president in an unopposed popular election. A prominent ex-communist reformer, Andrei Sangheli, was named prime minister in June 1992. Shortly afterward, the PFM speaker of parliament, Alexandru Mosanu, was replaced by ex-reform communist Petru Lucinschi. The PFM majority in parliament fractured and crumbled, leaving the terrain open to Agrarian and Socialist deputies, who benefited from public disappointment with the previous nationalist administration.

The new government presented itself as favoring inter-ethnic reconciliation and a measured economic reform program that would protect the weaker segments of society. Snegur and his colleagues also favored a "two states" position, in which close ties would be established with Romania without surrendering the country's newly acquired sovereignty. This gained him significant backing among broad sectors of society and helped his Agrarian Democratic Party (ADP) win the parliamentary elections on 27 February 1994 with 43% of the vote and an absolute majority of 56 out of 104 seats. The PFM factions gained only 20 seats in the legislature. The size of the new parliament had been reduced from 380 to 104 deputies in order to bolster its efficiency and legislative effectiveness.

The 1994 elections also produced a new, pro-Moscow and anti-Moldovanist movement, the Socialist Unity Bloc (SUB), which captured 22% of the national vote and 28 parliamentary seats, thus constituting the second largest legislative faction. The Bloc was composed of two main organizations, the Socialist Party (SP)—the chief heir to the old Communist Party—

and the *Edinstvo* movement. Its leaders, many of whom were former conservative Communist Party officials, called for the restoration of Russian as Moldova's official language. They benefited from the frustration evident among pensioners and in other social sectors where living standards had declined, especially in the urban areas. Nine other parties and alliances failed to win the 4% minimum vote necessary to gain parliamentary seats.

The new government coalition included the ADP, which advocated an independent Moldova, economic reform, and closer economic ties with Russia and the CIS (Commonwealth of Independent States). Their support for permanent Moldovan independence was radically different from the pro-Romanian views that had dominated the parliament before 1994; in the latter, independence was perceived as a stepping-stone toward outright unification with Romania. The staunchly pro-independence but non-Romanian position evidently enabled the government to negotiate on a sounder footing with the country's separatist groups. The new administration made several moves to defuse inter-ethnic tensions—for example, by suspending mandatory language tests for state employees and by virtually ensuring that Moldova became a bilingual state. A referendum on 6 March 1994 also served to calm tensions, as 95% of voters rejected unification with Romania in favor of an independent Moldova: the turnout was estimated at 75.1% of registered voters.

Snegur lost the presidential elections in November–December 1996 to Petru Lucinschi, who captured 54% of the vote to 46% for Snegur. President Lucinschi had been the penultimate first secretary of the Moldovan Communist Party, and a speaker of the Moldovan parliament who wanted to improve relations with Moscow. He presented himself as a moderate reformer seeking ethnic and international accommodation. The Sangheli cabinet resigned on 2 December 1996 in order to allow for the formation of a government that was more in tune with the new Moldovan president. Snegur himself subsequently altered his political stripes and established a new alliance with the former PFM and stood for parliamentary elections on 22 March 1998 with former Front leader Iurie Rosca.

The March 1998 legislative elections were won by the reconstructed Party of Moldovan Communists (PMC), which gained 30% of the vote and 40 seats. The PMC was led by Vladimir Voronin, a former leader of the *Interfront* movement. It was the most successful successor of the defunct Moldovan Communist Party, especially following the virtual collapse of the Socialist Unity Bloc after the 1995 local elections and the eclipse of the Agrarian Democrats. The Communists campaigned on a welfarist and protectionist platform in a country that was experiencing a major economic downturn. But it did not oppose Moldovan statehood or press for the re-creation of the Soviet state.

The pro-Romanian Democratic Convention of Moldova (DCM), which had merged with Snegur's Party of Renewal and Accord of Moldova (PRAM), captured only 19% of the vote and 26 seats. Only two other parties were represented in the new parliament: the Bloc for a Democratic and Prosperous

Moldova (BDPM), with 24 seats, and the Party of Democratic Forces (PDF), with 11 seats. The BDPM was composed predominantly of supporters of President Lucinschi. The PDF was the successor of a PFM splinter group, the Congress of Intellectuals (CI).

The new government of Prime Minister Ion Ciubuc consisted of the three minority parties, the MDPM, the DCM, and PDF, and it managed to exclude the Communists from forming a government. Ciubuc was replaced as premier in early 1999 by Ion Sturza, who endeavored to maintain the cohesion of the often-rancorous three-party agreement. According to observers, Moldova's electoral system discouraged the creation of stable parties with clear-cut constituencies.[4] The proportional representation system operated on the basis of a closed party list ballot, providing little incentive for parties to lobby among distinct constituencies. Moreover, patronage and cronyism were rampant, and economic networks sprang up, determined to defend their economic interests through political and party channels and by participation in the national parliament.

Moldova held a new series of presidential elections in December 2000. Under the new constitutional framework, the country had changed its election procedures. Instead of selecting the president by popular plebiscite, in July 2000 parliament implemented an indirect ballot inside the legislature. A presidential candidate needed to receive 61 of 101 possible votes in parliament to be elected. In the first ballot, on 1 December 2000, Communist Party leader Vladimir Voronin ran against the compromise centrist candidate Pavel Barbalat, the chief judge of the constitutional court. Neither of the two candidates managed to capture the 61 required votes. Voronin was locked at 48 votes and Barbalat gathered 37 votes; fifteen ballots were declared invalid. In the second round, on 4 December 2000, none of the candidates succeeded in gaining the required number of seats; and a third ballot, on 6 December 2000, was also unsuccessful.

The failure to elect a President after several rounds of voting, resulted in the dissolution of the legislature and early parliamentary polls. In November 2000, President Petru Lucinschi had asserted that he refused to run for reelection because he was strongly against the limitation on presidential powers and the indirect election process. At the end of December 2000, Lucinschi signed a decree dissolving parliament and setting new elections for February 2001. Lucinschi's term in office ended in mid-January, but he was scheduled to remain in his post until a new parliament was in place together with a new head of state. He claimed that the new parliament would decide whether to abolish the decision to transform Moldova into a presidential republic subsequent to a public referendum.

In parliamentary elections on 25 February 2001, the Party of Moldovan Communists (PMC) obtained slightly over 50% of the vote and gained over 71 out of 101 legislative seats. The newly formed Braghis Alliance of outgoing premier Dumitru Braghis, captured 13.36% of the vote and 19 seats, and the Christian Democratic People's Party only 8.24% and 11 seats. The Moldovan Party of Renewal and Accord led by former President Mircea Snegur failed to clear the 6% hurdle for parliamentary representation. With an overwhelming Communist majority, parliament easily elected the PMC leader Vladimir Voronin as the country's new President on 4 April 2001.

The Communists had regained power in Moldova largely because of widespread disillusionment with the economic performance of the outgoing coalition government. However, party leaders pledged themselves to maintaining a pluralistic political system and working with international institutions in the pursuit of economic reforms. The PMC government also asserted that it would redouble its efforts to resolve the Transnistrian dispute. Moldova's opposition expressed concerns that the new administration would press for membership in the Russia-Belarus Union and thereby undermine the country's European orientation.

Moldova signed the Alma-Ata declaration creating the Commonwealth of Independent States (CIS) on 31 December 1991 and took part in the CIS's economic components. However, it also developed good relations with other European nations and refused to sign agreements that would have strengthened ties and dependencies among the CIS states. Moldova also initiated a series of economic, social, and political reform programs. Its new constitution, which defined Moldova's sovereignty, neutrality, and dedication to democracy, was promulgated in July 1994.

Moldova maintained a largely agro-industrial economy. Agriculture accounted for 34% of the GDP (gross domestic product) and employed roughly 700,000 people. Industry in Moldova was weakened after independence because many of the industrial plants were located within the areas of separatist conflict in Transnistria. The search for alternative energy sources and attempts to create its own energy supplies were also critical for Moldova, to counter overwhelming dependence on Russian energy. The breakup of the Soviet Union contributed to energy shortages that resulted in a decline in industrial productivity. Although the CIS accounted for the majority of its foreign trade, Moldova's Western exports steadily increased as it struggled to transform its centralized state economy.[6]

About 3.2 million of the country's population were ethnic Moldovans, constituting nearly three-quarters of the republic's total, and another 800,000 inhabited the northern Bukovina and southern Danubian districts of Ukraine. Approximately one-third of the Moldovan population consisted of Ukrainian, Russian, and Gagauz Turkish minorities. Most of the 600,000 Ukrainians inhabited the west bank of the Dniestr River; but the 170,000 in Transnistria formed a more compact population. Russians were the second largest minority, with 562,000 inhabitants, primarily concentrated in the major cities and industrial areas of Transnistria. Approximately 154,000 Gagauz or Christian Turks lived in Moldova, primarily in the southern *raion*s or districts, in a region historically known as the Bugeac, or Budjak. About

88,400 Bulgarians also lived in Moldova, mostly in the southern districts alongside the Gagauz, and they also called for some limited self-government in the Taraclia region.

Even before attaining independence, Moldova confronted serious problems with its largest regional minorities. Gagauz leaders pressed for greater local rights in culture and education and the devolution of power to their region. They were clearly fearful that Moldovan independence would undermine their position and even extinguish their distinct identity. During 1989, activists established the *Gagauz Halki* (Gagauz People) association to campaign for their interests, and it initially cooperated with the Popular Front of Moldova. With the PFM adopting a staunchly pro-Romanian position, Gagauz leaders feared that their local power base would be threatened. In response to the PFM's Moldovization campaign, in August 1990 an autonomous Republic of Gagauzia was declared in five southern districts of the country (Besarabeasca, Comrat, Ciadir-Lunga, Taraclia, and Vulcanesti), with its center in Comrat, and headed by Stepan Topal. The Moldovan government promptly outlawed *Gagauz Halki*. Escalating tensions came close to a civil war in the fall of 1990, when the Gagauz formed their own "self-defense" units.

The standoff between Chişinău and Comrat continued through the early 1990s, with the Gagauz demanding control over local resources but not outright secession from Moldova. After the February 1994 elections, the new government, led by the Agrarian Democratic Party, finally settled its differences with Comrat with the passage of a law that gave the Gagauz a substantial degree of territorial autonomy and the right to secede if Moldova were to merge with another state. The law on Gagauz autonomy was adopted by parliament in December 1994 and promulgated by President Snegur in January 1995. In effect, a *Gagauz Yeri* (Gagauz Land) "autonomous territorial unit" was created in which wide-ranging powers were given to local officials and Gagauz became one of the official languages.[7]

The pro-Romanian political forces warned that Gagauz autonomy signaled the thin end of the wedge in the breakup of the state. However, Gagauz leaders pledged to respect the country's territorial integrity and the overarching authority of the Moldovan government. Indeed, the Gagauz population participated in all subsequent local and national elections, although the most influential party in the region after 1995 was the Party of Moldovan Communists (PMC), which accounted for nearly all Gagauz deputies in the Moldovan parliament. Chişinău clearly hoped that the Gagauz model of devolution would prove appealing to the more militant separatists in Transnistria.

While the Moldovan government declared the country's independence in August 1991, Russian and Ukrainian separatist leaders proclaimed their own Transnistrian Republic, carved out of the eastern sector of Moldova that was initially part of the pre–World War II Moldovan Autonomous Republic and was attached to the MSSR after the war. By 1989, about one-quarter of the region's 600,000 inhabitants were ethnic Russians, and Slavs predominated in the cities. Moldovans formed about 60% of the rural dwellers and 40% of the total Transnistrian population.

Protests against the Moldovization of the republic were evident in the late 1980s among Transnistrian communist officials, local government leaders, and military commanders. To counteract moves toward Moldovan sovereignty, they established a Soviet-style Union of Moldovan Working People (UMWP). These regional elites felt their positions were threatened by the government in Chişinău and sought to gain guarantees of local autonomy and to ensure their control over local resources. The dispute was framed in ethnic terms with the claim that the government in Chişinău wanted to turn non-Moldovans into second-class citizens. Such assertions were voiced despite the fact that the majority of Moldovan Slavs inhabited the Bessarabian region outside of Transnistria and were not involved in the conflict. In reality, ethnicity was used as a cover for local communists to seize and control Transnistria's political and economic resources.[8]

In January 1990, local leaders organized a referendum on Transnistrian autonomy, which was allegedly supported by 96% of voters. Following Chişinău's declaration of Moldovan sovereignty, on 2 September 1990 local communist activists proclaimed the Dnestr Moldovan Republic (DMR) with its capital in Tiraspol, and established "self-defense units" in case of a Moldovan government assault. The leadership pledged to uphold the principles of "Soviet power." In November 1990, the Transnistrians created a local parliament, which proclaimed that the territory was no longer part of Moldova. The local leader was Igor Smirnov, who had been elected chair of the United Council of Work Collectives, a body that organized strikes and demonstrations against the Moldovan authorities. Smirnov and his comrades were assisted by commanders of the Soviet-Russian army stationed in Moldova.

By early 1991, most of the Transnistrian region was no longer under Chisinau's control. Armed clashes between Moldovan police units, interior ministry troops, armed civilians, and Transnistrian separatist forces were sporadic during 1991. But they intensified after the failed hard-line coup attempt in Moscow in August 1991, during which Moldova declared its independence. The Transnistrian authorities were also severely criticized for arresting and imprisoning a group of Moldovan activists, the "Ilascu Group," in May 1992. The activists were charged with terrorism and assassination, but the real motive for their incarceration was clearly political.

A full-scale civil war erupted in the first half of 1992 as the government in Chişinău pledged to disarm the rebel militias by force. Russian military units directly assisted the Transnistrian units against Moldovan attacks, on the pretext that they were defending the threatened Slavic population. The Moldovan defeat in the city of Bendery in July 1992 effectively stalemated the conflict, which left more than 1,000 dead or wounded and displaced about 130,000 residents from their homes. Although there was no major outbreak of violence after 1992, the dispute over the status of the separatist territory continued through the end of the 1990s.

Throughout the decade, the Transnistrians benefited from the presence of the Russian 14th Army, which had transferred some of its weapons to the local defense forces and proved a strong deterrent to any Moldovan government attempt to retake the territory. Although negotiations between Chişinău and Tiraspol, with Moscow's mediation, continued for several years, no resolution to the standoff could be found, even when compromise agreements appeared to be in sight. While Chişinău supported far-reaching autonomy, Transnistrian leaders dismissed any arrangement short of a loose Moldovan confederation between two independent states, a formula that was repeatedly rejected by Chişinău.[9] The Moldovan authorities vigorously objected to the presence of Russian forces in Transnistria that effectively defended the separatist administration. Chişinău sought a reduction and demobilization of these units to promote the reintegration of the territory.

The Moldovan authorities charged Moscow and conservative communist forces with encouraging and aiding Transnistria's separatist forces. Meanwhile, local Russian and Ukrainian leaders accused Moldova of seeking reunification with Romania, even though the administration had approached the question with some caution and underscored the republic's independence and self-determination. Paradoxically, pressures for the separation of Transnistria actually encouraged calls for Romanian-Moldovan unification in both states, because of fears of renewed Russian domination. Concurrently, the government in Bucharest came under increasing domestic pressure to support the Moldovan authorities and adopt a more forthright anti-Russian position.

Chişinău offered various compromises to the Transnistrian leadership, including guarantees of far-reaching regional autonomy, similar to the arrangements reached with the Gagauz and approved by parliament in 1995. These offers were rejected by Tiraspol, which passed a separate constitution, approved a Transnistrian flag and currency, and held its own elections for a regional president and parliament and for local governments. It also disallowed any voting in Transnistria for Moldovan institutions, although it permitted residents to cross over into Moldovan-held territory if they wished to participate in any elections. Powerful pro-Russian and ultra-leftist groups remained influential on the territory, especially in the larger cities of Tiraspol and Bendery. They included the chief ideologist Valerii Yakovlev, the Transnistrian President Smirnov, and the Transnistrian Supreme Soviet Chairman Grigorii Marakutsa.

With the passage of a new Moldovan constitution by parliament on 29 July 1994 and the inauguration of a moderate government, Chişinău sought to defuse ethnic tensions. Moldova was no longer referred to as a "national" state; the constitution focused on citizenship, not ethnicity, as the locus of state sovereignty. This reinforced Moldova's citizenship law adopted in 1991, which allowed all persons living in the country at the time of independence to become citizens regardless of ethnicity, language, or length of residence. The new constitution also established a semi-presidential system of government and a strong constitutional court. However, it rejected President Snegur's proposals for the creation of a "presidential republic." The president was empowered to call for referenda, to suspend acts of government that he felt contravened the law, and to dissolve parliament after 45 days if a government was not formed or if the passage of a law was blocked for three months. Nevertheless, parliament retained its sovereignty and legislative authority.

The new constitution also declared Moldova's permanent neutrality and banned the stationing of foreign troops on the country's territory. On the ethnic front, it declared autonomy for special regions such as Transnistria and the Gagauz area. It also formally recognized Russian and the other languages spoken in the country, in order to assuage minority fears about linguistic discrimination.

Moldovan-Romanian relations at the governmental level continued to evolve steadily. President Snegur enunciated the doctrine of "one people, two states," or "two states cooperating with each other," a principle that became the cornerstone of Moldovan relations with Bucharest. In Moldova itself, organizations such as the PFM called for speedy reunification with Romania and disagreed with Snegur's measured approach. Meanwhile, government leaders in Romania adopted a gradualist policy: they essentially supported Chişinău's stance on Moldovan independence and the "two states" doctrine, and they accepted Moldovan statehood, deferring the possibility of reunification to a distant future.

Romanian President Ion Iliescu envisaged a gradual evolution of interstate relations, beginning with the consolidation of Moldova's republican status and a Romanian-Moldovan rapprochement through "practical steps" to develop direct relations in all fields, primarily economic and cultural. The Iliescu administration attempted to find a middle ground between domestic expectations of rapid progress toward reunification and Moldova's insistence on its permanent independence. Nevertheless, the escalation of armed insurgency in Transnistria, supported by Russia's 14th Army, helped consolidate security links between Romania and Moldova and injected nationalist and revanchist sentiments into the political debate in Romania.[10]

Most of Romania's political groups, including a substantial sector of the democratic opposition, a part of the National Salvation Front, and the extraparliamentary opposition, rejected Snegur's "two-states" doctrine and insisted on prompt reunification. The main opposition parties as well as former premier Petre Roman occasionally injected the Moldovan issue into domestic politics and sought to use it as a weapon against the Iliescu administration. They accused Iliescu of sabotaging reunification, and denounced Snegur's administration for promoting separate Moldovan statehood. Nationalists envisaged resolving this issue through Moldovan self-determination within the framework of full Romanian control over its former provinces.

Several Romanian nationalist organizations campaigned for reunification with Moldova, together with the return of Romanian provinces lost to Ukraine after World War II. They organized rallies and other protest actions and demanded that the Romanian government and parliament take a more active role in defending Moldovan and Bukovinan interests. The Romanian Ecologist Movement and a number of nationalist parties tried to enlist Mircea Druc, a former Moldovan prime minister, to run on their party ticket for the Romanian presidential elections in September 1992. Although they were unsuccessful, the move indicated the importance attached to reunification by some sectors of the Romanian electorate. Relations between Moldova and Romania were not always smooth, as many Moldovan leaders rejected what they perceived as Bucharest's objective to eventually absorb the new state and to establish a uniform culture and political system. Meanwhile, the victory of the Agrarian Democrats after 1994 was negatively viewed in Bucharest as a step away from eventual unification.

In general, Moldova's political party structure remained weak and restricted. Most parties possessed little organizational structure beyond the capital and a few major cities. Rather than constituency-based formations, parties were interest-based and revolved around the country's elites. They maintained a parliamentary organization but did not seek to mobilize the electorate in any structured manner. Only a handful of parties displayed long-term cohesion and organizational abilities, including the Agrarian Democratic Party, which maintained a network of activists and supporters in Moldova's sizeable agro-industrial complex.

POLITICAL PARTIES

Socialists and Social Democrats

Democratic Labor Party (DLP)
Partidul Democrat al Muncii (PDM)

The Democratic Labor Party (DLP) was formed in 1993 around the interests of Moldova's large state-owned industries. The party became a base of support for engineers, technicians, and industrial managers. It claimed that the incumbent government was unable to assure the true independence of the state, the integrity of its territory, an active and flexible foreign policy, or the real protection of the people. Headed by the former parliament presidium member Aleandru Arseni, the party chiefly represented industrial enterprises seeking closer trade ties but not reunification with Romania.[11] In the parliamentary elections in February 1994, the DLP only gained 2.77% of the vote and no legislative seats.

According to the DLP platform, there was an urgent need to adopt a new constitution that would ensure a real division of powers, political pluralism, free mass media, and unconditional respect for human rights. Regarding the Transnistrian and Gagauz questions, the DLP sought to resolve the situation on the basis of internationally recognized rights, the de-centralization of state power, and the expansion of the prerogatives of local self-administrative bodies. The party considered it necessary to build multilateral relations with the European Union while preserving economic relations with the CIS countries.

The DLP supported a gradual transition to a market economy that would take account of Moldova's "specific features." Party leaders believed that there was an urgent need for real land reform, liberalization of various sectors, the stimulation of exports, the promotion of a flexible tax policy, the creation of a monetary and credit system that would benefit manufactures, the "consolidation" of the national currency, and the protection of consumers. In the March 1998 elections, the DLP failed once again to gain any legislative seats.[12]

Social Democratic Party of Moldova (SDPM)
Partidul Social Democrat din Republica Moldova (PSDM)

This party was formed in 1990 in the wake of the breakdown of the Popular Front of Moldova and was led by Oazu Nantoi. It was multi-ethnic and composed mostly of representatives of educated professional and managerial groups. Despite its social democratic label, the Social Democratic Party of Moldova (SDPM) proved strongly pro-market and liberal in its economic policies and enjoyed a good relationship with international agencies and Western governments. The Social Democrats enjoyed some influence in foreign and economic affairs despite their small representation in parliament. However, the party failed to attract any significant number of voters, especially in the countryside and among working class residents. In the February 1994 elections, it only gained 3.66% of the vote and failed to obtain any parliamentary representation.

In 1996, the SDPM became a member of the Socialist International. It engaged in extra-parliamentary opposition activity until March 1998, when it ran for elections and managed to win only 1.86% of the popular vote, again failing to garner parliamentary representation. In 1997 the SDPM joined a political formation called the United Social Democratic Party (USDP) *(Partidul Social Democrat Unit, PSDU),* together with the Party of Social Progress, the Republican Party, the Party of Social Action, and the Party of Economic Rebirth.

The SDPM rejected shock therapy in the pursuit of economic reform, and the concentration of property and capital in the hands of what it perceived as a small social group. It also supported Moldova's neutrality and opposed the country's proposed federalization. For the 23 May 1999 local elections, the SDPM entered an alliance with the *"Furnica"* Civic Alliance for Reforms

(CAR) and the Professionals Movement of Moldova (PMM). The alliance was styled as the Social Democratic Union of Moldova (SDUM) *(Uniunea Social Democrata din Moldova, USDM)*—a small and essentially centrist bloc.

United Labor Party of Moldova (ULPM)
Partidul Uniunii Muncii din Moldova (PUMM)

Established on 19 February 1997 by 400 delegates, including delegates from Transnistria, the United Labor Party of Moldova (ULPM) became a centrist party in its economic orientation. Although it favored market reforms, it also promoted a high level of social protection. According to its leader Andrei Safonov, a prominent political scientist from the Transnistrian region, the ULPM was a "centrist party" promoting the legendary "third way" between communism and capitalism. Safonov was a deputy in the Soviet-era Moldovan parliament and then an education minister in the government of the breakaway Transnistrian republic. However, he began to represent organizations that were in opposition to the separatist authorities. The ULPM favored market reforms alongside "high social protection." It also sought to preserve Moldova's position outside any military alliance. The ULPM was in many respects an experimental party, given that its membership encompassed people from both Moldova and Transnistria. Its leaders hoped that there would be a gradual shift of power in Moldova to new political forces that were not directly responsible for the negative phenomena of the Soviet and post-Soviet periods.

Movement for a Democratic and Prosperous Moldova (MDPM)
Pentru o Moldova Democrată şi Prospera (PMDP)

The Movement for a Democratic and Prosperous Moldova (MDPM) was established in 1996 to promote President Lucinschi's policy platform. It described itself as a centrist organization with some affinities to both the moderate left and the right.[13] Although the Movement supported the President, it pledged to oppose him in the future if it disagreed with his policies. Its main goal was to stabilize the sociopolitical situation and to restore "harmony" in society, based on "social and economic progress." It attempted to unite people with differing political outlooks and ethnic affiliations, and created sections for women, youth, veterans, and businessmen.

In 1998, the party reorganized and took the name of Party for a Democratic and Prosperous Moldova (PDPM) *(Partidul Pentru o Moldova Democrată şi Prospera, PPMD)* under the leadership of Dumitru Diacov, the former head of staff of Lucinschi's presidential campaign. The party's honorary chairman was Eugen Gladun.

The PDPM established a centrist alliance called the Bloc for a Democratic and Prosperous Moldova (BDPM) *(Blocul Pentru o Moldova Democrată şi Prospera,*

BPMDP), in alliance with the Civic Party of Moldova (CPM) led by Vladimir Solonari, the Popular Democratic Party (PDP) led by Serghei Scripnic, the New Force Movement (NFM) led by Valeriu Plesca, and the National League of Moldova's Youth (NLMY) led by Valeriu Strelet. In the March 1998 elections, it received 18.16% of the votes and 24 seats in Moldova's 101-member legislature. PDPM members were entrusted with several key cabinet positions, including the ministries of economy, finance, and agriculture. In October 1998, the PDPM formed a political alliance with other centrist parties.

Liberals

Democratic Convention of Moldova (DCM)
Convenţia Democrată din Moldova (CDM)

The Democratic Convention of Moldova (DCM) alliance was created in 1997 by Iurie Rosca's Christian Democratic Popular Front (CDPF) *(Frontul Popular Creştin Democrat, FPCD)*, Mircea Snegur's Moldovan Party of Renewal and Accord (MPRA) *(Partidul Renaşterii si Concilierii din Moldova, PRCM)*, and the Ecological Party of Moldova (EPM) *(Partidul Ecologist din Moldova, PEM)*, and other small political groups. The main purpose of the DCM was to "replace the vestiges of communism." It also sought closer links with Romania and faster integration into the European Union. Among other priorities, the DCM sought to accelerate the privatization process and to cut off ties to the CIS and to Russia in general. The CDM's electoral sign was a clock showing five minutes to twelve, and its electoral slogan was: "Faith, Justice, Modernity."

The DCM included the Moldovan Party of Renewal and Accord (MPRA) and the Popular Front of Moldova. The MPRA was led by the country's former President Mircea Snegur, who gave up his communist identity in 1990. He was the chairman of the Moldovan Supreme Soviet in July 1989 and Central Committee secretary after 1985. Other founders of the Movement included former deputies of the Agrarian Democratic Party of Moldova. The DCM followed centrist economic policies and favored civic and ethnic conciliation. It also supported rapid unification with Romania and the return to Moldova of northern and southern territories that were a part of Ukraine. In the March 1998 parliamentary elections, the DCM finished second, winning 19.42 % of the votes and capturing 26 seats. In 1999, in the wake of a governmental crisis triggered by the resignation of Ion Ciubuc's cabinet, the Christian Democratic Popular Front withdrew from the DCM.

Alliance for Democracy and Reforms (ADR)
Alianţa Pentru Democraţia şi Reforme (ADR)

On 28 April 1998, a parliamentary coalition was formed combining the Democratic Convention of Moldova (DCM), the Party of Democratic Forces (PDF), and the Bloc for a Democratic and Prosperous Moldova (BDPM), entitled the Alliance for Democracy and Reforms (ADR). The creation of the ADR meant that the country obtained a ruling majority, which Moldova lacked in the previous three years. These varied formations managed to overcome their differences and to unify their efforts principally with regard to economic issues. According to observers, the agreement was an important step in the reconciliation of Moldovan society, which remained split after the second round of the November–December 1996 presidential elections. The accord also ensured reconciliation between the two most influential Moldovan politicians, President Petru Lucinschi and his predecessor Mircea Snegur.

Party of Democratic Forces (PDF)
Partidul Forţelor Democrate (PFD)

The Party of Democratic Forces (PDF) was a rightist political party supportive of state independence and national unity within a united Europe. It was one of the successors to the Movement of Rebirth and National Freedom (MRNF). It brought together members of the Moldovan Popular Front (1993) with its initial name being the Congress of Intellectuals (CI). The CI included several prominent ex-PFM leaders, including the former chairman of parliament Aleksandru Mosanu. As a result of fusion with some other factions, the PDF changed its name to the United Democratic Congress (UDC) in June 1994. In October 1995 it opted to reinstate the PDF name. Its electoral platform was similar to that of the Democratic Convention of Moldova (DCM). It backed the eventual unification of Moldova with Romania in a gradual and long-term fashion.

In the March 1998 parliamentary elections, the PDF won 8.83% of the national vote and garnered eleven parliamentary seats. It joined the DCM and the Bloc for a Democratic and Prosperous Moldova (BDPM), with which it formed the Alliance for Democracy and Reforms (ADR). The Alliance constructed a centrist majority government with 61 out of the 101 legislative seats. Although the Party of Moldovan Communists (PMC) gained 40 seats and captured a plurality of deputies in the legislature, it proved unable to form a coalition government.

Alliance of Democratic Forces (ADF)
Alianţa Forţelor Democratice (AFD)

This electoral bloc was set up in January 1995 by nine Moldovan opposition parties in preparation for the local elections in April 1995. It brought together the Moldovan Liberal Party (MLP), led by Mircea Rusu; the Moldovan National Peasant Party (MNPP), chaired by Semion Certan; the Moldovan National Liberal Party (MNLP), led by Andrei Iuri Apostol; the Free Peasants Alliance (FPA); the United Democratic Congress (UDC); the Christian Democratic Women's League (CDWL); and sectors of the Ecologist, Reform, Christian Democratic Peasants, and Teachers League parties. The Alliance of Democratic Forces (ADF) followed a center-right orientation and was evidently open to other political parties. In the March 1998 elections, the ADF coalition received 2.24% of the popular vote and did not gain any seats in parliament.[14] However, some parties allied with ADF did receive mandates in coalition with the Bloc for a Democratic and Prosperous Moldova.

Civic Alliance for Reforms (CAR)
Alianţa Civica Pentru Reforme (ACR)

The socio-political movement the Civic Alliance for Reforms (CAR) was constituted in Chişinău in April 1997. The CAR wanted to protect the interests of businesspeople and domestic producers. The manager of the Chişinău Tractor Plant, Aleksandru Oleinic, who was also a leader of the CAR, stated at its constitutional congress that the movement aimed at the "consolidation of private property and support of local producers." Oleinic claimed that under the prevailing economic policy, Moldovan producers lost both the external and home markets, and the CIS countries imposed "biting and unjustified taxes." Sergiu Certan, leader of the Moldovan Movement of Shareholders (MMS) and former minister of economics, stated that his party welcomed the appearance of the CAR. According to Certan, "There are three million shareholders and 140,000 private or joint enterprises whose interests are defended by none of the political parties." According to its statute, the CAR also aimed at the "removal of geopolitical interests from the economy; stimulation of local businesses and producers; reform in agriculture and the sale of land; and the removal of the state monopoly in the acquisition of agricultural products."

Congress of Peasants and Intellectuals (CPI)
Congresul Ţăranilor şi Intelectualilor (CTI)

Headed by the Congress of Intellectuals, a group that split from the Popular Front of Moldova in 1992, the Congress of Peasants and Intellectuals (CPI) officially formed in 1993. Centered around the Writers Union and Romanian literary circles, the Congress joined forces during the February 1994 elections with the Alliance of Free Peasants (AFP), the Christian Democratic Party (CDP), the National Liberty Party (NLP), and the Christian League of Women (CLW). The Congress claimed a moderate pro-unification and pro-Romanian platform. According to party leader Valeriu Matei, the CPI visualized the inevitability of reunification with Romania within the context of Moldova's integration into European structures. Its economic platform called for accelerated privatization and the full implementation of Moldova's land reforms, which would allow peasants to claim ownership of a portion of the land in their collective farms.[15] In the February 1994 elections, the CPI received 9.21%

of the votes, and 11 seats in parliament. By 1996, leaders of the Congress of Peasants and Intellectuals had reorganized into the Party of Democratic Forces (PDF) *(Partidul Forțelor Democrate, PFD)*, with parliamentary deputy Valeriu Matei as chairman. The PDF gained 8.83% of the popular vote in the March 1998 elections and accumulated eleven parliamentary seats.

United Democratic Congress (UDC)
Congresul Democrat Unit (CDU)

The United Democratic Congress (UDC) was launched in June 1994 as an alliance of moderate pan-Romanian parties, notably the Congress of Intelligentsia (CI), the Christian Democratic Party (CDP), and the Democratic Party (DP). Derived from the former Popular Front of Moldova, the UDC contested the February 1994 election within the Congress of Peasants and Intellectuals, embracing the CDP as well as the Alliance of Free Peasants (AFP) and the National Liberal Party (NLP). The AFP consisted mainly of farm sector bureaucrats rather than actual peasants, and the Congress failed to dent the rural support base of the Agrarian Democratic Party, winning eleven seats on a 9.2% vote share. The DP had been allied with the anti-separatist Gagauz People's Party (GPP), a group that proved unable to reach the 4% threshold in parliamentary ballots. Leaders of the UDC included Aleksandru Mosanu and Gheorghe Ghimpu.

Moldovan Party of Renewal and Accord (MPRA)
Partidul Renașterii și Concilierii din Moldova (PRCM)

The Moldovan Party of Renewal and Accord (MPRA) was launched by the former President Mircea Snegur on 15 July 1995, shortly after his resignation from the Agrarian Democratic Party of Moldova (ADPM), which he had accused of sabotaging his policies, particularly with regard to economic reform. Joined by 11 of the 56 Agrarian deputies, the MPRA declared itself to be a mass party of the center, seeking to unify all the "healthy" political forces in the country on the basis of a presidential rather than a parliamentary system of government. Its leaders included Snegur, the party chairman, and Nicolae Andonic, deputy chairman of parliament and deputy chairman of the party. It soon claimed a membership of some 5,000 people. The MPRA became a classic presidential party, favoring the creation of a presidential republic with a bicameral and weakened parliament.[16] In 1997 the MPRA helped to establish the Democratic Convention of Moldova (DCM), a rightist political bloc, together with the Christian Popular Front (CPF) and the Ecological Party (EP). The DCM managed to receive 19.42% of the vote in the March 1998 parliamentary elections and 26 legislative seats. According to the party congress, a key goal of the MPRA was to establish a broad rightist alliance similar to what had been created by centrist and leftist forces.

Party of Reform (PR)
Partidul Reformei (PR)

Registered in 1993, this pro-market and pro-independence party, despite benefiting from substantial funding, won only 2.36% of the vote in the February 1994 balloting and failed to gain representation in the legislature. It subsequently initiated moves to create a broader grouping of reformist movements. Its principal focus was the establishment of a prosperous middle class through individual entrepreneurship.[17] The Party of Reform (PR) leadership included Anatol Salaru, the chairman. According to its self-definition, the party constituted the only truly rightist-conservative party that wanted to adopt a new constitution. The electoral program of the PR focused on reforming the judiciary, the educational system, and economic ownership.

The PR considered that Moldova's main problems were economic. It concentrated its attention on creating the necessary conditions for the establishment of a broad middle class that would guarantee the country's stability and independence. The goals of the party in the economic arena included the equalization of rights of private and state property; a constitutional right to private property; "real privatization" as a means of economic reconstruction; a new investment policy oriented toward foreign business; financial support for the private sector; promotion of a tax policy that would stimulate economic growth; the development of agriculture; the diversification of energy resources; a basic reform of the wage system; revision of the social protection and insurance system; and the setting up of state insurance together with a private system for health assistance. The party also viewed the territorial integrity of Moldova as a critical task but supported the decentralization of state power and local autonomy for Transnistria and for localities densely populated by the Gagauz minority. In the March 1998 elections, the PR was unable to gain any parliamentary seats.

"Furnica" Civic Alliance Bloc (FCAB)
Blocul Alianţa Civica "Furnica" (BACF)

This bloc was formed in 1997 by the Civic Alliance for Reforms (CAR), the Civic Unity Movement (CUM), the Moldovan Progressive Party (MPP), and the Moldovan Centrist Democratic Party of Rebirth (MCDPR). Its leader was Adrian Usatii. "Furnica" Civic Alliance Bloc (FCAB) cast itself as a centrist coalition whose leading members were entrepreneurs and the self-employed. The bloc proposed extensive market reforms that would purportedly help create a new "social order" in the country. The FCAB received only 3.29 % of the March 1998 electoral votes and failed to garner any parliamentary seats. Among other liberal and centrist parties formed in the 1990s were the Moldovan Republican Party (MRP) and the Party of Civic Dignity (PCD), both registered in October 1999. The MRP described itself as a centrist organization supporting a presidential form of government. A National Salvation Movement (NSM) was formed in February 2000, following a schism within the small National Liberal Party (NLP). The new party's coordinating council included Andrei Groza, the pro-unification activist. While the NLP opposed a political union with Romania, the NSM favored it in its party platform.

Christian Democrats

Christian Democratic Popular Front (CDPF)
Frontul Popular Creştin-Democrat (FPCD)

The Christian Democratic Popular Front (CDPF) was a continuation of the Popular Front of Moldova (PFM), which had briefly dominated political life in the country following the end of Communist Party rule in 1990. The CDPF was created in May 1989 and soon adopted a strong anti-communist orientation. Its leaders supported Moldova's union with Romania through a democratic process. The PFM transformed itself into the CDPF at its third congress, in February 1992. The original PFM platform had focused on autonomy from the Soviet Union and on the rights of Moldova's ethnic Romanian population as well as on steps toward Moldovan-Romanian unification. The PFM's/CDPF's support for pan-Romanianism alienated many of its initial supporters and weakened its organizational base. Several leading Front members who were dissatisfied with its militancy and falling popularity left the movement in the early 1990s to create new political parties. These included the Congress of the Intelligentsia (CI) formed in April 1993, which was re-christened the Party of Democratic Forces (PDF) in 1996.

Ion Hadarca resigned as chairman of the PFM in protest against its stated goals. In May 1992 the party's executive committee replaced former Prime Minister Druc, who had become a Romanian citizen, with Iurie Roşca as chairman. Druc subsequently stood as an independent candidate in the Romanian presidential elections. In the February 1994 Moldovan elections, the CDPF obtained nine parliamentary seats and a popular vote of 7.53%. One of its previous major goals, unification with Romania, had decreased in importance in the party's priorities.

The CDPF became a member of the European Christian Democratic Union and promoted policies furthering European integration, gradual disengagement from the Commonwealth of the Independent States (CIS), and the shedding of ties binding Moldova's economy to that of Russia. In 1997 the CDPF was the main force in the newly established Democratic Convention of Moldova (DCM), from which it withdrew in 1999 over disagreements about the representation of its members in the formation of the government headed by Prime Minister Ion Sturza.[18]

Other Christian Democrat formations in Moldova included the Alliance of the Christian Democratic Popular Front (ACDPF) *(Alianţa Frontul Popular*

Creştin şi Democrat, FPCD), composed of the CDPF and its two affiliated youth organizations; the National Christian Party (NCP), which favored immediate unification with Romania and the merger of the Romanian and Moldovan Orthodox Churches; and the Moldovan Christian Democratic Peasant Party (MCDPP) *(Partidul Ţăranesc Creştin Democrat din Moldova, PTCDM)* established in 1994 and led by Vladimir Reus.[19]

Agrarians

Agrarian Democratic Party of Moldova (ADPM)
Partidul Democrat Agrar din Moldova (PDAM)

Formed in November 1991, the Agrarian Democratic Party of Moldova (ADPM) was the core of the Sangheli government of national unity formed in mid-1992. It included reform communists, agricultural managers, and collective farmers who supported Moldovan independence but not unification with Romania. Favoring continued Moldovan statehood and participation in the CIS economic structures (although not military or political integration into the CIS), the ADPM won a narrow overall parliamentary majority in the February 1994 parliamentary elections, with 43.18% of the vote and 56 out of 104 seats. It benefited from public disquiet with the staunchly pro-Romanian PFM government and adopted a moderate approach to nationality issues. The party was weakened by the departure of President Snegur and his formation of the rival Moldovan Party of Renewal and Accord (MPRA) in July 1995, thereby losing its absolute parliamentary majority. Nevertheless, it remained the dominant political grouping in the country.[20]

The ADPM's 1994 parliamentary success was a turning point for Moldovan politics. The new legislature was able to make compromises between ethnic Romanians and ethnic Slavs, enabling it to pass legislation and set a more moderate tone for governing the country. Although there were rumors of splits within the party, these were refuted by Dumitri Motpan, the party chairman and parliamentary speaker. Other major ADPM leaders included former prime minister, Andrei Sangheli, and Moldova's President Petru Lucinschi.

The ADPM was a moderately conservative party but lacked a clearly defined ideological and political base. The party promoted the concept of a "Moldovan identity," which in the early 1990s was a significant political issue debated by President Snegur and Prime Minister Sangheli. After its parliamentary victory, the party consolidated its position in the spring 1995 municipal elections. However, in 1995 the ADPM split following bitter disputes among its leaders, including Snegur, Lucinschi, and Sangheli. It subsequently began to disintegrate into rival power blocs despite attempts to revive its program and popularity.

The party failed to win any seats in the March 1998 parliamentary elections, gaining only 3.63% of the vote, and virtually disappeared from the political scene. The core of the party was taken over by hard-liners such as Anatol Papusoi and Aurel Talmatchi, who had little public support. In the aftermath of its defeat, negotiations were initiated for a merger with the Party of Moldovan Communists (PMC) and other leftist formations. Other agrarian based political groupings included the Moldovan National Peasant Party (MNPP) (*Partidul Naţional Ţărănesc din Moldova, PNTM*) led by Ilie Untila.

Greens

Ecological Party–Green Alliance (EP-GA)
Partidul Ecologic–Alianţa Verde (PE-AV)

The Ecological Party–Green Alliance (EP-GA) was established in 1992, and its leadership included Ion Dediu and Mircea Ciuhrii. In the February 1994 elections, the environmentalist coalition gained only 0.4% of the national vote and no parliamentary seats. In 1997 the Ecological Party joined the Democratic Convention of Moldova (DCM), a rightist political bloc that obtained 26 seats after the March 1998 ballot. Environmental issues did not figure prominently on Moldova's political agenda, but the green movement remained closely tied to the campaign for Moldova's statehood and eventual unification with Romania.

Communists

Socialist Unity Bloc (SUB)
Blocul Unitatea Socialista (BSU)

As an alliance of former *Interfront* and pro-Soviet parliamentarians, the Socialist Unity Bloc (SUB) was composed primarily of ethnic Russians, with a few prominent Moldovan figures in leadership positions. The SUB promoted "fully developed socialism" in the traditional Soviet style.[21] The SUB coalition was founded in 1992 and was supported by the Alliance for Concord and Progress (ACP), the Unity Movement (UM), and the Union of Veterans of War and Labor. Although the SUB was predominantly Russian, the Veterans Union was multi-ethnic. The Bloc was supported by some industrial workers as well as by people disaffected with the economic changes since the early 1990s.[22]

The Bloc favored a mixed economy and heavy reliance on the state to regulate the economy and control prices. It also supported restrictions on the privatization of the service sector; subsidized rental housing; and restored full employment. On non-economic issues, it called for making Russian the second state language, acceptance of dual citizenship, and the pursuit of Moldova's political and military integration into the CIS. It also favored Chişinău's recognition of the institutions already in place in Transnistria, and the confederalization of Moldova. In the February 1994 general elections, the Bloc received 28 seats, with 22% of the popular vote, and became the second largest formation in parliament. In the March 1998 national elections, the SUB only managed 1.83% of the vote and failed to qualify for any parliamentary seats.

Socialist Party (SP)
Partidul Socialist (PS)

The Socialist Party (SP) was a pro-Russian successor to the former Communist Party of Moldova, whose activity was suspended by the authorities in Chisinau between August 1991 and October 1993. The SP ran in an alliance in the February 1994 elections with the Unity Movement (UM) *(Mişcarea Unitatea-Edinstvo, MU-E)*, led by Petr Shornikov, who was banned from participating because he had allegedly backed the Transnistria Republic separatists. The alliance, which also included the Union of Veterans of War and Labor, won 28 legislative seats, with 22% of the vote, thus becoming the second largest formation in parliament.

The leader of the SP was Valeri Senic, and its support base included industrial workers, pensioners, and veterans, but few agricultural workers (they gravitated toward the ADPM). The SP was predominantly Russian in its membership and it campaigned on an economic platform that called for a mixed economy and retaining a heavy reliance on the state to regulate the economy and control prices. It sought to restrict private ownership to the service sector. The Socialists also sought to restore full employment and subsidize rental housing.

On non-economic issues, the SP supported making Russian a second state language, the acceptance of dual citizenship, Moldova's return to the ruble zone, and the country's political and military accession to the Commonwealth of Independent States (CIS). It also called for the legal recognition of the institutions already in place in Transnistria, the confederalization of Moldova, and the permanent stationing of the Russian 14th Army in Moldova.

During 1996, a party faction broke away to form the Moldovan Socialist Party (MSP). This new grouping favored a "democratic" form of socialism. Members of the party who defected from the SP claimed that they left because the *Edinstvo* bloc, which included the SP, was based on empty promises and the ethnic division of society. They also charged it with lacking ties with Western socialist and social democratic parties.

Party of Moldovan Communists (PMC)
Partidul Comunistilor din Moldova (PCM)

In August 1991 the Communist Party of Moldova (CPM) was suspended and its role was taken over by the Russophone *Interfront* movement, later to become the *Edinstvo* (Unity) Movement, which combined elements of communism and nationalism. Most of the communist *nomenklatura* in the rural areas reorganized itself into the Agrarian Democratic Party of Moldova (ADPM). In early 1994, the former Communist Party was re-legalized by the Agrarian-dominated parliament, and reemerged under the leadership of Vladimir Voronin. It united approximately 11,000 active members, grouped in 612 basic organizations.[23]

The party was renamed the Party of Moldovan Communists (PMC) in 1994 by former leaders and members of the CPM. Some 60 delegates attended the party's constituent conference. It continued to be led by Voronin, a former leader of the *Interfront* movement, and by Florin Christev, the former head of the Soviet-era Communist Party of Moldova. It proved to be the most successful successor of the defunct CPM in gaining support and influence. The PMC initially sought to reconstruct the Soviet Union under "new principles" and to increase the role of the state in administrating and regulating the economy. Party leaders believed that negative pressures were being exerted by Western financial circles on the Moldovan state. They opposed the land reform program, favored slower steps toward privatization, and supported the maintenance of state pricing on staple products. The PMC also demanded tighter relations between Moldova and the members of the Commonwealth of Independent States (CIS)—especially Russia.

The PMC electoral mascot was a hammer and a sickle below an open book. The PMC tried to appeal to a broader cross-section of Moldovan voters than the traditional industrial and urban base of the Socialist Unity Bloc and the various ethnic minority organizations. From the mid-1990s onwards, the party reached out across ethnic lines in an attempt to gain support among all Moldovan citizens who were dissatisfied with economic conditions and falling living standards. In 1996, the PMC backed Lucinschi in the second round of the presidential elections, calculating that he would seek to restore closer links with Moscow and enable the party to regain power.

In the March 1998 parliamentary elections, the PMC finished first, with 30.01% of the popular vote and 40 out of 101 seats. Nevertheless, the party failed to establish a governing majority, and a coalition of center-right political forces eventually formed the new Moldovan administration. The Communists overwhelmingly won the February 2001 parliamentary elections with 71 of 101 seats and established the new government. Other small orthodox communist parties during the 1990s included the Independent Communist Party of Moldova, ICPM (*Partidul Comunist Independent din Moldova, PCIM*), among whose leaders were the hard-liners A. Gavrilov, A. Gradzheiru, and A. Muntyann.

Nationalists

National Christian Party (NCP)
Partidul Naţional Creştin (PNC)

In addition to the pro–Romanian unification Popular Front of Moldova (PFM), several smaller Moldovan nationalist and ultra-nationalist parties became active during the 1990s. They benefited from only limited public support and failed to obtain any legislative seats. The National Christian Party (NCP) openly campaigned for reunification with Romania, and it also called for the abolition of the results of the Molotov-Ribbentrop Pact, which ceded Moldova to the Soviet Union. Its leaders included D. Todike, M. Baraga, and V. Niku. In contrast, the Republican Party (RP) *(Partidul Republican, PR),* founded in 1993 by parliamentary Vice-Chairman Victor Puscas, viewed Moldova as "neither a Russian nor a Romanian province" and was therefore strongly Moldovanist.[24] Its leaders included Victor Puscas.

Moldovan nationalists or "unionists" who supported unification with Romania and the creation of a "Greater Romania" were divided into two broad groupings: national radicals and moderates. The radicals were proponents of immediate and unconditional unification with Romania. They were represented by several political and social organizations, which formed the Christian Democratic Alliance "1 October." They included the Christian Democratic People's Front (CDPP), the Christian Democratic League of Moldovan Women (CDLMW), the Organization of Christian Democratic Youth (OCDY), the National Christian Party of Moldova (NCPM), and the Moldovan Intellectual Congress (MIC).

Moderate nationalists proposed the gradual unification of Moldova and Romania, and established Romanian sociocultural socialization as a means of achieving their goal. The following political parties represented this tendency: the Christian Democratic Party of Moldova (CDPM), the Ecological Party—Green Alliance (EP-GA), the National Liberal Party (NLP), the Free Peasants Alliance (FPA), the Party of Reform (PR), the Democratic Labor Party (DLP), and the Congress of Peasants and Intellectuals (CPI). Although their goals resembled those of the radical nationalists, the moderates disagreed with the radicals' methods and terms of unification.

Ethnic Minority and Religious Parties

Gagauz People (GP)
Gagauz Halki (GH)

This minority political group was formed in 1989 to represent the 153,000 Gagauz people in Moldova. It was led by S. Gulgar. At the outset it cooperated with the Popular Front of Moldova (PFM). As the PFM adopted a staunchly pro-Romanian position, Gagauz leaders feared that their local power base would be threatened. Like the Russian-speaking community in Transnistria, with whom they became close political allies, Gagauz nationalists gained control over local government in five *raions* in the south of the country, where the population was concentrated. They demanded far-reaching autonomy for these areas and expressed fears about potential Moldovan assimilationism that would allegedly eradicate their culture, language, and identity.

Former communist activists sponsored by the Transnistrian separatist leaders and by imperial circles in Moscow sought to exploit the Gagauz issue to create problems for the Chişinău government. In August 1990 an autonomous Republic of Gagauzia was declared in five southern districts of the country (Besarabeasca, Comrat, Ciadir-Lunga, Taraclia, and Vulcanesti), with its center in the largest city of Comrat, and headed by the militant Stepan Topal. The Moldovan government outlawed the Gagauz People (GP), and growing tensions almost precipitated a civil war in the fall of 1990, when the Gagauz formed their own "self-defense" units.

The standoff between Chişinău and Comrat continued through the early 1990s, with the Gagauz demanding control over local resources but not outright secession from Moldova. After the February 1994 elections, the new administration led by the Agrarians settled its differences with Comrat with the passage of legislation that gave the Gagauz a substantial degree of territorial autonomy and the right to secede if Moldova merged with another state. The Gagauz autonomy law was adopted by parliament in December 1994 and promulgated by President Snegur in January 1995. A *Gagauz Yeri* (Gagauz Land) "autonomous territorial unit" was created in which wide-ranging powers were given to local officials and Gagauz was designated as one of the official languages.[25] Chişinău calculated that the Gagauz model of devolution would prove appealing to the more militant separatists in Transnistria, but this supposition was mistaken.

Pro-Romanian political forces warned that Gagauz autonomy signaled the impending disintegration of the state. In reality, Gagauz leaders pledged to respect the country's territorial integrity and the authority of the Moldovan government. The Gagauz population participated in all subsequent local and national elections. The most popular party in the region after 1995 was the Party of Moldovan Communists (PMC), which accounted for nearly all Gagauz deputies in the Moldovan parliament.

On 7 August 1996, a "civic movement" among the Gagauz was formed that supported incumbent President Mircea Snegur's candidacy in the November 1996 presidential elections. This movement included 17 parties, organizations and associations, among which were Snegur's Moldovan Party of Renewal and Accord, the Alliance of Democratic Forces, the Christian Democratic Popular Front, the Gagauz People's Party, and the Christian Democratic Peasant Party. Among other Gagauz political formations established in the 1990s were the Democratic Party of the Gagauz (DPG) *(Partidul Democrat al Gagauzilor, PDG)* chaired by G. Savostin.

Moldova's smaller ethnic minorities, including Bulgarians, also formed their own political organizations and interest groups, but they did not obtain seats in the national parliament as ethnic parties. Nonetheless, minority representatives were able to become deputies through affiliation with the larger Moldovan parties.

Regionalist Separatists

Union of Patriotic Forces (UPF)
Uniunea Forţelor Patriotice (UFP)

In July 1989, Slavic activists in the Transnistrian region established the
Edinstvo (Unity) movement as a Moldovan branch of the Soviet-wide *Interfront*
organization, which campaigned for the preservation of the USSR. *Edinstvo*
or the Movement for Unity (MFU), *(Mişcarea Unitatea, MU),* led by Petr
Shornikov and Vasilii Iakovlev, benefited from the support of local party officials, industrial managers, and Soviet military officers. The pro-Russian
Union of Patriotic Forces (UPF), whose leaders included Vasily Yakovlev
and Igor Smirnov (Smirnov was also chairman of the United Council of Labor Collectives [UCLC] and became the initial leader of the breakaway
Transnistrian region), dominated the region's politics for much of the 1990s
and sought to build the underpinnings, institutions, and symbols of an independent Transnistrian state. In addition to its separatist and pro-Moscow political agenda, the UPF maintained an ultra-leftist and essentially communist
social and economic program. It sought to preserve the offices and privileges
of the old communist *nomenklatura* by appealing to Soviet nostalgia, ethnic
sentiments, and defensive nationalism against alleged Moldovan-Romanian
assimilationism and expansionism.

Unity–Transnistria Region (U-TR)
Edinstvo Pridnestrovye (EP)

The party of Russian President Vladimir Putin, Unity, set up its branch in the
Transnistria region in July 2000. A constitutional congress of the party branch
was held on 22 July 2000 in the city of Bendery (Tighina). According to the
Tiraspol-based Tiras-Media Center, the branch was called Unity–Transnistria
Region (U-TR). It was established by the local Union of Industrialists, Agri-
culturists, and Entrepreneurs. The congress was attended by 322 delegates
from all districts of the secessionist Transnistrian enclave. Though he was
invited, the leader of the Tiraspol administration, Igor Smirnov, did not participate in the congress. The congress was conducted under strongly pro-
Transnistrian and pro-Russian slogans. Speakers claimed that the party should
become a "political bridge" between the Russian Federation and the Transnistrian
republic. Vladimir Belitcenko, the director of the metallurgic plant in Ribniţa,
one of the leaders of the new formation, called on Moscow "to show courage
and recognize the Dniestr republic." The Transnistrian branch of Unity was to
become part of the Moscow territorial organization of the Unity Party.

Earlier in the 1990s, the ultra-nationalist Russian political leader
Vladimir Zhirinovsky had created a branch of his Liberal Democratic
Party (LDP) in Transnistria. Several other essentially Russian parties and

groupings also were active in Transnistria for much of the 1990s, viewing the region as a beacon of Russian grandeur that openly promoted the restoration of an imperial state.

Independents and Miscellaneous

Among various independent political movements or social groups in Moldova with political ambitions it is worth mentioning the Association of Victims of the Totalitarian Communist Regime (AVTCR) *(Asociaţia Victimelor Regimului Totalitar Comunist, AVRTC)*, led by Mihail Morosanu, which received 0.9% of the vote in the February 1994 parliamentary elections; the Association of Women (AW) *(Asociaţia Femeilor, AF)*, which received 2.83% of the 1994 vote and whose leaders included Liudmila Scalnii; the League of Moldovan Women (LMW) *(Liga Creştin-Democrata a Femeilor din Moldova, LCDFM)*, established in 1992 and led by Ala Mandacanu; and the "Dignity" Left-Bank Democratic Movement (DLBDM), an essentially anti-separatist Transnistrian party.

POLITICAL DATA

Name of State: Republic of Moldova *(Republica Moldova)*
Form of Government: Presidential republic
Structure of Legislature: Unicameral legislature *(Parlamentul)* with 104 seats elected for four-year terms by proportional representation.
Size of Territory: 13,067 square miles
Size of Population: 4,431,570 (2001)

Composition of Population:

Ethnic Group	Number	% of Population
Moldavians/Romanians	2,795,00	64.50
Ukrainians	600,000	13.80
Russians	562,000	13.00
Gagauz	153,000	3.50
Bulgarians	88,000	2.00
Jews	66,000	1.50
Belarussians	20,000	0.45
Roma	9,000	0.20
Germans	7,000	0.15
Others	41,000	0.90
Total	4,341,000	100.00

Source: CIA World Fact Book 2001.

ELECTION RESULTS

Presidential Election (Indirect), 4 April 2001

Candidate	Votes*	% of Vote
Vladimir Voronin	71	70.0
Dumitru Braghiş	15	15.0
Valerian Cristea	3	3.0
Absent or abstained	12	12.0
Total	101	100.0

*Sixty-one votes required to win.
Sources: BBC Worldwide Monitoring, Kyiv Unit, 5 April 2001; and Agence France-Presse, 4 April 2001.

Presidential Election, 17 November and 1 December 1996

Turnout: 68.13%

First Round, 17 November 1996

Candidate	Votes	% of Vote
Mircea Snegur	603,652	38.74
Petru Lucinschi	430,836	27.66
Vladimir Voronin	159,393	10.23
Andrei Sangheli	147,555	9.47
Valeriu Matei	138,605	8.90
Marina Levitchi	33,119	2.13
Anatol Plugaru	28,159	1.81
Iulia Gorea Costin	9,926	0.64
Veronica Abramciuc	6,619	0.42
Total	1,557,860	100.00

Second Round, 1 December 1996

Turnout: 71.61%

Candidate	Votes	% of Vote
Petru Lucinschi	919,831	54.02
Mircea Snegur	782,933	45.98
Total	1,702,764	100.00

Source: IFES, Moldova, Book 96, Republic of Moldova, Presidential Elections, 17 November and 1 December 1996 (CD).

Presidential Election, 8 December 1991

Turnout: 83%

Candidate	Votes	% of Vote
Mircea Snegur	1,911,490	98.17
Total	1,950,500	100.00

Source: www.bsos.umd.edu/cidcm/mar/molslavs.htm.

Parliamentary Elections, 25 February 2001

Turnout: 67.52%

Party/Coalition	Votes	% of Vote	Seats
Party of Moldovan Communists	794,808	50.07	71
The Braghiş Alliance	212,071	13.36	19
Christian-Democratic People's Party	130,810	8.24	11
Moldovan Party of Renewal and Accord	91,894	5.80	—
Democratic Party	79,757	5.02	—
Social Democratic Party of Moldova	39,247	2.47	—
Other	238,679	15.04	—
Total:	1,587,257	100.00	101

Source: International Foundation for Election Systems. http://www.ifes.org/eguide/resultsum/moldovares2.htm.

Parliamentary Elections, 22 March 1998

Turnout: 69.12%

Party/Coalition	Votes	% of Vote	Seats
Party of Moldovan Communists	487,002	30.01	40
Democratic Convention of Moldova	315,206	19.42	26
Bloc for a Democratic and Prosperous Moldova	294,691	18.16	24
Party of Democratic Forces	143,428	8.83	11
Agrarian Democratic Party	58,874	3.63	—
"Furnica" Civic Alliance Electoral Bloc	53,338	3.29	—
Alliance of Democratic Forces Electoral Bloc	36,344	2.24	—
Social Democratic Party	29,647	1.89	—
Socialist Unity Electoral Bloc	30,169	1.83	—
"Speranta" Social Democratic Electoral Bloc	21,282	1.31	—
Party of Socialists	9,514	0.59	—

Party of Reform	8,844	0.54	—
Christian Democratic Union	8,342	0.51	—
United Party of Labor	3,124	0.19	—
Independent Candidates	90,997	5.61	—
Other	32,185	1.98	—
Total	1,622,987	97.73	101

Source: IFES, Moldova, Book 98, Republic of Moldova, Parliamentary Elections, 22 March 1998 (CD).

Parliamentary Elections, 27 February 1994

Turnout: 79.31%

Party/Coalition	Votes	% of Vote	Seats
Agrarian Democratic Party of Moldova	766,589	43.18	56
Socialist Unity Bloc	390,584	22.00	28
Congress of Peasants and Intellectuals	163,513	9.21	11
Christian Democratic Popular Front	133,606	7.53	9
Social Democratic Party	65,028	3.66	—
Association of Women	50,243	2.83	—
Democratic Labor Party	49,210	2.77	—
Party of Reform	41,980	2.36	—
Democratic Party	23,368	1.32	—
Victims of the Totalitarian Communist Regime	16,672	0.94	—
Republican Party	16,529	0.93	—
Ecological Party–Green Alliance	7,025	0.40	—
National Christian Party	5,878	0.33	—
Independents	45,152	2.54	—
Total	1,7775,377	100.00	104

Source: University of Essex, www.2.essex.ac.uk/elect.

NOTES

1. For recent histories of Moldova see Charles King, *The Moldovans: Romania, Russia, and the Politics of Culture*, Stanford: Hoover Institution Press, 1999; George Cioranesco, *Bessarabia: Disputed Land Between East and West*, Munich: Editura Ion Dumitru, 1985; Ian Bremmer and Ray Taras (Eds.), *Nations and Politics in the Soviet Successor States*, Cambridge, England: Cambridge University Press, 1993; Jeff Chinn and Robert Kaiser, *Russians as the New Minority: Ethnicity and Nationalism in the Soviet Successor States*, Boulder, Colorado: Westview Press, 1996; Nicholas Dima, *From Moldavia to Moldova: The Soviet-Romanian Territorial Dispute*, Boulder, Colorado: East European Monographs, 1991; and Donald Dyer (Ed.), *Studies in Moldovan: The History, Culture, Language, and Contemporary Politics of the People of Moldova*, Boulder, Colorado: East European Monographs, 1996.

2. A valuable analysis of Moldova's transformation can be found in William Crowther, "The Politics of Democratization in Postcommunist Moldova," in Karen Dawisha and Bruce Parrott (Eds.), *Democratic Changes and Authoritarian Reactions in Russia, Ukraine, Belarus, and Moldova*, Cambridge: Cambridge University Press, 1997, pp. 282–329. See also Charles King, *Post-Soviet Moldova: A Borderland in Transition*, London: Royal Institute of International Affairs, 1995.

3. For discussion on national mobilization in Moldova see William Crowther, "Ethnic Politics and the Post-Communist Transition in Moldova," *Nationalities Papers*, 26, No. 1, 1998, pp. 147–164. For a useful summary of the language dispute consult Dan Ionescu, "Back to Romanian?" *Transition*, Vol. 1, No. 15, 25 August 1995, pp. 54–57.

4. See Charles King, 1999, pp. 160–161. Also check Vladimir Socor, "Moldova's Political Landscape: Profiles of the Parties," Radio Free Europe/Radio Liberty, *Research Report*, Vol. 3, No. 14, 11 March 1994.

5. "Presidential Election Begins," in Moldovan Parliament, at htpp://news.ournet.md/2000/12/01/en/1.html.

6. Arthur Banks (Ed.), *Political Handbook of the World*, CSA Publications, State University of New York at Binghamton, p. 625.

7. For details on the Gagauz issue see Vladimir Socor, "Moldova Granting Autonomy to Gagauz" Radio Free Europe/Radio Liberty, *Research Report*, No. 143, 29 July 1994; Jeff Chinn and Steven D. Roper, "Territorial Autonomy in Gagauzia," *Nationalities Papers*, 26, No. 1, 1998, pp. 87–101; and Charles King, "Gagauz Yeri and the Dilemmas of Self-Determination," *Transition*, Vol. 1, No. 19, 20 October 1995, pp. 21–25.

8. Information on the Transnistrian conflict can be found in Stuart J. Kaufman and Stephen R. Bowers, "Transnational Dimensions of the Transnistrian Conflict," and Pal Kolste and Andras Malgin, "The Transnistrian Republic: A Case of Politicized Regionalism," *Nationalities Papers*, 26, No. 1, 1998, pp. 129–146, and pp. 104–127. Also consult Erica Dailey, *Human Rights in Moldova: The Turbulent Dniester*, New York: Helsinki Watch, 1993.

9. Consult Dan Ionescu, "Playing the 'Dniester Card' In and After the Russian Election," *Transition*, Vol. 2, No. 17, 23 August 1996, pp. 26–28; and Gottfried Hanne, "Playing Two Different Tunes, as Usual, in Moldova," *Transitions*, Vol. 4, No. 7, December 1997, pp. 68–71.

10. Vladimir Socor, "Moldovan-Romanian Relations Are Slow to Develop," RFE/RL, *Research Report*, Vol. 1, No. 26, 26 June 1992.

11. CSCE , Report on Moldovan Parliamentary Elections, April 1994, p. 6.

12. IFES (International Foundation for Electoral Systems), Report on Moldova, "The Moldovan Parliamentary Elections," Washington, D.C., 1994.

13. http://194.196.235.201/bin/OMRI.acgi$main_search, Daily Digest, 10 February 1997.

14. http://www.agora.stm.it/elections/election/ moldova.htm.

15. IFES, "The Moldovan Parliamentary Elections Report," 27 February 1994: Appendix 20:25. See also www.european forum.bot-consult.se/cup/moldova/parties.

16. Consult Dan Ionescu and Igor Munteanu, "Likely Presidential Rivals Gear Up for Elections," *Transition*, Vol. 2, No. 2, 26 January 1996, pp. 50–52.

17. CSCE, Report on Moldovan Parliamentary Elections, April 1994, p. 6.

18. Andrei Brezianu, *Historical Dictionary of the Republic of Moldova*, Lanham, Maryland, and London: Scarecrow Press, 2000.

19. European Forum, "The Political Landscape of Moldova," http://www.europeanforum.bot-consult.se/cup/moldova/parties.htm.

20. Check Dan Ionescu, "Moldova Slides Back and to the Left," *Transition*, Vol. 3, No. 2, 7 February 1997, pp. 55–56.

21. CSCE, Report on the Moldovan Parliamentary Elections, April 1994, p. 6.

22. IFES, "The Moldovan Parliamentary Elections Report," 27 February 1994: Appendix 20:26.

23. http://www.odci.gov/cia/publications/95fact/md.html.

24. CSCE, "Report on the Moldovan Parliamentary Elections," April 1994, p. 6.

25. For details on the Gagauz issue see Jeff Chinn and Steven D. Roper, "Territorial Autonomy in Gagauzia," *Nationalities Papers*, 26, No. 1, 1998, pp. 87–101; and Charles King, "Gagauz Yeri and the Dilemmas of Self-Determination," *Transition*, Vol. 1, No. 19, 20 October 1995, pp. 21–25.

Ukraine

HISTORICAL OVERVIEW

Eastern Slavic tribes settled present-day Ukraine in the sixth century AD. Here, one of the most powerful states of medieval Europe, Kyivan Rus', was founded during the ninth. Kyivan Rus' included the cities of Kyiv, Novgorod, Chernihiv, Halych, Polotsk, Smolensk, Rostov, Suzdal, and later, Moscow. It constituted a huge expanse of territory between the Baltic and the Black Seas and the Kuban River, and from Transcarpathia to the Volga. The Dnipro river trade route from Scandinavia to Byzantium passed through Kyiv. In 988 AD, Prince Volodymyr introduced Christianity as the official state religion, and the formal christening of Kyivan Rus' took place on the banks of the Dnipro river. At the time of Kyivan Rus', Kyiv was one of the richest and most developed cities in Europe, with numerous architectural accomplishments, including St. Sofia's Cathedral and the Golden Gate of Kyiv. Although under the ecclesiastical jurisdiction of Constantinople, Rus' was not isolated from Latin and West European influences, political and religious authorities remained separated and autonomous.

In 1240, Mongol invaders captured Kyiv. Thousands of inhabitants were killed and much of the city was destroyed. Kyiv fell into a prolonged period of decline, as the Mongols ruled the territory for almost three centuries, and the most important trading routes were severed. The Kyivan Rus' state disintegrated and some of its lands eventually came under the rule of either Moscow or the Grand Duchy of Lithuania, Rus', and Samogitia. Ukrainians subsequently claimed the independent Galician-Volhynian state of the thirteenth and fourteenth centuries as part of their national and state heritage. This essentially feudal state structure collapsed, due largely to outside pressures, and was incorporated into the Grand Duchy.

As the Mongol Empire disintegrated, one of its successor states—the Crimean Khanate, which became a vassal of the Ottoman Empire in the fifteenth century—staged regular raids on Slavic Ukrainian territories, in search of slaves. However, the major part of Ukrainian ethnic territory came under the control of the Grand Duchy of Lithuania, Rus´, and Samogitia. At the end of the fifteenth century, Ukrainian Cossack territories in the eastern borderlands remained outside the control of any outside powers.[1] The Cossack phenomenon was essentially an organization of military self-defense of the Ukrainian peasantry in the exposed southern and eastern frontier zones. After the Union of Lublin in 1569 between Poland and Lithuania, Ukraine was incorporated into the Polish Commonwealth. However, the new government was unable to offer the Ukrainian peasantry effective protection against Tatar raids; and in a social structure controlled by nobles, demands for an emancipated and armed peasantry were combated. Polish attempts to suppress the Cossack military led to a more general Ukrainian uprising in 1648.

Between 1648 and 1654, Cossack armies, headed by *Hetman* (Cossack leader) Bohdan Khmelnytsky, waged several wars against Polish rule in order to liberate Ukrainian territories and establish a new administrative structure in areas under Cossack control. An independent Ukrainian Cossack state was created, officially named the Zaporizhzhian Army, while the name "Ukraine" (borderland) was widely adopted in all areas controlled by the Cossacks and gradually replaced the traditional designation of "Rus´," derived from the medieval state.

Confronted by the armies of Polish and Lithuanian feudal lords, Khmelnytsky sought the protection of the Russian tsar through the Treaty of Pereiaslav in 1654. The Cossacks sought to avoid fighting a war on two fronts simultaneously and to expand their territories westward. However, as a result of the Pereiaslav agreement, Ukraine accepted Muscovite overlordship and was pushed into a long period of domination by the Russian Empire. The autonomy of Cossack Ukraine was undermined and eventually extinguished by Moscow. At the end of the eighteenth century, the Crimean Khanate was also destroyed by Moscow, and Ukrainian peasants permanently settled the Black Sea region. Cossack forces continued to struggle for independence; but following a major defeat at the battle of Poltava in 1709, Ukraine was permanently incorporated into the Russian Empire and its autonomy was eliminated.

Despite such repression and severe tsarist autocratic rule during the seventeenth and eighteenth centuries, Ukraine managed to preserve its culture and folk traditions. The Mohyla Academy, founded by Metropolitan Petro Mohyla in the seventeenth century, was one of the first universities in Eastern Europe. Books were printed, philosophy was studied, and music, literature, and painting flourished. The first constitution appeared in Ukraine during the Cossack period, in 1711. Throughout the nineteenth century, Ukrainian movements of cultural and national revival continued to be active despite the prevailing current of repression and Russification. Political and cultural groups had to operate illegally and underground, as virtually all Russian political leaders denied the existence of a distinct Ukrainian nationality.

By contrast, in the Galician region, occupied by Austria after the 1848 nationalist revolutions, the Ukrainian population was able to take part in elections. It possessed a parliamentary representation, several political parties, an indigenous press, and a number of cultural and civic organizations. The Greek Catholic (Uniate) Church also played a major role in Ukraine's cultural and national revival. The Church was a bulwark against both Polish and Russian assimilation. The Uniate clergy became the leaders of the Ukrainian community, which increasingly asserted its identity throughout the nineteenth century. The role of Andrei Sheptysky, the Metropolitan of Galicia, was especially important in the independence struggle, and Galicia itself became the sanctuary of the Ukrainian national movement.

In January 1918, when the Russian Empire collapsed, national activists proclaimed the independence of Ukraine, and the Ukrainian National Republic was established. Mykhaylo Hrushevsky became the first President of Ukraine. But at that time Ukrainian statehood was not adequately defended, and Bolshevik forces rapidly overran the country. Russian military conquest was depicted by communist propaganda as "fraternal aid" for the Ukrainian people.

After a brief period of "indigenization" in the 1920s, the Soviet regime eliminated all vestiges of Ukrainian statehood and self-determination. Under Lenin, the Ukrainian Soviet Republic enjoyed some vestiges of autonomy in cultural and linguistic matters, and Moscow's New Economic Policy, designed to stimulate production, revived the Ukrainian economy. But Stalin's reign of terror during the 1930s destroyed the remnants of Ukrainian self-determination. In particular, the forced collectivization of the Ukrainian peasantry, and the artificially induced famine in 1933, led to the death of over five million people in the countryside.[2] Furthermore, Stalin's repression destroyed Ukraine's intellectual elites as well as the indigenous communist leadership, which Moscow considered to be too independently minded.

The Nazi German invasion of the Soviet Union in 1941 was viewed by the majority of Ukrainians as an opportunity for national liberation. However, they were quickly disillusioned as the Germans imposed a virtual colonial regime throughout the Ukrainian territories. A Ukrainian guerrilla movement sprang up that battled both Nazi and Soviet forces throughout the 1940s. As a result of World War II, the Soviet Union annexed the territories of Galicia, Subcarpathia, and Bukovyna (containing Ukrainian majorities) from Poland, Czechoslovakia, and Romania respectively, and incorporated them in the Ukrainian Soviet Socialist Republic.

In the post-war years, Ukraine had little opportunity for autonomy or the development of its national culture. Although not as brutal as the Stalinist terror, the post-Stalin regimes maintained a tight grip over Ukrainian society through their communist surrogates in Kyiv. Dissident groups emerged in the 1960s and 1970s, but they were generally small and uninfluential because of persistent state repression. Most notable among them was the Ukrainian

Helsinki Group, which was formed in 1976 to monitor Kyiv's compliance with the recently signed Helsinki Accords. The majority of new dissidents were essentially democrats seeking the restoration of human rights and Ukrainian sovereignty through peaceful means, as well as full disclosure about the "ethnocide" of the Ukrainian nation under Stalinist rule. However, the bulk of the population was highly atomized and politically passive. Political opponents of the communist regime fell into two main camps: those who wanted Ukraine to achieve genuine autonomy within the Soviet Union, and "integral nationalists," who sought complete independence.

Ukraine's conservative communist elite was taken by surprise with the launching of Gorbachev's *perestroika* campaign in 1987. Under the rule of Volodymyr Shcherbytskyi, the communist political class controlled the Ukrainian state and economy as their private fiefdom. Leonid Kravchuk, the ideological secretary of the party, declared that a popular front was unnecessary to reform and modernize the country. This stimulated the defection of many communist intellectuals and other dissatisfied elements to new liberal groupings such as the Ukrainian Popular Movement for Restructuring (UPMR), subsequently known as *Rukh*, which was inaugurated on 8 September 1989. *Rukh* initially presented itself as a movement that recognized the leading role of the Communist Party. But unlike in the Baltic states, Ukrainian rulers were not interested in reaching accommodation with democratic forces. Indeed, they deliberately obstructed the country's democratization, calculating that Gorbachev's reform policies would soon be reversed.

POST-COMMUNIST DEVELOPMENTS

Events moved swiftly during 1990–1991, regardless of the objectives of the hard-line communist leadership. On 4 March 1990, Ukraine held its first multi-candidate national ballot for the republican parliament and elected a bloc of deputies favoring Ukrainian statehood. Benefiting from large-scale coal miners' strikes in the summer of 1989, *Rukh* constructed a coalition of nationalists, moderates, and working-class dissenters to challenge communist rule. Although the Communist Party of Ukraine (CPU) had surrendered its sole leading role, there was insufficient time to register new parties or for democrats to gain access to the mass media. In a clearly flawed election process, the CPU won 373 of the 450 parliamentary seats.

Although in the major cities the embryonic Democratic Bloc did gain seats, in sum, the pro-reform coalition only managed to claim 25 out of 450 parliamentary deputies. They included the *Rukh*-led coalition, which garnered one quarter of legislative seats. Under both public and party pressure, Leonid Kravchuk replaced the hard-liner Volodymyr Ivashko as head of parliament.

Following protest actions by students and workers in support of Ukrainian sovereignty, Prime Minister Vitalii Masol resigned in October 1990.

On 24 August 1991, following the failed coup attempt by pro-Soviet hardliners in Moscow, the parliament, or Supreme Council (*Verkhovna Rada*), voted to declare the country's independence by initiating the Act of Declaration of the Independence of Ukraine. The implementation of this declaration was made contingent upon ratification in a popular referendum. Observers believed that the communist *nomenklatura* actually feared that the democratization and marketization process in Russia could sweep over Ukraine and dislodge them from their privileged positions. As a result, they cynically turned toward independence and nationalism in a move designed primarily to preserve as much of their power base as possible.

In a public referendum on 1 December 1991, the overwhelming majority of voters opted for independence: 84.1% of eligible voters took part, and 90.3% of those—or 76% of the total electorate—supported parliament's August declaration. Only 7.6% of citizens voted against independence. However, some significant regional variations were registered in the ballot. In the west and center of the country, over 95% of the electorate voted for independence; in the east, the figures ranged from 75% to 90%. In the Crimean peninsula, only 54% voted positively.[3] Ukrainian statehood thereby gained a solid base in the west and center, areas with a briefer experience of Sovietization and Russification, than in the east and south, where support for independence appeared to be conditioned on the performance of the post-Soviet government. The election results, as one analyst pointed out, indicated that "the road from external independence to *bona fide* internal unity remained rocky: much turbulence lies ahead."[4]

In the first presidential elections, held on 1 December 1991, Leonid Kravchuk was elected to office in competition with five other candidates—three nationalists and two centrists. Kravchuk had been head of the ideology department of the Communist Party of Ukraine and a member of the party's Politburo. He obtained 62% of the vote, with his nearest rival, the democratic nationalist Viacheslav Chornovil, receiving 23%. Kravchuk represented the "nationalist communist" stream in the CPU, which veered increasingly toward a pro-independence position as the Soviet Union unraveled. However, Kravchuk proved unable to win majorities in all regions; he gained only 30% of the ballot in nationalist western Ukraine and also lost ground to the pro-Russian candidate Volodymyr Hrynov in southern and eastern Ukraine. His highest level of support was in the country's central regions, including the capital, Kyiv.

During his term in office, President Kravchuk focused primarily on state building, on strengthening his own powers, and on ensuring the loyalty of the old *nomenklatura* by allowing it to benefit from the privatization of state assets. His support for independence won him the support of *Rukh* and several other nationalist groupings. With the split in *Rukh* at the end of 1992, the movement became increasingly marginalized, particularly as Kravchuk had virtually adopted its national program. Kravchuk's program did not involve wholesale market liberalization but the development of a patronage network and the dispensing of state property to specific economic elites. The country began to experience a major economic crisis in 1993 when Russia raised energy prices and freed most prices for raw materials on which Ukraine depended. The country was struck by hyperinflation and a wave of strikes by unpaid workers in the Donbas coal mines. Growing labor unrest led the Supreme Council to call for new parliamentary and presidential elections after the fall of the third government cabinet.

Legislative authority in Ukraine was located in the unicameral parliament *(Verkhovna Rada)*, consisting of 450 deputies elected for four-year terms.[5] The new election law, which created a mixed voting system, was adopted in October 1997. The law provided a framework in which 225 deputies were elected in single-mandate, majoritarian districts, and the remaining 225 were elected on party lists in proportion to the number of votes received after clearing a 4% threshold. Executive power was vested in the president and the prime minister. The president was elected by direct popular vote for a mandate of five years. With parliamentary approval, the president appointed the prime minister and members of the Cabinet of Ministers. Ukraine was a unitary state divided into 24 administrative regions *(oblasts)*, one autonomous republic (Crimea), and two cities with special status (Kyiv and Sevastopol).[6]

In the March 1994 parliamentary elections, half of the 450 deputies were elected on party lists, rather than as individual candidates running in districts, thus copying the Russian State *Duma* system. Before that, all Ukrainian deputies were elected in territorial districts, resulting in prominent local figures, usually with no party ties, winning seats, and political parties playing a weak role. Nevertheless, the electoral law still favored "independent" candidates rather than political parties. The former required the support of only 300 citizens in a district in order to secure nomination, whereas the registration of political parties was a long and laborious process. This undermined the development of political parties and favored the entrenched *nomenklatura*. The "independents," who were largely supportive of the *status quo*, received the largest bloc of votes in the ballot. Moreover, Ukraine had a weak tradition of political parties and few historical parties and institutions to draw upon. Compared with other postcommunist states, Ukraine witnessed a "chronic discontinuity in the national elite" because of prolonged Russian and Polish domination in its history.[7]

Even though 200,000 signatures were required to register for the 1994 elections, 30 parties and blocs qualified. Nevertheless, political parties in the commonly accepted sense hardly existed. They were not professionally organized, and their members were not loyal to their parties. In fact, most Ukrainian parties were based around regional or sectoral interest groups rather than political or ideological criteria. A majority of parties were weak and possessed a small and shifting popular base. Consequently, party affiliation and parliamentary groups were not fixed. In addition, the majority of election candidates did not consider themselves supporters of any particular party.[8]

Leonid Kuchma won the June–July 1994 presidential elections by defeating the incumbent Kravchuk. Kuchma ran on a program of closer links with Russia, against Kravchuk's largely nationalist appeal. Kuchma scored particularly well in eastern and southern Ukraine and among frustrated and underpaid workers. Nevertheless, the contest between Kuchma and Kravchuk "still represented an intra-clan feud within the party of power and not a contest between two political visions."[9] Kuchma focused more attention on economic stabilization than on state building, but his prescriptions did not diverge dramatically from those of his predecessor, and he did not challenge the economic stranglehold of the ex-*nomenklatura.*

Prior to the 1994 elections, two major political blocs emerged: the pro-Russian and socialist Interregional Bloc for Reforms, and the more nationalist Ukrainian Democratic Coalition. Before the March 1998 parliamentary ballot, several electoral alliances emerged, including the socialist Working Ukraine *(Trudova Ukraina)*, the Socialist and Peasant Union (SPU), the centrist Labor Party and Liberal Party Together *(Partiya Pratsi ta Liberalna Partiya-Razom)*, the Electoral Bloc of Democratic Parties *(Vyborchyy Blok Demokratychnykh Partiy)*, the Social Liberal Association, the Christian Democratic "Forward Ukraine" *(Vpred Ukraino)*, and the nationalist National Front *(Natsionalnyy Front)*. The parties ranged from Communist, Socialist, and Peasant on the "left" to the moderate nationalist *Rukh* and National Front and the extreme nationalist Ukrainian National Assembly on the "right." Most parties, including *Hromada*, remained in the center, but only a few of these were significant. In general, the Communists and Socialists consisted of pro-Russian groups with a strong base in eastern, Russian-speaking Ukraine. Their counterparts were the nationalist parties, whose main support came from western Ukraine. Both wings favored strong rule by the executive branch as an answer to social and economic problems. In both the 1994 and 1998 legislative elections, the leftist parties made a stronger showing than the center-rightist groups.

The centrists made half-hearted attempts to cooperate with each other, and also with Kuchma, who stated that he would not support any individual party but would work with all centrist forces in an effort to unite them against the communists. In early October 1998, Kuchma persuaded the heads of several centrist parties, including the Christian Democrats, Agrarians, and the Interregional Bloc of Reforms, to sign a "Memorandum on Joint Actions" for the upcoming election. Several centrist parties declined to sign, arguing that the memorandum committed them to supporting the President. Kuchma's cooperation with centrist parties notably excluded *Hromada*. The lines between government and opposition were blurred by the fact that some government officials ran on the tickets of opposition parties, suggesting that their opposition to Kuchma was not intense. The real opposition to Kuchma was from the Communists and *Hromada*, whose lists did not include any Kuchma officials.

An intensive struggle for power and predominance characterized Ukrainian politics in the 1990s. This was particularly visible in the conflict between president and parliament over the pace and implementation of the market reform program, the new post-Soviet constitution, and the country's election laws.[10] Kuchma demanded greater executive powers, but this was opposed by leftist deputies in the legislature. These disputes invariably paralyzed attempts at economic transformation; but unlike in Russia, they did not lead to outright violence and the forceful assertion of presidential powers.

The national constitution adopted on 28 June 1996, under the threat of a national referendum that Kuchma was confident of winning, defined the country as a unitary state in contradistinction to the federal system proposed by some regional interest groups. It created a stronger semi-presidential system but also included checks and balances among the three branches of power. For example, although the president nominated the premier, he had to obtain parliamentary approval for the candidate.[11] A unicameral legislative system was upheld, and the president was not given the right to dissolve parliament. The government established the long-delayed constitutional court, consisting of 18 members, with six each appointed by the president, parliament, and a congress of judges. However, the country failed to produce a truly independent judiciary, as the president and parliament remained deadlocked over the nominations. Kyiv was also accused of engaging in various human rights infractions, including the persecution of critical journalists through police and administrative measures and media censorship. However, the government stopped short of trying to impose an authoritarian system; indeed, attempted media censorship could be perceived as a sign of governmental insecurity and weakness.

Ukraine's new election law, implemented at the end of 1997, introduced a mixed voting system in which proportional party-list voting was combined with direct district races. It was intended to provide an important boost for the development of political parties, which had played a largely secondary role in Ukrainian politics. Parties were henceforth given a more prominent role in general elections. For the March 1998 elections, half of the 450 seats in parliament were elected on nationwide party lists, with parties entering the legislature needing to win at least 4% of the vote. The remaining half of the seats were allocated by single-mandate district races using a first-past-the-post system. Only eight parties cleared the election threshold. The centrist and rightist parties fared poorly and a leftist majority was installed in the legislature.[12]

On the left, the Communist Party took a total of 124 seats, the Socialist and Peasant bloc 35, the Progressive Socialists 16, and the United Social Democratic Party 18. At the center, the pro-Kuchma People's Democratic Party gained 28 seats, the *Hromada* opposition 23 seats, and the Green Party took 19 seats. The centrist parties remained in conflict and lacked unified interests and programs. On the center-right, *Rukh* managed to win only 46 seats, whereas 114 were won by nonaligned and independent candidates. The remainder of the seats were divided among representatives of smaller parties, including that of former Prime Minister Viktor Pynzenyk. The president concluded that the position of the new legislature would maintain political gridlock, and he pushed for changes in the constitution to give the prsidency greater powers.

Presidential elections were held on 31 October and 14 November 1999. In the second round of the ballot, incumbent Leonid Kuchma was victorious, having gained 56.25% of the vote, and his leftist rival Petro Symonenko obtained 37.8%. Elections revealed both the power of the political left and the ability of pro-reform center-right forces to coalesce and work together. The electoral process in 1999 could be divided into two periods: the first, from the beginning of the campaign until the results of the first ballot, was marked by fragmentation of both left and center; the second phase, during the subsequent round of elections, was signified by coalescing.

The first period showed a broad political spectrum represented by 15 presidential candidates ranging from Petro Symonenko on the extreme left to new candidates from the moderate right, such as Yuri Karmazin and Mykola Haber. During the second period, leftists grouped around the strongest candidate, Petro Symonenko. Centrist forces formed an ill-defined and seemingly unstable coalition around the most viable centrist candidate, Kuchma. This coalition highlighted the extreme positions of Symonenko on issues of property and economic development and generated fears of civil instability in the event of Symonenko's election.

The broad centrist coalition was probably the most important result of the elections, as it changed the parliamentary-presidential balance of power in favor of the President. The issue of strengthening presidential powers received a boost as President Kuchma attempted to use his more advantageous position after the elections. Ukraine held a referendum on 16 April 2000 to help define presidential powers. The Ukrainian constitution provided three grounds for a national referendum: it could be designated by the President or parliament, or result from "popular initiative," in which case it must be supported by no less than three million voters.[13]

Four questions were posited in the referendum: extending the President's power to dissolve parliament if it did not form a majority government within a month after elections or if it did not approve the state budget during a three-month period; restricting the immunity of parliamentary deputies; reducing the number of deputies from 450 to 300; and creating a second parliamentary chamber that would be composed of appointed regional leaders. Each question received a positive vote, especially as most voters had a negative view of the nation's squabbling parliament.[14] The referendum was a logical continuation of the political struggle between President and parliament, especially in the aftermath of the 1999 presidential elections, in which Kuchma sought to enhance presidential powers, in opposition to parliament's leftist majority elected in 1998, which continued to block market reforms. But despite the plebiscite, Ukrainian lawmakers failed to approve a bill on amending the constitution in line with the referendum, by the end of 2000. The voting was boycotted by Communist and Socialist parliamentarians.

The relative success of the new reformist Prime Minister Viktor Yushchenko during 2000 and early 2001 in stabilizing the economy and pursuing structural change was increasingly undermined by political uncertainty. President Kuchma stood accused by his opponents of cracking down on media freedoms and of playing a role in the murder of a critical journalist, Georgiy Gongadze. But despite protests in parliament and in the streets of Kyiv, Kuchma survived in office. In April 2001, parliament passed a vote of no-confidence in the Yushchenko government, which promptly resigned. The move led some analysts to conclude that oligarchic interest groups linked with the Communist Party were determined to sabotage or derail the Yushchenko program, which threatened their economic and business interests. Meanwhile, Kuchma was willing to sacrifice Yushchenko in order to remain President and to deflect attention from his own political problems. The government in Moscow also used the opportunity of Ukraine's political turmoil to offer support to President Kuchma, in an effort to draw the country into a tighter Russian orbit similar to that of neighboring Belarus.

Regional politics impinged on the progress of party formation and parliamentary performance. Ukraine's major regions produced political parties tied to specific powerful industrial, political, and business clans. This was the case especially with the heavily industrialized and economically powerful Dnipropetrovsk and Donetsk regions. The Dnipropetrovsk group included such notables as President Kuchma himself, former Prime Minister Pavlo Lazarenko, and Prosecutor-General Hryhorii Vorsinov. The Donetsk group included ex-Prime Minister and Donetsk Mayor Yukhym Zvyahilsky and businessman and clan leader Yevhen Shcherban, who was murdered in suspicious circumstances in November 1996. Zvyahilsky was forced to resign in June 1994, following persistent accusations of corruption and embezzlement of state funds.

The power of these regional "clans" stemmed from their control over the political process, industry, and trade.[15] After the collapse of centralized control from Moscow, and given the weakness of the government apparatus in Kyiv following independence, regional elites acquired control over local resources and formed alliances to better defend their interests. However, it was not in their interest to push for separation from Ukraine or formation of a new Soviet Union in which a stronger central government could exercise more stringent controls. Some analysts concluded that the focus on regional and sectoral interests also lessened the likelihood that ethnic cleavages would disrupt the country.

The Dnipropetrovsk "clan" remained in the ascendancy throughout the 1990s, particularly after the election of President Kuchma in July 1994 and with the appointment of Pavlo Lazarenko as Prime Minister in May 1996. The number of people from Dnipropetrovsk represented in the central political establishment increased substantially: observers estimated that there were 55 in high-level government positions in the late 1990s.[16] Furthermore, the persistence of elite interests and *"nomenklatura* privatization" camouflaged as democratization and reform stifled the emergence of a robust entrepreneurial middle class and a vibrant civil society. The majority of citizens remained disengaged from politics and distrustful of politicians and parties.

Following the collapse of the Soviet Union and the political emancipation of its constituent republics, problems of statehood and national identity preoccupied most of the newly independent countries. These issues became particularly poignant in republics such as Ukraine, which experienced brief interludes of sovereignty and contained sizable Russian or Russified populations. Problems of political democratization and economic reform became closely intertwined with the quest for national integration and state building. The uneven process of nation building and state construction, evident in persistent regional divisions, threatened to polarize national allegiances, derail the political and economic reform process, widen ethnic cleavages, fracture the country's territorial integrity, and even undermine its independent status. A commitment to Ukrainian independence was strongest in the western regions, the central provinces, and in Kyiv; it was weakest in the eastern areas, which had been more heavily Russified over the last three centuries. The problem was compounded by widespread opposition to fast-paced market reforms.

According to the last Soviet census figures, released in 1989, the population of Ukraine stood at 51,452,000.[17] Of this, 72.7%, or 37,419,000 persons, were registered as ethnic Ukrainians. Russians constituted the largest minority, with 11,358,000 residents, or 22% of the population. The remaining 5.2% of the population, or 2,675,000 persons, were of 108 different ethnic groups, including Jews, Tatars, Poles, Belarusians, Greeks, Romanians, and Moldovans. Some 4.6 million ethnic Ukrainians claimed Russian as their native language and were considered partially or wholly Russified. Whereas 87.7% of Ukrainian ethnics were principally Ukrainian speakers, and 12.3% were primarily Russian speakers, 98.4% of Russian ethnics declared Russian as their first or only language.

The accuracy of the Soviet census and its ethnic breakdown remained in serious doubt, particularly as it was never completed or fully interpreted and translated. Some analysts contended that the number of residents registered as Ukrainians was artificially or inadvertently reduced and the number of non-Ukrainian ethnics was inflated.[18] Nationality was self-defined in the census: individuals simply were asked to specify their ethnicity. Reportedly, many Ukrainians declared themselves Russian, for fear of potential discrimination under the prevailing process of Sovietization.

About 20% of marriages in Ukraine were mixed, and out of these unions most offspring identified themselves as Russian. Between 1970 and 1989, the proportion of Ukrainians decreased by 2.5%, while the proportion defining themselves as Russian increased by nearly 3%. Simultaneously, there was a decrease in the percentage of the population that considered Ukrainian its native language, in conditions where linguistic affiliation invariably shaped ethnic identity. Higher birth rates were recorded among Russians than among Ukrainians, and the inflow of non-indigenous ethnic groups increased. The post-1989 return of over 200,000 Crimean Tatars also had an impact on ethnic demographics.

One of the fundamental problems in Ukraine's state-and nation-building process was a persistent socio-psychological and political legacy. Ukrainians identified themselves as a minority in the Soviet Union and were subject to creeping Russification and de-ethnicization. Upon gaining national independence, they found themselves a majority but with a predominantly minority mentality, which precipitated confusion and a search for new bearings. Conversely, the Russians, who were formerly in the majority, suddenly found themselves a minority—a situation that invariably provoked uncertainty and a crisis of identity.[19] These contradictions were ripe for manipulation by nationalist and communist politicians intent on expanding their influence, as well as by local elites competing for offices and resources.

The new, post-independence Ukrainian political elite primarily consisted of a sector of the old ruling class, which adopted nationalist colors. With the escalating crisis in the USSR, they capitalized on an opportunity to retain their positions and to expand their autonomy as controls from Moscow progressively weakened.[20] The fracturing of the Soviet Union also had a ripple effect throughout the region, as local elites and industrial managers sought greater political and economic controls. Just as the "nationalized" Ukrainian *nomenklatura* preferred to be leaders of an independent state rather than provincial bosses of a centralized federation, so regional elites also sought to maximize their autonomy, especially in economic matters, rather than become mere administrators of a new political center. This process was facilitated by the Soviet heritage, whereby Kyiv exerted weak control over the regions because the previous lines of authority passed primarily through Moscow.

The unraveling of Kremlin controls under conditions of comprehensive and sometimes chaotic decentralization did not facilitate the emergence of a powerful new center, especially as Ukraine had limited experience of integral statehood. Not surprisingly, regions with contrasting historical, demographic, political, economic, and ethnic backgrounds developed differing levels of national consciousness and proved resistant to homogenization under conditions of expanding pluralism. Regional diversification was further encouraged by the slow pace of economic reform, the contrasting interests of the industrial and agricultural sectors, and the curtailment of the former Soviet market. The economic malaise during the first few years of independence tended to breed disillusionment with Kyiv and increased Russia's attractiveness for citizens in some regions, especially for Russified populations exhibiting only conditional loyalty toward the Ukrainian state.

Under the Kravchuk presidency, the Ukrainian government found it difficult to promote a unified, nationwide political ideology to encourage integration and loyalty to the new state. It proved both hesitant and hamstrung in imposing its authority in the eastern and southern regions, which pressed for far-reaching autonomy. Any forceful centralization during the slow process of statebuilding would have run counter to the prevailing climate of liberalization. It also could have been ultimately counterproductive, alienating important regional elites and buttressing public resistance toward the center.

A persistent problem was the growth of organized crime and corruption, which was invariably tied to regionally based interest groups in competition for resources and influence, whose loyalty to the central government remained tenuous. Striking an inter-regional balance between competing interest groups bedeviled Ukraine's political stability and state-building program. Supporters of extensive regionalism argued that economic reforms involving decentralization, marketization, and privatization should to be accompanied by administrative devolution and regional autonomy. From this perspective, regional autonomy would not challenge national integrity or state independence. On the contrary, delaying or preventing such a devolution actually contributed to separatist tendencies as resentment grew against state interference.[21]

The absence of a coherent economic program under the Kravchuk government and the slow pace of administrative reorganization encouraged regionalism and in some instances separatism. To counter such disintegrative trends, the consolidation of the state could actually be strengthened by granting regions greater powers, especially in the economic realm. Some observers contended that authentic self-government at the municipal level would undermine separatist tendencies among regional elites.[22] Integralists, or supporters of a unified state, remained wary that the varieties of autonomy were fracturing the new country. The government stood accused of lacking a program and instead was simply responding to pressures as local elites wrested power for themselves. Critics belied the phenomenon of "spontaneous regionalization," favoring instead a process of orderly decentralization in which the central government determined the pace of devolution.

The dispute between integralists and regionalists was evident in the debate between proponents of a unitary and a federalized state. In general, Ukrainian national democrats, centrists, and nationalists supported the maintenance of a unitary state with limited local autonomy, particularly in the political realm. Politicians upholding this position invariably represented Ukraine's western and central regions. They argued that Ukraine already had a federal-type structure in which several regions, particularly Crimea and the Donbas, were fully empowered and benefited from far-ranging political autonomy. By contrast, the center-left—communists, socialists, some liberals, and regional elites in southern and eastern Ukraine—tended to favor a federal system with more pronounced regional autonomy, especially in the economic arena. The disputes between integralists and federalists became somewhat muted during the Kuchma administration, particularly with the passage of the new Ukrainian constitution in June 1996, which defined Ukraine as a unitary state.

The unitarist-federalist dispute was impregnated with negative mutual perceptions between westerners and easterners. Ukrainians in the west tended to believe that easterners lacked a national identity and harbored a "sausage mentality," focusing their sights on material conditions rather than state sovereignty and national integrity. This left them susceptible to separatist agitation. From this perspective, support for federalization was largely a smokescreen for ultimate secession.

Politicians in western Ukraine believed that because the eastern half of the country was so comprehensively Russified, it would take time to construct a Ukrainian national identity and build allegiance to the new state. This would supposedly be accomplished through public education, the adoption of Ukrainian as a state language in all governmental offices, and more effective Ukrainian mass media. Such a process could take a generation to complete, but early results could be registered without surrendering the unitarist principle. Indeed, integralists in the west argued that regional autonomy, even in education, culture, and economic activities, could undermine this objective by reinforcing a Russified regional identity.

Among easterners, widespread suspicions were evident concerning the intentions of westerners. There was a pervasive belief that a process of "Ukrainianization" was underway, designed to construct a new ethno-national identity based on west Ukrainian principles. While this may have been evident under President Kravchuk, the Kuchma administration de-emphasized Ukrainianization. Regional elites in Donbas and Crimea feared a loss of political and economic influence if a federal solution were not implemented. They calculated that legislation on local administration did not go far enough in delegating power to the regions *(oblasti)*. The position of President Kuchma on the federal question remained unclear.[23] While he was overwhelmingly backed by east Ukrainians because of his support for closer relations with Russia, he also publicly expressed reservations about a federal-type arrangement that would weaken the center.

Kuchma moved to restrict the powers of regional governments that had been extended at the close of President Kravchuk's tenure. After the March 1994 parliamentary elections, the presidentially appointed local administrators were replaced by elected officials. Critics contended that this process of decentralization could foster the disintegration of the state, and Kuchma moved swiftly to reassert presidential authority. In October 1994, he submitted a draft law on local government according to which the President would obtain the power to veto decisions by the chairmen of *oblast* and city councils that contradicted the Ukrainian constitution.[24] Such legislation subordinated local bodies to the executive branch. Some regional leaders were opposed to these amendments, although there were indications that others would rather be answerable to the executive than to parliament. The parliamentary opposition criticized the notion of greater presidential controls over the regions. Presidential spokesmen attacked the latter for seeking the recreation of a Soviet-type system with parliament at the apex.

In September 1994, President Kuchma signed an edict creating a Council of Regions as a consultative and advisory organ. It comprised the chairmen of *oblast* councils and the city councils of Kyiv and Sevastopol (in Crimea), and answered directly to the presidency. Observers felt Kuchma would use the Council to counterbalance parliament and push for a package of amendments to the law on local councils, transforming *oblast* chairmen into full-fledged governors independent of parliament. The Council would thereby bypass a potentially anti-reformist legislature. The longer-term aim was to transform the Council of Regions into a second parliamentary chamber.[25]

The first independent Ukrainian government defined the country as a civic rather than an ethnic state; that is, in which citizenship was based on residence and not nationality.[26] The law on Ukrainian citizenship, passed in October 1991, declared all people living in Ukraine to be nationals, and imposed no onerous residency requirements. It declared Ukraine a territorial rather than an ethnic unit. Indeed, Kyiv tried to be accommodating on the question of minority rights and language use for non-Ukrainian speakers. In November 1991, the Declaration of the Rights of Nationalities guaranteed equal political, economic, social, and cultural rights to all individuals and nationalities. It guaranteed the existence of "national-administrative units" for the country's small but territorially compact minorities, and allowed for the language of any national group that was compactly settled in an administrative-territorial unit to function alongside the state language. This ruling clarified the July 1990 declaration of state sovereignty, which assured all nationalities the right to "national-cultural development."

However, the language issue and its potent symbolism as the expression and encapsulation of national identity bedeviled inter-ethnic and inter-regional relations. Soon after independence, the new government set out to restore Ukrainian as the sole state language. The application of this policy was often hampered by inertia fostered by decades of Russification. In some southern and eastern regions, the ensconced political apparatus ignored central directives and charged Kyiv with forcible Ukrainianization.[27] Such accusations were strenuously denied; for example, between 1988 and 1992 the proportion of children receiving instruction in Ukrainian grew by less than 2%, and the figure for Russian dropped by approximately the same amount. In addition, Russian speakers in southern and eastern Ukraine used their first language in all official discourse and benefited from a preponderance of Russian publications.[28]

The Ukrainian language law guaranteed all citizens the right to use their mother tongue. However, Russian did not achieve the status of a "state language" equal with Ukrainian, despite the protests of Russophone forces. Several Ukrainian organizations, including the Writers' Union and national democratic parties, expressed fears that amendments to the language law, which proposed to give Russian "official status" alongside Ukrainian, would undermine the national language and signal renewed Russian dominance.[29] Although such concerns appeared exaggerated, they indicated the continuing sensitivity of the language question. The new constitution confirmed Ukrainian as the sole state language. However, it also permitted *oblast*s to use two official languages in administrative affairs; in several regions, Russian was selected as a second language. Such measures seemed to appease much of the Russian-speaking population.

To strengthen the state's civic orientation, the authorities introduced enlightened legislation furthering non-discrimination toward ethnic minorities. In June 1992, parliament passed a law on national minorities in which it codified opportunities for cultural development and political participation. The constitution confirmed everyone's right to preserve and protect their national affiliation and to equality before the law regardless of nationality, language, religion, or race. It also specified a host of other civil, political, economic, and cultural rights and stressed the creation of a "civil society" based on equal rights, self-organization, and self-government, avoiding an exclusive focus on ethnicity or national identity.[30]

Kyiv established a fund for ethnic minorities, to promote their cultural, social, and economic development. But despite evident good intentions, and because of budgetary constraints and inflationary pressures, the sums were of limited practical value. Given this political context, ethnic relations in post-Soviet Ukraine could be assessed by reviewing the situation in several key regions where ethnic identity became politicized after the attainment of national independence.

In the eastern regions of Donbas and Luhansk there was no popular commitment to Ukrainian statehood and no strongly developed sense of national identity. However, it would be too simplistic to characterize the majority of inhabitants as secessionists or as seeking reintegration into Russia or the Commonwealth of Independent States (CIS).[31] Russian ethnics formed 43.6% of the population in Donetsk *oblast* and 44.8% in Luhansk *oblast*. Although the bulk of residents employed Russian as their first language, they did not display a strong loyalty toward Moscow and were not attracted to nationalist movements in Russia. Indeed, the population exhibited a tangible regional identity that was neither uni-ethnic nor multi-ethnic but rather a "de-ethnicized" identity in which Russian was the major language.

National identity in the Donbas was ambiguous and multi-layered: People viewed themselves simultaneously as Ukrainian, Russian, and Slavic; but the regional focus took priority. Some observers interpreted this as a "transitional identity," a flexibility stemming from centuries of intermarriage and intermixture as well as the privileged industrial-worker status the region was accorded under communist rule. Political and national allegiance was more dependent on local economic self-interest than on ethno-nationalist commitment, particularly after the collapse of communism. Since independence, there has been little evidence of ethnic polarization or conflict in the region, indicating that ethnic identity is not a prime concern for the majority of citizens.

Regional elites in Donbas and Luhansk, as well as moderate political forces, pushed for greater autonomy, particularly in the economic realm, but did not adopt the maximalist agenda of separation from Ukraine. Whereas the Ukrainian president appointed an executive for the Donbas region, under Kyiv's decentralization program initiated in 1993 several *oblast*s, including Donetsk, Luhansk, Dnipropetrovsk, and Zaporizhzhia, were given more extensive rights in managing state-controlled enterprises. In February 1994, President Kravchuk signed an edict granting a degree of regional self-government to these four eastern *oblast*s, specifically in the administration of state property.[32]

As an indication of further pressures toward autonomy, a "consultative poll" was conducted during the March 1994 parliamentary elections to test public support for a federative regional structure, for dual language use, and for full CIS membership. The overwhelming majority of voters—reportedly, more than 90%—supported each proposal.[33] Although the poll had no legal authority, it served as a warning to Kyiv that frustration with economic conditions could be exploited by pro-Russian forces. Nonetheless, the prominent position of cross-ethnic leftist parties and non-ethnic interest group structures undermined any potential secessionist tendencies.

Eastern elites also demanded greater autonomy to trade and re-establish direct relations with neighboring border regions in Russia, particularly as there remained a high degree of technical interdependence. In October 1994, Kharkiv *oblast* authorities signed a cooperation agreement with Moscow *oblast*. A large measure of illusion was evident in these proposals, which claimed that re-created economic links with Russian industry would significantly revive the local economy. They also indicated that pressures for interconnection stemmed from material rather than political objectives. Regional leaders and directors of large enterprises looked toward Russia for economic development, given the shortcomings of Kyiv's economic reform programs. Such expectations appeared overtly optimistic, as Ukraine had already lost much of its Russian market, which could not absorb a large volume of Ukrainian products.

The pursuit of economic reform by Kyiv, with the passage of market-oriented legislation in November 1994, also contributed to social unrest in Donbas, given that the heavily industrialized areas shouldered the burden of state budget cuts, plant closures, and unemployment. The danger remained that such industrial turmoil could be manipulated by separatist groupings. While communists, socialists, and regional leaders in the east favored economic autonomy, political devolution, and federalization, several pro-Russian groupings were more outspoken on regional self-determination and integration with Russia. The Civic Congress and the *Intermovement* of Donbas, with links to parts of the old *nomenklatura*, favored the restoration of a Russian-centered union and envisaged a step-by-step approach through economic union, a customs union, a ruble zone, and a military union, culminating in political unification.

Russophone leaders supported a regional autonomy similar to that which existed in Crimea, whereby Donbas would obtain its own legislature and executive able to forge direct agreements with Kyiv. The position of the Civic Congress and *Intermovement* was not identical with that of the Socialist or Communist parties or the "red directors" in industry and agriculture, who generally opposed Ukrainian partition and did not envisage the Donbas as a future appendage of Russia. Moreover, conflicts were evident even among Russophones, between proponents of a looser CIS-type union that incorporated all of Ukraine, and supporters of a Greater Russian federation that would annex eastern and southern territories following the partition of Ukraine.[34]

Separatists and Russian nationalists endeavored to push the Ukrainian authorities into defining the state on ethnic grounds, thus provocatively alienating the large segment of Russian-speakers. The Russophone lobby attempted to manipulate ethnic and linguistic distinctions, and raised the specter of forceful Ukrainianization to increase popular fears, mobilize public opinion behind their policies, and exacerbate opposition to Kyiv. The propaganda line asserted that the Ukrainian administration was dominated by nationalists who neglected the interests of Russian-speakers and were intent on "ethnicizing" them. Such allegations were grossly inflated, especially as Russian schools continued to function and there were more Russian-language publications available than demographic proportions alone would have warranted. Indeed, politicians in Kyiv proved cautious in pursuing Ukrainianization in the east, contending that the imposition of a west Ukrainian national consciousness would create resentment and ultimately backfire.[35]

The Crimean peninsula presented a more immediate problem for Kyiv, in that the majority of inhabitants identified themselves as ethnically Russian, and separatist forces were prominent. According to the 1989 census, 67.04% of the population of 2.43 million were Russian, and 25.7%, Ukrainian. Nearly half of the Ukrainian ethnics considered Russian their native language. Nonetheless, there was no popular unanimity supporting unification with Russia, and divisions were evident within the peninsula's political and economic elites. The majority of Crimeans participated in the March 1994 Ukrainian elections despite separatist calls for a boycott.

In January 1991, Crimea achieved the status of an autonomous republic within Ukraine after 93.3% of the electorate voted for such an arrangement, initially as a "subject of the USSR and a party to the Union Treaty." The Crimean *oblast* council ruled that Crimeans had the right to autonomous statehood, and asserted that the decree of the USSR's Supreme Soviet in June 1945 abolishing Crimea's autonomous status was unconstitutional. The Ukrainian parliament accepted the change of status in February 1991 and renewed Crimean autonomy "within the borders of the Ukrainian SSR."[36]

In September 1991, a week after Ukraine's declaration of independence, the Crimean parliament declared the state sovereignty of Crimea as a constituent part of Ukraine. Some deputies demanded the immediate declaration of separation and of continued membership in the Soviet Union and later the CIS. In April 1992, Kyiv passed a law delineating powers between state and republic, but it altered the version of the law approved by the Crimean authorities, reducing the powers initially granted to the Crimean capital, Simferopol. In retaliation, the Crimean parliament passed an independence declaration pending a public referendum. Kyiv proclaimed this action unconstitutional. Simferopol suspended its declaration, and renewed negotiations resulted in a revised law specifying the powers and responsibilities of the two political entities. But this arrangement failed to resolve the bitter political dispute over Crimea's status.

One of the major forces pushing for Crimean independence was the Republican Movement of Crimea, whose leader, Yuri Meshkov, was elected Crimea's president in March 1994, together with a largely Russophile parliament. The elections were accompanied by a non-binding referendum calling for a "treaty" between Ukraine and Crimea and for dual citizenship (Ukrainian and Russian). Some 75% of voters supported these proposals. Meshkov was propelled to office on a platform of closer links with Russia and independence for the peninsula. However, after the elections Meshkov tempered his separatist rhetoric and pressed instead for greater autonomy and more wide-ranging presidential powers.

Conflicts mounted between Meshkov and parliament and between various factions in the broad coalition, the Russia Bloc. This process culminated in mutual suspensions of presidential and parliamentary functions, the effective rescinding of Meshkov's powers, and even appeals to Kyiv to mediate the conflict. President Kuchma adroitly capitalized on these internal conflicts and showed no indication of surrendering Ukraine's territorial integrity. In November 1994, the Ukrainian parliament, with Kuchma's backing, annulled a series of laws adopted by Crimea that openly violated the country's constitution. He also appointed a presidential representative in the peninsula who wielded significant powers in the region.

Some nationalist forces even called for a dissolution of the Crimean parliament and the return of the peninsula to *oblast* status. Kuchma and a parliamentary majority opposed taking such a step, as they remained apprehensive of provoking a major confrontation. However, in March 1995, Kuchma abolished the Crimean presidency and annulled Crimea's separatist constitution. The Crimean prime minister and the parliamentary speaker were replaced with more accommodating figures. The new Ukrainian constitution afforded Crimea a significant degree of autonomy and its own regional constitution, both of which further undercut the separatist lobby. The Crimean government seemed committed to working within the parameters of the new Ukrainian constitution, and the majority of Crimeans understood that neither independence nor unification with Russia was on the political agenda.

Kyiv banked on continuing political infighting in Simferopol to draw Crimea away from a separatist platform and keep it from outright conflict with the center. It also calculated that Crimea's lack of viability as a separate state because of its total dependence on Ukraine for energy, water, and transportation links, as well as Russia's hesitancy to annex the peninsula, would bring Simferopol into line. Moscow's role in Crimea proved ambivalent. While some parliamentary factions and military leaders favored bringing the peninsula under Russian jurisdiction, the Yeltsin government avoided a direct conflict with Kyiv. Nonetheless, it periodically manipulated the Crimean issue to maintain political pressure on Kuchma. The activities of radical pro-Russian forces were carefully monitored by Kyiv, because the possibility of provocations in order to draw Moscow into a confrontation with Ukraine could not be discounted.[37] The pro-annexationist statements of some prominent Russian politicians, including the former presidential candidate Aleksander Lebed, as well as claims to Sevastopol by the Russian parliament, contributed to ongoing tensions.

Although inter-ethnic relations in Crimea were not overtly conflictive, Russophone nationalists sought to exploit the specter of Ukrainianization and a "Tatar invasion" to mobilize Russian ethnics against the Ukrainian state. Some Crimean-Russian politicians also attempted to alarm Ukrainians with the specter of Tatar separatism. After 1989, over 300,000 Tatars were resettled in Crimea, whence they had been deported under Stalin's orders during World War II. It was projected that another 120,000 would return by the end of the 1990s, at the invitation of the Ukrainian government. The Crimean authorities remained passive in assisting the Tatars in their resettlement, and in some cases obstructed the process.

The Tatar leadership supported Ukrainian independence but simultaneously demanded a greater role in the peninsula's government. The Tatar national council (*majlis*) promoted itself as a legitimate self-governing body that should be incorporated into Crimea's parliament as a second chamber representing "native peoples" and with a veto right over all legislation. When this proposal was rejected, the *majlis* sought a guaranteed third of all parliamentary seats. It eventually settled for an allocation of fourteen deputies in the 450-seat legislature.

Although the Tatar return has been supported by the Ukrainian authorities as a counterweight to the Russian-dominated Crimean government, Tatar numbers have not been large enough to be critical for the peninsula's ethnic and political balance. Moreover, Tatars have not been afforded substantial financial support from Kyiv in rebuilding their communities. Kyiv's Ministry of Nationalities and Migration is not well equipped to respond to Tatar needs and evidently does not consider these a high priority. Kyiv faces a major challenge in solving the social and economic problems of the Tatars' return to Crimea and of their integration into the political system, given the anti-Tatar policies of the Russian leadership.[38]

Ethnic Ukrainian leaders in Crimea complained that Kyiv had done little to foster a national Ukranian identity and had failed to establish a single Ukrainian-language school for 626,000 Crimean Ukrainians by the mid-1990s. At the same time, Crimean leaders accused Tatars of draining scarce resources from long-time residents, and prevented Tatars from reclaiming the most productive lands. Attempts were also made to evict Tatar families from new settlements, leading to clashes with police and local inhabitants and raising ethnic tensions on the peninsula. In general, the Tatar population has exhibited greater political mobilization than have Crimean Ukrainians. But leaders of the two groups have cooperated in opposition to the Russian parties.

The west Ukrainian *oblast*s were the first to push toward national independence. In March 1991, the local councils authorized a question on independence as an addition to Gorbachev's referendum to maintain the USSR as a federation. National democrats clustered around the *Rukh* movement gained important local government seats, and during the December 1991 referendum, sent nearly 20,000 activists to eastern and southern parts of the country to advocate Ukrainian independence. *Rukh* subsequently split into a number of parties and factions. The center-right bloc forged a working agreement with the "national communists" around President Kravchuk, in support of state independence. The more radical factions, including the Conservative Republicans, criticized the administration for unnecessarily making compromises with Moscow and the eastern elites, and for the slow pace of Ukrainianization.

Whereas *Rukh* generally displayed tolerance and moderation on the ethnic question, perceiving the danger of alienating eastern Ukrainians, the more radical local leaders in Haliczyna (western Ukraine, historically known as Galicia), some of whom were elected to parliament in March 1994, were less restrained in criticizing Russophone elements in eastern Ukraine. They demanded a government crackdown against separatist tendencies in Crimea and Donbas. Such pressures in turn fueled charges in Donetsk and Simferopol that a policy of coercive Ukrainianization was underway and was supported by the authorities in Kyiv.

An important factor in the self-identity of western Ukrainians has been the reinstated Greek Catholic or Uniate Church. It served as a pillar of resistance under Soviet and Russian rule but came under fire among some Orthodox congregations for advancing a nationalist anti-Russian agenda in education, culture, and the mass media. The revival of Ukrainian Catholicism and Ukrainian Autocephalous Orthodoxy, and the consequent reduction in the influence of the Russian Orthodox Church, particularly in western Ukraine, has had an important impact on national consciousness and inter-ethnic relations. Soon after the official restoration in June 1991, Cardinal Lyubachivskyi, the head of the Uniate Church, declared invalid Stalin's 1946 transfer of Church assets to the Russian Orthodox Church.

Simultaneously, there was a dramatic rise in Orthodox congregations opting for affiliation with the Ukrainian Autocephalous Orthodox Church or with the Ukrainian Orthodox Church–Kyiv Patriarchate, which did not recognize the authority of the Moscow patriarchate.[39] In western Ukraine, the Russian church effectively lost control over religious life and was denounced by local leaders as a tool of Russification, out of step with the Ukrainian national revival.[40] Disputes also surfaced between Greek Catholic and Ukrainian Orthodox leaders, as Uniates contended that the latter should focus their attention on the traditionally more Orthodox, eastern regions.

The struggle between the three Orthodox churches was particularly intense in central and eastern Ukraine, especially over territorial and property claims. It also had reverberations in political and regional conflicts. Observers grew concerned that the revival of independent churches could polarize ethno-regional divisions, especially where church leaders publicly supported specific political options. Indeed, in the March 1994 elections, the Uniate and Ukrainian Orthodox hierarchy explicitly backed centrist and national democrat candidates, while the Orthodox–Moscow Patriarchate attempted to stay out of the fray for fear of besmirching leftist and pro-Russian candidates in the public eye.[41]

Observers estimated that moderate nationalists and national democrats gained approximately eighty seats in the 1994 parliamentary elections, although many of these deputies canvassed as "independents." The ultranationalists did not perform well in the elections, obtaining a mere dozen seats in the 450-seat parliament.[42] However, their influence in parts of western Ukraine, in competition with the moderate national democrat majority, could expand in the event of deepening socioeconomic turmoil and increasing interregional and center-regional disputes.

As with several other Ukrainian regions, the Transcarpathian *oblast* council in western Ukraine canvassed to turn the area into a "special economic zone." It calculated that this would attract foreign investors, bypassing the Kyiv bureaucracy, and strengthen economic ties with neighboring Hungary and Slovakia.[43] Demands for economic autonomy in turn galvanized anti-Ruthenian sentiments among Ukrainian nationalists. Some Slavic residents of Transcarpathia identified themselves as Ruthenian, although the majority considered themselves Ukrainian ethnics. Disputes have raged since the collapse of the USSR on whether the Ruthenians were a separate ethno-linguistic group or merely a regional segment of the Ukrainian nation. In this context, economic emancipation for Transcarpathia was viewed by nationalists as anti-Ukrainian separatism, particularly as it allegedly had support among "international agencies" in Hungary and Slovakia.[44]

The development of ethnic relations in an independent Ukraine hinged on several key factors, including the impact of economic reforms, the extent of national political consensus, and the degree of regional stability. Unless the question of regional devolution is resolved to the satisfaction of western, eastern, and southern Ukrainian leaders, the danger of an escalating east-west conflict remains. The lines of confrontation could encompass a spectrum of contentious issues including economic programs, foreign policy and questions of language use and education.

President Kuchma, who was elected in July 1994 and re-elected in November 1999, succeeded to a greater degree than his predecessor, Kravchuk, in stabilizing the political situation by seeking to create a balance between centralism and regional decentralization. Whereas Kravchuk gained most of his votes in western regions, Kuchma managed to mobilize substantial support in the central and eastern areas. Although interregional disputes remain evident, they are focused less on questions of ethnic identity and state allegiance than on issues of economic interest.

During Kuchma's presidency, the ethnic question was largely defused in Ukrainian politics, and even the Crimean issue remained stable. Nonetheless, the potential for ethno-regional conflicts could not be completely discounted. A great deal depends on the success or failure of market reform and whether this promotes or dissipates popular loyalty to an integral Ukrainian state. In these conditions, the most important voting group is the Russian-speaking (Russophone) Ukrainians, who constitute about one third of all ethnic Ukrainians, and whose commitment to the new state continued to be tested throughout the 1990s.

POLITICAL PARTIES

Socialists and Social Democrats

Socialist Party of Ukraine (SPU)
Socialistychna Partiya Ukrainy (SPU)

The Socialist Party of Ukraine (SPU) was created by ex-communists when their party was banned in August 1991, with an initial membership of some 50,000. Their leader, Oleksandr Moroz, was the former head of the Communist majority in the Ukrainian parliament. The party's goal was to build a society founded on labor that ensured the principles of social justice regardless of nationality or religious or political conviction. In June 1992, the SPU initially declared its objectives to include the restoration of the USSR and the Ukrainian Soviet Socialist Republic, a return to a communist command economy, a state-controlled market, 90% income taxes on hard currency earnings, and a one-year moratorium on privatization.

During the early 1990s, the SPU evolved into a more center-left formation, rejecting communist calls for a restoration of the Soviet Union. It tried to blend leftist ideas with the principles of a market economy in which the state would play a regulating role favoring collective forms of ownership. How-

ever, it remained opposed to a strong presidency and sought presidential subordination to parliament. It also maintained a russocentric focus, calling for a
federal Ukraine, legal status for the Russian language, and dual citizenship
with the Russian Federation.

The SPU reconciled itself gradually to Ukrainian independence. In June 1993,
the SPU formed a close coalition with the People's Party and smaller leftist groups,
entitled "Working Ukraine." The SPU claimed the support of 38 parliamentary
deputies in 1992–1993, while it enjoyed the advantage of being the only organized leftist successor to the Communist Party. Its preeminence on the left disappeared with the rise of the restored Communist Party in 1993–1994, but it still
won 14 seats in the March 1994 elections. Moroz was elected chairman of parliament in April 1994. He also came in third behind Kuchma and Kravchuk in the
June–July 1994 presidential elections. The Socialist Party and the Peasant Party
formed an electoral bloc in November 1997, and in the March 1998 ballot it
obtained 8.6% of the vote and 35 parliamentary seats. Moroz also finished third
in the October 1999 presidential elections, with 11.75% of the popular vote. The
party's major publication was *Tovarysh* (Comrade).

United Social Democratic Party of Ukraine (USDPU)
Sotsial-Demokratychna Partiya Ukrainy "Obyednana" (SDPUO)

The United Social Democratic Party of Ukraine (USDPU) was established in
1997 by former Justice Minister Vasyl Onopenko, who became its chairman.
The major part of the party was rooted in the governmental bureaucracy. The
USDPU platform proclaimed social justice and well-being dependent on honest
work. In its pre-election program, the union supported private ownership and
a combination of a market economy with the effective social protection of
citizens. The party advocated state support for the domestic economy, especially of the agricultural sector, and the "balancing" of prices. In the political
sphere, it emphasized public control over the state and de-bureaucratization
of the administration. The USDPU called for building a "socially orientated
economy."[45] The party supported close relations with Russia, as well as European integration. Among its prominent members were former President Leonid Kravchuk and former Premier Yevhen Marchuk, who spoke up in support
of democratic socialism along the lines of West European leftist parties. The
party's support base was primarily in central and western Ukraine. In the
March 1998 parliamentary elections, the USDPU received 4% of votes and
18 seats in the Supreme Council.[46]

Labor Party of Ukraine (LPU)
Partiya Truda Ukrainy (PTU)

The Labor Party of Ukraine (LPU) was founded in December 1992 by the
Interregional Association of Industrialists, the main lobby for east Ukrainian

industry. Its leaders were Valentyn Landyk and Nikolai Azarov. Landyk was deputy prime minister in 1993–1994. The party had a strong position on the local councils of Donetsk and Luhansk, and long-standing links with the old official trade unions. It was the second strongest political formation in the Donetsk region, after the Communist Party, but was barely visible elsewhere in Ukraine. The LPU declared itself a centrist party standing for the equality of all forms of property and the union of state and market forms of regulation of the economy. The LPU also supported closer links between Ukraine and the CIS, and a system of several state languages in Ukraine. The party's main leaders were all elected as deputies in March 1994. Before the March 1998 legislative elections, the party joined with the Liberal Party to create the Labor-Liberal bloc, which captured only 1.9% of the popular vote.

Party of Democratic Rebirth of Ukraine (PDRU)
Partiya Demokratychna Vidrodzhennia Ukrainy (PDVU)

The Party of Democratic Rebirth of Ukraine (PDRU) was founded in 1990 as the Democratic Platform within the Communist Party by reform communists, mainly from Kharkiv and Zaporizhzhia, who regarded *Rukh* as too nationalistic and favored western Ukraine over other regions. Its principal leader was Volodymyr Filenko and its membership stood at 3,000. The PDRU advocated economic reforms leading to a market economy and privatization, and thus opposed President Kravchuk, who had been slow to implement such reforms. It also advocated close economic links with Russia and the CIS. The PDRU supported the further development of democracy and opposed any return to communist rule centered in Moscow. At the same time, it opposed Ukrainianization, as most of the PDRU members were Russian-speakers. The party's drift from the left toward the political center in 1993 cost it support in eastern Ukraine, and in the March 1994 elections, it won only four seats. The party merged with the Popular Democratic Party of Ukraine (PDPU) on 24 February 1996 but failed to garner any seats in the March 1998 parliamentary elections.

Social Democratic Party of Ukraine (SDPU)
Sotsial-Demokratychna Partiya Ukrainy (SDPU)

The Social Democratic Party of Ukraine (SDPU) was founded in May 1990, as a result of splits among social democratic forces. Its leaders included Mikalay Statkevic and Yurii Zbitniev, and its membership reached 2,900. Its main publication was *Sotsial-Demokrat Ukrainy* (Social Democrat of Ukraine). The SDPU opposed "traditional" socialism and advocated a social democratic system of government. In May 1992, the party splintered again on the question of joining the coalition New Ukraine. In order to form one social democratic movement, the SDPU explored ways to unite with other leftist formations, including the Party of Democratic Rebirth of Ukraine (PDRU). In late 1994, these efforts failed, but a small part of the SDPU joined the PDRU. In late 1993, the party announced its departure from the centrist New Ukraine coalition and moved back to the left. The SDPU won only one seat in the March 1994 elections. In the March 1998 elections, the SDPU won only 0.3% of votes and did not obtain any seats in the Supreme Council.

Bloc of Socialist and Peasant Party of Ukraine (SPPU)
Blok Sotsialistychna Partiya i Selyanska Partiya Ukrainy (SPU-SPU)

The 1998 electoral bloc, the Socialist and Peasant Party of Ukraine (SPPU), consisted of the Peasant and Socialist parties. In its election program, the bloc advocated effective state control in the sphere of banking activity and over strategic and highly profitable markets and the nationalization of privatized enterprises. Additionally, the bloc supported price regulation and a tax reduction for domestic goods producers. The bloc promised to undercut the influence of international financial institutions if it was elected. The SPPU placed the agriculture sector at the center of Ukrainian industry. According to its program, food imports should be stopped, domestic large-scale producers subsidized, and state purchases of bread, sugar beet, and sunflower extended. Furthermore, the SPPU pledged an increase in salaries, pensions, and social payments. The bloc rejected Ukraine's bid to join NATO, and instead supported good relationships with "the Slavic world." In the March 1998 elections, the bloc—led by one of Kuchma's chief opponents, Oleksandr Moroz—obtained 8.6% of the vote, and 35 seats in the Supreme Council.

Working Ukraine (WU)
Trudova Ukraina (TU)

The 1998 electoral bloc Working Ukraine (WU) was formed by the Ukrainian Party of Justice (UPJ), the Civic Congress of Ukraine (CCU), and by some large public associations. This radical socialist bloc proposed to restore the system of "workers' control" over enterprises by nationalizing strategically important, profitable, and "groundlessly" privatized enterprises, and by prohibiting the privatization of social assets in science and medicine. Additionally, the bloc advocated the establishment of a state monopoly on foreign trade transactions involving energy supplies, alcohol, and tobacco. The WU also proposed to prohibit foreigners from purchasing land. Working Ukraine campaigned for the restoration of wide-ranging economic relations with the CIS countries. In the March 1998 elections, the bloc received 3.1% of votes and obtained one seat in parliament.

Liberals

Interregional Bloc for Reforms (IBR)
Mizhrehionalnyi Blok Reformiv (MBR)

The Interregional Bloc for Reforms (IBR) was formed in December 1993, and its initial leaders included Leonid Kuchma and Volodymyr Hrynov. The Interregional Bloc for Reforms was primarily a parliamentary group of 34 members, with little party structure. The Bloc united directors of agricultural and industrial enterprises with liberal-centrist forces. The IBR favored economic cooperation with Russia and the CIS.[47] Most of its support came from the Russian-speaking regions of eastern and southern Ukraine, and from Crimea. In 1994, the IBR's slogan was "strength to the state, prosperity to the people, reason to power." The IBR had three main planks in its election program: more power to the Ukrainian regions, controlled market reforms, and a strategic alliance between Ukraine and Russia. Despite quarrels between Kuchma and Hrynov, the IBR managed to elect 25 supporters in the March 1994 elections, with many posing as "independents."

Under the leadership of Hrynov, the party joined with the Constitutional Democrats to create the Social Liberal Association (SLA) electoral bloc. In its pre-election program the bloc proposed liberal reforms, especially tax reduction, a decrease in state expenditures, a stable monetary policy, protection of private ownership, and the creation of good conditions for small businesses. The bloc demanded that Russian become an official language, and proposed the creation of an economic alliance with Russia to form a unified market for the free movement of people, goods, and capital. The bloc failed to win any seats in the March 1998 elections, gaining only 0.9% of the popular vote.[48]

All-Ukrainian Association "Community" (AUAC)
Vseukrainske Obyednannya "Hromada" (VOH)

The All-Ukrainian Association "Community" (AUAC) was the successor of the nineteenth-century emancipation movement. The original *Hromadas* emerged in Kyiv and St. Petersburg, the cultural and national centers of the Ukrainian intelligentsia. Among its spiritual leaders was poet Taras Shevchenko.[49] The modern All-Ukrainian Association *Hromada* was re-organized on an all-Ukrainian level at its statutory congress on 12 December 1993 and registered as a political association in March 1994.[50] The party was in direct opposition to the Kuchma government. It emphasized the rights of the individual and advocated the creation of a civic society in Ukraine. The party was rejuvenated when former Prime Minister Pavlo Lazarenko and former United Energy System chief Yulia Tymoshenko took control over the organization in 1996.[51]

Lazarenko declared the necessity of establishing an alliance of centrist and liberal forces with *Hromada* as its base. In its 1998 election program, *Hromada* supported extensive property rights and appropriate political, economic, and social conditions for satisfying the "spiritual and material interests of individuals." To lead Ukraine out of economic crisis, the AUAC advocated the protection of domestic producers and the creation of new regional markets. The party also urged public control over privatization and an increase in salaries for teachers, physicians, scholars, and cultural workers. In the March 1998 elections, *Hromada* gained 16 parliamentary seats.[52]

People's Democratic Party of Ukraine (PDPU)
Narodno-Demokratychna Partiya Ukrainy (NDPU)

The People's Democratic Party of Ukraine (PDPU) was established in February 1996 by politicians close to President Kuchma. It emerged from two centrist parties, the Party of Democratic Rebirth (PDR) and the Labor Congress of Ukraine (LCU). The group was widely labeled the "party of power." Various pro-presidential factions in parliament were linked to the PDPU, including the Inter-regional Deputies Group, Unity, and Center. The PDPU could be variously defined as centrist or liberal in its political orientation and program. It advocated the interests of the middle class but was primarily considered to be lobbying for the objectives of business groups in the Dnipropetrovsk region that were associated with or loyal to the president. Supporting domestic goods producers, the PDPU wanted to guarantee stable economic growth. In its program, the party promised the stabilization of prices on industrial and agricultural goods. The PDPU also emphasized the strict enforcement of law and order. It was led by chairman Anatoliy Matviyenko and included Prime Minister Valerii Pustovoitenko; President Kuchma's chief of staff, Yevhen Kushanriov; Anatolii Kinakh, the head of the Ukrainian Union of Industrialists and Entrepreneurs; and former parliamentary speaker Ivan Plyushch. The PDPU proved instrumental in forging a centrist consensus to pass the 1996 Ukrainian constitution. In the March 1998 elections, it obtained 28 seats in parliament.

Liberal Party of Ukraine (LPU)
Liberalna Partiya Ukrainy (LPU)

The Liberal Party of Ukraine (LPU) was founded in August 1991 in Donetsk by a local businessman and adviser to President Kravchuk, Ihor Markulov. The party claimed a membership of some 40,000. Its chief publications were *Liberalna Hazeta* (Liberal Gazette) and *Vzgliad* (View). The LPU was a centrist party, supported by resources from local Communists and from the former youth organization *Komsomol* as well as from wealthy Donetsk businessmen. It also had some backing from the local intelligentsia, students, and skilled workers. The LPU supported freedom of enterprise, freedom of movement of labor and capital, freedom of speech and expression, a federal system for Ukraine, and the openness of borders for the free exchange of goods and information between Ukraine and the countries of the former Soviet Union.

The LPU supported aggressive economic reforms and the creation of a legal basis for a market economy. The negative image of the LPU as the party of the rich contributed to its losses in the March 1994 elections. However, the LPU's youth auxiliary became the fastest-growing youth movement in Ukraine. Volodymyr Nakonechny was the party's leader until mid-1997, when he was replaced by Volodymyr Shcherban, the former governor of Donetsk *oblast,* who was fired by Kuchma. Before the March 1998 election, the party joined the Labor Party to create the Labor-Liberal bloc, but it failed to take any parliamentary seats. One of the primary representatives of the Liberals was ex–Prime Minister Yevhen Marchuk, who fell out of favor with President Kuchma in 1995 and who headed the Social Market Choice faction in the Ukrainian parliament. As an interest group representing the Donetsk elite, the LPU excluded any cooperation with "centrist" formations from other regions, including the PDPU or the AUAC, and represented the chief center of opposition to President Kuchma.

The election bloc Labor Party and Liberal Party–Together (LPLP-T) *(Partiya Pratsia ta Liberalna Partiya–Razom, PPLP-R)* combined a mixture of liberal and social democratic notions. Its platform was based on the values of individual freedom, social justice, and responsibility. Its program emphasized respect for individual freedom in the political and economic spheres; support for the elderly, families, and invalids; and the provision of good conditions for education. In the March 1998 elections, the bloc failed to gain any seats in parliament, garnering only 1.9% of the vote.

Liberal Democratic Party of Ukraine (LDPU)
Liberalno-Demokratychna Partiya Ukrainy (LDPU)

The Liberal Democratic Party of Ukraine (LDPU) was founded in July 1992 and aimed to attract a base membership of entrepreneurs. It also sought to form coalitions and blocs with similar political entities in order to support an economic policy protecting human rights. It was led by Volodymyr Klymchuk, and attained only a small membership. Its publications included *Polslova.* Unlike Vladimir Zhirinovsky's nationalist LDP in Russia, the LDPU supported moderate, centrist positions. It favored a managed transition to a market economy, greater stress on individual rights, and friendly relations with Russia. The LDPU supported a strong state that would provide the opportunity for "uninhibited creative expression" by the Ukrainian people. It viewed the existing government apparatus as basically corrupt and tainted by totalitarianism. In November 1997, the party joined the Ukrainian Peasant Democratic Party to create European Choice. This new bloc supported the

"Europeanization" of Ukraine and was favorably disposed toward President Kuchma.[53]

Reforms and Order Party (ROP)
Partiya "Reformy i Poryadok" (PRP)

The Reforms and Order Party (ROP) was founded in July 1997 by prominent liberal reformer Viktor Pynzenyk, who twice served as deputy Prime Minister, under President Kravchuk and President Kuchma. On both occasions he resigned from government because he charged that his economic reform program was not being implemented. The ROP's program reflected the far-reaching structural economic reforms that Pynzenyk promoted, including tax liberalization, strict monetary policies, and the implementation of a market economy. Observers believed the party was established to promote Pynzenyk in the March 1998 general elections. ROP was the only centrist-liberal party with a concrete economic program. Its members consisted primarily of reformist economists, young politicians, and entrepreneurs. The ROP captured three seats in the March 1998 parliamentary elections, with 3.1% of the popular vote.

Christian Democrats

Ukrainian Christian Democratic Party (UCDP)
Ukrainska Khrystiyansko-Demokratychna Partiya (UKDP)

The Ukrainian Christian Democratic Party (UCDP) was created in 1990 and pursued the establishment of a Christian Democratic Front. Its leader was Volodymyr Zhuravskyi, and it claimed a membership of 30,000 people. The party represented the tradition of humanistic Christian democracy, and its goals included facilitating the renewal of Ukrainian sovereignty and the creation of a democratic state. The UCDP primarily represented Orthodox Christians in central and eastern Ukraine, a majority of whom were Russian speakers. In its program, the UCDP stood for an independent, democratic, multi-ethnic, multi-religious, and nuclear-free Ukraine. It concentrated on the development of the nation-state, a new constitution and legal system, and the privatization of land and economic enterprises. The UCDP maintained branches in 20 of Ukraine's 25 provinces. In the March 1994 elections, the UCDP won one seat in parliament. In the March 1998 elections, the UCDP received only 1.3% of the vote and did not obtain a single seat in the People's Council.

The UCDP formed an election bloc in 1998 called "Forward Ukraine" (FU) *(Vpred Ukraino, VU)* with the Christian Popular Union Party (CPUP). It was headed by the leader of the UCDP at that time, O.F. Serhienko, and CPUP leader H.P. Tkachenko. The bloc spoke out for Christian values in a liberal-oriented society. During the March 1998 elections, the bloc assembled 1.7% of the popular vote.

Agrarians

Peasant Party of Ukraine (PPU)
Selianska Partiya Ukrainy (SPU)

The roots of the Peasant Party of Ukraine (PPU) were based in the traditional rural Communist Party organizations, which established the party in January 1992. Serhii Dovhan was chairman. The PPU claimed a membership of 65,000, and was basically a party of collective farm *(kolkhoz)* chairmen with a powerful parliamentary lobby, headquartered in the city of Kherson. Most collective farm chairmen preferred to remain non-party, but nearly all supported the Peasant Party in practice because of its opposition to market reform in the agricultural sector. The conservatism of rural voters, and the position of farm chairmen, ensured the PPU a large voting bloc.

Ukrainian peasants became a powerful force supporting the maintenance of huge subsidies to the agricultural sector and obstructing plans for land privatization. Many of their leaders opposed market reforms and the privatization of *kolkhoz* land, and advocated the retention of the collective farm system. They also called for the preservation of an economic zone within the CIS. The party was considered anti-nationalist. In alliance with the Socialist Party, the PPU polled strongly in the March 1994 elections, winning 19 seats in conservative rural areas. It also dominated the faction Rural Ukraine, which claimed 36 parliamentary members. However, the PPU found it difficult to maintain organizational unity. In the fall of 1995, about half of the party's parliamentary group left the organization to form the centrist Agrarians for Reform (AR), which later was transformed into the Agrarian Party of Ukraine (APU). Before the March 1998 elections, the PPU joined with the Socialist Party to create the Electoral Bloc of Socialist and Peasant Parties, which took 8.6% of the popular vote and 35 legislative seats. It thereby became the third strongest force in parliament.

Agrarian Party of Ukraine (APU)
Ahrarna Partiya Ukrainy (APU)

The Agrarian Party of Ukraine (APU) was created in September 1996, when Pavlo Lazarenko was prime minister. The party was considered to be pro-Kuchma and pro-reformist. After the March 1994 elections, it claimed 24 incumbent *Verkhovna Rada* (Supreme Council) deputies and many top local government officials, such as Odessa Governor Ruslan Bodelan, Crimean premier Anatoliy Franchuk, the governors of Rivne and Zhytomyr, and several deputy governors. In the March 1998 elections, the APU garnered 3.7% of the national vote and obtained 8 parliamentary seats. Other agricultural or rural-based parties have included the more liberal-nationalist Ukrainian Peasant Democratic Party (UPDP), which became a part of the European Choice electoral bloc.

Greens

Green Party of Ukraine (GPU)
Partiya Zelenykh Ukrainy (PZU)

Because of public reaction to the 1986 Chornobyl accident, the environmental association *Zelenyi Svit* (Green World) was one of the first opposition groups to emerge in the late 1980s. It held its initial congress in 1989, during which it was decided to establish a separate party for explicitly political activities. The Green Party of Ukraine (GPU) leaders were Yurii Shcherbak and Vitalii Kononov, with a party membership of some 3,500. The GPU, initially supported by elements within the Communist Party, first proposed a leftist program of "eco-socialism," but its leaders fell under the influence of more liberal and rightist elements. The GPU then became informally linked to the centrist New Ukraine group and was a firm supporter of Ukrainian independence.

The Green Party remained focused on a concern for the environment "in the name of the dignified existence of today's and future generations." Its fundamental principles included the primacy of ecology over economy and politics, international participation in deciding ecological questions, and the combining of academic and humanist principles. It supported the development of alternative sources of energy and industry. The GPU also promoted the creation of independent social and community groups. It wanted to liquidate nuclear weapons but did not want them turned over to Russia. Party leaders worked together with Kravchuk's government and avoided adopting an anti-establishment stance. Because of shallow public support, the GPU was unable to send any of members to the March 1994 parliament. The party maintained a steady support base, and in the March 1998 elections it captured 5.4% of the vote and gained 19 parliamentary seats. Its major publication is *Zelenyi Svit* (Green World).

Communists

Communist Party of Ukraine (CPU)
Komunistychna Partiya Ukrainy (KPU)

The Communist Party of Ukraine (CPU) was formally banned in August 1991, but a campaign for its revival began in the summer of 1992, culminating in two restoration congresses in Donetsk, in March and June 1993. Its leader was Petro Symonenko, its membership reportedly stood at 122,560 people, and its main publication was *Kommunist* (Communist). The party claimed to be the legal successor to the defunct Communist Party of the Ukrainian Soviet Socialist Republic; however, it was unable to reclaim former CPU property.

The CPU was officially registered in October 1993. It remained aggressively anti-capitalist and anti-nationalist and stood for the restoration of state control over the economy and for a confederal union between Ukraine and Russia. The CPU blamed the country's problems principally on market reforms and the collapse of the Soviet Union, and its leaders asserted that they intended to restore the previous system. Unlike many former communist parties in Eastern Europe, the CPU did not renounce its Leninist ideology, its hierarchical internal structure, or its statist economic prescriptions.

The CPU's populist and collectivist nostalgia rapidly gained it support in economically troubled industrial areas of eastern Ukraine, especially in the Donbas. It also benefited from the small and fragmented nature of the national and democratic parties, which failed to properly articulate popular concerns and aspirations. The CPU emerged as the largest party in the Ukrainian parliament after the March–April 1994 elections, obtaining over 12% of the votes and 86 seats in the first round. It received most of its support in eastern and southern Ukraine. In the March 1998 parliamentary elections, the CPU obtained 24.7% of the votes and 124 seats in the Supreme Council. The Communists remain the largest party in parliament, and the party is the most extensive political formation in Ukraine. Most of its supporters are believed to be pensioners, who account for about 14 million of Ukraine's population of some 51 million. Factional divisions have become increasingly noticeable in the party, between the more orthodox Marxist-Leninists and adherents of "national communism," who accepted the independence of Ukraine.

Progressive Socialist Party (PSP)
Prohresyvna Sotsialistychna Partiya (PSP)

The Progressive Socialist Party (PSP) was led by radical socialist Natalya Vitrenko, who was known as a prominent representative of the "hard left," and by Volodymyr Marchenko. The PSP was formed by orthodox leftists who broke with the Socialist Party in 1995, in protest against their leaders' willingness to seek compromises with President Kuchma. The PSP supported a return to the "radiant past" of the early Soviet Union and the establishment of closer ties with Russia and Belarus. It opposed the institution of the presidency, and Vitrenko called for a return to "Soviet power." The party's platform included proposals for "confiscatory monetary reform and nationalization of national security enterprises." Its pre-election program also advocated a strengthening of Ukraine's defense system and the expulsion of international organizations from the country. The party opposed links with the North Atlantic Treaty Organization (NATO) and was vehemently against the International Monetary Found (IMF) and the World Bank. In the March 1998 election, the party obtained 4% of the votes and 17 seats in the Supreme Council.

Nationalists

National Movement of Ukraine (NMU)
Populat Rukh Ukraine (PRU)

The National Movement of Ukraine (NMU), popularly known as *Rukh*, was founded in September 1989 in Galicia, in an attempt to unite all the Ukrainian opposition groups. Its leader was Hennadiy Udovenko, and it published *Narodna Hazeta* (National Gazette). As the Soviet Union began to dissolve, *Rukh* increasingly shifted its emphasis from the defense of human rights and democracy to a stress on national independence. After its inception, however, *Rukh* lost its role as the sole opposition group. Other political parties began to appear, and *Rukh* fell increasingly under the control of its nationalist wing. The Movement split at its third congress in February 1992, with the more nationalist wing leaving to found the Congress of National Democratic Forces (CNDF) in August 1992. The majority of delegates supported the "constructive opposition" to Kravchuk, led by Vyacheslav Chornovil, who was intent on securing *Rukh* as his political base for the next presidential elections. The Chornovil camp adopted a stridently anti-communist line, maintaining that independence had been stolen by Kravchuk and other "sovereign communists." The minority, on the other hand, insisted that cooperation with the former communists was necessary during the early stages of establishing an independent state.

At the fourth congress of *Rukh,* in December 1992, the movement underwent another split. Chornovil transformed *Rukh* into a political party and was elected as *Rukh*'s leader by an overwhelming majority of delegates. The congress also adopted a wide-ranging program for enhancing state building, which would serve as *Rukh*'s political platform in the next parliamentary elections. *Rukh* took a centrist-nationalist line on most questions. It supported market reforms and a liberal democratic state united around territorial rather than ethnic patriotism. It wanted a strong national defense and Ukraine's immediate departure from the CIS.

With 52,000 full members and 100,000 associate members, *Rukh* was the largest mass political organization in Ukraine in early 1990s. But its support base began to contract throughout the decade, as new political formations emerged across the nationalist and centrist spectrums. It was unable to transform itself into a viable political party with nationwide appeal, and even lost much of its support base in western Ukraine.

Rukh became the strongest player in the Ukrainian Democratic Coalition (UDC), formed by the former ambassador to Canada, Levko Lukyanenko, before the March 1994 elections. The bloc united most of the national democratic parties and some nationalist radical parties. It was supported mainly in western Ukraine and Kyiv, and won 20 seats in the balloting. But its fortunes subsequently declined as a result of internal disputes and inter-party competition. In the March 1998 elections, *Rukh* obtained 9.4% of votes and 46 seats in the Supreme Council.

The Movement splintered into two factions in 1999 and diminished further as a factor on the political scene. On 19 February 1999, the majority of *Rukh*'s parliamentary faction elected Yuri Kostenko as their new leader. Vyacheslav Chornovil disagreed with the decision and thus precipitated a major split within the Movement. Among the influential deputies who followed Kostenko were Dmytro Pavlychko, Vitaly Shevchenko, Ivan Drach, Vyacheslav Kyrylenko, Ivan Zayets, and Oleksandr Lavrynovych. Hennadiy Udovenko, Lilia Hryhorovych, Mykhailo Kosiv, Vyacheslav Koval, and Les Taniuk supported Chornovil. The situation further deteriorated after Chornovil's tragic death in a car accident.

In December 1999, *Rukh* held a "constituent and unifying congress," in which the faction leader and the party's legal head, Hennadiy Udovenko, did not participate. Persistent attempts were made to unite the disparate *Rukh* factions, especially the organization's two largest offshoots—the People's *Rukh* of Ukraine, led by Udovenko, and Yuri Kostenko's Ukrainian People's *Rukh*.[54] Indeed, some *Rukh* activists resolved to establish a new political formation called "For Unity of *Rukh*," which would combine both factions and seek to elicit public support in the campaign for the scheduled parliamentary elections in 2002. By the close of 2000, this new entity possessed three co-chairs: a member of the *Rukh* parliamentary faction Bohdan Boiko, non-faction deputy Georgy Filipchuk, and Eduard Krech.

Congress of National Democratic Forces (CNDF)
Kongres Natsionalno-Demokratychnykh Syl (KNDS)

Led by Mykhailo Horyn, the Congress of National Democratic Forces (CNDF) was inaugurated in August 1992 as a result of the fractures in the *Rukh* organization. CNDF became an umbrella organization representing parties and organizations of a national democratic orientation, including the Ukrainian Republican Party (URP), the Democratic Party (DP), and a variety of like-minded social organizations, such as the Union of Ukrainian Students, and the Ukrainian language society *Prosvita*. Before the March 1998 elections the URP and the DP joined with other blocs, but the CNDF did not participate in the national ballot.

The CNDF proved more nationalistic than *Rukh*, arguing for the "national character" of Ukrainian statehood and the Ukrainianization of the state, schools, armed forces, and public administration. It also stood for a unitary state system and opposed concessions to ethnic minorities in eastern Ukraine, Crimea, and Transcarpathia. The CNDF supported a strong national defense and the retention of nuclear weapons in the face of Russian threats to Ukrainian security. The CNDF wanted Ukraine to leave the CIS and lead an anti-Russian "Baltic–Black Sea Alliance." In the economic sphere, the CNDF supported the creation of a society of property owners and opposed "wild privatization" that favored the old communist *nomenklatura*. The CNDF faction *Derzhavnist* (Statehood) obtained 25 members in parliament following the March 1994 elections.

Democratic Party of Ukraine (DPU)
Demokratychna Partiya Ukrainy (DPU)

The Democratic Party of Ukraine (DPU) became the main party of the nationalist Ukrainian intelligentsia, many of whom were the original founders of *Rukh*.[55] It was led by Volodymyr Yavorivskyi and included well-known dissidents Ivan Drach and Dmytro Pavlychko, with a membership of some 3,000. It published *Demokrat* (Democrat). It supported a civic and territorial definition of the nation, favored a unitary state, and opposed autonomy for Ukraine's ethnic minorities. Under the party's first leader, Yurii Badzio, the DP moved to the "right" and into a close alliance with the Ukrainian Republican Party (URP). However, after Badzio was replaced by Yavorivskyi as party leader, the DPU moved back toward the political center. It supported a strong national defense, Ukraine's prompt departure from the CIS, and a social market economy. At the same time it placed greater emphasis on human rights than did the URP. Party leaders also believed that former communists could be converted to the national democratic cause, and the DPU thereby differed with other nationalist formations. The DPU had 23 deputies in the 1990–1994 parliament; but with a poor organizational structure, its representation collapsed to only two deputies during 1994.

The Bloc of Democratic Parties–People, Economy, and Order (BDP-PEO) (*Vyborchyy Blok Demokratychnykh Partiy, VBDP-NEP*) was created during the 1998 election campaign by the DPU and the Party of Economic Rebirth of Crimea (PERC). Its pre-election program included a mixture of rightist and leftist ideas. The bloc supported economic freedom and private business, and was Western-oriented. Its platform emphasized the "social wealth" of citizens, especially a guarantee of minimal wages and pensions, health reform, family support, and free education. The Bloc advocated the enhancement of Ukraine's role and influence in the regional cooperation structures of the CIS. In the March 1998 elections, the bloc obtained one parliamentary seat and gathered 1.2% of the popular vote.

Ukrainian Republican Party (URP)
Ukrainska Respublikanska Partiya (URP)

In April 1990, the Ukrainian Republican Party (URP), led by Mykhailo Horyn and Levko Lukyanenko, and with a claimed membership of 13,000 people, was the first modern non-communist political party to be officially formed in Ukraine. It was also the first party to be officially registered, in November 1990. The URP was a direct successor of the Ukrainian Helsinki Union. In the early 1990s, it was the best-organized nationalist party, despite its lack of support from the intelligentsia, which supported the Democratic Party of Ukraine instead. The URP advocated a tolerant approach to the civic rights of ethnic minorities. However, the party always had more radical elements within its ranks. After independence, the URP became a strong supporter of the Ukrainian authorities, and it stood for a resolute national defense, immediate departure from the CIS, and a strong, unitary, and presidential republic. In the economic sphere, the URP favored the creation of a society of property owners but opposed socially unjust privatization and backed a policy of priority support for national industry. The party performed poorly in the March 1994 parliamentary elections, as it was tainted by its uncritical support for the Ukrainian authorities. Only eight party members were elected. For the March 1998 election, the party joined the National Front, but garnered only 2.7% of the national vote, without gaining any legislative seats. Its major publications included *Samostiina Ukraina* (Independent Ukraine) and *Rozbudova Derzhavy* (Development of the State).

Ukrainian Conservative Republican Party (UCRP)
Ukrainska Konservatyvna Respublikanska Partiya (UKRP)

The Ukrainian Conservative Republican Party (UCRP) was created in May 1992, after being forced out of the Republican Party for its more radical nationalist views. It was led by Stepan Khmara. The party's initial membership totaled about 1,000 people. The UCRP was vehemently anti-Russian and was strongly opposed to any compromises with former Communists such as Kravchuk and Kuchma, whom it described as traitors to Ukrainian national interests. The UCRP openly supported a nuclear Ukraine and the rights of ethnic Ukrainians in neighboring Russian territories. The UCRP one seat in the post-1994 parliament. Before the March 1998 elections, the party joined with the URP to create the National Front, which garnered 2.7% of the vote and 5 parliamentary seats. Its publications have included *Klych* (Key). Like other staunchly nationalist groupings, the UCRP advocated a more pronounced state role in fostering Ukrainian education and language use in order to promote a uniform Ukrainian culture and to marginalize the Russian population.

Congress of Ukrainian Nationalists (CUN)
Kongres Ukrainskykh Natsionalistiv (KUN)

Led by Slava Stetsko and with a membership of some 5,000, the Congress of Ukrainian Nationalists (CUN) was established by the emigré Organization of Ukrainian Nationalists (OUN) in 1992 as a means to attract various small nationalist groups into OUN ranks. The CUN supported democratic nationalism and a strong nation-state independent from Russia. The CUN urged the elimination of all groups and forces seeking to destabilize Ukraine's eastern border regions. Economically, the CUN veered between the strongly pro-capitalist orientation of its emigré members and calls for state protection of the Ukrainian economy. The CUN, together with the Organization of Ukrainian Nationalists, won considerable support in western Ukraine, and it elected five deputies to parliament in March 1994. Before the March 1998 election, the party joined the National Front *(Natsionalnyy Front, NF)*. Its chief publication was *Shliakh Peremohy* (Way of Victory).

Another nationalist electoral bloc, "Less Talk," was created during the 1998 election campaign by the Social Nationalist Party and by the State Independence for Ukraine Party. Its pre-election program argued for the creation of criminal and anti-corruption courts and the enforcement of single terms for parliamentary deputies. It failed to obtain any seats in the legislature, with a mere 0.2% of the vote.

Neo-Fascists

Social Nationalist Party (SNP)
Sotsial Natsionalna Partiya (SNP)

The Social Nationalist Party (SNP) was an openly neo-fascist and ethnocentric party based in Lviv, in western Ukraine, which favored the expansion of the Ukrainian state to include the territory controlled by the early medieval kingdom of Kyivan Rus´. It was led by Yaroslav Andrushkiv and had a membership of 200. The party also claimed to have a paramilitary wing. The SNP tried to take over the Lviv branch of *Rukh* in October 1992, and it successfully recruited new members as economic conditions deteriorated in the early 1990s. Its 19 candidates in Lviv during the 1994 elections won 2.5% of the local vote. Before the March 1998 elections, the party joined the "Less Talk" electoral bloc. The SNP and other ethno-nationalist formations constituted part of the "integral nationalist" tradition, which rejected civil rights and a pluralistic and multi-ethnic political system. Instead, they promoted revolutionary violence and the dictatorship of a single vanguard party that would purportedly lead Ukrainian society to salvation.

State Independence for Ukraine (SIU)
Derzhavna Samostiinist Ukrainy (DSU)

State Independence for Ukraine (SIU) formed as a radical splinter from the Ukrainian Helsinki Union in 1990, and registered at the national level in March 1993. Its leadership included Ivan Kandyba, Roman Koval, and Volodymyr Shlemko, and its membership totaled about 600 people. The SIU stood for a powerful Ukrainian nation-state within its ethnographic borders, including territories in Poland, Belarus, and Russia. Membership was not open to non-Ukrainians and former members of the Communist Party. Some party leaders called for the "ethnic cleansing" of Russians and Jews from Ukraine. Before the March 1998 election, the party joined with the neo-fascist Social National Party (SNP) to create the "Less Talk" electoral bloc, which stridently opposed liberalism and socialism. Its publications have included *Neskorenna Natsiia* (Unbeatable Nation) and *Napriam* (Direction), and it was reported to operate a small paramilitary structure and security service.

Ukrainian National Assembly (UNA)
Ukrainska Natsionalna Assembleya (UNA)

The Ukrainian National Assembly (UNA), led initially by Yurii Shukhevych and Dmytro Korchinski, was a radical nationalist group that supported building a "neo-imperial" Ukrainian state, independent of both Russia and the West. Its membership reportedly reached about 14,000 in the mid-1990s. The UNA created a paramilitary wing, the Ukrainian People's Self-Defense (UPSD), which claimed to have over 5,000 men under arms. It participated in the conflicts in Transdnistria (Moldova), and Abkhazia (Georgia), as well as in violent attacks on separatist organizations in Ukraine. In 1993, the Ukrainian parliament outlawed paramilitary groups but the UPSD continued its activities. The UNA took advantage of the radicalization of the public mood in western Ukraine, where three of its members were elected to parliament. The party was well organized and tightly disciplined and was able to adapt its policies to the major political and social issues confronting the country.[56]

The UNA was staunchly anti-Russian and envisaged politics essentially as a struggle between Ukrainians and Russians. At the same time, it wanted to rebuild a pan-Slavic state centered on Kyiv with its own military-political bloc that would transcend narrow ethnic criteria. The party's registration was repealed in 1996 because of its radical views. After a split between top party officials Dmytro Korchinski and Yurii Shukhevych, Oleg Vitovych became party chairman. In February 1997, the UNA expelled some of its extreme members in a bid to become a parliamentary party.[57] Its publications included *Holos Natsiy* (Voice of the Nation), and *Ukrainski Obrii,* (Ukrainian Horizons). During the March 1998 election campaign, the party advocated military reform and a "Ukrainianized" army. The UNA failed to obtain any seats in parliament, garnering only 0.4% of the national vote.

Ethnic Minority and Religious Parties

Democratic Union of Hungarians in Ukraine (DUHU)
Demokratychnyy Soyuz Ugortsiv v Ukrayini (DSUU)

Hungarian community leaders in Transcarpathia, where Magyars accounted for 12.55% of the region's population, were active in campaigning for an "autonomous district" in the Berehiv *raion* (region), which contained the highest concentration of ethnic Hungarians in Ukraine. The Democratic Union of Hungarians in Ukraine (DUHU) organized a poll in 1992 about granting Berehiv a special "national district" status; 81% of voters approved of this measure.[58] The DUHU also supported autonomy for the whole of Transcarpathia within an independent Ukraine. The authorities in Kyiv proved fairly accommodating to the Hungarian minority, acceding to calls for a "special status" for the Berehiv district; but they were opposed to granting autonomous status to Transcarpathia, for fear of initiating a domino effect in Crimea. Ukrainian authorities did not perceive Magyars as a threat to national integrity but as a bridge toward establishing cooperative ties with Hungary and as a potential lever against the more strident Ruthenian demands for regional autonomy. The DUHU, chaired by Mihály Tóth, supported individual and cultural autonomy for the Hungarian minority in western Ukraine, and the establishment of regional "self-rule" in Subcarpathia.[59]

Another Hungarian organization, the Cultural Alliance of Hungarians in Subcarpathia (CAHS), chaired by Miklós Kovács, supported national minority self-rule. It proposed to create a regional-level public administrative unit called *Tisza*, which would incorporate Hungarians presently living in four districts. By 2000, the Ukrainian government had not responded to this proposal. The CAHS was also concerned with the brain drain from Hungarian-populated areas. The Alliance offered financial support to students who promised to return from Hungary after the completion of their studies.[60] Its major publication was *Kárpátaljai Szemle* (Carpathian Review).

Christian Democratic Alliance of Romanians in Ukraine (CDARU)
Hristiansko-Demokratychny Allians Ruminiv na Ukraini (HDARU)

Led by Ivan Popescu, the Christian Democratic Alliance of Romanians in Ukraine (CDARU) represented the interests of 190,000 Romanians and Moldovans who lived in the Chernivtsi region of western Ukraine. The CDARU's official program called for greater cultural and linguistic autonomy for the Romanian minority, but some of its militants openly called for the region to be rejoined with Romania, which ruled the area from 1918 to 1940. One deputy from CDARU was elected to parliament in the March 1994 elections. Its publications included *Plai Românesc* (Romanian Land). In October 1993, the local authorities attempted to suppress the publication, accusing it of fermenting separatist sentiment.

Eminescu Society (ES)
Spilka Eminescu (SE)

The Bukovina region in southwestern Ukraine also exhibited some autonomous trends. A rift developed between western, pro-Haliczyna *raions* and eastern, conservative raions. The former favored more extensive economic decentralization and the creation of a "free economic zone." Divisions have also appeared between Ukrainian majority *raions* and those with substantial Romanian and Moldovan populations. Approximately 20% of the total population of the *oblast* were registered as Romanians and Moldovans.

The minority Eminescu Society (ES) became very active in the region and lodged various proposals for improving the position of the Romanian community, including the establishment of a Romanian university in Chernivtsi and even dual Ukrainian-Romanian citizenship. This was interpreted by some Ukrainian spokesman as creeping ethno-territorial separatism aided and abetted by revisionist circles in Romania. Indeed, the more outspoken minority leaders supported an eventual merger of Bukovina with Romania. Under the inspiration of nationalist and separatist forces, minority leaders called for a boycott of the December 1991 referendum on Ukrainian independence, and some local village councils reportedly hoisted the Romanian flag and adopted other Romanian or Moldovan symbols.[61]

Kyiv initially proved less accommodating to the Romanian minority than to the Hungarian, clearly fearful that aspirations toward autonomy could result in a major confrontation with Bucharest over several territories annexed from Romania at the close of World War II, including Bukovina and the southern Danubian counties in the Odesa *oblast*. Nevertheless, the Romanian-Moldovan population has been granted local self-government in districts where it predominates.

Regionalists

Communist Party of Crimea (CPC)
Komunistychna Partiya Kryma (KPK)

Led by Leonid Grach and with a membership of 30,000, the Communist Party of Crimea (CPC) was a regional communist organization that was folded into the Union of Communists of Crimea (UCC) in June 1992. In June 1993, the union formally renamed itself the Communist Party of Crimea (CPC). The party stood for a revived USSR and wanted to become a part of the re-created Communist Party of the Soviet Union. The CPC maintained close links with the Russian Communist Party. Communist and socialist organizations existed all over the peninsula, headed by council chairmen and executive committees. The party won four seats in the Ukrainian elections of March 1994, but only three in the elections to the Crimean parliament, and subsequently entered the opposition there. Its major publication was *Kommunist Kryma* (Crimean Communist).

Party of Economic Rebirth of Crimea (PERC)
Partiia Ekonomicheskogo Vozrozhdeniia Kryma (PEVK)

Led by Vladimir Sheviov and with a membership of 30,000, the Party of Economic Rebirth of Crimea (PERC) held its first conference in November

1992, and constituted itself as a political party in May 1993. The PERC was backed by local export and import businesses and by tourism. It established a strong presence in the Crimean parliament, gaining 60 out of 196 seats. The party supported market reforms within the framework of an economically independent Crimea and was recognized as a pragmatic centrist party. In 1993, the PERC formulated plans for Crimean fiscal independence and a Crimean central bank. The PERC's relations with the local communist and republican parties remained poor. The party's close association with the Crimean leadership under Mykola Bagrov led to a heavy defeat in the Crimean elections in 1994, when the party gained only two seats. Before the March 1998 elections, the PERC joined with the Democratic Party of Ukraine, but it failed to win any seats in the national parliament.

Republican Party of Crimea (RPC)
Respublikanska Partiya Kryma (RPK)

The Republican Party of Crimea (RPC) was formed in August 1991 by local deputy Yurii Meshkov to campaign against Ukrainian independence and for the maintenance of the USSR. Subsequently, it favored Crimean independence. The RPC's petition campaign to force the Crimean authorities to hold a referendum on Crimean independence collected 246,000 signatures. In 1993, the RPC organized a second petition campaign to force the resignation of the leader of the Crimean parliament, Mykola Bagrov, as well as the local parliament itself. In the campaign to elect a Crimean president, Meshkov defeated Bagrov by a wide margin. Meshkov urged local voters to boycott the Ukrainian elections of March 1994. The RPC's political platform was dominated by the single theme of securing Crimean independence, and its economic policy was a mixture of populist measures to lower food prices, together with plans for Crimean economic independence. Its fortunes declined during the latter half of the 1990s as President Kuchma successfully played off factional infighting in Crimea to undermine the drive for separation from Ukraine.

People's Party of Crimea (PPC)
Narodna Partiya Kryma (NPK)

Led by Viktor Mezhak, and with a membership of about 1,000, the People's Party of Crimea (PPC) was originally formed as a moderate alternative to the Republican Party of Crimea. In November 1993, it splintered from the original Republican Movement of Crimea. The PPC stood for a confederation among Crimea, Russia, and Ukraine rather than outright Crimean independence or simple reunion with Russia. In January 1994, the PPC joined the Republican Party to form the "Russia" bloc, which won 54 out of 94 seats in the Crimean elections in the spring of 1994.

Other centrist forces were also active on the peninsula. The Democratic

Party of Crimea (DPC) *(Demokraticheska Partiia Kryma, DPK)* was led by Anatolii Filatov and had 200 members. It was based mainly in rural regions and amongst the Yalta intelligentsia in Crimea. The DPC favored a policy of national reconciliation in Crimea and allied itself with moderate Crimean Tatar groups. The DPC also favored Crimean autonomy but believed that the peninsula should remain part of the Ukrainian state. The Union in Support of the Republic of Crimea (USRC) *(Soiuz v Podderzhku Respubliki Kryma, SPRK)*, under the leadership of Sergei Kunitsyn, represented traditional industrial interests in the Crimea. The USRC took a relatively moderate line toward relations with the government in Kyiv and with the local authorities. In the spring of 1994, the USRC formed "Unity" *(Yednist)*, a coalition between the Crimean Tatar *Majlis* and centrist parties, but it had little impact in the 1994 elections and won less than 3% of the vote.

Russian Party of Crimea (RPC)
Russka Partiya Kryma (RPK)

The Russian Party of Crimea, led by Sergei Shuvainikov was a splinter group from Meshkov's Republican Party of Crimea. Its membership stood at about 1,000 people. It was more radically anti-Ukrainian than the Republicans and was supported by Zhirinovsky's Liberal Democratic Party in Russia. The RPC was mostly composed of ethnic Russians; but unlike the Republicans, it favored union between Russia and Crimea rather than a fully independent Crimea. Shortly before the 1994 Crimean elections, the leader of the Russian party was accused of personal corruption, and the party won only one seat in the balloting. The RPC's chief publication was *Rossiiskii Krym* (Russian Crimea).

Ukrainian Civic Congress of Crimea (UCCC)
Ukrainskyi Hromadskyi Kongres Kryma (UHKK)

Under the leadership of Serhii Lytvyn and Ihor Banakh, the Ukrainian Civic Congress of Crimea (UCCC) was formed in November 1993 by the local Ukrainian community in Crimea, in order to oppose the region's separatist movements. The UCCC demanded that the Crimean constitution and laws be brought into line with those of Ukraine as a whole. The UCCC condemned the Crimean elections of 1994 and called on local Ukrainians to boycott the vote. The UCCC was unable to elect any deputies in the spring 1994 elections either to the Ukrainian or the Crimean parliament.

National Movement of Crimean Tatars (NMCT)
Natsionalnoe dvizhenie Krymskikh Tatar (NDKT)

The National Movement of Crimean Tatars (NMCT) was the oldest Crimean Tatar organization. Under the leadership of Vashti Abduraiimov, it was the most moderate of the three main Crimean Tatar organizations. The NMCT favored cooperation and dialogue with the Crimean authorities and rejected the claim to Tatar sovereignty over the whole of Crimea. The NMCT was soundly defeated in the special elections for the Crimean Tatars, winning only 5.5% of the vote and no seats in the local parliament. The Movement's main publication was *Areket*.

Organization of the Crimean Tatar National Movement (OCTNM)
Organizatsiia Krymskotatarskogo Natsionalnogo Dvizheniia (OKND)

Under the leadership of Rejep Khairedinov and with approximately 800 members, the Organization of the Crimean Tatar National Movement (OCTNM) was the largest Crimean Tatar party. It was mostly composed of mainstream Crimean Tatar activists and the leaders of the *Majlis*—the Tatar a representative parliamentary body. The OCTNM stood for the restoration of national statehood to the Crimean Tatars in their historic homeland. Together with the *Majlis*, the OCTNM won 90% of the Crimean Tatar vote in the Crimean parliamentary elections and all 14 of the seats reserved for the Tatars. Its publications included *Avdet*, *Kirim Sedasi*, and *Kyrym*.

In May 1999 the Crimean Tatar National Assembly (CTNA), with chairman Julrem Abljamitor, staged a protest against the expulsion of Tatars from the Crimea during World War II, in an attempt to focus attention on the minority's current problems. Abljamitor rejected accusations of "radical nationalism," claiming that his party was not among those taking a radical approach to the Tatar issue. The party was apparently only demanding the passage of laws that would be helpful to the Tatar people, and aimed to find a solution to ethnic and economic problems in the Crimea.[62]

National Party (NP)
Milli Firka (MF)

Under the leadership of Ilmy Umerov and with a small membership of 100, the National Party (NP) was a radical Crimean Tatar group that rejected all ideas of compromise with the authorities in the Crimea and in Kyiv. It sought to establish an ethnic Crimean Tatar republic in the Crimea in which the Tatar language, culture, and religion would predominate. The party also supported direct, extra-parliamentary methods of struggle where necessary. Umerov became a Crimean parliamentary deputy in March 1994. Another nationalist grouping was the *Adalet* or Justice party, which took a hard-line stance vis-à-vis the central government on the question of Crimean sovereignty.

Democratic Movement of Donbas (DMD)
Demokraticheskoe Dvizhenie Donbassa (DDD)

The Democratic Movement of Donbas (DMD), under the leadership of Dmitrii Kornilov and with a membership of 3,000, was formed in the largely Russian-speaking Donbas region in December 1990. It campaigned against the introduction of Ukrainian as the official state language. The DMD opposed Ukrainian independence, and subsequently called for an autonomous Donbas within a federalized Ukraine, local "state" status for the Russian language, and dual citizenship arrangements between Russia and Ukraine. Because the Ukrainian electoral law attempted to prevent overtly regional groups from standing for parliament, the DMD was instrumental in creating a broader Civic Congress of Ukraine in 1992, into which its efforts were subsumed. The DMD's major publication was *Nash Donbas* (Our Donbas).

Society of Carpathian Ruthenians (SCR)
Spilka Karpatskyh Rusyniv (SKR)

Autonomist tendencies were visible in Transcarpathia during the 1990s, with several groups pressing for varying degrees of self-determination. In December 1990, even before Ukrainian independence, the Society of Carpathian Ruthenians (SCR), formed initially as a cultural-educational group, demanded the "return of the status of an autonomous republic" to the Transcarpathian *oblast*. The SCR sought autonomy similar to that possessed by the semi-independent Subcarpathian Ruthenia in October 1938, following the dismemberment of Czechoslovakia. Such autonomist voices had some resonance among local *oblast* leaders, who called for full autonomy along Crimean lines but underlined their intent to remain a constituent part of Ukraine. They also raised the prospect of conducting public plebiscites on the question of autonomy and "self-governing" status for the region. Indeed, in a regional referendum in December 1991, 78% of the population favored the creation of a "special self-governing administrative territory" for the Transcarpathian *oblast* within an independent Ukraine.[63]

Subcarpathian Republican Party (SRP)
Zakarpatska Respublikanska Partiya (ZRP)

More radical groups have also emerged in the Carpathian region, including the Subcarpathian Republican Party (SRP), which called for the transformation of the region into an independent state. However, their popular influence has been limited, and their objectives are rejected by the regional government. Under the leadership of Vasyl Zaiats, the SRP argued that the Slavic population of the Transcarpathian region in western Ukraine formed a distinct ethnic group—the Rusyns, or Ruthenians. It started its campaign for Transcarpathian autonomy with an informal referendum endorsed by local voters in December 1991. After that time, Kyiv repeatedly delayed plans to turn Transcarpathia into a free economic zone, calculating that this could escalate autonomist and secessionist demands among Ruthenian activists. Some of the more radical members of the SRP have openly called for Transcarpathia to be returned to Hungary, which ruled the region before 1918 and between 1938 and 1945.

POLITICAL DATA

Name of State: Ukraine *(Ukrayina)*
Form of Government: Parliamentary democracy
Structure of Legislature: Unicameral Supreme Council *(Verkhovna Rada)*, 450 seats; half of seats allocated on a proportional basis to parties gaining 4% of the national vote; 225 members elected in single-mandate constituencies. (first used in the 1998 election).
Size of Territory: 233,000 square miles
Population: 51,867,828 (1995 estimate); 49,811,174 (1999 estimate)

Source: http:www.odci.gov/cia/publications/factbook/up.html#people.

Composition of Population (1991):

Ethnic Group	Number	% of Population
Ukrainian	37,763,000	72.7
Russian	11,480,000	22.1
Jewish	468,000	0.9
Belarusian	467,000	0.9
Moldovan	312,000	0.6
Bulgarian	260,000	0.5
Polish	208,000	0.4
Hungarian	156,000	0.3
Romanian	155,000	0.3
Crimean Tatar	135,000	0.2
Greek	104,000	0.2
Other	467,000	0.9
Total	51,965,000	100.0

Source: http://www.bsos.umd.edu/cidcm/mar/ukrcrus.htm.

ELECTION RESULTS

Presidential Election, 31 October 1999 and 14 November 1999

First Round, 31 October 1999

Turnout: 70.15%

Candidate	Votes	% of Vote
Leonid Kuchma	9,598,672	37.99
Petro Symonenko	5,849,077	23.15
Oleksandr Moroz	2,969,896	11.75
Natalya Vitrenko	2,886,972	11.43
Yevhen Marchuk	2,138,356	8.46
Yuri Kostenko	570,623	2.26
Hennadiy Udovenko	319,778	1.27
Vasyl Onopenko	124,040	0.49
Oleksandr Rzhavskiy	96,515	0.38

Yuriy Karmazin	90,793	0.36
Vitali Kononov	76,832	0.30
Oleksandr Bazyliuk	36,012	0.14
Mykola Haber	31,829	0.13
Votes against all candidates	477,019	1.89
Total	25,266,414	100.00

Second Round, 14 November 1999

Turnout: 74.87%

Candidate	Votes	% of Vote
Leonid Kuchma	15,870,722	56.25
Petro Symonenko	10,665,420	37.80
Votes against all candidates	970,181	5.95
Total	27,506,323	100.00

Sources: http://www.ourworld.compuserve.com/homepages/bohdans/ukre1991.htm, and International Foundation for Election systems - www.ifes-ukraine.org.

Presidential Election, 26 June 1994 and 10 July 1994

First Round, 26 June 1994

Turnout: 69%

Candidate	Votes	% of Vote
Leonid Kravchuk	9,977,766	38.36
Leonid Kuchma	8,107,626	31.17
Oleksandr Moroz	3,466,541	13.33
Volodymyr Lanovy	2,483,986	9.44
Valeriy Babych	644,263	2.48
Ivan Plyushch	321,886	1.24
Petro Talanchuk	143,361	0.55
Votes against all candidates	892,740	3.43
Total	26,038,169	100.00

Second Round, 10 July 1994

Turnout: 70%

Candidate	Votes	% of Vote
Leonid Kuchma	14,016,850	52.14
Leonid Kravchuk	12,111,603	45.06
Votes against all candidates	751,380	2.80
Total	26,879,833	100.00

Source: http://www.ifes ukraine.org/english/Elections1994/Presidential/Results/.

Presidential Election, 1 December 1991

Turnout: 84.16%

Candidate	Votes	% of Vote
Leonid Kravchuk	n/a	61.59
Vyacheslav Chornovil	n/a	23.27
Levko Lukyanenko	n/a	4.49
Volodymyr Hrynov	n/a	4.17
Ihor Yukhnovsky	n/a	1.74
Leopold Taburiansky	n/a	0.57
Total	n/a	95.83

Parliamentary Elections, 29 March 1998

Turnout: 70.78%

Party/Coalition	Votes	% of Vote	Seats
Communist Party of Ukraine	6,550,353	24.7	124
National Movement of Ukraine (*Rukh*)	2,498,262	9.4	46
Socialist Party/Peasant Party	2,273,788	8.6	35
Green Party of Ukraine	1,444,264	5.4	19
People's Democratic Party of Ukraine	1,331,460	5.0	28
All-Ukrainian Union *Hromada*	1,242,235	4.7	23
United Social Democratic Party of Ukraine	1,066,113	4.0	18
Progressive Socialist Party	1,075,118	4.0	17
Agrarian Party of Ukraine	978,330	3.7	8
Reforms and Order Party	832,574	3.1	3
Working Ukraine	813,326	3.1	1
National Front	721,966	2.7	5
Labor Party and Liberal Party	502,969	1.9	1
Forward Ukraine	461,924	1.7	2
Christian Democratic Party of Ukraine	344,826	1.3	2
Democratic Party of Ukraine	326,489	1.2	1
Other	n/a	15.5	117
Total	25,749,574	100.0	450

Sources: Wilfried Derksen's Electoral web sites: http://www.agora.stm.it/elections/election/ukraine.htm; and http://www-public.rz.uni-duesseldorf.de/~nordsiew/ukraine2.html, and International Foundation for Election Systems.

Parliamentary Elections, 27 March and November 1994

First Round, 27 March 1994

Turnout: 75.81%

Party/Coalition	Votes	% of Vote	Seats
Independents	14,894,269	66.48	168
Communist Party of Ukraine	3,683,332	12.72	86
National Movement of Ukraine (*Rukh*)	1,491,164	5.15	20

Peasant Party of Ukraine	794,614	2.74	19
Socialist Party of Ukraine	895,830	3.09	14
Ukranian Republican Party	728,614	2.52	8
Congress of Ukrainian Nationalists	361,352	1.25	5
Party of Democratic Rebirth	239,763	0.83	4
Labor Party of Ukraine	114,409	0.40	4
Democratic Party of Ukraine	312,842	1.08	2
Organization of Ukrainian Nationalists	48,239	0.51	1
Social Democratic Party	104,204	0.36	2
Christian Democratic Party	100,007	0.35	1
Civic Congress	72,473	0.25	2
Ukrainian Conservative Republican Party	99,028	0.34	2
Other	—	1.93	—
Total	27,142,632	100.00	338

Source: http://www2.essex.ac.uk/elect/electer/ukr_er_nl.htm.

The 1994 Ukrainian parliamentary elections took several rounds to complete due to insufficient votes. As a result, there is no single source that provides complete election data. Rounds of voting occured between March and November 1994.

Parliamentary Elections, 1994

Final seates after three subsequent rounds of voting in July, August and November.

Party/Coalition	Votes	% of Vote	Seats
Communist Party of Ukraine	n/a	n/a	90
National Movement of Ukraine (*Rukh*)	n/a	n/a	20
Peasant Party of Ukraine	n/a	n/a	19
Socialist Party of Ukraine	n/a	n/a	15
Ukrainian Republican Party	n/a	n/a	11
Congress of Ukrainian Nationalists	n/a	n/a	5
Inter-Regional Bloc for Reform	n/a	n/a	5
Others	n/a	n/a	12
Independent Candidates	n/a	n/a	228
Vacant	n/a	n/a	45
Total	n/a	n/a	450

Source: www.ipu.org.80/cgi.

Some candidates crossed party lines in the multiple rounds of voting and have been counted in varying ways depending upon the source consulted.

NOTES

1. For recent histories of Ukraine consult: Orest Subtelny, *Ukraine: A History,* Toronto: University of Toronto Press, 1988; Ivan L. Rudnytsky, *Essays in Modern Ukrainian History,* Edmonton: University of Alberta, Canadian Institute of Ukrainian Studies,1987; and Albert Seaton, *The Horsemen of the Steppes: The Story of the Cossacks*, London: Bodley Head, 1985.

2. See Robert Conquest, *The Harvest of Sorrow: Soviet Collectivization and the Terror-Famine*, New York: Oxford University Press, 1986.

3. See the *Report on Ukraine's Referendum on Independence and Presidential Election*, CSCE, 1 December 1991, U.S. Congress, CSCE Committee, Washington, D.C., 20 December 1991.

4. Henry R. Huttenbach, "The (Re)Birth of Ukraine," *Analysis of Current Events,* Vol. 3, No. 3, December 1991.

5. See the Constitution of Ukraine, Articles 75 and 76, at http://www.infoukes.com/history/constitution/index-en.html#r4.

6. Refer to CSCE Bulletin on Ukraine's Parliamentary Elections, April 1994, p. 7.

7. Ilya Prizel, "Ukraine Between Proto-Democracy and 'Soft' Authoritarianism," in Karen Dawisha and Bruce Parrott (Eds.), *Democratic Changes and Authoritarian Reactions in Russia, Ukraine, Belarus, and Moldova*, Cambridge, U.K.: Cambridge University Press, 1997, pp. 330–369.

8. In the March 1994 elections, 3,633 individual candidates (more than 90% of the total number of candidates) considered themselves independent. See The European Forum, *The Political Landscape of Ukraine*, June 1997, at http://www.europeanforum.bot-consult.se/cup/ukraine/parties.htm.

9. Prizel, 1997, p. 355.

10. Concerning the struggle over the Ukrainian constitution see Ustina Markus, "Rivals Compromise on Constitution," *Transition*, Vol. 2, No. 15, 26 July 1996, pp. 36–37.

11. For details on the 1996 constitution see Kataryna Wolczuk, "The Politics of Constitution Making in Ukraine," in Taras Kuzio (Ed.), *Contemporary Ukraine: Dynamics of Post-Soviet Transformation*, Armonk: M.E. Sharpe, 1998, pp. 118–138; and Chrystyna Lapychak and Ustina Markus, "Ukraine's Continuing Evolution," *Transition*, Vol. 3, No. 2, 7 February 1997, pp. 29–32.

12. Check Katya Gorchinskaya, "Ukraine Joins the Party," *Transition*, Vol. 5, No. 5, May 1998, pp. 54–61.

13. For more information on the referendum consult President Kuchma's edict "On Declaration of an All-Ukrainian Referendum on Popular Initiative," at http://www.brama.com/ua-consulate/ukaz_ref.html; the "Constitutional Court Ruling on Referendum," in Uryadovyy Kur'er at http://www.brama.com/ua-consulate/refer_ksud.html, and the Report of the European Commission for Democracy Through Law (Venice Commission), "Constitutional Referendum in Ukraine," Venice, 31 March 2000.

14. The results of the April 2000 referendum were as follows: 1. To reduce the total number of seats in the Supreme Council from 450 to 300—Yes: 84.77%, No: 13.89%; 2. To divide the unicameral Supreme Council into two separate chambers, one of nationally elected officials and the other of regional officials appointed by the President—Yes: 89.11%, No: 9.65%; 3. To outlaw legal immunity for deputies—Yes: 90.02%, No: 8.75%; 4. To give President Kuchma the power to disband parliament if it is unable to come to consensus within a month or pass a budget within three months—Yes: 81.78%, No:16.82%. The data are taken from the International Foundation for Election Systems website at http://www.ifes.org/eguide/resultsum/ukraine2res.htm.

15. See Oleg Varfolomeyev, "Rival 'Clans' Mix Business, Politics, and Murder," *Transition*, Vol. 3, No. 6, 4 April 1997, pp. 31–34; and Oleg Varfolomeyev, "Ukrainian Party Politics Gets a Boost," *Transition*, Vol. 5, No. 1, January 1998, pp. 80–85.

16. For an analysis of Ukrainian politics throughout the Kuchma era see Roman Solchanyk, "The Post-Soviet Transition in Ukraine: Prospects for Stability," in Taras Kuzio (Ed.), *Contemporary Ukraine: Dynamics of Post-Soviet Transformation*, Armonk: M.E. Sharpe, 1998, pp. 17–40.

17. For census statistics see Derzhkomstat, *Naselennya Ukrayinskoyi RSR (Za Dannymy Vsesoyuzneko Perepuso Naselennya)*, 1989 (Kyiv: Derzhkomstat, 1990), pp. 144, 153–161.

18. Consult Natalya Lakiza-Sachuk, "Front-Page Topic," *Demokratychna Ukrayina*, 28 May 1994, in Foreign Broadcast Information Service (FBIS), *Daily Reports, Central Eurasia*, *FBIS-USR-94–066*, 21 June 1994. See also Stephen Rapawy, "Socio-Economic Indicators for Ukraine," Soviet Branch, Center for International Research, U.S. Bureau of the Census, Washington, D.C., April 1992.

19. A valuable analysis of ethnic attitudes in Ukraine can be found in Ian Bremmer, "The Politics of Ethnicity: Russians in the New Ukraine," *Europe-Asia Studies,* Vol. 46, No. 2, (1994), pp. 261–283. See also Valeri Khmelko and Andrew Wilson, "Regionalism and Linguistic Cleavages in Ukraine," in Taras Kuzio (Ed.), *Contemporary Ukraine: Dynamics of Post-Soviet Transformation*, Armonk: M.E. Sharpe, 1998, pp. 60–80. See also Janusz Bugajski, "Ethnic Relations and Regional Problems in Independent Ukraine," in Sharon Wolchik and Volodymyr Zviglyanich (Eds.), *Ukraine: The Search for National Identity*, London: Rowman & Littlefield, 1999.

20. Consult Eugene B. Rumer, "Eurasia Letter: Will Ukraine Return to Russia?" *Foreign Policy*, No. 96, Fall 1994, pp. 129–144.

21. See Stanislav Gorlobokov, "Praise for Autonomy," *Pravda Ukrainy*, Kyiv, 6 August 1993, in *FBIS-USR-93–116*, 7 September 1993.

22. Check "The Absence of Self-Government Is the Cause of the Regionalization of Ukraine," *Holos Ukrainy*, Kyiv, 25 January 1994, in *FBIS-USR-94–018*, 28 February 1994.

23. For an analysis of the elections see Dominique Arel and Andrew Wilson, "Ukraine Under Kuchma: Back to Eurasia?" *Radio Free Europe/Radio Liberty (RFE/RL) Research Report*, Vol. 3, No. 32, 19 August 1994, pp. 1–12.

24. See the Ukrinform Report, "Leonid Kuchma Proposes to Bring Order to the Executive Chain of Command," *Donbas*, Donetsk, 18 October 1994, in *FBIS-USR-94–115*, 25 October 1994.

25. Oleh Shmid, "One Element Is Lacking in the Unfinished Report of Leonid Kuchma: The Price Has Not Been Indicated in It," *Post-Postup*, Lviv, 29 September–5 October 1994, in *FBIS-USR-94–116*, 27 October 1994.

26. See Roman Szporluk, "Reflections on Ukraine After 1994: The Dilemmas of Nationhood," *Harriman Review*, Vol. 7, Nos. 7–9, March–May 1994, pp. 1–10.

27. For a useful discussion on the context of "Ukrainianization," see Ivan Z. Holowinsky, "Linguistic Policy as a Political Weapon," *Ukrainian Quarterly*, Vol. 2, No. 1, Spring 1994, pp. 13–20.

28. See the paper delivered by Natalia Lakiza-Sachuk, "The Current Situation and Perspectives of Ethnic Policy in Ukraine as a Factor of International Security," Tallinn, Estonia, 14–18 October 1993.

29. Consult "Protest of the Union of Writers of Ukraine," *Literaturna Ukrayina*, Kyiv, 21 July 1994, in *FBIS-USR-94–083*, 2 August 1994.

30. For the text of the October 1993 draft of the Constitution of Ukraine, see the Special Supplement to *Holos Ukrainy*, Kyiv, 30 October 1993, in *FBIS-USR-93–148*, 22 November 1993.

31. Based on extensive interviews during the author's visit to the Donbas region in July 1994. Also see "Focus on Serious Challenges Facing Ukraine," Briefing of the Commission on Security and Cooperation in Europe, Washington, D.C., May 1994.

32. See Tetyana Khomych, "The Counselor of Rutskyy Teaches Us to Live," *Moloda Ukrainy*, Kyiv, 1 March 1994, in *FBIS-USR-94–024*, 14 March 1994.

33. Check the results of the "advisory plebiscite" in *Unian*, Kyiv, 31 March 1994, in *FBIS-SOV-94–063*, 1 April 1994.

34. Some militant separatists have proposed reviving the short-lived Donetsk–Krivoi Rog Republic of 1918, as a Donetsk-Dniepr or Dniepr autonomous republic. Russophile regionalism has also been evident in Odessa, where autonomists have campaigned for "special state status" for four southern *oblasts* in the historical boundaries of "Novorossiia." For details see Roman Solchanyk, "The Politics of State Building: Centre-Periphery Relations in Post-Soviet Ukraine," *Europe-Asia Studies,* Vol. 46, No. 1, 1994, pp. 47–68. See also Sarah Birch and Ihor Zinko, "The Dilemma of Regionalism," *Transition*, Vol. 2, No. 22, 1 November 1996, pp. 22–25, 64.

35. See the interview with Taras Stetskiv, "New Wave Politicians Already Know That the Ukrainian Superidea Hidden in Conservatism's Coffer Cannot Be Unlocked with a Liberal Key," *Post-Postup*, Lviv, 10–16 June 1994, in *FBIS-USR-94–075*, 14 July 1994.

36. See Roman Solchanyk, "Centrifugal Movements in Ukraine on the Eve of the Independence Referendum," *RFE/RL Report on the USSR*, Vol. 3, No. 48, 29 November 1991, pp. 8–13.

37. For useful background on the Russian minority see William D. Jackson, "Russia After the Crisis, Imperial Temptation: Ethnics Abroad," *Orbis*, Vol. 38, No. 1, Winter 1994, pp. 1–17. Delays in signing the Ukrainian-Russian state treaty also encouraged separatist voices in Crimea and elsewhere. See *Unian*, Kyiv, 12 October 1994, in *FBIS-SOV-94–198*, 13 October 1994.

38. For a valuable overview of Crimean Tatar issues see "The Crimean Tatar Dilemma," *Research Update*, Vol. 6, No. 168, 10 April 2000, Ukrainian Center for Independent Political Research (UCIPR), Kyiv, Ukraine.

39. In June 1992, the Ukrainian Autocephalous Orthodox Church and the Ukrainian Orthodox Church were united to form the Ukrainian Orthodox Church–Kyiv Patriarchate. The UOC declared its autocephaly from Moscow in November 1991. See Anatoliy Kolosha, "The Kyiv Patriarchate: A Difficult Path to Unity," *Holos Ukrainy*, Kyiv, 31 July 1993, in *FBIS-USR-93–121*, 20 September 1993. Despite this official merger, conflicts persisted between the two hierarchies, preventing the emergence of a truly unified Church. Consult Jaroslaw Martyniuk, "The State of the Orthodox Church in Ukraine," *RFE/RL Research Report,* Vol. 3, No. 7, 18 February 1994.

40. See Kathleen Mihalisko, "Cardinal Lyubachivskyi Takes Up Permanent Residence in Ukraine," *RFE/RL Report on the USSR*, Vol. 3, No. 28, 12 July 1991, pp.19–20.

41. For a useful summary of inter-church conflicts see Victor Yelenskyy, "The Crusaders: Ukrainian Churches and Great Politics," *Post-Postup*, Lviv, 11–16 May 1994, in *FBIS-USR-94–060*, 8 June 1994.

42. Check Dominique Arel and Andrew Wilson, "The Ukrainian Parliamentary Elections," *RFE/RL Research Report,* Vol. 3, No. 26, 1 July 1994; Ivan Bilaniuk, "Plus 60 Deputies: An Analysis of the Parliamentary By-election Results and Their Implications," *Ukrainian Legal and Economic Bulletin*, September 1994; and Ustina Markus, "Results of Ukrainian Parliamentary Elections," *RFE/RL Daily Report*, 22 November 1994.

43. See Ivan Chopordya, *Novyny Zakarpattya*, Uzhhorod, 21 October 1993, in *FBIS-SOV-93–215*, 9 November 1993.

44. See Andriy Rak, "Separatists Are Causing Trouble in Transcarpathia," *Ukrayinska Hazeta*, No. 20 (40), 2–15 December 1993: 4, in *FBIS-SOV-93–239*, 15 December 1993.

45. Check http://www.house.gov/csce/ukrelect98.htm.

46. See the party pre-election program and 1998 election results at the International Foundation for Election Systems, http://ifes.ipri.kiev.ua/Elections98/index.phtml.

47. See The European Forum, *The Political Landscape of Ukraine*, June 1997, http://www.europeanforum.bot-consult.se/cup/ukraine/parties.htm.

48. International Foundation for Election Systems, http://ifes.ipri.kiev.ua/Elections98/index.phtml.

49. Check C. A. Manning, *Outline of Ukrainian History*, University of Manitoba, Center for Ukrainian Canadian Studies, Winnipeg, Canada, 1949.

50. http://www.hromada.relc.com/eng/history.htm.

51. http://www.house.gov.csce.ukrelect98.htm.

52. International Foundation for Election Systems, http://ifes.ipri.kiev.ua/Elections98/index.phtml.

53. See BRAMA, *Parties Registered for the March 1998 Election in Ukraine*, at http://www.brama.com/ua-gov/pol-detl.html.

54. See the Ukrainian Center for Independent Political Research (UCIPR), *Research Update*, Kyiv, Vol. 6, No. 199, 11 December 2000.

55. gopher://infomeister.osc.edu.

56. For an analysis of Ukrainian radicalism see Roman Solchanyk, "The Radical Right in Ukraine," in Sabrina P. Ramet (Ed.), *The Radical Right in Central and Eastern Europe Since 1989*, University Park, Pennsylvania: Pennsylvania State University Press, 1999, pp. 279–296.

57. See http://www.europeanforum.bot-consult.se/cup/ukraine/parties.htm.

58. The compact Bulgarian population in the Bolhrad *raion* of Odessa *oblast* also voted in favor of forming a Bolhrad national district. See Solchanyk, *op. cit.*, 1994, p. 65.

59. Consult www.htmh.hu.dokumentok/repukr-e.hu.

60. See http://www.hhrf.org/monitor/.

61. See Volodymyr Stafanets, "Reunification of Bukovyna with Romania Landed in Court," *Post-Postup*, Lviv, 26 May–2 June 1994. One additional complication was the dispute between Romanian and Moldovan nationalists within the minority community in Bukovina: the former promoted the restoration of a Greater Romania; the latter, of a Greater Moldova.

62. See http://www.rferl.org/nca/features/1999/05/F.RU.990506124203.html.

63. For more details on the Hungarian minority in Ukraine see Alfred A. Reisch, "Transcarpathia's Hungarian Minority and the Autonomy Issue," *RFE/RL Research Report*, Vol. 1, No. 6, 7 February 1992, pp. 17–23.

Conclusion: Roads to Democracy

The primary prerequisite for sustained domestic development and international integration for all the East European states is the consolidation and legitimation of pluralistic and democratic political systems. Political structures must ensure an effective and efficient separation of powers by which the various branches of government check and balance one another. In this context, the development of strong and representative political parties is important for anchoring public participation in the evolving system of political pluralism.

For democracy to function, a range of political parties mandated by a broad spectrum of constituencies, ideologies, and policy prescriptions need to be represented in state institutions. They must be enabled to compete fairly and freely through regular national, regional, and local elections. To maximize public inputs into the political process, strong governing parties and coalitions should be counterbalanced by a credible and vibrant political opposition in all parliamentary bodies and by a politically engaged and publicly energized civil society.

Each administration will need to promote consensus on the most vital reform issues. They must ensure a measure of programmatic continuity so that the reform process does not veer between unpredictable periods of progress and reversal. A cross-party commitment to the goal of institutional reform is necessary whatever differences may exist between specific political formations. Successful political stabilization requires the consolidation of stable and authoritative democratic institutions based on constitutional principles.

Governments have to focus on improving efficiency, competence, and professionalism among officials and the civil service. Indeed, a core civic administration needs to be developed that provides continuity and credibility regardless of changes in government, and one that is based on merit and not on patronage and political subservience. Concurrently, the judicial system must become both independent and competent—a system in which equality before the law is guaranteed, regardless of ethnicity, gender, or creed. A fully independent judiciary will give substance to individual rights and liberties without governmental or political interference.

Extremist political formations advocating dictatorship, authoritarianism, ultra-nationalism, xenophobia, and racism need to be exposed, marginalized, and prevented from threatening by nondemocratic means the stability of the political system and the success of the transformation process. Although no opinions should be prohibited in a developing democracy, hate propaganda and racist attacks must be answered and countered by responsible politicians, civic activists, and media outlets.

National and ethnic minorities must be involved in political decision-making through their inclusion in parliaments as well as in local and regional governments. Through a process of administrative decentralization, local and municipal authorities must be empowered to function and to effectively canvass for and represent the interests of their constituents. The question of minority rights needs to be comprehensively tackled, whether through the granting of cultural and educational autonomy, some measure of territorial self-administration, or regional decentralization, or through a guaranteed proportion of parliamentary seats. The protection of minority rights is not the exclusive preserve of national governments but has become a legitimate component of international human rights conventions. Hence, each state must pass legislation and pursue policies that comply with its international obligations.

Each state needs to develop predictable, authoritative, and participatory democratic institutions based on constitutional principles. Government organs must benefit from overwhelming public confidence and the commitment of all the major political players. The military, police, and intelligence forces must remain under strict governmental control and supervision. At the same time, they must have the authority and capability to engender popular trust in the system of justice and law enforcement as well as the capability to improve their effectiveness. Civic confidence in the police forces will grow as their success in fighting crime and maintaining law and order increases. Furthermore, civil-military relations need to be comprehensively restructured to meet the appropriate NATO criteria and to enable absolute governmental controls over the country's armed forces.

Public security organs must be empowered to deal with a dominating and growing problem throughout much of the East European region—organized crime and corruption. The breadth and scope of these phenomena present a direct challenge to both domestic and regional stability. They also confront the international community with serious regional security problems.

The pervasiveness of politically connected corruption and criminality threatens to obstruct the reform process in the region's fragile democracies. It contributes to the consolidation of special interest groups, corrodes democratic institutions, encourages polarization and radicalism, dissipates public support for the transformation process, and jeopardizes economic stability, competition, and marketization. To combat crime, appropriate laws must be passed and enforced, and the police must be provided with relevant training, manpower, and equipment. No government official, manager, or businessman can stand above the law.

All states can make significant strides in enshrining the full array of human rights, including freedom of expression, conscience, assembly, association, movement, and worship. Each country must develop effective and robust alternative media as well as professional, state-funded media outlets. Equally important are a broad range of influential and participatory interest groups representing entrepreneurs; consumers; women; ethnic, religious, regional, and cultural minorities; environmentalists; taxpayers; and other sectors of society or issue-focused groupings. The activism of these constituencies will significantly enhance the democratization process.

Public participation in political and decision-making processes is evident in the media, in local and regional governments, and in the activities of a range of civic organizations. Such participation greatly enriches the emerging democracies by enabling public input into decisionmaking and by cultivating a new generation of politicians and businessmen. Democratic politics does not revolve solely around the activities and ambitions of political leaders and parties, but needs to be aimed at maximizing public input into the decision- and policy-making processes at local, regional, and national levels.

The development of a multi-faceted and multi-organizational civil society will restrain the tendency to focus on exclusivist ethnic and national questions. Encouraging popular participation in a broad range of civic groups and voluntary organizations will in turn greatly enhance public confidence in the reform agenda and in the legitimacy of the political system. A significant change in each nation's political culture is necessary: one that counters decades of anti-democratic ideology and nationalist extremism, transforms public institutions and public perceptions, and injects tolerance, dialogue, and compromise into the political process.

During the next decade, the most advanced states will successfully construct a functioning market economy. The state sector will need to be limited to a few strategic industries and to the provision of essential welfare benefits, and governmental regulations must be designed principally to ensure fair economic competition and the protection of consumers. Business activities must be regulated by effective laws to minimize the opportunities for corruption, nepotism, and monopolization. If it is to meet the challenges of European Union (EU) integration, each successive government cannot compromise on the most essential components of a viable market economy, including limitations on state subsidies to enterprises; a balanced national budget; a transparent and open privatization process; fair business competition; and the combating of cronyism and criminality.

All too often in the past decade, vested interest groups, including elements of the old communist *nomenklatura*, have stalled or diverted the reform process to their advantage. Alternatively, numerous politicians have compromised on many essential market components by maintaining state subsidies to unprofitable enterprises, favoring graft and corruption, and failing to ensure the transparent privatization of the state sector. A serious and far-reaching reform program cannot be held hostage by any political party, criminal cartel, economic lobby, trade union, or industrial sector. No program of economic transformation will gain easy popularity for any government; indeed, most administrations may face the challenges of widespread public disquiet. Nevertheless, a reformist government has to weather such storms and ensure that popular unrest is not exploited by radical anti-democratic and ultra-nationalist elements, nor degenerates into wholesale social and political breakdown.

Significant success also needs to be registered in building social support for the transformation program and in fully respecting private property rights. Such an objective can be furthered through a credible media campaign on the benefits of liberalism, competitive capitalism, and foreign investment, as well an astute promotion of successful new businesses. An appropriate business culture needs to be developed throughout the region, in which investment and hard work overcome the negative ethics of dead-weight statism, egalitarian disincentives, robber capitalism, or uncontrolled criminality among new entrepreneurs.

It is imperative that economic investment and some forms of direct assistance be afforded to those states that have made firm commitments to market reform, democratization, and regional stability. In some countries, more resolute support should be provided to democratic forces struggling against essentially authoritarian regimes or seeking to build functioning public institutions. In potential regional trouble spots, international institutions need to be more actively involved in conflict prevention, the buttressing of democratic bodies, and the enforcement of viable political solutions that would inhibit ethnopolitical conflicts, eliminate authoritarian temptations, and curtail the spillover of instability.

Eastern Europe's political systems resemble proto-democracies at various stages of development that have become increasingly diversified over the past decade. Although democratic institutions are largely in place in most countries in the region, a fully "democratic culture" has yet to evolve. Numerous impediments continue to obstruct this process, ranging from constitutional confusion, bureaucratism, public apathy, and corruption, to various forms of extremism, populism, and radicalism.

The dangers of radicalism should not be lightly dismissed. If the postcommunist governments fail to gain the confidence and commitment of sufficiently wide sectors of society, the electorate may turn to more extreme political solutions and militant party formations. This may be especially destabilizing where both right-of-center and left-of-center governments have failed to gain sufficient public credibility. Some sectors of society may be particularly prone to manipulation by populist, nationalist, or authoritarian forces. If public identification with distinct political parties remains fragile and transient in a disruptive economic environment, widespread alienation and frustration could be manifest either in disengagement from the transformation process or in growing support for militant or "strong-arm" political alternatives.

A breakdown of any tentative reform process could precipitate a resurgence of populism, nationalism, and authoritarianism. This in turn could provoke ethnic, religious, and regional conflicts inside several countries and spur cross-border confrontations. Democratic reform, economic development, and market transformation should not be seen merely as a domestic but as a region-wide concern. The failure of democratization and marketization, a social breakdown, or the rise of authoritarianism in any specific country will directly challenge all neighboring states. Such factors could reverse reformist efforts by exacerbating regional instabilities and distracting attention from domestic agendas. Hence, emphasis must be placed on building regional security systems and economic networks that serve to enhance security, stability, and reconstruction while promoting membership in all the major international institutions.

In a broader strategic perspective, the aspirations of the former hegemon Russia toward the East European region need to be carefully scrutinized. There are strong indications that the regime in Moscow is seeking to rebuild a broad sphere of influence in parts of Central and Southeastern Europe by forging closer alliances with unstable, authoritarian, anti-American, or criminally connected governments and political forces. For much of the 1990s, Milošević's Serbia constituted the most useful wedge for Russia in exploiting the Balkan conflicts to its advantage by creating disputes between the United States and its European allies and in weakening the case for further NATO involvement and institutional expansion.

There is wide suspicion among democrats in Southeastern Europe and in the Baltic region concerning Moscow's objectives. Although the Kremlin is unable to block or veto further NATO enlargement, the Vladimir Putin presidency has seemed to be primarily interested in disqualifying the major contenders from attaining NATO membership. Moscow has endeavored to subvert their political and economic institutions, to consolidate links with anti-reformist interest groups, to exploit any significant ethnic and religious differences, and to promote organized criminality. Indeed, it would be safe to conclude that the Kremlin will endeavor to keep pro-NATO governments off balance even if it cannot dislodge them from power. This serves Russia's "national security interest" because it keeps Moscow involved, creates complications for the Alliance, stirs controversies between America and its European allies, and thrusts Moscow forward as a "mediator" or "partner" in resolving security problems.

In the years ahead, Russian politics could undergo a more fundamental nationalist radicalization accompanied by a more aggressive foreign policy.

Russia's return to an assertive authoritarianism simply cannot be ruled out, given the country's unstable and unpredictable political and economic climate. Moscow may then pursue more sustained efforts to bring the states excluded from NATO or inhabiting the European periphery into a closer Russian orbit. In stark contrast to that of Russia, it is clearly in America's "national interest" to have secure, democratic, and law-abiding countries throughout the eastern half of Europe that will assume membership in international institutions and enable Washington gradually to disengage militarily from the region without precipitating any new insecurities. But to guarantee such a scenario, the United States must remain closely engaged in the developmental process over the coming years and not abandon its interests either to Russian ambitions or to European Union fickleness.

In sum, different East European states are moving at different speeds in consolidating pluralistic liberal democracies. In some countries, the process has developed more smoothly and comprehensively. In others, the evolution of liberal democracies has been stalled for several years and may prove that much more difficult to restart or accelerate in the midst of wrenching but necessary structural economic reforms. Democratic transformations are clearly a long-term project. There are no simple remedies that can be automatically applied to all states in this increasingly diversified region, and each incumbent government will face both challenges and opportunities for the foreseeable future.

List of Abbreviations of East European Political Party Names

AASz	1956–os Antifasiszta és Antibolseviszta Szövetség (1956 Anti-Fascist and Anti-Bolshevik Association) (Hung.)
ACR	Alianţa Civica Pentru Reforme (Civic Alliance for Reforms) (Mold.)
ADPB	Abyadnanaya Demokratichnaya Partiya Belarusi (Democratic Party of Belarus) (Bel.)
ADR	Alianţa Pentru Democraţia şi Reforme (Alliance for Democracy and Reforms) (Mold.)
ADS	Aleanca Demokratike e Shqipërisë (Albanian Democratic Alliance Party) (Alb.)
ADS-LP	Albansko Demokratski Sojuz-Liberalna Partija (Albanian Democratic Union-Liberal Party) (Maced.)
AFD	Alianţa Forţelor Democratice (Alliance of Democratic Forces) (Mold.)
AGP	Abyadnanaya Grazhdanskaya Partiya (United Civic Party) (Bel.)
AP	Arengupartei (Progressive Party) (Est.)
APBB	Asociaţia Pro-Basarabia şi Bucovina (Pro-Bessarabia and Bukovina Association) (Rom.)
APR	Alianţa Pentru România (Alliance For Romania) (Rom.)
APU	Ahrarna Partiya Ukrainy (Agrarian Party of Ukraine) (Ukr.)
ASB	Agrarny Sayuz Belarusi (Agrarian Union of Belarus) (Bel.)
ASH	Akcija Socijaldemokrata Hrvatske (Action of Social Democrats of Croatia) (Croatia)
AWS	Akcja Wyborcza Solidarność (Solidarity Electoral Action) (Pol.)
AYD-MPP	Fiatal Demokraták Szövetsége-Magyar Polgári Párt (Alliance of Young Democrats-Hungarian Civic Party) (Hung.)
BACF	Blocul Alianţa Civica "Furnica" ("Furnica" Civic Alliance Bloc) (Mold.)
BBB	Bulgarski Biznes Blok (Bulgarian Business Bloc) (Bulg.)
BBWR	Bezpartyjny Blok Wspierania Reform (Non-Party Bloc for the Support of Reforms) (Pol.)
BDMG	Bashkimi Demokratik i Minoritetit Grek "Omonia" (Democratic Union of the Greek Minority "Omonia") (Alb.)

BDN	Bashkimi i të Drejtave të Njeriut (Unity Party for Human Rights) (Alb.)
BEL	Bulgarska Evrolevitsa (Bulgarian Euro-Left) (Bulg.)
BEP	Belaruskaya Ekalagichnaya Partiya (Belarusian Ecological Party) (Bel.)
BES	Belarusky Ekalagichny Sayuz (Belarusian Ecological Union) (Bel.)
BK	Balli Kombëtar (National Front) (Alb.)
BKDZ	Belaruskaya Khrystsiyanska Demakratychnaya Zluchnasts (Belarusian Christian Democratic Association) (Bel.)
BKP	Bulgarska Komunisticheska Partiya (Bulgarian Communist Party) (Bulg.)
BLP	Bulgarska Liberalna Partiya (Bulgarian Liberal Party) (Bulg.)
BM	Bokaljska Mornarica (Boka Mariner's Association) (Mont.)
BNF	Belaruski Narodni Front (Belarusian Popular Front) (Bel.)
BNP	Belaruskaya Natsianalistychnaya Partiya (Belarusian Nationalist Party) (Bel.)
BNRP	Bulgarska Natsional Radikalna Partia (Bulgarian National Radical Party) (Bulg.)
BO	Bošnjačka Organizacija (Bosniak Organization) (B-H)
BPP	Belaruskaya Partiya Pratsy (Belarusian Party of Labor) (Bel.)
BPR	Belaruski Patryatychny Rukh (Belarusian Patriotic Movement) (Bel.)
BPUAZ	Belaruskaya Partiya Usebelaruskaga Adzinstva i Zhody (All-Belarusian Party for Unity and Accord) (Bel.)
BPZ	Belaruskaya Partiya Zhanchyn "Nadzeya" (Belarusian Women's Party "Hope") (Bel.)
BPZ	Belaruskaya Partiya Zyalyonykh (Green Party of Belarus) (Bel.)
BRP	Belaruskaya Respublikanskaya Partiya (Belarusian Republican Party) (Bel.)
BSDH	Belaruskaya Satsiyal Demakratychnaya "Hramada" (Belarusian Social Democratic Union) (Bel.)
BSDP	Belaruskaya Satsiyal Demakratychnaya Partiya (Belarusian Social Democratic Party) (Bel.)
BSDP	Bulgarska Sotsialdemokraticheska Partiya (Bulgarian Social Democratic Party) (Bulg.)
BSP	Belaruskaya Syalanskaya Partiya (Belarusian Peasant Party) (Bel.)
BSP	Bulgarska Sotsialisticheska Partiya (Bulgarian Socialist Party) (Bulg.)
BSSH	Bashkimi Socialdemokrat i Shqipërisë (Social Democratic Union of Albania) (Alb.)
BSU	Blocul Unitatea Socialista (Socialist Unity Bloc) (Mold.)
BZD	Białoruskie Zjednoczenie Demokratyczne (Belarusian Democratic Union) (Pol.)
BZNS-AS	Bulgarski Zemedelski Naroden Sayuz–Aleksandar Stamboliyski (Bulgarian Agrarian National Union–Aleksandar Stamboliyski) (Bulg.)
BZNS-NP	Bulgarski Zemedelski Naroden Sayuz–Nikola Petkov (Bulgarian Agrarian National Union–Nikola Petkov) (Bulg.)

BZP	Bulgarska Zelena Partiya (Bulgarian Green Party) (Bulg.)
CDM	Convenţiă Democrată din Moldova (Democratic Convention of Moldova) (Mold.)
CDR	Convenţiă Democrată din România (Democratic Convention of Romania) (Rom.)
CDU	Congresul Democrat Unit (United Democratic Congress) (Mold.)
CMUS	Českomoravská Unie Stredu (Bohemian-Moravian Union of the Center) (Cz.)
CMUS	Českomoravská Unie Stredu (Czech- Moravian Center Union) (Cz.)
CSNS	Ceská Strana Národne Sociální (Czech People's Social Party)
CSSD	Česká Strana Socialna Demokratická (Czech Social Democratic Party) (Cz.)
CTI	Congresul Ţaranilor şi Intelectualilor (Congress of Peasants and Intellectuals) (Mold.)
DA	Dalmatinska Akcija (Dalmatian Action) (Croatia)
DA	Demokratska Alternativa (Democratic Alternative) (Maced.)
DA	Demokratska Alternativa (Democratic Alternative) (Serbia)
DAR	Demokratichna Alternativa za Republika (Democratic Alternative for the Republic) (Bulg.)
DDD	Demokraticheskoe Dvizhenie Donbassa (Democratic Movement of Donbas) (Ukr.)
DEMOS	Demokratska Opozicija Slovenije (Democratic Opposition of Slovenia) (Slovenia)
DeSUS	Demokratska Stranka Upokojencev Slovenije (Democratic Party of Pensioners of Slovenia) (Slovenia)
DEU	Demokratická Unie (Democratic Union) (Cz.)
DNS	Dalmatinska Narodna Stranka (Dalmatian National Party) (Croatia)
DNSU	Domovinsko Nepartijsko Srpsko Udruženje (Homeland Non-Party Serbian Association) (Serbia)
DP	Demokrātiku Partija (Democratic Party) (Latv.)
DP	Demokraticheska Partiya (Democratic Party) (Bulg.)
DP	Demokratska Partija (Democratic Party) (Maced.)
DPA	Demokratska Partija na Albancite (Democratic Party of Albanians) (Maced.)
DPM	Demokratska Partija na Makedonija (Democratic Party of Macedonia) (Maced.)
DPPR	Demokratska Politička Partija Roma (Democratic Political Party of Roma) (Serbia)
DPPRM	Demokratska Progresivna Partija na Romite vo Makedonija (Democratic Progressive Party of Roma in Macedonia) (Maced.)
DPS	Demokrātiskā Partija "Saimnieks" (Democratic Party "Master") (Latv.)
DPS	Demokratska Partija na Srbite (Democratic Party of Serbs) (Maced.)
DPS	Demokratska Partija Socijalista (Democratic Party of Socialists) (Mont.)
DPS	Dvizhenie za Prava i Svobodi (Movement for Rights and Freedoms) (Bulg.)

DPT	Demokratska Partija na Turcite (Democratic Party of Turks) (Maced.)
DPTs	Demokratichna Partiya Tsenter (Democratic Center Party) (Bulg.)
DPU	Demokratychna Partiya Ukrainy (Democratic Party of Ukraine) (Ukr.)
DS	Demohrišćanska Stranka (Christian Democratic Party) (Serbia)
DS	Demokratická Strana (Democratic Party) (Slovakia)
DS	Demokratska Stranka (Democratic Party) (B-H)
DS	Demokratska Stranka (Democratic Party) (Mont.)
DS	Demokratska Stranka (Democratic Party) (Serbia)
DS	Makedonski Savez (Macedonian Alliance) (Maced.)
DSA	Demokratski Savez Albanaca (Democratic Alliance of Albanians) (B-H)
DSBJ	Demokratski Savez Bugara Jugoslavije (Democratic Union of Bulgarians in Yugoslavia) (Serbia)
DSCG	Demokratski Savez Crne Gore (Democratic Alliance of Montenegro) (Mont.)
DSHV	Demokratski Savez Hrvata u Vojvodini (Democratic Alliance of Croats in Vojvodina) (Serbia)
DS-PZ	Demokratski Sojuz- Partija na Zemjodelcite (Democratic Alliance-Party of Farmers) (Maced.)
DSRV	Demokratski Savez Rumuna Vojvodine (Democratic Alliance of Vojvodina Romanians) (Serbia)
DSS	Demokratična Stranka Slovenije (Democratic Party of Slovenia) (Slovenia)
DSS	Demokratska Stranka Srbije (Democratic Party of Serbia) (Serbia)
DSU	Derzhavna Samostiinist Ukrainy (State Independence for Ukraine) (Ukr.)
DSUU	Demokratychnyy Soyuz Ugortsiv v Ukrayini (Democratic Union of Hungarians in Ukraine) (Ukr.)
DUA	Demokratska Unija Albanaca (Democratic Union of Albanians) (Mont.)
DUS	Demokratická Únia Slovenska (Democratic Union of Slovakia) (Slovakia)
DZJ	Dùchodci za Životní Jistoty (Pensioners for Secure Living) (Cz.)
DZMV	Demokratska Zajednica Madjara Vojvodine (Democratic Community of Vojvodina Hungarians) (Serbia)
DZRS	Demokratický Zväz Rómov na Slovensku (Democratic Union of Roma in Slovakia) (Slovakia)
EDO	Eesti Demokraatlik Õiglusliit (Estonian Democratic Justice Union) (Est.)
EDT	Eesti Demokraatlik Tööpartei (Estonian Democratic Workers' Party) (Est.)
EEE	Eesti Ettevõtjate Erakond (Estonian Entrepreneurs Party) (Est.)
EK	Eesti Keskerakond (Estonian Center Party) (Est.)
EK	Eesti Kodanik (Estonian Citizen) (Est.)
EK	Eesti Kodu (Estonian Home) (Est.)
EK	Eesti Koonderakond (Estonian Coalition Party) (Est.)

EKDE	Eesti Kristlik Demokraatlik Erakond (Estonian Christian Democratic Party) (Est.)
EKDL	Eesti Kristlik Demokraatlik Liit (Estonian Christian Democratic Union) (Est.)
EKR	Eesti Konservatiivne Rahvaerakond (Estonian Conservative People's Party) (Est.)
ELP	Eesti Liberaaldemokraatlik Partei (Estonian Liberal Democratic Party) (Est.)
EM	Eesti Maaliit (Estonian Rural Union) (Est.)
EME	Eesti Maarahva Erakond (Estonian Rural People's Party) (Est.)
EME	Eesti Metsnike Erakond (Estonian Foresters Party) (Est.)
EMK	Eesti Maa Keskerakond (Estonian Rural Center Party) (Est.)
EP	Edinstvo-Pridnestrovye (Unity-Transnistria Region) (Mold.)
ER	Eesti Rahvarinne (Popular Front of Estonia) (Est.)
ER	Eesti Reformierakond (Estonian Reform Party) (Est.)
ER	Eesti Rohelised (Estonian Greens) (Est.)
ERE	Eesti Rahvuslik Eduerakond (Estonian National Progress Party) (Est.)
ERKE	Eesti Rahvusliku Kaitse Erakond (Estonian National Protection Party) (Est.)
ERP	Eesti Roheline Partei (Estonian Green Party) (Est.)
ERSP	Eesti Rahvusliku Sõltumatuse Partei (Estonian National Independence Party) (Est.)
ES	Economistu Savienība (Union of Economists) (Latv.)
ESDP	Estonian Social Democratic Party (ESDP), Eesti Sotsiaaldemokraatlik Partei (ESDP) (Est.)
ESDTP	Eesti Sotsiaaldemokraatiik Tööpartei (Estonian Social Democratic Labor Party) (Est.)
ESE	Eesti Sinine Erakond (Estonian Blue Party) (Est.)
ETE	Eesti Talurahva Erakond (Estonian Farmers' Party) (Est.)
EÜRP	Eestimaa Ühendatud Rahvapartei (Estonian United People's Party) (Est.)
EVK	Eesti Vabariiklaste Koonderakond (Estonian Republican Coalition Party) (Est.)
FBK	Federatsiya "Tsarstvo Bulgaria" (Federation "Bulgarian Kingdom") (Bulg.)
FDGR	Forumul Democratic al Germanilor din România (Democratic Forum of Germans in Romania) (Rom.)
FKgP	Független Kisgazda Párt (Independent Smallholders' Party) (Hung.)
FNIF	Független Nemzeti Ifjúsági Front (Independent National Youth Front) (Hung.)
FPCD	Frontul Popular Creştin-Democrat (Christian Democratic Popular Front) (Mold.)
GH	Gagauz Halki (Gagauz People) (Mold.)
GLPM	Gradjansko-Liberalna Partija na Makedonija (Civil Liberal Party of Macedonia) (Maced.)
GSS	Gradjanski Savez Srbije (Civic Alliance of Serbia) (Serbia)

HDARU	Hristiansko-Demokratychny Allians Ruminiv na Ukraini (Christian Democratic Alliance of Romanians in Ukraine) (Ukr.)
HDC	Hrvatski Demokratski Centar (Croatian Democratic Center) (Croatia)
HDZ	Hrvatska Demokratska Zajednica (Croatian Democratic Union) (B-H)
HDZ	Hrvatska Demokratska Zajednica (Croatian Democratic Union) (Croatia)
HKDU	Hrvatščanska Demokratska Unija (Croatian Christian Democratic Union) (B-H)
HKDU	Hrvatska Kršćanska Demokratska Unija (Croatian Christian Democratic Union) (Croatia)
HMDS	Hrvatska Muslimanska Demokratska Stranka (Croatian Muslim Democratic Party) (Croatia)
HND	Hrvatski Nezavisni Demokrati (Croatian Independent Democrats) (Croatia)
HNS	Hnutie Nové Slovensko (New Slovakia Movement) (Slovakia)
HNS	Hnutie za Nezávislé Slovensko (Movement for an Independent Slovakia) (Slovakia)
HNS	Hrvatska Narodna Stranka (Croatian People's Party) (Croatia)
HSD-SMS	Hnutí za Samosprávnou Demokracii-Společnost pro Moravu a Slezsko (Movement for Self-Governing Democracy-Society for Moravia and Silesia) (Cz.)
HSLS	Hrvatska Socijalno Liberalna Stranka (Croatian Social Liberal Party) (Croatia)
HSP	Hrvatska Stranka Prava (Croatian Party of Right) (Croatia)
HSS	Hrvatska Seljačka Stranka (Croatian Peasant Party) (Croatia)
HSS	Hrvatska Seljačka Stranka (Croatian Peasants Party) (B-H)
HSZ	Hrvatska Stranka Zelenih (Croatian Green Party) (Croatia)
HZDS	Hnutie za Demokratické Slovensko (Movement for a Democratic Slovensko) (Slovakia)
I	Isamaaliit (Pro Patria Union) (Est.)
IDS	Istarski Demokratski Sabor (Istrian Democratic Assembly) (Croatia)
IRO	Istarska Radikalna Organizacija (Istrian Radical Organization) (Croatia)
ISMM	Interesna Skupnost Madžarske Manjšine (Interest Community of the Hungarian Minority) (Slovenia)
IZIR	Italijanska Zveza za Istro in Reko (Italian Union for Istria and Rijeka) (Slovenia)
JP	Jaunā Partija (New Party) (Latv.)
JUL	Jugoslovenska Ujedinjena Levica (Yugoslav United Left) (Mont.)
JUL	Jugoslovenska Ujedinjena Levica (Yugoslav United Left) (Serbia)
KAN	Klub Angažovaných Nestraníků (Club of Committed Non-Party Members) (Cz.)
KDH	Kresťanskodemokratické Hnutie (Christian Democratic Movement) (Slovakia)
KDNP	Keresztény Demokrata Néppárt (Christian Democratic People's Party) (Hung.)

KDP	Ukrainska Khrystiiansko-Demokratychna Partiya (Ukrainian Christian Democratic Party) (Ukr.)
KDS	Kresťanskodemokratická Strana (Christian Democratic Party) (Cz.)
KDU-CSL	Kresťanská a Demokratická Unie-Československá Strana Lidová (Christian and Democratic Union-Czechoslovak People's Party) (Cz.)
KK	Kisebbségi Kerekasztal (National Minority Roundtable) (Hung.)
KKPPSH	Këshilli Koordinues i Partive Politike Shqiptare (Coordinating Council of Albanian Political Parties) (Kos.)
KMDLNJ	Këshilli për Mbrojtjen e të Drejtave dhe Lirive të Njeriut (Council for the Protection of Human Rights and Freedoms) (Kos.)
KNDS	Kongres Natsionalno-Demokratychnykh Syl (Congress of National Democratic Forces) (Ukr.)
KNU	Keresztény Nemzeti Unió (Christian National Union) (Hung.)
KPB	Kamunistychnaya Partiya Belarusi (Communist Party of Belarus) (Bel.)
KPEiR	Krajowa Partia Emerytów i Rencistów (National Party of Senior Citizens and Pensioners) (Pol.)
KPK	Kommunisticheska Partiya Kryma (Communist Party of Crimea) (Ukr.)
KPN	Koła Przyjaźni Niemieckiej (German Friendship Circles) (Pol.)
KPN	Konfederacja Polski Niepodległej (Confederation for Independent Poland) (Pol.)
KPU	Komunistychna Partiya Ukrainy (Communist Party of Ukraine) (Ukr.)
KRP	Ukrainska Konservatyvna Respublikanska Partiya (Ukrainian Conservative Republican Party) (Ukr.)
KSCM	Komunistická Strana Čech a Moravy (Communist Party of Bohemia and Moravia) (Cz.)
KSS	Komunistická Strana Slovenska (Communist Party of Slovakia) (Slovakia)
KSU	Kresťansko Sociálná Unia (Christian Social Union) (Slovakia)
KUN	Kongres Ukrainskykh Natsionalistiv (Congress of Ukrainian Nationalists) (Ukr.)
KV	Koalicija Vojvodina (KV) (Serbia), Vojvodina Coalition (VC)
KZNI	Komitet za Zashtita na Natsionalnite Interesi (Committee for Defense of National Interests) (Bulg.)
KZP	Kaszubski Związek Pomorski (Kaszubian Pomeranian Union) (Pol.)
LB	Levý Blok (Left Bloc) (Cz.)
LBD	Lëvizja e Bashkuar Demokratike (United Democratic Movement) (Kos.)
LBO	Liberalna Bošnjačka Organizacija (Liberal Bosniak Organization) (Serbia)
LC	Latvijas Ceļš (Latvia's Way) (Latv.)
LCS	Lietuvos Centro Sąjunga (Lithuanian Center Union) (Lith.)
LDA	Liberalno Demokratichna Alternativa (Liberal Democratic Alternative) (Bulg.)
LDDP	Latvijas Demokrātiskā Darba Partija (Latvian Democratic Labor Party) (Latv.)

LDDP	Lietuvos Demokratinė Darbo Partija (Lithuanian Democratic Labor Party) (Lith.)
LDK	Lidhja Demokratike e Kosovës (Democratic League of Kosova) (Kos.)
LDP	Latgales Demokrātiskā Partija (Letgallian Democratic Party) (Latv.)
LDP	Liberalno-Demokratska Partija (Liberal Democratic Party) (Maced.)
LDP	Lietuvos Demokratų Partija (Lithuanian Democratic Party) (Lith.)
LDPB	Liberalna Demakratychnaya Partiya Belarusi (Liberal Democratic Party of Belarus) (Bel.)
LDPU	Liberalno-Demokratychna Partiya Ukrainy (Liberal Democratic Party of Ukraine) (Ukr.)
LDS	Liberalna Demokracija Slovenije (Liberal Democracy of Slovenia) (Slovenia)
LEKE	Lõuna Eesti Kodanike Erakond (Southern Estonia Citizens' Party) (Est.)
LKCK	Lëvizja Kombëtare për Çlirimin e Kosovës (National Movement for the Liberation of Kosova) (Kos.)
LKD	Latvijas Kristigo Demokratu (Christian People's Party) (Latv.)
LKDP	Lietuvos Krikščionių Demokratų Partija (Lithuanian Christian Democratic Party) (Lith.)
LKDS	Latvijas Kristīgo Demokrātu Savienība (Latvian Christian Democratic Party) (Latv.)
LKPP	Latvijas Krievu Pilsoņu Partija (Latvia's Russian Citizens' Party) (Latv.)
LKRS	Liberalno-Konserwatywny Ruch Stu (Liberal Conservative Movement of the One Hundred) (Pol.)
LLP	Latviešu Liberāla Partija (Latvian Liberal Party) (Latv.)
LLRA	Lietuvos Lenkų Rinkimų Akcija (Lithuanian Poles Electoral Action) (Lith.)
LLS	Lietuvos Liberalų Sąjunga (Lithuanian Liberal Union) (Lith.)
LNKP	Latvijas Nacionāli Konservatīvā Partija (Latvian National Conservative Party) (Latv.)
LNNK	Latvijas Nacionālas Neatkarības Kustiba (Latvian National Independence Movement) (Latv.)
LNP-JL	Lietuviu Nacionalinė Partija "Jaunoji Lietuva" (Lithuanian Nationalist Party "Young Lithuania") (Lith.)
LP	Liga Polska (Polish League) (Pol.)
LPK	Lëvizja Popullore e Kosovës (People's Movement of Kosova) (Kos.)
LPKTS	Lietuvos Politinių Kalinių Ir Tremtinių Sąjunga (Union of Political Prisoners and Deportees) (Lith.)
LPS	Lietuvos Persitvarkymo Sąjūdis (Lithuanian Restructuring Movement) (Lith.)
LPU	Liberalna Partiya Ukrainy (Liberal Party of Ukraine) (Ukr.)
LRS	Lietuvos Rusų Sąjunga (Union of Russians in Lithuania) (Lith.)
LS	Liberalna Stranka (Liberal Party) (Croatia)
LSDA	Latvijas Sociāldemokrātu Apvienība (Latvian Social Democratic Alliance) (Latv.)

LSCG	Liberalni Savez Crne Gore (Liberal Alliance of Montenegro) (Mont.)
LSDP	Lietuvos Socialdemokratų Partija (Lithuanian Social Democratic Party) (Lith.)
LSDSP	Latvijas Sociāldemokrātiska Stradnieku Partija (Latvian Social Democratic Workers' Party) (Latv.)
LSNS	Liberální Strana Národne Sociální (Liberal National Socialist Party) (Cz.)
LSP	Latvijas Sociālistiskā Partija (Latvian Socialist Party) (Latv.)
LSU	Liberálne Sociální Unie (Liberal Social Union) (Cz.)
LSV	Liga Socialdemokrata Vojvodine (League of Social Democrats of Vojvodina) (Serbia)
LTF	Latvijas Tautas Fronte (Latvian Popular Front) (Latv.)
LTS	Lietuviu Tautininkų Sąjunga (Lithuanian National Union) (Lith.)
LV	Liga na Vlasite (League of Vlachs) (Maced.)
LVP	Latvijas Vienības Partija (Latvian Unity Party) (Latv.)
LVP	Lietuvos Valstiečių Partija (Lithuanian Peasant's Party) (Lith.)
LZP	Latvijas Zaļā Partija (Latvian Green Party) (Latv.)
LZP	Lietuvos žaliujų Partija (Lithuanian Green Party) (Lith.)
LZS	Latvijas Zemnieku Savienība (Latvian Agrarian Union) (Latv.)
MAAK-KP	Dvizenje za Semakedonska Akcija-Konservativna Partija (Movement for All-Macedonian Action-Conservative Party) (Maced.)
MBO	Muslimanska Bošnjačka Organizacija (Muslim Bosnian Organization) (B-H)
MBR	Mizhrehionalnyi Blok Reformiv (Interregional Bloc for Reforms) (Ukr.)
MCDSz	Magyarországi Cigányok Demokratikus Szövetsége (Democratic Alliance of Hungarian Gypsies) (Hung.)
MCNU	Magyarországi Cigányok Nemzetiségi Uniója (Nationality Council of Gypsies in Hungary) (Hung.)
MDF	Magyar Demokrata Fórum (Hungarian Democratic Forum) (Hung.)
MDNP	Magyar Demokrata Néppárt (Hungarian Democratic People's Party) (Hung.)
MDS	Moravská Demokratická Strana (Moravian Democratic Party) (Cz.)
MDS	Muslimanska Demokratska Stranka (Muslim Democratic Party) (B-H)
MER	Mişcarea Ecologista din România (Romanian Ecologist Movement) (Rom.)
MF	Milli Firka (National Party) (Ukr.)
MHSz	Magyarországi Horvátok Szövetsége (Croatian Democratic Alliance) (Hung.)
MiéP	Magyar Igazság és élet Pártja (Hungarian Justice and Life Party) (Hung.)
MKDH	Madărské Krestănsko Demokratické Hnutie (Hungarian Christian Democratic Movement) (Slovakia)
MKE	Meie Kodu on Eestimaa (Our Home is Estonia) (Est.)
MLS	Madărská Ľudová Strana (Hungarian People's Party) (Slovakia)
MM	Magyar Munkáspárt (Hungarian Workers Party) (Hung.)

MMD	Makedonsko Mladezhko Druzhestvo (Macedonian Youth Society) (Bulg.)
MNF	Magyar Nemzeti Front (Hungarian National Front) (Hung.)
MNP	Magyar Néppárt (Hungarian People's Party) (Hung.)
MNS	Madjarska Narodna Stranka (Hungarian People's Party) (Croatia)
MNS	Moravská Národní Strana (Moravian National Party) (Cz.)
MNSz	Magyar Nemzeti Szövetség (Hungarian National Alliance) (Hung.)
MNSz	Magyarországi Németek Szövetsége (Association of Germans in Hungary) (Hung.)
MOS	Maďárská Občianska Strana (Hungarian Civic Party) (Slovakia)
MPR	Mişcarea Pentru România (Movement for Romania) (Rom.)
MRDSz	Magyarországi Románok Demokratikus Szövetsége (Democratic Association of Romanians in Hungary) (Hung.)
MRP	Magyarországi Romaparlament (Roma Parliament) (Hung.)
MS	Makedonski Sojuz (Macedonian Alliance) (Maced.)
MS	Matica Slovenská (Slovak Motherland) (Slovakia)
MSzDP	Magyarországi Szociáldemokrata Párt (Hungarian Social Democratic Party) (Hung.)
MSzP	Magyar Szociálista Párt (Hungarian Socialist Party) (Hung.)
MSzSz	Magyarországi Szlovákok Szövetsége (Democratic Union of Slovaks in Hungary) (Hung.)
MZsKE	Magyar Zsidók Kulturális Egyesülete (Jewish Cultural Federation) (Hung.)
N	Nezávislí (Independents) (Cz.)
NAS	Nová Agrárna Strana (New Agrarian Party) (Slovakia)
ND	Nova Demokratija (New Democracy) (Serbia)
NDKT	Natsionanyi Dvizheniia Krymskikh Tatar (National Movement of Crimean Tatars) (Ukr.)
ND-MP	Naujoji Demokratija-Moterų Partija (New Democracy-Women's Party) (Lith.)
NDP	Narodna Demokratska Partija (People's Democratic Party) (Maced.)
NDPB	Natsyianalnaya Demakratychnaya Partiya Belarusi (National Democratic Party of Belarus) (Bel.)
NDPU	Narodno-Demokratychna Partiya Ukrainy (People's Democratic Party of Ukraine) (Ukr.)
NDS	Narodna Demokratska Stranka (National Democratic Party) (Slovenia)
NDS	Narodna Demokratska Stranka (People's Democratic Party) (Mont.)
NFP	Narodowy Front Polski (Polish National Front) (Pol.)
NHI	Nova Hrvatska Inicijativa (New Croatian Initiative) (B-H)
NO	Narodowa Ofensywa (National Offensive) (Pol.)
NOP	Narodowe Odrodzenie Polski (National Rebirth of Poland) (Pol.)
NP	Nepriklausomybės Partija (Independence Party) (Lith.)
NPK	Narodna Partiya Kryma (People's Party of Crimea) (Ukr.)
NRM	Narodny Ruh Belarusi (Popular Movement of Belarus) (Bel.)
NS	Naroden Sayuz (Popular Union) (Bulg.)
NSCG	Narodna Stranka Crne Gore (People's Party of Montenegro) (Mont.)
NSS	Narodna Seljačka Stranka (People's Peasant Party) (Serbia)

NS-SL	Naujoji Sąjunga-Socialliberaliai (New Union-Social Liberals) (Lith.)
NZCH	Nacionalna Zajednica Crnogoraca Hrvatske (National Community of Croatian Montenegri) (Croatia)
OBS	Obshto-Bulgarski Sayuz (All-Bulgarian Union) (Bulg.)
ODA	Občanská Demokratická Aliance (Civic Democratic Alliance) (Cz.)
ODS	Občanská Demokratická Strana (Civic Democratic Party) (Cz.)
OKL	Obywatelski Krąg Lemków "Hospodar" (Citizens Circle of Lemkos "Hospodar") (Pol.)
OKND	Organizatsiia Krymskotatarskogo Natsionalnogo Dvizheniia (Organization of the Crimean Tatar National Movement) (Ukr.)
OK-PK	Občanská Koalice–Politický Klub (Citizen's Coalition-Political Club) (Cz.)
OMOI	Obedinena Makedonska Organizatsia Ilinden (United Macedonian Organization "Ilinden") (Bulg.)
ONS	Obedinenie za Natsionalno Spasenie (National Salvation Union) (Bulg.)
OOR	Obedinena Organizatsia Roma (United Roma Organization) (Bulg.)
OPO	Obshtestvo Peti Oktomvri (Fifth of October Society) (Bulg.)
OPT	Otechestvena Partiya na Truda (Fatherland Party of Labor) (Bulg.)
OPZZ	Ogólnopolskie Porozumienie Związków Zawodowych (All-Polish Accord of Trade Unions) (Pol.)
OSMS	Občanské Shromáždení Moravy a Slezska (Moravian-Silesian Citizen's Assembly) (Cz.)
OSNN	Osnivanje Slovačka Narodna Nasledstva (Slovak National Heritage Foundation) (Serbia)
OTE	Õigusliku Tasakaalu Erakond (Party for Legal Justice) (Est.)
PAC	Partidul Alianţei Civice (Civic Alliance Party) (Rom.)
PAP	Partiya Amatarau Piva (Beer Lovers' Party) (Bel.)
PAPCGS	Pokret za Autonomni Pristup Crne Gore u Srbiju (Movement for Montenegro's Autonomous Accession to Serbia) (Mont.)
PAS	Partie Agrare e Shqipërisë (Albanian Agrarian Party) (Alb.)
PB	Pravý Blok (Right Bloc) (Cz.)
PCER	Partija za Celosna Emancipacjia na Romite (Party for Complete Emancipation of Roma) (Maced.)
PCM	Partidul Comunistilor din Moldova (Party of Moldovan Communists) (Mold.)
PDAM	Partidul Democrat Agrar din Moldova (Agrarian Democratic Party of Moldova) (Mold.)
PDAR	Partidul Democrat Agrar din România (Agrarian Democratic Party of Romania) (Rom.)
PDC	Porozumienie Demokratyczne Centrum (Center Democratic Accord) (Pol.)
PDD	Partia Demokratike e Djathtë (Democratic Party of the Right) (Alb.)
PD-FSN	Partidul Democrat-Frontul Salvării Naţionale (Democratic Party-National Salvation Front) (Rom.)
PDM	Partidul Democrat al Muncii (Democratic Labor Party) (Mold.)
PDN	Partidul Dreapta Naţională (Party of National Right) (Rom.)

PDP	Partija Demokratskog Progresa (Party of Democratic Progress) (B-H)
PDP	Partija za Demokratski Prosperitet (Party for Democratic Prosperity) (Maced.)
PDS	Pokret za Demokratsku Srbiju (Movement for Democratic Serbia) (Serbia)
PDSH	Partia Demokratike e Shqipërisë (Albanian Democratic Party) (Alb.)
PDSH	Partia Demokristiane e Shqipërisë (Christian Democratic Party) (Alb.)
PDSR	Partidul Democratiei Sociale din România (Party of Social Democracy in Romania) (Rom.)
PDV	Partiya Demokratychna Vidrodzhennia Ukrainy (Party of Democratic Rebirth of Ukraine) (Ukr.)
PDV	Partiya za Demokraticheski Vazkhod (Party for Democratic Prosperity) (Bulg.)
PDZ	Polskaye Demakratychnaye Zhurtavanne (Polish Democratic Union) (Bel.)
PE-AV	Partidul Ecologic–Alianţa Verde (Ecological Party-Green Alliance) (Mold.)
PEKE	Põhja Eesti Kodanike Erakond (Northern Estonia Citizens' Party) (Est.)
PER	Partidul Ecologist Român (Romanian Ecologist Party) (Rom.)
PES	Partia Ekologjike e Shqipërisë (Albanian Ecological Party) (Alb.)
PEVK	Partiya Ekonomivheskogo Vozrozhdeniya Kryma (Party of Economic Rebirth of Crimea) (Ukr.)
PFCSz	"Phralipe" (Testvériség) Független Cigány Szervezet ("Phralipe" Independent Gypsy Association) (Hung.)
PFD	Partidul Forţelor Democrate (Party of Democratic Forces) (Mold.)
PGSiT	Porozumienie Górnośląskich Stowarzyszeń i Towarzystw (Alliance of Upper Silesian Societies and Associations) (Pol.)
PKB	Partiya Kamunistau Belarusi (Party of Communists of Belarus) (Bel.)
PKE	Politicheski Klub "Ekoglasnost" (Political Club "Ecoglasnost") (Bulg.)
PKS	Partia Komuniste Shqiptare (Albanian Communist Party) (Alb.)
PL	Partidul Liberal (Liberal Party) (Rom.)
PL	Porozumienie Ludowe (Peasant Alliance) (Pol.)
PL-93	Partidul Liberal 1993 (Liberal Party 1993) (Rom.)
PLL	Partia Lëvizja e Legalitetit (Movement of Legality Party) (Alb.)
PLP-SESG	Pokret za Ljudska Prava-Stranka Ekološki Svjesnih Gradana (Movement for Human Rights-Party of Environmentally Conscious Citizens) (Croatia)
PMDP	Pentru o Moldova Democrată şi Prosperă (Movement for a Democratic and Prosperous Moldova) (Mold.)
PNŢCD	Partidul Naţional Ţaranesc-Creştin şi Democrat (Christian and Democratic National Peasants' Party) (Rom.)
PNC	Partidul Naţional Creştin (National Christian Party) (Mold.)
PNL	Partidul Naţional Liberal (National Liberal Party) (Rom.)
PNL-CD	Partidul Naţional Liberal-Convenţia Democratica (National Liberal Party-Democratic Convention) (Rom.)

PNR	Partidul Naţional Român (National Romanian Party) (Rom.)
PNR	Partidul Naţionala din România (Romanian National Party) (Rom.)
PNRC	Partidul Noua Românie Creştină (New Christian Romania Party) (Rom.)
PNZ	Partiya Narodnay Zhody (Party of National Accord) (Bel.)
PPDK	Partia e Progresit Demokratik të Kosovës (Party of Democratic Progress of Kosova) (Kos.)
PPK	Partia Parlamentare e Kosovës (Parliamentary Party of Kosova) (Kos.)
PPPP	Polska Partia Przyjaciół Piwa (Polish Beer Lovers Party) (Pol.)
PPZ	Polska Partia Zielonych (Polish Green Party) (Pol.)
PR	Partidul Reformei (Party of Reform) (Mold.)
PRAS	Ruch na Rzecz Autonomii Śląska (Movement for Silesian Autonomy) (Pol.)
PRCM	Partidul Renaşterii şi Concilierii din Moldova (Party of Revival and Reconciliation of Moldova) (Mold.)
PRK	Respublikanska Partiya Kryma (Republican Party of Crimea) (Ukr.)
PRK	Russka Partiya Kryma (Russian Party of Crimea) (Ukr.)
PRM	Partidul România Mare (Greater Romania Party) (Rom.)
PRN	Partidul Pentru Reunire Naţionala (National Reunification Party) (Rom.)
PRP	Partiya Reformy i Poryadok (Reforms and Order Party) (Ukr.)
PRSH	Partia Republikane e Shqipërisë (Albanian Republican Party) (Alb.)
PRU	Populat Rukh Ukraine (National Movement of Ukraine) (Ukr.)
PS	Partidul Socialist (Socialist Party) (Mold.)
PS	Partidul Socialist (Socialist Party) (Rom.)
PSDM	Partidul Social Democrat din Republica Moldova (Social Democratic Party of Moldova) (Mold.)
PSDR	Partidul Social Democrat Român (Romanian Social Democratic Party) (Rom.)
PSDS	Partia Socialdemokratike e Shqipërisë (Social Democratic Party of Albania) (Alb.)
PSHDK	Partia Shqiptare Demokristiane e Kosovës (Christian Democratic Party of Kosova) (Kos.)
PSJ	Stranka Srpskog Jedinstva (Party of Serbian Unity) (Serbia)
PSL	Polskie Stronnictwo Ludowe (Polish Peasant Party) (Pol.)
PSL-M	Polskie Stronnictwo Ludowe-Mikołajczykowskie (Polish Peasant Party-Mikołajczyk) (Pol.)
PSM	Partidul Socialist al Muncii (Socialist Labor Party) (Rom.)
PSP	Prohresyvna Sotsialistychna Partiya (Progressive Socialist Party) (Ukr.)
PSS	Partia Socialiste e Shqipërisë (Albanian Socialist Party) (Alb.)
PSSKCwNT	Podhalańskie Stowarzyszenie Społeczno-Kulturalne Cyganów w Nowym Targu (Podhale Social-Cultural Association of Gypsies in Nowy Targ) (Pol.)
PTU	Partiya Truda Ukrainy (Labor Party of Ukraine) (Ukr.)
PUK	Partia e Unitetit Kombëtar (Albanian National Unity Party) (Alb.)

PUMM	Partidul Uniunii Muncii din Moldova (United Labor Party of Moldova) (Mold.)
PUNR	Partidul Unităţii Naţionale Române (Romanian National Unity Party) (Rom.)
PWN-PSN	Polska Wspólnota Narodowa-Polskie Stronnictwo Narodowe (Polish National Commonwealth-Polish National Party) (Pol.)
PZU	Partiya Zelenykh Ukrainy (Green Party of Ukraine) (Ukr.)
PZZ-RPS	Polski Zwiâzek Zachodni—Ruch Polskiego Śląska (Polish Western Union-Movement of Polish Silesia) (Pol.)
RdR	Ruch dla Rzeczypospolitej (Movement for the Republic) (Pol.)
RDS	Riječki Demokratski Savez (Rijeka Democratic Alliance) (Croatia)
RDSV	Reformsko Demokratska Stranka Vojvodine (Reformist Democratic Party of Vojvodina) (Serbia)
RE	Rahvaerakond (People's Party) (Est.)
RHDP	Romska Hristiyan Demokraticheska Partiya (Romani Christian Democratic Party) (Bulg.)
RM	Rahvapartei Mõõdukad (People's Party "Moderates") (Est.)
RMN	Rada Mniejszości Narodowych (National Minorities Council) (Pol.)
RN	Ruch Narodowy (National Movement) (Pol.)
RNK	Romský Národní Kongres (Romani National Congress) (Cz.)
RO	Rusínska Obroda (Ruthenian Revival) (Slovakia)
ROI	Rómská Občanská lniciatíva (Romani Civic Initiative) (Cz.)
ROP	Ruch Odbudowy Polski (Movement for Reconstruction of Poland) (Pol.)
RP	Rada Poláku (Polish Council) (Cz.)
RP	Republikanska Partija (Republican Party) (Maced.)
RS	Republikanska Stranka (Republican Party) (B-H)
RSNP	Radikalna Stranka Nikola Pašić (Radical Party Nikola Pašić) (Serbia)
RZOCZ	Rada Židovských Obcí Českých Zemí (Council of Jewish Communities in the Czech Lands) (Cz.)
S	Smer (Direction) (Slovakia)
S	Spolužitie (Coexistence) (Slovakia)
SAP	Savez za Promene (Alliance for Change) (Serbia)
SAS	Shqata e Arumunëve të Shqipërisë (Association of Arumanians in Albania) (Alb.)
SB-H	Stranka za Bosnu i Hercegovinu (Party for Bosnia-Herzegovina) (B-H)
SCA	Societatea Culturală Aromână (Arumanian Cultural Society) (Rom.)
SD	Socijaldemokratija (Social Democracy) (Serbia)
SD	Svobodní Demokraté (Free Democrats) (Cz.)
SDA	Partija za Demokratska Akcija (Party for Democratic Action) (Maced.)
SDA	Stranka Demokratske Akcije (Party of Democratic Action) (B-H)
SDA	Stranka Demokratske Akcije (Party of Democratic Action) (Serbia)
SDA-CG	Stranka Demokratske Akcije-Crna Gora (Party of Democratic Action-Montenegro) (Mont.)
SDAK	Stranka Demokratske Akcije Kosova (Party of Democratic Action for Kosova) (Kos.)

SDF	Srpski Demokratski Forum (Serbian Democratic Forum) (Croatia)
SDK	Slovenská Demokratická Koalicia (Slovak Democratic Coalition) (Slovakia)
SDL	Strana Demokratické Levice (Democratic Left Party) (Cz.)
SDL	Strana Demokratickej Ľavice (Party of the Democratic Left) (Slovakia)
SD-LSNS	Svobodní Demokraté–Liberální Strana Národne Sociální (Free Democrats-Liberal National Socialist Party) (Cz.)
SDP	Socijaldemokratska Partija (Social Democratic Party) (Mont.)
SDPH	Socijaldemokratska Partija Hrvatske (Social Democratic Party of Croatia) (Croatia)
SDPU	Sotsial Demokratychna Partiya Ukrainy (Social Democratic Party of Ukraine) (Ukr.)
SDPU"O"	Sotsial Demokratychna Partiya Ukrainy "Obyednana" (United Social Democratic Party of Ukraine) (Ukr.)
SDR	Stranka Demokratskih Reform (Party of Democratic Reform) (Slovenia)
SdRP	Socjaldemokracja Rzeczpospolitej Polskiej (Social Democracy of the Republic of Poland) (Pol.)
SDS	Sayuz na Demokratichnite Sili (Union of Democratic Forces) (Bulg.)
SDS	Socialdemokratska Stranka (Social Democratic Party) (B-H)
SDS	Socialdemokratska Stranka Slovenije (Social Democratic Party of Slovenia) (Slovenia)
SDS	Srpska Demokratska Stranka (Serbian Democratic Party) (B-H)
SDS	Srpska Demokratska Stranka (Serbian Democratic Party) (Croatia)
SDS	Strana Demokratického Socialismu (Party of Democratic Socialism) (Cz.)
SDSCG	Srpska Demokratska Stranka Crne Gore (Serbian Democratic Party of Montenegro) (Mont.)
SDSM	Socijaldemokratski Sojuz Makedonije (Social Democratic Alliance of Macedonia) (Maced.)
SDSS	Socialno Demokratická Strana Slovenska (Social Democratic Party of Slovakia) (Slovakia)
SDU	Socijaldemokratska Unija (Social Democratic Union) (Serbia)
SDZMS	Sociálny a Demokratický Zväz Madärov na Slovensku (Social and Democratic Union of Hungarians in Slovakia) (Slovakia)
SE	Spilka Eminescu (Eminescu Society) (Ukr.)
SK	Sõltumatud Kuningriiklased (Independent Royalists) (Est.)
SKD	Slovenski Krščanski Demokrati (Slovenian Christian Democrats) (Slovenia)
SKDS	Slovenská Krestănskodemokratická Strana (Slovak Christian Democratic Party) (Slovakia)
SKL	Stronnictwo Konserwatywno-Ludowe (Conservative Peasant Party) (Pol.)
SKM	Sojuz na Komunistite na Makedonija (League of Communists of Macedonia) (Maced.)
SK-PJ	Savez Komunista-Pokret za Jugoslaviju (League of Communists-Movement for Yugoslavia) (Mont.)

SKR	Spilka Karpatskyh Rusyniv (Society of Carpathian Ruthenians) (Ukr.)
SK-SDP	Savez Komunista–Socijalisticka Demokratska Partija (League of Communists—Social Democratic Party) (B-H)
SL	Stowarzyszenie Lemków (Lemko Association) (Pol.)
SLD	Sojusz Lewicy Demokratycznej (Democratic Left Alliance) (Pol.)
SLP	Stowarzyszenie Litwinów w Polsce (Association of Lithuanians in Poland) (Pol.)
SLS	Slovenska Ljudska Stranka (Slovenian People's Party) (Slovenia)
SM	Shoqata e Malazezëve (Association of Montenegrins) (Alb.)
SM	Stowarzyszenie Mazurskie (Mazurian Association) (Pol.)
SMK	Strana Maďarskej Koalície (Party of the Hungarian Coalition) (Slovakia)
SN	Stronnictwo Narodowe (National Party) (Pol.)
SND	Stronnictwo Narodowo-Demokratyczne (National Democratic Party) (Pol.)
SNDH	Slovenské Národné Demokratické Hnutie (Slovak National Democratic Movement) (Slovakia)
SNI	Sayuz Nov Izbor ("New Choice" Union) (Bulg.)
SNJ	Stranka Narodne Jednakosti (Party of National Equality) (Mont.)
SNKO	Svaz Nemeckých Kulturních Organizací (Union of German Cultural Associations) (Cz.)
SNO	Srpska Narodna Obnova (Serbian National Renewal) (Serbia)
SNP	Socjalistička Narodna Partija (Socialist Peoples' Party) (Mont.)
SNP	Sotsial Natsionalna Partiya (Social Nationalist Party) (Ukr.)
SNS	Slovenská Národná Strana (Slovak National Party) (Slovakia)
SNS	Slovenska Nacionalna Stranka (Slovenian National Party) (Slovenia)
SNS	Srpska Narodna Stranka (Serbian National Party) (Croatia)
SNS	Srpski Narodni Savez (Serbian People's Union) (B-H)
SNSD	Stranka Nezavisna Socijalitička Demokratska (Independent Social Democratic Party) (B-H)
SOP	Strana Občianskeho Porozumenia (Party of Civic Understanding) (Slovakia)
SPAC	Shoqata Patriotike Atdhetare "Çamëria" (Çamëria Political and Patriotic Association) (Alb.)
SPAK	Shoqata Patriotike Atdhetare Kosova (Kosova Patriotic and Political Association) (Alb.)
SPB	Satsiyalistychnaya Partiya Belarusi (Socialist Party of Belarus)
SPCG	Socijalistička Partija Crne Gore (Socialist Party of Montenegro) (Mont.)
SPM	Shoqata Politike "Mëmëdheu" (Motherland Political Association) (Alb.)
SPM	Socijalisticka Partija na Makedonija (Socialist Party Of Macedonia) (Maced.)
SPO	Srpski Pokret Otpora (Serbian Resistance Movement) (Kos.)
SPO	Srpski Pokret Obnove (Serbian Renewal Movement) (Serbia)
SPO	Strana Podnikatelů a Obchodníků (Party of Businessmen and Tradesmen) (Czech Republic)

SPR-RSC	Sdružení Pro Republiku-Republikánská Strana Československa (Association for the Republic-Republican Party of Czechoslovakia) (Cz.)
SPRS	Socijalistička Partija Republike Srpske (Socialist Party of the Serb Republic) (B-H)
SPS	Socialistička Partija Srbije (Socialist Party of Serbia) (Serbia)
SPU	Selianska Partiya Ukrainy (Peasant Party of Ukraine) (Ukr.)
SPU	Socialistychna Partiya Ukrainy (Socialist Party of Ukraine) (Ukr.)
SPU-SPU	Sotsialistychnoi Partii ta Selyanskoi Partii Ukrainy (Socialist and Peasant Party of Ukraine) (Ukr.)
SRH	Stranka Roma Hrvatske (Romani Party of Croatia) (Croatia)
SRI	Strana za Rómsku Integráciu (Party for Romani Integration) (Slovakia)
SRS	Srpska Radikalna Stranka (Serbian Radical Party) (B-H)
SRS	Srpska Radikalna Stranka (Serbian Radical Party) (Mont.)
SRS	Srpska Radikalna Stranka (Serbian Radical Party) (Serbia)
SRSJ	Savez Reformskih Snaga Jugoslavije (Alliance of Reform Forces of Yugoslavia) (B-H)
SRU	Savez Rutenca i Ukrajinca (Alliance of Ruthenians and Ukrainians) (Serbia)
SS	Sdružení Slováku (Union of Slovaks) (Cz.)
SS	Společnost Slováku (Community of Slovaks) (Cz.)
SSBR	Slavyansky Sabor, Belaia Rus (Slavic Assembly, White Russia) (Bel.)
SSV	Seljačka Stranka Vojvodine (Farmers Party of Vojvodina) (Serbia)
SV	Spoločná Voľba (Common Choice) (Slovakia)
SVM	Savez Vojvodjanskih Madjara (Alliance of Vojvodina Hungarians) (Serbia)
SZ	Slovenska Zveza (Slovenian Alliance) (Slovenia)
SZ	Srbija Zajedno (Serbia Together) (Serbia)
SZ	Strana Zelených (Green Party) (Cz.)
SZDSz	Szabad Demokraták Szövetsége (Alliance of Free Democrats) (Hung.)
SzDSz	Szerb Demokratikus Szövetség (Democratic Federation of Serbs) (Hung.)
SZS	Strana Zelených na Slovensku (Green Party of Slovakia) (Slovakia)
SzT	Szentkorona Társulat (Holy Crown Society) (Hung.)
TDP	Turska Demokraticheska Partiya (Turkish Democratic Party) (Bulg.)
TKL-ZP	Tautas Kustība Latvijai-Zīgerista Partija (National Movement For Latvia-Siegerist's Party) (Latv.)
TP	Tautas Partija (People's Party) (Latv.)
TP	Tulevikupartei (Estonian Future Party) (Est.)
TPA	Tastsaimnieku Politiska Apvienība (Political Union of Economists) (Latv.)
TSKCiSwP	Towarzystwo Społeczno-Kulturalne Czechów i Słowaków w Polsce (Cultural-Social Society of Czechs and Slovaks in Poland) (Pol.)
TSKMNSO	Towarzystwo Społeczno-Kulturalne Mniejszości Niemieckiej na śląsku Opolskim (Social-Cultural Association of the German Minority in Silesian Opole) (Pol.)

TSKZwP	Towarzystwo Społeczno-Kulturalne Żydów w Polsce (Socio-Cultural Society of Jews in Poland) (Pol.)
TS-LK	Tėvynės Sąjunga-Lietuvos Konservatoriai (Homeland Union-Lithuanian Conservatives) (Lith.)
TSP	Tautas Saskaņas Partija (National Harmony Party) (Latv.)
TU	Trudova Ukraina (Working Ukraine) (Ukr.)
TVB	'Tēvzemei un Brīvībai' (For Fatherland and Freedom) (Latv.)
UDMR	Uniunea Democrată Maghiară din România (Democratic Union of Hungarians in Romania) (Rom.)
UDRR	Uniunea Democratică a Romilor din România (Democratic Union of Roma in Romania) (Rom.)
UDS	Uniunea Democratică a Sîrbilor (Democratic Union of Serbs) (Rom.)
UDSC	Uniunea Democratică a Slovacilor şi Cehilor (Democratic Union of Slovaks and Czechs) (Rom.)
UFP	Uniunea Forţelor Patriotice (Union of Patriotic Forces) (Mold.)
UHKK	Ukrainskyi Hromadsyi Kongres Kryma (Ukrainian Civic Congress of Crimea) (Ukr.)
UMDSJ	Udruženje Madjara za Našu Domovinu, Srbiju i Jugoslaviju (Association of Hungarians for Our Fatherland Serbia and Yugoslavia) (Serbia)
UNA	Ukrainska Natsionalna Assembleya (Ukrainian National Assembly) (Ukr.)
UP	Unia Pracy (Union of Labor) (Pol.)
UPR	Unia Polityki Realnej (Union of Real Politics) (Pol.)
URP	Ukrainska Respublikanska Partiya (Ukrainian Republican Party) (Ukr.)
US	Unie Svobody (Freedom Union) (Cz.)
USD	Uniunea Social Democrat (Social Democratic Union) (Rom.)
UTDM	Uniunea Tineretului Democratic Maghiar (Union of Hungarian Democratic Youth) (Rom.)
UUR	Uniunea Ucrainienilor din România (Union of Ukrainians in Romania) (Rom.)
UW	Unia Wolności (Freedom Union) (Pol.)
VEE	Vene Erakond Eestis (Russian Party in Estonia) (Est.)
VKR	Vavariiklaste ja Konservatiivne Rahvaerakond-Parampoolsed (Republican and Conservative People's Party-Right Wingers) (Est.)
VMRO-DOM	VMRO-Dvizenje za Obnova na Makedonija (IMRO-Movement for Restoration of Macedonia) (Maced.)
VMRO-DP	Vnatresna Makedonska Revolucionerna Organizacija-Demokratska Partija (Internal Macedonian Revolutionary Organization-Democratic Party) (Maced.)
VMRO-DPMNE	Vnatresna Makedonska Revolucionerna Organizacija Demokratska Partija za Makedonsko Nacionalno Edinstvo (Internal Macedonian Revolutionary Organization-Democratic Party for Macedonian National Unity) (Maced.)

VMRO-N	Vatreshna Makedonska Revolyutsionna Organizatsia–Nezavisim (Internal Macedonian Revolutionary Organization–Independent) (Bulg.)
VMRO-OMD	Vatreshna Makedonska Revolyutsionna Organizatsia–Obedinenie na Makedonskite Druzhestva (Internal Macedonian Revolutionary Organization–Union of Macedonian Societies) (Bulg.)
VOH	Vseukrainske Obyednannya "Hromada"(All-Ukrainian Association "Community") (Ukr.)
VP	Vojvodjanski Pokret (Vojvodina Movement) (Serbia)
VR	Vatra Românească (Romanian Hearth) (Rom.)
Z	Zöldek (Greens) (Hung.)
ZChN	Zjednoczenie Chrześcijańsko-Narodowe (Christian National Union) (Pol.)
ZE	Zdruzenie na Egipjanite (Egyptian Association of Citizens) (Maced.)
ZG	Związek Górnośląski (Upper Silesian Union) (Pol.)
ZL	Zjednoczenie Łemków (Lemko Union) (Pol.)
ZLSD	Združena Lista Socialnih Demokratov (United List of Social Democrats) (Slovenia)
ZMM	Zdruzenie na Makedonci Muslimani (Association of Macedonian Muslims) (Maced.)
ZNSSKP	Związek Niemieckich Stowarzyszeń Społeczno-Kulturalnych w Polsce (Union of German Socio-Cultural Associations in Poland) (Pol.)
ZRP	Zakarpatska Respublikanska Partiya (Subcarpathian Republican Party) (Ukr.)
ZRS	Združenie Robotníkov Slovenska (Association of Slovak Workers) (Slovakia)
ZS	Zelena Stranka (Ecological Party) (B-H)
ZS	Zelena Stranka (Green Party) (Croatia)
ZS	Zemědelská Strana (Agricultural Party) (Cz.)
ZS-ESS	Zeleni Slovenije-Ekološko Socialna Stranka (Greens of Slovenia-Ecological Social Party) (Slovenia)
ZSN	Zemské Shromáždeni Nemců (German Landowner's Assembly) (Cz.)
ZSS	Zelena Stranka Srbije (Serbian Green Party) (Serbia)
ZUP	Związek Ukraińców w Polsce (Union of Ukrainians in Poland) (Pol.)
ZURCS	Zväz Ukrajincov a Rusínov v Česko-Slovensku (Union of Ukrainians and Ruthenians in Czechoslovakia) (Slovakia)

Index of Names

Index of Party Names

Janusz Bugajski is director of the Eastern Europe Project at the Center for Strategic and International Studies and currently runs the South-Central Europe area studies program at the Foreign Service Institute (FSI), U.S. Department of State. Dr. Bugajski has served as a consultant for the U.S. Department of Defense, the U.S. Agency for International Development (USAID), the International Research and Exchanges Board (IREX), and the International Republican Institute (IRI), and as a project director for the Council of Foreign Relations. In 1998 he received the Distinguished Public Service Award granted jointly by the U.S. Department of State, the U.S. Agency for International Development, the U.S. Information Agency, and the Arms Control and Disarmament Agency. His books include *Ethnic Politics in Eastern Europe: A Guide to Nationality Policies, Organizations, and Parties* (1994) and *Nations in Turmoil: Conflict and Cooperation in Eastern Europe* (1995). Dr. Bugajski is a regular contributor to newspapers in the West and in Eastern Europe, and publishes in several international journals.